Silverplated Flatware

An Identification & Value Guide

Revised 4th Editon

By Tere Hagan

Drawings By Alfred J. Hagan

COLLECTOR BOOKS
A Division of Schroeder Publishing Co., Inc.

The current values in this book should be used only as a guide. They are not intended to set prices, which vary from one section of the country to another. Auction prices as well as dealer prices vary greatly and are affected by condition as well as demand. Neither the Author nor the publisher assumes responsiblity for any losses that might be incurred as a result of consulting this guide.

Additional copies of this book may be ordered from:

COLLECTOR BOOKS
P.O. Box 3009
Paducah, Kentucky 42002-3009
or
Tere Hagan
P.O. Box 25487
Tempe, Arizona 85285

@ $14.95 Add $2.00 for postage and handling.

1 2 3 4 5 6 7 8 9 0

Printed by IMAGE GRAPHICS, Paducah, Kentucky

This, the fourth edtion, as well as prior editions of this book, are dedicated to my husband, Al, who patiently drew picture after picture, as well as our two sons, Michael & Matthew, who endured patiently our many long hours completing each edition.

HOW TO USE THIS BOOK

This book is organized alphabetically by firm. Patterns are illustrated in chronological order by introduction date. All dates of introduction are circa dates. These firms are listed in the Index of Manufacturers. The various marks of the firms are listed in the Index of Marks.

In order to identify the piece of silverplated flatware, begin with the Index of Marks, page 369. After finding the mark, proceed to the proper part of the book and locate the pattern. If the pattern is 19th Century, check the 19th Century section of patterns, page 9, before proceeding to the specific section of the book indicated by the Index of Marks. Included in this section are thirteen patterns that were made in the latter half of the 19th Century by almost every maker of silverplated flatware. There will be slight variation in the patterns, so the backstamp should always be noted when referring to the pattern.

In this 4th edition, patterns placed in production after 1984 for ALL manufacturers are illustrated beginning on page 344. BE SURE TO CHECK THIS SECTION OF THE BOOK.

If the piece of flatware is prior to about 1915 and the mark cannot be found, it may be a mark of a retail firm in which case it may be necessary to check each mark in the book, but especially American Silver Company, Rogers & Brothers, etc., E.H.H. Smith, Rockford, Towle, and Williams. Some retail marks are included in the Index of Marks and that also will be a clue where to look for the pattern.

If the pattern cannot be found after identifying the mark, check the Index of Manufacturers and find the other marks of that firm and check those marks also. Different marks on the same pattern have been cross indexed. If the pattern still cannot be found, turn to the Unidentified Patterns. Shown are twenty-one unidentified patterns beginning on page 339.

Many pattern names are repeated by many of the firms as well as often repeated within a particular firm. For this reason, when describing the pattern, it is important to note the backstamp of the pattern. If this book shows an "aka" (also known as), use both names (or sometimes more than two names). When a pattern name is used more than once with the same backstamp and does not have an "aka" to set it apart, the name of the pattern with the year of introduction is shown. This again, is another way to identify the particular pattern. An example would be Community's Patrician - 1914 and Patrician - 1975.

Generally in this book the various backstamps of the firms have been separated. The exceptions are some of the backmarks of International. There is so much duplication of these backmarks on the same patterns that the most practical way of setting up the book was to combine these marks of International. Usage of the book will determine whether or not this is indeed the most practical solution to the problem of different backstamps on the same pattern.

Notice that the term "not in full line" appears after the date of introduction of some patterns. Perhaps only serving pieces were made or perhaps only some place pieces were made, but at any rate a full service in these patterns cannot be found. Other patterns will have the term "multi-motif" behind the date of introduction. This means that different motifs appear on the various place and serving pieces in that pattern.

The Index of Marks is not set up strictly alphabetically. Included are retailer marks which can be used as an additional aid in locating patterns. There are quite a few probable retailer marks and all are listed under the first letter of the mark. Another deviation from strictly alphabetical is the various Rogers marks of both Oneida and International. They are all together under Rogers.

With the above comments in mind, hopefully, the reader's pattern can be identified. If not, the author welcomes a photocopy of the pattern and will aid in identification. Also, if there is a pattern that is not included in this book and the pattern name is known, contact the author for possible inclusion in another book. In the meantime, ENJOY YOUR SILVERPLATED FLATWARE!

TABLE OF CONTENTS

The information given with each pattern includes a code as follows:

P = pattern presently in production
M = pattern most extremely collectible
E = pattern extremely collectible
H = pattern highly collectible
C = pattern collectible
S = pattern seldom collectible

The prices of presently made silverplated flatware patterns vary quite a bit from firm to firm and even within different lines of the same firm. A middle of the line price has been chosen for the price guide. However, for new flatware, prices can be more or less than the listed price. Values here are average for silverplated flatware.

At the present time, there are no generally accepted prices set on various pieces of silverplated flatware. Prices vary a great deal from dealer to dealer throughout the country. Listed are reasonable average prices in the price guide. Furthermore, a reasonable price to pay could vary 20% or more in either direction from the prices given. Some pieces and patterns are more difficult to find than others and that has an effect upon prices also.

The pattern code shown is the author's perception of a pattern's collectibility based upon inquiries received. Each dealer is going to receive somewhat different inquiries and it is quite likely that some dealers would classify some of the patterns differently. Some individuals collect a pattern for the sake of the pattern itself. Other individuals are trying to complete sets that they have inherited or bought before the pattern was discontinued. Both of these interests were taken into consideration in determining prices. Perhaps popularity of a pattern would be a better choice of words than collectibility.

A price guide should also include an idea of what a dealer will pay for an item. Again, this will vary from dealer to dealer, and often, even for a particular dealer, will vary with time depending upon his own needs at the moment. If a dealer is buying in quantity, the following is a probable range for flatware in LIKE NEW condition with NO MONOGRAM.

P = $1.50 - $2.50 per piece.
M = $5.00 + -- per piece -- offer will probably be about 40% of what the dealer perceives as retail.
E= $4.00 - $7.00 per piece --offer will probably be about 40% of what the dealer perceives as retail.
H = $2.50 - $5.00 per piece -- offer will probably be about 30% of what the dealer perceives as retail.
C = $1.50 - $2.50 per piece --offer will probably be about 25% of what the dealer perceives as retail.
S = $ .50 - $1.50 per piece -- offer will probably be about 12½% of what the dealer perceives as retail.

Let's look at the reasons for the prices paid by dealers. Assume an entire set of a "C" pattern is bought. Some pieces in that set will be sold rather rapidly as they have a relatively high turnover. Other pieces even in a collectible pattern will not sell rapidly. If the dealer can pick and choose from what the seller wants to sell, the seller will get more for certain pieces that sell rapidly. He is then left with what will sell slowly for a dealer. When the less popular pieces are sold, the price received will be lower than average.

Notice the prices are for flatware that has a like-new condition with no monogram. If the piece is worn or if it has a monogram, the price offered by the dealer will be substantially less. There exists a very thin (practically non-existent) market for worn or monogramed pieces. If the pattern is either an E or M pattern, it is usually profitable to have them restored. However, it is not cheap to restore flatware and furthermore, contrary to a belief held by many persons, not all pieces can be restored. If the fork tines are uneven, the bowls of spoons are worn down from stirring, or if the hollow handles are dented, restoration is not successful.

Many individuals think that if a pattern is old, it has to be valuable. This is not always true. Some old patterns are in either the C, H, E, or M category, but many of them are in the S category also. Just because it is old, does not mean it is good, which is true of most areas of collecting. In fact, most interest these days is in the patterns that are not extremely old. For one thing, extremely old patterns are very difficult to find and to find them in good condition is even more difficult. Evidently, it is for this reason that people have turned to more obtainable patterns.

Most patterns is this edition indicate the retail price for a dinner knife, dinner fork and teaspoon. Some patterns are marked "thin market." Although a price could have been given, it was decided that more information could be given to the reader in this fashion. If you want to collect these patterns, it will be a long, slow process for not many of these patterns appear on the secondary market. A few patterns have a price for only a dinner fork and a teaspoon. Although knives may have been made in these patterns, again few, if any, show up on the secondary market. Notice also, that in some of the older patterns, the knives varied from the dinner forks and teaspoons. Old catalogs have proven that these indeed are the knives of that particular pattern.

As you look over the prices of a dinner knife, dinner fork and teaspoon in each pattern, you will see that some are lower or higher than the price guide on the following page. The prices on the following page are by necessity averages. An individual pattern price is determined by quality of the plate, availability in the secondary market and many other factors.

Type of Piece	S	C	H	E	M
Three piece carving set	15.00-25.00	40.00-50.00	60.00-95.00	125.00-150.00	195.00-225.00
Ice Cream Fork	8.00-12.00	12.00-15.00	15.00-20.00	35.00- 40.00	60.00- 65.00
Cocktail Fork	6.00- 8.00	9.00-12.00	15.00-20.00	20.00- 25.00	35.00- 40.00
Individual Butter Spreader	5.00- 6.00	7.00- 9.00	10.00-15.00	20.00- 25.00	35.00- 40.00
Ice Cream Spoon	8.00-12.00	12.00-14.00	15.00-20.00	30.00- 35.00	50.00- 55.00
Bouillon Spoon	6.00- 8.00	8.00-10.00	9.00-12.00	20.00- 25.00	35.00- 40.00
Fruit Spoon	6.00- 8.00	8.00-10.00	12.00-15.00	20.00- 25.00	40.00- 45.00
Salad Fork	6.00- 8.00	10.00-12.00	20.00-25.00	35.00- 40.00	60.00- 70.00
Iced Tea Spoon	6.00- 8.00	9.00-12.00	18.00-20.00	40.00- 45.00	60.00- 70.00
Two Piece Carving Set	15.00-20.00	30.00-45.00	45.00-75.00	95.00-125.00	145.00-175.00
Bent Handle Baby Spoon	8.00-10.00	12.00-15.00	18.00-25.00	30.00- 35.00	40.00- 45.00
Baby Fork	5.00- 6.00	7.00- 9.00	12.00-15.00		
Baby Spoon	5.00- 6.00	7.00- 9.00	12.00-15.00		
Jam Spoon	8.00-10.00	10.00-15.00	18.00-20.00		
Pickle Fork	8.00-10.00	12.00-18.00	18.00-20.00	25.00- 30.00	55.00- 60.00
Sugar Spoon	5.00- 6.00	6.00- 8.00	15.00-18.00	20.00- 25.00	25.00- 30.00
Lemon Fork	10.00-12.00	12.00-18.00	18.00-20.00		
Master Butter Knife	5.00- 6.00	6.00- 8.00	12.00-15.00	15.00- 20.00	25.00- 30.00
Olive Spoon	10.00-12.00	12.00-18.00	20.00-25.00		
Jelly Server	8.00-10.00	12.00-15.00	20.00-25.00	45.00- 50.00	65.00- 75.00
Sugar Tongs	10.00-15.00	15.00-20.00	25.00-30.00	45.00- 50.00	75.00- 85.00
Cold Meat Fork	12.00-15.00	25.00-30.00	30.00-35.00	40.00- 45.00	65.00- 75.00
Cream Ladle	12.00-15.00	20.00-25.00	25.00-30.00	35.00- 40.00	50.00- 55.00
Pastry Server	12.00-15.00	30.00-35.00	30.00-35.00	45.00- 50.00	70.00- 75.00
Berry Spoon	12.00-15.00	30.00-40.00	40.00-45.00	50.00- 55.00	65.00- 75.00
Gravy Ladle	12.00-15.00	30.00-40.00	40.00-45.00	45.00- 50.00	65.00- 75.00
Cheese Knife	8.00-12.00	15.00-20.00	20.00-25.00	35.00- 40.00	50.00- 60.00
Tomato Server	12.00-15.00	30.00-40.00	40.00-45.00	65.00- 75.00	115.00-125.00
Dessert Server	12.00-15.00	30.00-40.00	40.00-45.00	50.00- 60.00	70.00- 75.00
Youth Fork	6.00- 8.00	7.00- 9.00	12.00-15.00	15.00- 18.00	20.00- 25.00
Youth Spoon	5.00- 6.00	7.00- 9.00	12.00-15.00	15.00- 18.00	20.00- 25.00
Youth Knife	6.00- 8.00	7.00- 9.00	12.00-15.00	18.00- 20.00	25.00- 30.00
Demitasse Spoon	4.00- 6.00	8.00-12.00	12.00-15.00	15.00- 20.00	25.00- 30.00
5 O'Clock Spoon	4.00- 6.00	8.00-10.00	12.00-15.00	15.00- 18.00	20.00- 25.00
Teaspoon	4.00- 6.00	6.00- 8.00	12.00-15.00	15.00- 18.00	18.00- 20.00
Oval Soup or Place Spoon	4.00- 6.00	7.00- 8.00	12.00-15.00	15.00- 18.00	18.00- 20.00
Round Soup Spoon	5.00- 6.00	7.00- 9.00	15.00-18.00	18.00- 20.00	25.00- 30.00
Luncheon or Place Fork	7.00- 8.00	10.00-15.00	15.00-18.00	18.00- 20.00	20.00- 25.00
Dinner Fork	7.00- 8.00	10.00-15.00	15.00-18.00	18.00- 20.00	20.00- 25.00
Grill or Viande Fork	7.00- 8.00	10.00-15.00			
Luncheon or Place Knife	7.00- 8.00	10.00-15.00	15.00-18.00	25.00- 30.00	35.00- 40.00
Dinner Knife	7.00- 8.00	10.00-15.00	15.00-18.00	25.00- 30.00	35.00- 40.00
Grill or Viande Knife	7.00- 8.00	10.00-15.00			
Tablespoon	8.00-10.00	10.00-15.00	15.00-18.00	18.00- 20.00	20.00- 25.00
Soup Ladle	20.00-30.00	50.00-75.00	60.00-95.00	125.00-150.00	275.00-300.00

AN UPDATE - SILVERPLATED FLATWARE - 1990

As we enter a new decade, the problems facing the flatware industry do not seem to be diminishing. Rather, if anything, the problems in the secondary market seem to be increasing.

The problems of consumer confusion due to "sale" marketing techniques and the financial problems of the silver manufacturers still exist today. These problems were well described in the third edition update.

Silverplated flatware reaching the secondary market has diminished in quantity and quality. It would appear as if there are several reasons for this to be happening. First, many of the popular patterns from the 1940's and 1950's are now 40 to 50 years old. The sets have been used and often abused. Twenty years ago, it would have been unthinkable to put the Sunday best in the dishwasher. Such is not the case today. It is unusual today to find NOS (new old stock) or very lightly used merchandise in the popular patterns.

Secondly, the last several years have seen the growth of an industry using silverplated flatware in large, large quantities. These people use the popular patterns to make razors, make-up brushes and many, many more gift items. Huge quantities of flatware have thus disappeared from the secondary market. Furthermore, the patterns most desired by these manufacturers are the ones in demand for filling out sets i.e., the very popular patterns of the turn of the century and the late 1940's and 1950's.

The above factors have had an impact on prices charged to the customer for any top quality non-monogrammed flatware. The prices of most pieces in the popular fancy patterns have increased perhaps 20 percent in the last couple of years. The very plain patterns have seen a decrease in price due to lack of demand. These patterns, although not plentiful, were generally not the quality of the popular patterns. Therefore, not as much has survived and even if it has, most people do not choose to replace or increase their sets. The fancy patterns of poorer quality have maintained more or less the same pricing structure of the previous edition. Because these patterns are in demand by the gift product industry, pieces are difficult to find and owners of these patterns are most likely to want to replace or increase their set because the pattern is attractive.

This decade should also see the passing down of sets from the 1960's and 1970's. As one reviews the text, one will see that not many patterns were produced in these two decades and as we look at the situation historically, not as much silverplated flatware was produced in the 1940's and 1950's.

Finally, as I talk to personnel at the various silver flatware manufacturing firms they see a return to at-home entertaining. They also see a trend to the so-called finer things of life as far as the home is concerned. If this is the case, we will see increased interest in tabletop items from all age groups.

The following thirteen patterns were made in the latter half of the 19th century and into the early 20th century by virtually every manufacturer of silverplated flatware. There will be slight variation in the patterns, so the backstamp should always be noted when referring to the pattern. By the standards of today, these patterns, with the exception of Kings which was used by the United States Navy, were not full line. Dinner and luncheon forks, serving, soup and teaspoons as well as some serving pieces were made in these patterns.

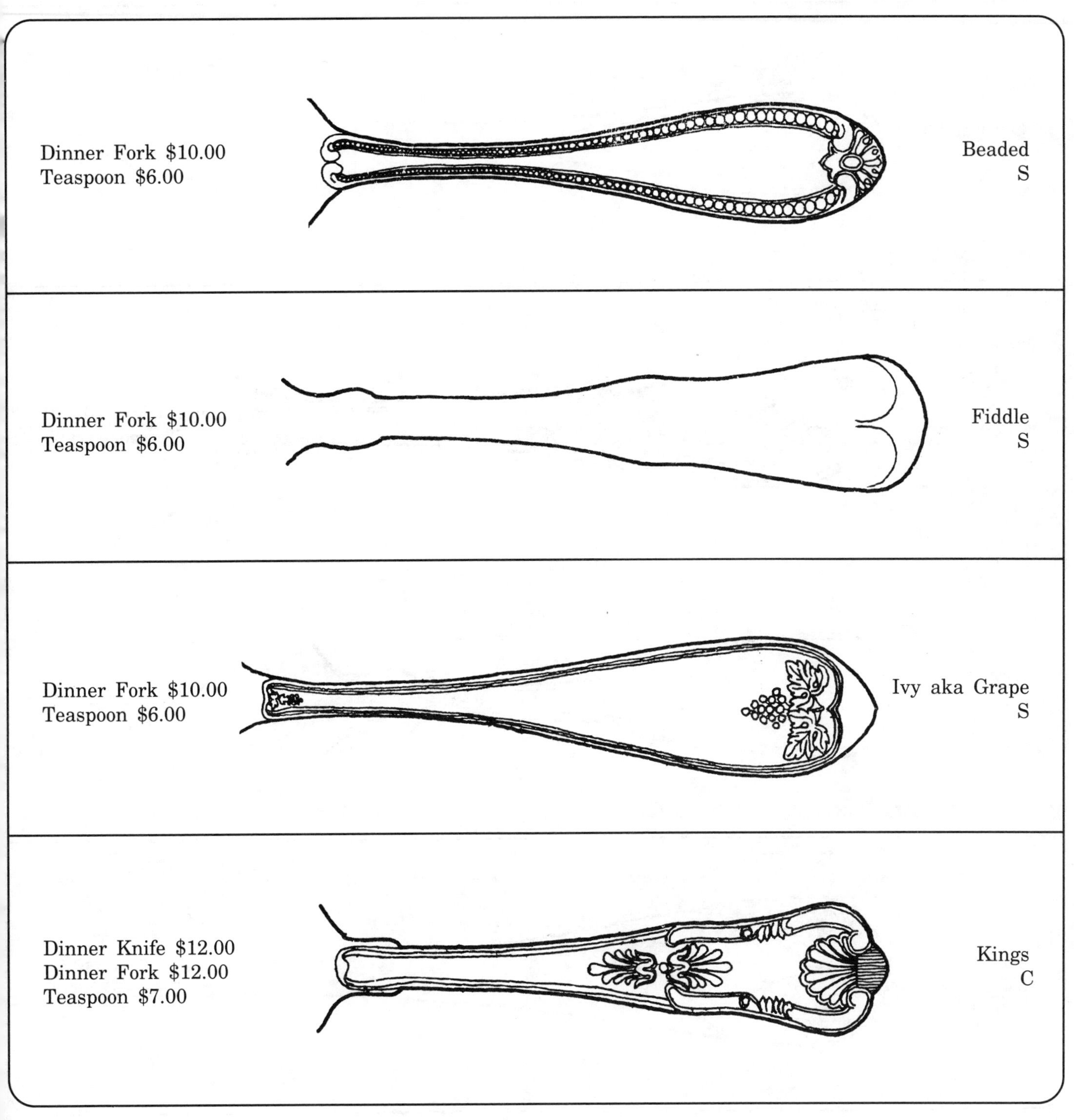

Please refer to "How To Use This Book" page 4.

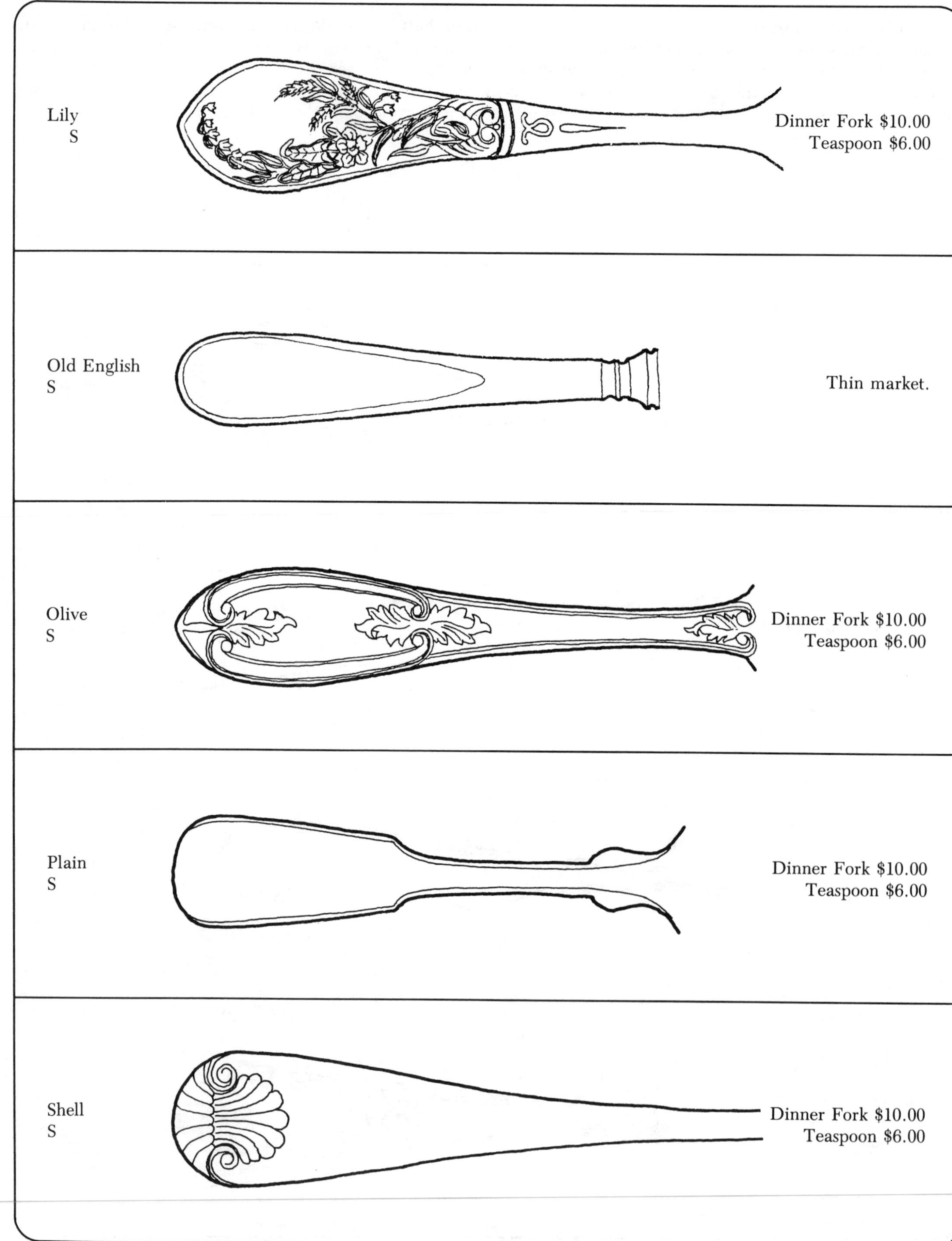

Please refer to "How To Use This Book" page 4.

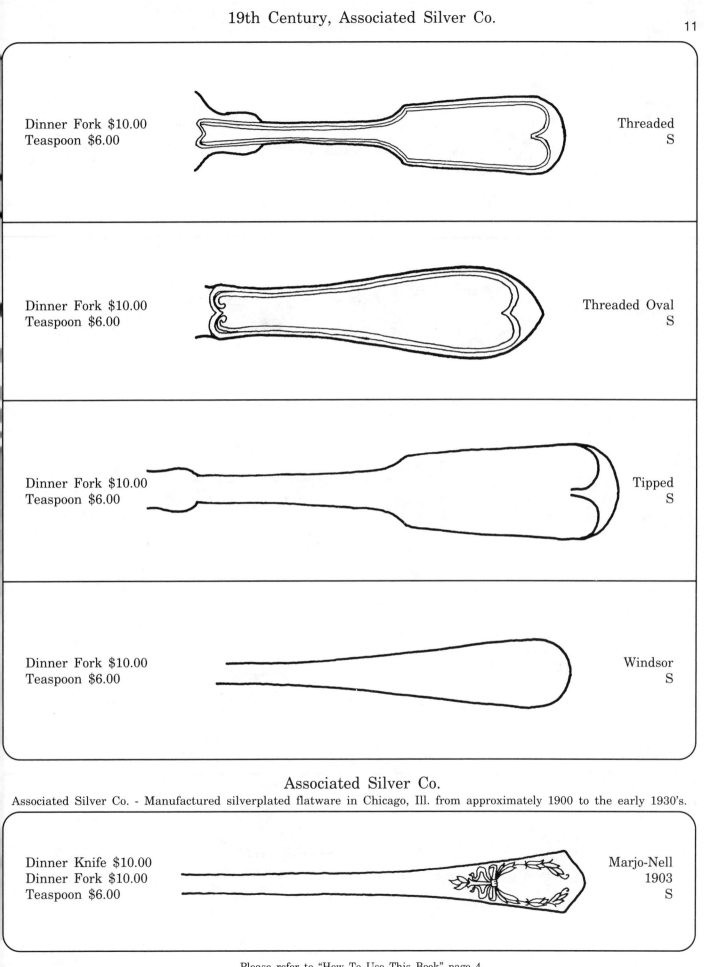

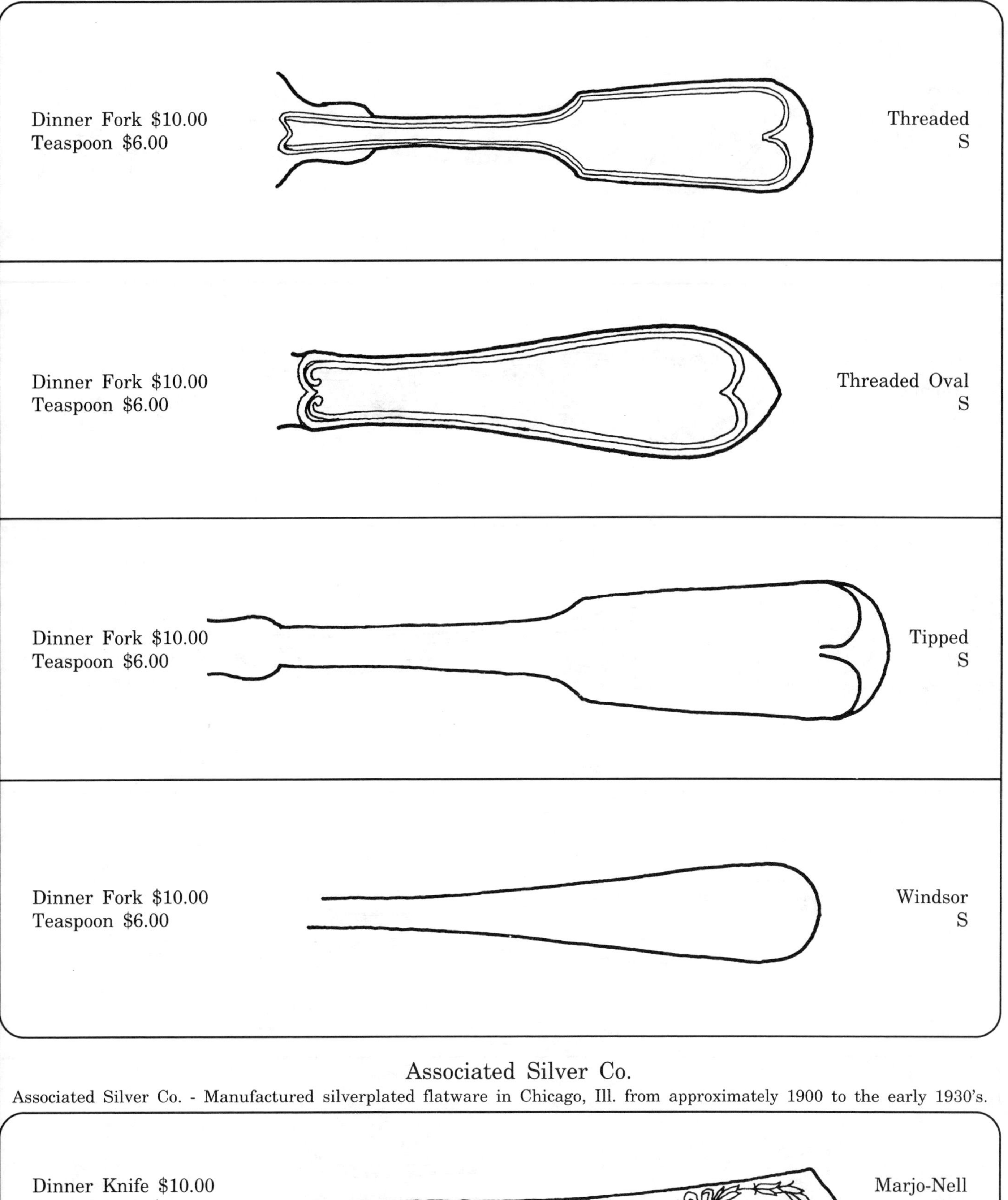

Dinner Fork $10.00
Teaspoon $6.00

Threaded
S

Dinner Fork $10.00
Teaspoon $6.00

Threaded Oval
S

Dinner Fork $10.00
Teaspoon $6.00

Tipped
S

Dinner Fork $10.00
Teaspoon $6.00

Windsor
S

Associated Silver Co.

Associated Silver Co. - Manufactured silverplated flatware in Chicago, Ill. from approximately 1900 to the early 1930's.

Dinner Knife $10.00
Dinner Fork $10.00
Teaspoon $6.00

Marjo-Nell
1903
S

Please refer to "How To Use This Book" page 4.

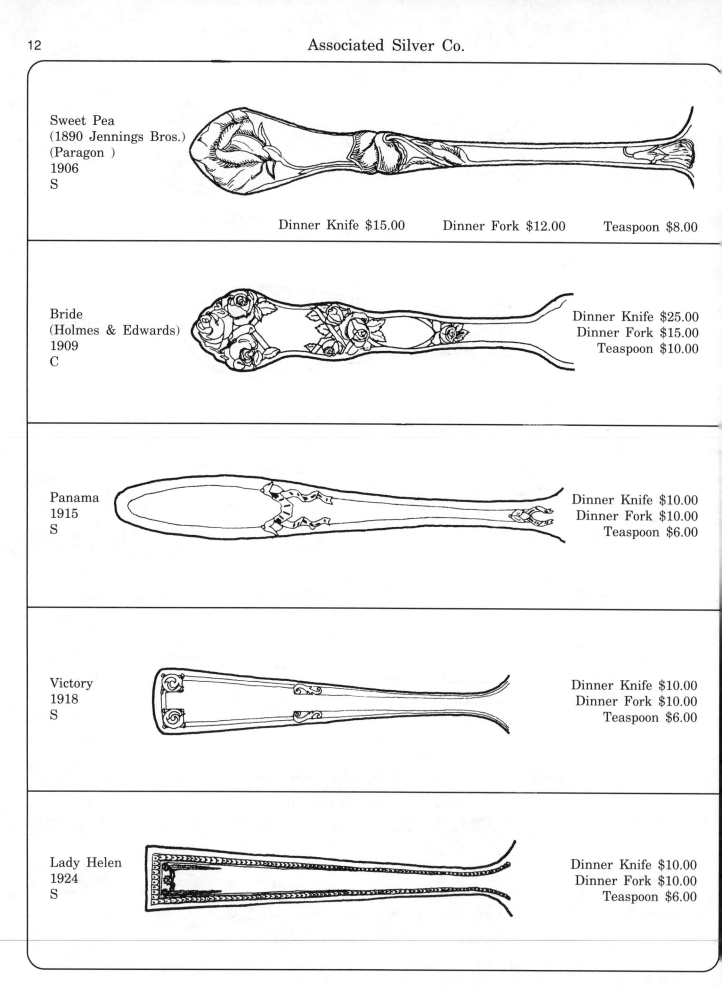

Sweet Pea
(1890 Jennings Bros.)
(Paragon)
1906
S

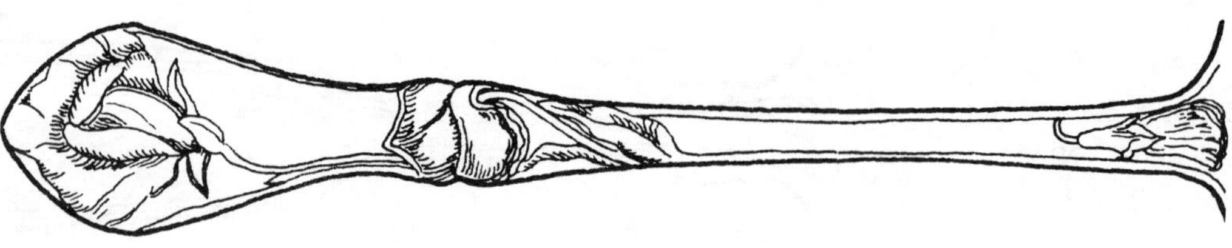

Dinner Knife $15.00 Dinner Fork $12.00 Teaspoon $8.00

Bride
(Holmes & Edwards)
1909
C

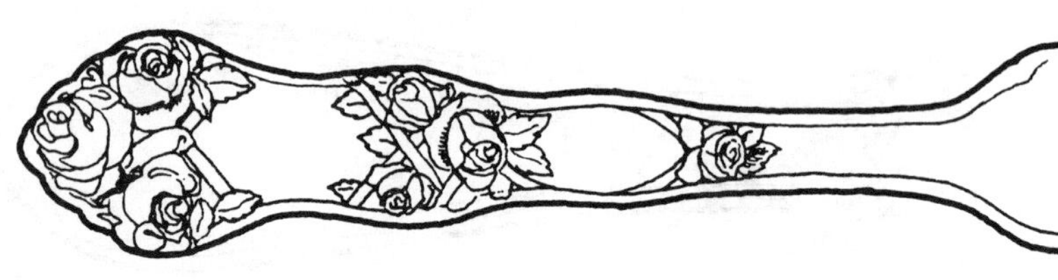

Dinner Knife $25.00
Dinner Fork $15.00
Teaspoon $10.00

Panama
1915
S

Dinner Knife $10.00
Dinner Fork $10.00
Teaspoon $6.00

Victory
1918
S

Dinner Knife $10.00
Dinner Fork $10.00
Teaspoon $6.00

Lady Helen
1924
S

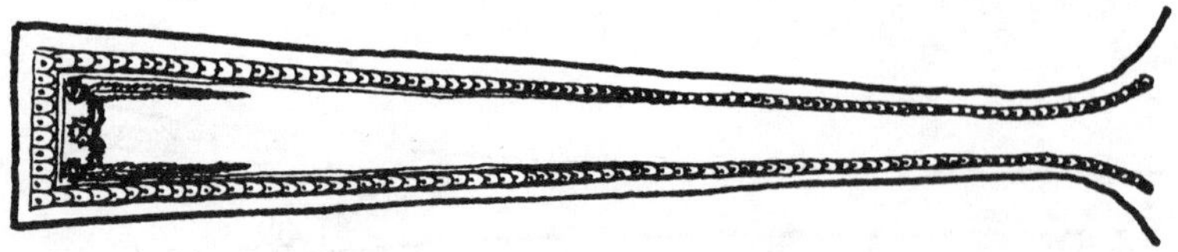

Dinner Knife $10.00
Dinner Fork $10.00
Teaspoon $6.00

Please refer to "How To Use This Book" page 4.

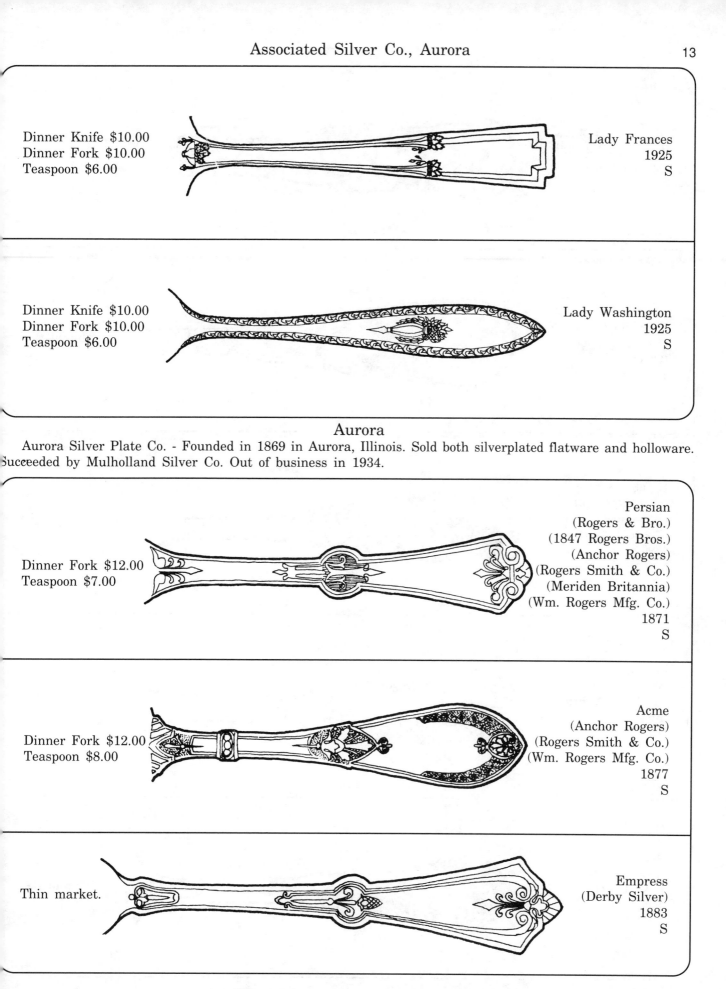

Dinner Knife $10.00
Dinner Fork $10.00
Teaspoon $6.00

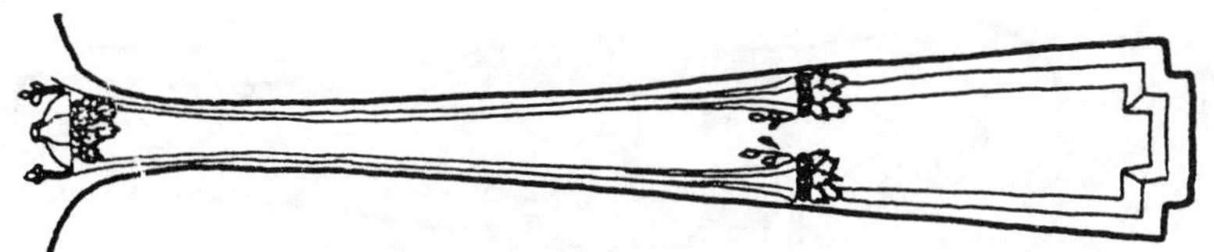

Lady Frances
1925
S

Dinner Knife $10.00
Dinner Fork $10.00
Teaspoon $6.00

Lady Washington
1925
S

Aurora

Aurora Silver Plate Co. - Founded in 1869 in Aurora, Illinois. Sold both silverplated flatware and holloware. Succeeded by Mulholland Silver Co. Out of business in 1934.

Dinner Fork $12.00
Teaspoon $7.00

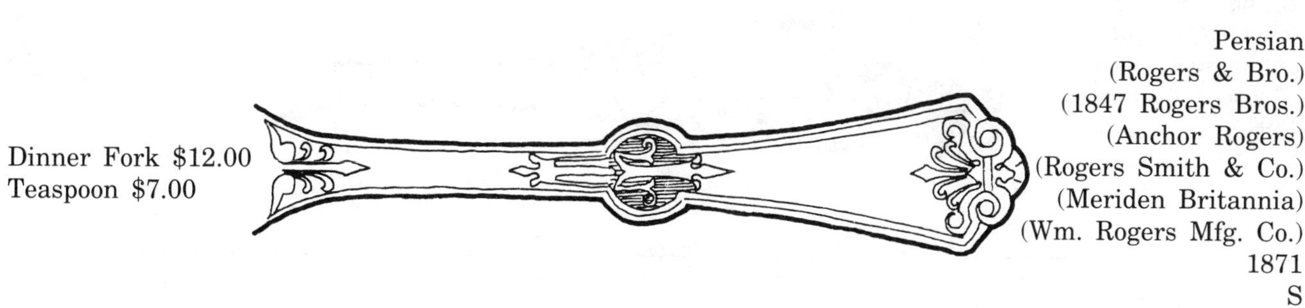

Persian
(Rogers & Bro.)
(1847 Rogers Bros.)
(Anchor Rogers)
(Rogers Smith & Co.)
(Meriden Britannia)
(Wm. Rogers Mfg. Co.)
1871
S

Dinner Fork $12.00
Teaspoon $8.00

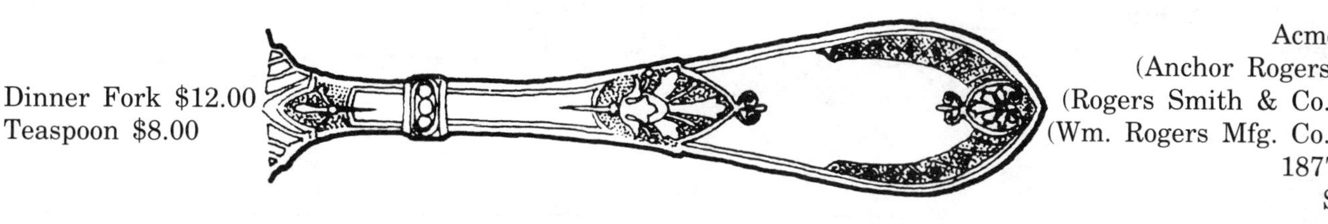

Acme
(Anchor Rogers)
(Rogers Smith & Co.)
(Wm. Rogers Mfg. Co.)
1877
S

Thin market.

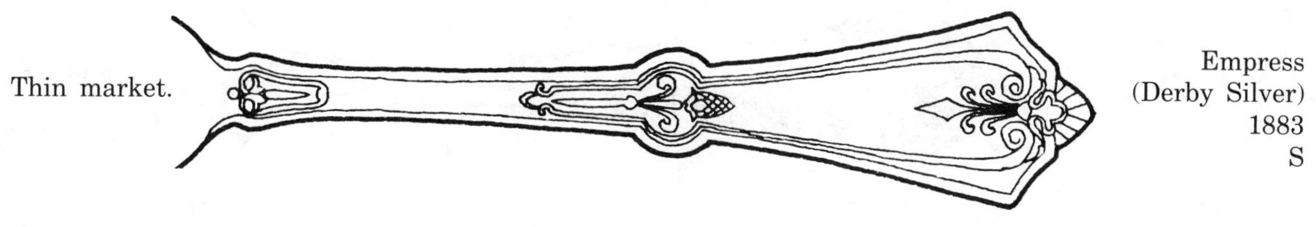

Empress
(Derby Silver)
1883
S

Please refer to "How To Use This Book" page 4.

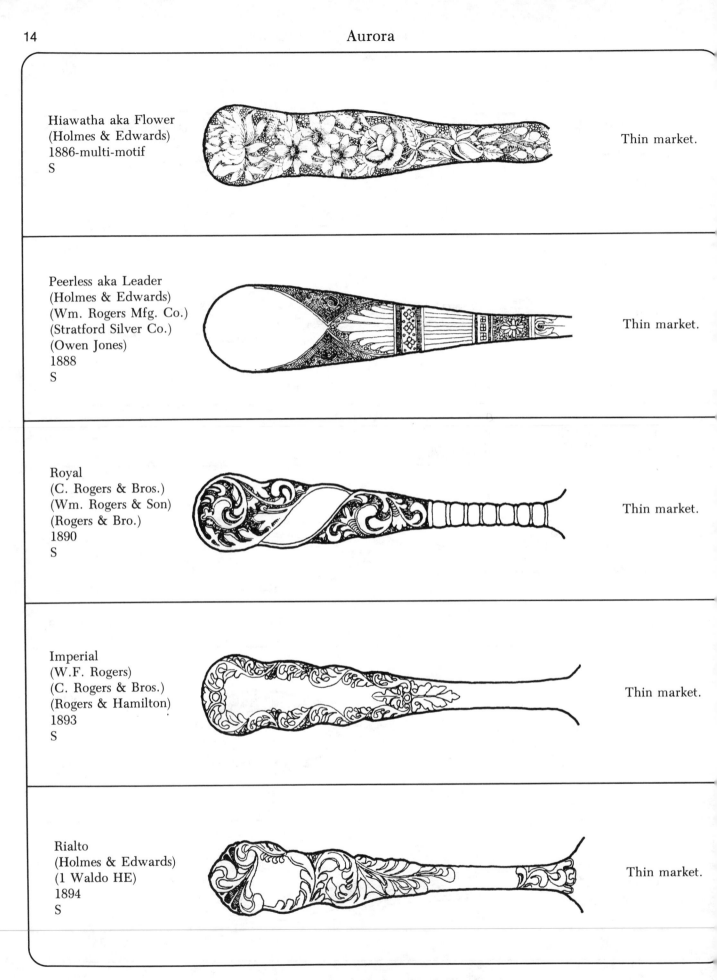

Hiawatha aka Flower
(Holmes & Edwards)
1886-multi-motif
S

Thin market.

Peerless aka Leader
(Holmes & Edwards)
(Wm. Rogers Mfg. Co.)
(Stratford Silver Co.)
(Owen Jones)
1888
S

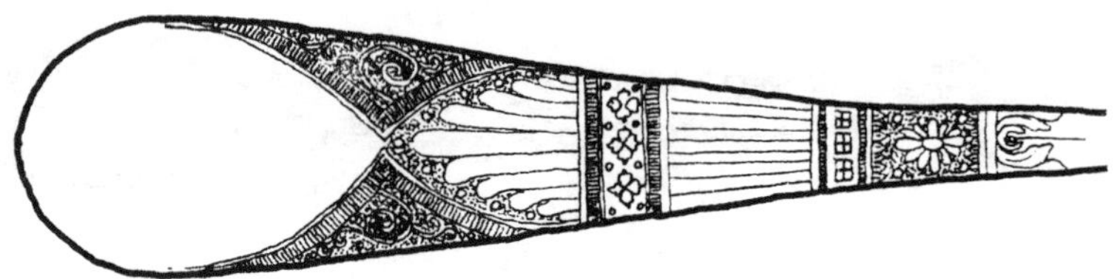

Thin market.

Royal
(C. Rogers & Bros.)
(Wm. Rogers & Son)
(Rogers & Bro.)
1890
S

Thin market.

Imperial
(W.F. Rogers)
(C. Rogers & Bros.)
(Rogers & Hamilton)
1893
S

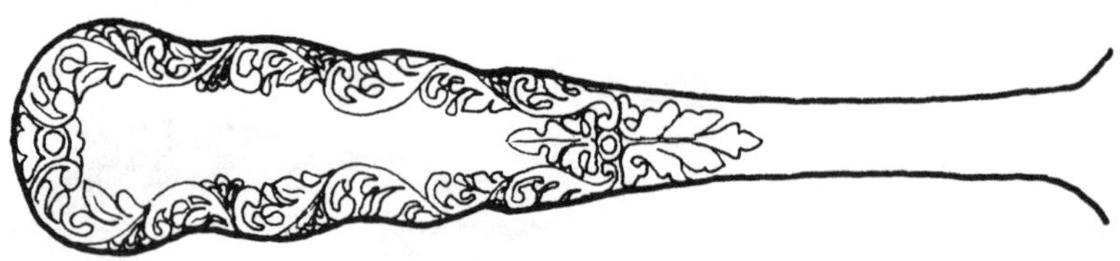

Thin market.

Rialto
(Holmes & Edwards)
(1 Waldo HE)
1894
S

Thin market.

Please refer to "How To Use This Book" page 4.

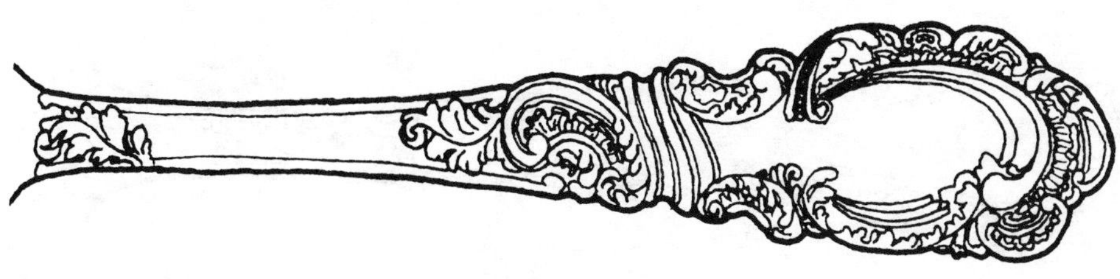

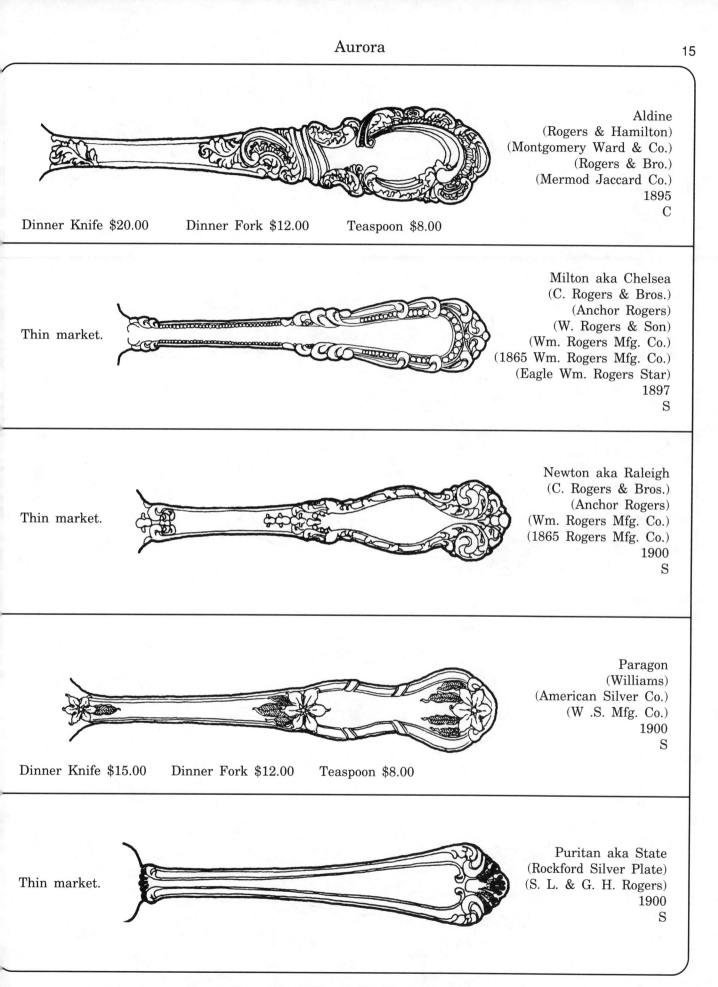

Aldine
(Rogers & Hamilton)
(Montgomery Ward & Co.)
(Rogers & Bro.)
(Mermod Jaccard Co.)
1895
C

Dinner Knife $20.00 Dinner Fork $12.00 Teaspoon $8.00

Thin market.

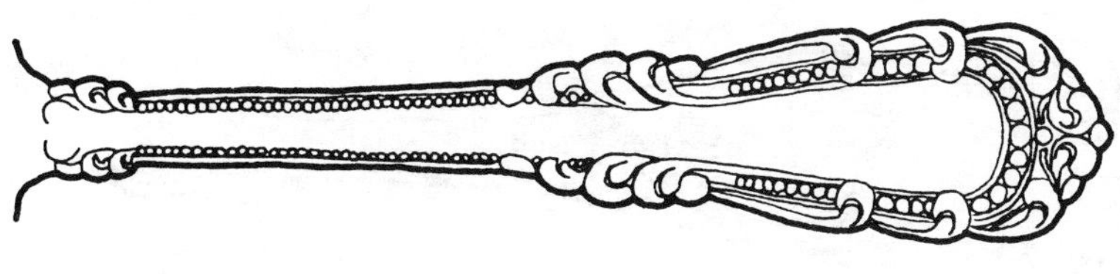

Milton aka Chelsea
(C. Rogers & Bros.)
(Anchor Rogers)
(W. Rogers & Son)
(Wm. Rogers Mfg. Co.)
(1865 Wm. Rogers Mfg. Co.)
(Eagle Wm. Rogers Star)
1897
S

Thin market.

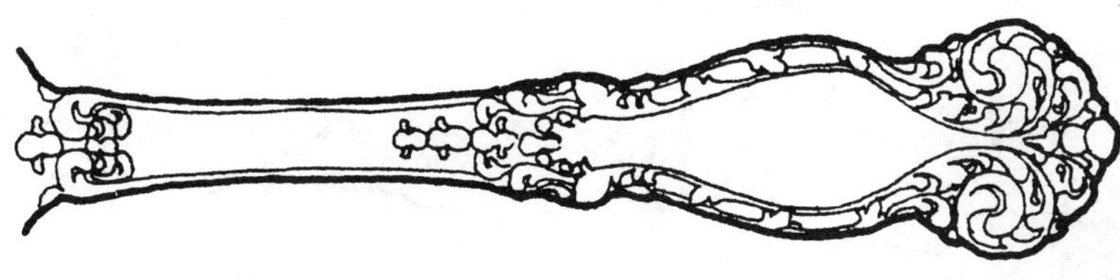

Newton aka Raleigh
(C. Rogers & Bros.)
(Anchor Rogers)
(Wm. Rogers Mfg. Co.)
(1865 Rogers Mfg. Co.)
1900
S

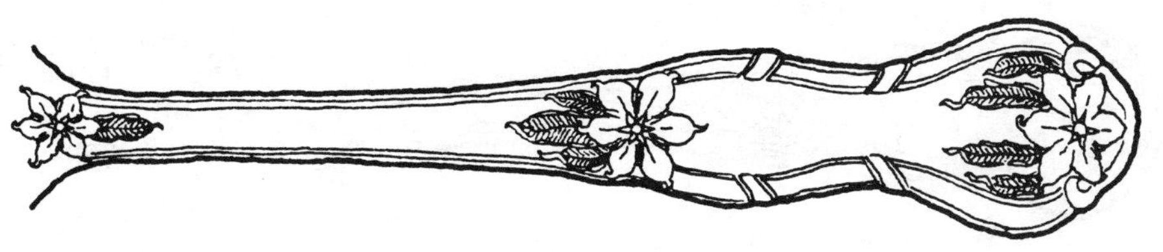

Paragon
(Williams)
(American Silver Co.)
(W .S. Mfg. Co.)
1900
S

Dinner Knife $15.00 Dinner Fork $12.00 Teaspoon $8.00

Thin market.

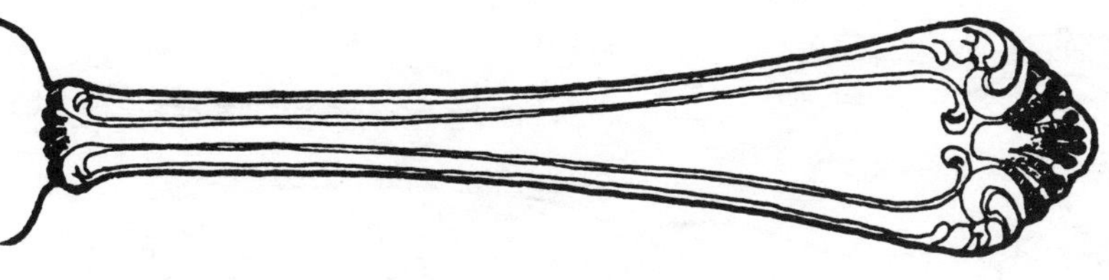

Puritan aka State
(Rockford Silver Plate)
(S. L. & G. H. Rogers)
1900
S

Please refer to "How To Use This Book" page 4.

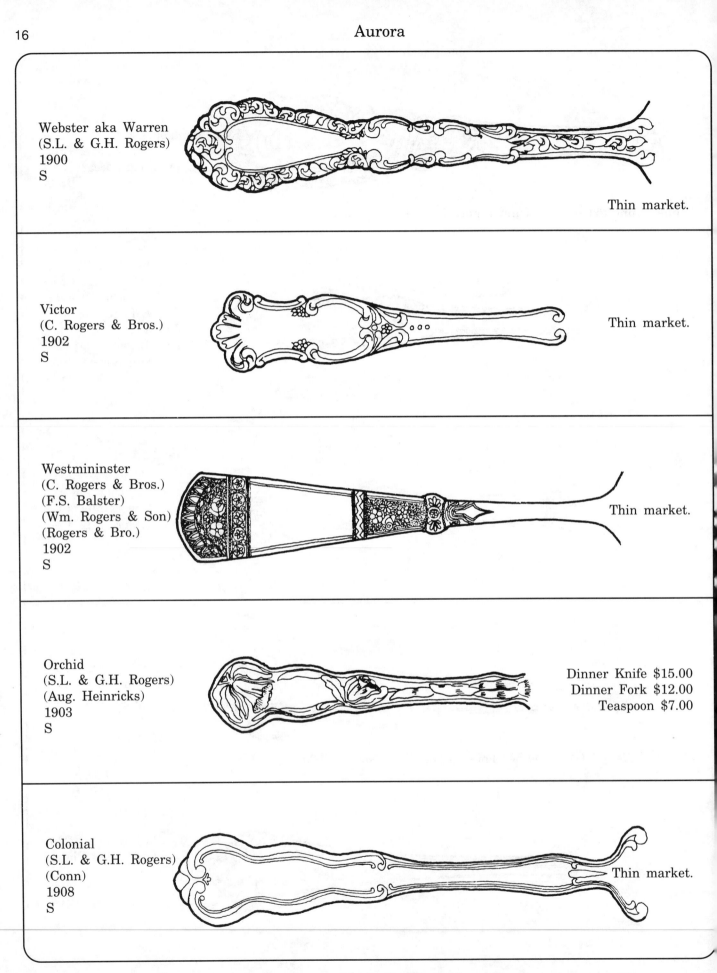

Webster aka Warren
(S.L. & G.H. Rogers)
1900
S

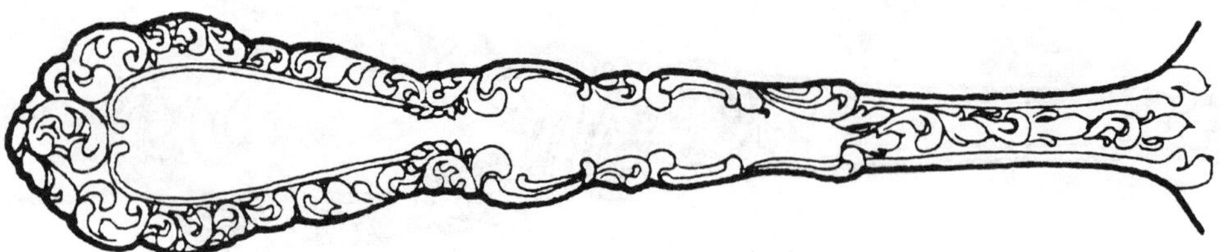

Thin market.

Victor
(C. Rogers & Bros.)
1902
S

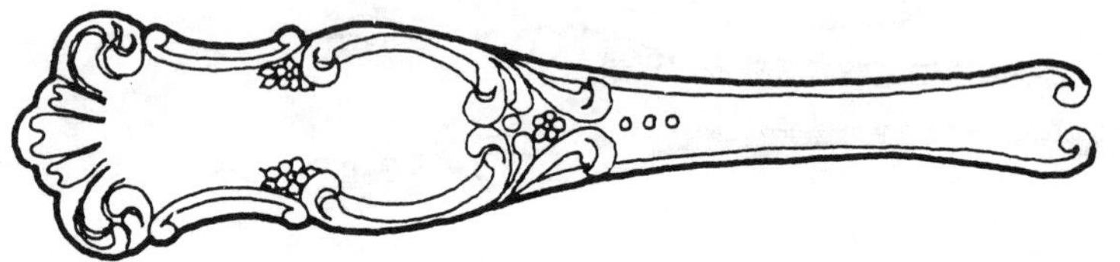

Thin market.

Westmininster
(C. Rogers & Bros.)
(F.S. Balster)
(Wm. Rogers & Son)
(Rogers & Bro.)
1902
S

Thin market.

Orchid
(S.L. & G.H. Rogers)
(Aug. Heinricks)
1903
S

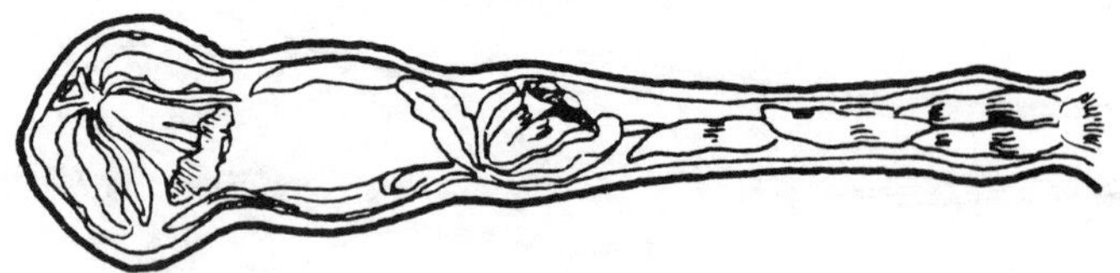

Dinner Knife $15.00
Dinner Fork $12.00
Teaspoon $7.00

Colonial
(S.L. & G.H. Rogers)
(Conn)
1908
S

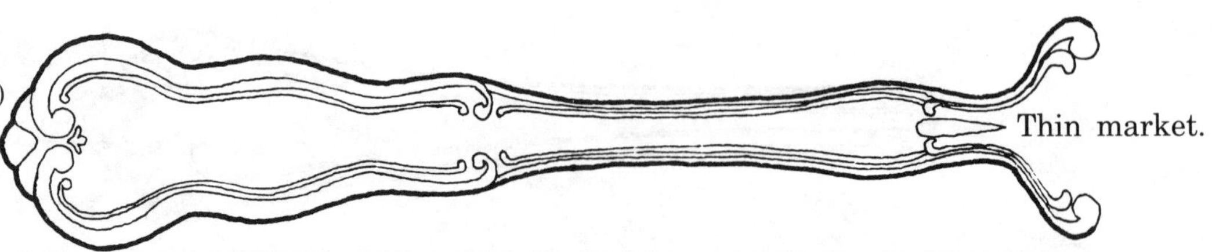

Thin market.

Please refer to "How To Use This Book" page 4.

Baroness Silver Plate

No information available about the user of this backstamp.

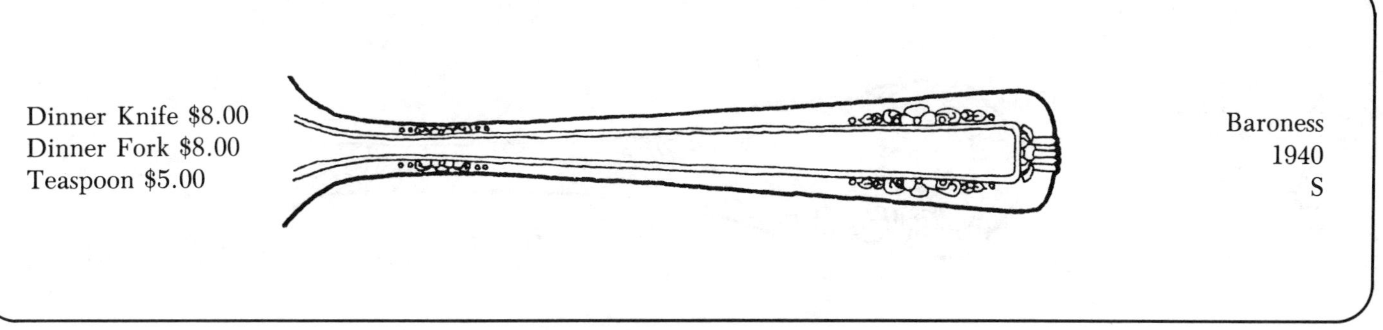

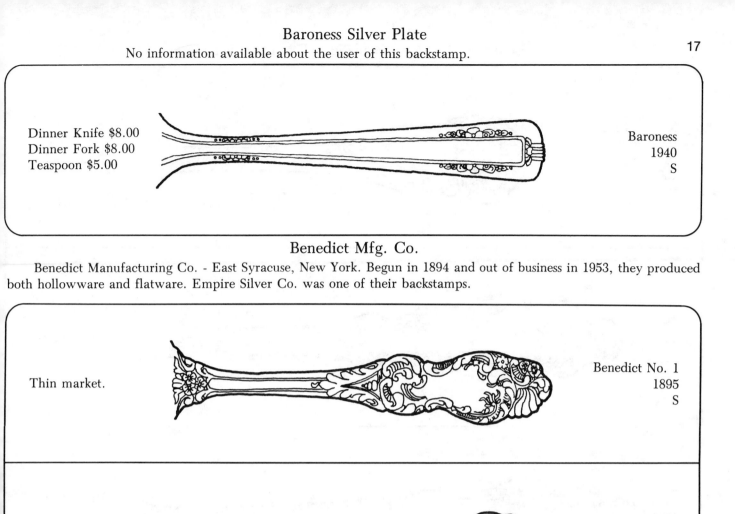

Dinner Knife $8.00
Dinner Fork $8.00
Teaspoon $5.00

Baroness
1940
S

Benedict Mfg. Co.

Benedict Manufacturing Co. - East Syracuse, New York. Begun in 1894 and out of business in 1953, they produced both hollowware and flatware. Empire Silver Co. was one of their backstamps.

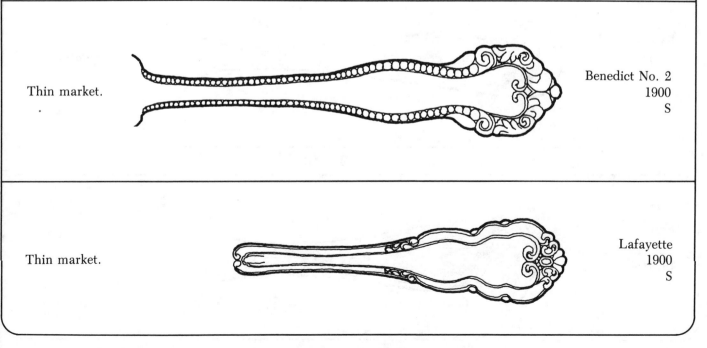

Thin market.

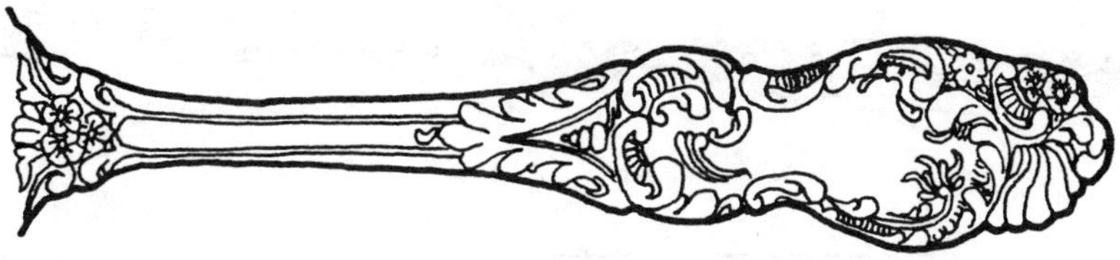

Benedict No. 1
1895
S

Thin market.

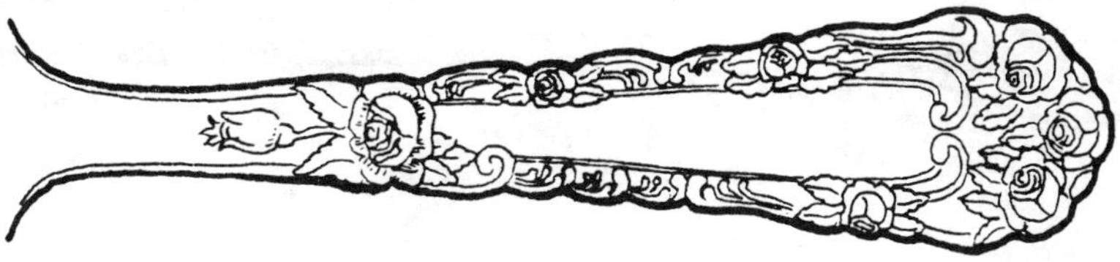

American Beauty
(Royal Plate)
(Crown Silver Plate)
1900
S

Thin market.

Benedict No. 2
1900
S

Thin market.

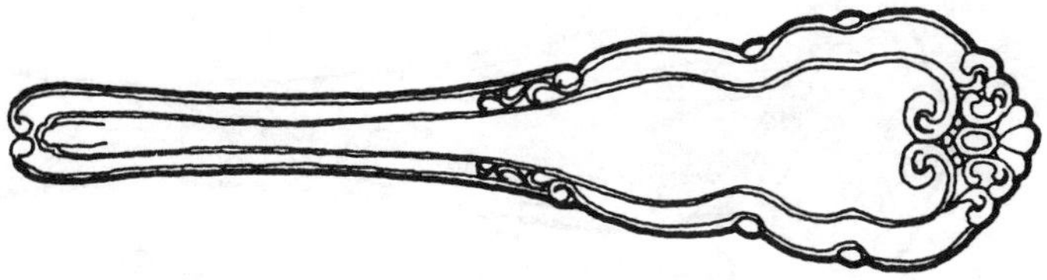

Lafayette
1900
S

Please refer to "How To Use This Book" page 4.

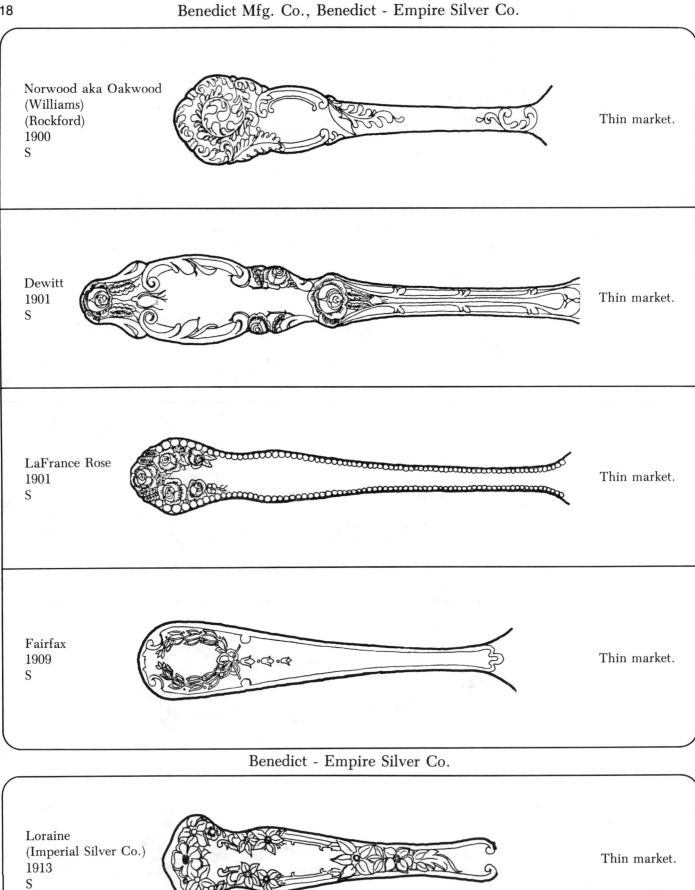

Norwood aka Oakwood
(Williams)
(Rockford)
1900
S

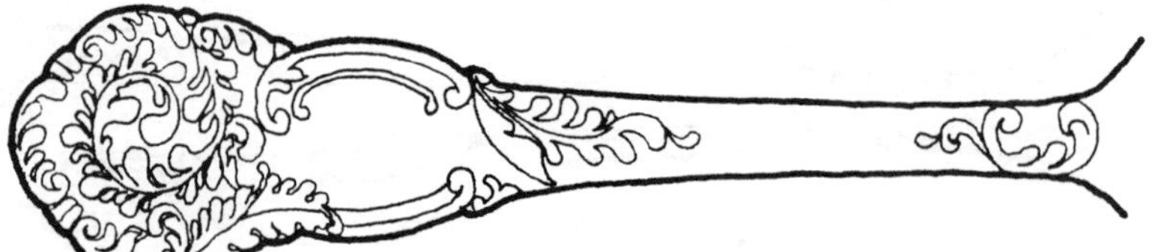

Thin market.

Dewitt
1901
S

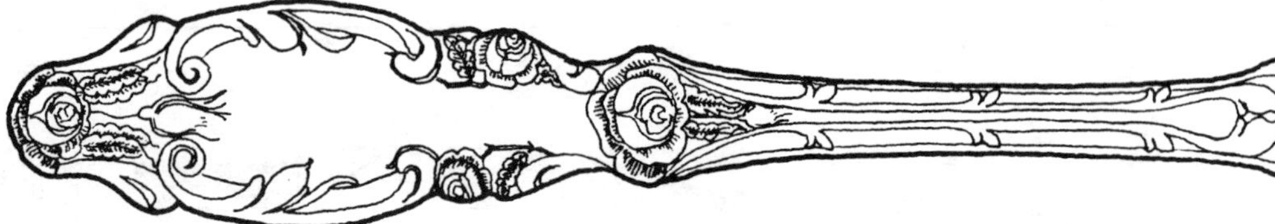

Thin market.

LaFrance Rose
1901
S

Thin market.

Fairfax
1909
S

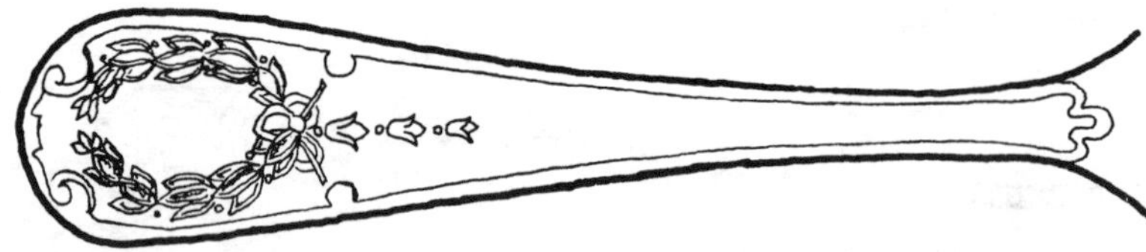

Thin market.

Benedict - Empire Silver Co.

Loraine
(Imperial Silver Co.)
1913
S

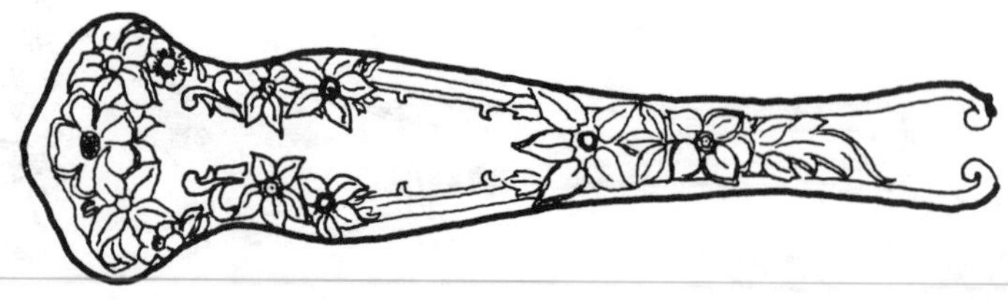

Thin market.

Please refer to "How To Use This Book" page 4.

E.A. Bliss Co., L. Boardman & Son, Crosby Silverplate

E.A. Bliss Co.

E.A. Bliss Co. - Founded in 1875 in North Attleboro, Massachusetts as Carpenter & Bliss. E.A. Bliss was the firm name from 1883 until 1920. Eventually became the Napier Company in 1922. The factory moved to Meriden, Conn. in 1890.

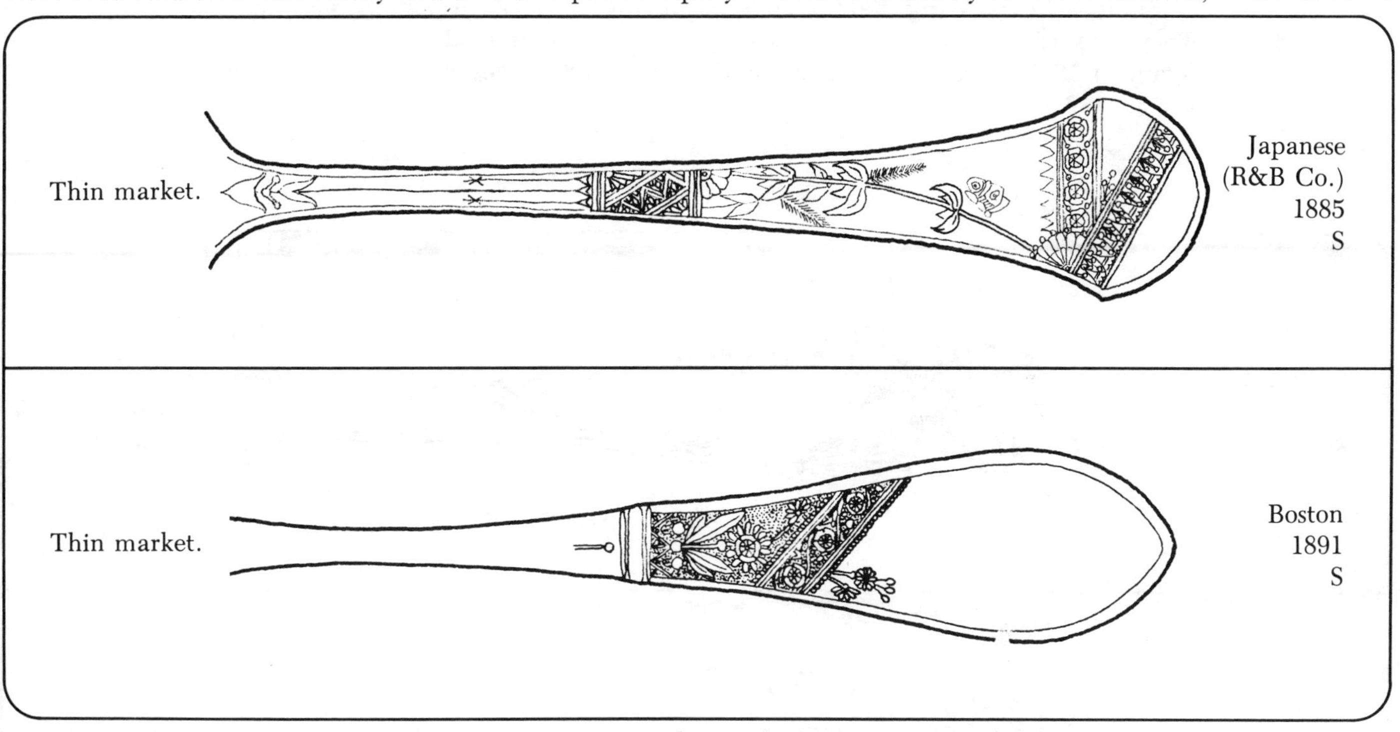

L. Boardman & Son

Luther Boardman & Son - This firm was founded in the 1820's and was out of business by 1905. The firm was located in East Haddam, Connecticut.

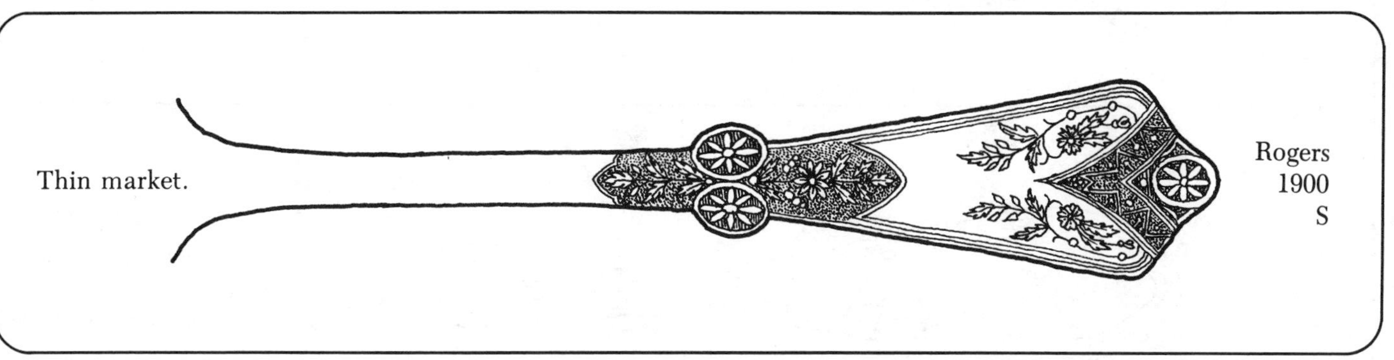

Crosby Silverplate

Crosby Silverplate is a backstamp of A Cohen & Sons of New York, New York. Founded in 1911, they wholesale silverplated flatware and hollowware which is made for them.

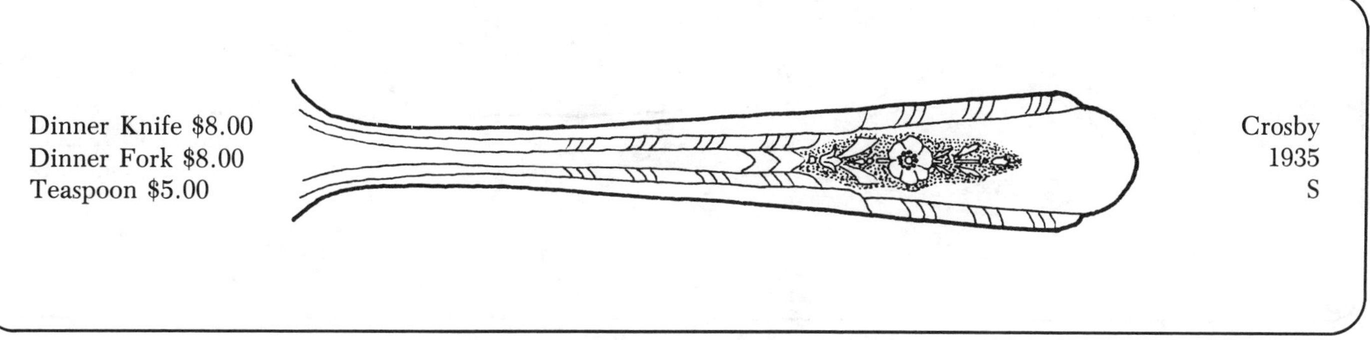

Please refer to "How To Use This Book" page 4.

Gorham - Alvin Silver Plate

The Gorham Div. of Textron, Inc., Providence, Rhode Island traces its beginnings to the early 1800's. They began producing silverplated items in 1865. They discontinued production of silverplated flatware in 1962 but began production again in 1977. Production was discontinued in 1986. They purchased Alvin Silver Co. in 1928.

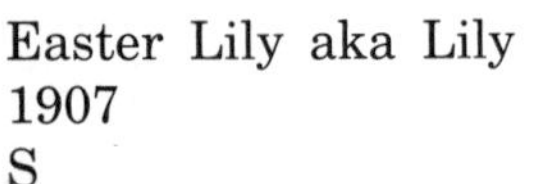

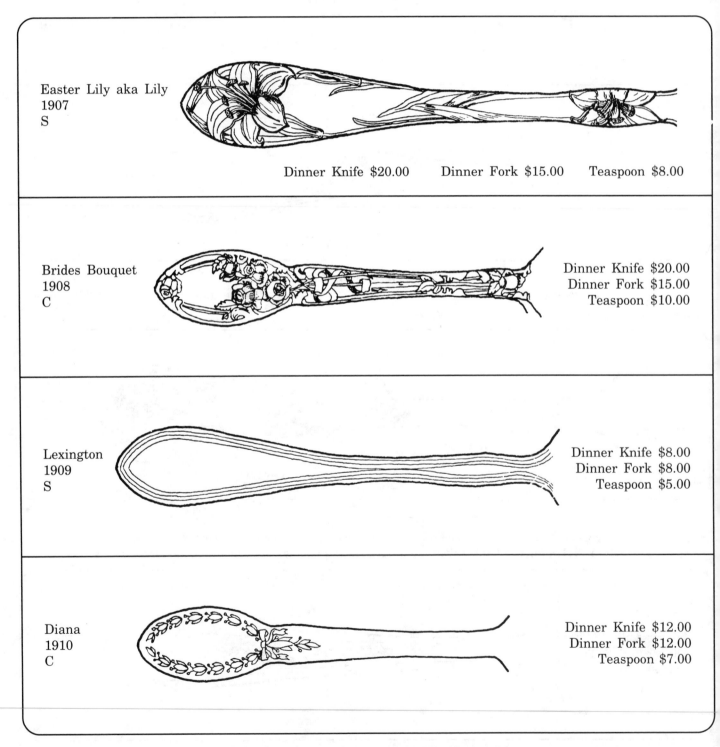

Easter Lily aka Lily
1907
S

Dinner Knife $20.00 Dinner Fork $15.00 Teaspoon $8.00

Brides Bouquet
1908
C

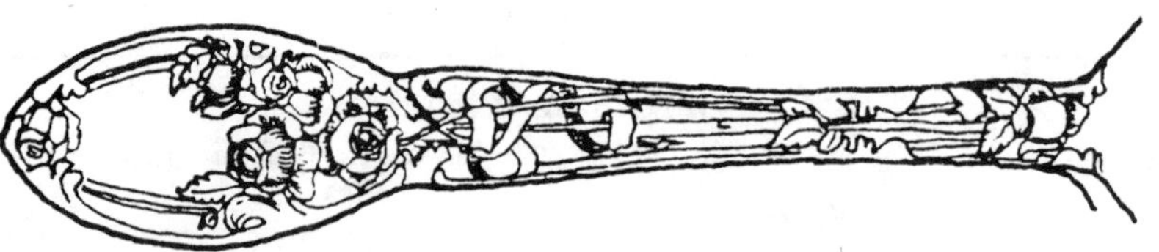

Dinner Knife $20.00
Dinner Fork $15.00
Teaspoon $10.00

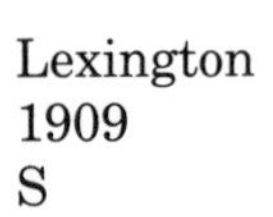

Lexington
1909
S

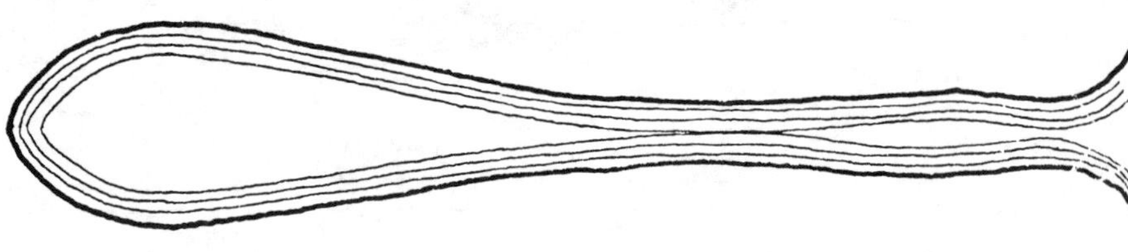

Dinner Knife $8.00
Dinner Fork $8.00
Teaspoon $5.00

Diana
1910
C

Dinner Knife $12.00
Dinner Fork $12.00
Teaspoon $7.00

Please refer to "How To Use This Book" page 4.

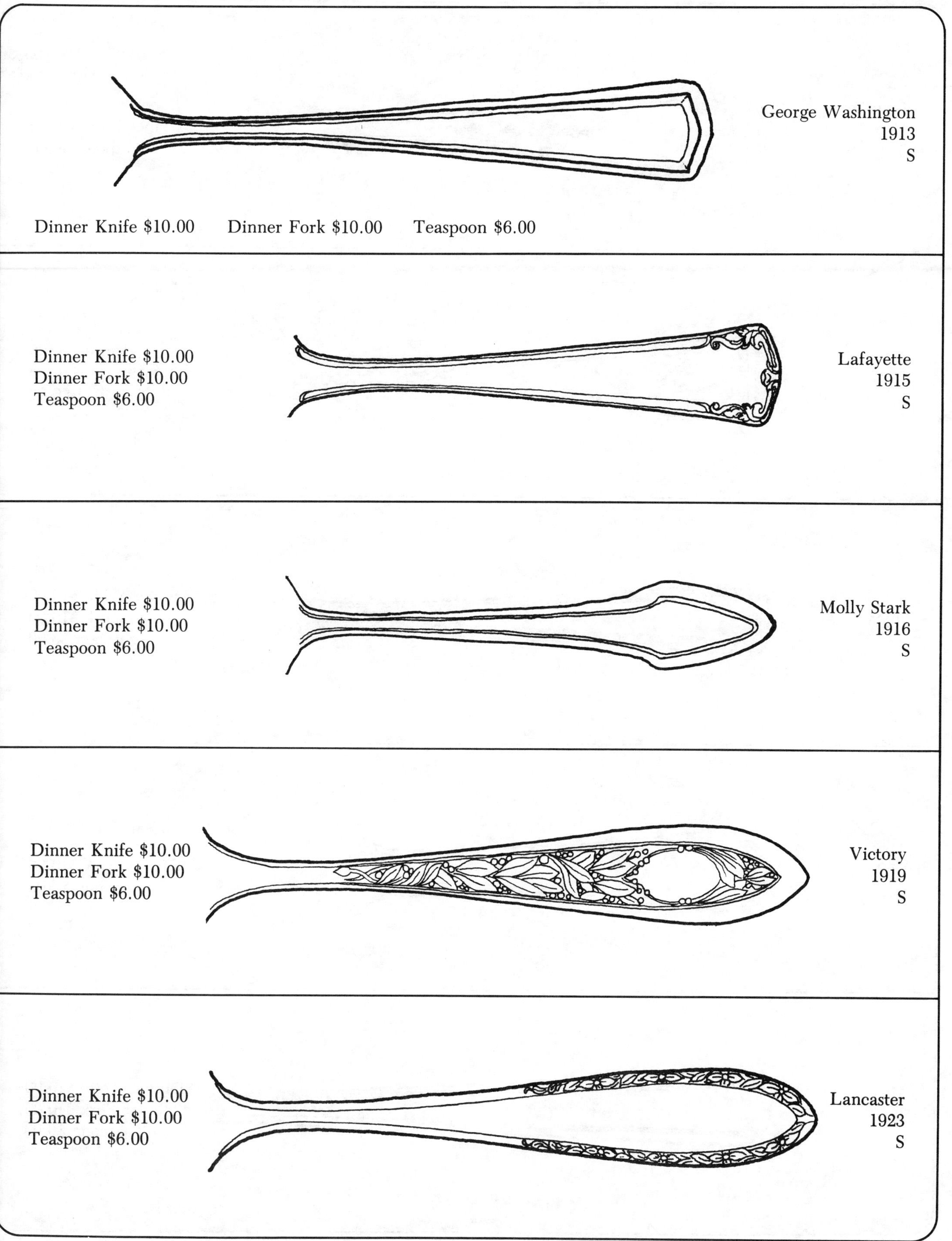

George Washington
1913
S

Dinner Knife $10.00 Dinner Fork $10.00 Teaspoon $6.00

Lafayette
1915
S

Dinner Knife $10.00
Dinner Fork $10.00
Teaspoon $6.00

Molly Stark
1916
S

Dinner Knife $10.00
Dinner Fork $10.00
Teaspoon $6.00

Victory
1919
S

Dinner Knife $10.00
Dinner Fork $10.00
Teaspoon $6.00

Lancaster
1923
S

Dinner Knife $10.00
Dinner Fork $10.00
Teaspoon $6.00

Please refer to "How To Use This Book" page 4.

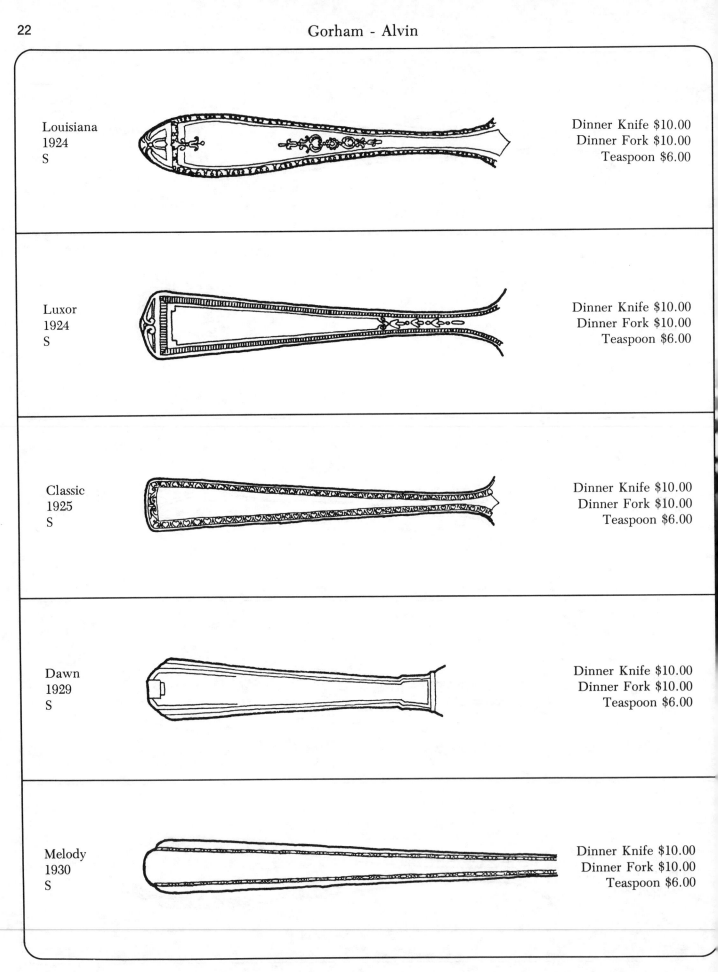

Louisiana
1924
S

Dinner Knife $10.00
Dinner Fork $10.00
Teaspoon $6.00

Luxor
1924
S

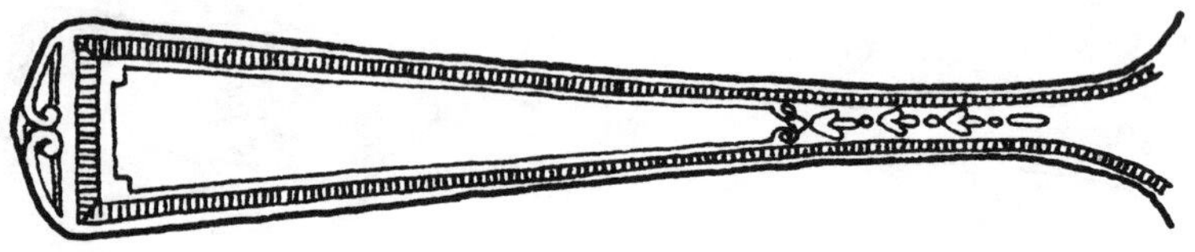

Dinner Knife $10.00
Dinner Fork $10.00
Teaspoon $6.00

Classic
1925
S

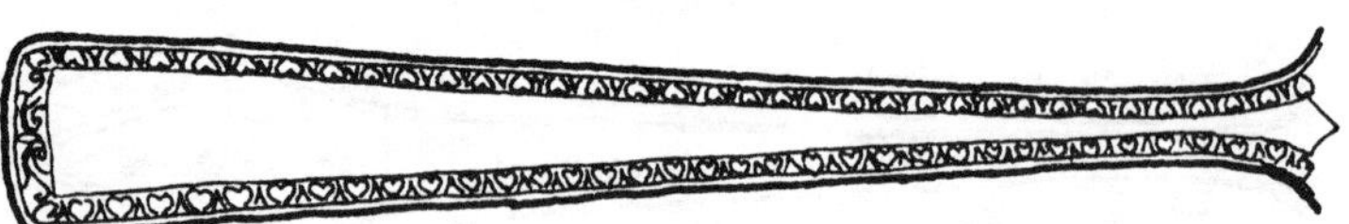

Dinner Knife $10.00
Dinner Fork $10.00
Teaspoon $6.00

Dawn
1929
S

Dinner Knife $10.00
Dinner Fork $10.00
Teaspoon $6.00

Melody
1930
S

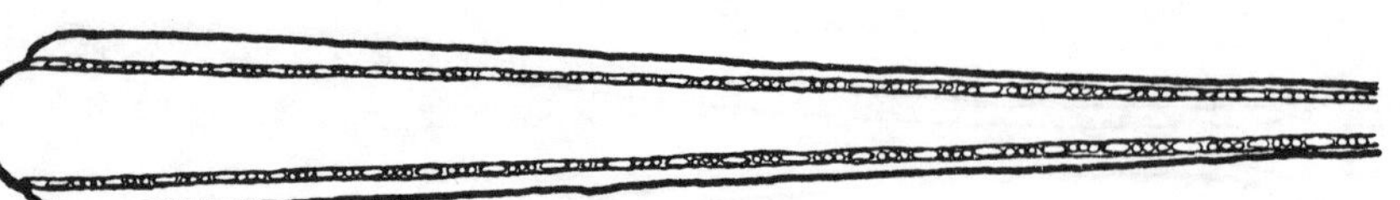

Dinner Knife $10.00
Dinner Fork $10.00
Teaspoon $6.00

Please refer to "How To Use This Book" page 4.

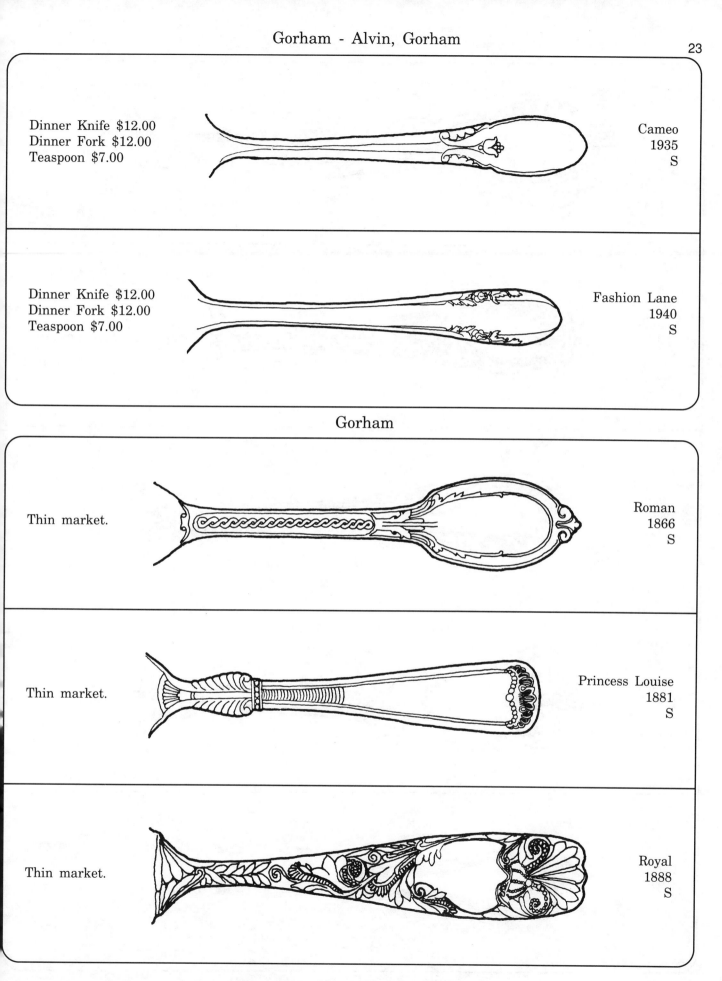

Dinner Knife $12.00
Dinner Fork $12.00
Teaspoon $7.00

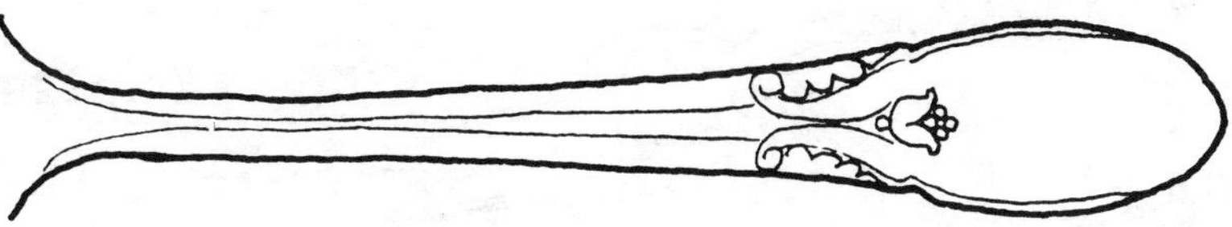

Cameo
1935
S

Dinner Knife $12.00
Dinner Fork $12.00
Teaspoon $7.00

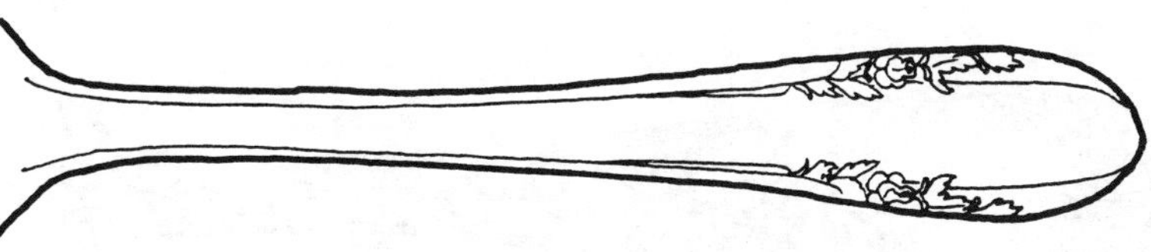

Fashion Lane
1940
S

Gorham

Thin market.

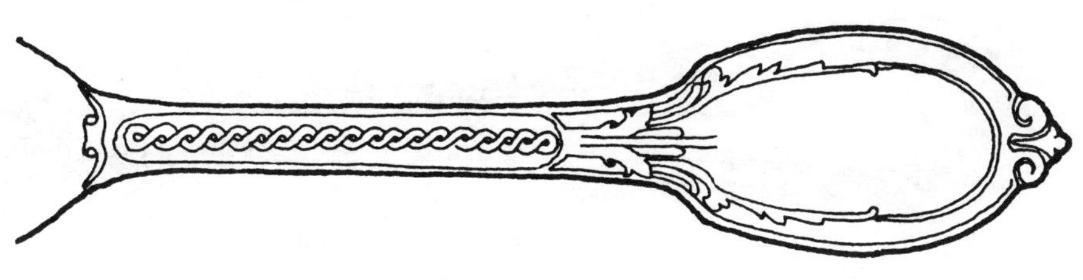

Roman
1866
S

Thin market.

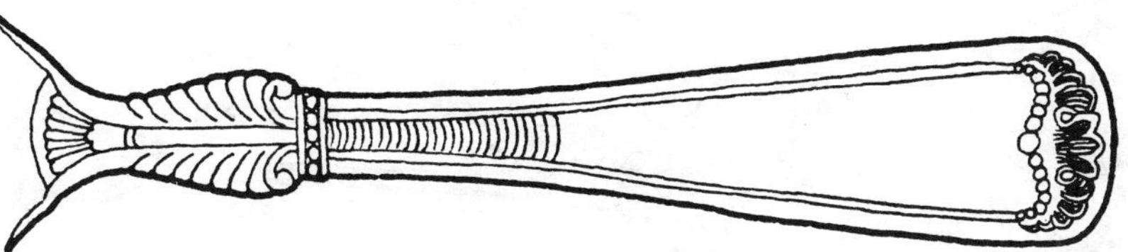

Princess Louise
1881
S

Thin market.

Royal
1888
S

Please refer to "How To Use This Book" page 4.

Saxony
1891
S

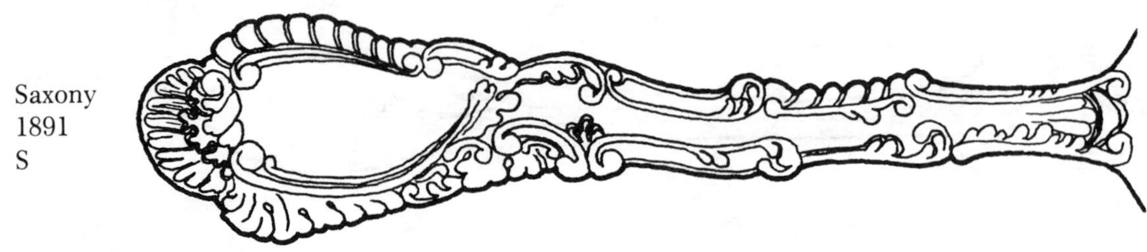

Thin market.

Carolina
1895
S

Thin market.

Winthrop
1896
S

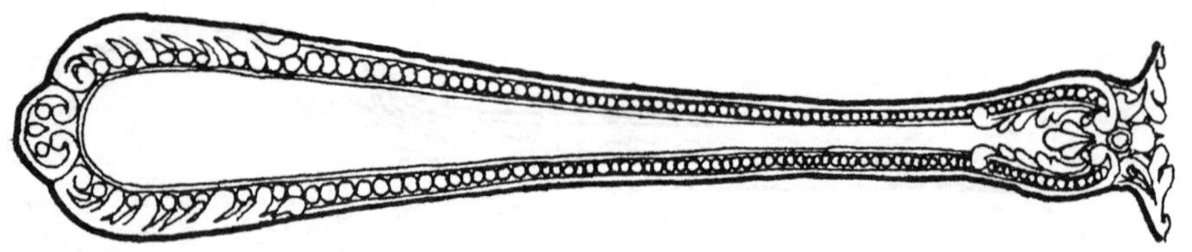

Thin market.

Richmond
1897
S

Thin market.

Radisson
1900
S

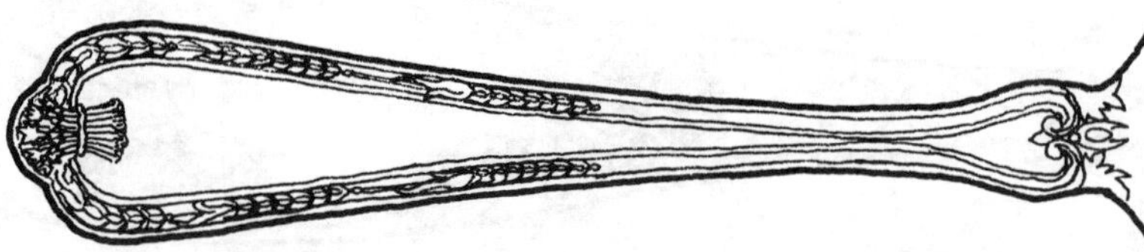

Thin market.

Please refer to "How To Use This Book" page 4.

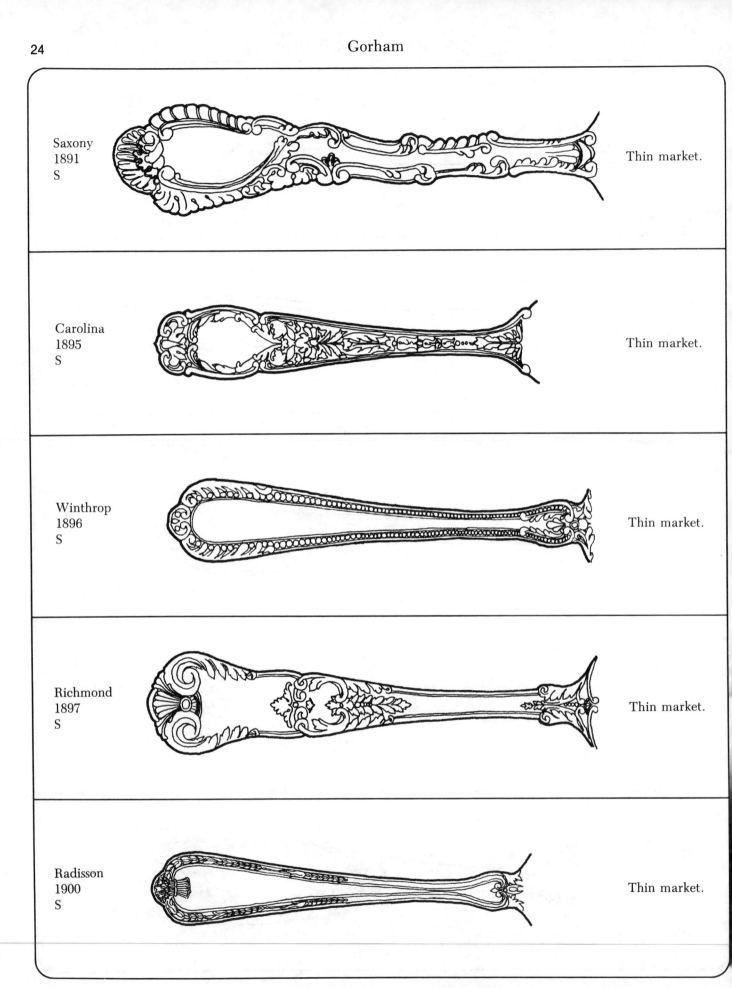

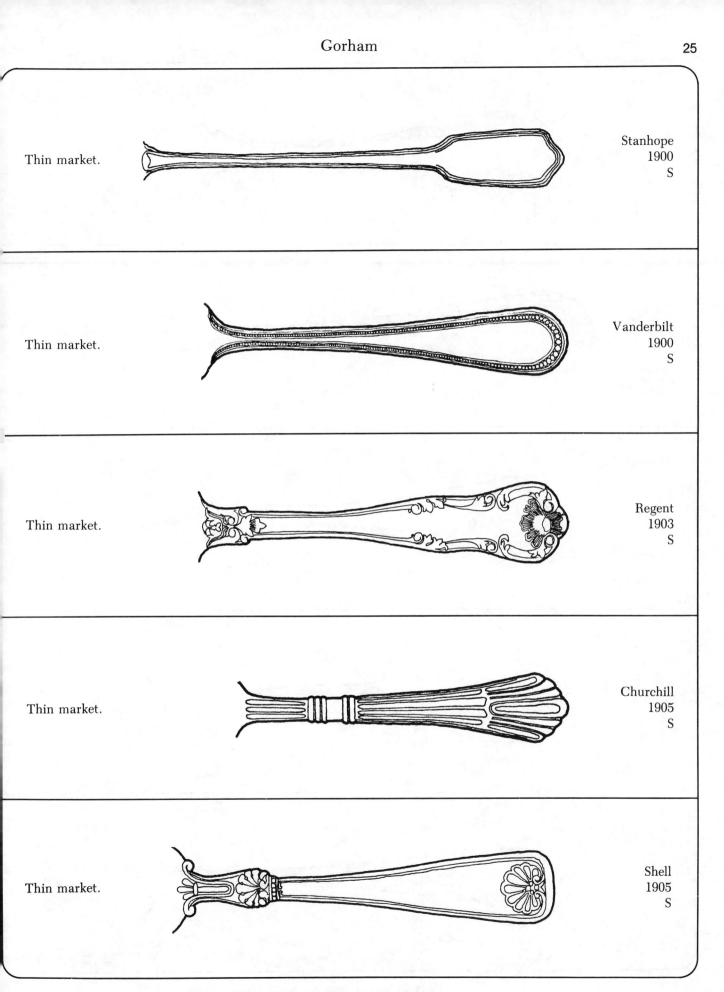

Thin market.	Stanhope 1900 S
Thin market.	Vanderbilt 1900 S
Thin market.	Regent 1903 S
Thin market.	Churchill 1905 S
Thin market.	Shell 1905 S

Please refer to "How To Use This Book" page 4.

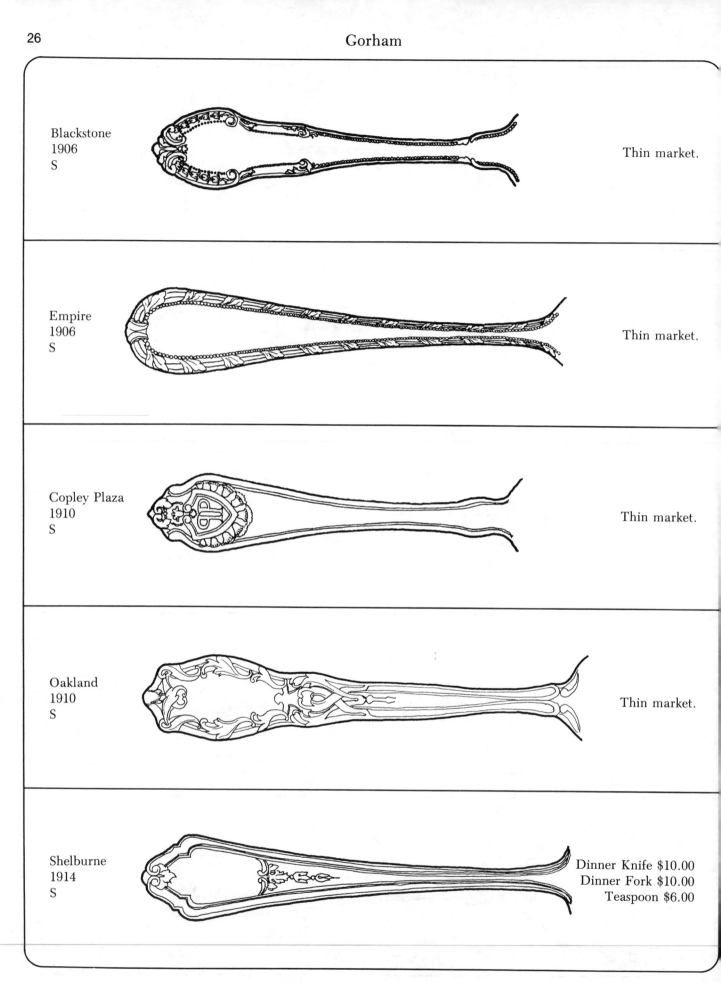

Blackstone
1906
S

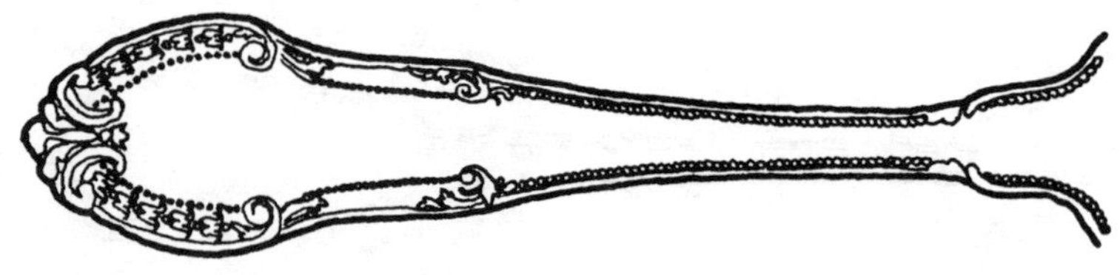

Thin market.

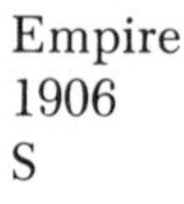

Empire
1906
S

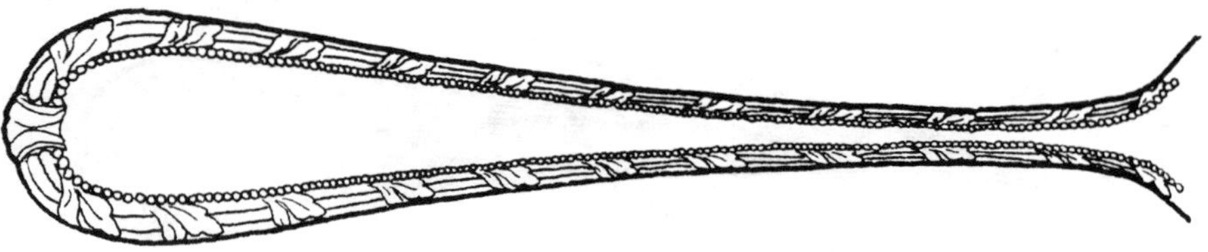

Thin market.

Copley Plaza
1910
S

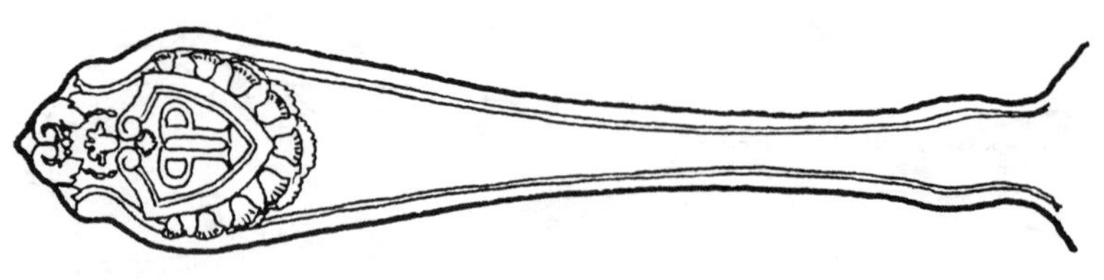

Thin market.

Oakland
1910
S

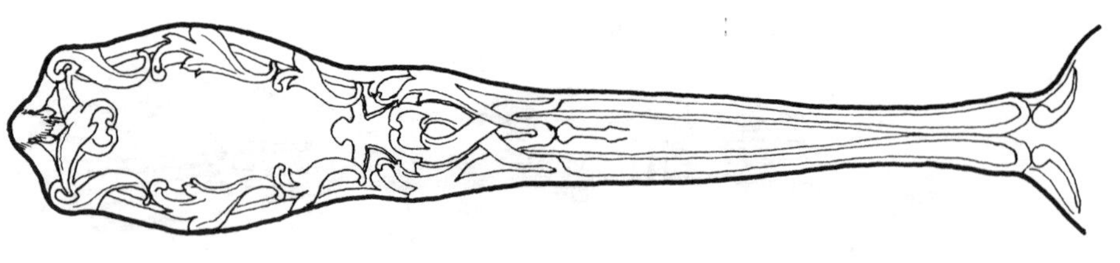

Thin market.

Shelburne
1914
S

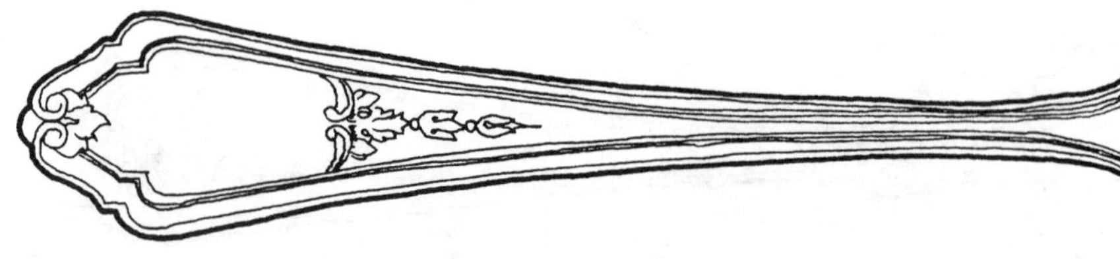

Dinner Knife $10.00
Dinner Fork $10.00
Teaspoon $6.00

Please refer to "How To Use This Book" page 4.

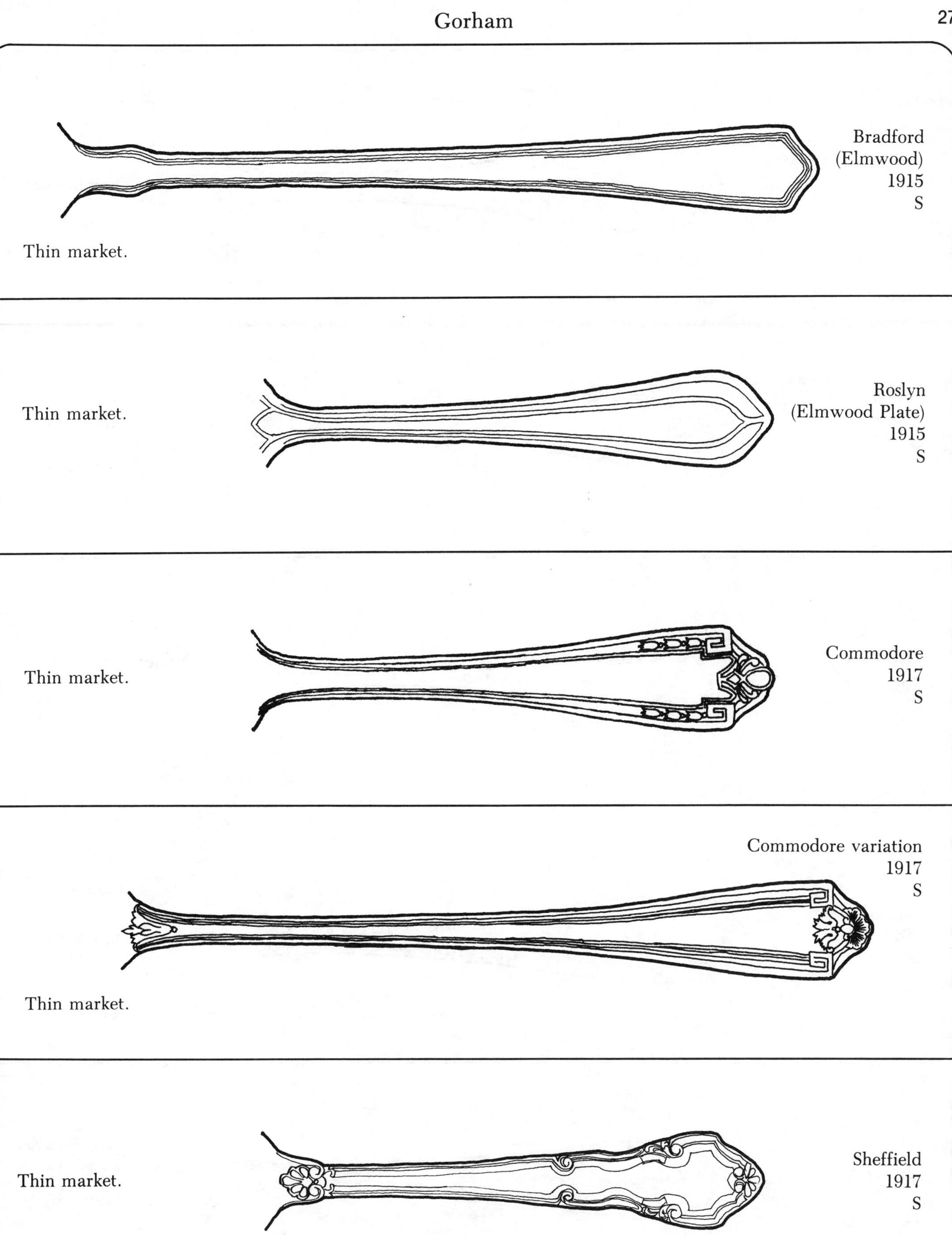
Bradford
(Elmwood)
1915
S
Thin market.
Thin market.
Roslyn
(Elmwood Plate)
1915
S
Thin market.
Commodore
1917
S
Commodore variation
1917
S
Thin market.
Thin market.
Sheffield
1917
S

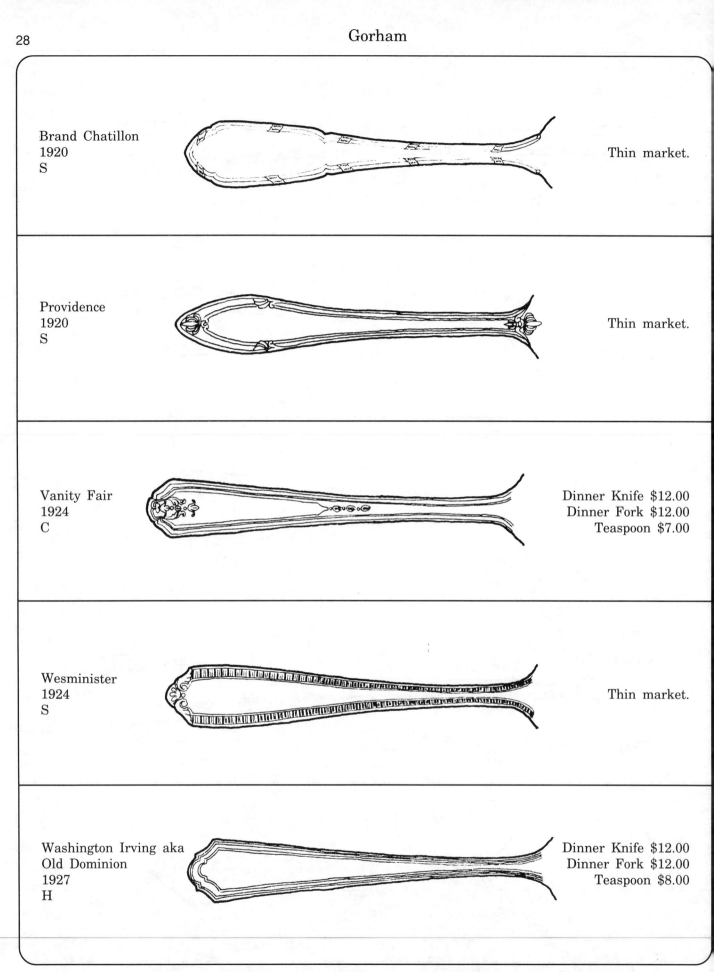

Brand Chatillon
1920
S

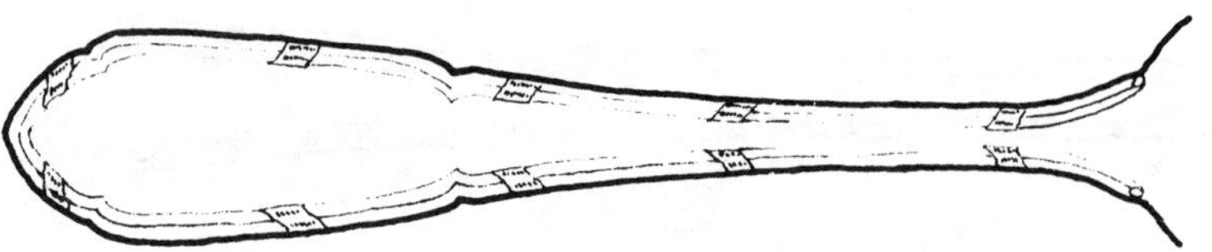

Thin market.

Providence
1920
S

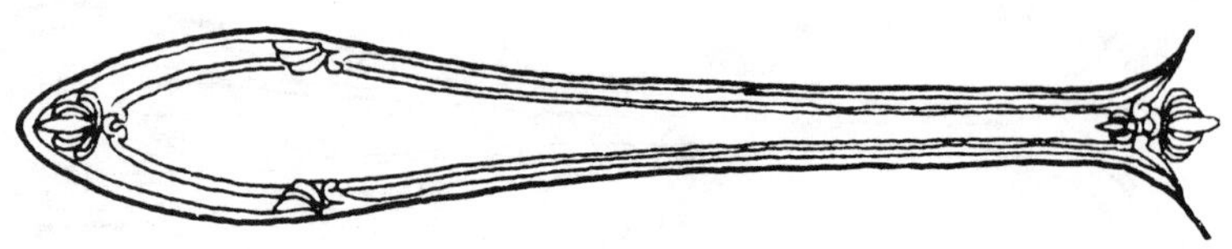

Thin market.

Vanity Fair
1924
C

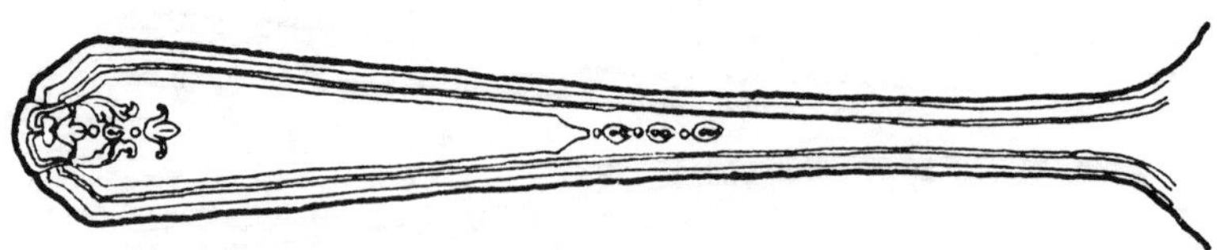

Dinner Knife $12.00
Dinner Fork $12.00
Teaspoon $7.00

Wesminister
1924
S

Thin market.

Washington Irving aka
Old Dominion
1927
H

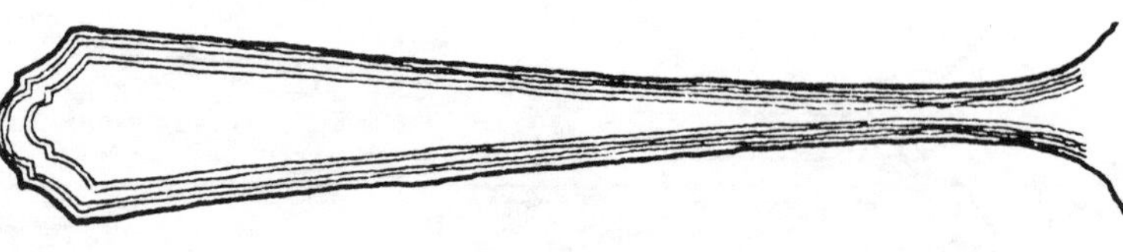

Dinner Knife $12.00
Dinner Fork $12.00
Teaspoon $8.00

Please refer to "How To Use This Book" page 4.

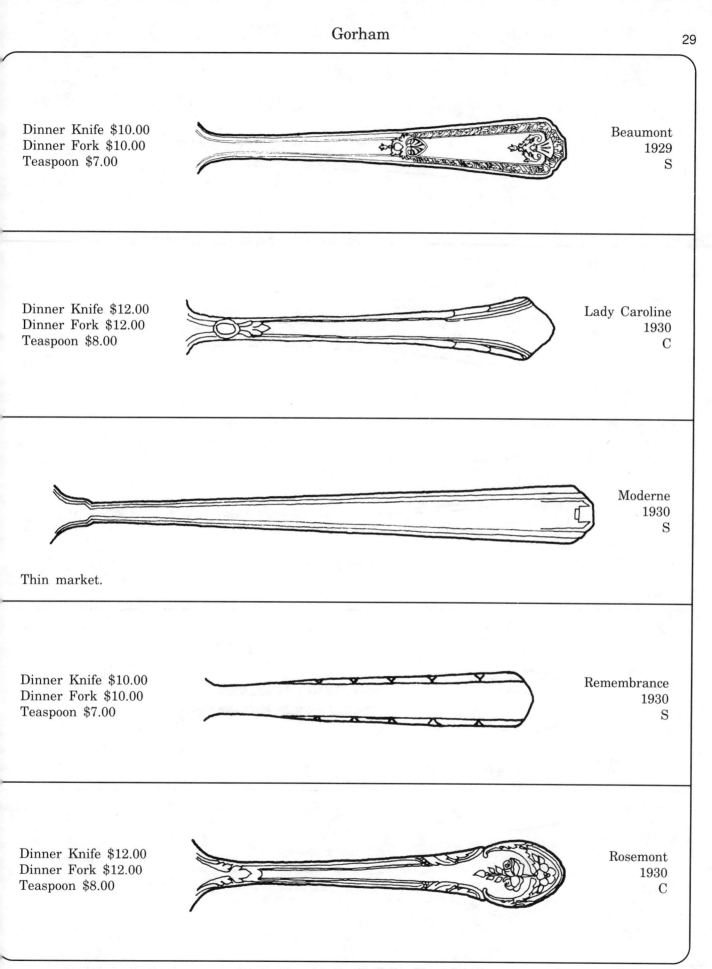

Dinner Knife $10.00
Dinner Fork $10.00
Teaspoon $7.00

Beaumont
1929
S

Dinner Knife $12.00
Dinner Fork $12.00
Teaspoon $8.00

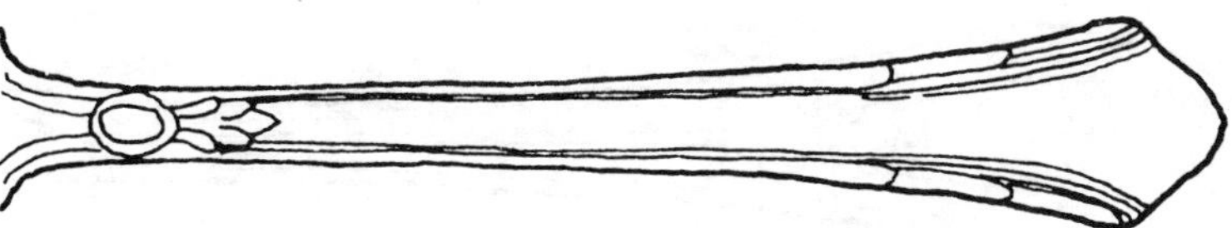

Lady Caroline
1930
C

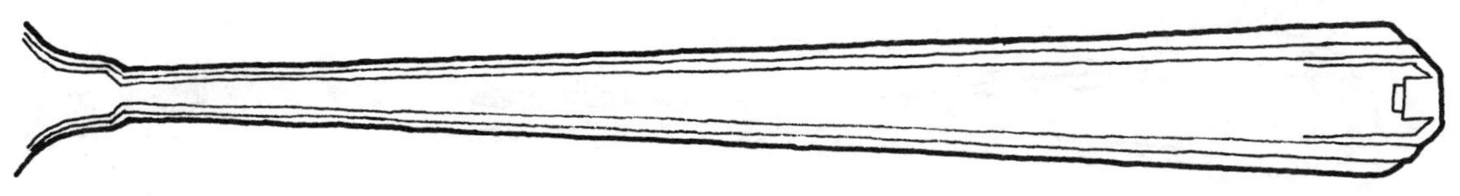

Moderne
1930
S

Thin market.

Dinner Knife $10.00
Dinner Fork $10.00
Teaspoon $7.00

Remembrance
1930
S

Dinner Knife $12.00
Dinner Fork $12.00
Teaspoon $8.00

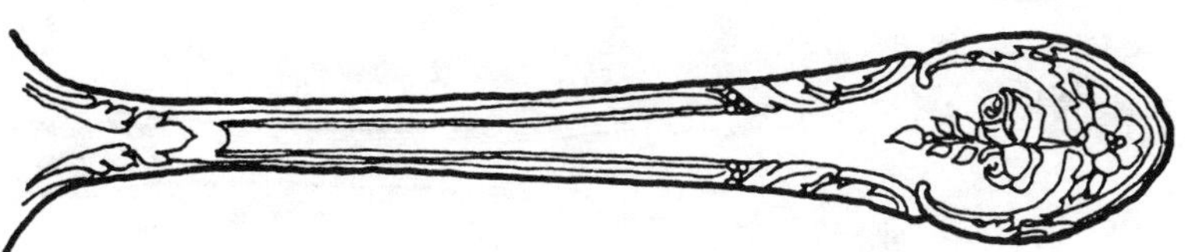

Rosemont
1930
C

Please refer to "How To Use This Book" page 4.

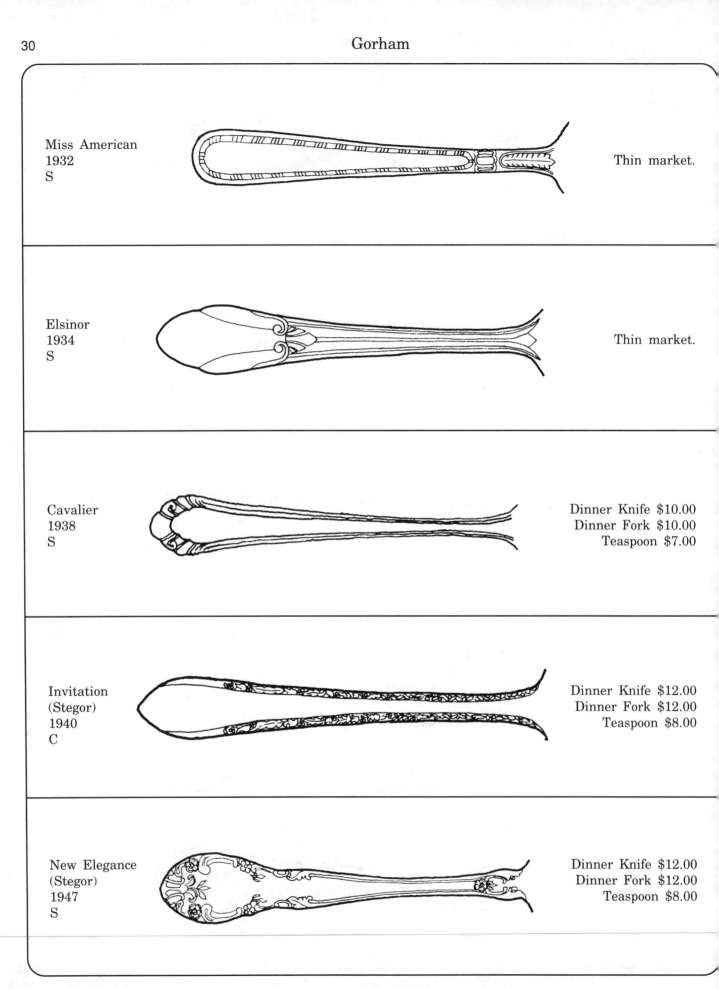

Miss American
1932
S

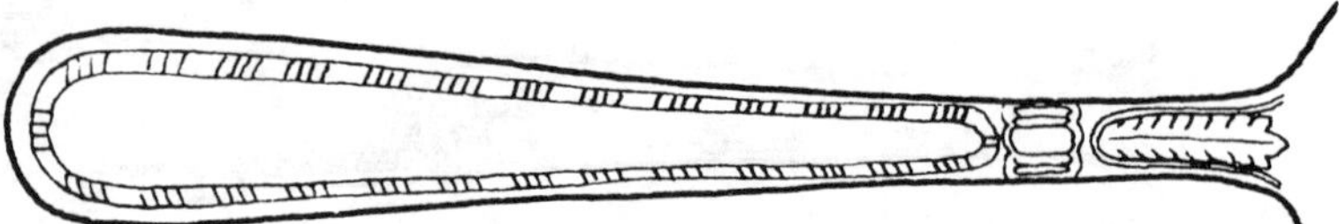

Thin market.

Elsinor
1934
S

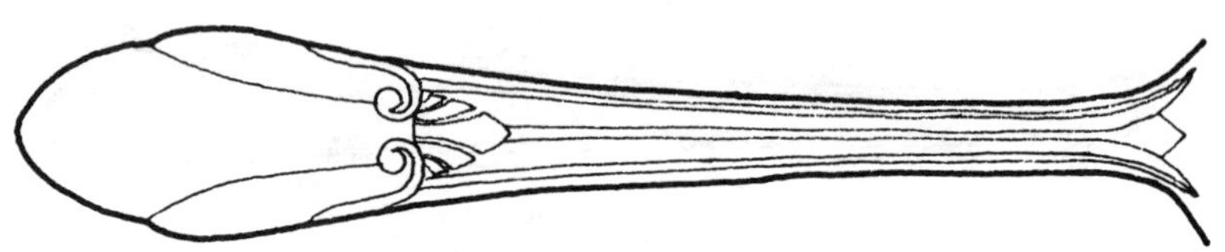

Thin market.

Cavalier
1938
S

Dinner Knife $10.00
Dinner Fork $10.00
Teaspoon $7.00

Invitation
(Stegor)
1940
C

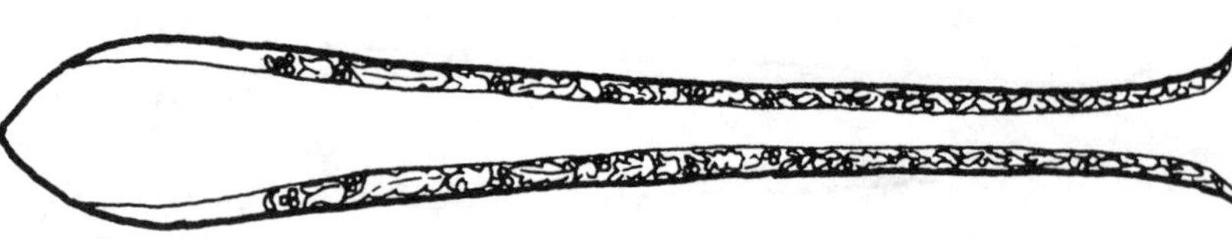

Dinner Knife $12.00
Dinner Fork $12.00
Teaspoon $8.00

New Elegance
(Stegor)
1947
S

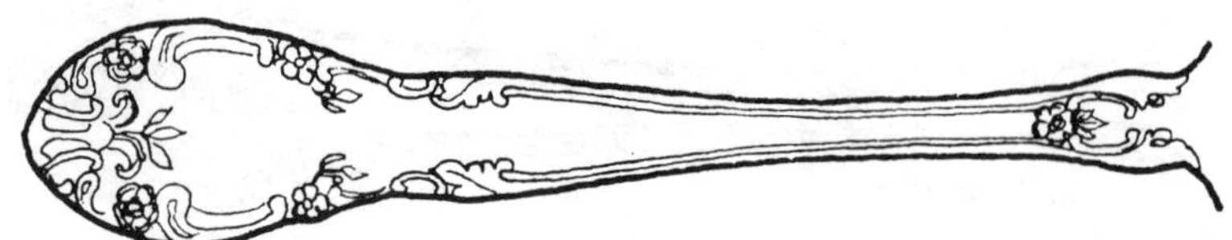

Dinner Knife $12.00
Dinner Fork $12.00
Teaspoon $8.00

Please refer to "How To Use This Book" page 4.

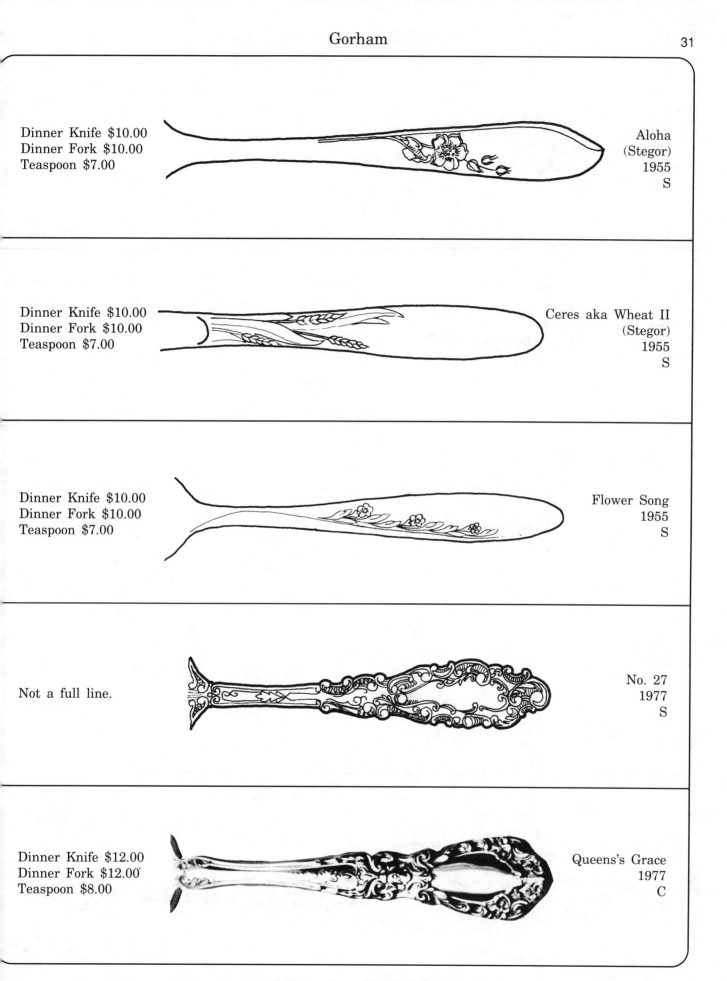

Dinner Knife $10.00
Dinner Fork $10.00
Teaspoon $7.00

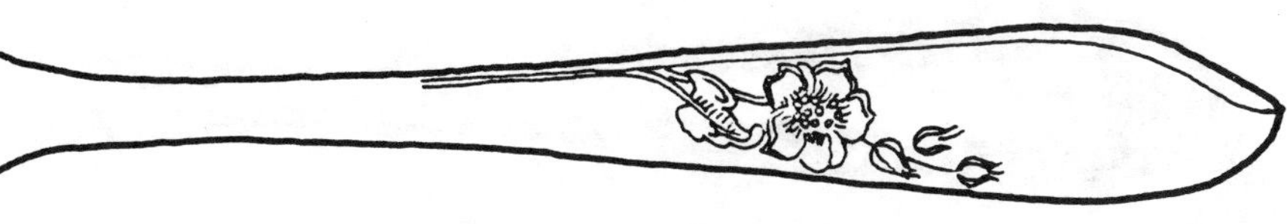

Aloha
(Stegor)
1955
S

Dinner Knife $10.00
Dinner Fork $10.00
Teaspoon $7.00

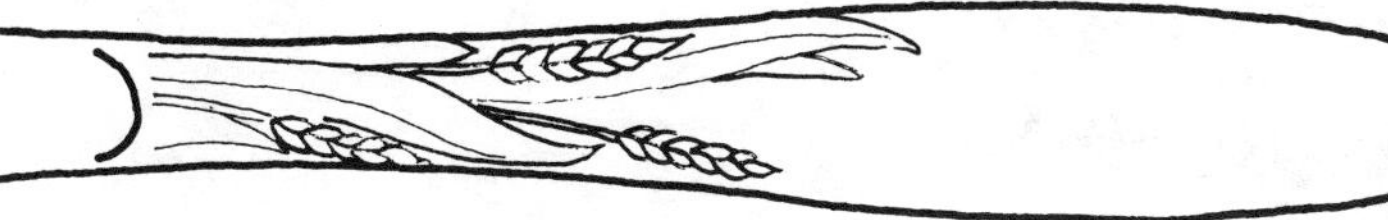

Ceres aka Wheat II
(Stegor)
1955
S

Dinner Knife $10.00
Dinner Fork $10.00
Teaspoon $7.00

Flower Song
1955
S

Not a full line.

No. 27
1977
S

Dinner Knife $12.00
Dinner Fork $12.00
Teaspoon $8.00

Queens's Grace
1977
C

Please refer to "How To Use This Book" page 4.

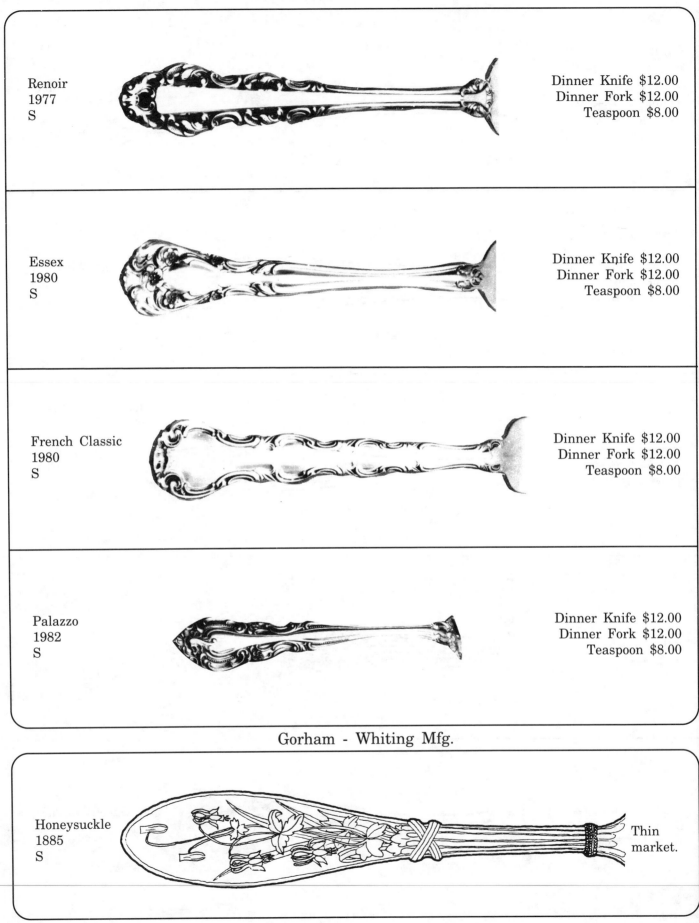

Renoir
1977
S

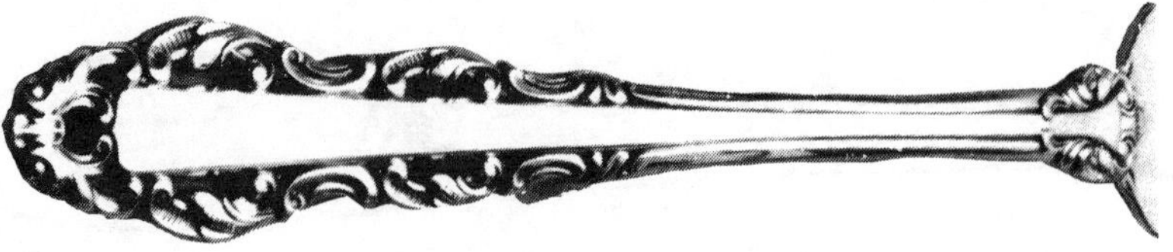

Dinner Knife $12.00
Dinner Fork $12.00
Teaspoon $8.00

Essex
1980
S

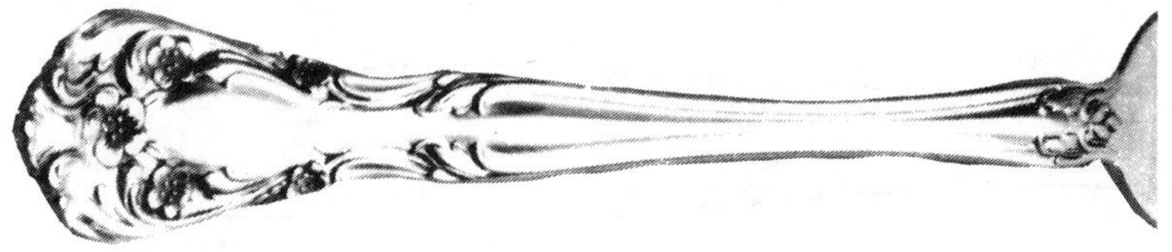

Dinner Knife $12.00
Dinner Fork $12.00
Teaspoon $8.00

French Classic
1980
S

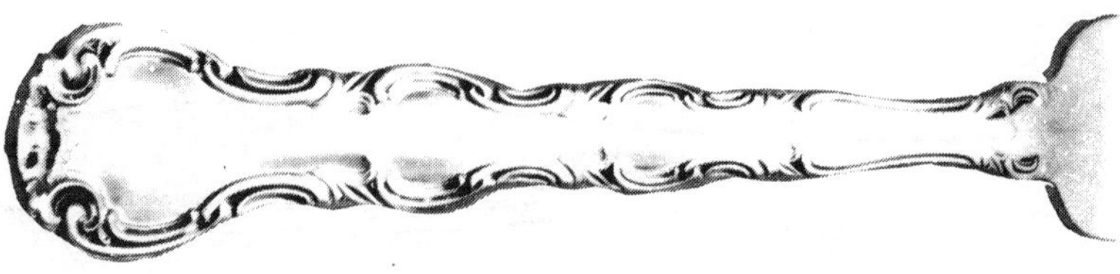

Dinner Knife $12.00
Dinner Fork $12.00
Teaspoon $8.00

Palazzo
1982
S

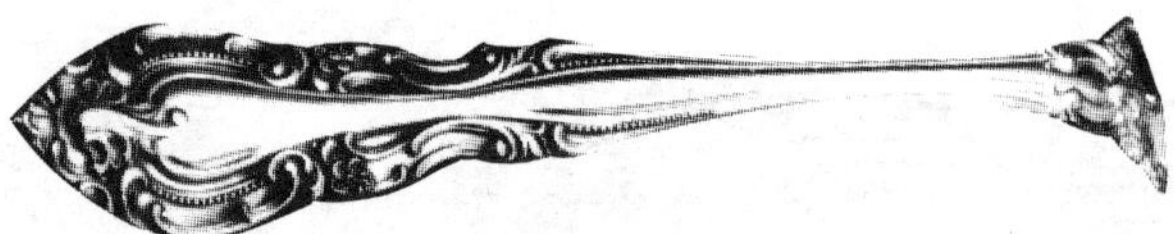

Dinner Knife $12.00
Dinner Fork $12.00
Teaspoon $8.00

Gorham - Whiting Mfg.

Honeysuckle
1885
S

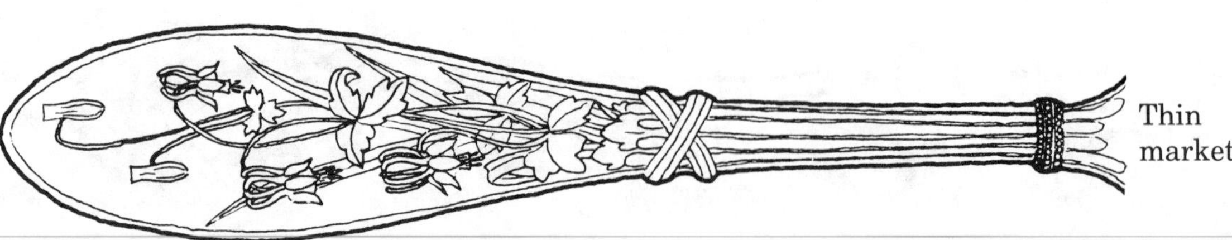

Thin market.

Please refer to "How To Use This Book" page 4.

Heritage Quadruple Plate, Hibbard Spencer Bartlett & Co. - Our Very Best

No information available about the user of this backstamp.

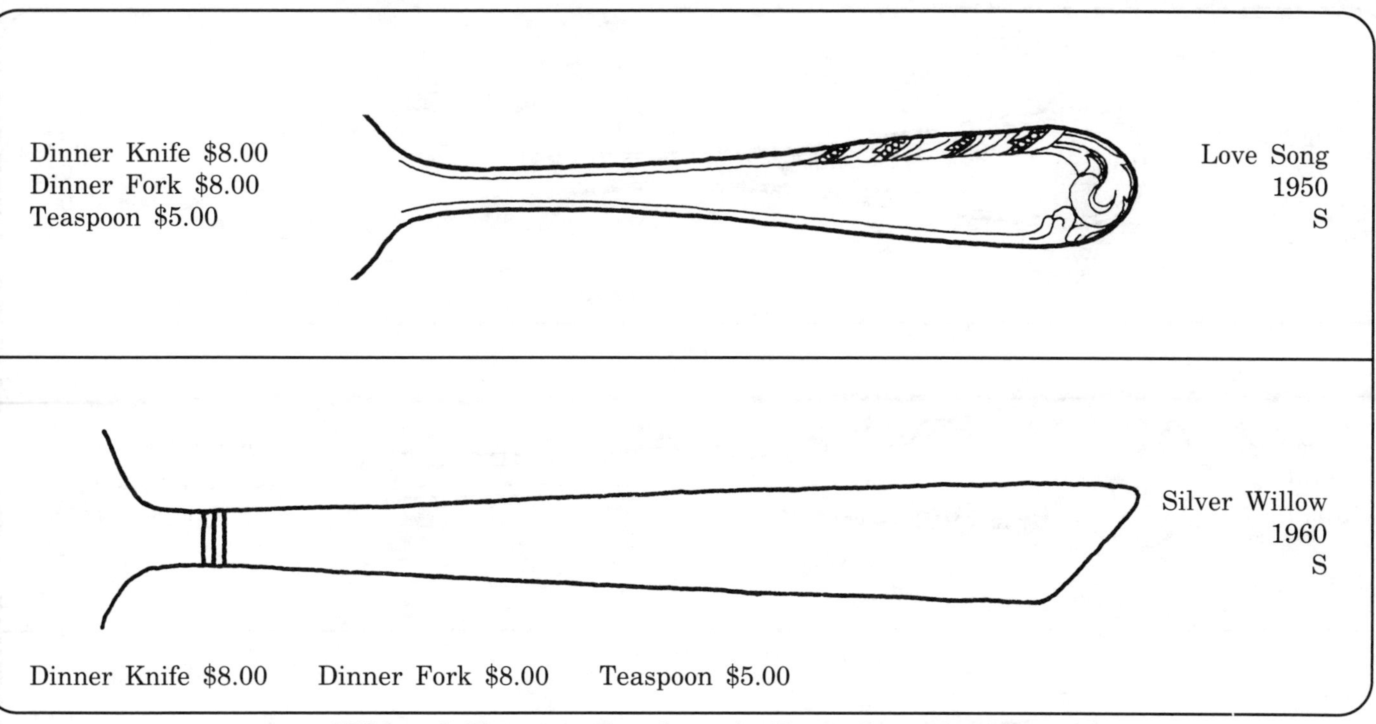

Dinner Knife $8.00
Dinner Fork $8.00
Teaspoon $5.00

Love Song
1950
S

Silver Willow
1960
S

Dinner Knife $8.00 Dinner Fork $8.00 Teaspoon $5.00

Hibbard Spencer Bartlett & Co. - Our Very Best

Hibbard, Spencer Bartlett & Co. - Chicago, Illinois. A hardware firm that used the backstamp "Our Very Best" on plated flatware and hollowware.

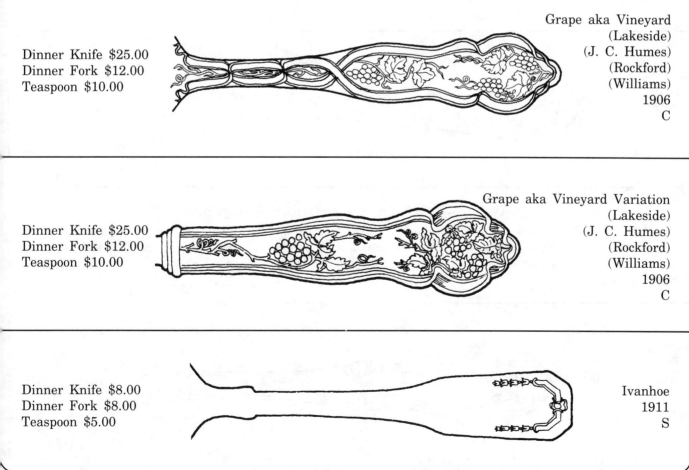

Dinner Knife $25.00
Dinner Fork $12.00
Teaspoon $10.00

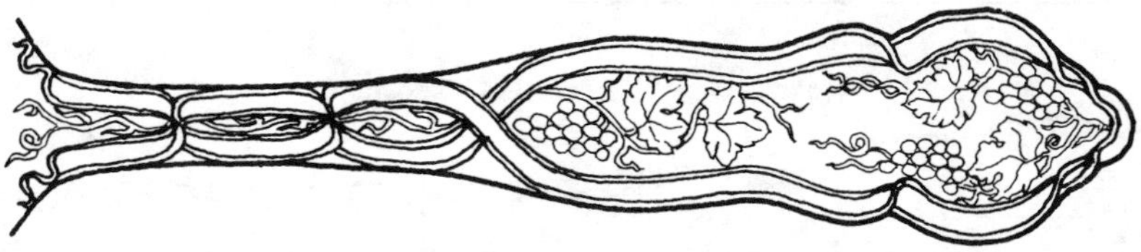

Grape aka Vineyard
(Lakeside)
(J. C. Humes)
(Rockford)
(Williams)
1906
C

Dinner Knife $25.00
Dinner Fork $12.00
Teaspoon $10.00

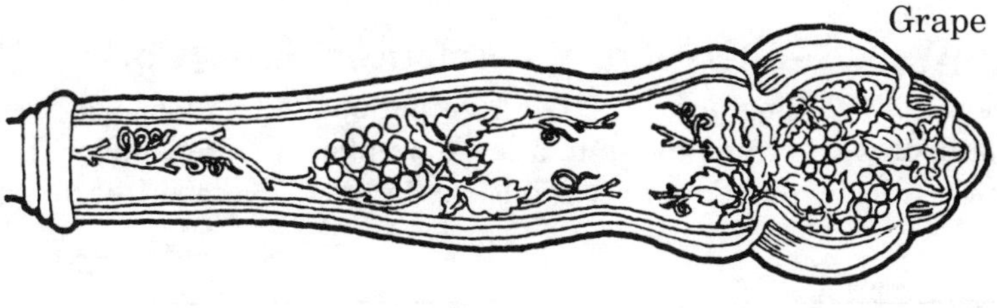

Grape aka Vineyard Variation
(Lakeside)
(J. C. Humes)
(Rockford)
(Williams)
1906
C

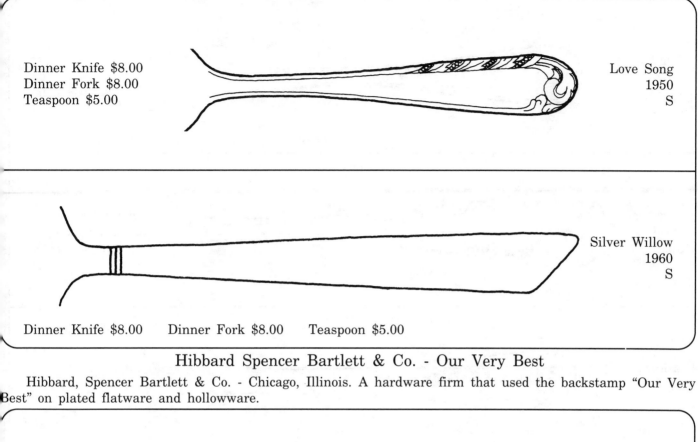

Dinner Knife $8.00
Dinner Fork $8.00
Teaspoon $5.00

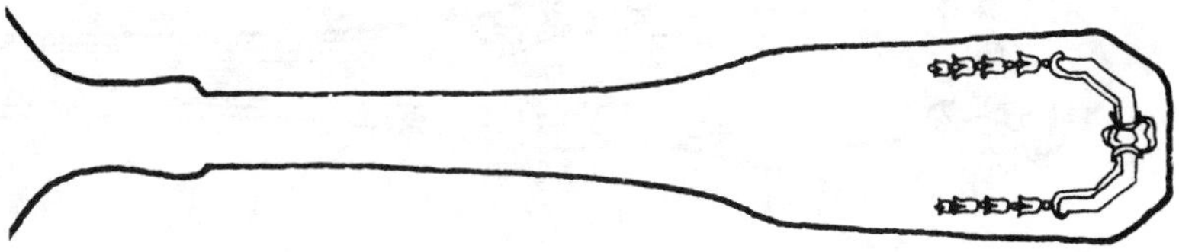

Ivanhoe
1911
S

Please refer to "How To Use This Book" page 4.

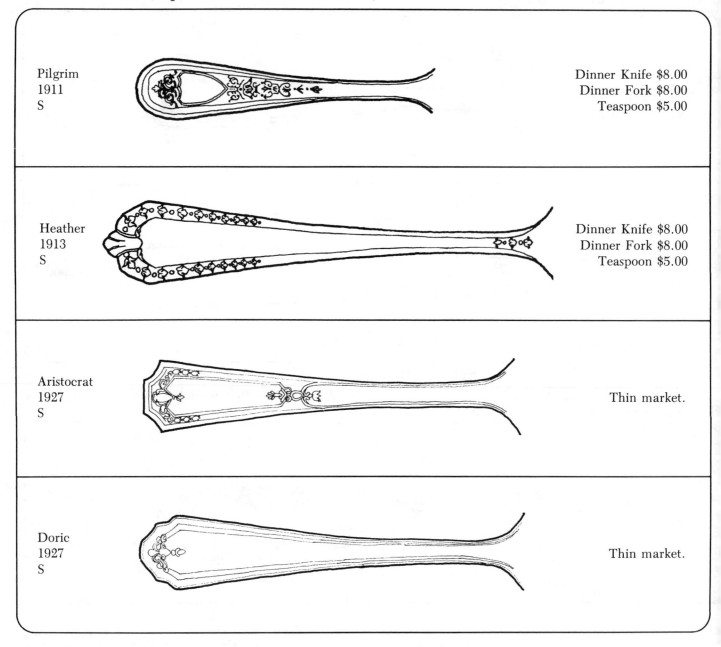

Pilgrim 1911 S	Dinner Knife $8.00 Dinner Fork $8.00 Teaspoon $5.00
Heather 1913 S	Dinner Knife $8.00 Dinner Fork $8.00 Teaspoon $5.00
Aristocrat 1927 S	Thin market.
Doric 1927 S	Thin market.

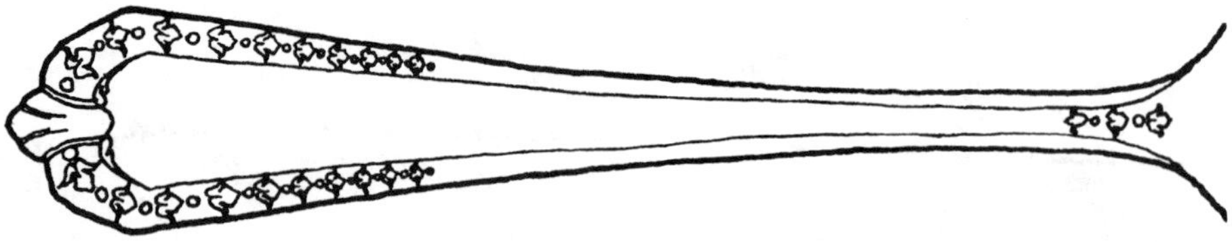

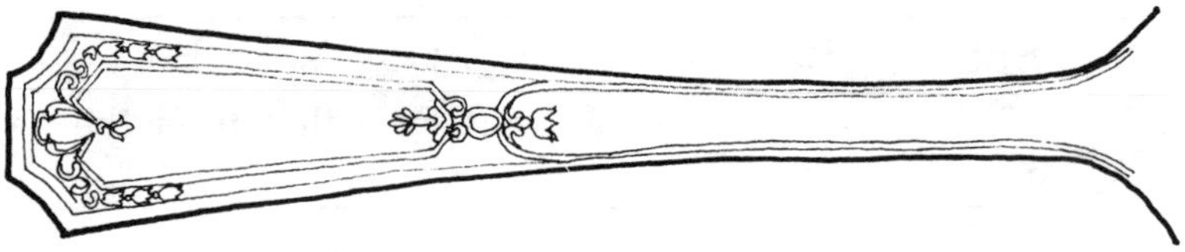

Wallace-International - American Silver Co.

Wallace-International Silver Co. - Wallingford, CT. The International Silver Co. was incorporated in 1898.It could trace its origins to the early 1800's. It was formed by quite a large number of independent firms. Both the International Silver Co. and Wallace Silversmiths were acquired by Katy Industries in 1984. Wallace-International was sold to an investor group late in 1986.

Berlin
(1897 Butler Bros.)
1889
S

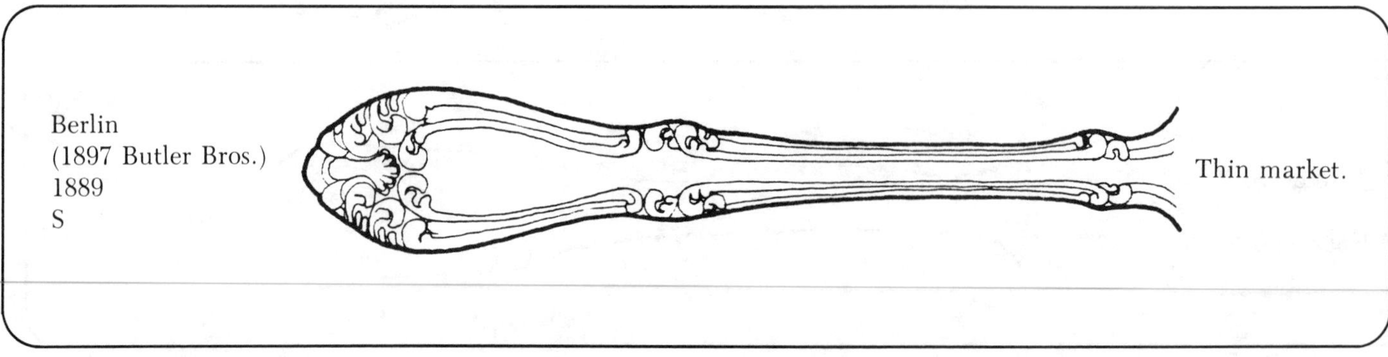

Thin market.

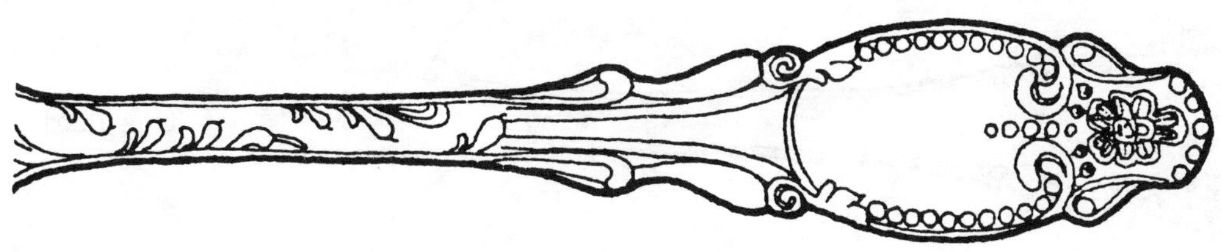

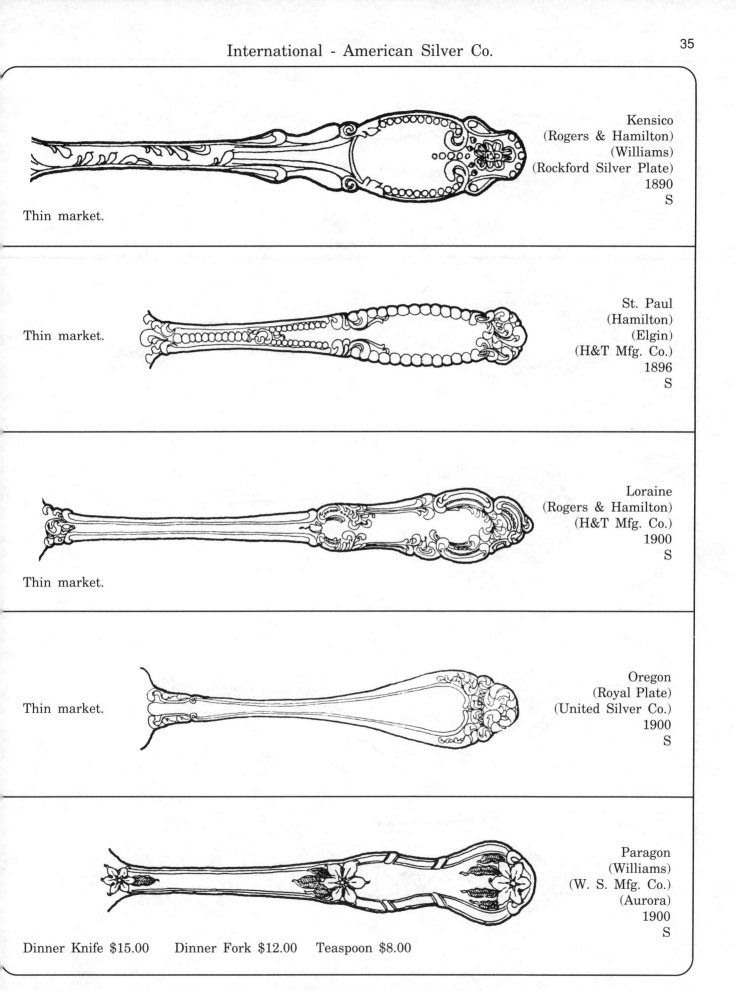

Kensico
(Rogers & Hamilton)
(Williams)
(Rockford Silver Plate)
1890
S

Thin market.

Thin market.

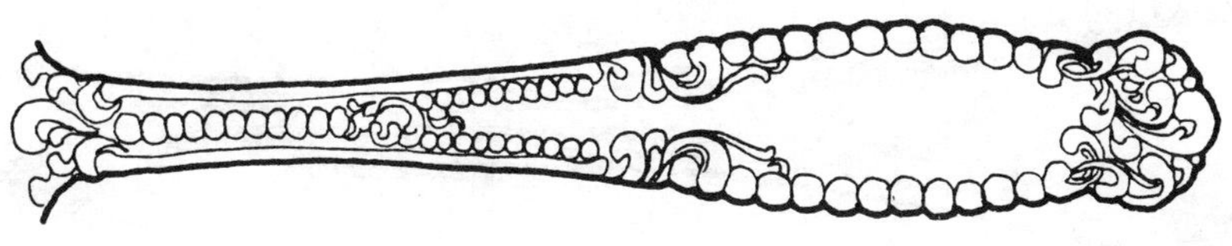

St. Paul
(Hamilton)
(Elgin)
(H&T Mfg. Co.)
1896
S

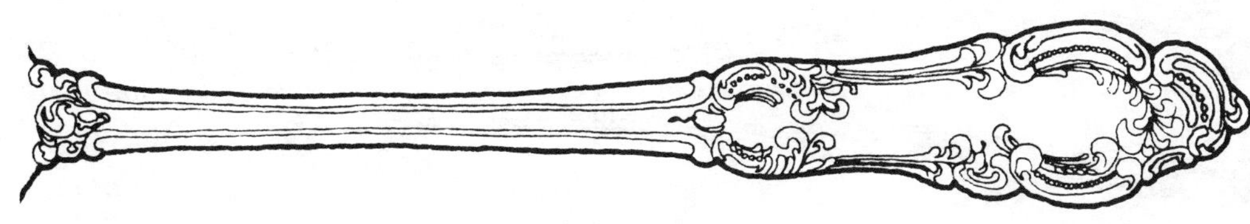

Loraine
(Rogers & Hamilton)
(H&T Mfg. Co.)
1900
S

Thin market.

Thin market.

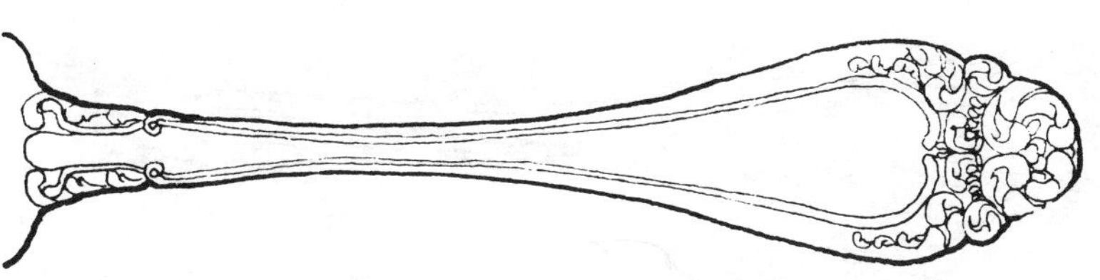

Oregon
(Royal Plate)
(United Silver Co.)
1900
S

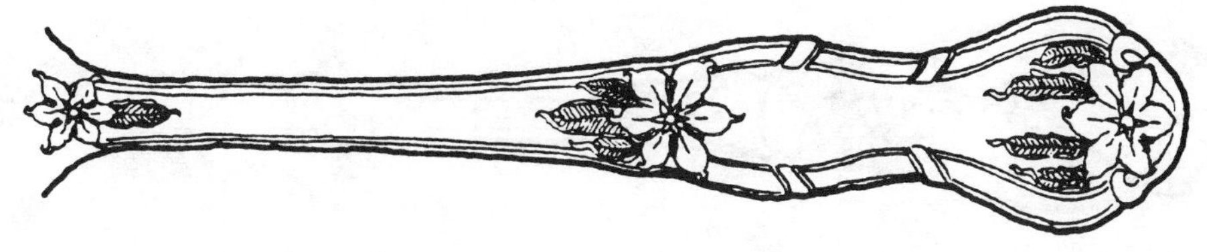

Paragon
(Williams)
(W. S. Mfg. Co.)
(Aurora)
1900
S

Dinner Knife $15.00 Dinner Fork $12.00 Teaspoon $8.00

Please refer to "How To Use This Book" page 4.

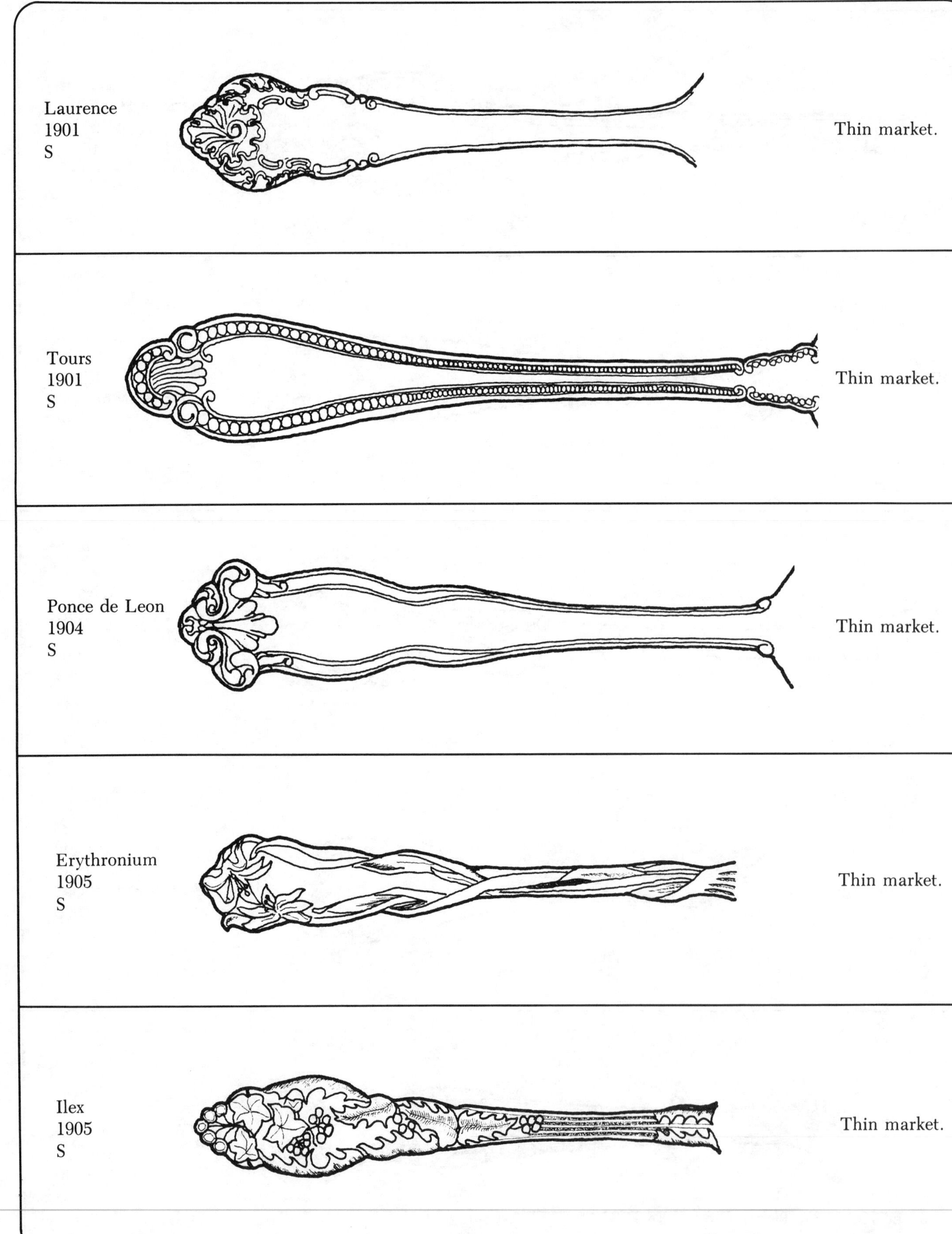

Please refer to "How To Use This Book" page 4.

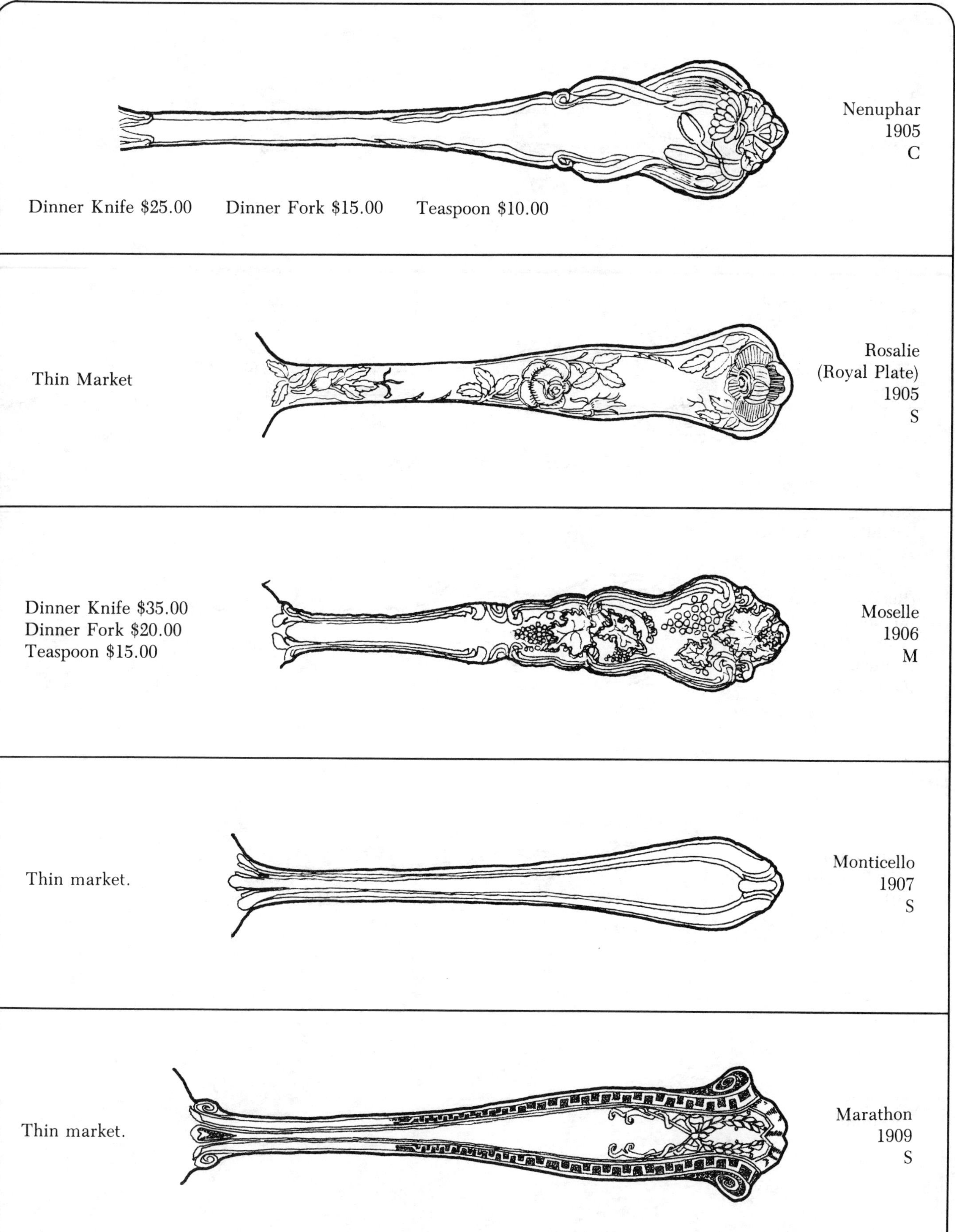

Nenuphar
1905
C

Dinner Knife $25.00 Dinner Fork $15.00 Teaspoon $10.00

Rosalie
(Royal Plate)
1905
S

Thin Market

Moselle
1906
M

Dinner Knife $35.00
Dinner Fork $20.00
Teaspoon $15.00

Monticello
1907
S

Thin market.

Marathon
1909
S

Thin market.

Please refer to "How To Use This Book" page 4.

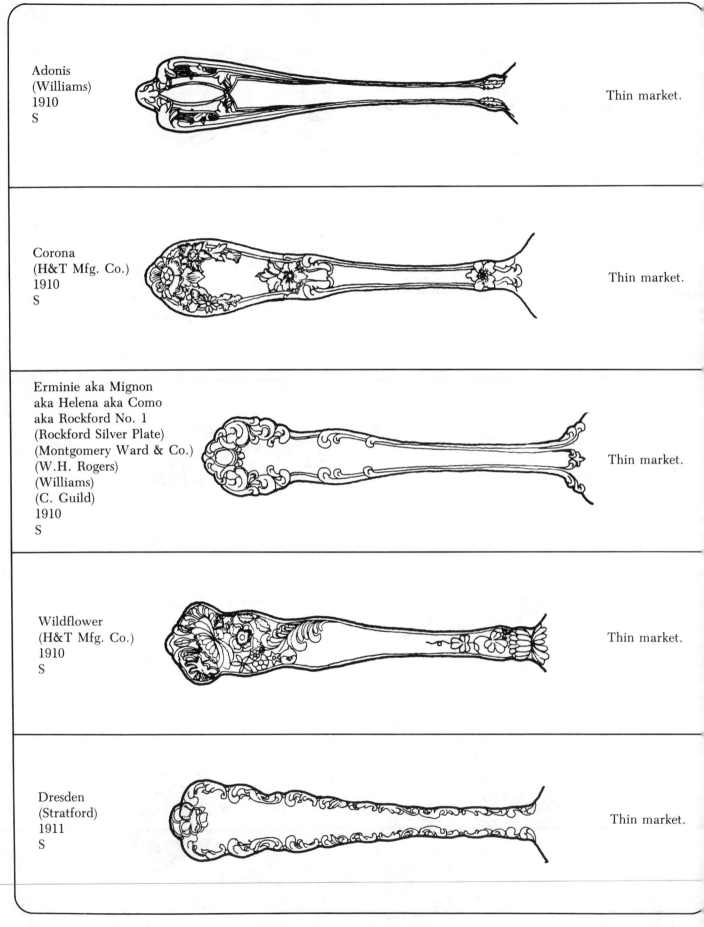

Adonis
(Williams)
1910
S

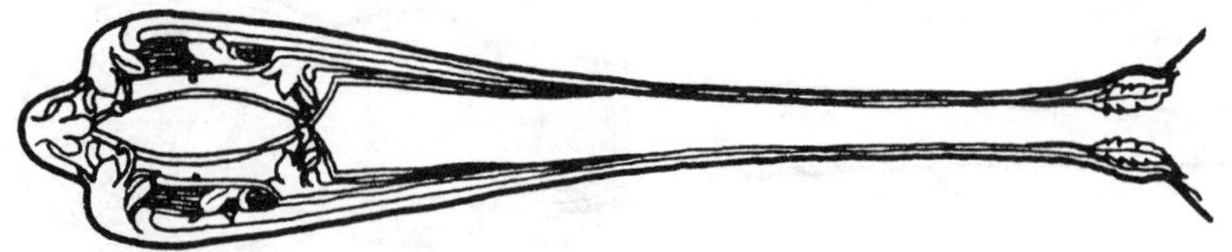

Thin market.

Corona
(H&T Mfg. Co.)
1910
S

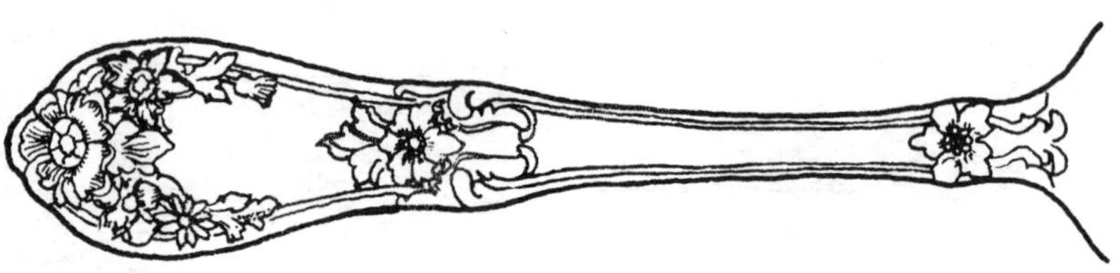

Thin market.

Erminie aka Mignon
aka Helena aka Como
aka Rockford No. 1
(Rockford Silver Plate)
(Montgomery Ward & Co.)
(W.H. Rogers)
(Williams)
(C. Guild)
1910
S

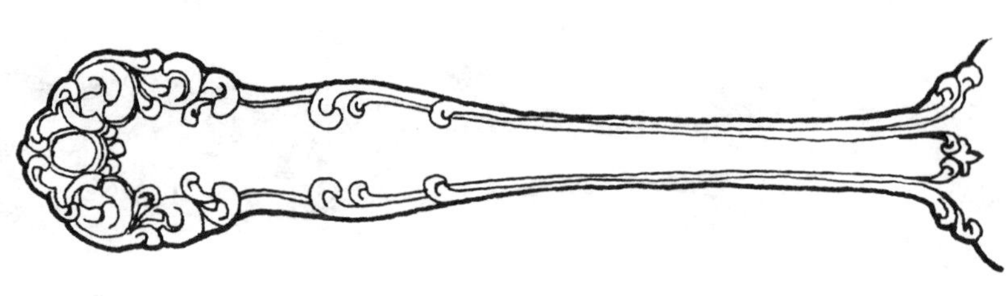

Thin market.

Wildflower
(H&T Mfg. Co.)
1910
S

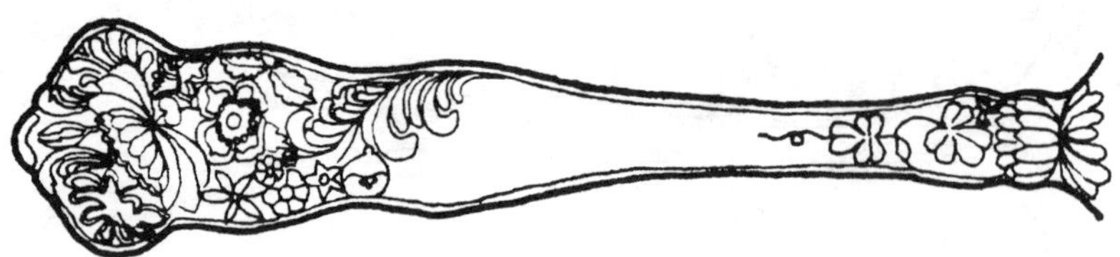

Thin market.

Dresden
(Stratford)
1911
S

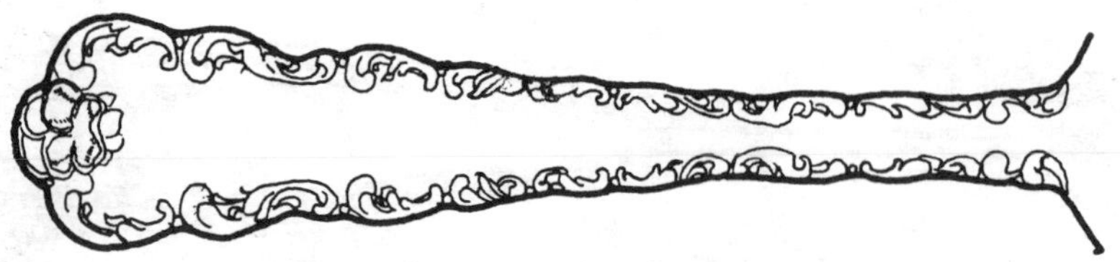

Thin market.

Please refer to "How To Use This Book" page 4.

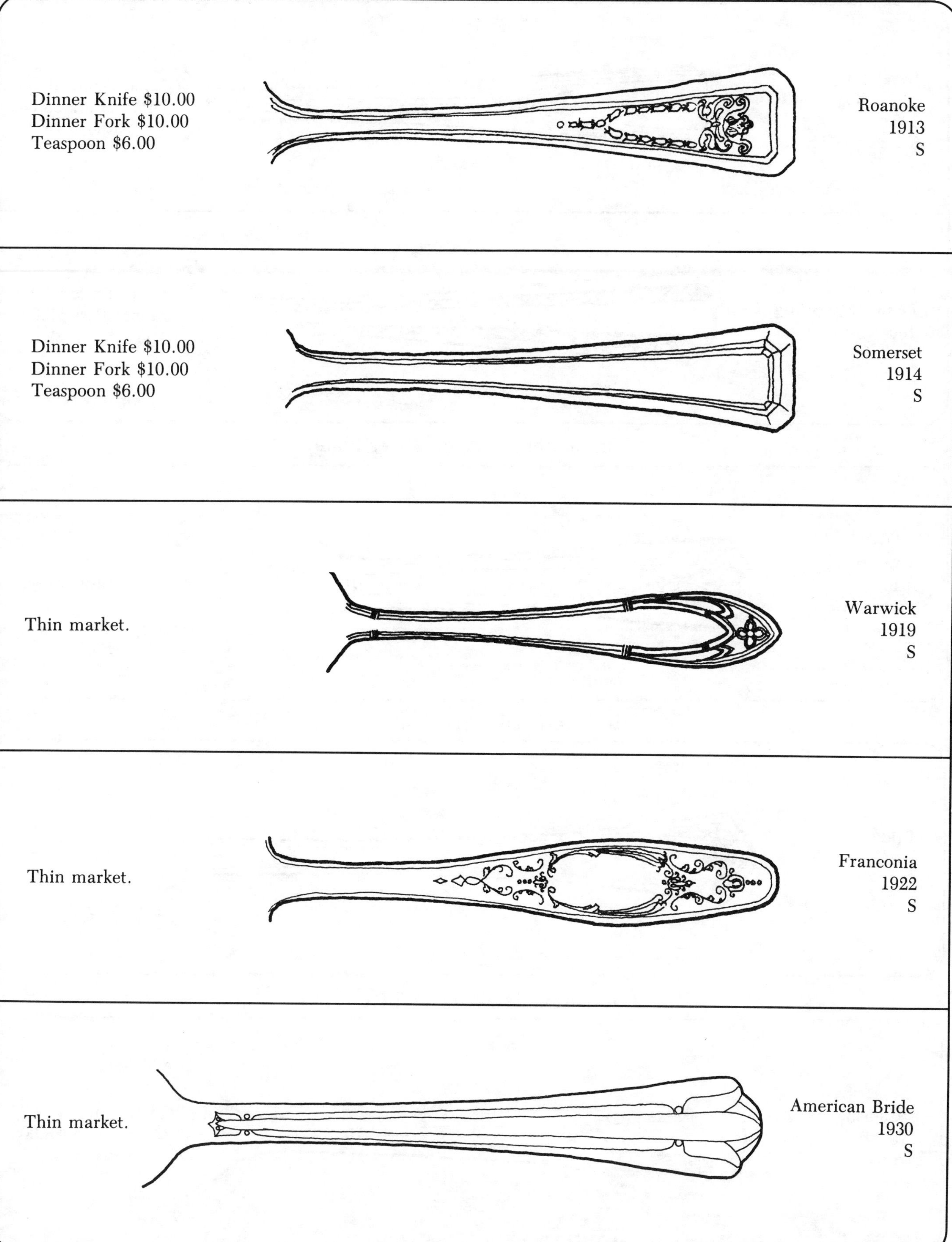

Dinner Knife $10.00
Dinner Fork $10.00
Teaspoon $6.00

Roanoke
1913
S

Dinner Knife $10.00
Dinner Fork $10.00
Teaspoon $6.00

Somerset
1914
S

Thin market.

Warwick
1919
S

Thin market.

Franconia
1922
S

Thin market.

American Bride
1930
S

Please refer to "How To Use This Book" page 4.

International - American Silver Co., International - Avon Silver Plate
International - Bride Silver Plate, International - Camelia Silver Plate

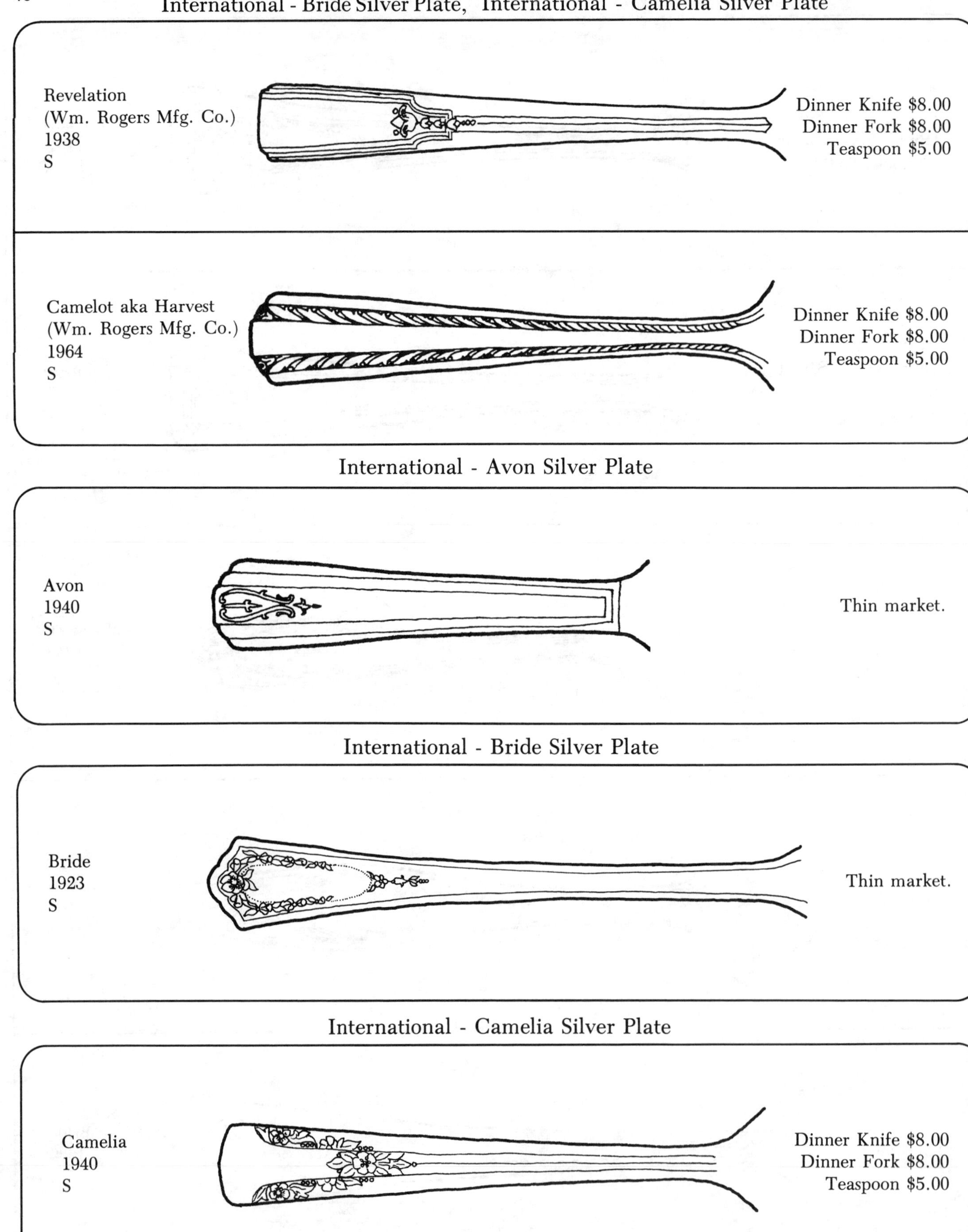

Revelation
(Wm. Rogers Mfg. Co.)
1938
S

Dinner Knife $8.00
Dinner Fork $8.00
Teaspoon $5.00

Camelot aka Harvest
(Wm. Rogers Mfg. Co.)
1964
S

Dinner Knife $8.00
Dinner Fork $8.00
Teaspoon $5.00

International - Avon Silver Plate

Avon
1940
S

Thin market.

International - Bride Silver Plate

Bride
1923
S

Thin market.

International - Camelia Silver Plate

Camelia
1940
S

Dinner Knife $8.00
Dinner Fork $8.00
Teaspoon $5.00

Please refer to "How To Use This Book" page 4.

International - Court Silver Plate

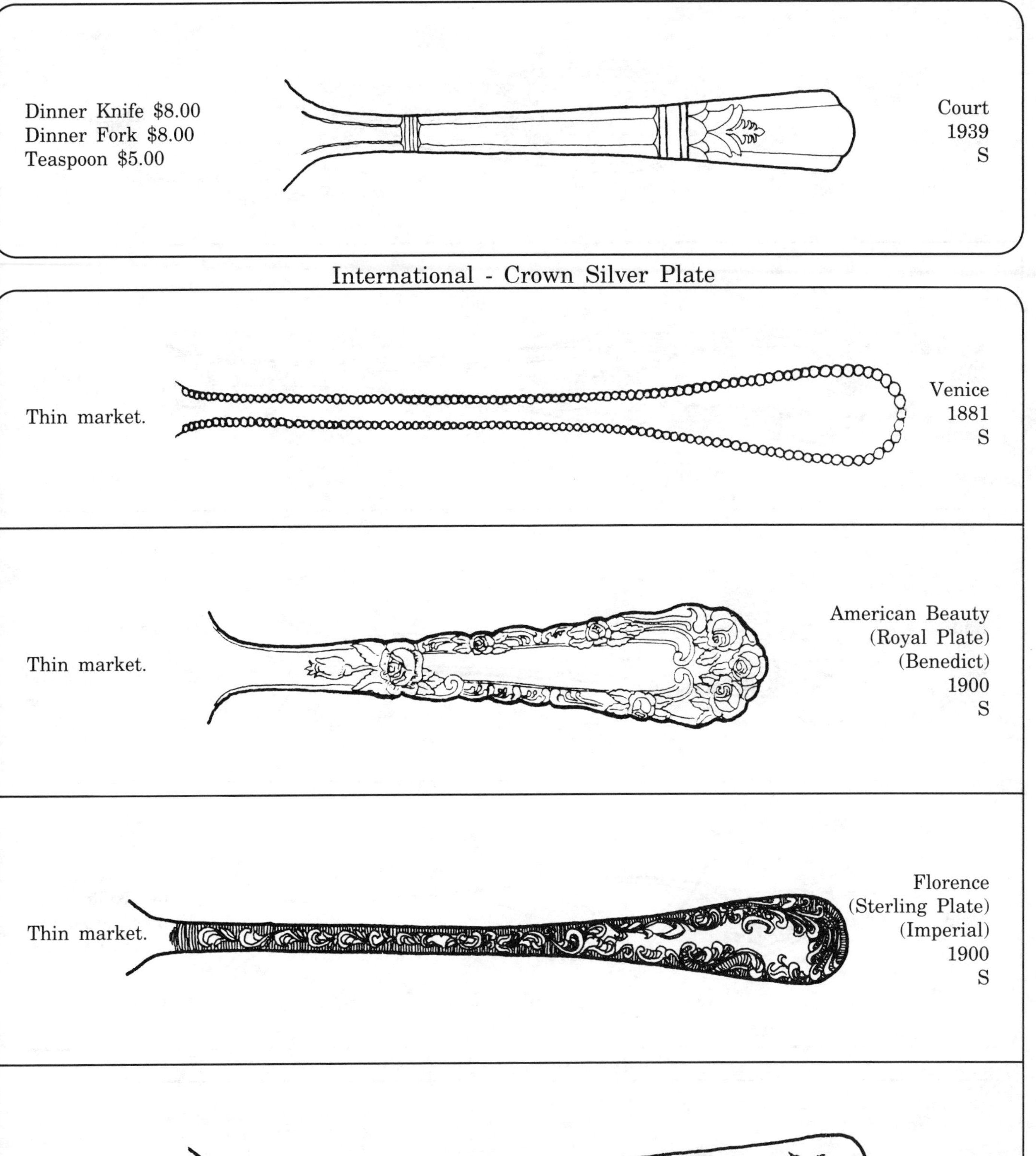

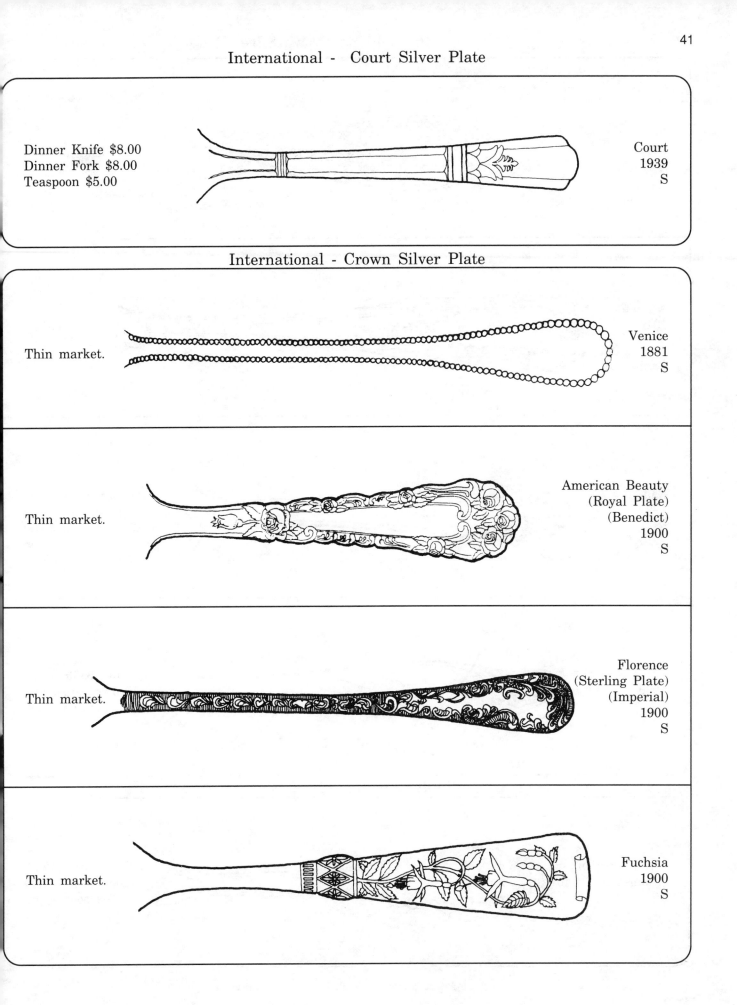

Dinner Knife $8.00
Dinner Fork $8.00
Teaspoon $5.00

Court
1939
S

International - Crown Silver Plate

Thin market.

Venice
1881
S

Thin market.

American Beauty
(Royal Plate)
(Benedict)
1900
S

Thin market.

Florence
(Sterling Plate)
(Imperial)
1900
S

Thin market.

Fuchsia
1900
S

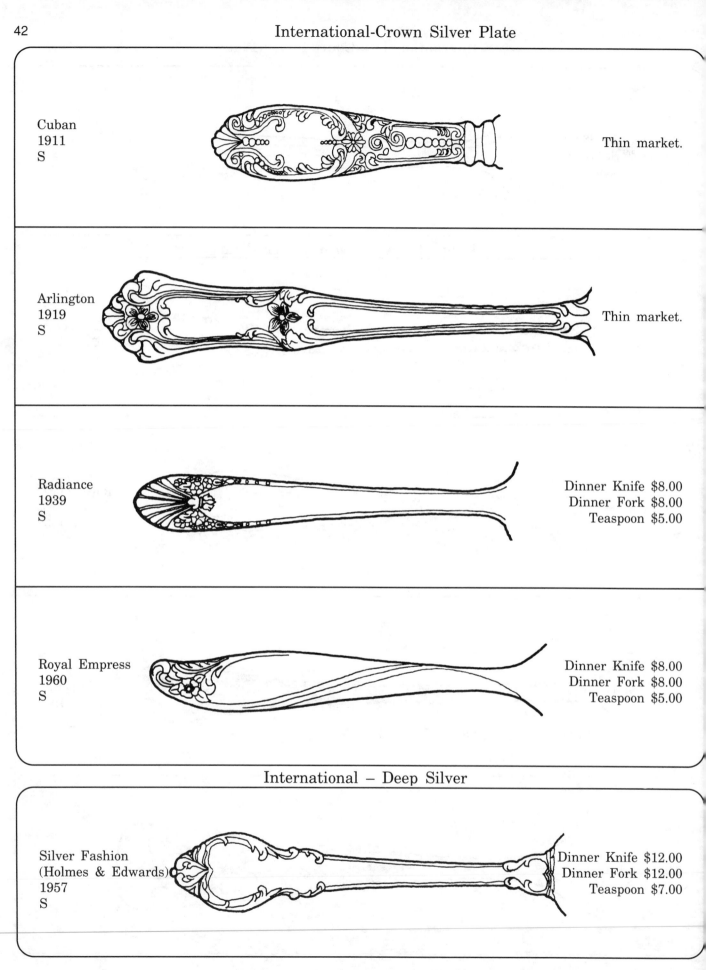

Cuban
1911
S

Thin market.

Arlington
1919
S

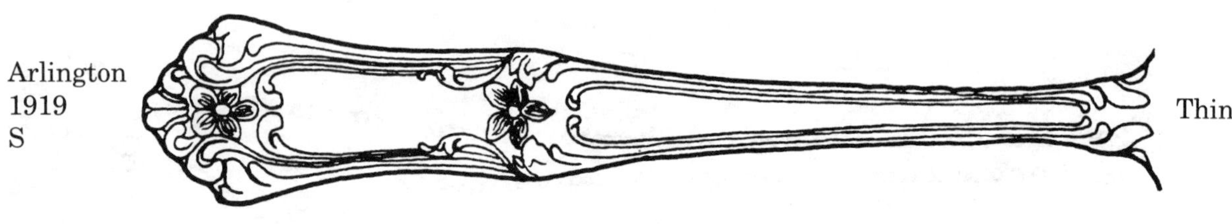

Thin market.

Radiance
1939
S

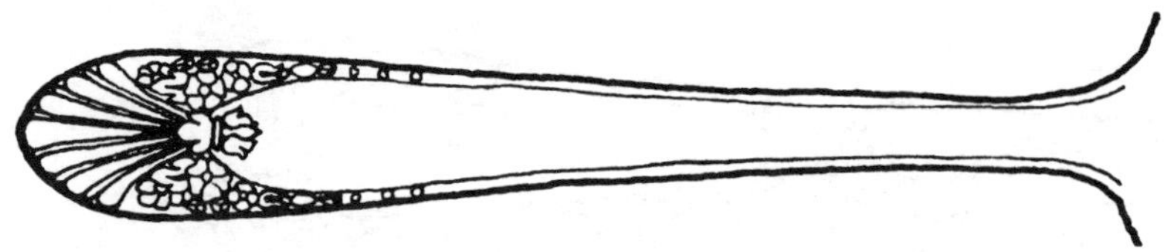

Dinner Knife $8.00
Dinner Fork $8.00
Teaspoon $5.00

Royal Empress
1960
S

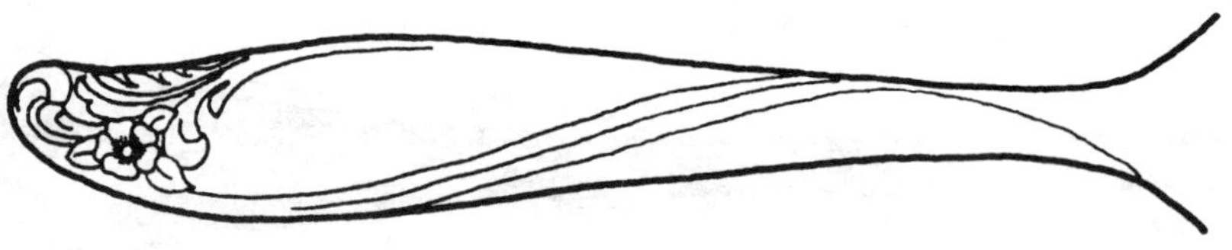

Dinner Knife $8.00
Dinner Fork $8.00
Teaspoon $5.00

International – Deep Silver

Silver Fashion
(Holmes & Edwards)
1957
S

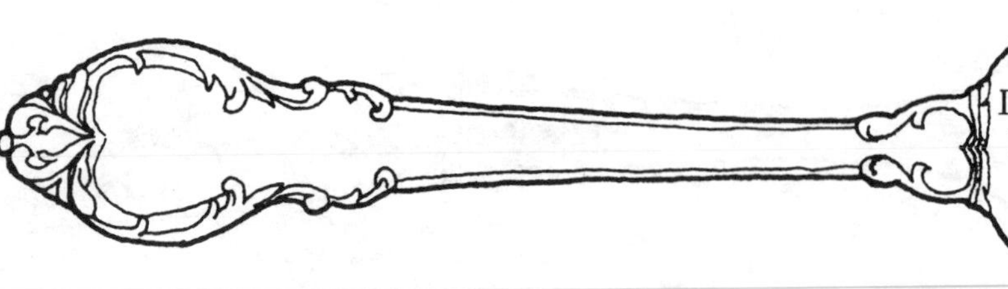

Dinner Knife $12.00
Dinner Fork $12.00
Teaspoon $7.00

Please refer to "How To Use This Book" page 4.

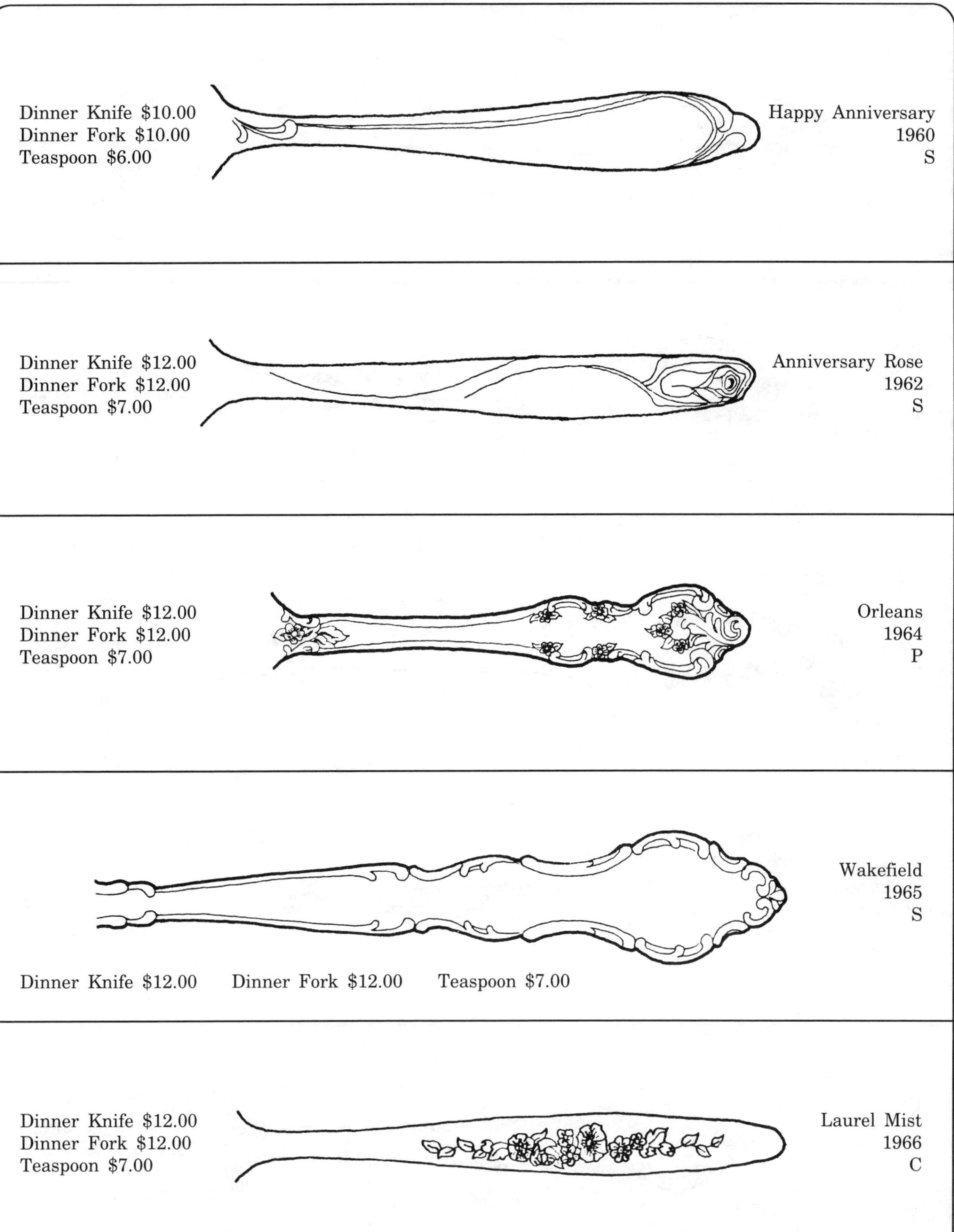

Dinner Knife $10.00
Dinner Fork $10.00
Teaspoon $6.00

Happy Anniversary
1960
S

Dinner Knife $12.00
Dinner Fork $12.00
Teaspoon $7.00

Anniversary Rose
1962
S

Dinner Knife $12.00
Dinner Fork $12.00
Teaspoon $7.00

Orleans
1964
P

Wakefield
1965
S

Dinner Knife $12.00 Dinner Fork $12.00 Teaspoon $7.00

Dinner Knife $12.00
Dinner Fork $12.00
Teaspoon $7.00

Laurel Mist
1966
C

Please refer to "How To Use This Book" page 4.

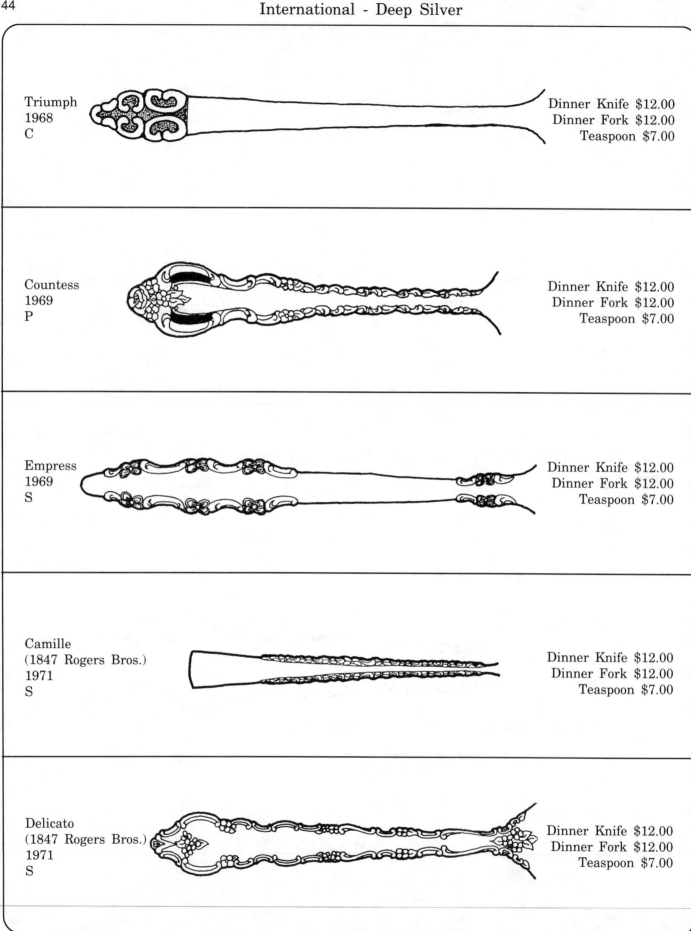

Triumph
1968
C

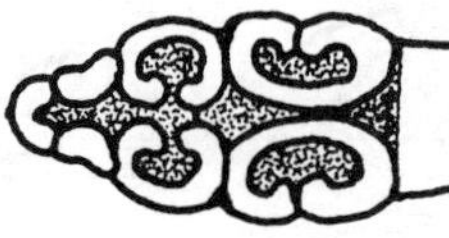

Dinner Knife $12.00
Dinner Fork $12.00
Teaspoon $7.00

Countess
1969
P

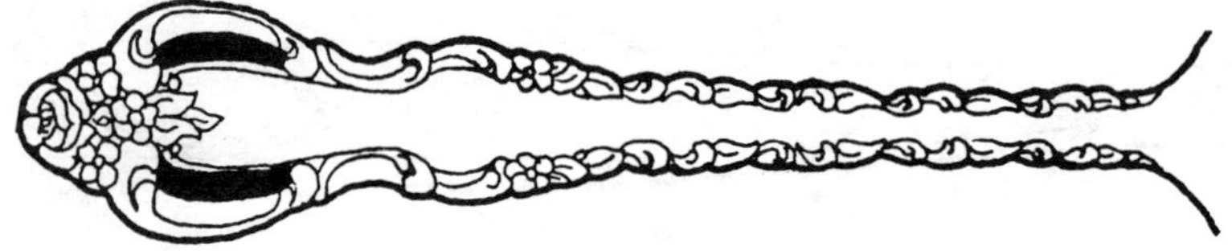

Dinner Knife $12.00
Dinner Fork $12.00
Teaspoon $7.00

Empress
1969
S

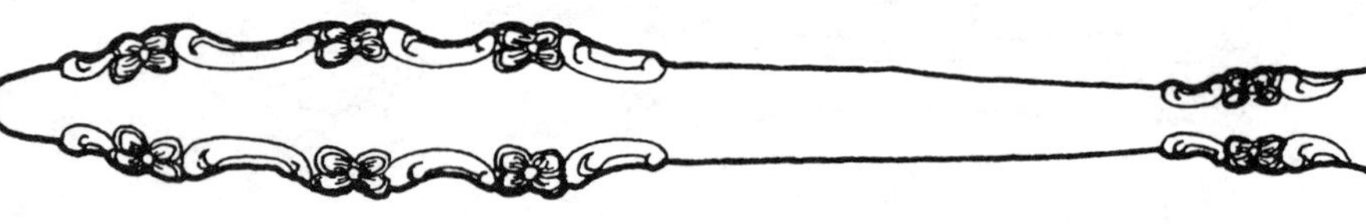

Dinner Knife $12.00
Dinner Fork $12.00
Teaspoon $7.00

Camille
(1847 Rogers Bros.)
1971
S

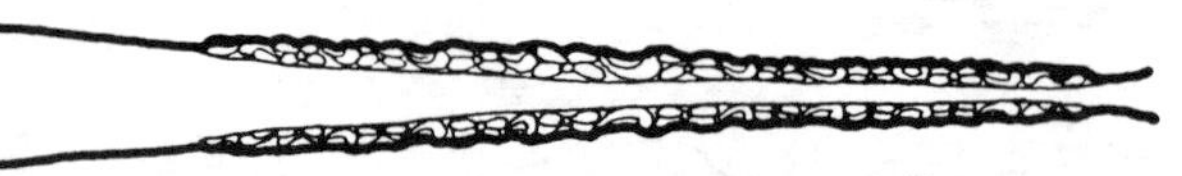

Dinner Knife $12.00
Dinner Fork $12.00
Teaspoon $7.00

Delicato
(1847 Rogers Bros.)
1971
S

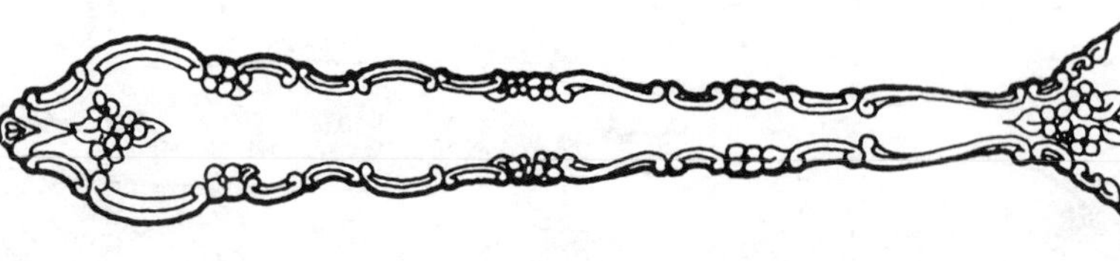

Dinner Knife $12.00
Dinner Fork $12.00
Teaspoon $7.00

Please refer to "How To Use This Book" page 4.

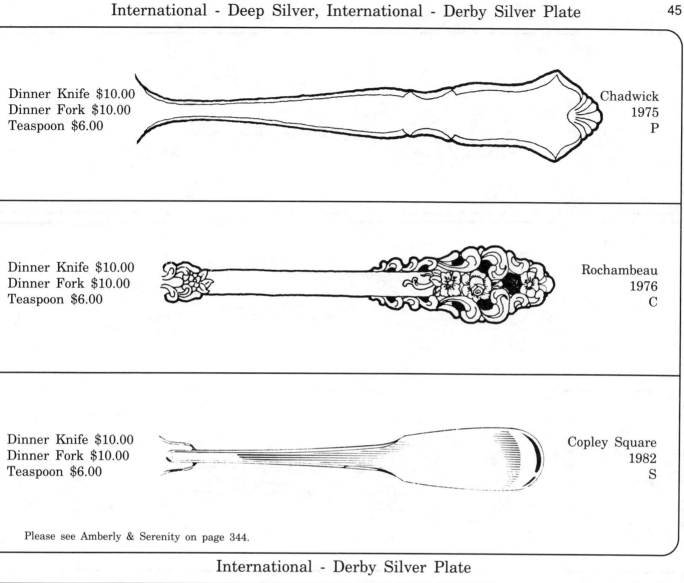

Dinner Knife $10.00
Dinner Fork $10.00
Teaspoon $6.00

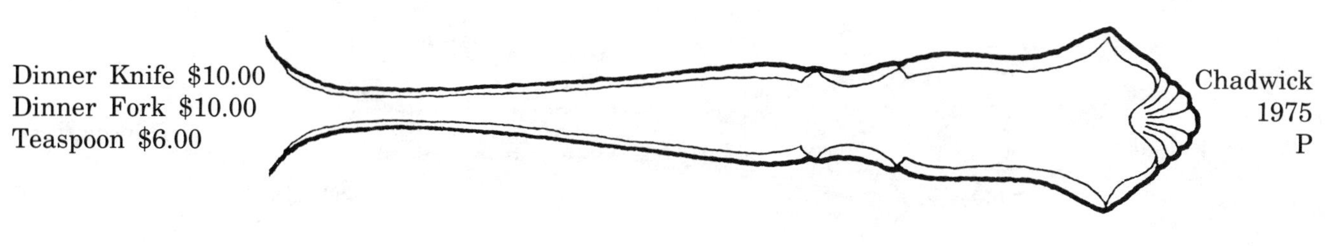

Chadwick
1975
P

Dinner Knife $10.00
Dinner Fork $10.00
Teaspoon $6.00

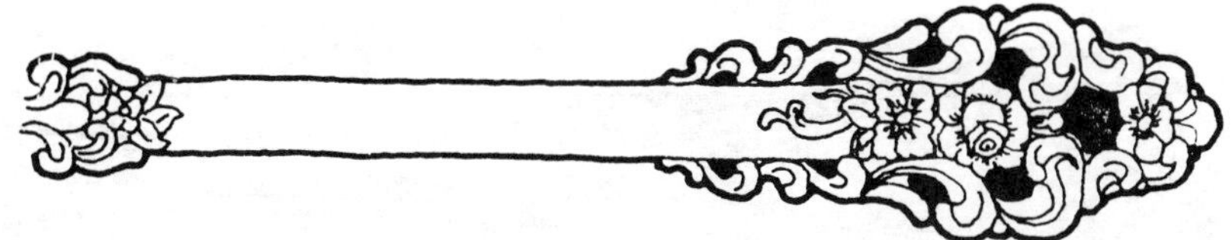

Rochambeau
1976
C

Dinner Knife $10.00
Dinner Fork $10.00
Teaspoon $6.00

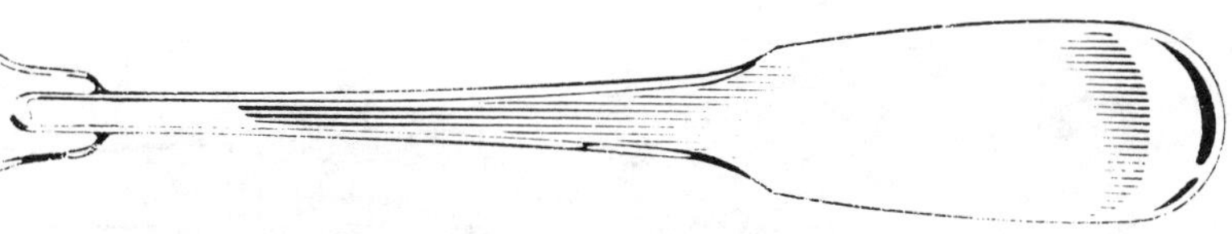

Copley Square
1982
S

Please see Amberly & Serenity on page 344.

International - Derby Silver Plate

Thin market.

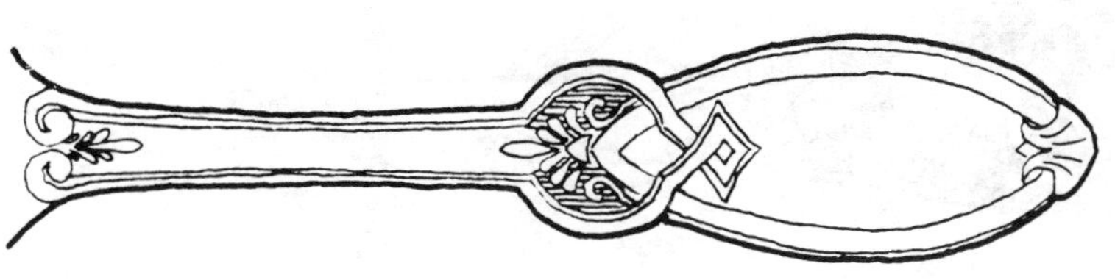

Roman
(1847 Rogers Bros.)
(Anchor Rogers)
(Rogers & Bro.)
(Rogers Smith & Co.)
1865
S

Thin market.

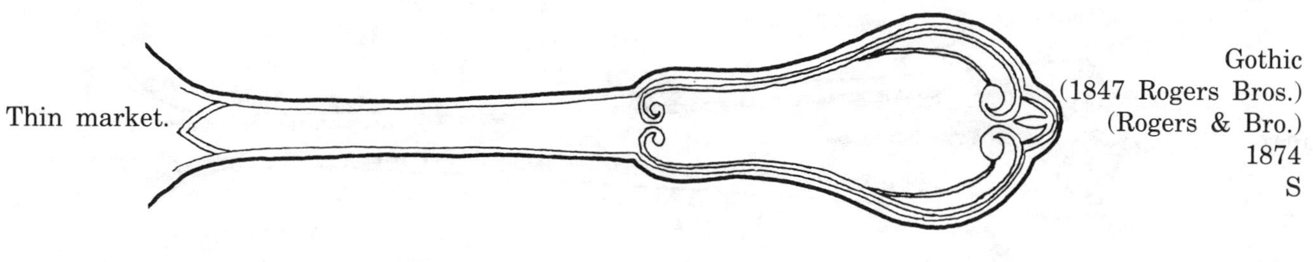

Gothic
(1847 Rogers Bros.)
(Rogers & Bro.)
1874
S

Please refer to "How To Use This Book" page 4.

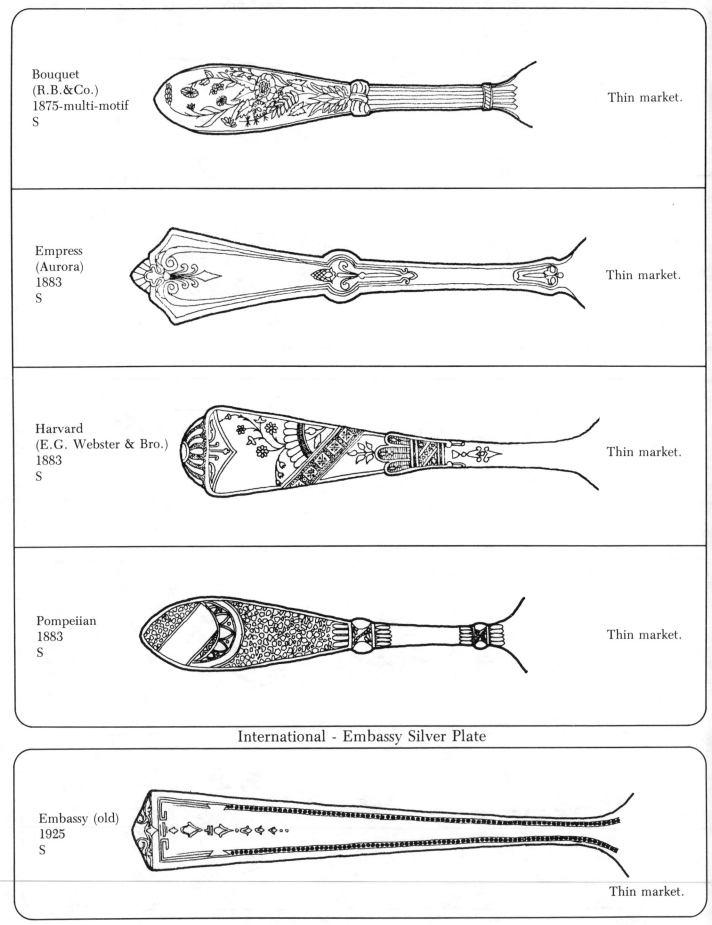

Bouquet
(R.B.&Co.)
1875-multi-motif
S

Thin market.

Empress
(Aurora)
1883
S

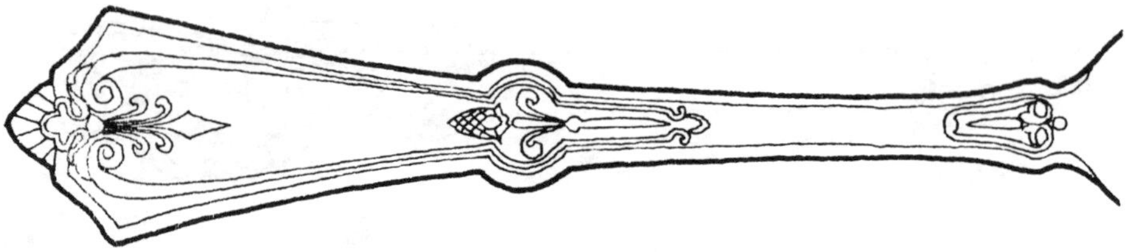

Thin market.

Harvard
(E.G. Webster & Bro.)
1883
S

Thin market.

Pompeiian
1883
S

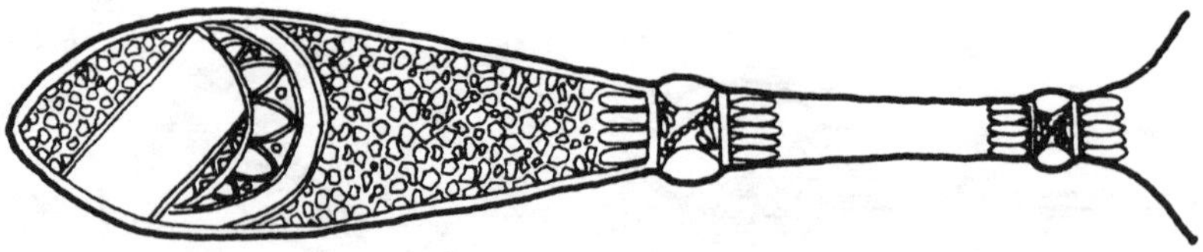

Thin market.

International - Embassy Silver Plate

Embassy (old)
1925
S

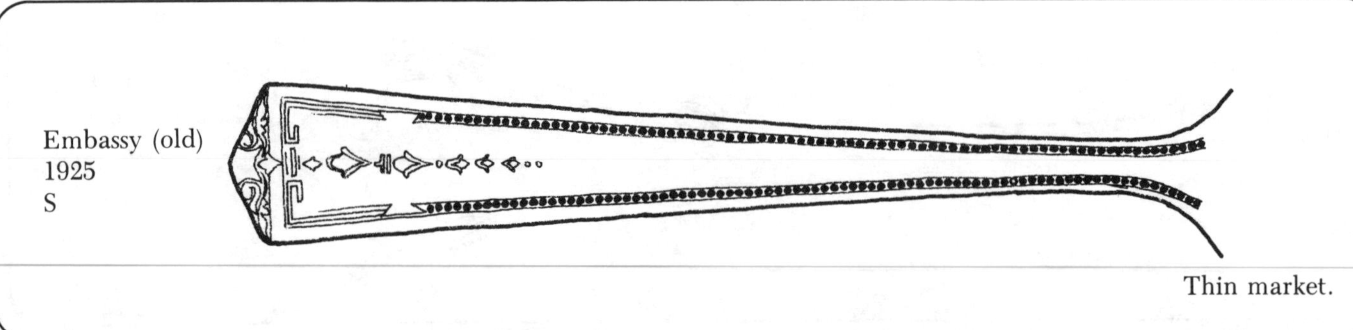

Thin market.

Please refer to "How To Use This Book" page 4.

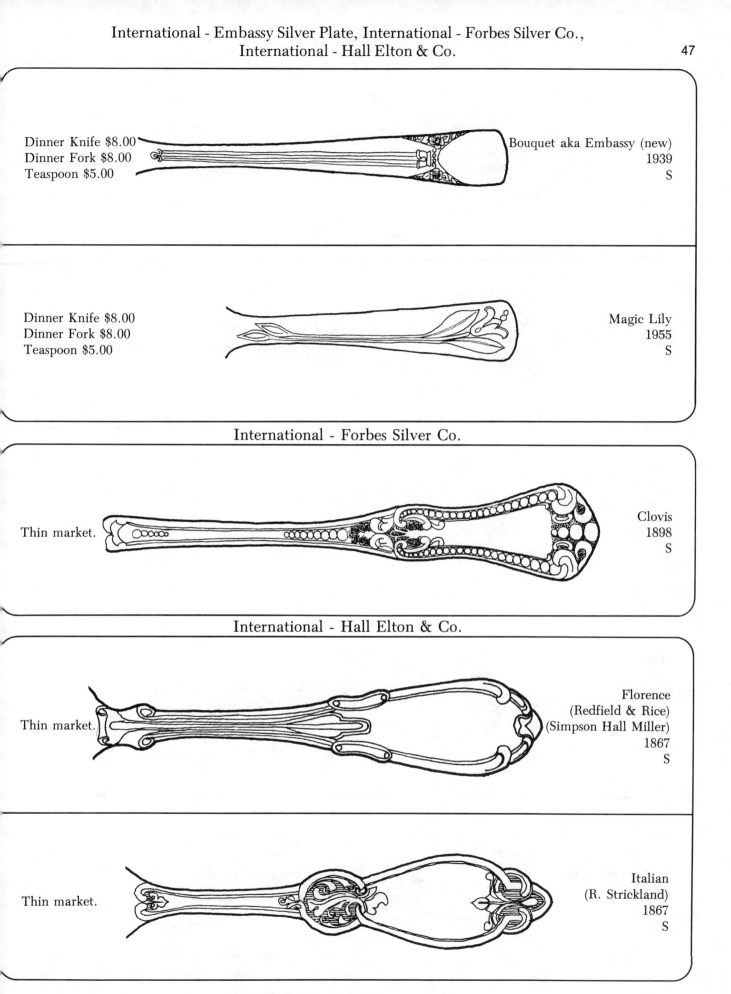

Dinner Knife $8.00
Dinner Fork $8.00
Teaspoon $5.00

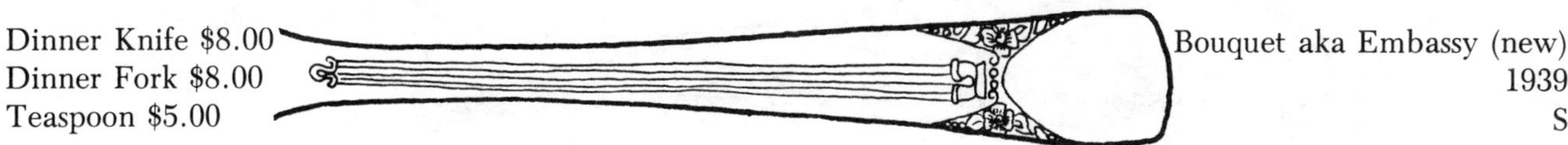

Bouquet aka Embassy (new)
1939
S

Dinner Knife $8.00
Dinner Fork $8.00
Teaspoon $5.00

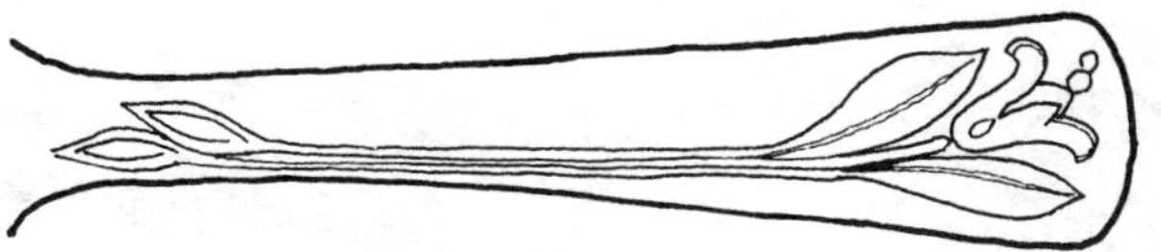

Magic Lily
1955
S

International - Forbes Silver Co.

Thin market.

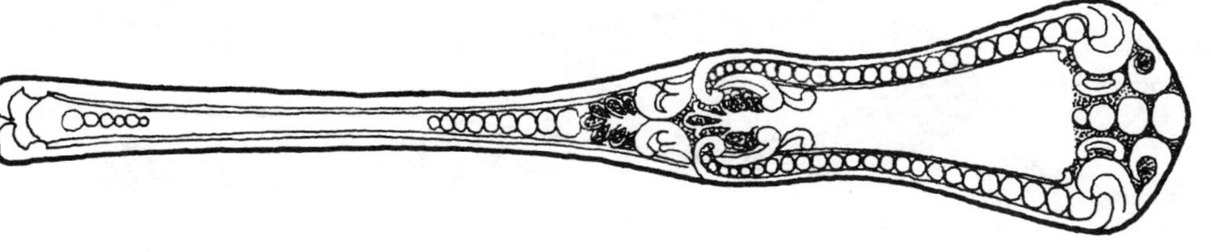

Clovis
1898
S

International - Hall Elton & Co.

Thin market.

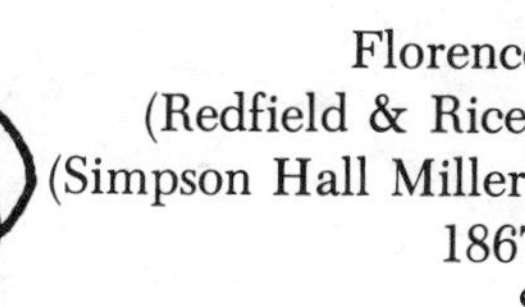

Florence
(Redfield & Rice)
(Simpson Hall Miller)
1867
S

Thin market.

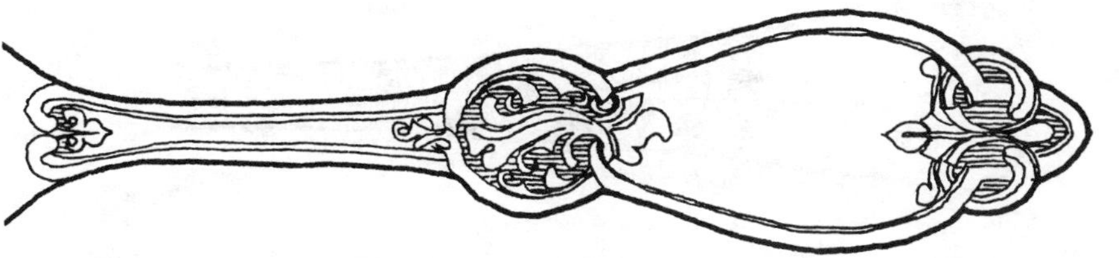

Italian
(R. Strickland)
1867
S

Please refer to "How To Use This Book" page 4.

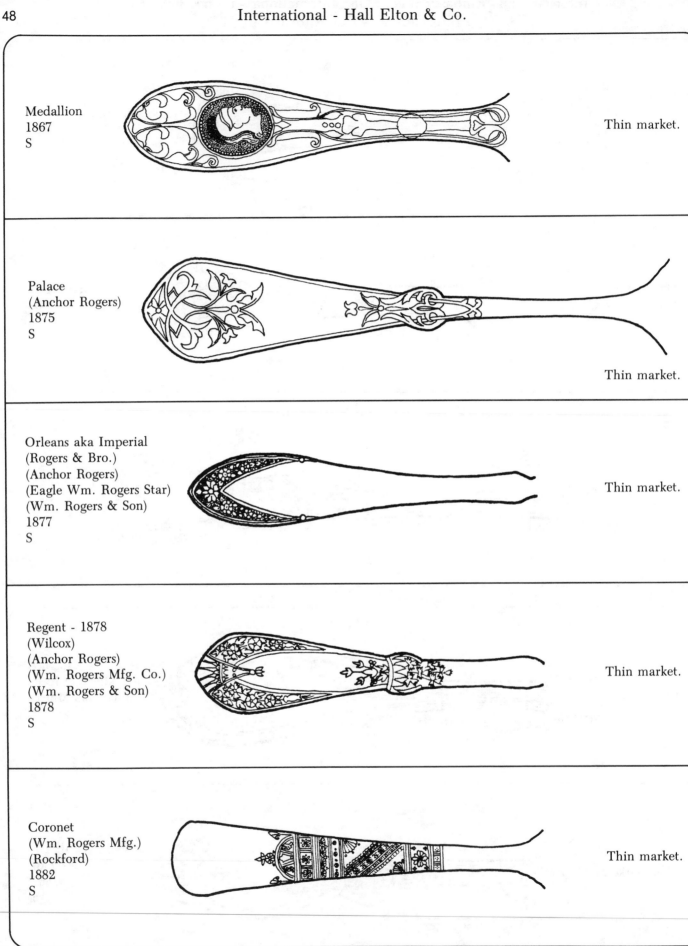

Medallion
1867
S

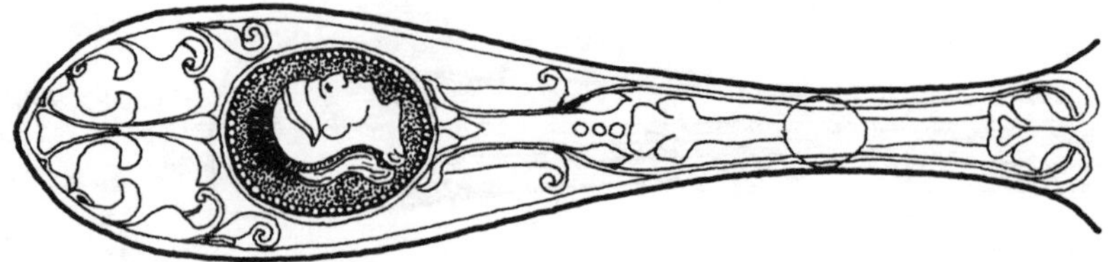

Thin market.

Palace
(Anchor Rogers)
1875
S

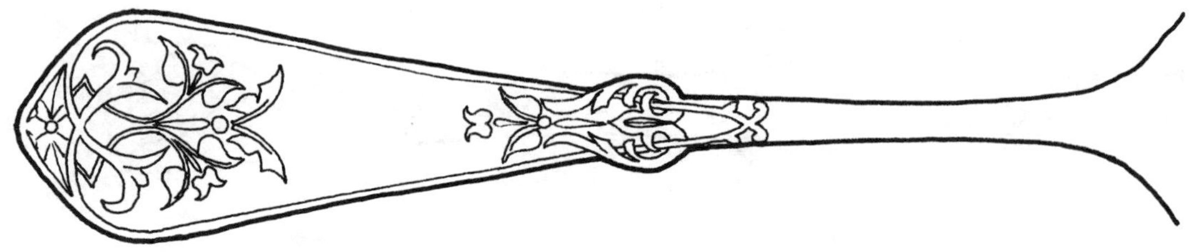

Thin market.

Orleans aka Imperial
(Rogers & Bro.)
(Anchor Rogers)
(Eagle Wm. Rogers Star)
(Wm. Rogers & Son)
1877
S

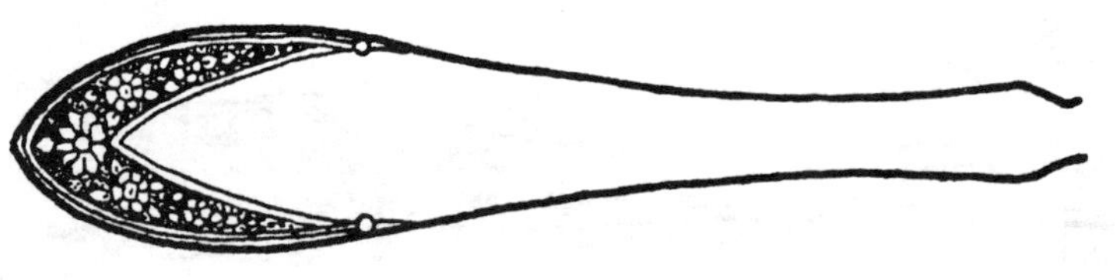

Thin market.

Regent - 1878
(Wilcox)
(Anchor Rogers)
(Wm. Rogers Mfg. Co.)
(Wm. Rogers & Son)
1878
S

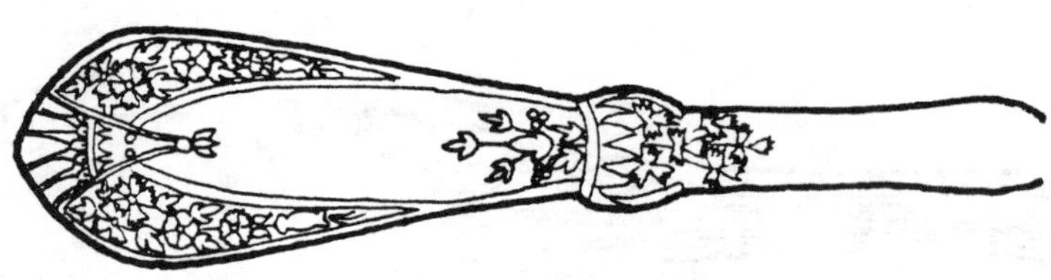

Thin market.

Coronet
(Wm. Rogers Mfg.)
(Rockford)
1882
S

Thin market.

Please refer to "How To Use This Book" page 4.

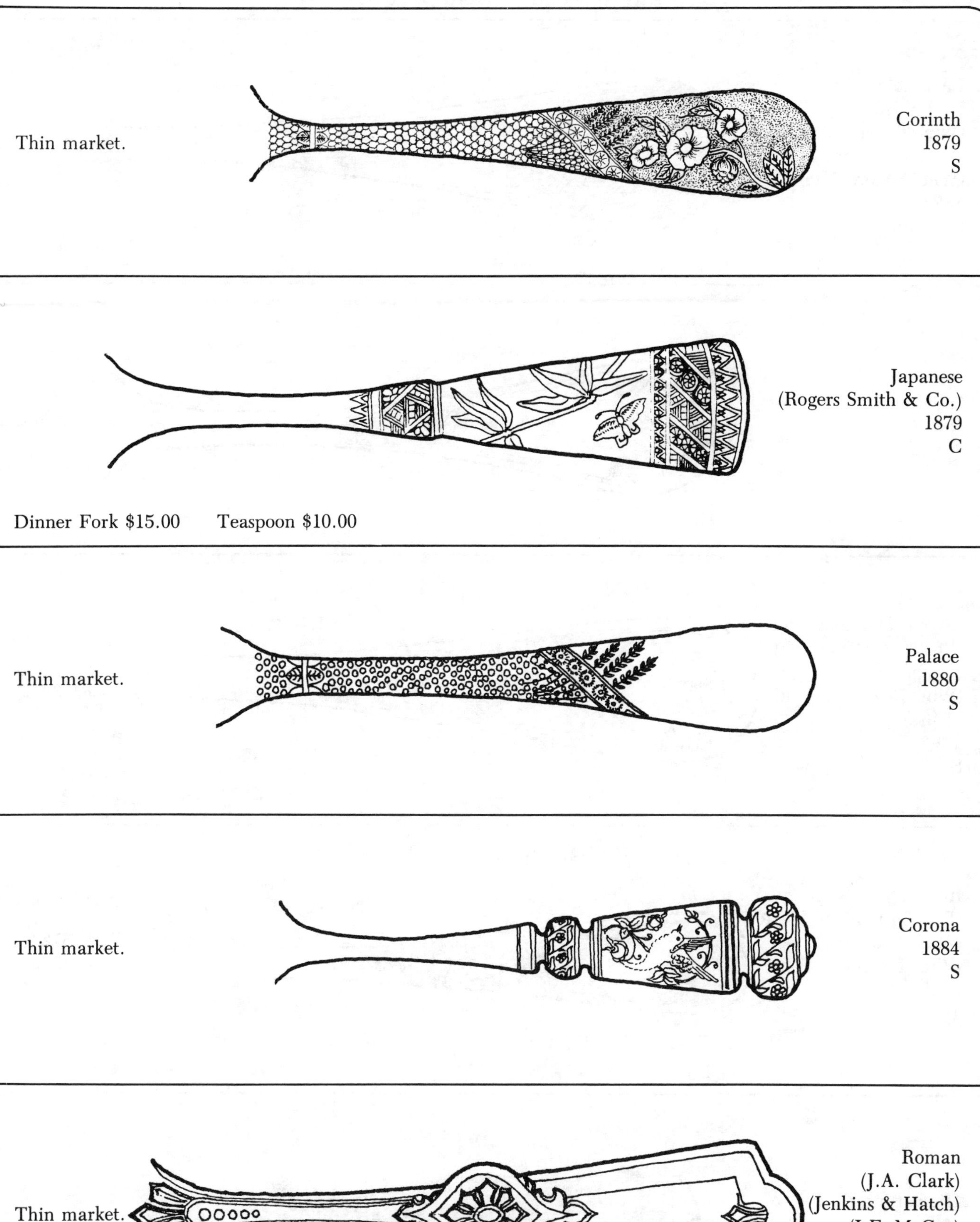

Thin market.

Corinth
1879
S

Japanese
(Rogers Smith & Co.)
1879
C

Dinner Fork $15.00 Teaspoon $10.00

Thin market.

Palace
1880
S

Thin market.

Corona
1884
S

Thin market.

Roman
(J.A. Clark)
(Jenkins & Hatch)
(J.F. McCoy)
1884
S

Please refer to "How To Use This Book" page 4.

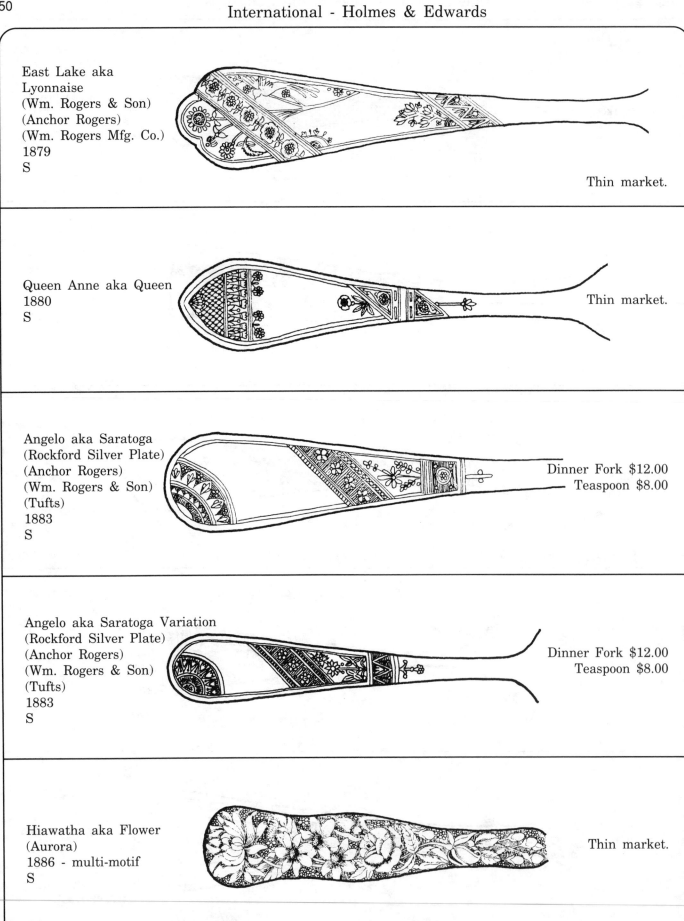

East Lake aka
Lyonnaise
(Wm. Rogers & Son)
(Anchor Rogers)
(Wm. Rogers Mfg. Co.)
1879
S

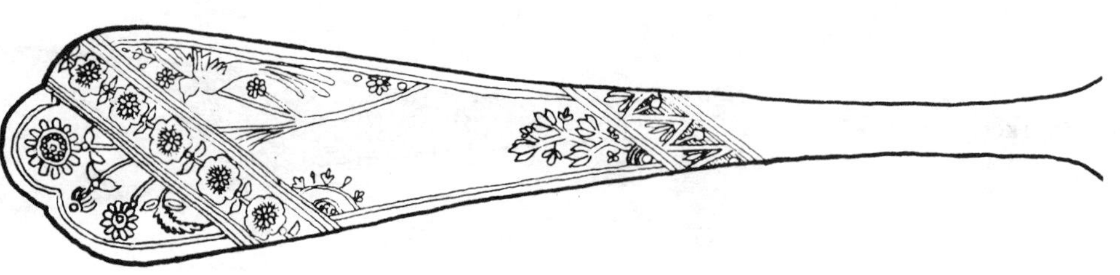

Thin market.

Queen Anne aka Queen
1880
S

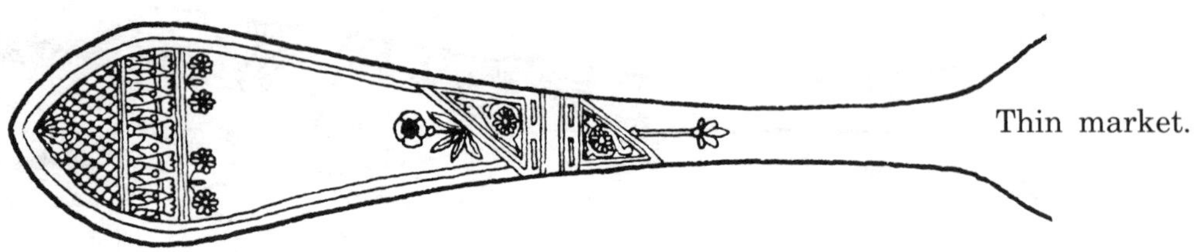

Thin market.

Angelo aka Saratoga
(Rockford Silver Plate)
(Anchor Rogers)
(Wm. Rogers & Son)
(Tufts)
1883
S

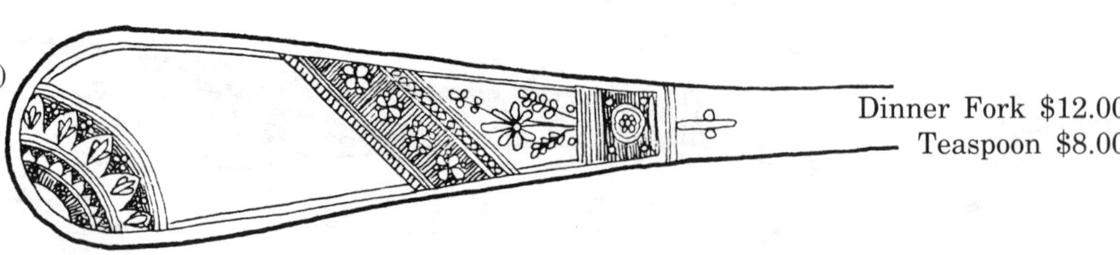

Dinner Fork $12.00
Teaspoon $8.00

Angelo aka Saratoga Variation
(Rockford Silver Plate)
(Anchor Rogers)
(Wm. Rogers & Son)
(Tufts)
1883
S

Dinner Fork $12.00
Teaspoon $8.00

Hiawatha aka Flower
(Aurora)
1886 - multi-motif
S

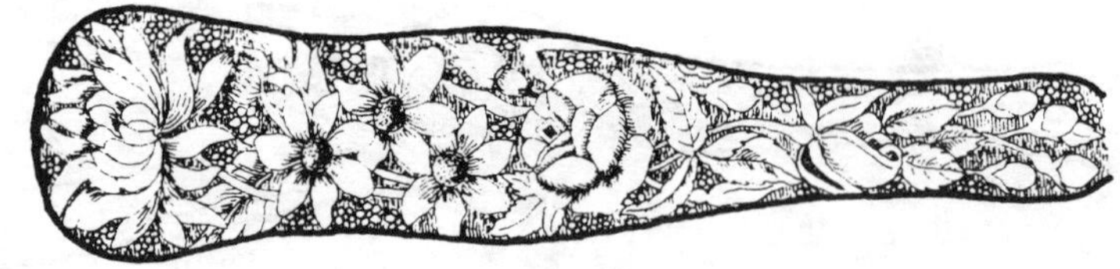

Thin market.

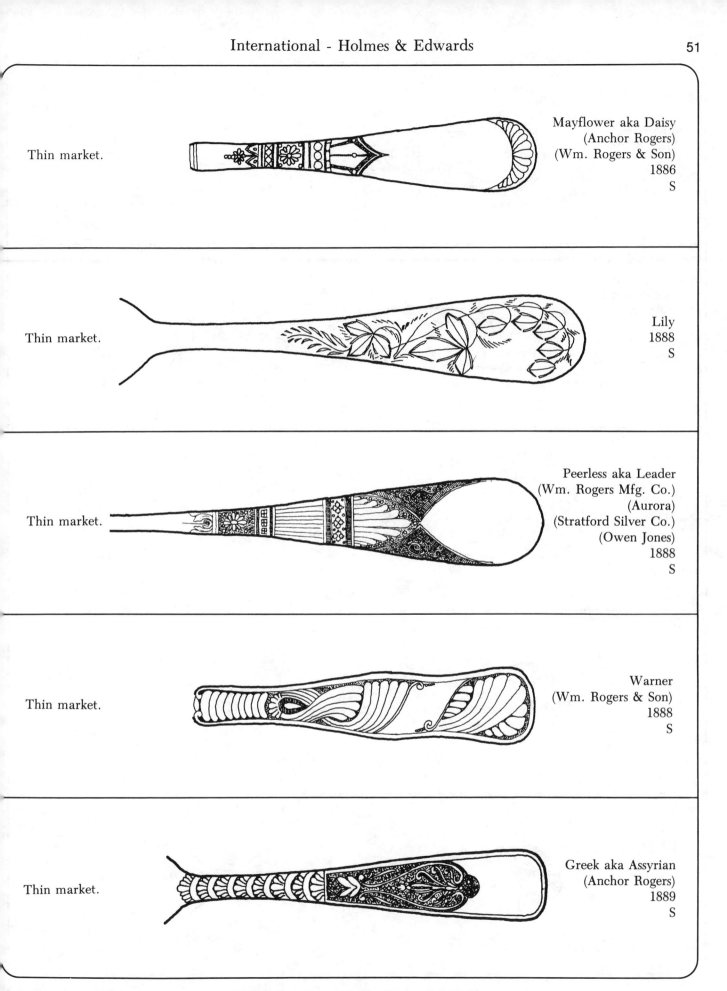

Thin market.

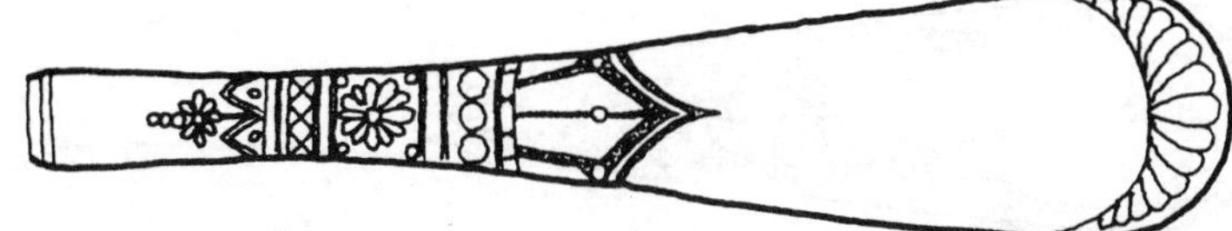

Mayflower aka Daisy
(Anchor Rogers)
(Wm. Rogers & Son)
1886
S

Thin market.

Lily
1888
S

Thin market.

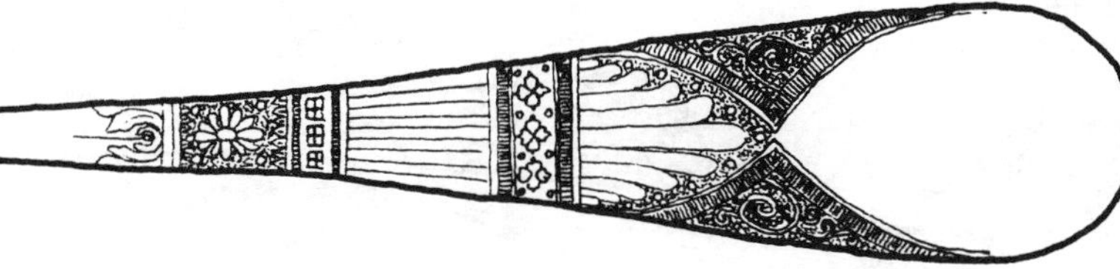

Peerless aka Leader
(Wm. Rogers Mfg. Co.)
(Aurora)
(Stratford Silver Co.)
(Owen Jones)
1888
S

Thin market.

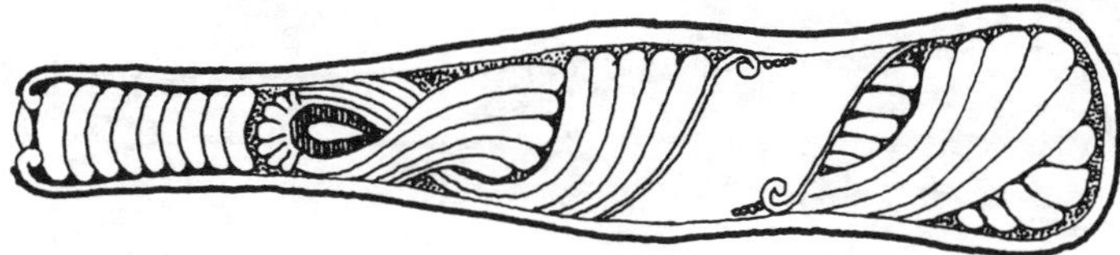

Warner
(Wm. Rogers & Son)
1888
S

Thin market.

Greek aka Assyrian
(Anchor Rogers)
1889
S

Please refer to "How To Use This Book" page 4.

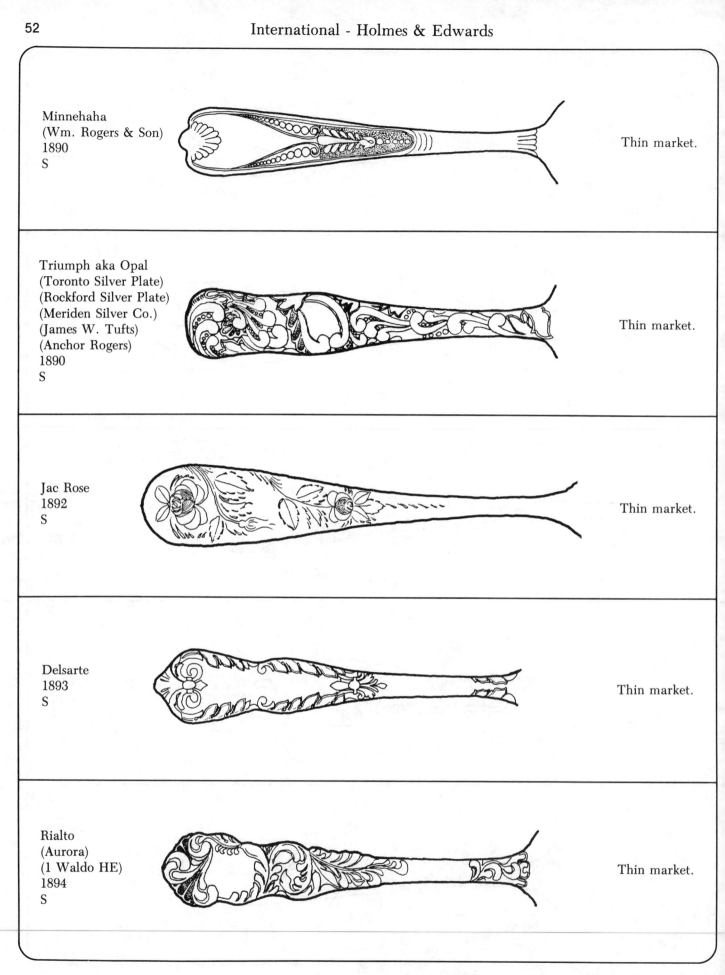

Minnehaha
(Wm. Rogers & Son)
1890
S

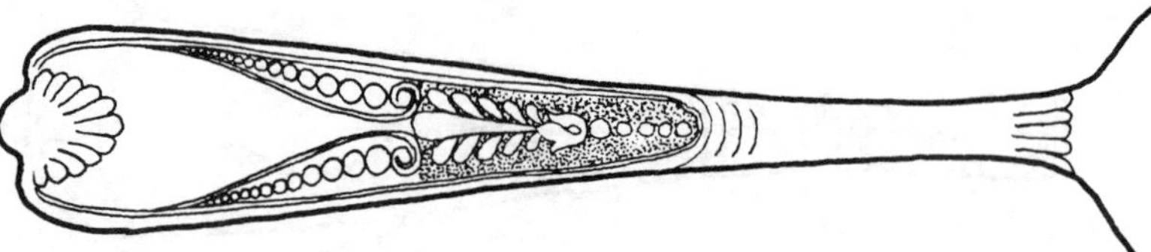

Thin market.

Triumph aka Opal
(Toronto Silver Plate)
(Rockford Silver Plate)
(Meriden Silver Co.)
(James W. Tufts)
(Anchor Rogers)
1890
S

Thin market.

Jac Rose
1892
S

Thin market.

Delsarte
1893
S

Thin market.

Rialto
(Aurora)
(1 Waldo HE)
1894
S

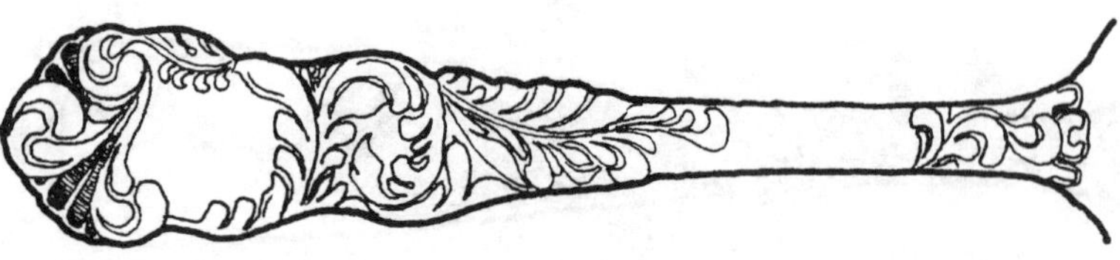

Thin market.

Please refer to "How To Use This Book" page 4.

Thin market.

Waldorf
1894
S

Thin market.

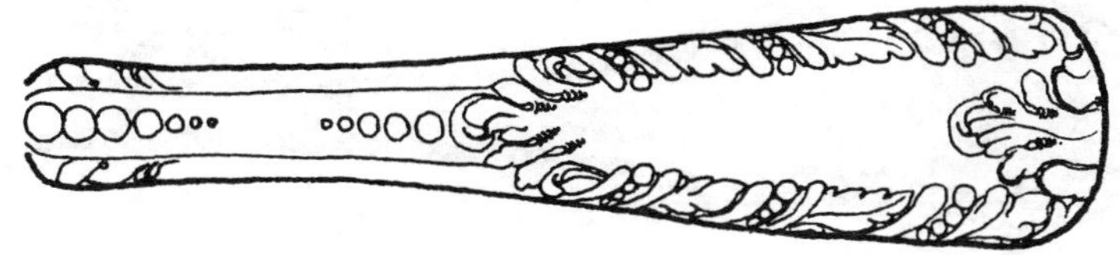

Irving
(New Haven Silver Plate)
(B.S. Co.)
1895
S

Thin market.

Liberty
1895
S

Thin market.

Lincoln
1895
S

Thin market.

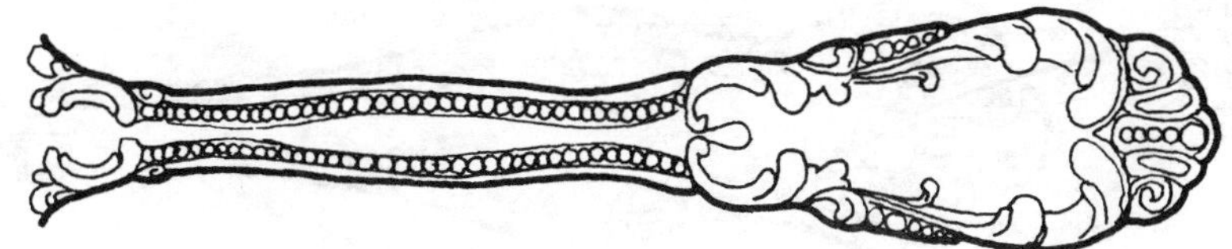

Marina
1896
S

Please refer to "How To Use This Book" page 4.

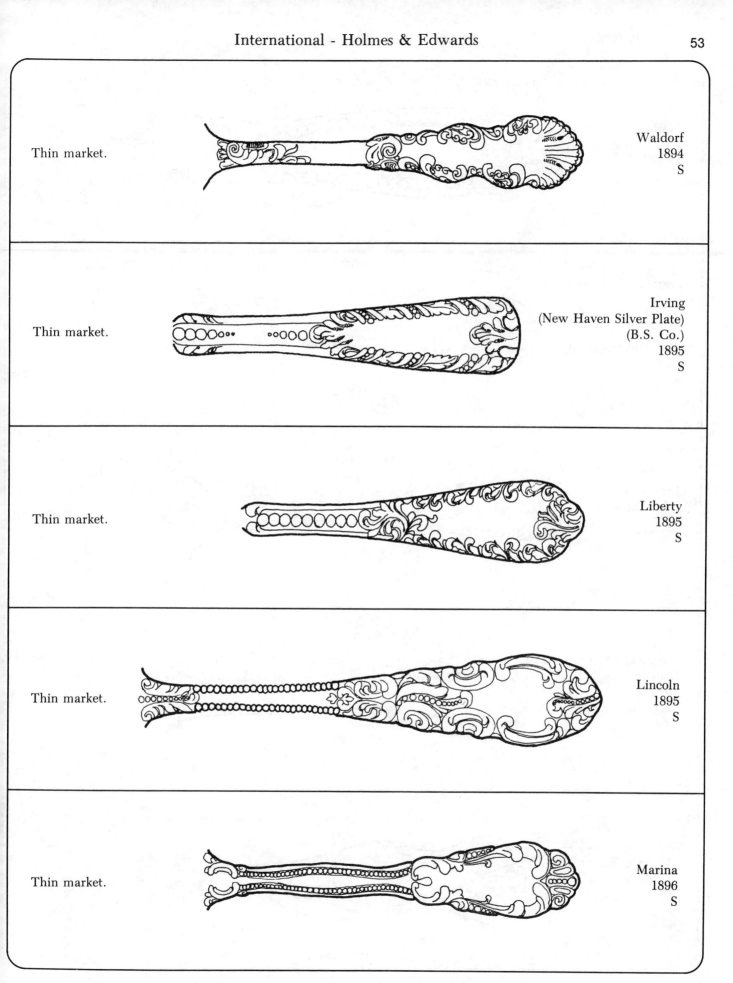

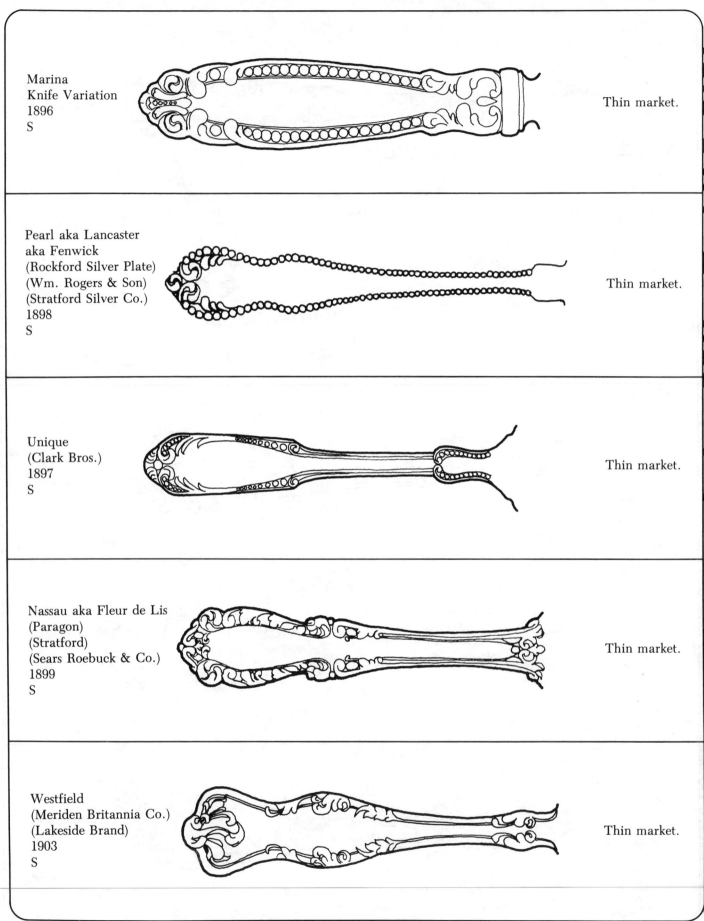

Marina
Knife Variation
1896
S

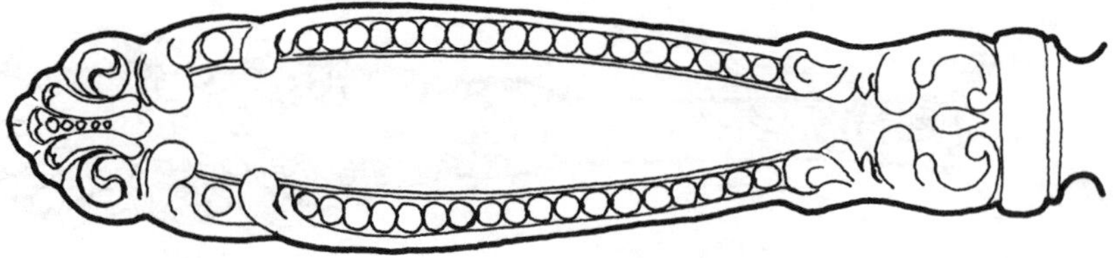

Thin market.

Pearl aka Lancaster
aka Fenwick
(Rockford Silver Plate)
(Wm. Rogers & Son)
(Stratford Silver Co.)
1898
S

Thin market.

Unique
(Clark Bros.)
1897
S

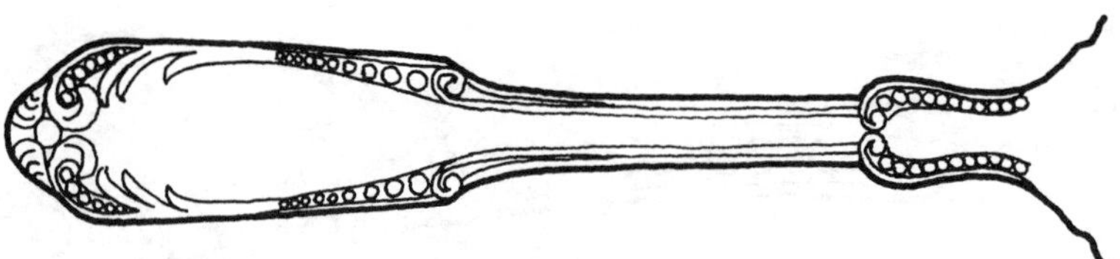

Thin market.

Nassau aka Fleur de Lis
(Paragon)
(Stratford)
(Sears Roebuck & Co.)
1899
S

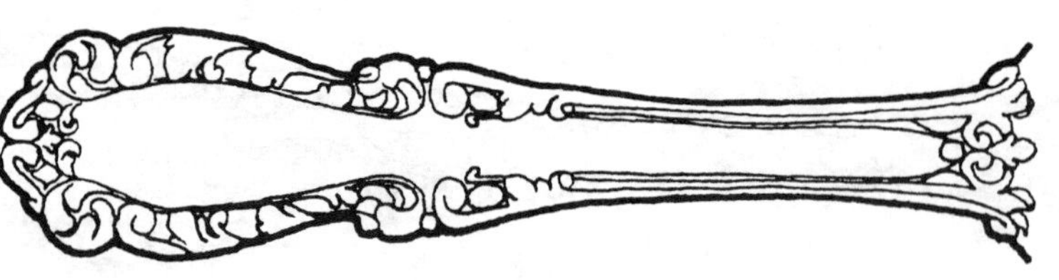

Thin market.

Westfield
(Meriden Britannia Co.)
(Lakeside Brand)
1903
S

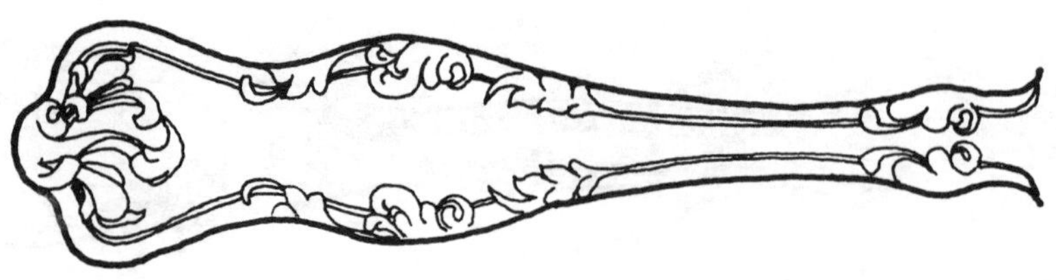

Thin market.

Please refer to "How To Use This Book" page 4.

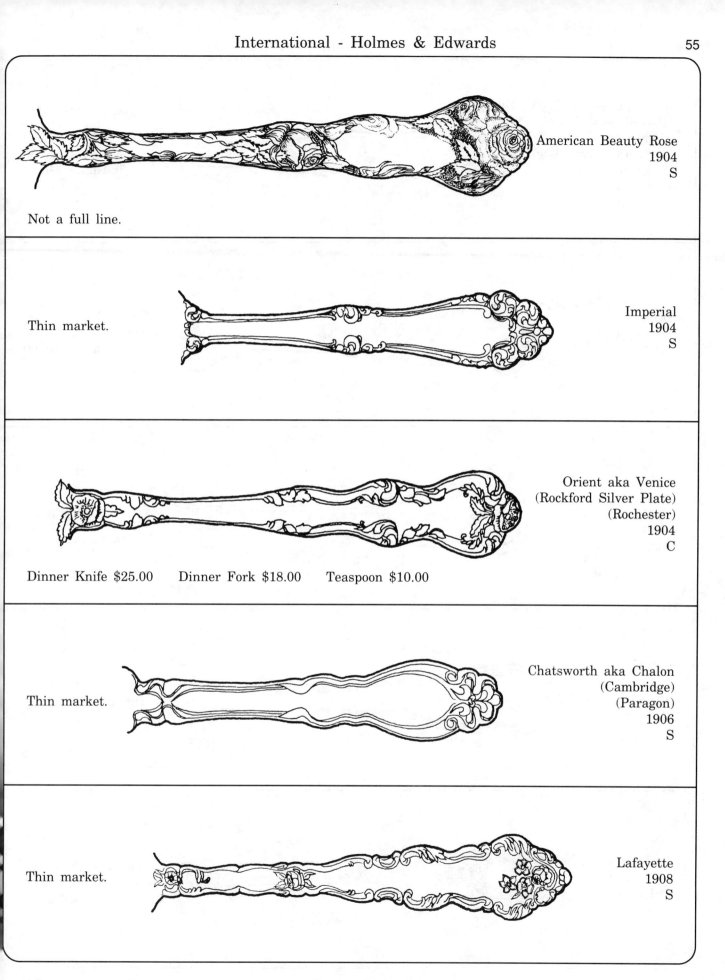

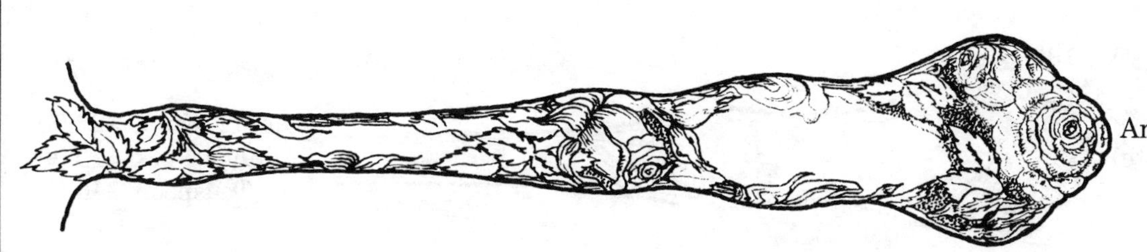

American Beauty Rose
1904
S

Not a full line.

Thin market.

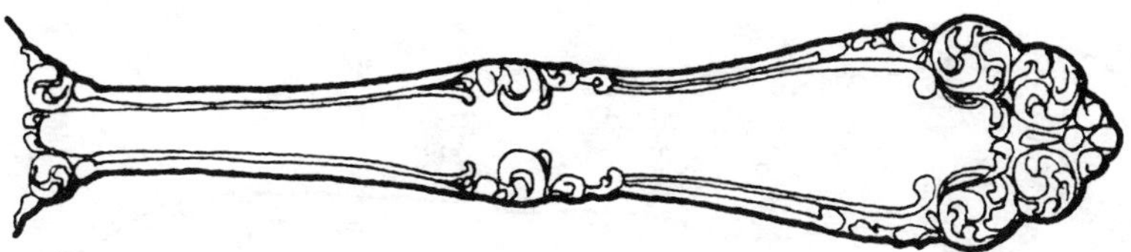

Imperial
1904
S

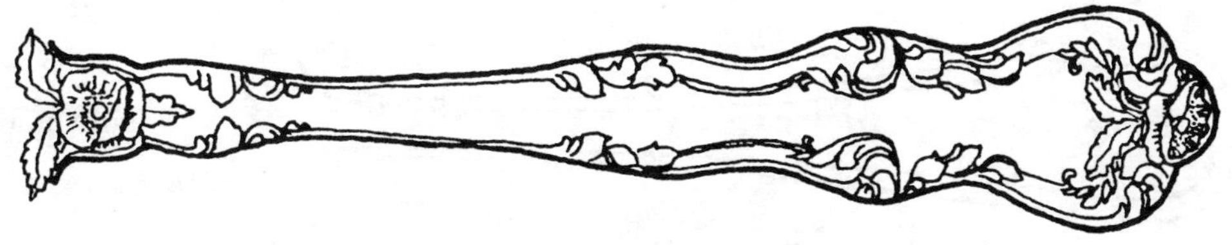

Orient aka Venice
(Rockford Silver Plate)
(Rochester)
1904
C

Dinner Knife $25.00 Dinner Fork $18.00 Teaspoon $10.00

Thin market.

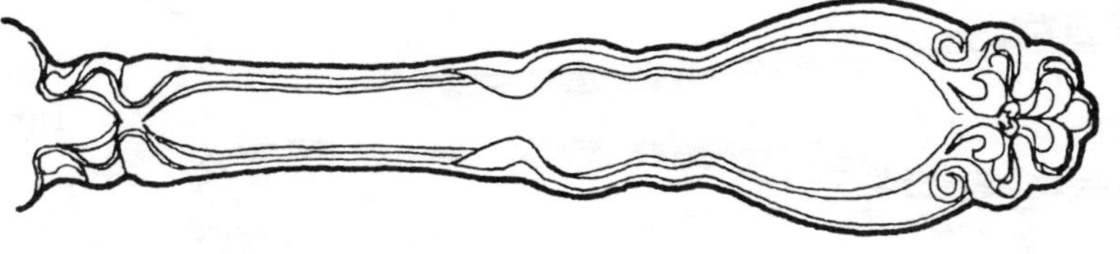

Chatsworth aka Chalon
(Cambridge)
(Paragon)
1906
S

Thin market.

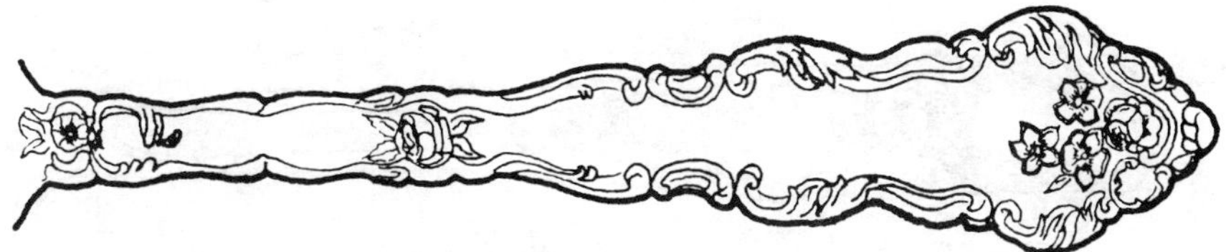

Lafayette
1908
S

Please refer to "How To Use This Book" page 4.

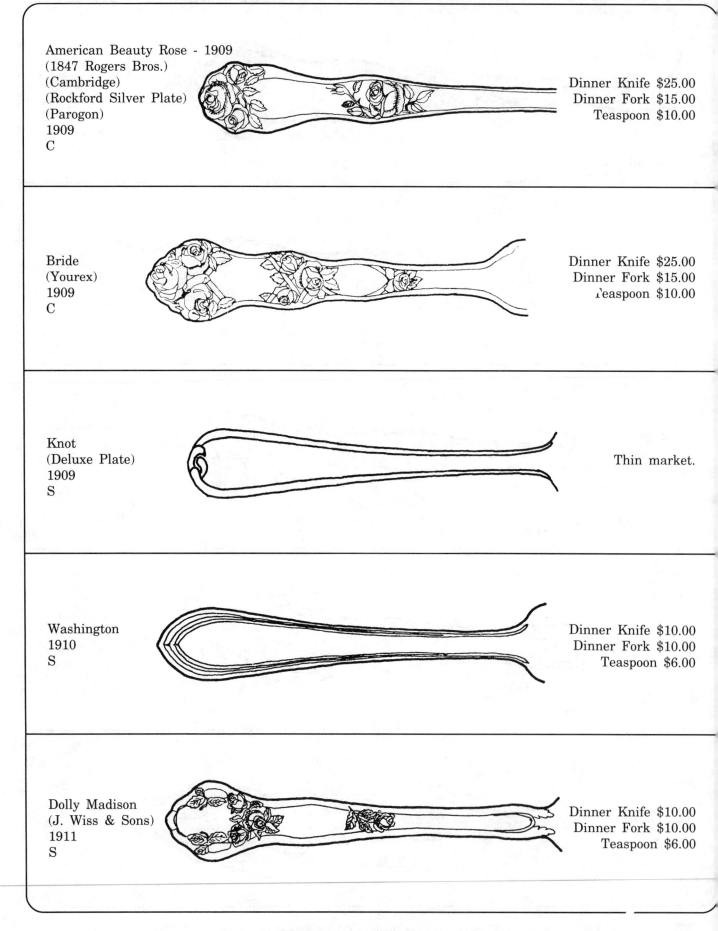

American Beauty Rose - 1909
(1847 Rogers Bros.)
(Cambridge)
(Rockford Silver Plate)
(Parogon)
1909
C

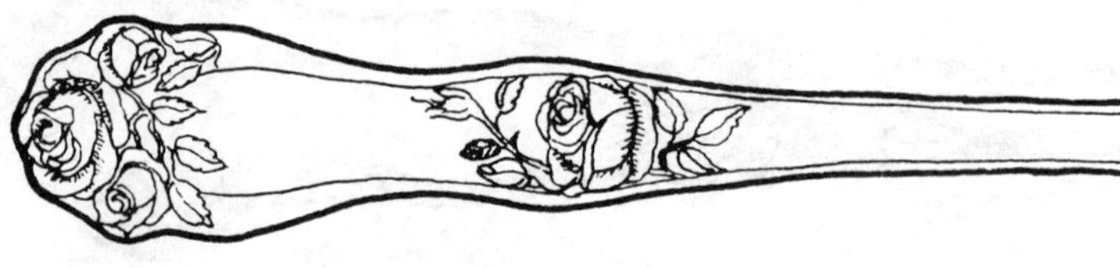

Dinner Knife $25.00
Dinner Fork $15.00
Teaspoon $10.00

Bride
(Yourex)
1909
C

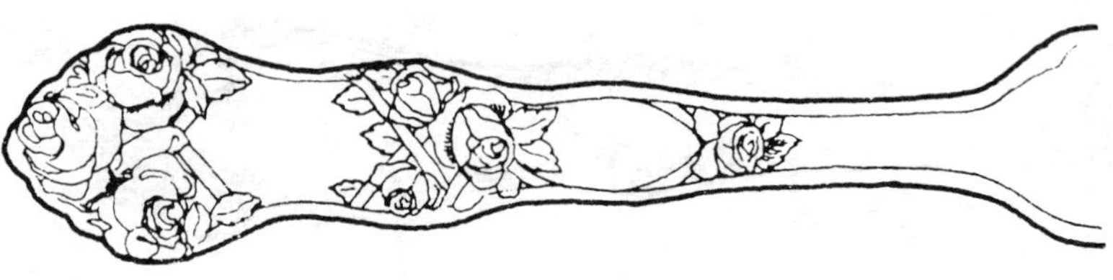

Dinner Knife $25.00
Dinner Fork $15.00
Teaspoon $10.00

Knot
(Deluxe Plate)
1909
S

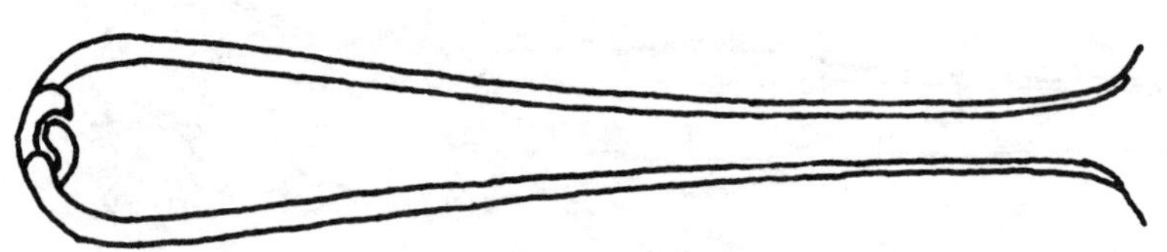

Thin market.

Washington
1910
S

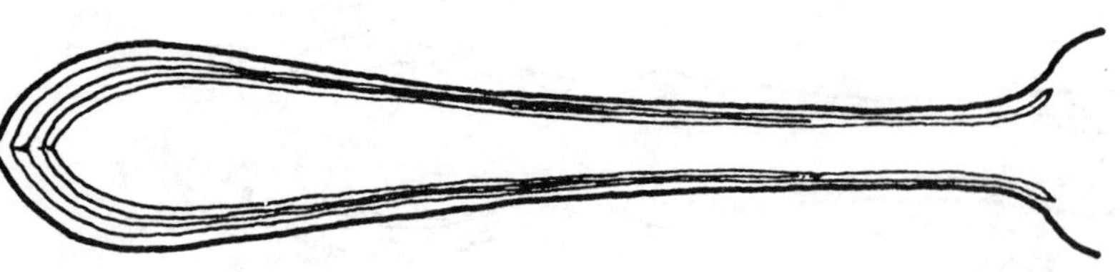

Dinner Knife $10.00
Dinner Fork $10.00
Teaspoon $6.00

Dolly Madison
(J. Wiss & Sons)
1911
S

Dinner Knife $10.00
Dinner Fork $10.00
Teaspoon $6.00

Please refer to "How To Use This Book" page 4.

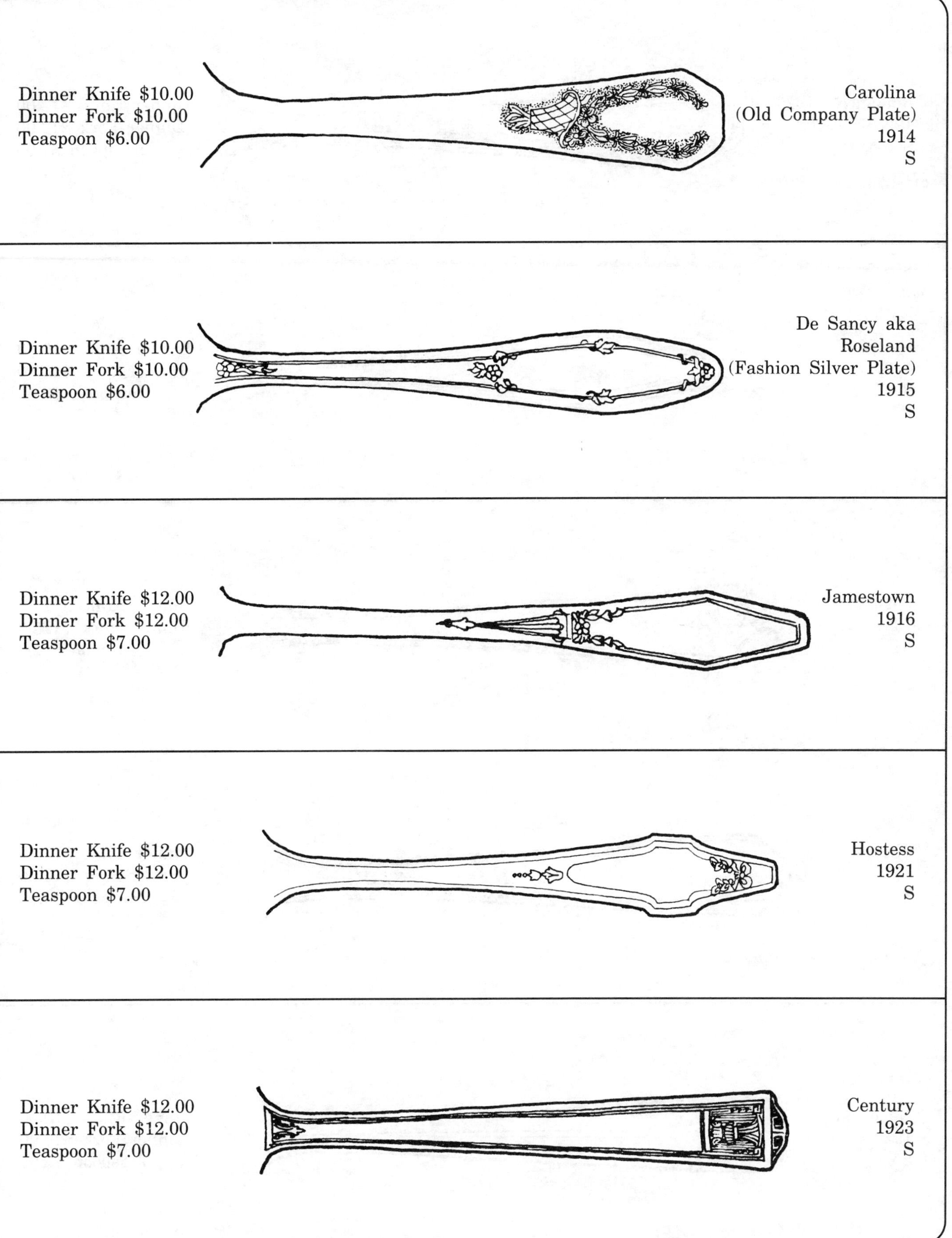

Dinner Knife $10.00
Dinner Fork $10.00
Teaspoon $6.00

Carolina
(Old Company Plate)
1914
S

Dinner Knife $10.00
Dinner Fork $10.00
Teaspoon $6.00

De Sancy aka
Roseland
(Fashion Silver Plate)
1915
S

Dinner Knife $12.00
Dinner Fork $12.00
Teaspoon $7.00

Jamestown
1916
S

Dinner Knife $12.00
Dinner Fork $12.00
Teaspoon $7.00

Hostess
1921
S

Dinner Knife $12.00
Dinner Fork $12.00
Teaspoon $7.00

Century
1923
S

Please refer to "How To Use This Book" page 4.

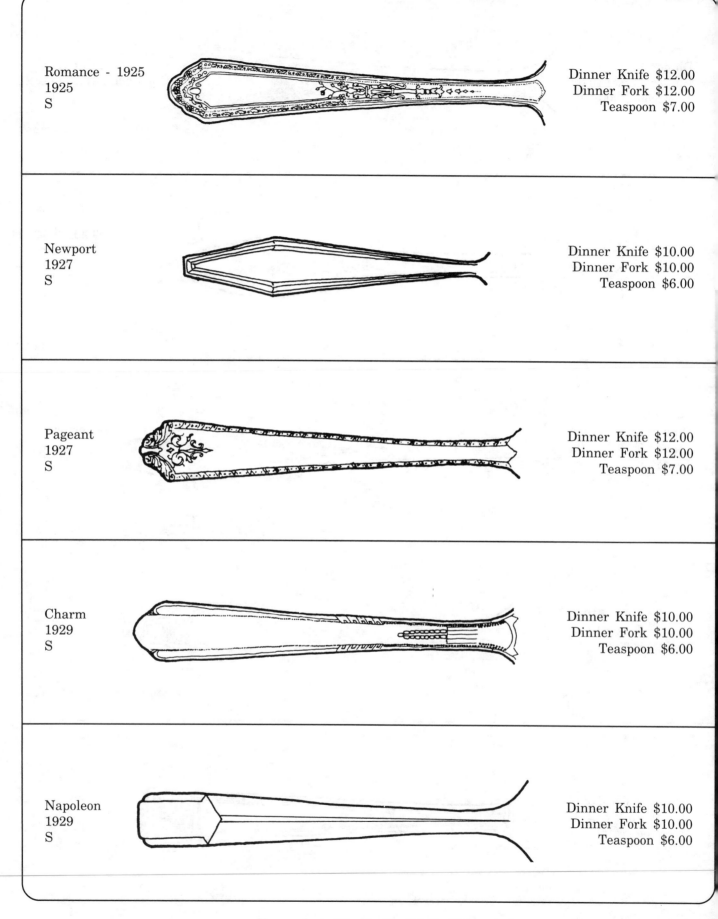

Romance - 1925
1925
S

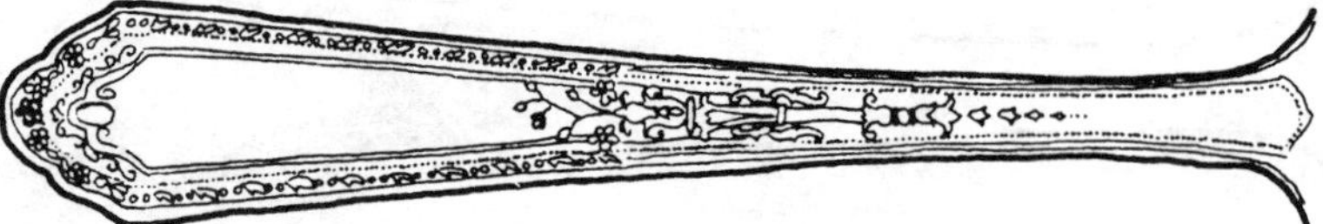

Dinner Knife $12.00
Dinner Fork $12.00
Teaspoon $7.00

Newport
1927
S

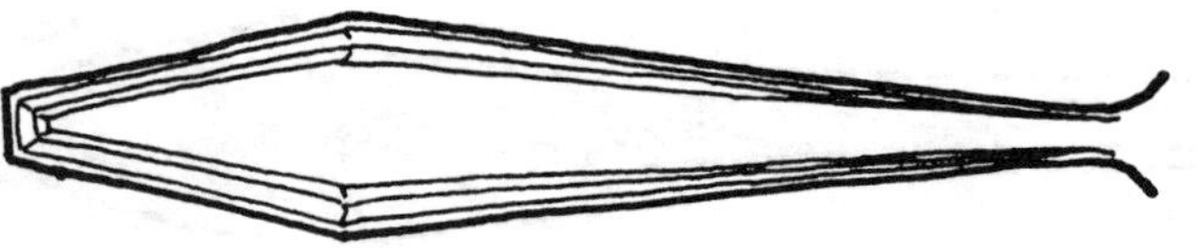

Dinner Knife $10.00
Dinner Fork $10.00
Teaspoon $6.00

Pageant
1927
S

Dinner Knife $12.00
Dinner Fork $12.00
Teaspoon $7.00

Charm
1929
S

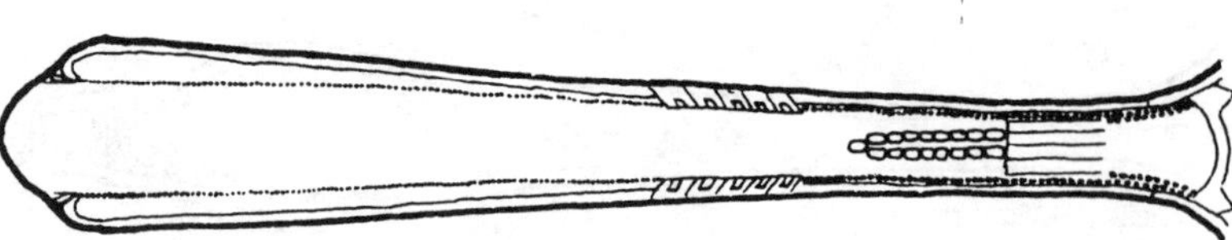

Dinner Knife $10.00
Dinner Fork $10.00
Teaspoon $6.00

Napoleon
1929
S

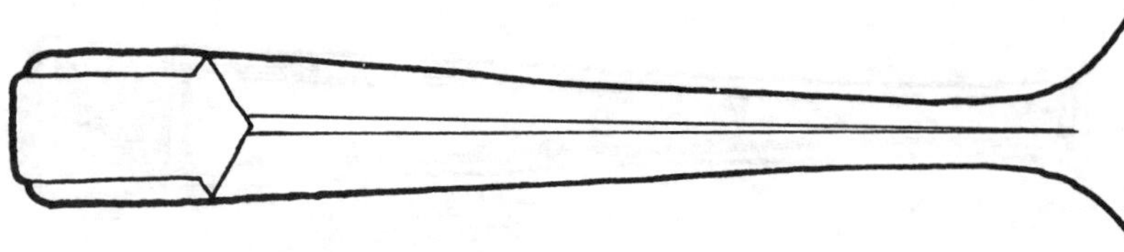

Dinner Knife $10.00
Dinner Fork $10.00
Teaspoon $6.00

Please refer to "How To Use This Book" page 4.

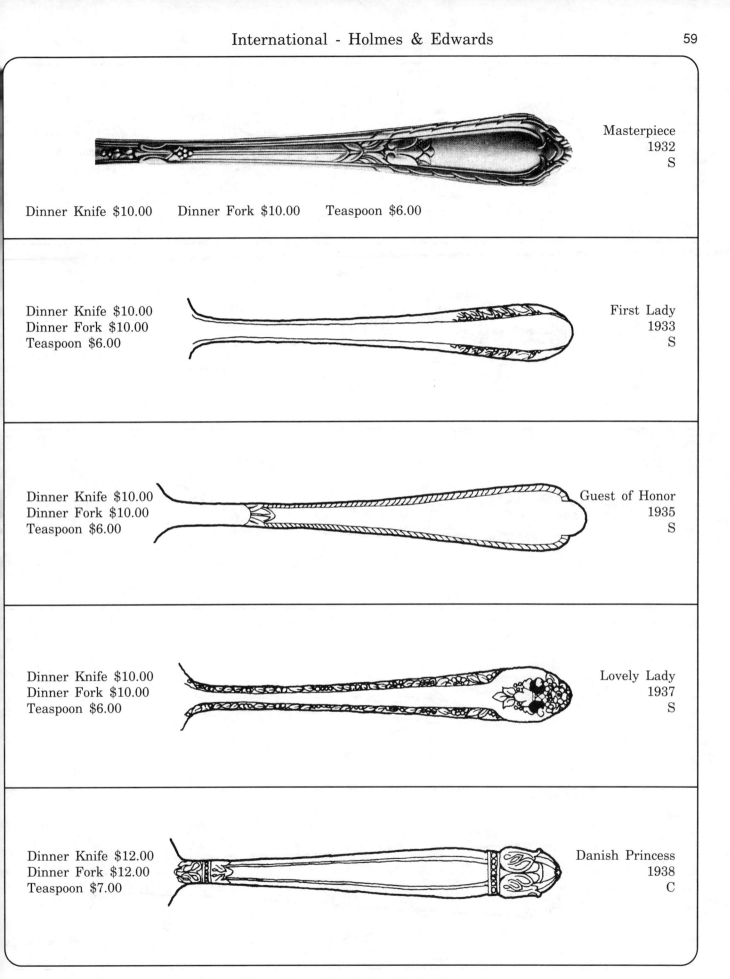

Masterpiece
1932
S

Dinner Knife $10.00 Dinner Fork $10.00 Teaspoon $6.00

Dinner Knife $10.00
Dinner Fork $10.00
Teaspoon $6.00

First Lady
1933
S

Dinner Knife $10.00
Dinner Fork $10.00
Teaspoon $6.00

Guest of Honor
1935
S

Dinner Knife $10.00
Dinner Fork $10.00
Teaspoon $6.00

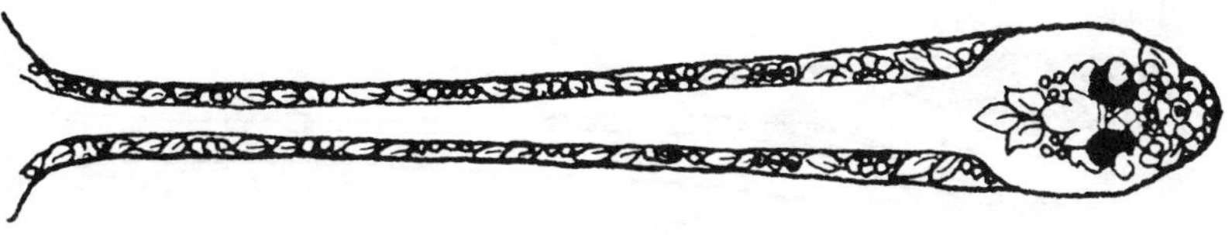

Lovely Lady
1937
S

Dinner Knife $12.00
Dinner Fork $12.00
Teaspoon $7.00

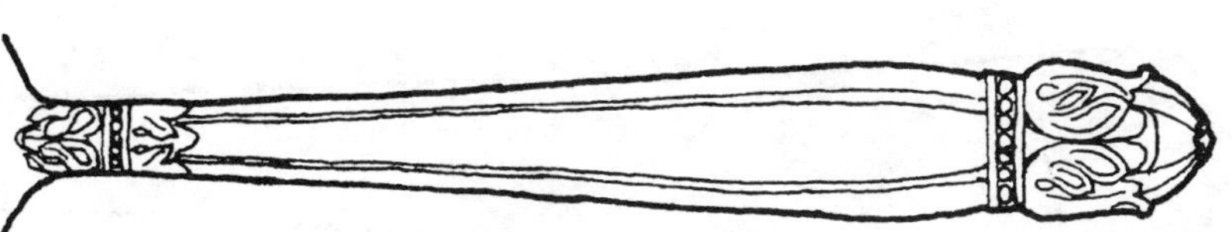

Danish Princess
1938
C

Please refer to "How To Use This Book" page 4.

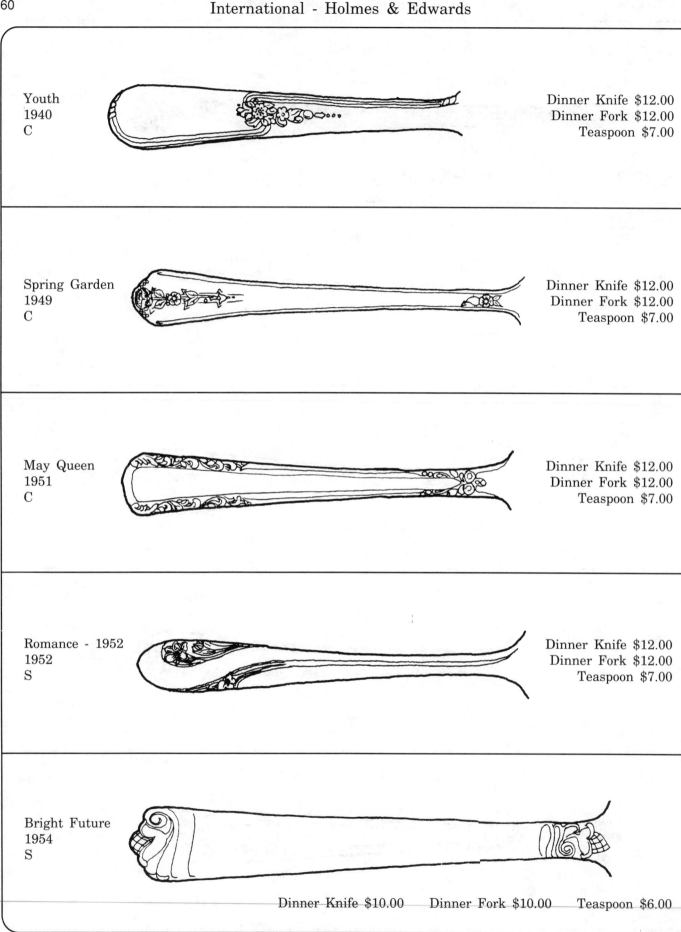

Youth
1940
C

Dinner Knife $12.00
Dinner Fork $12.00
Teaspoon $7.00

Spring Garden
1949
C

Dinner Knife $12.00
Dinner Fork $12.00
Teaspoon $7.00

May Queen
1951
C

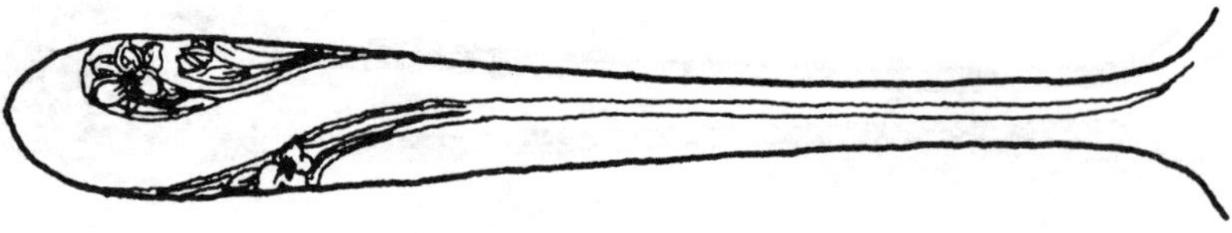

Dinner Knife $12.00
Dinner Fork $12.00
Teaspoon $7.00

Romance - 1952
1952
S

Dinner Knife $12.00
Dinner Fork $12.00
Teaspoon $7.00

Bright Future
1954
S

Dinner Knife $10.00 Dinner Fork $10.00 Teaspoon $6.00

Please refer to "How To Use This Book" page 4.

Dinner Knife $10.00
Dinner Fork $10.00
Teaspoon $6.00

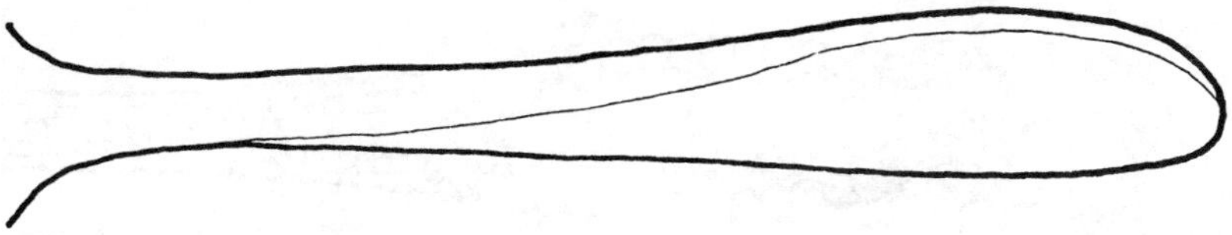

Rhythmic
1957
S

Dinner Knife $12.00
Dinner Fork $12.00
Teaspoon $7.00

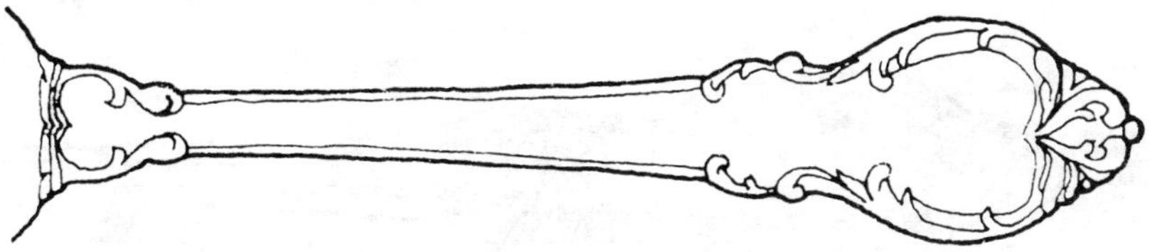

Silver Fashion
(Deep Silver)
1957
S

Dinner Knife $10.00
Dinner Fork $10.00
Teaspoon $6.00

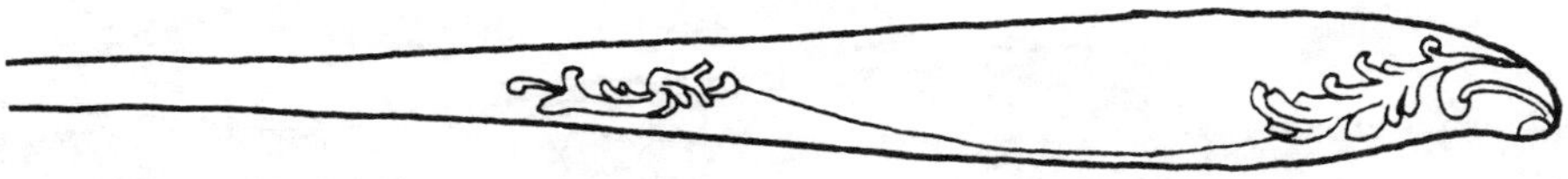

Woodsong
1958
S

International - Hollyhock Silver Plate

Dinner Knife $8.00
Dinner Fork $8.00
Teaspoon $5.00

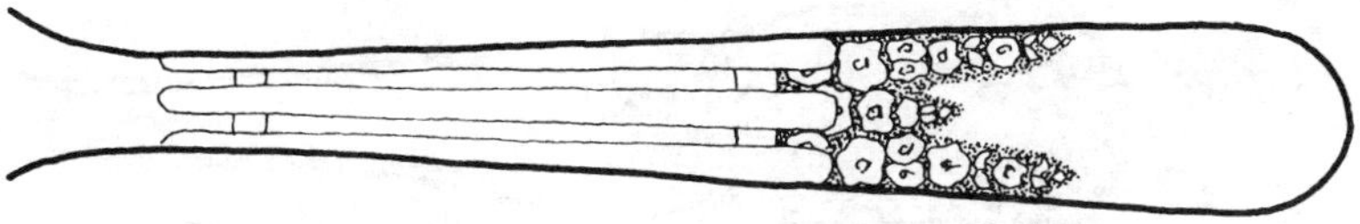

Hollyhock
1940
S

International - Hope Chest

Dinner Knife $8.00
Dinner Fork $8.00
Teaspoon $5.00

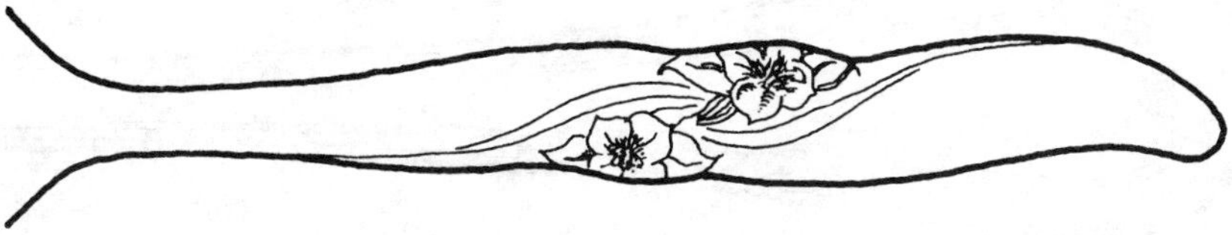

Silver Wind
1955
S

Please refer to "How To Use This Book" page 4.

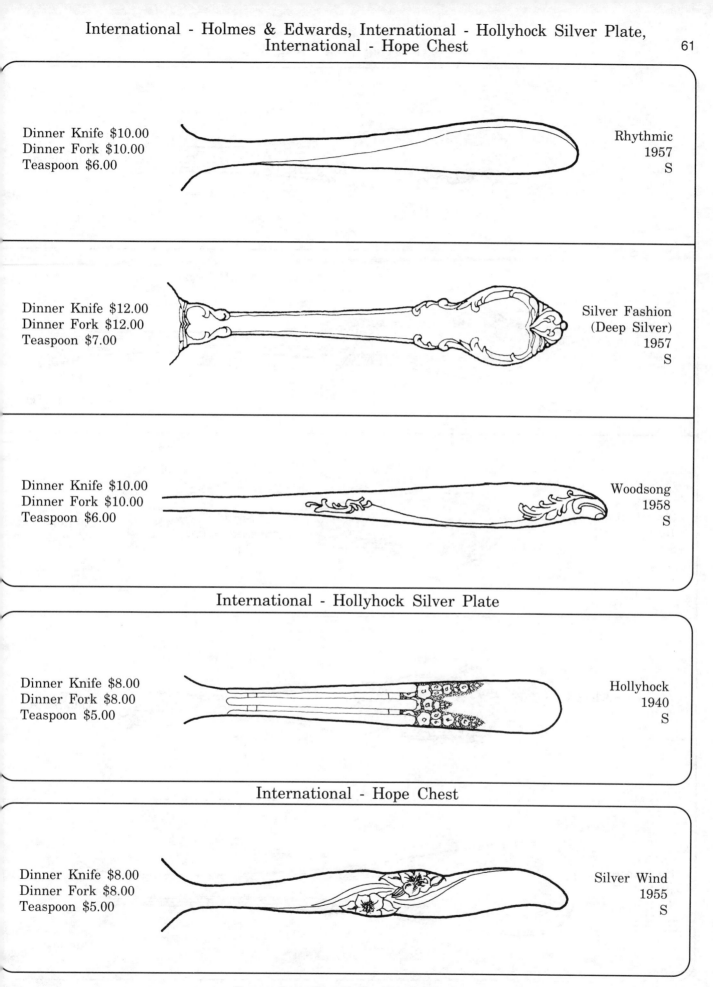

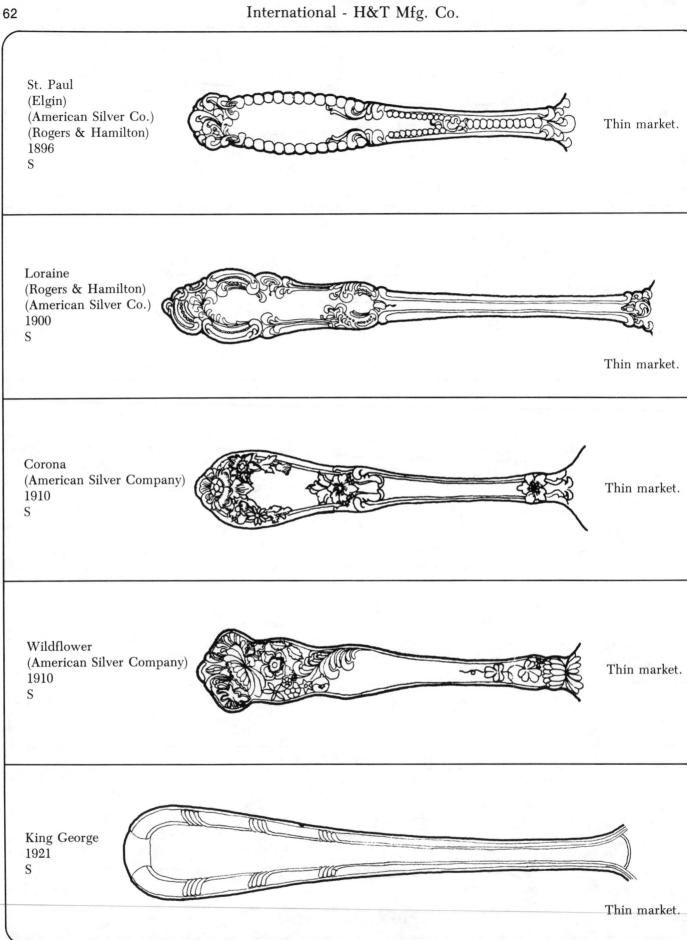

St. Paul
(Elgin)
(American Silver Co.)
(Rogers & Hamilton)
1896
S

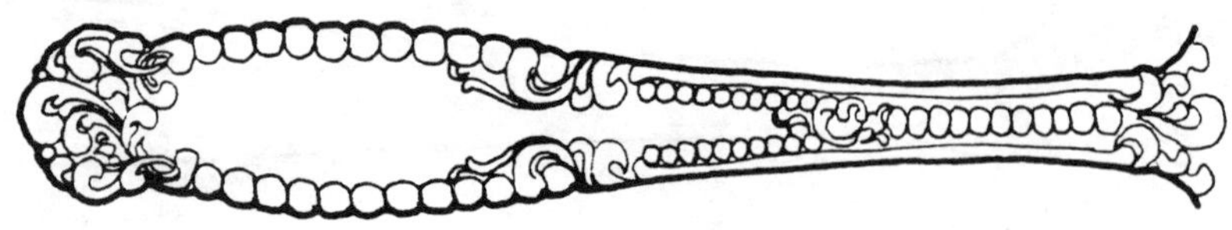

Thin market.

Loraine
(Rogers & Hamilton)
(American Silver Co.)
1900
S

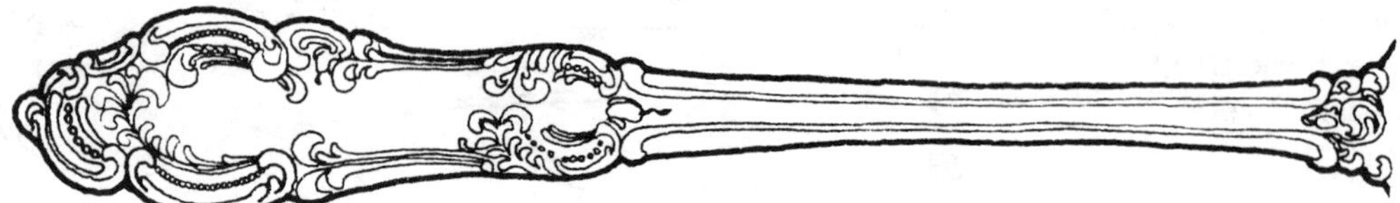

Thin market.

Corona
(American Silver Company)
1910
S

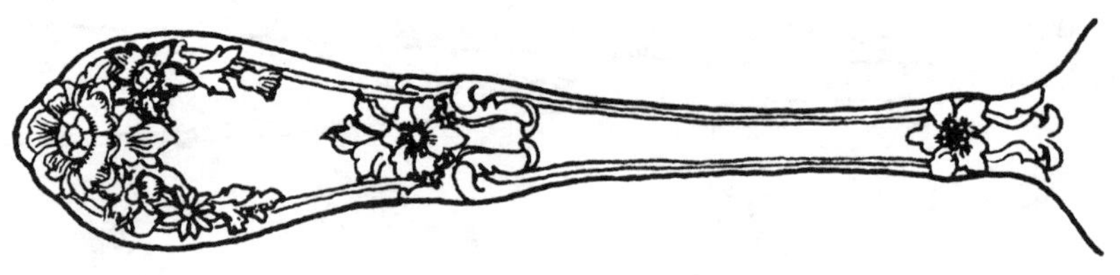

Thin market.

Wildflower
(American Silver Company)
1910
S

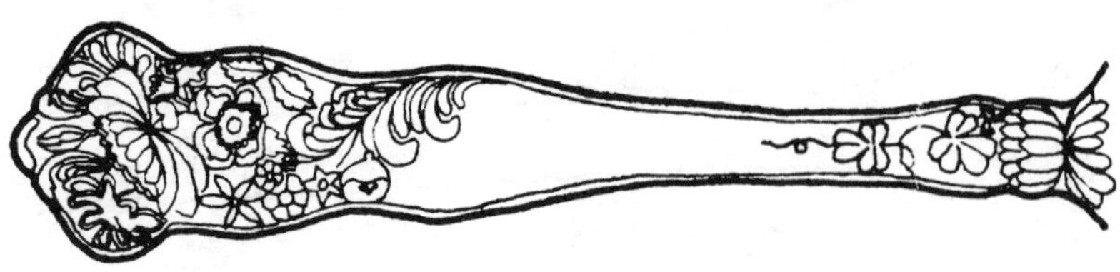

Thin market.

King George
1921
S

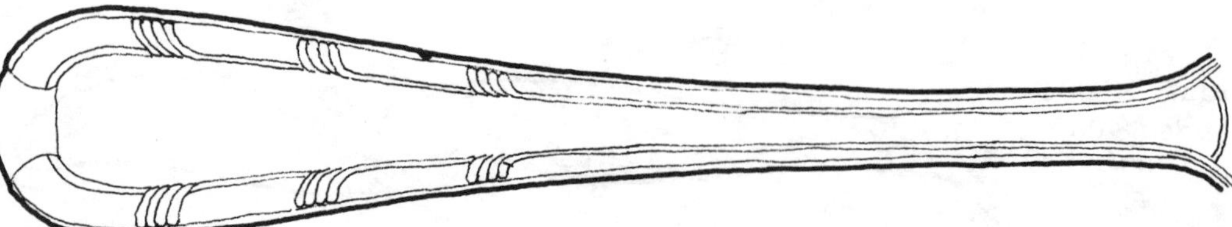

Thin market.

Please refer to "How To Use This Book" page 4.

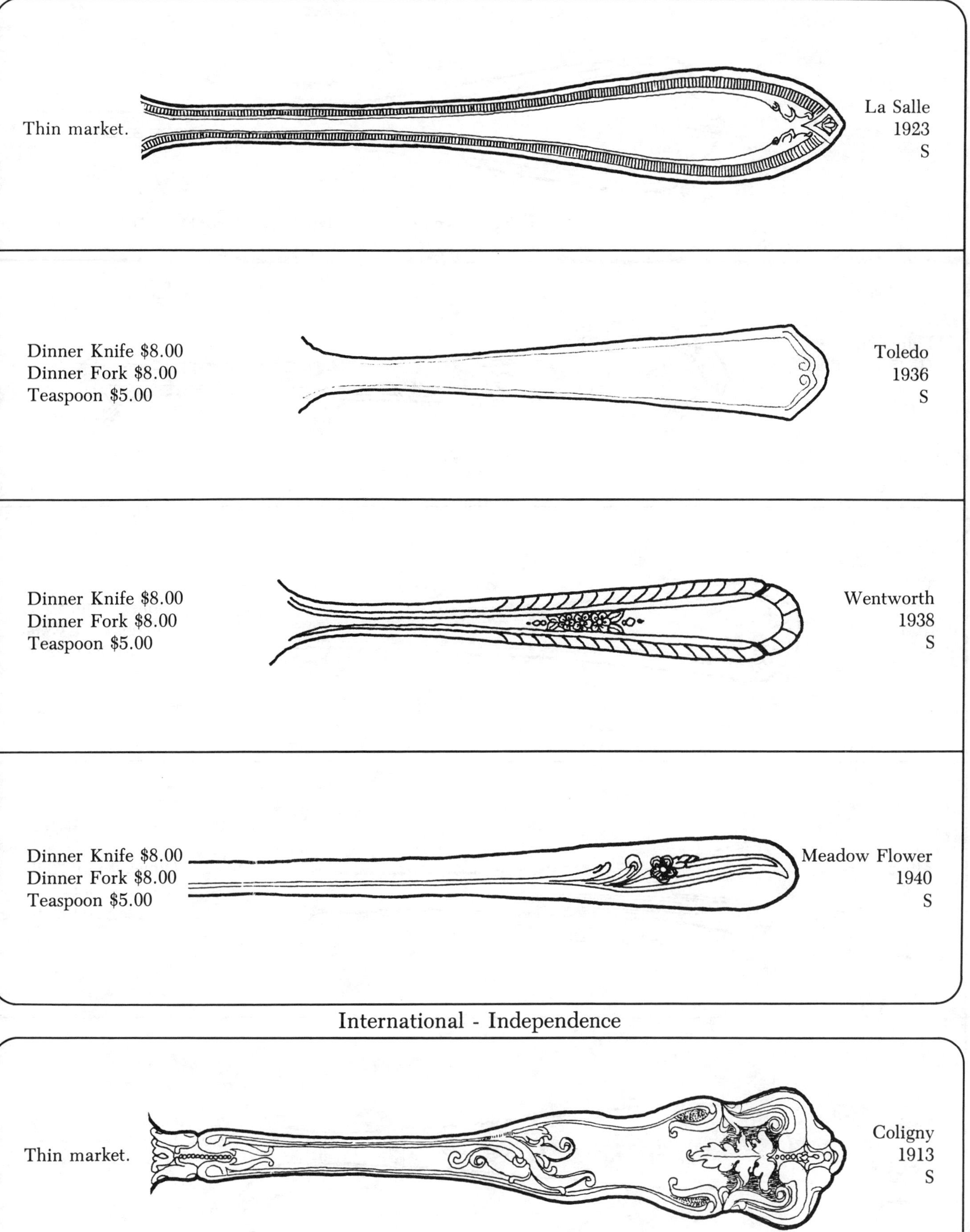

Thin market.

La Salle
1923
S

Dinner Knife $8.00
Dinner Fork $8.00
Teaspoon $5.00

Toledo
1936
S

Dinner Knife $8.00
Dinner Fork $8.00
Teaspoon $5.00

Wentworth
1938
S

Dinner Knife $8.00
Dinner Fork $8.00
Teaspoon $5.00

Meadow Flower
1940
S

International - Independence

Thin market.

Coligny
1913
S

Please refer to "How To Use This Book" page 4.

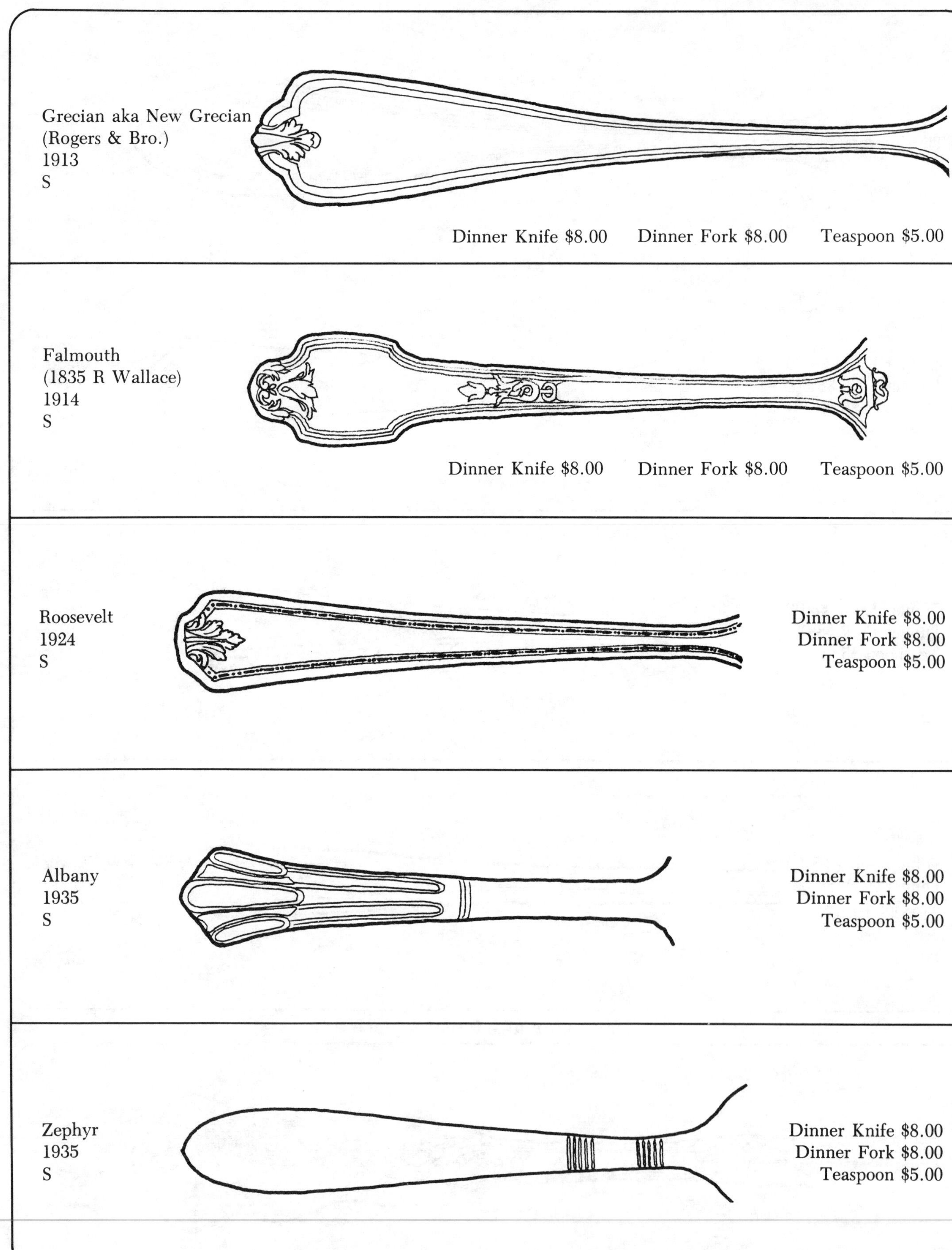

Grecian aka New Grecian
(Rogers & Bro.)
1913
S

Dinner Knife $8.00 Dinner Fork $8.00 Teaspoon $5.00

Falmouth
(1835 R Wallace)
1914
S

Dinner Knife $8.00 Dinner Fork $8.00 Teaspoon $5.00

Roosevelt
1924
S

Dinner Knife $8.00
Dinner Fork $8.00
Teaspoon $5.00

Albany
1935
S

Dinner Knife $8.00
Dinner Fork $8.00
Teaspoon $5.00

Zephyr
1935
S

Dinner Knife $8.00
Dinner Fork $8.00
Teaspoon $5.00

Please refer to "How To Use This Book" page 4.

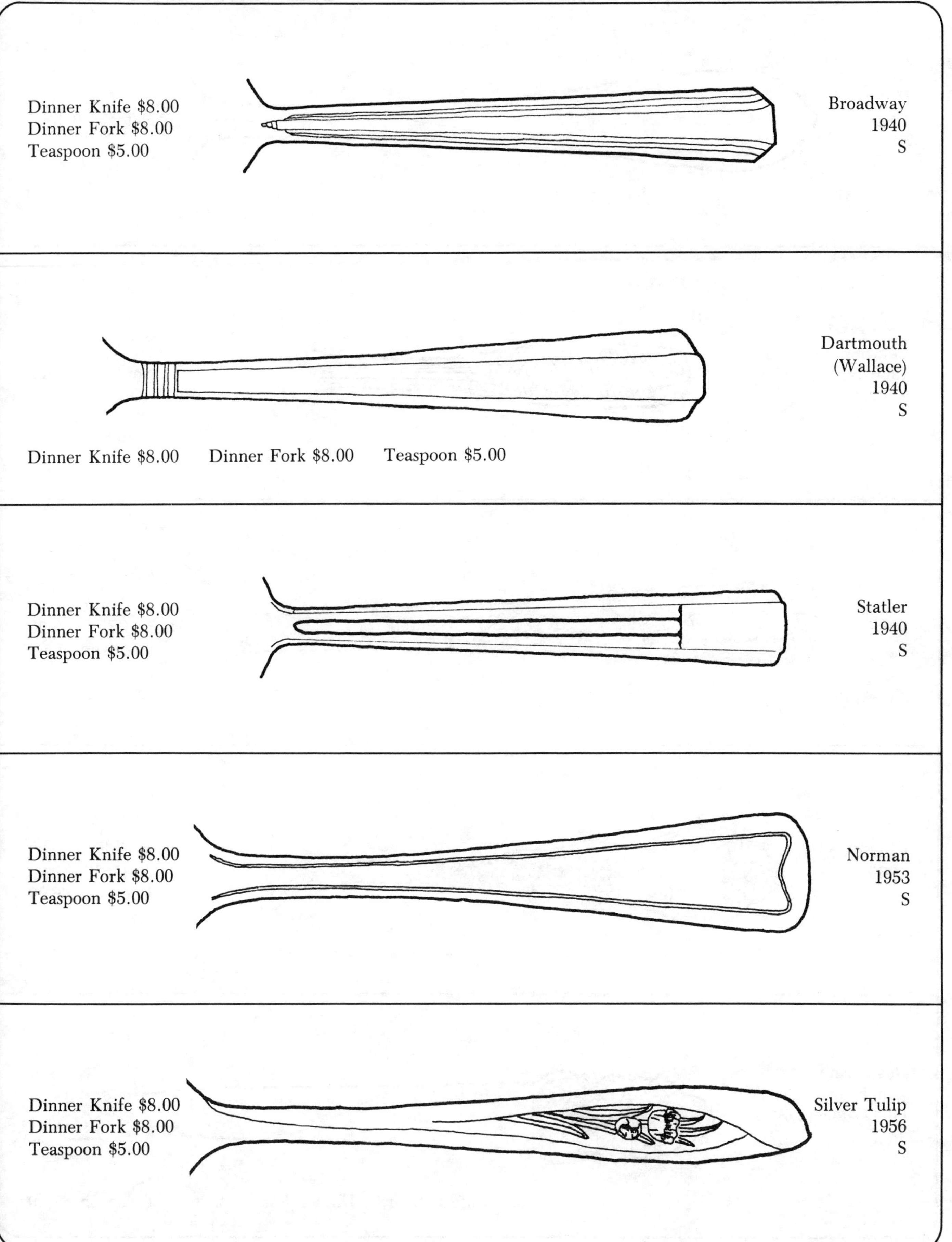

Dinner Knife $8.00
Dinner Fork $8.00
Teaspoon $5.00

Broadway
1940
S

Dartmouth
(Wallace)
1940
S

Dinner Knife $8.00 Dinner Fork $8.00 Teaspoon $5.00

Dinner Knife $8.00
Dinner Fork $8.00
Teaspoon $5.00

Statler
1940
S

Dinner Knife $8.00
Dinner Fork $8.00
Teaspoon $5.00

Norman
1953
S

Dinner Knife $8.00
Dinner Fork $8.00
Teaspoon $5.00

Silver Tulip
1956
S

Please refer to "How To Use This Book" page 4.

Hutton
1960
S

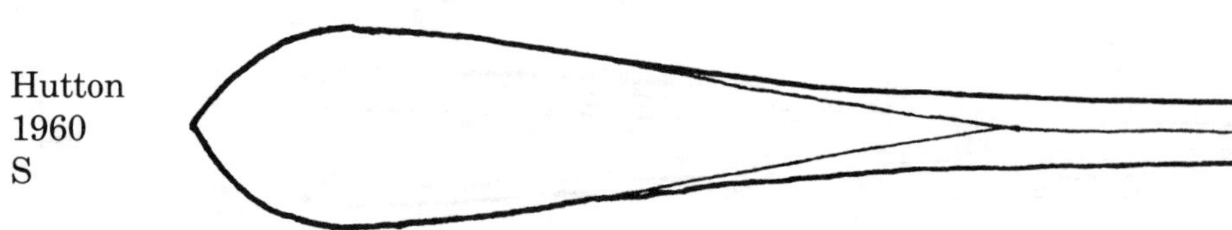

Not a full line.

Century Moritz
1966
S

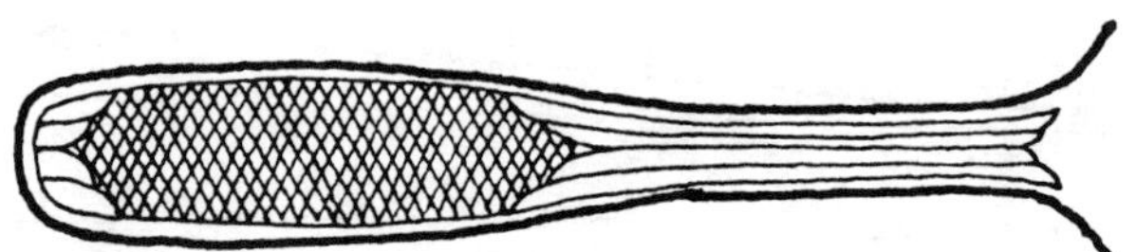

Not a full line.

Vintage
1968
S

Dinner Knife $8.00
Dinner Fork $8.00
Teaspoon $5.00

Chalfonte
1969
S

Dinner Knife $10.00
Dinner Fork $10.00
Teaspoon $6.00

Royal Empress
aka King Frederik
(1847 Rogers Bros.)
1969
C

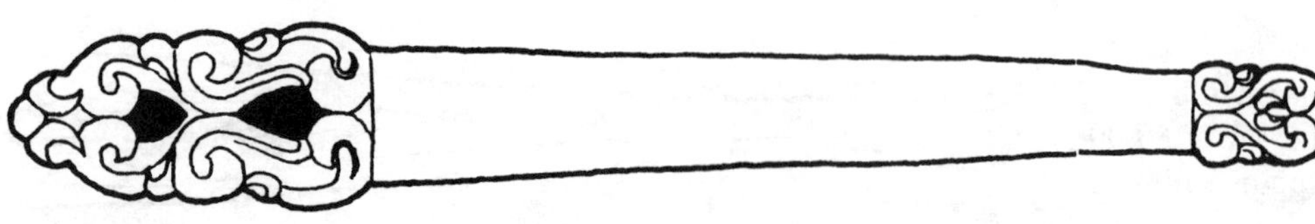

Dinner Knife $12.00 Dinner Fork $12.00 Teaspoon $7.00

Please refer to "How To Use This Book" page 4.

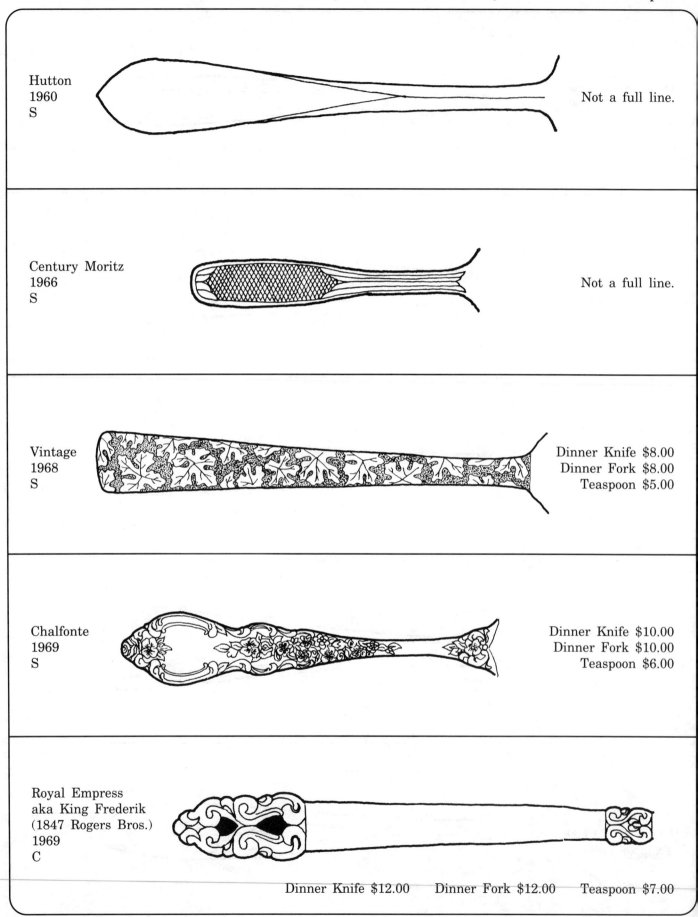

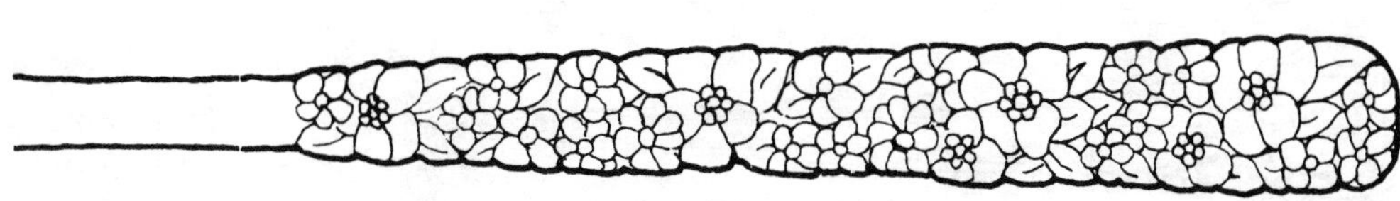

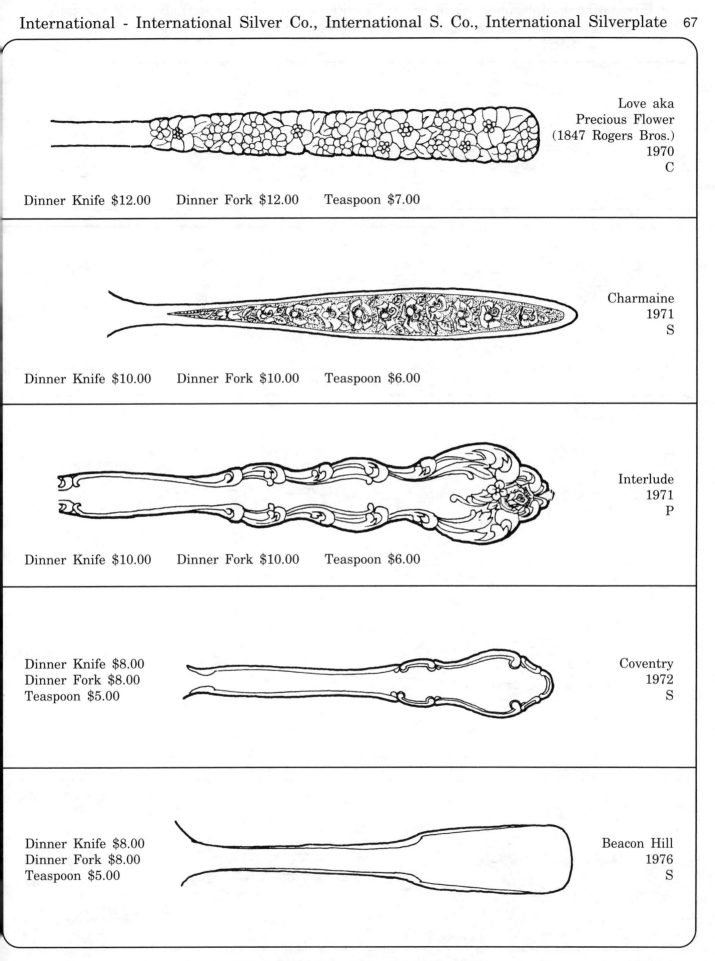

Love aka
Precious Flower
(1847 Rogers Bros.)
1970
C

Dinner Knife $12.00 Dinner Fork $12.00 Teaspoon $7.00

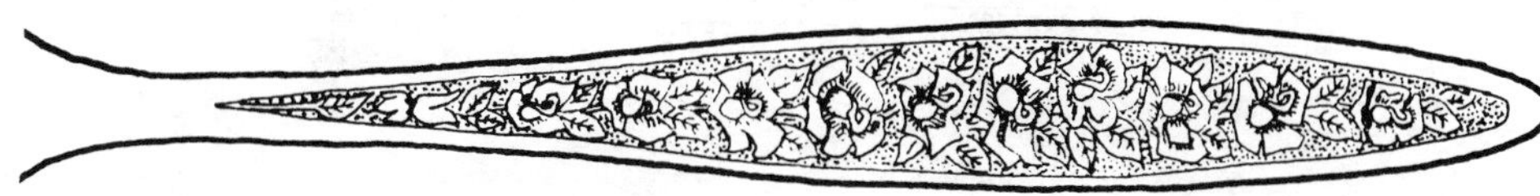

Charmaine
1971
S

Dinner Knife $10.00 Dinner Fork $10.00 Teaspoon $6.00

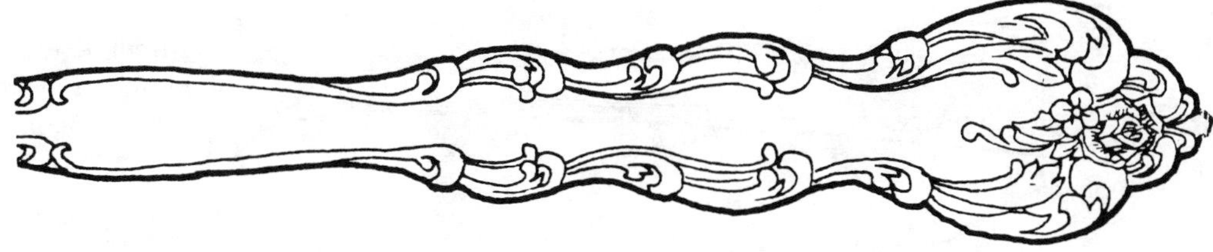

Interlude
1971
P

Dinner Knife $10.00 Dinner Fork $10.00 Teaspoon $6.00

Dinner Knife $8.00
Dinner Fork $8.00
Teaspoon $5.00

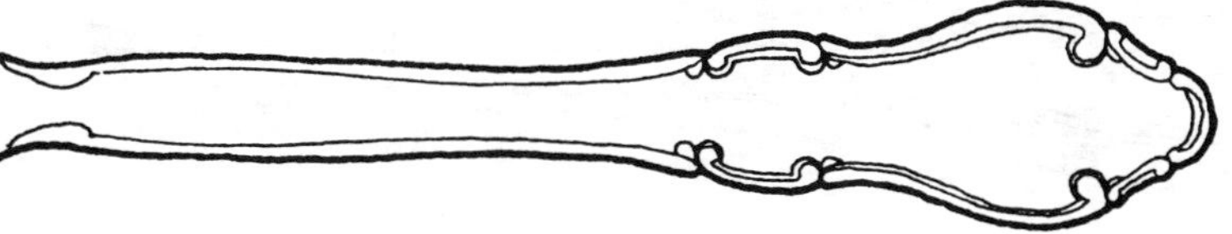

Coventry
1972
S

Dinner Knife $8.00
Dinner Fork $8.00
Teaspoon $5.00

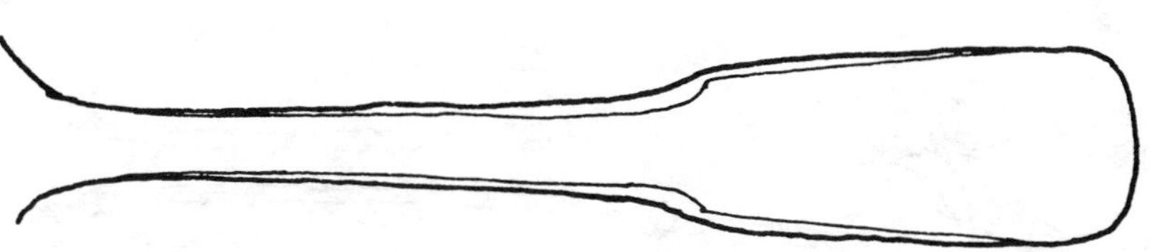

Beacon Hill
1976
S

Please refer to "How To Use This Book" page 4.

International - International Silver Co., International S. Co., International Silverplate, International - Kensington Silver Plate, International - Lady Betty Silver Plate

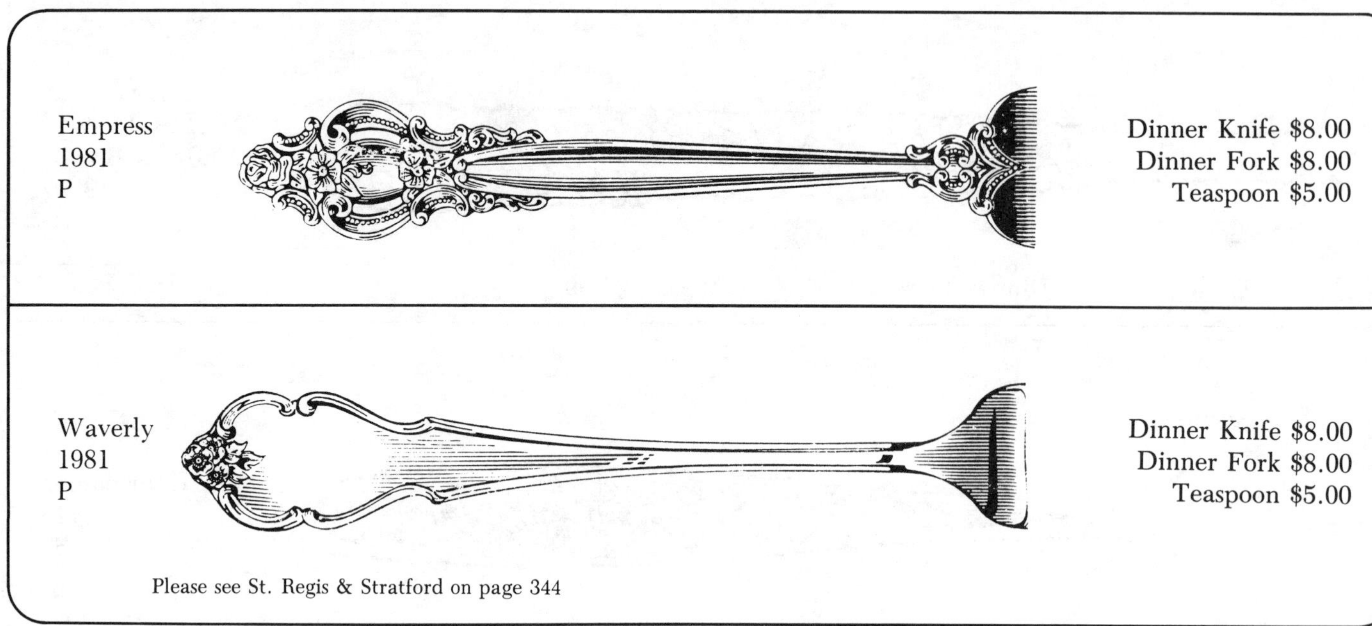

Empress
1981
P

Dinner Knife $8.00
Dinner Fork $8.00
Teaspoon $5.00

Waverly
1981
P

Dinner Knife $8.00
Dinner Fork $8.00
Teaspoon $5.00

Please see St. Regis & Stratford on page 344

International - Kensington Silver Plate

Sheldon
1920
S

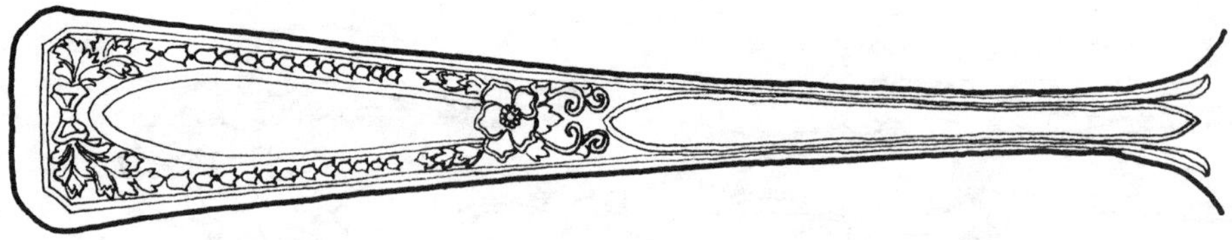

Dinner Knife $8.00
Dinner Fork $8.00
Teaspoon $5.00

International - Lady Betty Silverplate

Lady Betty
1940
S

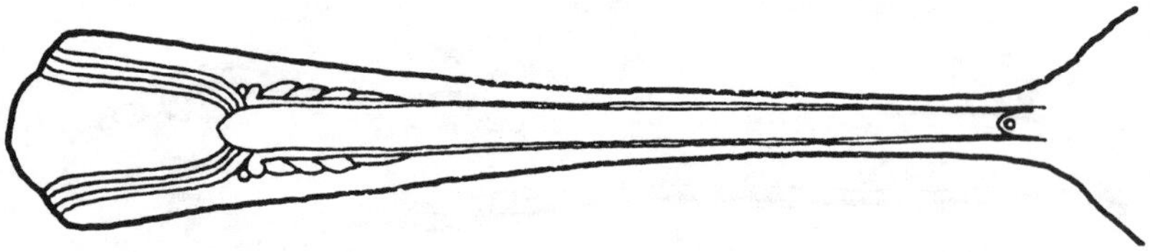

Dinner Knife $8.00
Dinner Fork $8.00
Teaspoon $5.00

International - Melody Silver Plate

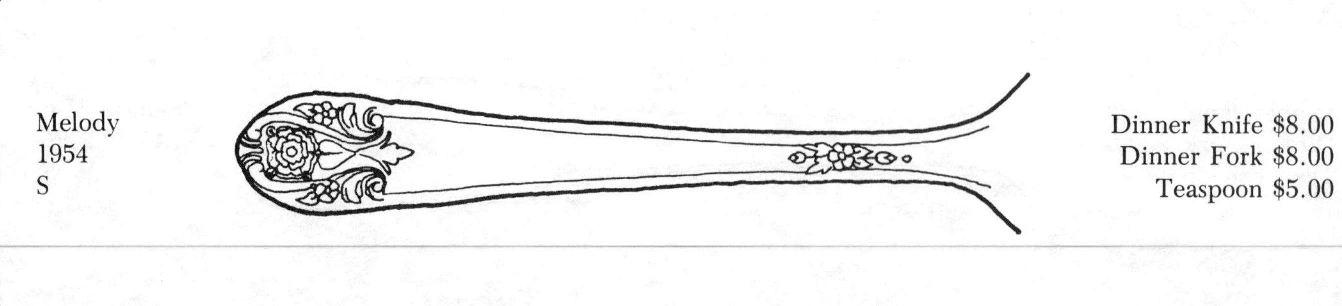

Melody
1954
S

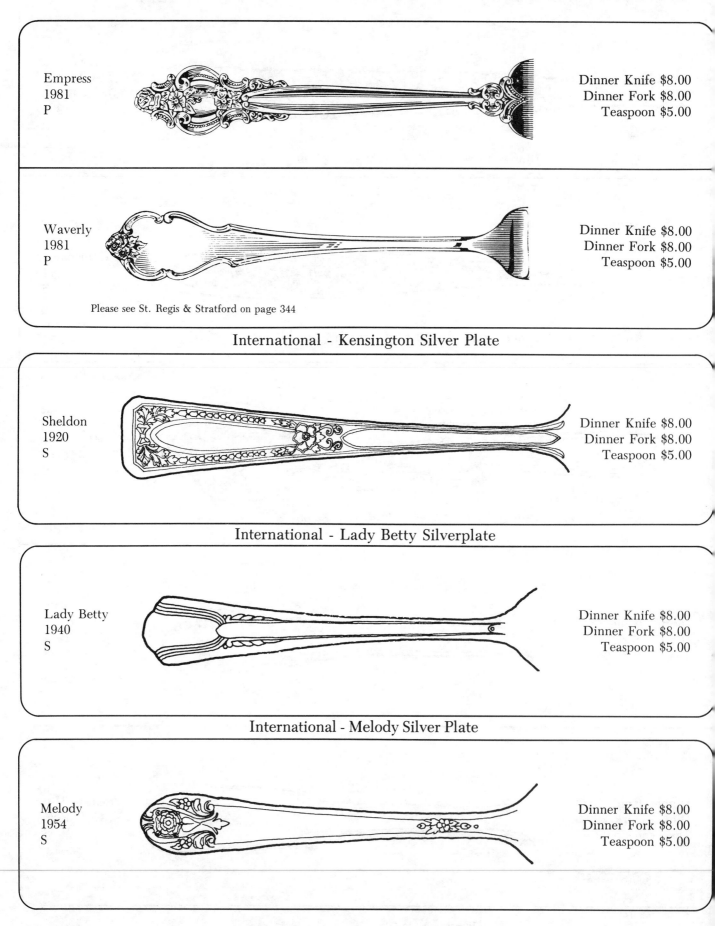

Dinner Knife $8.00
Dinner Fork $8.00
Teaspoon $5.00

Please refer to "How To Use This Book" page 4.

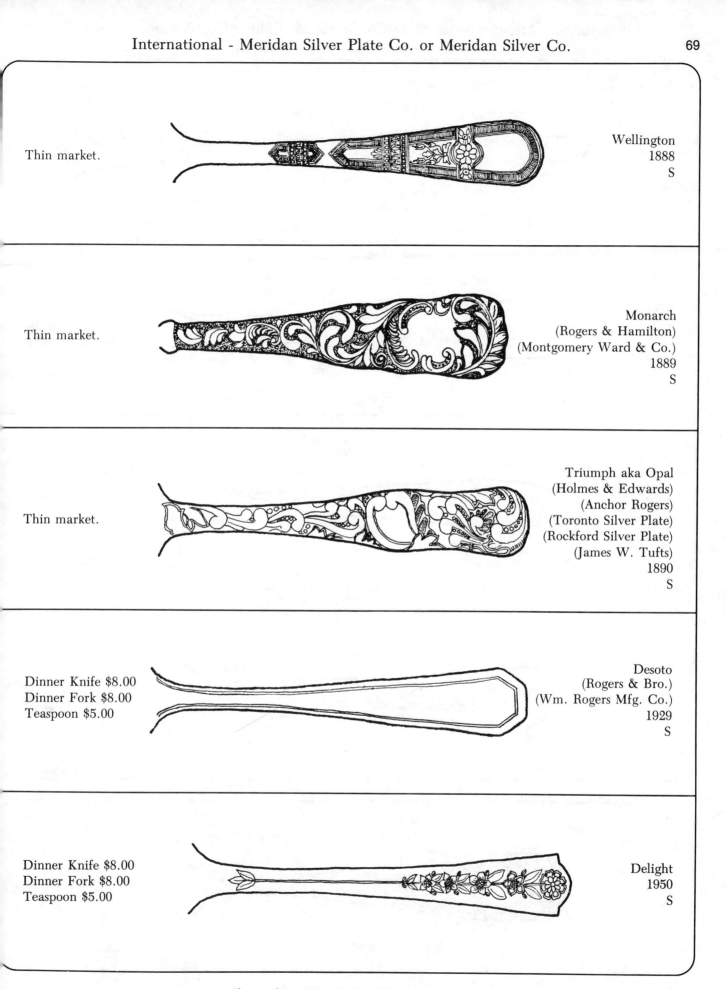

Thin market.

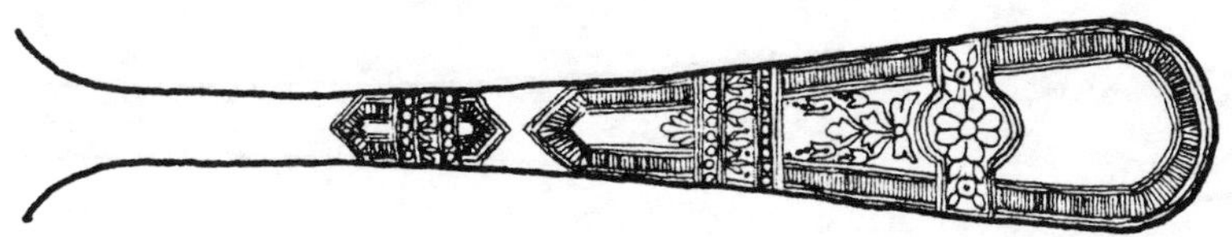

Wellington
1888
S

Thin market.

Monarch
(Rogers & Hamilton)
(Montgomery Ward & Co.)
1889
S

Thin market.

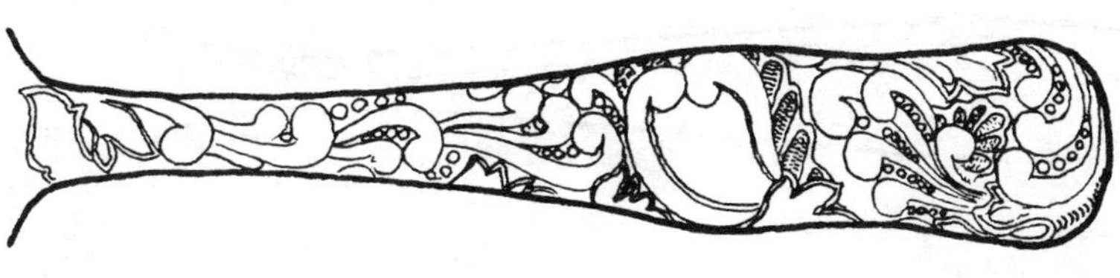

Triumph aka Opal
(Holmes & Edwards)
(Anchor Rogers)
(Toronto Silver Plate)
(Rockford Silver Plate)
(James W. Tufts)
1890
S

Dinner Knife $8.00
Dinner Fork $8.00
Teaspoon $5.00

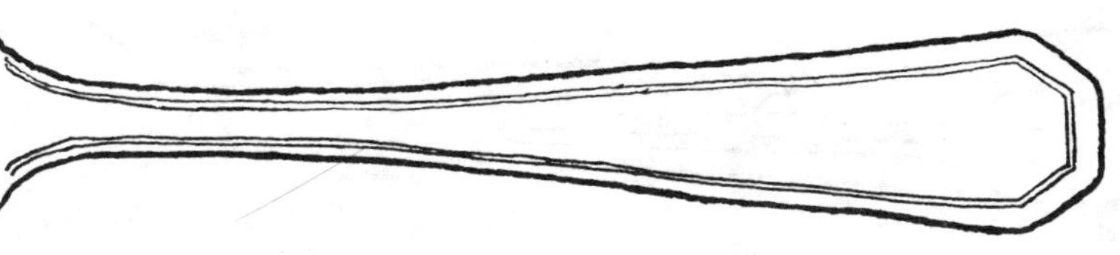

Desoto
(Rogers & Bro.)
(Wm. Rogers Mfg. Co.)
1929
S

Dinner Knife $8.00
Dinner Fork $8.00
Teaspoon $5.00

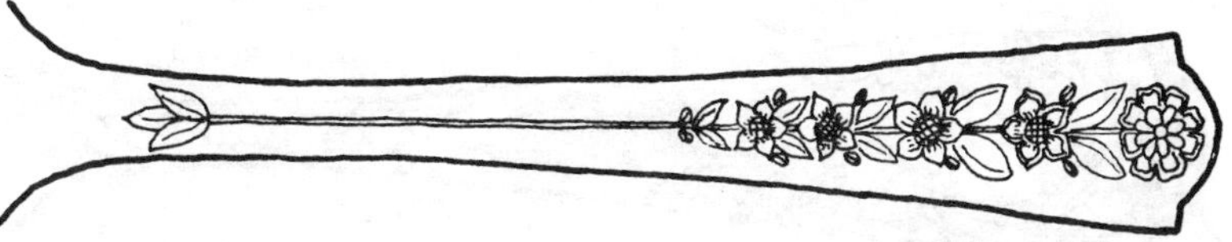

Delight
1950
S

Please refer to "How To Use This Book" page 4.

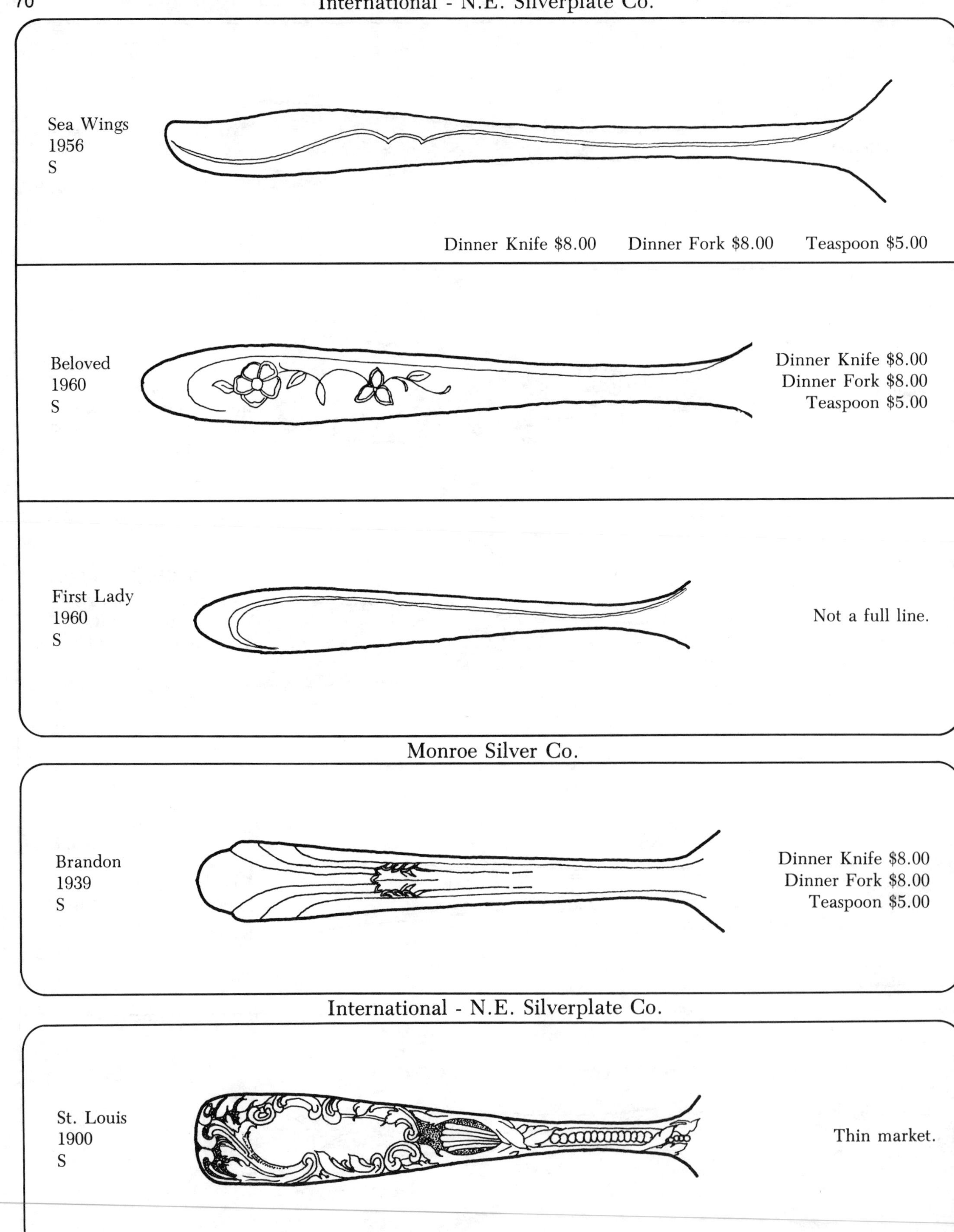

Sea Wings
1956
S

Dinner Knife $8.00 Dinner Fork $8.00 Teaspoon $5.00

Beloved
1960
S

Dinner Knife $8.00
Dinner Fork $8.00
Teaspoon $5.00

First Lady
1960
S

Not a full line.

Monroe Silver Co.

Brandon
1939
S

Dinner Knife $8.00
Dinner Fork $8.00
Teaspoon $5.00

International - N.E. Silverplate Co.

St. Louis
1900
S

Thin market.

Please refer to "How To Use This Book" page 4.

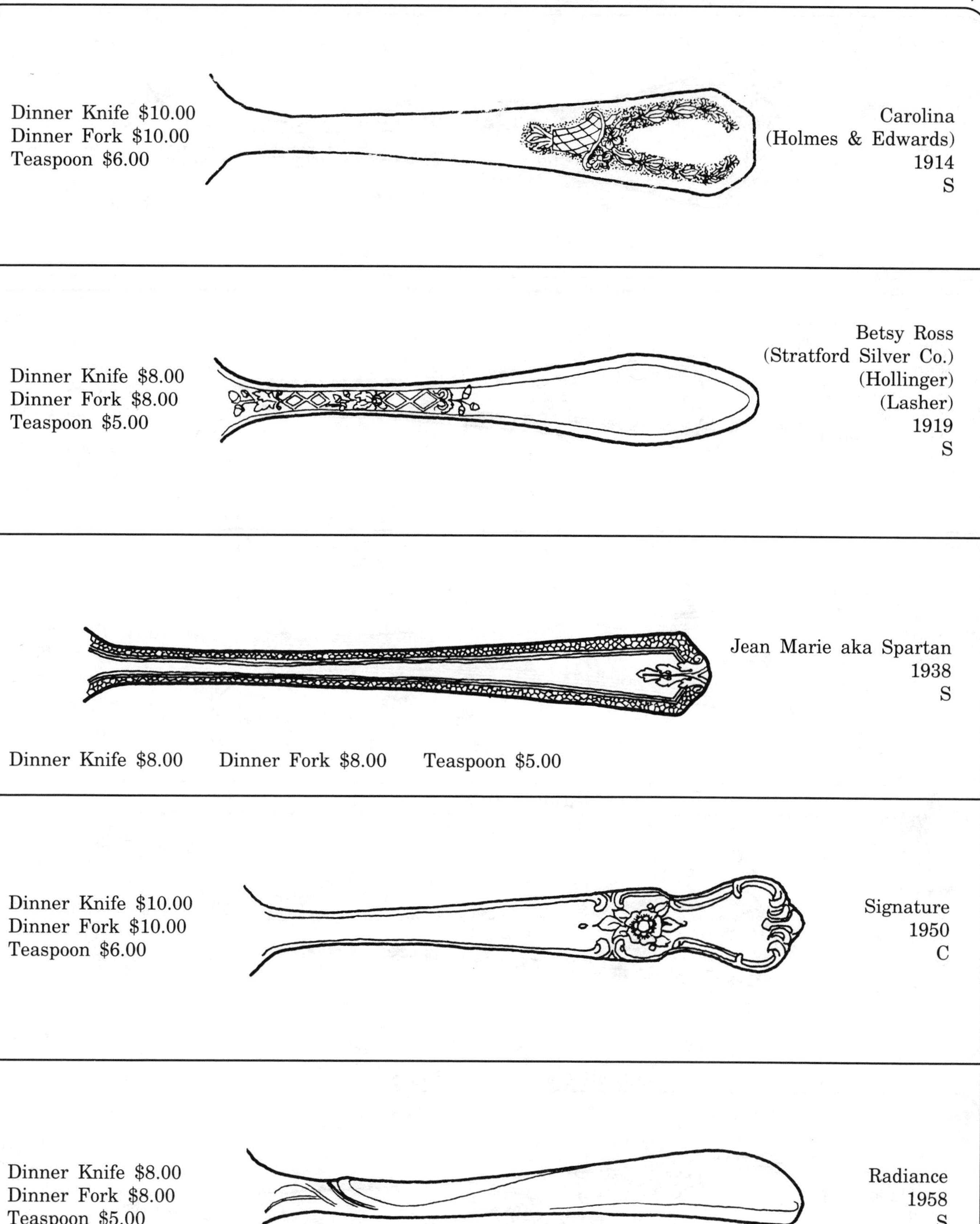

Dinner Knife $10.00
Dinner Fork $10.00
Teaspoon $6.00

Carolina
(Holmes & Edwards)
1914
S

Dinner Knife $8.00
Dinner Fork $8.00
Teaspoon $5.00

Betsy Ross
(Stratford Silver Co.)
(Hollinger)
(Lasher)
1919
S

Jean Marie aka Spartan
1938
S

Dinner Knife $8.00 Dinner Fork $8.00 Teaspoon $5.00

Dinner Knife $10.00
Dinner Fork $10.00
Teaspoon $6.00

Signature
1950
C

Dinner Knife $8.00
Dinner Fork $8.00
Teaspoon $5.00

Radiance
1958
S

Please refer to "How To Use This Book" page 4.

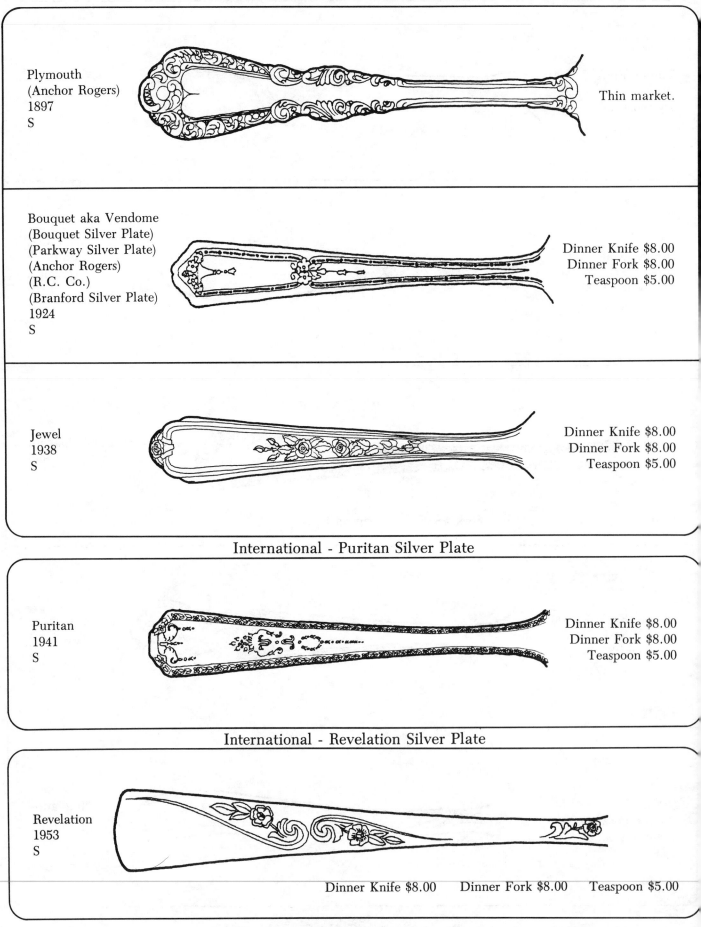

Plymouth
(Anchor Rogers)
1897
S

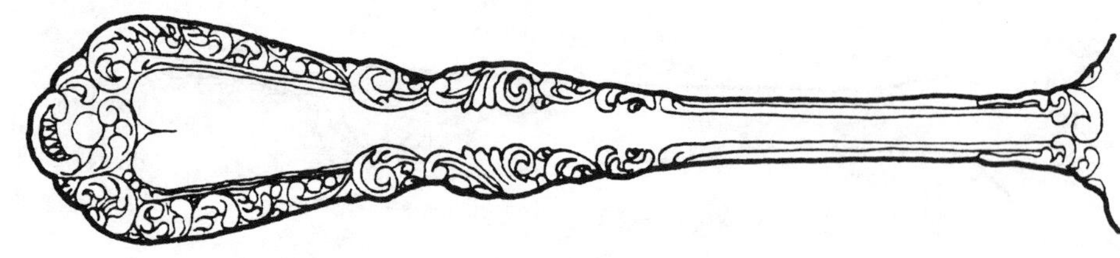

Thin market.

Bouquet aka Vendome
(Bouquet Silver Plate)
(Parkway Silver Plate)
(Anchor Rogers)
(R.C. Co.)
(Branford Silver Plate)
1924
S

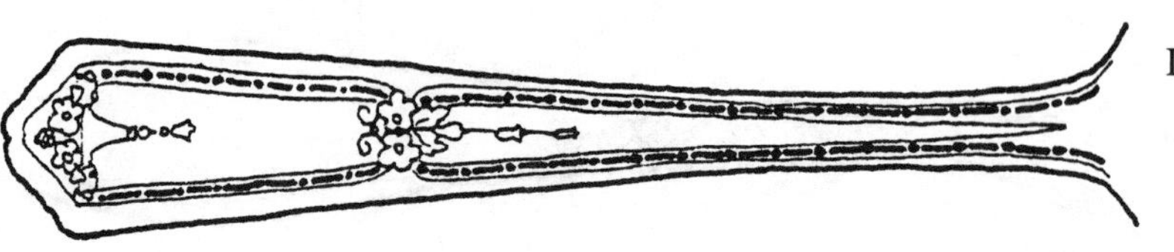

Dinner Knife $8.00
Dinner Fork $8.00
Teaspoon $5.00

Jewel
1938
S

Dinner Knife $8.00
Dinner Fork $8.00
Teaspoon $5.00

International - Puritan Silver Plate

Puritan
1941
S

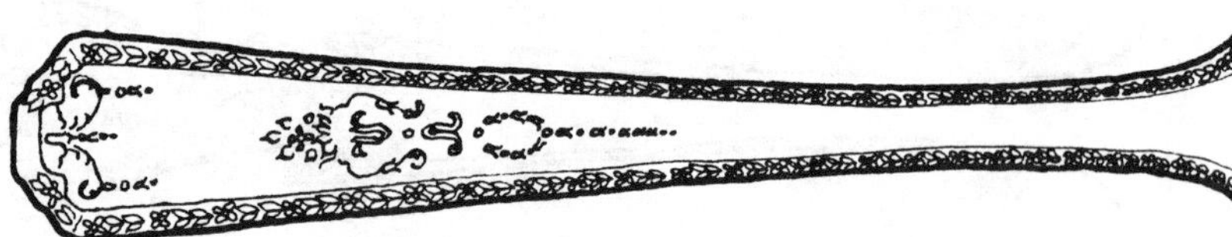

Dinner Knife $8.00
Dinner Fork $8.00
Teaspoon $5.00

International - Revelation Silver Plate

Revelation
1953
S

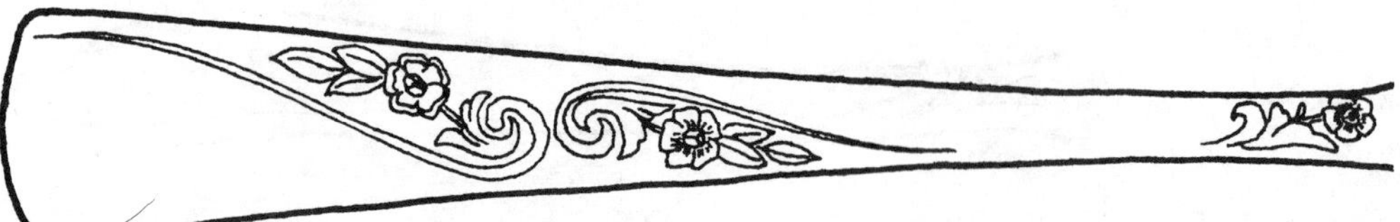

Dinner Knife $8.00 Dinner Fork $8.00 Teaspoon $5.00

Please refer to "How To Use This Book" page 4.

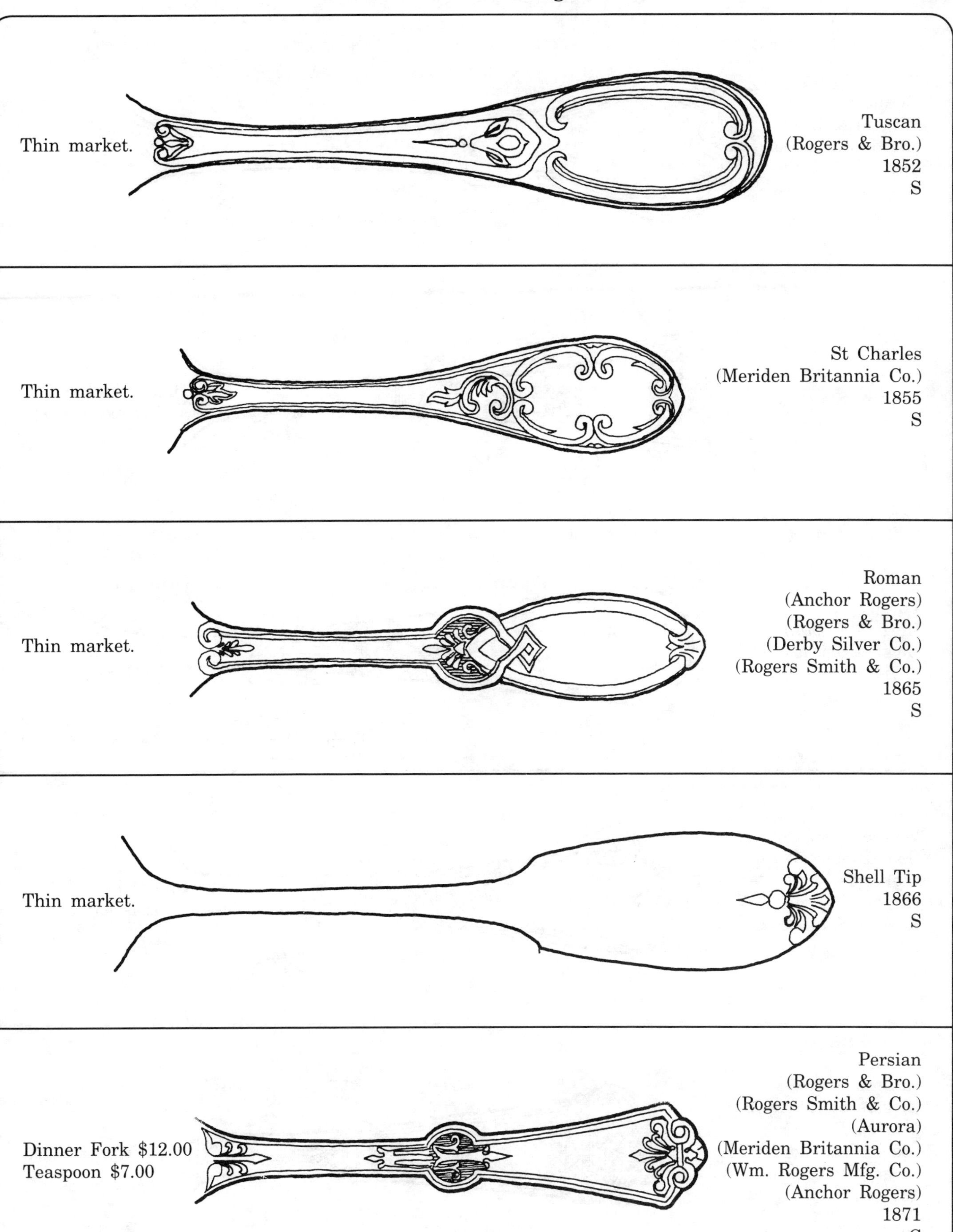

Thin market.

Tuscan
(Rogers & Bro.)
1852
S

Thin market.

St Charles
(Meriden Britannia Co.)
1855
S

Thin market.

Roman
(Anchor Rogers)
(Rogers & Bro.)
(Derby Silver Co.)
(Rogers Smith & Co.)
1865
S

Thin market.

Shell Tip
1866
S

Dinner Fork $12.00
Teaspoon $7.00

Persian
(Rogers & Bro.)
(Rogers Smith & Co.)
(Aurora)
(Meriden Britannia Co.)
(Wm. Rogers Mfg. Co.)
(Anchor Rogers)
1871
C

Please refer to "How To Use This Book" page 4.

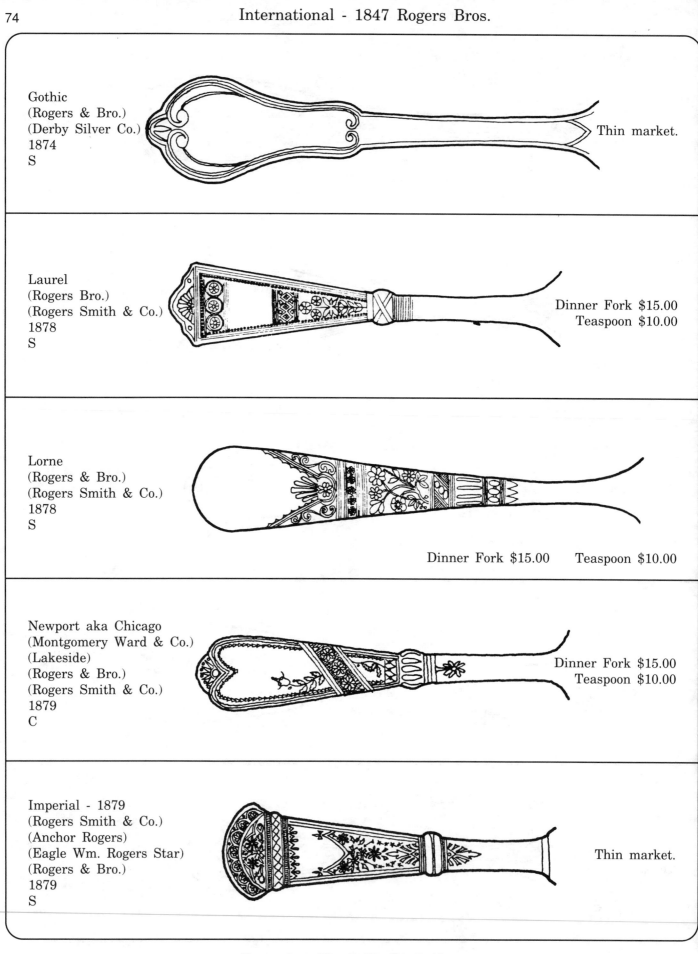

Gothic
(Rogers & Bro.)
(Derby Silver Co.)
1874
S

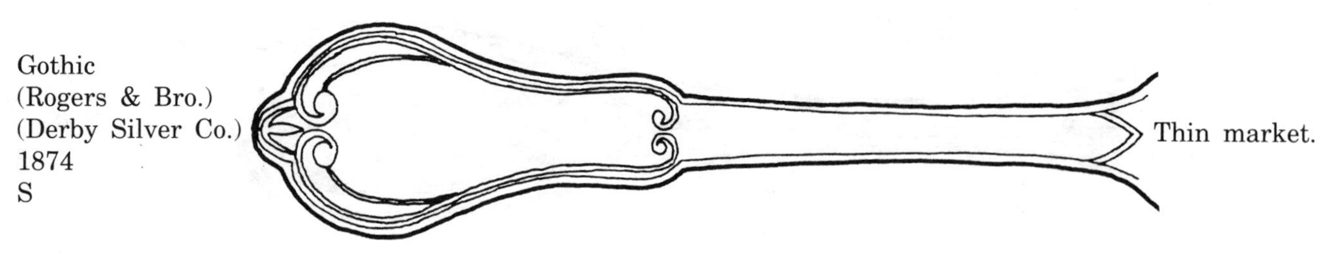

Thin market.

Laurel
(Rogers Bro.)
(Rogers Smith & Co.)
1878
S

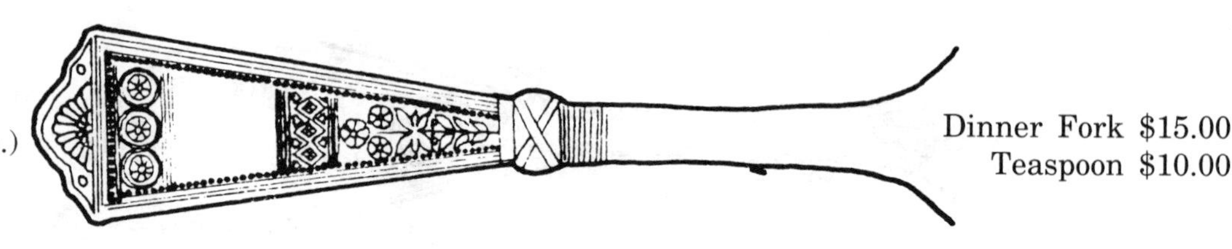

Dinner Fork $15.00
Teaspoon $10.00

Lorne
(Rogers & Bro.)
(Rogers Smith & Co.)
1878
S

Dinner Fork $15.00 Teaspoon $10.00

Newport aka Chicago
(Montgomery Ward & Co.)
(Lakeside)
(Rogers & Bro.)
(Rogers Smith & Co.)
1879
C

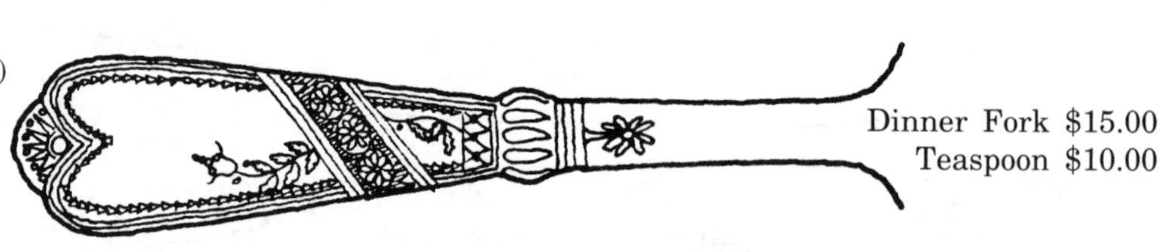

Dinner Fork $15.00
Teaspoon $10.00

Imperial - 1879
(Rogers Smith & Co.)
(Anchor Rogers)
(Eagle Wm. Rogers Star)
(Rogers & Bro.)
1879
S

Thin market.

Please refer to "How To Use This Book" page 4.

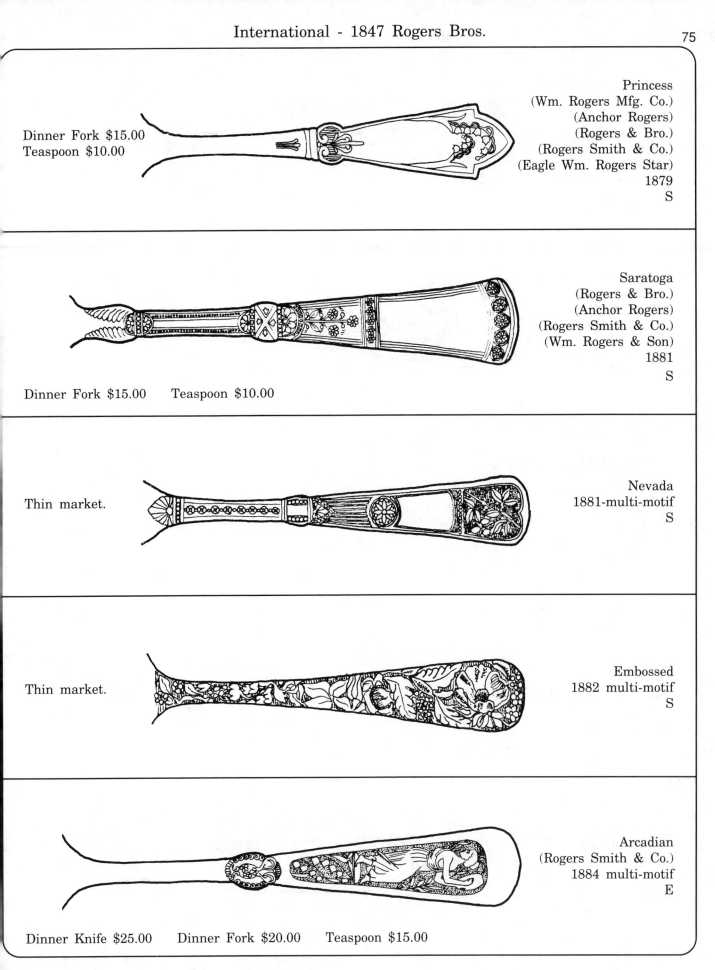

Dinner Fork $15.00
Teaspoon $10.00

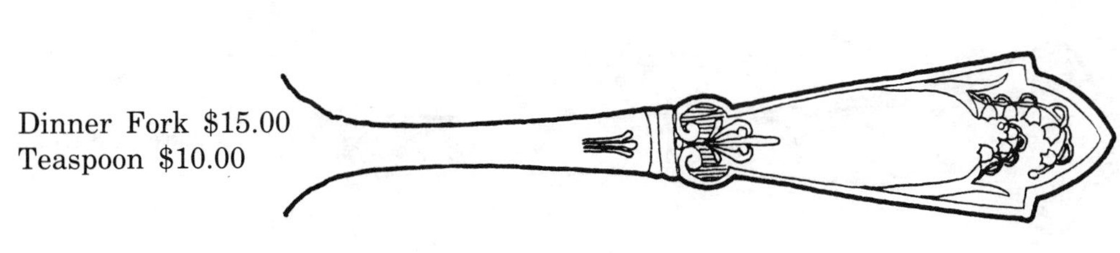

Princess
(Wm. Rogers Mfg. Co.)
(Anchor Rogers)
(Rogers & Bro.)
(Rogers Smith & Co.)
(Eagle Wm. Rogers Star)
1879
S

Saratoga
(Rogers & Bro.)
(Anchor Rogers)
(Rogers Smith & Co.)
(Wm. Rogers & Son)
1881
S

Dinner Fork $15.00 Teaspoon $10.00

Thin market.

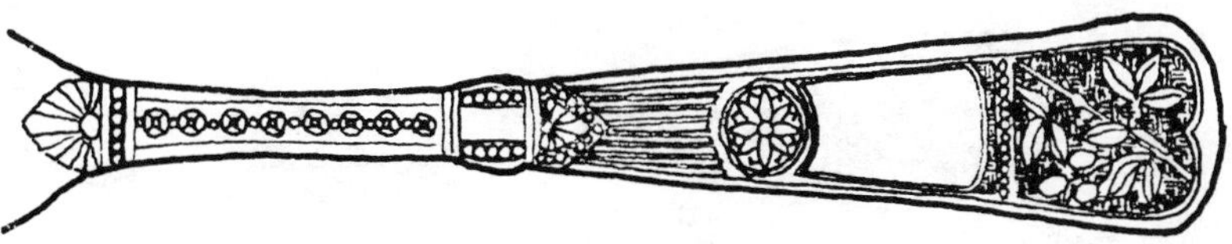

Nevada
1881-multi-motif
S

Thin market.

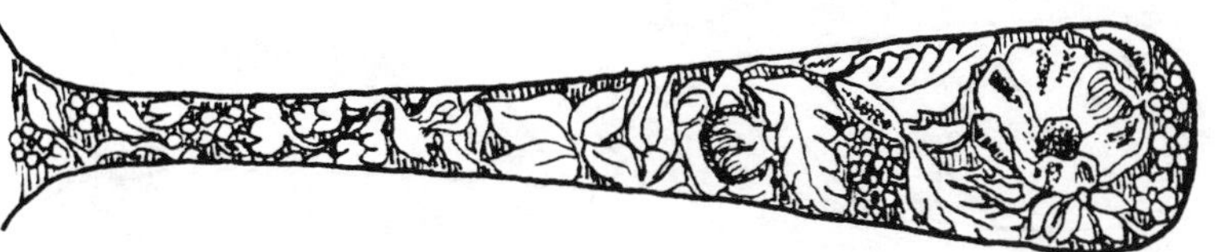

Embossed
1882 multi-motif
S

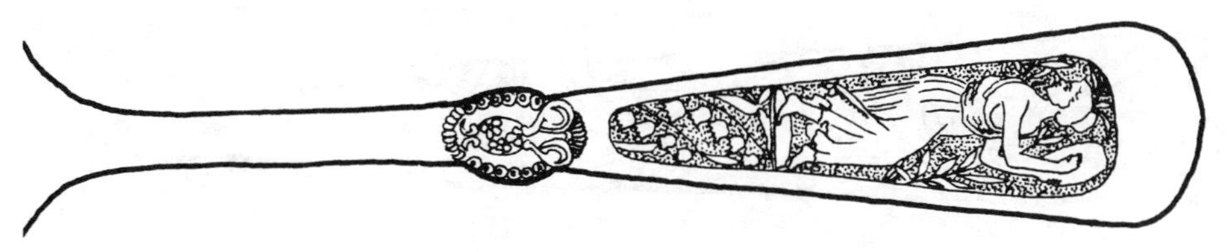

Arcadian
(Rogers Smith & Co.)
1884 multi-motif
E

Dinner Knife $25.00 Dinner Fork $20.00 Teaspoon $15.00

Please refer to "How To Use This Book" page 4.

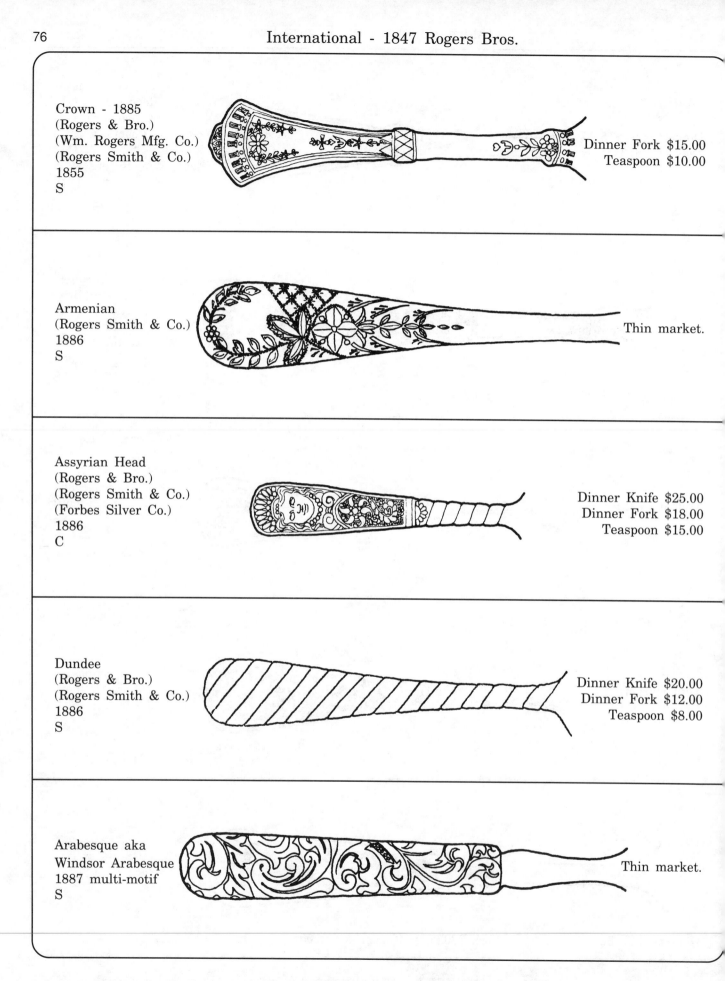

Crown - 1885
(Rogers & Bro.)
(Wm. Rogers Mfg. Co.)
(Rogers Smith & Co.)
1855
S

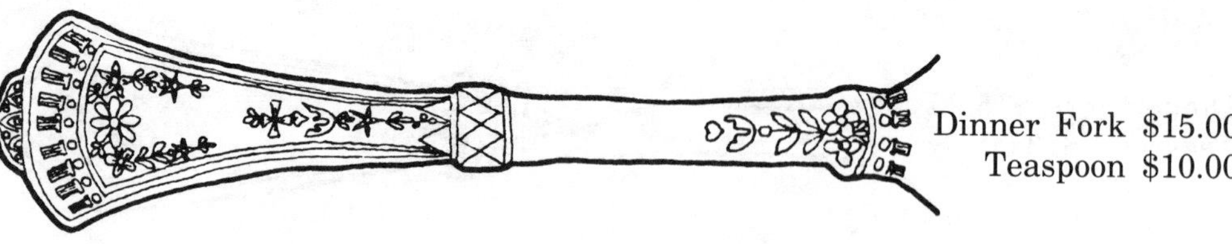

Dinner Fork $15.00
Teaspoon $10.00

Armenian
(Rogers Smith & Co.)
1886
S

Thin market.

Assyrian Head
(Rogers & Bro.)
(Rogers Smith & Co.)
(Forbes Silver Co.)
1886
C

Dinner Knife $25.00
Dinner Fork $18.00
Teaspoon $15.00

Dundee
(Rogers & Bro.)
(Rogers Smith & Co.)
1886
S

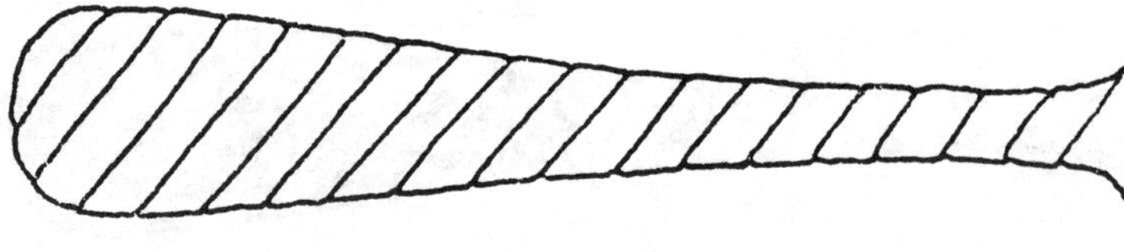

Dinner Knife $20.00
Dinner Fork $12.00
Teaspoon $8.00

Arabesque aka
Windsor Arabesque
1887 multi-motif
S

Thin market.

Please refer to "How To Use This Book" page 4.

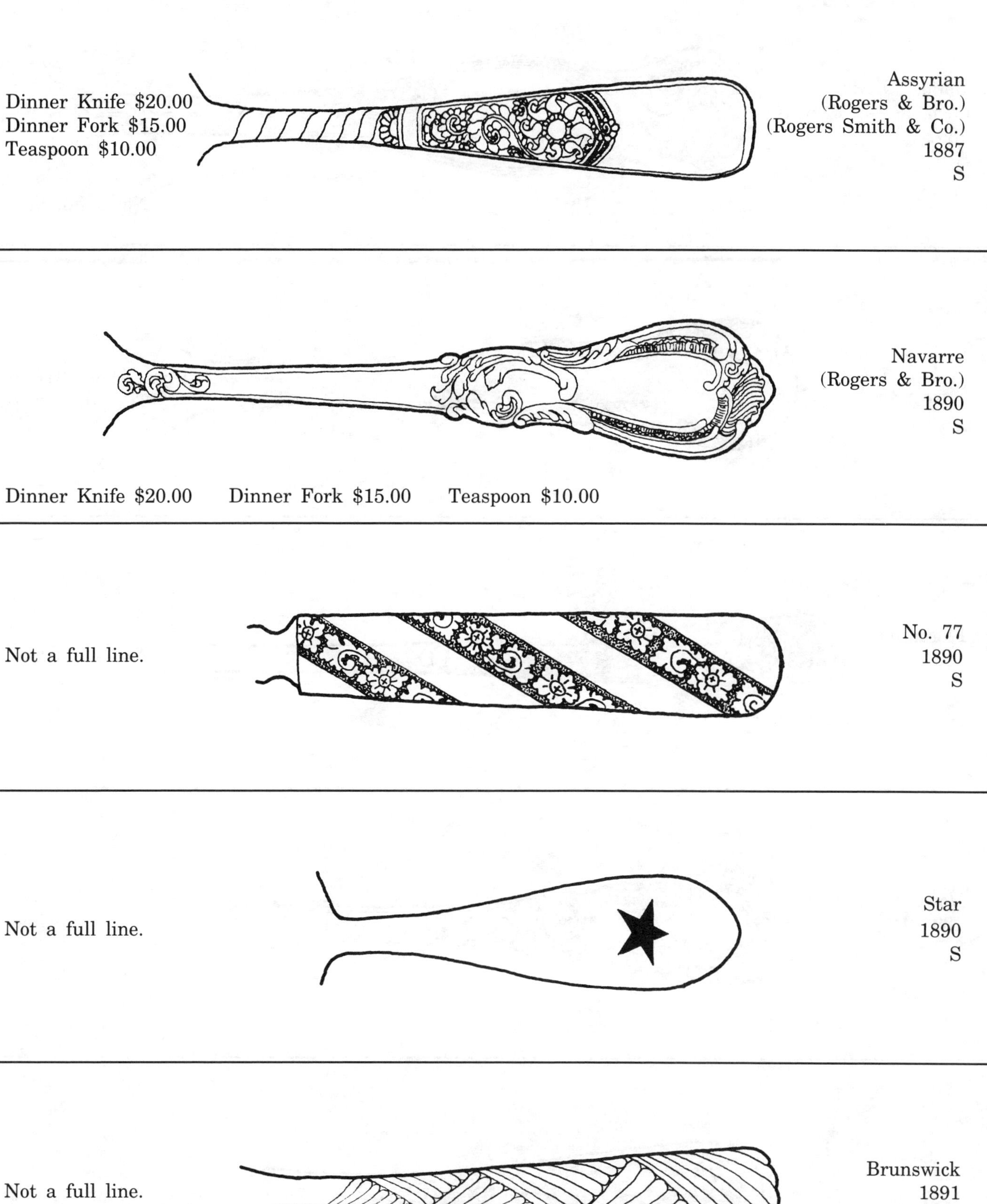

Dinner Knife $20.00
Dinner Fork $15.00
Teaspoon $10.00

Assyrian
(Rogers & Bro.)
(Rogers Smith & Co.)
1887
S

Navarre
(Rogers & Bro.)
1890
S

Dinner Knife $20.00 Dinner Fork $15.00 Teaspoon $10.00

Not a full line.

No. 77
1890
S

Not a full line.

Star
1890
S

Not a full line.

Brunswick
1891
S

Please refer to "How To Use This Book" page 4.

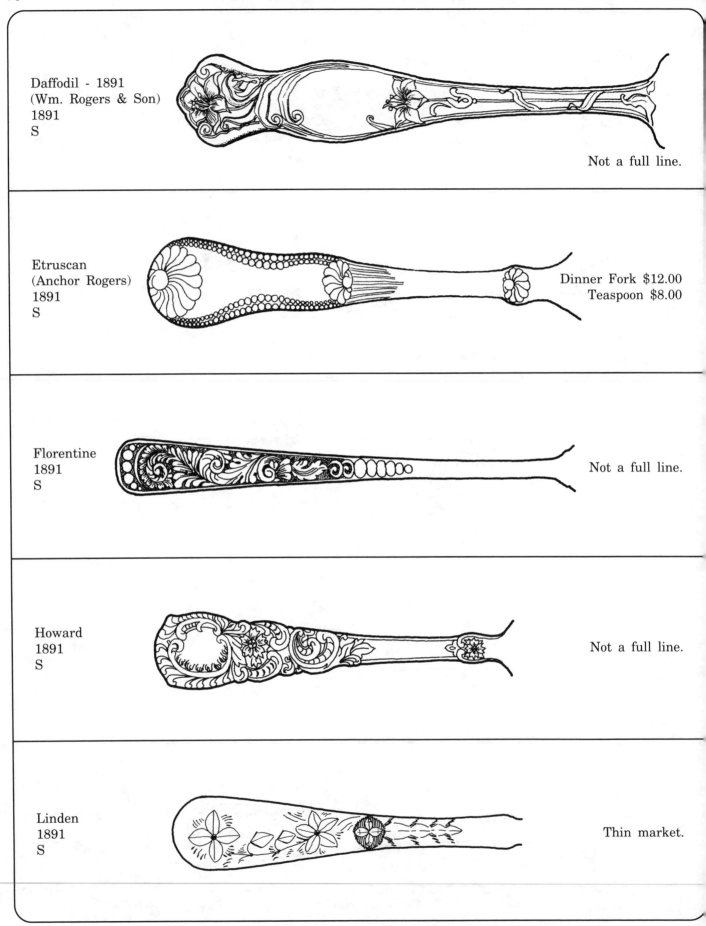

Daffodil - 1891
(Wm. Rogers & Son)
1891
S

Not a full line.

Etruscan
(Anchor Rogers)
1891
S

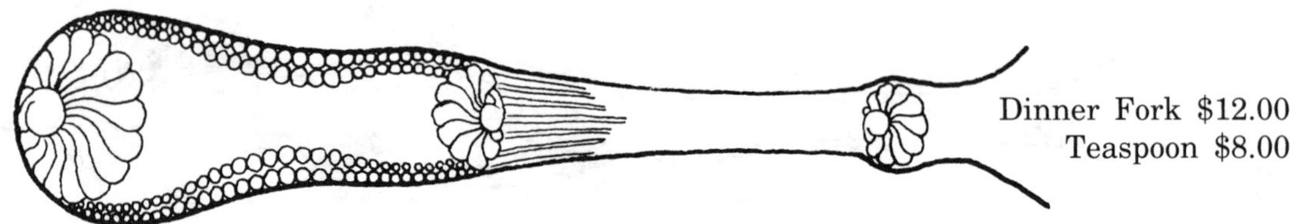

Dinner Fork $12.00
Teaspoon $8.00

Florentine
1891
S

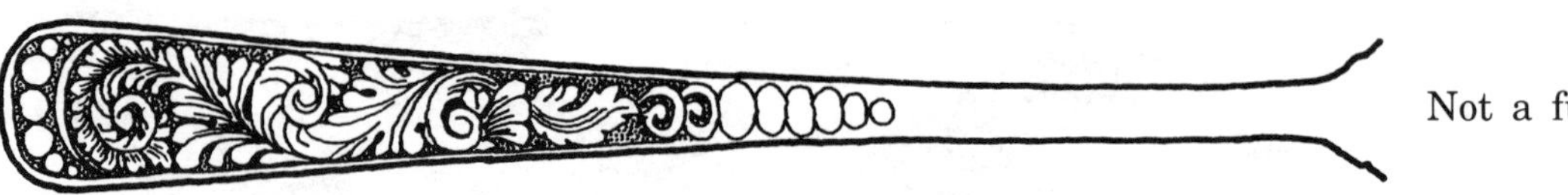

Not a full line.

Howard
1891
S

Not a full line.

Linden
1891
S

Thin market.

Please refer to "How To Use This Book" page 4.

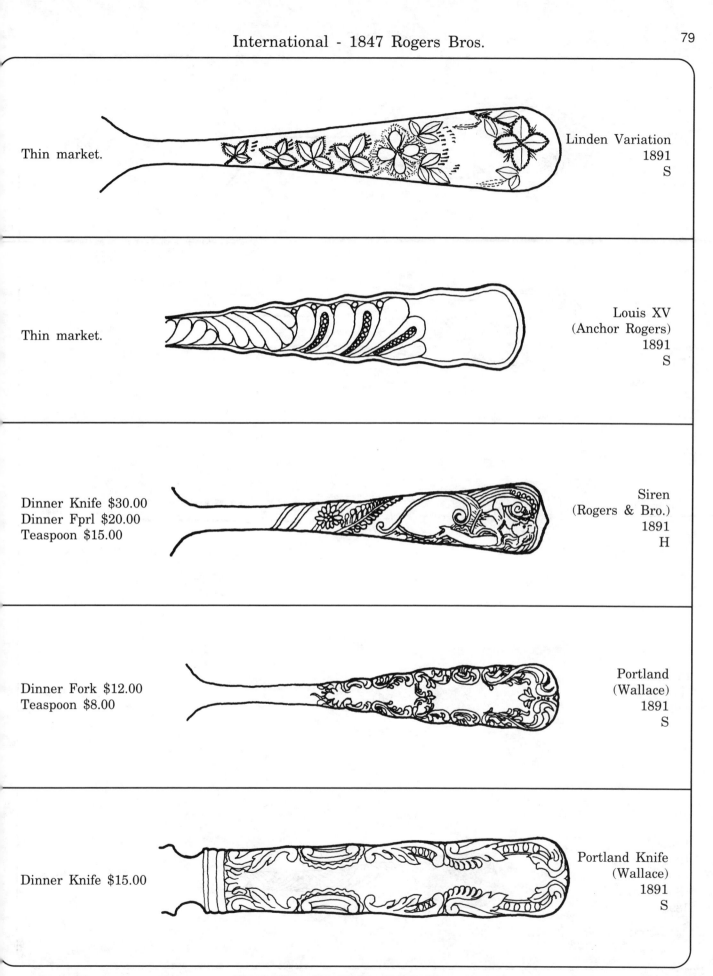

Thin market.

Linden Variation
1891
S

Thin market.

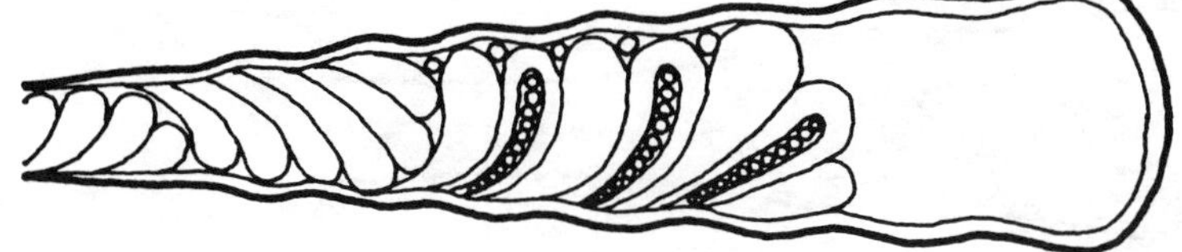

Louis XV
(Anchor Rogers)
1891
S

Dinner Knife $30.00
Dinner Fprl $20.00
Teaspoon $15.00

Siren
(Rogers & Bro.)
1891
H

Dinner Fork $12.00
Teaspoon $8.00

Portland
(Wallace)
1891
S

Dinner Knife $15.00

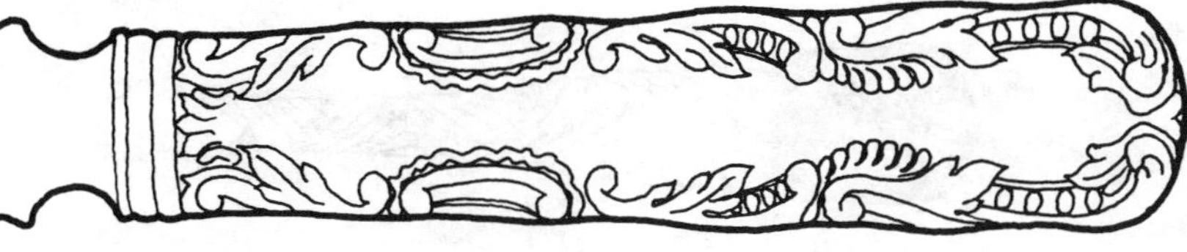

Portland Knife
(Wallace)
1891
S

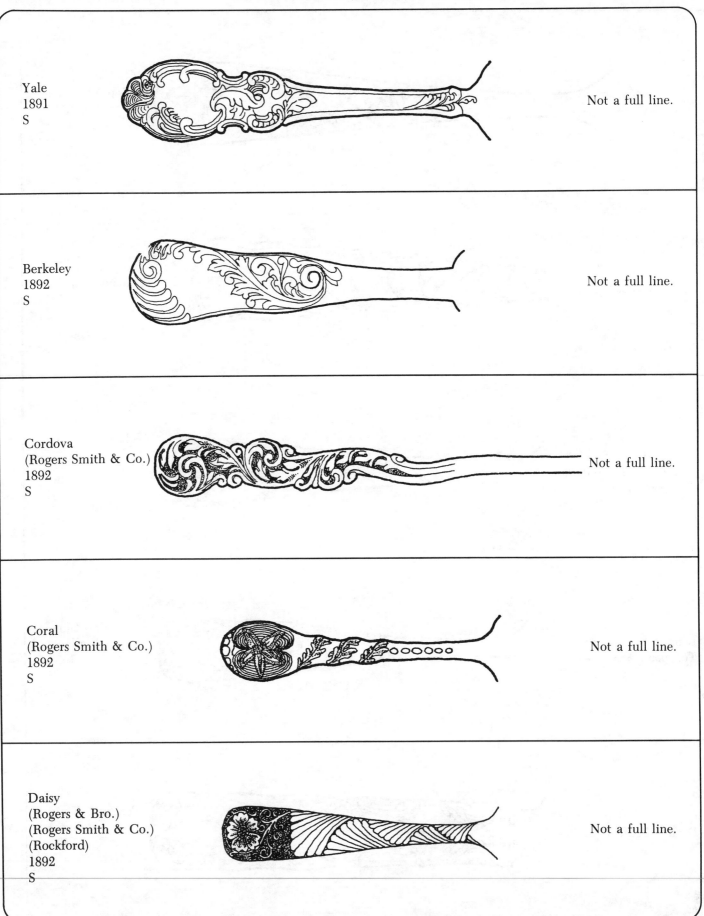

Yale
1891
S

Not a full line.

Berkeley
1892
S

Not a full line.

Cordova
(Rogers Smith & Co.)
1892
S

Not a full line.

Coral
(Rogers Smith & Co.)
1892
S

Not a full line.

Daisy
(Rogers & Bro.)
(Rogers Smith & Co.)
(Rockford)
1892
S

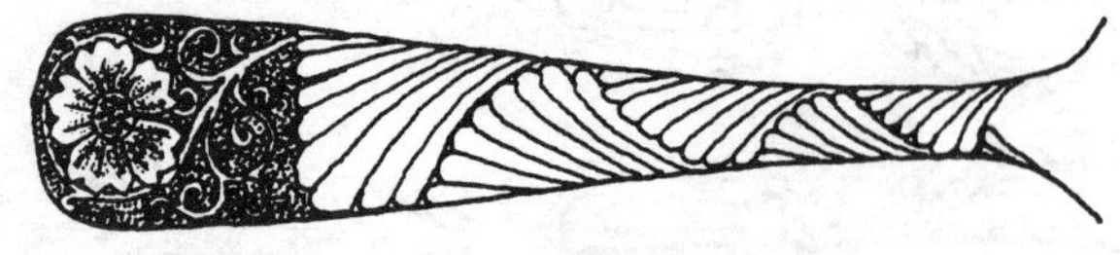

Not a full line.

Please refer to "How To Use This Book" page 4.

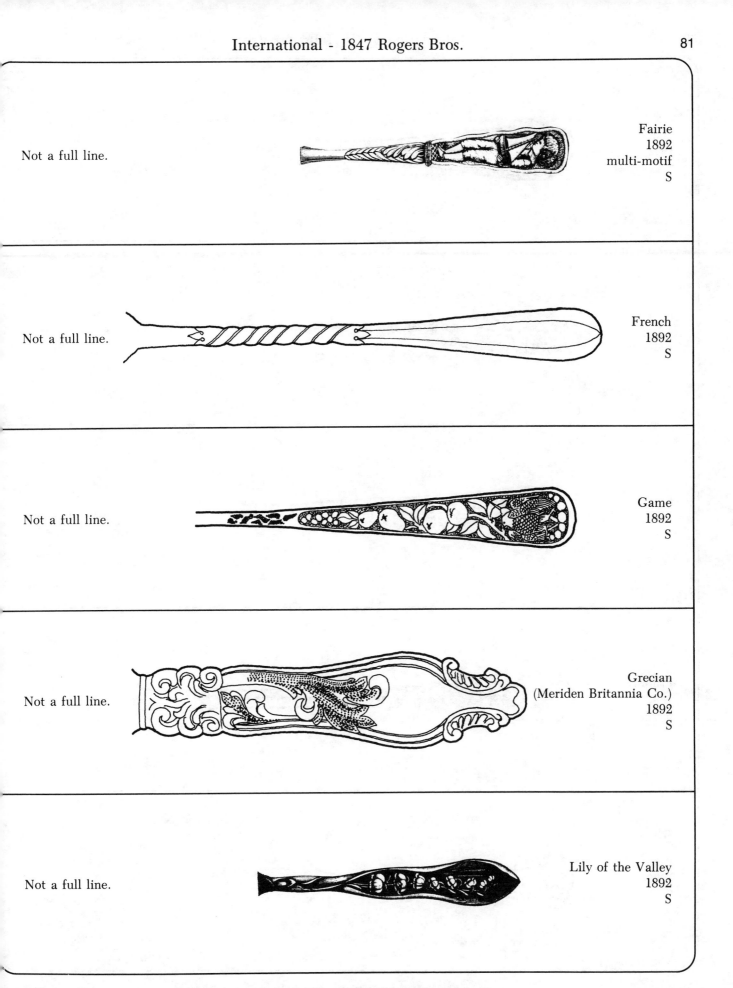

Not a full line.

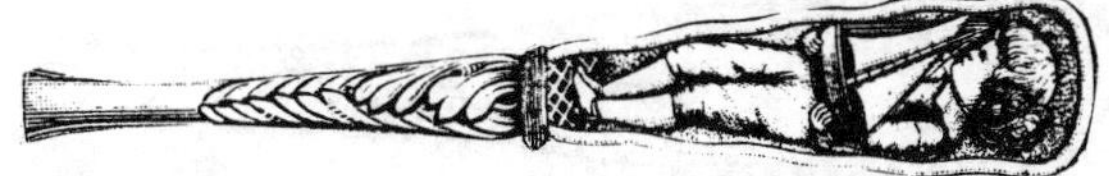

Fairie
1892
multi-motif
S

Not a full line.

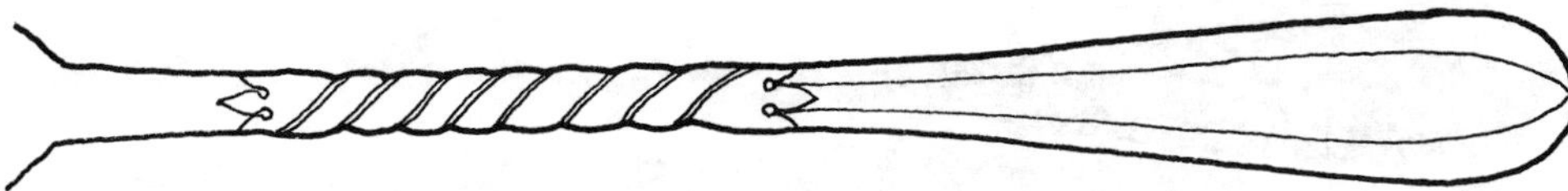

French
1892
S

Not a full line.

Game
1892
S

Not a full line.

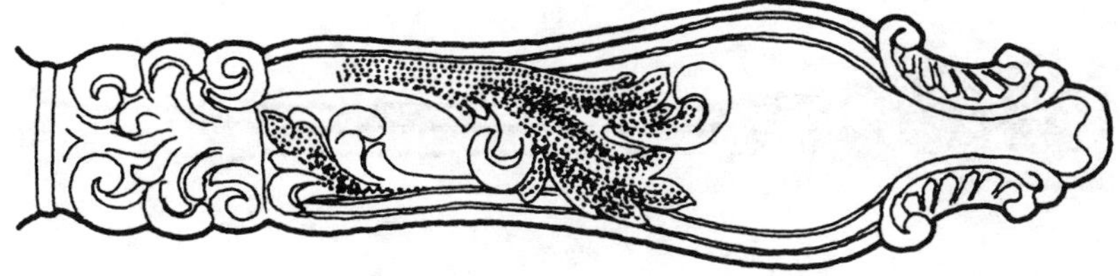

Grecian
(Meriden Britannia Co.)
1892
S

Not a full line.

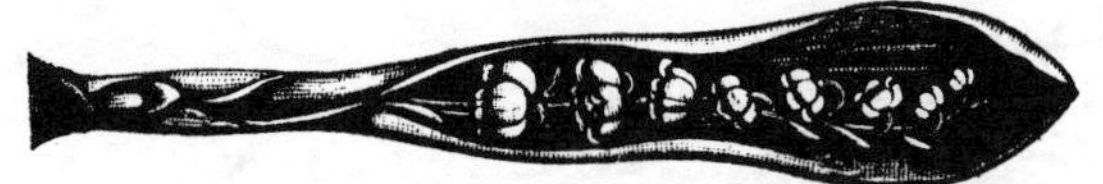

Lily of the Valley
1892
S

Please refer to "How To Use This Book" page 4.

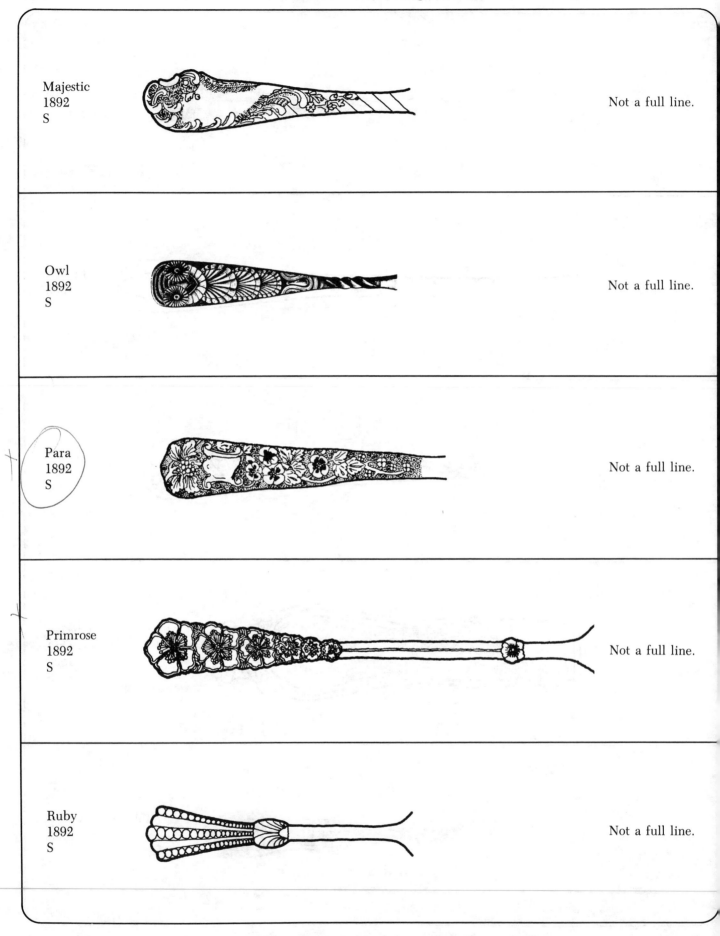

Majestic
1892
S

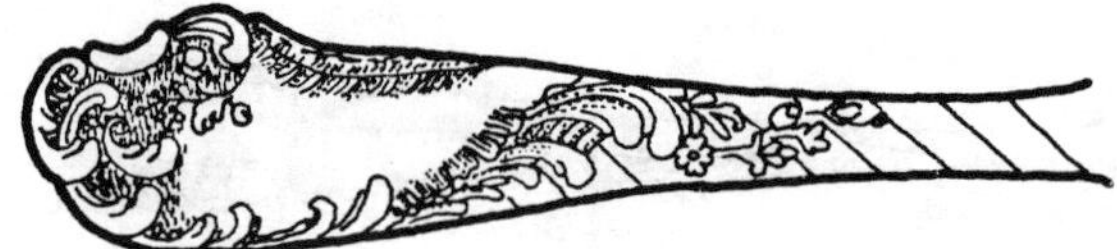

Not a full line.

Owl
1892
S

Not a full line.

Para
1892
S

Not a full line.

Primrose
1892
S

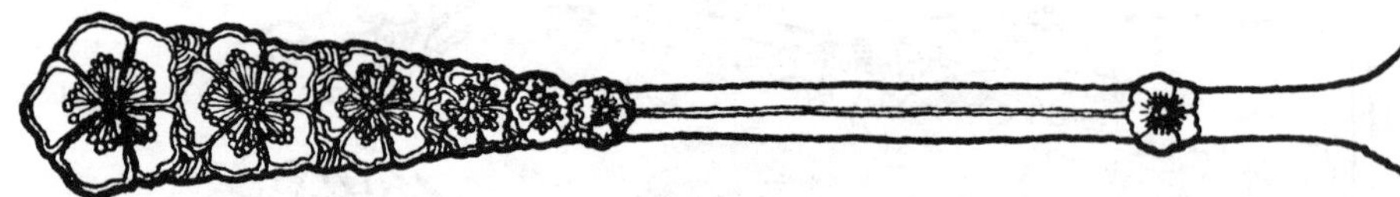

Not a full line.

Ruby
1892
S

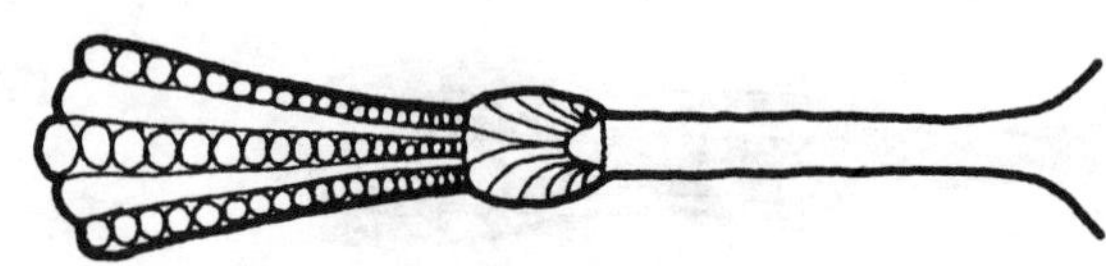

Not a full line.

Please refer to "How To Use This Book" page 4.

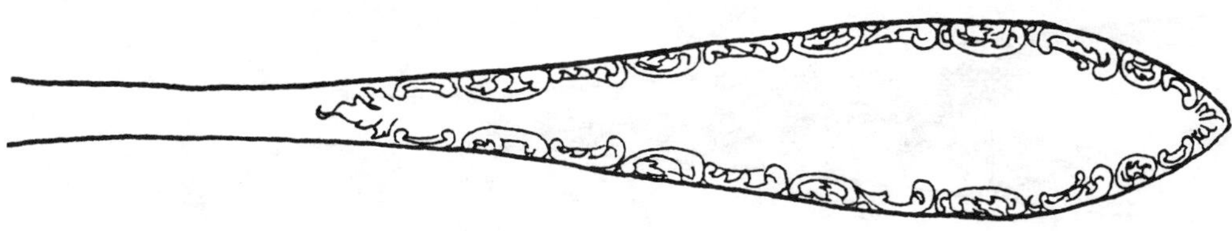

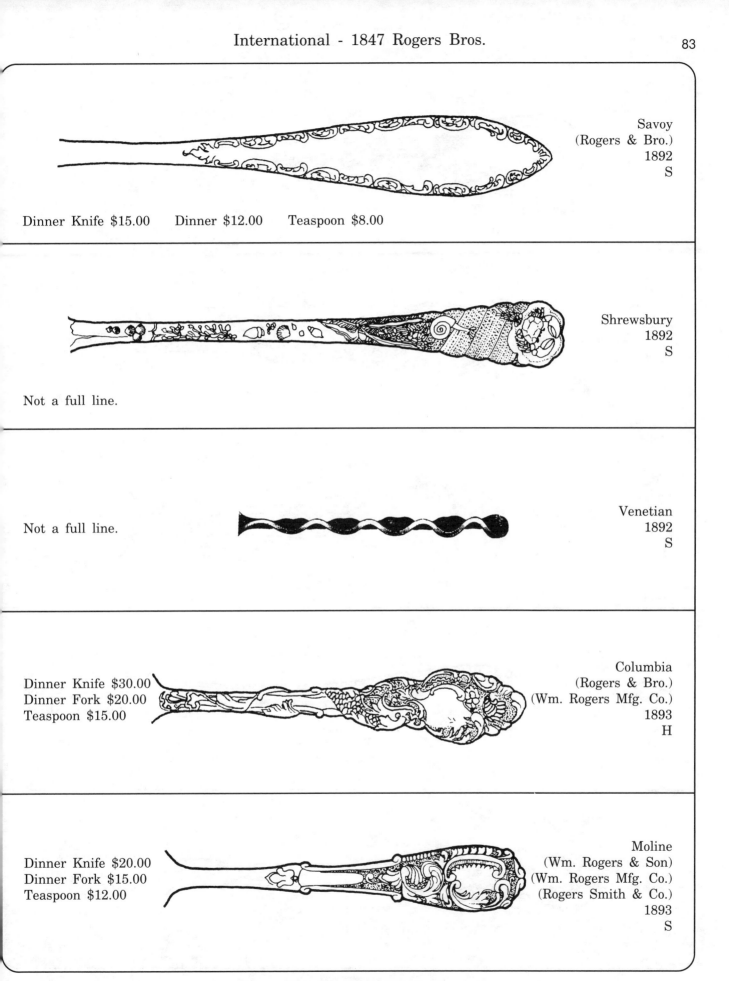

Savoy
(Rogers & Bro.)
1892
S

Dinner Knife $15.00 Dinner $12.00 Teaspoon $8.00

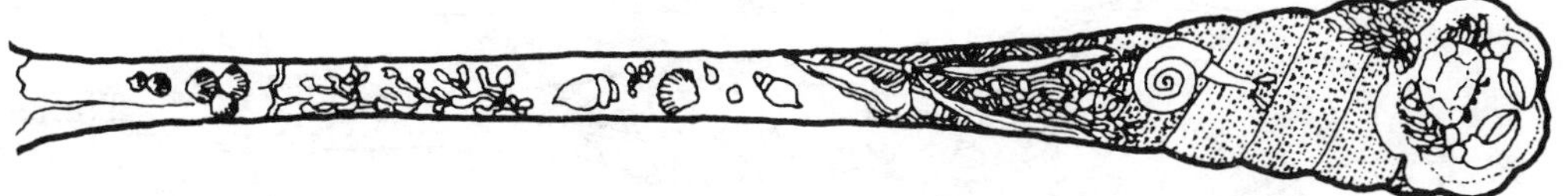

Shrewsbury
1892
S

Not a full line.

Not a full line.

Venetian
1892
S

Dinner Knife $30.00
Dinner Fork $20.00
Teaspoon $15.00

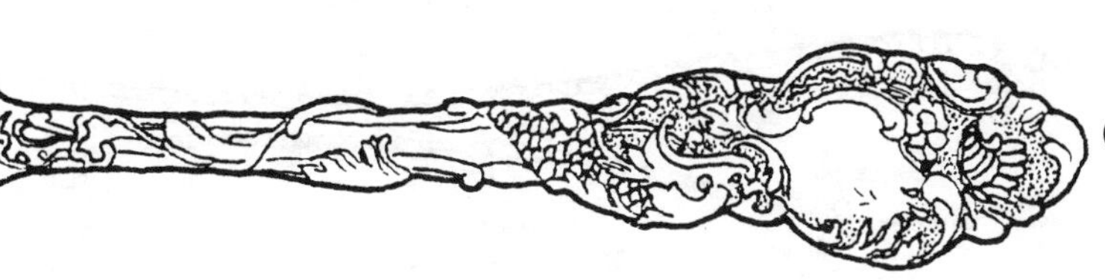

Columbia
(Rogers & Bro.)
(Wm. Rogers Mfg. Co.)
1893
H

Dinner Knife $20.00
Dinner Fork $15.00
Teaspoon $12.00

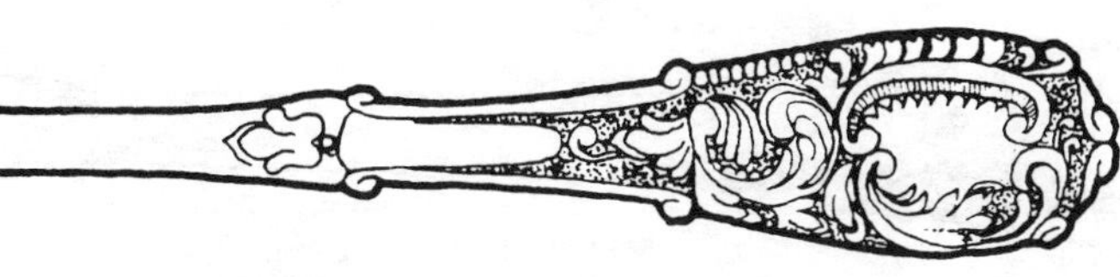

Moline
(Wm. Rogers & Son)
(Wm. Rogers Mfg. Co.)
(Rogers Smith & Co.)
1893
S

Please refer to "How To Use This Book" page 4.

Diana
1894
S

Thin market.

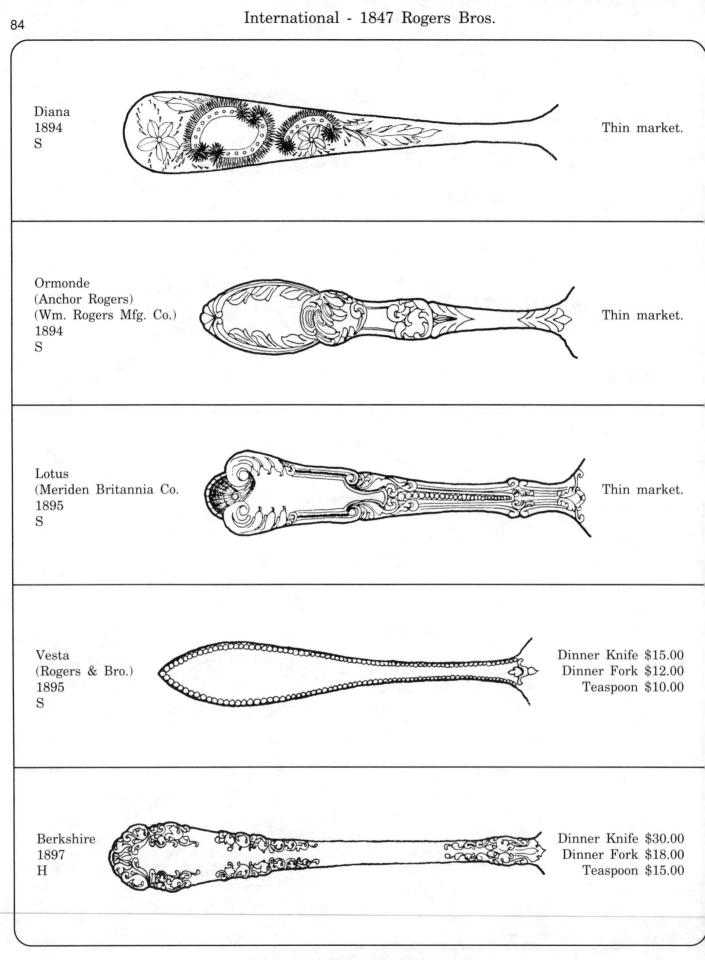

Ormonde
(Anchor Rogers)
(Wm. Rogers Mfg. Co.)
1894
S

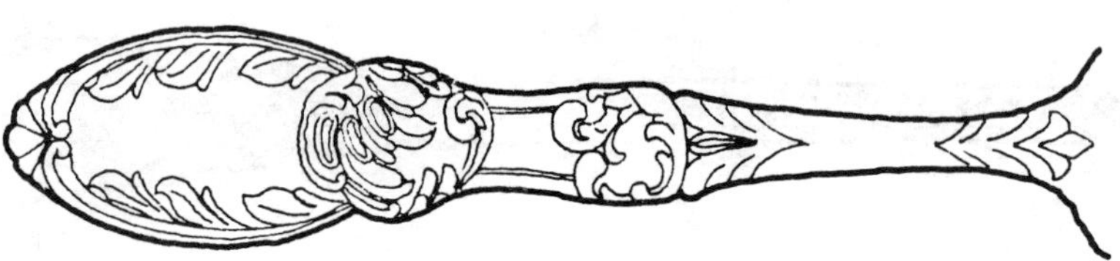

Thin market.

Lotus
(Meriden Britannia Co.
1895
S

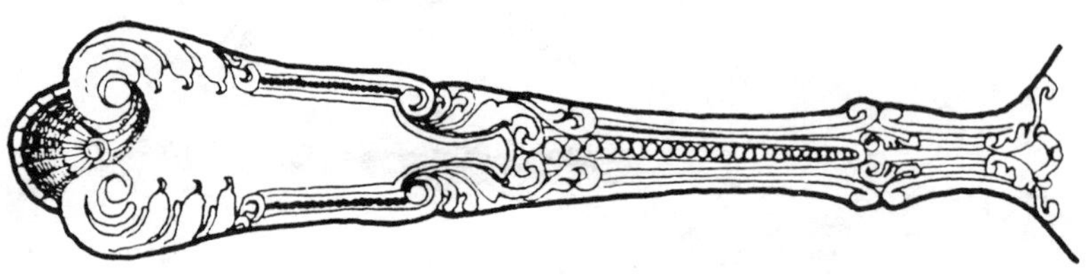

Thin market.

Vesta
(Rogers & Bro.)
1895
S

Dinner Knife $15.00
Dinner Fork $12.00
Teaspoon $10.00

Berkshire
1897
H

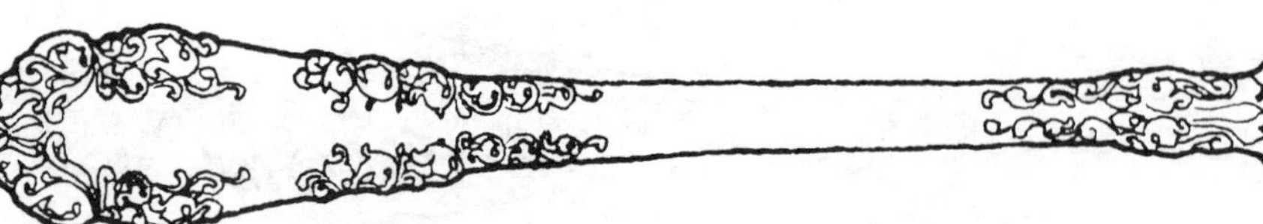

Dinner Knife $30.00
Dinner Fork $18.00
Teaspoon $15.00

Please refer to "How To Use This Book" page 4.

Thin market.

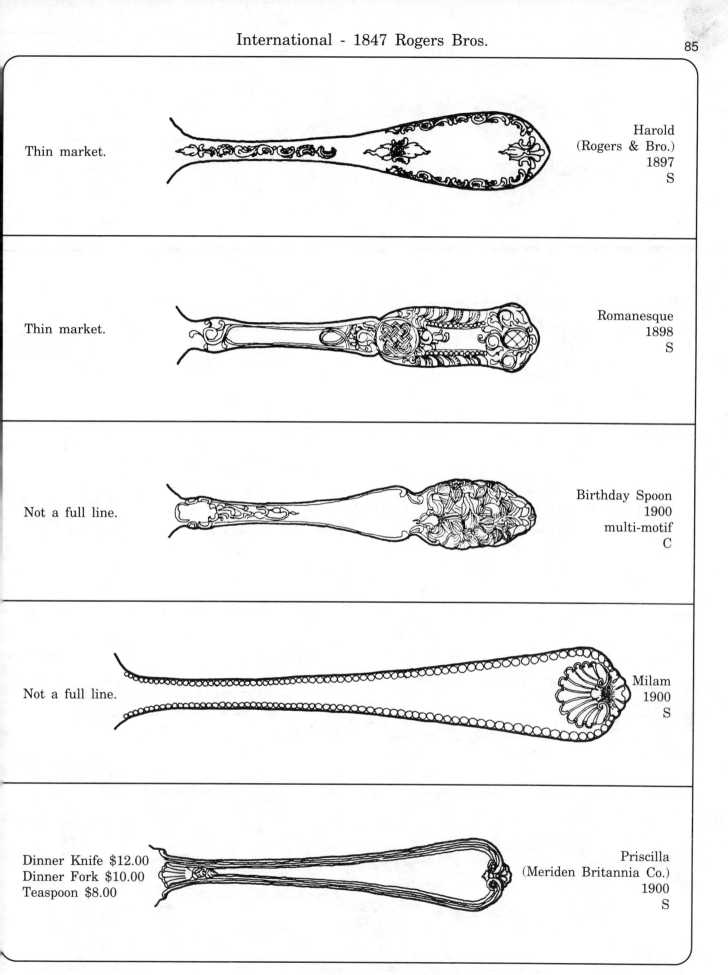

Harold
(Rogers & Bro.)
1897
S

Thin market.

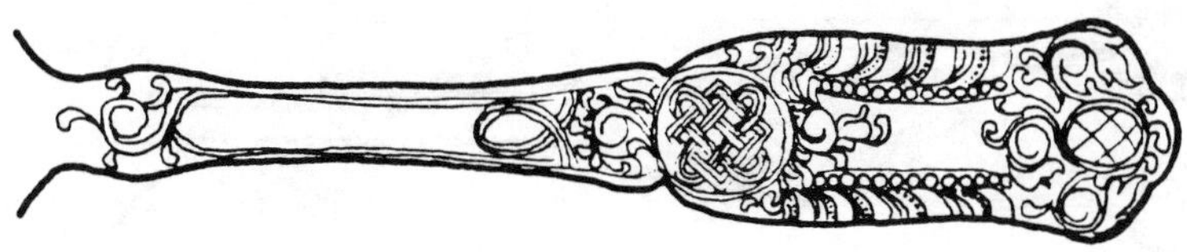

Romanesque
1898
S

Not a full line.

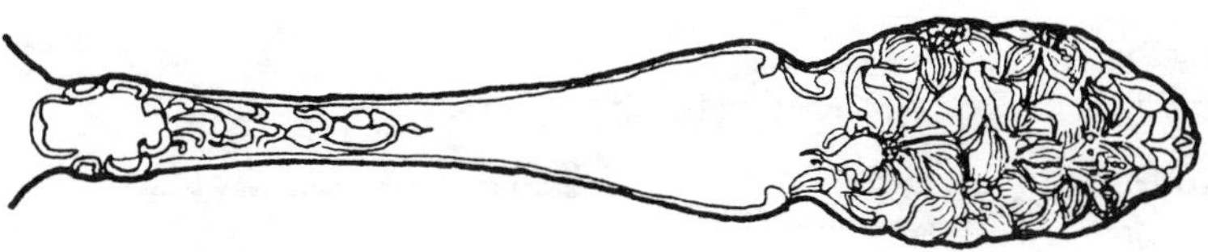

Birthday Spoon
1900
multi-motif
C

Not a full line.

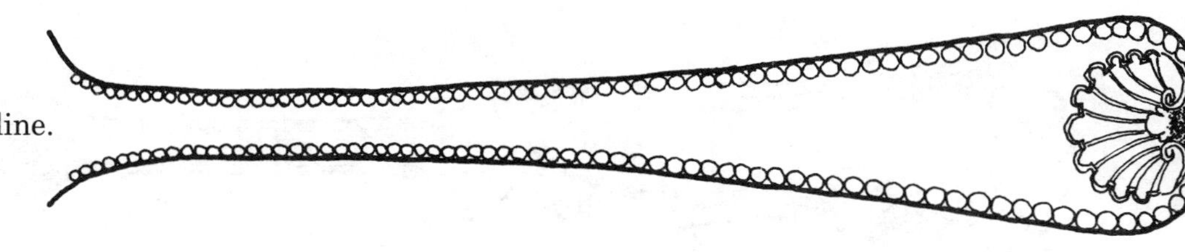

Milam
1900
S

Dinner Knife $12.00
Dinner Fork $10.00
Teaspoon $8.00

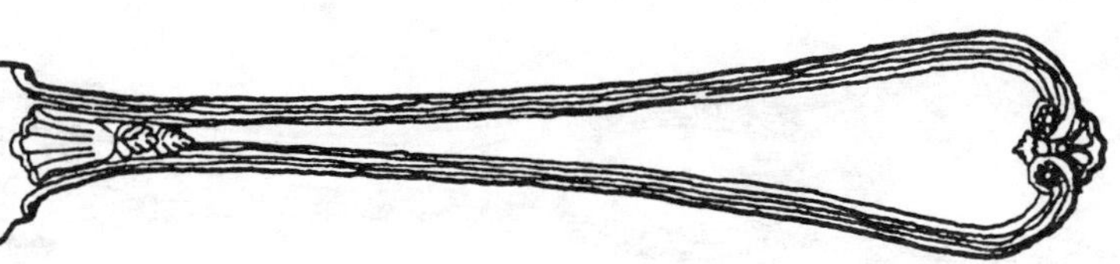

Priscilla
(Meriden Britannia Co.)
1900
S

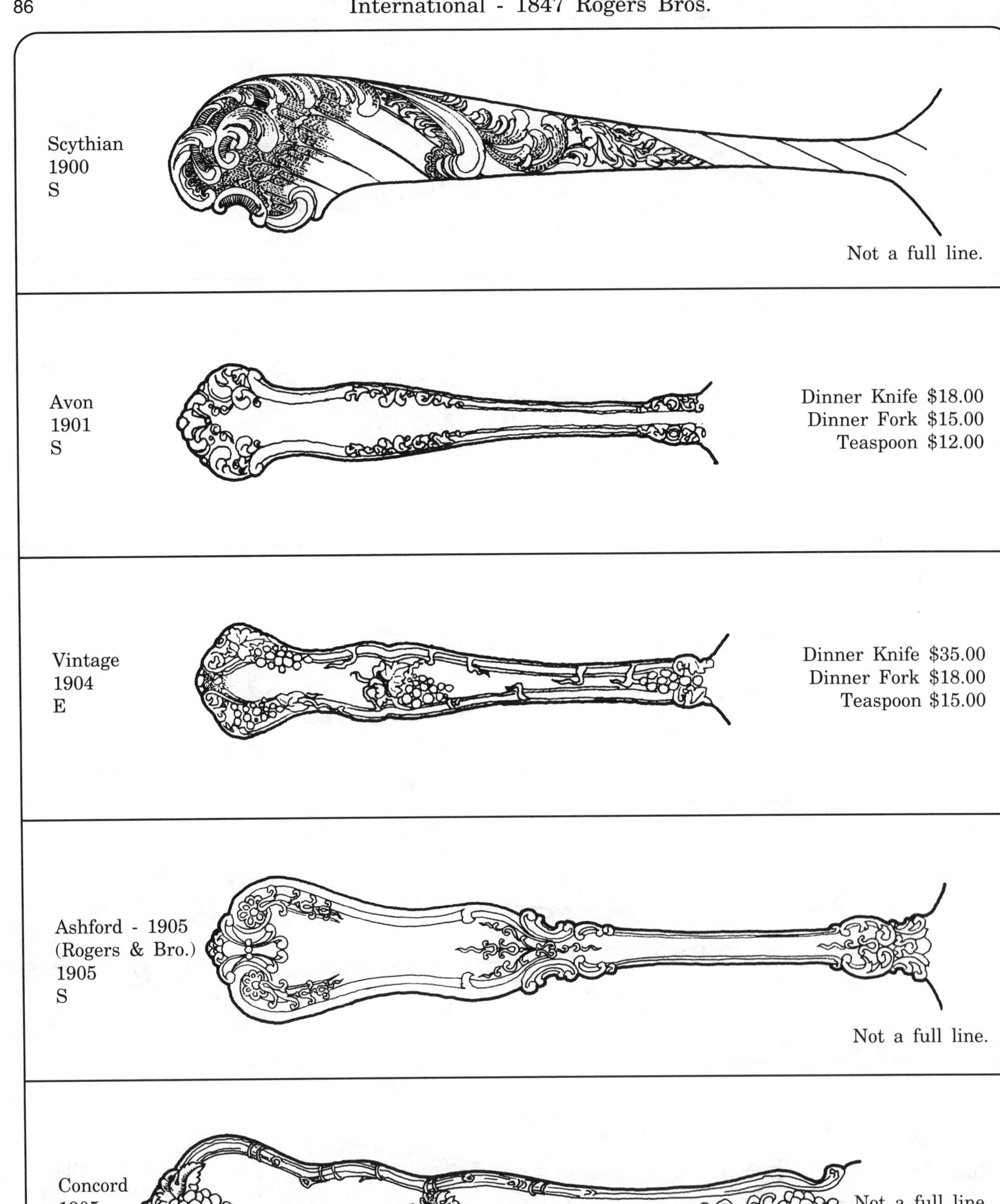

Scythian
1900
S

Not a full line.

Avon
1901
S

Dinner Knife $18.00
Dinner Fork $15.00
Teaspoon $12.00

Vintage
1904
E

Dinner Knife $35.00
Dinner Fork $18.00
Teaspoon $15.00

Ashford - 1905
(Rogers & Bro.)
1905
S

Not a full line.

Concord
1905
S

Not a full line.

Please refer to "How To Use This Book" page 4.

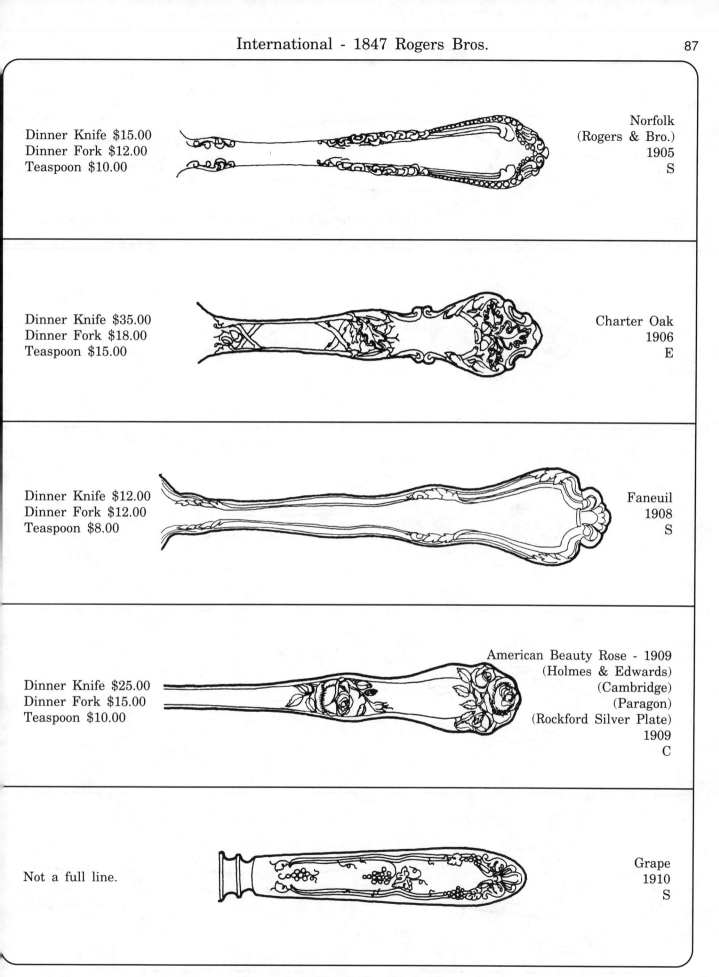

Dinner Knife $15.00
Dinner Fork $12.00
Teaspoon $10.00

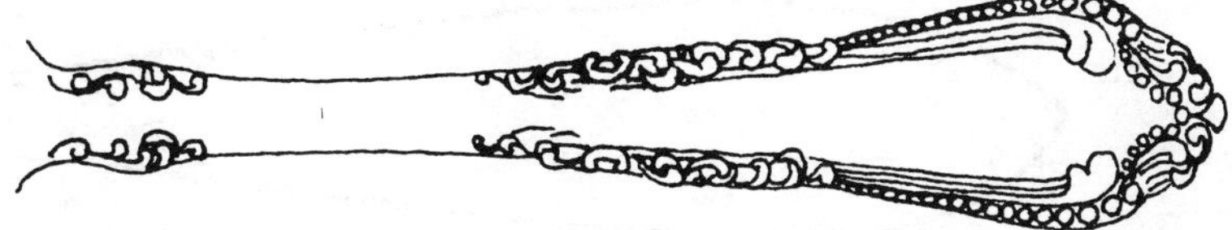

Norfolk
(Rogers & Bro.)
1905
S

Dinner Knife $35.00
Dinner Fork $18.00
Teaspoon $15.00

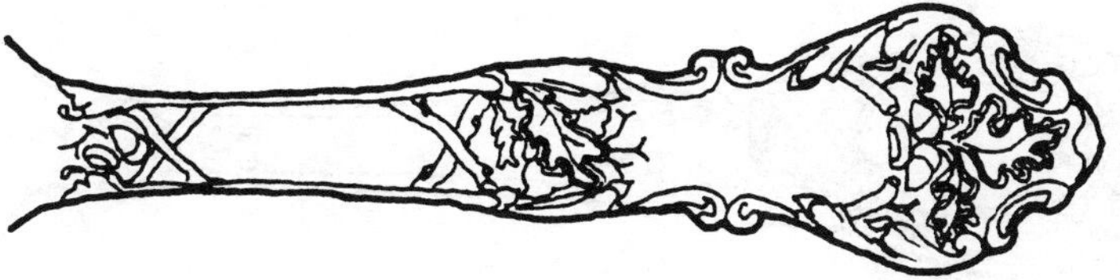

Charter Oak
1906
E

Dinner Knife $12.00
Dinner Fork $12.00
Teaspoon $8.00

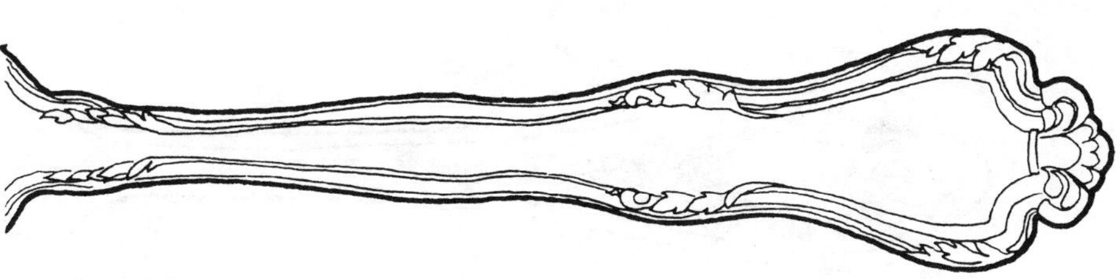

Faneuil
1908
S

Dinner Knife $25.00
Dinner Fork $15.00
Teaspoon $10.00

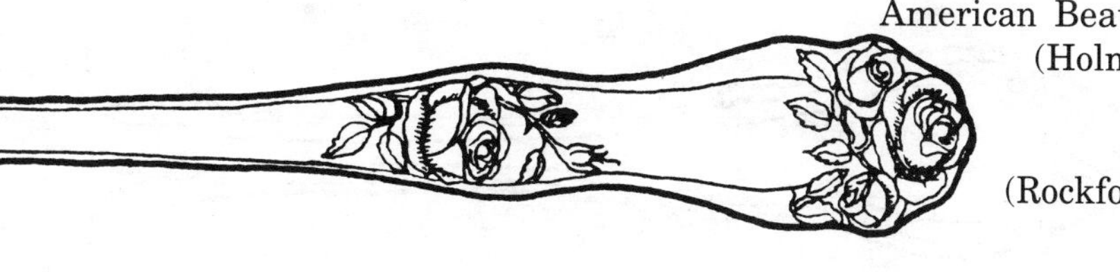

American Beauty Rose - 1909
(Holmes & Edwards)
(Cambridge)
(Paragon)
(Rockford Silver Plate)
1909
C

Not a full line.

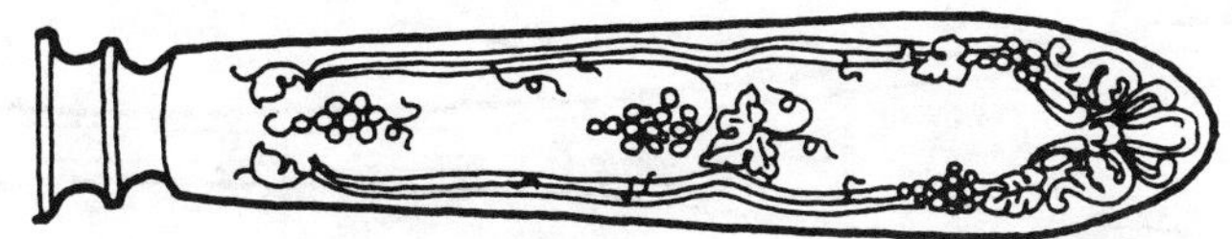

Grape
1910
S

Please refer to "How To Use This Book" page 4.

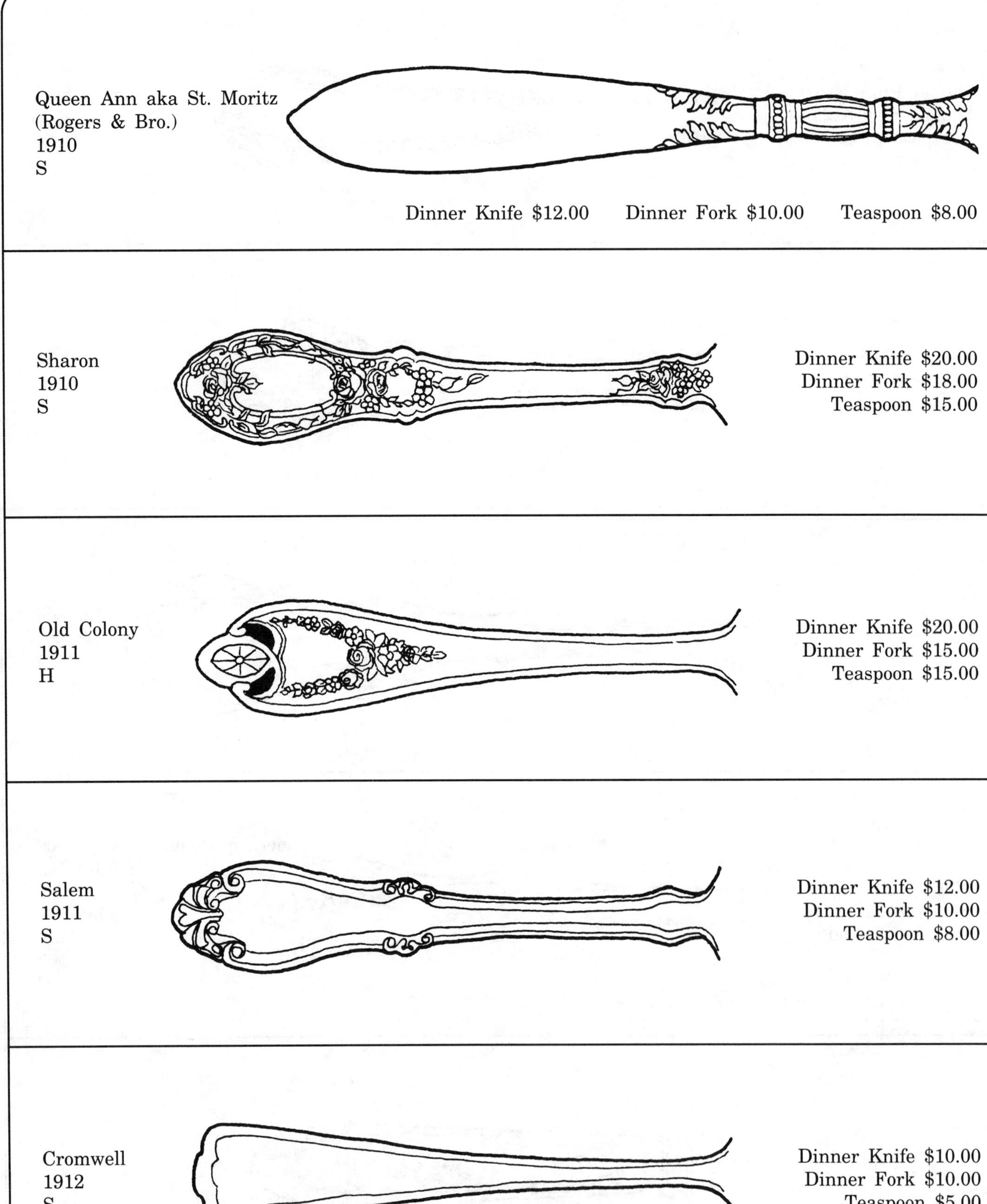

Queen Ann aka St. Moritz
(Rogers & Bro.)
1910
S

Dinner Knife $12.00 Dinner Fork $10.00 Teaspoon $8.00

Sharon
1910
S

Dinner Knife $20.00
Dinner Fork $18.00
Teaspoon $15.00

Old Colony
1911
H

Dinner Knife $20.00
Dinner Fork $15.00
Teaspoon $15.00

Salem
1911
S

Dinner Knife $12.00
Dinner Fork $10.00
Teaspoon $8.00

Cromwell
1912
S

Dinner Knife $10.00
Dinner Fork $10.00
Teaspoon $5.00

Please refer to "How To Use This Book" page 4.

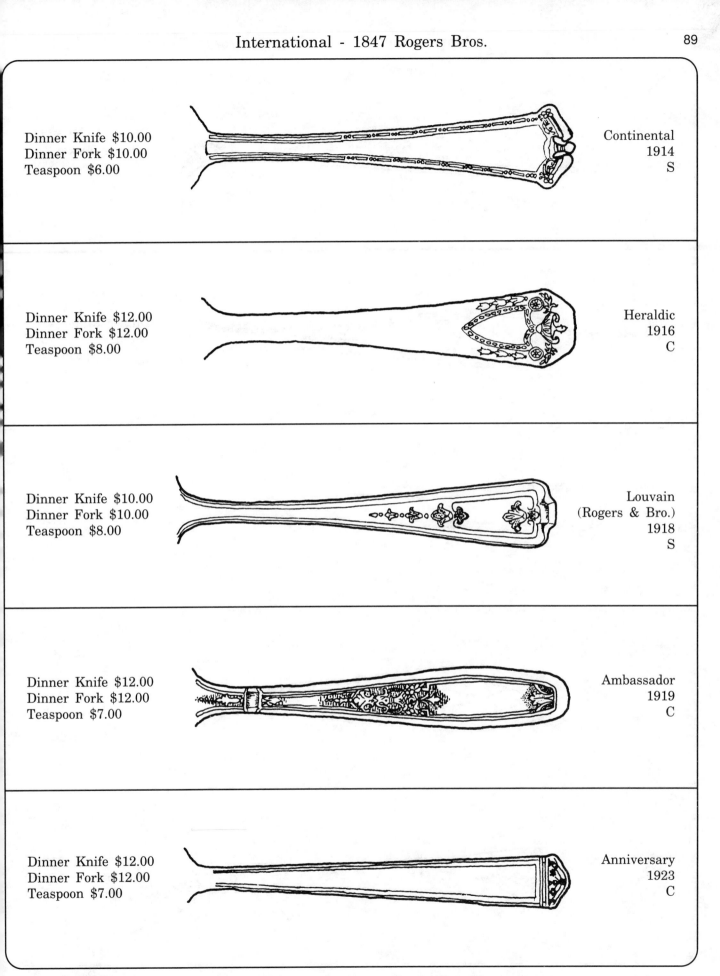

Dinner Knife $10.00
Dinner Fork $10.00
Teaspoon $6.00

Continental
1914
S

Dinner Knife $12.00
Dinner Fork $12.00
Teaspoon $8.00

Heraldic
1916
C

Dinner Knife $10.00
Dinner Fork $10.00
Teaspoon $8.00

Louvain
(Rogers & Bro.)
1918
S

Dinner Knife $12.00
Dinner Fork $12.00
Teaspoon $7.00

Ambassador
1919
C

Dinner Knife $12.00
Dinner Fork $12.00
Teaspoon $7.00

Anniversary
1923
C

Please refer to "How To Use This Book" page 4.

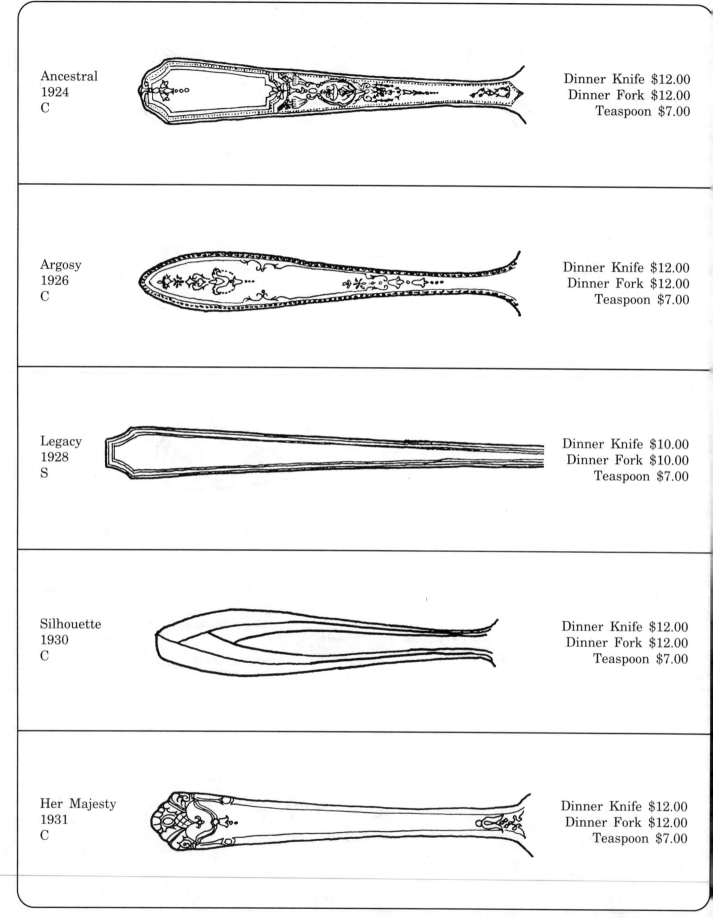

Ancestral
1924
C

Dinner Knife $12.00
Dinner Fork $12.00
Teaspoon $7.00

Argosy
1926
C

Dinner Knife $12.00
Dinner Fork $12.00
Teaspoon $7.00

Legacy
1928
S

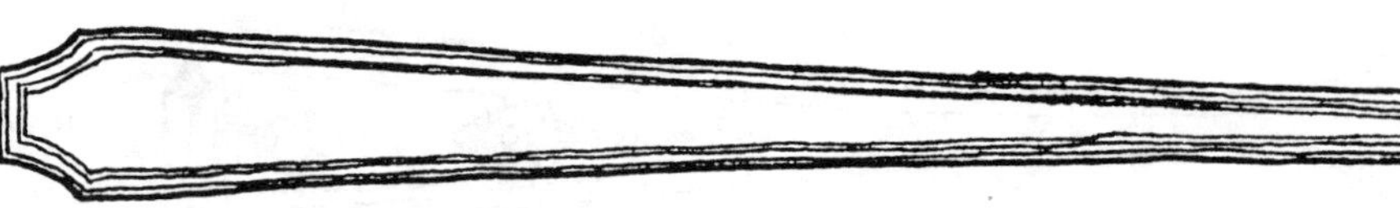

Dinner Knife $10.00
Dinner Fork $10.00
Teaspoon $7.00

Silhouette
1930
C

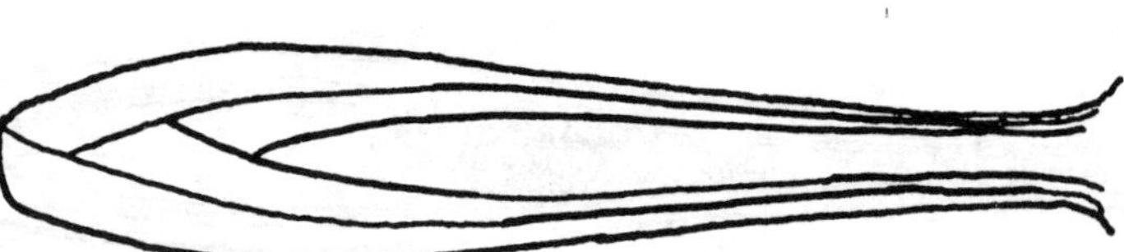

Dinner Knife $12.00
Dinner Fork $12.00
Teaspoon $7.00

Her Majesty
1931
C

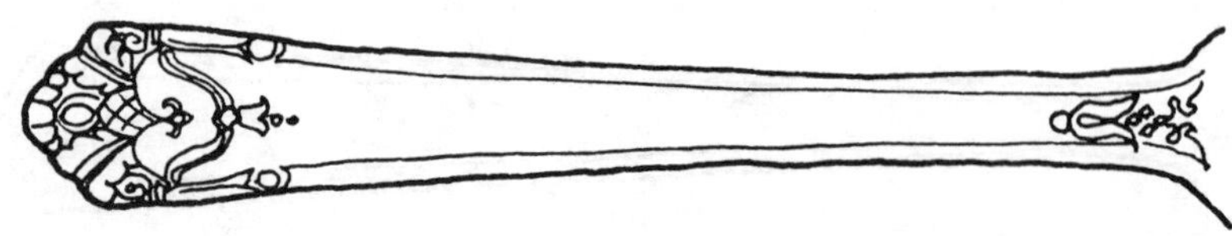

Dinner Knife $12.00
Dinner Fork $12.00
Teaspoon $7.00

Please refer to "How To Use This Book" page 4.

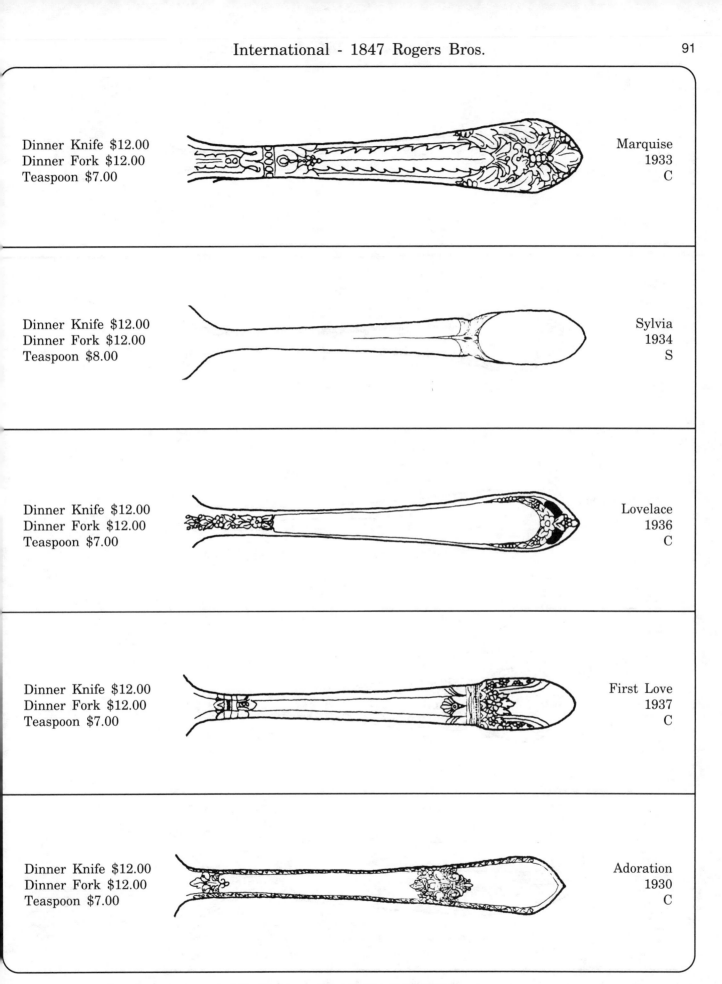

Dinner Knife $12.00
Dinner Fork $12.00
Teaspoon $7.00

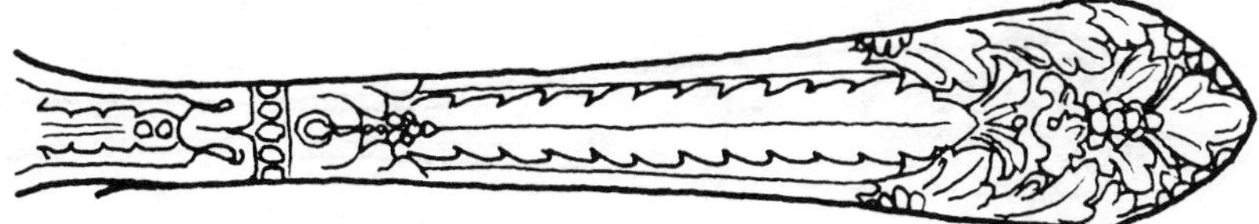

Marquise
1933
C

Dinner Knife $12.00
Dinner Fork $12.00
Teaspoon $8.00

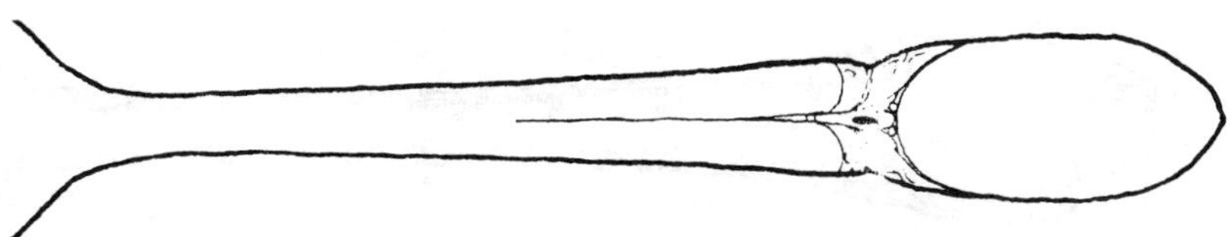

Sylvia
1934
S

Dinner Knife $12.00
Dinner Fork $12.00
Teaspoon $7.00

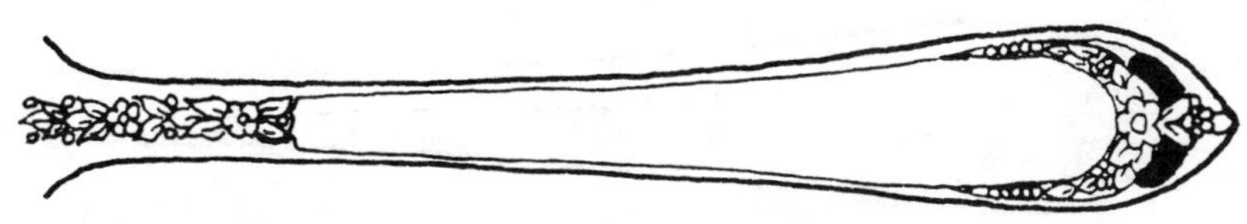

Lovelace
1936
C

Dinner Knife $12.00
Dinner Fork $12.00
Teaspoon $7.00

First Love
1937
C

Dinner Knife $12.00
Dinner Fork $12.00
Teaspoon $7.00

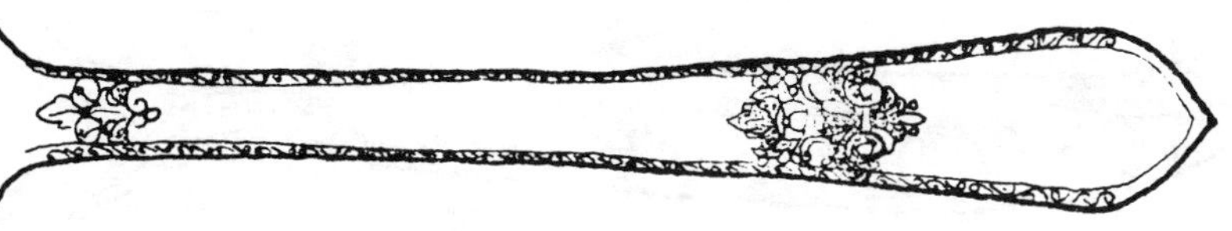

Adoration
1930
C

Please refer to "How To Use This Book" page 4.

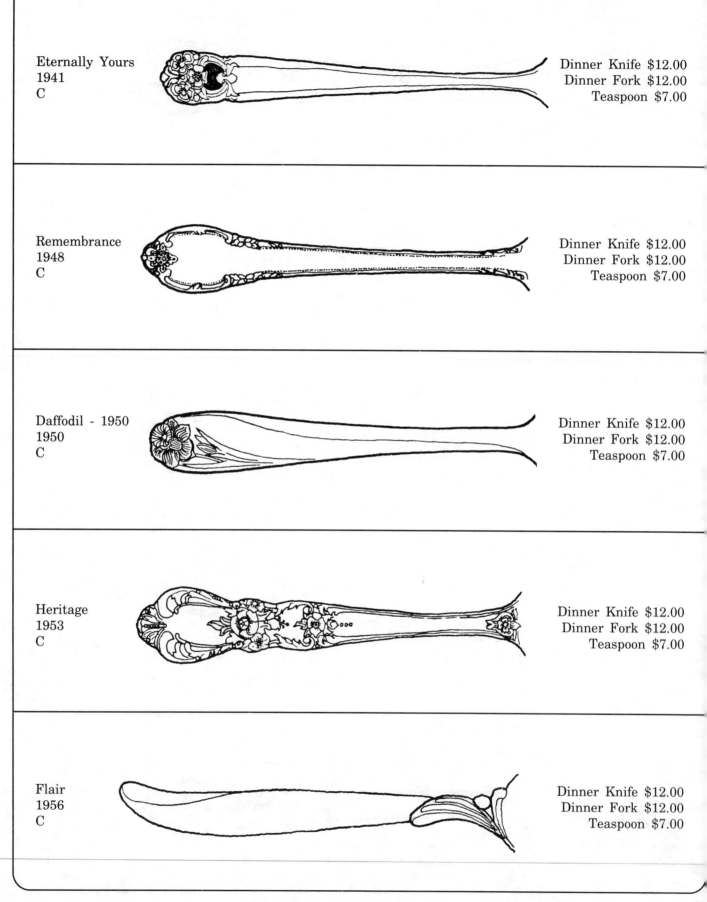

Eternally Yours
1941
C

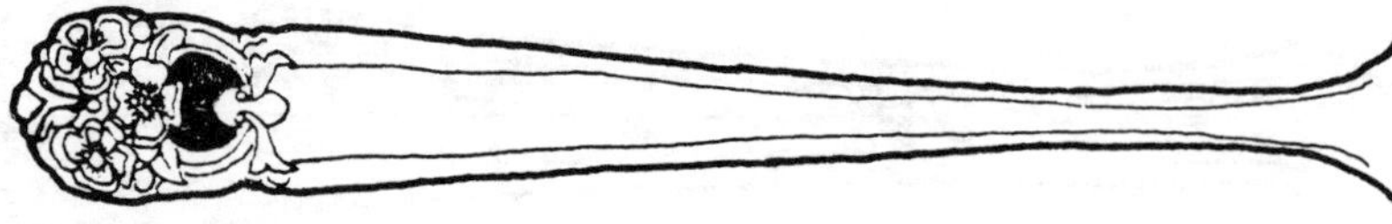

Dinner Knife $12.00
Dinner Fork $12.00
Teaspoon $7.00

Remembrance
1948
C

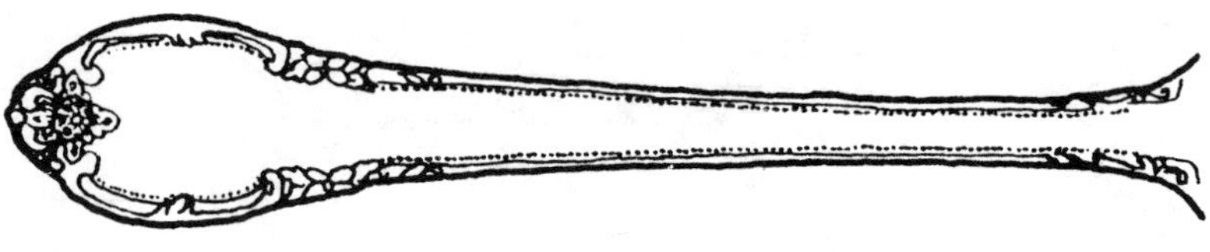

Dinner Knife $12.00
Dinner Fork $12.00
Teaspoon $7.00

Daffodil - 1950
1950
C

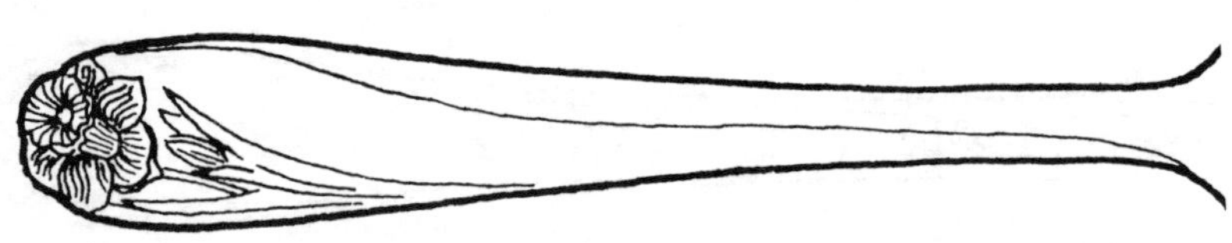

Dinner Knife $12.00
Dinner Fork $12.00
Teaspoon $7.00

Heritage
1953
C

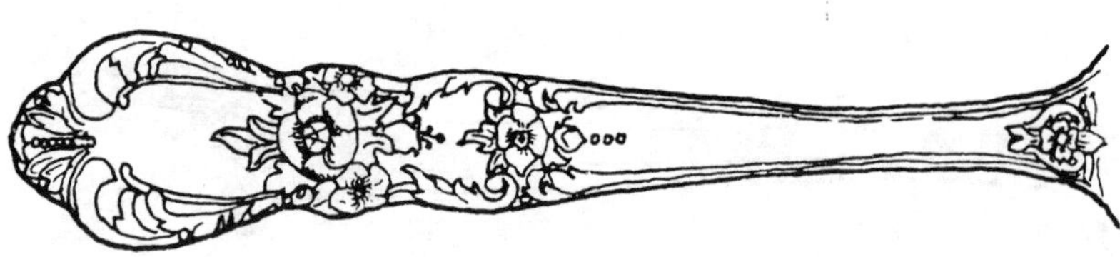

Dinner Knife $12.00
Dinner Fork $12.00
Teaspoon $7.00

Flair
1956
C

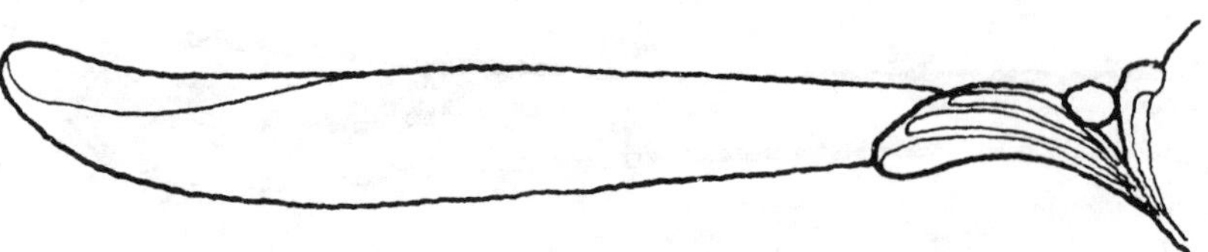

Dinner Knife $12.00
Dinner Fork $12.00
Teaspoon $7.00

Please refer to "How To Use This Book" page 4.

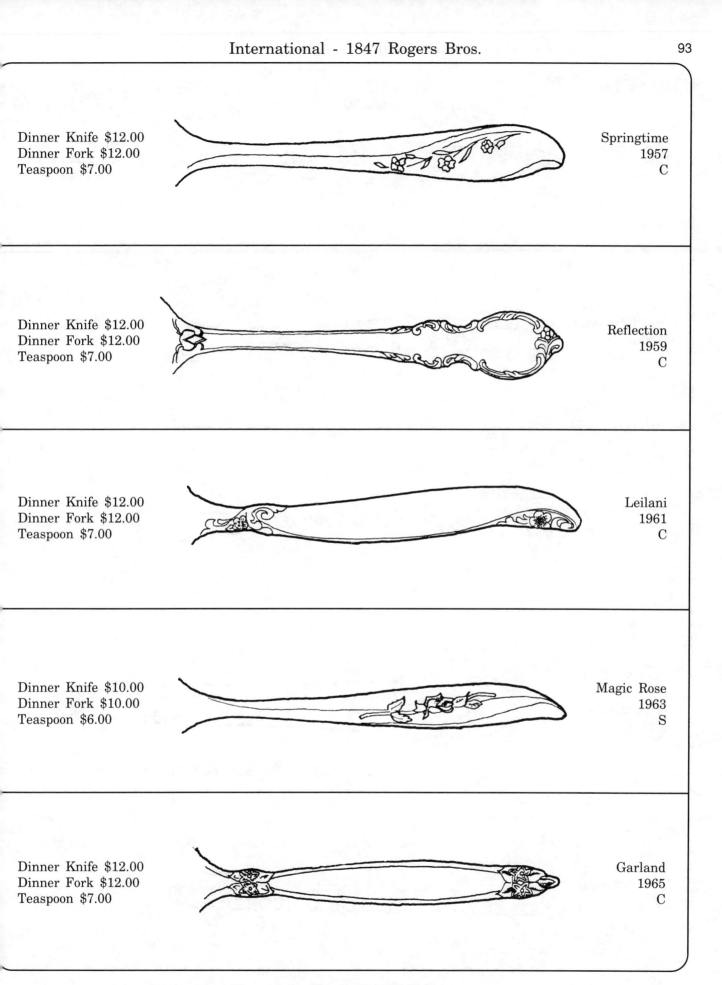

Dinner Knife $12.00
Dinner Fork $12.00
Teaspoon $7.00

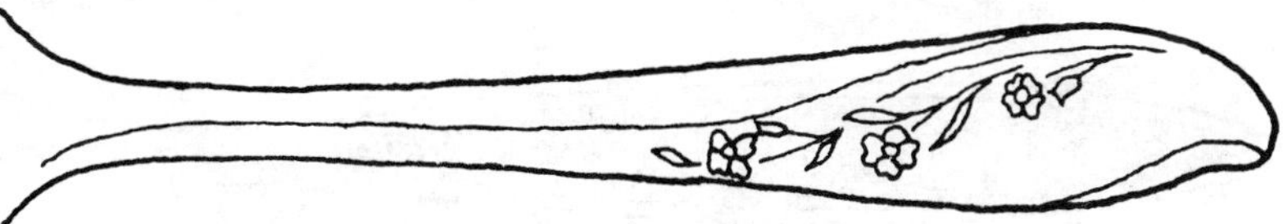

Springtime
1957
C

Dinner Knife $12.00
Dinner Fork $12.00
Teaspoon $7.00

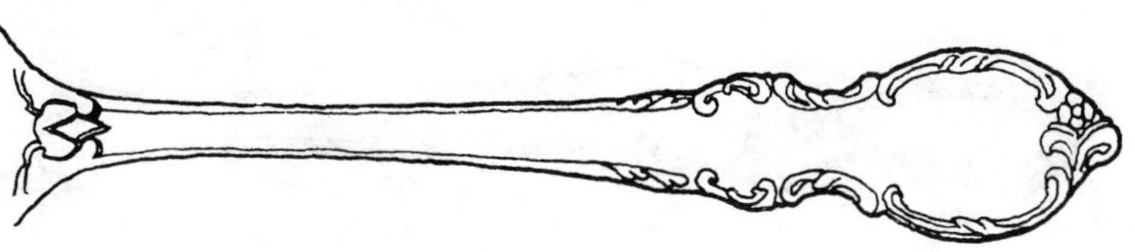

Reflection
1959
C

Dinner Knife $12.00
Dinner Fork $12.00
Teaspoon $7.00

Leilani
1961
C

Dinner Knife $10.00
Dinner Fork $10.00
Teaspoon $6.00

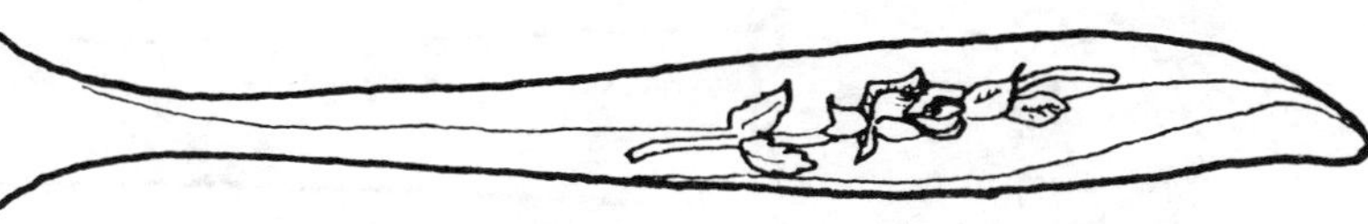

Magic Rose
1963
S

Dinner Knife $12.00
Dinner Fork $12.00
Teaspoon $7.00

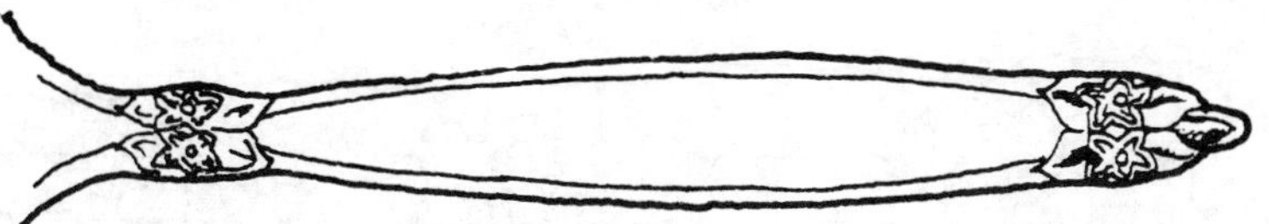

Garland
1965
C

Please refer to "How To Use This Book" page 4.

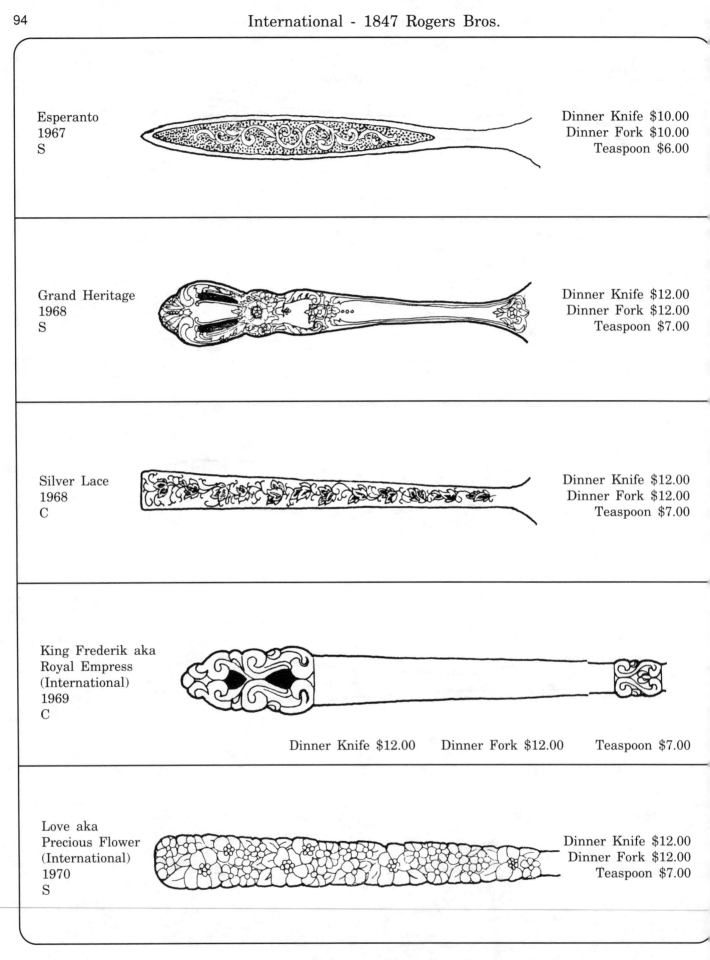

Esperanto
1967
S

Dinner Knife $10.00
Dinner Fork $10.00
Teaspoon $6.00

Grand Heritage
1968
S

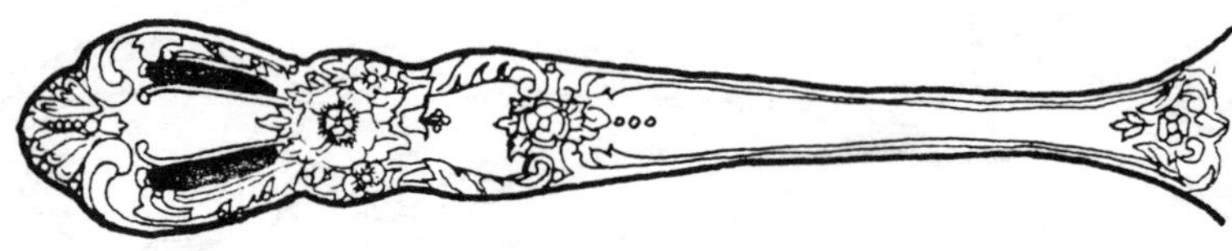

Dinner Knife $12.00
Dinner Fork $12.00
Teaspoon $7.00

Silver Lace
1968
C

Dinner Knife $12.00
Dinner Fork $12.00
Teaspoon $7.00

King Frederik aka
Royal Empress
(International)
1969
C

Dinner Knife $12.00 Dinner Fork $12.00 Teaspoon $7.00

Love aka
Precious Flower
(International)
1970
S

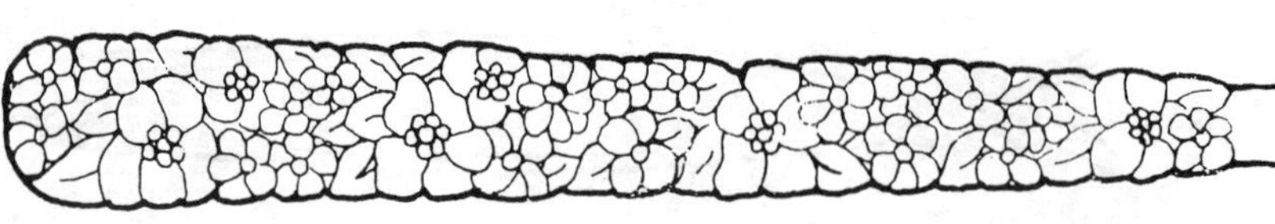

Dinner Knife $12.00
Dinner Fork $12.00
Teaspoon $7.00

Please refer to "How To Use This Book" page 4.

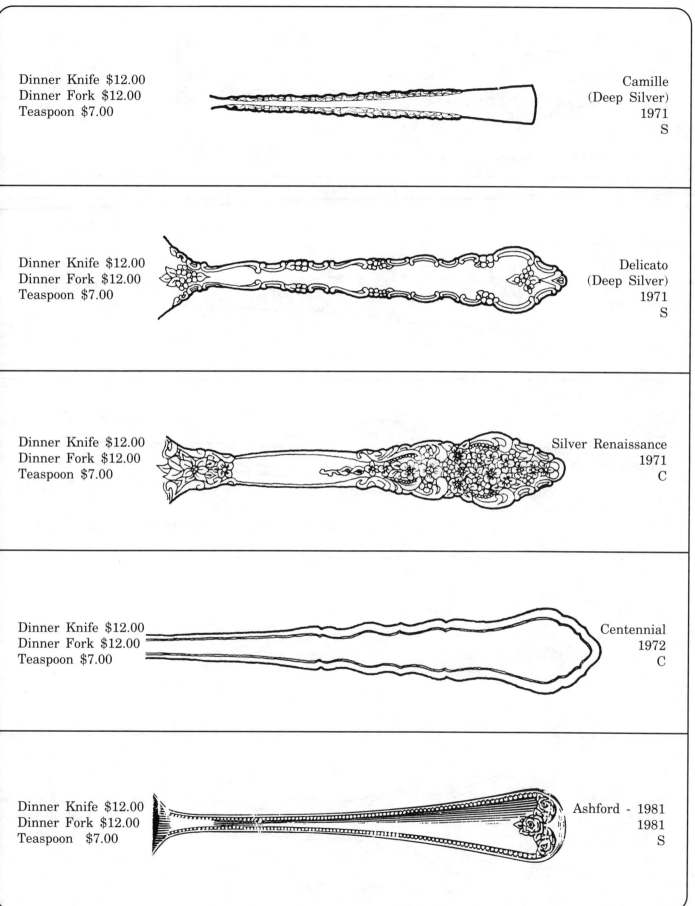

Dinner Knife $12.00
Dinner Fork $12.00
Teaspoon $7.00

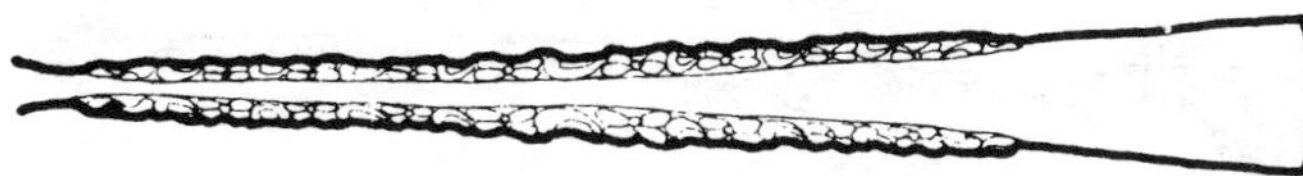

Camille
(Deep Silver)
1971
S

Dinner Knife $12.00
Dinner Fork $12.00
Teaspoon $7.00

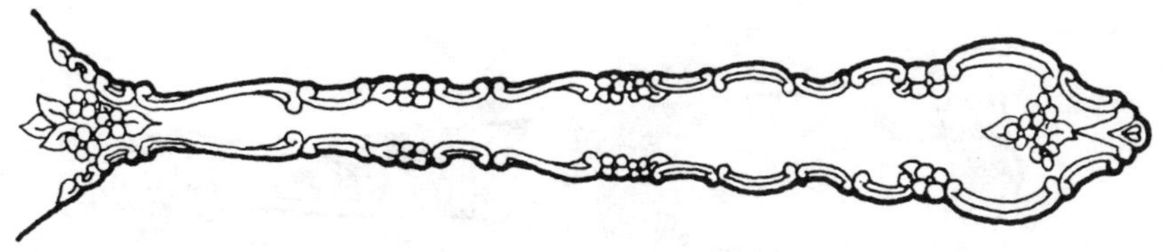

Delicato
(Deep Silver)
1971
S

Dinner Knife $12.00
Dinner Fork $12.00
Teaspoon $7.00

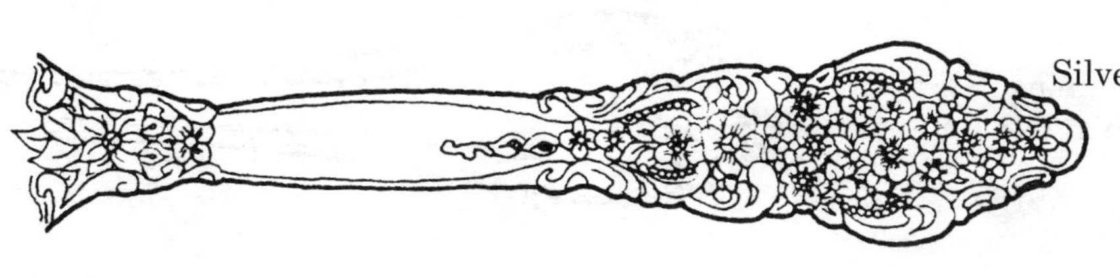

Silver Renaissance
1971
C

Dinner Knife $12.00
Dinner Fork $12.00
Teaspoon $7.00

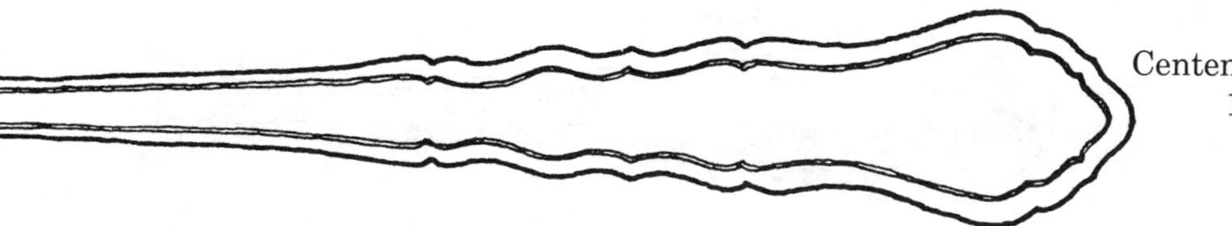

Centennial
1972
C

Dinner Knife $12.00
Dinner Fork $12.00
Teaspoon $7.00

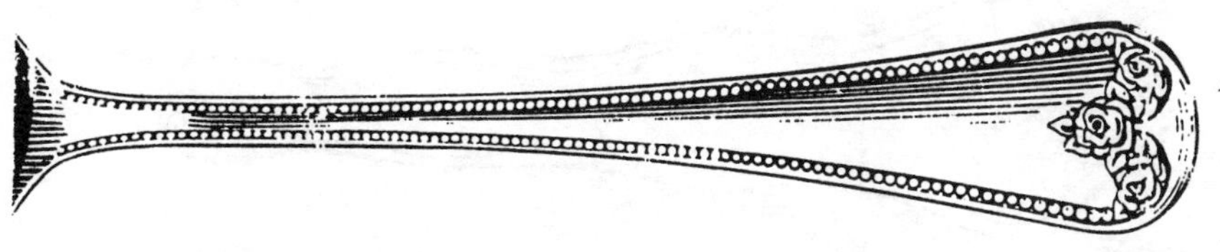

Ashford - 1981
1981
S

Please refer to "How To Use This Book" page 4.

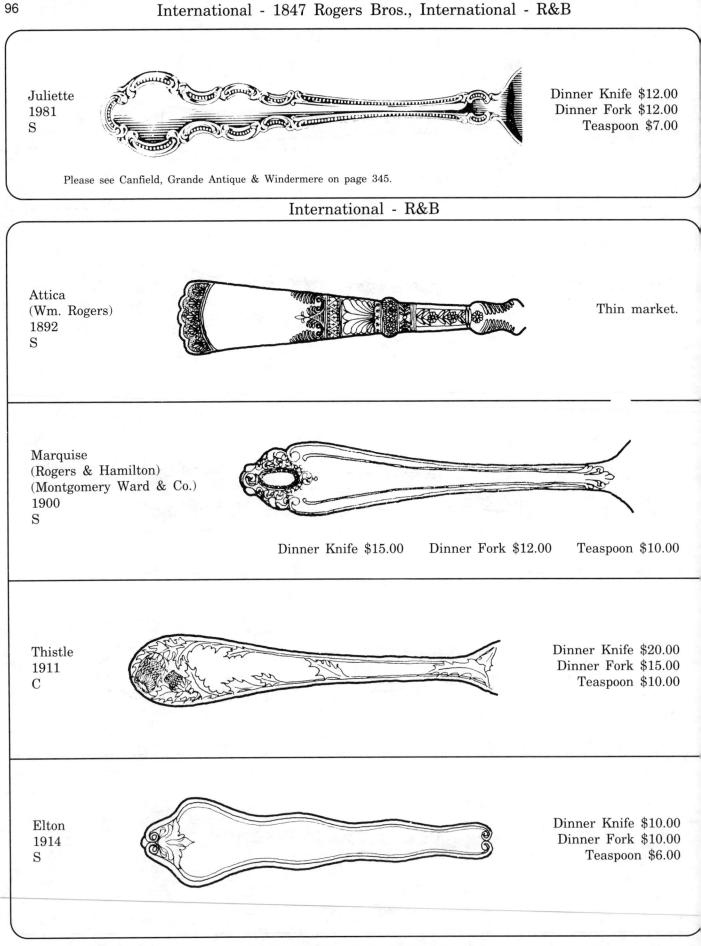

Juliette
1981
S

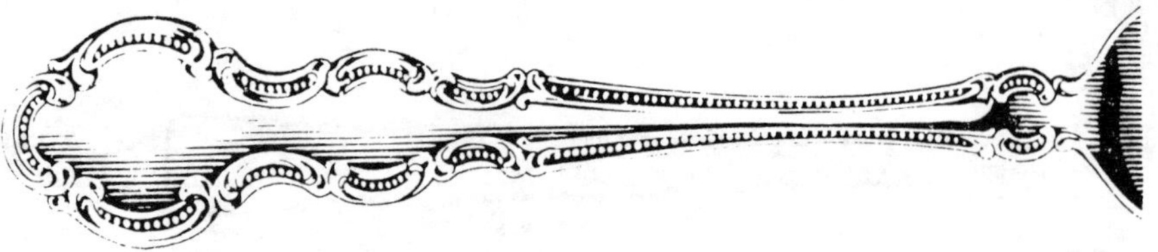

Dinner Knife $12.00
Dinner Fork $12.00
Teaspoon $7.00

Please see Canfield, Grande Antique & Windermere on page 345.

International - R&B

Attica
(Wm. Rogers)
1892
S

Thin market.

Marquise
(Rogers & Hamilton)
(Montgomery Ward & Co.)
1900
S

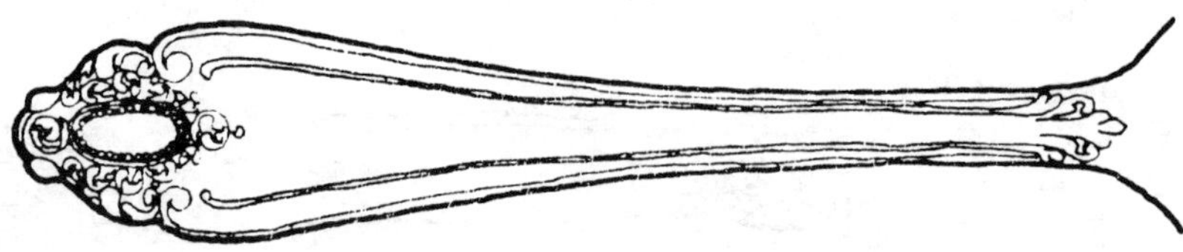

Dinner Knife $15.00 Dinner Fork $12.00 Teaspoon $10.00

Thistle
1911
C

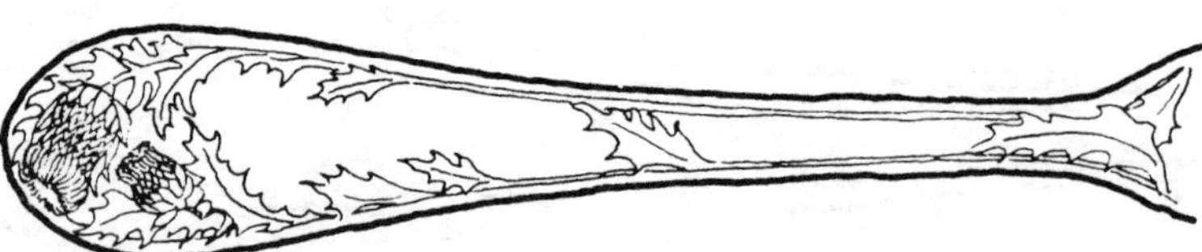

Dinner Knife $20.00
Dinner Fork $15.00
Teaspoon $10.00

Elton
1914
S

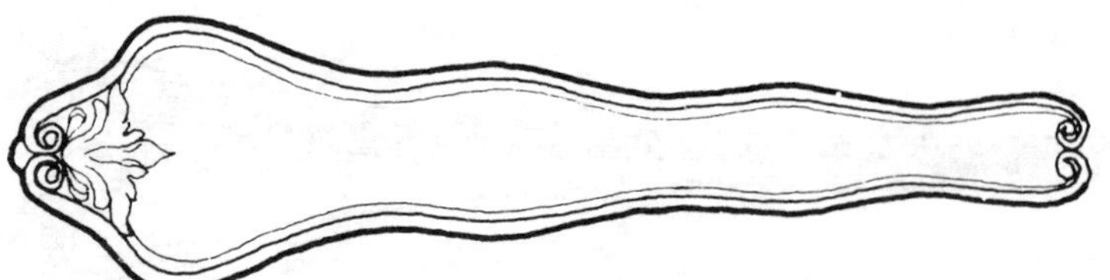

Dinner Knife $10.00
Dinner Fork $10.00
Teaspoon $6.00

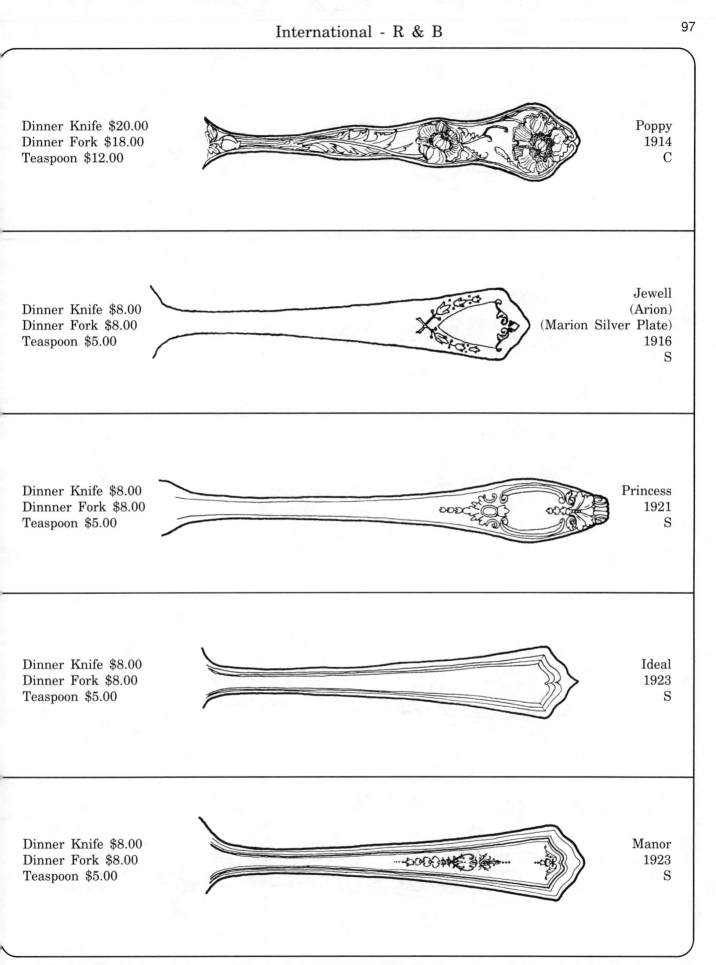

Dinner Knife $20.00
Dinner Fork $18.00
Teaspoon $12.00

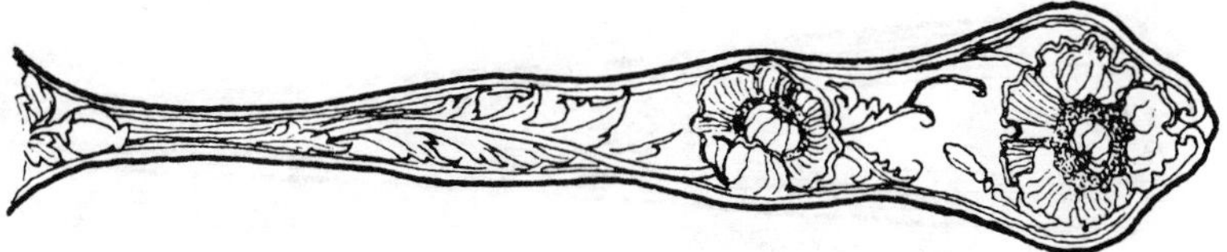

Poppy
1914
C

Dinner Knife $8.00
Dinner Fork $8.00
Teaspoon $5.00

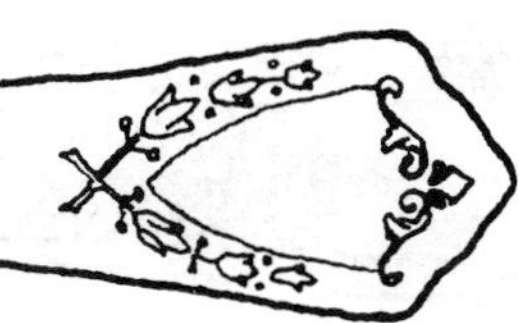

Jewell
(Arion)
(Marion Silver Plate)
1916
S

Dinner Knife $8.00
Dinnner Fork $8.00
Teaspoon $5.00

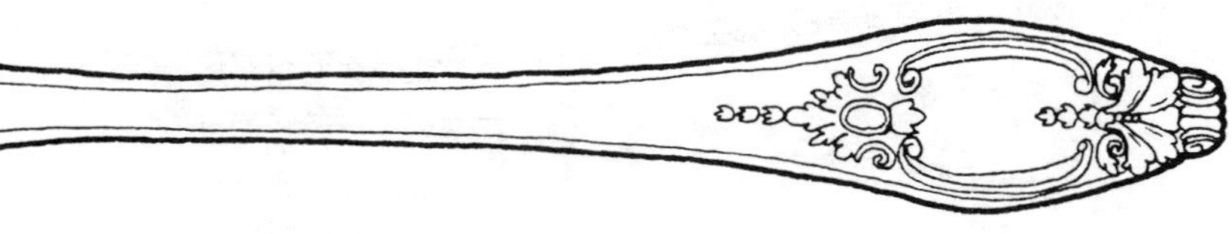

Princess
1921
S

Dinner Knife $8.00
Dinner Fork $8.00
Teaspoon $5.00

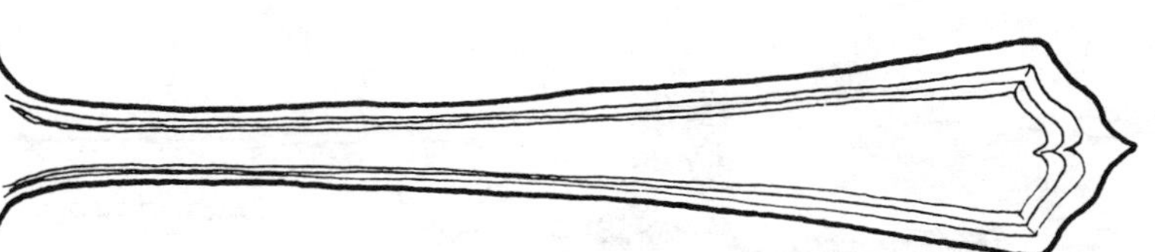

Ideal
1923
S

Dinner Knife $8.00
Dinner Fork $8.00
Teaspoon $5.00

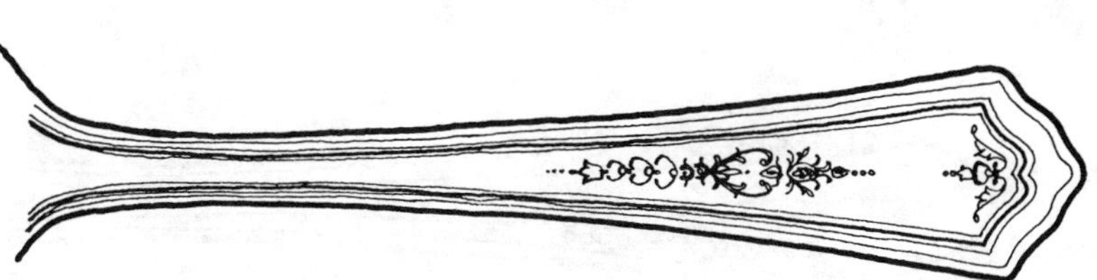

Manor
1923
S

Please refer to "How To Use This Book" page 4.

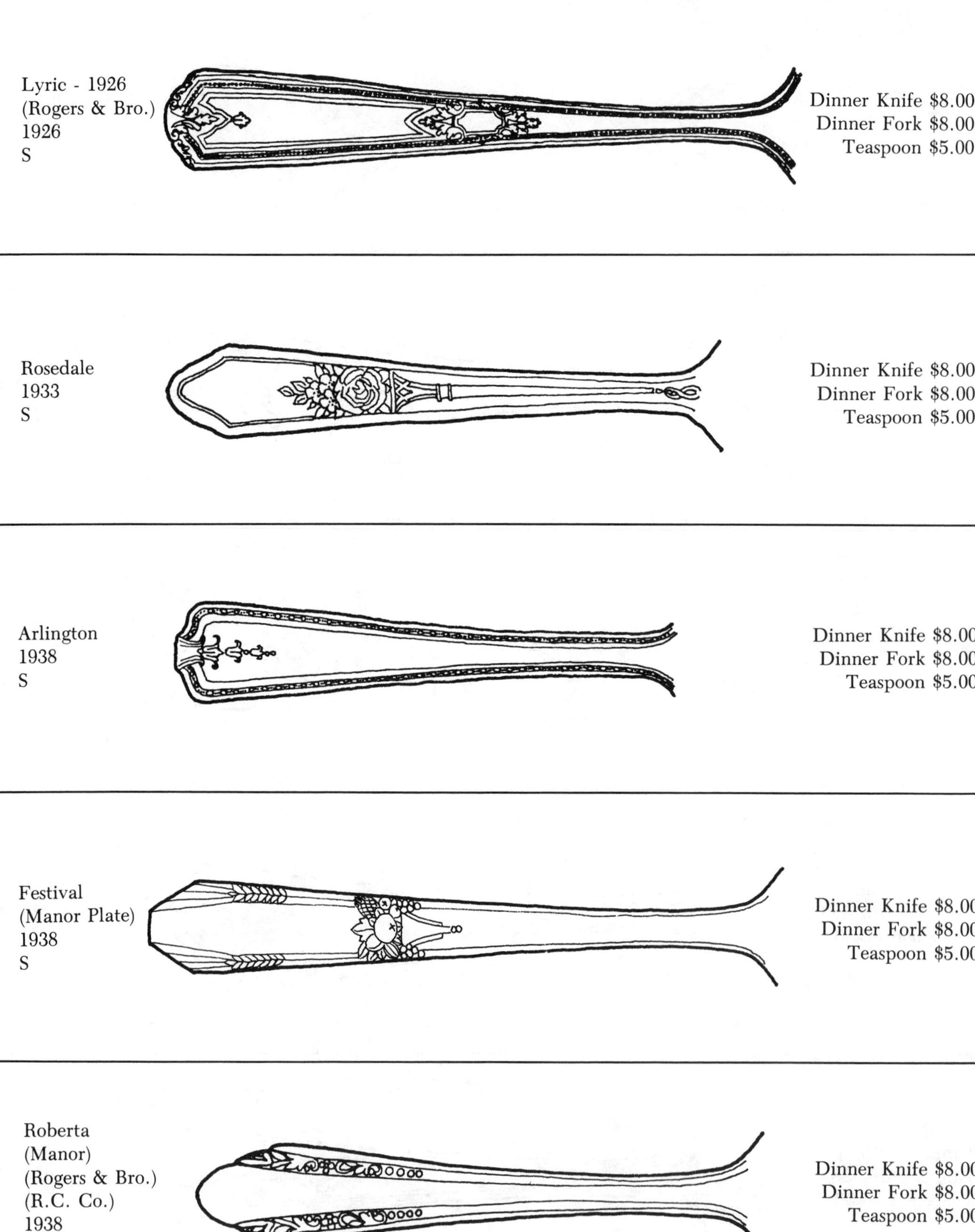

Lyric - 1926
(Rogers & Bro.)
1926
S

Dinner Knife $8.00
Dinner Fork $8.00
Teaspoon $5.00

Rosedale
1933
S

Dinner Knife $8.00
Dinner Fork $8.00
Teaspoon $5.00

Arlington
1938
S

Dinner Knife $8.00
Dinner Fork $8.00
Teaspoon $5.00

Festival
(Manor Plate)
1938
S

Dinner Knife $8.00
Dinner Fork $8.00
Teaspoon $5.00

Roberta
(Manor)
(Rogers & Bro.)
(R.C. Co.)
1938
S

Dinner Knife $8.00
Dinner Fork $8.00
Teaspoon $5.00

Please refer to "How To Use This Book" page 4.

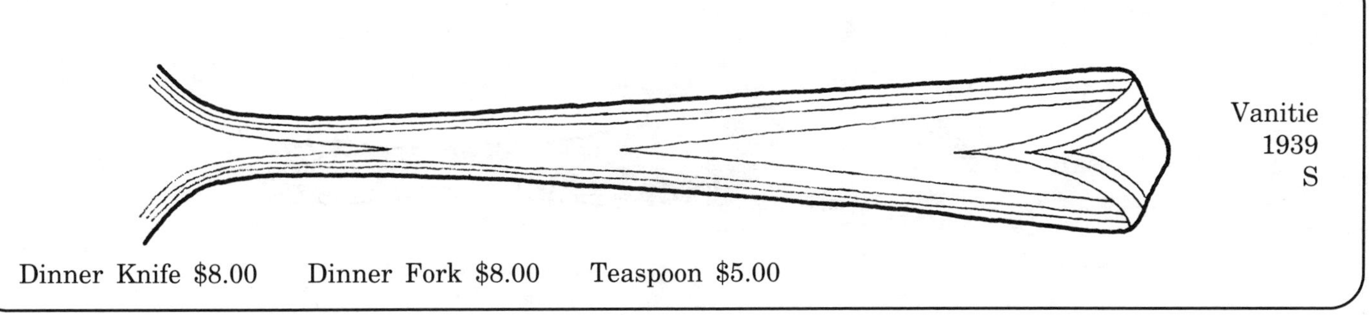

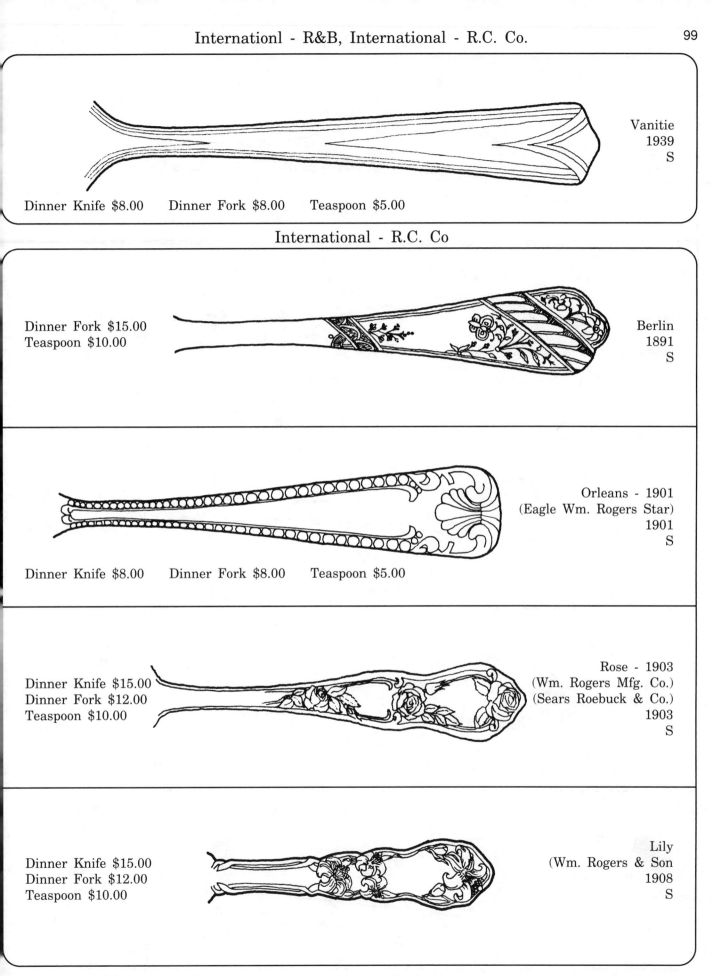

Vanitie
1939
S

Dinner Knife $8.00 Dinner Fork $8.00 Teaspoon $5.00

International - R.C. Co

Dinner Fork $15.00
Teaspoon $10.00

Berlin
1891
S

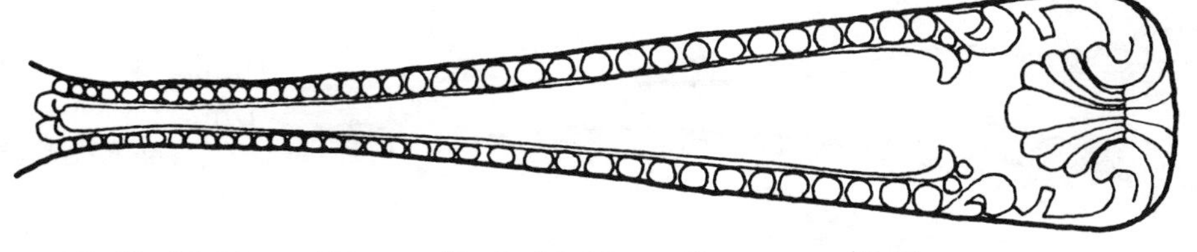

Orleans - 1901
(Eagle Wm. Rogers Star)
1901
S

Dinner Knife $8.00 Dinner Fork $8.00 Teaspoon $5.00

Dinner Knife $15.00
Dinner Fork $12.00
Teaspoon $10.00

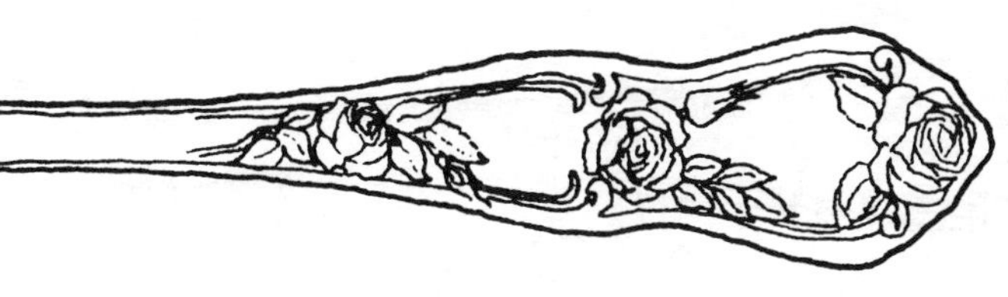

Rose - 1903
(Wm. Rogers Mfg. Co.)
(Sears Roebuck & Co.)
1903
S

Dinner Knife $15.00
Dinner Fork $12.00
Teaspoon $10.00

Lily
(Wm. Rogers & Son
1908
S

Please refer to "How To Use This Book" page 4.

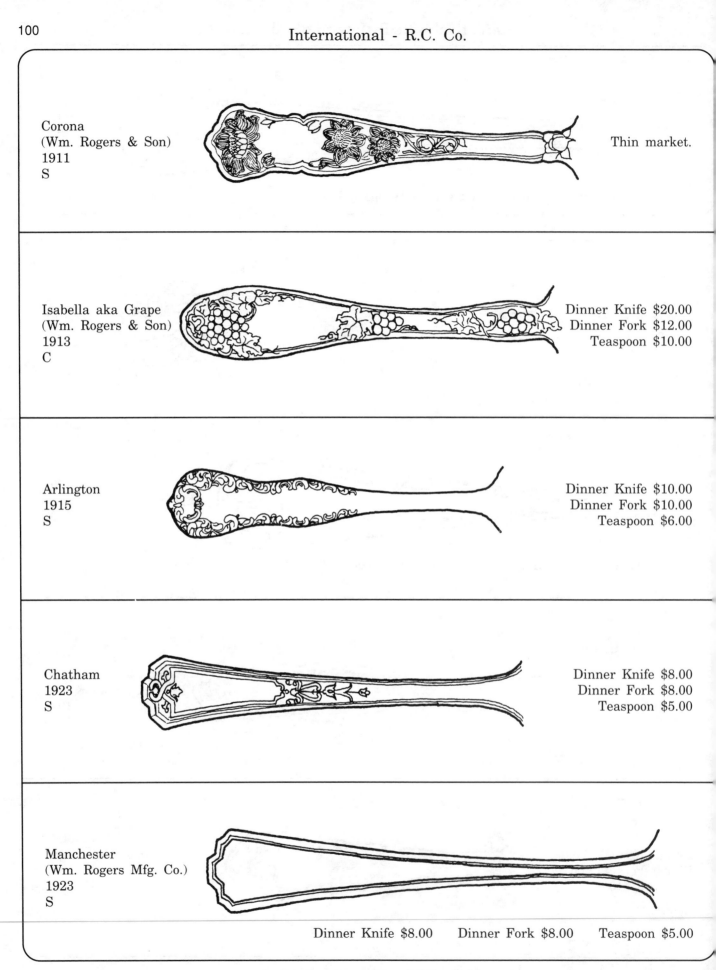

Corona
(Wm. Rogers & Son)
1911
S

Thin market.

Isabella aka Grape
(Wm. Rogers & Son)
1913
C

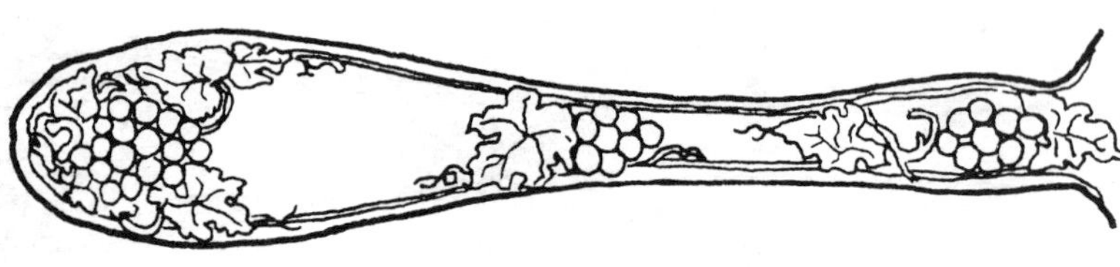

Dinner Knife $20.00
Dinner Fork $12.00
Teaspoon $10.00

Arlington
1915
S

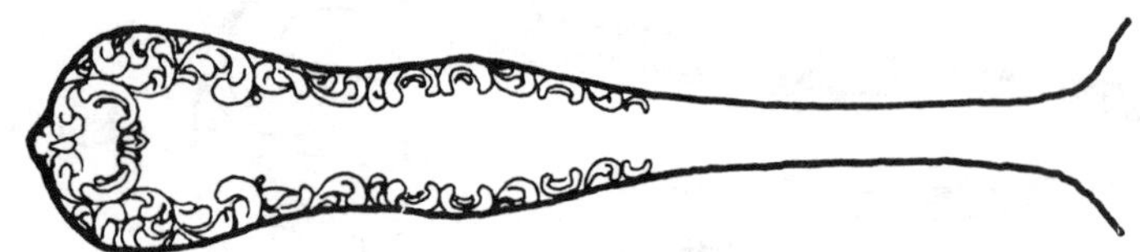

Dinner Knife $10.00
Dinner Fork $10.00
Teaspoon $6.00

Chatham
1923
S

Dinner Knife $8.00
Dinner Fork $8.00
Teaspoon $5.00

Manchester
(Wm. Rogers Mfg. Co.)
1923
S

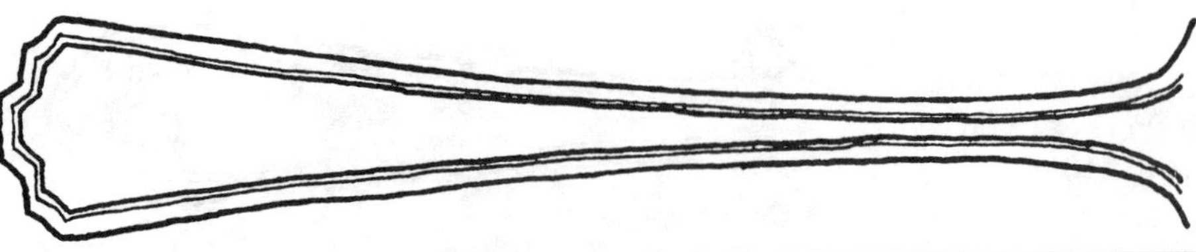

Dinner Knife $8.00 Dinner Fork $8.00 Teaspoon $5.00

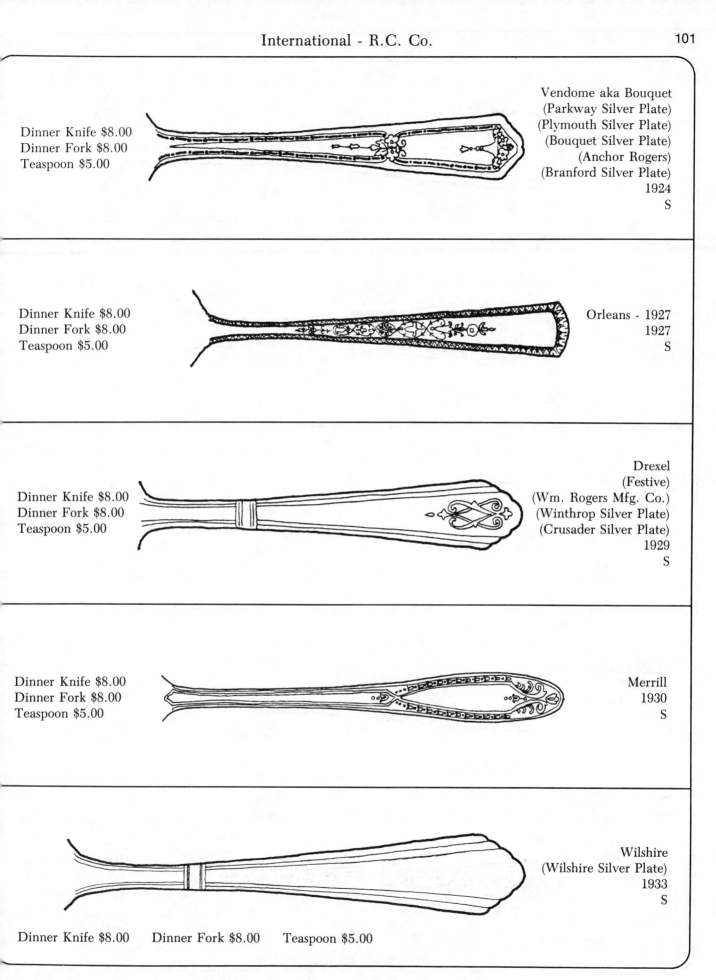

Dinner Knife $8.00
Dinner Fork $8.00
Teaspoon $5.00

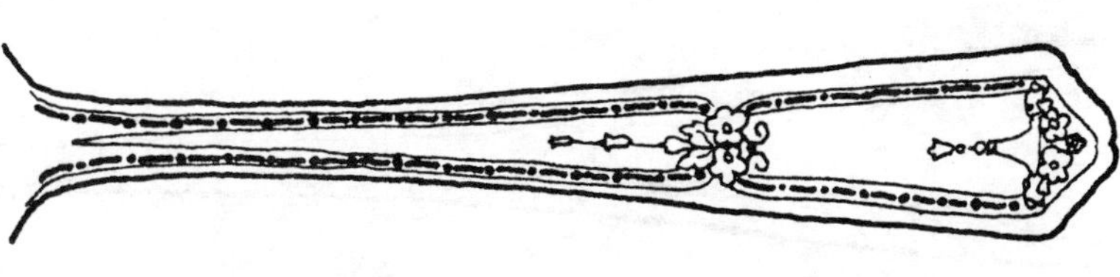

Vendome aka Bouquet
(Parkway Silver Plate)
(Plymouth Silver Plate)
(Bouquet Silver Plate)
(Anchor Rogers)
(Branford Silver Plate)
1924
S

Dinner Knife $8.00
Dinner Fork $8.00
Teaspoon $5.00

Orleans - 1927
1927
S

Dinner Knife $8.00
Dinner Fork $8.00
Teaspoon $5.00

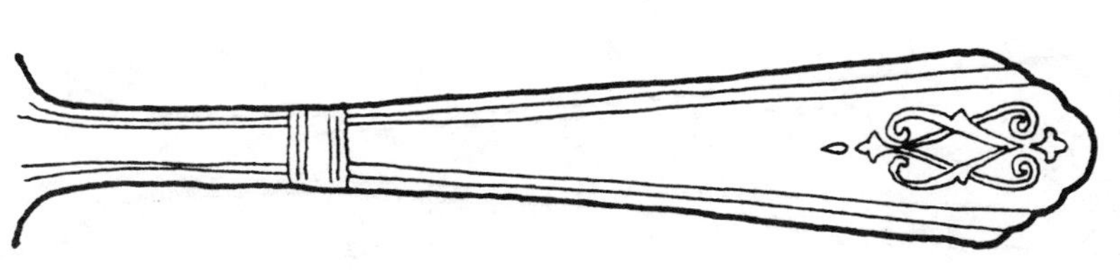

Drexel
(Festive)
(Wm. Rogers Mfg. Co.)
(Winthrop Silver Plate)
(Crusader Silver Plate)
1929
S

Dinner Knife $8.00
Dinner Fork $8.00
Teaspoon $5.00

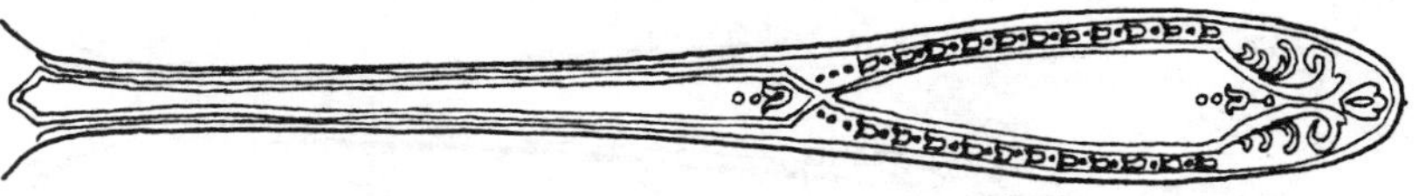

Merrill
1930
S

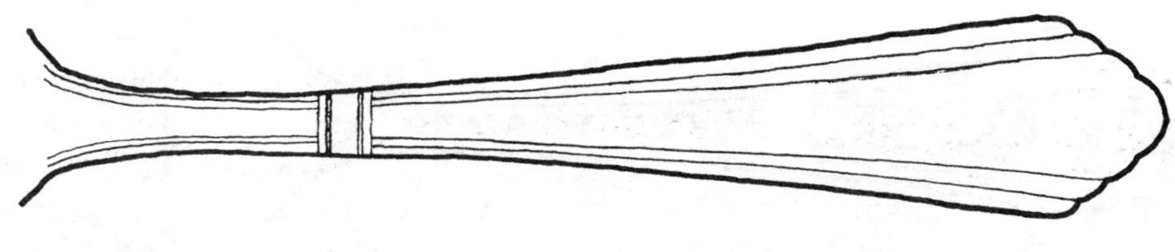

Wilshire
(Wilshire Silver Plate)
1933
S

Dinner Knife $8.00 Dinner Fork $8.00 Teaspoon $5.00

Please refer to "How To Use This Book" page 4.

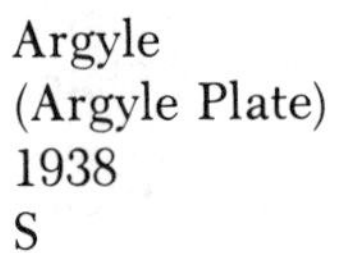

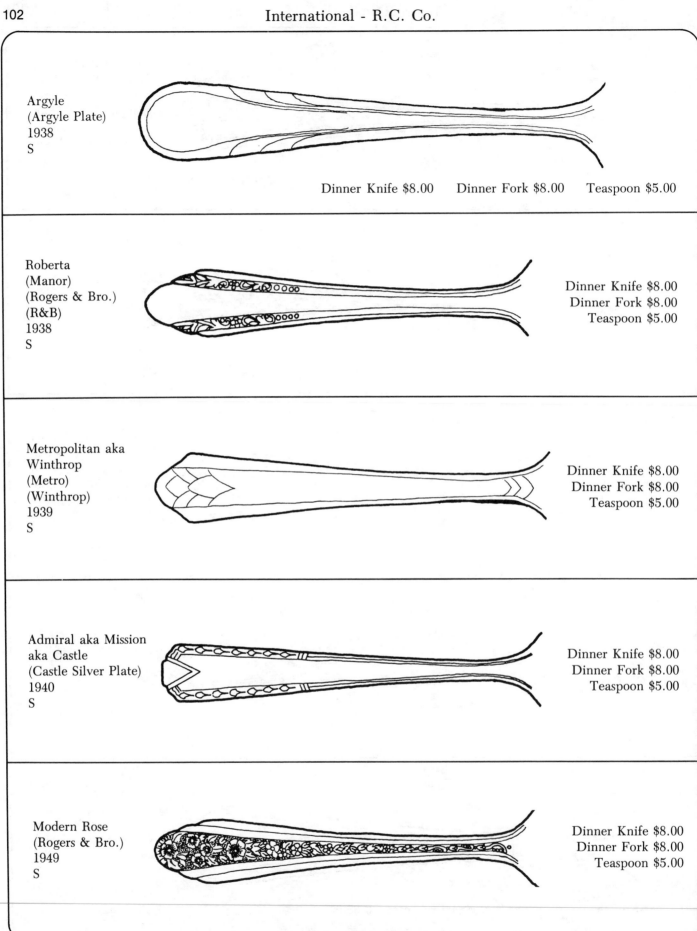

Argyle
(Argyle Plate)
1938
S

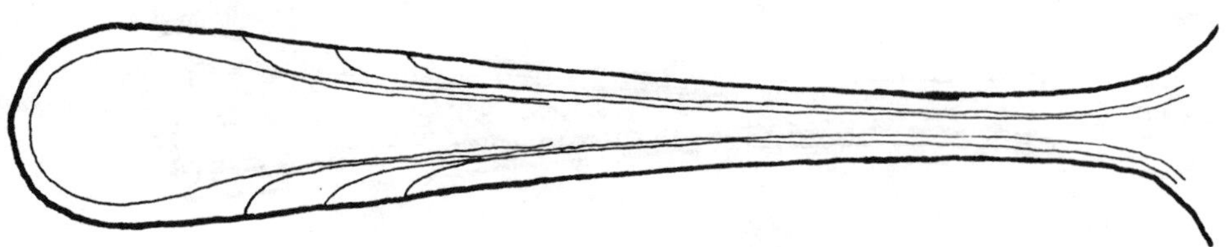

Dinner Knife $8.00 Dinner Fork $8.00 Teaspoon $5.00

Roberta
(Manor)
(Rogers & Bro.)
(R&B)
1938
S

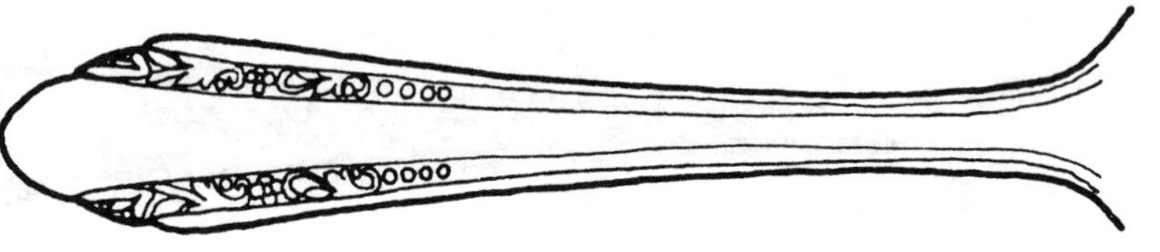

Dinner Knife $8.00
Dinner Fork $8.00
Teaspoon $5.00

Metropolitan aka
Winthrop
(Metro)
(Winthrop)
1939
S

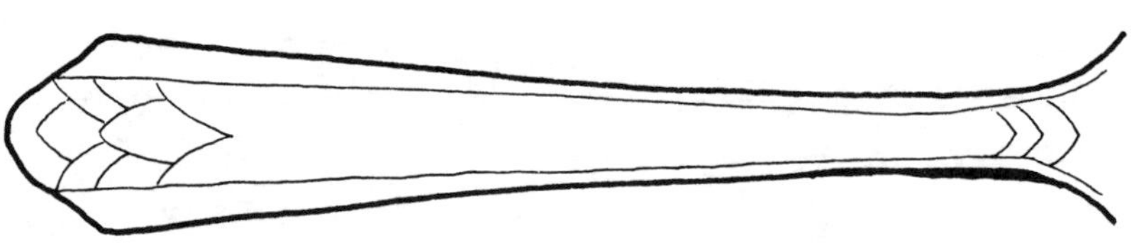

Dinner Knife $8.00
Dinner Fork $8.00
Teaspoon $5.00

Admiral aka Mission
aka Castle
(Castle Silver Plate)
1940
S

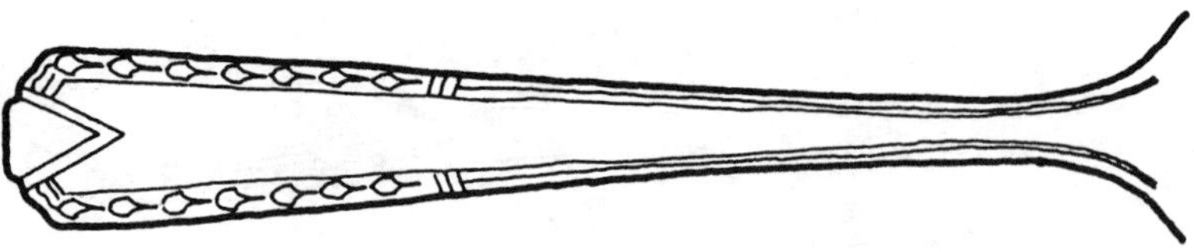

Dinner Knife $8.00
Dinner Fork $8.00
Teaspoon $5.00

Modern Rose
(Rogers & Bro.)
1949
S

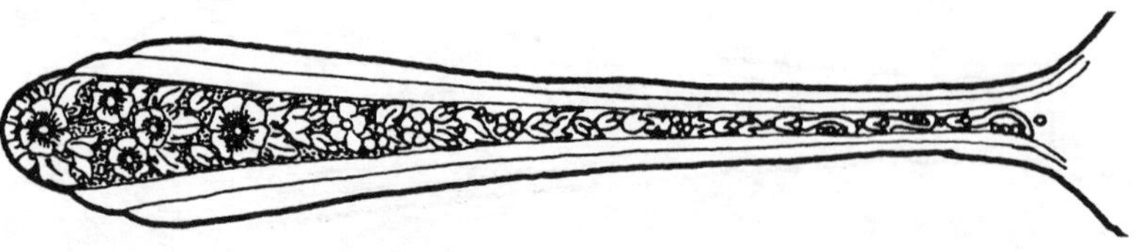

Dinner Knife $8.00
Dinner Fork $8.00
Teaspoon $5.00

Please refer to "How To Use This Book" page 4.

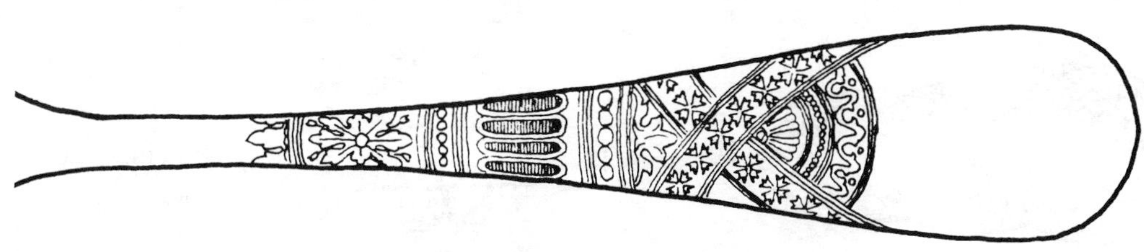

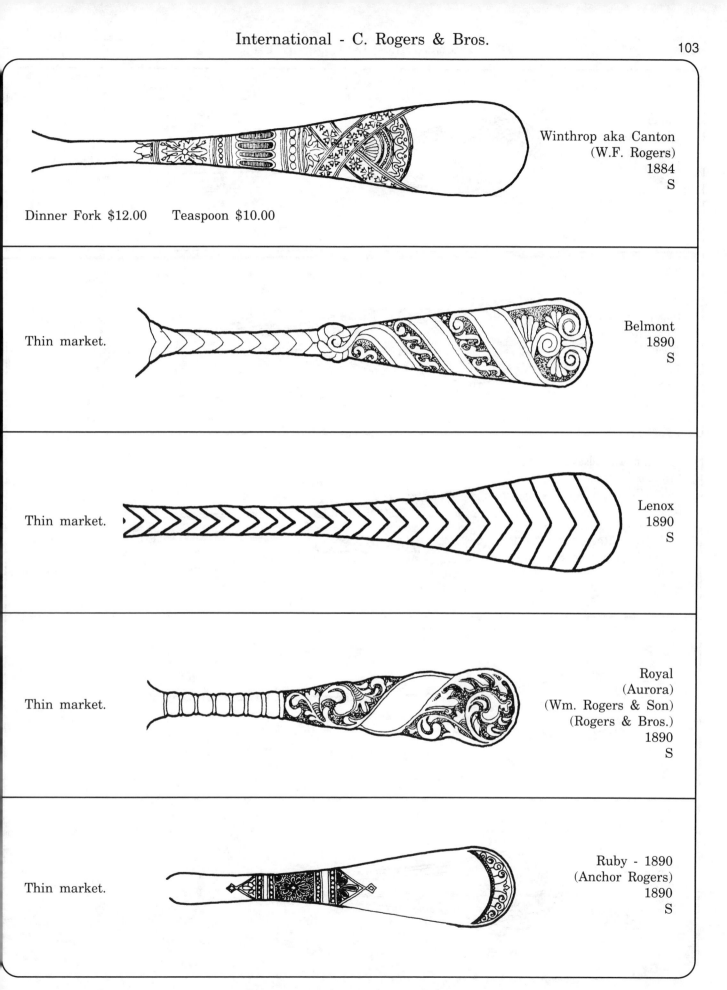

Winthrop aka Canton
(W.F. Rogers)
1884
S

Dinner Fork $12.00 Teaspoon $10.00

Thin market.

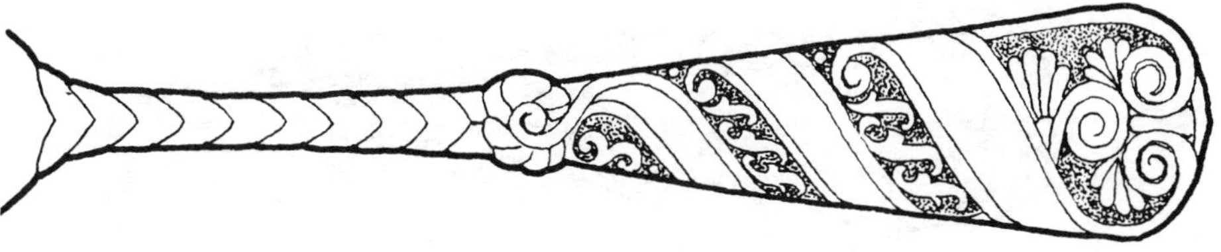

Belmont
1890
S

Thin market.

Lenox
1890
S

Thin market.

Royal
(Aurora)
(Wm. Rogers & Son)
(Rogers & Bros.)
1890
S

Thin market.

Ruby - 1890
(Anchor Rogers)
1890
S

Please refer to "How To Use This Book" page 4.

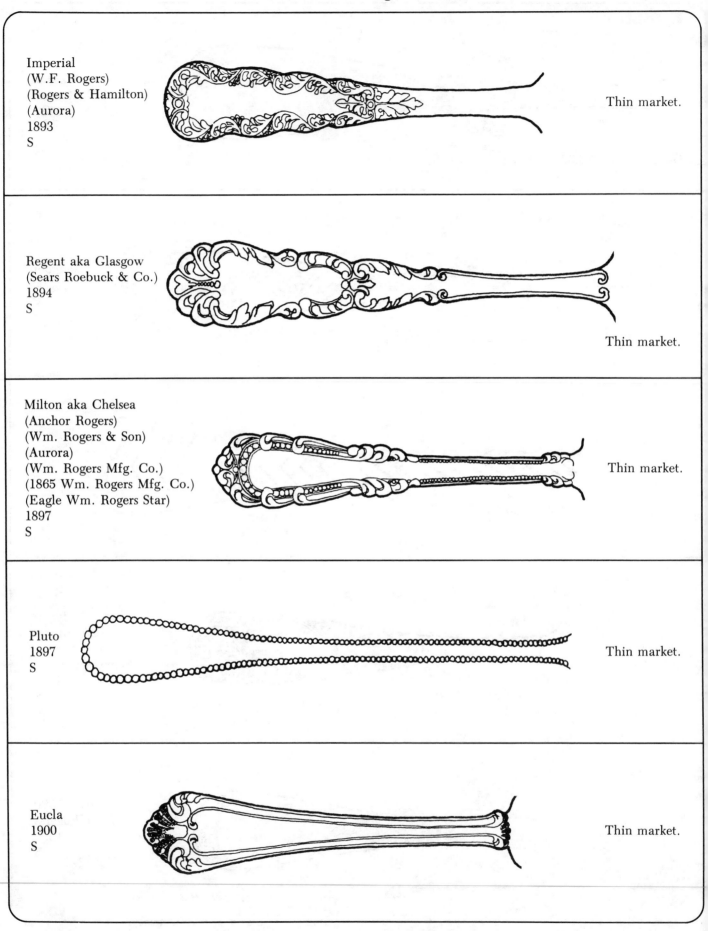

Imperial
(W.F. Rogers)
(Rogers & Hamilton)
(Aurora)
1893
S

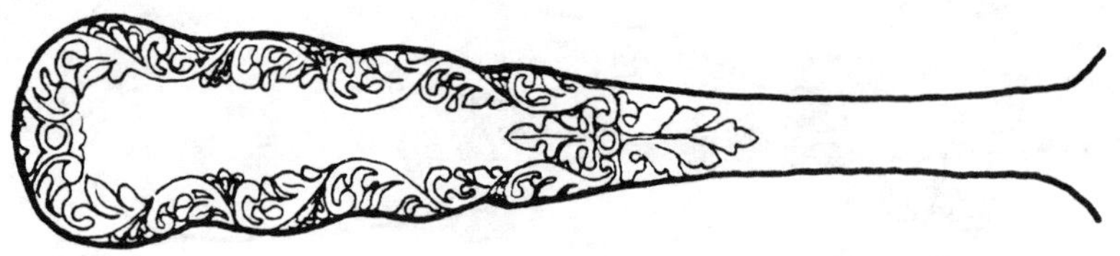

Thin market.

Regent aka Glasgow
(Sears Roebuck & Co.)
1894
S

Thin market.

Milton aka Chelsea
(Anchor Rogers)
(Wm. Rogers & Son)
(Aurora)
(Wm. Rogers Mfg. Co.)
(1865 Wm. Rogers Mfg. Co.)
(Eagle Wm. Rogers Star)
1897
S

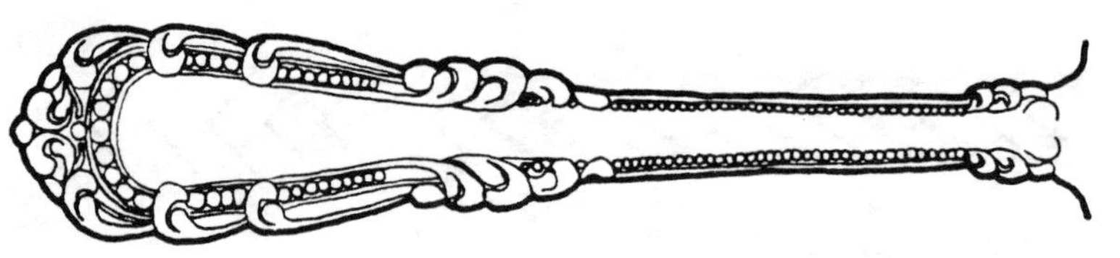

Thin market.

Pluto
1897
S

Thin market.

Eucla
1900
S

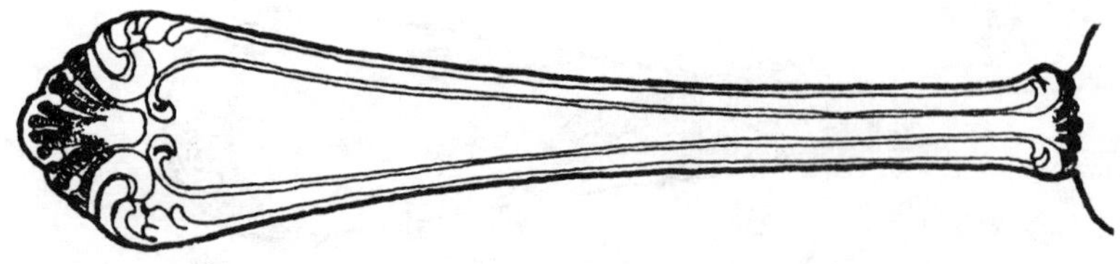

Thin market.

Please refer to "How To Use This Book" page 4.

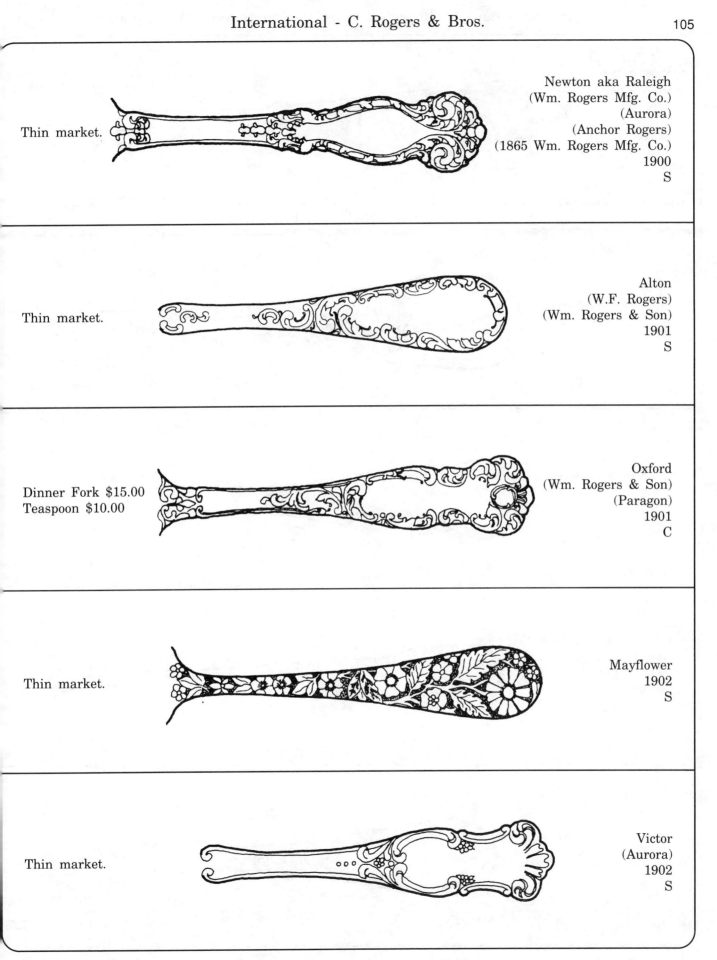

Thin market.

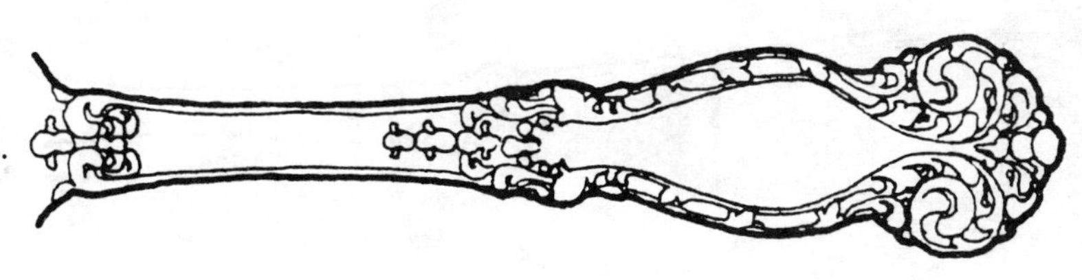

Newton aka Raleigh
(Wm. Rogers Mfg. Co.)
(Aurora)
(Anchor Rogers)
(1865 Wm. Rogers Mfg. Co.)
1900
S

Thin market.

Alton
(W.F. Rogers)
(Wm. Rogers & Son)
1901
S

Dinner Fork $15.00
Teaspoon $10.00

Oxford
(Wm. Rogers & Son)
(Paragon)
1901
C

Thin market.

Mayflower
1902
S

Thin market.

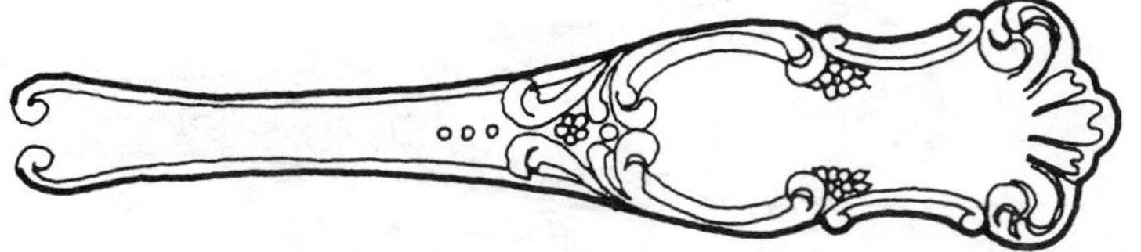

Victor
(Aurora)
1902
S

Please refer to "How To Use This Book" page 4.

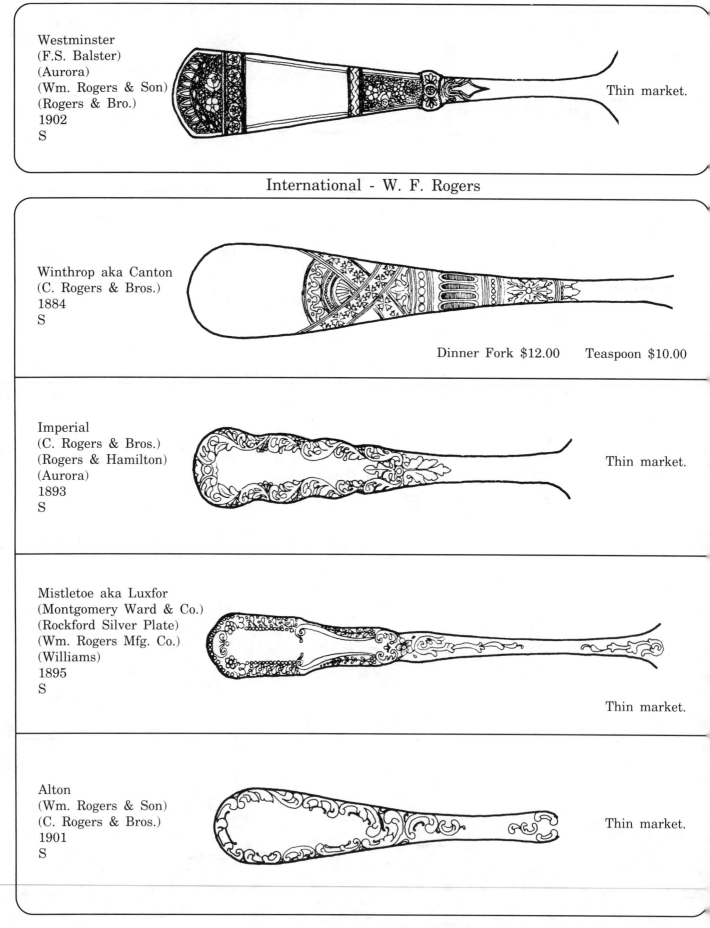

Westminster
(F.S. Balster)
(Aurora)
(Wm. Rogers & Son)
(Rogers & Bro.)
1902
S

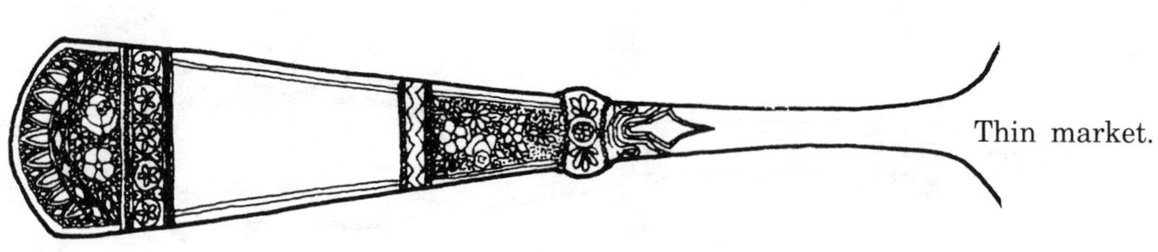

Thin market.

International - W. F. Rogers

Winthrop aka Canton
(C. Rogers & Bros.)
1884
S

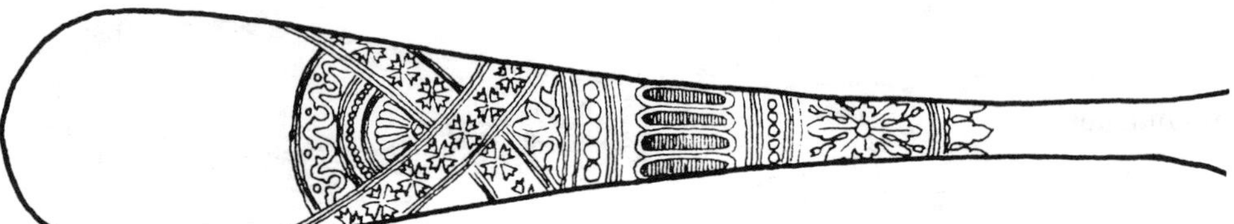

Dinner Fork $12.00 Teaspoon $10.00

Imperial
(C. Rogers & Bros.)
(Rogers & Hamilton)
(Aurora)
1893
S

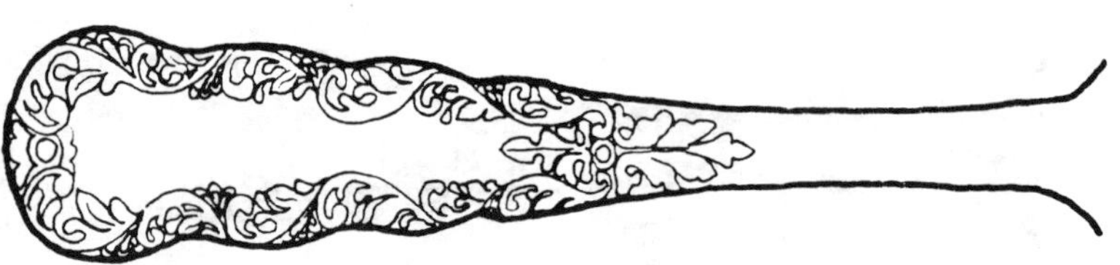

Thin market.

Mistletoe aka Luxfor
(Montgomery Ward & Co.)
(Rockford Silver Plate)
(Wm. Rogers Mfg. Co.)
(Williams)
1895
S

Thin market.

Alton
(Wm. Rogers & Son)
(C. Rogers & Bros.)
1901
S

Thin market.

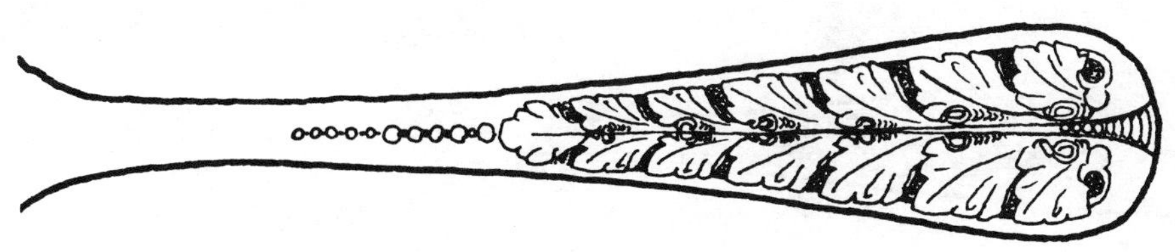

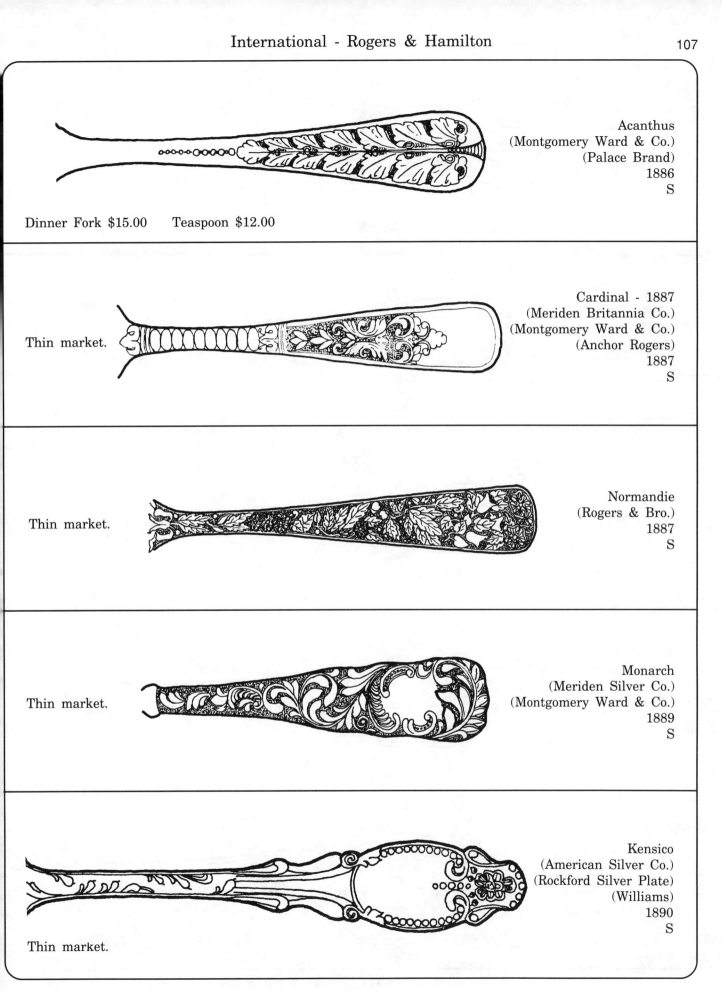

Acanthus
(Montgomery Ward & Co.)
(Palace Brand)
1886
S

Dinner Fork $15.00 Teaspoon $12.00

Thin market.

Cardinal - 1887
(Meriden Britannia Co.)
(Montgomery Ward & Co.)
(Anchor Rogers)
1887
S

Thin market.

Normandie
(Rogers & Bro.)
1887
S

Thin market.

Monarch
(Meriden Silver Co.)
(Montgomery Ward & Co.)
1889
S

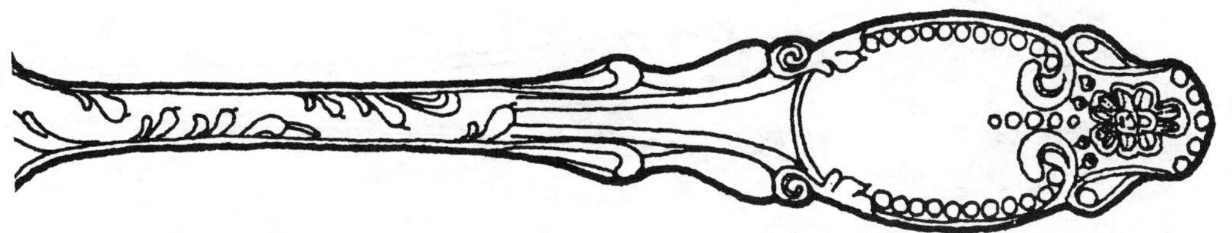

Kensico
(American Silver Co.)
(Rockford Silver Plate)
(Williams)
1890
S

Thin market.

Please refer to "How To Use This Book" page 4.

Czar
1891
S

Thin market.

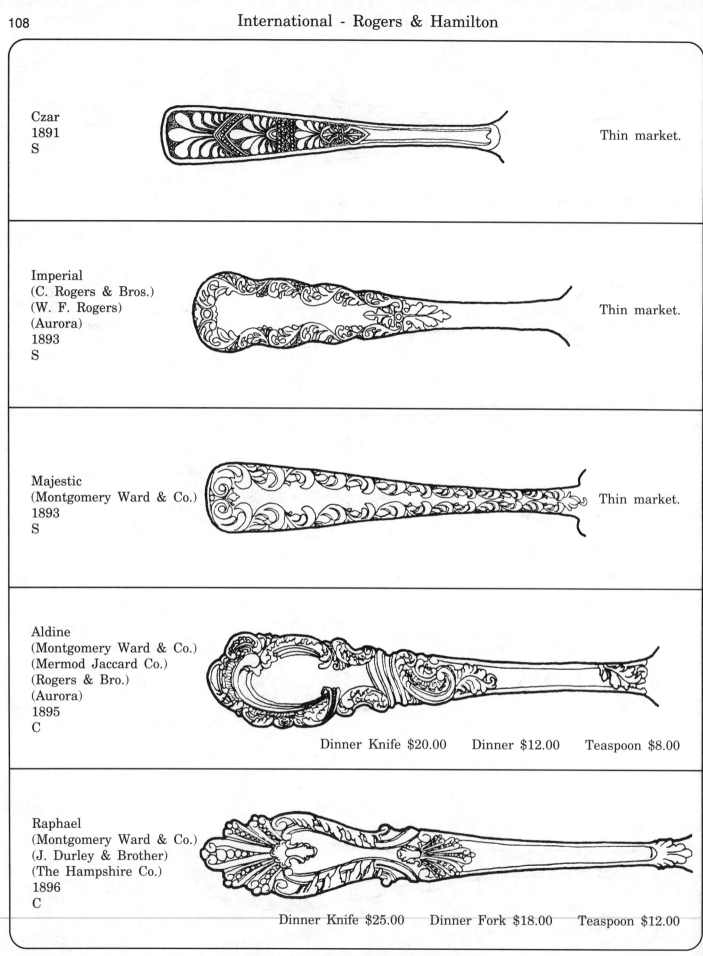

Imperial
(C. Rogers & Bros.)
(W. F. Rogers)
(Aurora)
1893
S

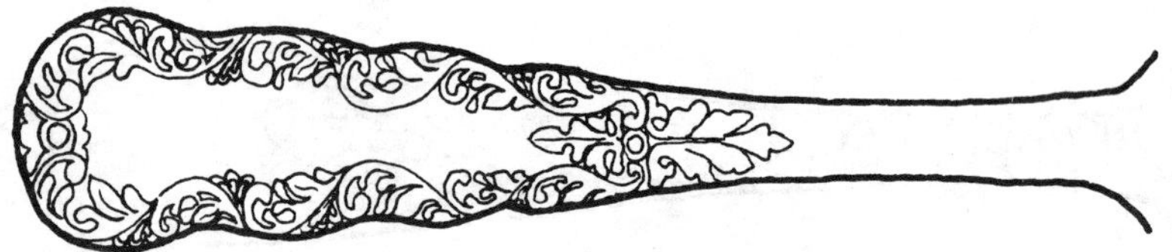

Thin market.

Majestic
(Montgomery Ward & Co.)
1893
S

Thin market.

Aldine
(Montgomery Ward & Co.)
(Mermod Jaccard Co.)
(Rogers & Bro.)
(Aurora)
1895
C

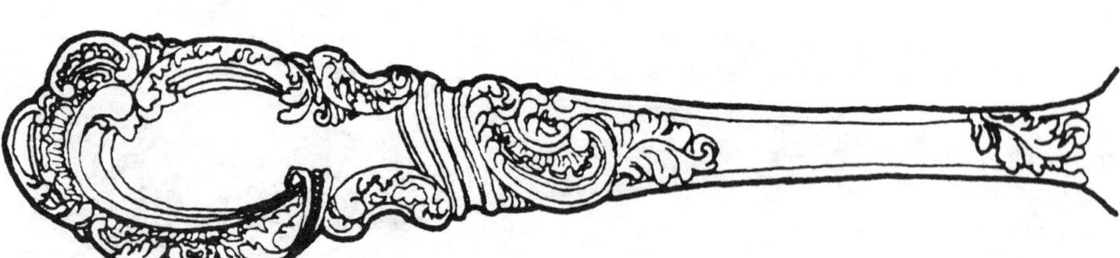

Dinner Knife $20.00 Dinner $12.00 Teaspoon $8.00

Raphael
(Montgomery Ward & Co.)
(J. Durley & Brother)
(The Hampshire Co.)
1896
C

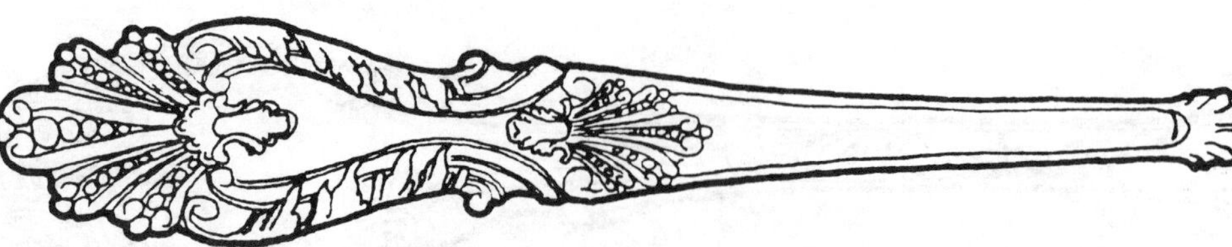

Dinner Knife $25.00 Dinner Fork $18.00 Teaspoon $12.00

Please refer to "How To Use This Book" page 4.

Thin market.

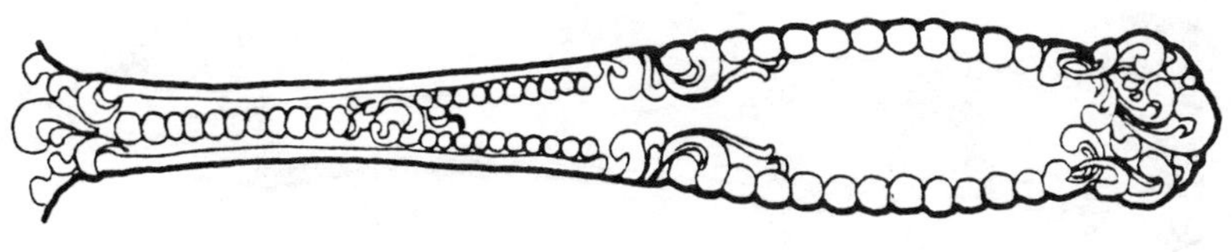

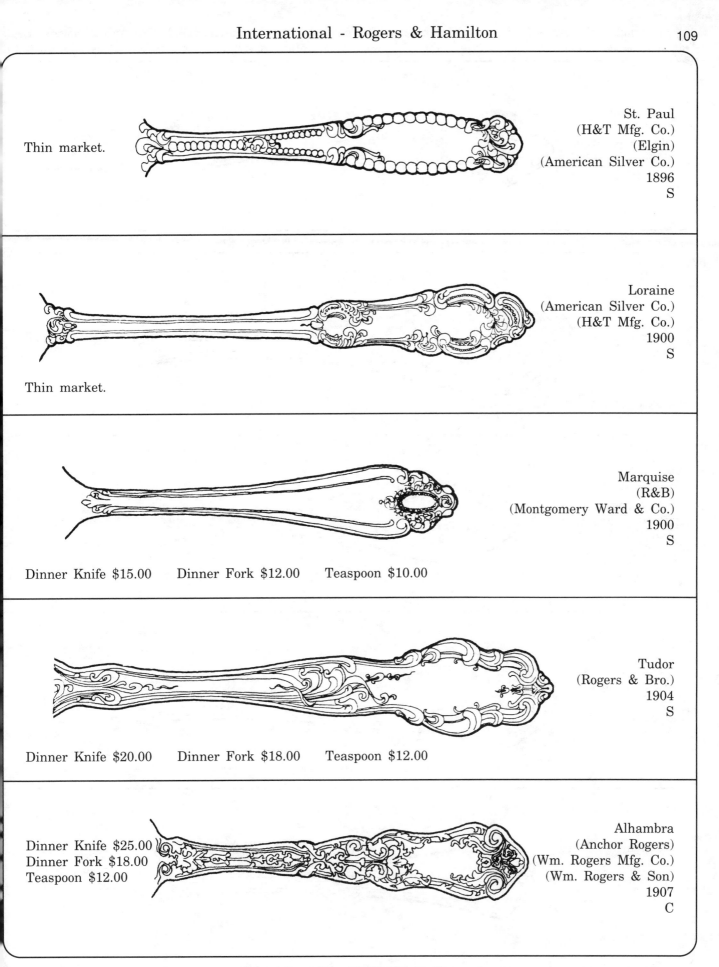

St. Paul
(H&T Mfg. Co.)
(Elgin)
(American Silver Co.)
1896
S

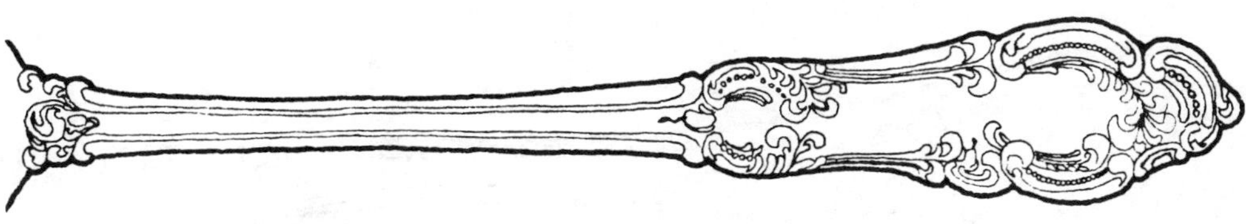

Loraine
(American Silver Co.)
(H&T Mfg. Co.)
1900
S

Thin market.

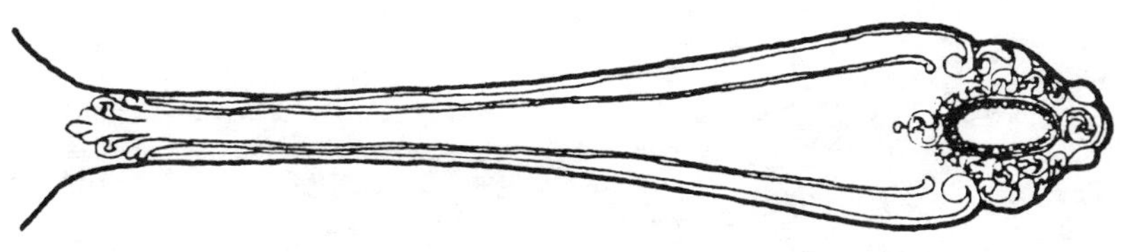

Marquise
(R&B)
(Montgomery Ward & Co.)
1900
S

Dinner Knife $15.00 Dinner Fork $12.00 Teaspoon $10.00

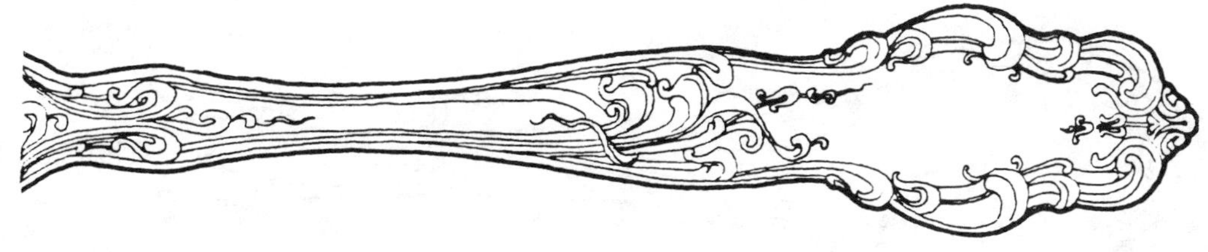

Tudor
(Rogers & Bro.)
1904
S

Dinner Knife $20.00 Dinner Fork $18.00 Teaspoon $12.00

Dinner Knife $25.00
Dinner Fork $18.00
Teaspoon $12.00

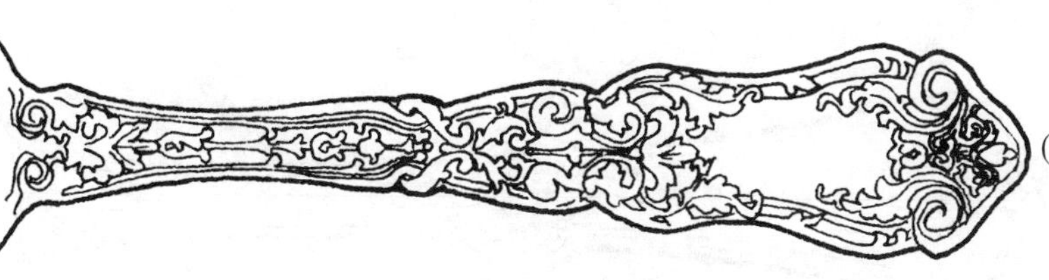

Alhambra
(Anchor Rogers)
(Wm. Rogers Mfg. Co.)
(Wm. Rogers & Son)
1907
C

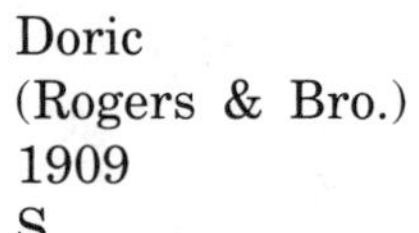

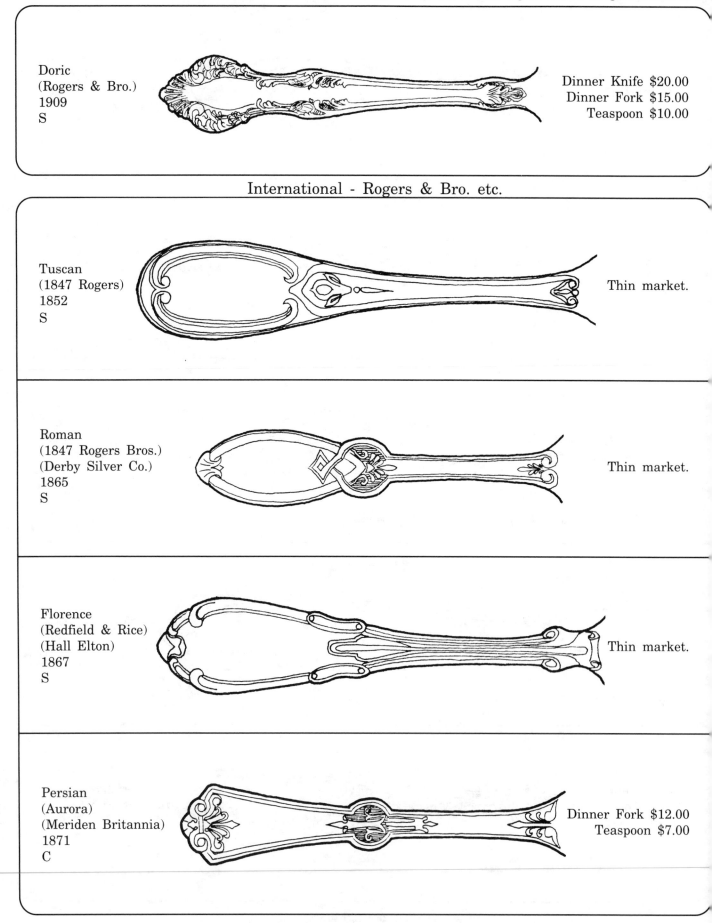

Doric
(Rogers & Bro.)
1909
S

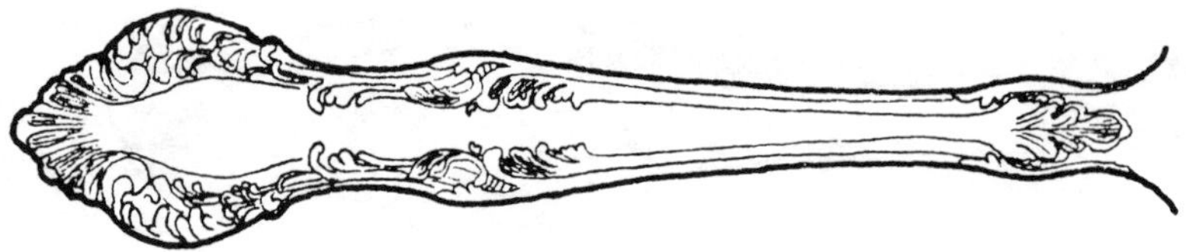

Dinner Knife $20.00
Dinner Fork $15.00
Teaspoon $10.00

International - Rogers & Bro. etc.

Tuscan
(1847 Rogers)
1852
S

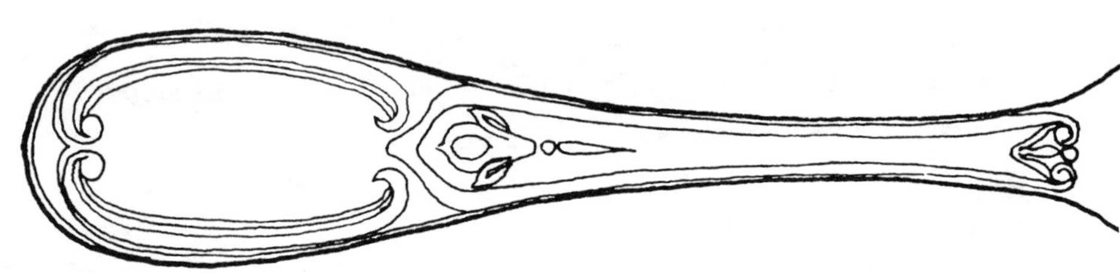

Thin market.

Roman
(1847 Rogers Bros.)
(Derby Silver Co.)
1865
S

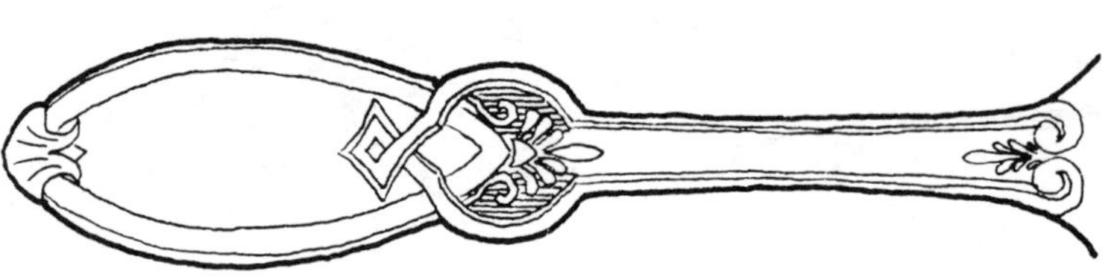

Thin market.

Florence
(Redfield & Rice)
(Hall Elton)
1867
S

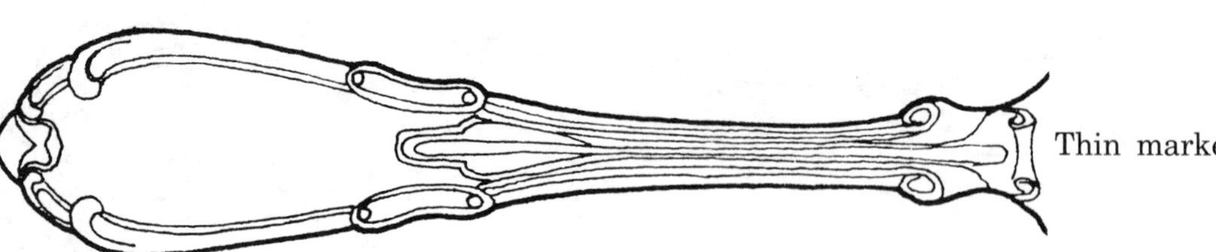

Thin market.

Persian
(Aurora)
(Meriden Britannia)
1871
C

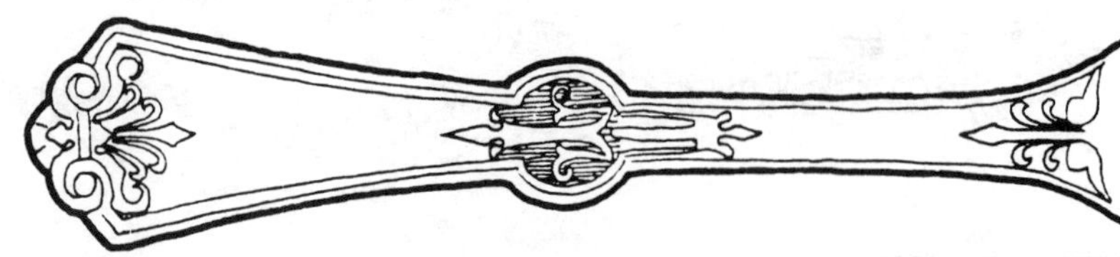

Dinner Fork $12.00
Teaspoon $7.00

Please refer to "How To Use This Book" page 4.

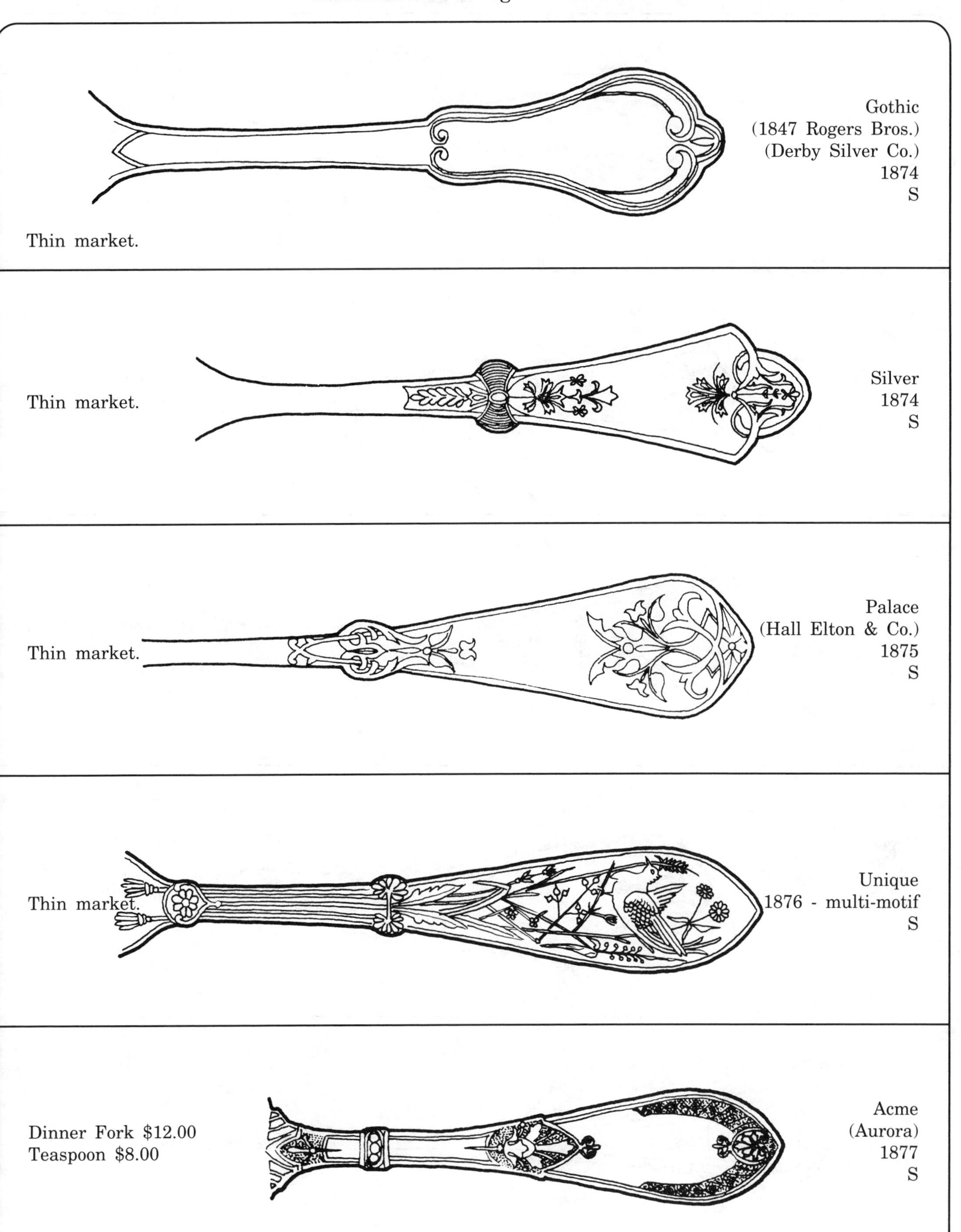

Gothic
(1847 Rogers Bros.)
(Derby Silver Co.)
1874
S

Thin market.

Silver
1874
S

Thin market.

Palace
(Hall Elton & Co.)
1875
S

Thin market.

Unique
1876 - multi-motif
S

Thin market.

Acme
(Aurora)
1877
S

Dinner Fork $12.00
Teaspoon $8.00

Please refer to "How To Use This Book" page 4.

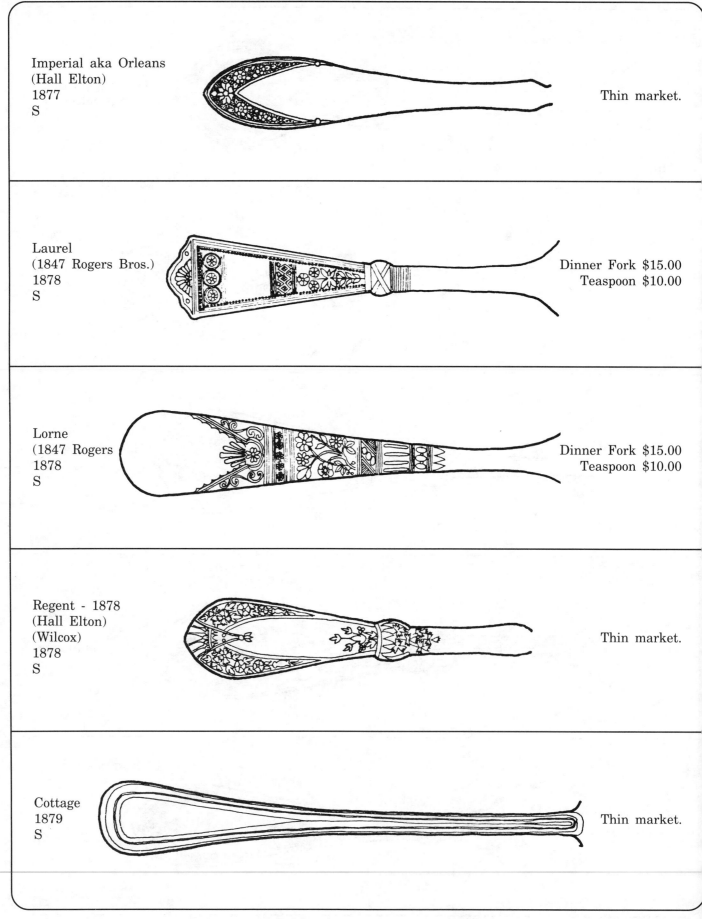

Imperial aka Orleans
(Hall Elton)
1877
S

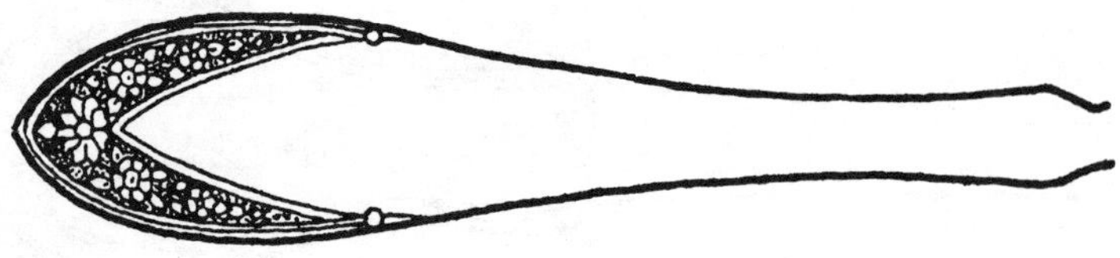

Thin market.

Laurel
(1847 Rogers Bros.)
1878
S

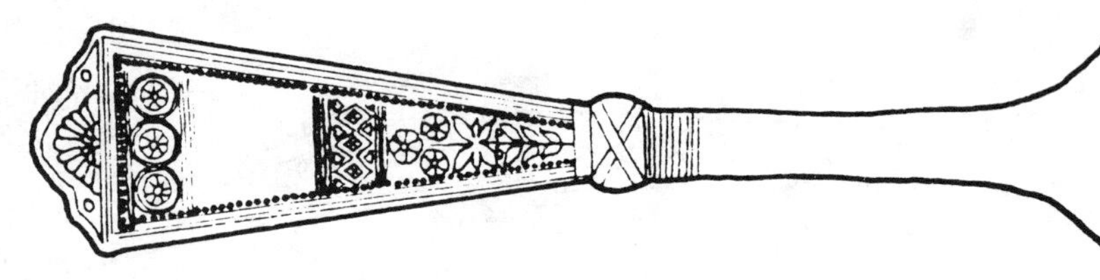

Dinner Fork $15.00
Teaspoon $10.00

Lorne
(1847 Rogers
1878
S

Dinner Fork $15.00
Teaspoon $10.00

Regent - 1878
(Hall Elton)
(Wilcox)
1878
S

Thin market.

Cottage
1879
S

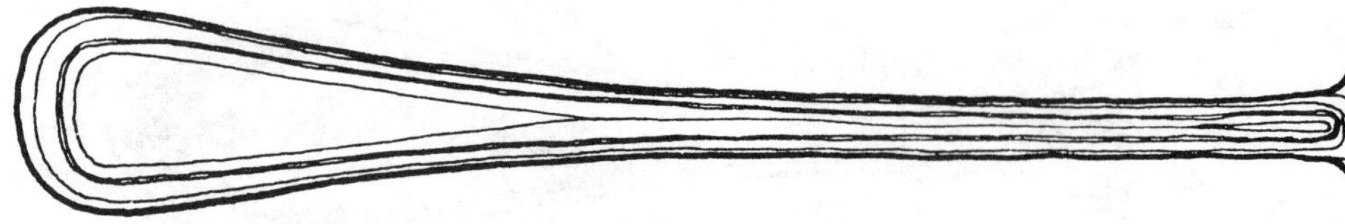

Thin market.

Please refer to "How To Use This Book" page 4.

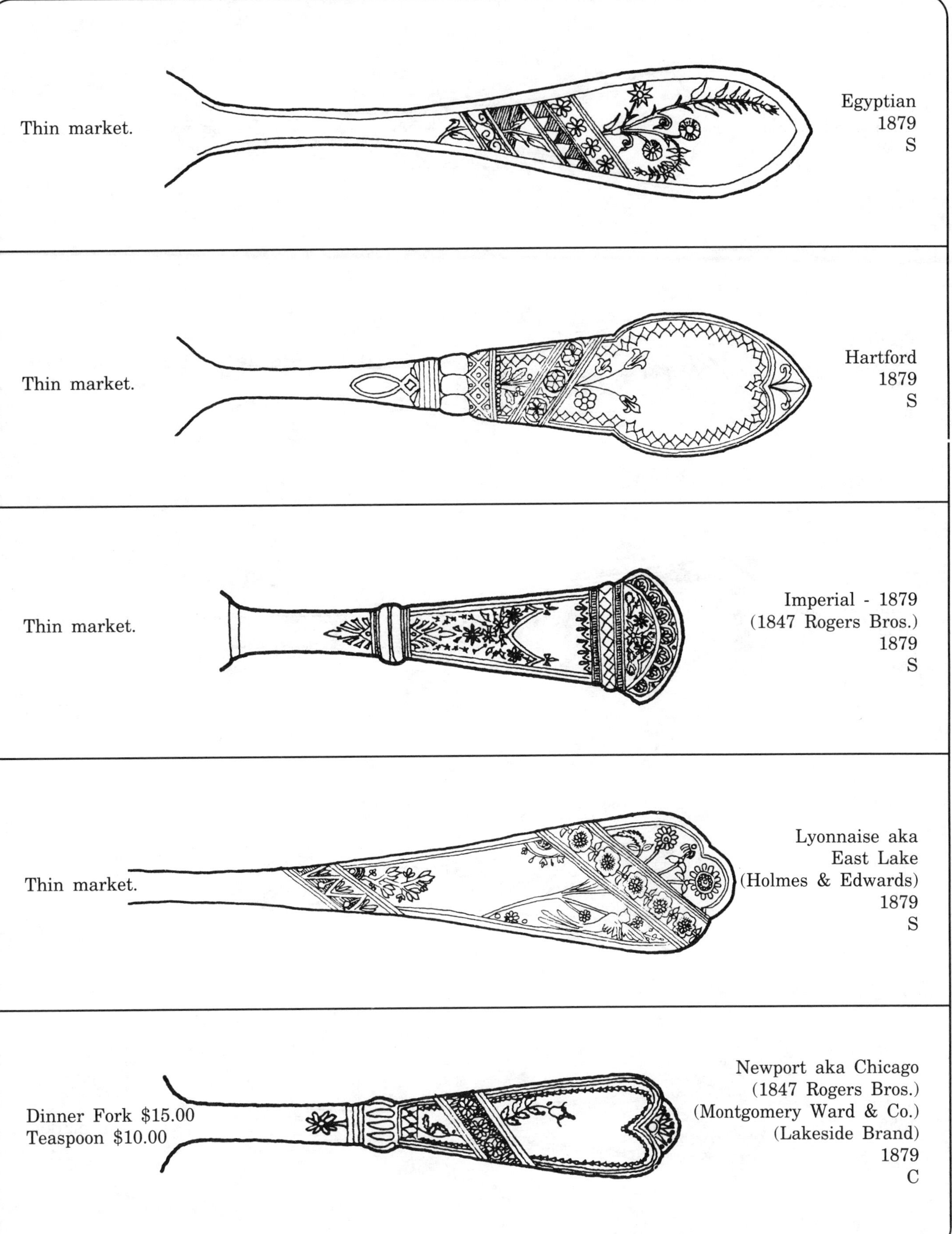

Thin market.

Egyptian
1879
S

Thin market.

Hartford
1879
S

Thin market.

Imperial - 1879
(1847 Rogers Bros.)
1879
S

Thin market.

Lyonnaise aka
East Lake
(Holmes & Edwards)
1879
S

Dinner Fork $15.00
Teaspoon $10.00

Newport aka Chicago
(1847 Rogers Bros.)
(Montgomery Ward & Co.)
(Lakeside Brand)
1879
C

Please refer to "How To Use This Book" page 4.

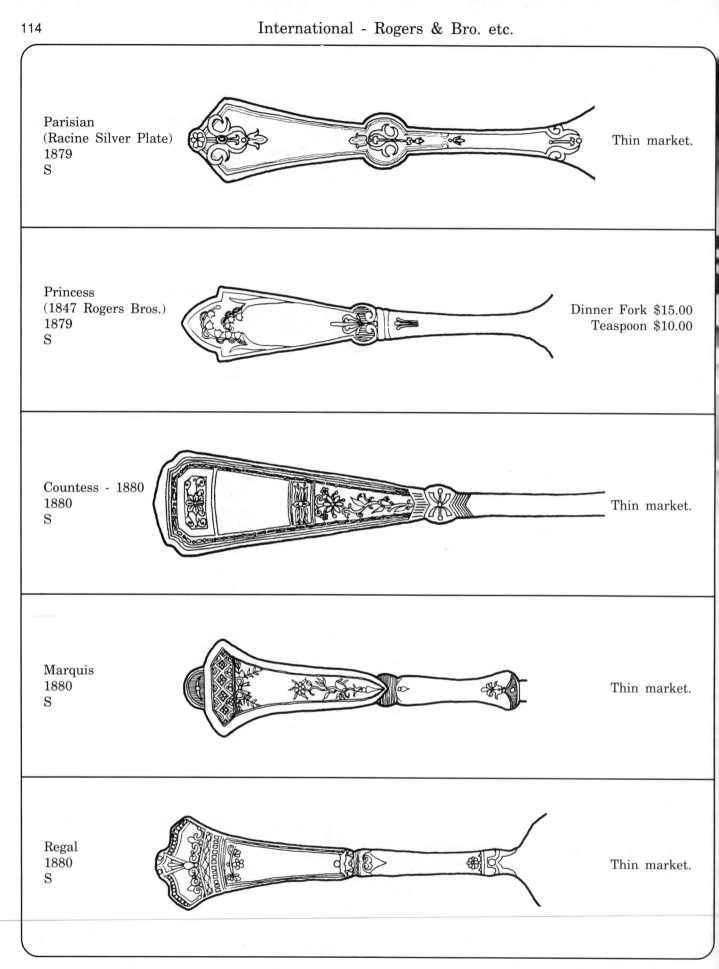

Parisian
(Racine Silver Plate)
1879
S

Thin market.

Princess
(1847 Rogers Bros.)
1879
S

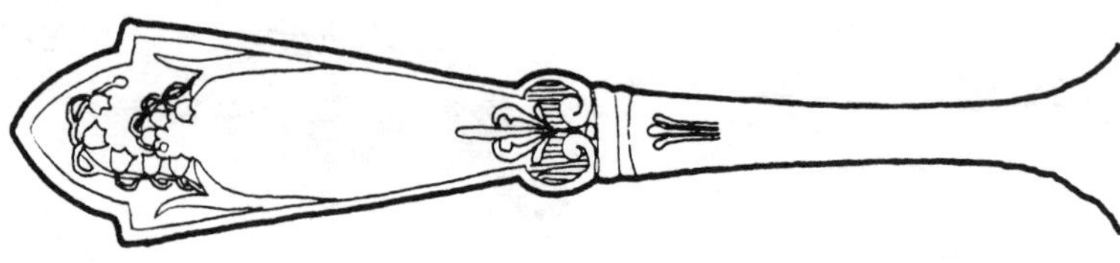

Dinner Fork $15.00
Teaspoon $10.00

Countess - 1880
1880
S

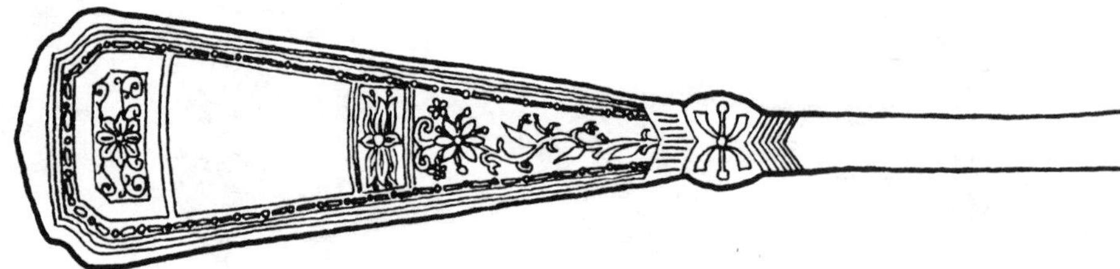

Thin market.

Marquis
1880
S

Thin market.

Regal
1880
S

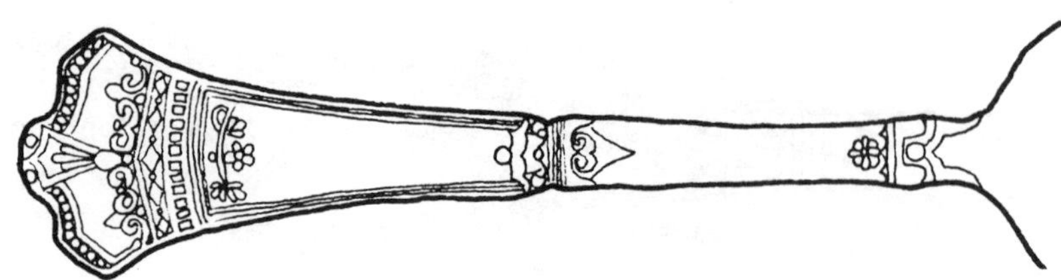

Thin market.

Please refer to "How To Use This Book" page 4.

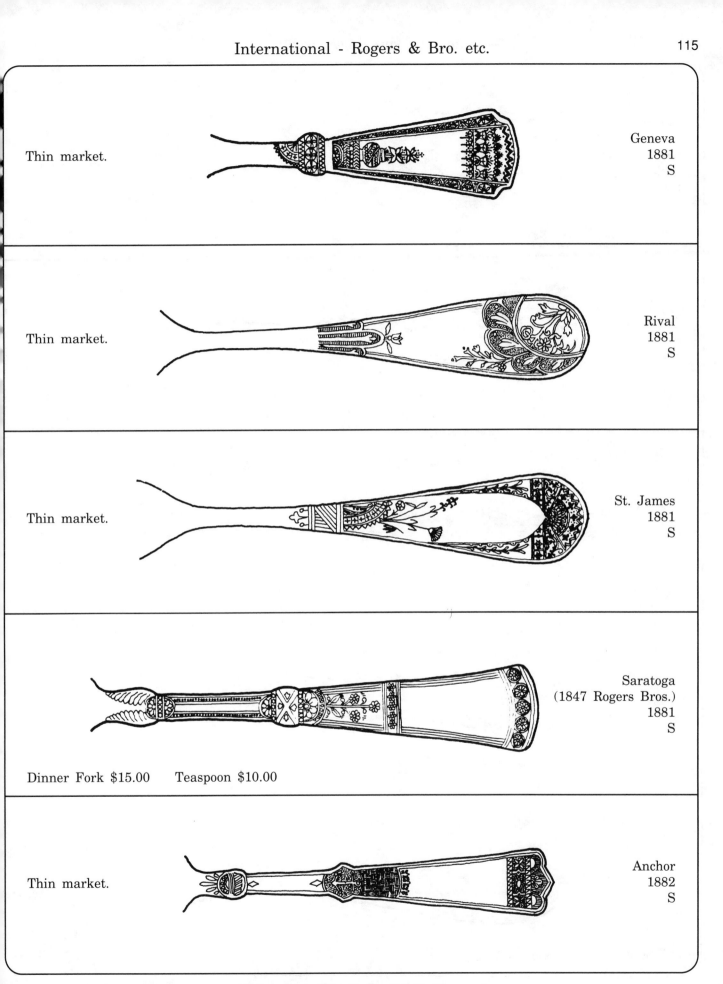

Thin market.

Geneva
1881
S

Thin market.

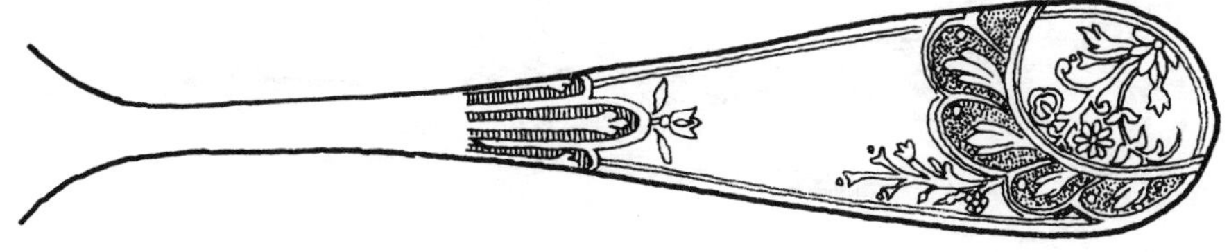

Rival
1881
S

Thin market.

St. James
1881
S

Saratoga
(1847 Rogers Bros.)
1881
S

Dinner Fork $15.00 Teaspoon $10.00

Thin market.

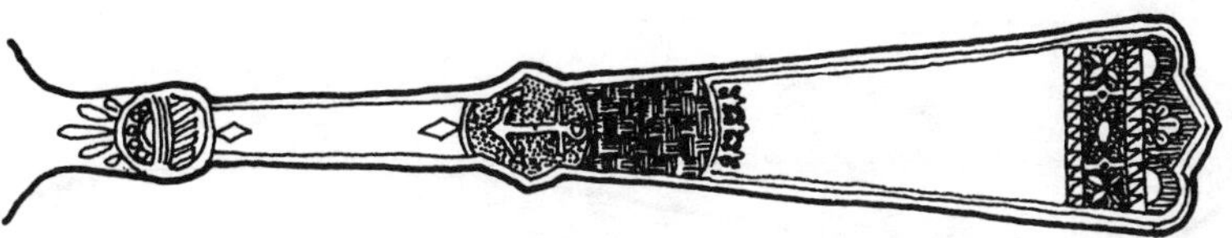

Anchor
1882
S

Please refer to "How To Use This Book" page 4.

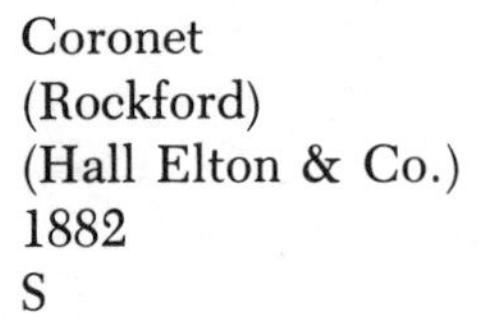

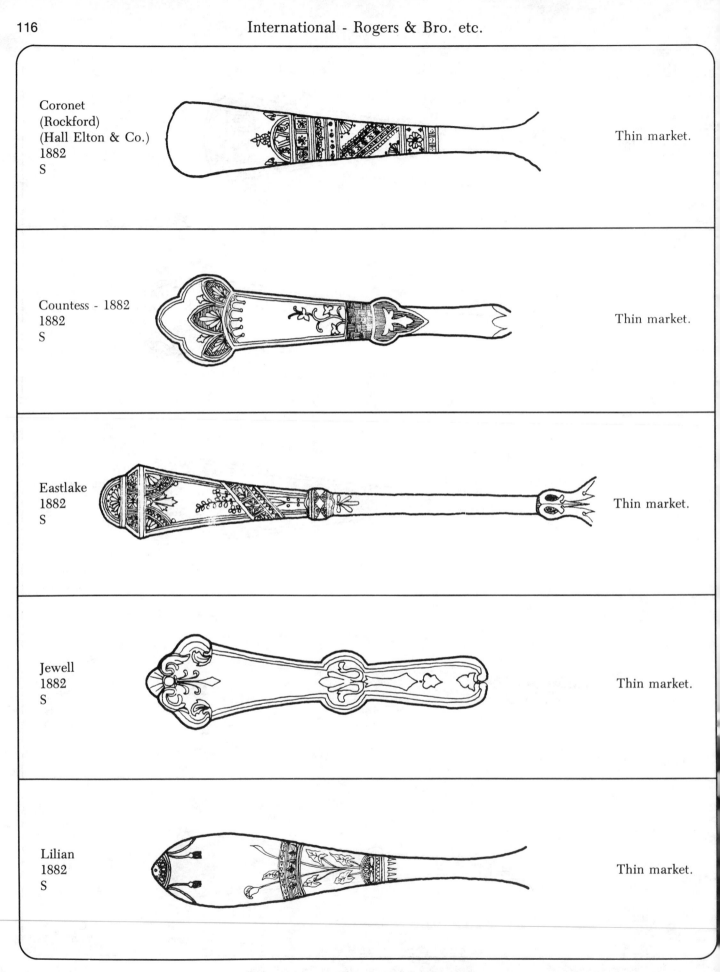

Coronet
(Rockford)
(Hall Elton & Co.)
1882
S

Thin market.

Countess - 1882
1882
S

Thin market.

Eastlake
1882
S

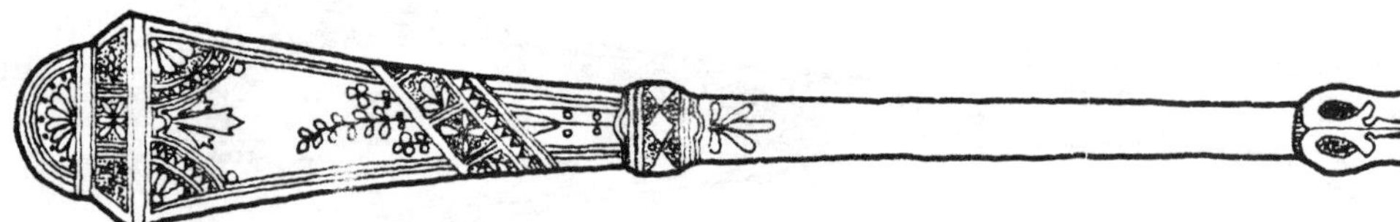

Thin market.

Jewell
1882
S

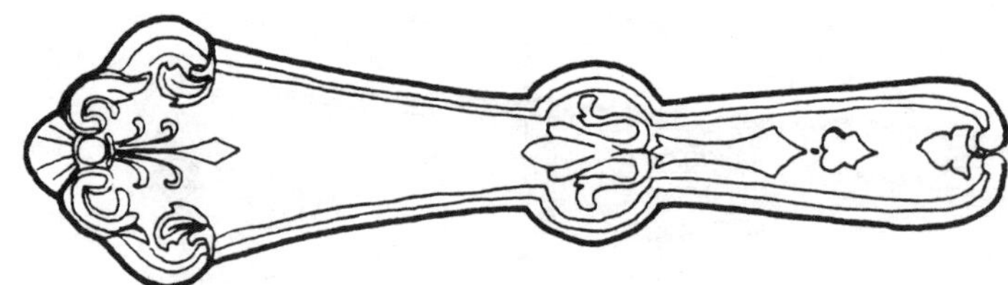

Thin market.

Lilian
1882
S

Thin market.

Please refer to "How To Use This Book" page 4.

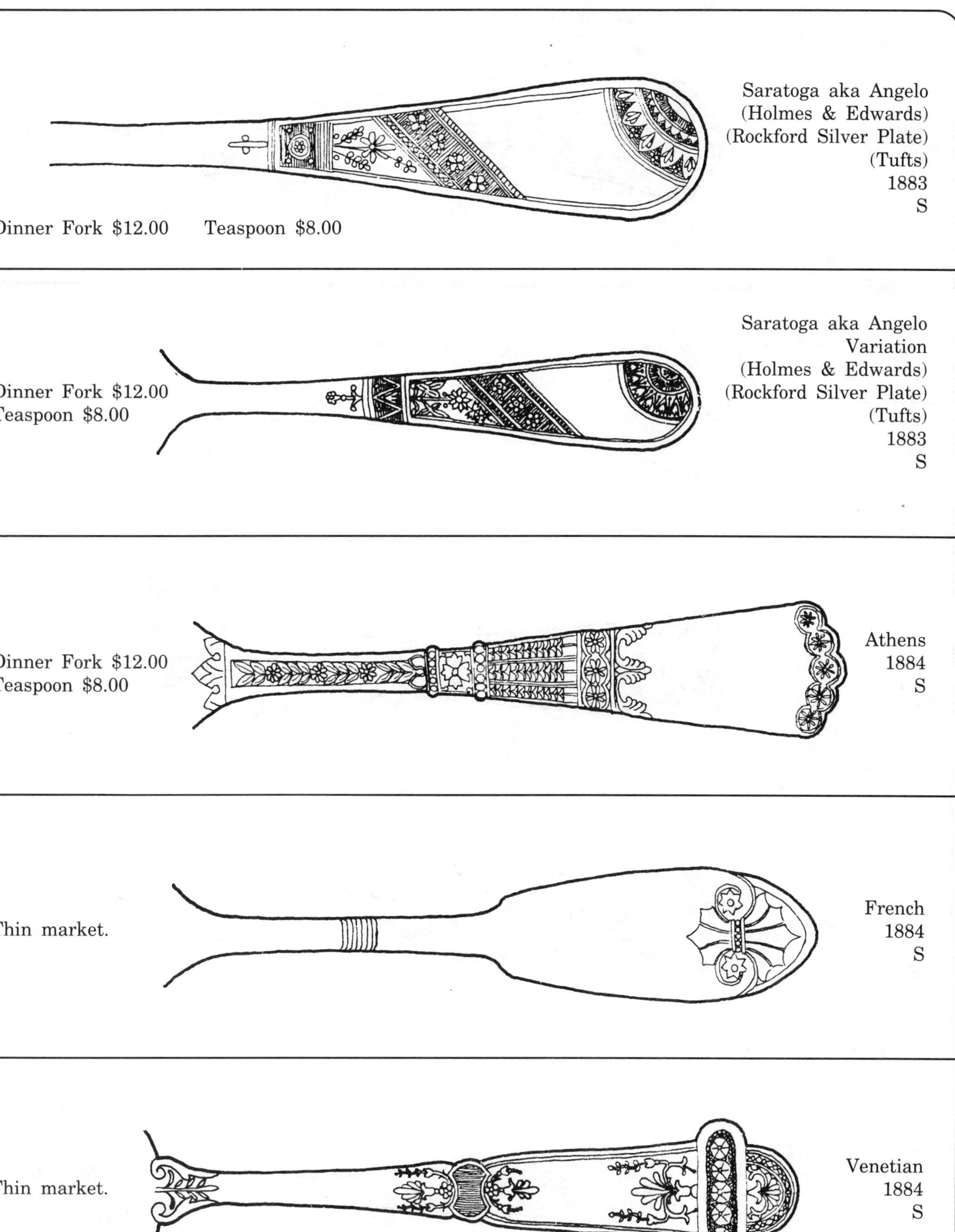

Saratoga aka Angelo
(Holmes & Edwards)
(Rockford Silver Plate)
(Tufts)
1883
S

Dinner Fork $12.00 Teaspoon $8.00

Saratoga aka Angelo
Variation
(Holmes & Edwards)
(Rockford Silver Plate)
(Tufts)
1883
S

Dinner Fork $12.00
Teaspoon $8.00

Athens
1884
S

Dinner Fork $12.00
Teaspoon $8.00

French
1884
S

Thin market.

Venetian
1884
S

Thin market.

Please refer to "How To Use This Book" page 4.

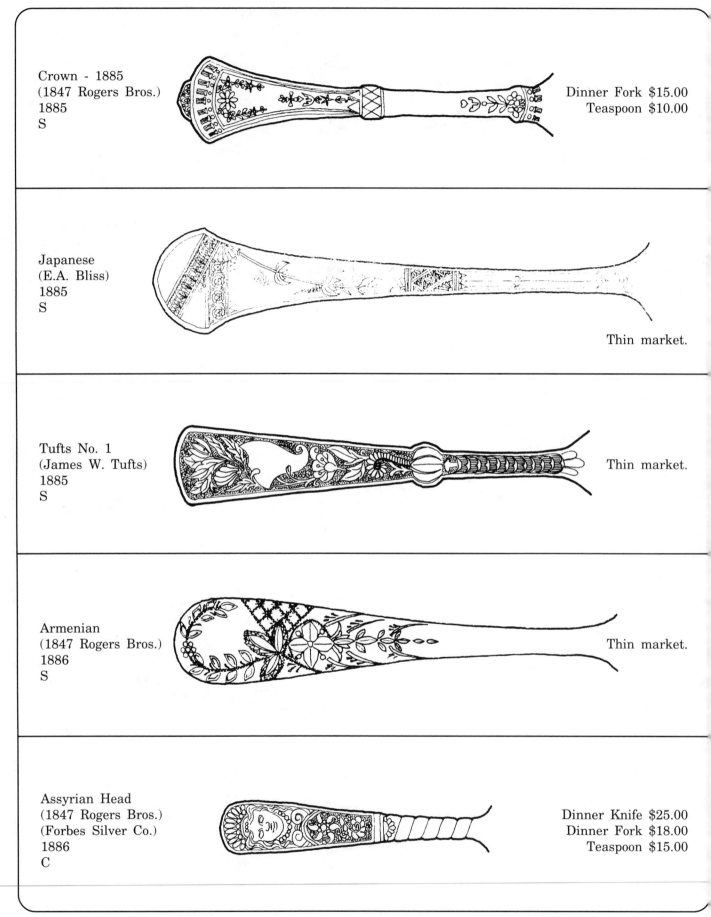

Crown - 1885
(1847 Rogers Bros.)
1885
S

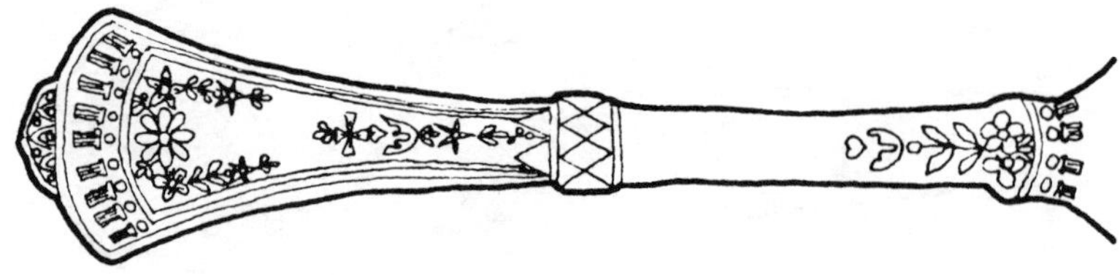

Dinner Fork $15.00
Teaspoon $10.00

Japanese
(E.A. Bliss)
1885
S

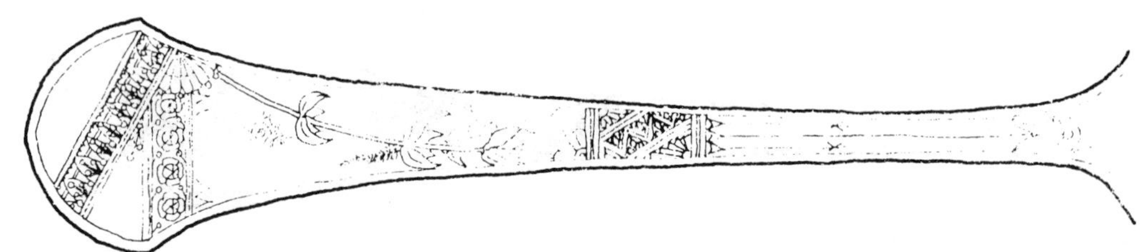

Thin market.

Tufts No. 1
(James W. Tufts)
1885
S

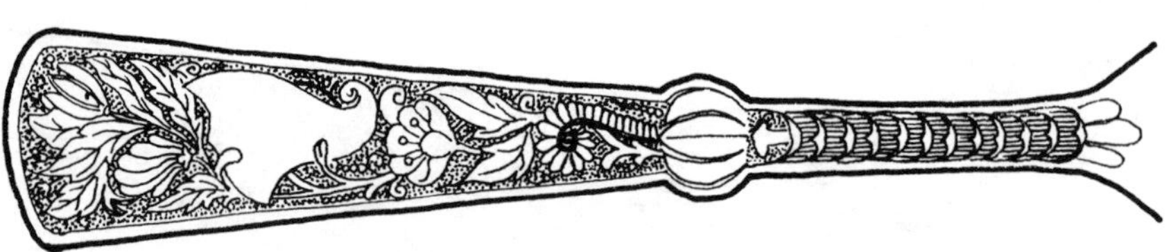

Thin market.

Armenian
(1847 Rogers Bros.)
1886
S

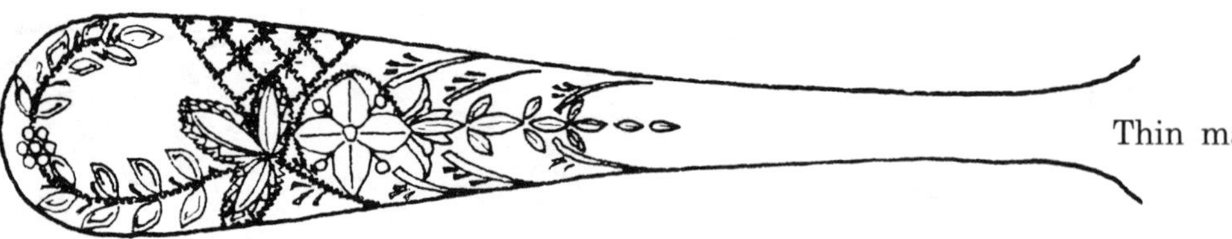

Thin market.

Assyrian Head
(1847 Rogers Bros.)
(Forbes Silver Co.)
1886
C

Dinner Knife $25.00
Dinner Fork $18.00
Teaspoon $15.00

Please refer to "How To Use This Book" page 4.

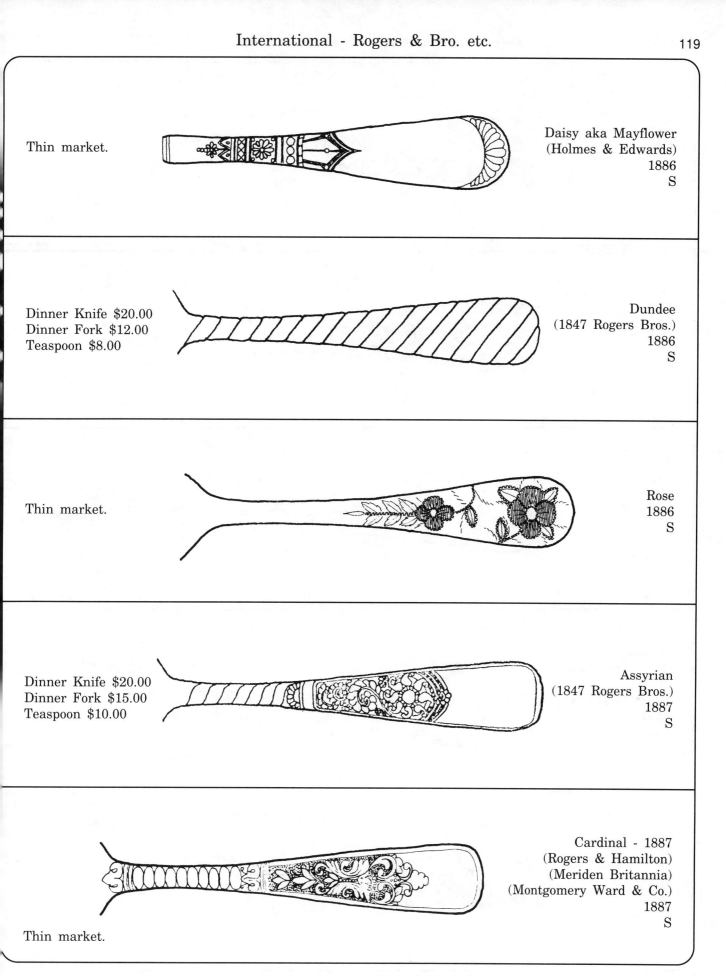

Thin market.

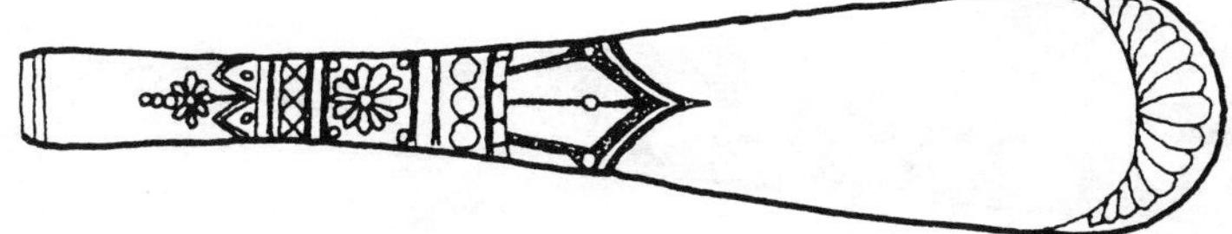

Daisy aka Mayflower
(Holmes & Edwards)
1886
S

Dinner Knife $20.00
Dinner Fork $12.00
Teaspoon $8.00

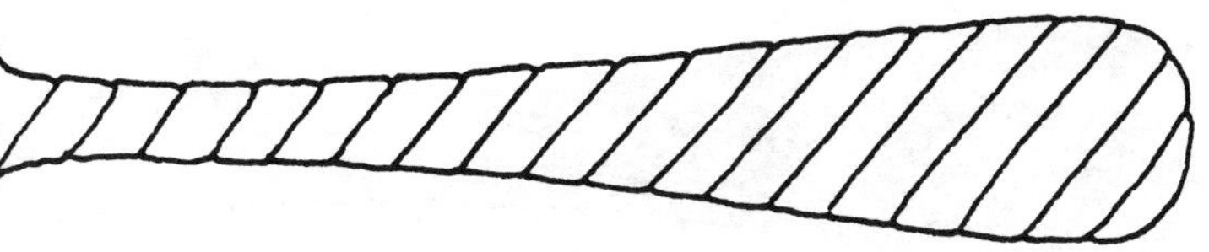

Dundee
(1847 Rogers Bros.)
1886
S

Thin market.

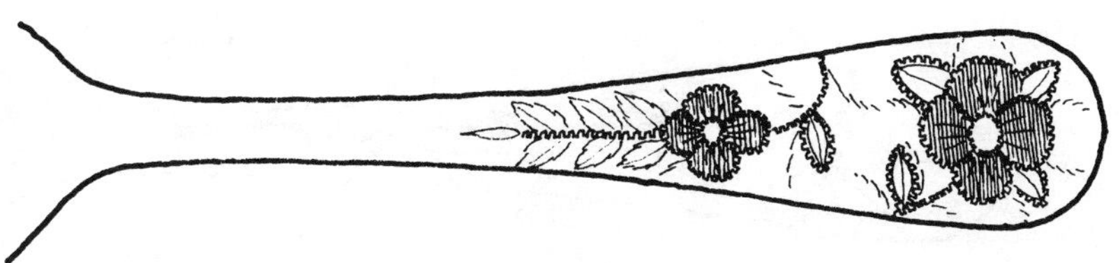

Rose
1886
S

Dinner Knife $20.00
Dinner Fork $15.00
Teaspoon $10.00

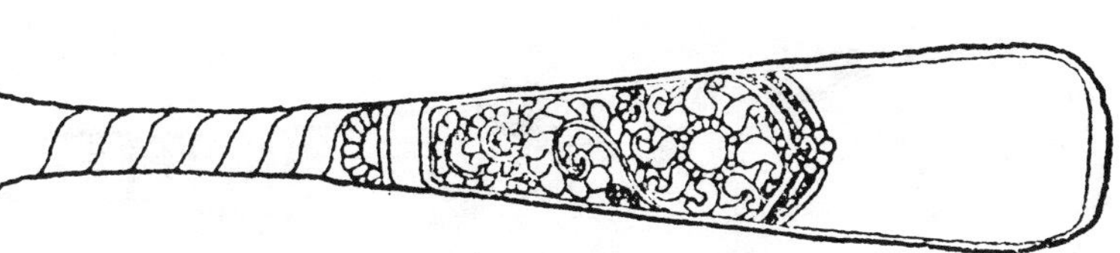

Assyrian
(1847 Rogers Bros.)
1887
S

Cardinal - 1887
(Rogers & Hamilton)
(Meriden Britannia)
(Montgomery Ward & Co.)
1887
S

Thin market.

Please refer to "How To Use This Book" page 4.

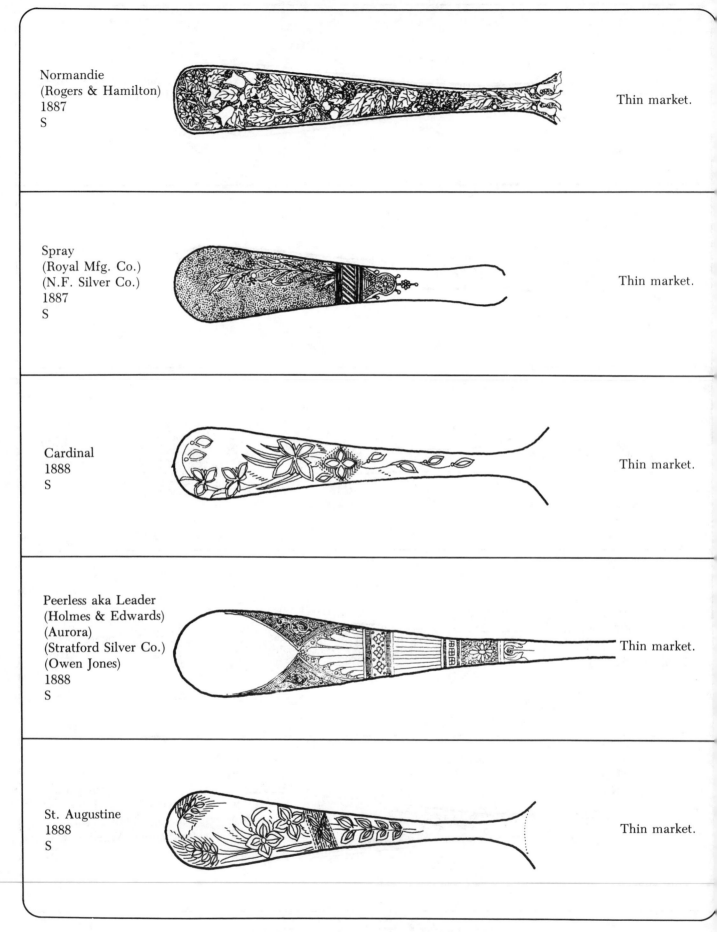

Normandie
(Rogers & Hamilton)
1887
S

Thin market.

Spray
(Royal Mfg. Co.)
(N.F. Silver Co.)
1887
S

Thin market.

Cardinal
1888
S

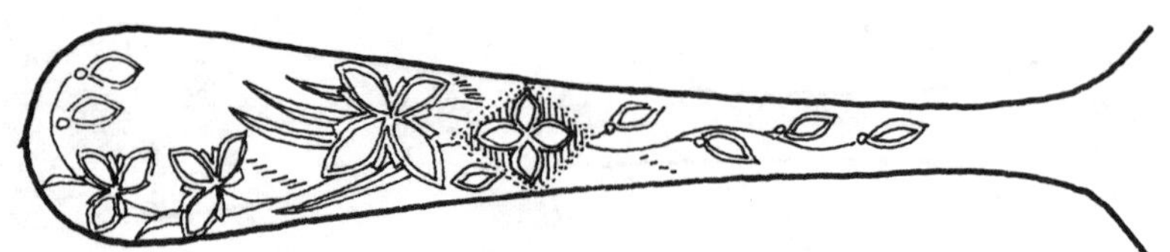

Thin market.

Peerless aka Leader
(Holmes & Edwards)
(Aurora)
(Stratford Silver Co.)
(Owen Jones)
1888
S

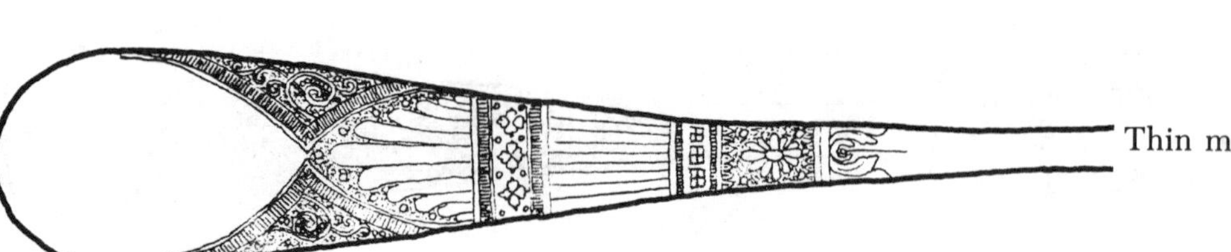

Thin market.

St. Augustine
1888
S

Thin market.

Please refer to "How To Use This Book" page 4.

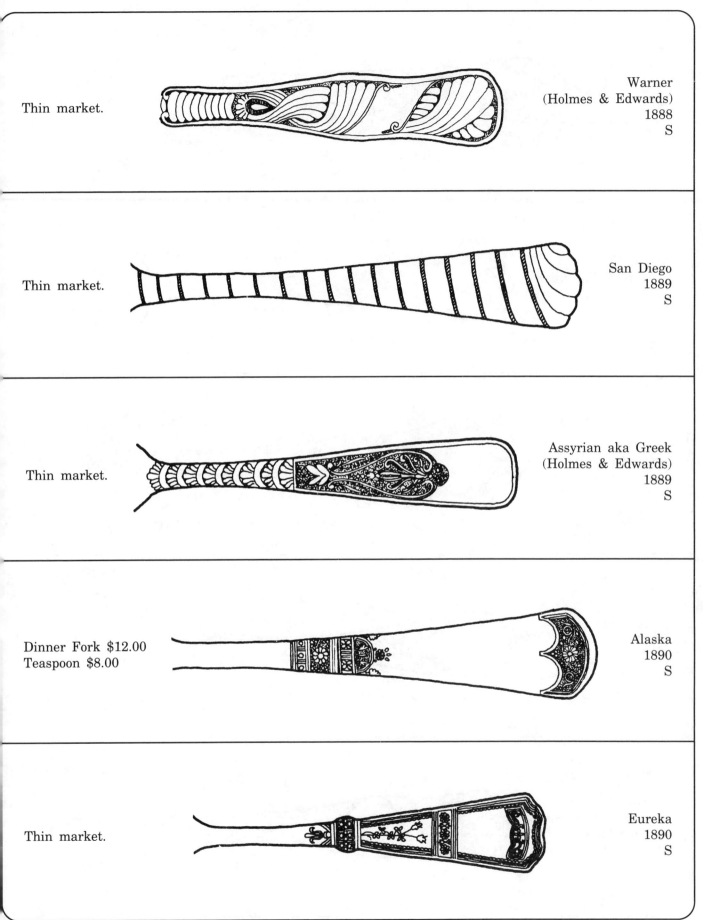

Thin market.

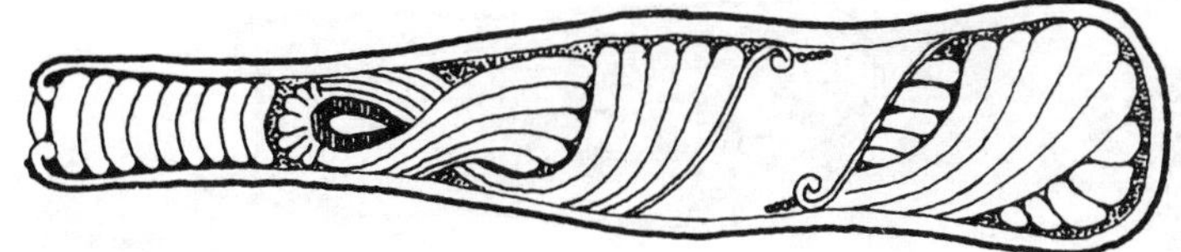

Warner
(Holmes & Edwards)
1888
S

Thin market.

San Diego
1889
S

Thin market.

Assyrian aka Greek
(Holmes & Edwards)
1889
S

Dinner Fork $12.00
Teaspoon $8.00

Alaska
1890
S

Thin market.

Eureka
1890
S

Please refer to "How To Use This Book" page 4.

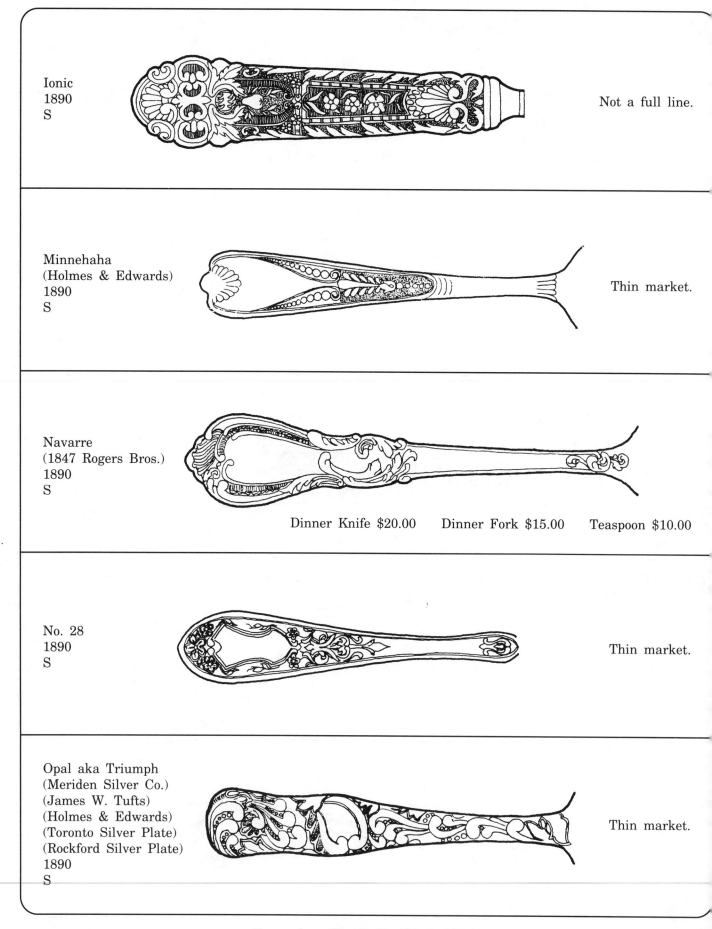

Ionic
1890
S

Not a full line.

Minnehaha
(Holmes & Edwards)
1890
S

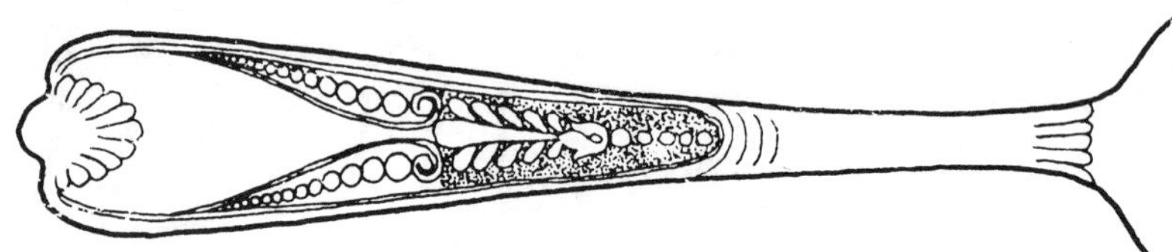

Thin market.

Navarre
(1847 Rogers Bros.)
1890
S

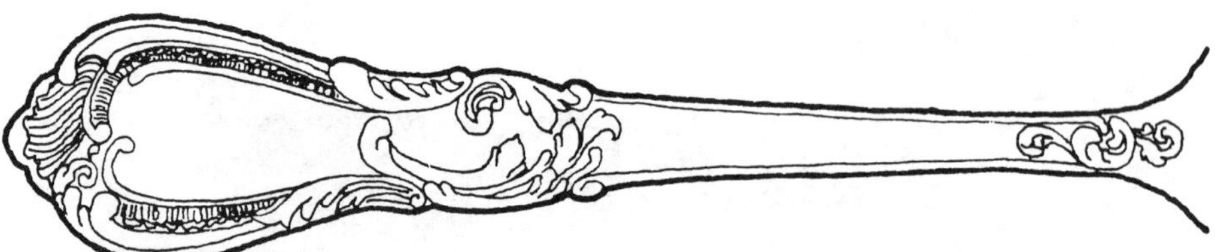

Dinner Knife $20.00 Dinner Fork $15.00 Teaspoon $10.00

No. 28
1890
S

Thin market.

Opal aka Triumph
(Meriden Silver Co.)
(James W. Tufts)
(Holmes & Edwards)
(Toronto Silver Plate)
(Rockford Silver Plate)
1890
S

Thin market.

Please refer to "How To Use This Book" page 4.

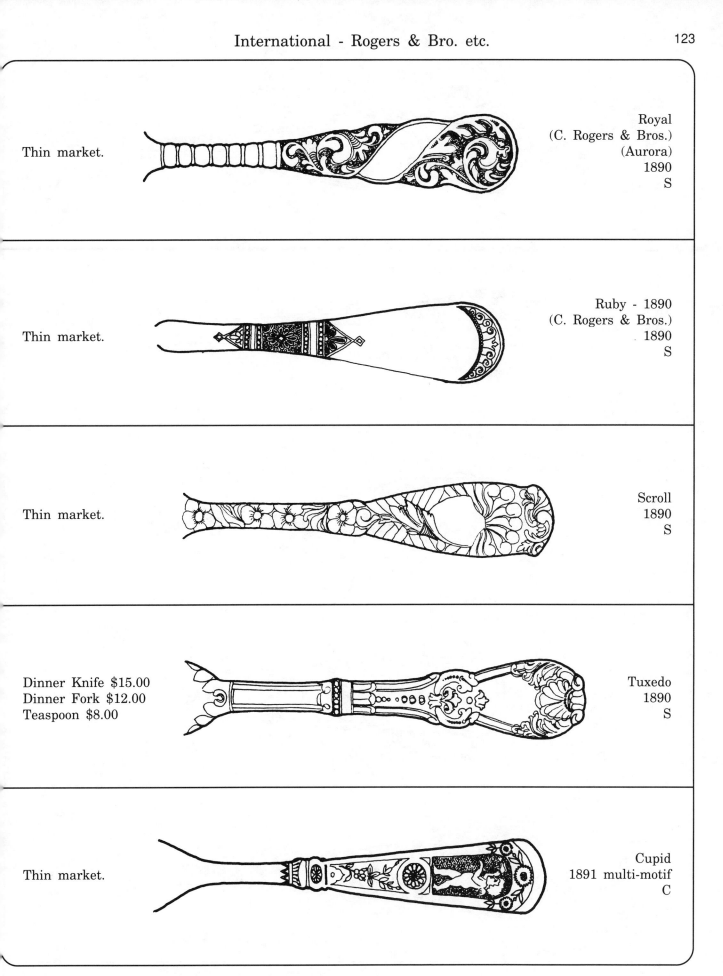

Thin market.

Royal
(C. Rogers & Bros.)
(Aurora)
1890
S

Thin market.

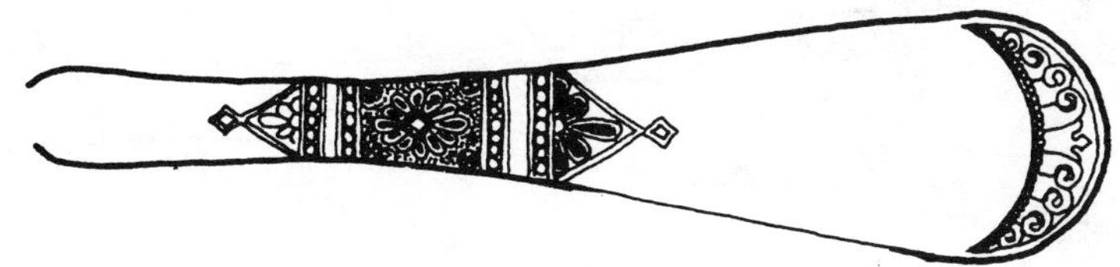

Ruby - 1890
(C. Rogers & Bros.)
1890
S

Thin market.

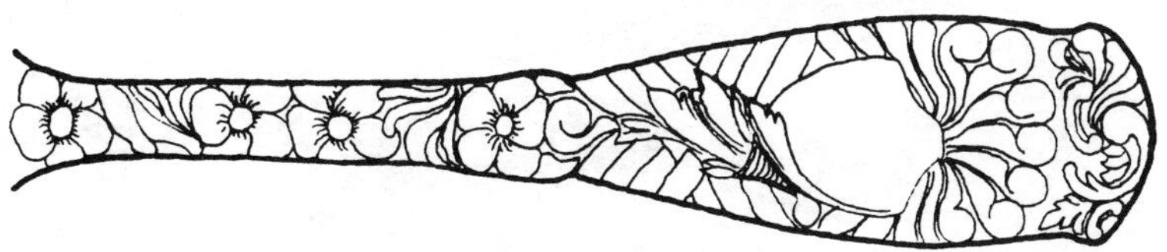

Scroll
1890
S

Dinner Knife $15.00
Dinner Fork $12.00
Teaspoon $8.00

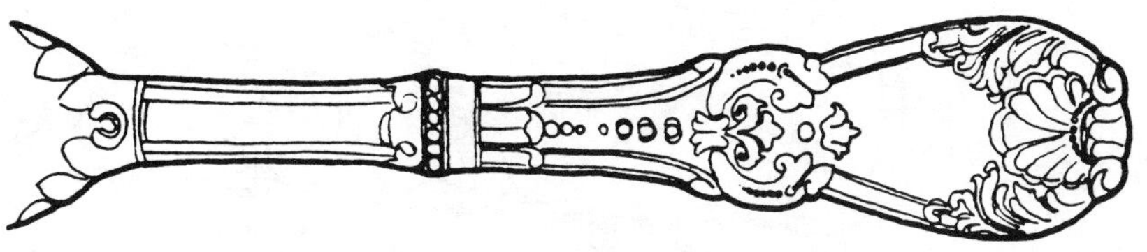

Tuxedo
1890
S

Thin market.

Cupid
1891 multi-motif
C

Please refer to "How To Use This Book" page 4.

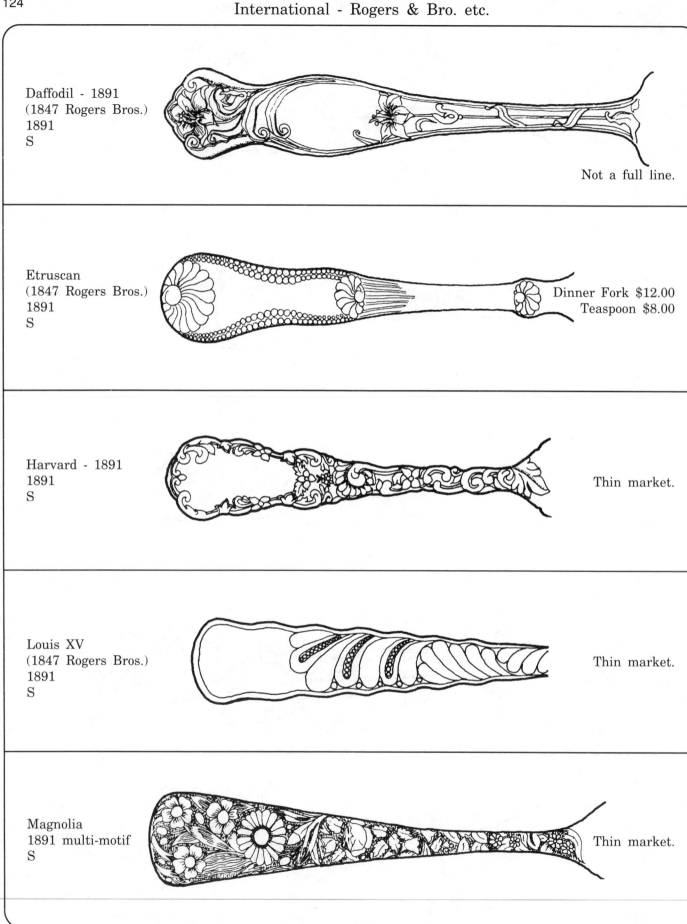

Daffodil - 1891
(1847 Rogers Bros.)
1891
S

Not a full line.

Etruscan
(1847 Rogers Bros.)
1891
S

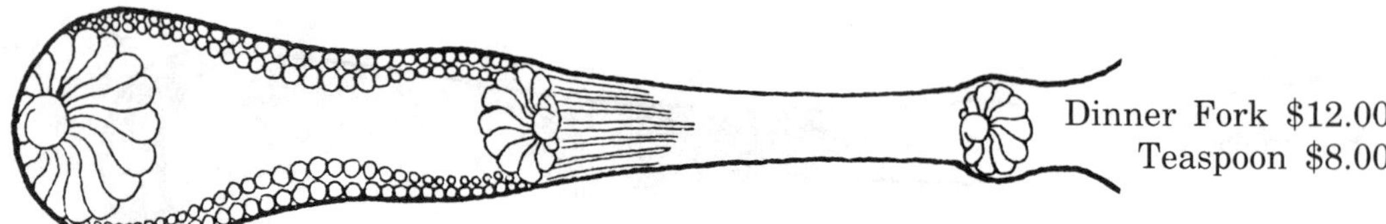

Dinner Fork $12.00
Teaspoon $8.00

Harvard - 1891
1891
S

Thin market.

Louis XV
(1847 Rogers Bros.)
1891
S

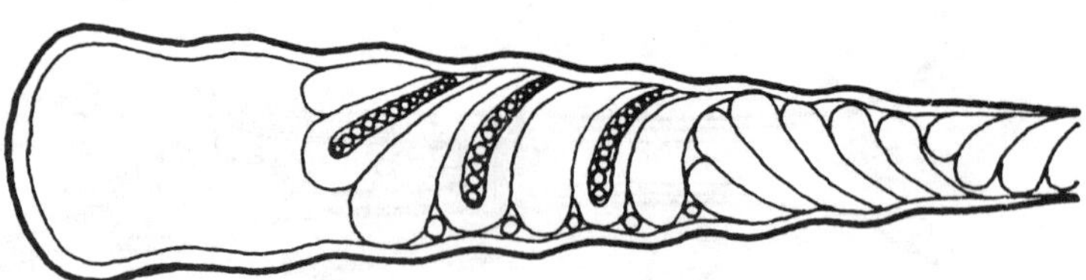

Thin market.

Magnolia
1891 multi-motif
S

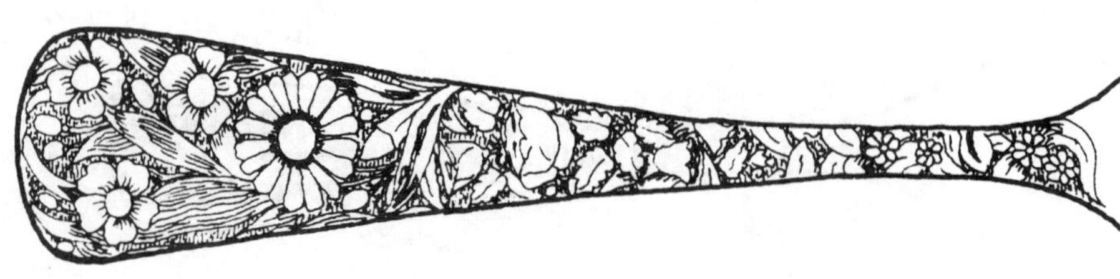

Thin market.

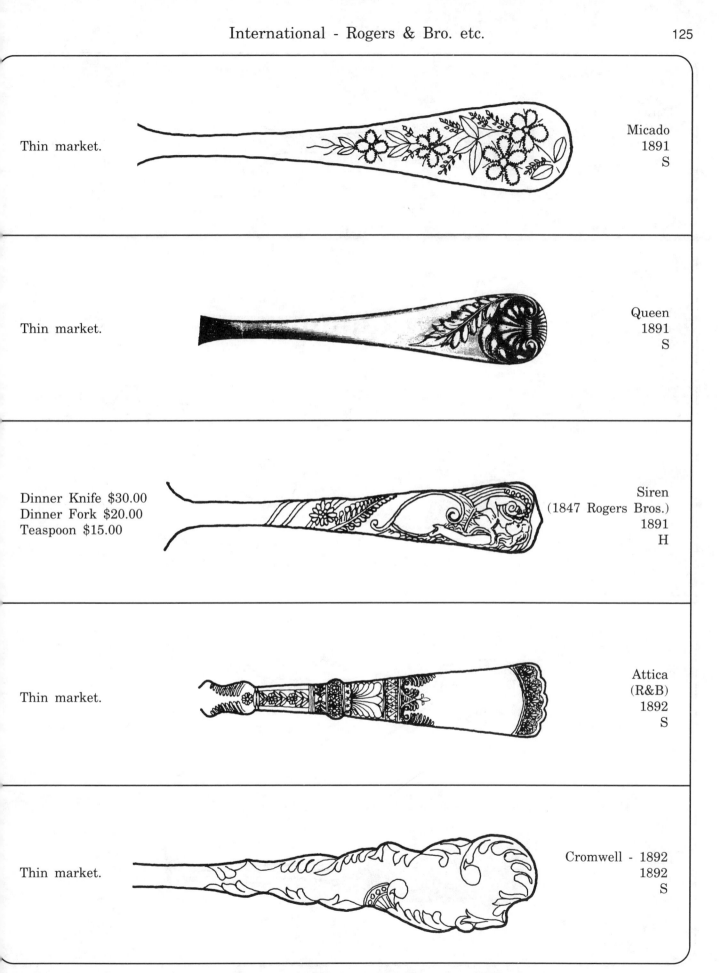

Thin market.

Micado
1891
S

Thin market.

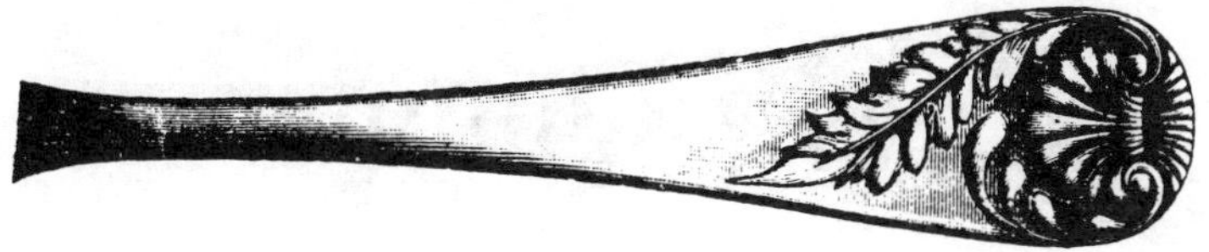

Queen
1891
S

Dinner Knife $30.00
Dinner Fork $20.00
Teaspoon $15.00

Siren
(1847 Rogers Bros.)
1891
H

Thin market.

Attica
(R&B)
1892
S

Thin market.

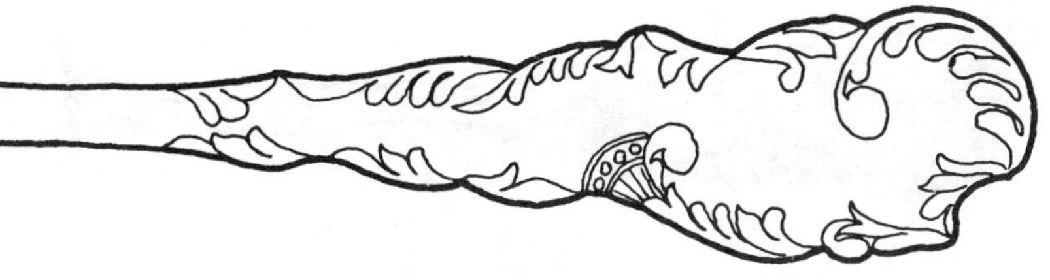

Cromwell - 1892
1892
S

Please refer to "How To Use This Book" page 4.

Daisy (1847 Rogers Bros.) (Rockford) 1892 S	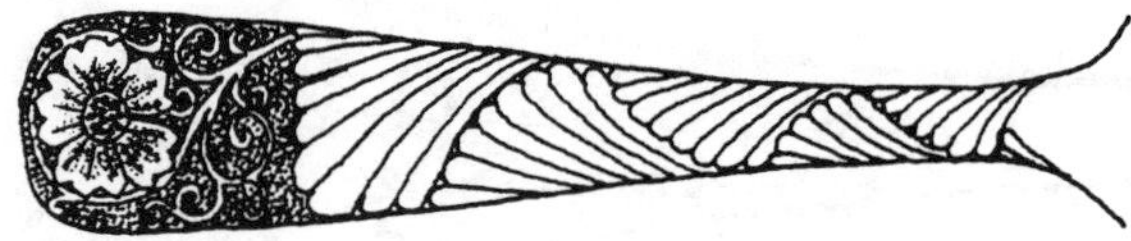	Not a full line.
Florida - 1892 1892 S	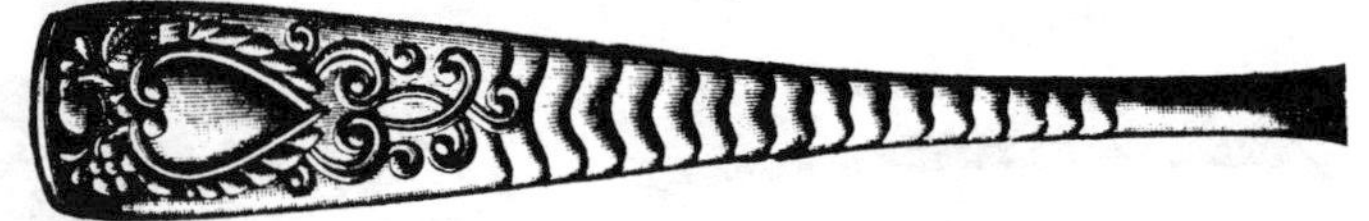	Not a full line.
Gem 1892 S		Thin market.
Pequot 1892 S	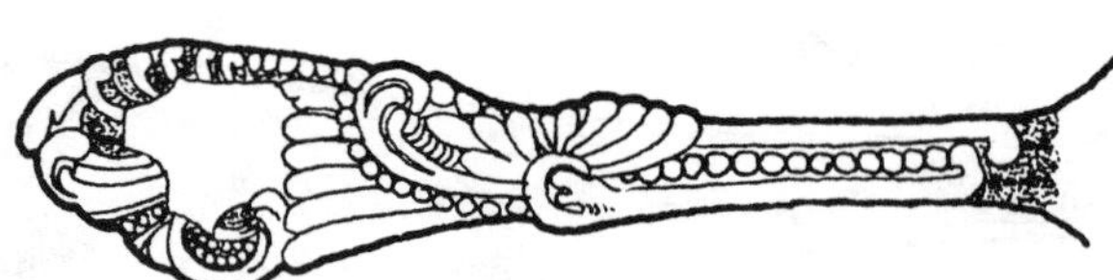	Thin market.
Princeton 1892 S	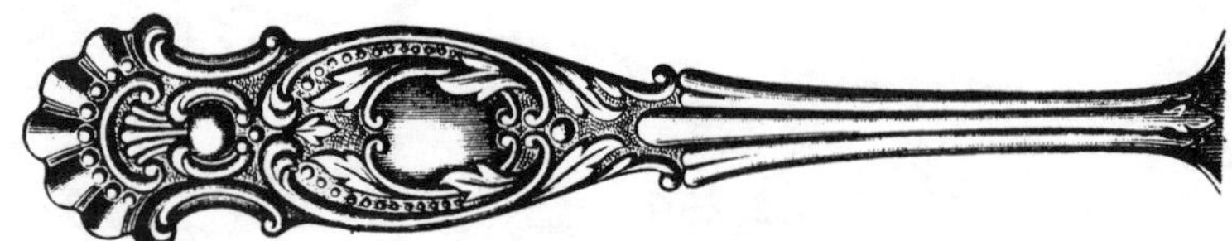	Thin market.

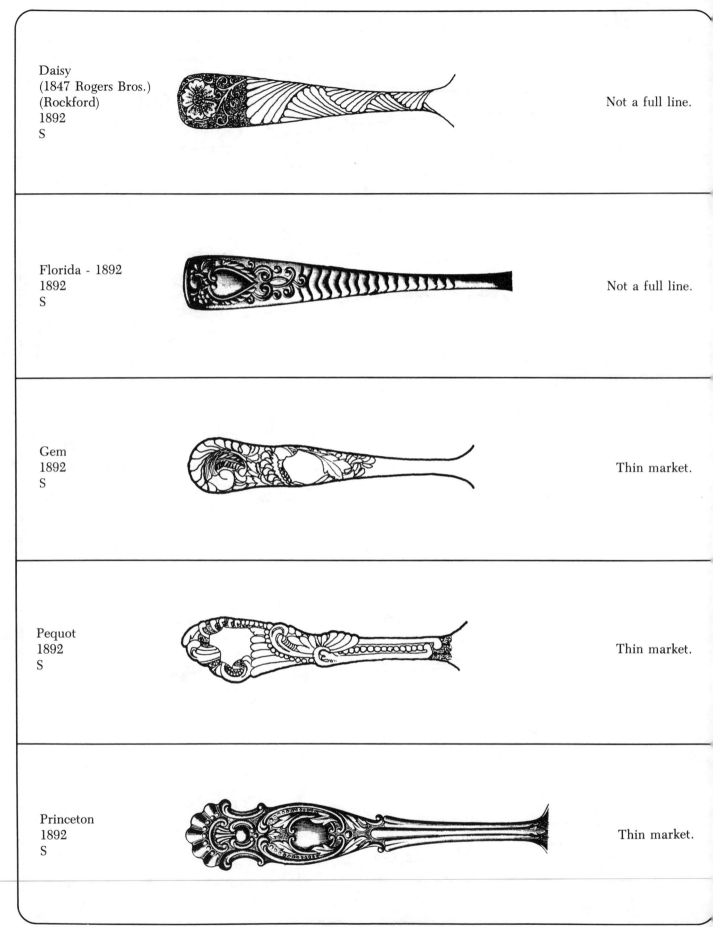

Please refer to "How To Use This Book" page 4.

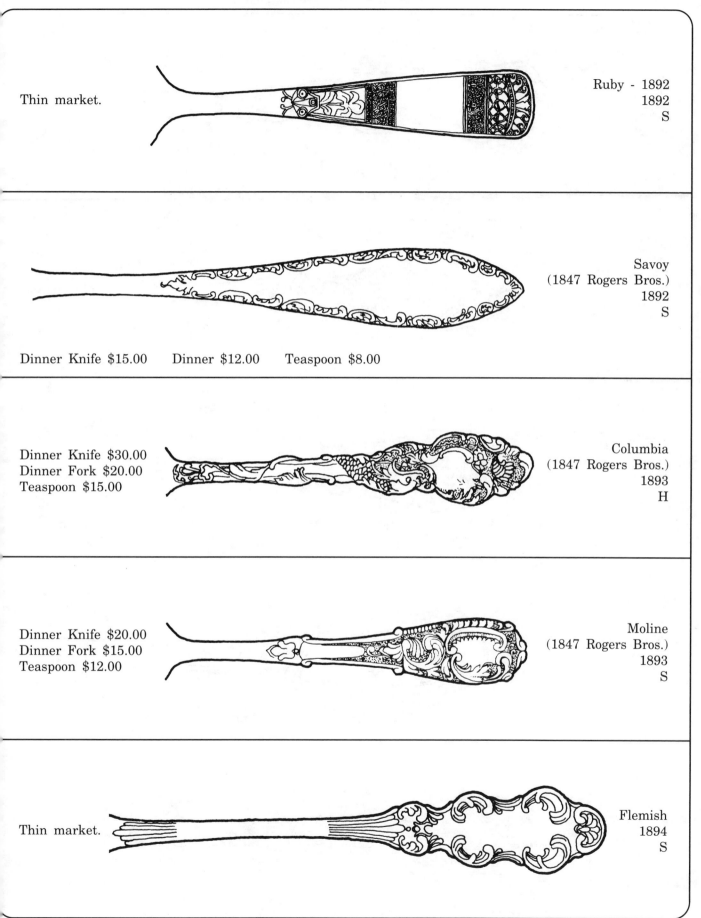

Thin market.

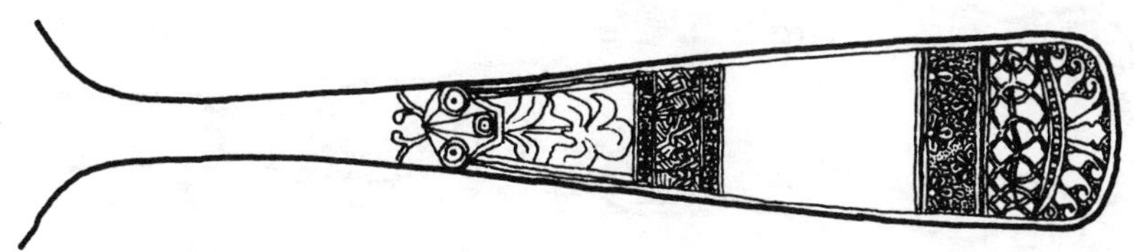

Ruby - 1892
1892
S

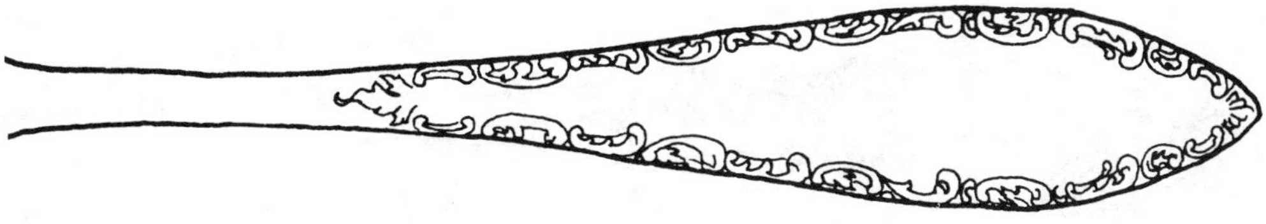

Savoy
(1847 Rogers Bros.)
1892
S

Dinner Knife $15.00 Dinner $12.00 Teaspoon $8.00

Dinner Knife $30.00
Dinner Fork $20.00
Teaspoon $15.00

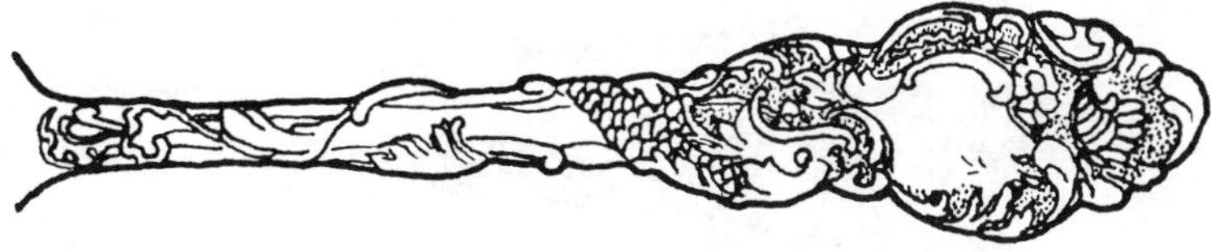

Columbia
(1847 Rogers Bros.)
1893
H

Dinner Knife $20.00
Dinner Fork $15.00
Teaspoon $12.00

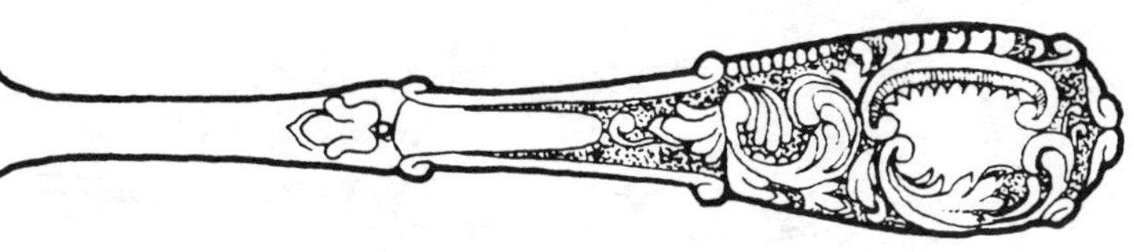

Moline
(1847 Rogers Bros.)
1893
S

Thin market.

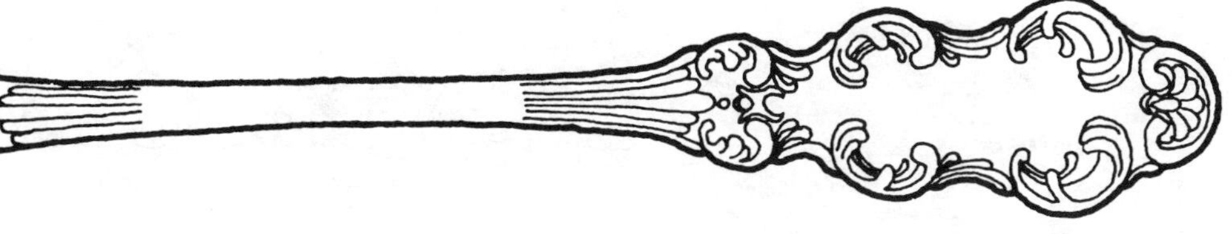

Flemish
1894
S

Please refer to "How To Use This Book" page 4.

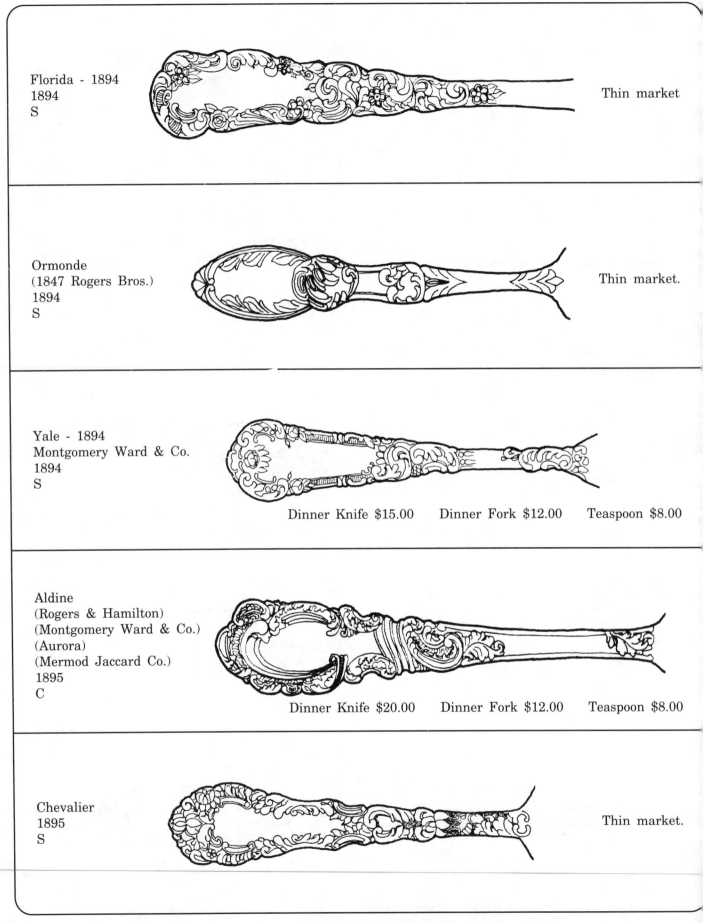

Florida - 1894
1894
S

Thin market

Ormonde
(1847 Rogers Bros.)
1894
S

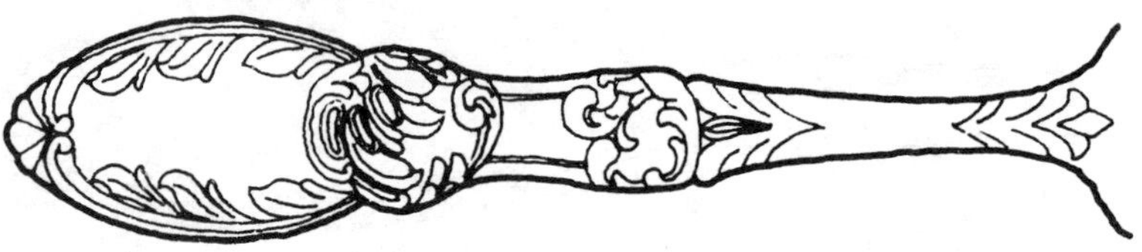

Thin market.

Yale - 1894
Montgomery Ward & Co.
1894
S

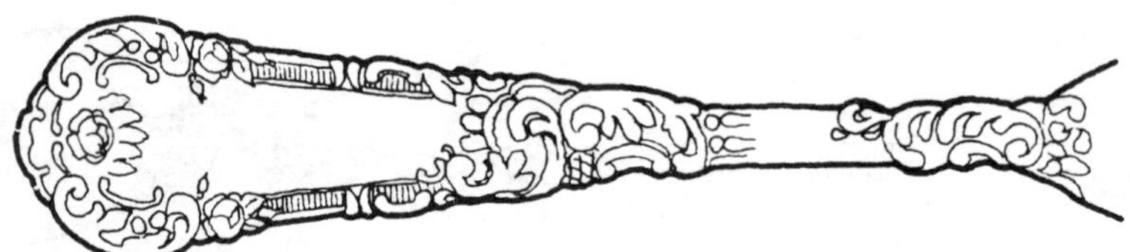

Dinner Knife $15.00 Dinner Fork $12.00 Teaspoon $8.00

Aldine
(Rogers & Hamilton)
(Montgomery Ward & Co.)
(Aurora)
(Mermod Jaccard Co.)
1895
C

Dinner Knife $20.00 Dinner Fork $12.00 Teaspoon $8.00

Chevalier
1895
S

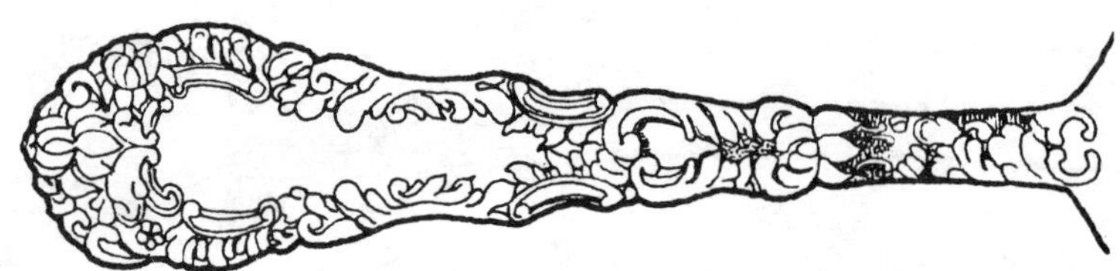

Thin market.

Please refer to "How To Use This Book" page 4.

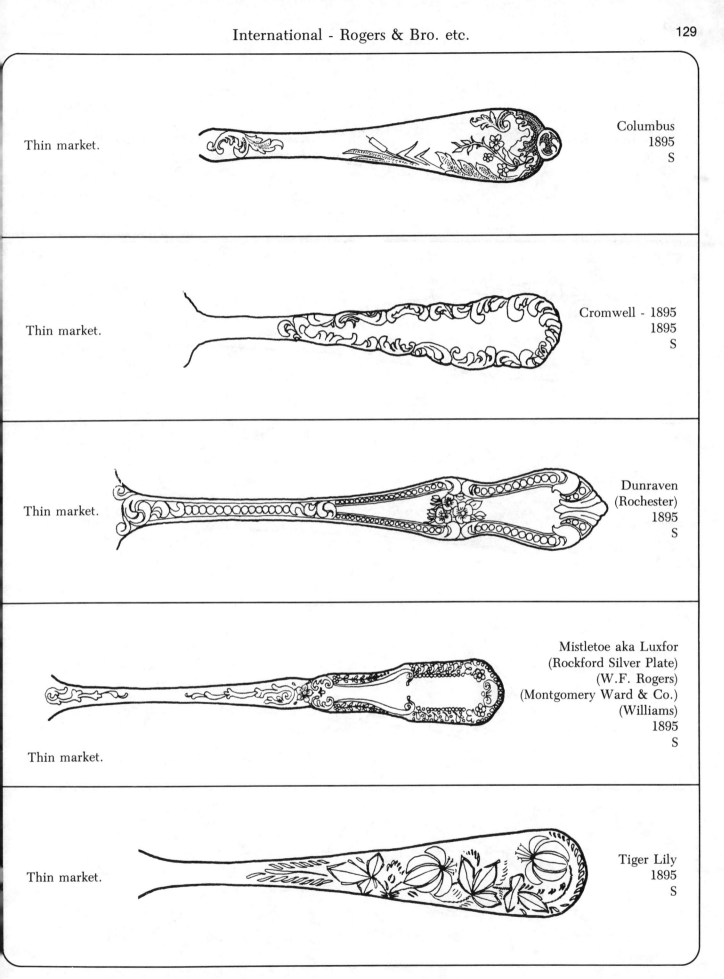

Thin market.

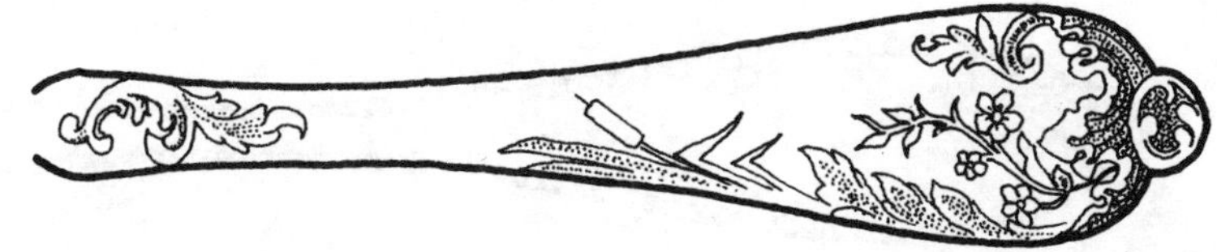

Columbus
1895
S

Thin market.

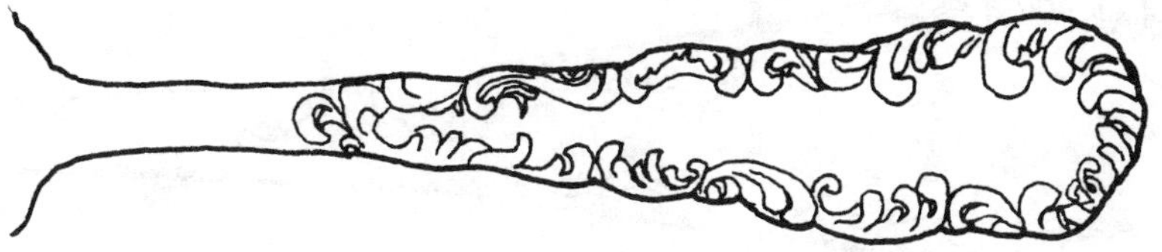

Cromwell - 1895
1895
S

Thin market.

Dunraven
(Rochester)
1895
S

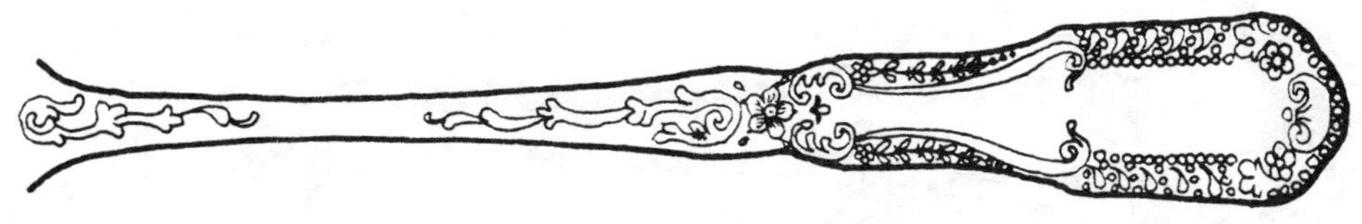

Mistletoe aka Luxfor
(Rockford Silver Plate)
(W.F. Rogers)
(Montgomery Ward & Co.)
(Williams)
1895
S

Thin market.

Thin market.

Tiger Lily
1895
S

Please refer to "How To Use This Book" page 4.

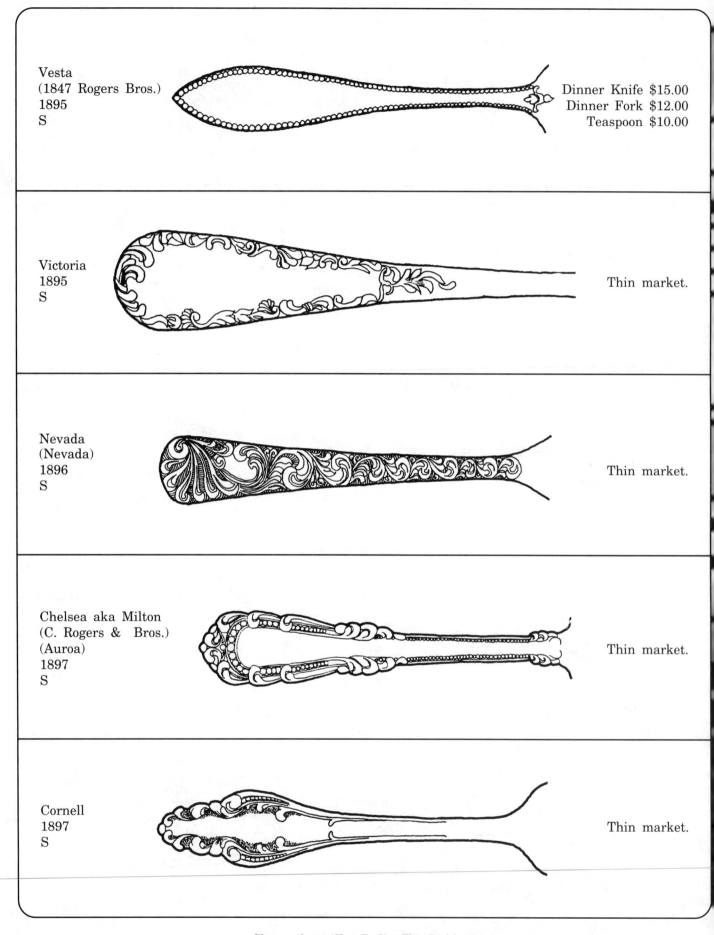

Vesta
(1847 Rogers Bros.)
1895
S

Dinner Knife $15.00
Dinner Fork $12.00
Teaspoon $10.00

Victoria
1895
S

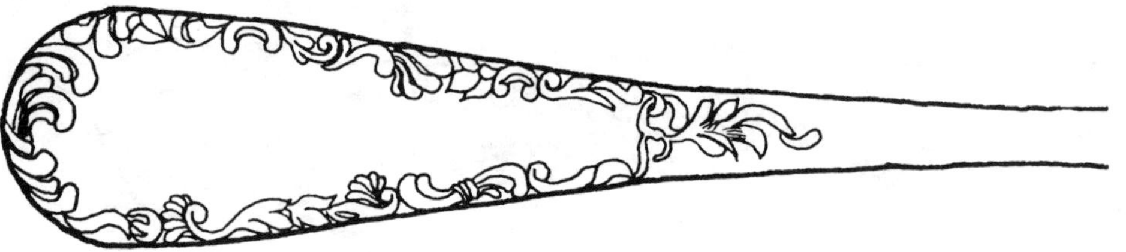

Thin market.

Nevada
(Nevada)
1896
S

Thin market.

Chelsea aka Milton
(C. Rogers & Bros.)
(Auroa)
1897
S

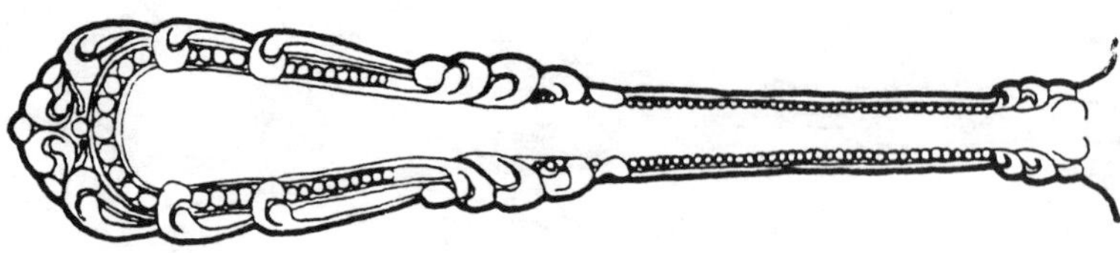

Thin market.

Cornell
1897
S

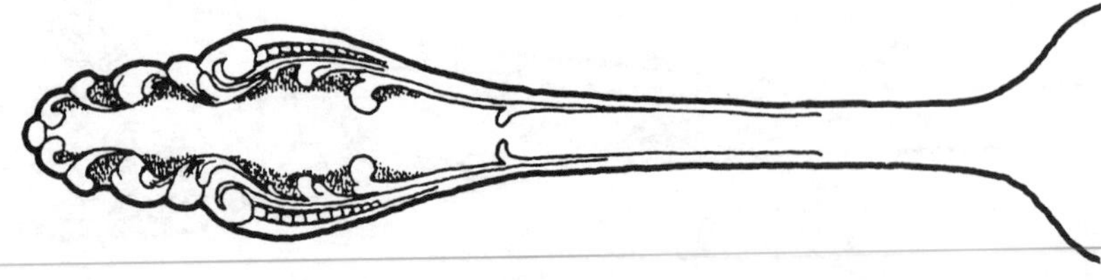

Thin market.

Please refer to "How To Use This Book" page 4.

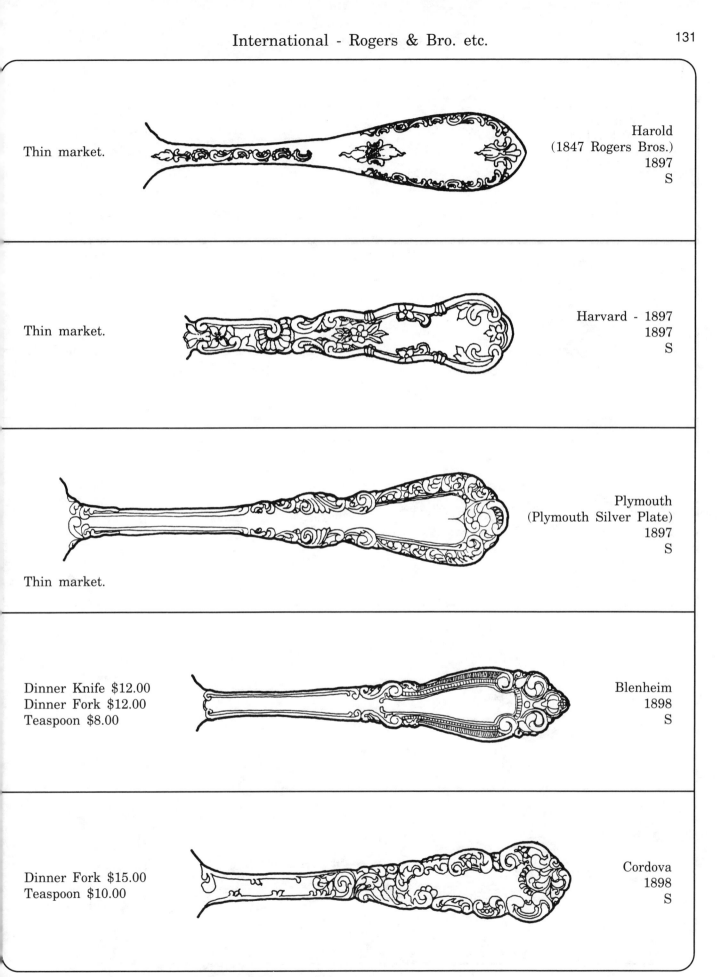

Thin market.

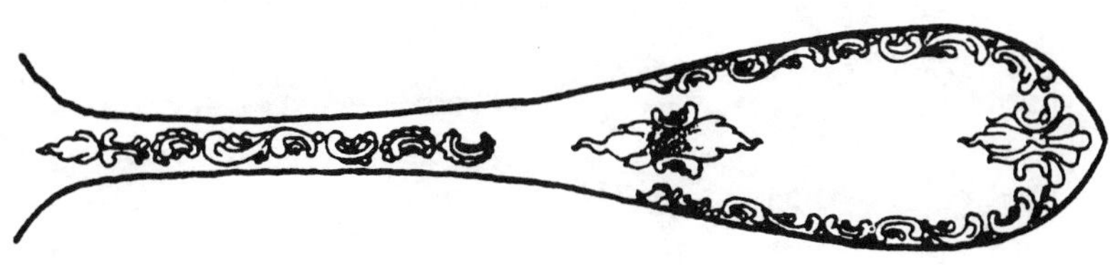

Harold
(1847 Rogers Bros.)
1897
S

Thin market.

Harvard - 1897
1897
S

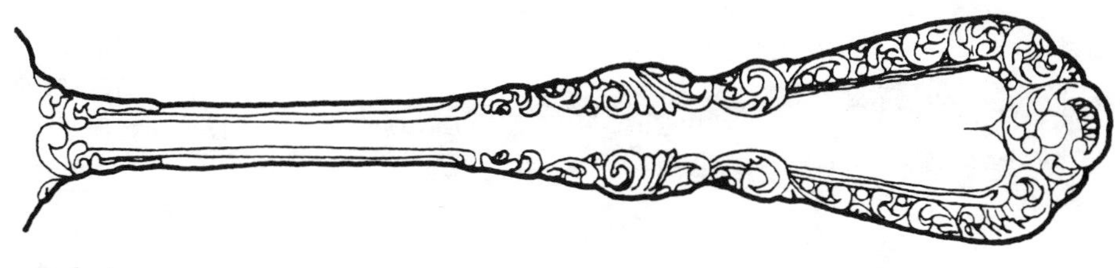

Thin market.

Plymouth
(Plymouth Silver Plate)
1897
S

Dinner Knife $12.00
Dinner Fork $12.00
Teaspoon $8.00

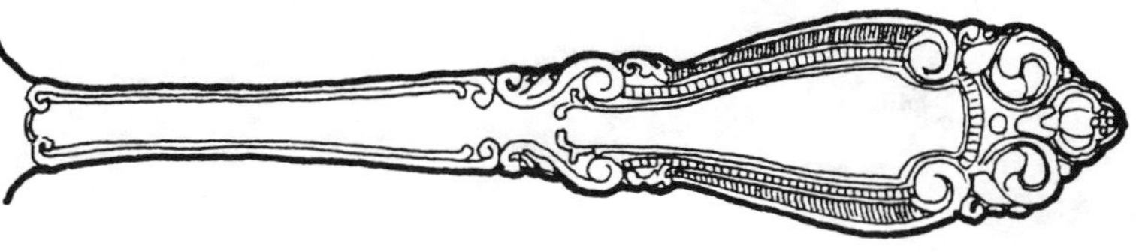

Blenheim
1898
S

Dinner Fork $15.00
Teaspoon $10.00

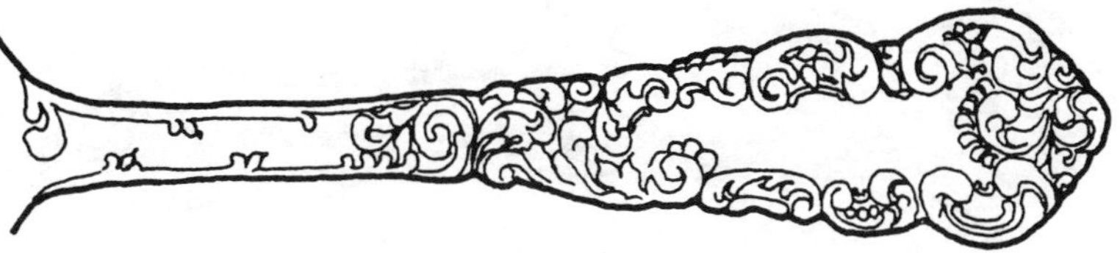

Cordova
1898
S

Please refer to "How To Use This Book" page 4.

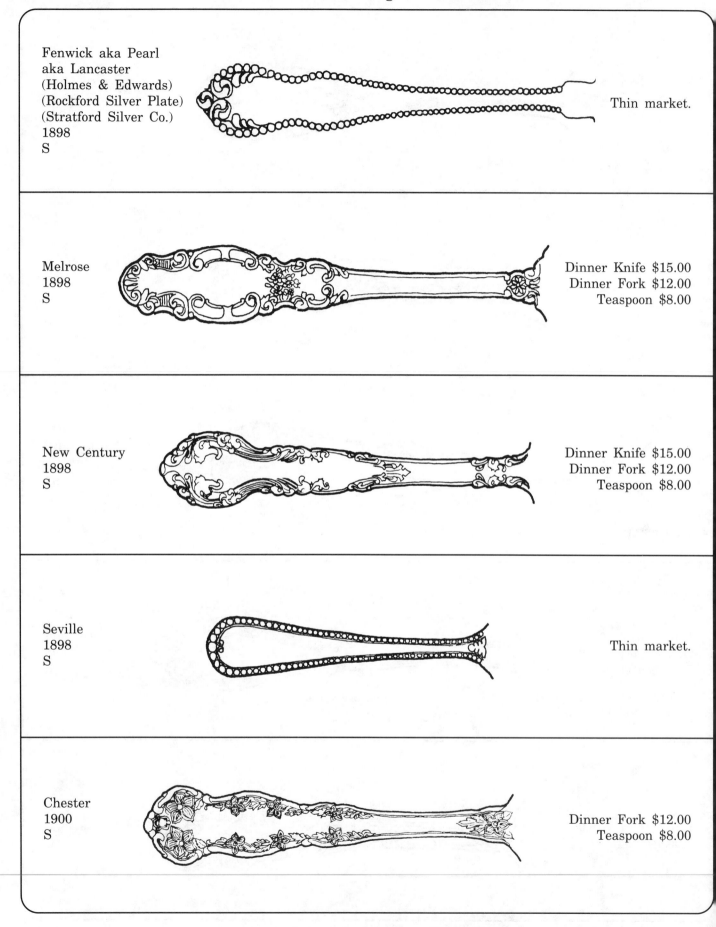

Fenwick aka Pearl
aka Lancaster
(Holmes & Edwards)
(Rockford Silver Plate)
(Stratford Silver Co.)
1898
S

Thin market.

Melrose
1898
S

Dinner Knife $15.00
Dinner Fork $12.00
Teaspoon $8.00

New Century
1898
S

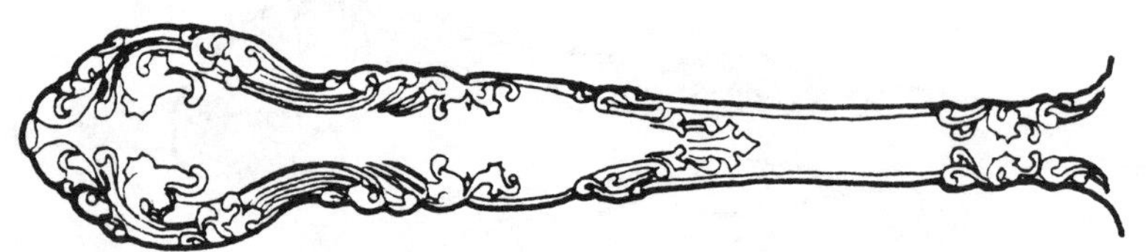

Dinner Knife $15.00
Dinner Fork $12.00
Teaspoon $8.00

Seville
1898
S

Thin market.

Chester
1900
S

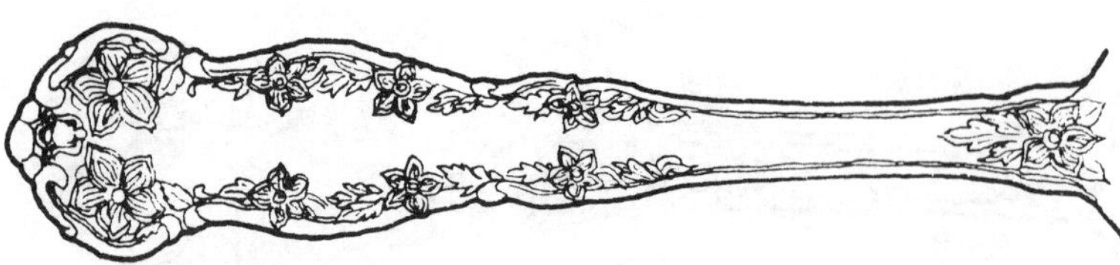

Dinner Fork $12.00
Teaspoon $8.00

Please refer to "How To Use This Book" page 4.

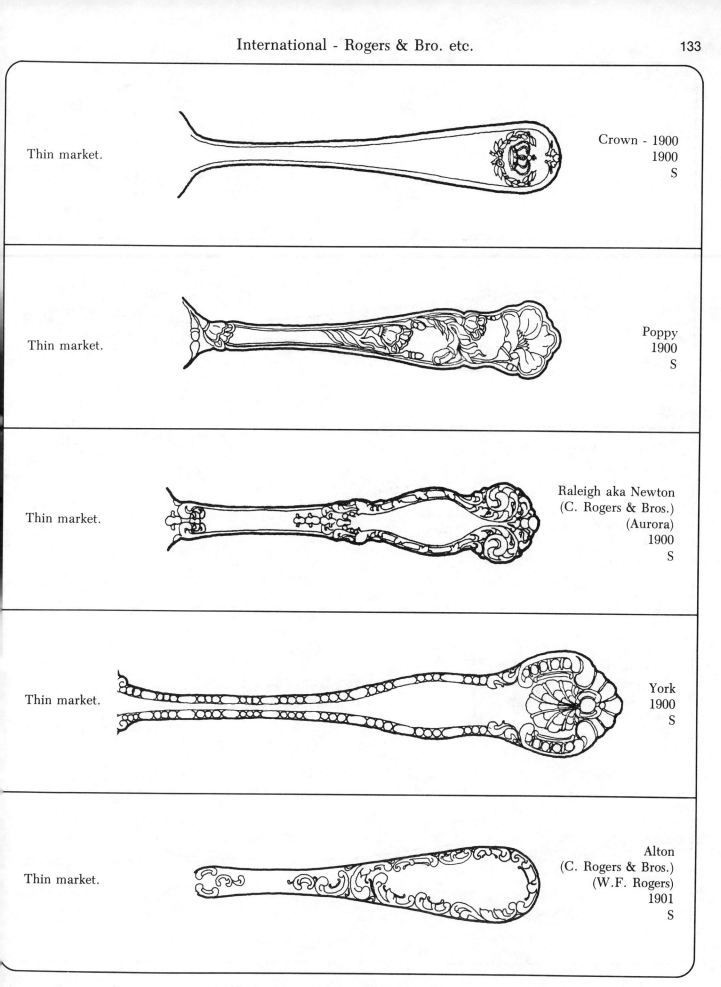

Thin market.	Crown - 1900 1900 S
Thin market.	Poppy 1900 S
Thin market.	Raleigh aka Newton (C. Rogers & Bros.) (Aurora) 1900 S
Thin market.	York 1900 S
Thin market.	Alton (C. Rogers & Bros.) (W.F. Rogers) 1901 S

Please refer to "How To Use This Book" page 4.

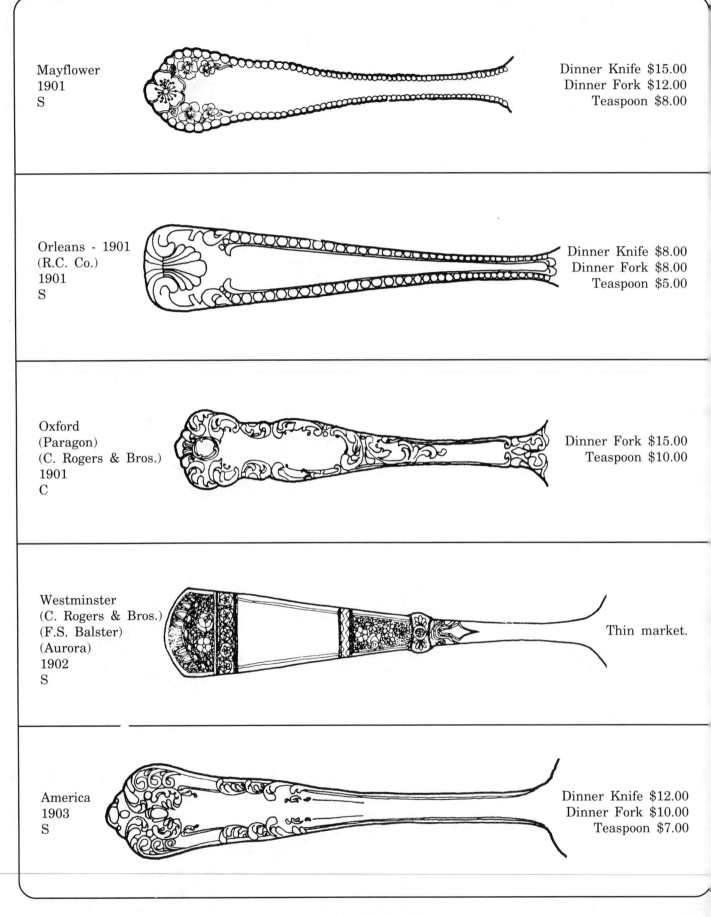

Mayflower
1901
S

Dinner Knife $15.00
Dinner Fork $12.00
Teaspoon $8.00

Orleans - 1901
(R.C. Co.)
1901
S

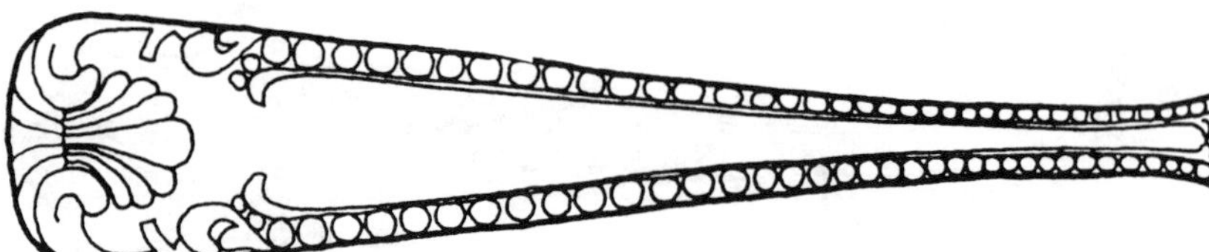

Dinner Knife $8.00
Dinner Fork $8.00
Teaspoon $5.00

Oxford
(Paragon)
(C. Rogers & Bros.)
1901
C

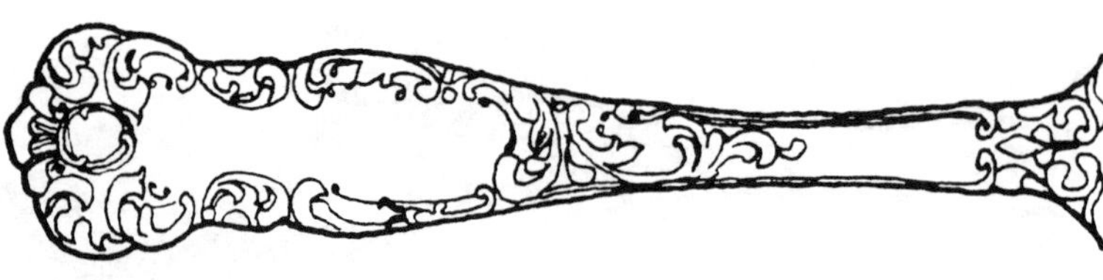

Dinner Fork $15.00
Teaspoon $10.00

Westminster
(C. Rogers & Bros.)
(F.S. Balster)
(Aurora)
1902
S

Thin market.

America
1903
S

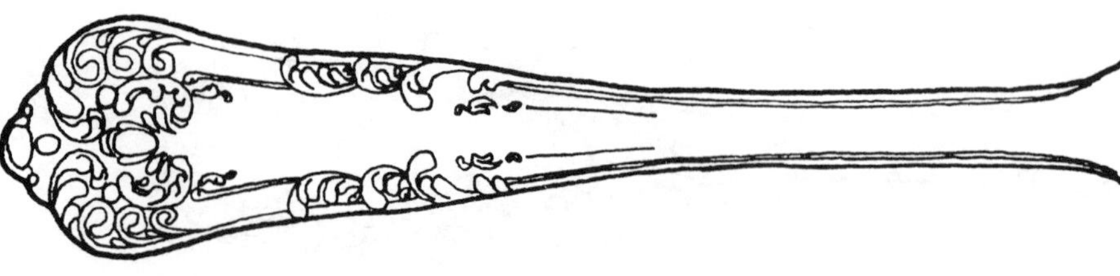

Dinner Knife $12.00
Dinner Fork $10.00
Teaspoon $7.00

Please refer to "How To Use This Book" page 4.

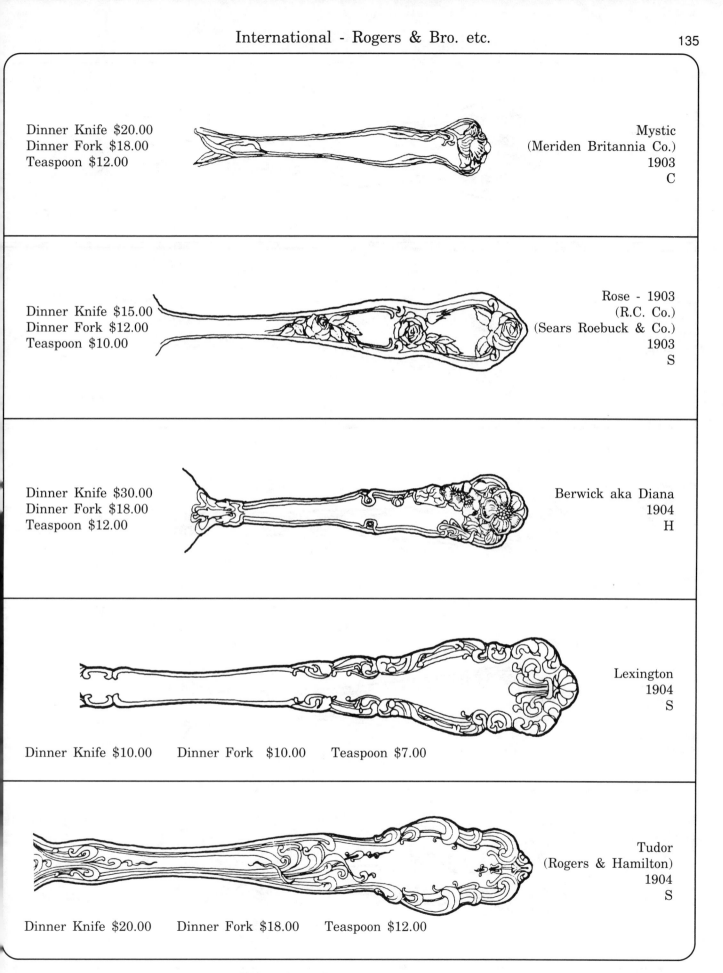

Dinner Knife $20.00
Dinner Fork $18.00
Teaspoon $12.00

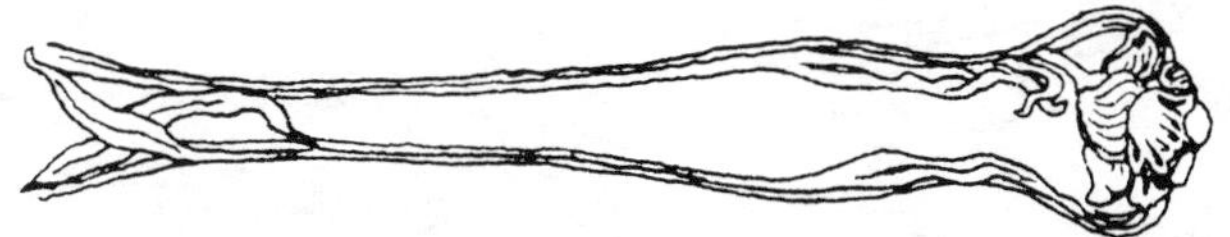

Mystic
(Meriden Britannia Co.)
1903
C

Dinner Knife $15.00
Dinner Fork $12.00
Teaspoon $10.00

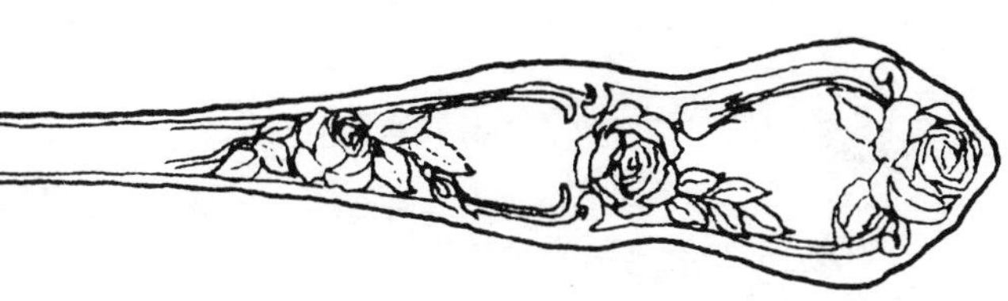

Rose - 1903
(R.C. Co.)
(Sears Roebuck & Co.)
1903
S

Dinner Knife $30.00
Dinner Fork $18.00
Teaspoon $12.00

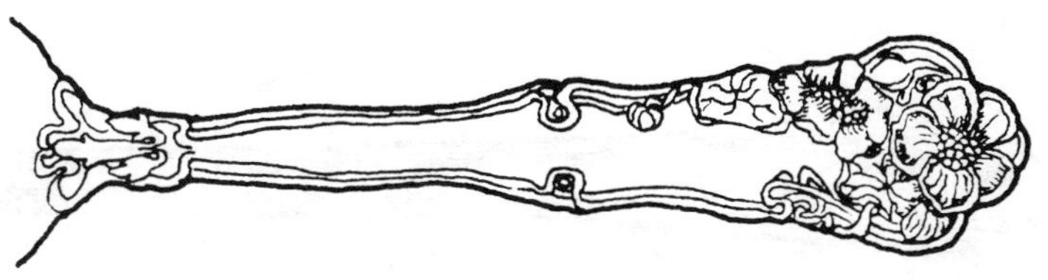

Berwick aka Diana
1904
H

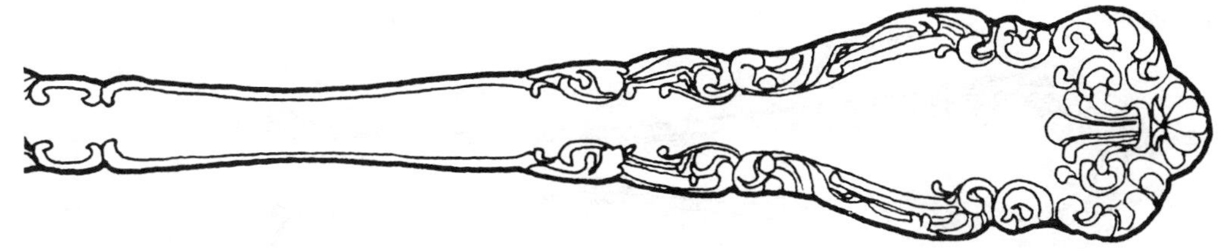

Lexington
1904
S

Dinner Knife $10.00 Dinner Fork $10.00 Teaspoon $7.00

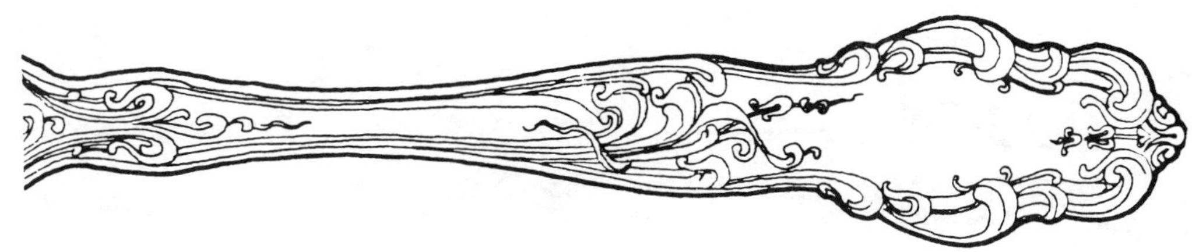

Tudor
(Rogers & Hamilton)
1904
S

Dinner Knife $20.00 Dinner Fork $18.00 Teaspoon $12.00

Please refer to "How To Use This Book" page 4.

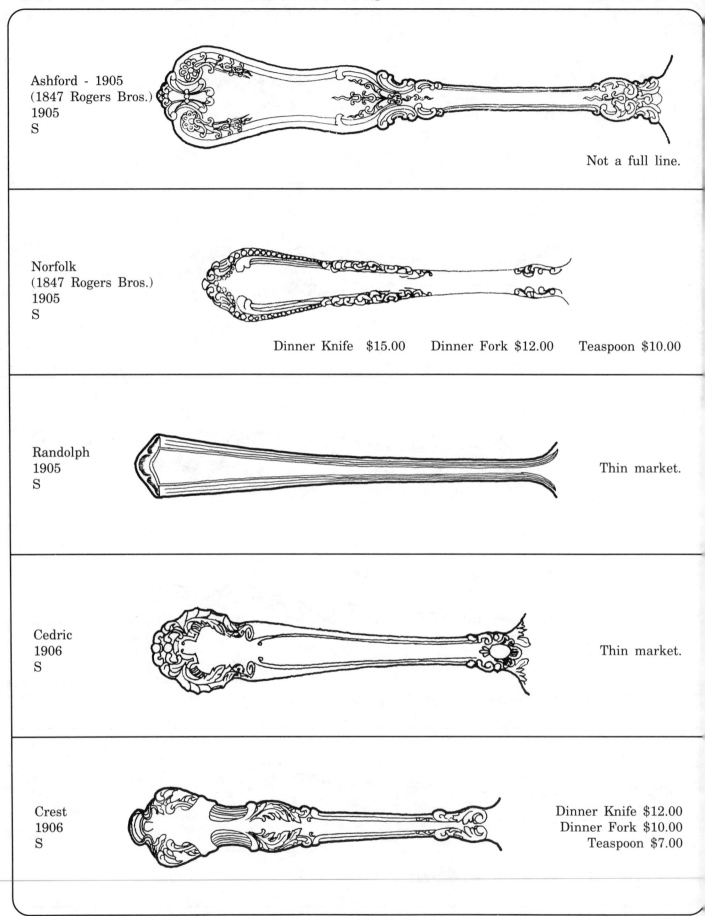

Ashford - 1905
(1847 Rogers Bros.)
1905
S

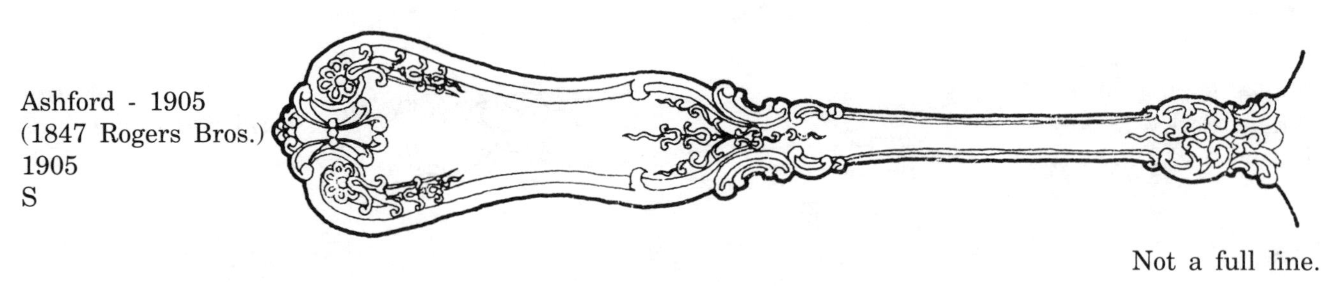

Not a full line.

Norfolk
(1847 Rogers Bros.)
1905
S

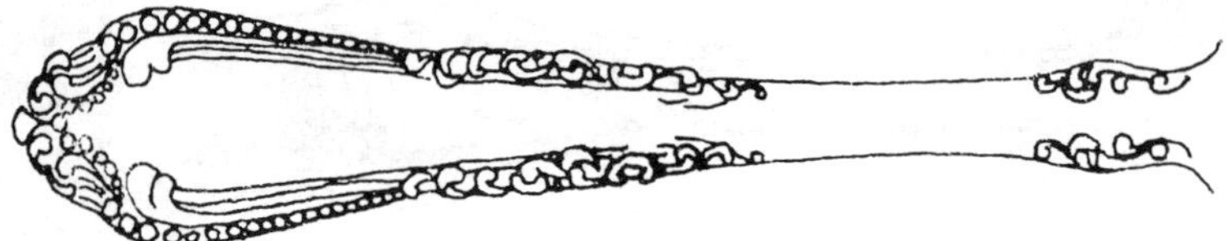

Dinner Knife $15.00 Dinner Fork $12.00 Teaspoon $10.00

Randolph
1905
S

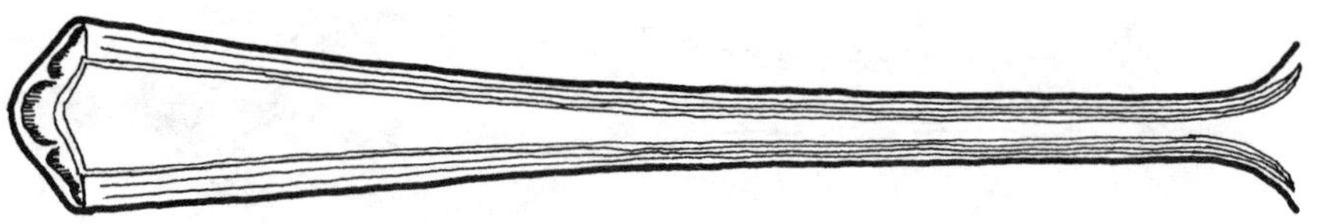

Thin market.

Cedric
1906
S

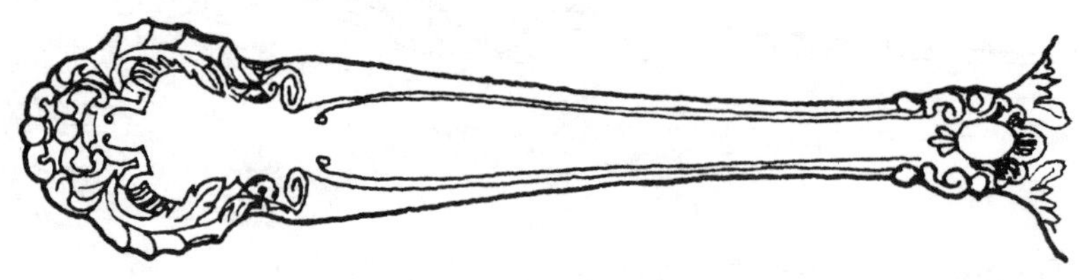

Thin market.

Crest
1906
S

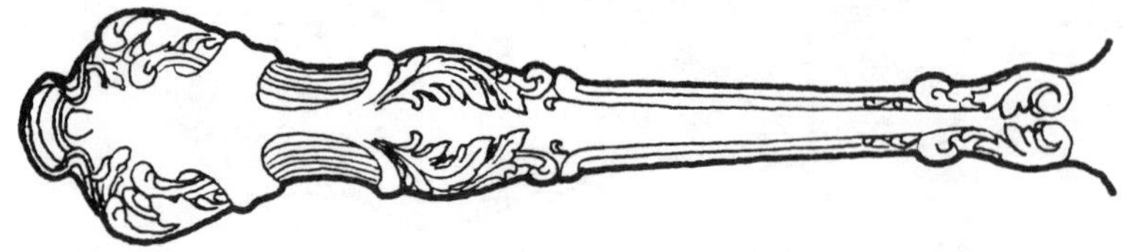

Dinner Knife $12.00
Dinner Fork $10.00
Teaspoon $7.00

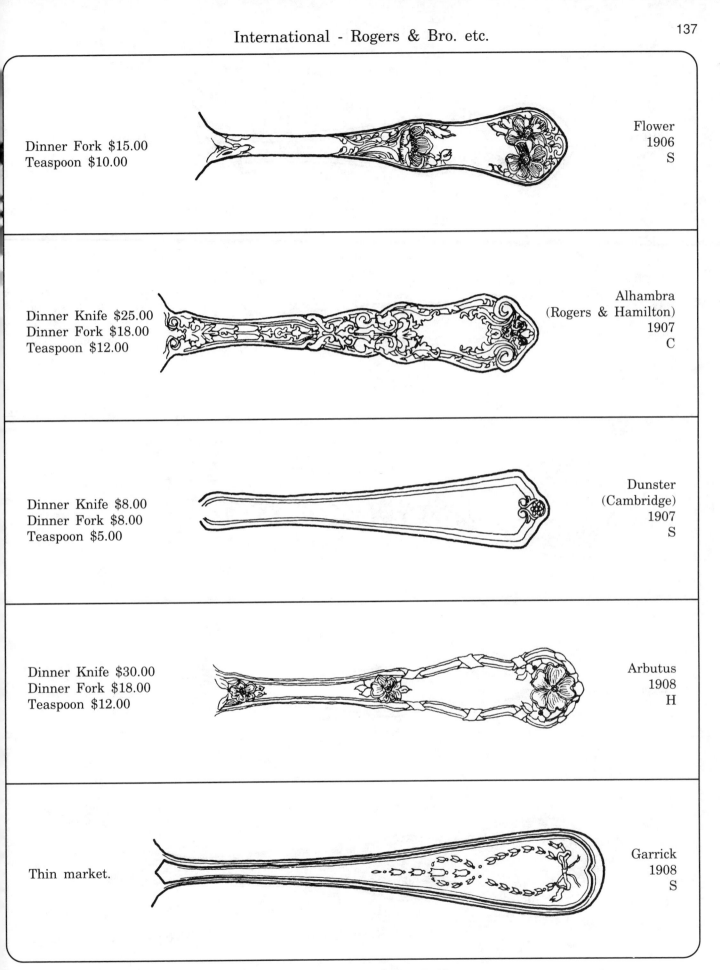

Dinner Fork $15.00
Teaspoon $10.00

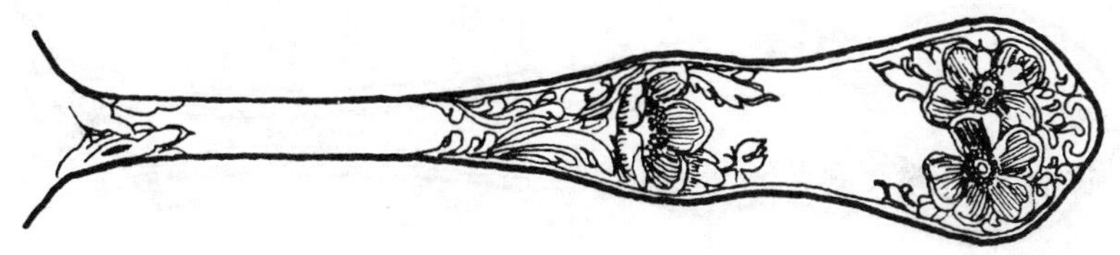

Flower
1906
S

Dinner Knife $25.00
Dinner Fork $18.00
Teaspoon $12.00

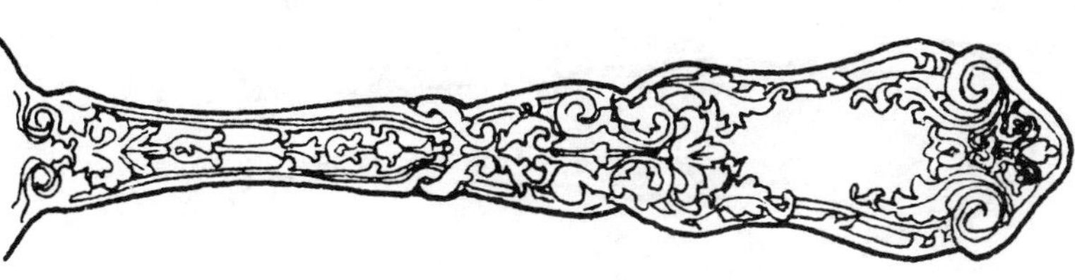

Alhambra
(Rogers & Hamilton)
1907
C

Dinner Knife $8.00
Dinner Fork $8.00
Teaspoon $5.00

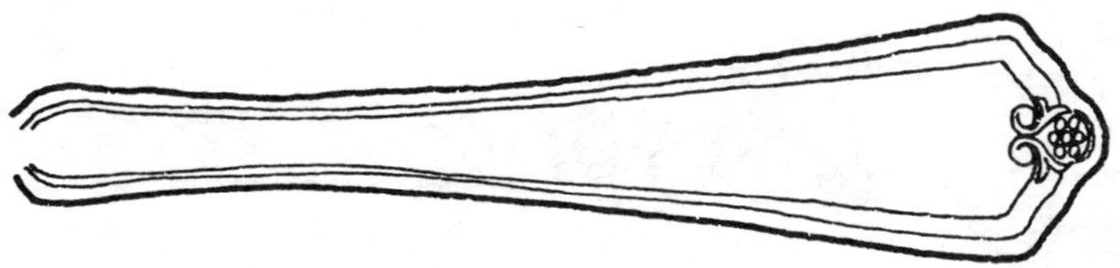

Dunster
(Cambridge)
1907
S

Dinner Knife $30.00
Dinner Fork $18.00
Teaspoon $12.00

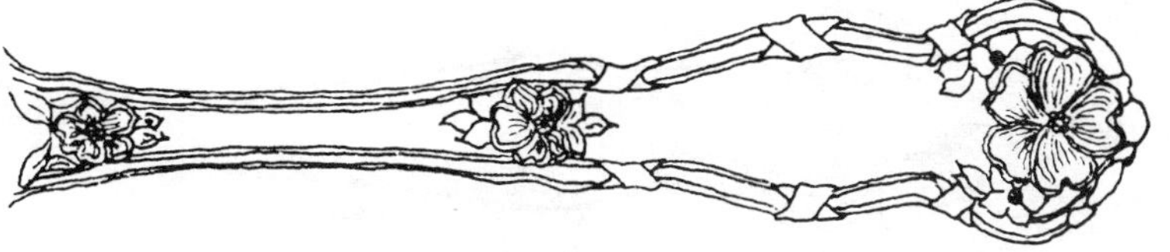

Arbutus
1908
H

Thin market.

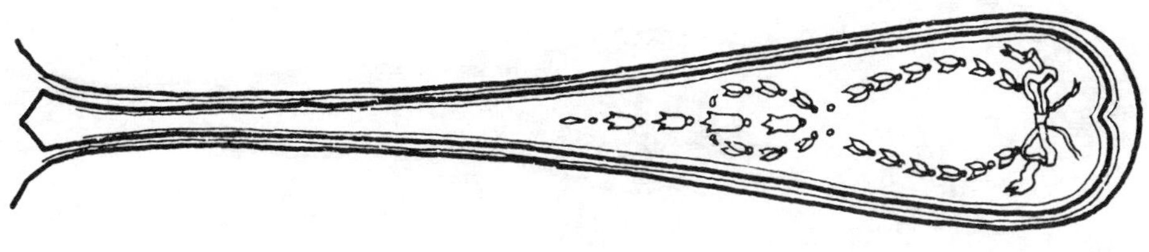

Garrick
1908
S

Please refer to "How To Use This Book" page 4.

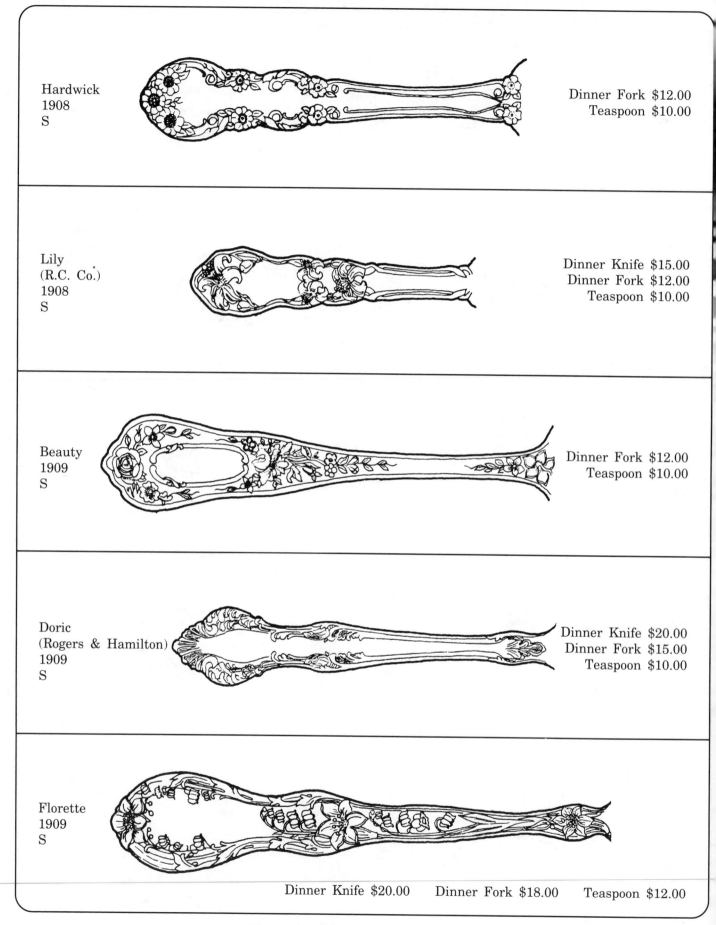

Hardwick
1908
S

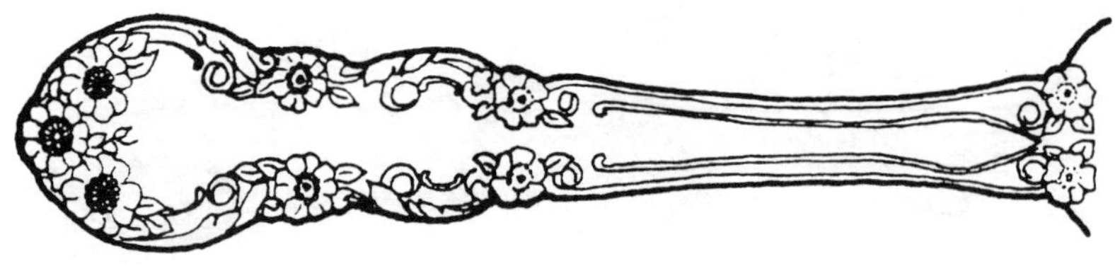

Dinner Fork $12.00
Teaspoon $10.00

Lily
(R.C. Co.)
1908
S

Dinner Knife $15.00
Dinner Fork $12.00
Teaspoon $10.00

Beauty
1909
S

Dinner Fork $12.00
Teaspoon $10.00

Doric
(Rogers & Hamilton)
1909
S

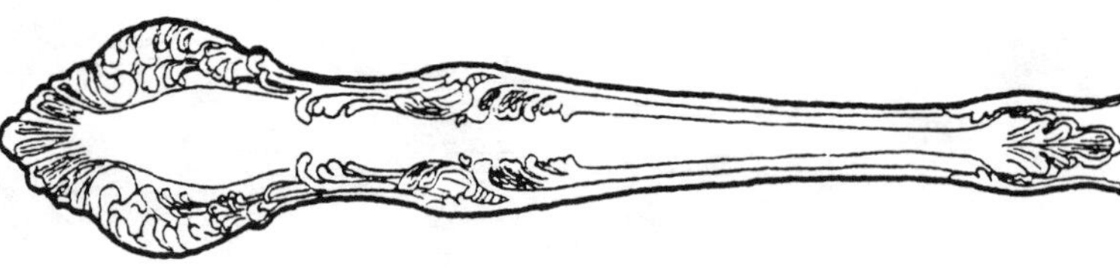

Dinner Knife $20.00
Dinner Fork $15.00
Teaspoon $10.00

Florette
1909
S

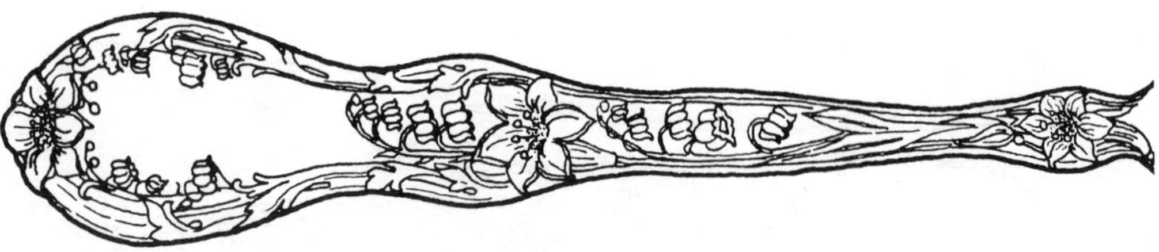

Dinner Knife $20.00 Dinner Fork $18.00 Teaspoon $12.00

Please refer to "How To Use This Book" page 4.

Dinner Knife $15.00
Dinner Fork $12.00
Teaspoon $10.00

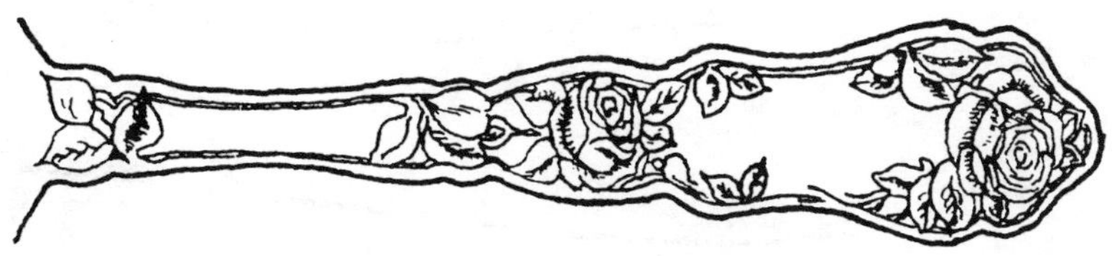

Rose - 1909
1909
S

Beaded aka Essex
1910
S

Thin market.

Thin market.

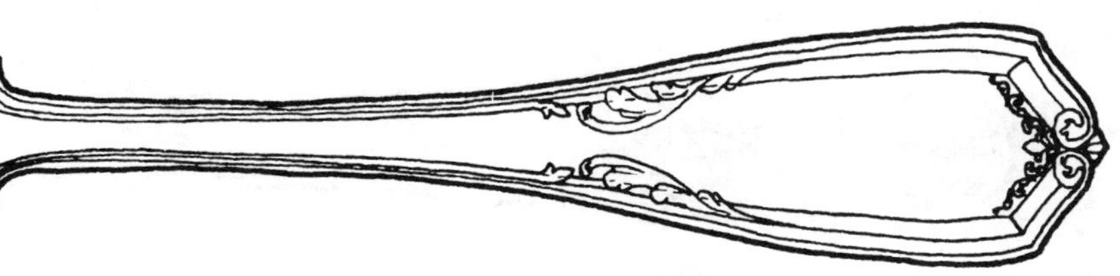

Concord
1910
S

Dinner Knife $15.00
Dinner Fork $12.00
Teaspoon $10.00

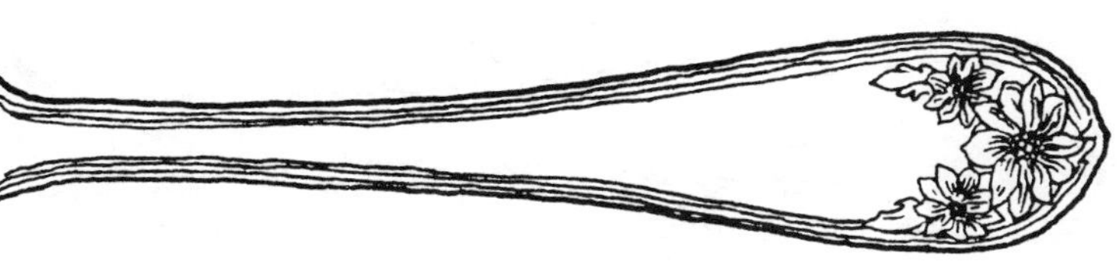

Daisy aka New Daisy
1910
S

Dinner Knife $35.00
Dinner Fork $15.00
Teaspoon $10.00

Orange Blossom
1910
H

Please refer to "How To Use This Book" page 4.

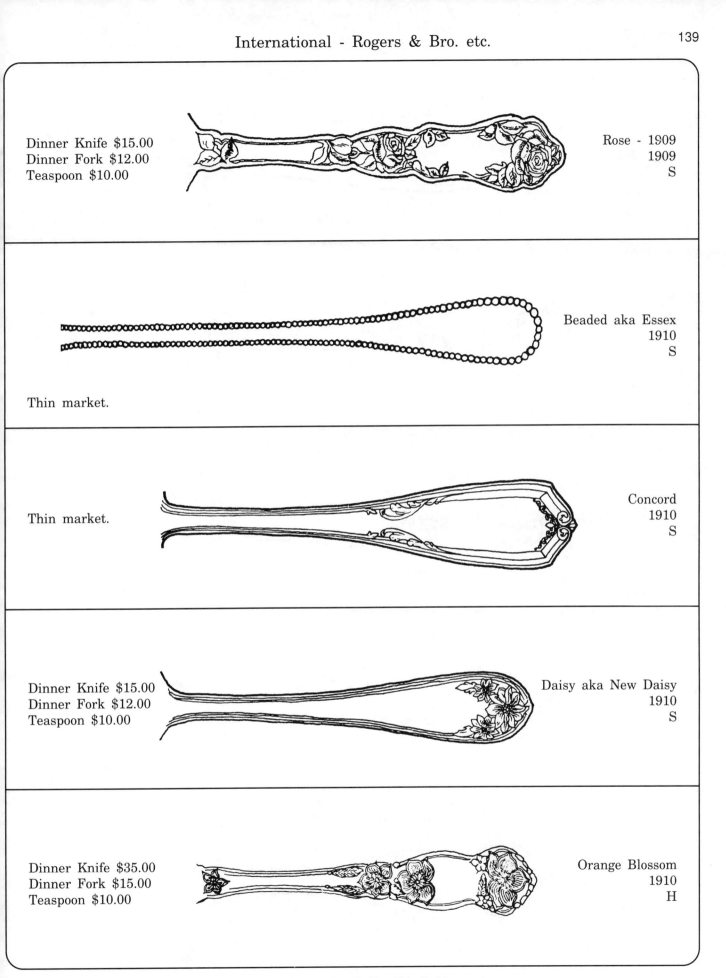

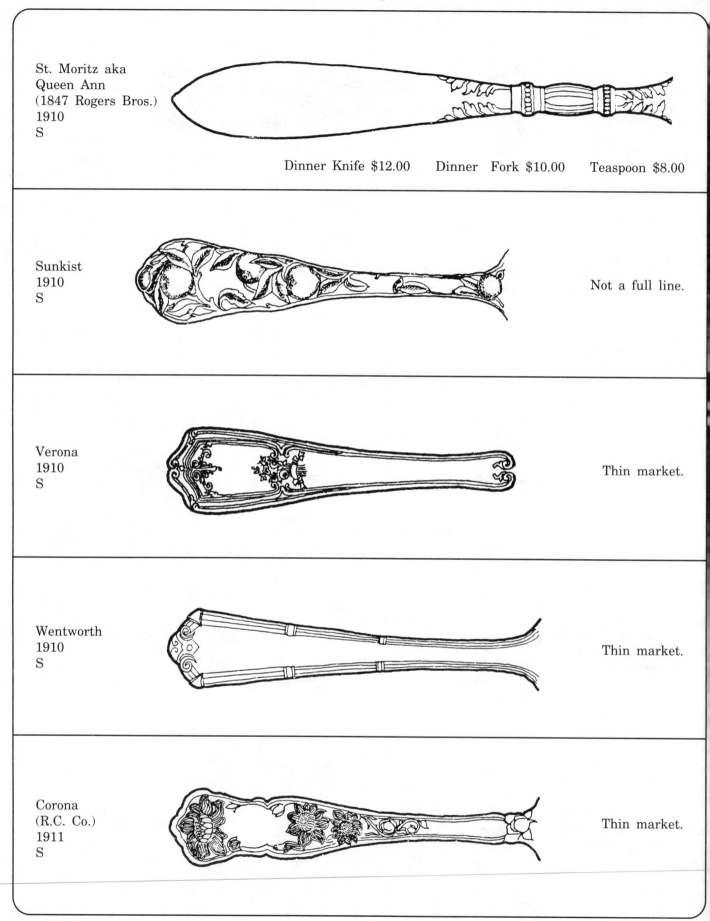

St. Moritz aka
Queen Ann
(1847 Rogers Bros.)
1910
S

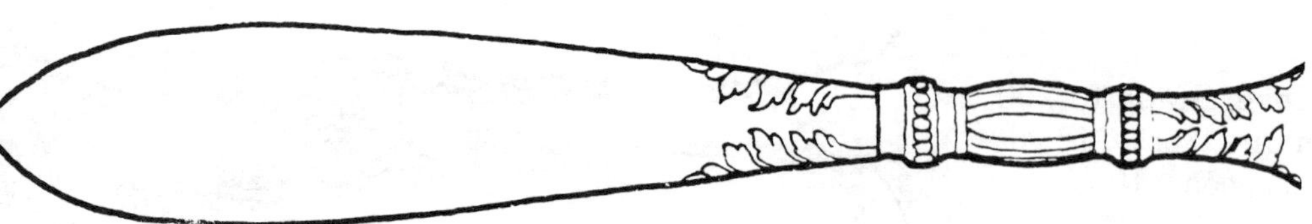

Dinner Knife $12.00 Dinner Fork $10.00 Teaspoon $8.00

Sunkist
1910
S

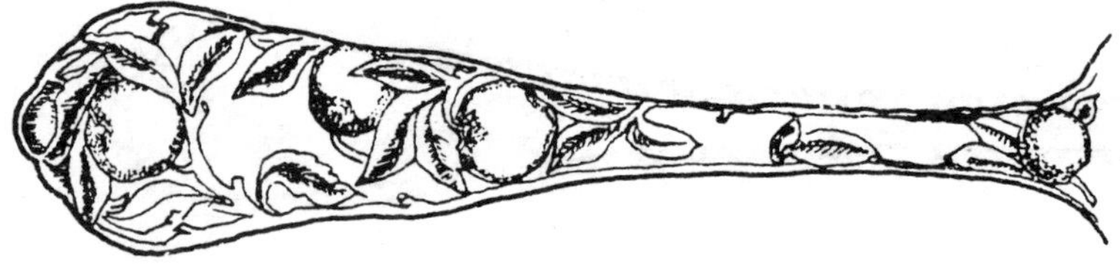

Not a full line.

Verona
1910
S

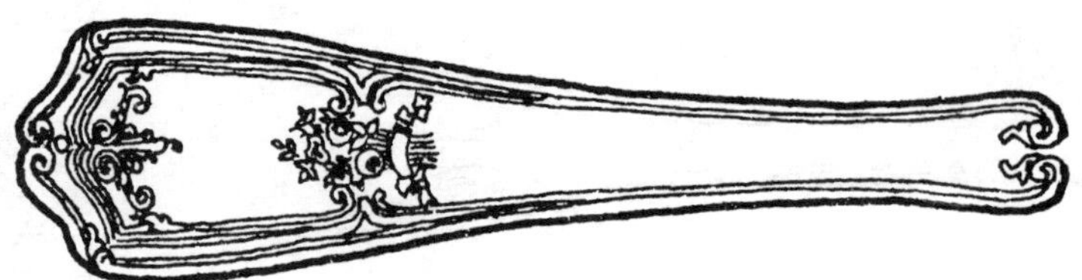

Thin market.

Wentworth
1910
S

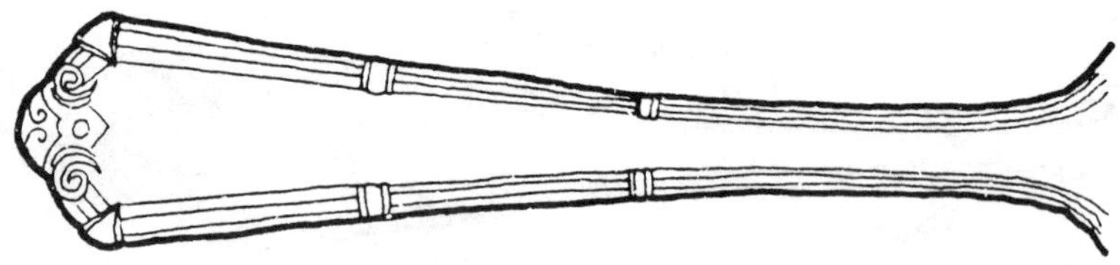

Thin market.

Corona
(R.C. Co.)
1911
S

Thin market.

Please refer to "How To Use This Book" page 4.

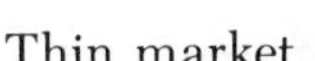

Thin market.

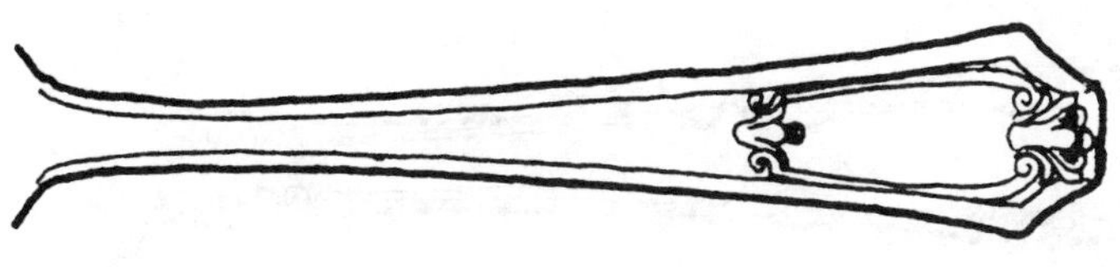

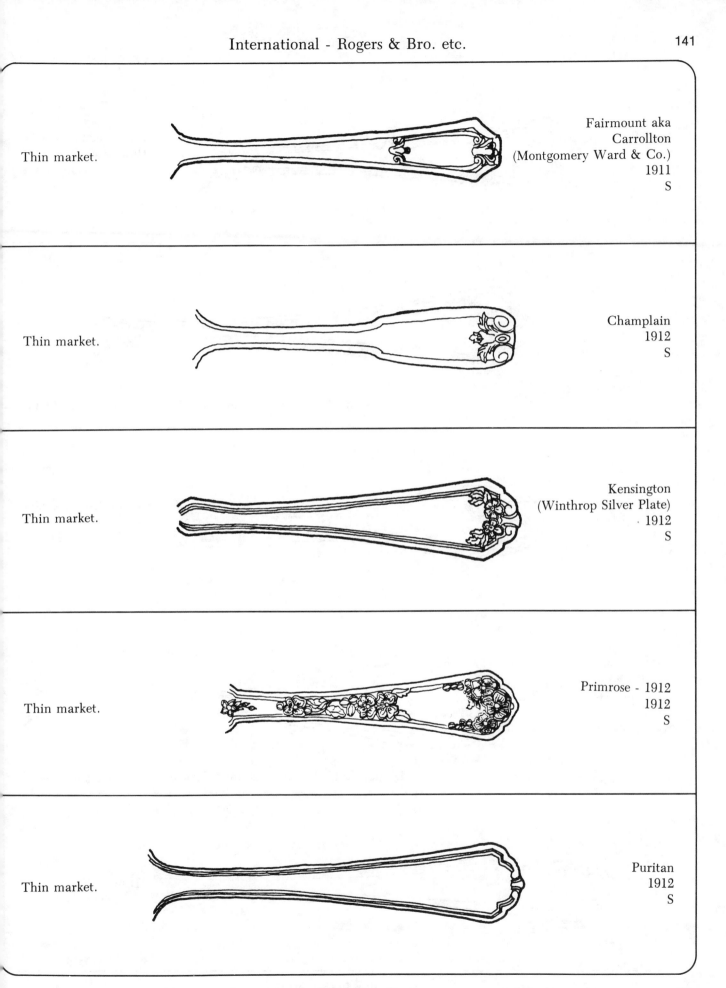

Fairmount aka
Carrollton
(Montgomery Ward & Co.)
1911
S

Thin market.

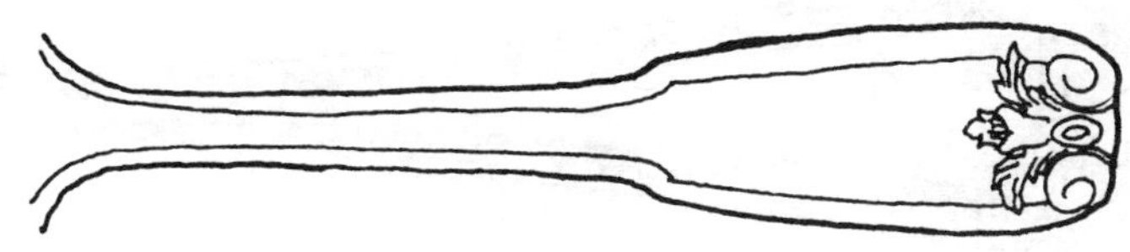

Champlain
1912
S

Thin market.

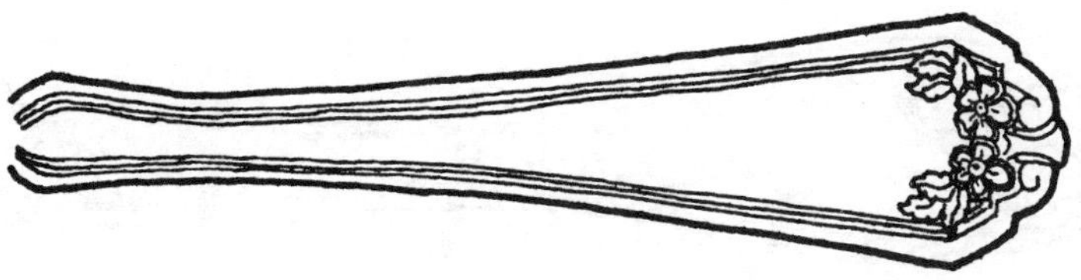

Kensington
(Winthrop Silver Plate)
1912
S

Thin market.

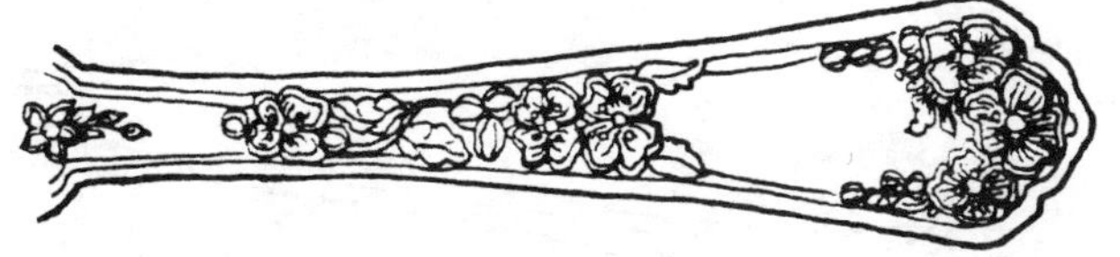

Primrose - 1912
1912
S

Thin market.

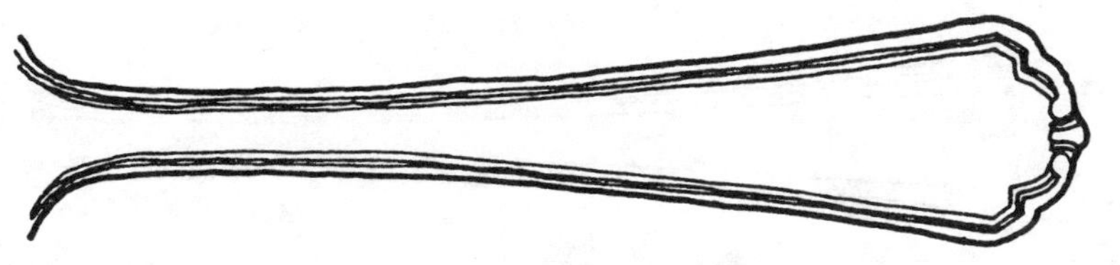

Puritan
1912
S

Please refer to "How To Use This Book" page 4.

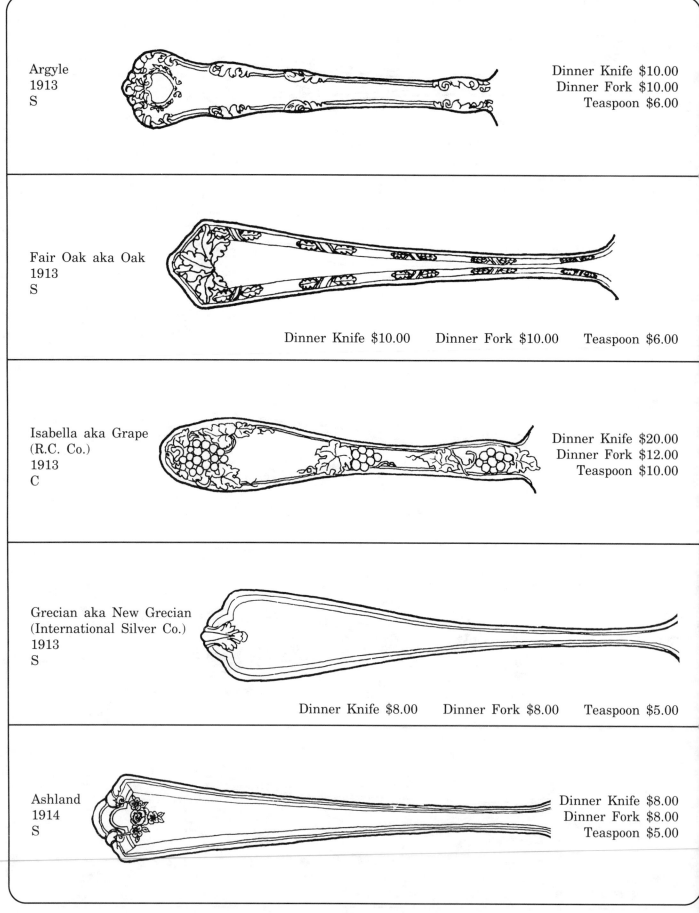

Argyle
1913
S

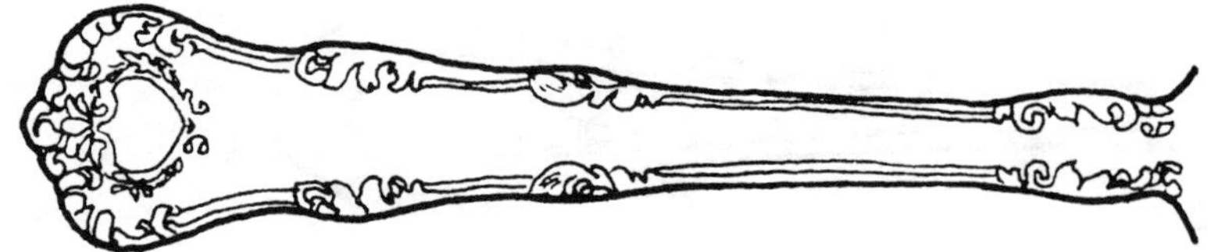

Dinner Knife $10.00
Dinner Fork $10.00
Teaspoon $6.00

Fair Oak aka Oak
1913
S

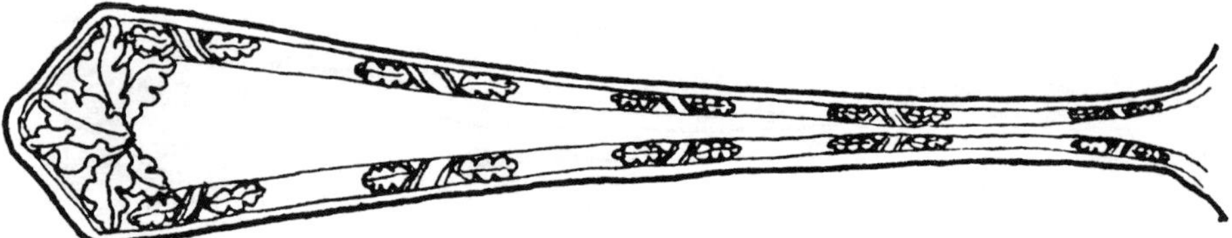

Dinner Knife $10.00 Dinner Fork $10.00 Teaspoon $6.00

Isabella aka Grape
(R.C. Co.)
1913
C

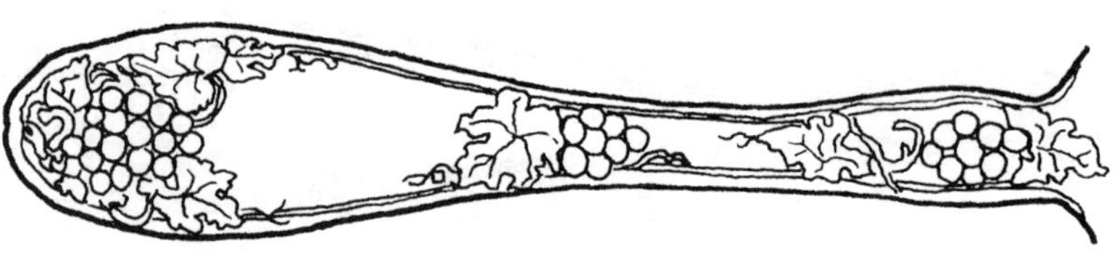

Dinner Knife $20.00
Dinner Fork $12.00
Teaspoon $10.00

Grecian aka New Grecian
(International Silver Co.)
1913
S

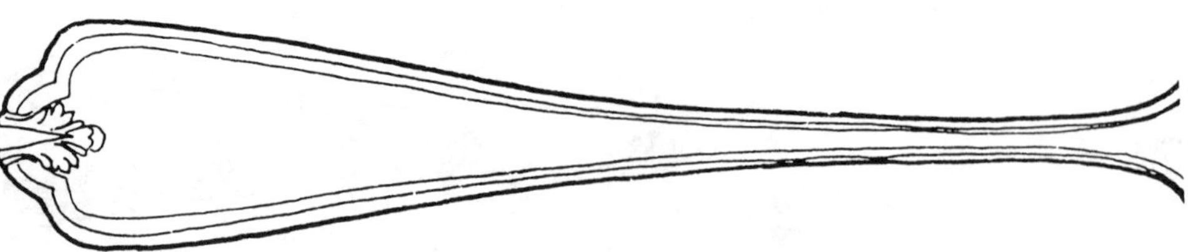

Dinner Knife $8.00 Dinner Fork $8.00 Teaspoon $5.00

Ashland
1914
S

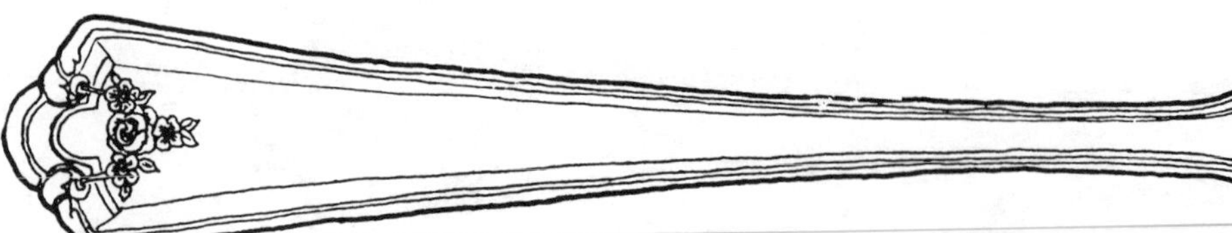

Dinner Knife $8.00
Dinner Fork $8.00
Teaspoon $5.00

Please refer to "How To Use This Book" page 4.

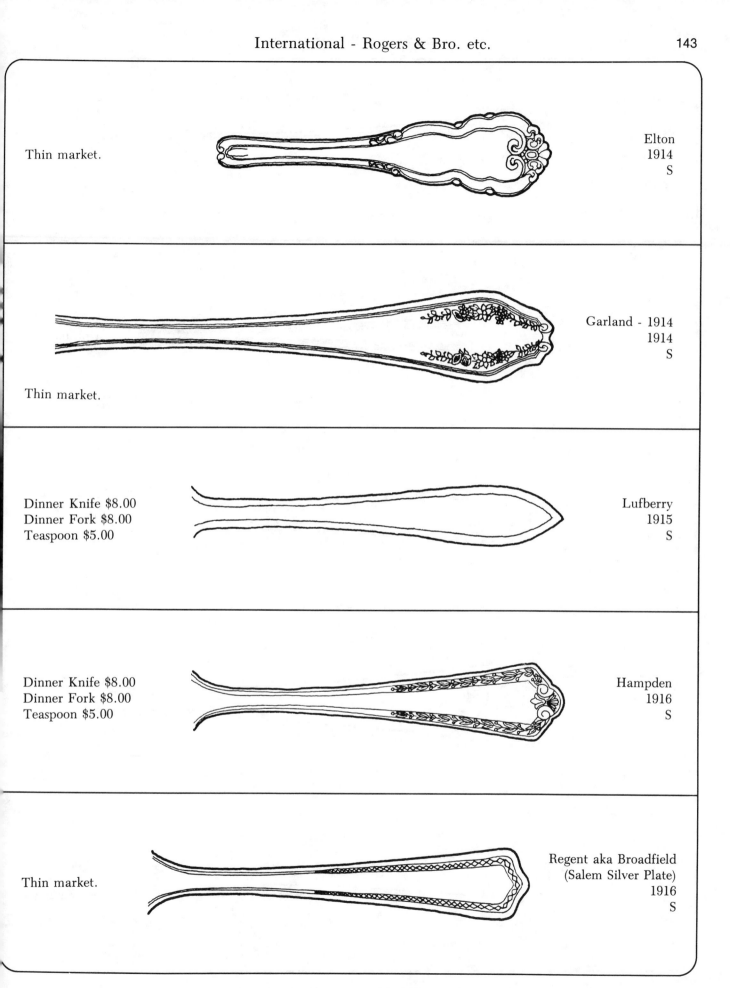

Thin market.

Elton
1914
S

Garland - 1914
1914
S

Thin market.

Dinner Knife $8.00
Dinner Fork $8.00
Teaspoon $5.00

Lufberry
1915
S

Dinner Knife $8.00
Dinner Fork $8.00
Teaspoon $5.00

Hampden
1916
S

Thin market.

Regent aka Broadfield
(Salem Silver Plate)
1916
S

Please refer to "How To Use This Book" page 4.

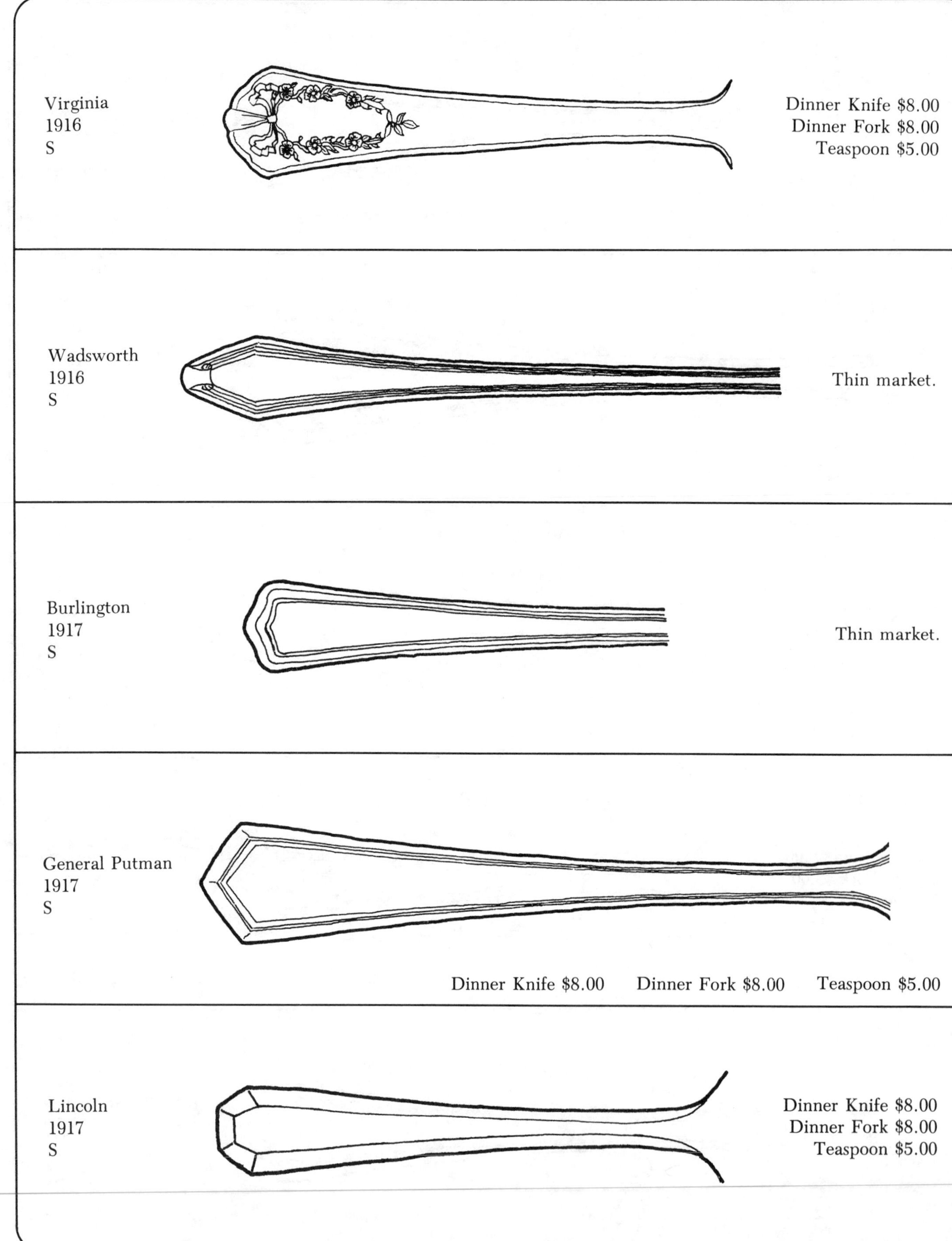

Virginia
1916
S

Dinner Knife $8.00
Dinner Fork $8.00
Teaspoon $5.00

Wadsworth
1916
S

Thin market.

Burlington
1917
S

Thin market.

General Putman
1917
S

Dinner Knife $8.00 Dinner Fork $8.00 Teaspoon $5.00

Lincoln
1917
S

Dinner Knife $8.00
Dinner Fork $8.00
Teaspoon $5.00

Please refer to "How To Use This Book" page 4.

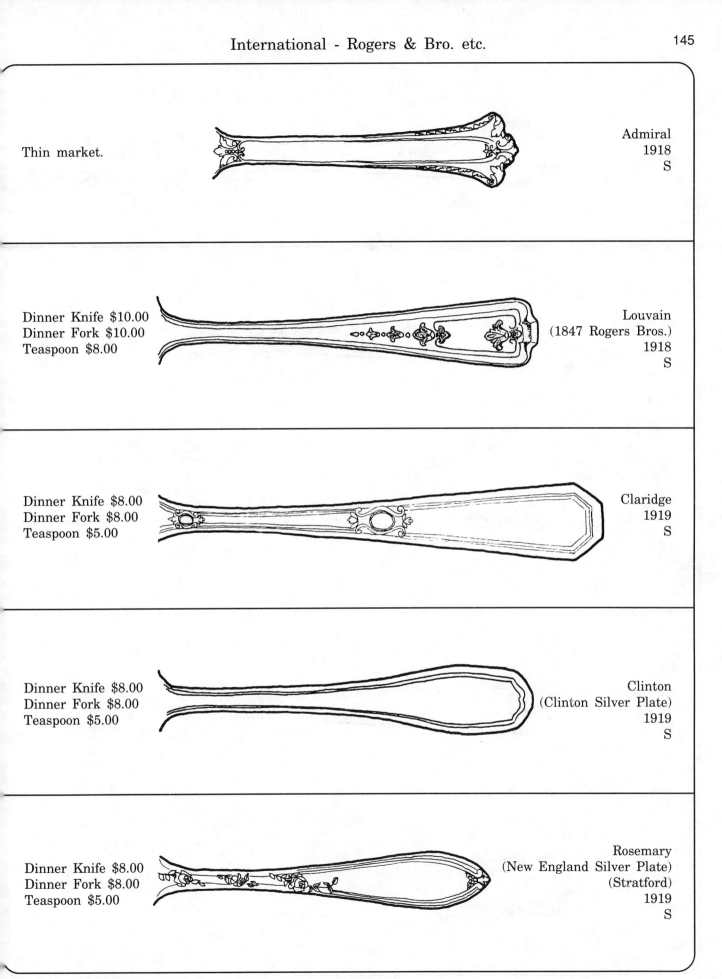

Thin market.

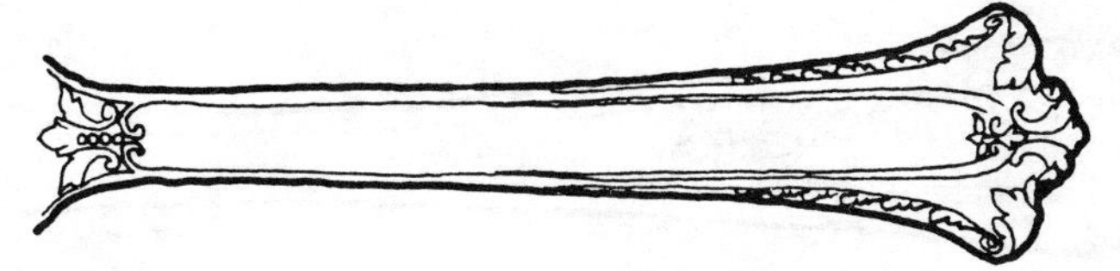

Admiral
1918
S

Dinner Knife $10.00
Dinner Fork $10.00
Teaspoon $8.00

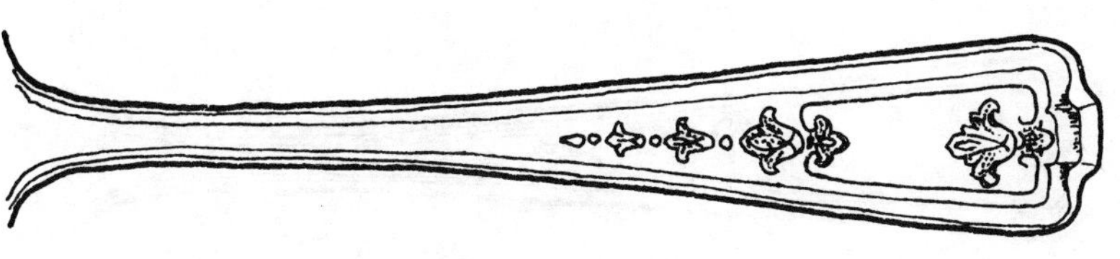

Louvain
(1847 Rogers Bros.)
1918
S

Dinner Knife $8.00
Dinner Fork $8.00
Teaspoon $5.00

Claridge
1919
S

Dinner Knife $8.00
Dinner Fork $8.00
Teaspoon $5.00

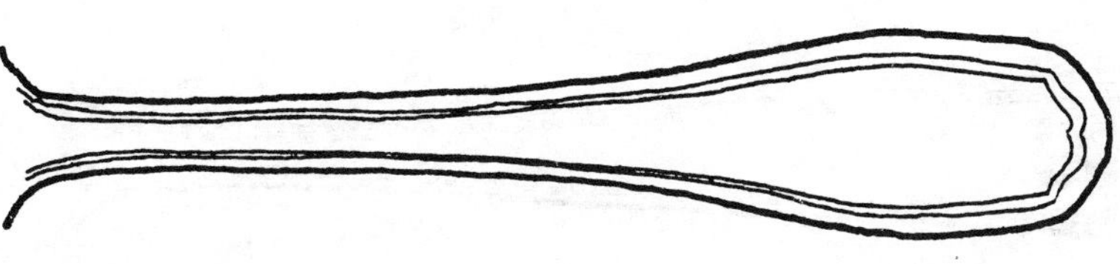

Clinton
(Clinton Silver Plate)
1919
S

Dinner Knife $8.00
Dinner Fork $8.00
Teaspoon $5.00

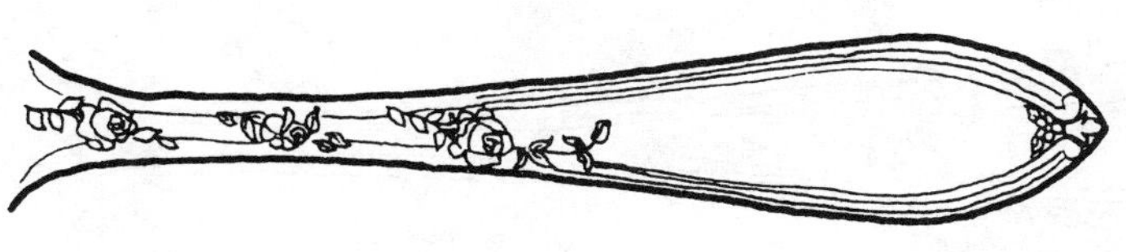

Rosemary
(New England Silver Plate)
(Stratford)
1919
S

Please refer to "How To Use This Book" page 4.

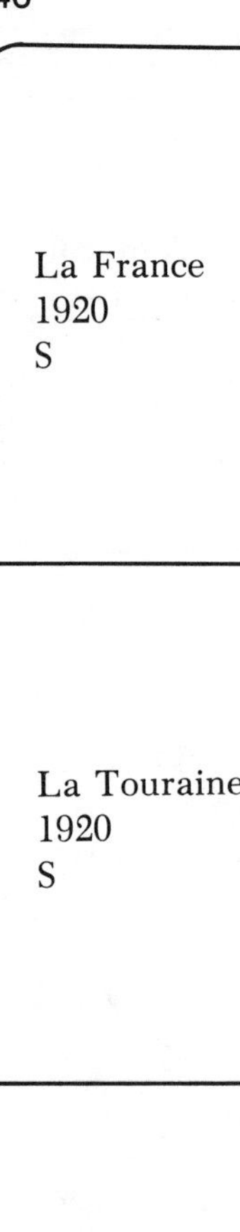

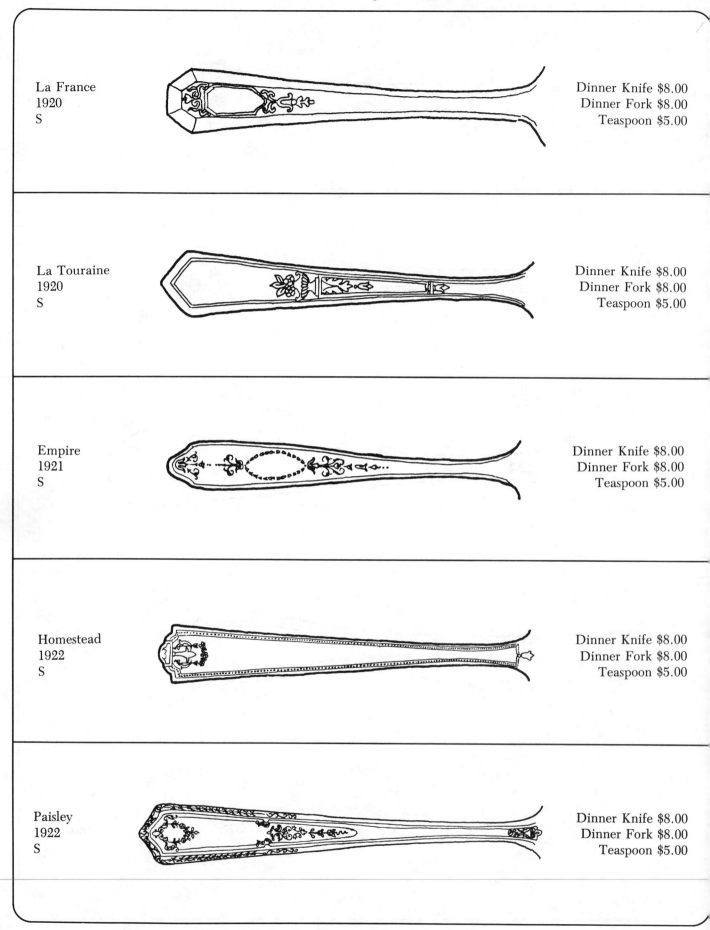

La France
1920
S

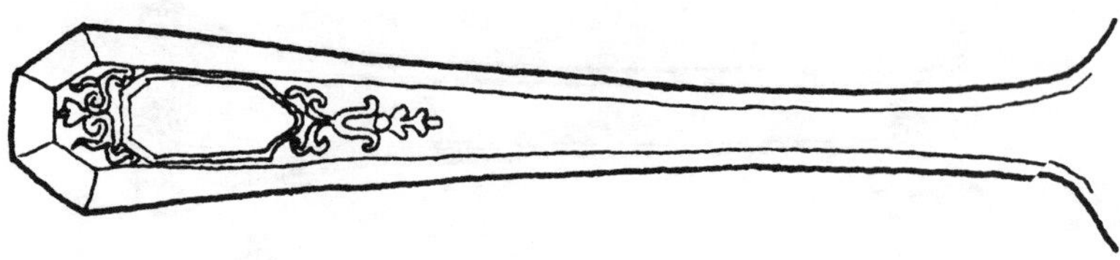

Dinner Knife $8.00
Dinner Fork $8.00
Teaspoon $5.00

La Touraine
1920
S

Dinner Knife $8.00
Dinner Fork $8.00
Teaspoon $5.00

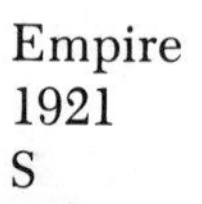

Empire
1921
S

Dinner Knife $8.00
Dinner Fork $8.00
Teaspoon $5.00

Homestead
1922
S

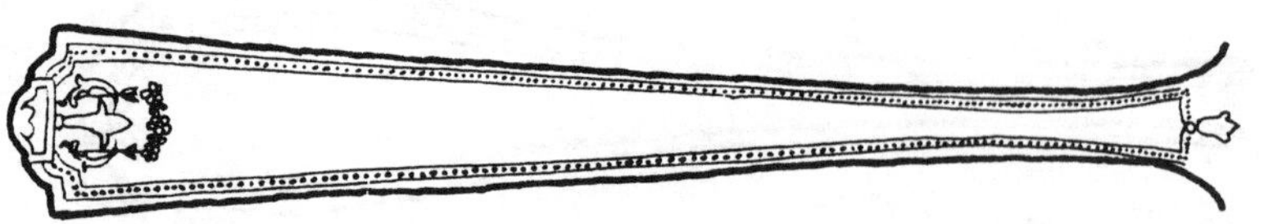

Dinner Knife $8.00
Dinner Fork $8.00
Teaspoon $5.00

Paisley
1922
S

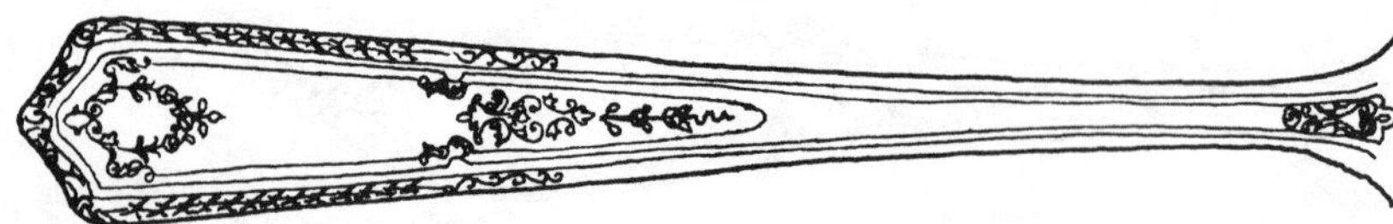

Dinner Knife $8.00
Dinner Fork $8.00
Teaspoon $5.00

Please refer to "How To Use This Book" page 4.

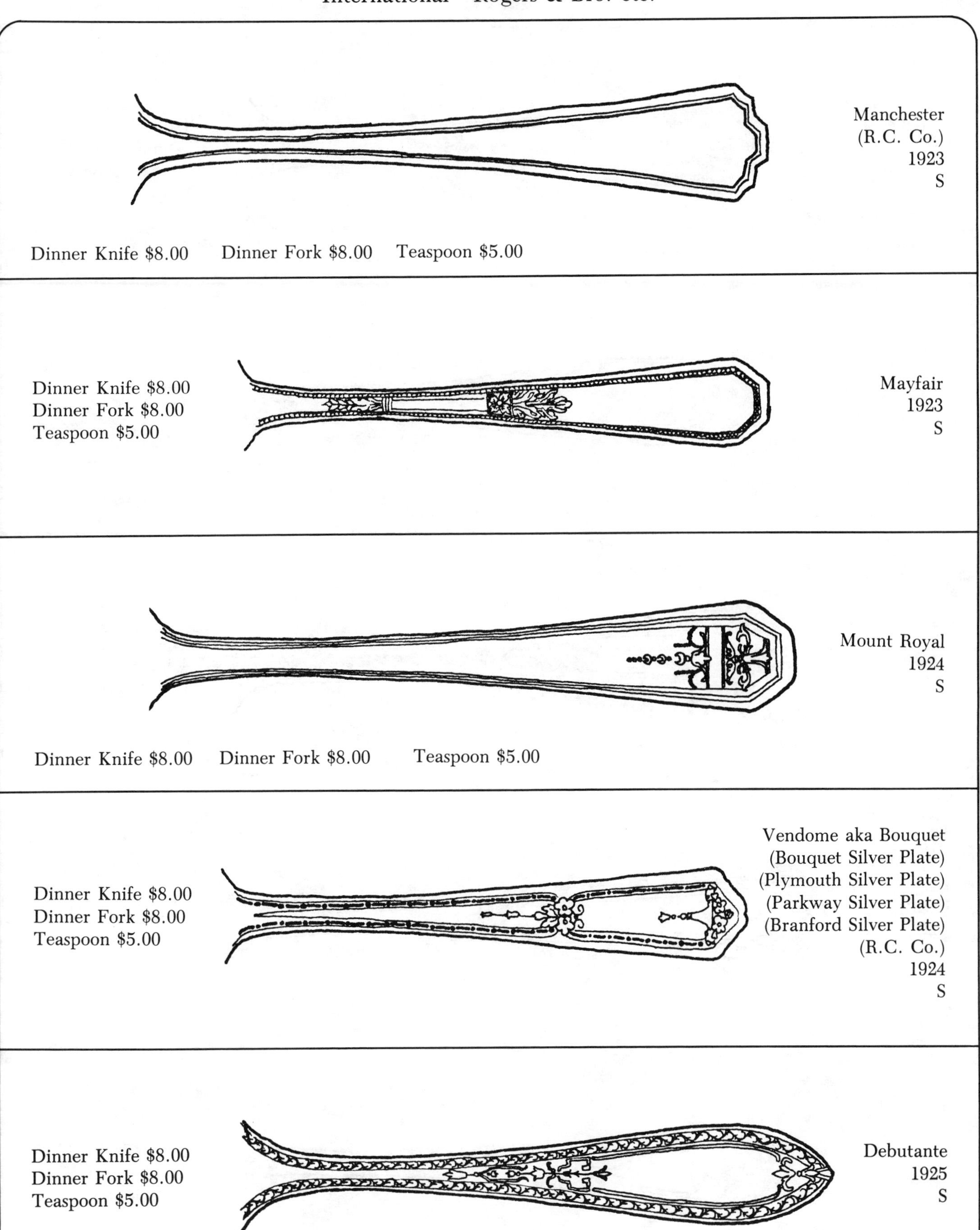

Manchester
(R.C. Co.)
1923
S

Dinner Knife $8.00 Dinner Fork $8.00 Teaspoon $5.00

Dinner Knife $8.00
Dinner Fork $8.00
Teaspoon $5.00

Mayfair
1923
S

Mount Royal
1924
S

Dinner Knife $8.00 Dinner Fork $8.00 Teaspoon $5.00

Dinner Knife $8.00
Dinner Fork $8.00
Teaspoon $5.00

Vendome aka Bouquet
(Bouquet Silver Plate)
(Plymouth Silver Plate)
(Parkway Silver Plate)
(Branford Silver Plate)
(R.C. Co.)
1924
S

Dinner Knife $8.00
Dinner Fork $8.00
Teaspoon $5.00

Debutante
1925
S

Please refer to "How To Use This Book" page 4.

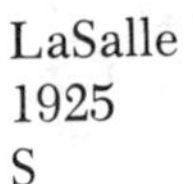

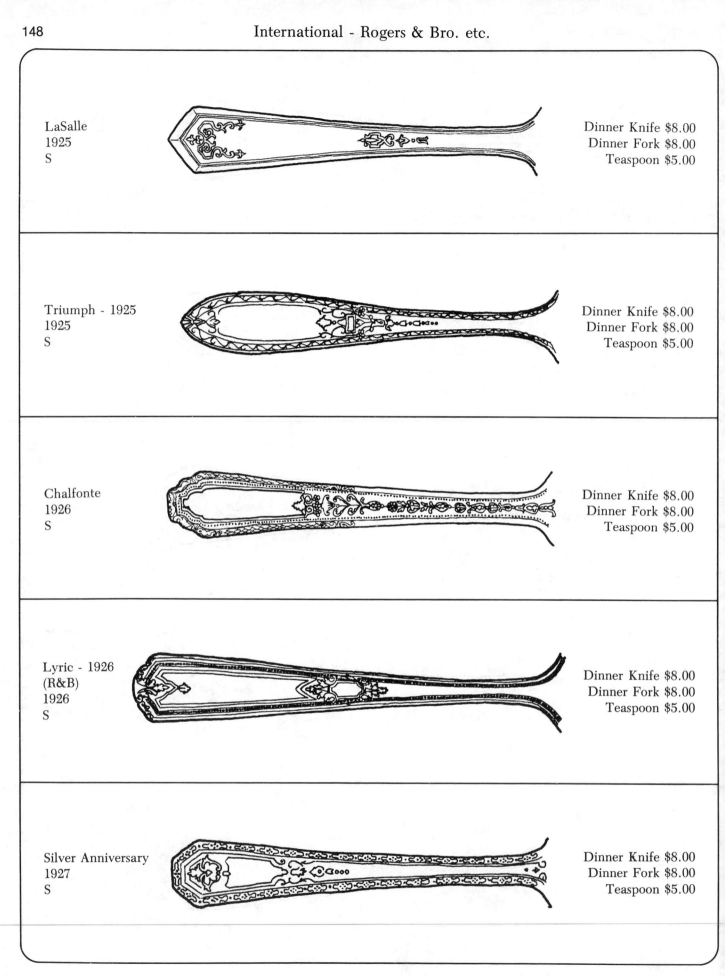

LaSalle
1925
S

Dinner Knife $8.00
Dinner Fork $8.00
Teaspoon $5.00

Triumph - 1925
1925
S

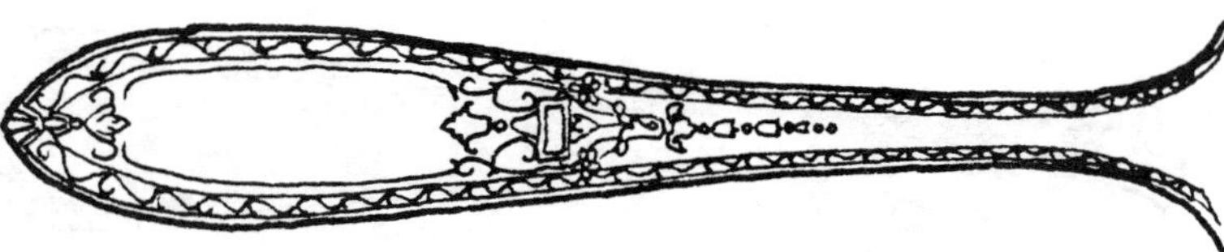

Dinner Knife $8.00
Dinner Fork $8.00
Teaspoon $5.00

Chalfonte
1926
S

Dinner Knife $8.00
Dinner Fork $8.00
Teaspoon $5.00

Lyric - 1926
(R&B)
1926
S

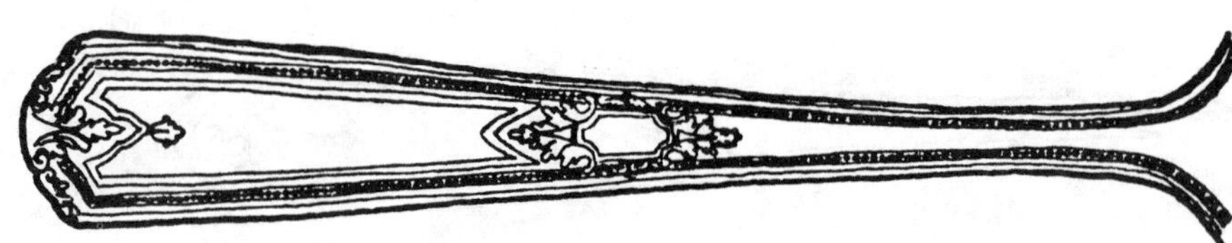

Dinner Knife $8.00
Dinner Fork $8.00
Teaspoon $5.00

Silver Anniversary
1927
S

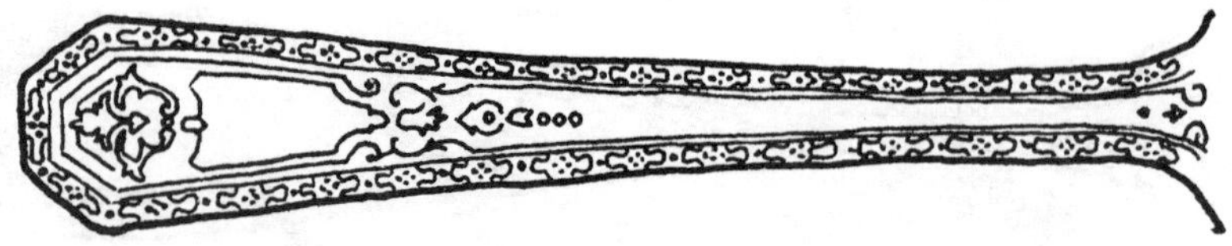

Dinner Knife $8.00
Dinner Fork $8.00
Teaspoon $5.00

Please refer to "How To Use This Book" page 4.

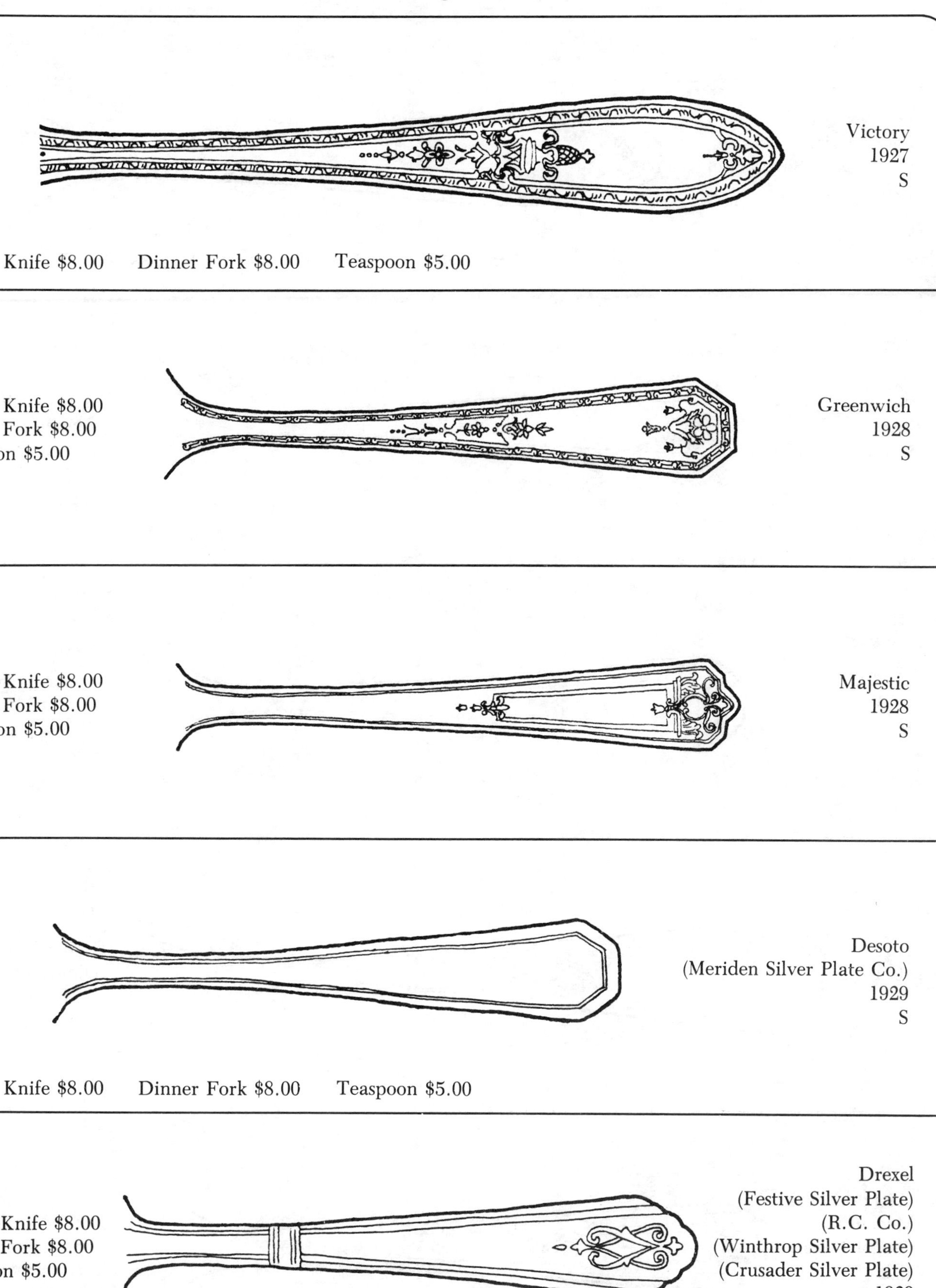

Victory
1927
S

Dinner Knife $8.00 Dinner Fork $8.00 Teaspoon $5.00

Greenwich
1928
S

Dinner Knife $8.00
Dinner Fork $8.00
Teaspoon $5.00

Majestic
1928
S

Dinner Knife $8.00
Dinner Fork $8.00
Teaspoon $5.00

Desoto
(Meriden Silver Plate Co.)
1929
S

Dinner Knife $8.00 Dinner Fork $8.00 Teaspoon $5.00

Drexel
(Festive Silver Plate)
(R.C. Co.)
(Winthrop Silver Plate)
(Crusader Silver Plate)
1929
S

Dinner Knife $8.00
Dinner Fork $8.00
Teaspoon $5.00

Please refer to "How To Use This Book" page 4.

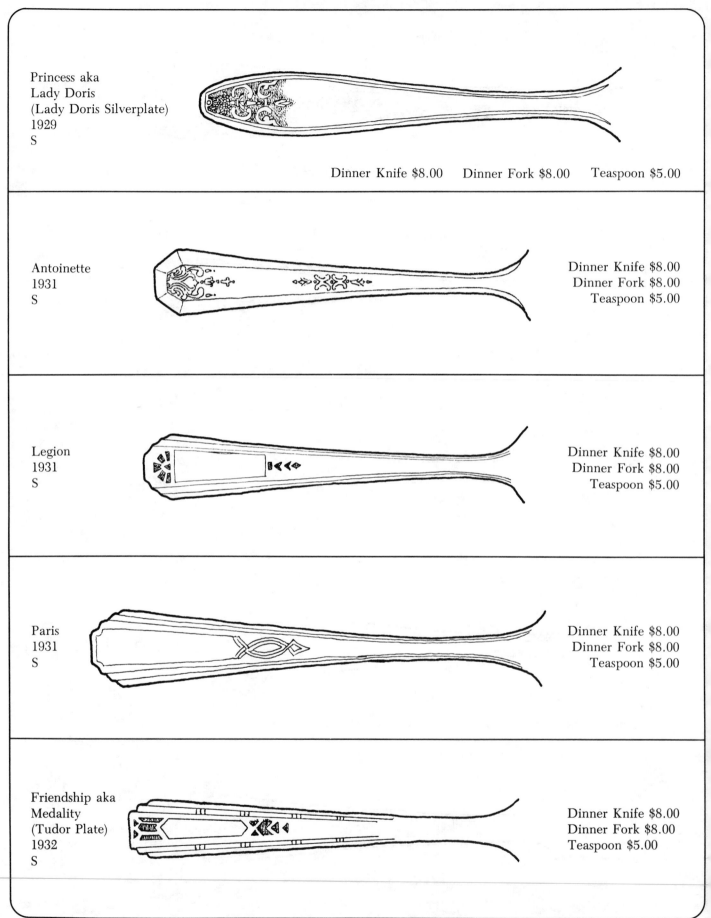

Princess aka
Lady Doris
(Lady Doris Silverplate)
1929
S

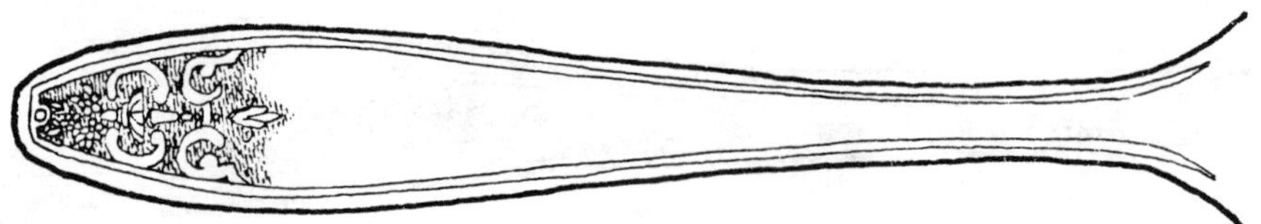

Dinner Knife $8.00 Dinner Fork $8.00 Teaspoon $5.00

Antoinette
1931
S

Dinner Knife $8.00
Dinner Fork $8.00
Teaspoon $5.00

Legion
1931
S

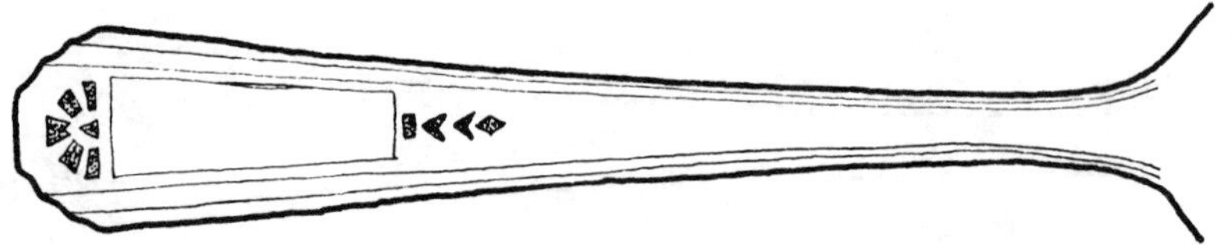

Dinner Knife $8.00
Dinner Fork $8.00
Teaspoon $5.00

Paris
1931
S

Dinner Knife $8.00
Dinner Fork $8.00
Teaspoon $5.00

Friendship aka
Medality
(Tudor Plate)
1932
S

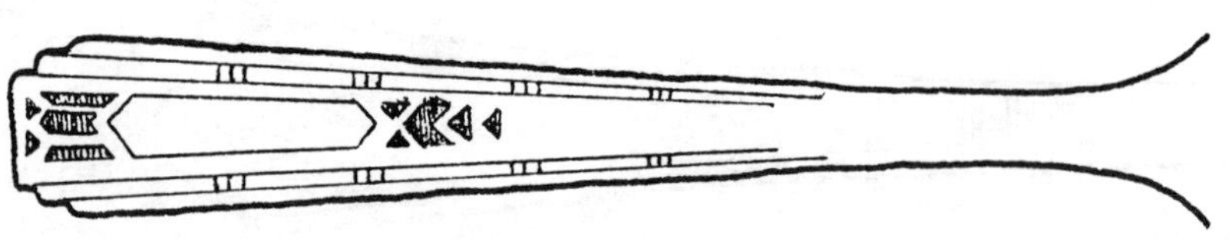

Dinner Knife $8.00
Dinner Fork $8.00
Teaspoon $5.00

Please refer to "How To Use This Book" page 4.

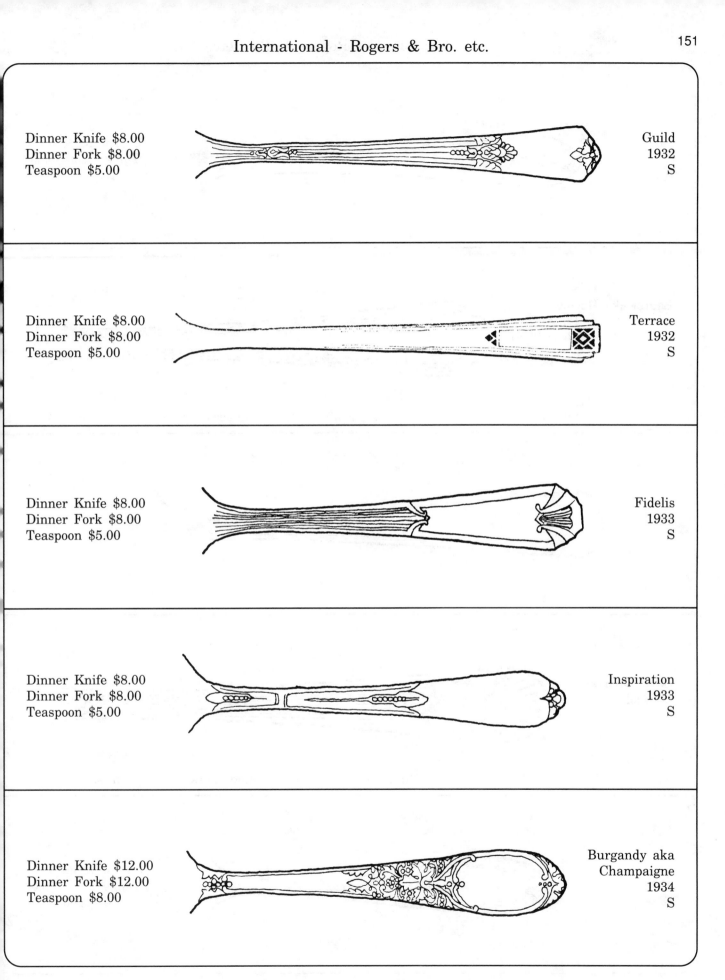

Dinner Knife $8.00
Dinner Fork $8.00
Teaspoon $5.00

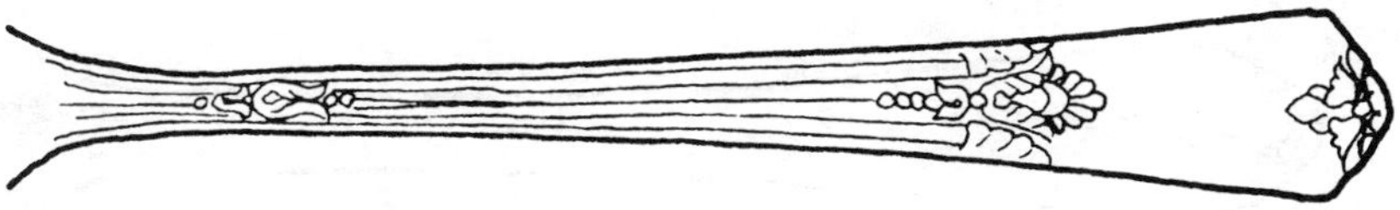

Guild
1932
S

Dinner Knife $8.00
Dinner Fork $8.00
Teaspoon $5.00

Terrace
1932
S

Dinner Knife $8.00
Dinner Fork $8.00
Teaspoon $5.00

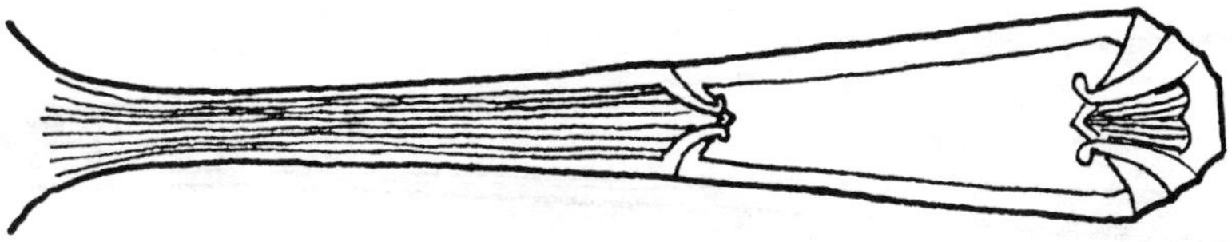

Fidelis
1933
S

Dinner Knife $8.00
Dinner Fork $8.00
Teaspoon $5.00

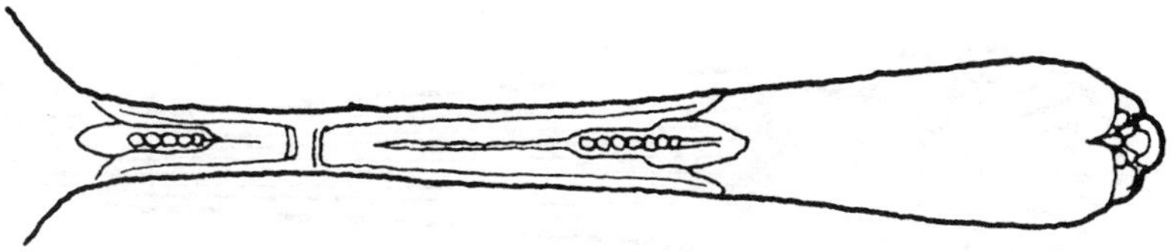

Inspiration
1933
S

Dinner Knife $12.00
Dinner Fork $12.00
Teaspoon $8.00

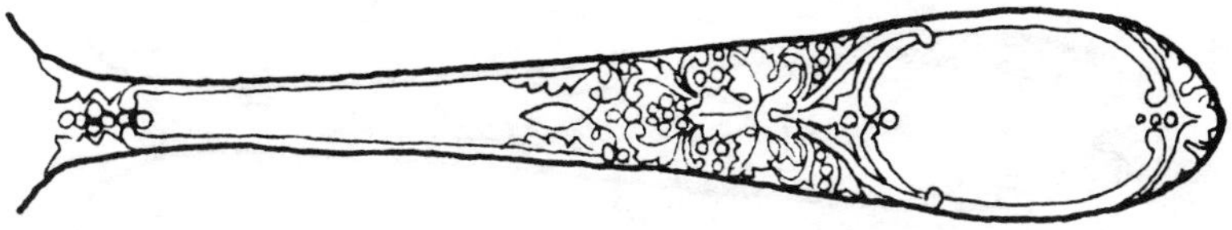

Burgandy aka
Champaigne
1934
S

Please refer to "How To Use This Book" page 4.

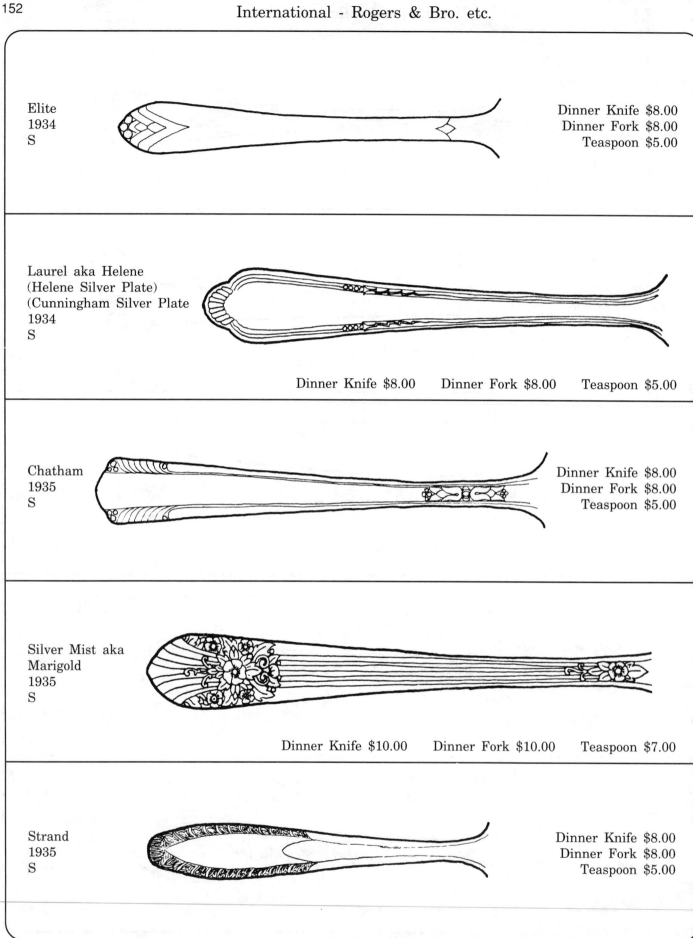

Elite
1934
S

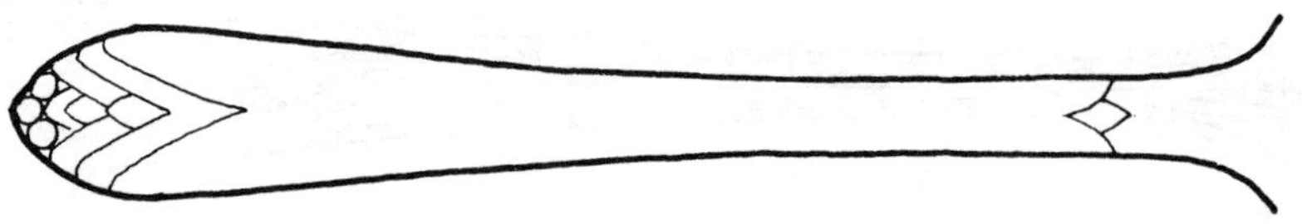

Dinner Knife $8.00
Dinner Fork $8.00
Teaspoon $5.00

Laurel aka Helene
(Helene Silver Plate)
(Cunningham Silver Plate
1934
S

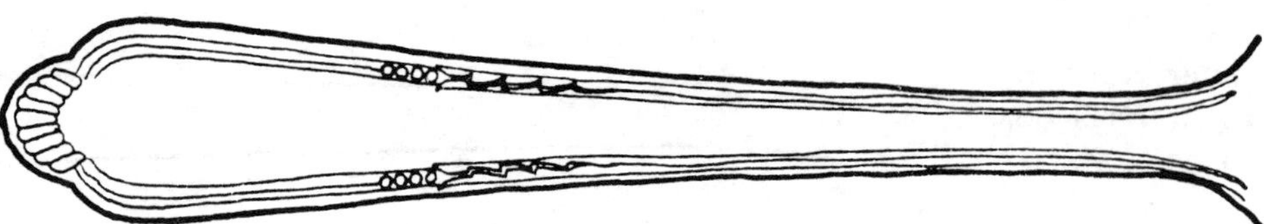

Dinner Knife $8.00 Dinner Fork $8.00 Teaspoon $5.00

Chatham
1935
S

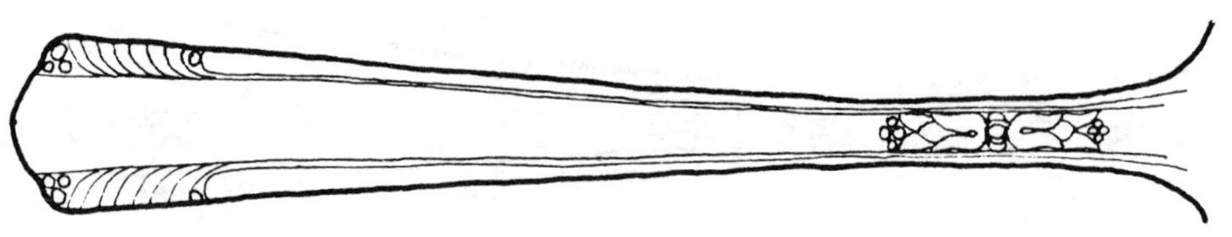

Dinner Knife $8.00
Dinner Fork $8.00
Teaspoon $5.00

Silver Mist aka
Marigold
1935
S

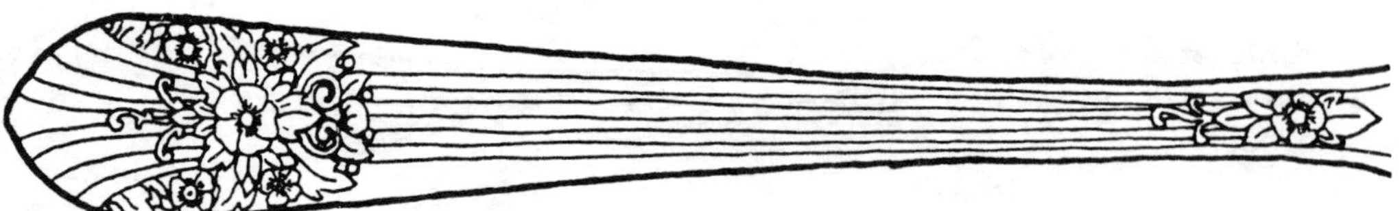

Dinner Knife $10.00 Dinner Fork $10.00 Teaspoon $7.00

Strand
1935
S

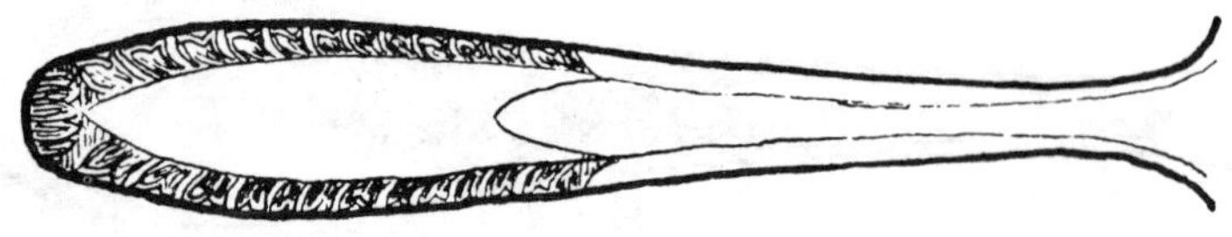

Dinner Knife $8.00
Dinner Fork $8.00
Teaspoon $5.00

Please refer to "How To Use This Book" page 4.

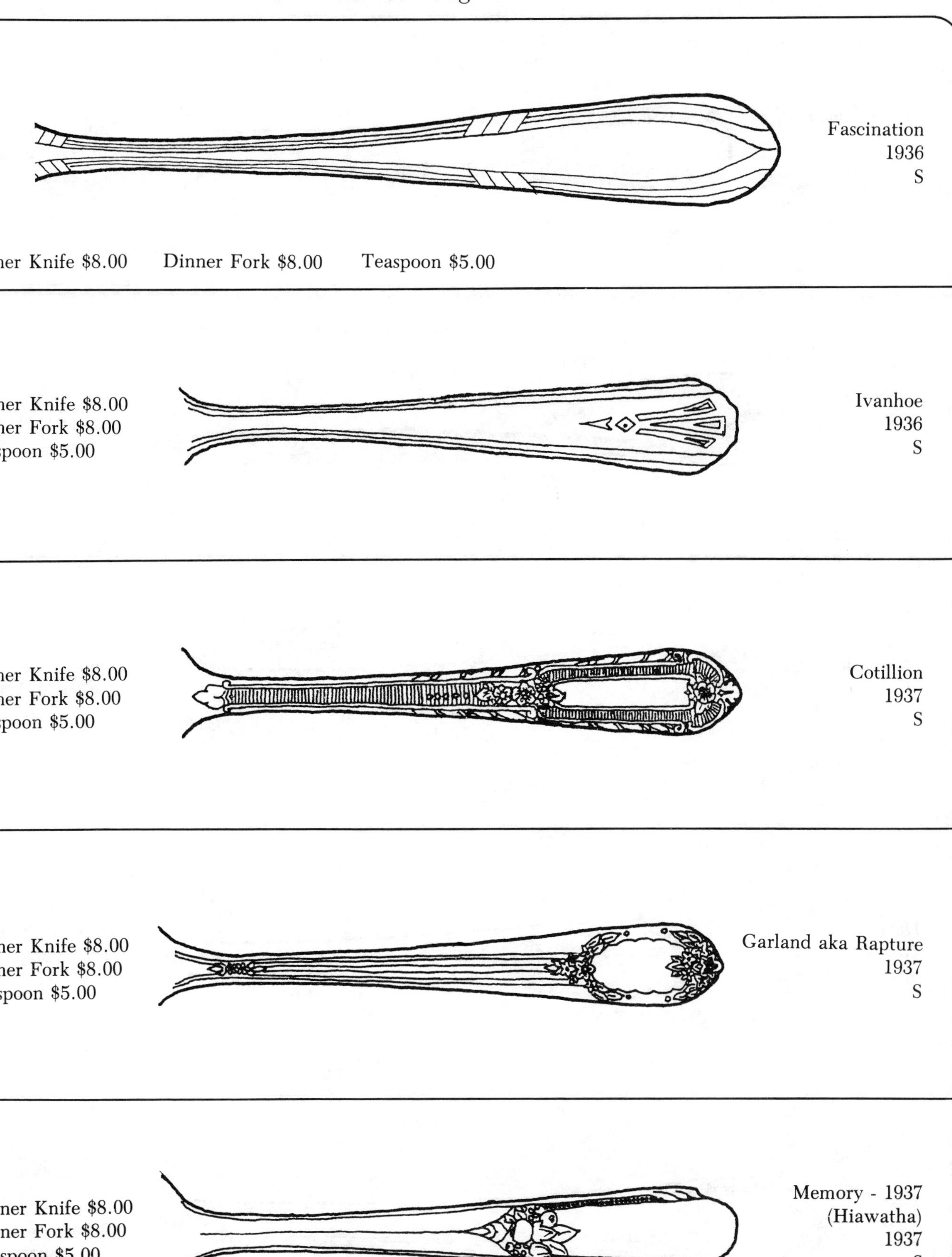

Fascination
1936
S

Dinner Knife $8.00 Dinner Fork $8.00 Teaspoon $5.00

Ivanhoe
1936
S

Dinner Knife $8.00
Dinner Fork $8.00
Teaspoon $5.00

Cotillion
1937
S

Dinner Knife $8.00
Dinner Fork $8.00
Teaspoon $5.00

Garland aka Rapture
1937
S

Dinner Knife $8.00
Dinner Fork $8.00
Teaspoon $5.00

Memory - 1937
(Hiawatha)
1937
S

Dinner Knife $8.00
Dinner Fork $8.00
Teaspoon $5.00

Please refer to "How To Use This Book" page 4.

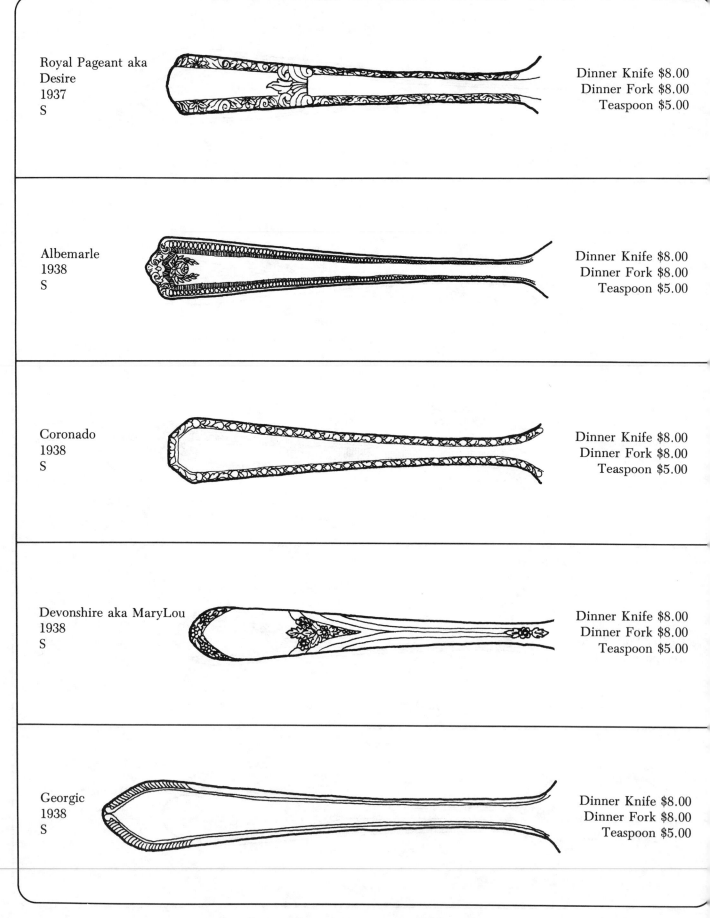

Royal Pageant aka Desire
1937
S

Dinner Knife $8.00
Dinner Fork $8.00
Teaspoon $5.00

Albemarle
1938
S

Dinner Knife $8.00
Dinner Fork $8.00
Teaspoon $5.00

Coronado
1938
S

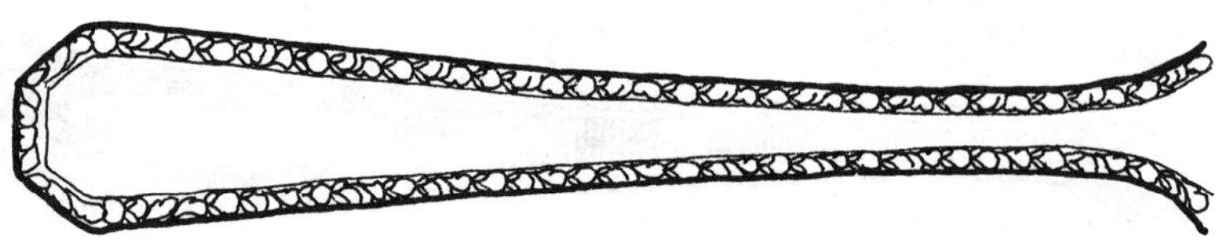

Dinner Knife $8.00
Dinner Fork $8.00
Teaspoon $5.00

Devonshire aka MaryLou
1938
S

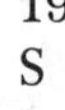

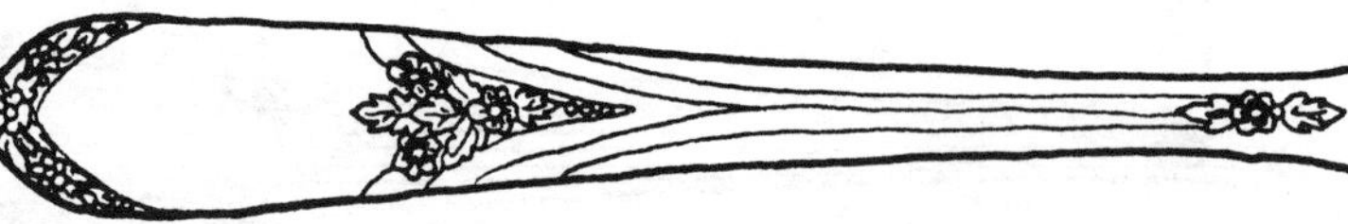

Dinner Knife $8.00
Dinner Fork $8.00
Teaspoon $5.00

Georgic
1938
S

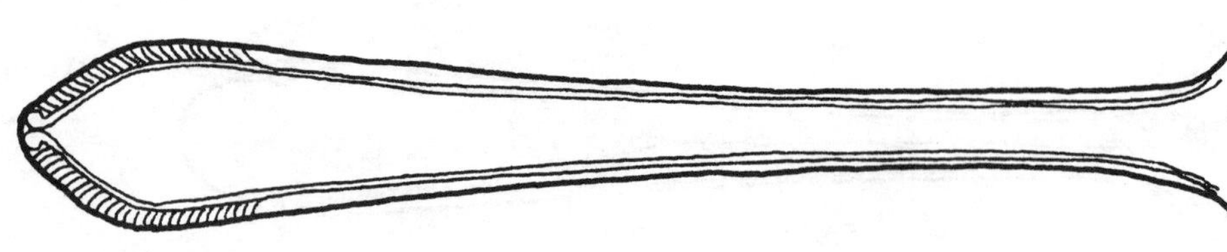

Dinner Knife $8.00
Dinner Fork $8.00
Teaspoon $5.00

Please refer to "How To Use This Book" page 4.

Dinner Knife $8.00
Dinner Fork $8.00
Teaspoon $5.00

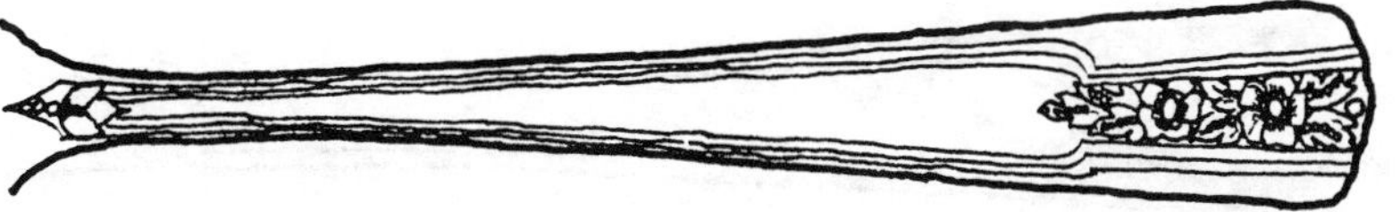

Louisiane
1938
S

Dinner Knife $8.00
Dinner Fork $8.00
Teaspoon $5.00

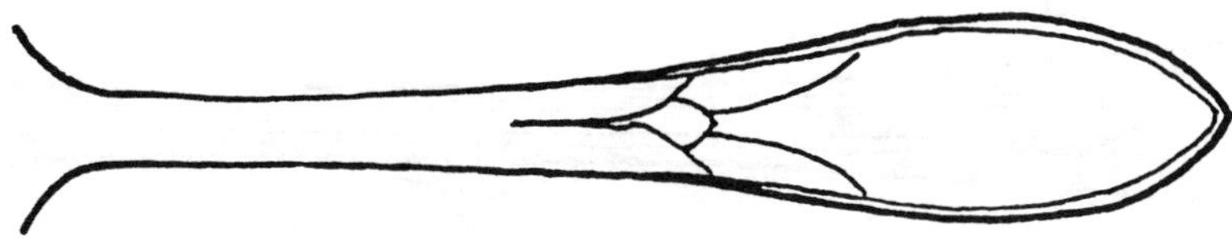

Pickwick
1938
S

Dinner Knife $8.00
Dinner Fork $8.00
Teaspoon $5.00

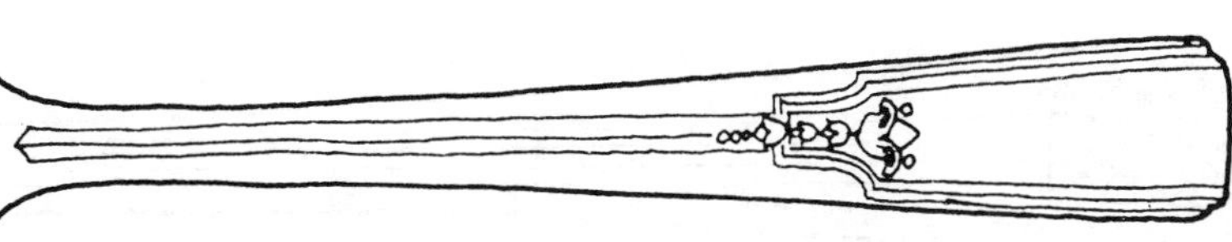

Revelation
(American Silver Co.)
1938
S

Dinner Knife $8.00
Dinner Fork $8.00
Teaspoon $5.00

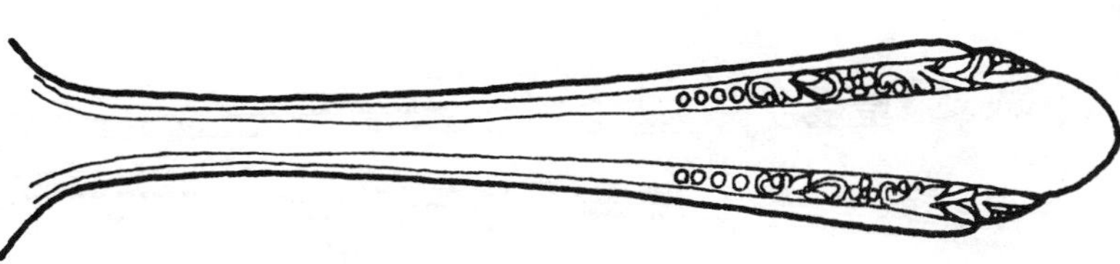

Roberta
(R&B)
(R.C. Co.)
(Manor)
1938
S

Dinner Knife $8.00
Dinner Fork $8.00
Teaspoon $5.00

Rosalind
1938
S

Please refer to "How To Use This Book" page 4.

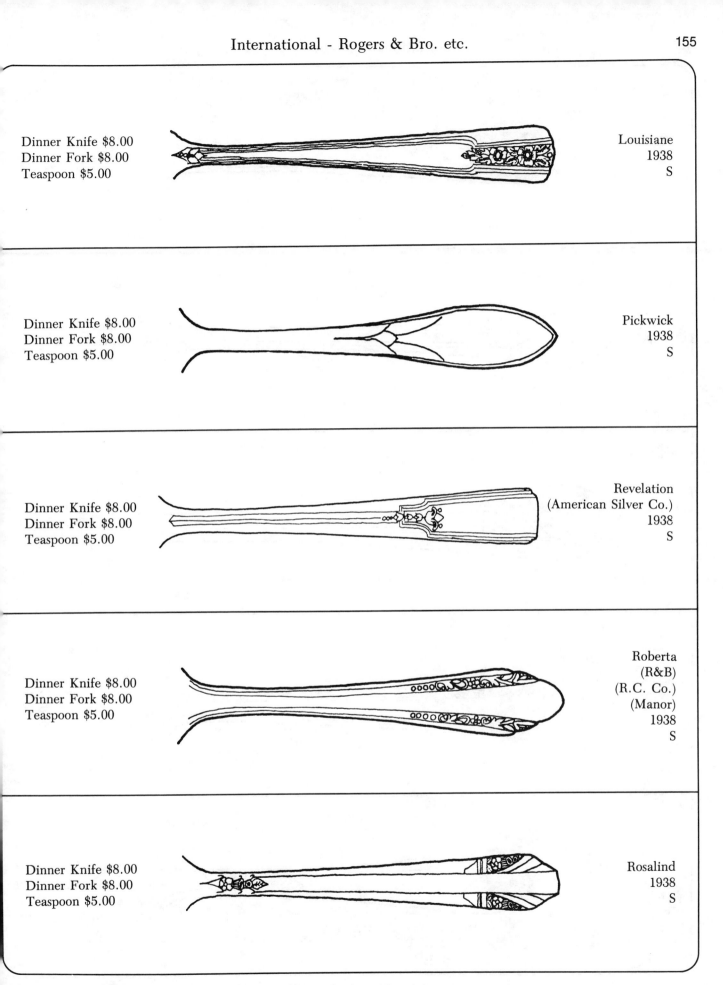

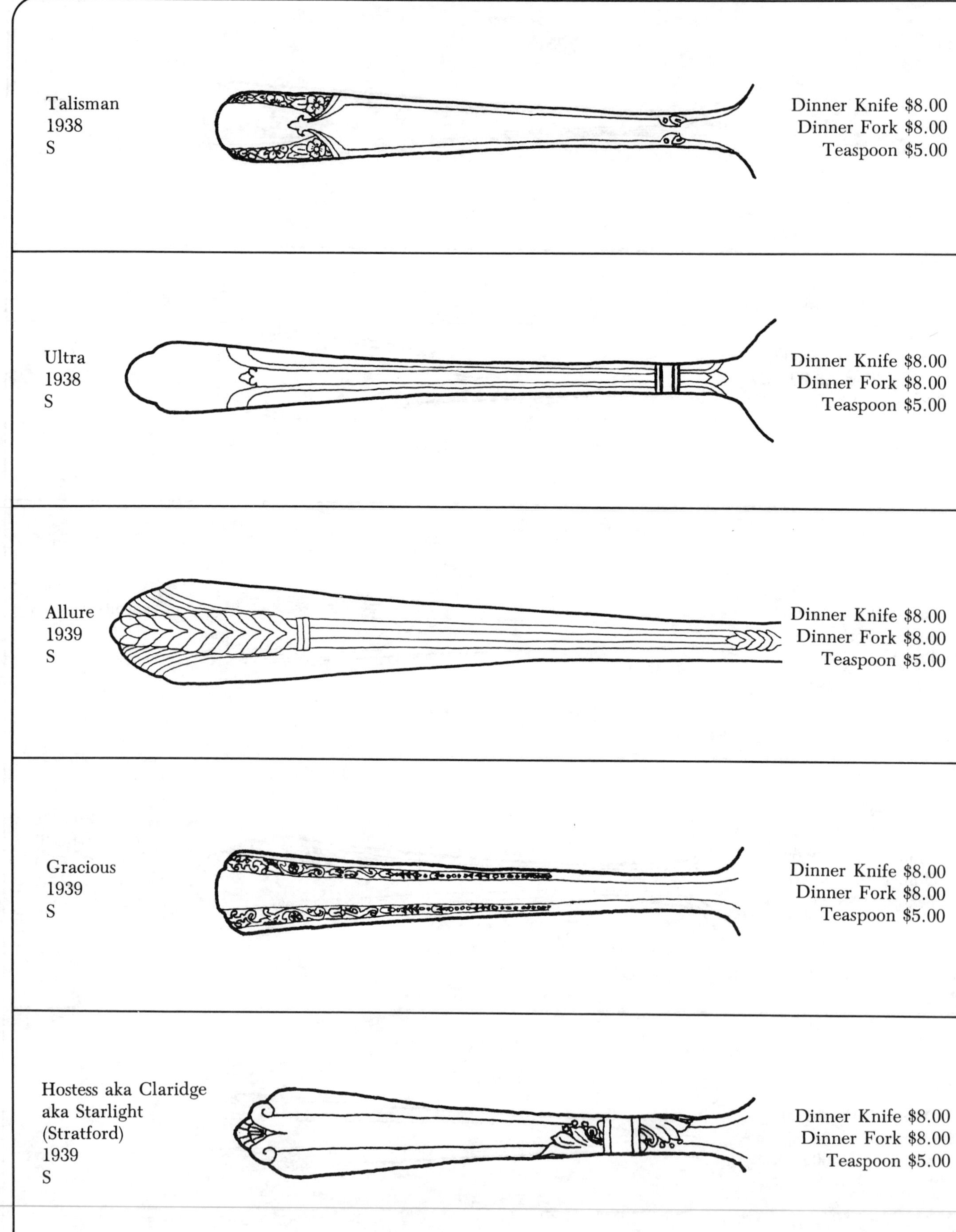

Talisman
1938
S

Dinner Knife $8.00
Dinner Fork $8.00
Teaspoon $5.00

Ultra
1938
S

Dinner Knife $8.00
Dinner Fork $8.00
Teaspoon $5.00

Allure
1939
S

Dinner Knife $8.00
Dinner Fork $8.00
Teaspoon $5.00

Gracious
1939
S

Dinner Knife $8.00
Dinner Fork $8.00
Teaspoon $5.00

Hostess aka Claridge
aka Starlight
(Stratford)
1939
S

Dinner Knife $8.00
Dinner Fork $8.00
Teaspoon $5.00

Please refer to "How To Use This Book" page 4.

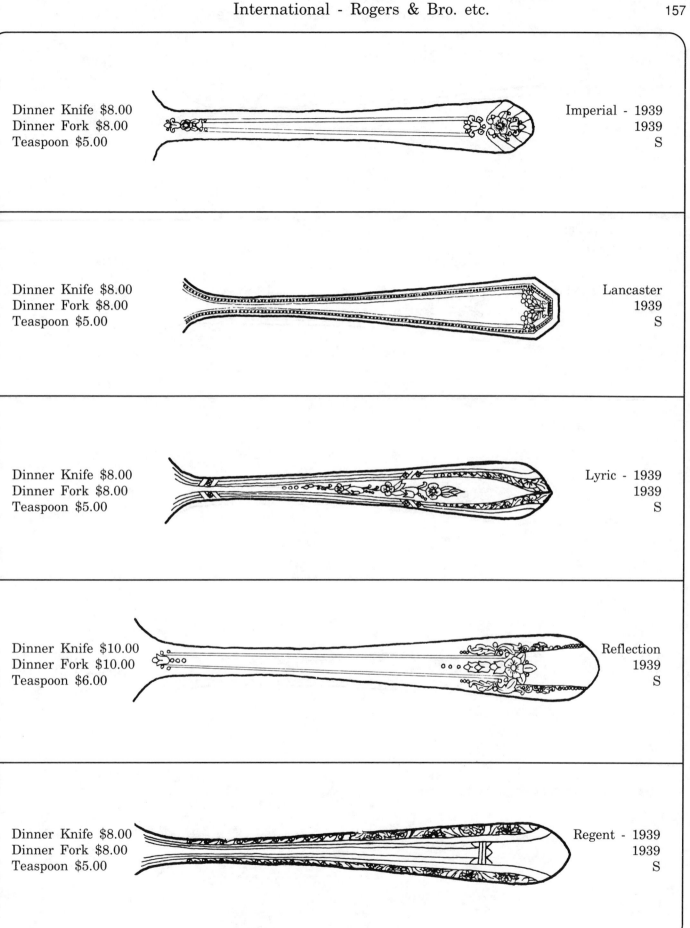

Dinner Knife $8.00
Dinner Fork $8.00
Teaspoon $5.00

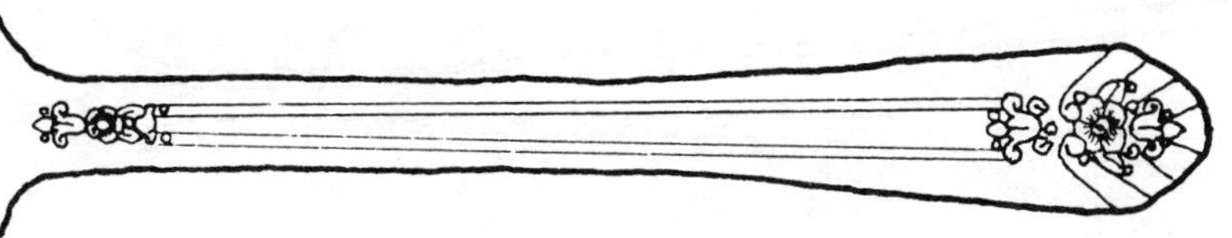

Imperial - 1939
1939
S

Dinner Knife $8.00
Dinner Fork $8.00
Teaspoon $5.00

Lancaster
1939
S

Dinner Knife $8.00
Dinner Fork $8.00
Teaspoon $5.00

Lyric - 1939
1939
S

Dinner Knife $10.00
Dinner Fork $10.00
Teaspoon $6.00

Reflection
1939
S

Dinner Knife $8.00
Dinner Fork $8.00
Teaspoon $5.00

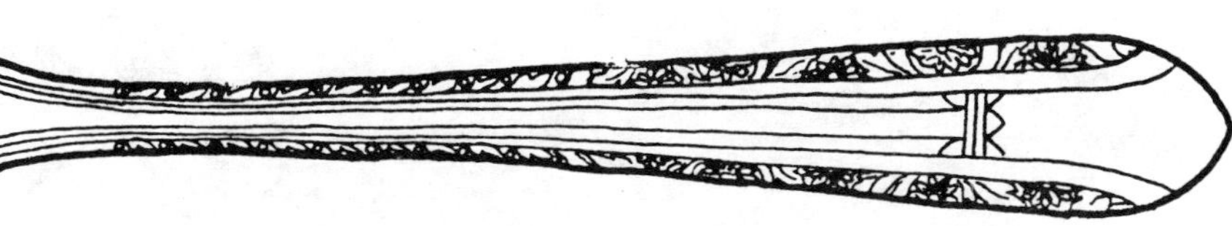

Regent - 1939
1939
S

Please refer to "How To Use This Book" page 4.

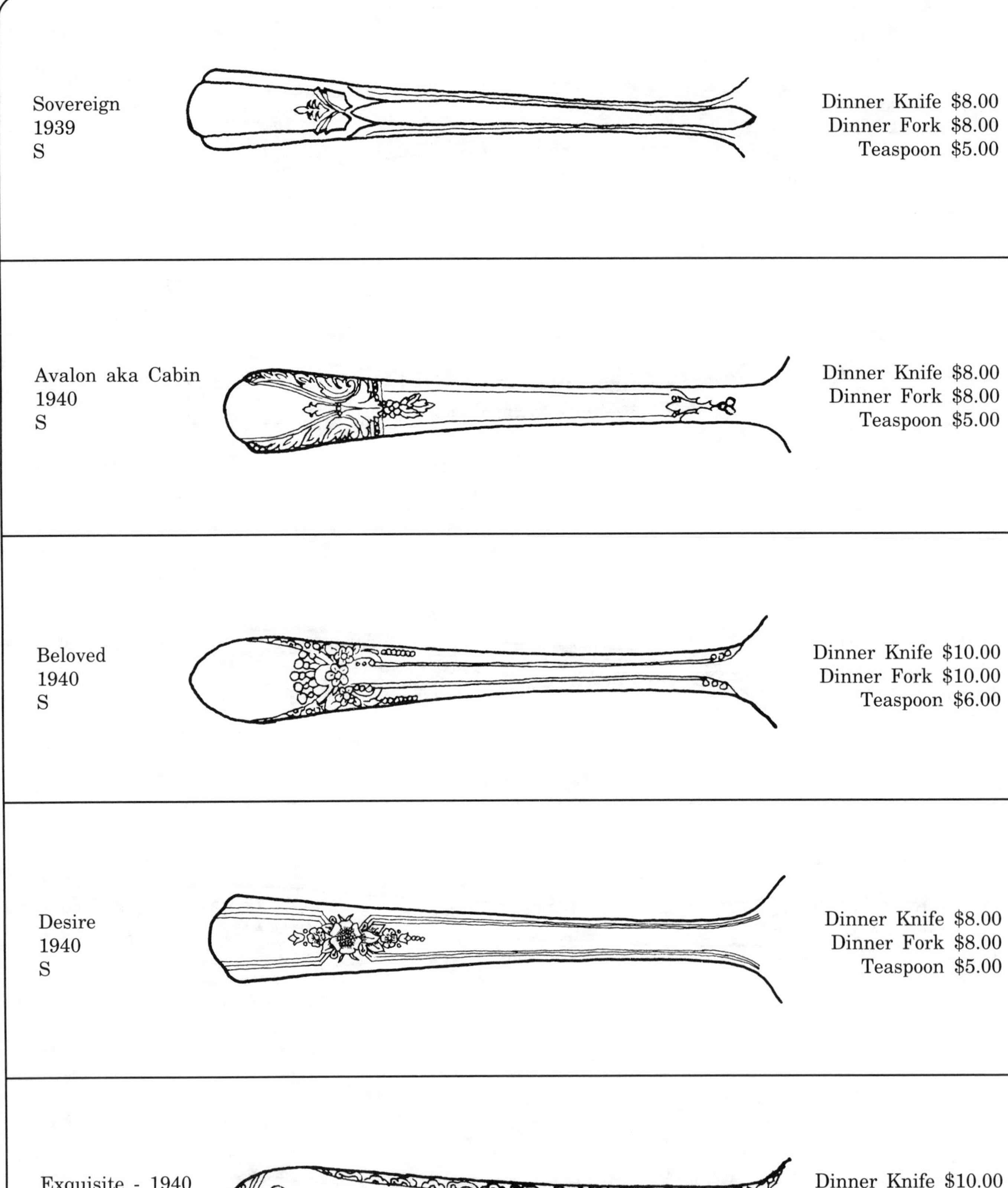

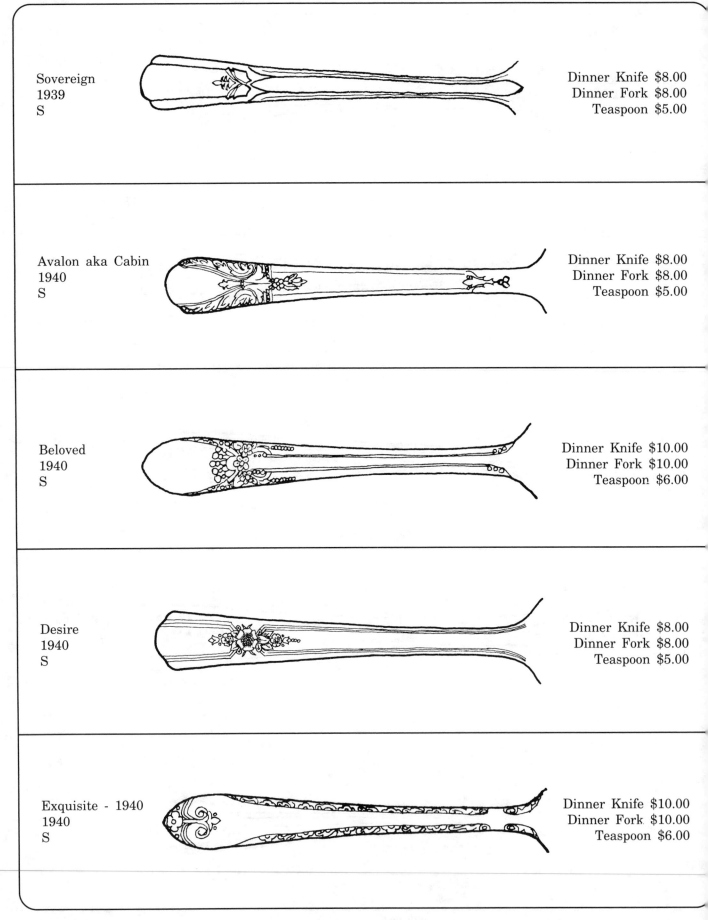

Sovereign
1939
S

Dinner Knife $8.00
Dinner Fork $8.00
Teaspoon $5.00

Avalon aka Cabin
1940
S

Dinner Knife $8.00
Dinner Fork $8.00
Teaspoon $5.00

Beloved
1940
S

Dinner Knife $10.00
Dinner Fork $10.00
Teaspoon $6.00

Desire
1940
S

Dinner Knife $8.00
Dinner Fork $8.00
Teaspoon $5.00

Exquisite - 1940
1940
S

Dinner Knife $10.00
Dinner Fork $10.00
Teaspoon $6.00

Please refer to "How To Use This Book" page 4.

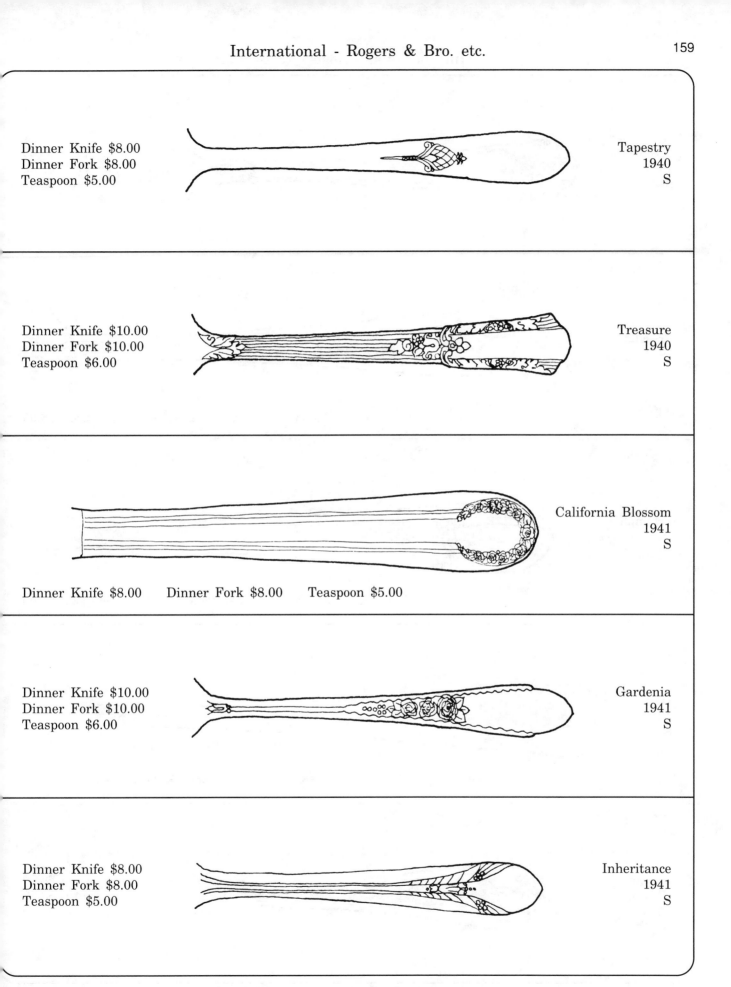

Dinner Knife $8.00
Dinner Fork $8.00
Teaspoon $5.00

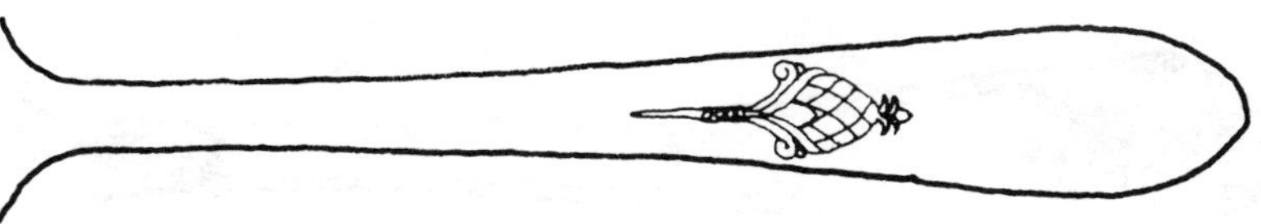

Tapestry
1940
S

Dinner Knife $10.00
Dinner Fork $10.00
Teaspoon $6.00

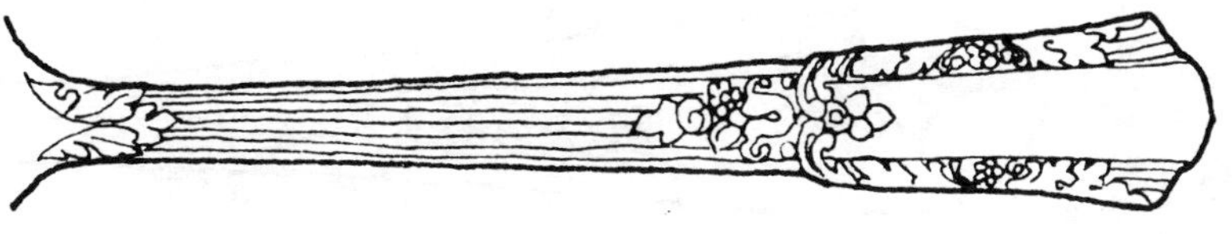

Treasure
1940
S

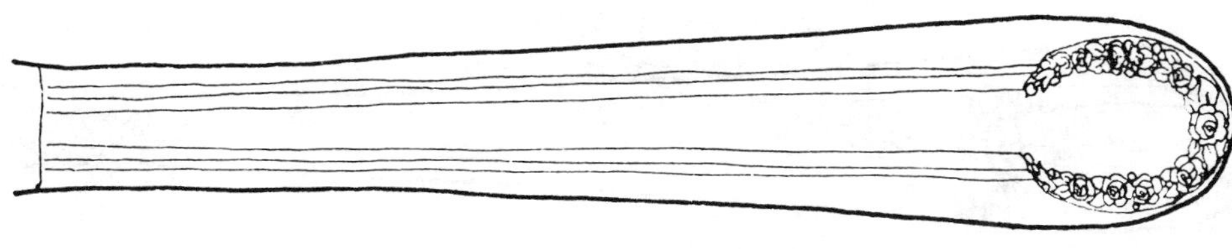

California Blossom
1941
S

Dinner Knife $8.00 Dinner Fork $8.00 Teaspoon $5.00

Dinner Knife $10.00
Dinner Fork $10.00
Teaspoon $6.00

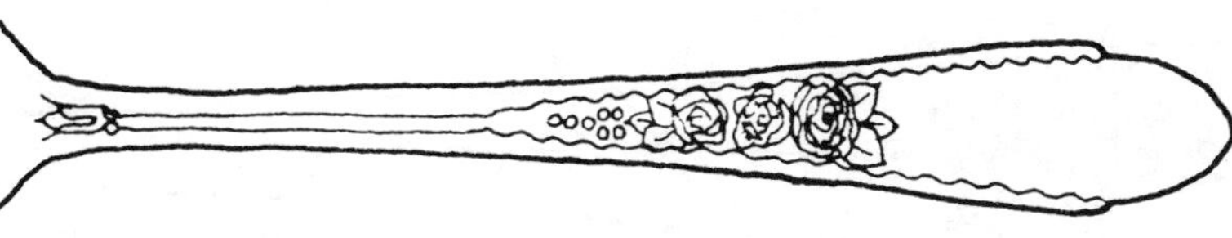

Gardenia
1941
S

Dinner Knife $8.00
Dinner Fork $8.00
Teaspoon $5.00

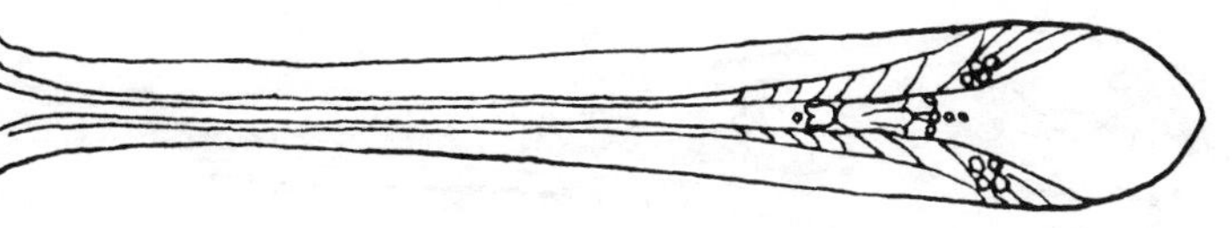

Inheritance
1941
S

Please refer to "How To Use This Book" page 4.

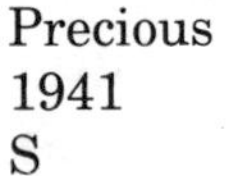

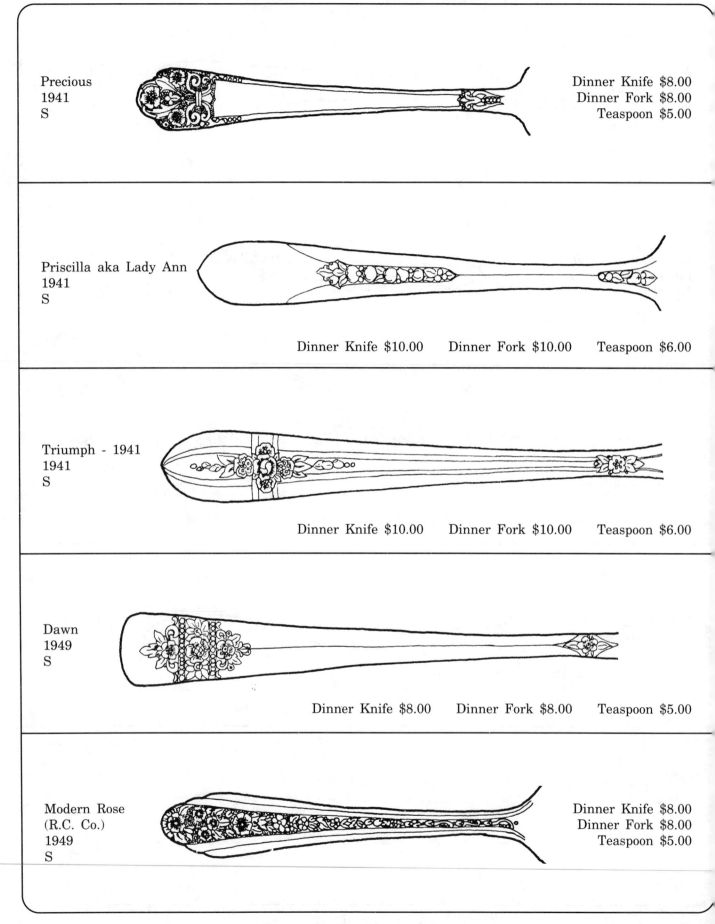

Precious
1941
S

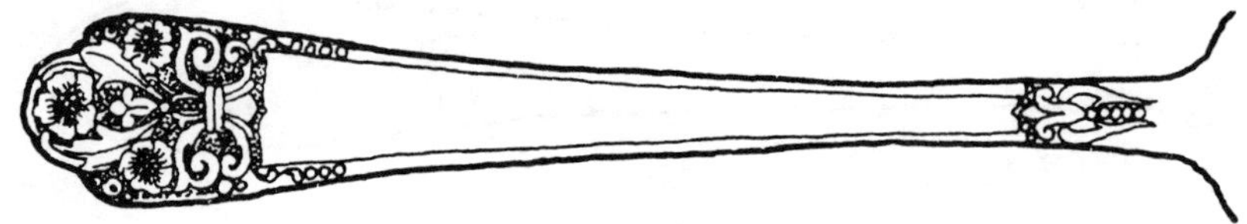

Dinner Knife $8.00
Dinner Fork $8.00
Teaspoon $5.00

Priscilla aka Lady Ann
1941
S

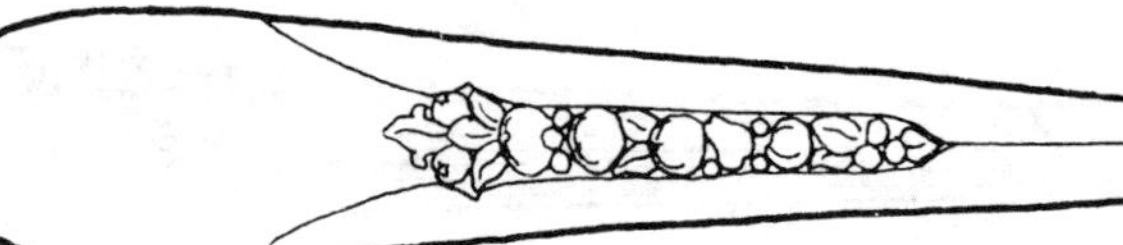

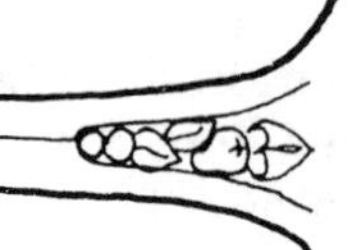

Dinner Knife $10.00 Dinner Fork $10.00 Teaspoon $6.00

Triumph - 1941
1941
S

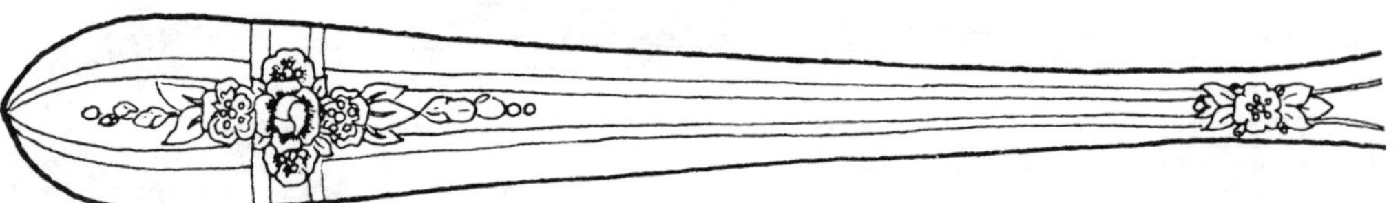

Dinner Knife $10.00 Dinner Fork $10.00 Teaspoon $6.00

Dawn
1949
S

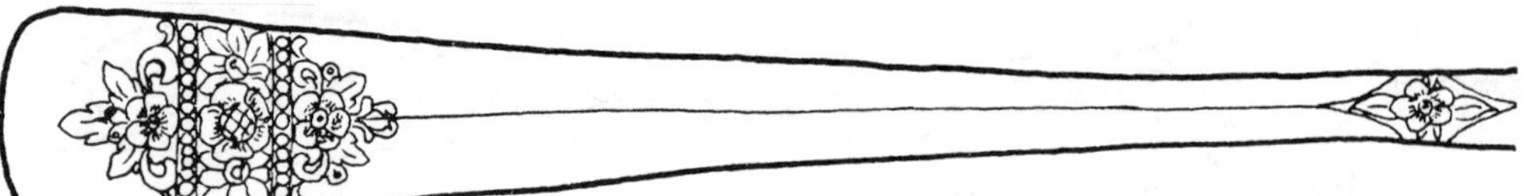

Dinner Knife $8.00 Dinner Fork $8.00 Teaspoon $5.00

Modern Rose
(R.C. Co.)
1949
S

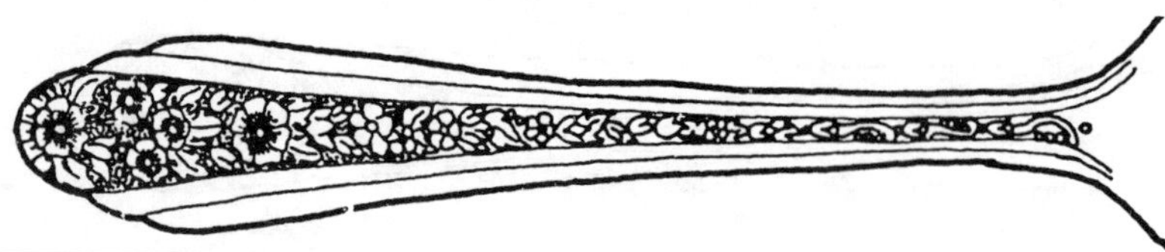

Dinner Knife $8.00
Dinner Fork $8.00
Teaspoon $5.00

Please refer to "How To Use This Book" page 4.

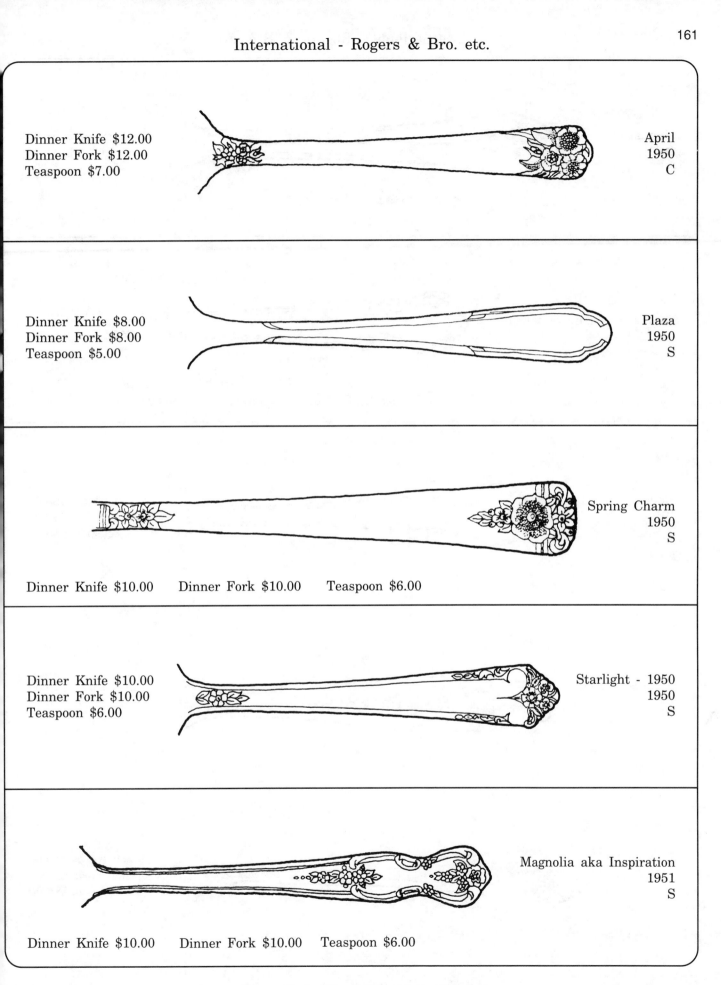

Dinner Knife $12.00
Dinner Fork $12.00
Teaspoon $7.00

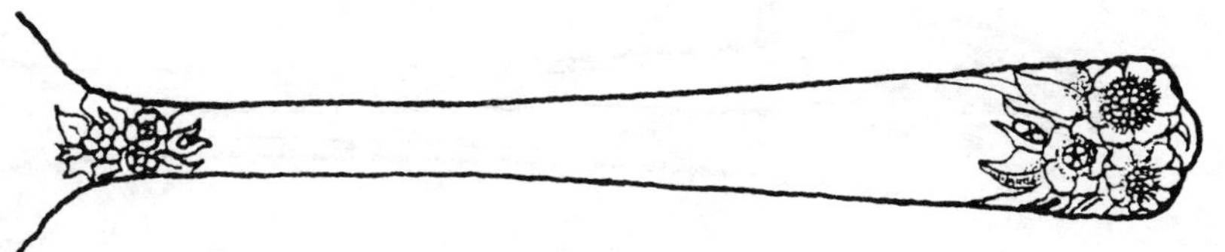

April
1950
C

Dinner Knife $8.00
Dinner Fork $8.00
Teaspoon $5.00

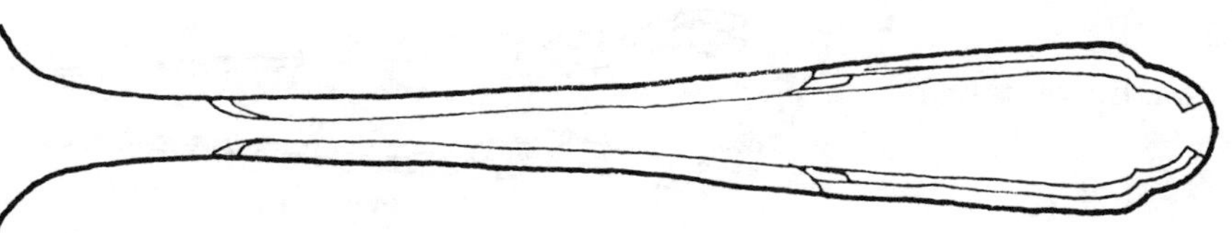

Plaza
1950
S

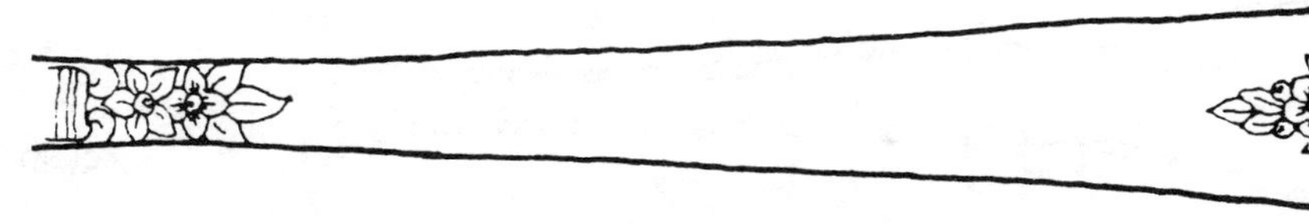

Spring Charm
1950
S

Dinner Knife $10.00 Dinner Fork $10.00 Teaspoon $6.00

Dinner Knife $10.00
Dinner Fork $10.00
Teaspoon $6.00

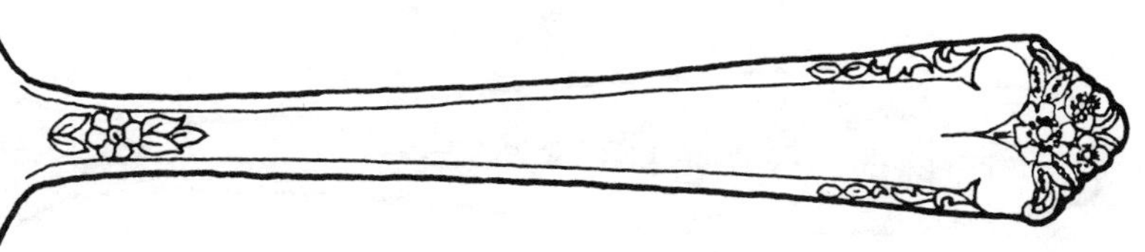

Starlight - 1950
1950
S

Magnolia aka Inspiration
1951
S

Dinner Knife $10.00 Dinner Fork $10.00 Teaspoon $6.00

Please refer to "How To Use This Book" page 4.

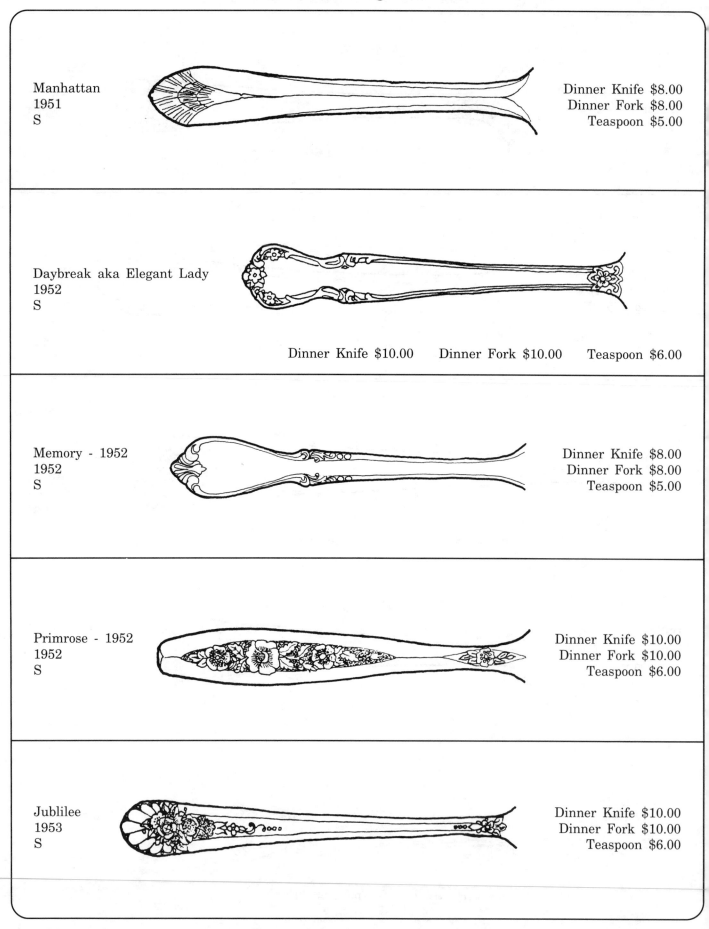

Manhattan
1951
S

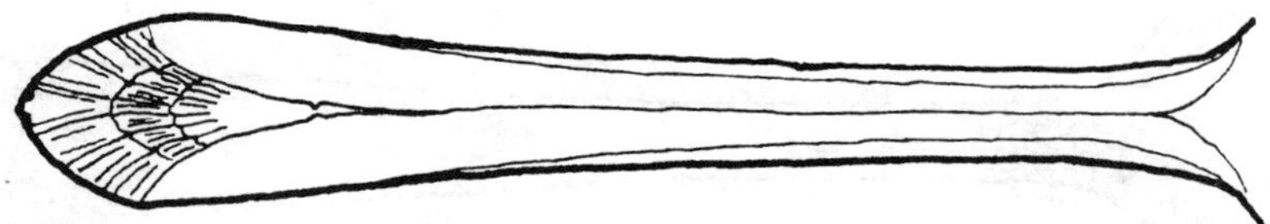

Dinner Knife $8.00
Dinner Fork $8.00
Teaspoon $5.00

Daybreak aka Elegant Lady
1952
S

Dinner Knife $10.00 Dinner Fork $10.00 Teaspoon $6.00

Memory - 1952
1952
S

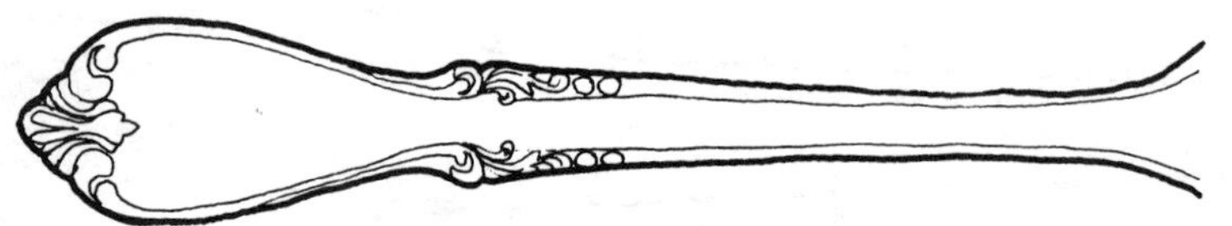

Dinner Knife $8.00
Dinner Fork $8.00
Teaspoon $5.00

Primrose - 1952
1952
S

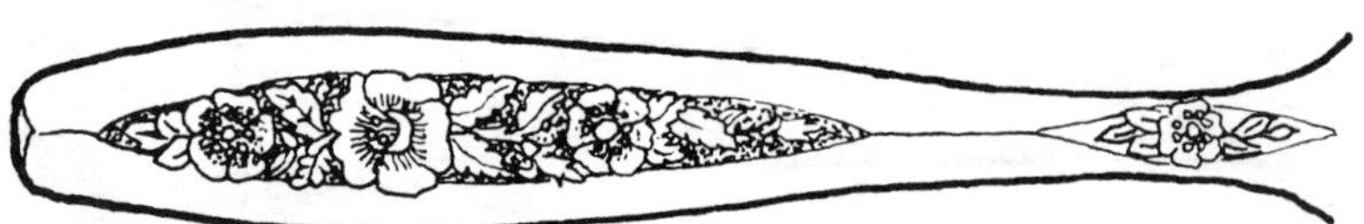

Dinner Knife $10.00
Dinner Fork $10.00
Teaspoon $6.00

Jublilee
1953
S

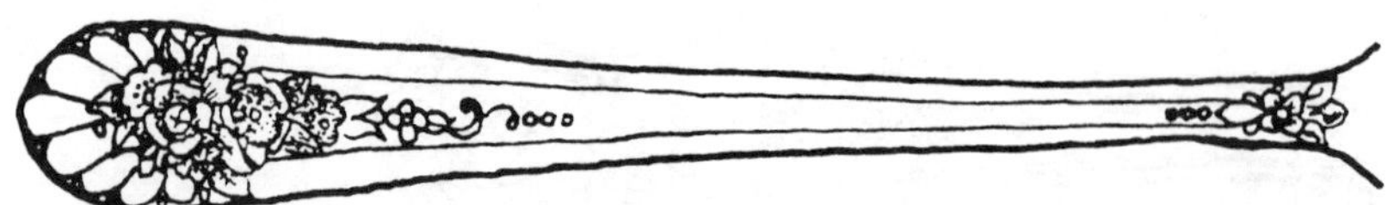

Dinner Knife $10.00
Dinner Fork $10.00
Teaspoon $6.00

Please refer to "How To Use This Book" page 4.

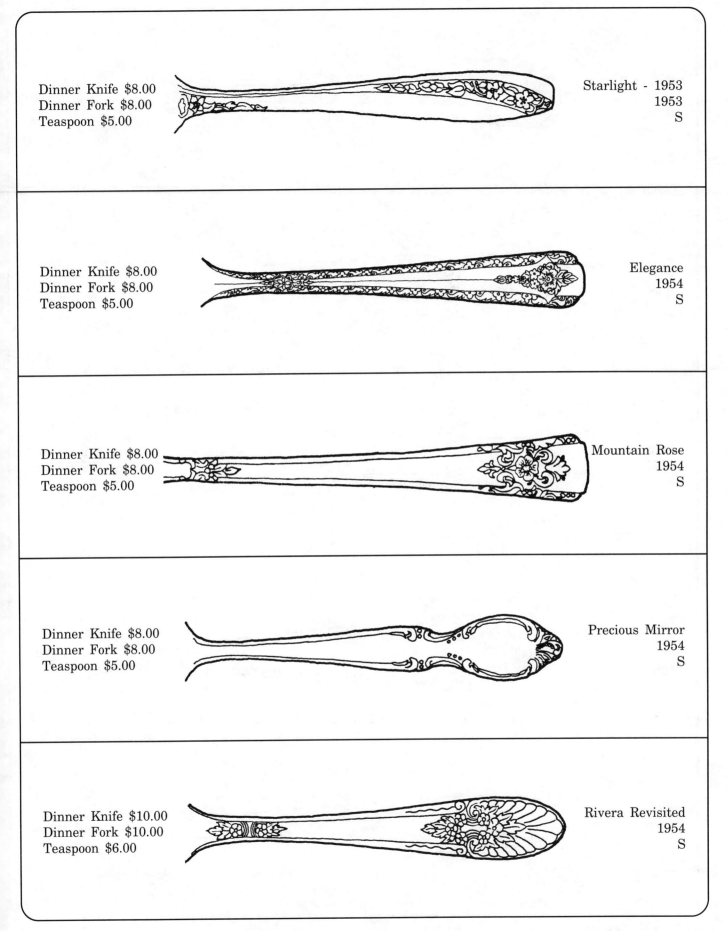

Dinner Knife $8.00
Dinner Fork $8.00
Teaspoon $5.00

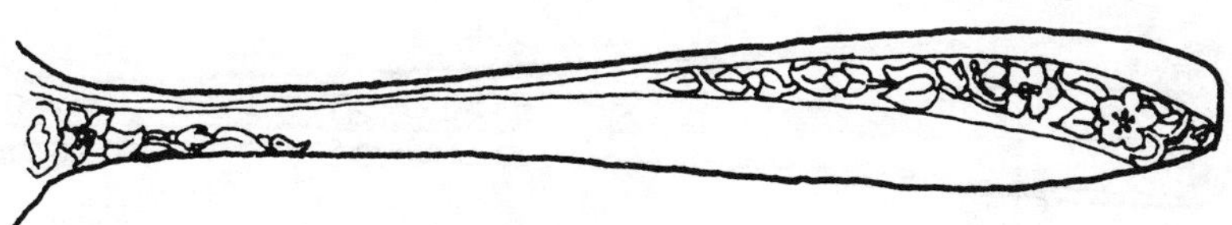

Starlight - 1953
1953
S

Dinner Knife $8.00
Dinner Fork $8.00
Teaspoon $5.00

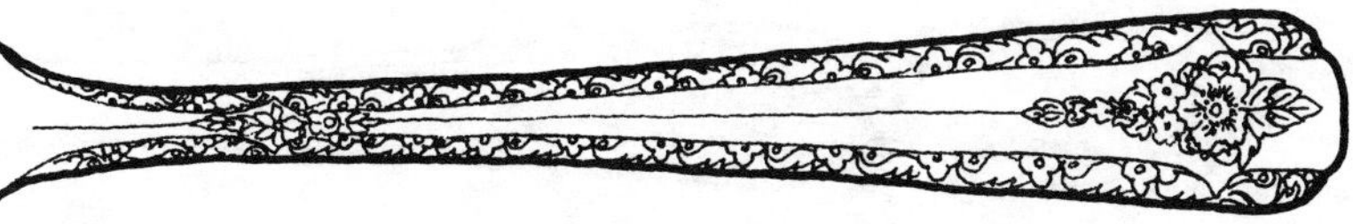

Elegance
1954
S

Dinner Knife $8.00
Dinner Fork $8.00
Teaspoon $5.00

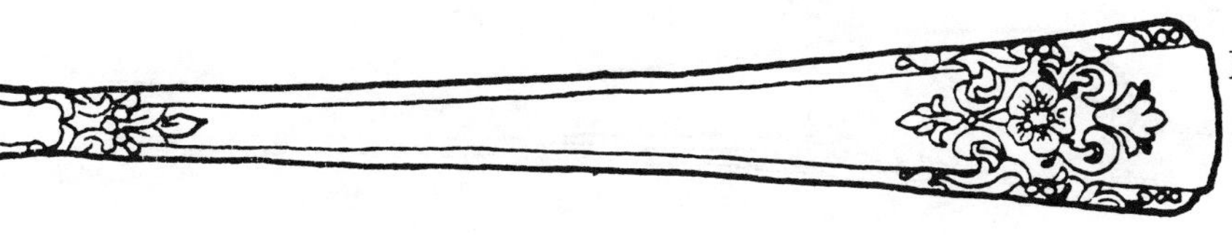

Mountain Rose
1954
S

Dinner Knife $8.00
Dinner Fork $8.00
Teaspoon $5.00

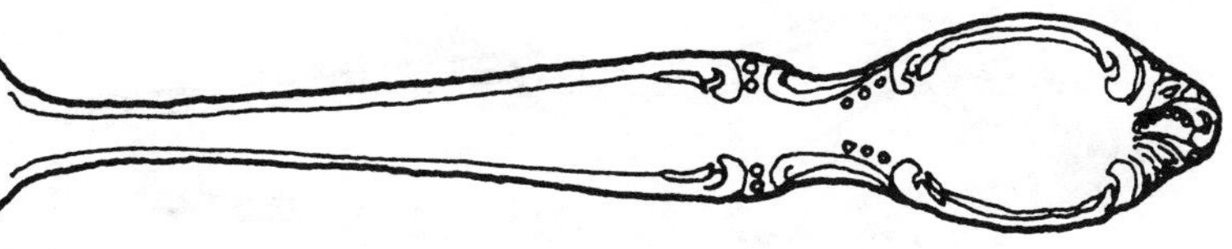

Precious Mirror
1954
S

Dinner Knife $10.00
Dinner Fork $10.00
Teaspoon $6.00

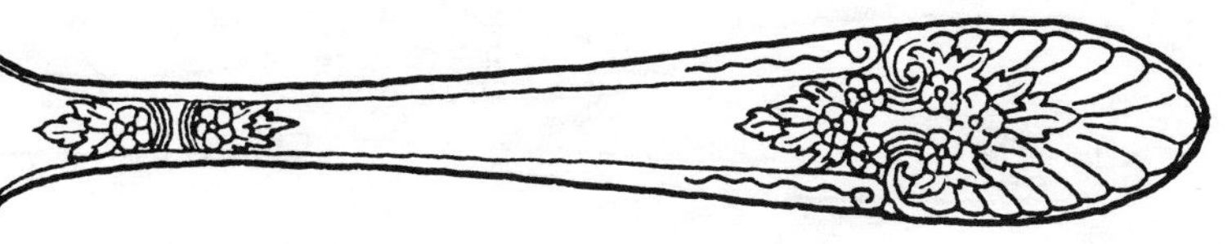

Rivera Revisited
1954
S

Please refer to "How To Use This Book" page 4.

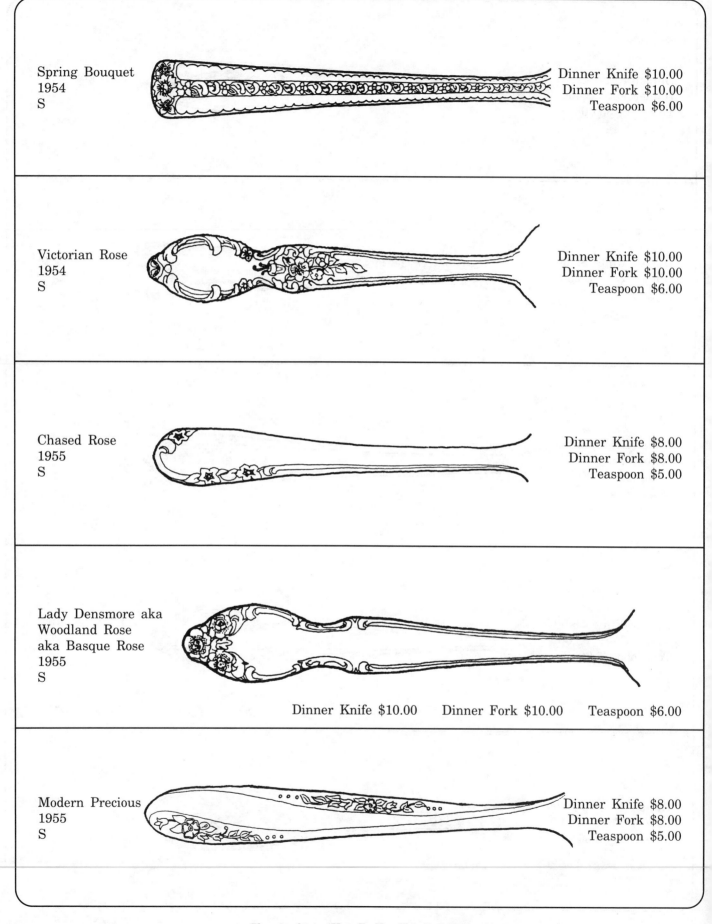

Spring Bouquet
1954
S

Dinner Knife $10.00
Dinner Fork $10.00
Teaspoon $6.00

Victorian Rose
1954
S

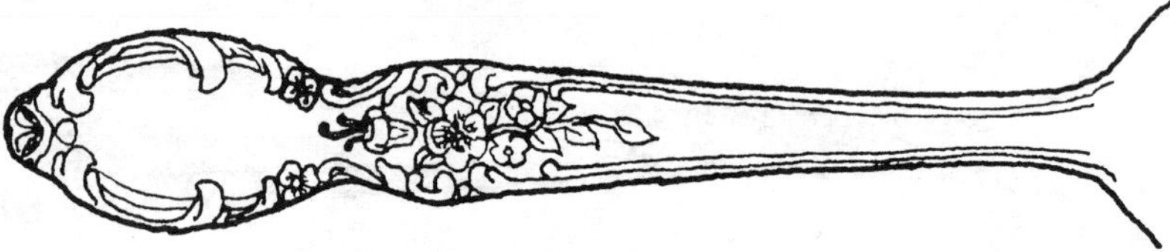

Dinner Knife $10.00
Dinner Fork $10.00
Teaspoon $6.00

Chased Rose
1955
S

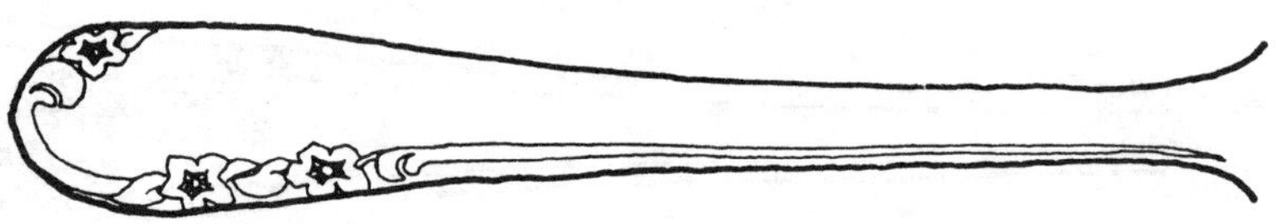

Dinner Knife $8.00
Dinner Fork $8.00
Teaspoon $5.00

Lady Densmore aka
Woodland Rose
aka Basque Rose
1955
S

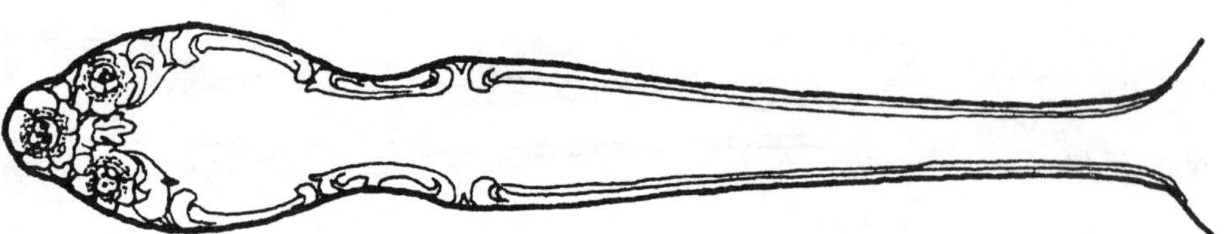

Dinner Knife $10.00 Dinner Fork $10.00 Teaspoon $6.00

Modern Precious
1955
S

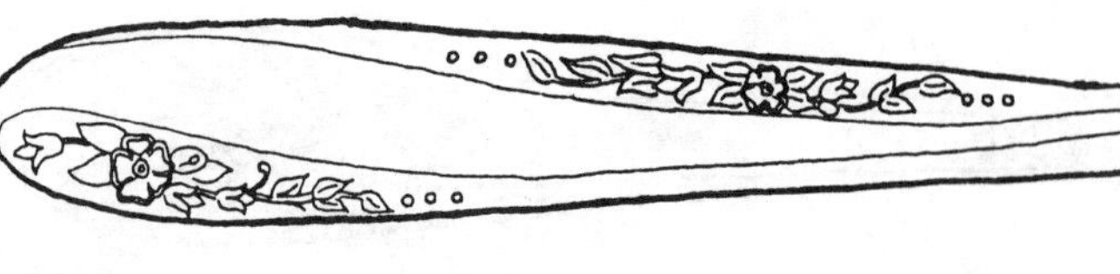

Dinner Knife $8.00
Dinner Fork $8.00
Teaspoon $5.00

Please refer to "How To Use This Book" page 4.

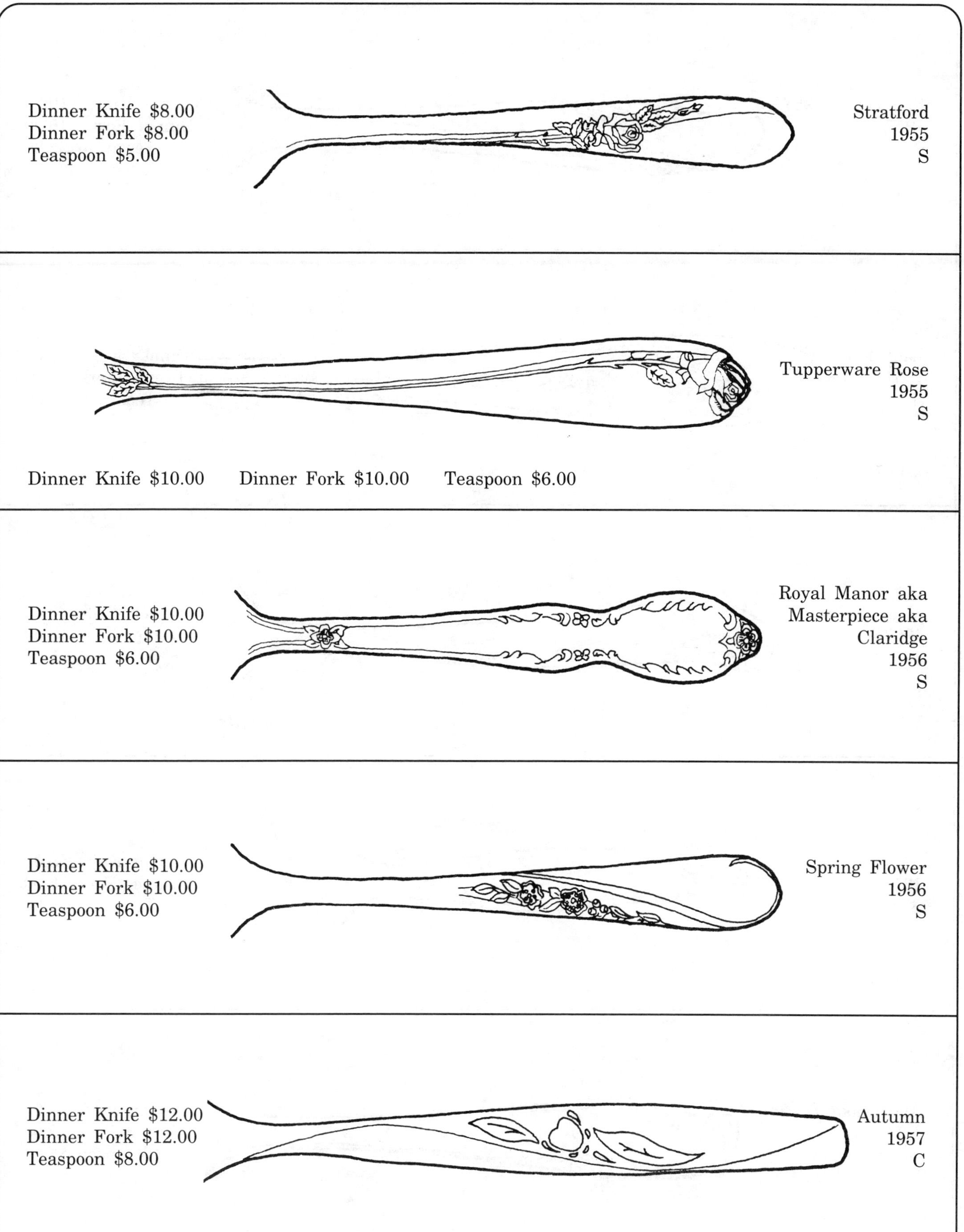

Dinner Knife $8.00
Dinner Fork $8.00
Teaspoon $5.00

Stratford
1955
S

Tupperware Rose
1955
S

Dinner Knife $10.00 Dinner Fork $10.00 Teaspoon $6.00

Dinner Knife $10.00
Dinner Fork $10.00
Teaspoon $6.00

Royal Manor aka
Masterpiece aka
Claridge
1956
S

Dinner Knife $10.00
Dinner Fork $10.00
Teaspoon $6.00

Spring Flower
1956
S

Dinner Knife $12.00
Dinner Fork $12.00
Teaspoon $8.00

Autumn
1957
C

Please refer to "How To Use This Book" page 4.

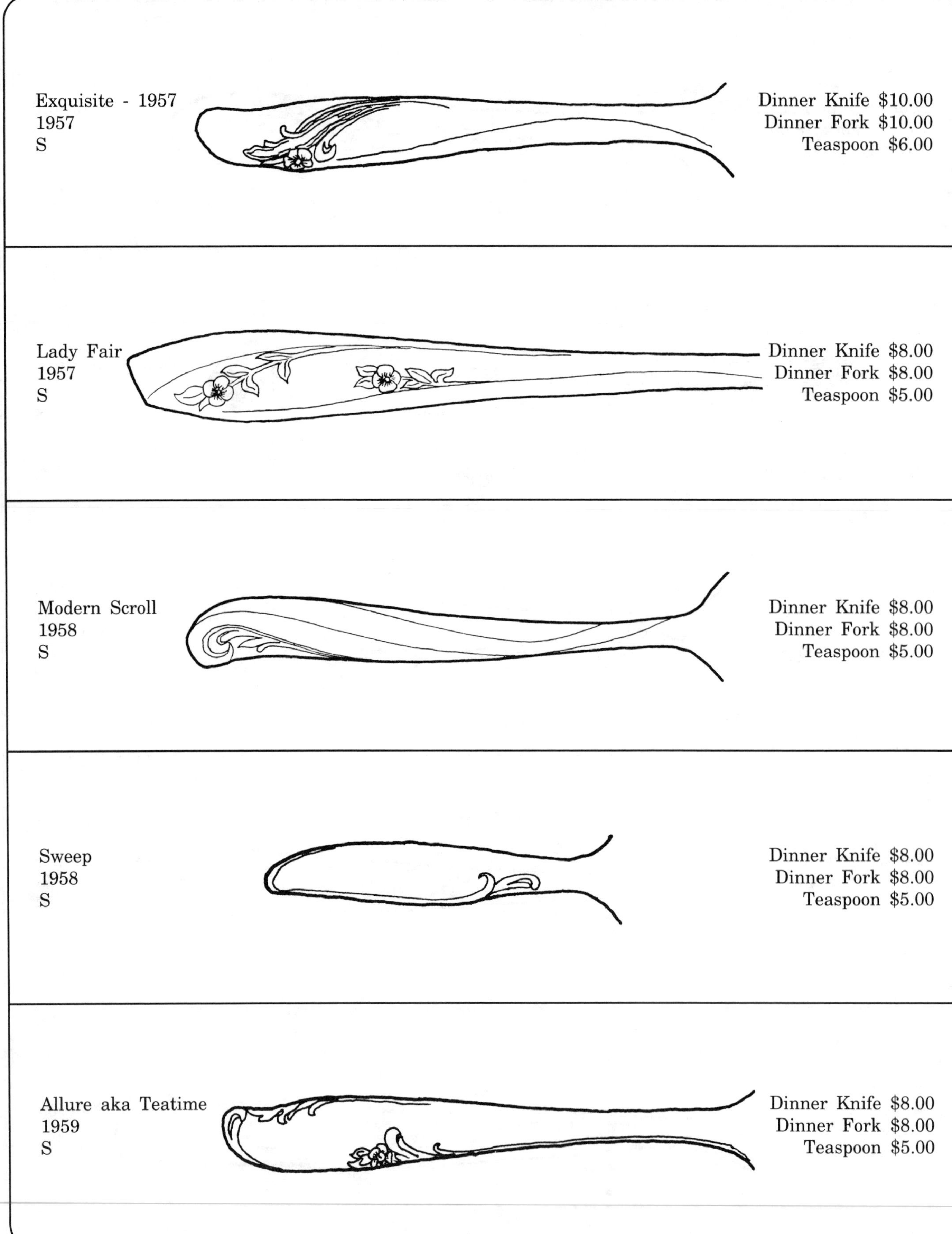

Exquisite - 1957
1957
S

Dinner Knife $10.00
Dinner Fork $10.00
Teaspoon $6.00

Lady Fair
1957
S

Dinner Knife $8.00
Dinner Fork $8.00
Teaspoon $5.00

Modern Scroll
1958
S

Dinner Knife $8.00
Dinner Fork $8.00
Teaspoon $5.00

Sweep
1958
S

Dinner Knife $8.00
Dinner Fork $8.00
Teaspoon $5.00

Allure aka Teatime
1959
S

Dinner Knife $8.00
Dinner Fork $8.00
Teaspoon $5.00

Please refer to "How To Use This Book" page 4.

Dinner Knife $8.00
Dinner Fork $8.00
Teaspoon $5.00

Celebration
1959
S

Dinner Knife $10.00
Dinner Fork $10.00
Teaspoon $6.00

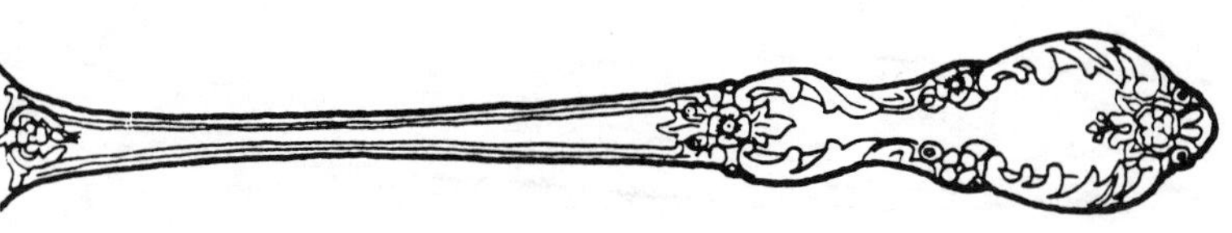

Grand Elegance
aka Southern Manor
1959
S

Dinner Knife $8.00
Dinner Fork $8.00
Teaspoon $5.00

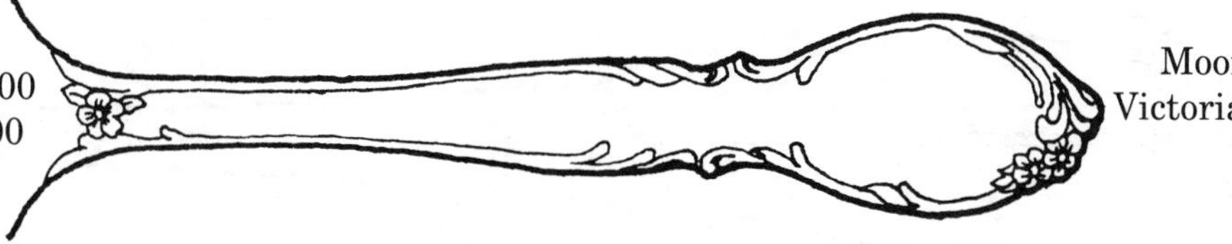

Moonlight aka Royal
Victorian aka Lovelight
1959
S

Dinner Knife $10.00
Dinner Fork $10.00
Teaspoon $6.00

Floral Bouquet
aka Silver Bouquet
1960
S

Not a full line.

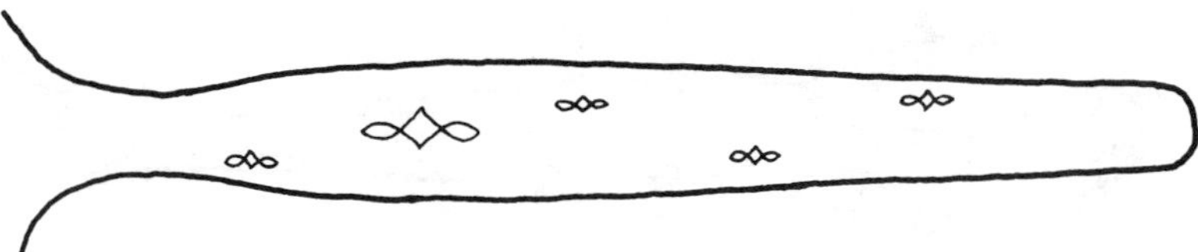

Grapefruit
1960
S

Please refer to "How To Use This Book" page 4.

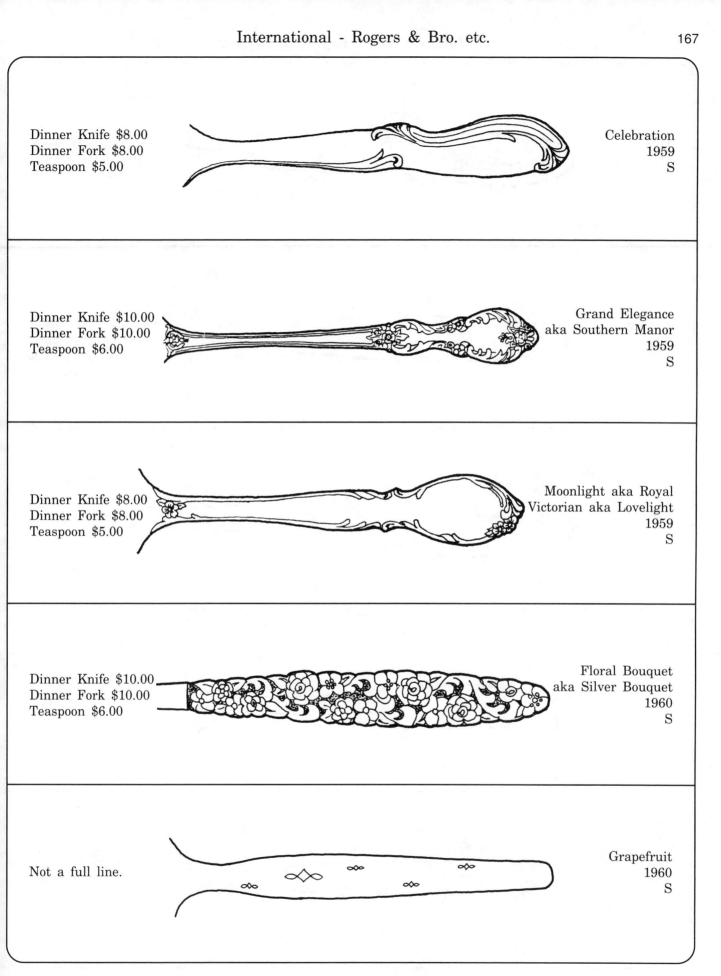

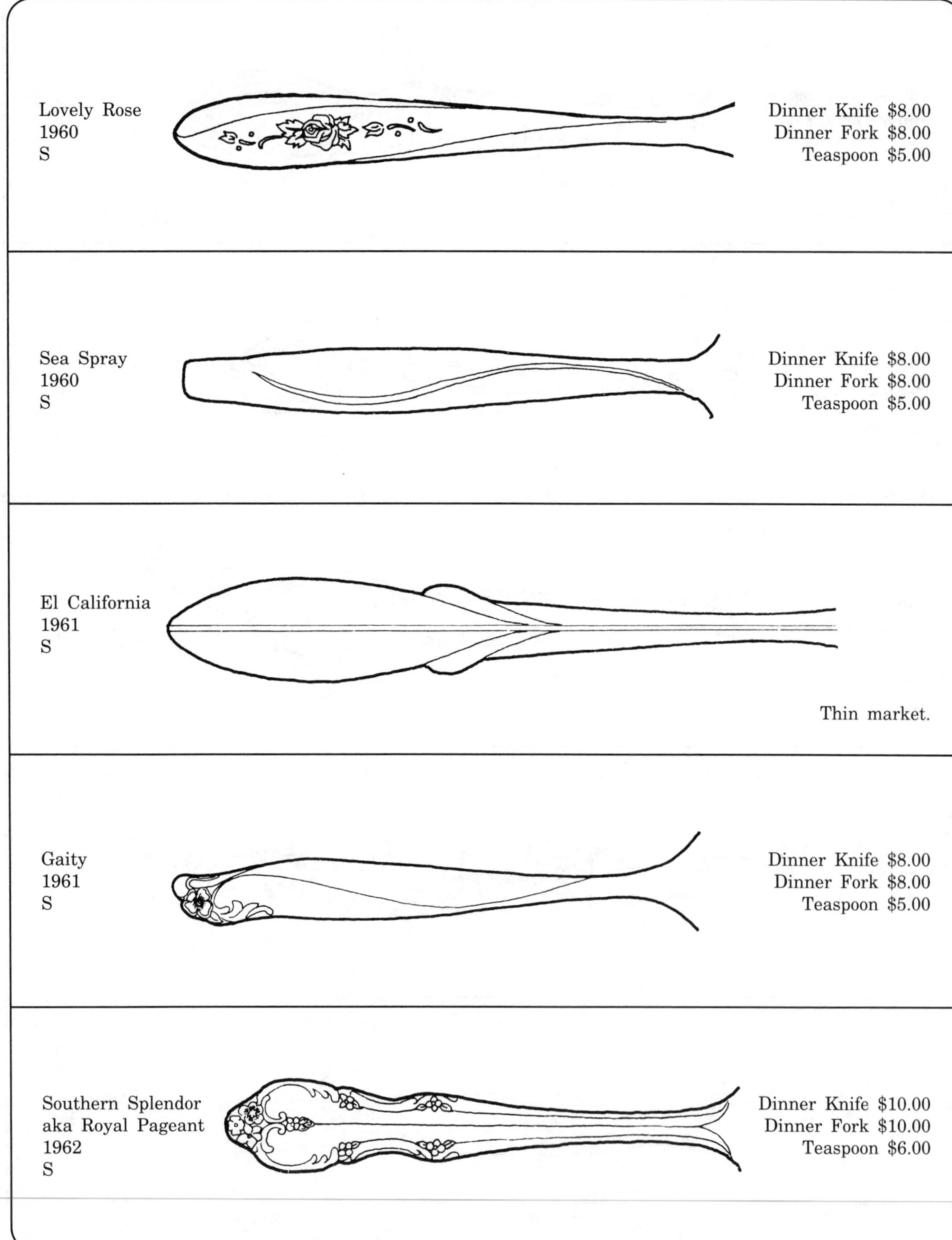

Lovely Rose
1960
S

Dinner Knife $8.00
Dinner Fork $8.00
Teaspoon $5.00

Sea Spray
1960
S

Dinner Knife $8.00
Dinner Fork $8.00
Teaspoon $5.00

El California
1961
S

Thin market.

Gaity
1961
S

Dinner Knife $8.00
Dinner Fork $8.00
Teaspoon $5.00

Southern Splendor
aka Royal Pageant
1962
S

Dinner Knife $10.00
Dinner Fork $10.00
Teaspoon $6.00

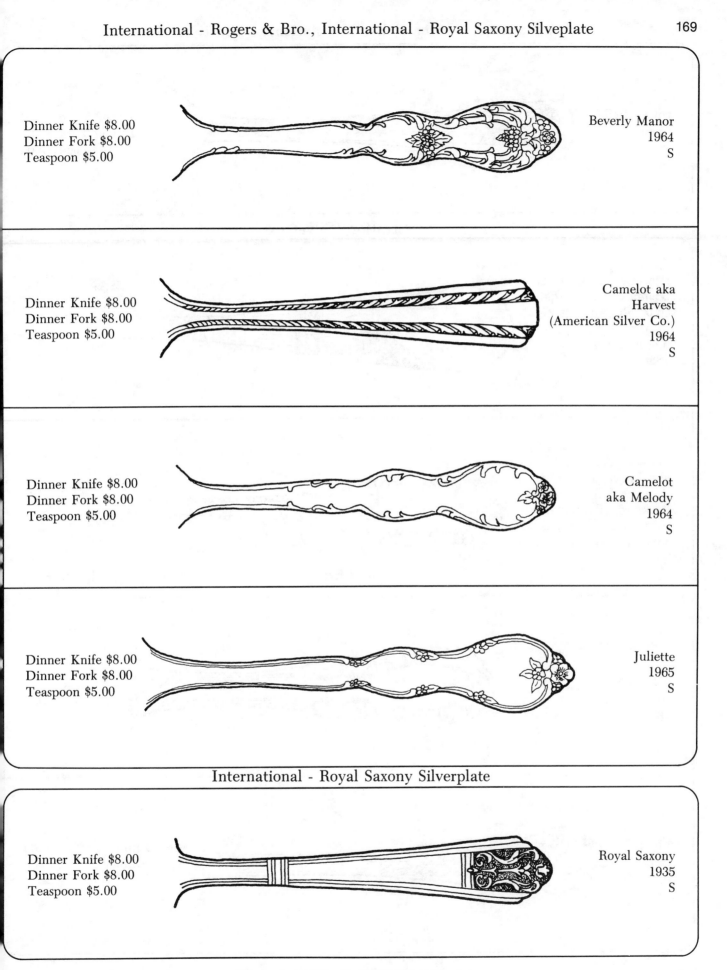

Dinner Knife $8.00
Dinner Fork $8.00
Teaspoon $5.00

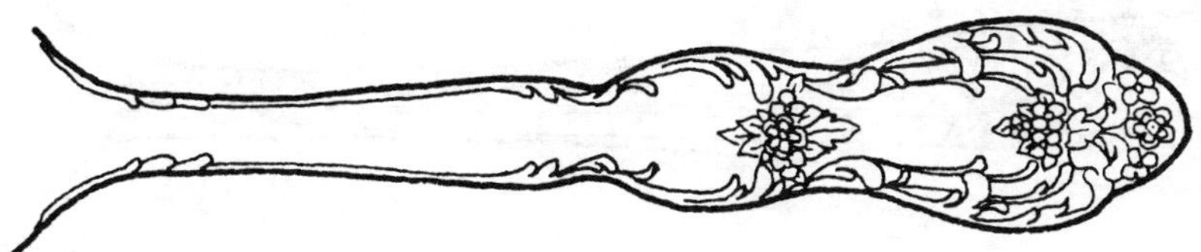

Beverly Manor
1964
S

Dinner Knife $8.00
Dinner Fork $8.00
Teaspoon $5.00

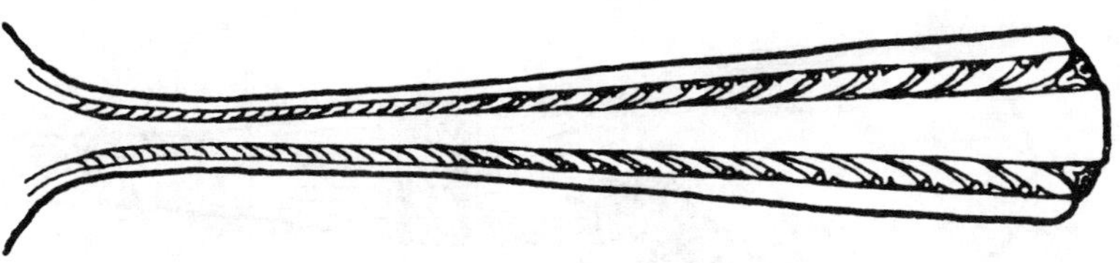

Camelot aka
Harvest
(American Silver Co.)
1964
S

Dinner Knife $8.00
Dinner Fork $8.00
Teaspoon $5.00

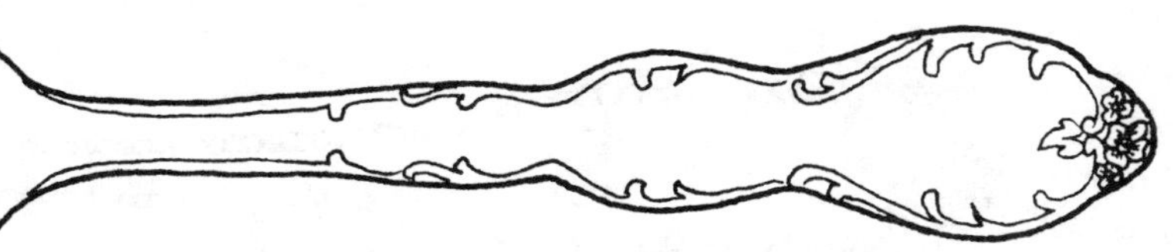

Camelot
aka Melody
1964
S

Dinner Knife $8.00
Dinner Fork $8.00
Teaspoon $5.00

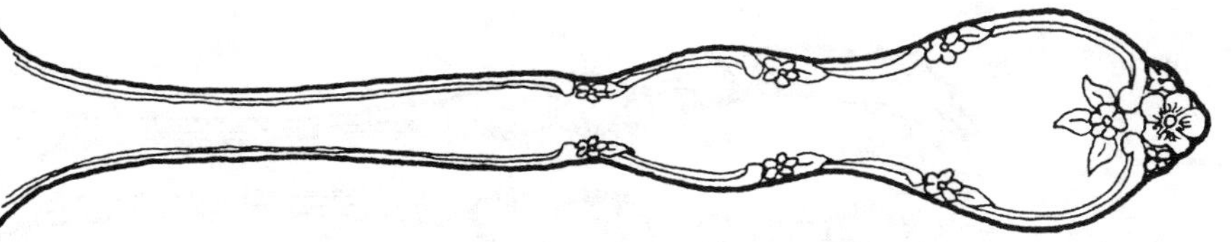

Juliette
1965
S

International - Royal Saxony Silverplate

Dinner Knife $8.00
Dinner Fork $8.00
Teaspoon $5.00

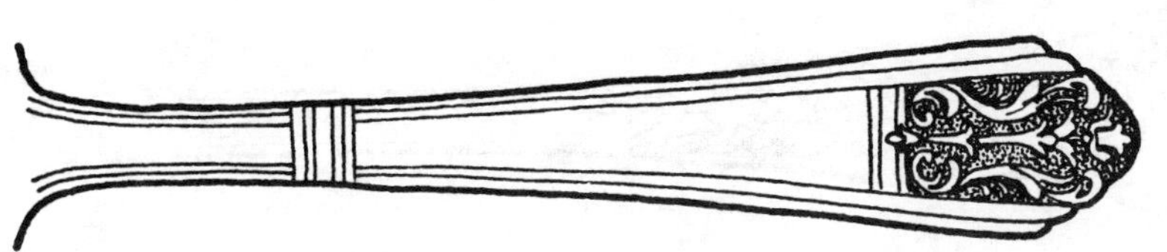

Royal Saxony
1935
S

Please refer to "How To Use This Book" page 4.

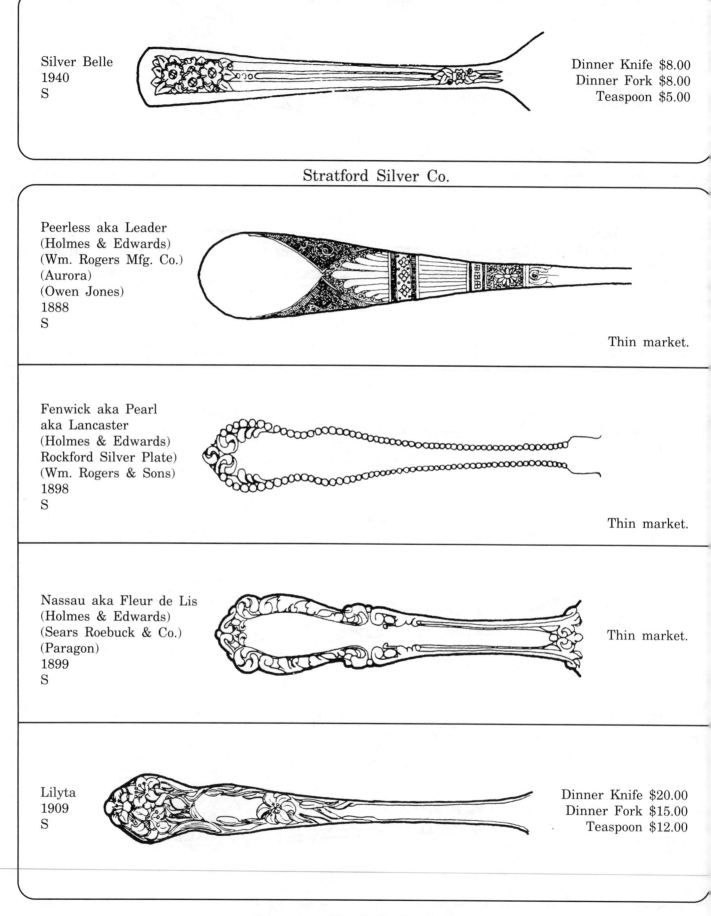

Silver Belle
1940
S

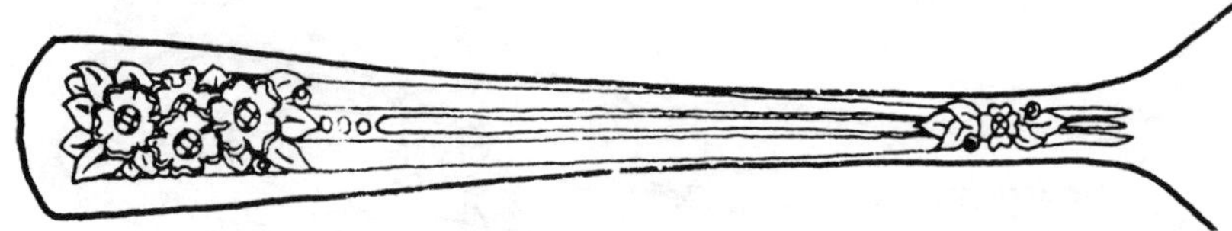

Dinner Knife $8.00
Dinner Fork $8.00
Teaspoon $5.00

Stratford Silver Co.

Peerless aka Leader
(Holmes & Edwards)
(Wm. Rogers Mfg. Co.)
(Aurora)
(Owen Jones)
1888
S

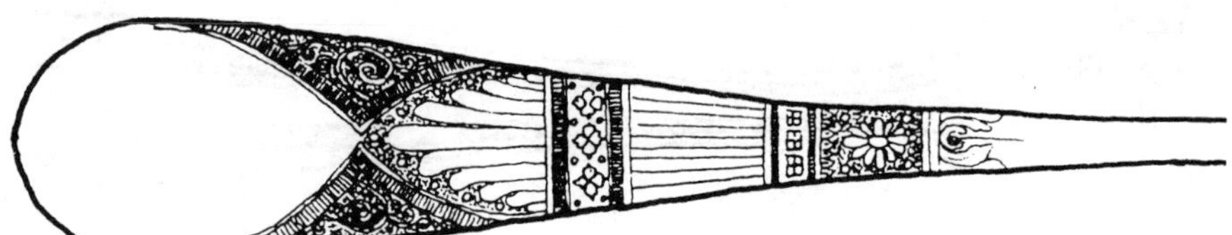

Thin market.

Fenwick aka Pearl
aka Lancaster
(Holmes & Edwards)
Rockford Silver Plate)
(Wm. Rogers & Sons)
1898
S

Thin market.

Nassau aka Fleur de Lis
(Holmes & Edwards)
(Sears Roebuck & Co.)
(Paragon)
1899
S

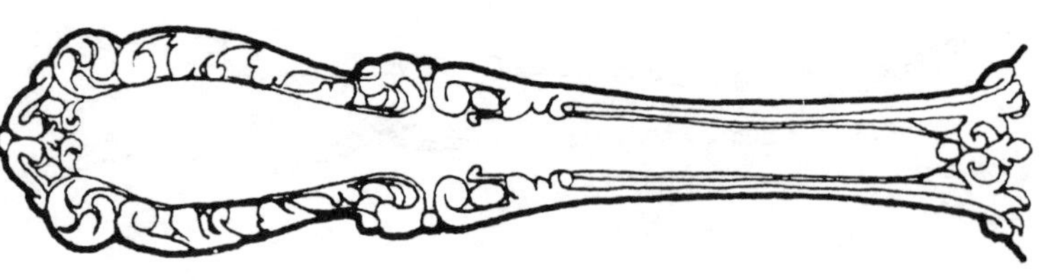

Thin market.

Lilyta
1909
S

Dinner Knife $20.00
Dinner Fork $15.00
Teaspoon $12.00

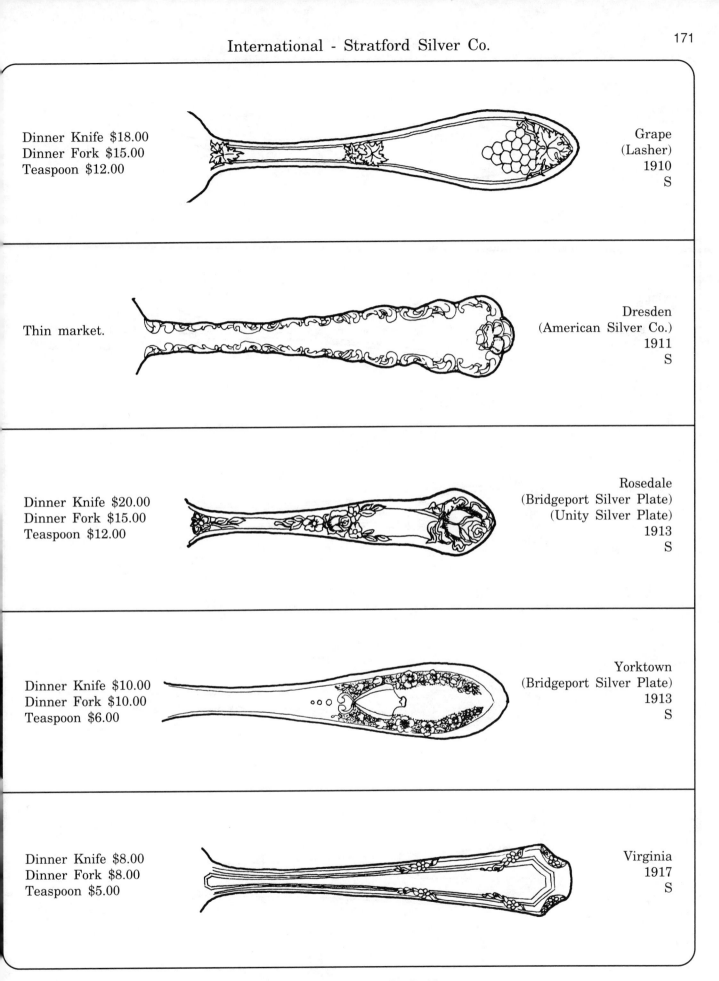

Dinner Knife $18.00
Dinner Fork $15.00
Teaspoon $12.00

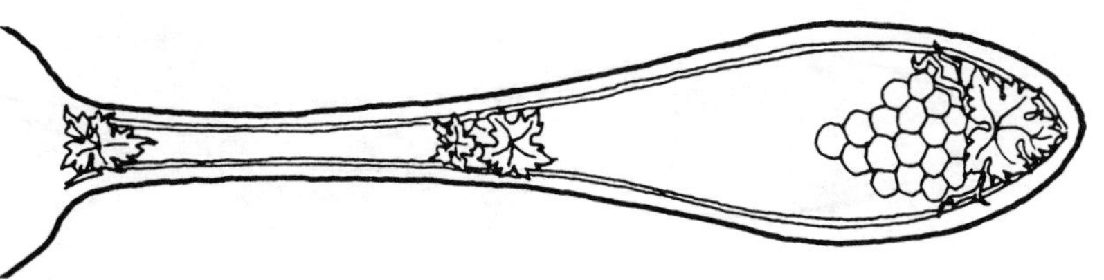

Grape
(Lasher)
1910
S

Thin market.

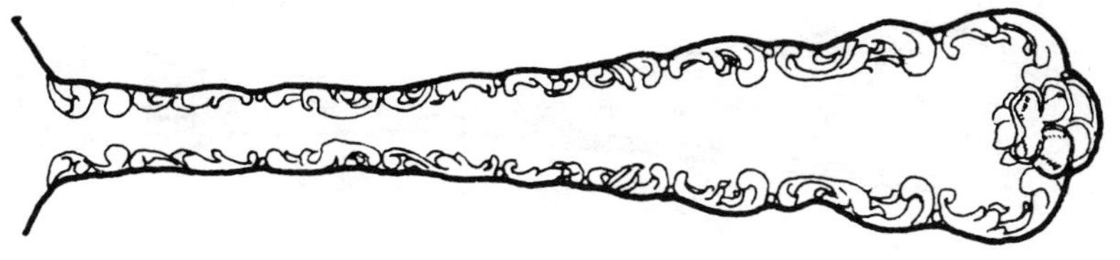

Dresden
(American Silver Co.)
1911
S

Dinner Knife $20.00
Dinner Fork $15.00
Teaspoon $12.00

Rosedale
(Bridgeport Silver Plate)
(Unity Silver Plate)
1913
S

Dinner Knife $10.00
Dinner Fork $10.00
Teaspoon $6.00

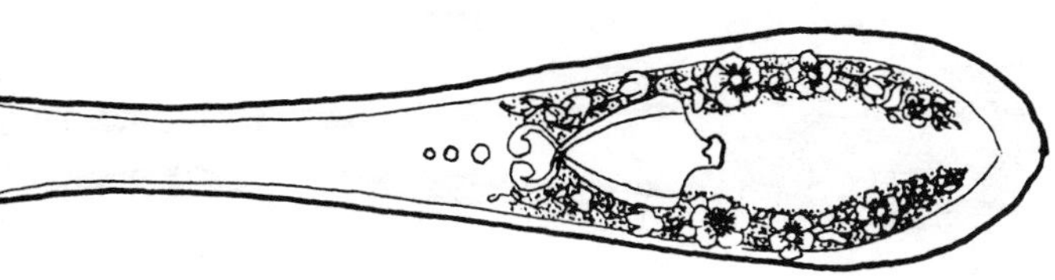

Yorktown
(Bridgeport Silver Plate)
1913
S

Dinner Knife $8.00
Dinner Fork $8.00
Teaspoon $5.00

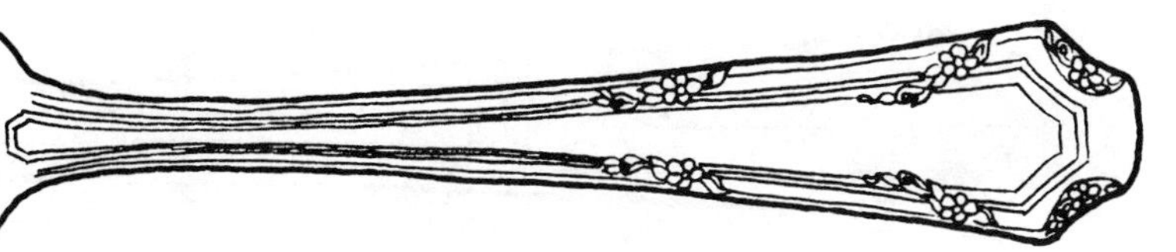

Virginia
1917
S

Please refer to "How To Use This Book" page 4.

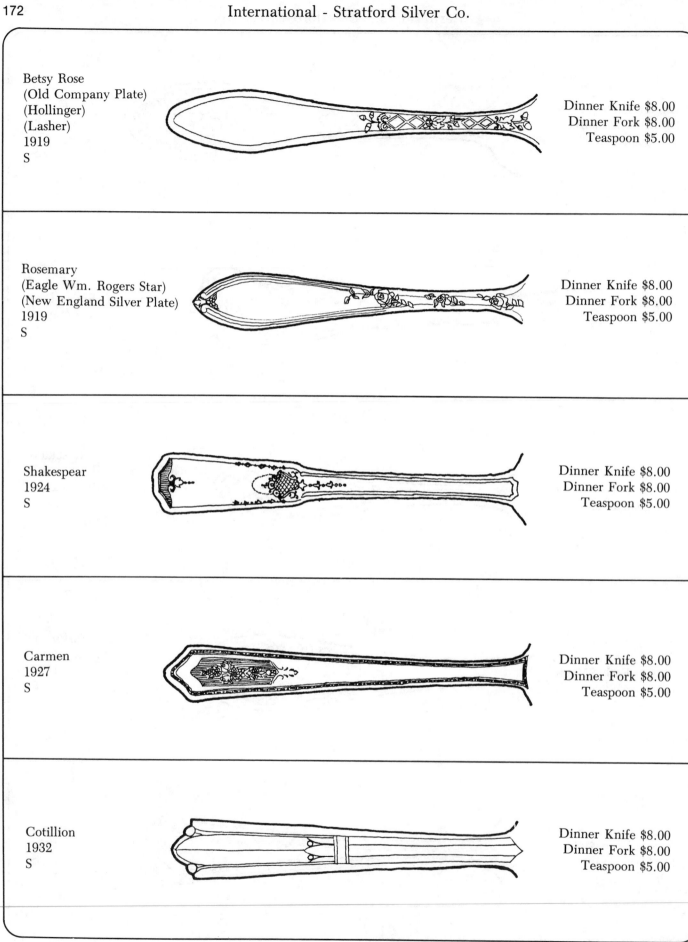

Betsy Rose
(Old Company Plate)
(Hollinger)
(Lasher)
1919
S

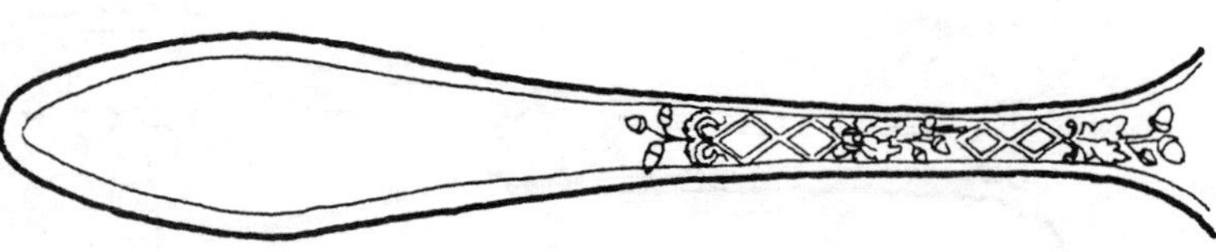

Dinner Knife $8.00
Dinner Fork $8.00
Teaspoon $5.00

Rosemary
(Eagle Wm. Rogers Star)
(New England Silver Plate)
1919
S

Dinner Knife $8.00
Dinner Fork $8.00
Teaspoon $5.00

Shakespear
1924
S

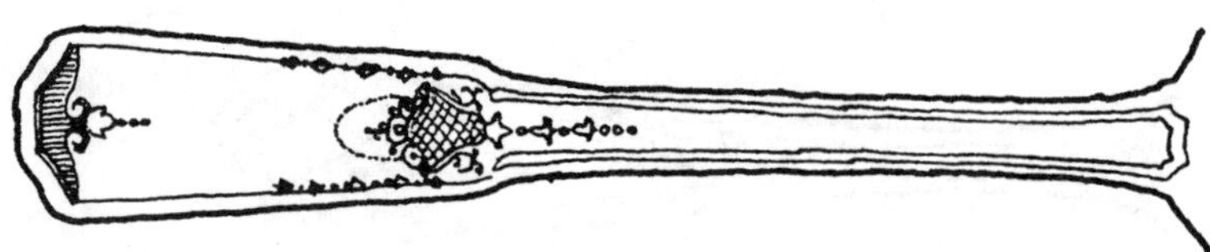

Dinner Knife $8.00
Dinner Fork $8.00
Teaspoon $5.00

Carmen
1927
S

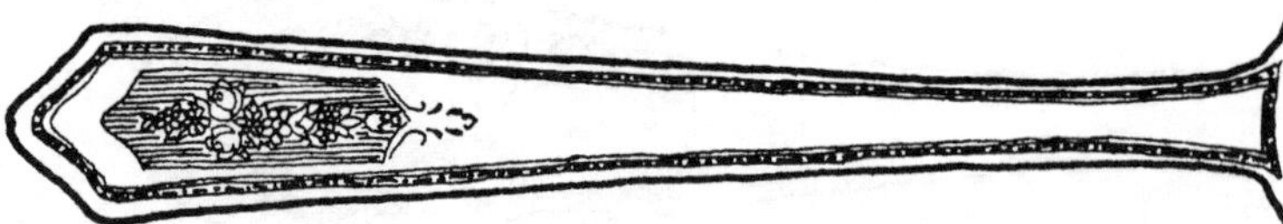

Dinner Knife $8.00
Dinner Fork $8.00
Teaspoon $5.00

Cotillion
1932
S

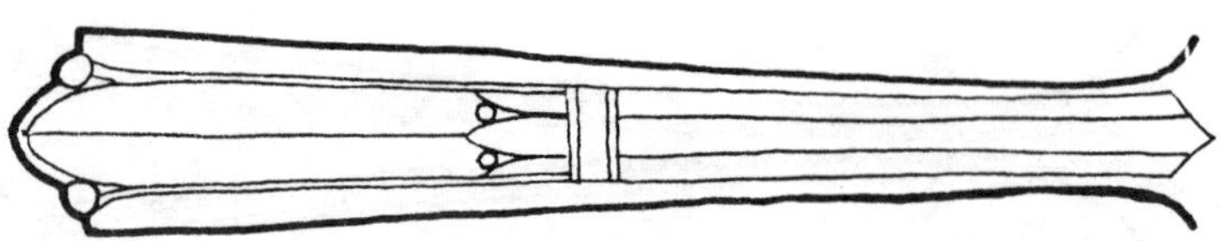

Dinner Knife $8.00
Dinner Fork $8.00
Teaspoon $5.00

Please refer to "How To Use This Book" page 4.

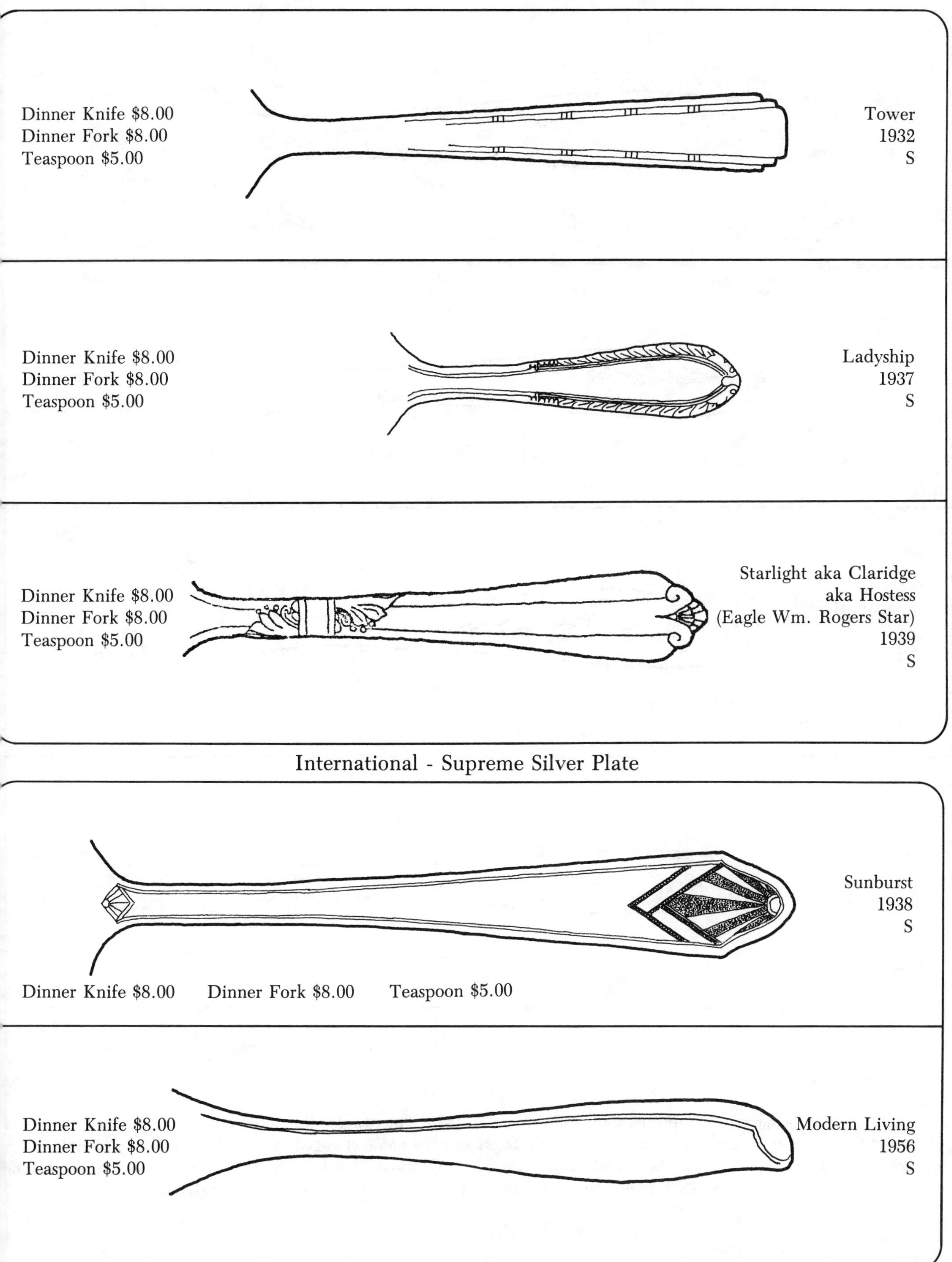

Dinner Knife $8.00
Dinner Fork $8.00
Teaspoon $5.00

Tower
1932
S

Dinner Knife $8.00
Dinner Fork $8.00
Teaspoon $5.00

Ladyship
1937
S

Dinner Knife $8.00
Dinner Fork $8.00
Teaspoon $5.00

Starlight aka Claridge
aka Hostess
(Eagle Wm. Rogers Star)
1939
S

International - Supreme Silver Plate

Sunburst
1938
S

Dinner Knife $8.00 Dinner Fork $8.00 Teaspoon $5.00

Dinner Knife $8.00
Dinner Fork $8.00
Teaspoon $5.00

Modern Living
1956
S

Please refer to "How To Use This Book" page 4.

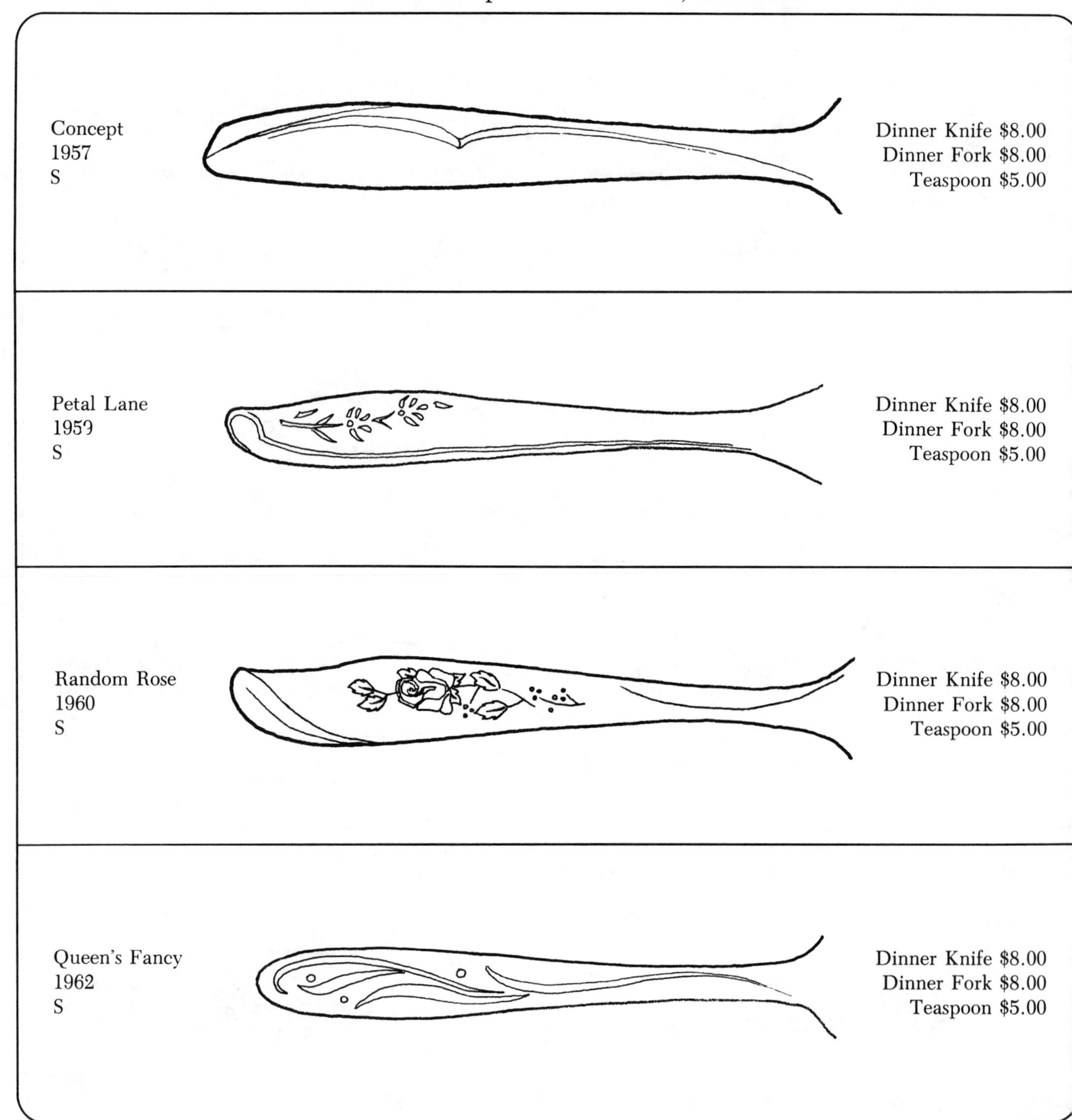

Kirk Stieff

Samuel Kirk opened a silversmithing shop in Baltimore in 1815. The firm has long been noted for superb sterling silver. The Stieff Company was begun in 1892 by Charles C. Stieff and the name changed to the Stieff Company in 1904. They, too, have been known for their excellent sterling flatware and holloware. Shortly after the two companies joined together as Kirk Stieff, they introduced four silverplated flatware patterns, all originally designed for sterling.

Please refer to "How To Use This Book" page 4.

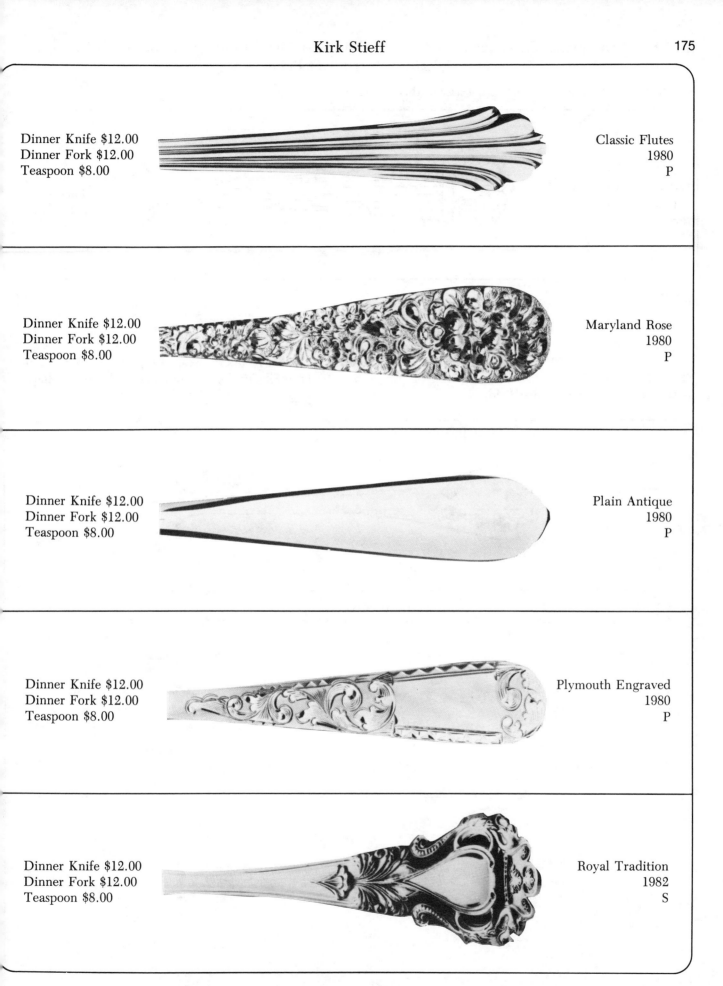

Dinner Knife $12.00
Dinner Fork $12.00
Teaspoon $8.00

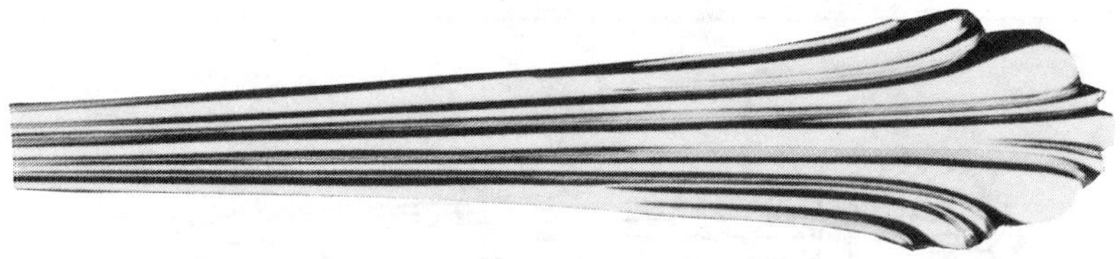

Classic Flutes
1980
P

Dinner Knife $12.00
Dinner Fork $12.00
Teaspoon $8.00

Maryland Rose
1980
P

Dinner Knife $12.00
Dinner Fork $12.00
Teaspoon $8.00

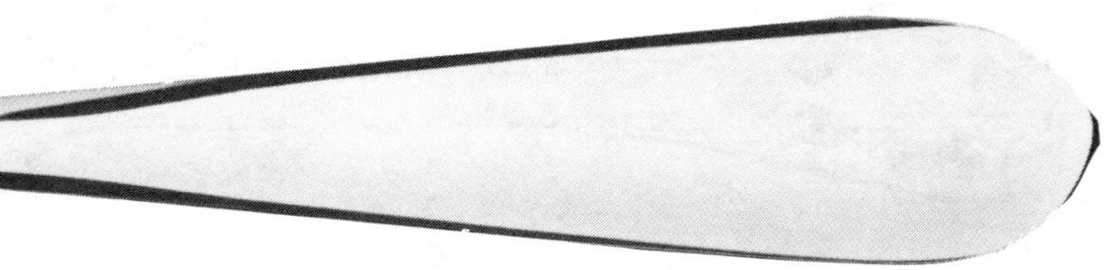

Plain Antique
1980
P

Dinner Knife $12.00
Dinner Fork $12.00
Teaspoon $8.00

Plymouth Engraved
1980
P

Dinner Knife $12.00
Dinner Fork $12.00
Teaspoon $8.00

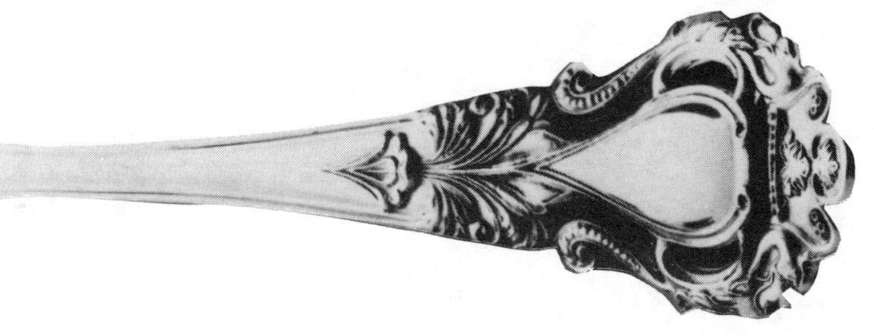

Royal Tradition
1982
S

Please refer to "How To Use This Book" page 4.

Lady Esther Silver Plate

No information available about the user of this backstamp.

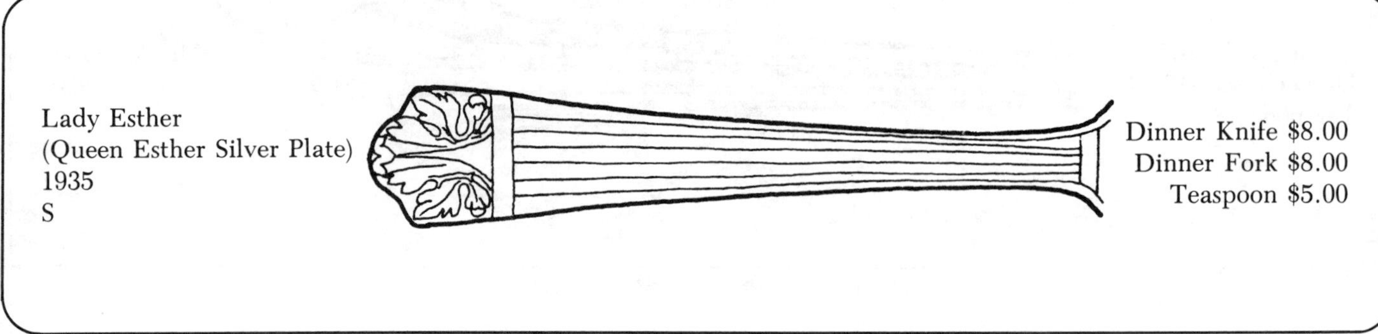

Lady Esther
(Queen Esther Silver Plate)
1935
S

Dinner Knife $8.00
Dinner Fork $8.00
Teaspoon $5.00

Lunt - Franklin Silver Plate

In 1902 the Rogers, Lunt & Bowlen Co., commonly known as Lunt Silversmiths acquired the A.F. Towle & Son Co. which had begun in 1880. In about 1922 Lunt acquired the Franklin Silver Plate Company of Greenfield, Massachusetts. The 1834 J. Russell & Co. backstamp can also be traced to Lunt. Lunt Silversmiths began making silverplated flatware in 1980 and is located in Greenfield, Massachusetts. It is interesting to note the Towle owl trademark belongs to Lunt.

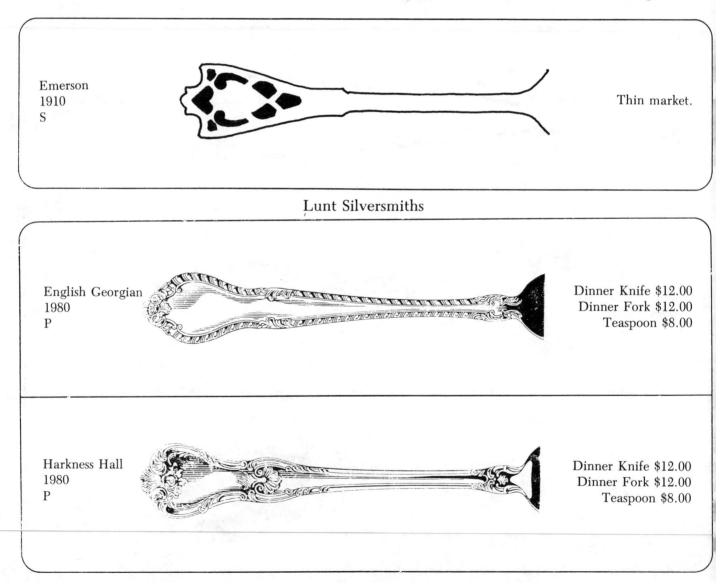

Emerson
1910
S

Thin market.

Lunt Silversmiths

English Georgian
1980
P

Dinner Knife $12.00
Dinner Fork $12.00
Teaspoon $8.00

Harkness Hall
1980
P

Dinner Knife $12.00
Dinner Fork $12.00
Teaspoon $8.00

Please refer to "How To Use This Book" page 4.

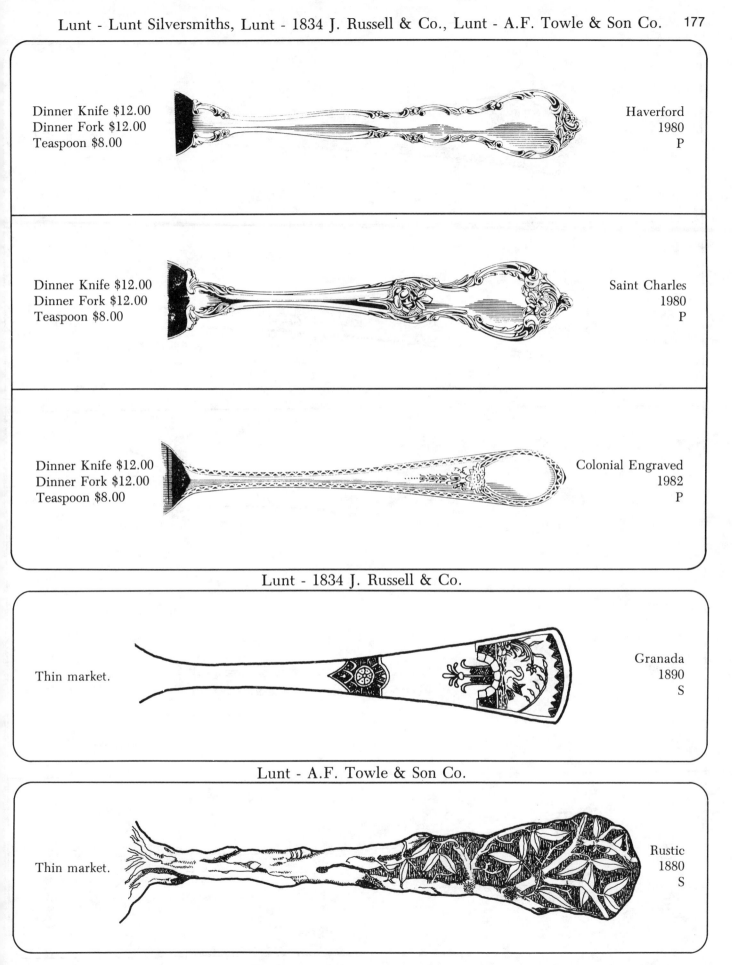

Dinner Knife $12.00
Dinner Fork $12.00
Teaspoon $8.00

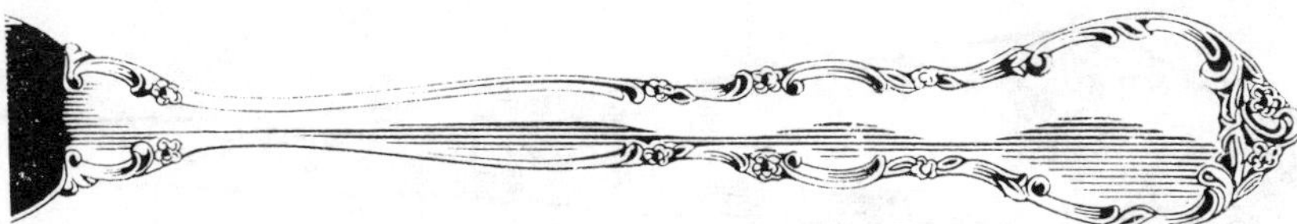

Haverford
1980
P

Dinner Knife $12.00
Dinner Fork $12.00
Teaspoon $8.00

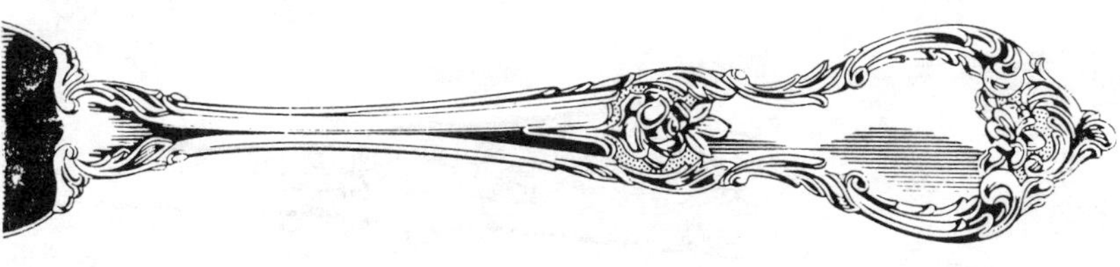

Saint Charles
1980
P

Dinner Knife $12.00
Dinner Fork $12.00
Teaspoon $8.00

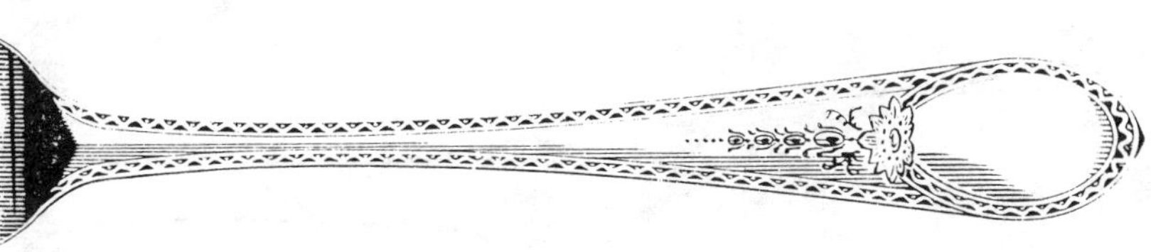

Colonial Engraved
1982
P

Lunt - 1834 J. Russell & Co.

Thin market.

Granada
1890
S

Lunt - A.F. Towle & Son Co.

Thin market.

Rustic
1880
S

Please refer to "How To Use This Book" page 4.

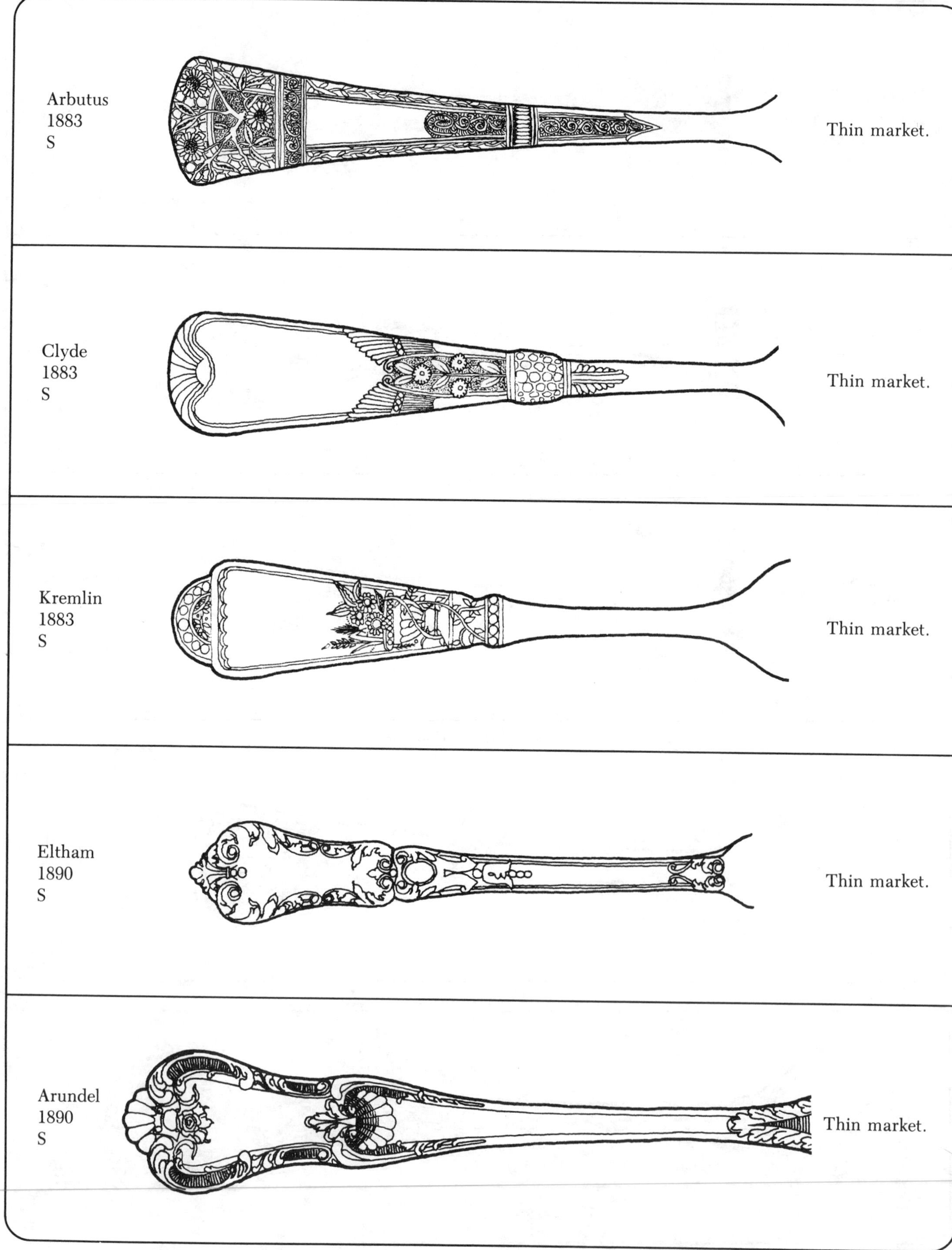

Please refer to "How To Use This Book" page 4.

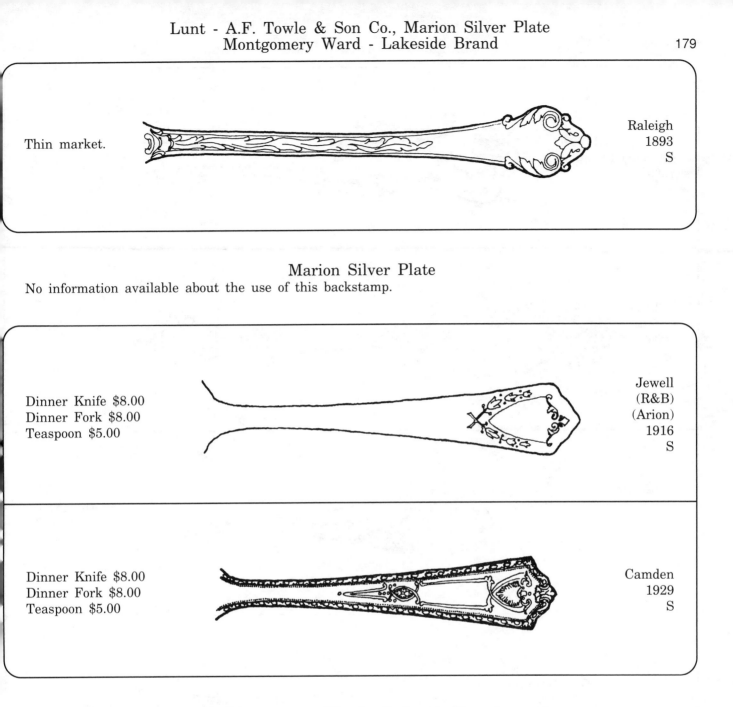

Thin market.

Raleigh
1893
S

Marion Silver Plate

No information available about the use of this backstamp.

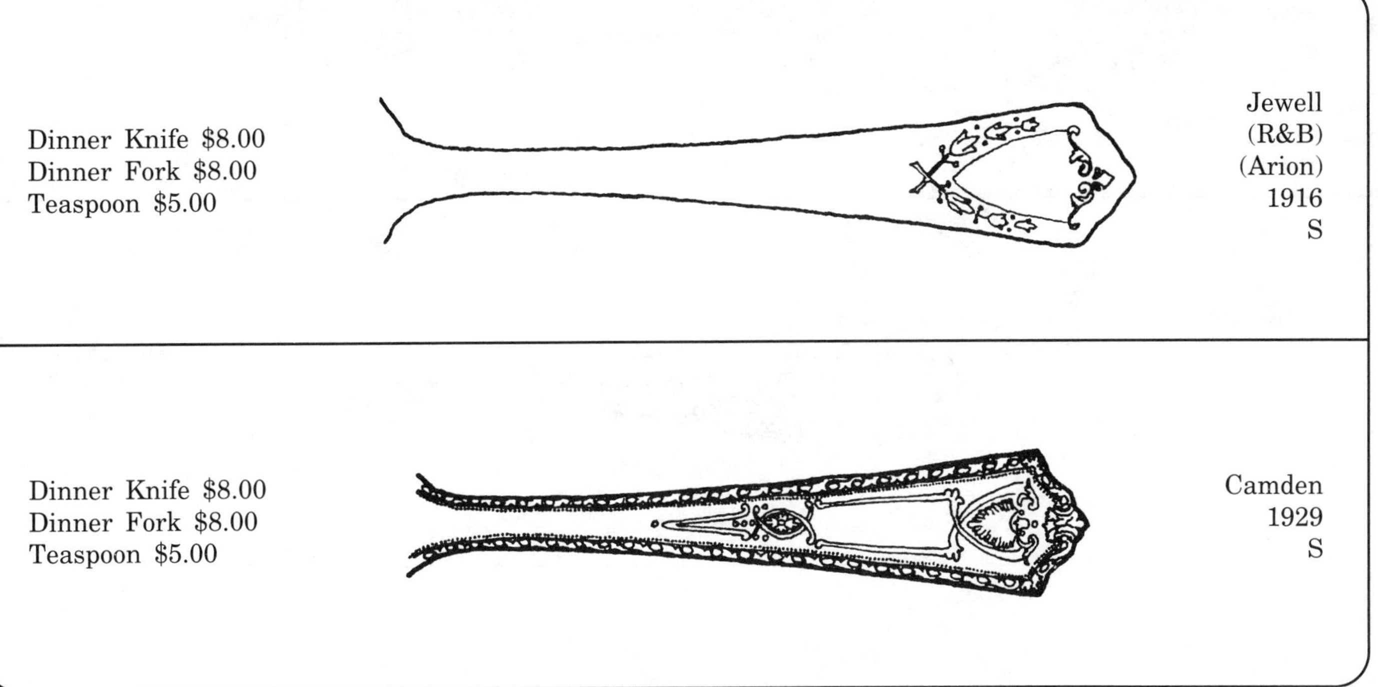

Dinner Knife $8.00
Dinner Fork $8.00
Teaspoon $5.00

Jewell
(R&B)
(Arion)
1916
S

Dinner Knife $8.00
Dinner Fork $8.00
Teaspoon $5.00

Camden
1929
S

Montgomery Ward - Lakeside Brand

Many different manufacturers of silverplated flatware made flatware for the well-known retailer - Montgomery Ward - to sell through their outlets.

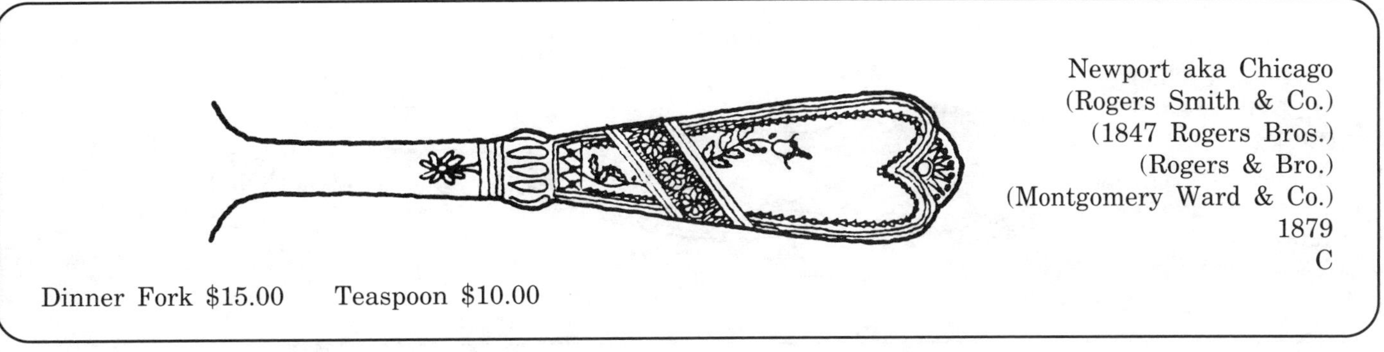

Newport aka Chicago
(Rogers Smith & Co.)
(1847 Rogers Bros.)
(Rogers & Bro.)
(Montgomery Ward & Co.)
1879
C

Dinner Fork $15.00 Teaspoon $10.00

Please refer to "How To Use This Book" page 4.

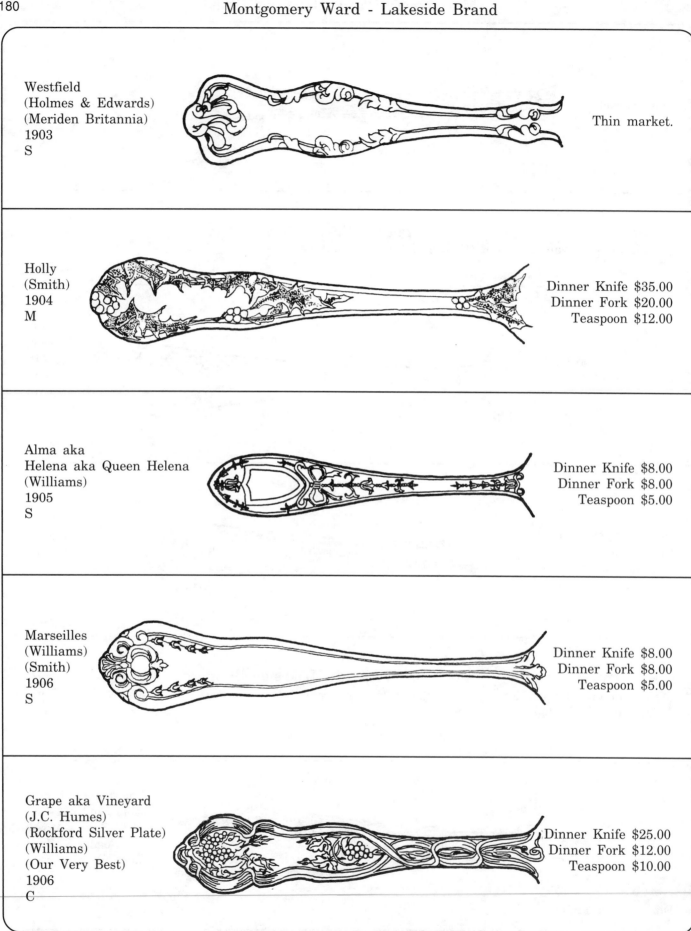

Westfield
(Holmes & Edwards)
(Meriden Britannia)
1903
S

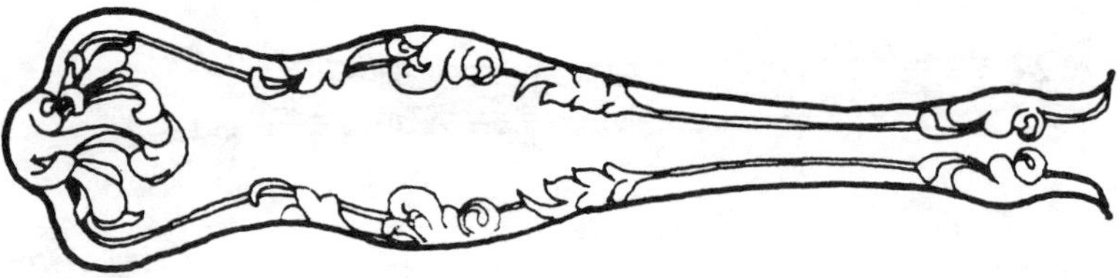

Thin market.

Holly
(Smith)
1904
M

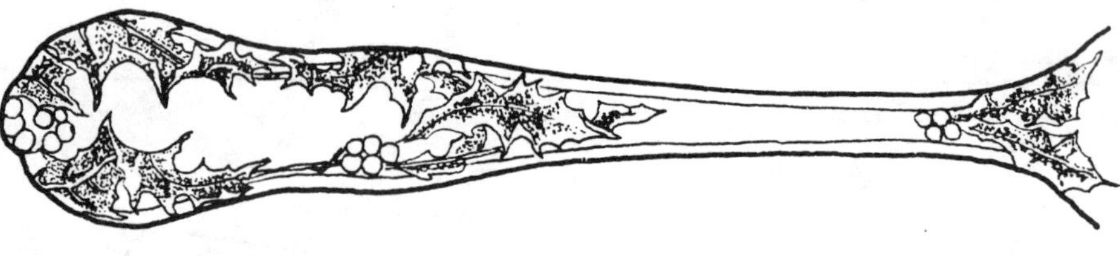

Dinner Knife $35.00
Dinner Fork $20.00
Teaspoon $12.00

Alma aka
Helena aka Queen Helena
(Williams)
1905
S

Dinner Knife $8.00
Dinner Fork $8.00
Teaspoon $5.00

Marseilles
(Williams)
(Smith)
1906
S

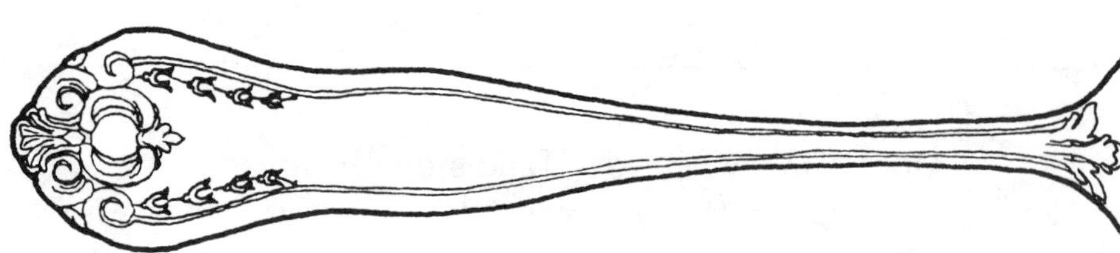

Dinner Knife $8.00
Dinner Fork $8.00
Teaspoon $5.00

Grape aka Vineyard
(J.C. Humes)
(Rockford Silver Plate)
(Williams)
(Our Very Best)
1906
C

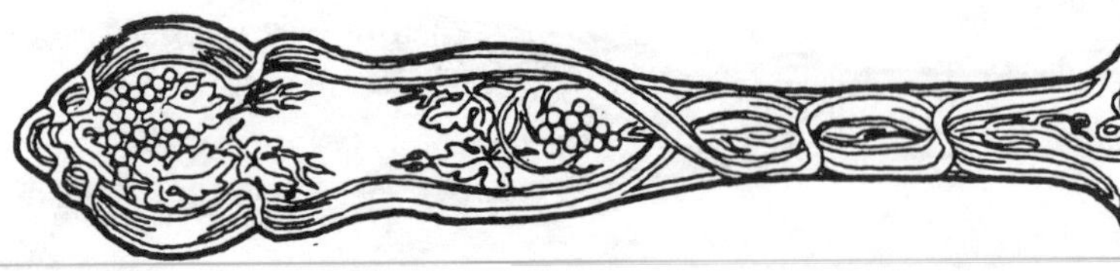

Dinner Knife $25.00
Dinner Fork $12.00
Teaspoon $10.00

Please refer to "How To Use This Book" page 4.

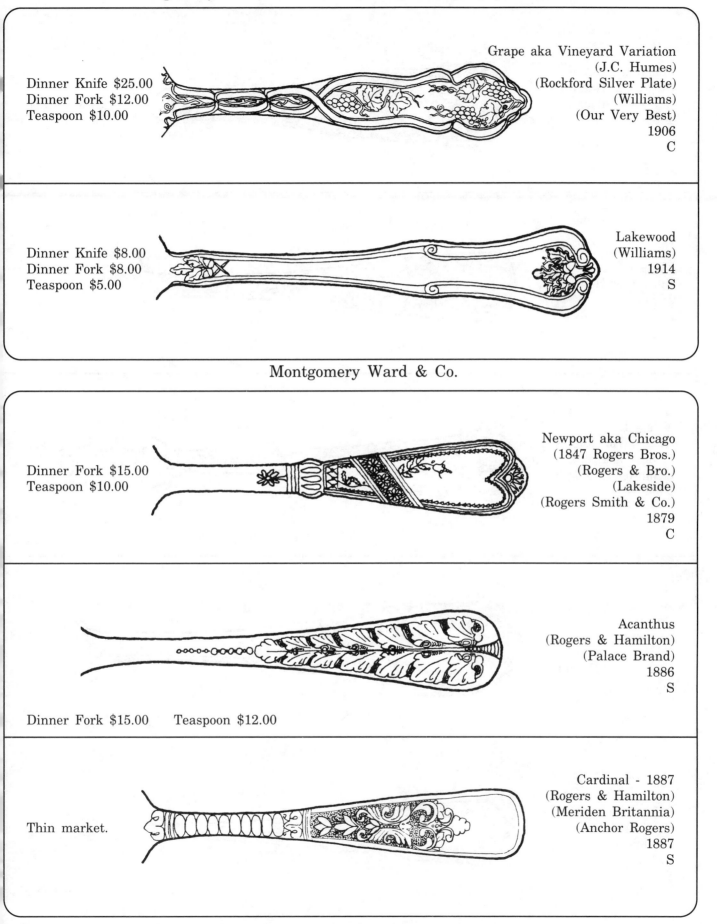

Dinner Knife $25.00
Dinner Fork $12.00
Teaspoon $10.00

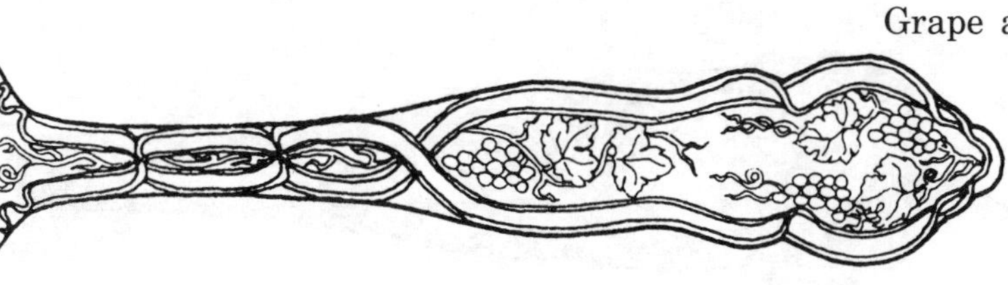

Grape aka Vineyard Variation
(J.C. Humes)
(Rockford Silver Plate)
(Williams)
(Our Very Best)
1906
C

Dinner Knife $8.00
Dinner Fork $8.00
Teaspoon $5.00

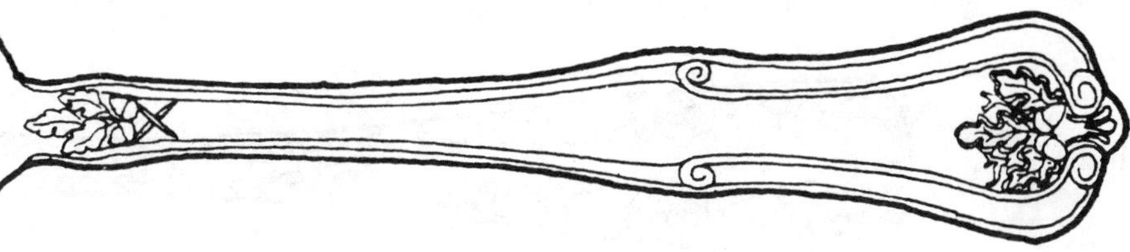

Lakewood
(Williams)
1914
S

Montgomery Ward & Co.

Dinner Fork $15.00
Teaspoon $10.00

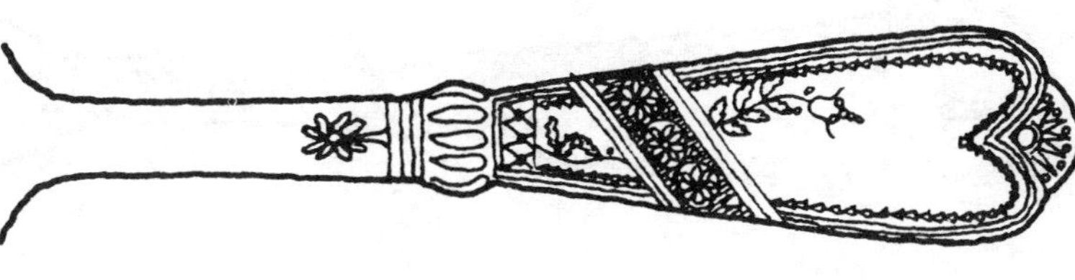

Newport aka Chicago
(1847 Rogers Bros.)
(Rogers & Bro.)
(Lakeside)
(Rogers Smith & Co.)
1879
C

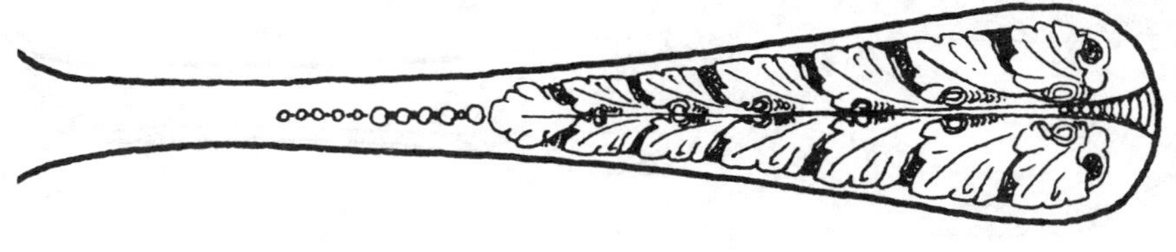

Acanthus
(Rogers & Hamilton)
(Palace Brand)
1886
S

Dinner Fork $15.00 Teaspoon $12.00

Thin market.

Cardinal - 1887
(Rogers & Hamilton)
(Meriden Britannia)
(Anchor Rogers)
1887
S

Please refer to "How To Use This Book" page 4.

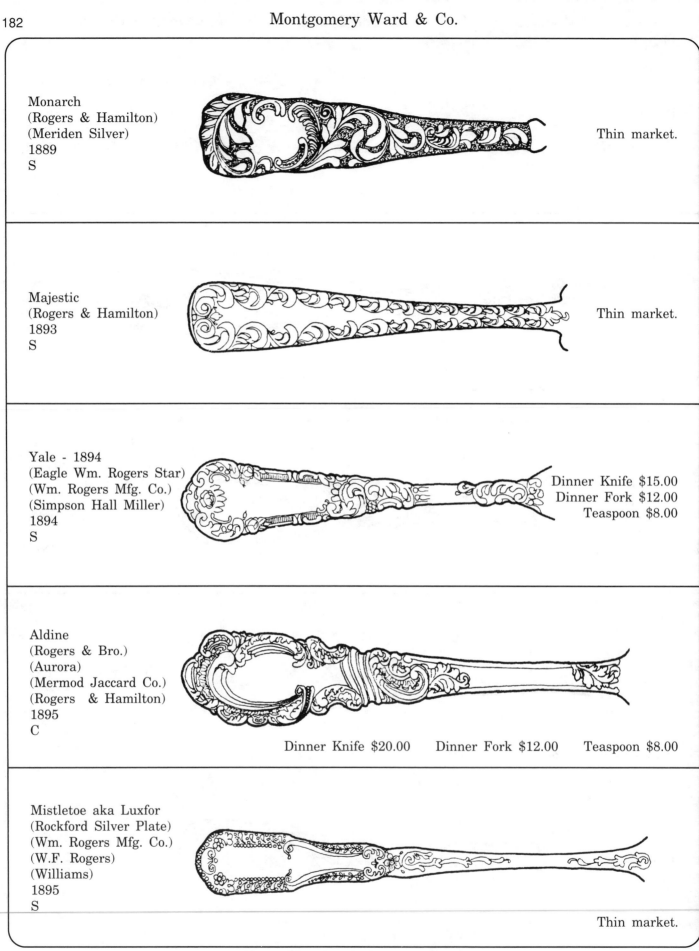

Monarch
(Rogers & Hamilton)
(Meriden Silver)
1889
S

Thin market.

Majestic
(Rogers & Hamilton)
1893
S

Thin market.

Yale - 1894
(Eagle Wm. Rogers Star)
(Wm. Rogers Mfg. Co.)
(Simpson Hall Miller)
1894
S

Dinner Knife $15.00
Dinner Fork $12.00
Teaspoon $8.00

Aldine
(Rogers & Bro.)
(Aurora)
(Mermod Jaccard Co.)
(Rogers & Hamilton)
1895
C

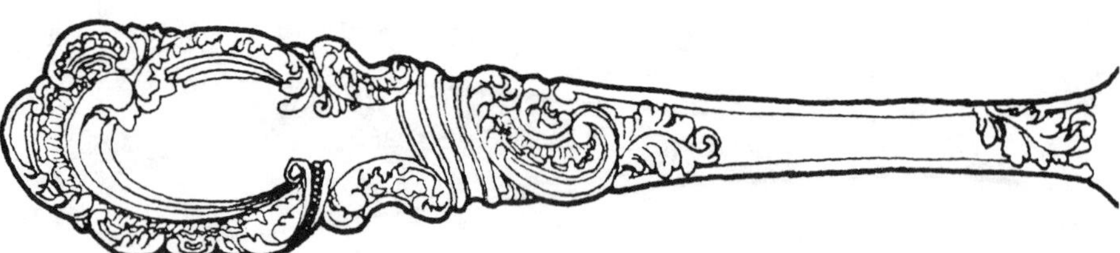

Dinner Knife $20.00 Dinner Fork $12.00 Teaspoon $8.00

Mistletoe aka Luxfor
(Rockford Silver Plate)
(Wm. Rogers Mfg. Co.)
(W.F. Rogers)
(Williams)
1895
S

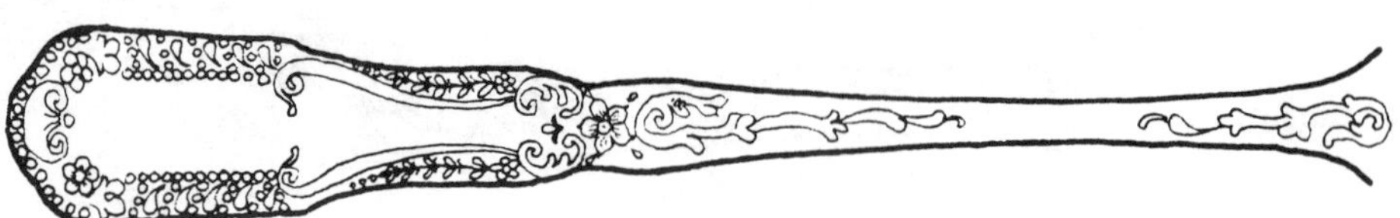

Thin market.

Please refer to "How To Use This Book" page 4.

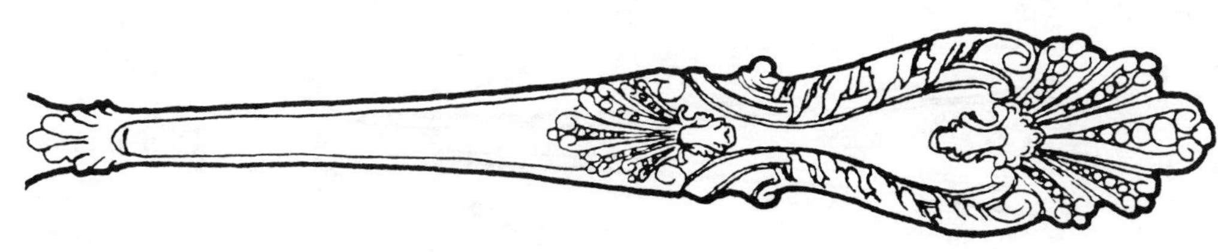

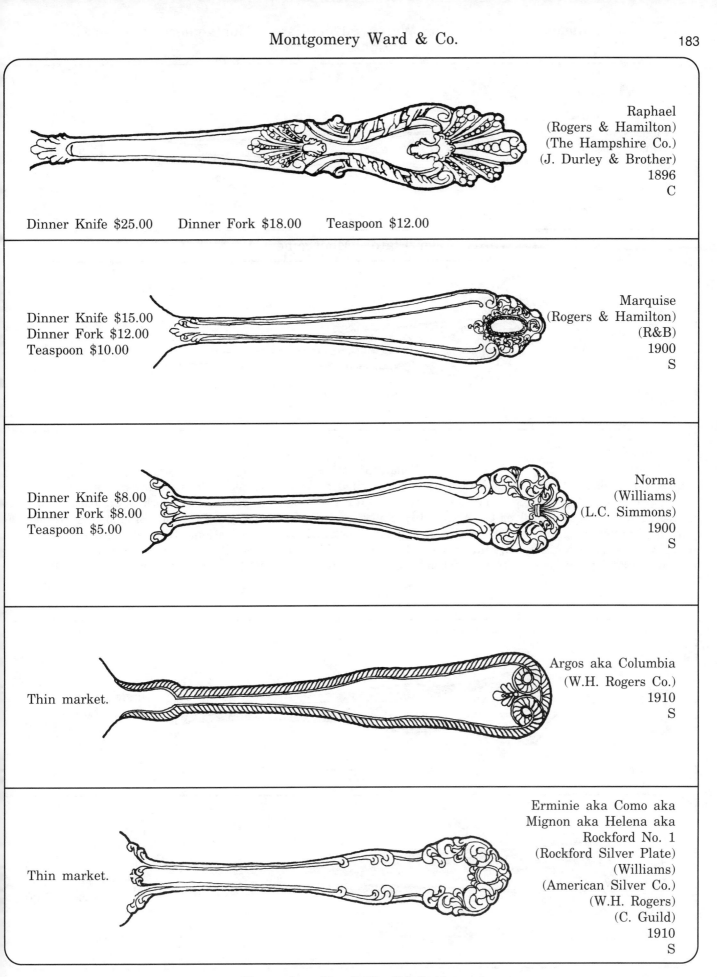

Raphael
(Rogers & Hamilton)
(The Hampshire Co.)
(J. Durley & Brother)
1896
C

Dinner Knife $25.00 Dinner Fork $18.00 Teaspoon $12.00

Dinner Knife $15.00
Dinner Fork $12.00
Teaspoon $10.00

Marquise
(Rogers & Hamilton)
(R&B)
1900
S

Dinner Knife $8.00
Dinner Fork $8.00
Teaspoon $5.00

Norma
(Williams)
(L.C. Simmons)
1900
S

Thin market.

Argos aka Columbia
(W.H. Rogers Co.)
1910
S

Thin market.

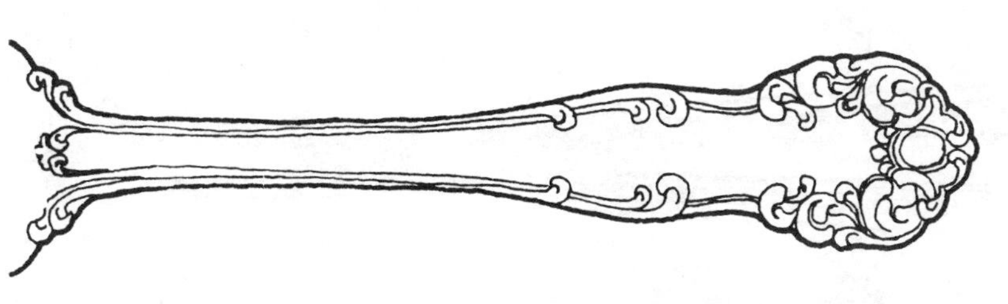

Erminie aka Como aka
Mignon aka Helena aka
Rockford No. 1
(Rockford Silver Plate)
(Williams)
(American Silver Co.)
(W.H. Rogers)
(C. Guild)
1910
S

Please refer to "How To Use This Book" page 4.

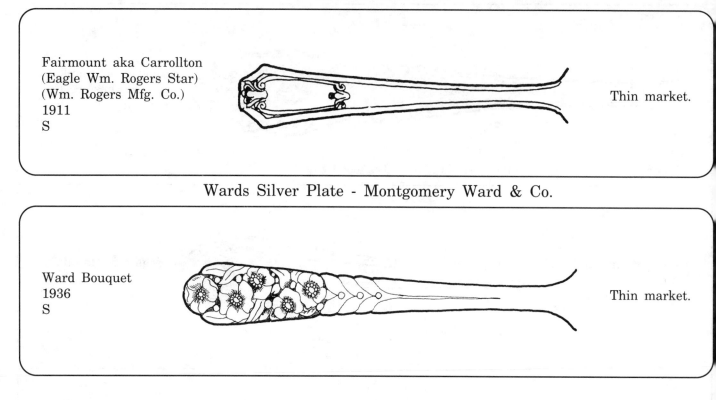

Fairmount aka Carrollton
(Eagle Wm. Rogers Star)
(Wm. Rogers Mfg. Co.)
1911
S

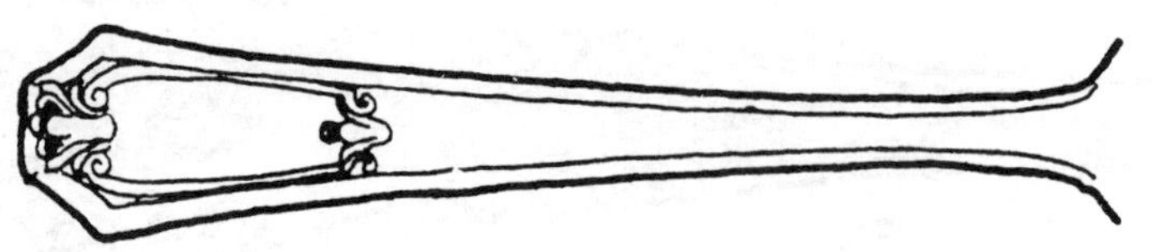

Thin market.

Wards Silver Plate - Montgomery Ward & Co.

Ward Bouquet
1936
S

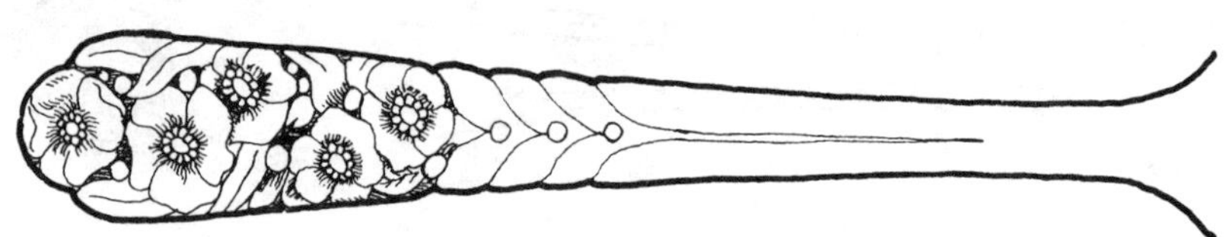

Thin market.

National Silver Co.

The National Silver Company of New York, discontinued making silverplate flatware in the late 1950's. They have since disposed of all records of their flatware. The E.H.H. Smith and the Albert Pick & Co. backstamps can be traced to the National Silver Co. The E.H.H. Smith Co. manufactured silverware for Simmons Hardware Co. and thus, Simmons Hardware, Co. (S.H. Co.) has been included under the National Silver Co. Other backstamps used by National are Mildred Quality Silver Plate, S.E.B., Monarch Silver Company and Viceroy Silver Co. The company traces their beginnings to 1890 and became known as the National Silver Company before 1904.

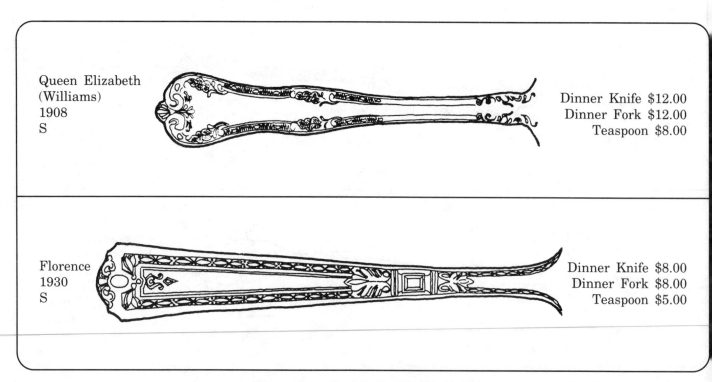

Queen Elizabeth
(Williams)
1908
S

Dinner Knife $12.00
Dinner Fork $12.00
Teaspoon $8.00

Florence
1930
S

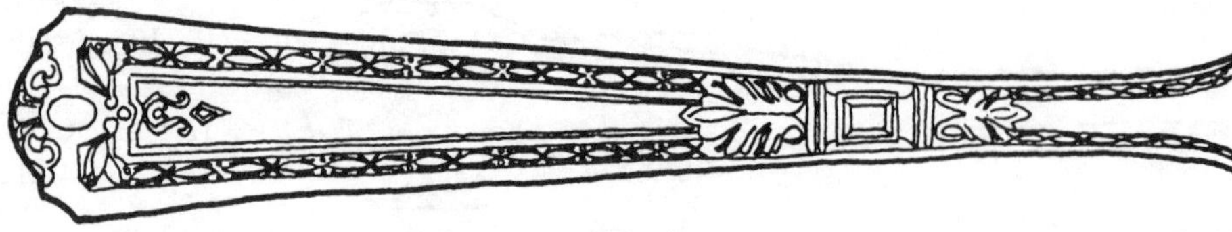

Dinner Knife $8.00
Dinner Fork $8.00
Teaspoon $5.00

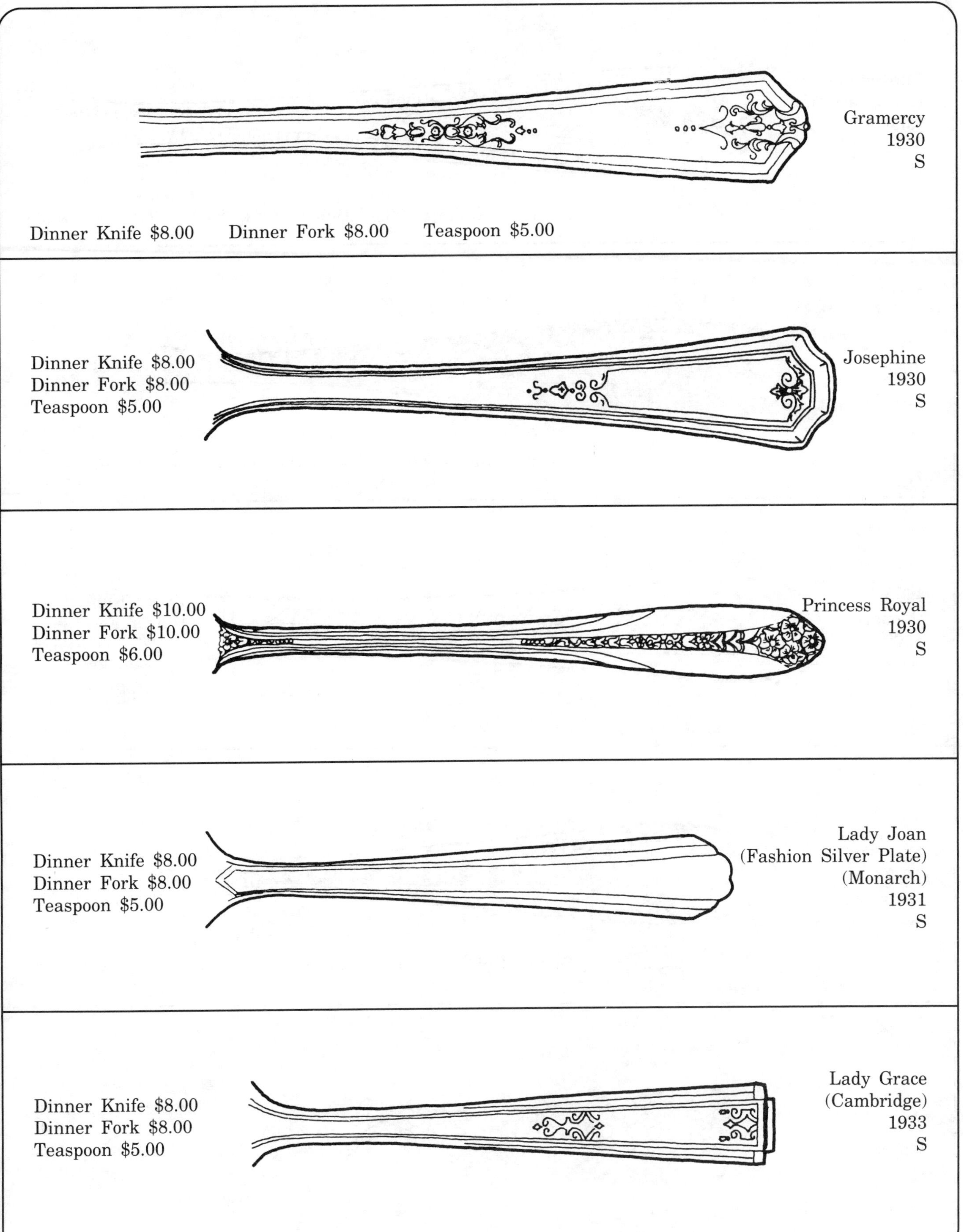

Please refer to "How To Use This Book" page 4.

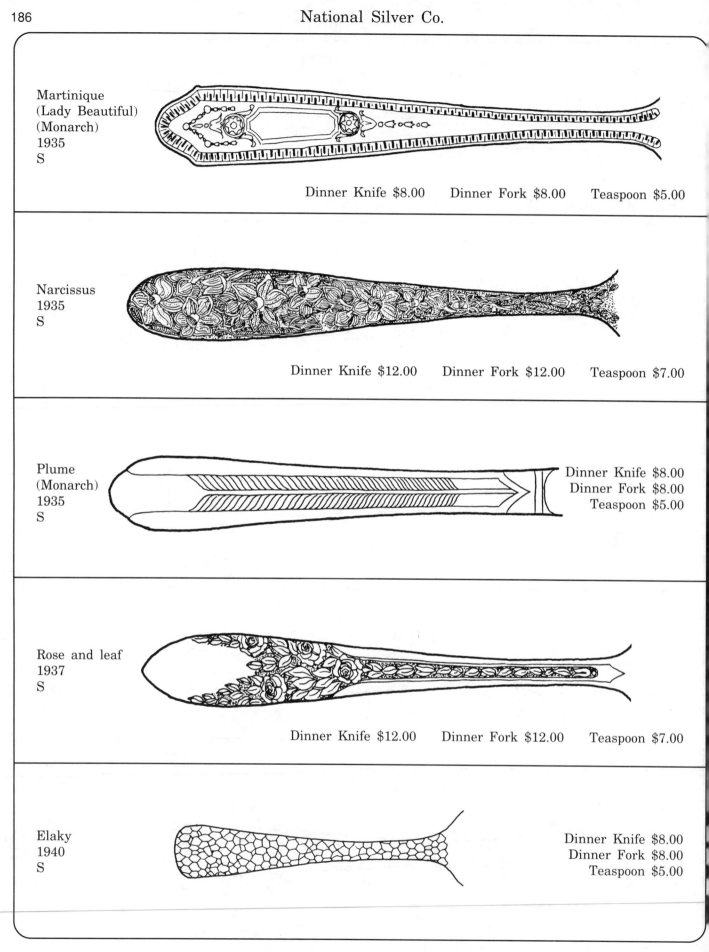

Martinique
(Lady Beautiful)
(Monarch)
1935
S

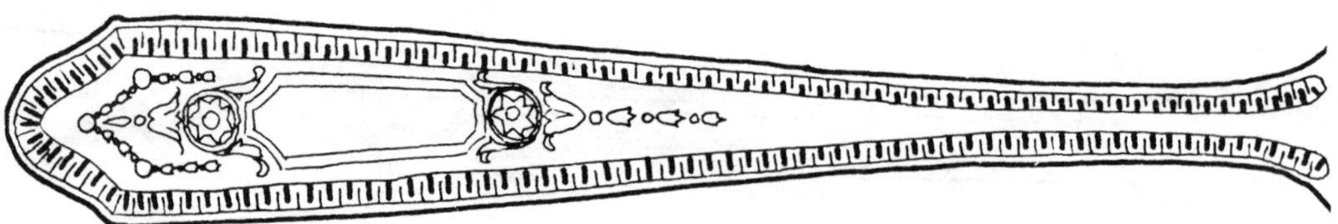

Dinner Knife $8.00 Dinner Fork $8.00 Teaspoon $5.00

Narcissus
1935
S

Dinner Knife $12.00 Dinner Fork $12.00 Teaspoon $7.00

Plume
(Monarch)
1935
S

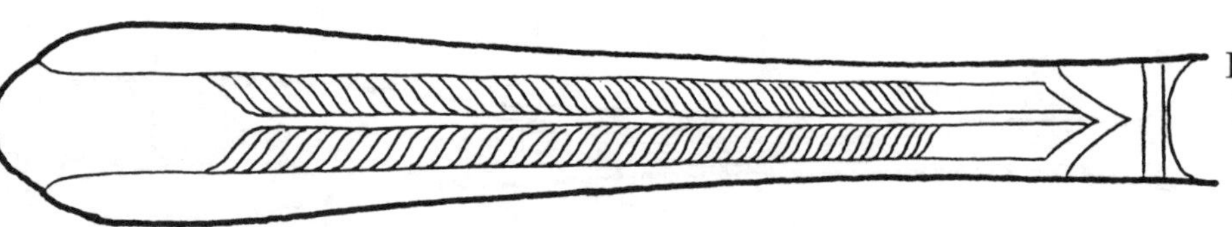

Dinner Knife $8.00
Dinner Fork $8.00
Teaspoon $5.00

Rose and leaf
1937
S

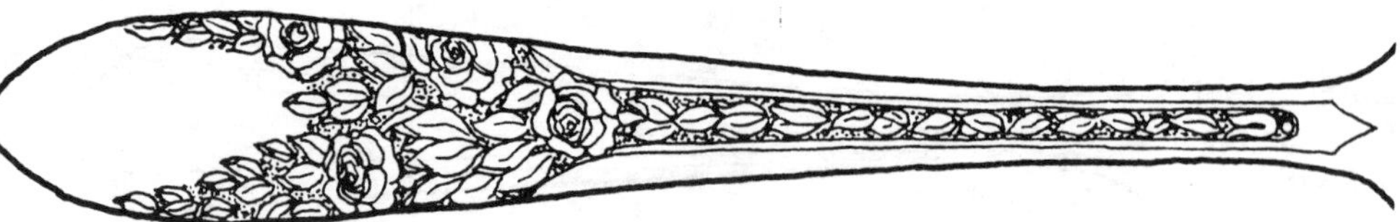

Dinner Knife $12.00 Dinner Fork $12.00 Teaspoon $7.00

Elaky
1940
S

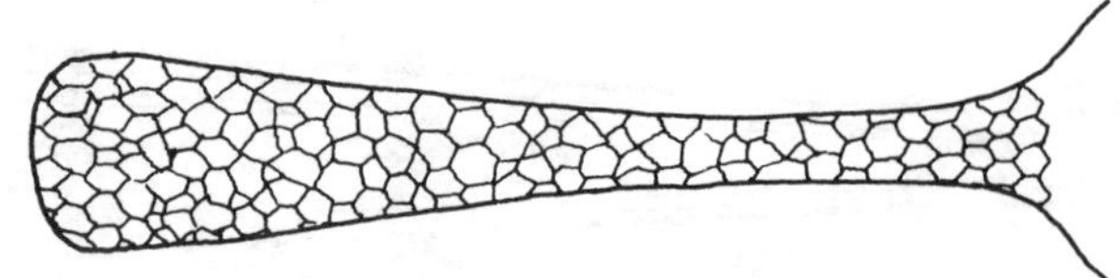

Dinner Knife $8.00
Dinner Fork $8.00
Teaspoon $5.00

Please refer to "How To Use This Book" page 4.

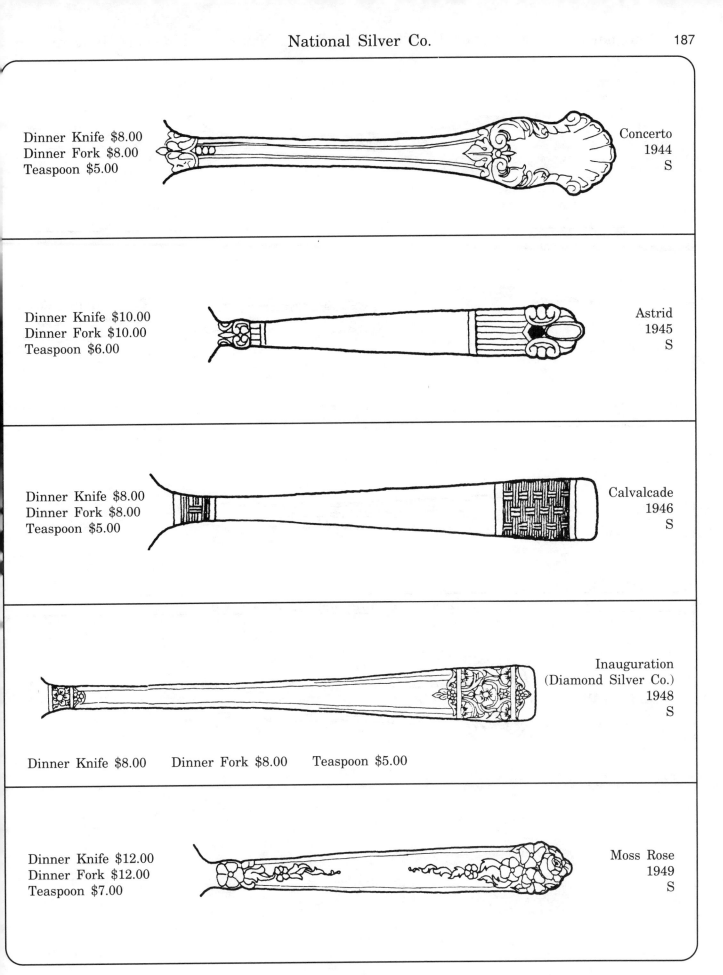

Dinner Knife $8.00
Dinner Fork $8.00
Teaspoon $5.00

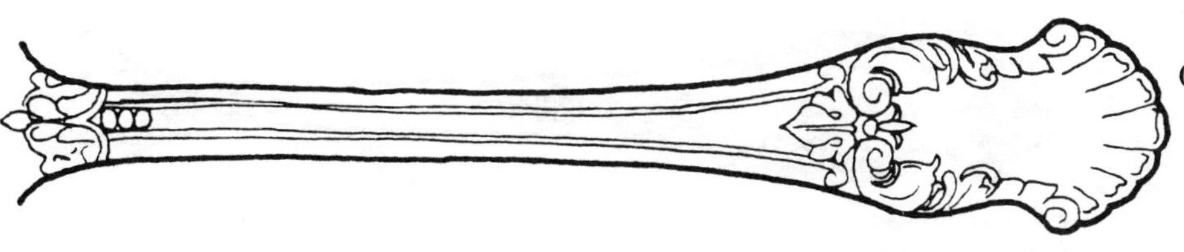

Concerto
1944
S

Dinner Knife $10.00
Dinner Fork $10.00
Teaspoon $6.00

Astrid
1945
S

Dinner Knife $8.00
Dinner Fork $8.00
Teaspoon $5.00

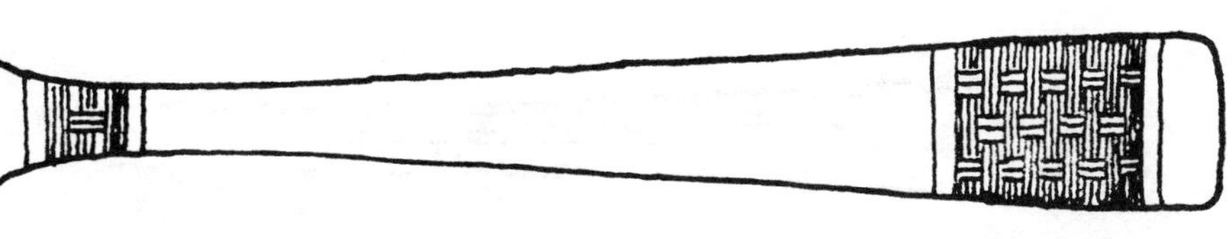

Calvalcade
1946
S

Inauguration
(Diamond Silver Co.)
1948
S

Dinner Knife $8.00 Dinner Fork $8.00 Teaspoon $5.00

Dinner Knife $12.00
Dinner Fork $12.00
Teaspoon $7.00

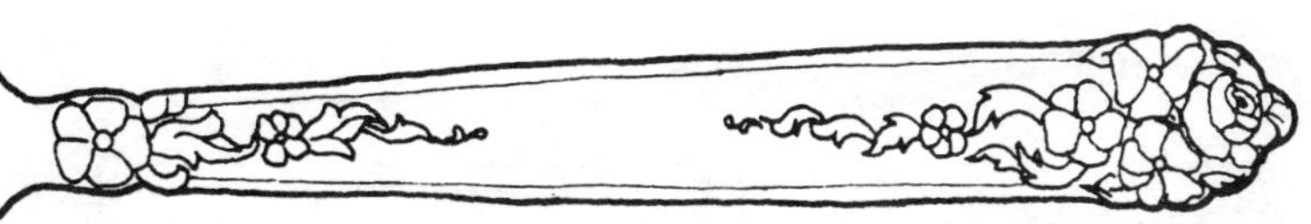

Moss Rose
1949
S

Please refer to "How To Use This Book" page 4.

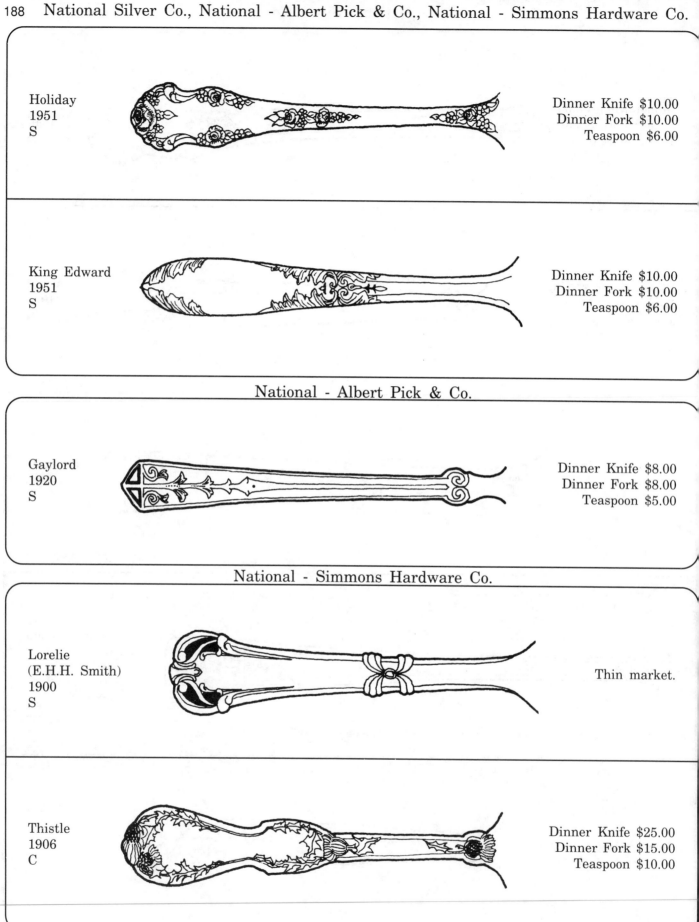

Holiday
1951
S

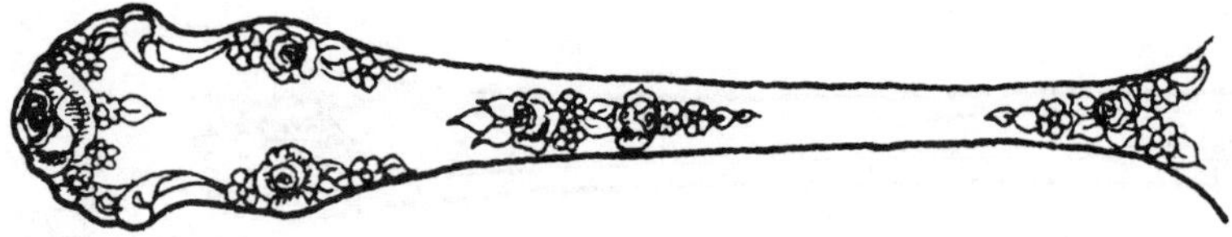

Dinner Knife $10.00
Dinner Fork $10.00
Teaspoon $6.00

King Edward
1951
S

Dinner Knife $10.00
Dinner Fork $10.00
Teaspoon $6.00

National - Albert Pick & Co.

Gaylord
1920
S

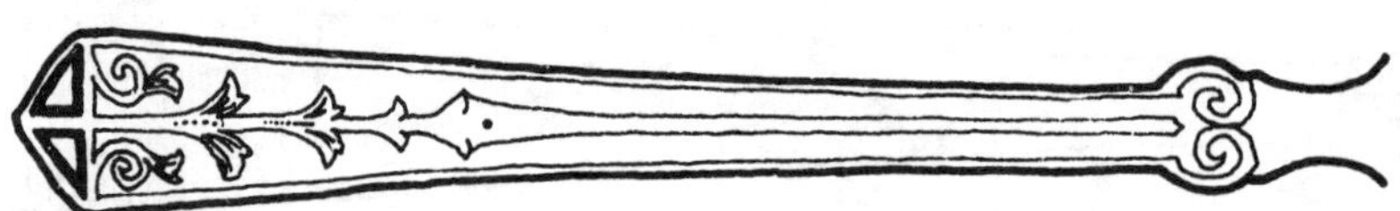

Dinner Knife $8.00
Dinner Fork $8.00
Teaspoon $5.00

National - Simmons Hardware Co.

Lorelie
(E.H.H. Smith)
1900
S

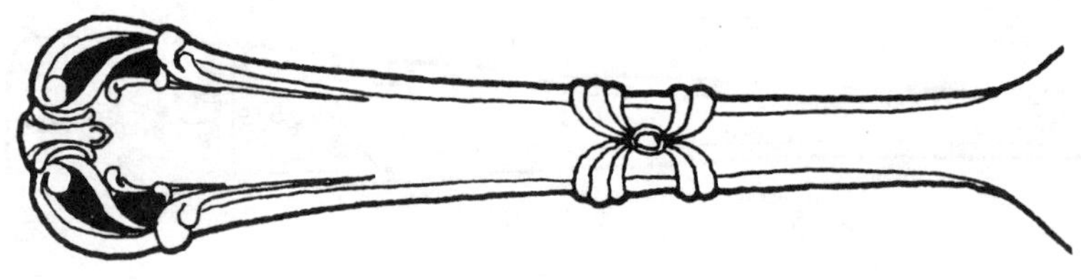

Thin market.

Thistle
1906
C

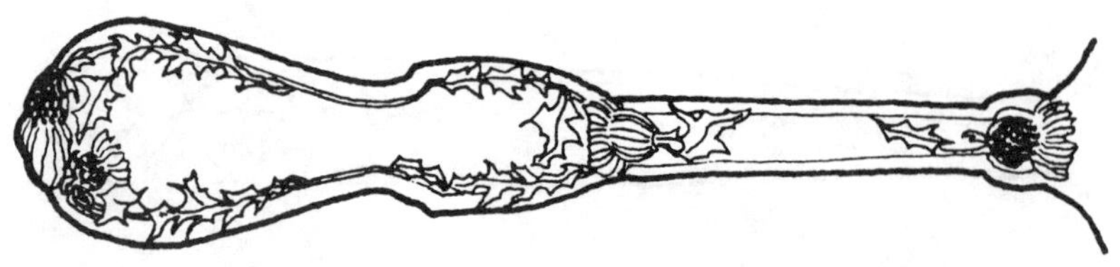

Dinner Knife $25.00
Dinner Fork $15.00
Teaspoon $10.00

Please refer to "How To Use This Book" page 4.

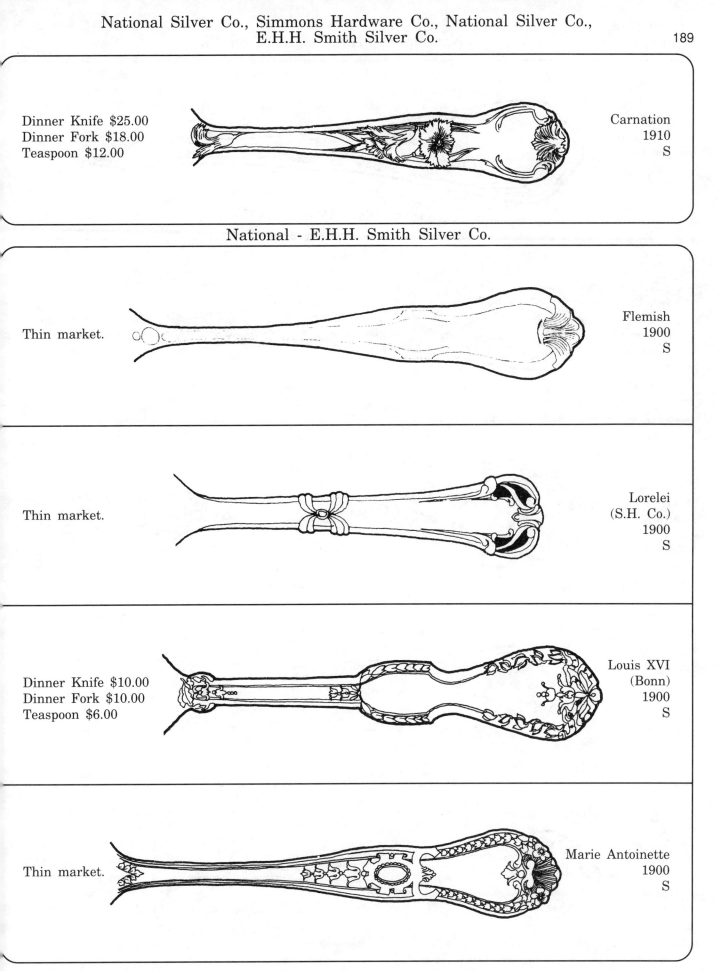

Dinner Knife $25.00
Dinner Fork $18.00
Teaspoon $12.00

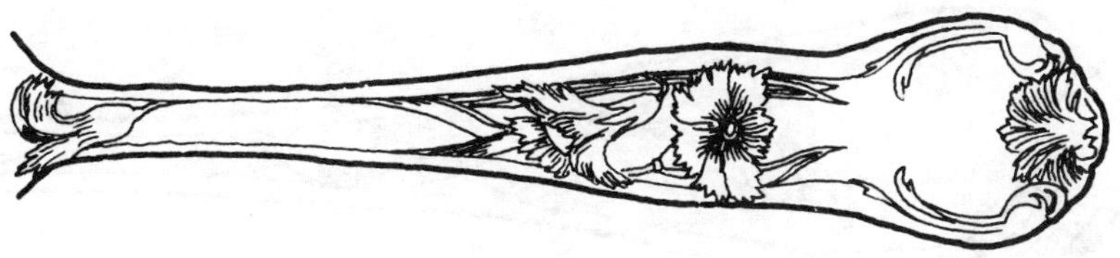

Carnation
1910
S

National - E.H.H. Smith Silver Co.

Thin market.

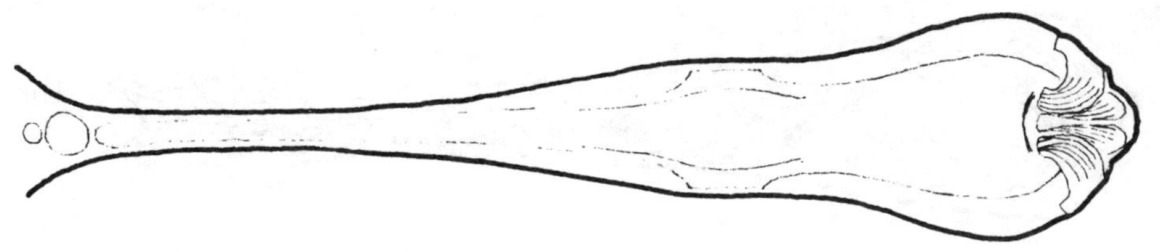

Flemish
1900
S

Thin market.

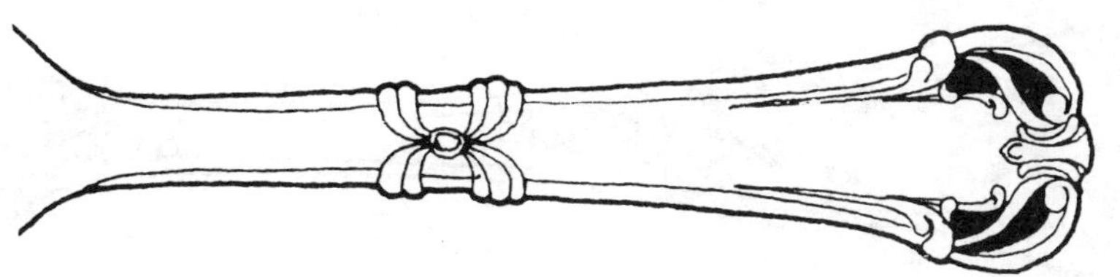

Lorelei
(S.H. Co.)
1900
S

Dinner Knife $10.00
Dinner Fork $10.00
Teaspoon $6.00

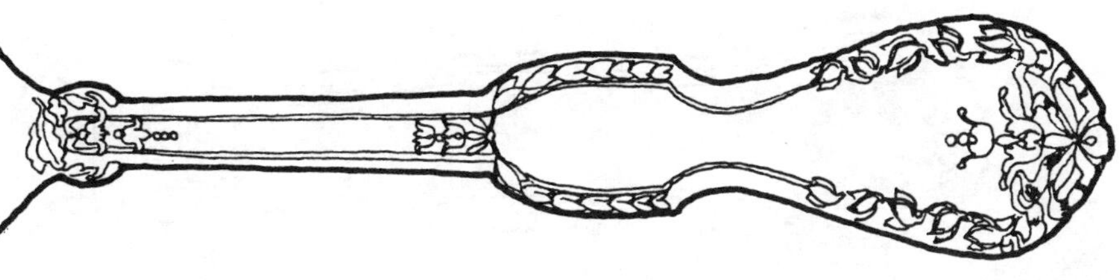

Louis XVI
(Bonn)
1900
S

Thin market.

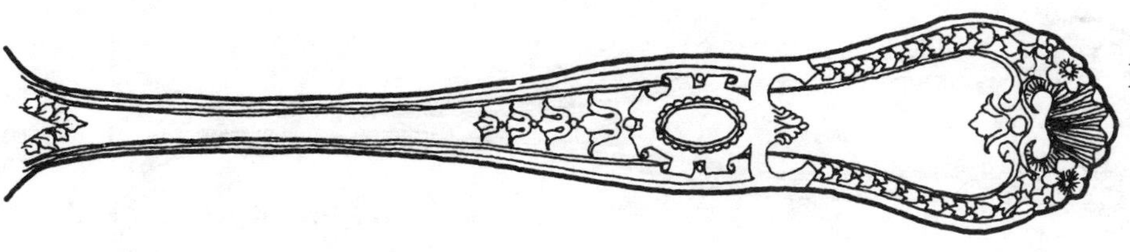

Marie Antoinette
1900
S

Please refer to "How To Use This Book" page 4.

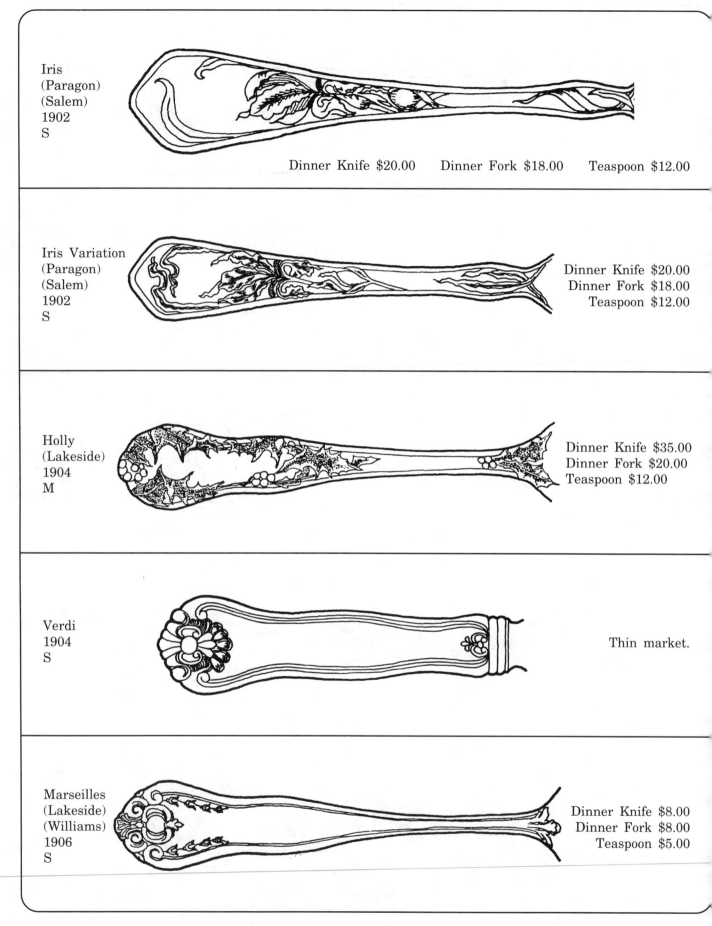

Iris
(Paragon)
(Salem)
1902
S

Dinner Knife $20.00 Dinner Fork $18.00 Teaspoon $12.00

Iris Variation
(Paragon)
(Salem)
1902
S

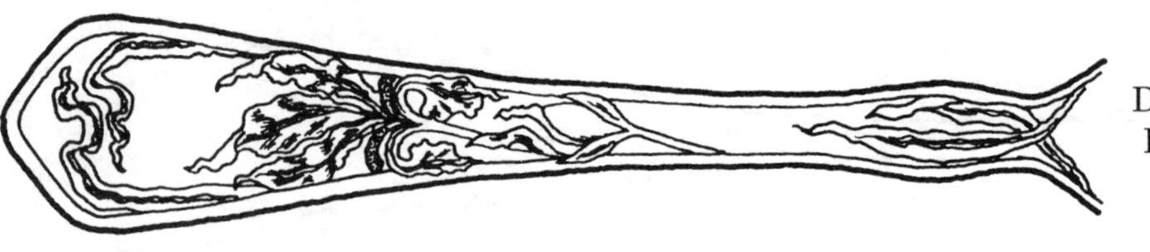

Dinner Knife $20.00
Dinner Fork $18.00
Teaspoon $12.00

Holly
(Lakeside)
1904
M

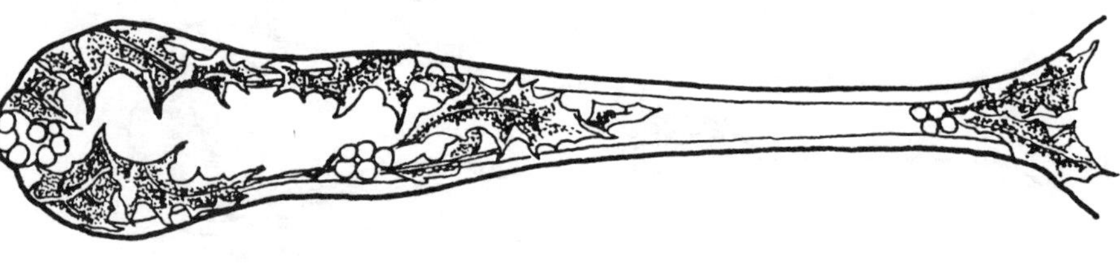

Dinner Knife $35.00
Dinner Fork $20.00
Teaspoon $12.00

Verdi
1904
S

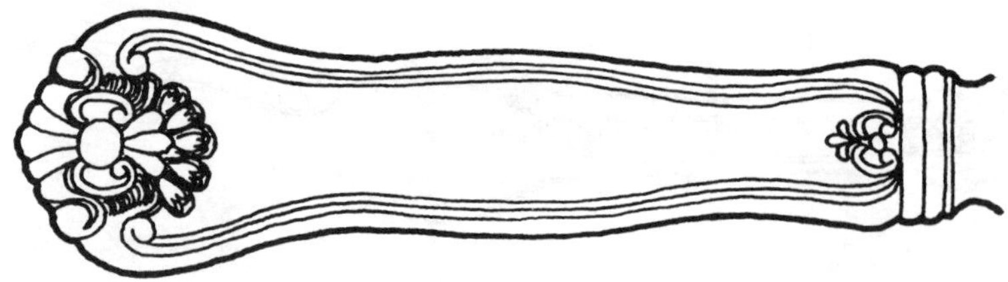

Thin market.

Marseilles
(Lakeside)
(Williams)
1906
S

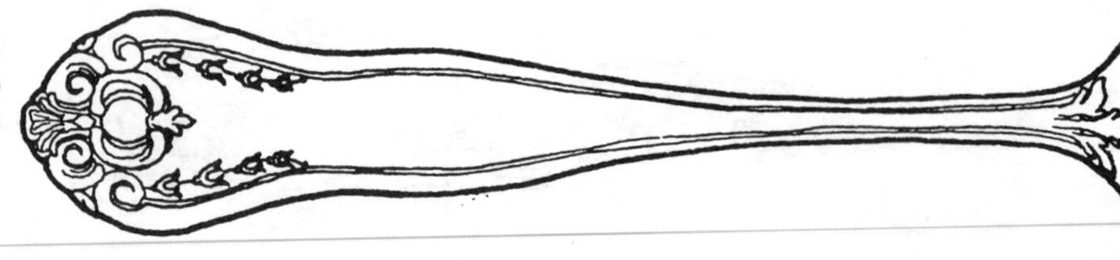

Dinner Knife $8.00
Dinner Fork $8.00
Teaspoon $5.00

Please refer to "How To Use This Book" page 4.

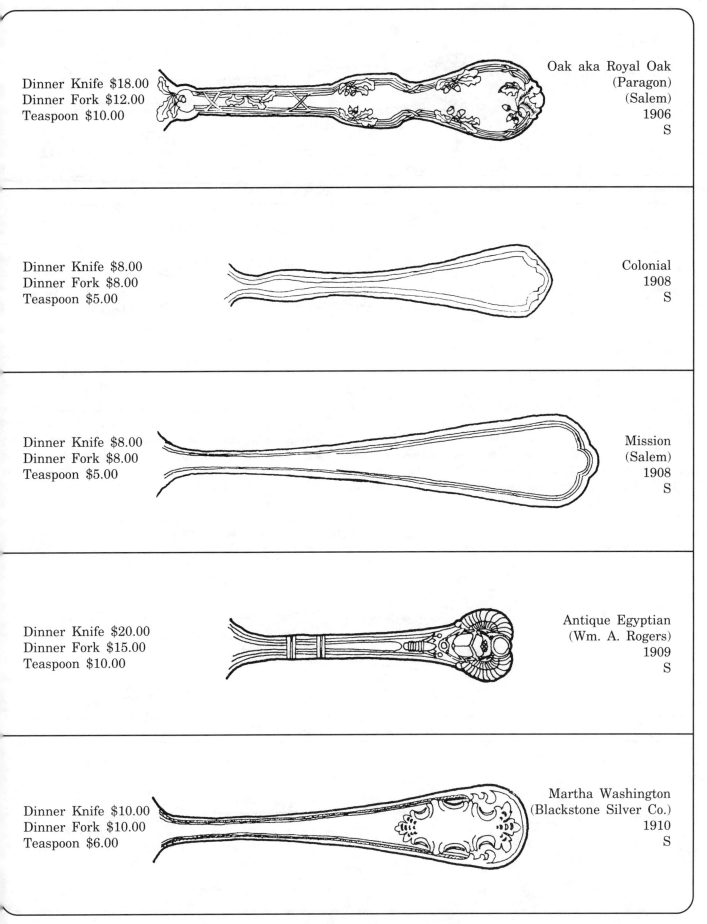

Dinner Knife $18.00
Dinner Fork $12.00
Teaspoon $10.00

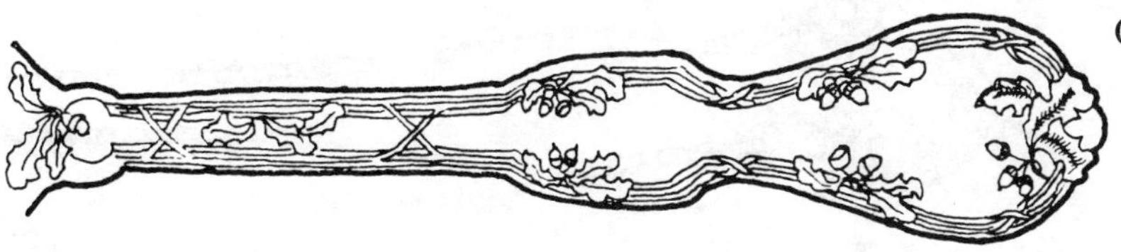

Oak aka Royal Oak
(Paragon)
(Salem)
1906
S

Dinner Knife $8.00
Dinner Fork $8.00
Teaspoon $5.00

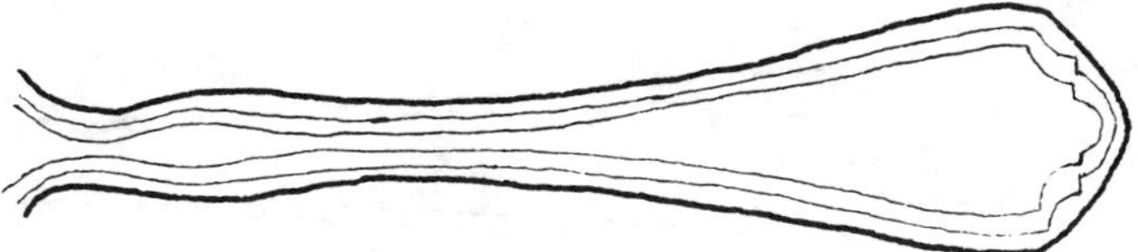

Colonial
1908
S

Dinner Knife $8.00
Dinner Fork $8.00
Teaspoon $5.00

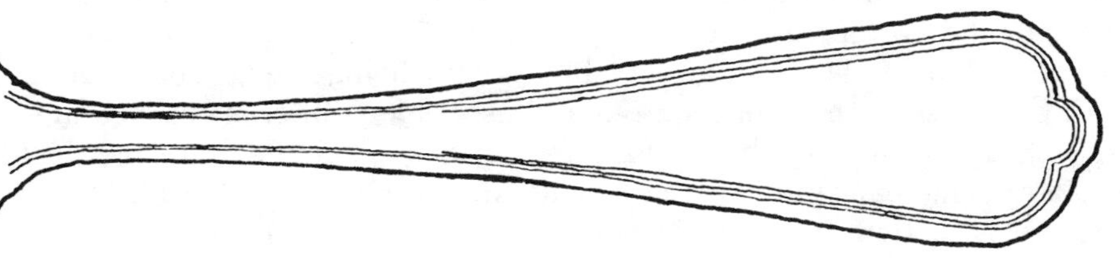

Mission
(Salem)
1908
S

Dinner Knife $20.00
Dinner Fork $15.00
Teaspoon $10.00

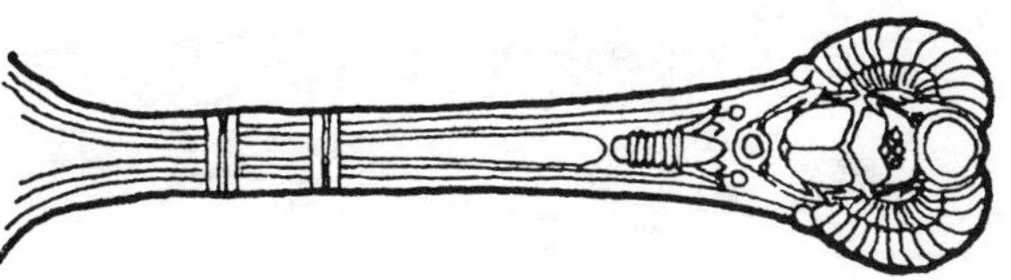

Antique Egyptian
(Wm. A. Rogers)
1909
S

Dinner Knife $10.00
Dinner Fork $10.00
Teaspoon $6.00

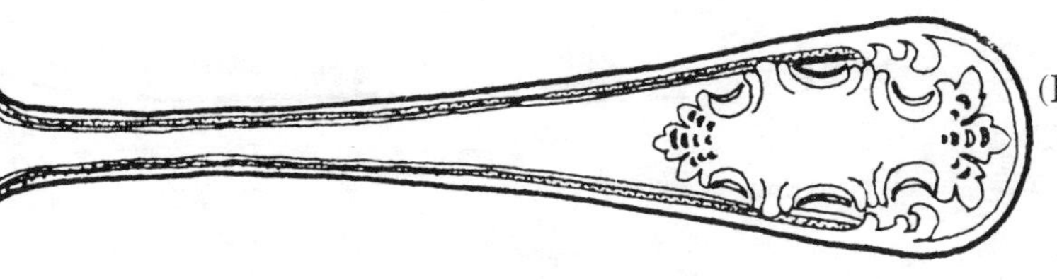

Martha Washington
(Blackstone Silver Co.)
1910
S

Please refer to "How To Use This Book" page 4.

Rose aka York Rose
(Rockford Silver Plate)
1910
S

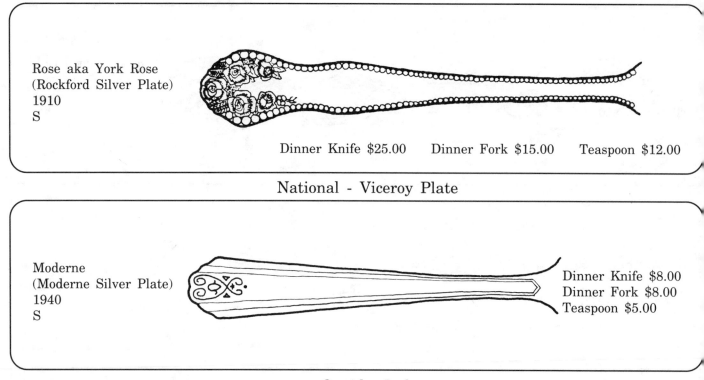

Dinner Knife $25.00 Dinner Fork $15.00 Teaspoon $12.00

National - Viceroy Plate

Moderne
(Moderne Silver Plate)
1940
S

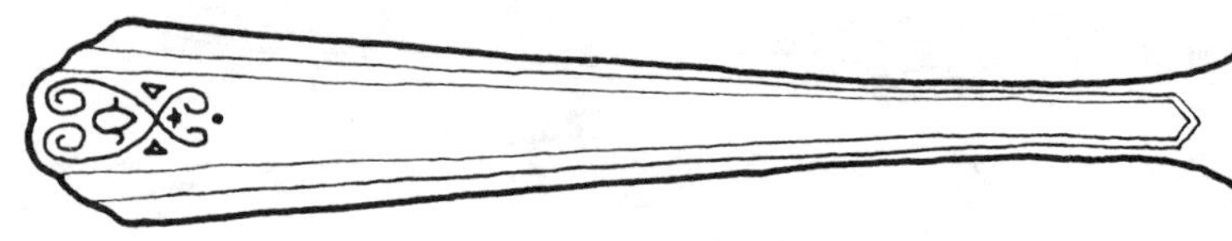

Dinner Knife $8.00
Dinner Fork $8.00
Teaspoon $5.00

Oneida, Ltd.

Oneida began as an experiment in community living in the late 1840's. The community began making flatware in the 1870's but they did not begin to make high quality flatware until they introduced the Community line in 1901 with the pattern Avalon. The Community line is still being made today and continues to be their quality line of flatware. Over the years the firm acquired and used many different backstamps on their flatware. The firm has made not only flatware but also hollowware and dishes. Their flatware has included sterling and stainless as well as silverplate. Some patterns have been made in a variety of materials. It can also be discovered looking at this section of the book that their patterns have had a variety of names and backstamps.

Oneida - Beacon Silver Plate

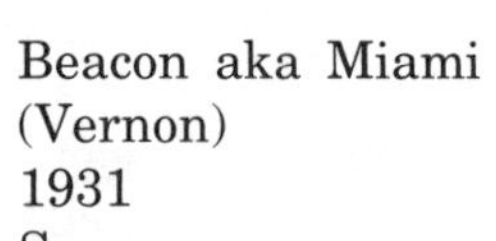

Beacon aka Miami
(Vernon)
1931
S

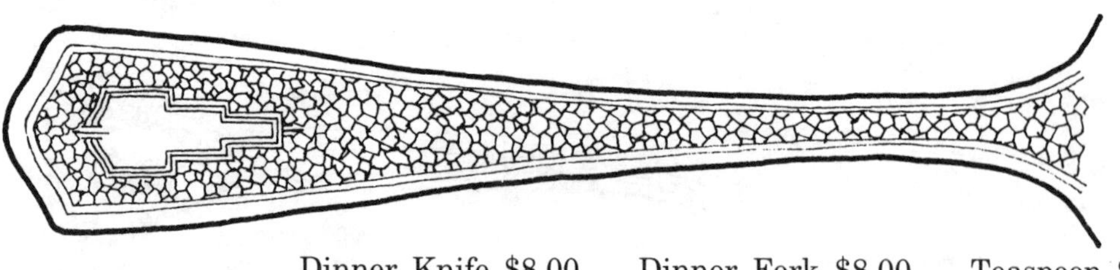

Dinner Knife $8.00 Dinner Fork $8.00 Teaspoon $5.00

Oneida - Camden Silver Plate

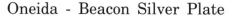

Birchmont
1933
S

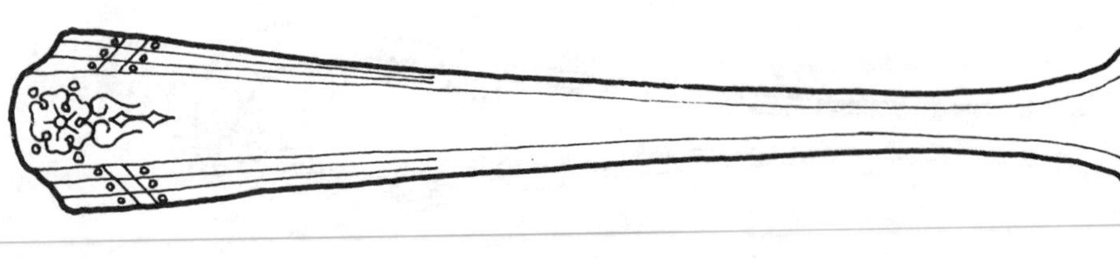

Dinner Knife $8.00
Dinner Fork $8.00
Teaspoon $5.00

Please refer to "How To Use This Book" page 4.

Dinner Knife $8.00
Dinner Fork $8.00
Teaspoon $5.00

Randolph
1929
S

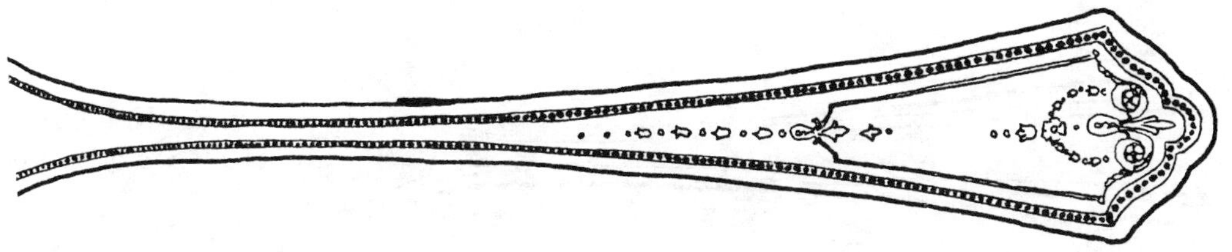

Winthrop
(Honor Plate)
1929
S

Dinner Knife $8.00 Dinner Fork $8.00 Teaspoon $5.00

Dinner Knife $8.00
Dinner Fork $8.00
Teaspoon $5.00

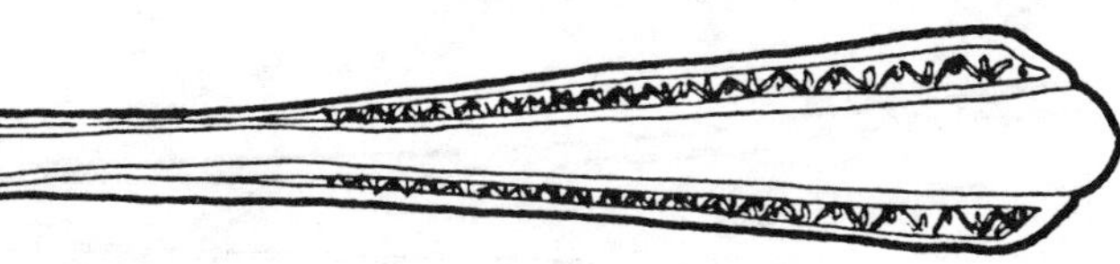

Mary Lee aka Croyden
(Wm. A. Rogers)
1932
S

Oneida - Carlton Silver Plate

Brentwood aka
Ramona aka Lakewood
(Wm. A. Rogers)
(Vernon)
1928
S

Dinner Knife $8.00 Dinner Fork $8.00 Teaspoon $5.00

Dinner Knife $8.00
Dinner Fork $8.00
Teaspoon $5.00

Thelma aka Hampton
(Vernon)
1928
S

Please refer to "How To Use This Book" page 4.

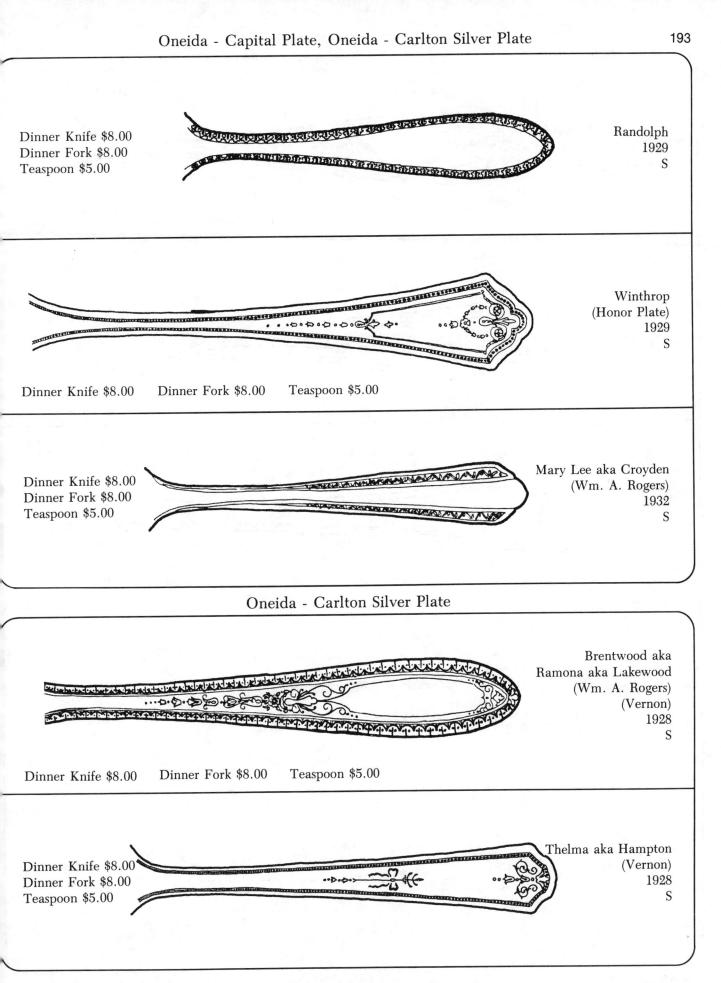

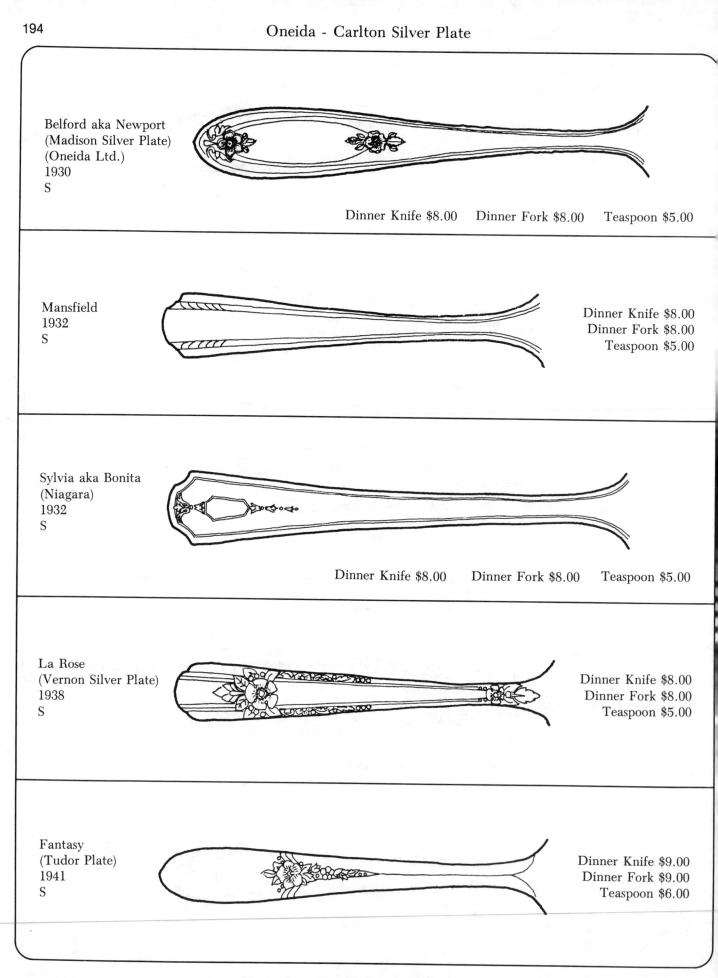

Belford aka Newport
(Madison Silver Plate)
(Oneida Ltd.)
1930
S

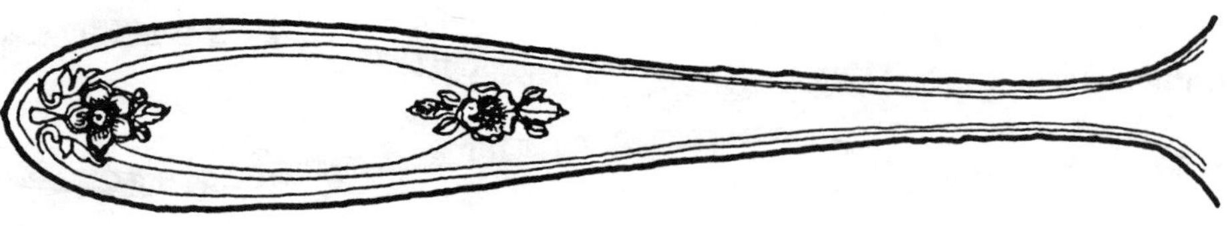

Dinner Knife $8.00 Dinner Fork $8.00 Teaspoon $5.00

Mansfield
1932
S

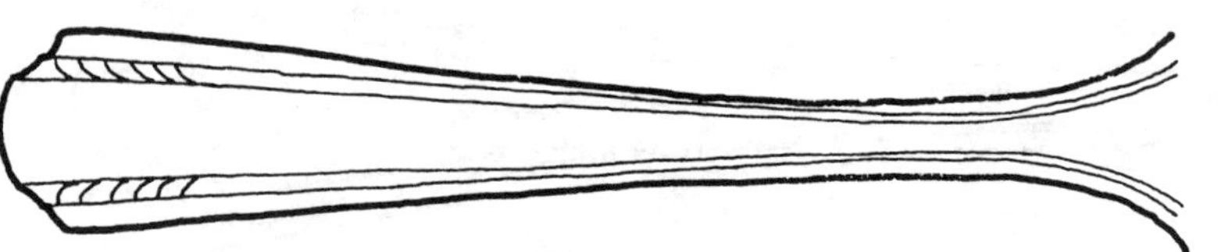

Dinner Knife $8.00
Dinner Fork $8.00
Teaspoon $5.00

Sylvia aka Bonita
(Niagara)
1932
S

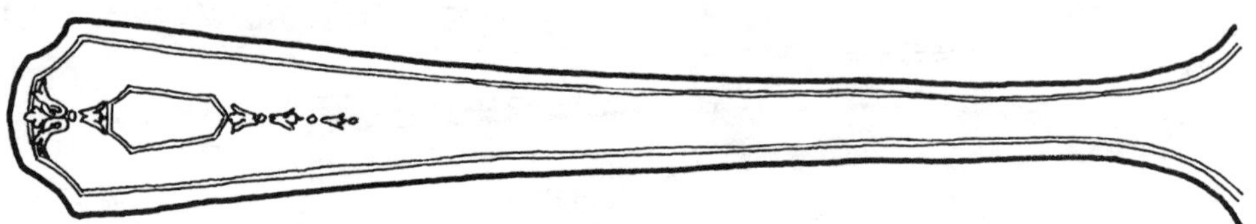

Dinner Knife $8.00 Dinner Fork $8.00 Teaspoon $5.00

La Rose
(Vernon Silver Plate)
1938
S

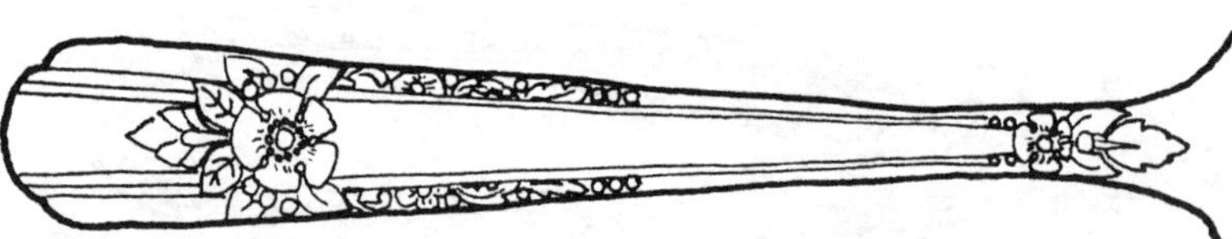

Dinner Knife $8.00
Dinner Fork $8.00
Teaspoon $5.00

Fantasy
(Tudor Plate)
1941
S

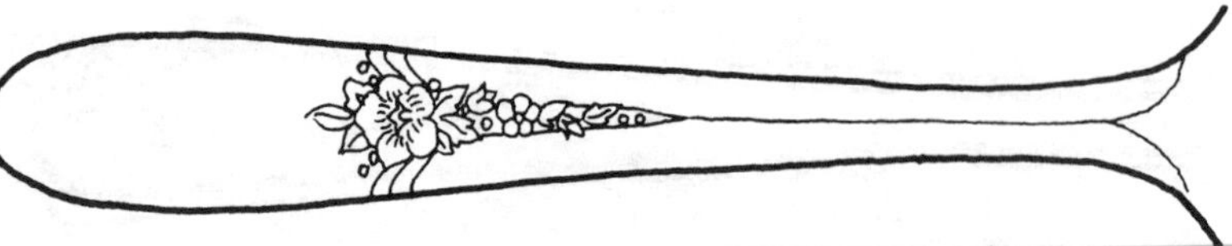

Dinner Knife $9.00
Dinner Fork $9.00
Teaspoon $6.00

Please refer to "How To Use This Book" page 4.

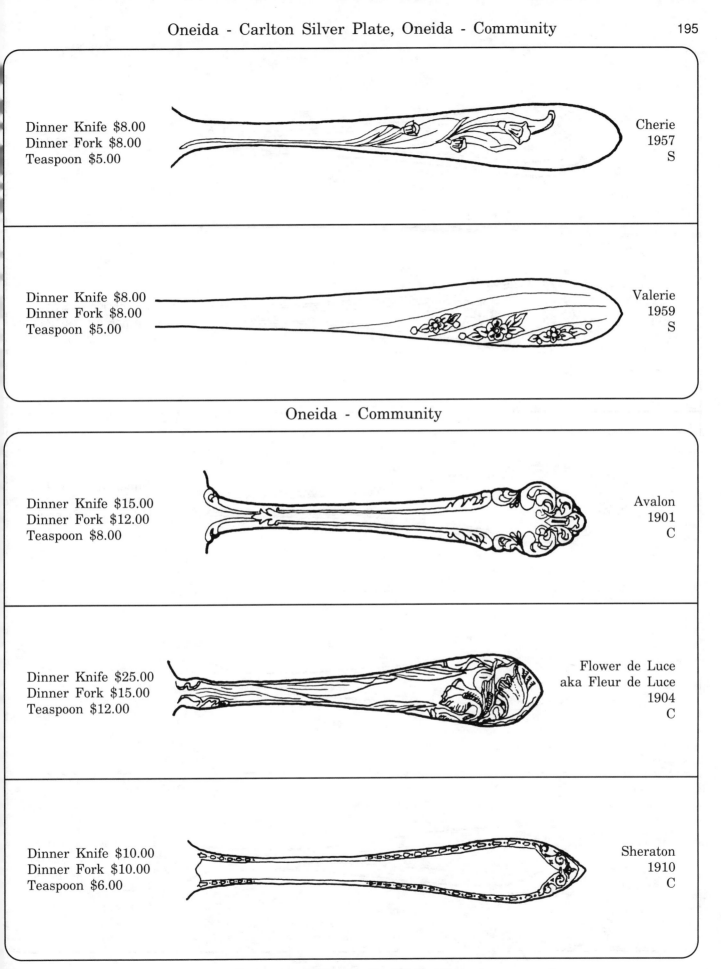

Dinner Knife $8.00
Dinner Fork $8.00
Teaspoon $5.00

Cherie
1957
S

Dinner Knife $8.00
Dinner Fork $8.00
Teaspoon $5.00

Valerie
1959
S

Oneida - Community

Dinner Knife $15.00
Dinner Fork $12.00
Teaspoon $8.00

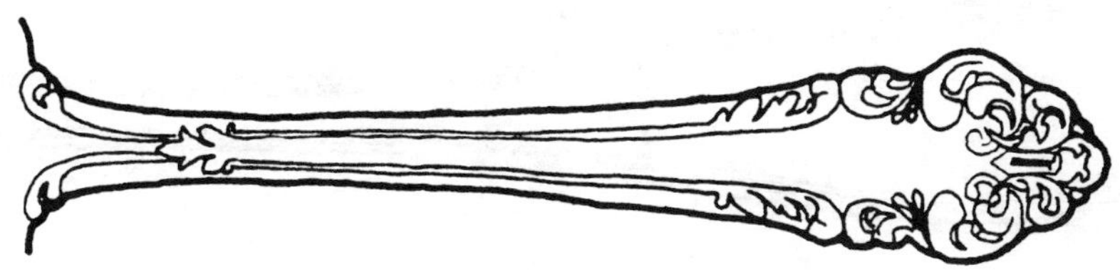

Avalon
1901
C

Dinner Knife $25.00
Dinner Fork $15.00
Teaspoon $12.00

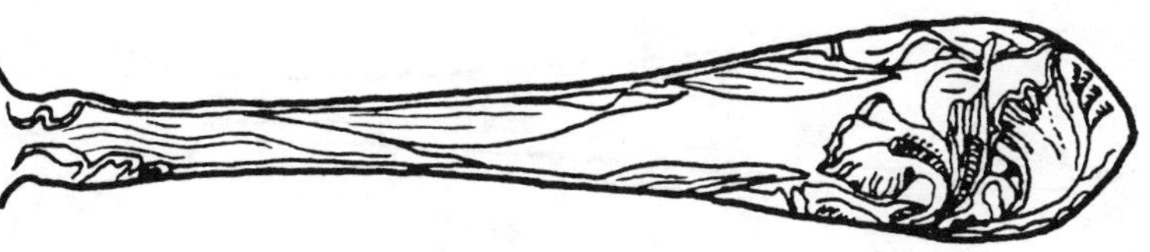

Flower de Luce
aka Fleur de Luce
1904
C

Dinner Knife $10.00
Dinner Fork $10.00
Teaspoon $6.00

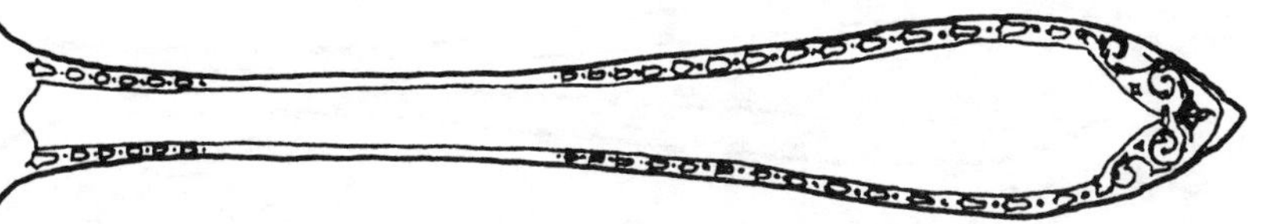

Sheraton
1910
C

Please refer to “How To Use This Book” page 4.

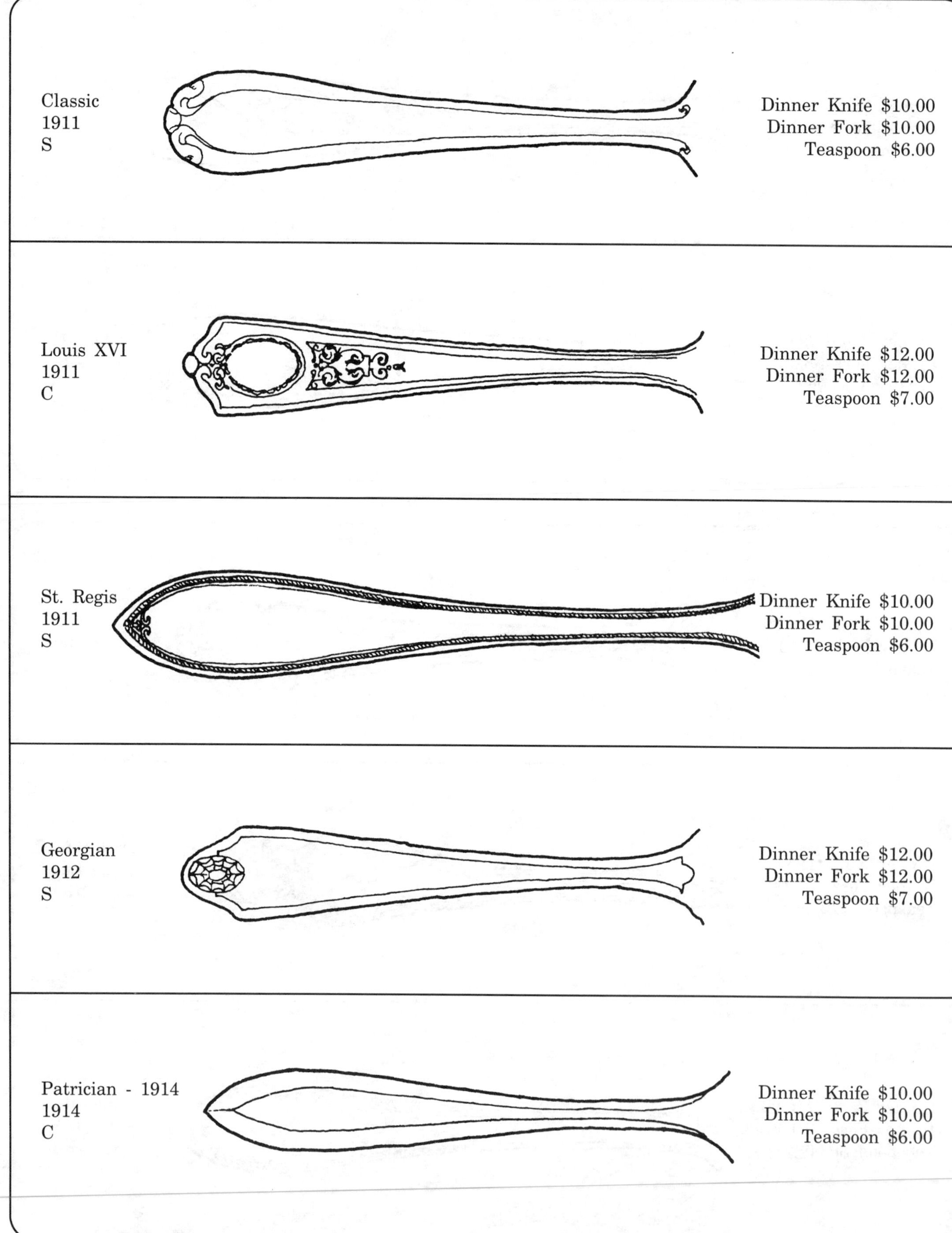

Classic
1911
S

Dinner Knife $10.00
Dinner Fork $10.00
Teaspoon $6.00

Louis XVI
1911
C

Dinner Knife $12.00
Dinner Fork $12.00
Teaspoon $7.00

St. Regis
1911
S

Dinner Knife $10.00
Dinner Fork $10.00
Teaspoon $6.00

Georgian
1912
S

Dinner Knife $12.00
Dinner Fork $12.00
Teaspoon $7.00

Patrician - 1914
1914
C

Dinner Knife $10.00
Dinner Fork $10.00
Teaspoon $6.00

Please refer to "How To Use This Book" page 4.

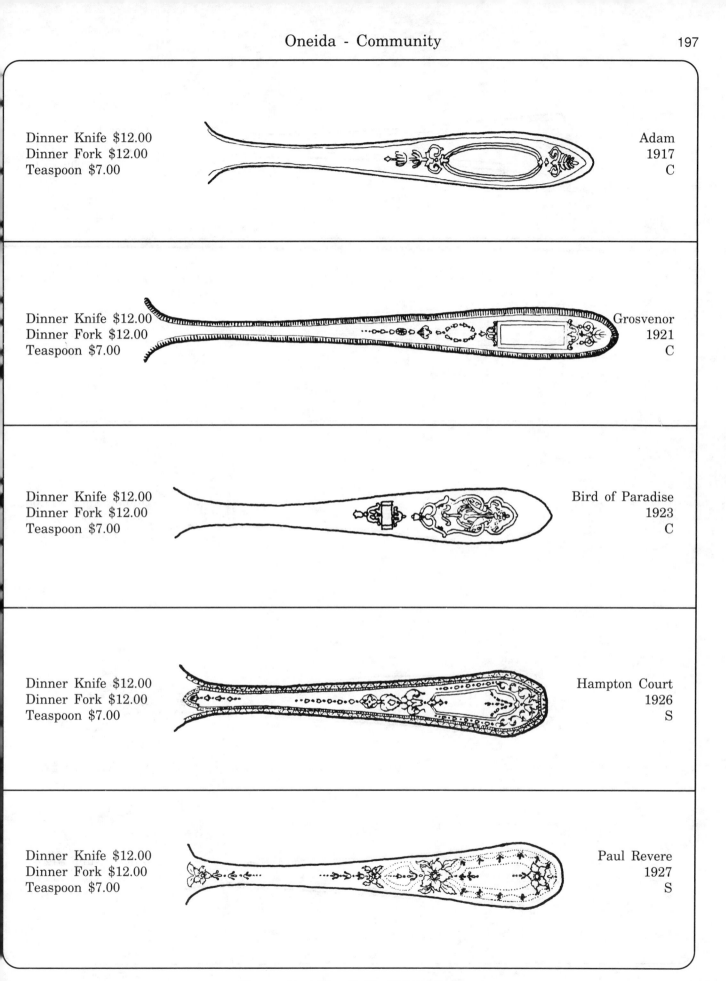

Dinner Knife $12.00
Dinner Fork $12.00
Teaspoon $7.00

Adam
1917
C

Dinner Knife $12.00
Dinner Fork $12.00
Teaspoon $7.00

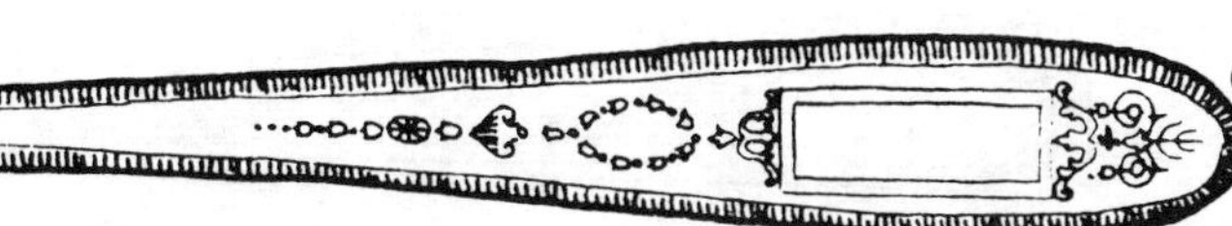

Grosvenor
1921
C

Dinner Knife $12.00
Dinner Fork $12.00
Teaspoon $7.00

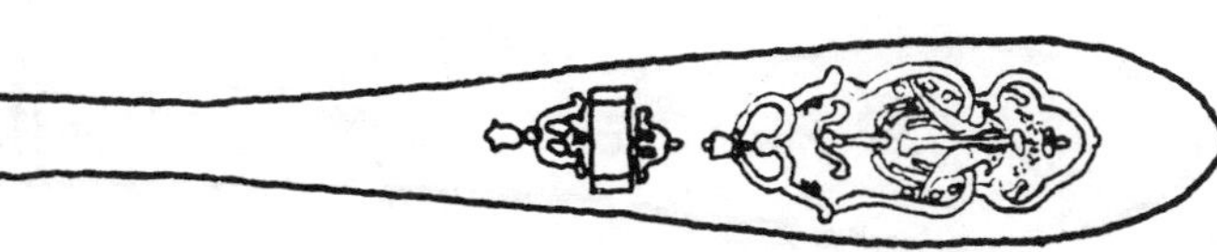

Bird of Paradise
1923
C

Dinner Knife $12.00
Dinner Fork $12.00
Teaspoon $7.00

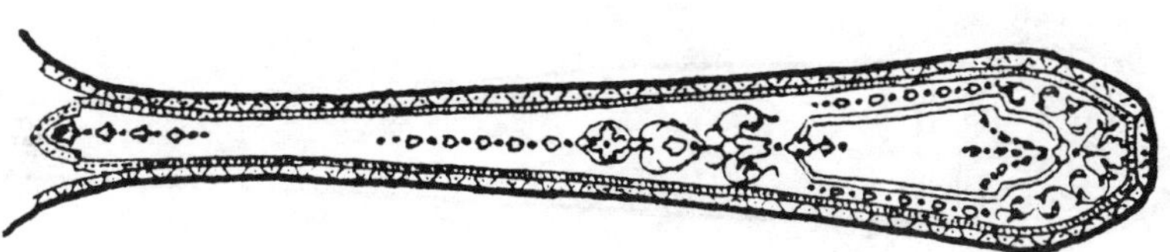

Hampton Court
1926
S

Dinner Knife $12.00
Dinner Fork $12.00
Teaspoon $7.00

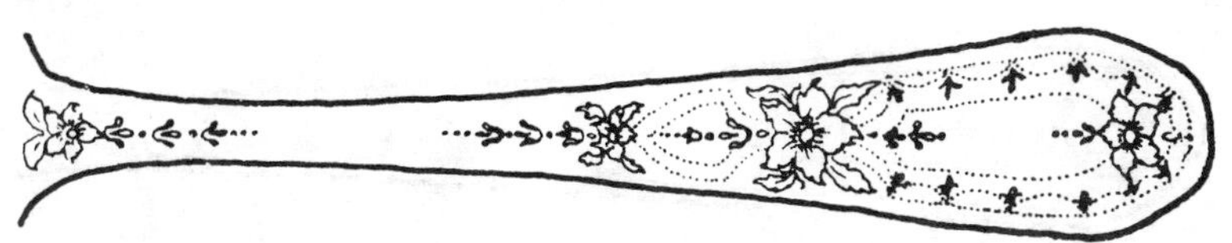

Paul Revere
1927
S

Please refer to "How To Use This Book" page 4.

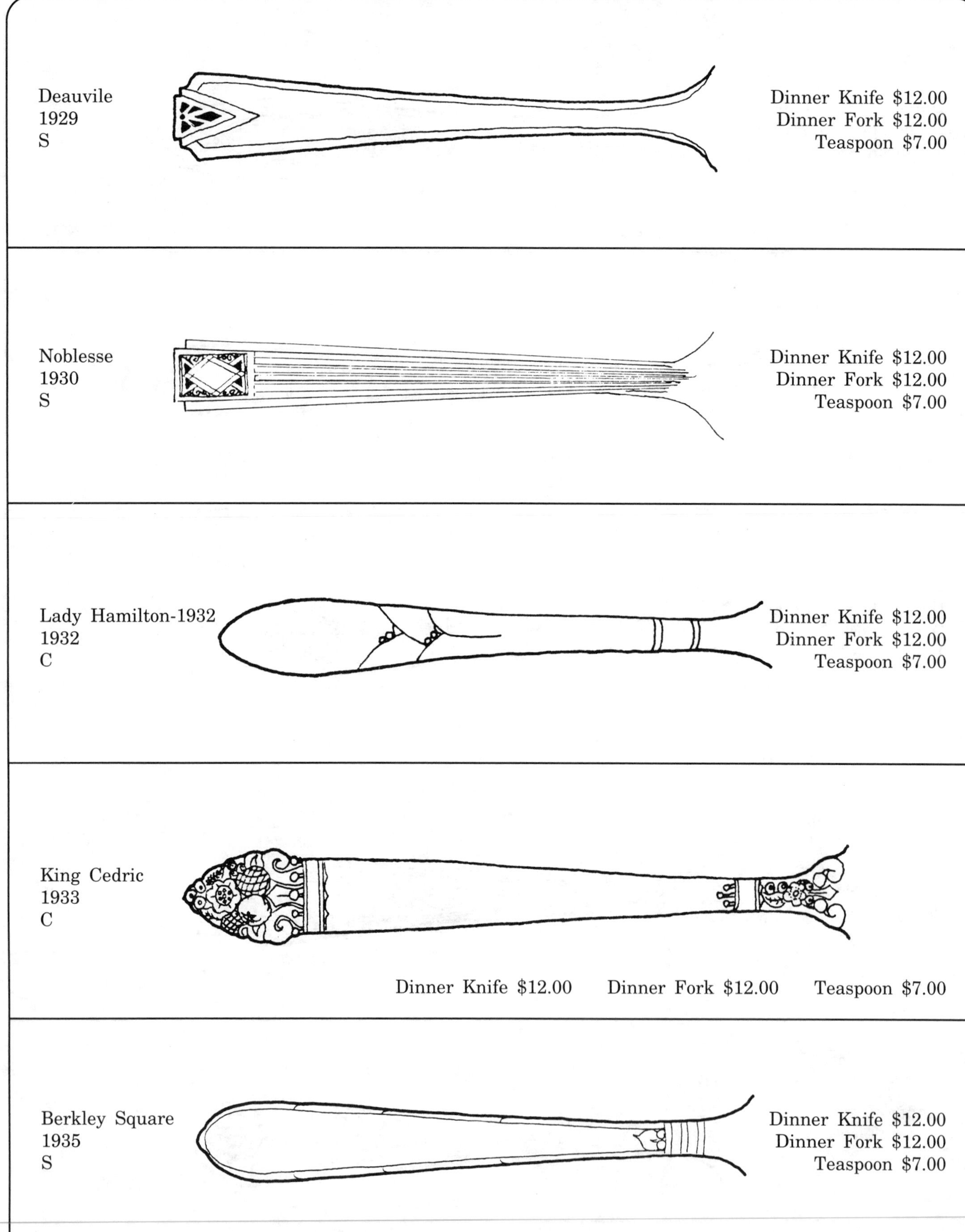

Deauvile
1929
S

Dinner Knife $12.00
Dinner Fork $12.00
Teaspoon $7.00

Noblesse
1930
S

Dinner Knife $12.00
Dinner Fork $12.00
Teaspoon $7.00

Lady Hamilton-1932
1932
C

Dinner Knife $12.00
Dinner Fork $12.00
Teaspoon $7.00

King Cedric
1933
C

Dinner Knife $12.00 Dinner Fork $12.00 Teaspoon $7.00

Berkley Square
1935
S

Dinner Knife $12.00
Dinner Fork $12.00
Teaspoon $7.00

Please refer to "How To Use This Book" page 4.

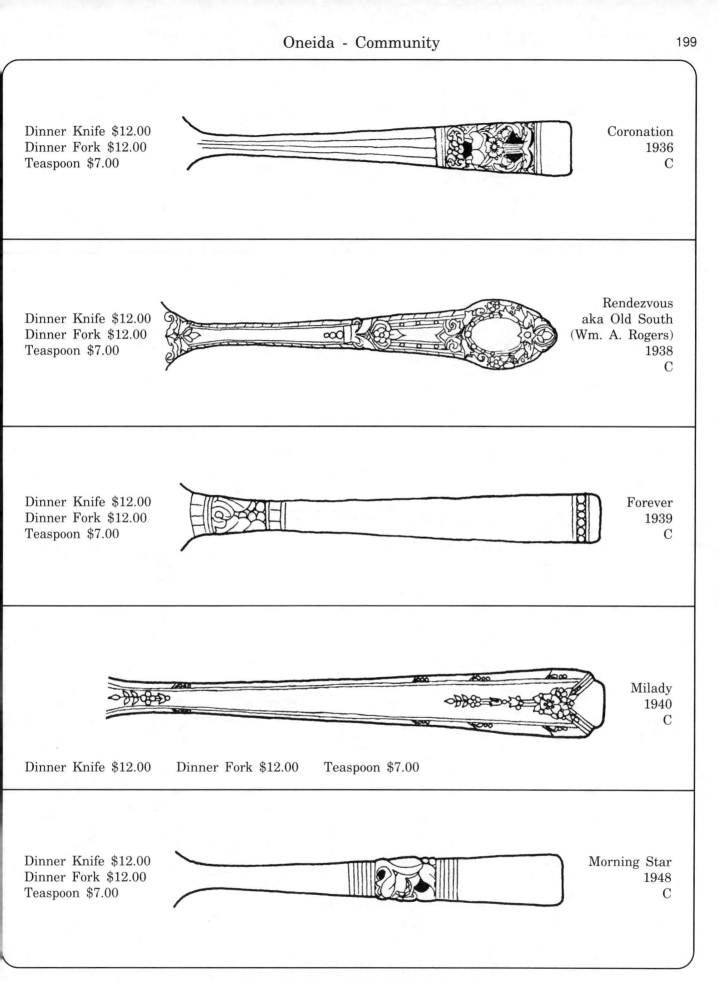

Dinner Knife $12.00
Dinner Fork $12.00
Teaspoon $7.00

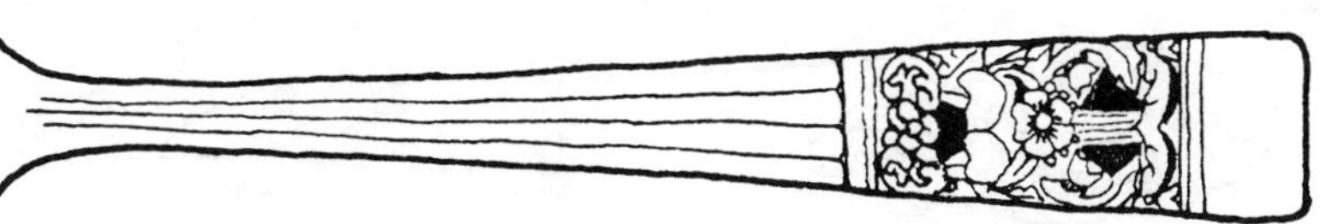

Coronation
1936
C

Dinner Knife $12.00
Dinner Fork $12.00
Teaspoon $7.00

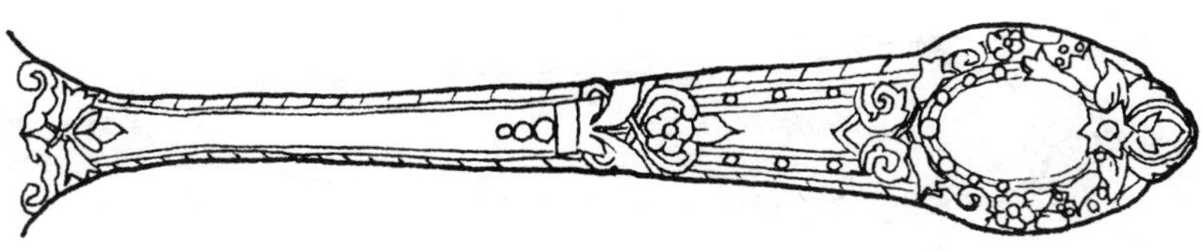

Rendezvous
aka Old South
(Wm. A. Rogers)
1938
C

Dinner Knife $12.00
Dinner Fork $12.00
Teaspoon $7.00

Forever
1939
C

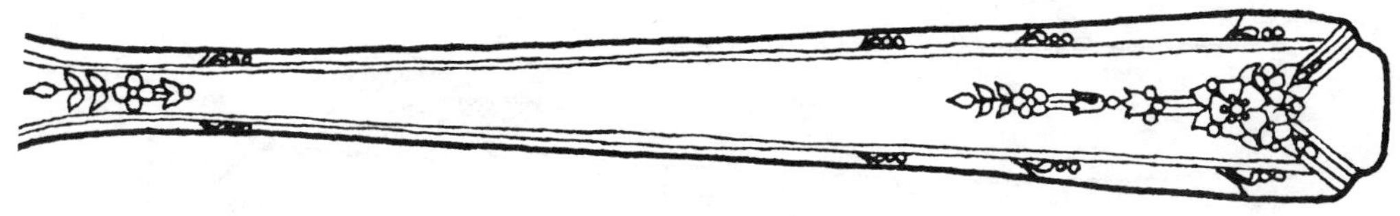

Milady
1940
C

Dinner Knife $12.00 Dinner Fork $12.00 Teaspoon $7.00

Dinner Knife $12.00
Dinner Fork $12.00
Teaspoon $7.00

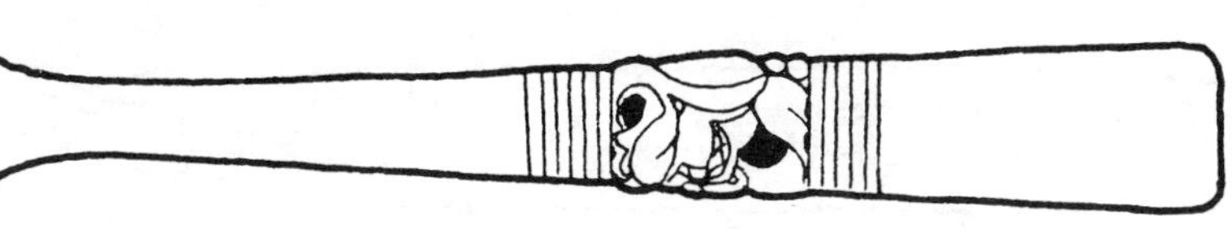

Morning Star
1948
C

Please refer to "How To Use This Book" page 4.

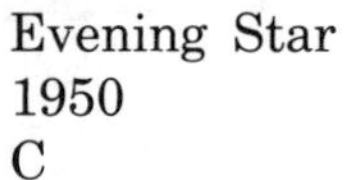

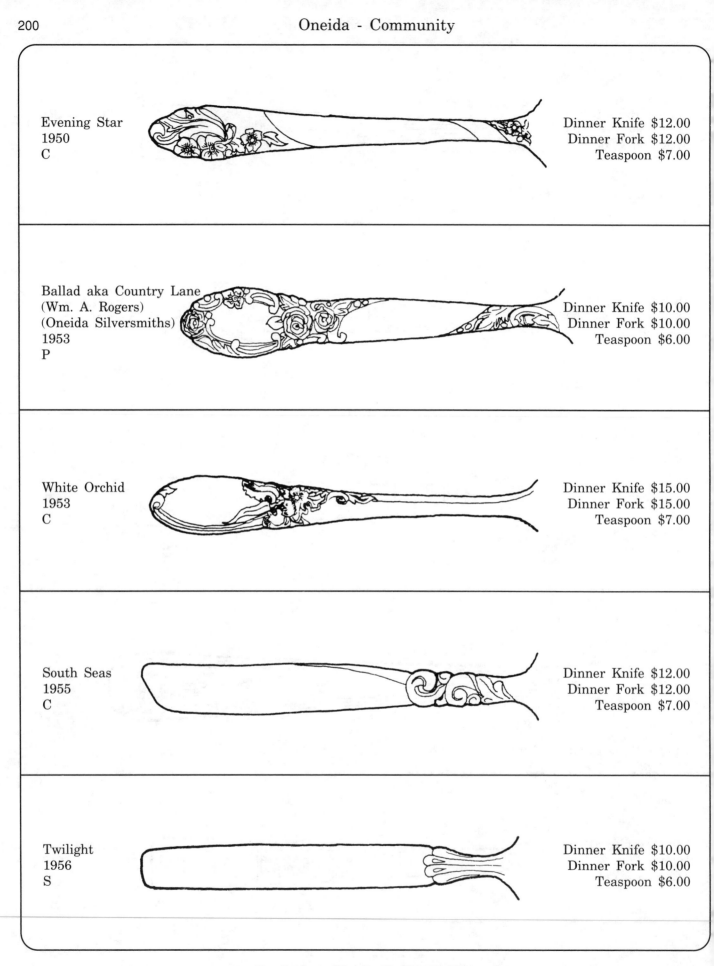

Evening Star
1950
C

Dinner Knife $12.00
Dinner Fork $12.00
Teaspoon $7.00

Ballad aka Country Lane
(Wm. A. Rogers)
(Oneida Silversmiths)
1953
P

Dinner Knife $10.00
Dinner Fork $10.00
Teaspoon $6.00

White Orchid
1953
C

Dinner Knife $15.00
Dinner Fork $15.00
Teaspoon $7.00

South Seas
1955
C

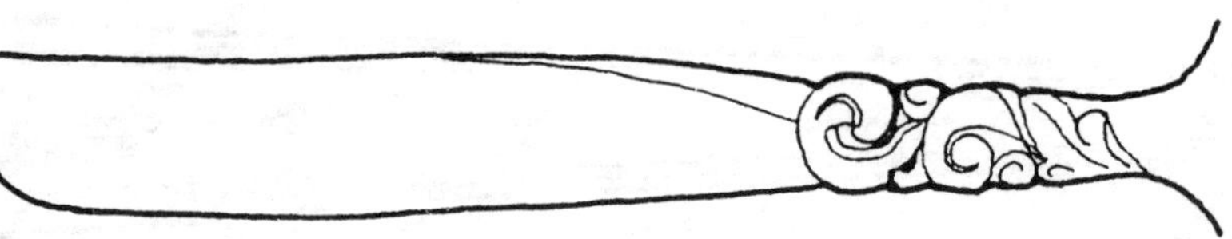

Dinner Knife $12.00
Dinner Fork $12.00
Teaspoon $7.00

Twilight
1956
S

Dinner Knife $10.00
Dinner Fork $10.00
Teaspoon $6.00

Please refer to "How To Use This Book" page 4.

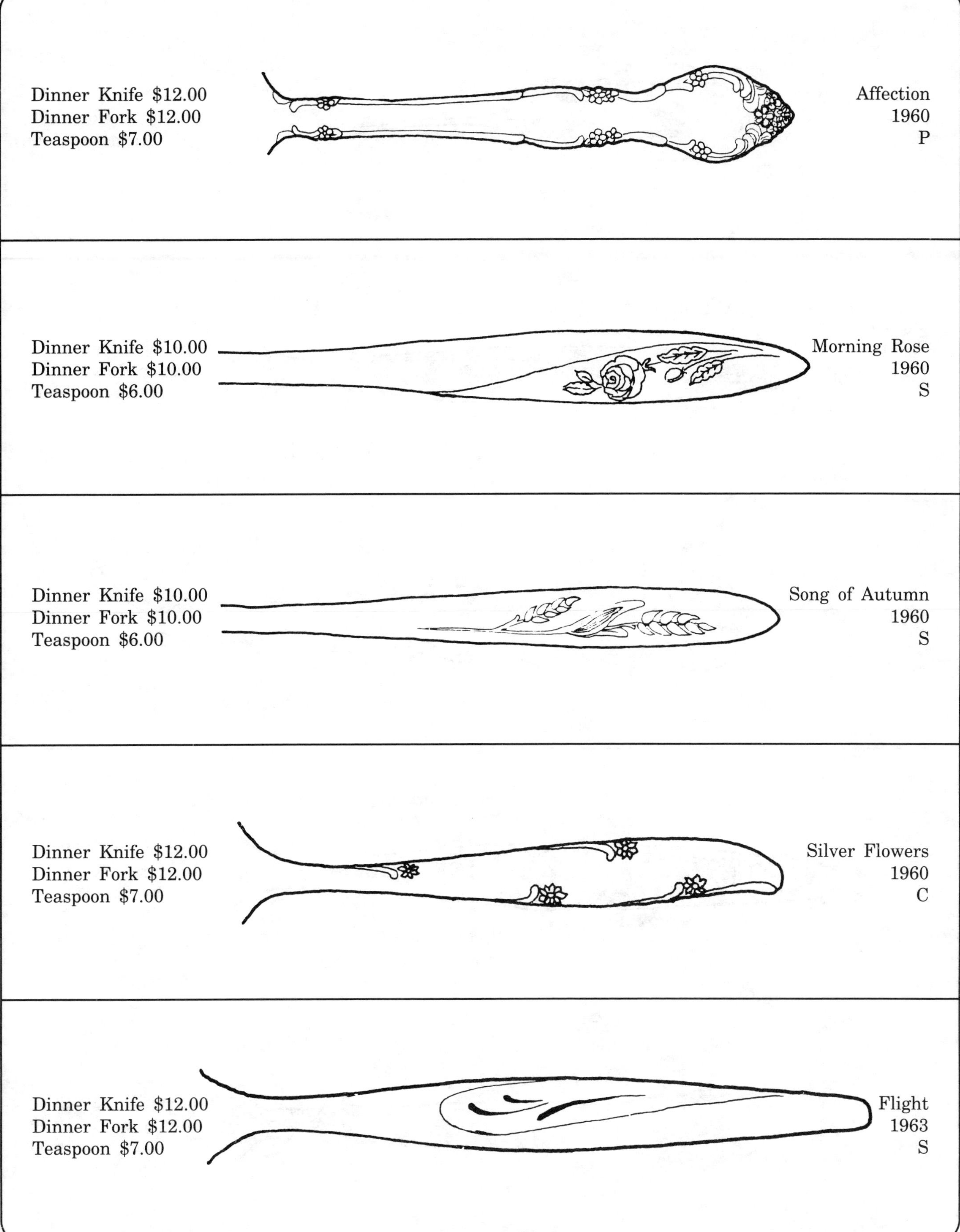

Please refer to "How To Use This Book" page 4.

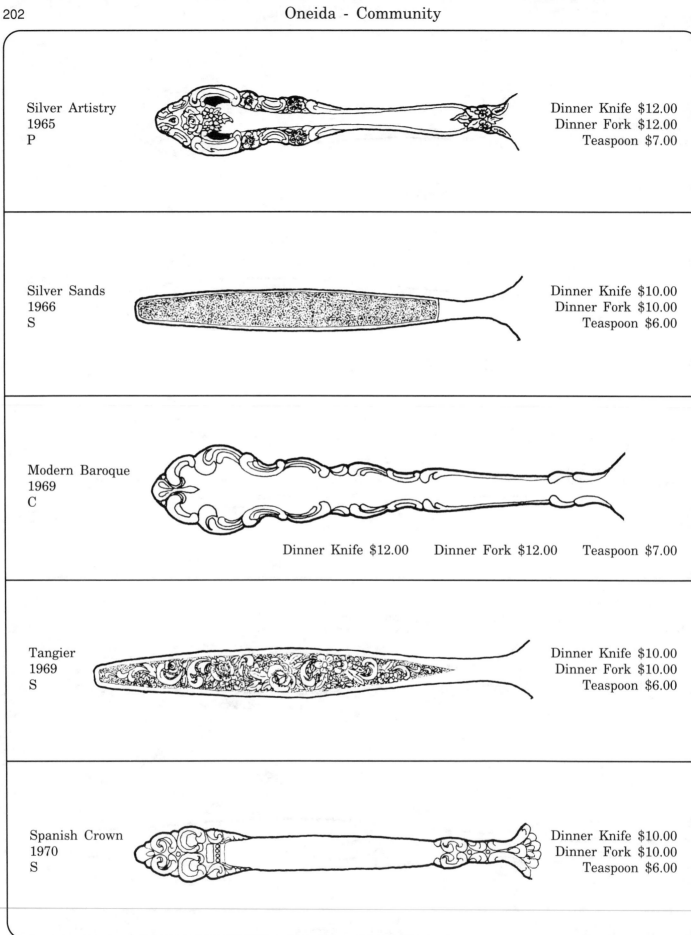

Silver Artistry
1965
P

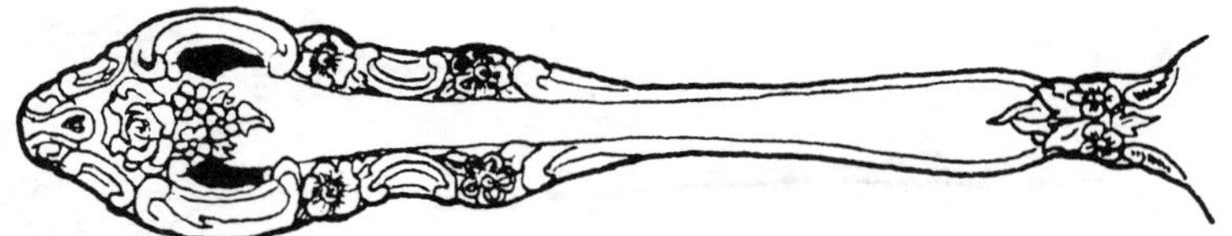

Dinner Knife $12.00
Dinner Fork $12.00
Teaspoon $7.00

Silver Sands
1966
S

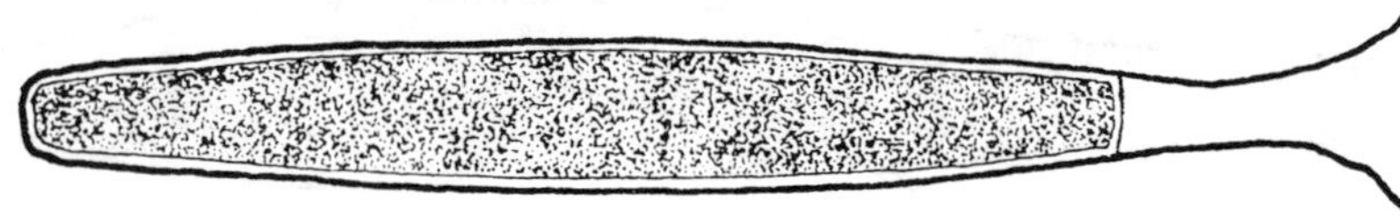

Dinner Knife $10.00
Dinner Fork $10.00
Teaspoon $6.00

Modern Baroque
1969
C

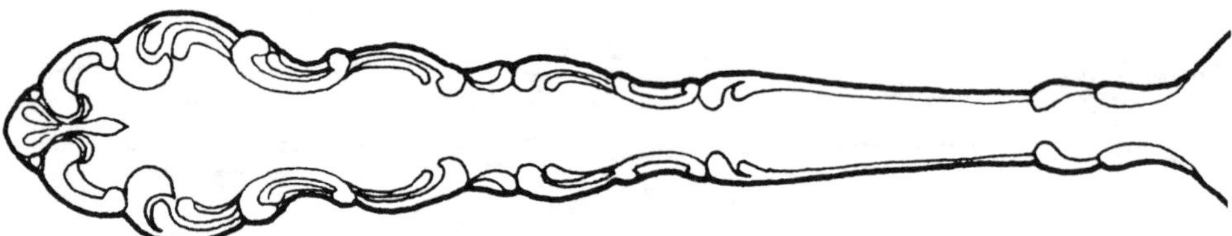

Dinner Knife $12.00 Dinner Fork $12.00 Teaspoon $7.00

Tangier
1969
S

Dinner Knife $10.00
Dinner Fork $10.00
Teaspoon $6.00

Spanish Crown
1970
S

Dinner Knife $10.00
Dinner Fork $10.00
Teaspoon $6.00

Please refer to "How To Use This Book" page 4.

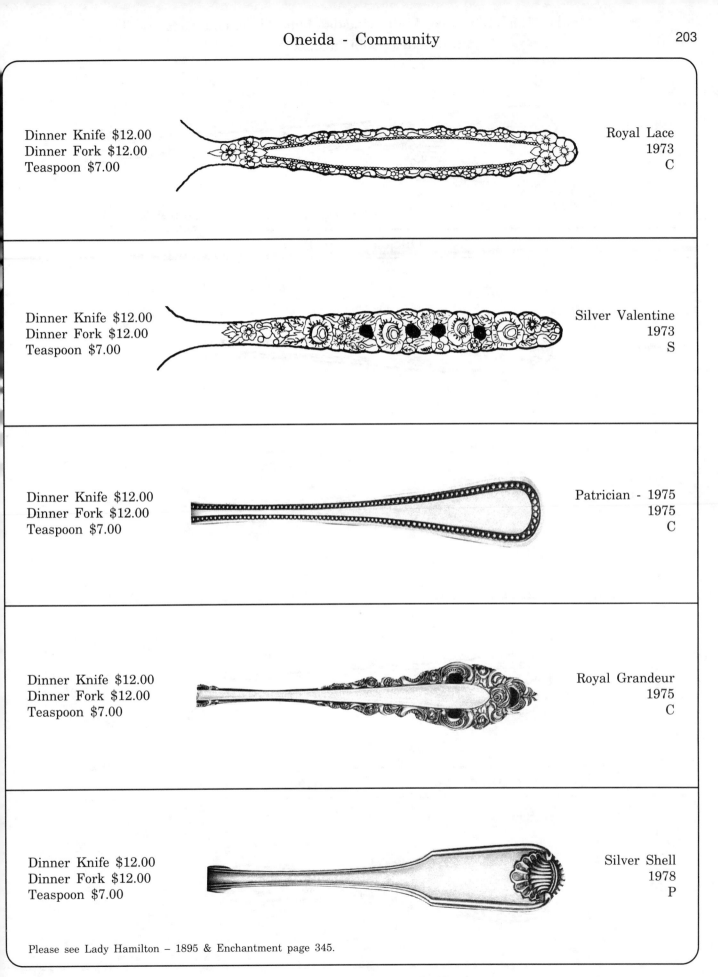

Dinner Knife $12.00
Dinner Fork $12.00
Teaspoon $7.00

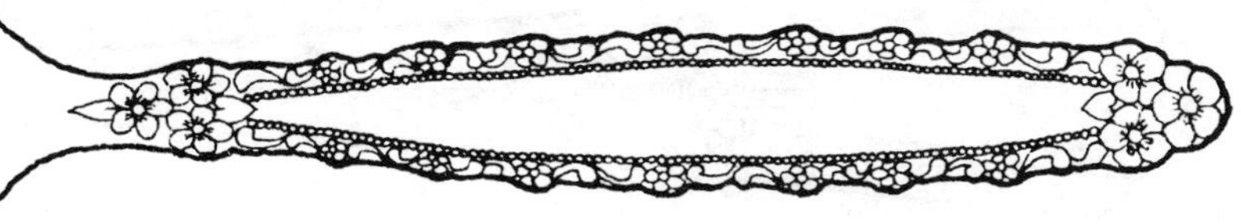

Royal Lace
1973
C

Dinner Knife $12.00
Dinner Fork $12.00
Teaspoon $7.00

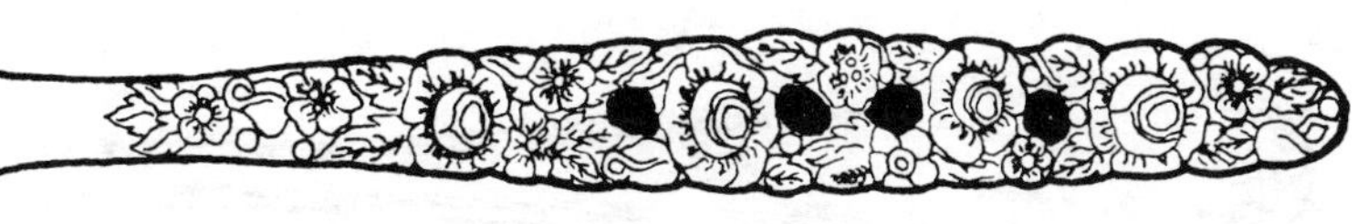

Silver Valentine
1973
S

Dinner Knife $12.00
Dinner Fork $12.00
Teaspoon $7.00

Patrician - 1975
1975
C

Dinner Knife $12.00
Dinner Fork $12.00
Teaspoon $7.00

Royal Grandeur
1975
C

Dinner Knife $12.00
Dinner Fork $12.00
Teaspoon $7.00

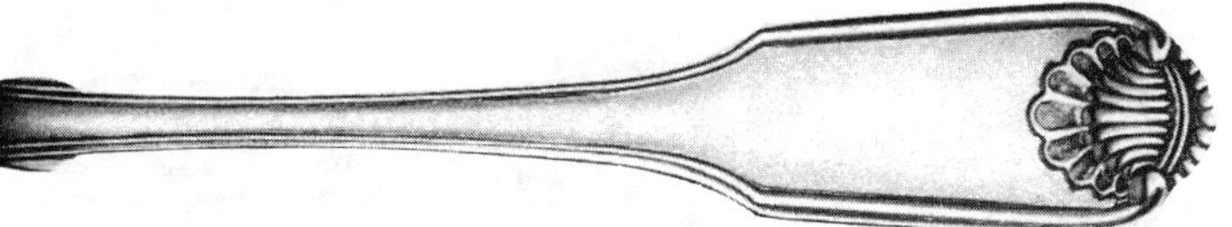

Silver Shell
1978
P

Please see Lady Hamilton – 1895 & Enchantment page 345.

Please refer to "How To Use This Book" page 4.

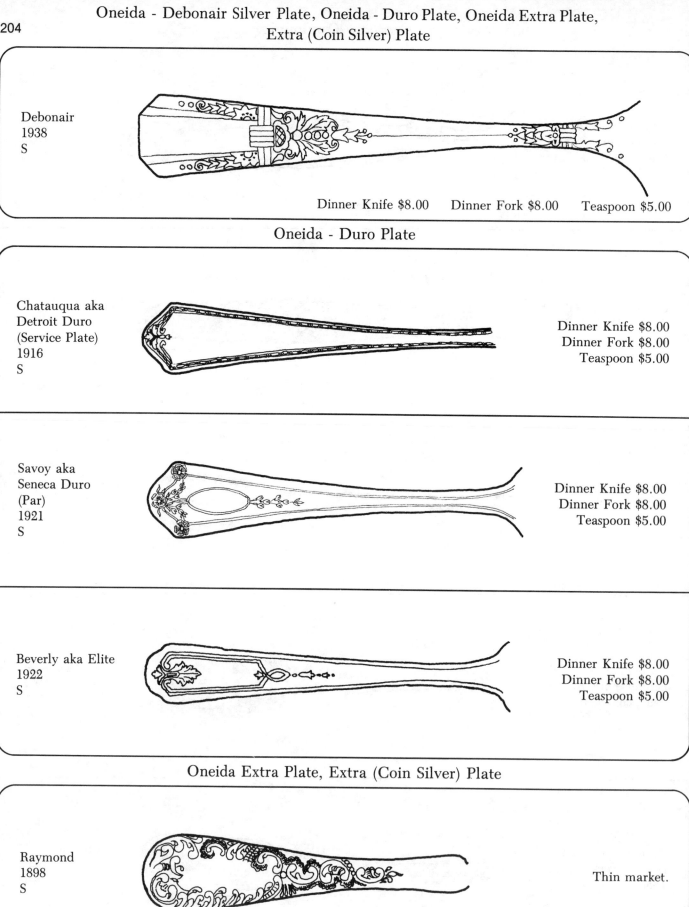

Debonair
1938
S

Dinner Knife $8.00 Dinner Fork $8.00 Teaspoon $5.00

Oneida - Duro Plate

Chatauqua aka
Detroit Duro
(Service Plate)
1916
S

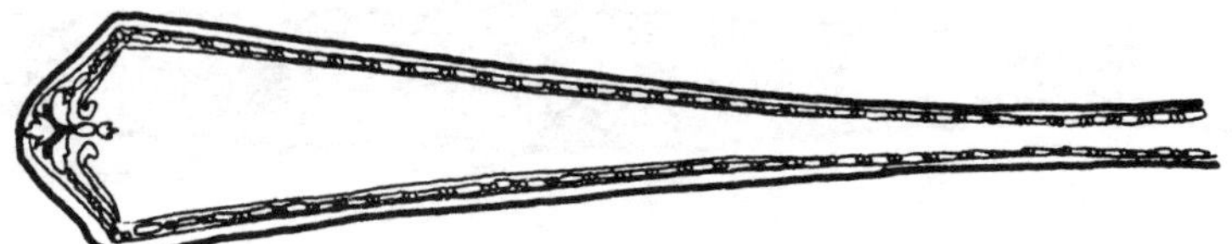

Dinner Knife $8.00
Dinner Fork $8.00
Teaspoon $5.00

Savoy aka
Seneca Duro
(Par)
1921
S

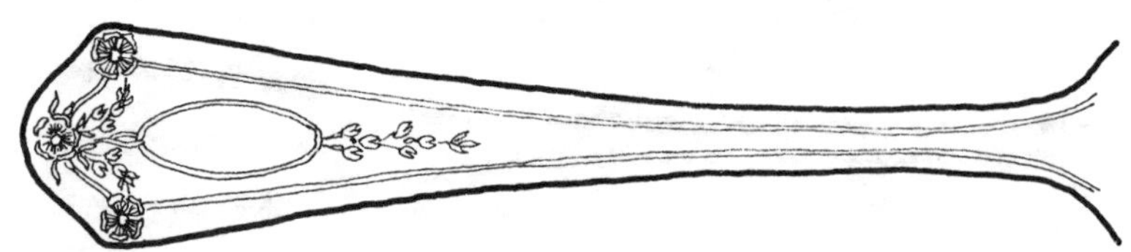

Dinner Knife $8.00
Dinner Fork $8.00
Teaspoon $5.00

Beverly aka Elite
1922
S

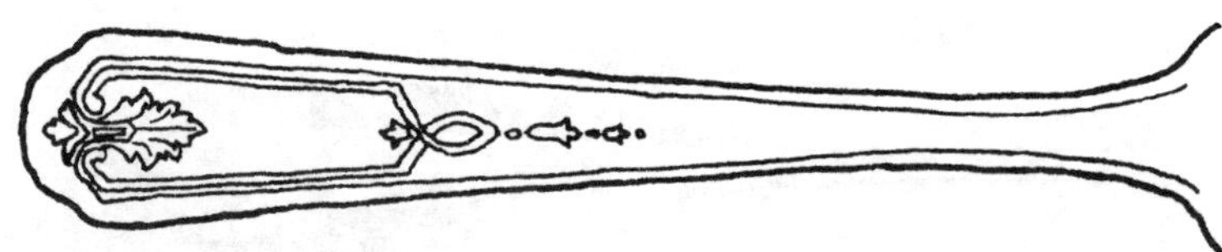

Dinner Knife $8.00
Dinner Fork $8.00
Teaspoon $5.00

Oneida Extra Plate, Extra (Coin Silver) Plate

Raymond
1898
S

Thin market.

Thin market.

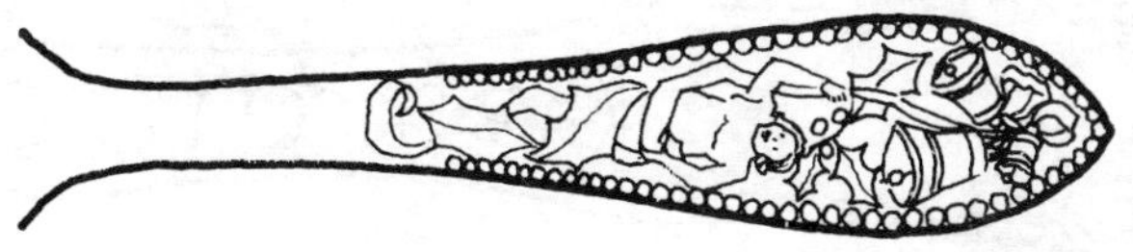

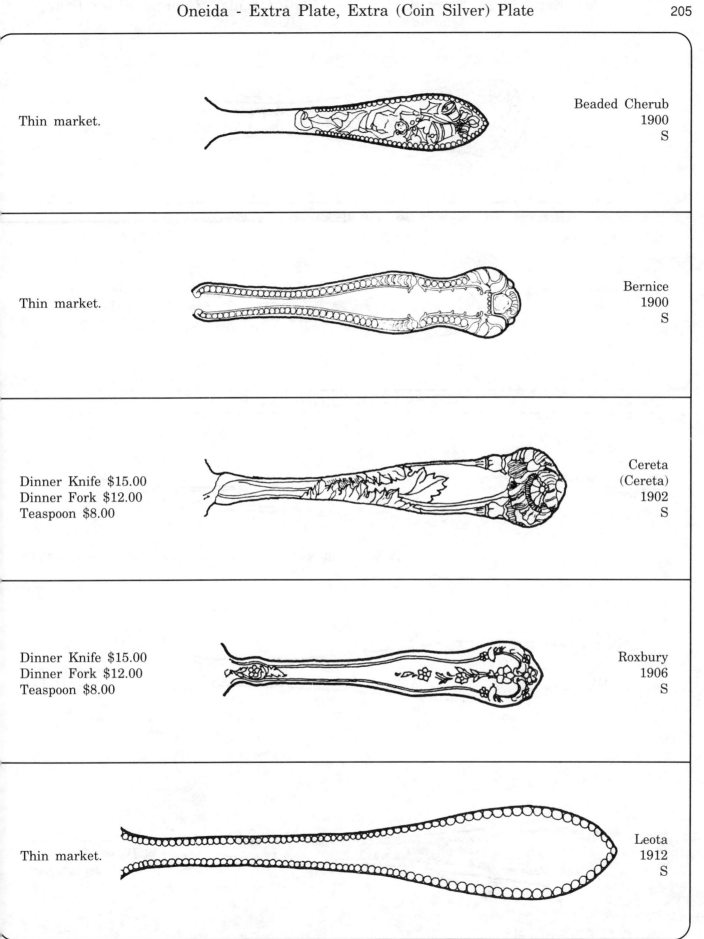

Beaded Cherub
1900
S

Thin market.

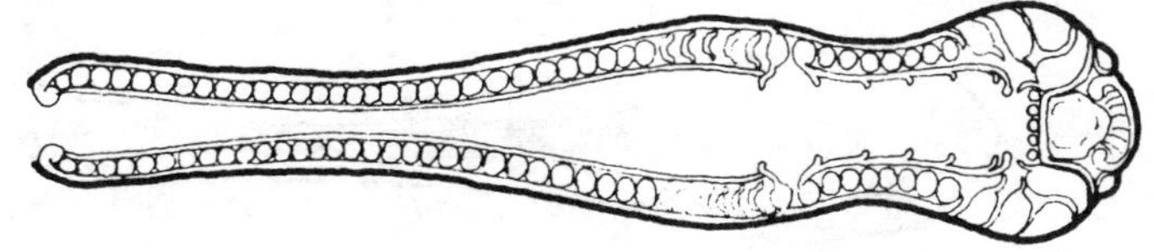

Bernice
1900
S

Dinner Knife $15.00
Dinner Fork $12.00
Teaspoon $8.00

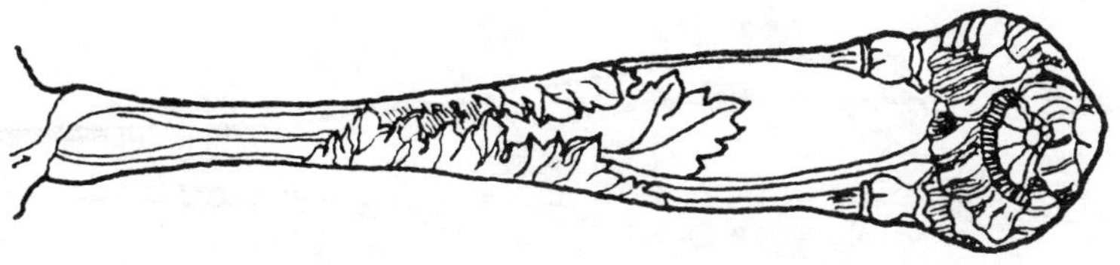

Cereta
(Cereta)
1902
S

Dinner Knife $15.00
Dinner Fork $12.00
Teaspoon $8.00

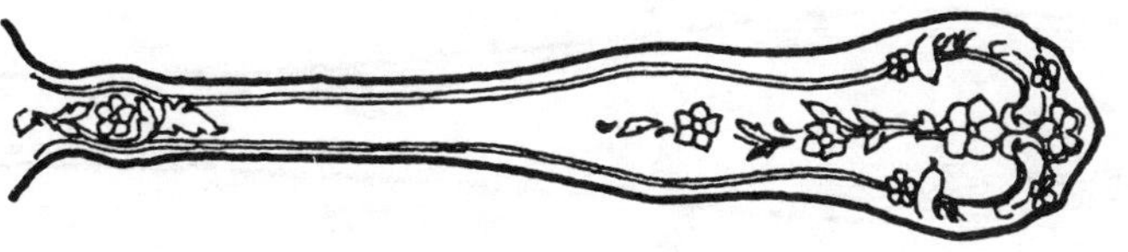

Roxbury
1906
S

Thin market.

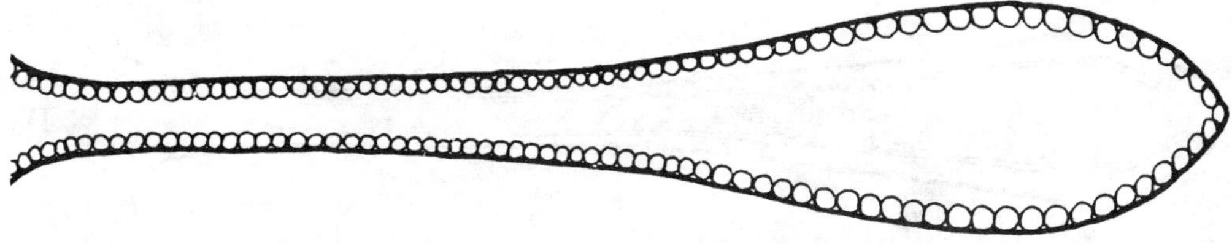

Leota
1912
S

Please refer to "How To Use This Book" page 4.

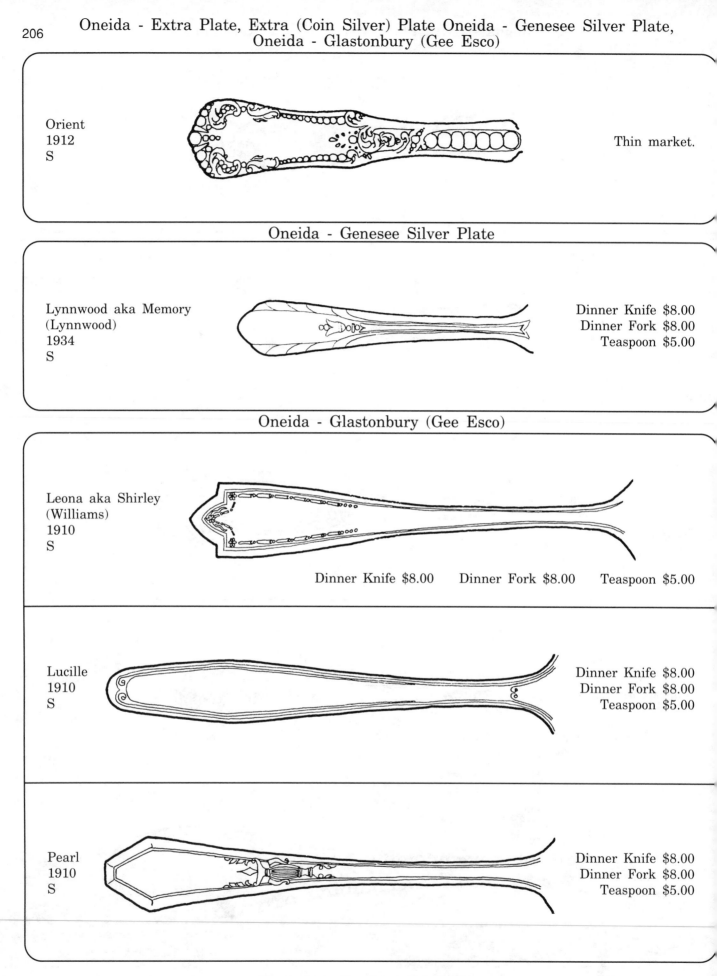

Orient
1912
S

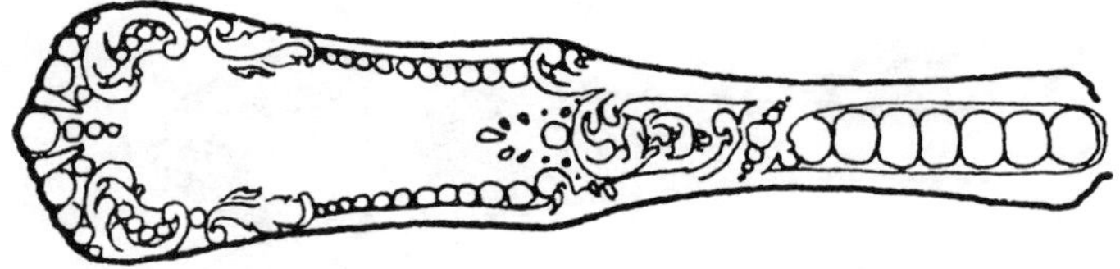

Thin market.

Oneida - Genesee Silver Plate

Lynnwood aka Memory
(Lynnwood)
1934
S

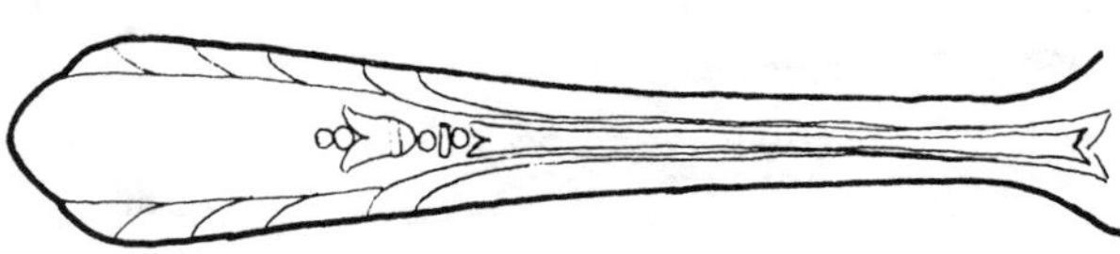

Dinner Knife $8.00
Dinner Fork $8.00
Teaspoon $5.00

Oneida - Glastonbury (Gee Esco)

Leona aka Shirley
(Williams)
1910
S

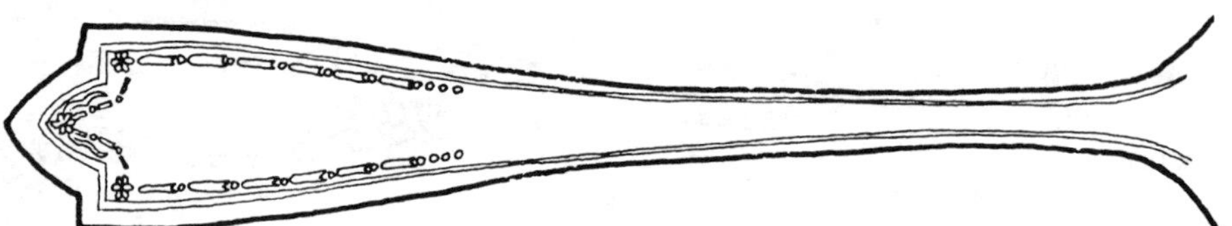

Dinner Knife $8.00 Dinner Fork $8.00 Teaspoon $5.00

Lucille
1910
S

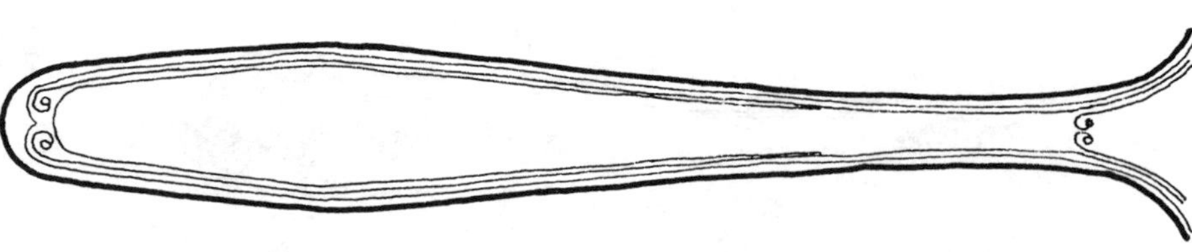

Dinner Knife $8.00
Dinner Fork $8.00
Teaspoon $5.00

Pearl
1910
S

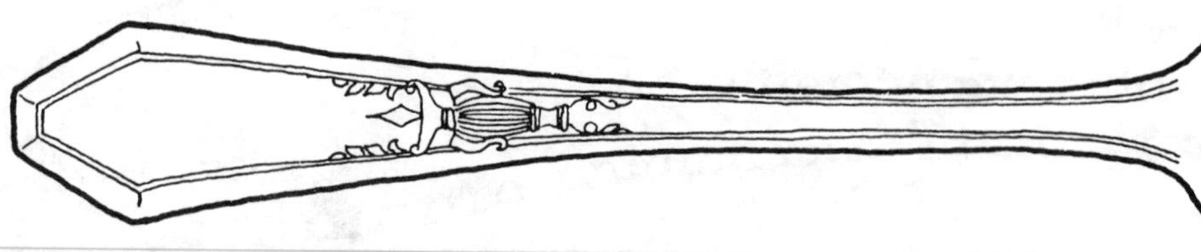

Dinner Knife $8.00
Dinner Fork $8.00
Teaspoon $5.00

Please refer to "How To Use This Book" page 4.

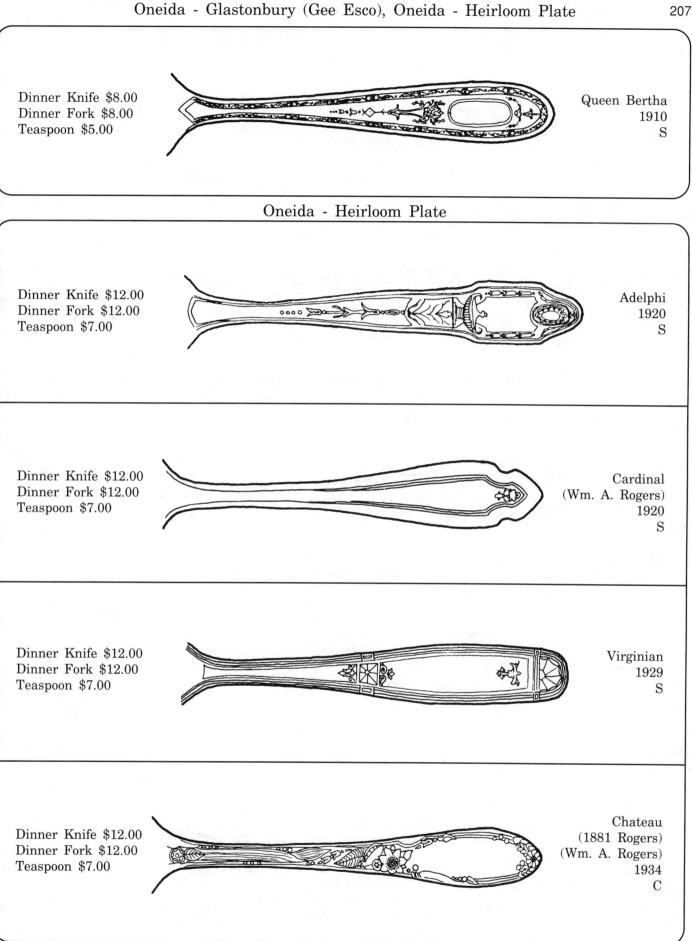

Dinner Knife $8.00
Dinner Fork $8.00
Teaspoon $5.00

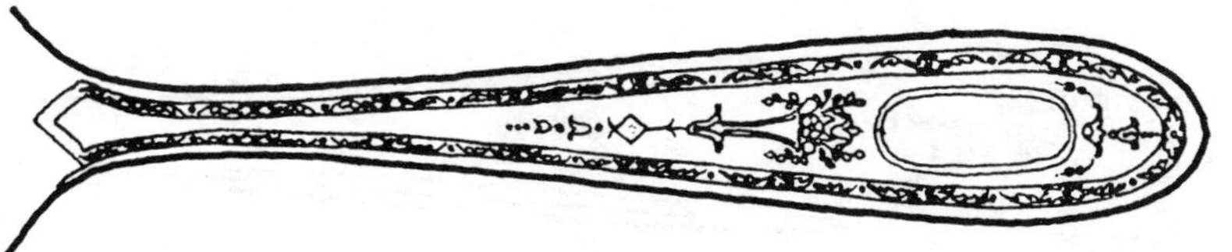

Queen Bertha
1910
S

Oneida - Heirloom Plate

Dinner Knife $12.00
Dinner Fork $12.00
Teaspoon $7.00

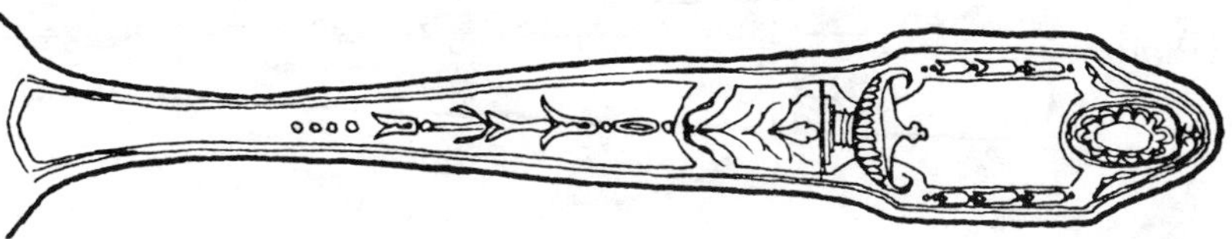

Adelphi
1920
S

Dinner Knife $12.00
Dinner Fork $12.00
Teaspoon $7.00

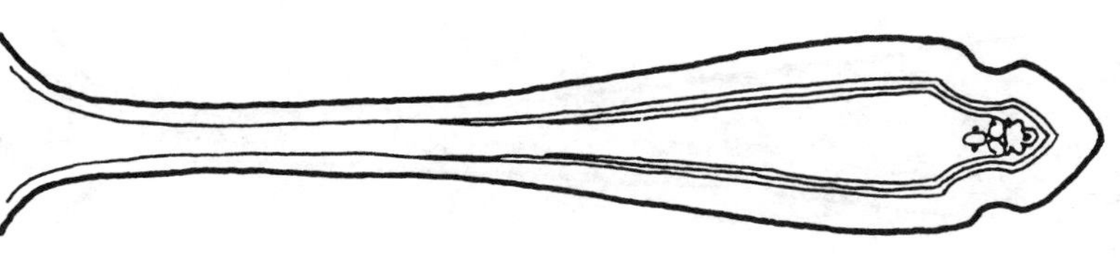

Cardinal
(Wm. A. Rogers)
1920
S

Dinner Knife $12.00
Dinner Fork $12.00
Teaspoon $7.00

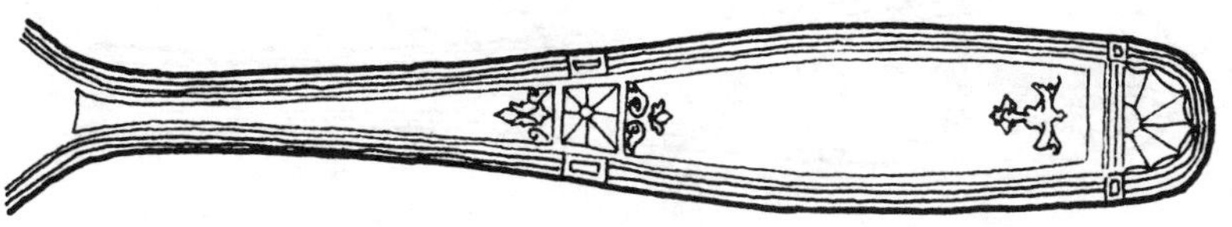

Virginian
1929
S

Dinner Knife $12.00
Dinner Fork $12.00
Teaspoon $7.00

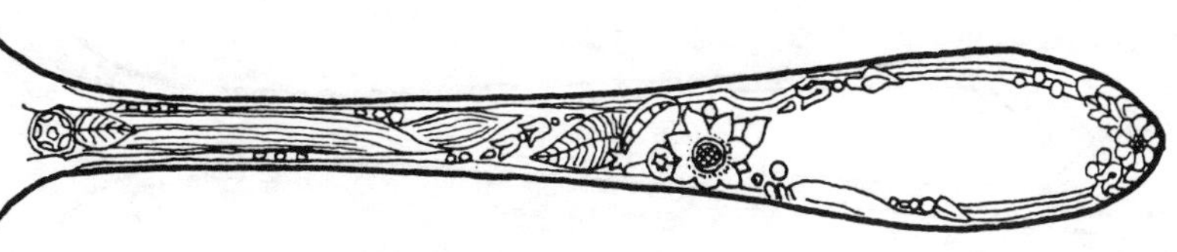

Chateau
(1881 Rogers)
(Wm. A. Rogers)
1934
C

Please refer to "How To Use This Book" page 4.

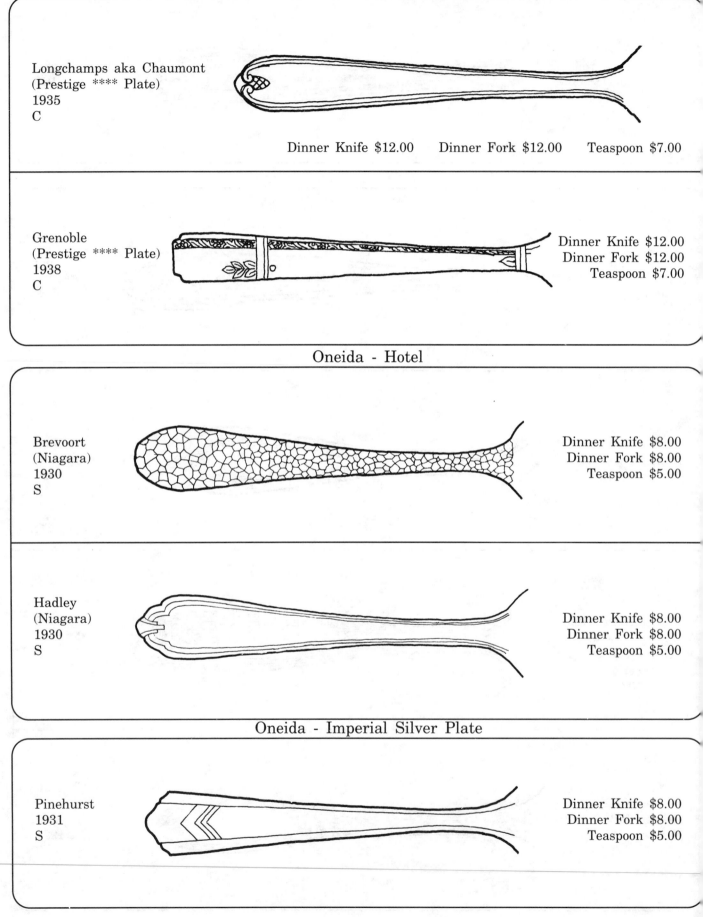

Longchamps aka Chaumont
(Prestige **** Plate)
1935
C

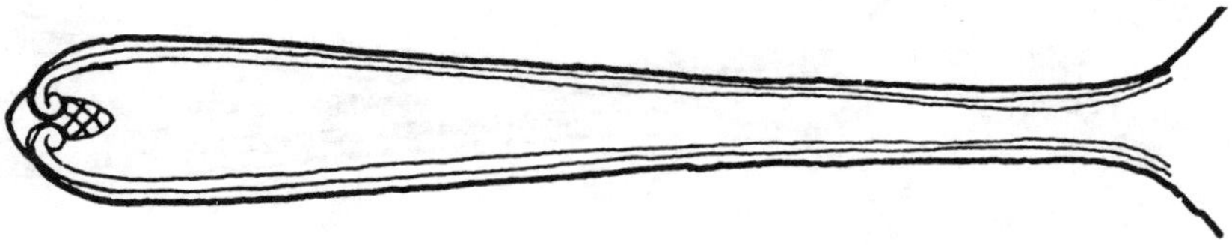

Dinner Knife $12.00 Dinner Fork $12.00 Teaspoon $7.00

Grenoble
(Prestige **** Plate)
1938
C

Dinner Knife $12.00
Dinner Fork $12.00
Teaspoon $7.00

Oneida - Hotel

Brevoort
(Niagara)
1930
S

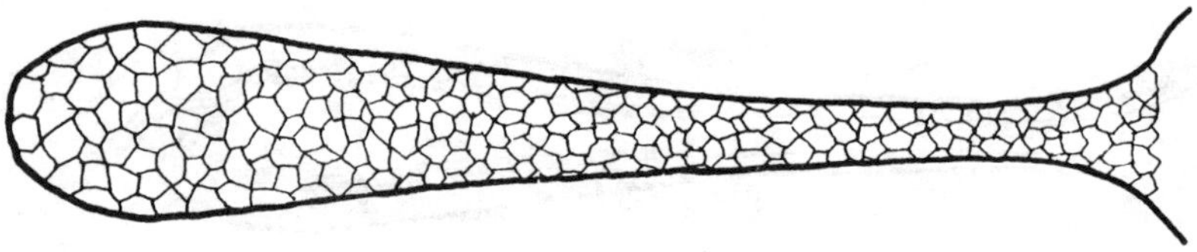

Dinner Knife $8.00
Dinner Fork $8.00
Teaspoon $5.00

Hadley
(Niagara)
1930
S

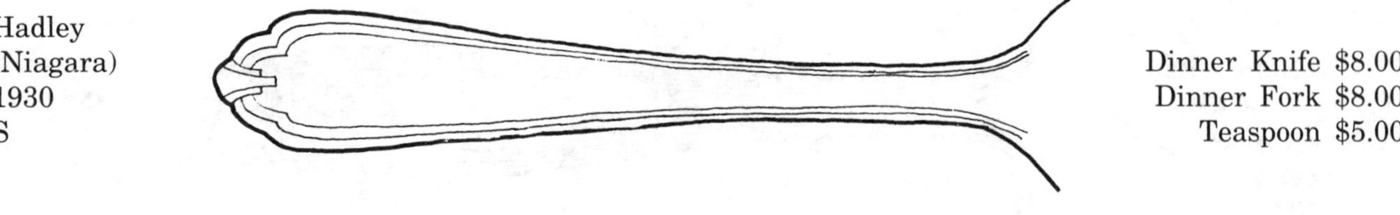

Dinner Knife $8.00
Dinner Fork $8.00
Teaspoon $5.00

Oneida - Imperial Silver Plate

Pinehurst
1931
S

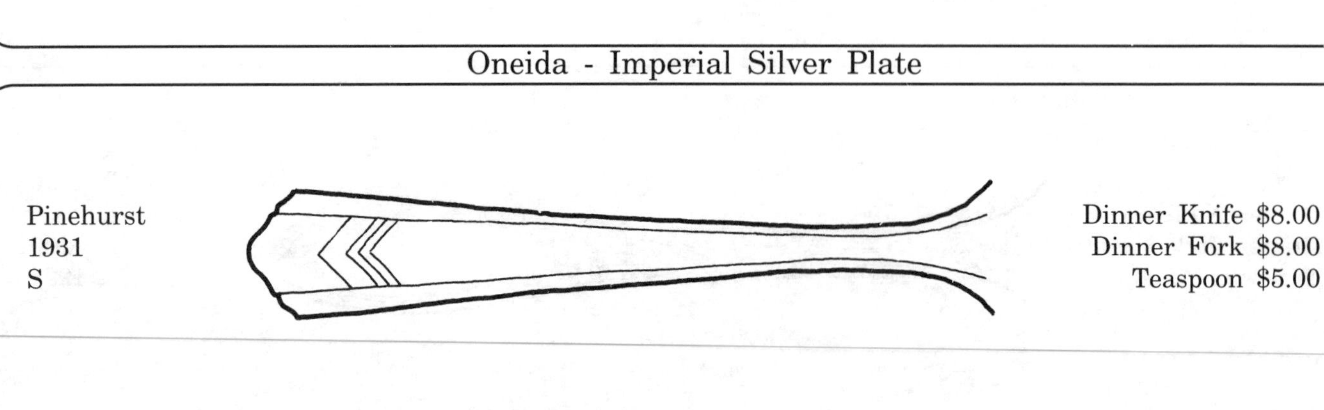

Dinner Knife $8.00
Dinner Fork $8.00
Teaspoon $5.00

Please refer to "How To Use This Book" page 4.

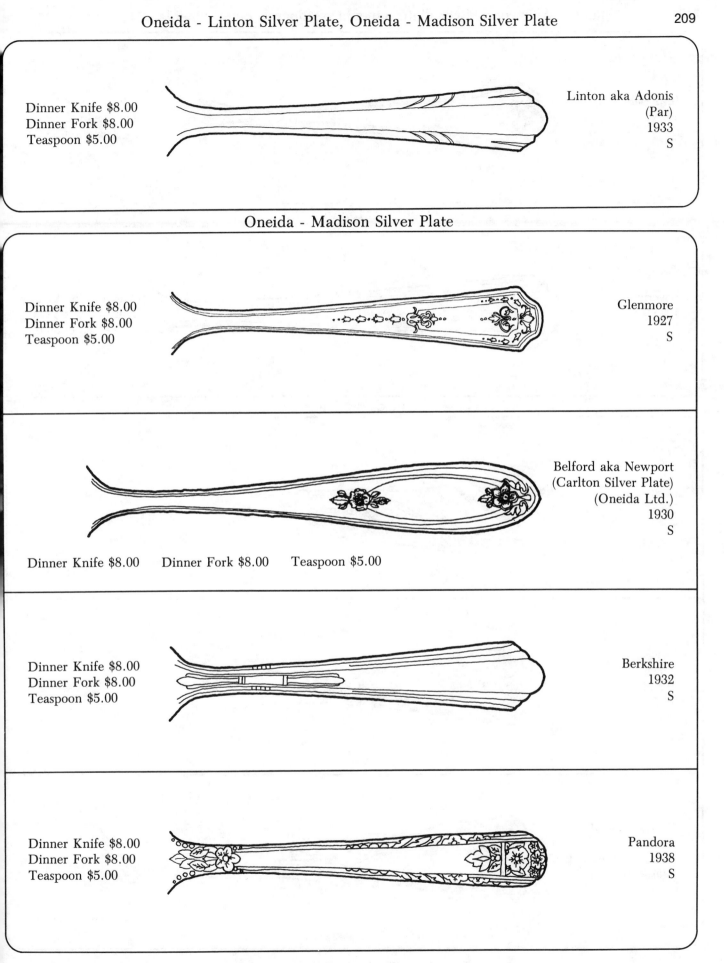

Dinner Knife $8.00
Dinner Fork $8.00
Teaspoon $5.00

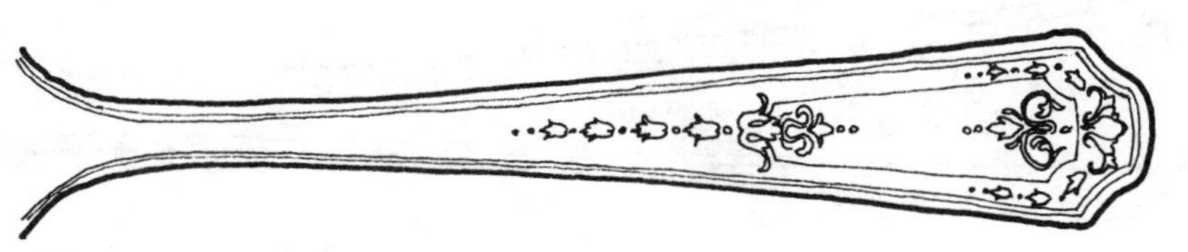

Linton aka Adonis
(Par)
1933
S

Oneida - Madison Silver Plate

Dinner Knife $8.00
Dinner Fork $8.00
Teaspoon $5.00

Glenmore
1927
S

Belford aka Newport
(Carlton Silver Plate)
(Oneida Ltd.)
1930
S

Dinner Knife $8.00 Dinner Fork $8.00 Teaspoon $5.00

Dinner Knife $8.00
Dinner Fork $8.00
Teaspoon $5.00

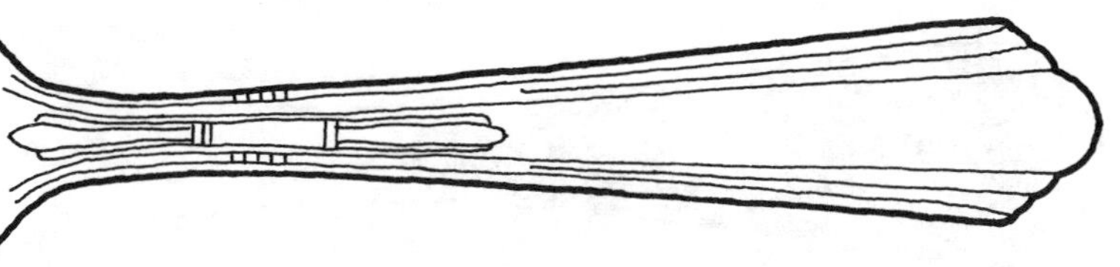

Berkshire
1932
S

Dinner Knife $8.00
Dinner Fork $8.00
Teaspoon $5.00

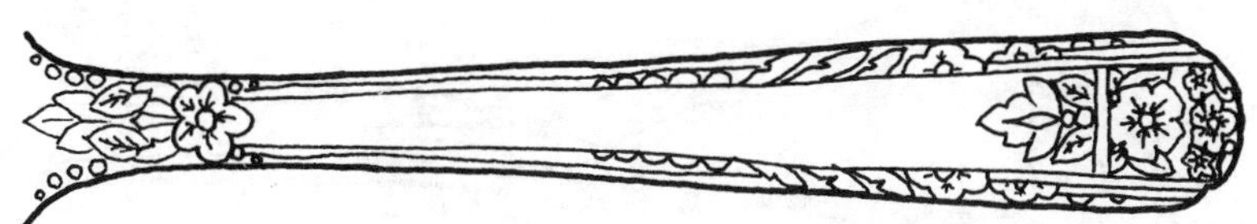

Pandora
1938
S

Please refer to "How To Use This Book" page 4.

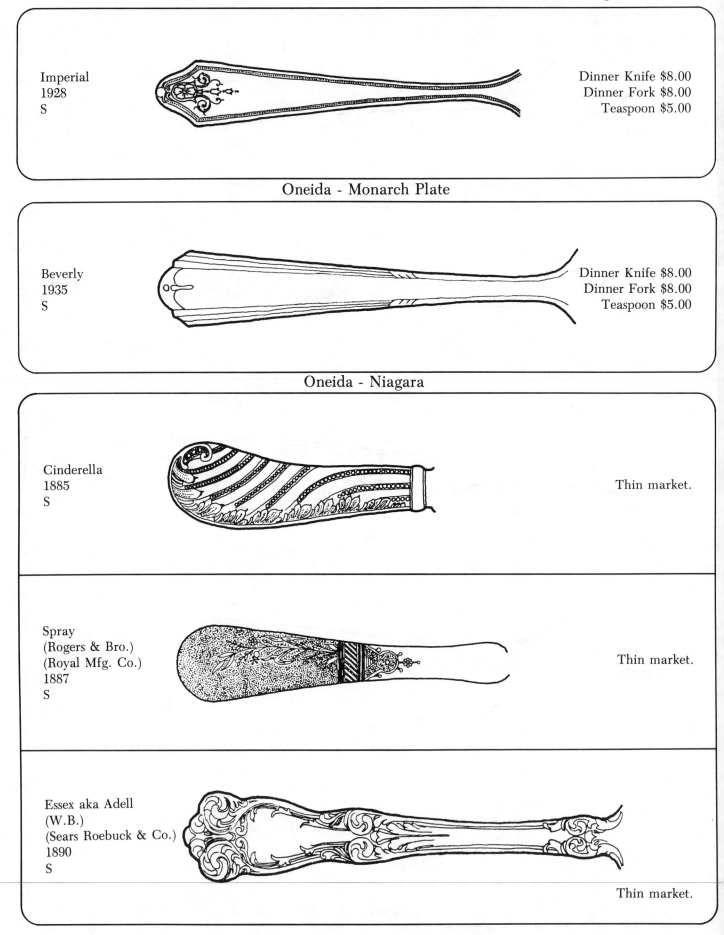

Imperial
1928
S

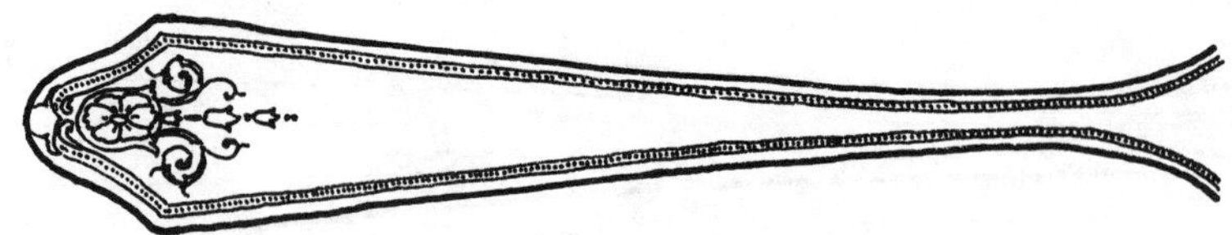

Dinner Knife $8.00
Dinner Fork $8.00
Teaspoon $5.00

Oneida - Monarch Plate

Beverly
1935
S

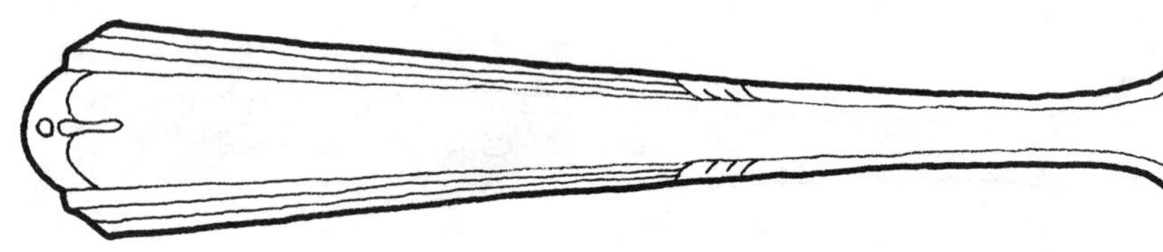

Dinner Knife $8.00
Dinner Fork $8.00
Teaspoon $5.00

Oneida - Niagara

Cinderella
1885
S

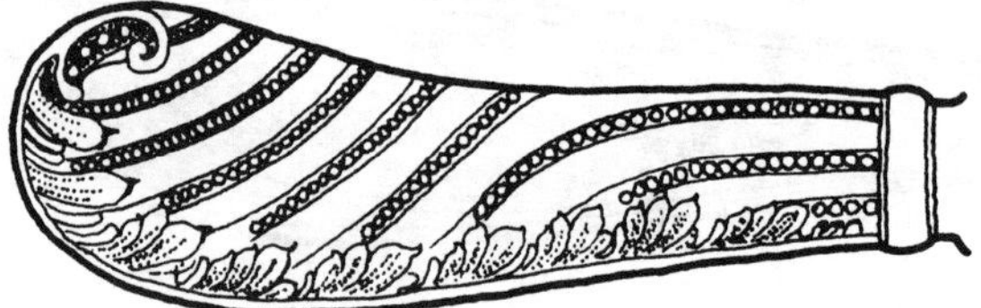

Thin market.

Spray
(Rogers & Bro.)
(Royal Mfg. Co.)
1887
S

Thin market.

Essex aka Adell
(W.B.)
(Sears Roebuck & Co.)
1890
S

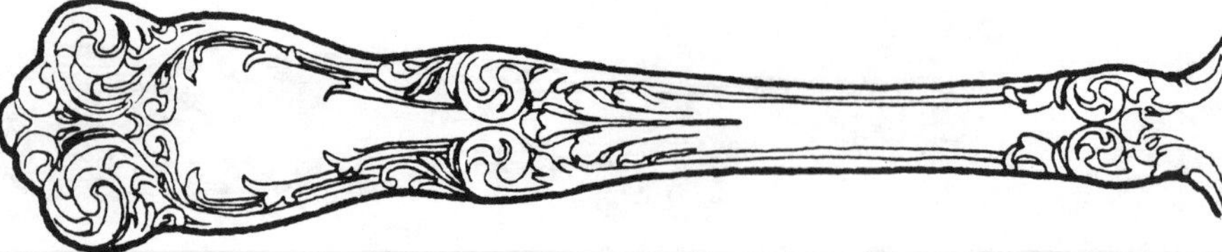

Thin market.

Please refer to "How To Use This Book" page 4.

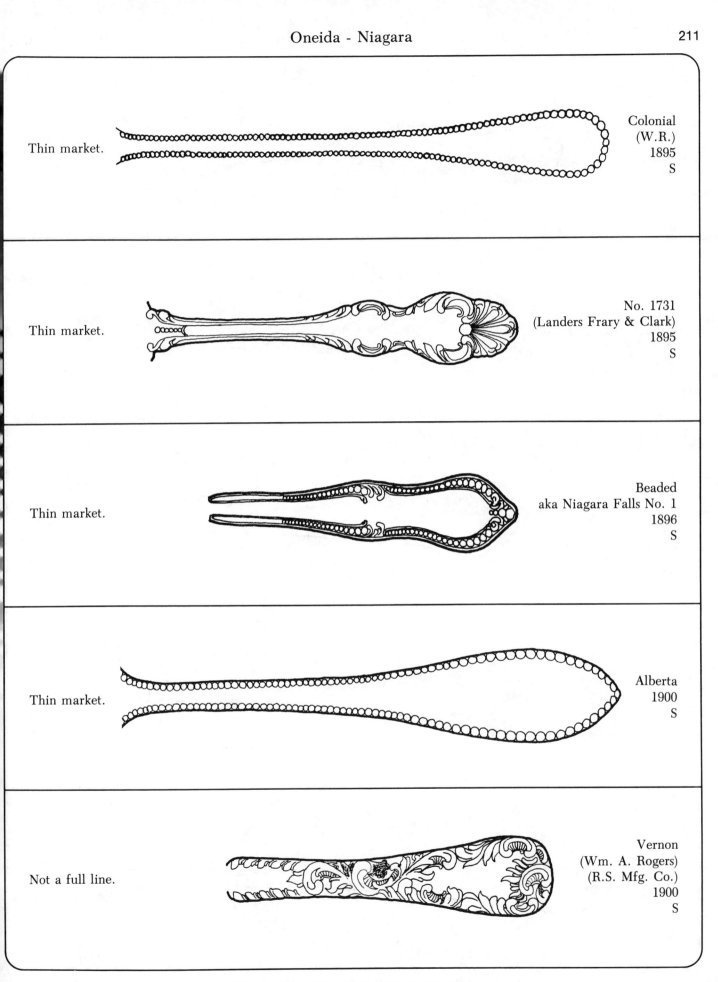

Thin market.	Colonial (W.R.) 1895 S
Thin market.	No. 1731 (Landers Frary & Clark) 1895 S
Thin market.	Beaded aka Niagara Falls No. 1 1896 S
Thin market.	Alberta 1900 S
Not a full line.	Vernon (Wm. A. Rogers) (R.S. Mfg. Co.) 1900 S

Please refer to "How To Use This Book" page 4.

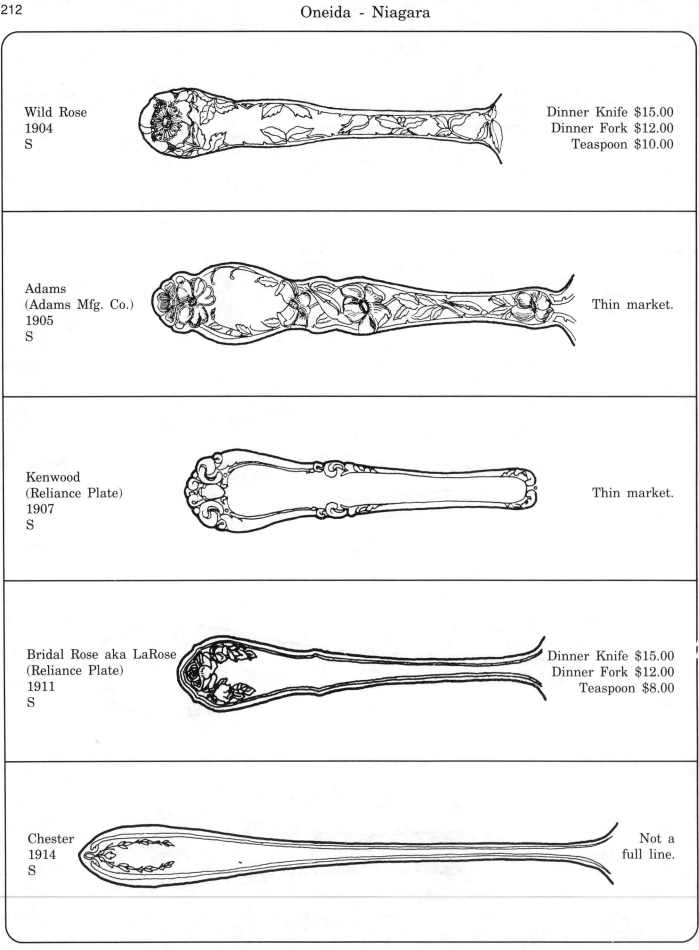

Wild Rose
1904
S

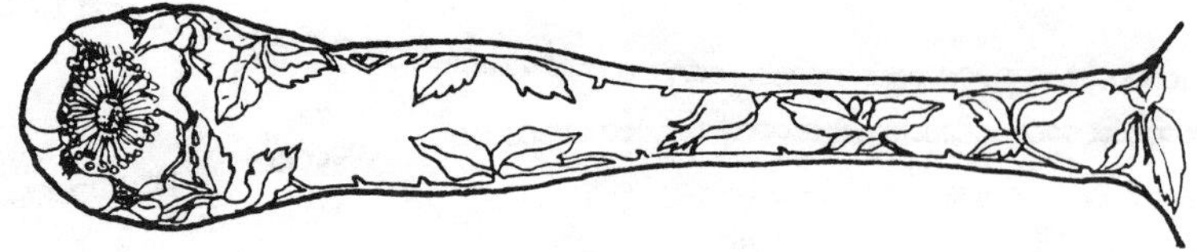

Dinner Knife $15.00
Dinner Fork $12.00
Teaspoon $10.00

Adams
(Adams Mfg. Co.)
1905
S

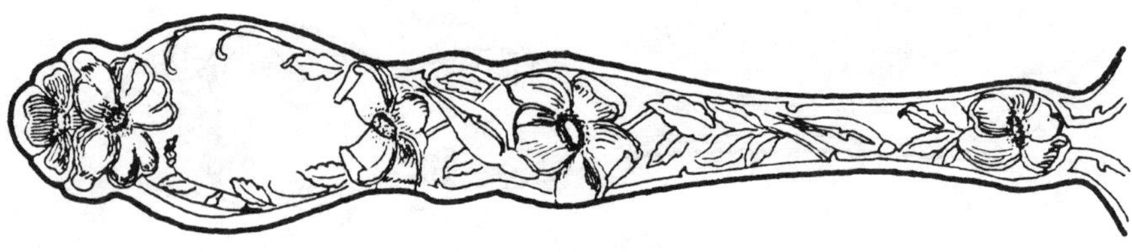

Thin market.

Kenwood
(Reliance Plate)
1907
S

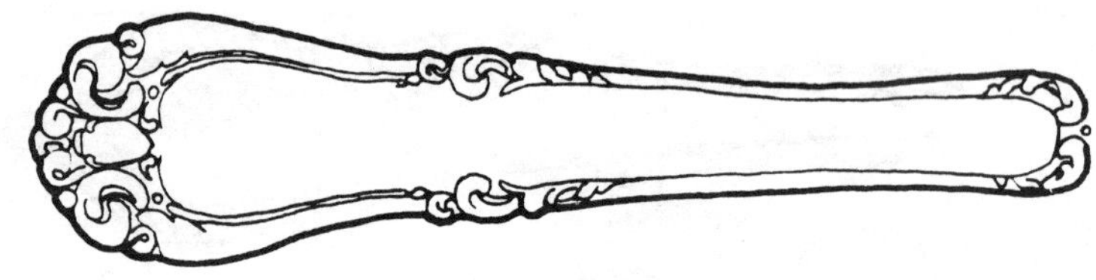

Thin market.

Bridal Rose aka LaRose
(Reliance Plate)
1911
S

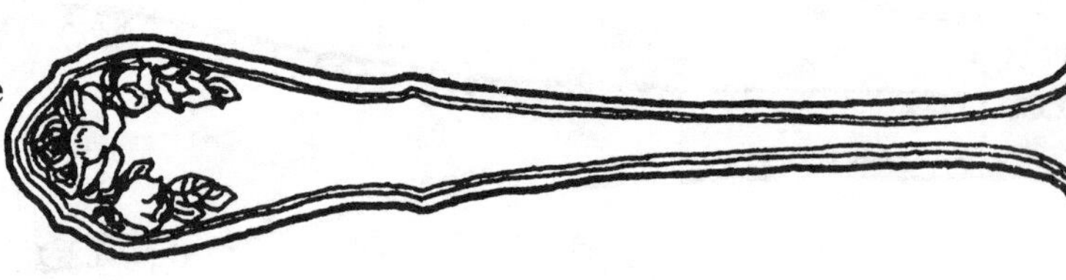

Dinner Knife $15.00
Dinner Fork $12.00
Teaspoon $8.00

Chester
1914
S

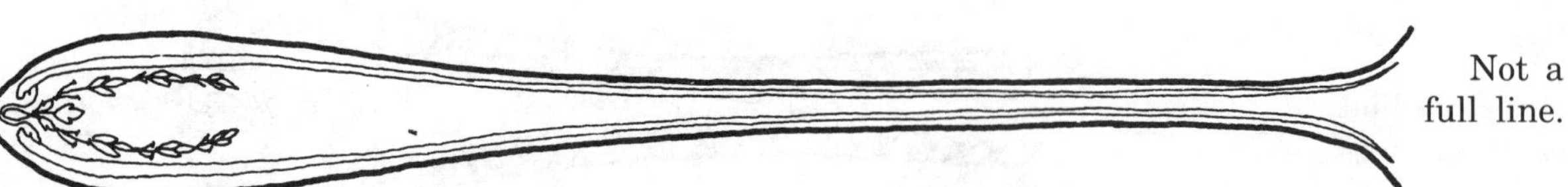

Not a full line.

Please refer to "How To Use This Book" page 4.

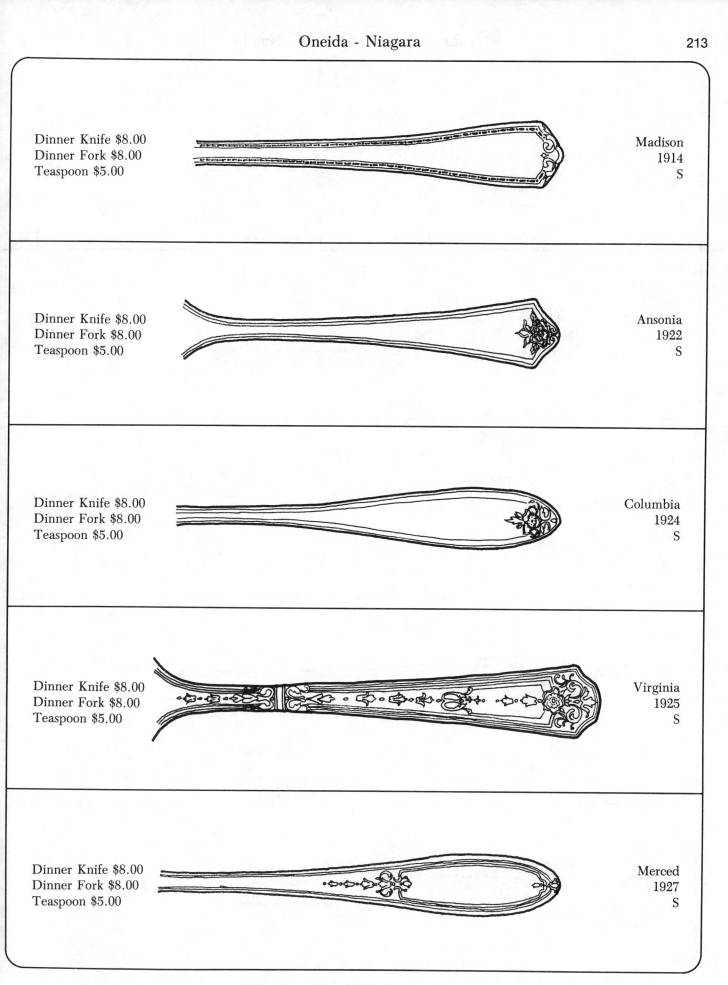

Dinner Knife $8.00 Dinner Fork $8.00 Teaspoon $5.00	Madison 1914 S
Dinner Knife $8.00 Dinner Fork $8.00 Teaspoon $5.00	Ansonia 1922 S
Dinner Knife $8.00 Dinner Fork $8.00 Teaspoon $5.00	Columbia 1924 S
Dinner Knife $8.00 Dinner Fork $8.00 Teaspoon $5.00	Virginia 1925 S
Dinner Knife $8.00 Dinner Fork $8.00 Teaspoon $5.00	Merced 1927 S

Please refer to "How To Use This Book" page 4.

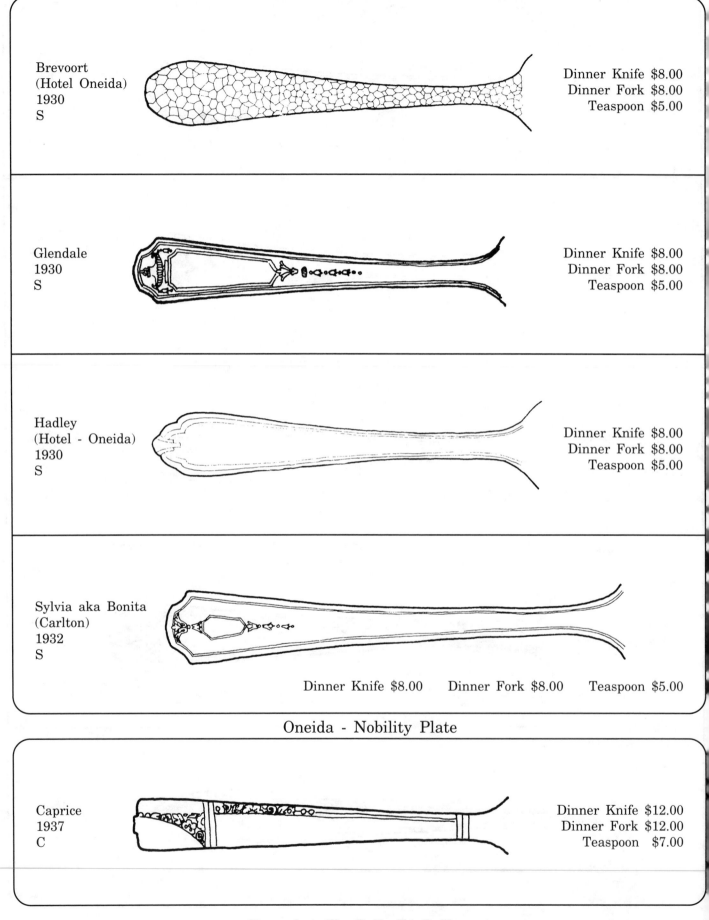

Brevoort
(Hotel Oneida)
1930
S

Dinner Knife $8.00
Dinner Fork $8.00
Teaspoon $5.00

Glendale
1930
S

Dinner Knife $8.00
Dinner Fork $8.00
Teaspoon $5.00

Hadley
(Hotel - Oneida)
1930
S

Dinner Knife $8.00
Dinner Fork $8.00
Teaspoon $5.00

Sylvia aka Bonita
(Carlton)
1932
S

Dinner Knife $8.00 Dinner Fork $8.00 Teaspoon $5.00

Oneida - Nobility Plate

Caprice
1937
C

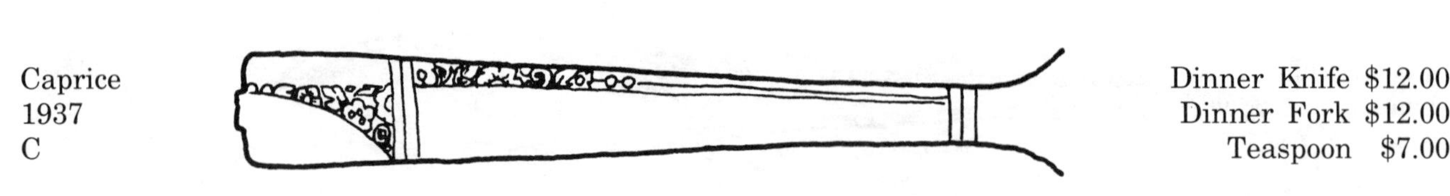

Dinner Knife $12.00
Dinner Fork $12.00
Teaspoon $7.00

Please refer to "How To Use This Book" page 4.

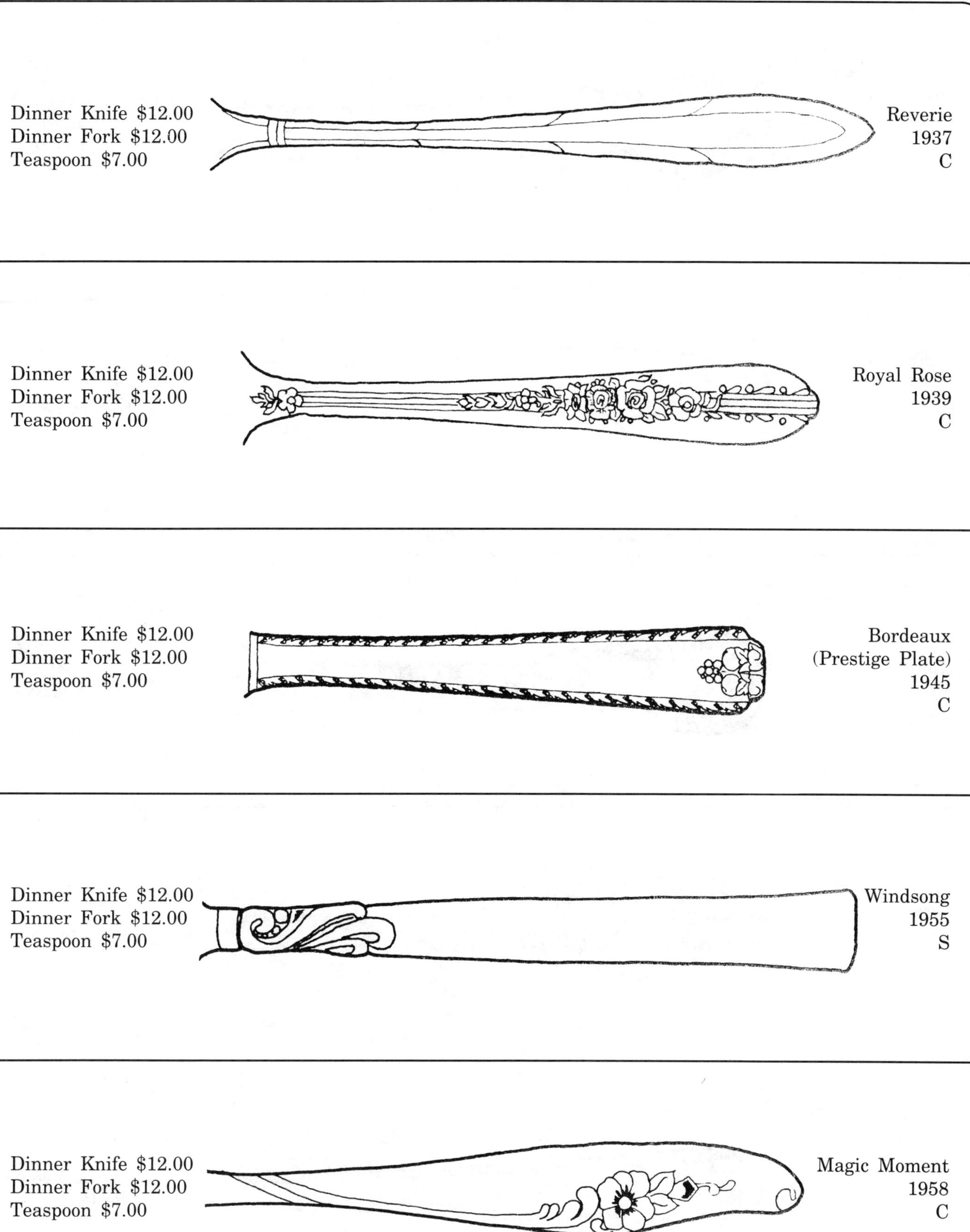

Dinner Knife $12.00
Dinner Fork $12.00
Teaspoon $7.00

Reverie
1937
C

Dinner Knife $12.00
Dinner Fork $12.00
Teaspoon $7.00

Royal Rose
1939
C

Dinner Knife $12.00
Dinner Fork $12.00
Teaspoon $7.00

Bordeaux
(Prestige Plate)
1945
C

Dinner Knife $12.00
Dinner Fork $12.00
Teaspoon $7.00

Windsong
1955
S

Dinner Knife $12.00
Dinner Fork $12.00
Teaspoon $7.00

Magic Moment
1958
C

Please refer to "How To Use This Book" page 4.

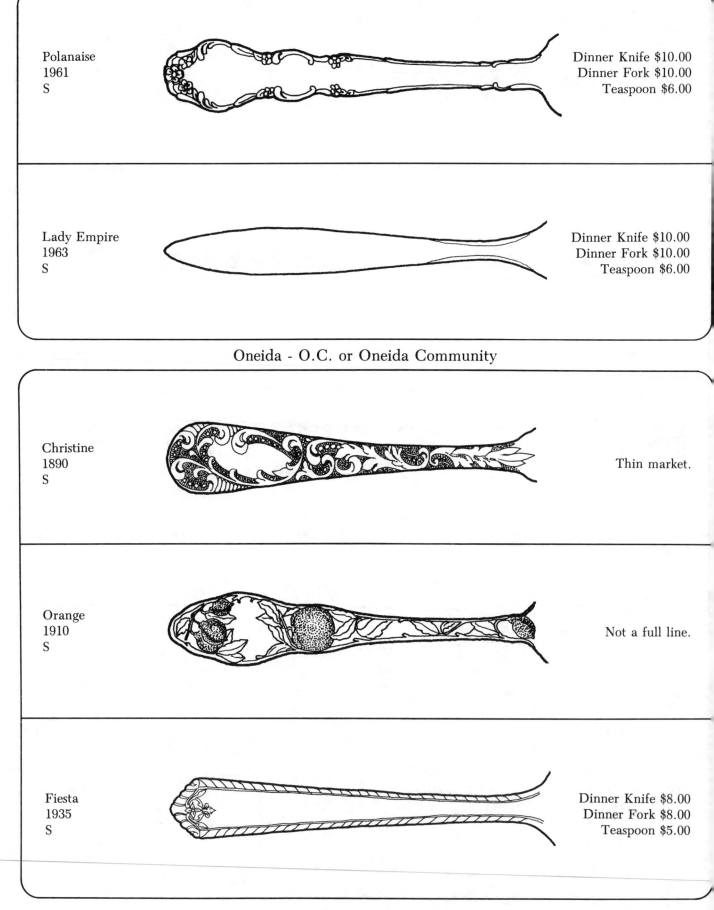

Polanaise
1961
S

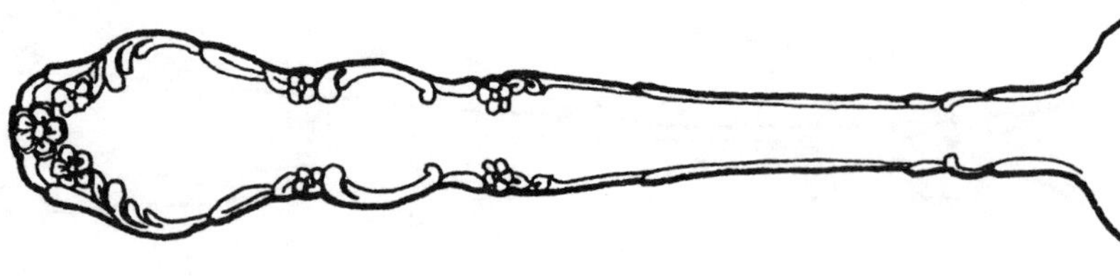

Dinner Knife $10.00
Dinner Fork $10.00
Teaspoon $6.00

Lady Empire
1963
S

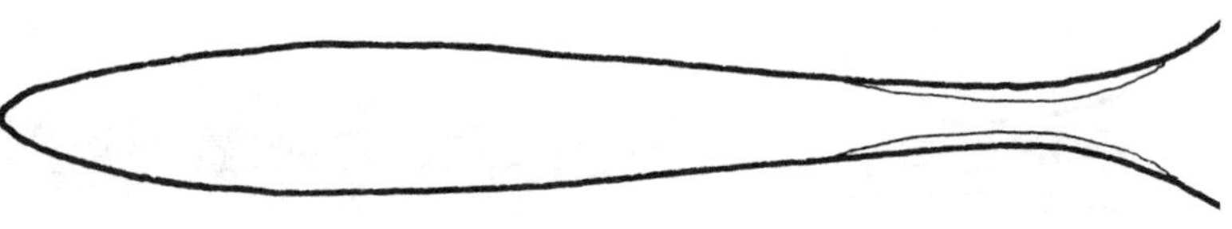

Dinner Knife $10.00
Dinner Fork $10.00
Teaspoon $6.00

Oneida - O.C. or Oneida Community

Christine
1890
S

Thin market.

Orange
1910
S

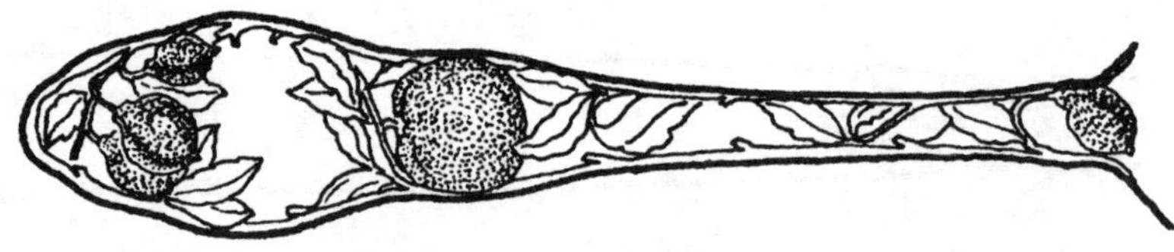

Not a full line.

Fiesta
1935
S

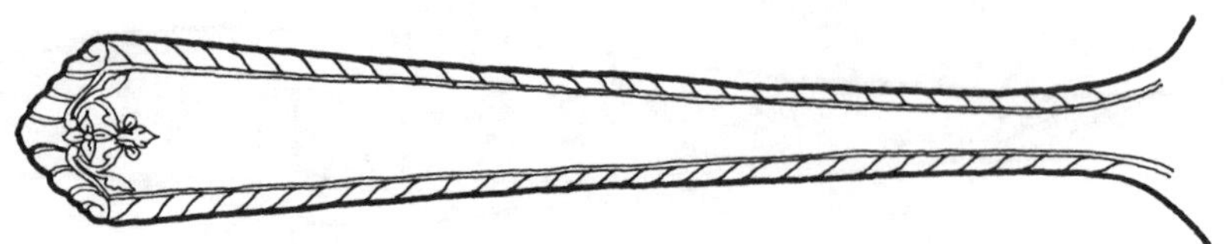

Dinner Knife $8.00
Dinner Fork $8.00
Teaspoon $5.00

Please refer to "How To Use This Book" page 4.

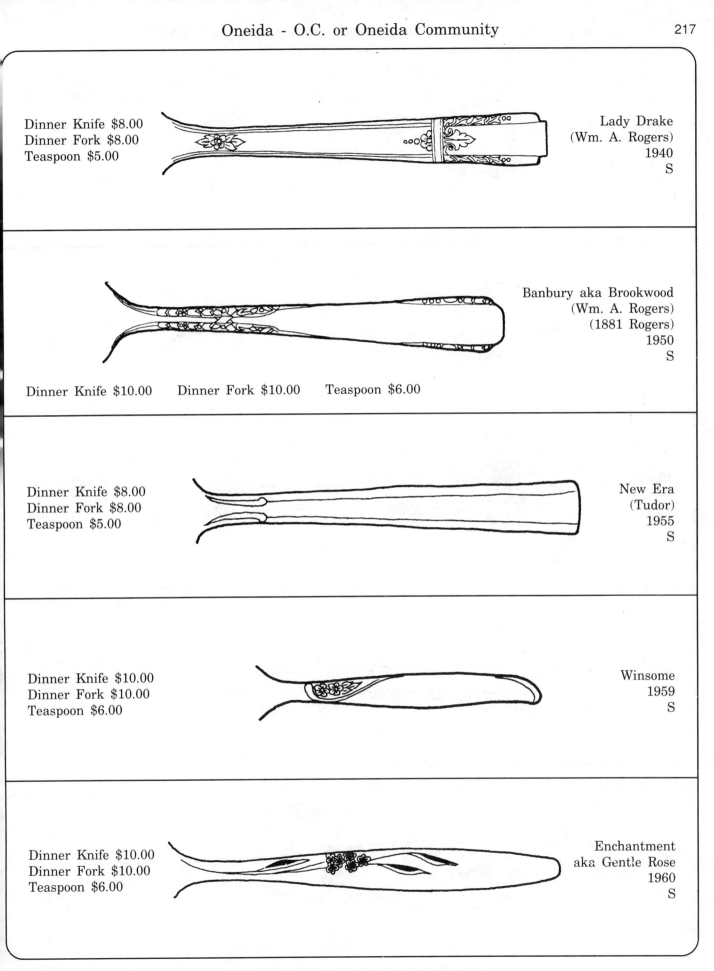

Dinner Knife $8.00
Dinner Fork $8.00
Teaspoon $5.00

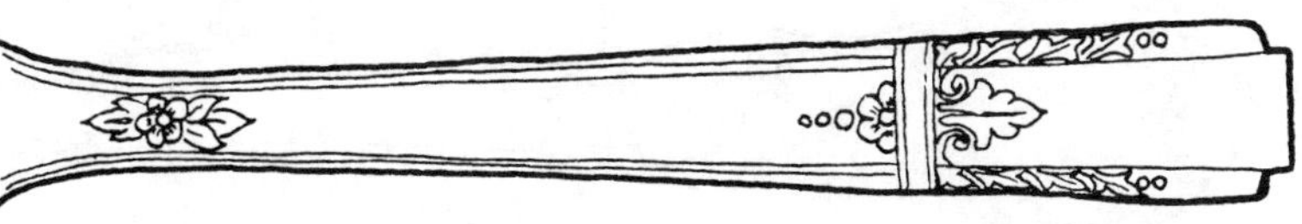

Lady Drake
(Wm. A. Rogers)
1940
S

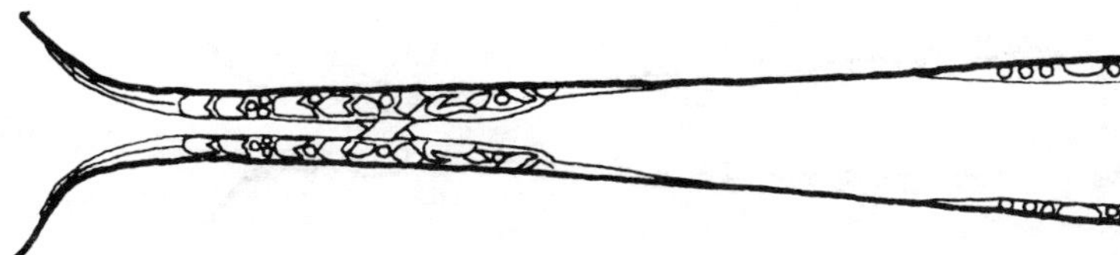

Banbury aka Brookwood
(Wm. A. Rogers)
(1881 Rogers)
1950
S

Dinner Knife $10.00 Dinner Fork $10.00 Teaspoon $6.00

Dinner Knife $8.00
Dinner Fork $8.00
Teaspoon $5.00

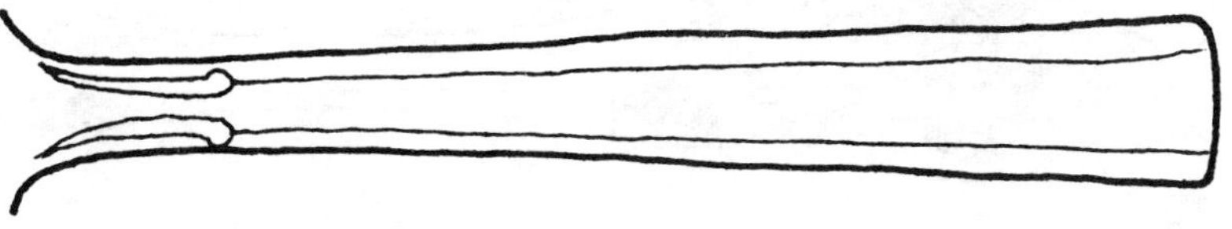

New Era
(Tudor)
1955
S

Dinner Knife $10.00
Dinner Fork $10.00
Teaspoon $6.00

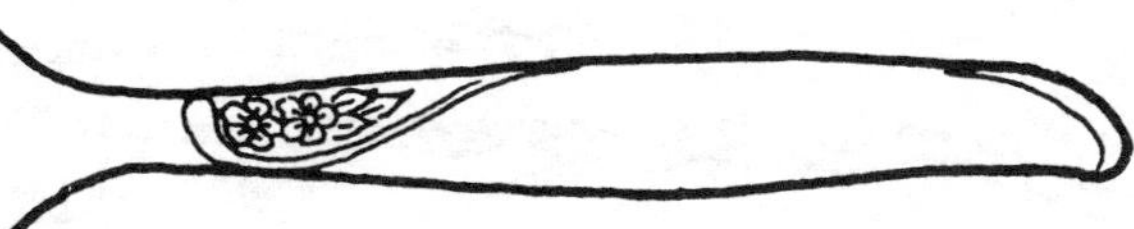

Winsome
1959
S

Dinner Knife $10.00
Dinner Fork $10.00
Teaspoon $6.00

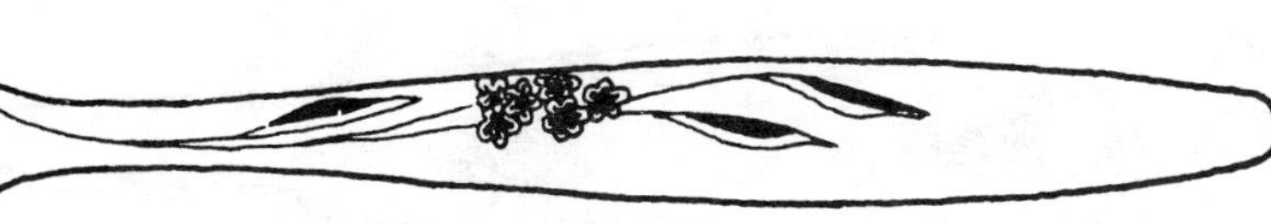

Enchantment
aka Gentle Rose
1960
S

Please refer to "How To Use This Book" page 4.

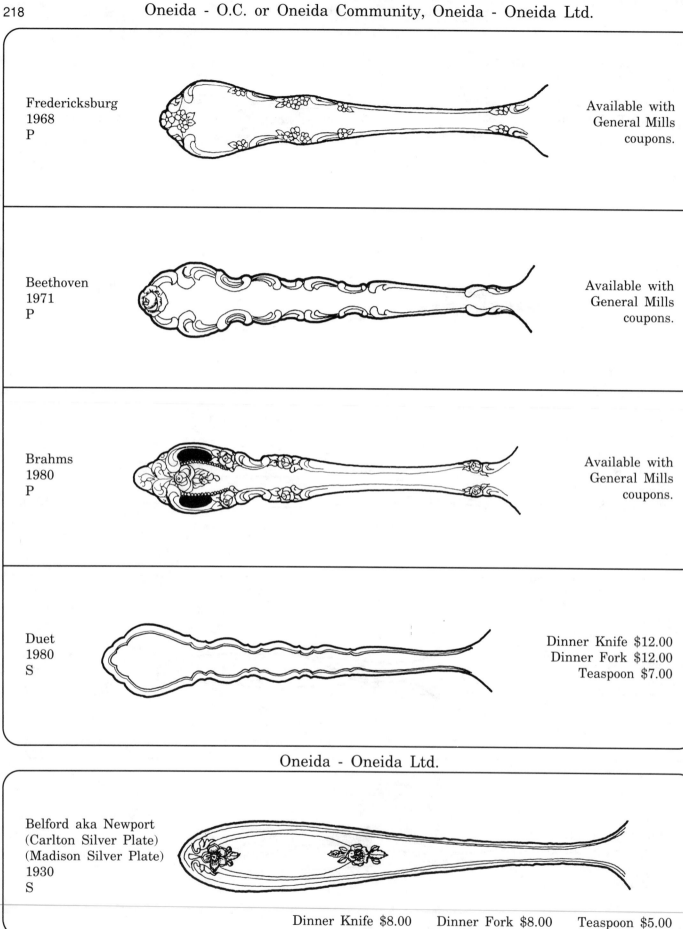

Fredericksburg
1968
P

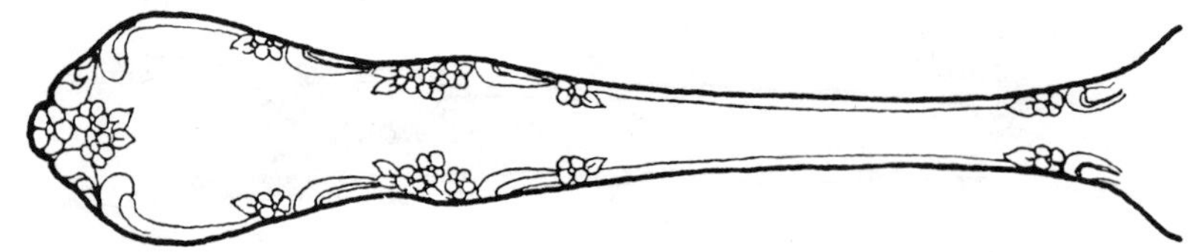

Available with General Mills coupons.

Beethoven
1971
P

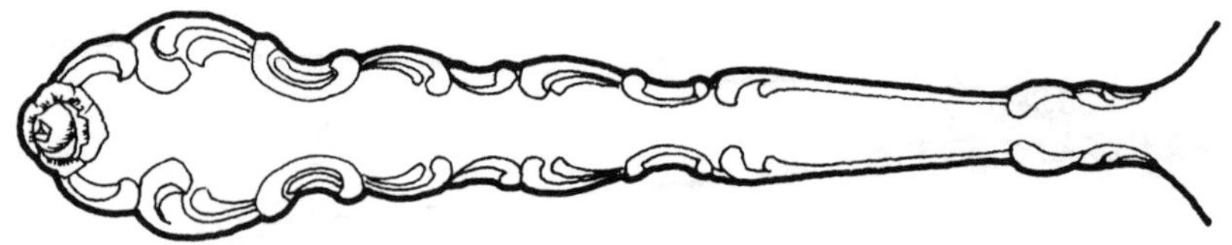

Available with General Mills coupons.

Brahms
1980
P

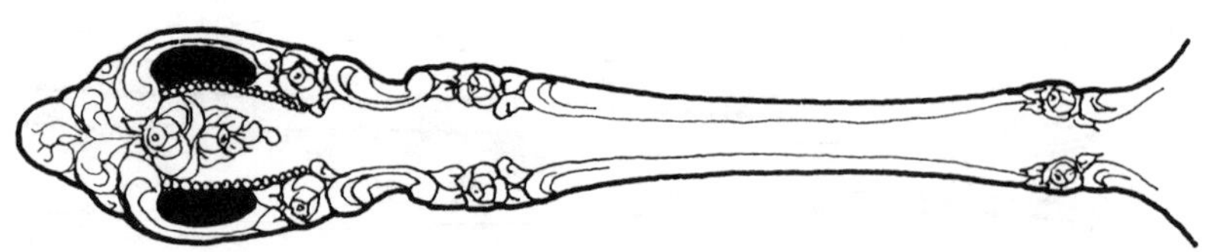

Available with General Mills coupons.

Duet
1980
S

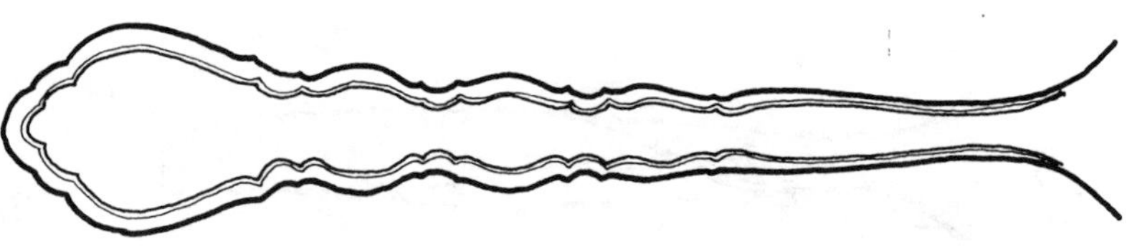

Dinner Knife $12.00
Dinner Fork $12.00
Teaspoon $7.00

Oneida - Oneida Ltd.

Belford aka Newport
(Carlton Silver Plate)
(Madison Silver Plate)
1930
S

Dinner Knife $8.00 Dinner Fork $8.00 Teaspoon $5.00

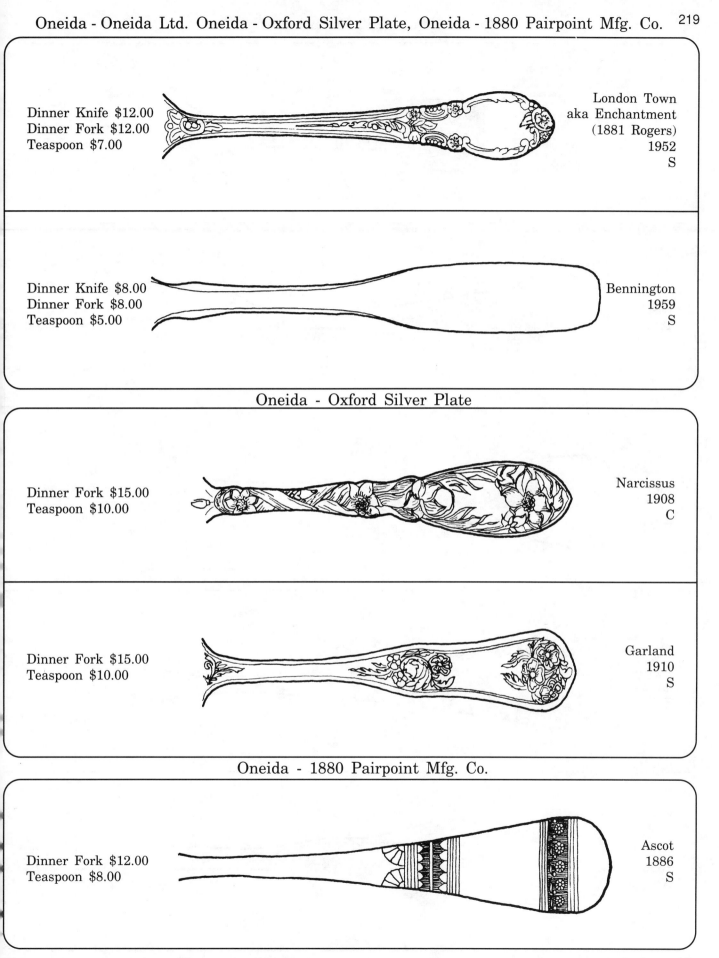

Dinner Knife $12.00
Dinner Fork $12.00
Teaspoon $7.00

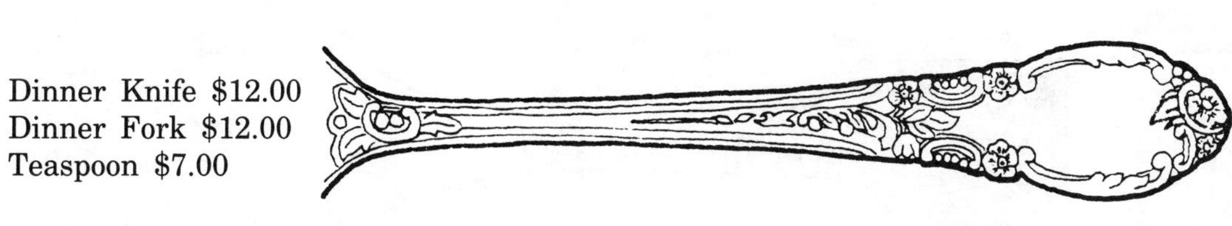

London Town
aka Enchantment
(1881 Rogers)
1952
S

Dinner Knife $8.00
Dinner Fork $8.00
Teaspoon $5.00

Bennington
1959
S

Oneida - Oxford Silver Plate

Dinner Fork $15.00
Teaspoon $10.00

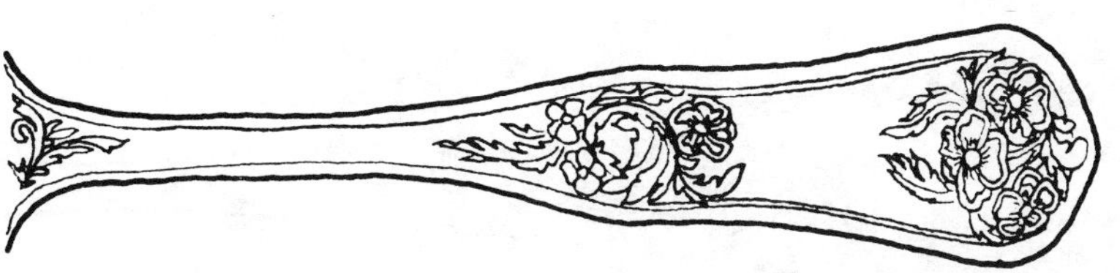

Narcissus
1908
C

Dinner Fork $15.00
Teaspoon $10.00

Garland
1910
S

Oneida - 1880 Pairpoint Mfg. Co.

Dinner Fork $12.00
Teaspoon $8.00

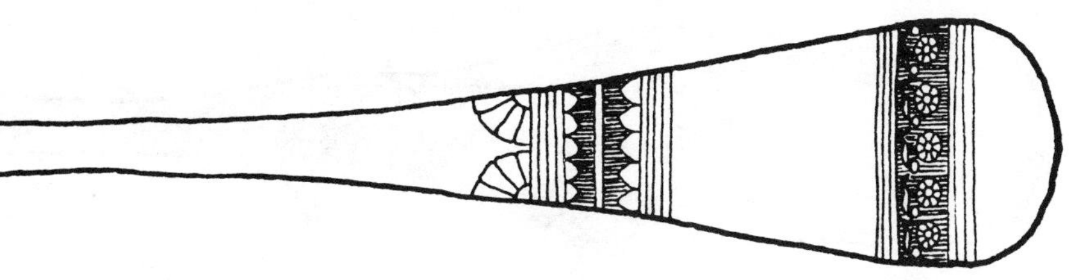

Ascot
1886
S

Please refer to "How To Use This Book" page 4.

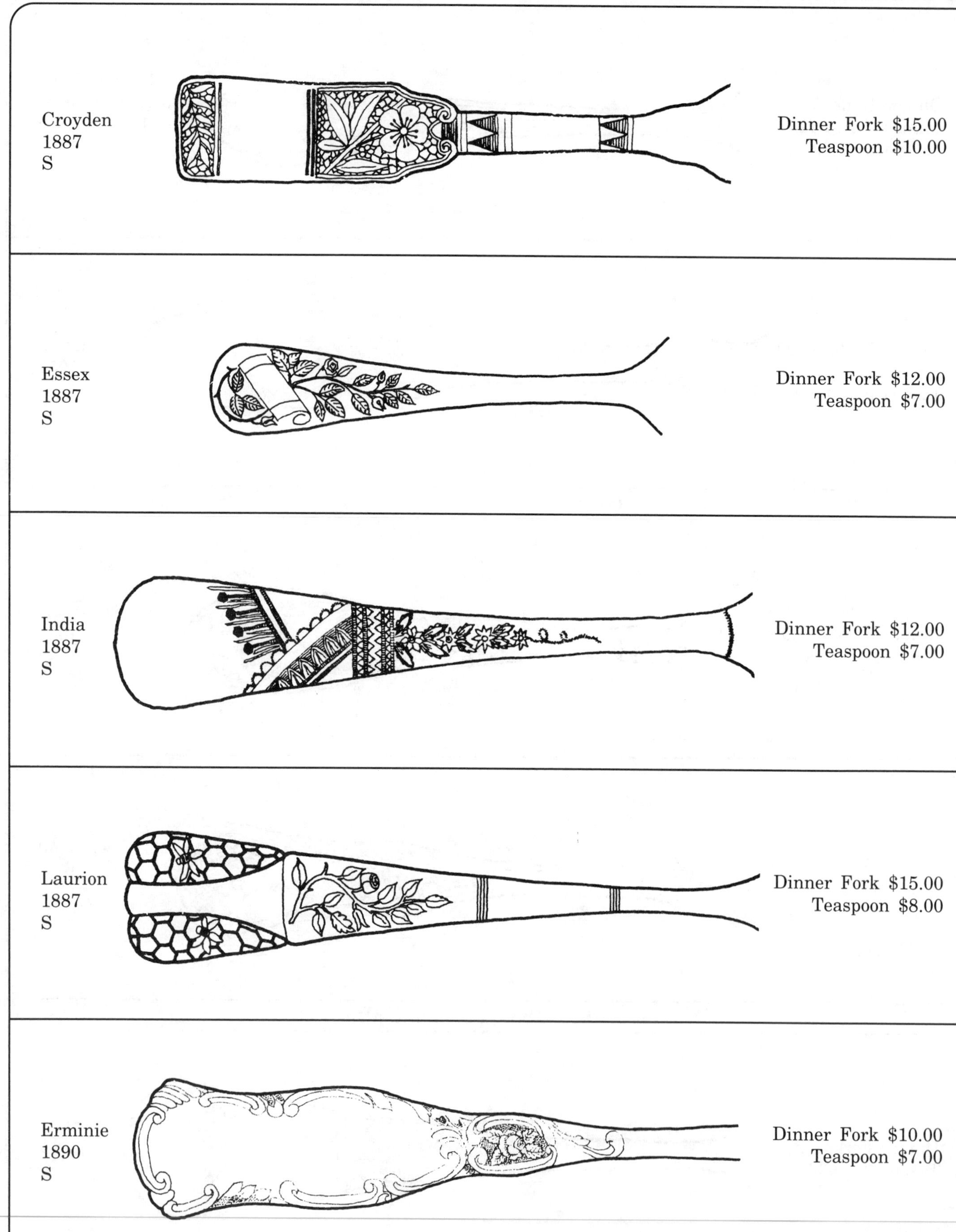

Croyden
1887
S

Dinner Fork $15.00
Teaspoon $10.00

Essex
1887
S

Dinner Fork $12.00
Teaspoon $7.00

India
1887
S

Dinner Fork $12.00
Teaspoon $7.00

Laurion
1887
S

Dinner Fork $15.00
Teaspoon $8.00

Erminie
1890
S

Dinner Fork $10.00
Teaspoon $7.00

Please refer to "How To Use This Book" page 4.

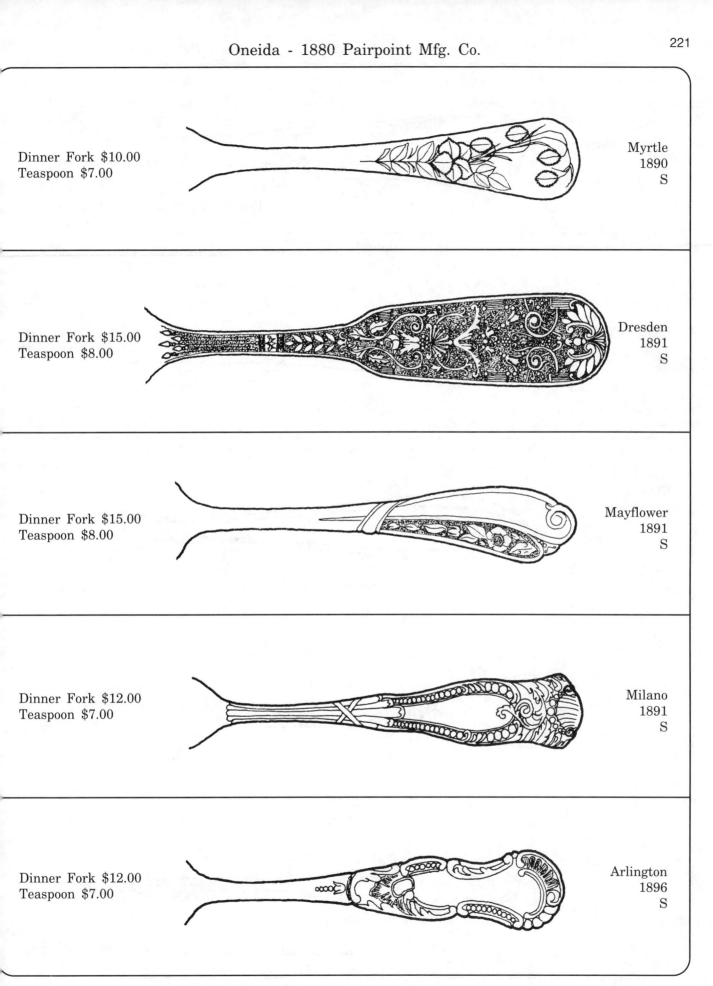

Dinner Fork $10.00
Teaspoon $7.00

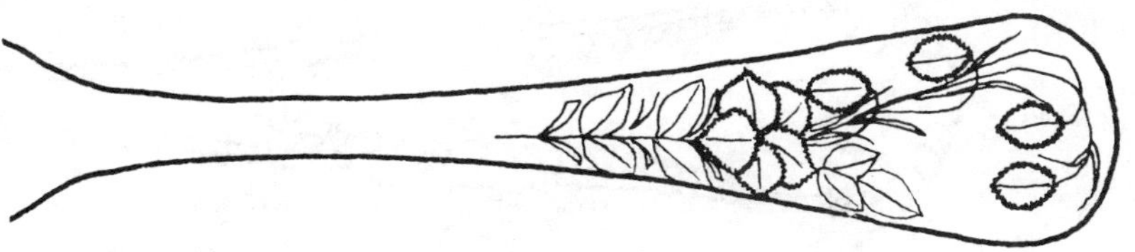

Myrtle
1890
S

Dinner Fork $15.00
Teaspoon $8.00

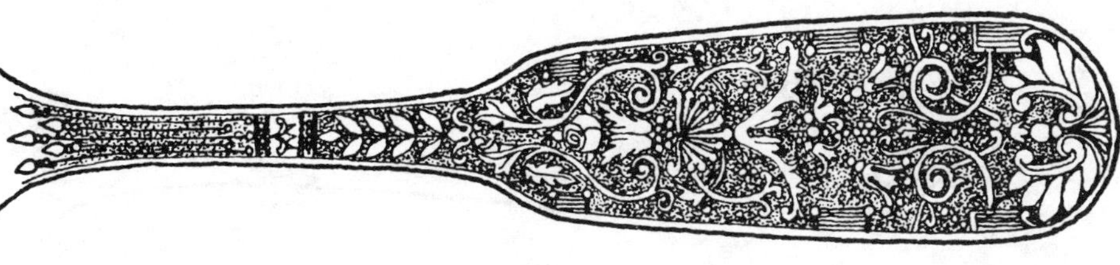

Dresden
1891
S

Dinner Fork $15.00
Teaspoon $8.00

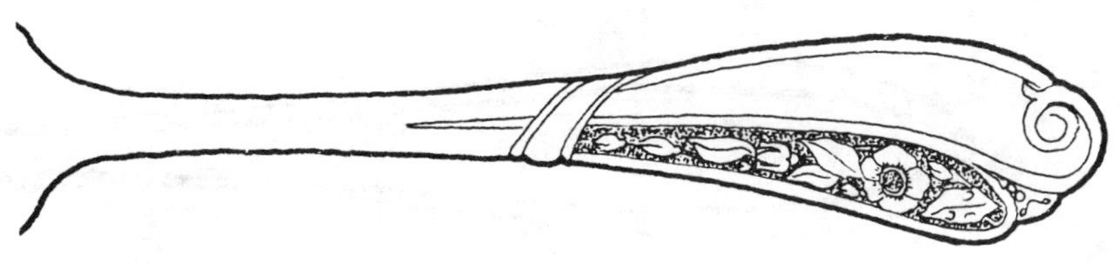

Mayflower
1891
S

Dinner Fork $12.00
Teaspoon $7.00

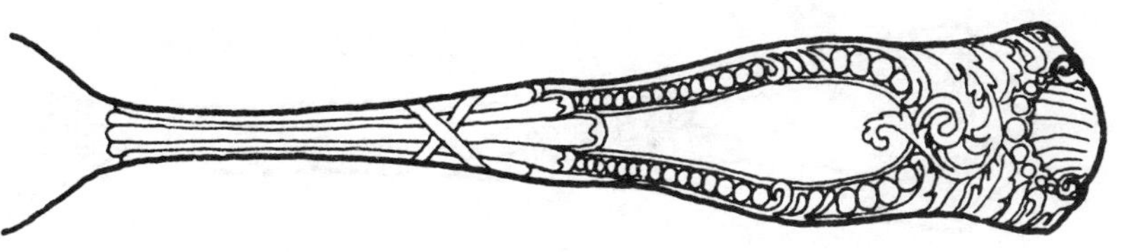

Milano
1891
S

Dinner Fork $12.00
Teaspoon $7.00

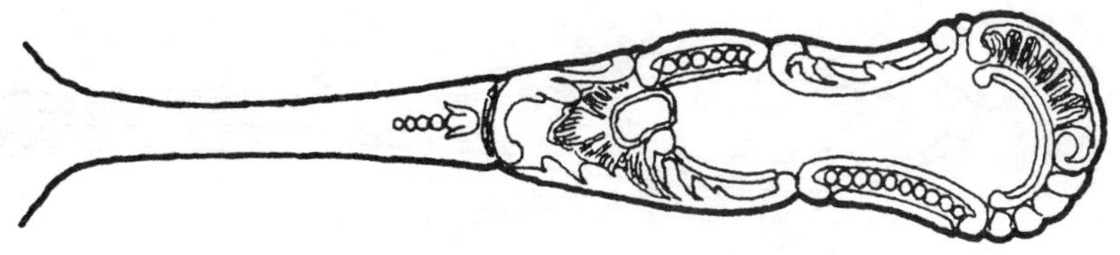

Arlington
1896
S

Please refer to "How To Use This Book" page 4.

Oneida - 1880 Pairpoint Mfg. Co., Oneida - Par Plate

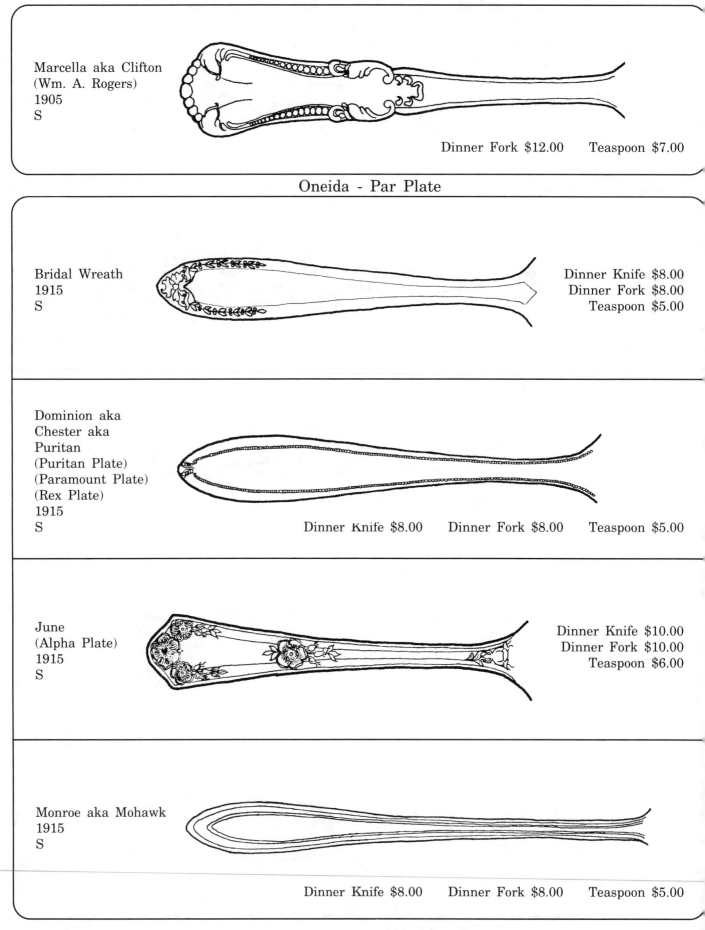

Marcella aka Clifton
(Wm. A. Rogers)
1905
S

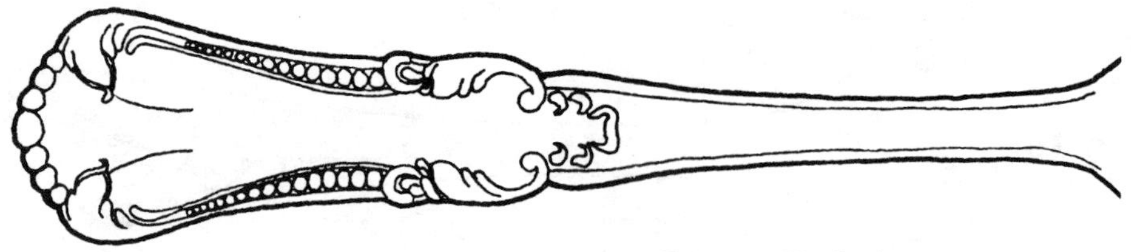

Dinner Fork $12.00 Teaspoon $7.00

Oneida - Par Plate

Bridal Wreath
1915
S

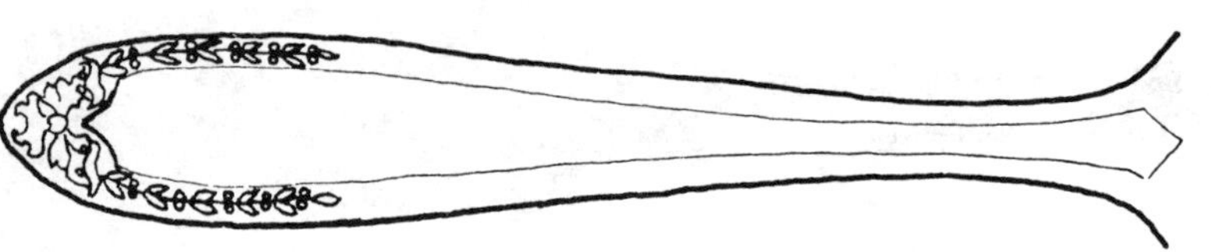

Dinner Knife $8.00
Dinner Fork $8.00
Teaspoon $5.00

Dominion aka
Chester aka
Puritan
(Puritan Plate)
(Paramount Plate)
(Rex Plate)
1915
S

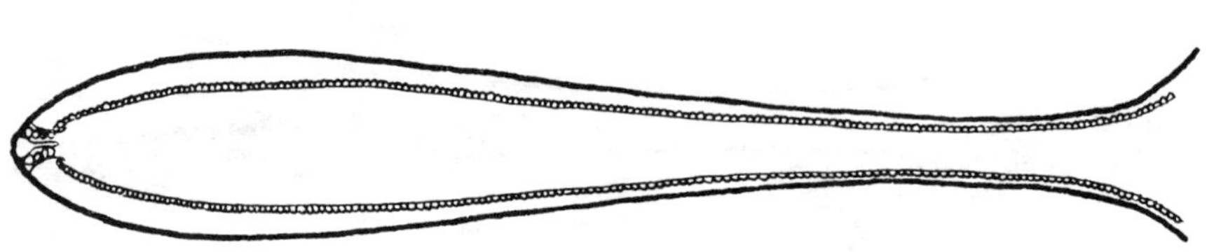

Dinner Knife $8.00 Dinner Fork $8.00 Teaspoon $5.00

June
(Alpha Plate)
1915
S

Dinner Knife $10.00
Dinner Fork $10.00
Teaspoon $6.00

Monroe aka Mohawk
1915
S

Dinner Knife $8.00 Dinner Fork $8.00 Teaspoon $5.00

Please refer to "How To Use This Book" page 4.

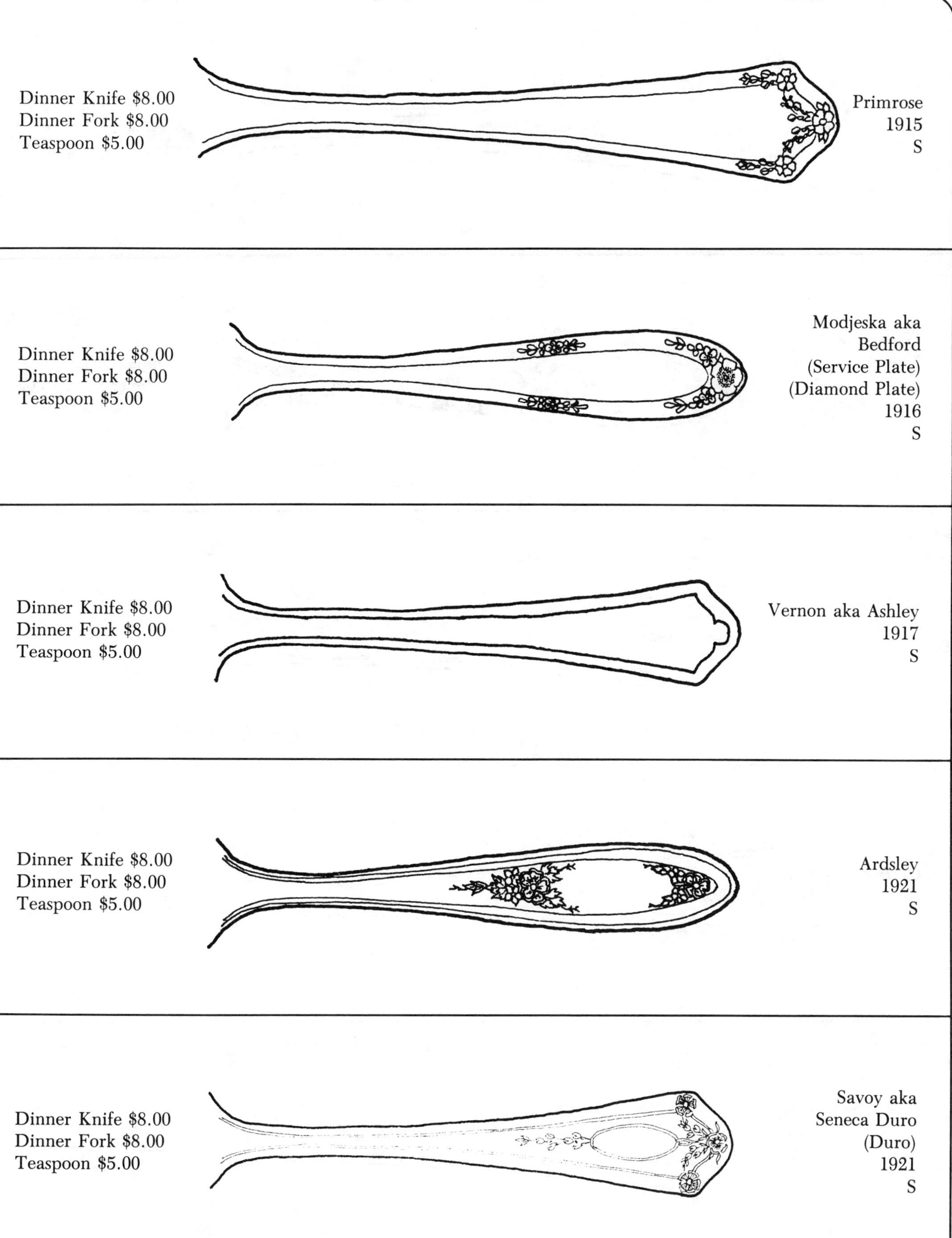

Dinner Knife $8.00
Dinner Fork $8.00
Teaspoon $5.00

Primrose
1915
S

Dinner Knife $8.00
Dinner Fork $8.00
Teaspoon $5.00

Modjeska aka
Bedford
(Service Plate)
(Diamond Plate)
1916
S

Dinner Knife $8.00
Dinner Fork $8.00
Teaspoon $5.00

Vernon aka Ashley
1917
S

Dinner Knife $8.00
Dinner Fork $8.00
Teaspoon $5.00

Ardsley
1921
S

Dinner Knife $8.00
Dinner Fork $8.00
Teaspoon $5.00

Savoy aka
Seneca Duro
(Duro)
1921
S

Please refer to "How To Use This Book" page 4.

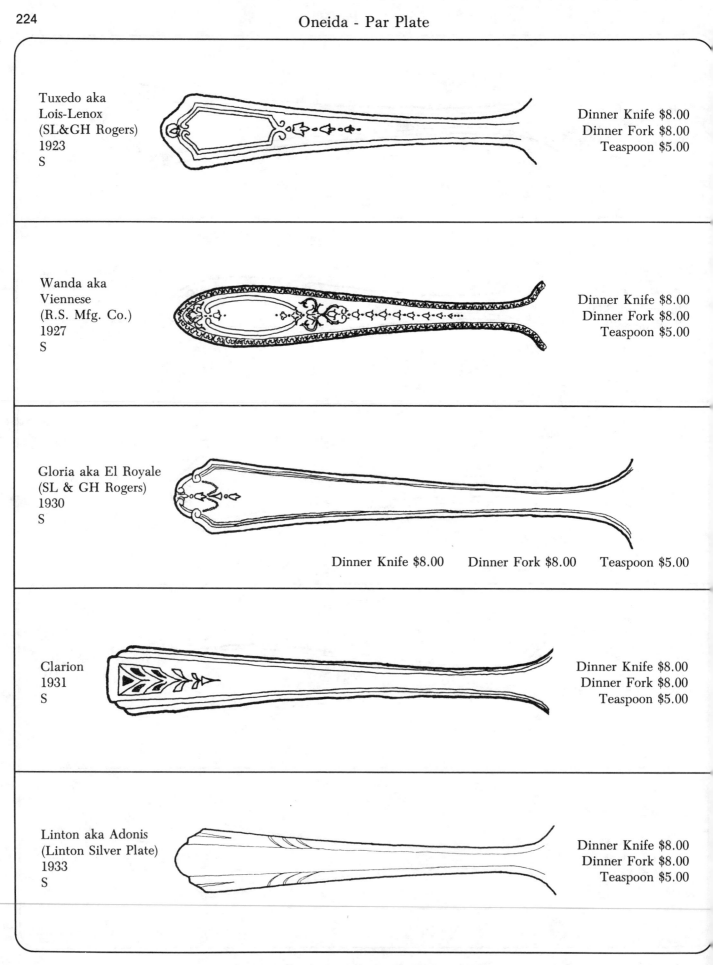

Tuxedo aka
Lois-Lenox
(SL&GH Rogers)
1923
S

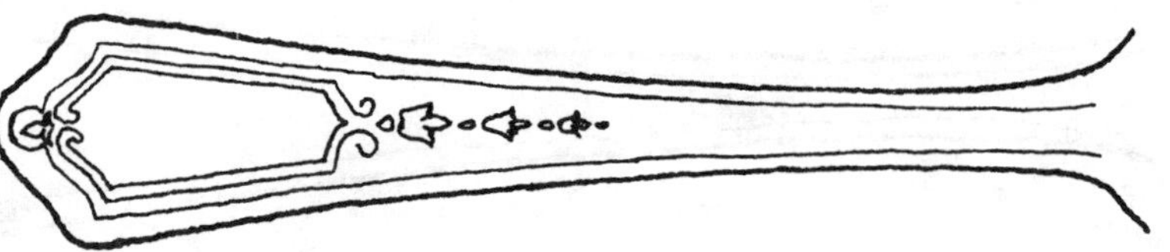

Dinner Knife $8.00
Dinner Fork $8.00
Teaspoon $5.00

Wanda aka
Viennese
(R.S. Mfg. Co.)
1927
S

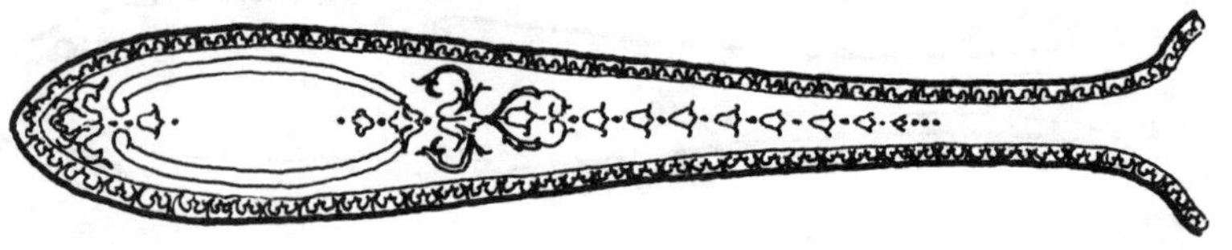

Dinner Knife $8.00
Dinner Fork $8.00
Teaspoon $5.00

Gloria aka El Royale
(SL & GH Rogers)
1930
S

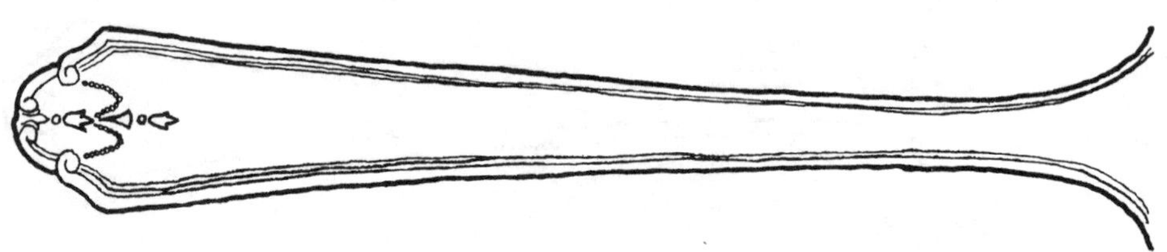

Dinner Knife $8.00 Dinner Fork $8.00 Teaspoon $5.00

Clarion
1931
S

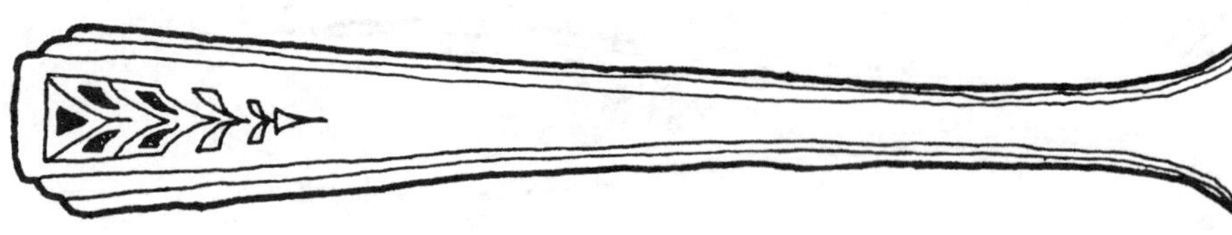

Dinner Knife $8.00
Dinner Fork $8.00
Teaspoon $5.00

Linton aka Adonis
(Linton Silver Plate)
1933
S

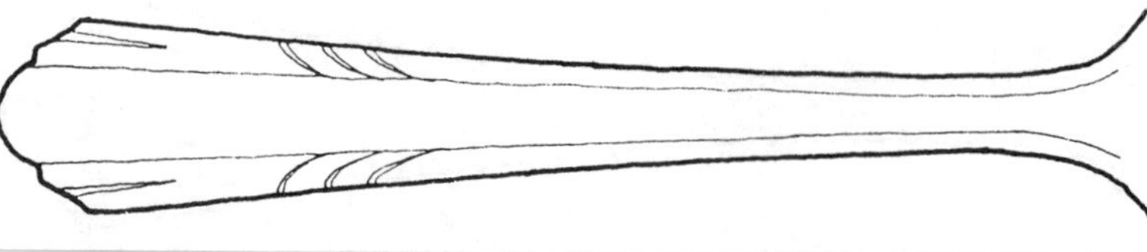

Dinner Knife $8.00
Dinner Fork $8.00
Teaspoon $5.00

Please refer to "How To Use This Book" page 4.

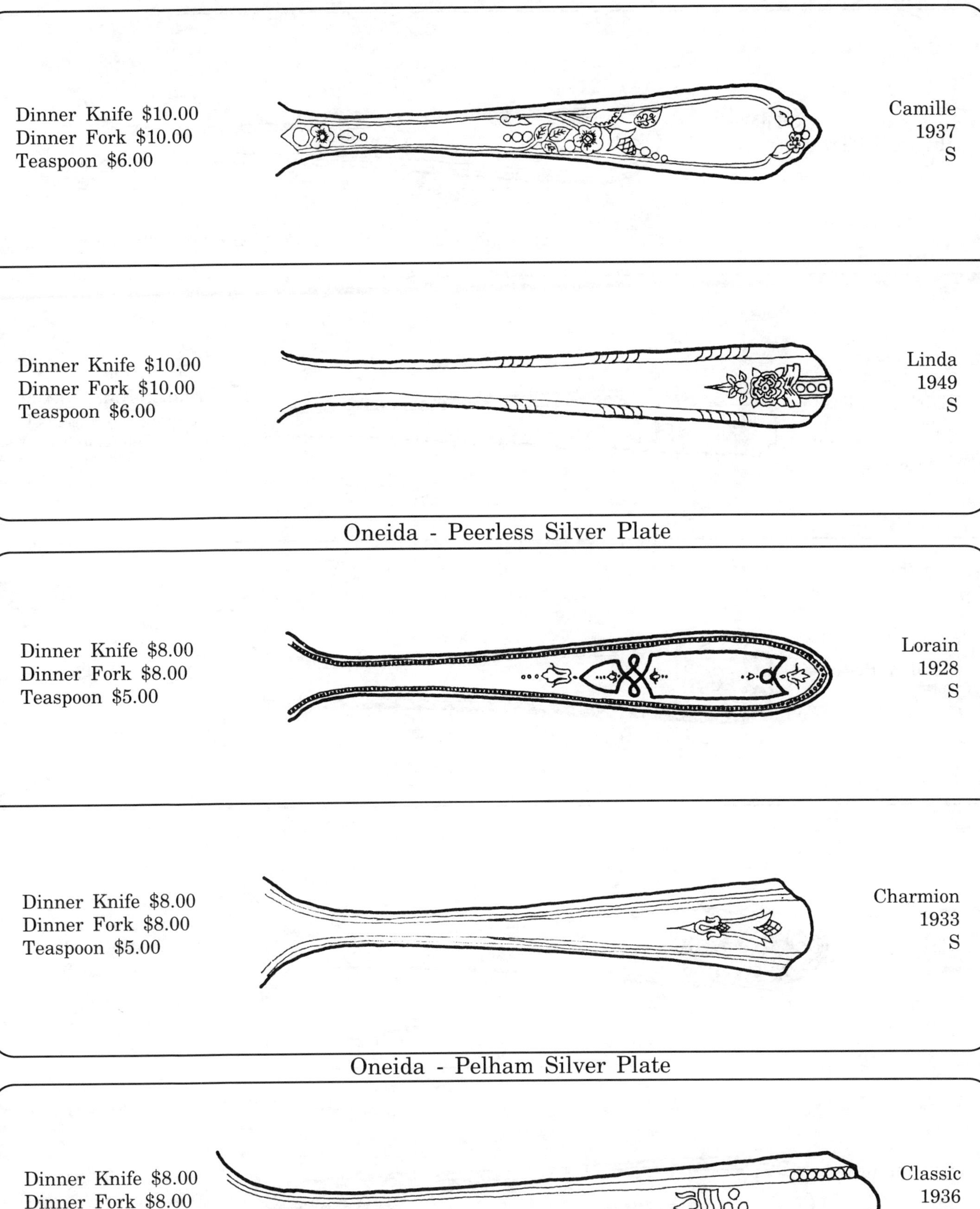

Dinner Knife $10.00
Dinner Fork $10.00
Teaspoon $6.00

Camille
1937
S

Dinner Knife $10.00
Dinner Fork $10.00
Teaspoon $6.00

Linda
1949
S

Oneida - Peerless Silver Plate

Dinner Knife $8.00
Dinner Fork $8.00
Teaspoon $5.00

Lorain
1928
S

Dinner Knife $8.00
Dinner Fork $8.00
Teaspoon $5.00

Charmion
1933
S

Oneida - Pelham Silver Plate

Dinner Knife $8.00
Dinner Fork $8.00
Teaspoon $5.00

Classic
1936
S

Please refer to “How To Use This Book” page 4.

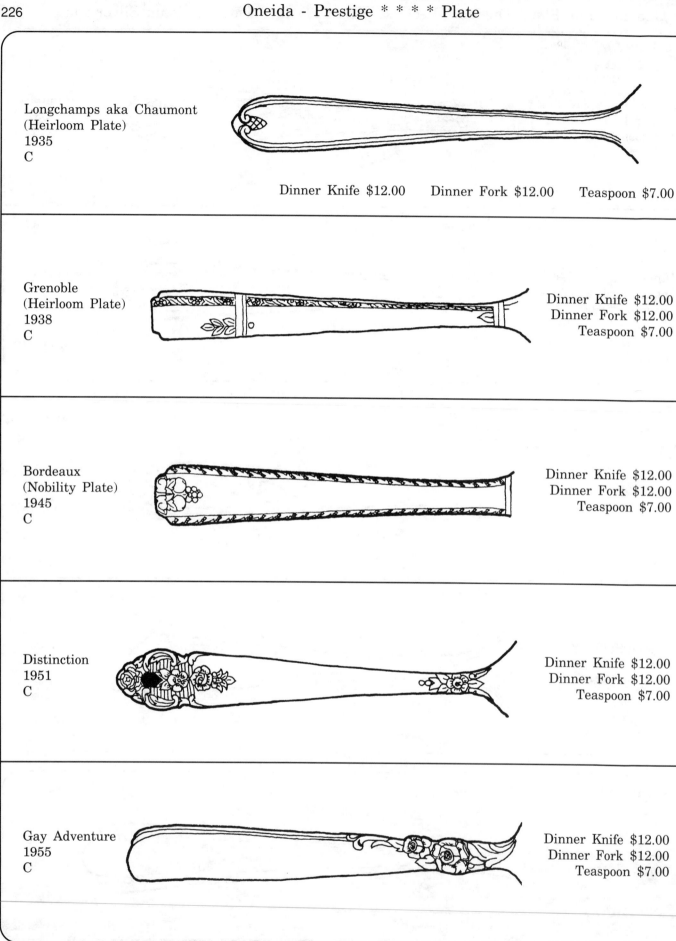

Longchamps aka Chaumont
(Heirloom Plate)
1935
C

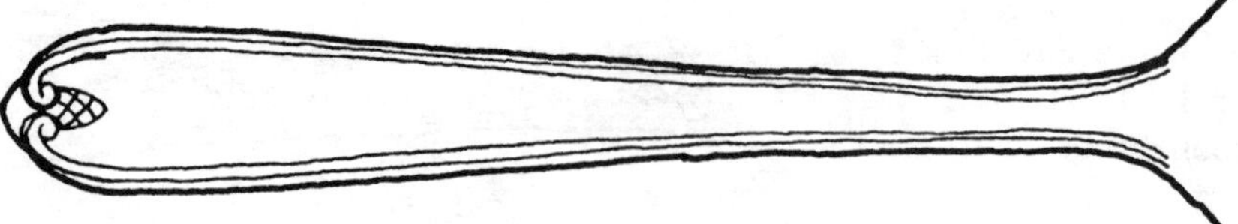

Dinner Knife $12.00 Dinner Fork $12.00 Teaspoon $7.00

Grenoble
(Heirloom Plate)
1938
C

Dinner Knife $12.00
Dinner Fork $12.00
Teaspoon $7.00

Bordeaux
(Nobility Plate)
1945
C

Dinner Knife $12.00
Dinner Fork $12.00
Teaspoon $7.00

Distinction
1951
C

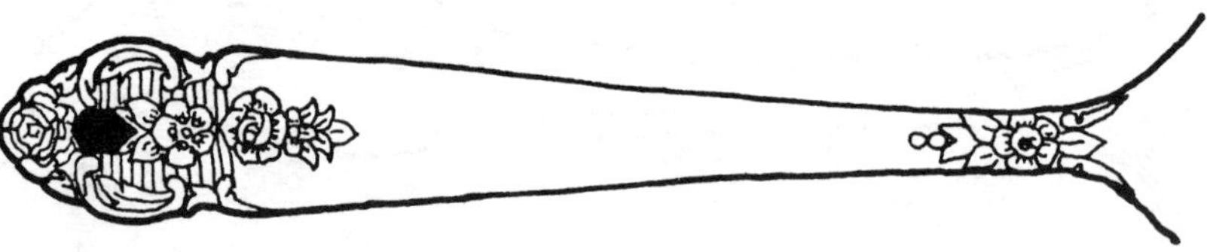

Dinner Knife $12.00
Dinner Fork $12.00
Teaspoon $7.00

Gay Adventure
1955
C

Dinner Knife $12.00
Dinner Fork $12.00
Teaspoon $7.00

Please refer to "How To Use This Book" page 4.

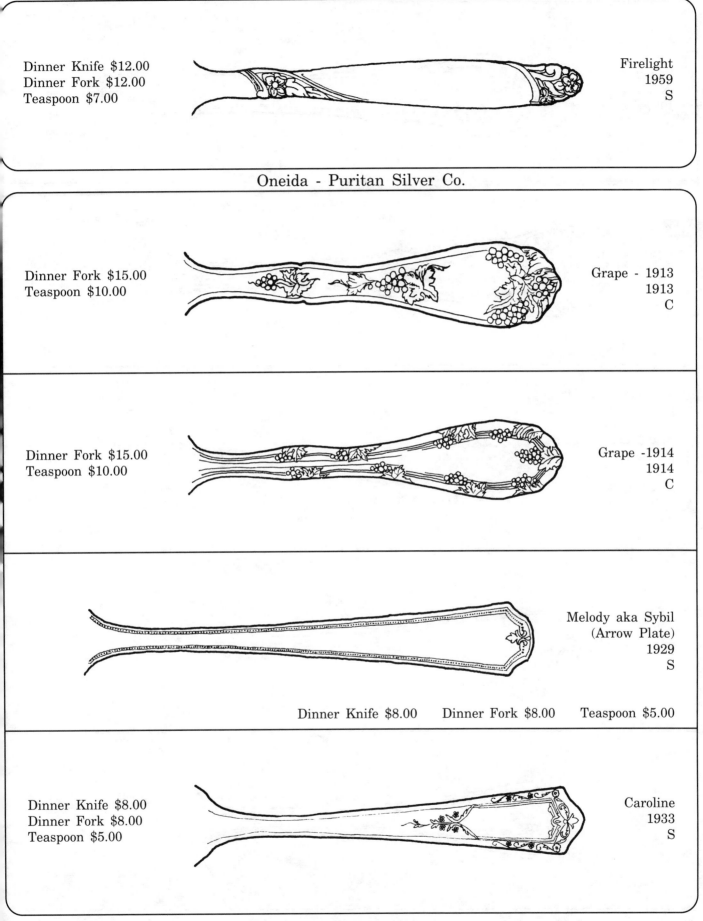

Dinner Knife $12.00
Dinner Fork $12.00
Teaspoon $7.00

Firelight
1959
S

Oneida - Puritan Silver Co.

Dinner Fork $15.00
Teaspoon $10.00

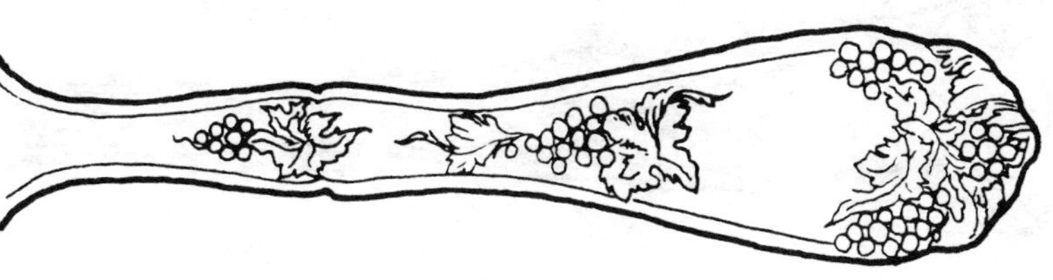

Grape - 1913
1913
C

Dinner Fork $15.00
Teaspoon $10.00

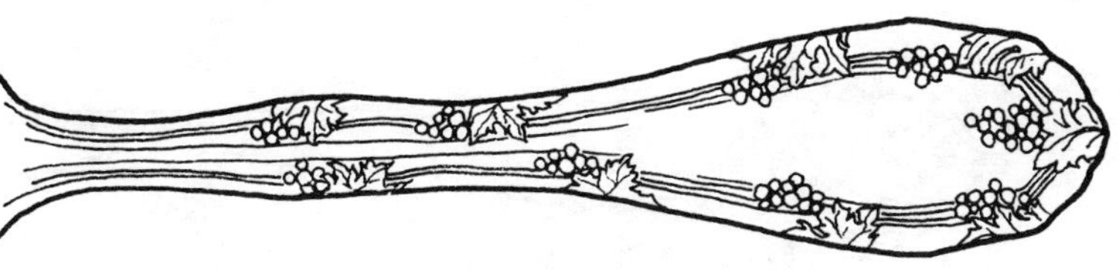

Grape -1914
1914
C

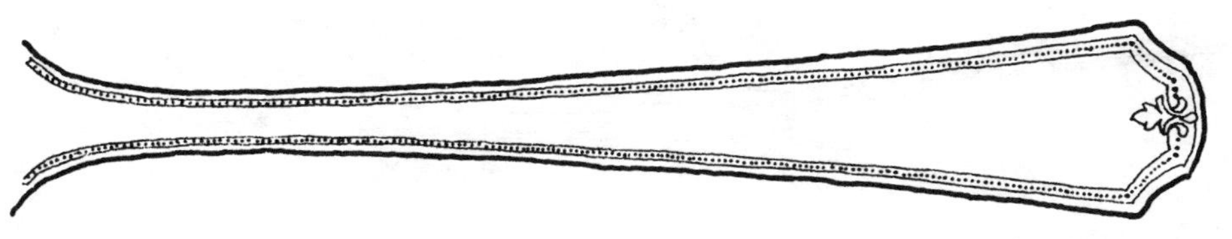

Melody aka Sybil
(Arrow Plate)
1929
S

Dinner Knife $8.00 Dinner Fork $8.00 Teaspoon $5.00

Dinner Knife $8.00
Dinner Fork $8.00
Teaspoon $5.00

Caroline
1933
S

Please refer to "How To Use This Book" page 4.

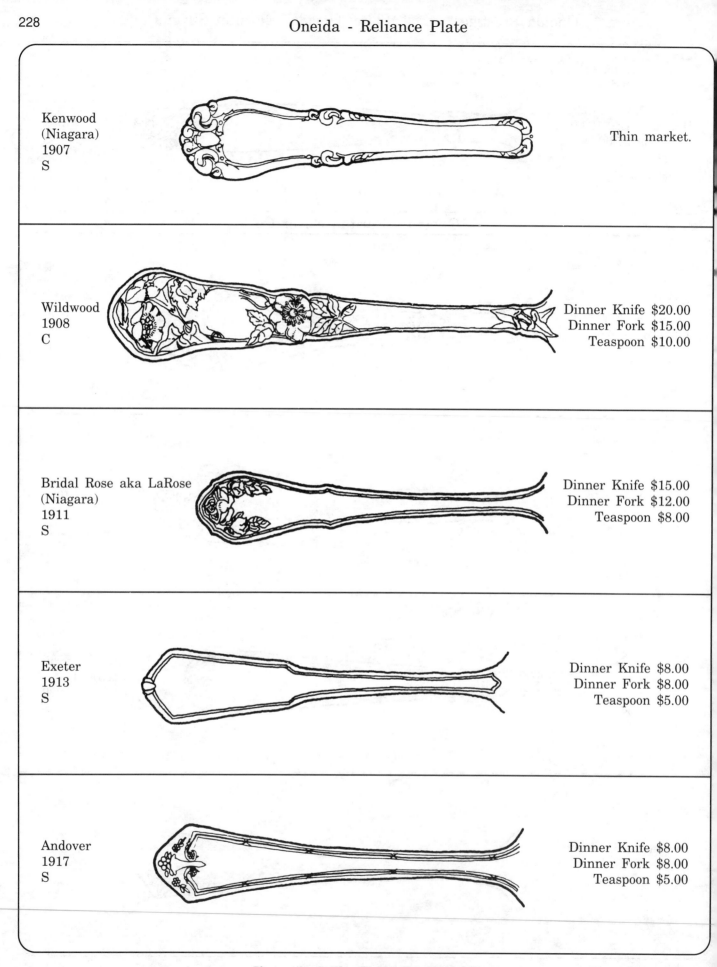

Kenwood
(Niagara)
1907
S

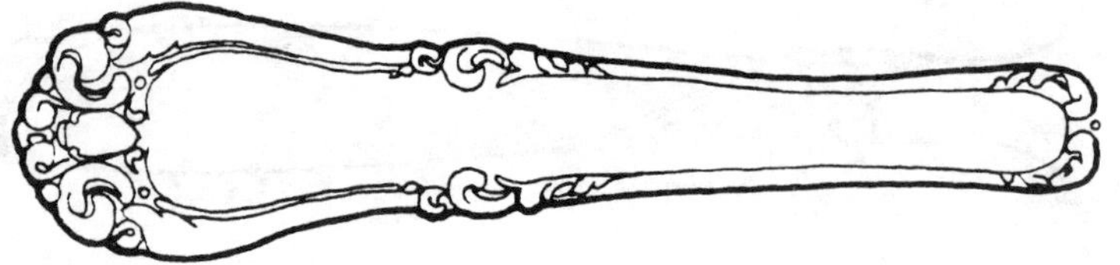

Thin market.

Wildwood
1908
C

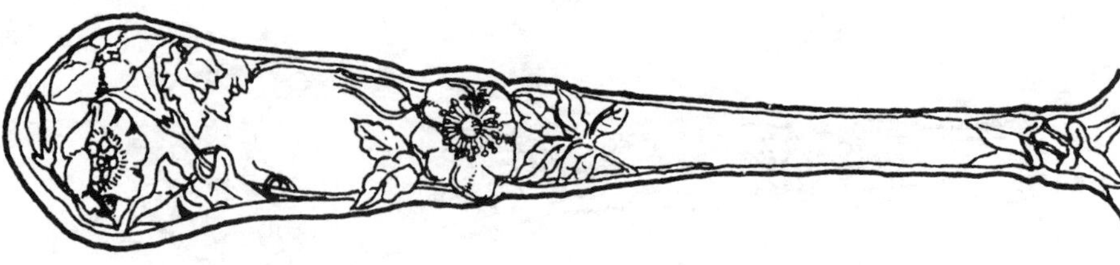

Dinner Knife $20.00
Dinner Fork $15.00
Teaspoon $10.00

Bridal Rose aka LaRose
(Niagara)
1911
S

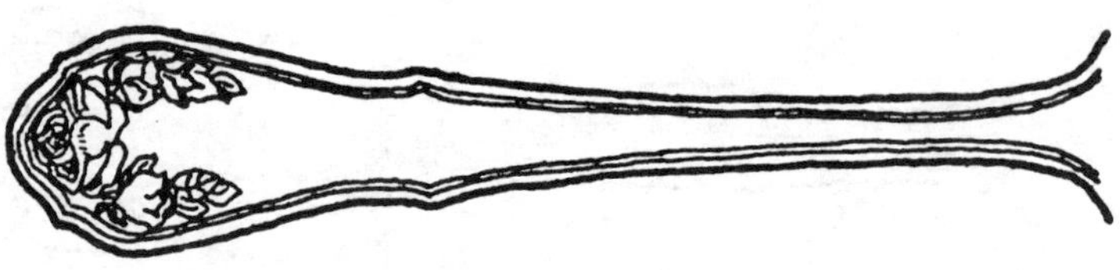

Dinner Knife $15.00
Dinner Fork $12.00
Teaspoon $8.00

Exeter
1913
S

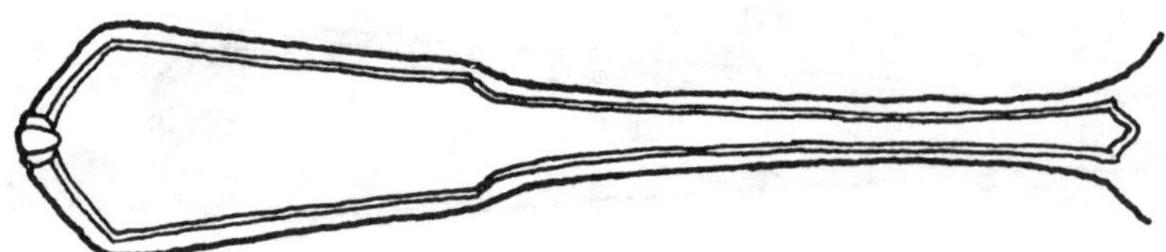

Dinner Knife $8.00
Dinner Fork $8.00
Teaspoon $5.00

Andover
1917
S

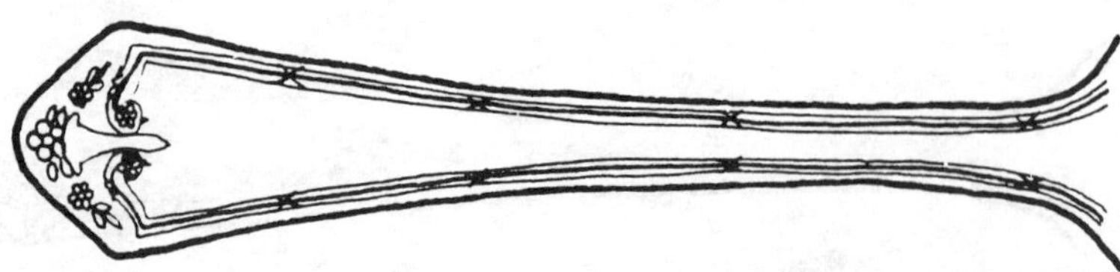

Dinner Knife $8.00
Dinner Fork $8.00
Teaspoon $5.00

Please refer to "How To Use This Book" page 4.

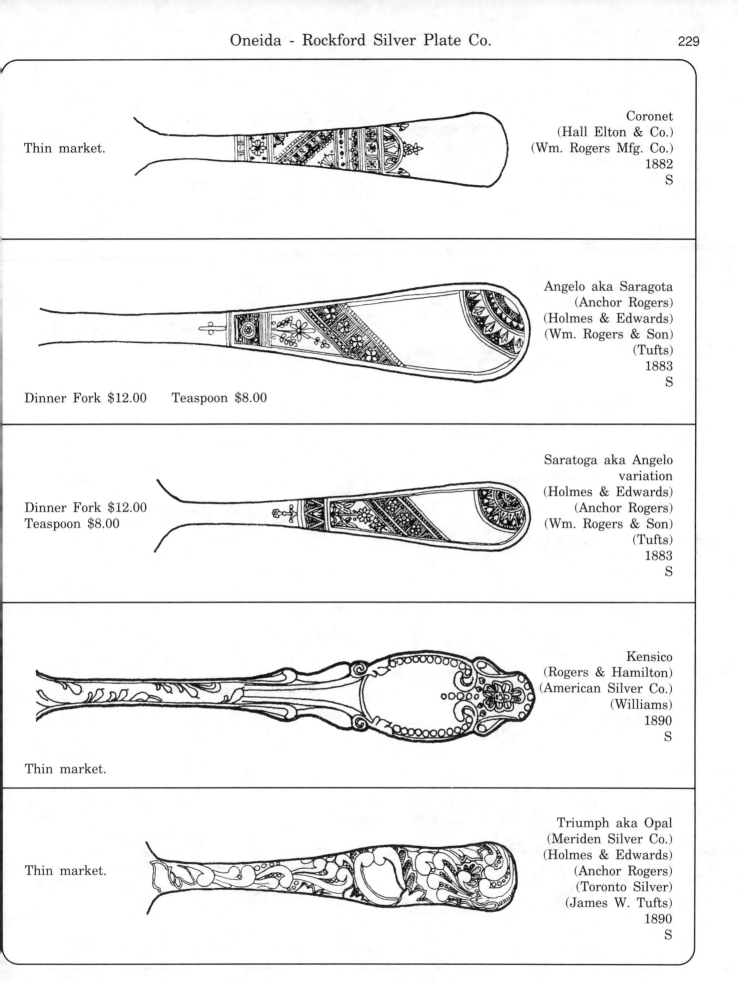

Thin market.

Coronet
(Hall Elton & Co.)
(Wm. Rogers Mfg. Co.)
1882
S

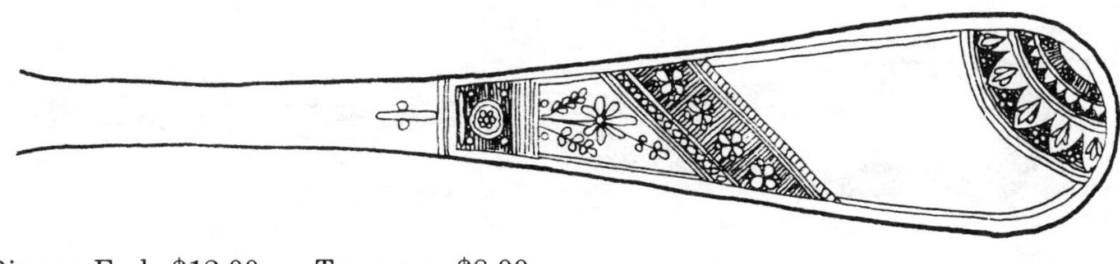

Angelo aka Saragota
(Anchor Rogers)
(Holmes & Edwards)
(Wm. Rogers & Son)
(Tufts)
1883
S

Dinner Fork $12.00 Teaspoon $8.00

Dinner Fork $12.00
Teaspoon $8.00

Saratoga aka Angelo variation
(Holmes & Edwards)
(Anchor Rogers)
(Wm. Rogers & Son)
(Tufts)
1883
S

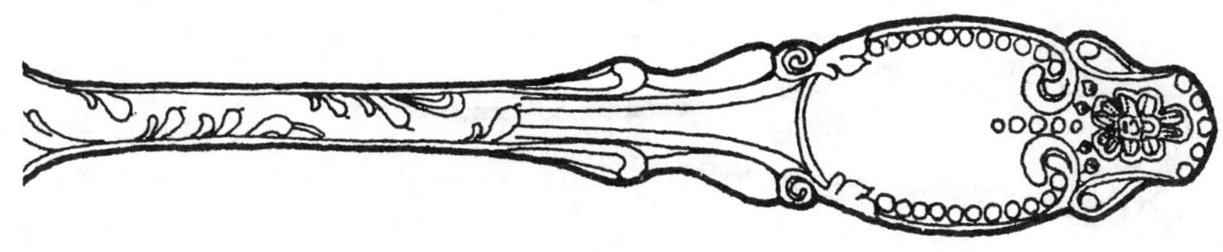

Kensico
(Rogers & Hamilton)
(American Silver Co.)
(Williams)
1890
S

Thin market.

Thin market.

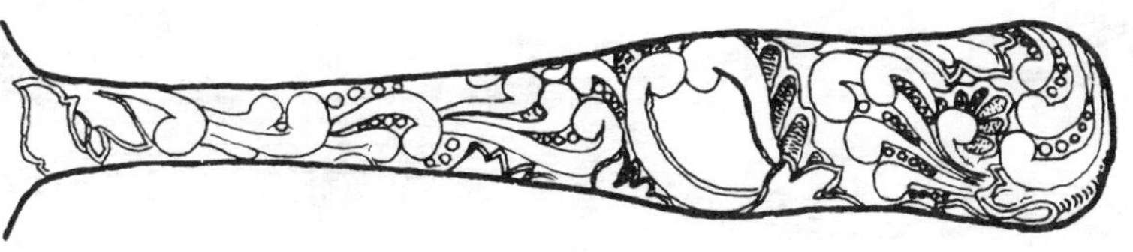

Triumph aka Opal
(Meriden Silver Co.)
(Holmes & Edwards)
(Anchor Rogers)
(Toronto Silver)
(James W. Tufts)
1890
S

Please refer to "How To Use This Book" page 4.

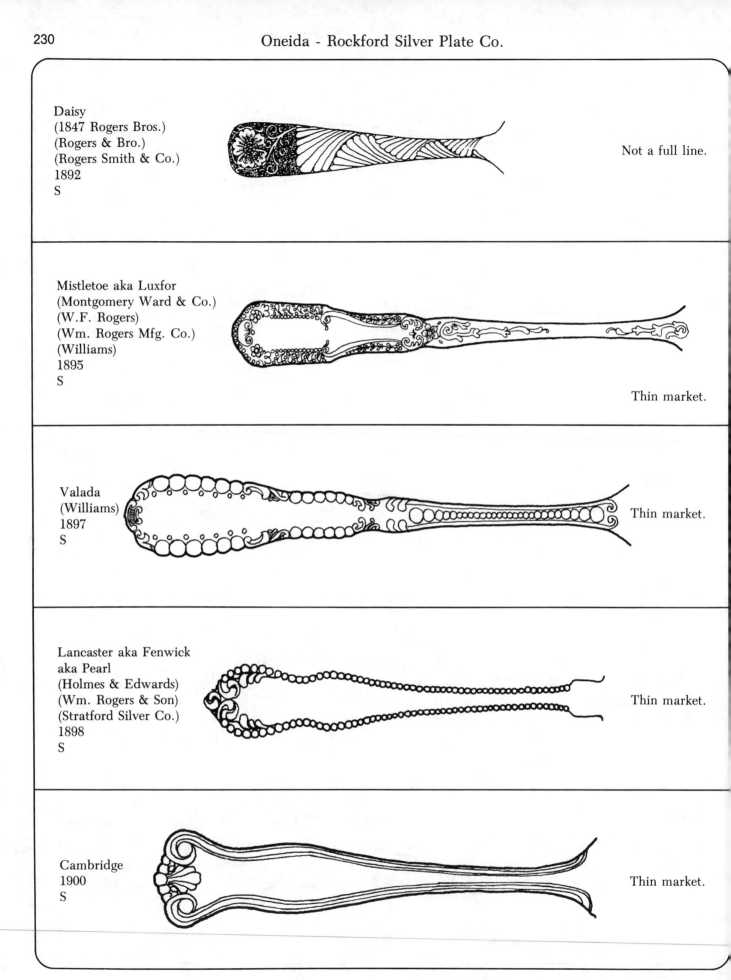

Daisy
(1847 Rogers Bros.)
(Rogers & Bro.)
(Rogers Smith & Co.)
1892
S

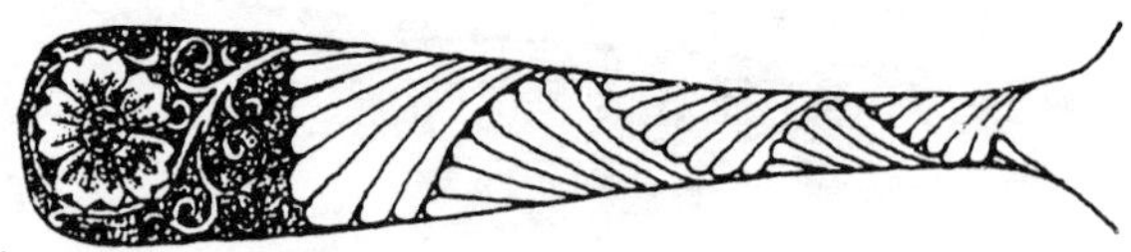

Not a full line.

Mistletoe aka Luxfor
(Montgomery Ward & Co.)
(W.F. Rogers)
(Wm. Rogers Mfg. Co.)
(Williams)
1895
S

Thin market.

Valada
(Williams)
1897
S

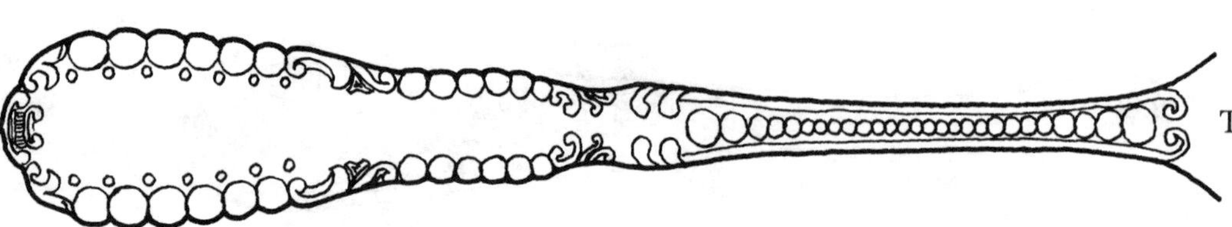

Thin market.

Lancaster aka Fenwick
aka Pearl
(Holmes & Edwards)
(Wm. Rogers & Son)
(Stratford Silver Co.)
1898
S

Thin market.

Cambridge
1900
S

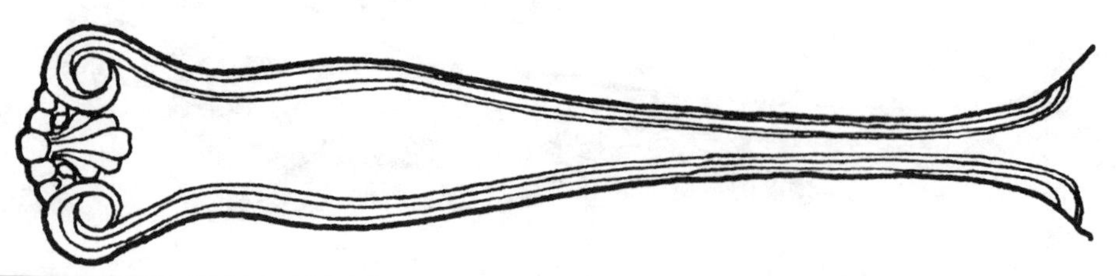

Thin market.

Please refer to "How To Use This Book" page 4.

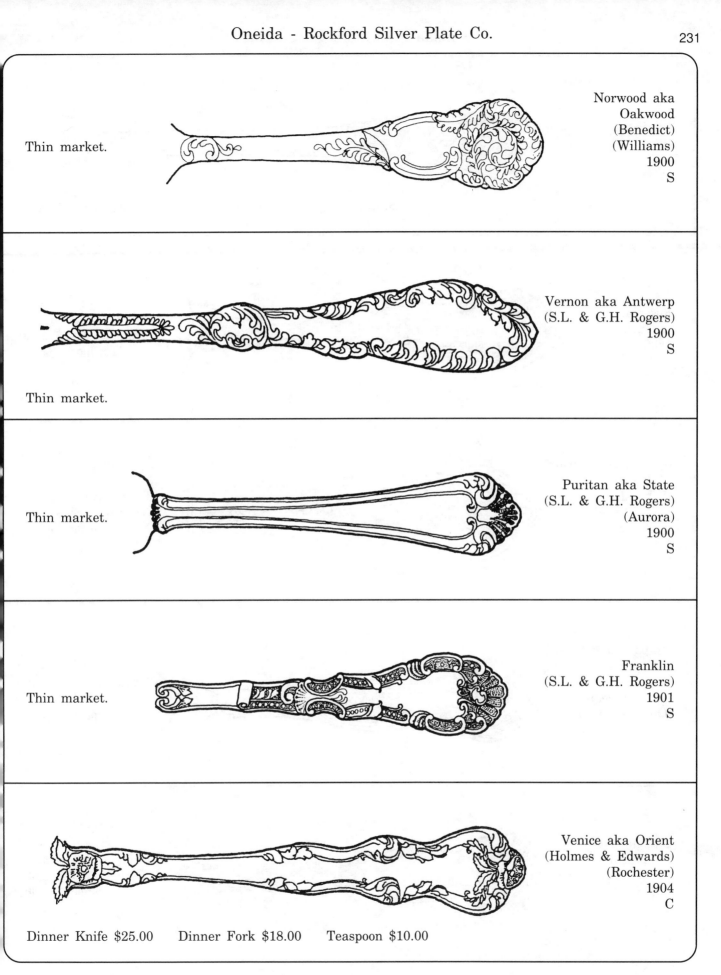

Thin market.

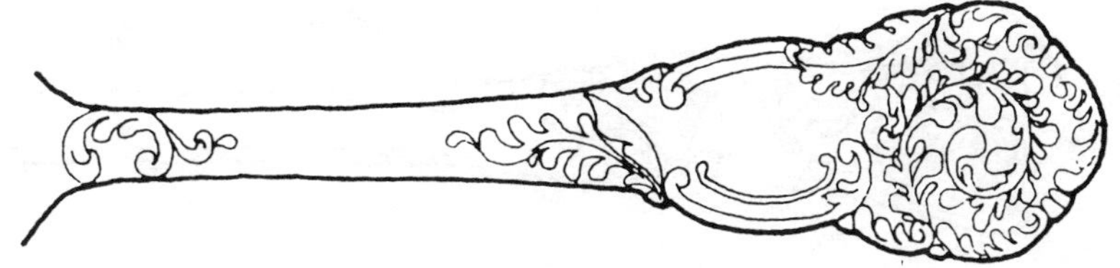

Norwood aka
Oakwood
(Benedict)
(Williams)
1900
S

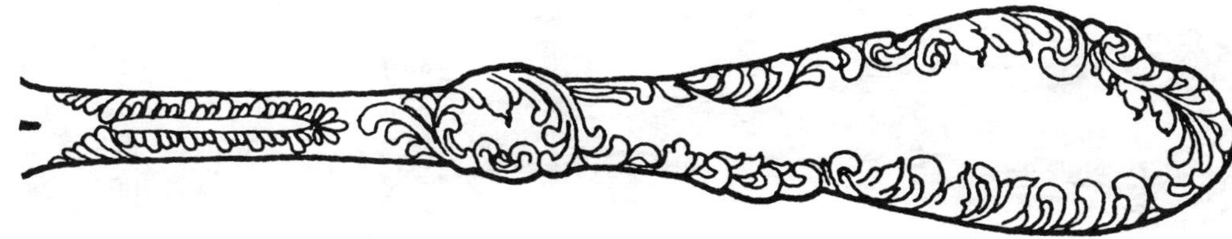

Vernon aka Antwerp
(S.L. & G.H. Rogers)
1900
S

Thin market.

Thin market.

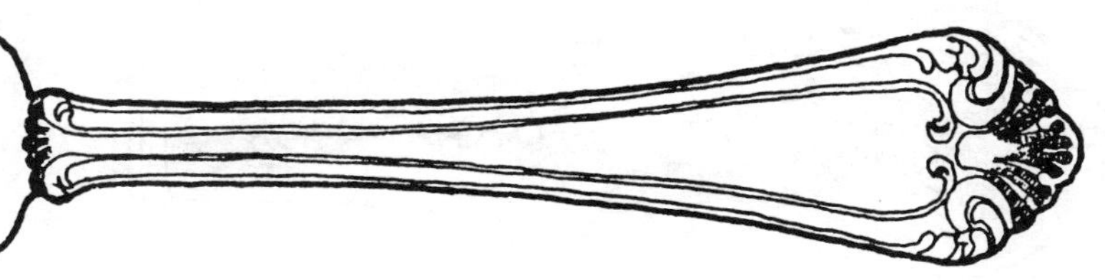

Puritan aka State
(S.L. & G.H. Rogers)
(Aurora)
1900
S

Thin market.

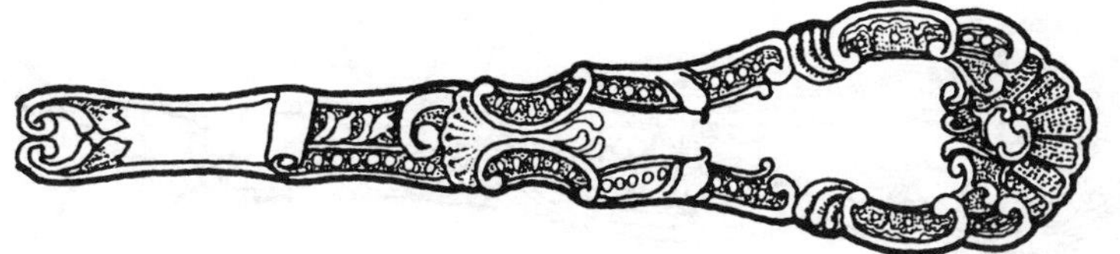

Franklin
(S.L. & G.H. Rogers)
1901
S

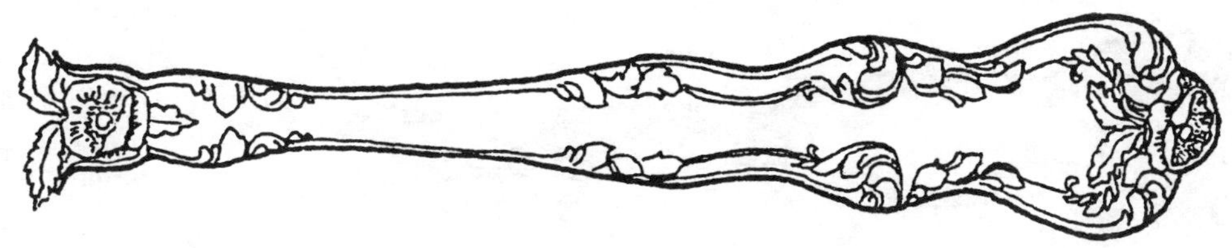

Venice aka Orient
(Holmes & Edwards)
(Rochester)
1904
C

Dinner Knife $25.00 Dinner Fork $18.00 Teaspoon $10.00

Please refer to "How To Use This Book" page 4.

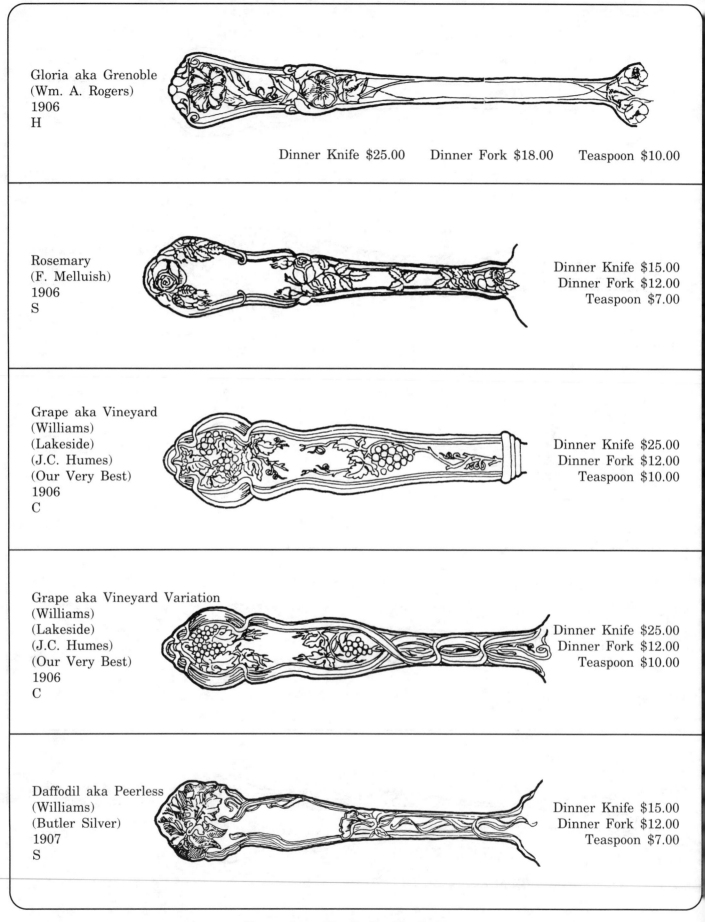

Gloria aka Grenoble
(Wm. A. Rogers)
1906
H

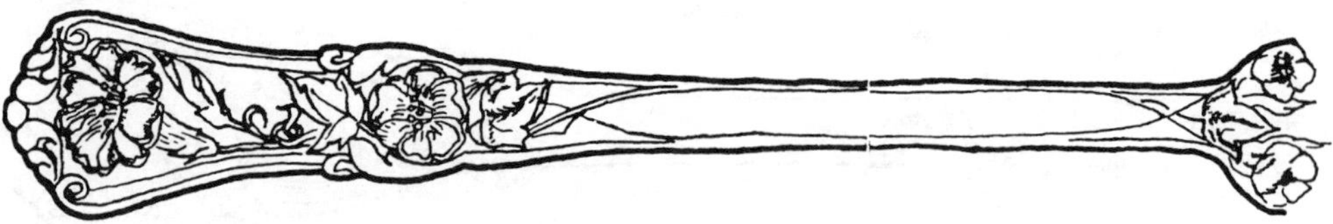

Dinner Knife $25.00 Dinner Fork $18.00 Teaspoon $10.00

Rosemary
(F. Melluish)
1906
S

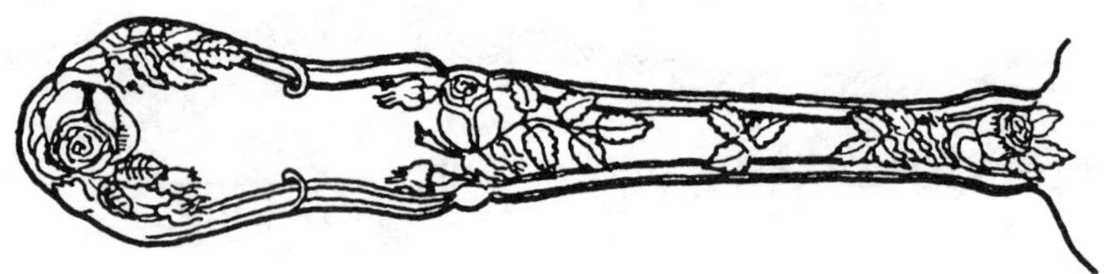

Dinner Knife $15.00
Dinner Fork $12.00
Teaspoon $7.00

Grape aka Vineyard
(Williams)
(Lakeside)
(J.C. Humes)
(Our Very Best)
1906
C

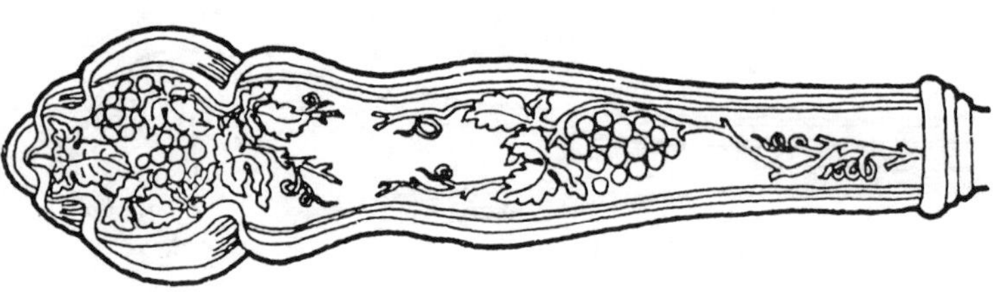

Dinner Knife $25.00
Dinner Fork $12.00
Teaspoon $10.00

Grape aka Vineyard Variation
(Williams)
(Lakeside)
(J.C. Humes)
(Our Very Best)
1906
C

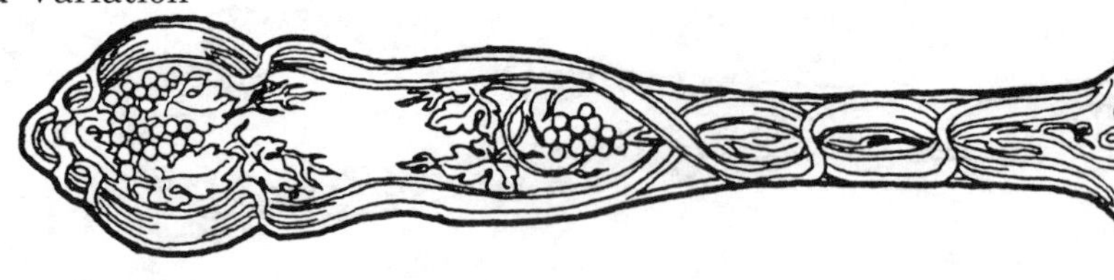

Dinner Knife $25.00
Dinner Fork $12.00
Teaspoon $10.00

Daffodil aka Peerless
(Williams)
(Butler Silver)
1907
S

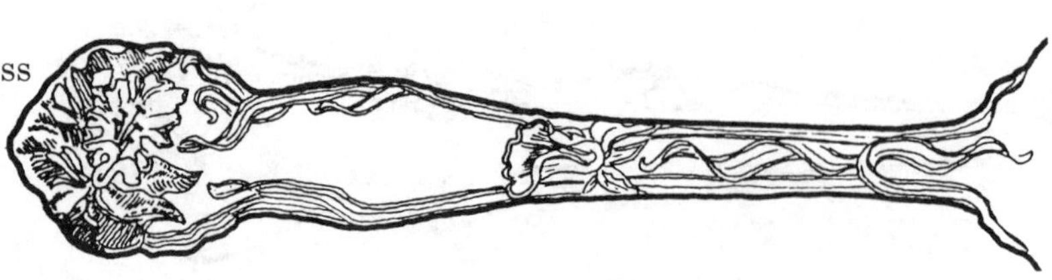

Dinner Knife $15.00
Dinner Fork $12.00
Teaspoon $7.00

Please refer to "How To Use This Book" page 4.

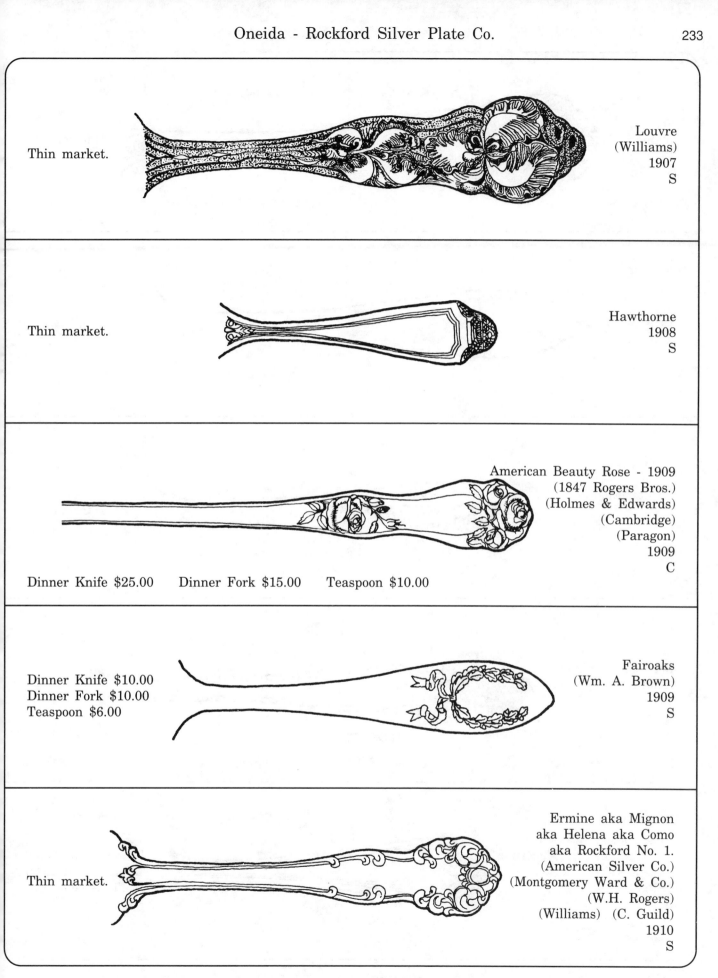

Thin market.

Louvre
(Williams)
1907
S

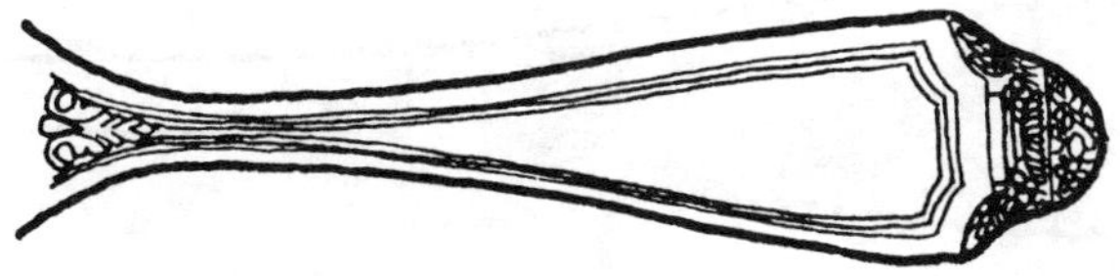

Thin market.

Hawthorne
1908
S

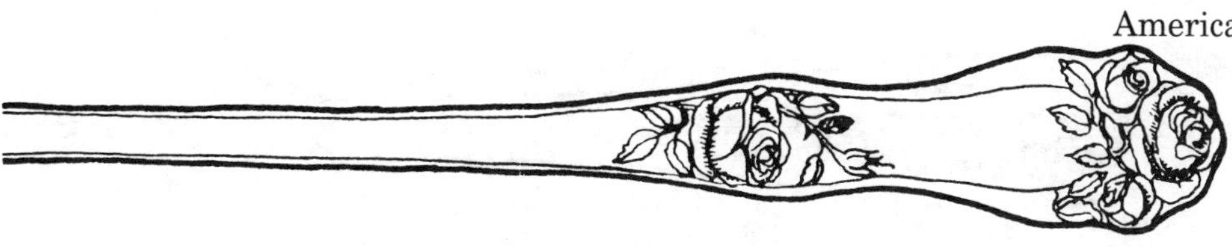

American Beauty Rose - 1909
(1847 Rogers Bros.)
(Holmes & Edwards)
(Cambridge)
(Paragon)
1909
C

Dinner Knife $25.00 Dinner Fork $15.00 Teaspoon $10.00

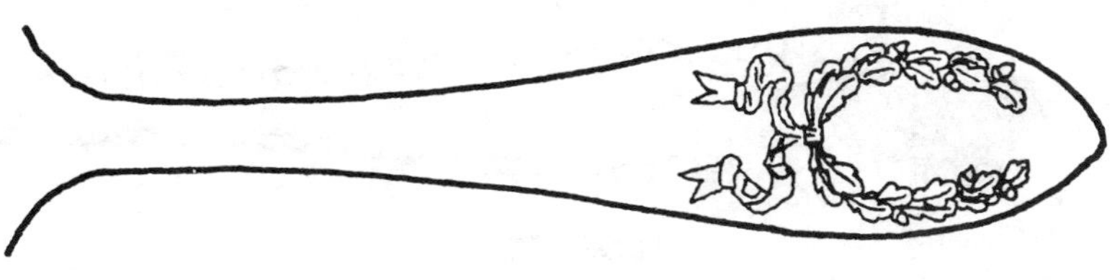

Dinner Knife $10.00
Dinner Fork $10.00
Teaspoon $6.00

Fairoaks
(Wm. A. Brown)
1909
S

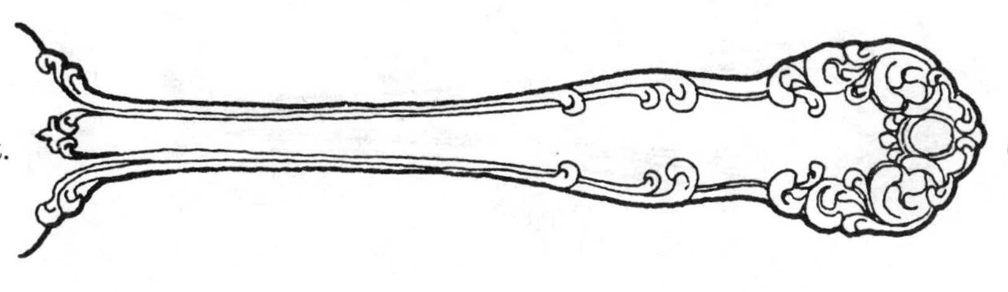

Thin market.

Ermine aka Mignon
aka Helena aka Como
aka Rockford No. 1.
(American Silver Co.)
(Montgomery Ward & Co.)
(W.H. Rogers)
(Williams) (C. Guild)
1910
S

Please refer to "How To Use This Book" page 4.

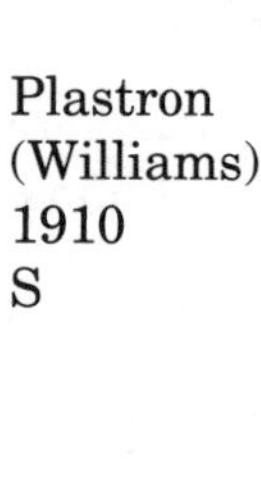

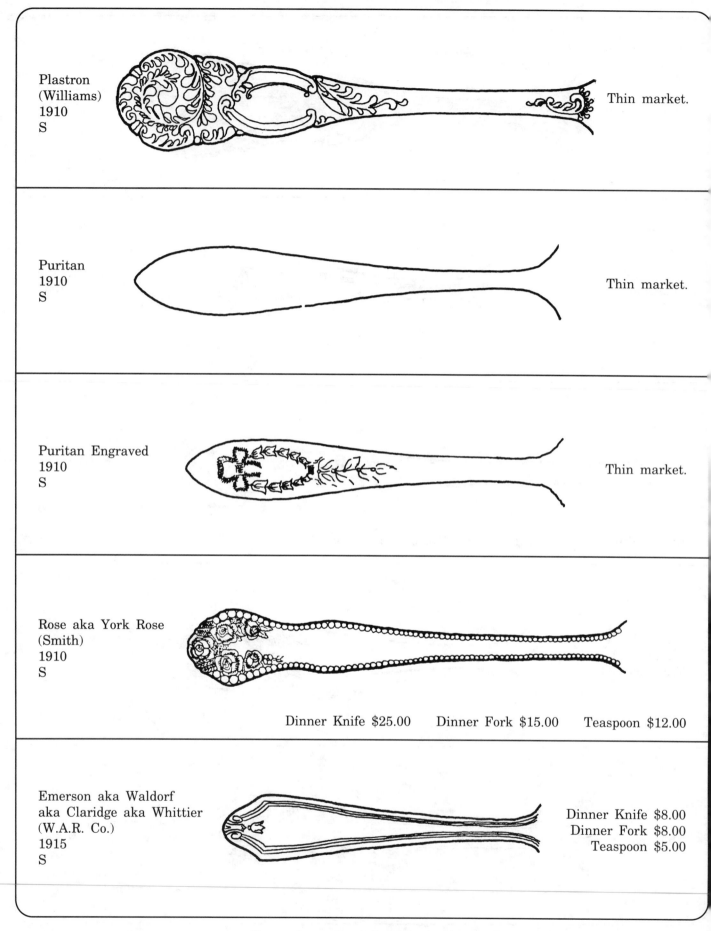

Plastron
(Williams)
1910
S

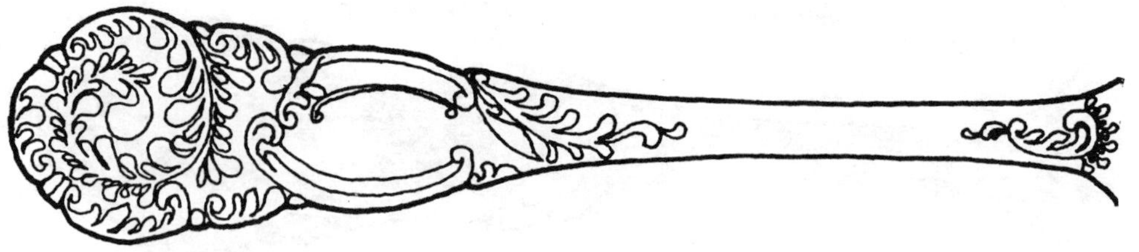

Thin market.

Puritan
1910
S

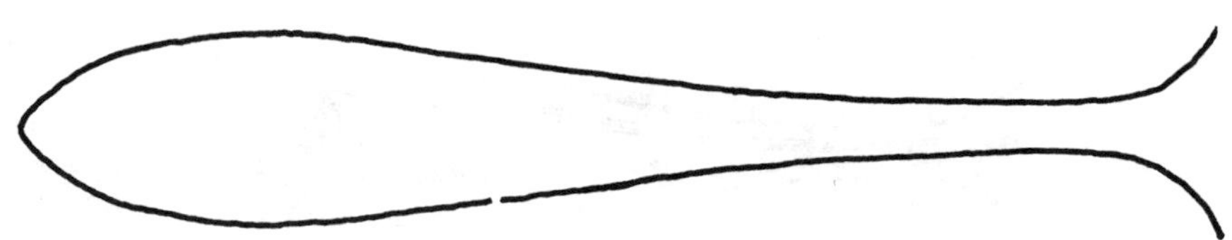

Thin market.

Puritan Engraved
1910
S

Thin market.

Rose aka York Rose
(Smith)
1910
S

Dinner Knife $25.00 Dinner Fork $15.00 Teaspoon $12.00

Emerson aka Waldorf
aka Claridge aka Whittier
(W.A.R. Co.)
1915
S

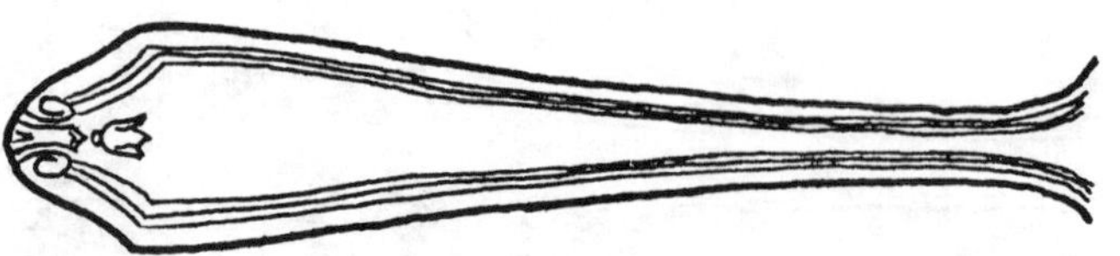

Dinner Knife $8.00
Dinner Fork $8.00
Teaspoon $5.00

Please refer to "How To Use This Book" page 4.

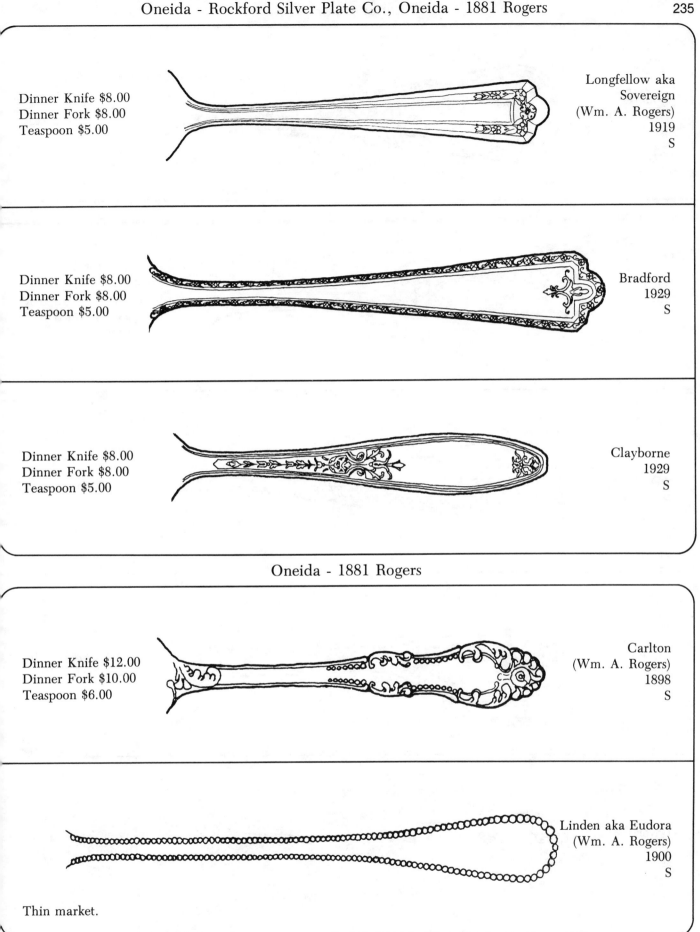

Dinner Knife $8.00
Dinner Fork $8.00
Teaspoon $5.00

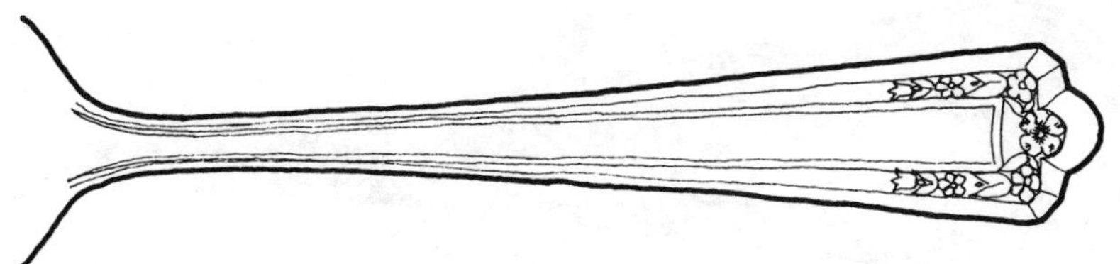

Longfellow aka Sovereign (Wm. A. Rogers) 1919 S

Dinner Knife $8.00
Dinner Fork $8.00
Teaspoon $5.00

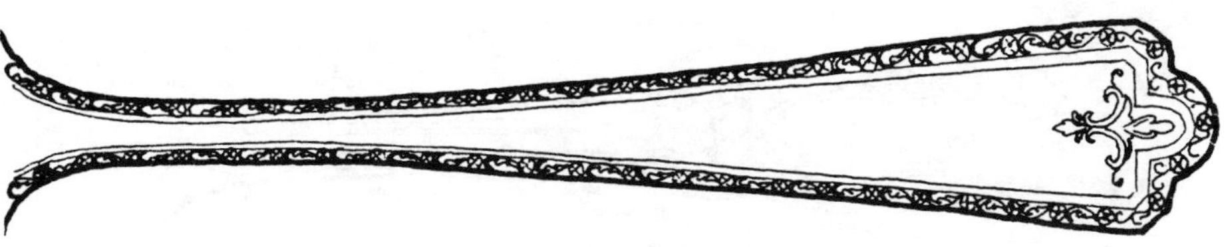

Bradford 1929 S

Dinner Knife $8.00
Dinner Fork $8.00
Teaspoon $5.00

Clayborne 1929 S

Oneida - 1881 Rogers

Dinner Knife $12.00
Dinner Fork $10.00
Teaspoon $6.00

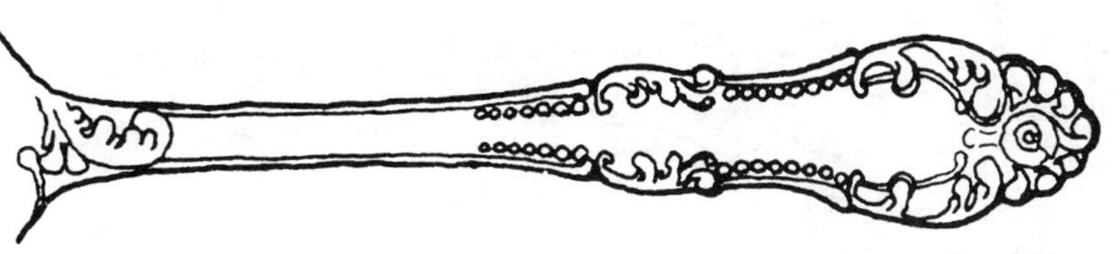

Carlton (Wm. A. Rogers) 1898 S

Linden aka Eudora (Wm. A. Rogers) 1900 S

Thin market.

Please refer to "How To Use This Book" page 4.

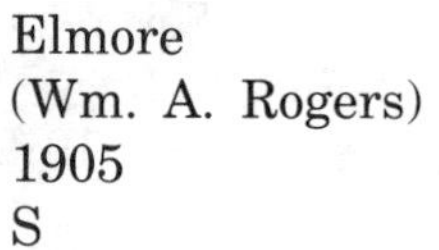

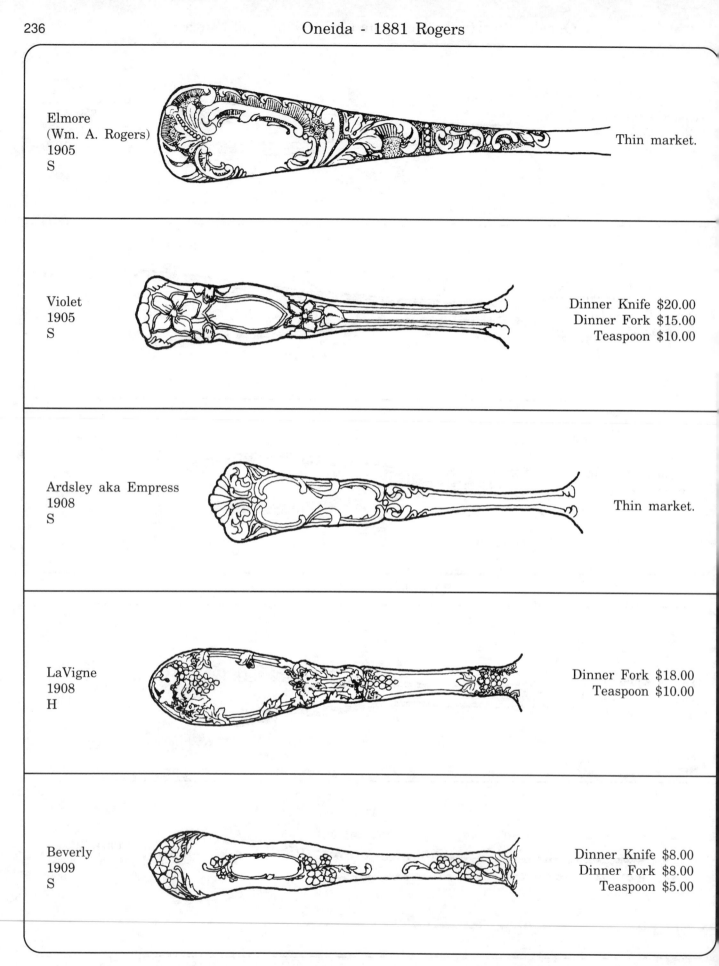

Elmore
(Wm. A. Rogers)
1905
S

Thin market.

Violet
1905
S

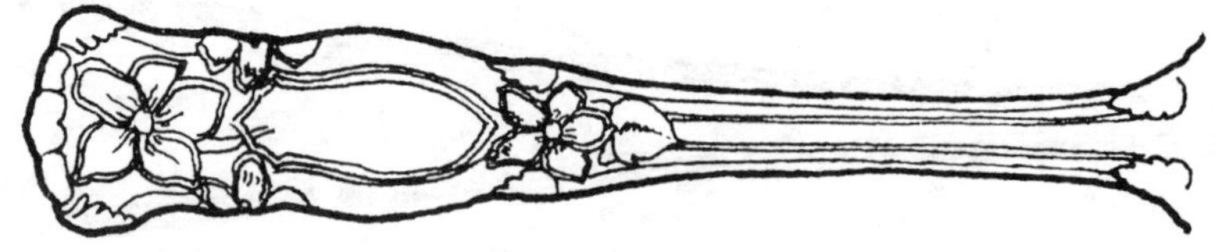

Dinner Knife $20.00
Dinner Fork $15.00
Teaspoon $10.00

Ardsley aka Empress
1908
S

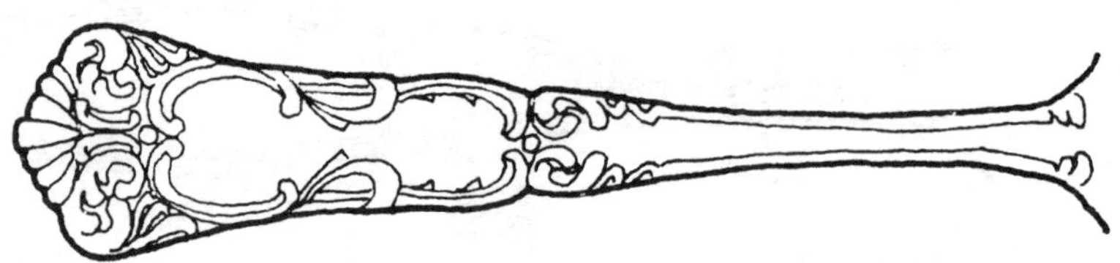

Thin market.

LaVigne
1908
H

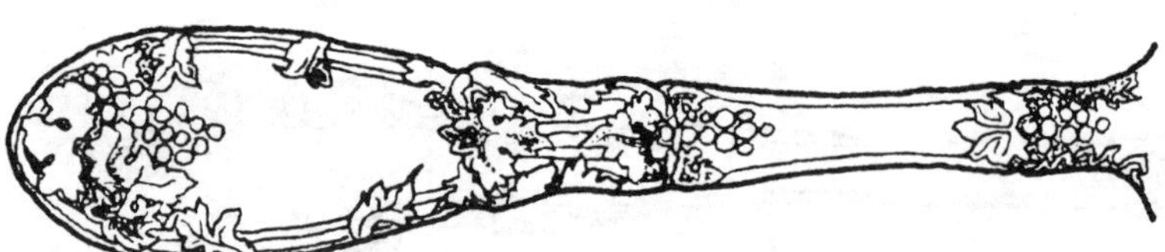

Dinner Fork $18.00
Teaspoon $10.00

Beverly
1909
S

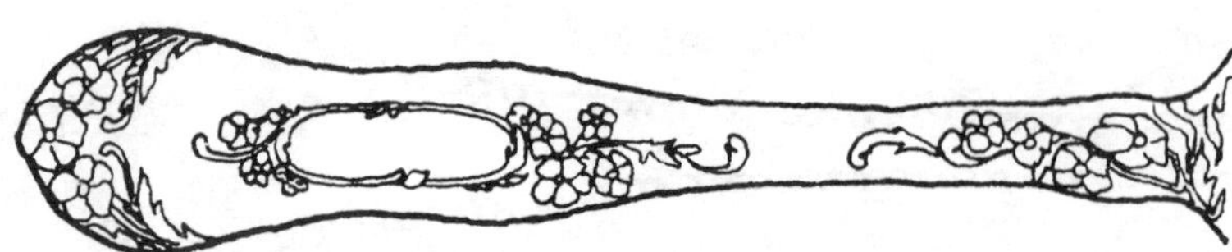

Dinner Knife $8.00
Dinner Fork $8.00
Teaspoon $5.00

Please refer to "How To Use This Book" page 4.

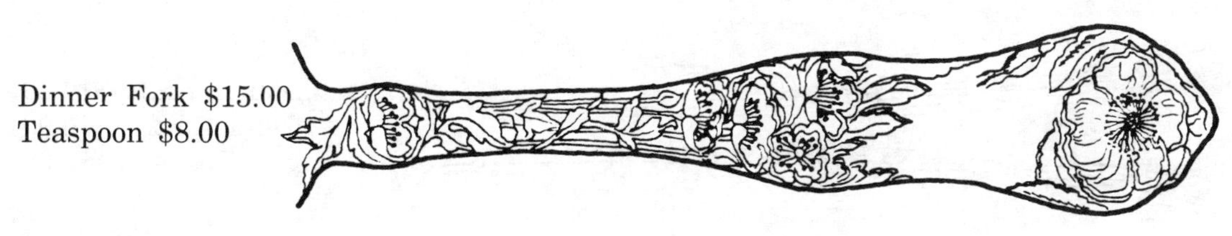

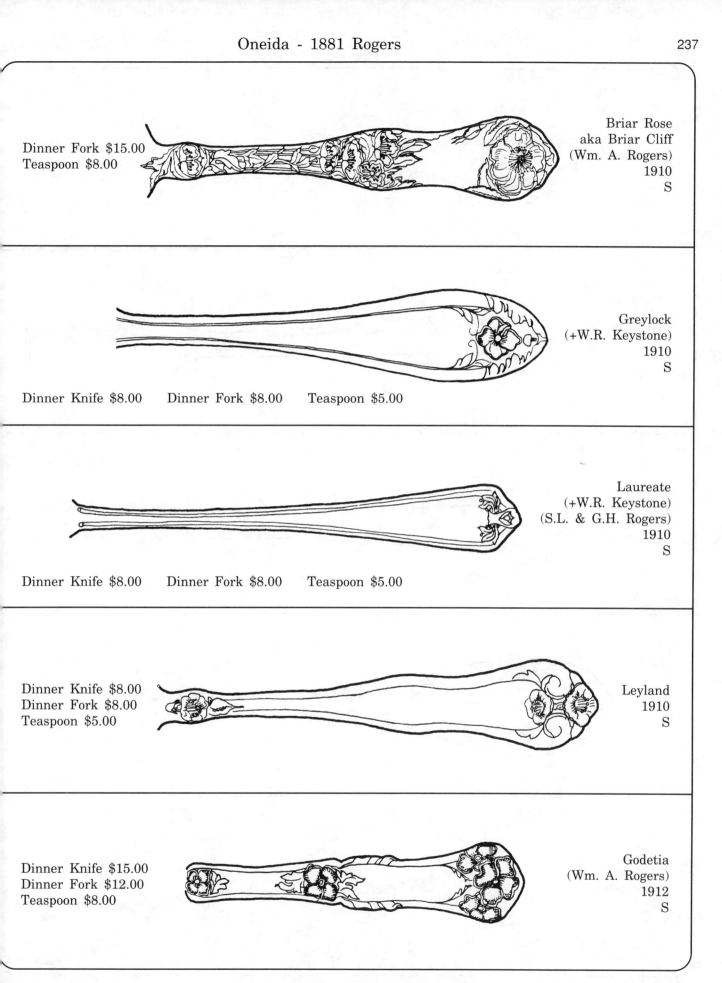

Dinner Fork $15.00
Teaspoon $8.00

Briar Rose
aka Briar Cliff
(Wm. A. Rogers)
1910
S

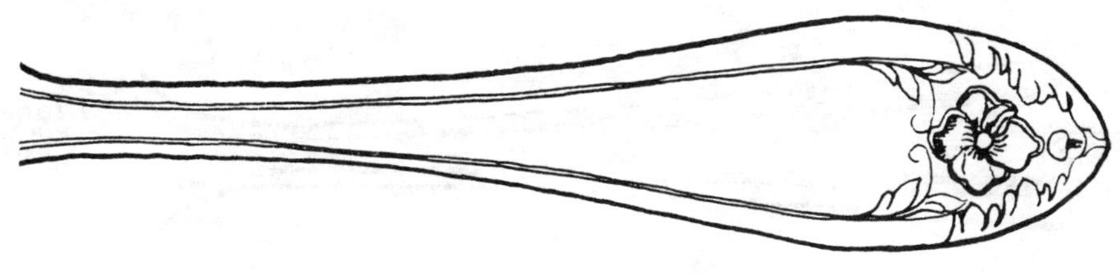

Greylock
(+W.R. Keystone)
1910
S

Dinner Knife $8.00 Dinner Fork $8.00 Teaspoon $5.00

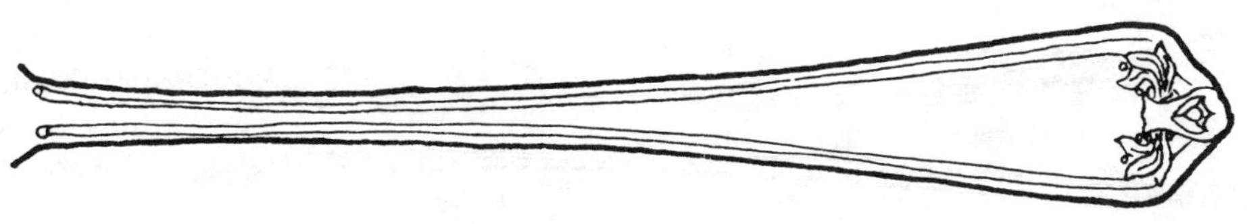

Laureate
(+W.R. Keystone)
(S.L. & G.H. Rogers)
1910
S

Dinner Knife $8.00 Dinner Fork $8.00 Teaspoon $5.00

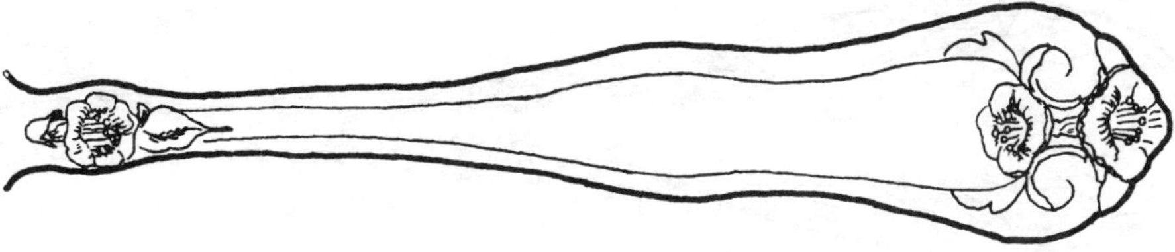

Dinner Knife $8.00
Dinner Fork $8.00
Teaspoon $5.00

Leyland
1910
S

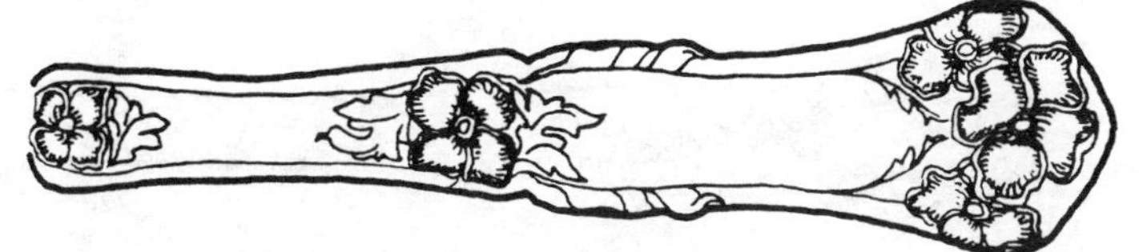

Dinner Knife $15.00
Dinner Fork $12.00
Teaspoon $8.00

Godetia
(Wm. A. Rogers)
1912
S

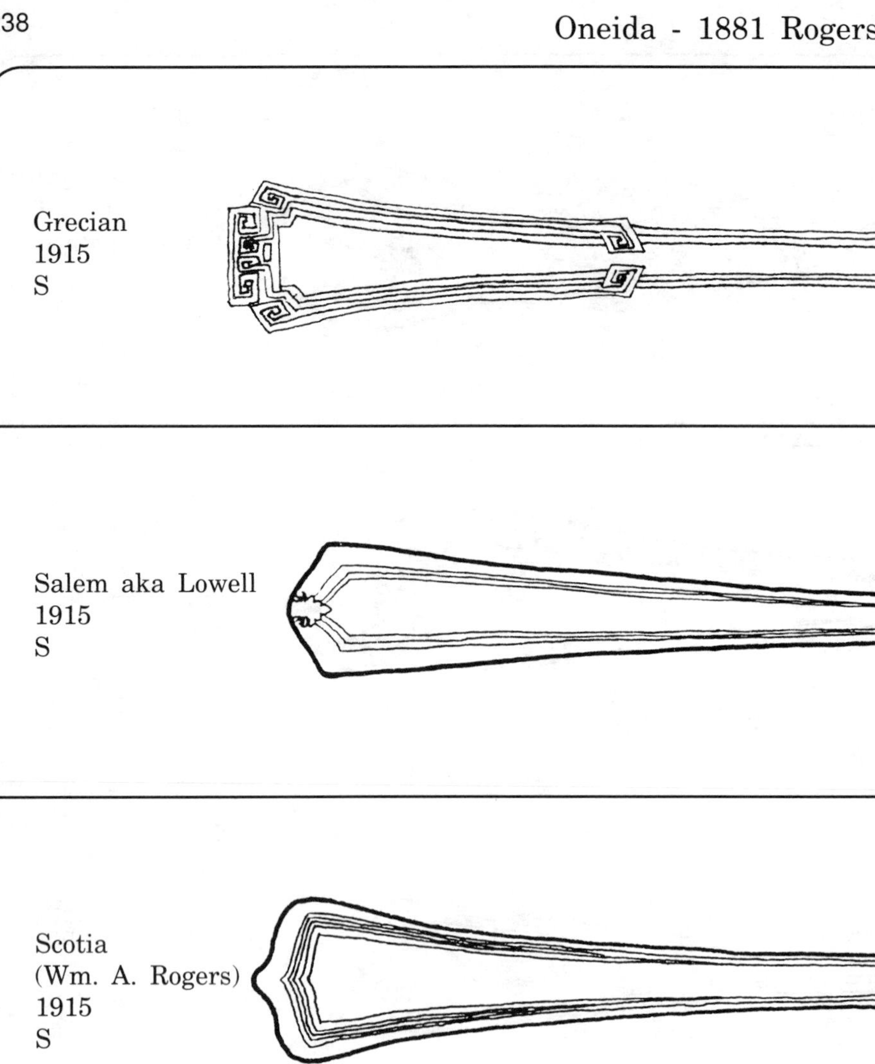

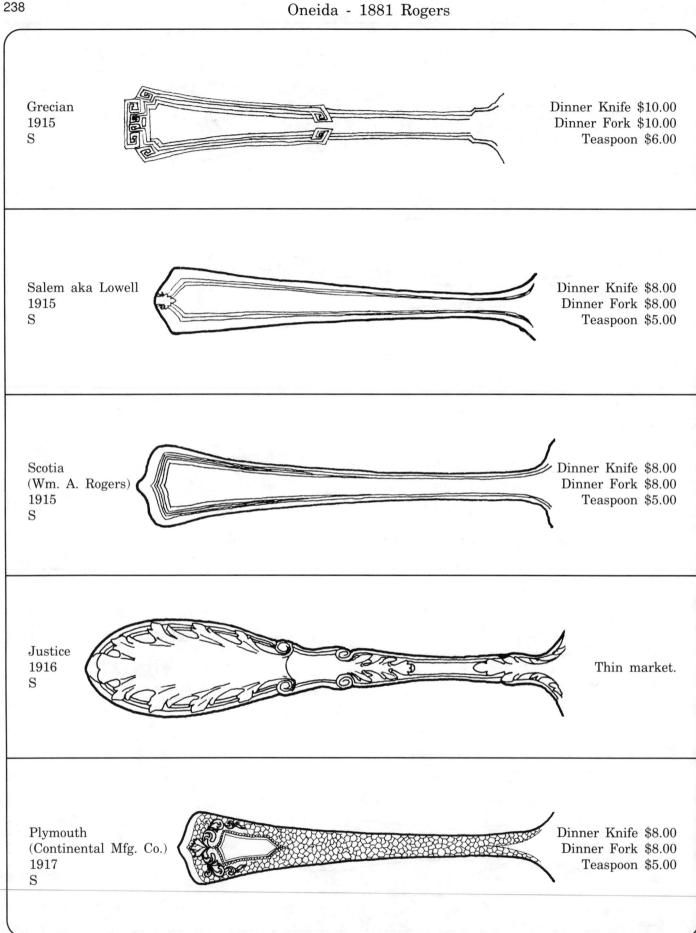

Grecian
1915
S

Dinner Knife $10.00
Dinner Fork $10.00
Teaspoon $6.00

Salem aka Lowell
1915
S

Dinner Knife $8.00
Dinner Fork $8.00
Teaspoon $5.00

Scotia
(Wm. A. Rogers)
1915
S

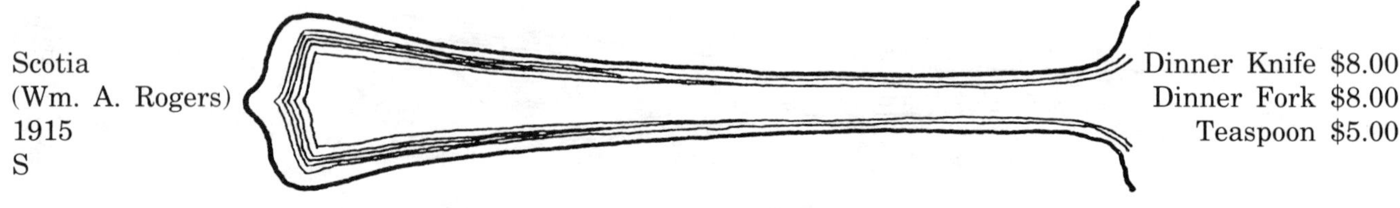

Dinner Knife $8.00
Dinner Fork $8.00
Teaspoon $5.00

Justice
1916
S

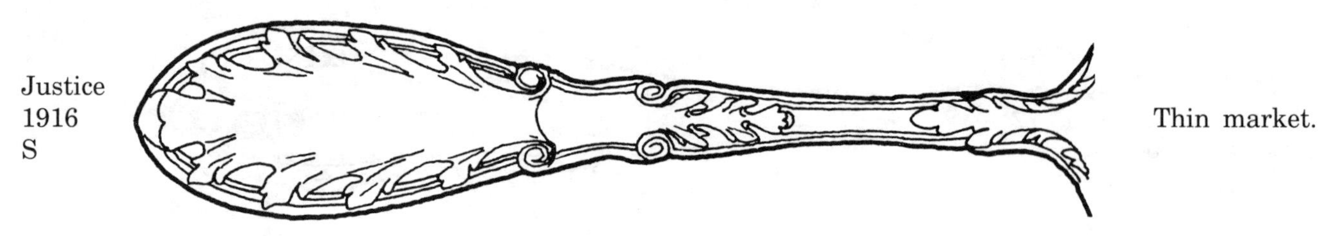

Thin market.

Plymouth
(Continental Mfg. Co.)
1917
S

Dinner Knife $8.00
Dinner Fork $8.00
Teaspoon $5.00

Please refer to "How To Use This Book" page 4.

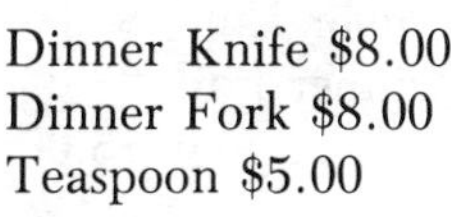

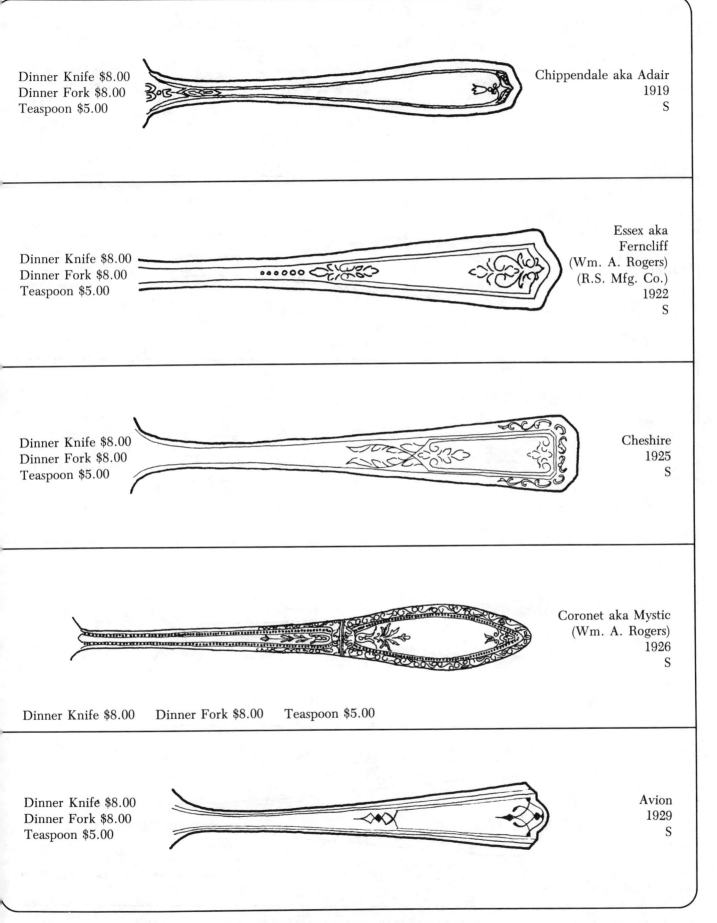

Dinner Knife $8.00
Dinner Fork $8.00
Teaspoon $5.00

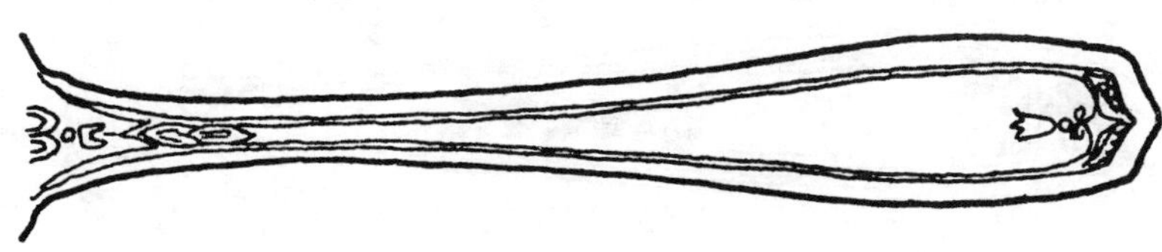

Chippendale aka Adair
1919
S

Dinner Knife $8.00
Dinner Fork $8.00
Teaspoon $5.00

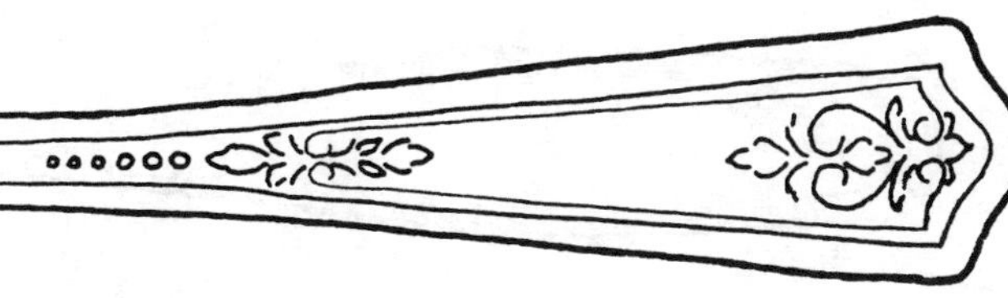

Essex aka
Ferncliff
(Wm. A. Rogers)
(R.S. Mfg. Co.)
1922
S

Dinner Knife $8.00
Dinner Fork $8.00
Teaspoon $5.00

Cheshire
1925
S

Coronet aka Mystic
(Wm. A. Rogers)
1926
S

Dinner Knife $8.00 Dinner Fork $8.00 Teaspoon $5.00

Dinner Knife $8.00
Dinner Fork $8.00
Teaspoon $5.00

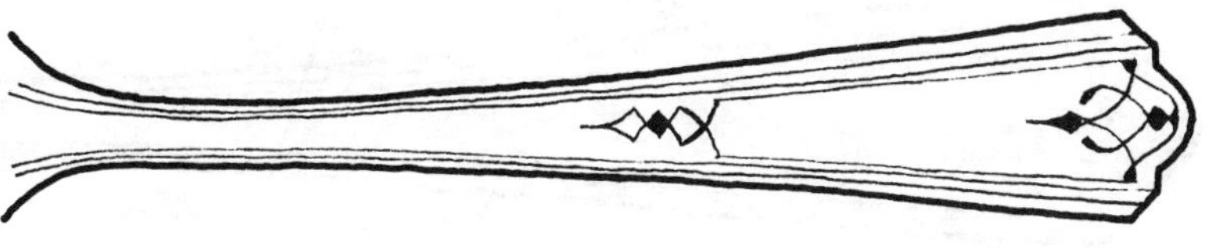

Avion
1929
S

Please refer to "How To Use This Book" page 4.

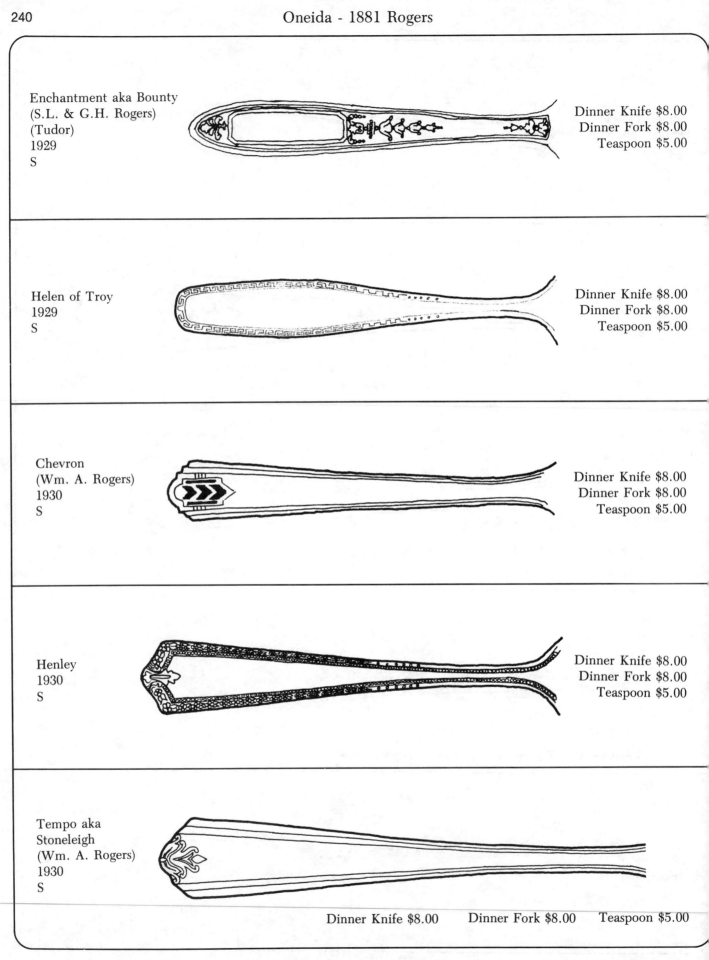

Enchantment aka Bounty
(S.L. & G.H. Rogers)
(Tudor)
1929
S

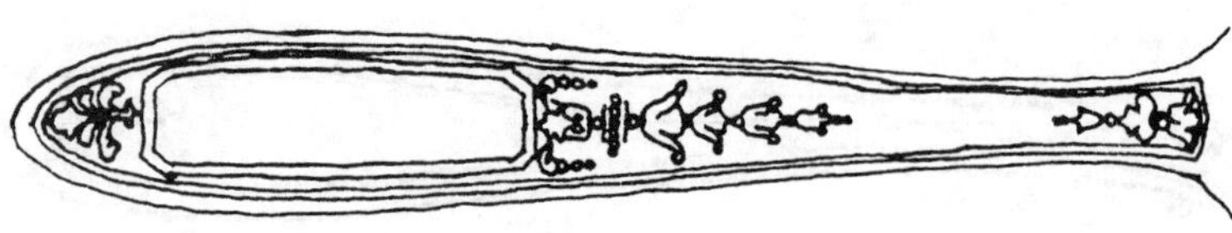

Dinner Knife $8.00
Dinner Fork $8.00
Teaspoon $5.00

Helen of Troy
1929
S

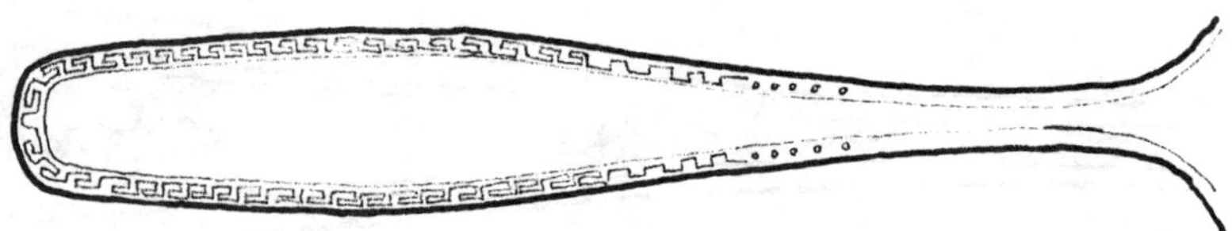

Dinner Knife $8.00
Dinner Fork $8.00
Teaspoon $5.00

Chevron
(Wm. A. Rogers)
1930
S

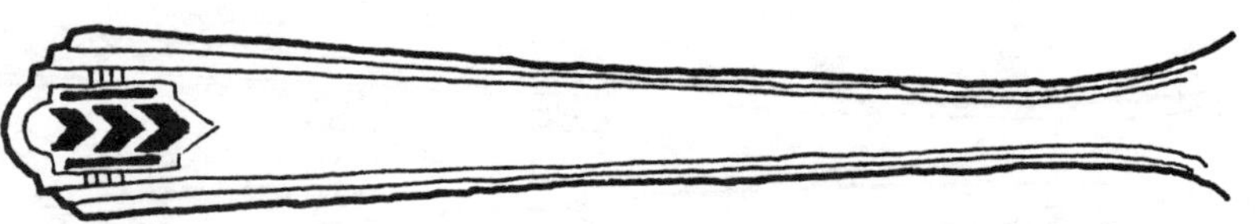

Dinner Knife $8.00
Dinner Fork $8.00
Teaspoon $5.00

Henley
1930
S

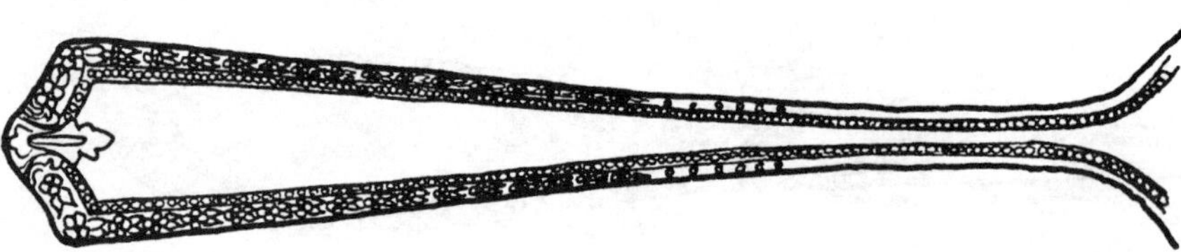

Dinner Knife $8.00
Dinner Fork $8.00
Teaspoon $5.00

Tempo aka
Stoneleigh
(Wm. A. Rogers)
1930
S

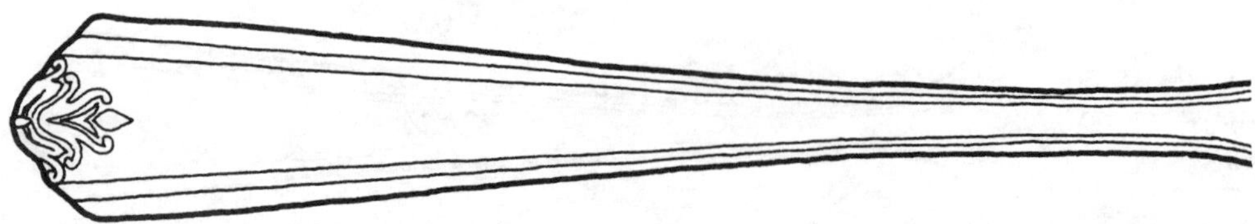

Dinner Knife $8.00 Dinner Fork $8.00 Teaspoon $5.00

Please refer to "How To Use This Book" page 4.

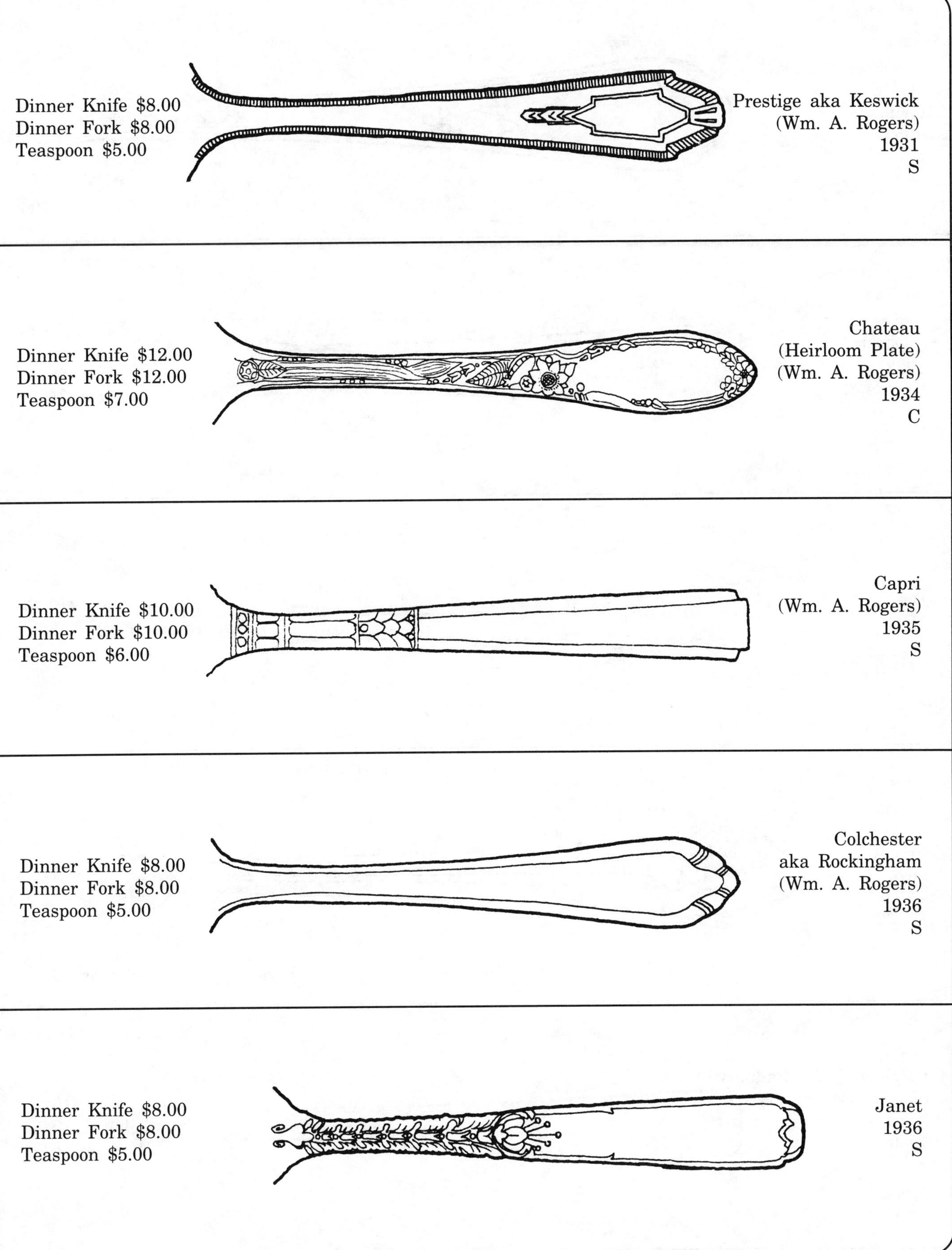

Dinner Knife $8.00
Dinner Fork $8.00
Teaspoon $5.00

Prestige aka Keswick
(Wm. A. Rogers)
1931
S

Dinner Knife $12.00
Dinner Fork $12.00
Teaspoon $7.00

Chateau
(Heirloom Plate)
(Wm. A. Rogers)
1934
C

Dinner Knife $10.00
Dinner Fork $10.00
Teaspoon $6.00

Capri
(Wm. A. Rogers)
1935
S

Dinner Knife $8.00
Dinner Fork $8.00
Teaspoon $5.00

Colchester
aka Rockingham
(Wm. A. Rogers)
1936
S

Dinner Knife $8.00
Dinner Fork $8.00
Teaspoon $5.00

Janet
1936
S

Please refer to “How To Use This Book” page 4.

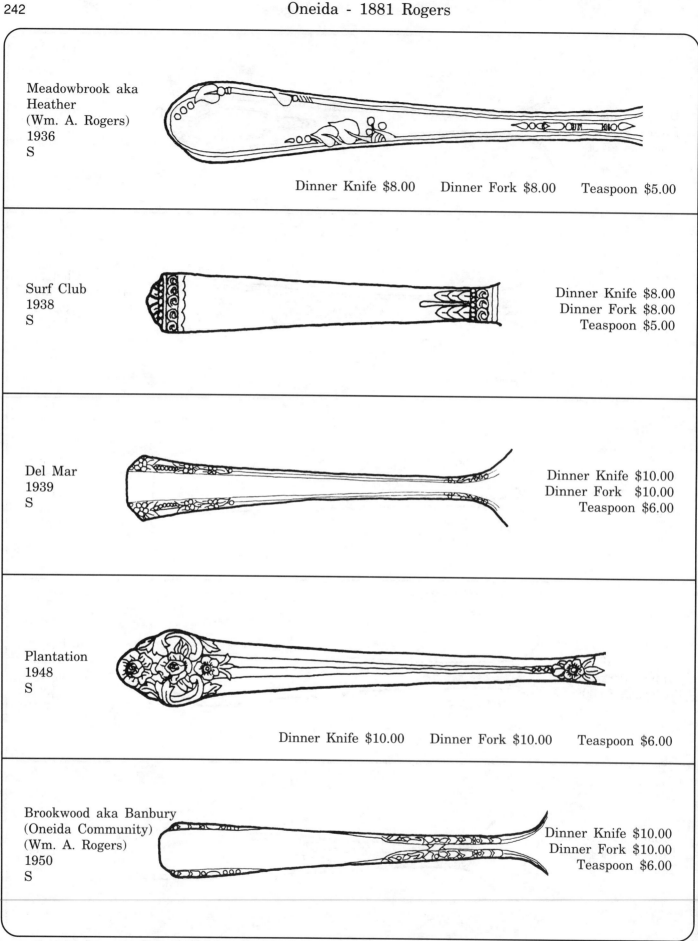

Meadowbrook aka
Heather
(Wm. A. Rogers)
1936
S

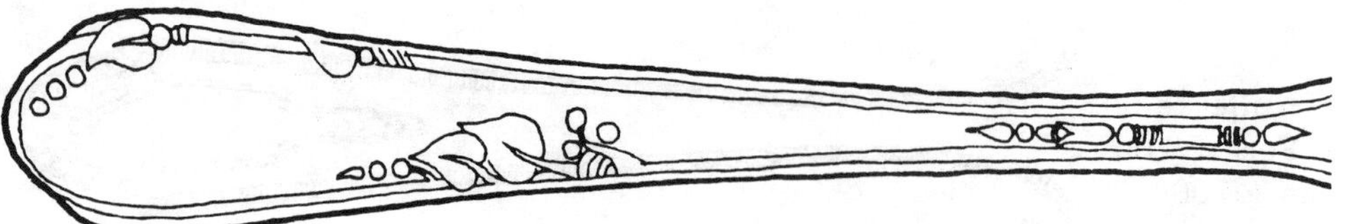

Dinner Knife $8.00 Dinner Fork $8.00 Teaspoon $5.00

Surf Club
1938
S

Dinner Knife $8.00
Dinner Fork $8.00
Teaspoon $5.00

Del Mar
1939
S

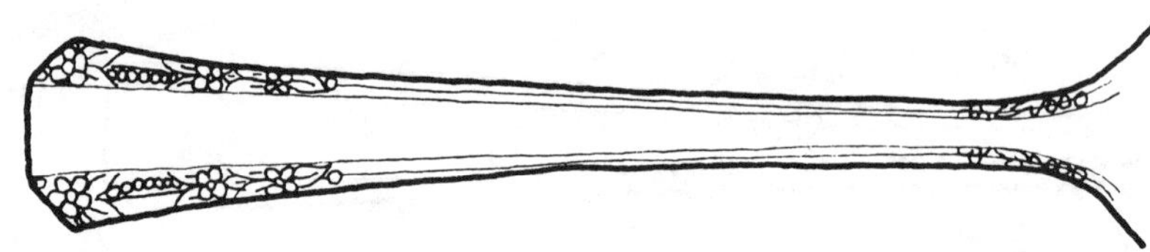

Dinner Knife $10.00
Dinner Fork $10.00
Teaspoon $6.00

Plantation
1948
S

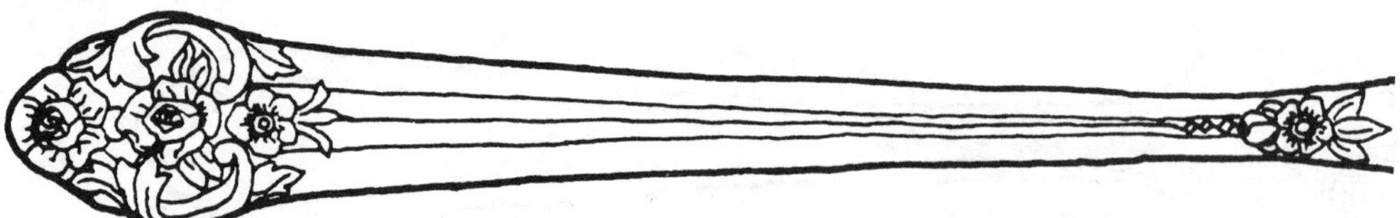

Dinner Knife $10.00 Dinner Fork $10.00 Teaspoon $6.00

Brookwood aka Banbury
(Oneida Community)
(Wm. A. Rogers)
1950
S

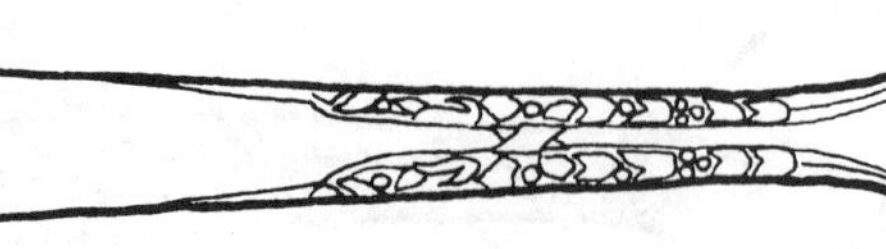

Dinner Knife $10.00
Dinner Fork $10.00
Teaspoon $6.00

Please refer to "How To Use This Book" page 4.

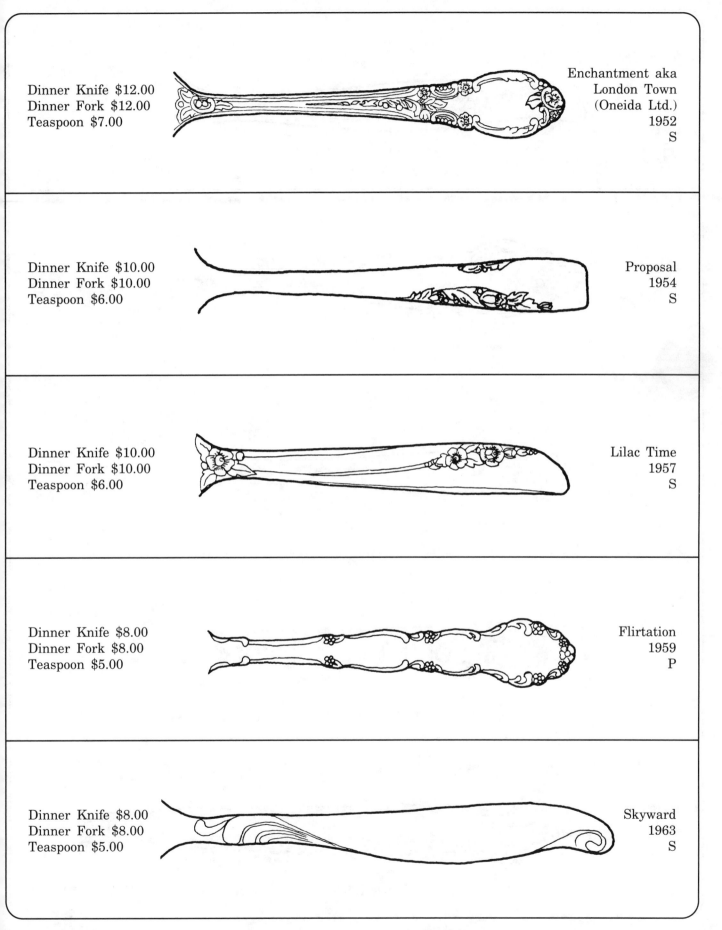

Dinner Knife $12.00
Dinner Fork $12.00
Teaspoon $7.00

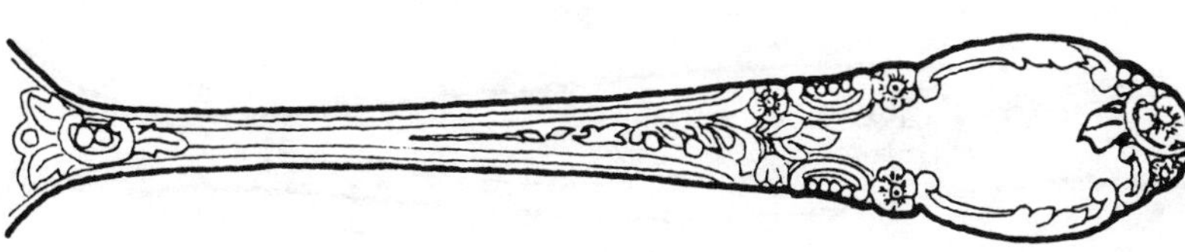

Enchantment aka London Town (Oneida Ltd.)
1952
S

Dinner Knife $10.00
Dinner Fork $10.00
Teaspoon $6.00

Proposal
1954
S

Dinner Knife $10.00
Dinner Fork $10.00
Teaspoon $6.00

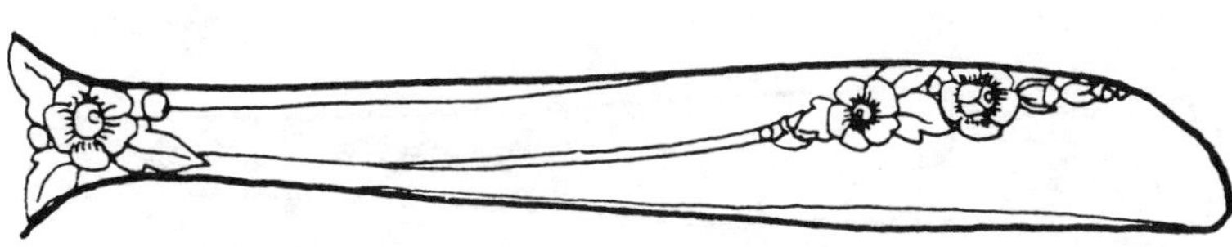

Lilac Time
1957
S

Dinner Knife $8.00
Dinner Fork $8.00
Teaspoon $5.00

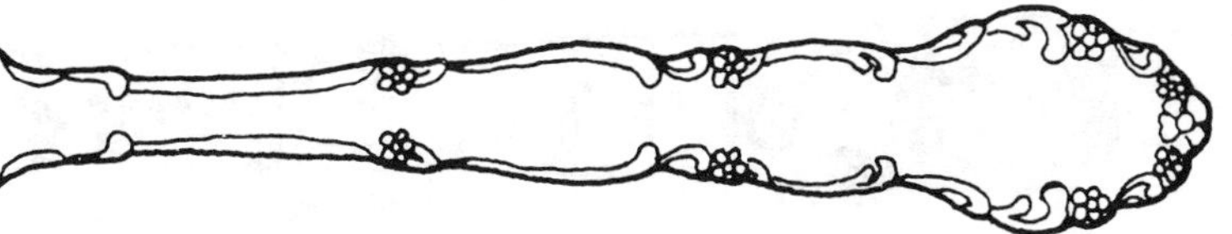

Flirtation
1959
P

Dinner Knife $8.00
Dinner Fork $8.00
Teaspoon $5.00

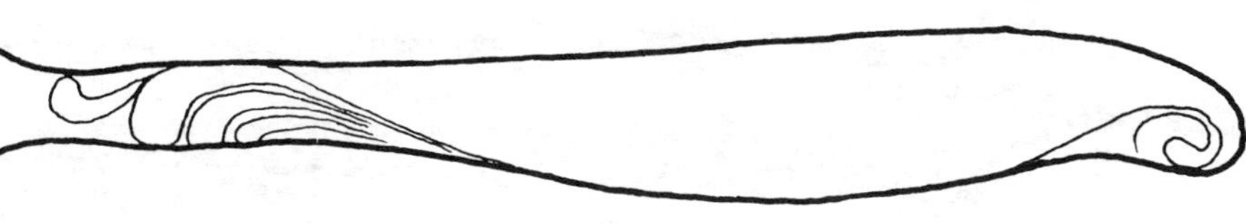

Skyward
1963
S

Please refer to "How To Use This Book" page 4.

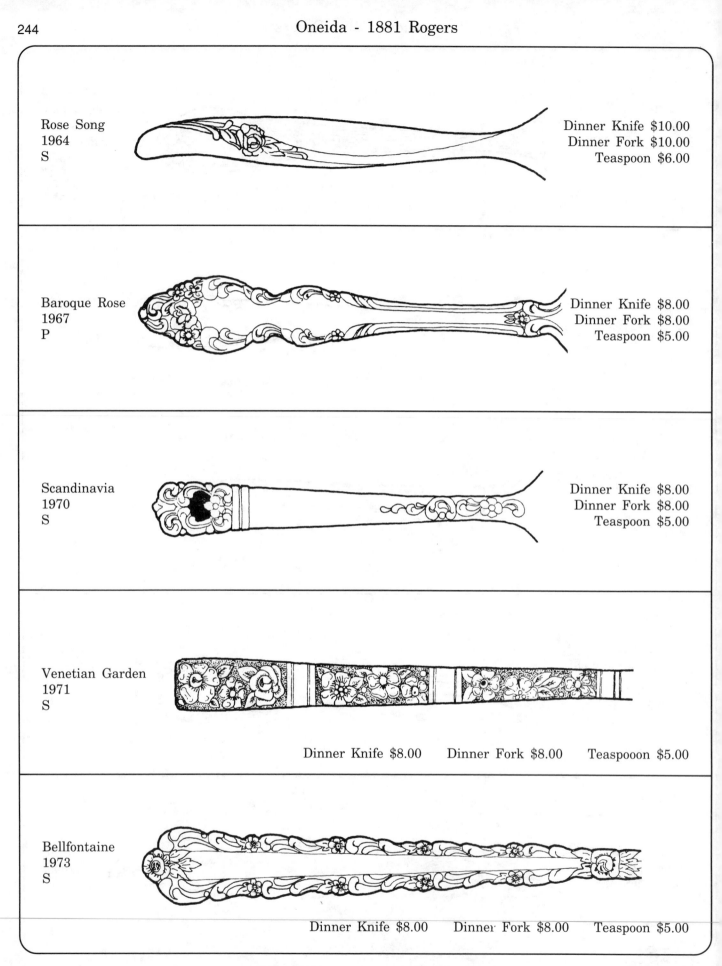

Rose Song
1964
S

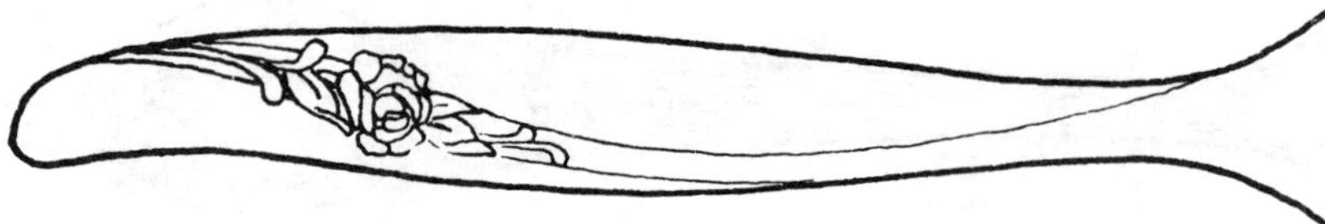

Dinner Knife $10.00
Dinner Fork $10.00
Teaspoon $6.00

Baroque Rose
1967
P

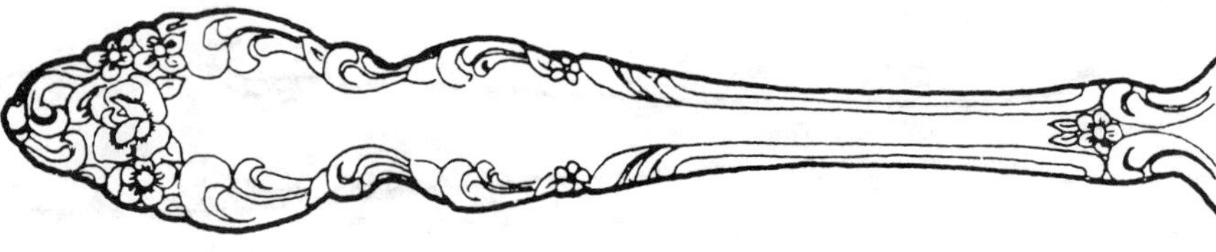

Dinner Knife $8.00
Dinner Fork $8.00
Teaspoon $5.00

Scandinavia
1970
S

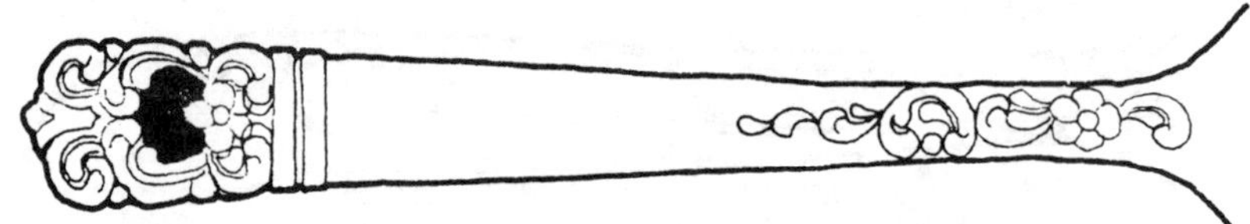

Dinner Knife $8.00
Dinner Fork $8.00
Teaspoon $5.00

Venetian Garden
1971
S

Dinner Knife $8.00 Dinner Fork $8.00 Teaspooon $5.00

Bellfontaine
1973
S

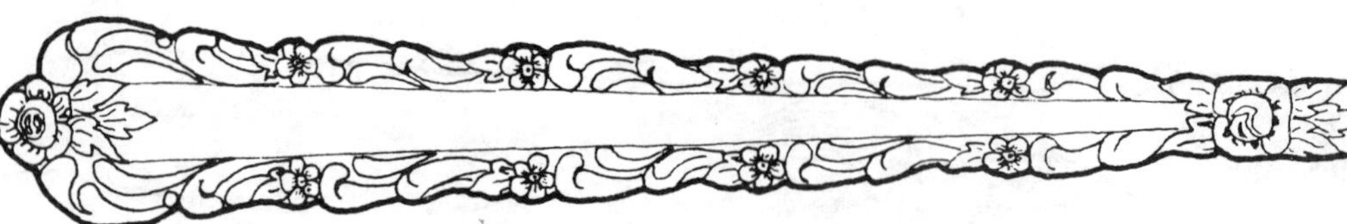

Dinner Knife $8.00 Dinner Fork $8.00 Teaspoon $5.00

Please refer to "How To Use This Book" page 4.

Dinner Knife $8.00
Dinner Fork $8.00
Teaspoon $5.00

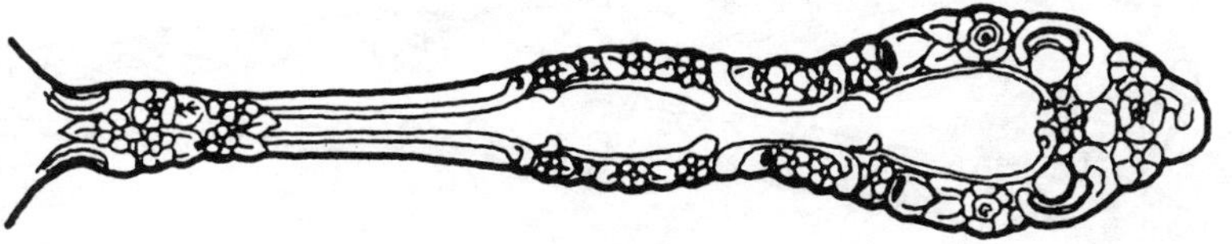

Victorian Classic
1973
S

Dinner Knife $8.00
Dinner Fork $8.00
Teaspoon $5.00

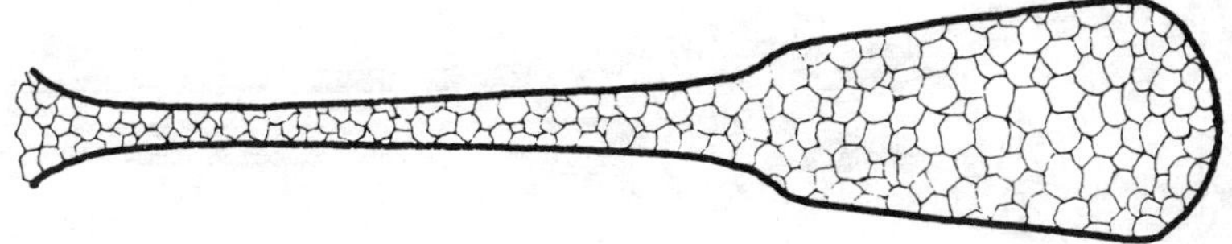

First Colony
1975
S

Dinner Knife $8.00
Dinner Fork $8.00
Teaspoon $5.00

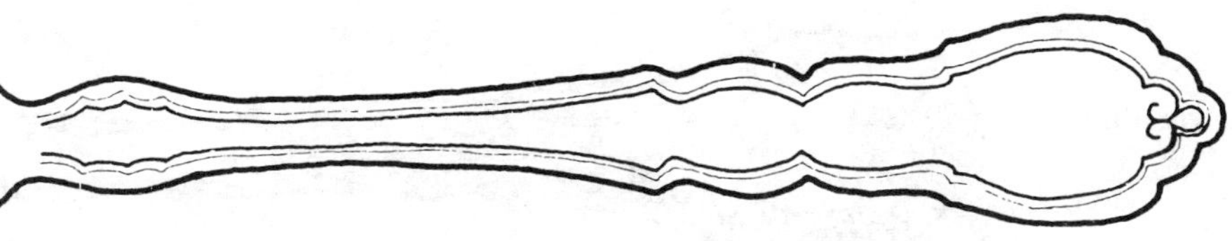

Alouette
1978
S

Please see King James on page 347.

Oneida - S.L. & G.H. Rogers

Thin market.

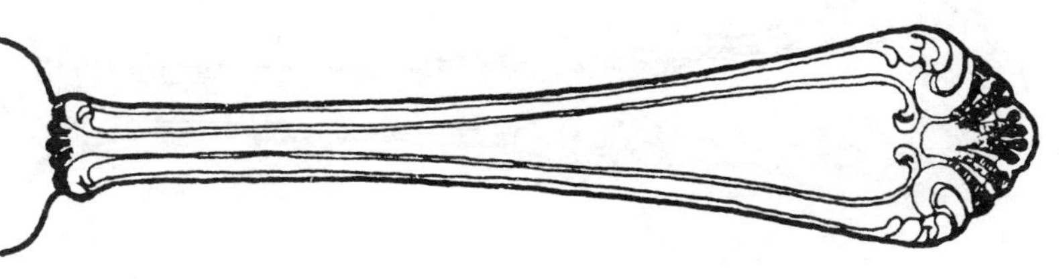

Puritan aka State
(Rockford Silver Plate)
(Aurora)
1900
S

Thin market.

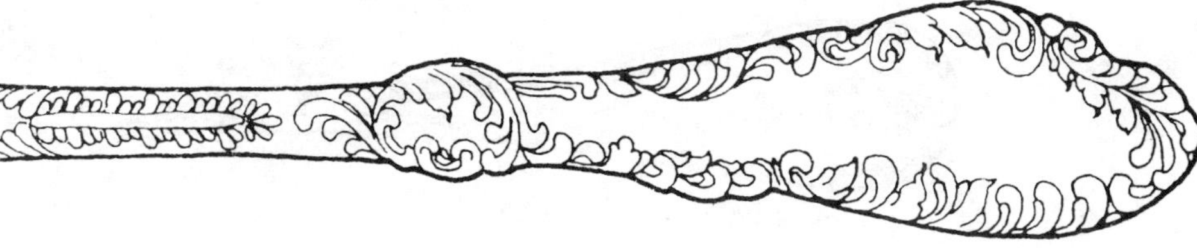

Vernon aka
Antwerp
(Rockford)
1900

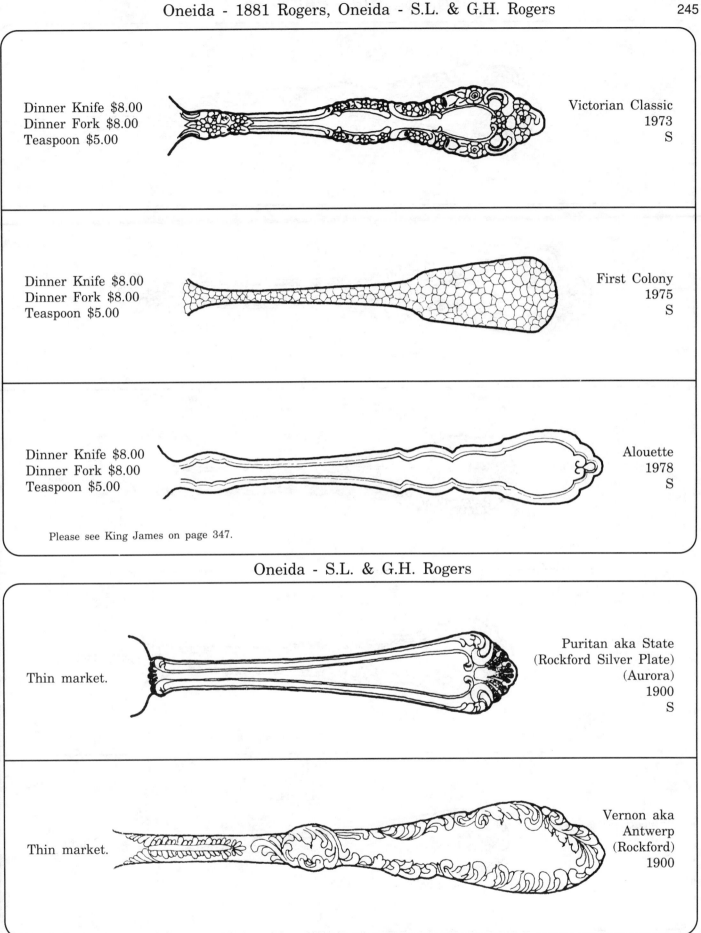

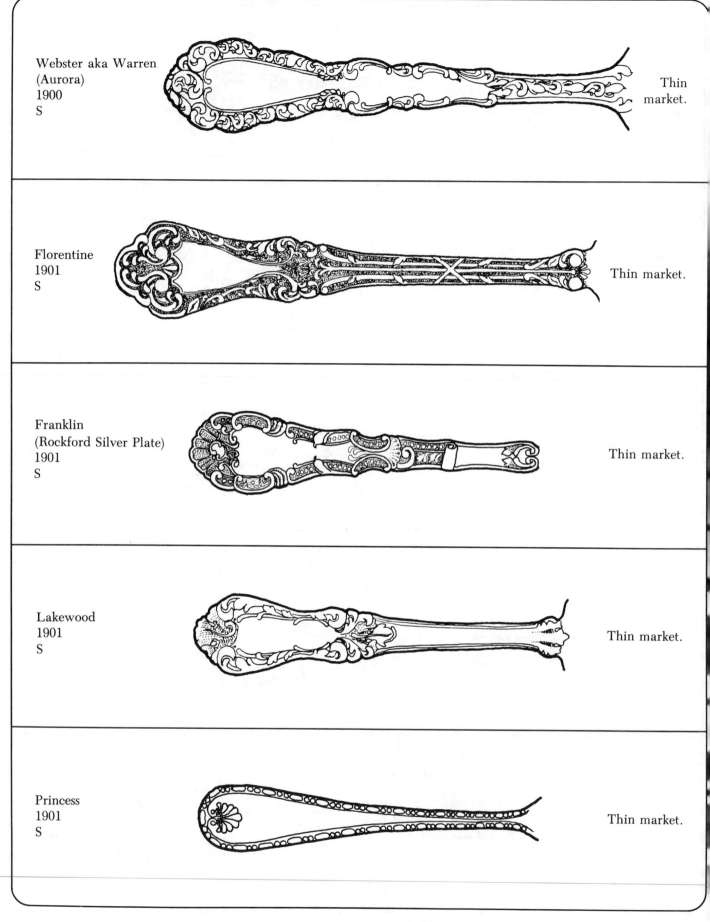

Webster aka Warren
(Aurora)
1900
S

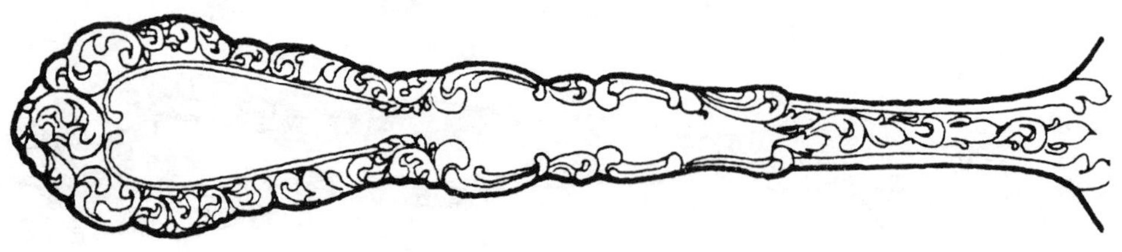

Thin market.

Florentine
1901
S

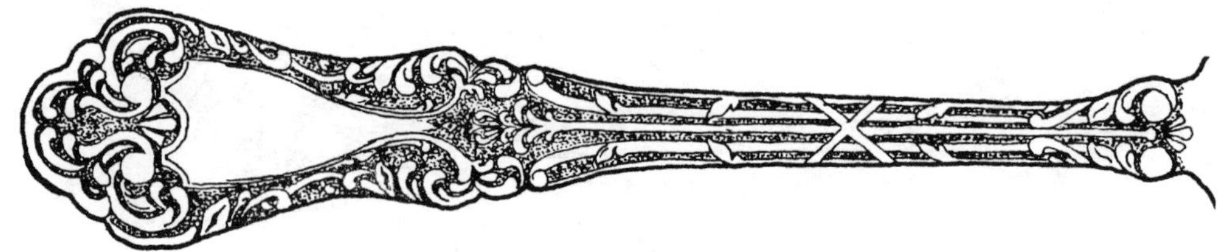

Thin market.

Franklin
(Rockford Silver Plate)
1901
S

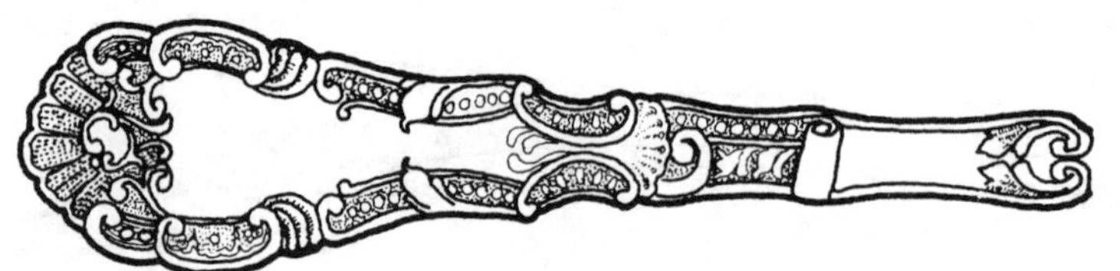

Thin market.

Lakewood
1901
S

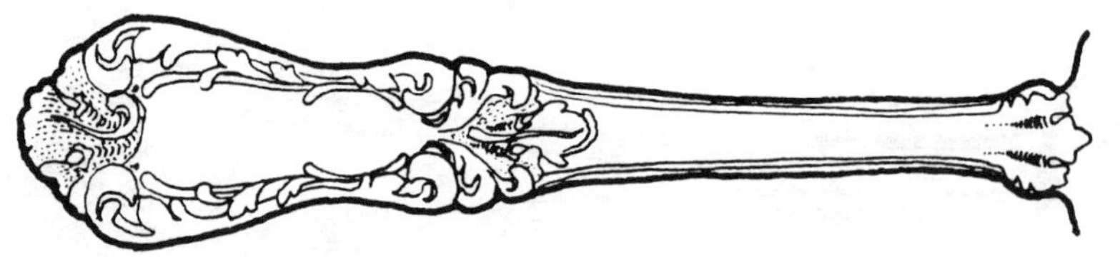

Thin market.

Princess
1901
S

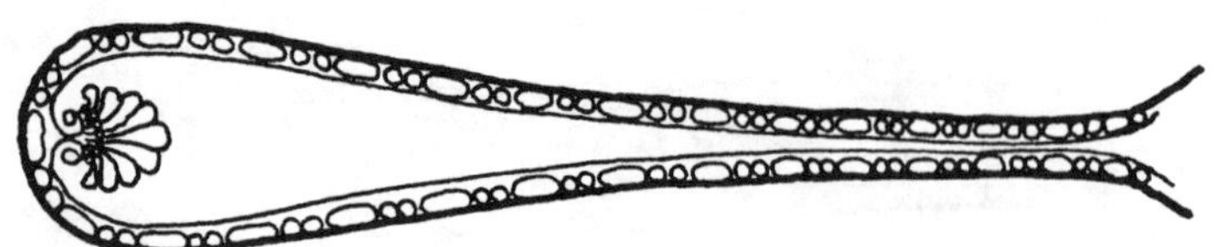

Thin market.

Please refer to "How To Use This Book" page 4.

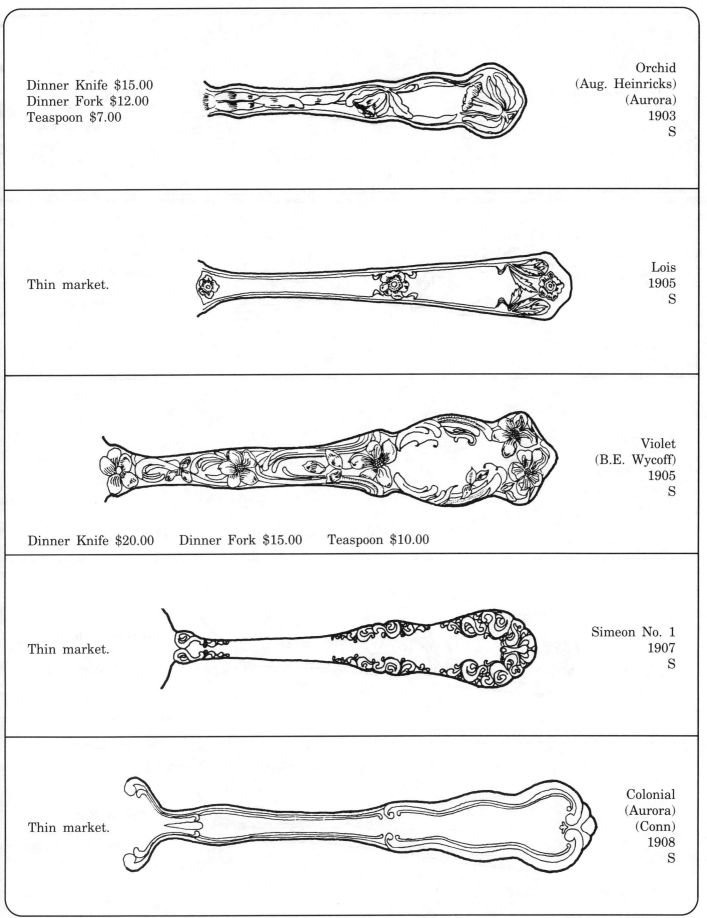

Dinner Knife $15.00
Dinner Fork $12.00
Teaspoon $7.00

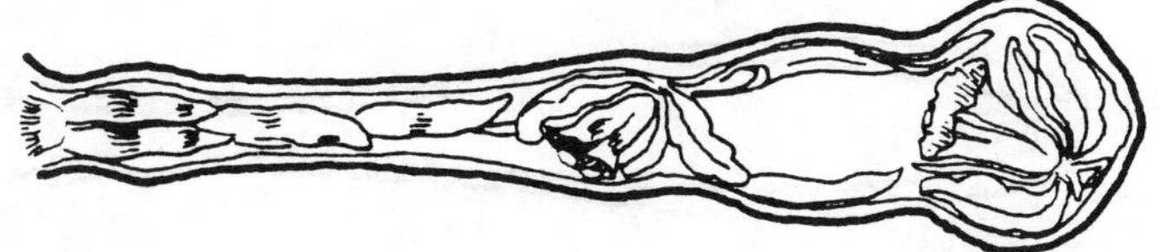

Orchid
(Aug. Heinricks)
(Aurora)
1903
S

Thin market.

Lois
1905
S

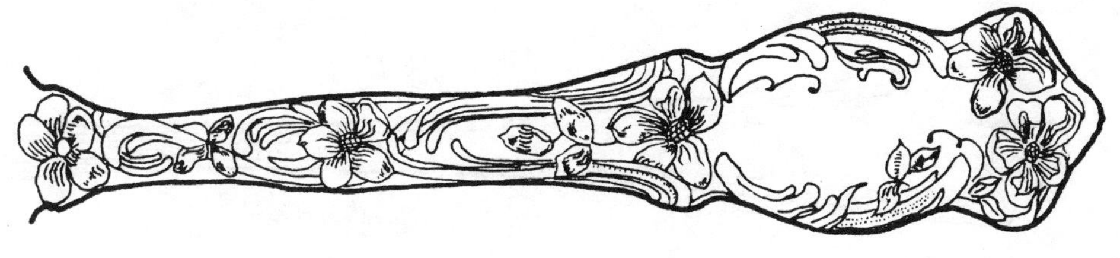

Violet
(B.E. Wycoff)
1905
S

Dinner Knife $20.00 Dinner Fork $15.00 Teaspoon $10.00

Thin market.

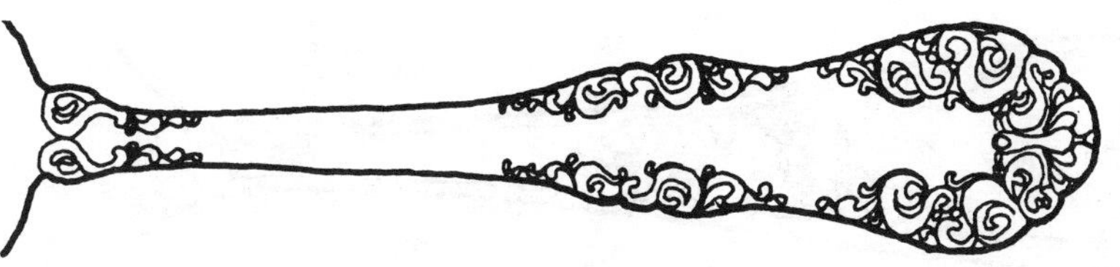

Simeon No. 1
1907
S

Thin market.

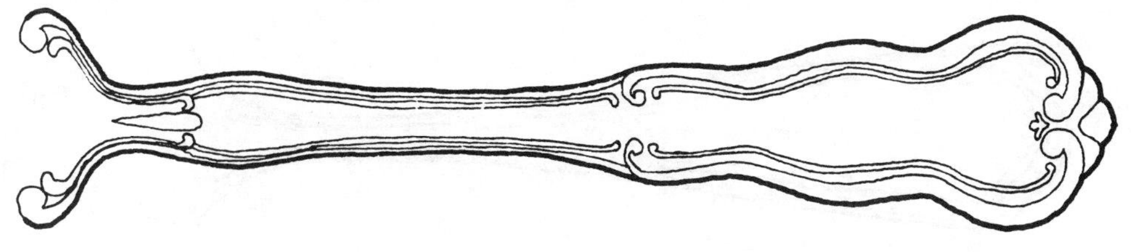

Colonial
(Aurora)
(Conn)
1908
S

Please refer to "How To Use This Book" page 4.

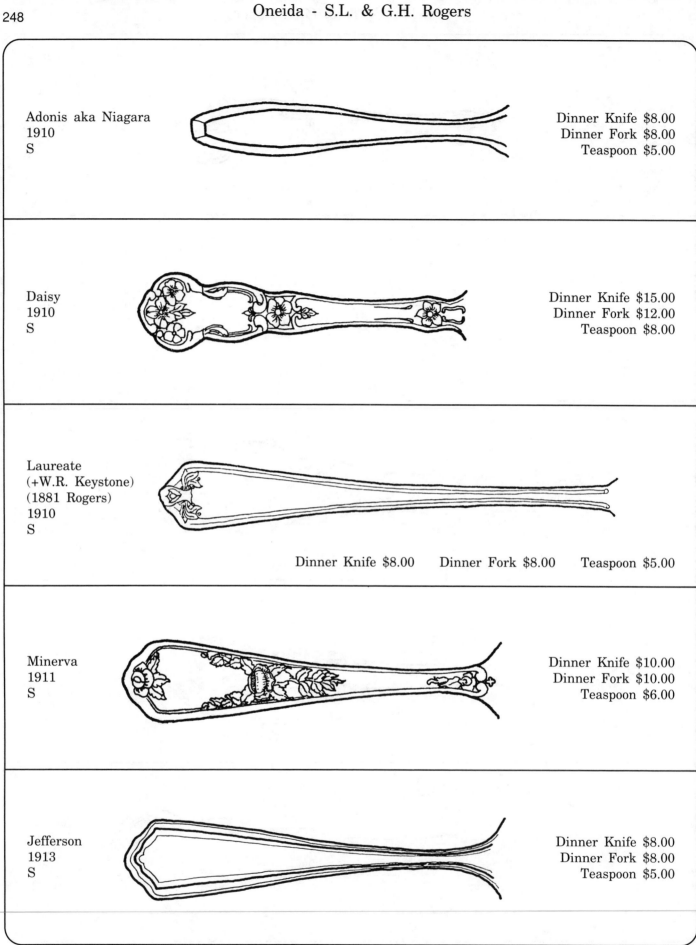

Adonis aka Niagara
1910
S

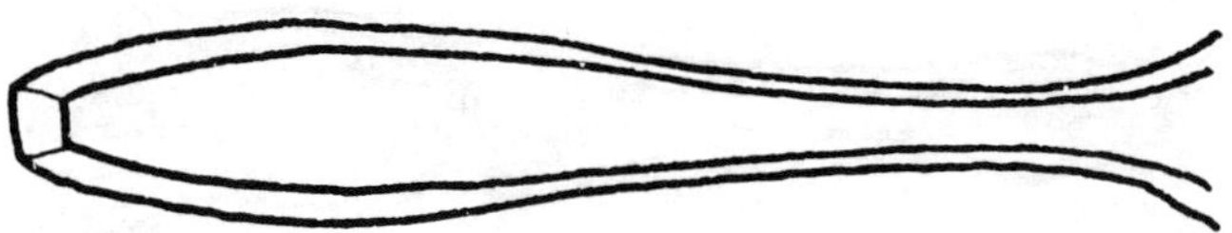

Dinner Knife $8.00
Dinner Fork $8.00
Teaspoon $5.00

Daisy
1910
S

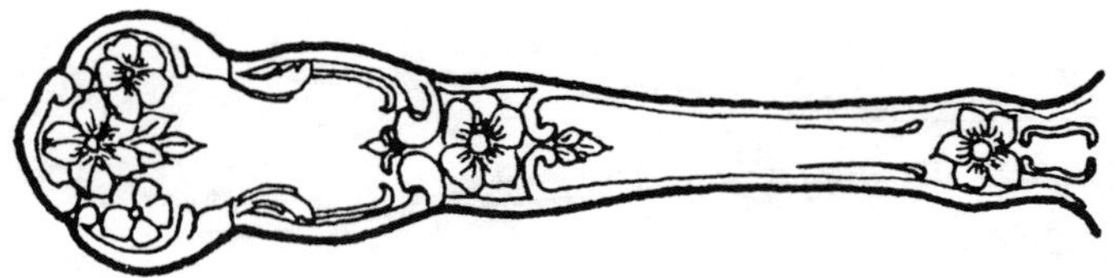

Dinner Knife $15.00
Dinner Fork $12.00
Teaspoon $8.00

Laureate
(+W.R. Keystone)
(1881 Rogers)
1910
S

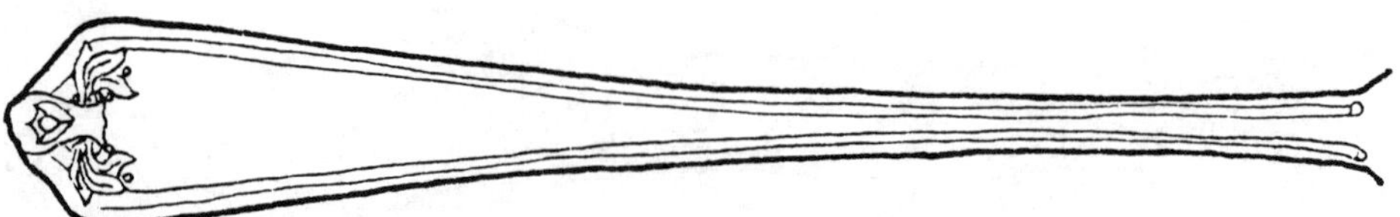

Dinner Knife $8.00 Dinner Fork $8.00 Teaspoon $5.00

Minerva
1911
S

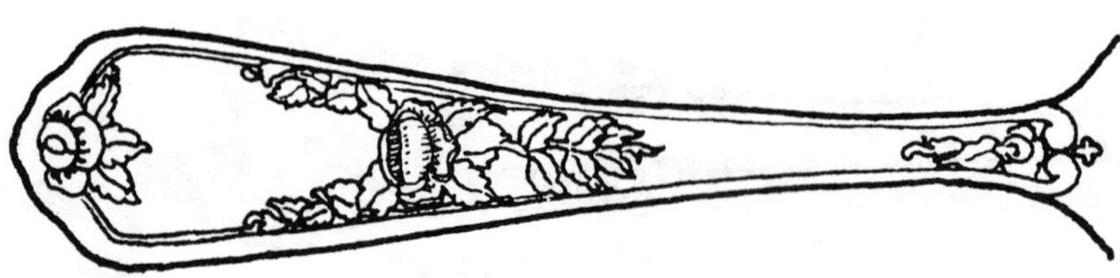

Dinner Knife $10.00
Dinner Fork $10.00
Teaspoon $6.00

Jefferson
1913
S

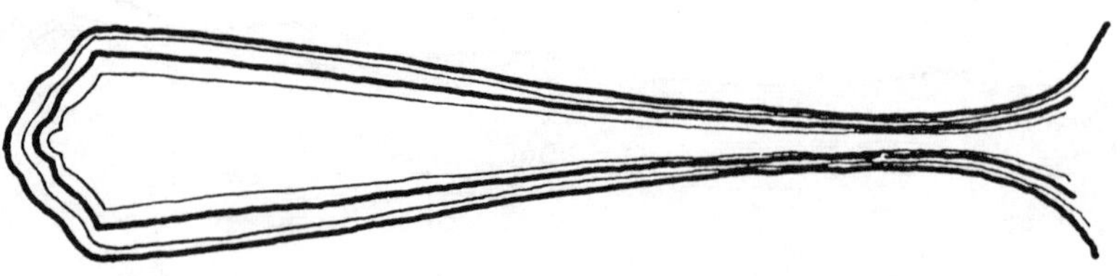

Dinner Knife $8.00
Dinner Fork $8.00
Teaspoon $5.00

Please refer to "How To Use This Book" page 4.

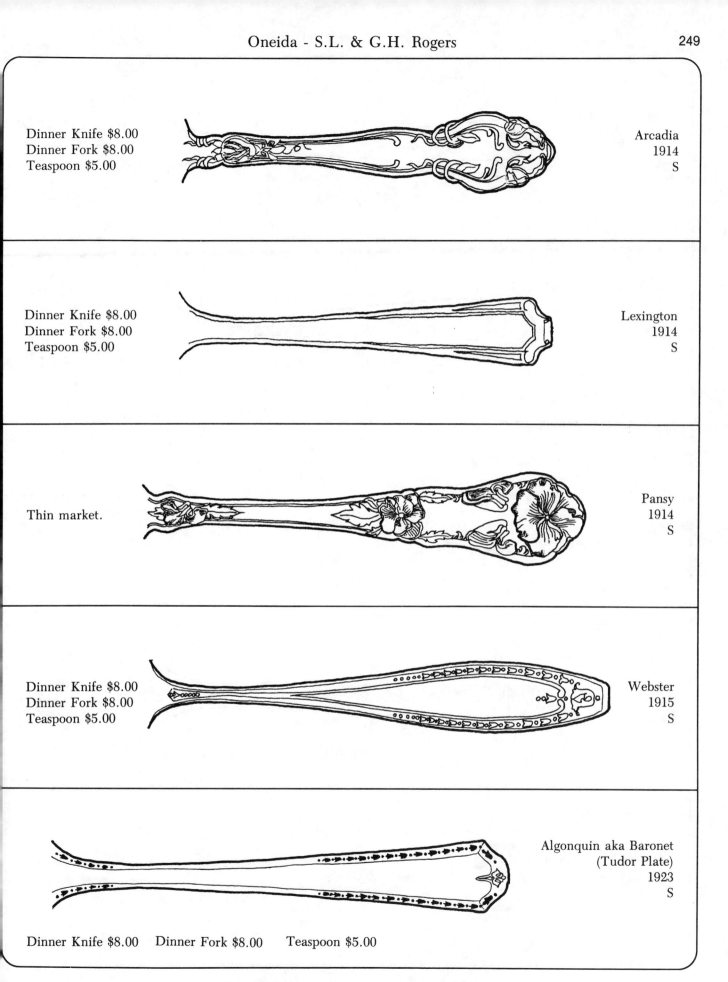

Dinner Knife $8.00
Dinner Fork $8.00
Teaspoon $5.00

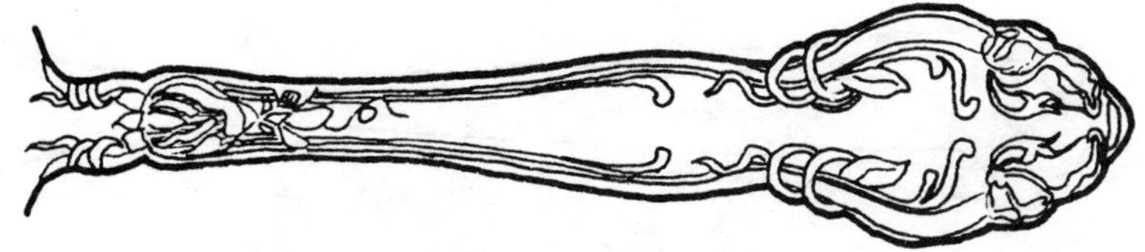

Arcadia
1914
S

Dinner Knife $8.00
Dinner Fork $8.00
Teaspoon $5.00

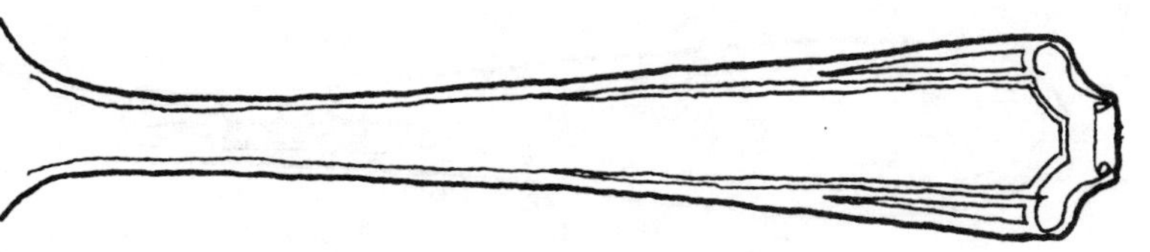

Lexington
1914
S

Thin market.

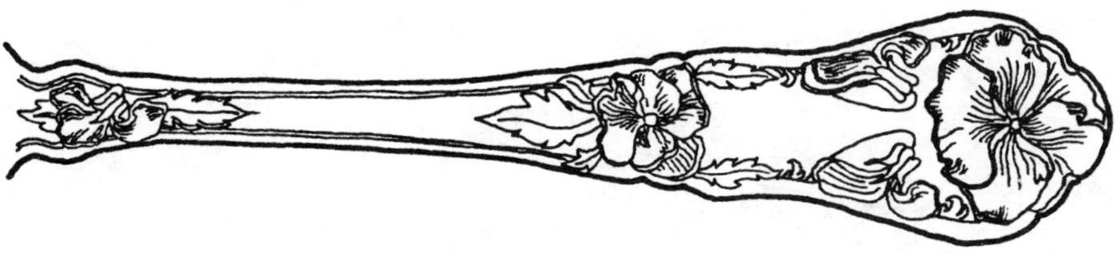

Pansy
1914
S

Dinner Knife $8.00
Dinner Fork $8.00
Teaspoon $5.00

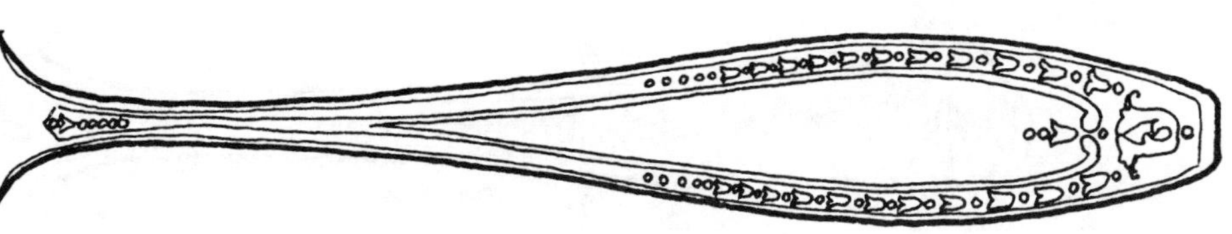

Webster
1915
S

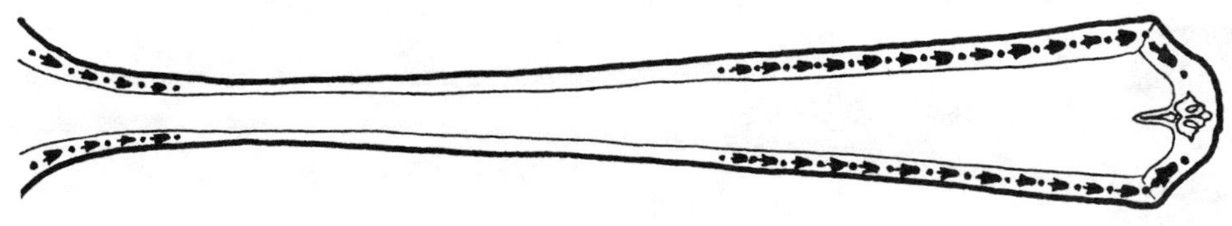

Algonquin aka Baronet
(Tudor Plate)
1923
S

Dinner Knife $8.00 Dinner Fork $8.00 Teaspoon $5.00

Please refer to "How To Use This Book" page 4.

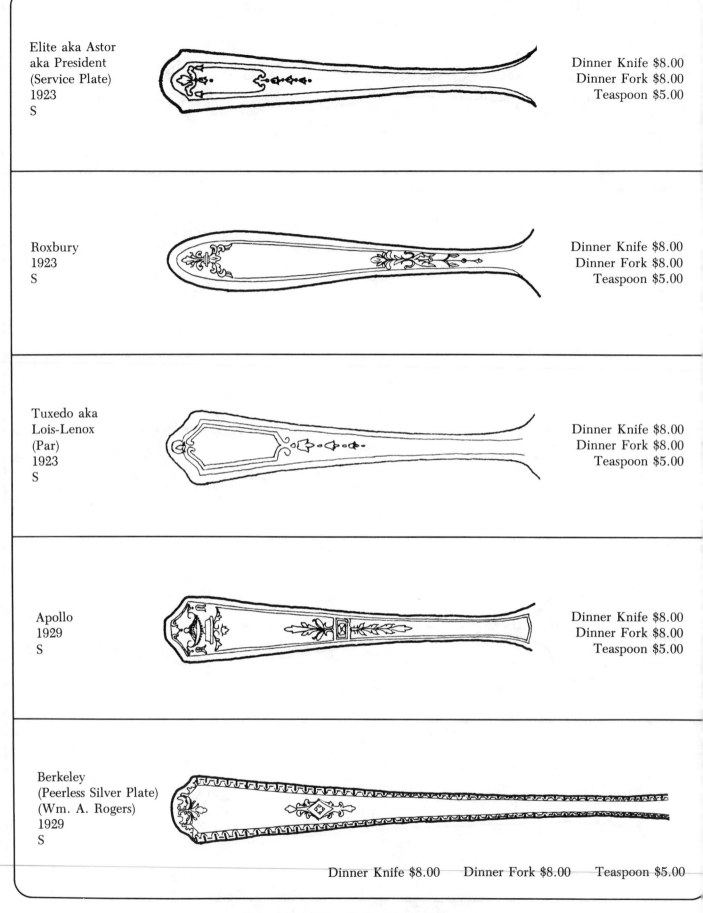

Elite aka Astor
aka President
(Service Plate)
1923
S

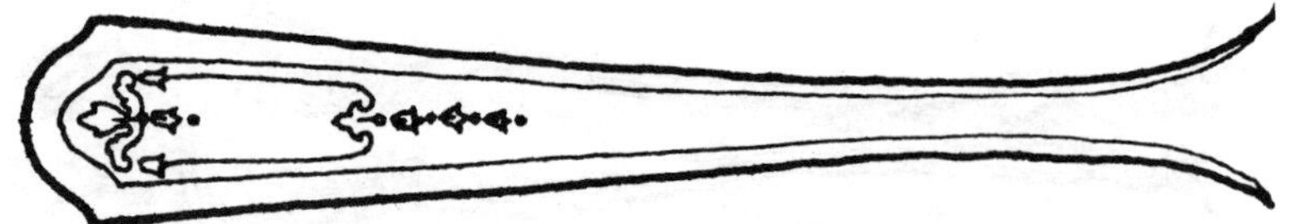

Dinner Knife $8.00
Dinner Fork $8.00
Teaspoon $5.00

Roxbury
1923
S

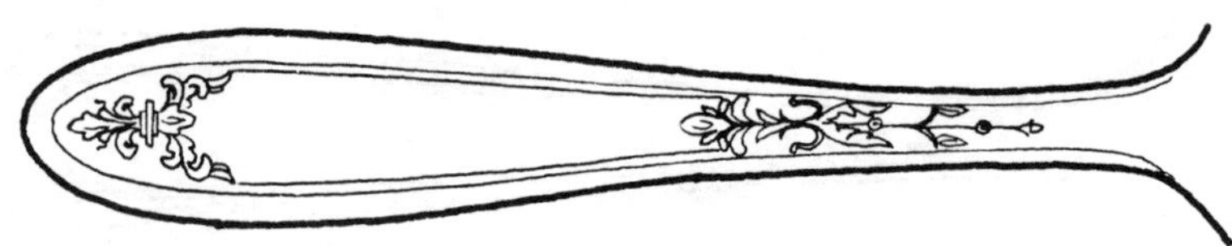

Dinner Knife $8.00
Dinner Fork $8.00
Teaspoon $5.00

Tuxedo aka
Lois-Lenox
(Par)
1923
S

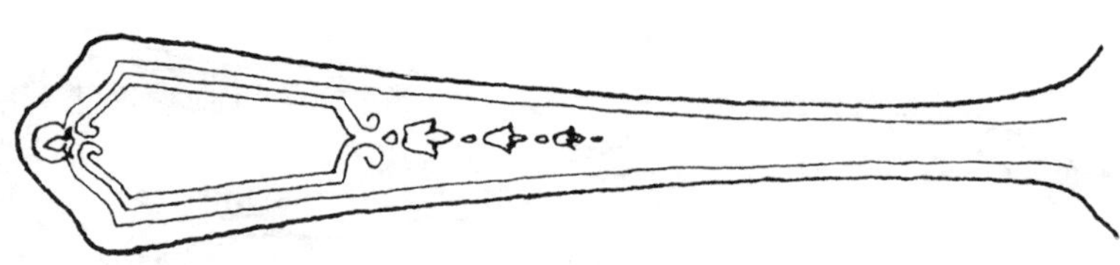

Dinner Knife $8.00
Dinner Fork $8.00
Teaspoon $5.00

Apollo
1929
S

Dinner Knife $8.00
Dinner Fork $8.00
Teaspoon $5.00

Berkeley
(Peerless Silver Plate)
(Wm. A. Rogers)
1929
S

Dinner Knife $8.00 Dinner Fork $8.00 Teaspoon $5.00

Please refer to "How To Use This Book" page 4.

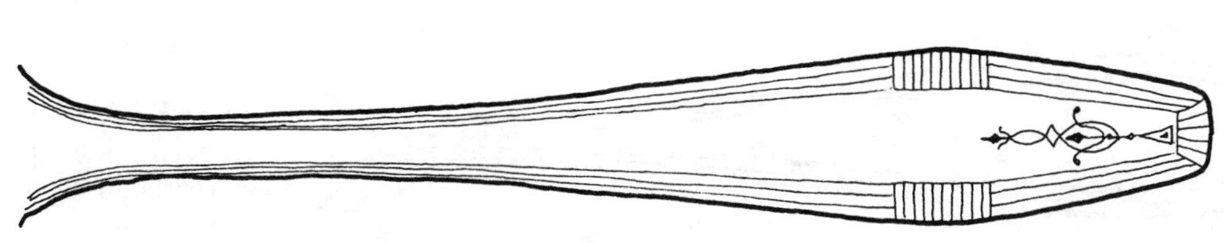

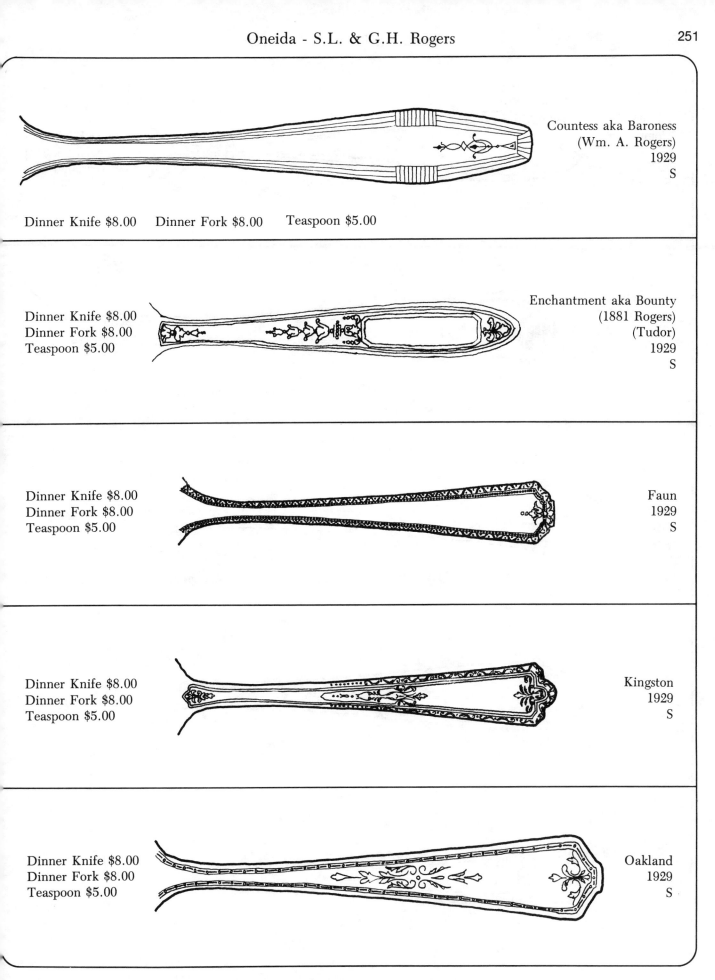

Countess aka Baroness
(Wm. A. Rogers)
1929
S

Dinner Knife $8.00 Dinner Fork $8.00 Teaspoon $5.00

Dinner Knife $8.00
Dinner Fork $8.00
Teaspoon $5.00

Enchantment aka Bounty
(1881 Rogers)
(Tudor)
1929
S

Dinner Knife $8.00
Dinner Fork $8.00
Teaspoon $5.00

Faun
1929
S

Dinner Knife $8.00
Dinner Fork $8.00
Teaspoon $5.00

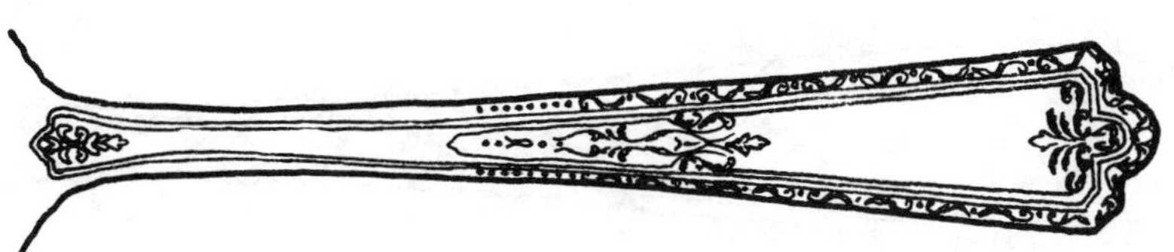

Kingston
1929
S

Dinner Knife $8.00
Dinner Fork $8.00
Teaspoon $5.00

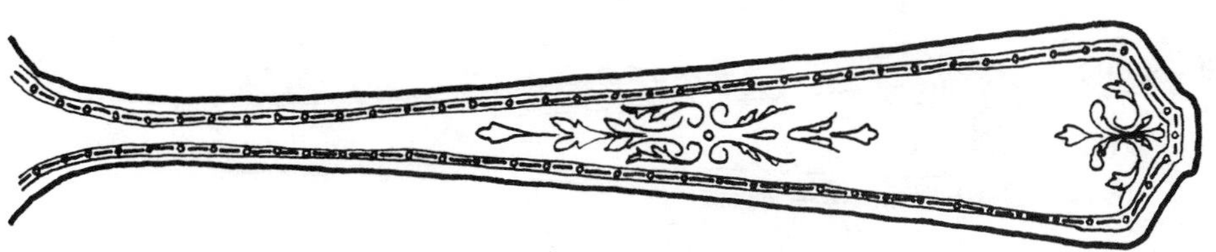

Oakland
1929
S

Please refer to "How To Use This Book" page 4.

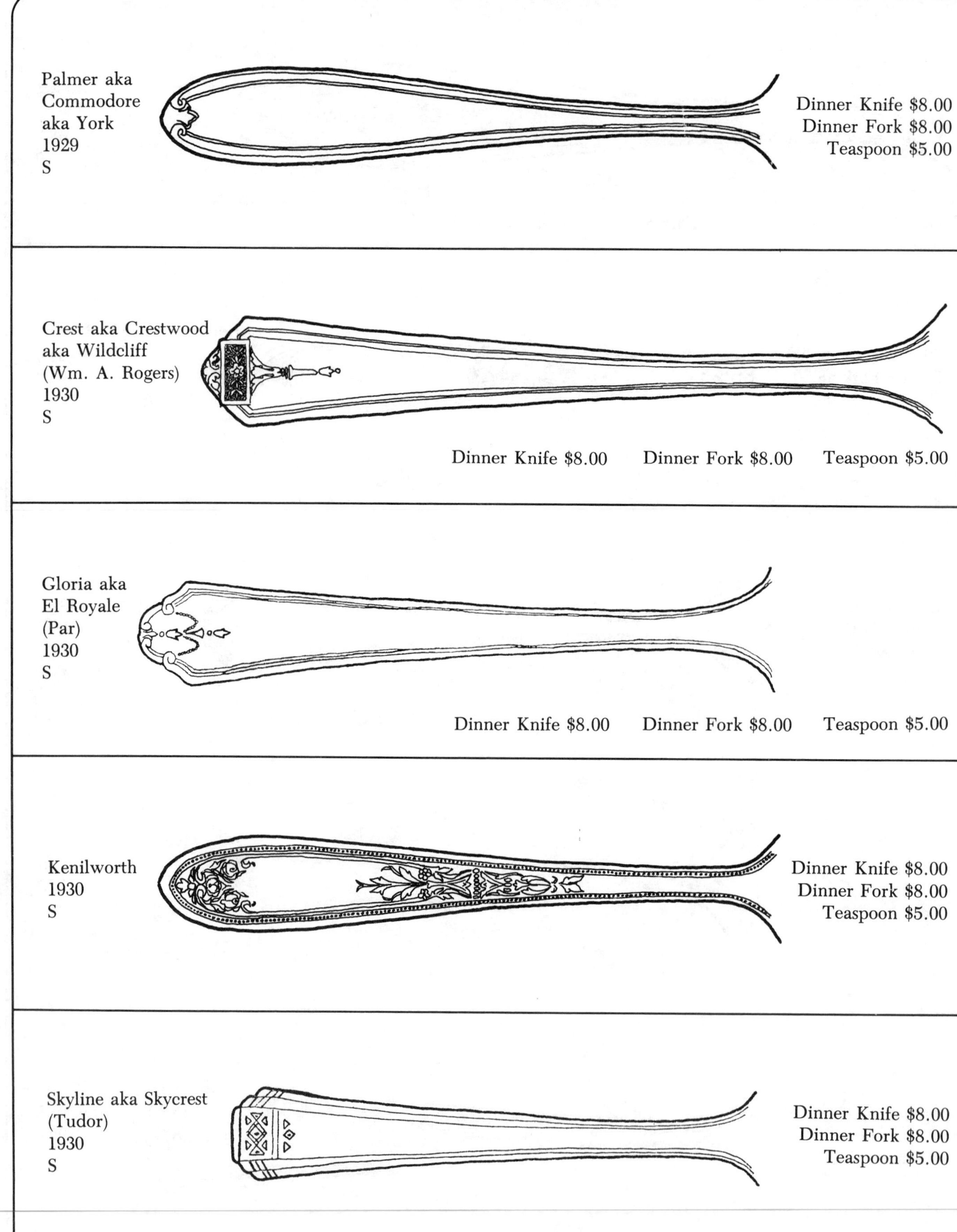

Palmer aka Commodore aka York
1929
S

Dinner Knife $8.00
Dinner Fork $8.00
Teaspoon $5.00

Crest aka Crestwood aka Wildcliff (Wm. A. Rogers)
1930
S

Dinner Knife $8.00 Dinner Fork $8.00 Teaspoon $5.00

Gloria aka El Royale (Par)
1930
S

Dinner Knife $8.00 Dinner Fork $8.00 Teaspoon $5.00

Kenilworth
1930
S

Dinner Knife $8.00
Dinner Fork $8.00
Teaspoon $5.00

Skyline aka Skycrest (Tudor)
1930
S

Dinner Knife $8.00
Dinner Fork $8.00
Teaspoon $5.00

Please refer to "How To Use This Book" page 4.

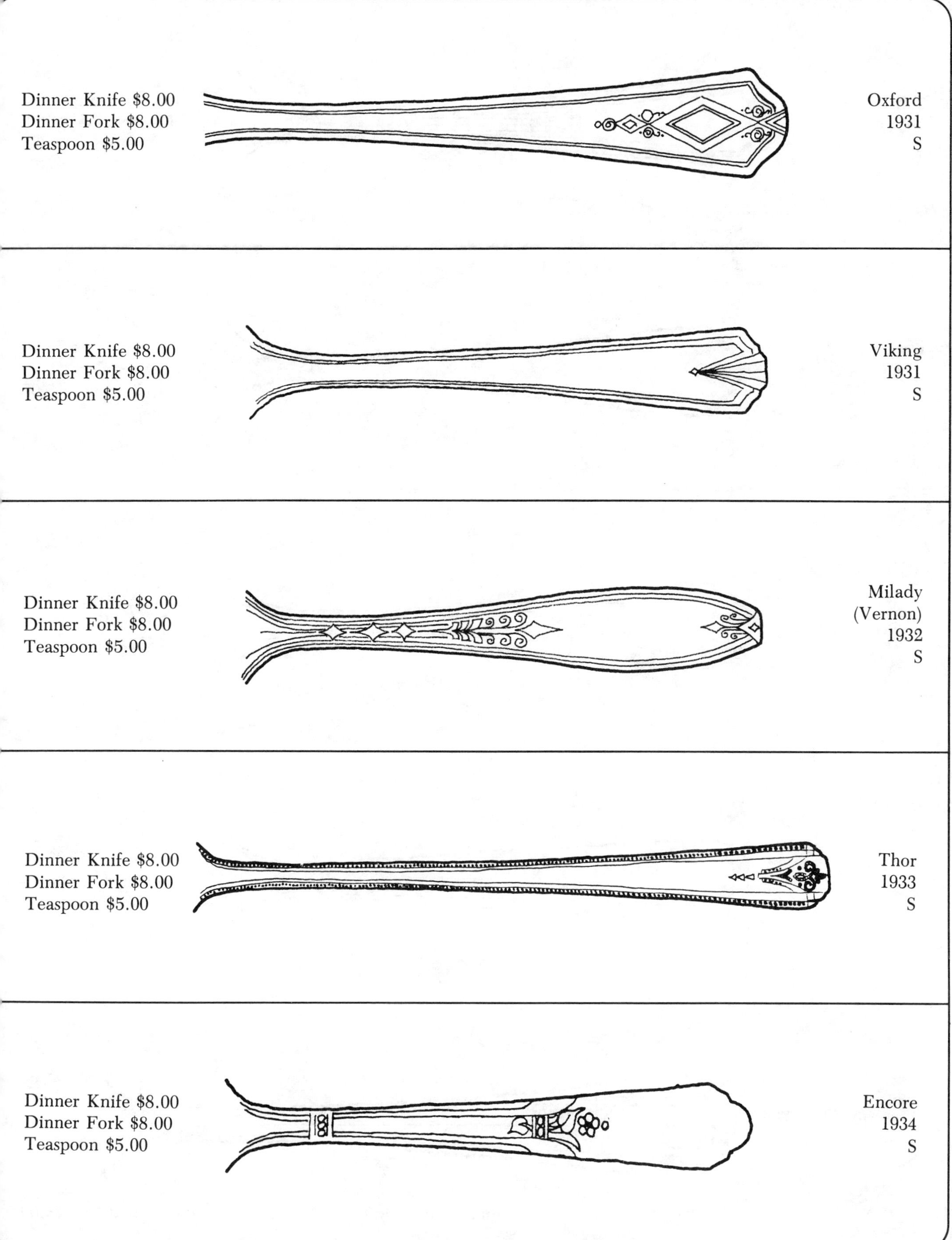

Dinner Knife $8.00
Dinner Fork $8.00
Teaspoon $5.00

Oxford
1931
S

Dinner Knife $8.00
Dinner Fork $8.00
Teaspoon $5.00

Viking
1931
S

Dinner Knife $8.00
Dinner Fork $8.00
Teaspoon $5.00

Milady
(Vernon)
1932
S

Dinner Knife $8.00
Dinner Fork $8.00
Teaspoon $5.00

Thor
1933
S

Dinner Knife $8.00
Dinner Fork $8.00
Teaspoon $5.00

Encore
1934
S

Please refer to "How To Use This Book" page 4.

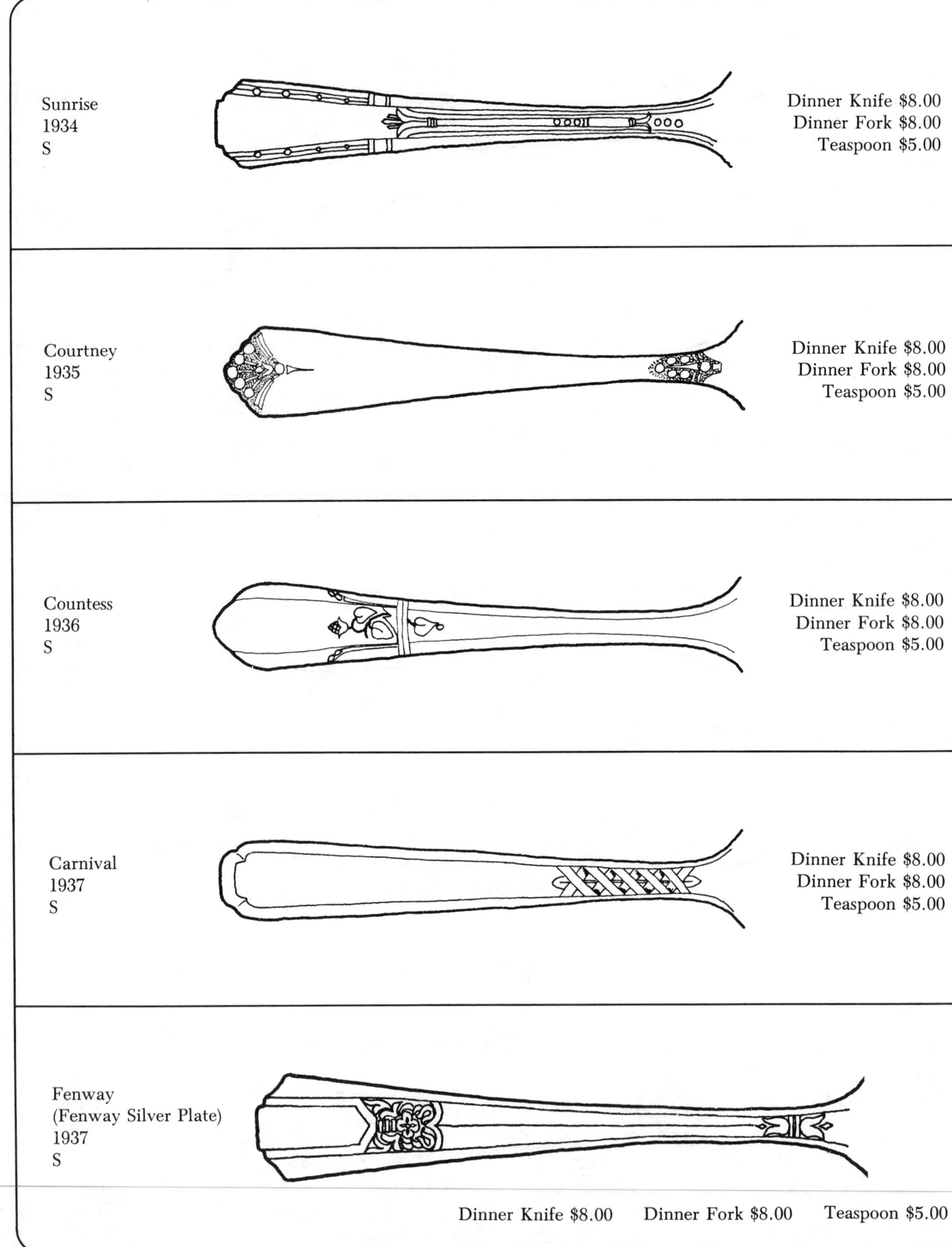

Sunrise
1934
S

Dinner Knife $8.00
Dinner Fork $8.00
Teaspoon $5.00

Courtney
1935
S

Dinner Knife $8.00
Dinner Fork $8.00
Teaspoon $5.00

Countess
1936
S

Dinner Knife $8.00
Dinner Fork $8.00
Teaspoon $5.00

Carnival
1937
S

Dinner Knife $8.00
Dinner Fork $8.00
Teaspoon $5.00

Fenway
(Fenway Silver Plate)
1937
S

Dinner Knife $8.00 Dinner Fork $8.00 Teaspoon $5.00

Please refer to "How To Use This Book" page 4.

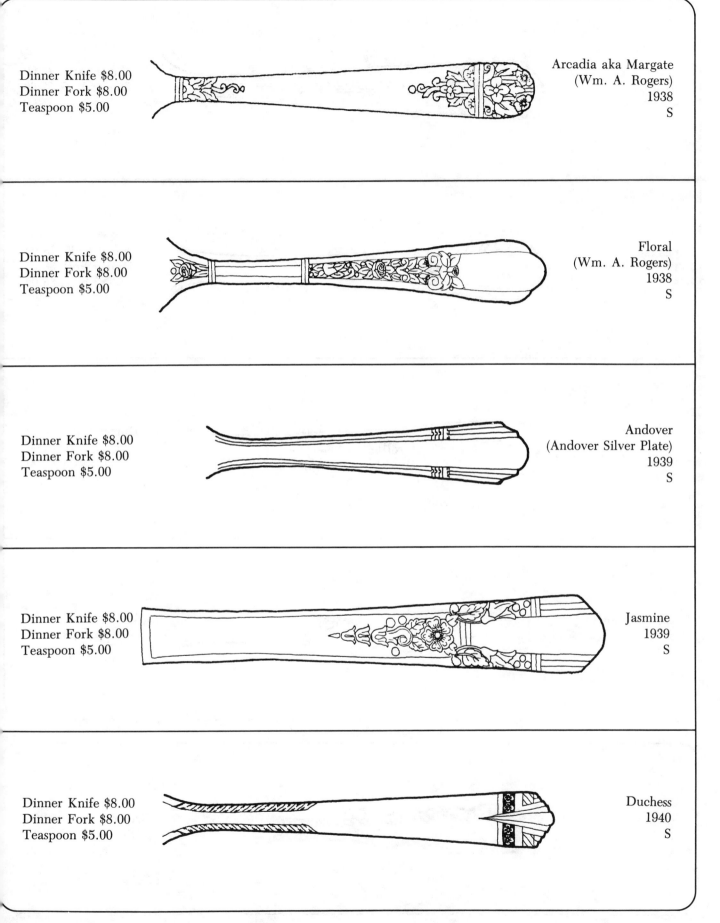

Dinner Knife $8.00
Dinner Fork $8.00
Teaspoon $5.00

Arcadia aka Margate
(Wm. A. Rogers)
1938
S

Dinner Knife $8.00
Dinner Fork $8.00
Teaspoon $5.00

Floral
(Wm. A. Rogers)
1938
S

Dinner Knife $8.00
Dinner Fork $8.00
Teaspoon $5.00

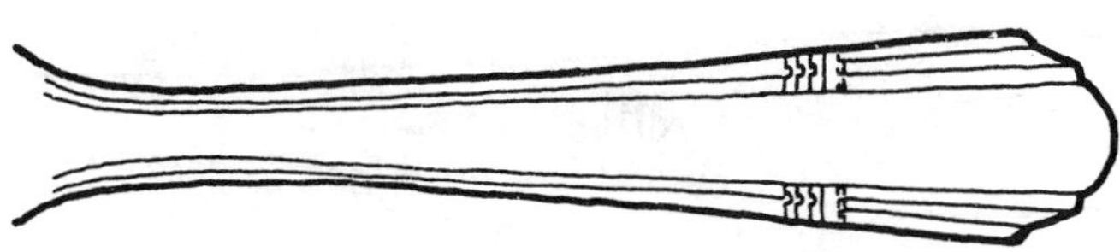

Andover
(Andover Silver Plate)
1939
S

Dinner Knife $8.00
Dinner Fork $8.00
Teaspoon $5.00

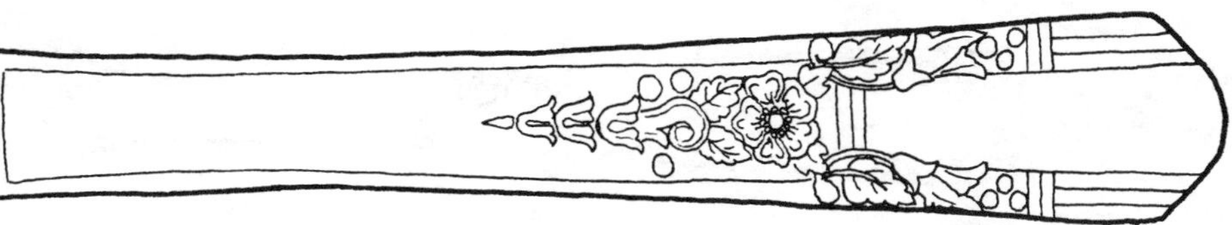

Jasmine
1939
S

Dinner Knife $8.00
Dinner Fork $8.00
Teaspoon $5.00

Duchess
1940
S

Please refer to "How To Use This Book" page 4.

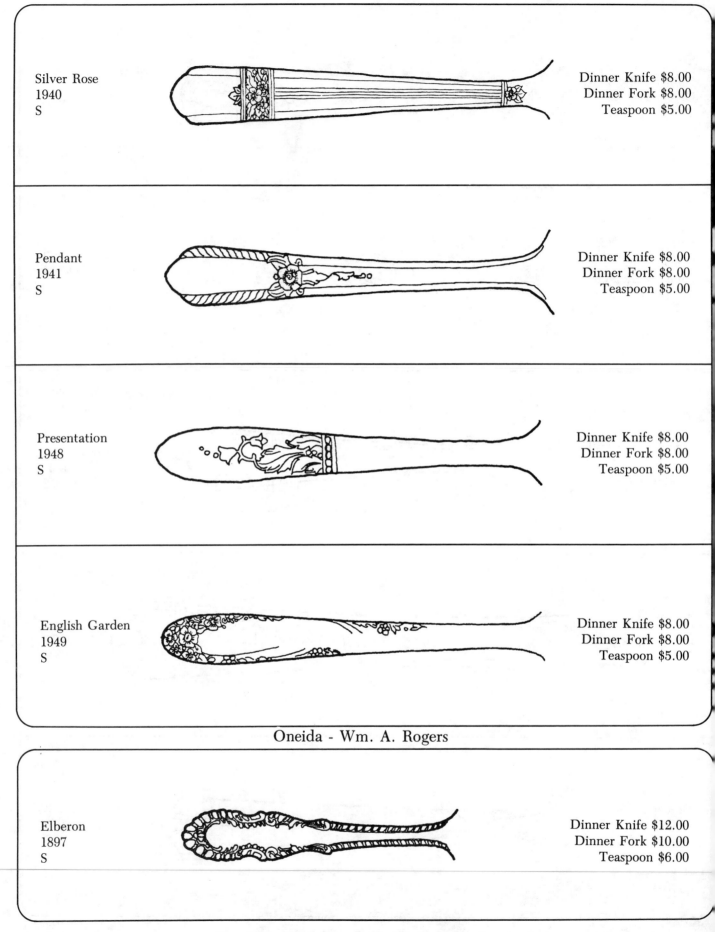

Silver Rose
1940
S

Dinner Knife $8.00
Dinner Fork $8.00
Teaspoon $5.00

Pendant
1941
S

Dinner Knife $8.00
Dinner Fork $8.00
Teaspoon $5.00

Presentation
1948
S

Dinner Knife $8.00
Dinner Fork $8.00
Teaspoon $5.00

English Garden
1949
S

Dinner Knife $8.00
Dinner Fork $8.00
Teaspoon $5.00

Oneida - Wm. A. Rogers

Elberon
1897
S

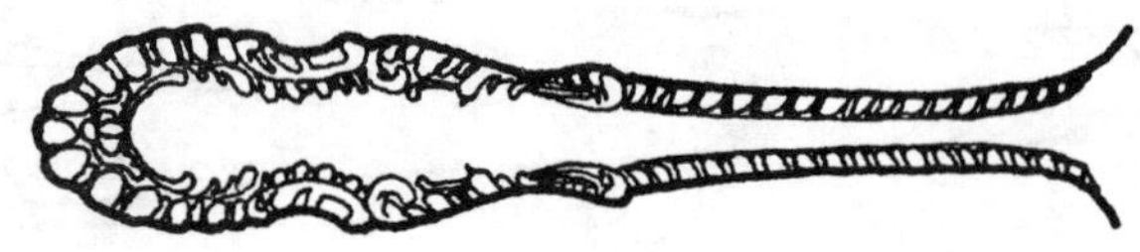

Dinner Knife $12.00
Dinner Fork $10.00
Teaspoon $6.00

Please refer to "How To Use This Book" page 4.

Oneida - Wm. A. Rogers

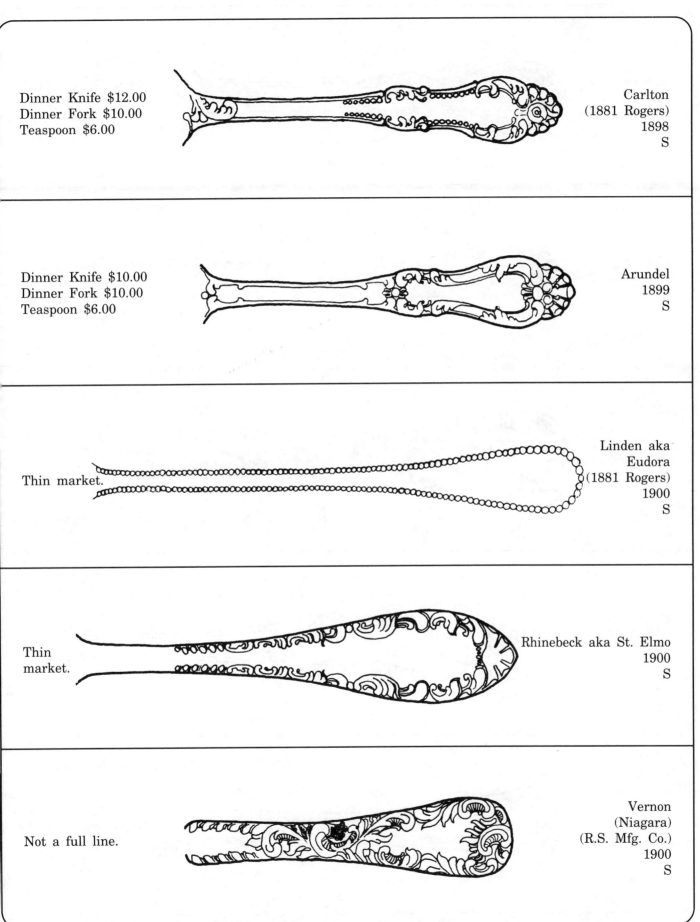

Dinner Knife $12.00
Dinner Fork $10.00
Teaspoon $6.00

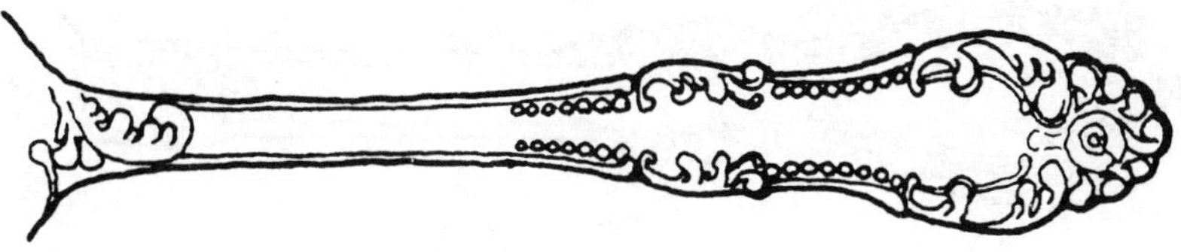

Carlton
(1881 Rogers)
1898
S

Dinner Knife $10.00
Dinner Fork $10.00
Teaspoon $6.00

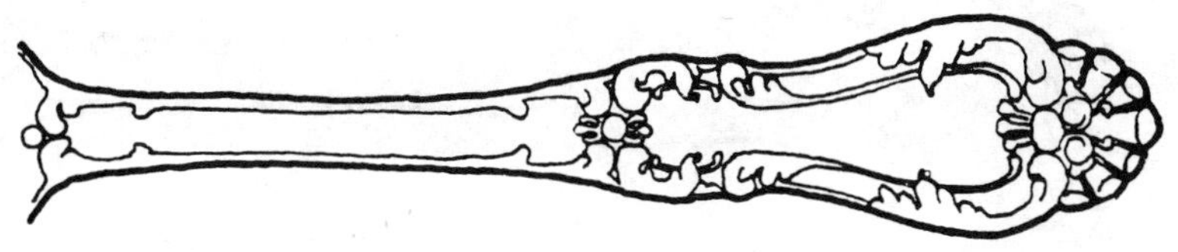

Arundel
1899
S

Thin market.

Linden aka Eudora
(1881 Rogers)
1900
S

Thin market.

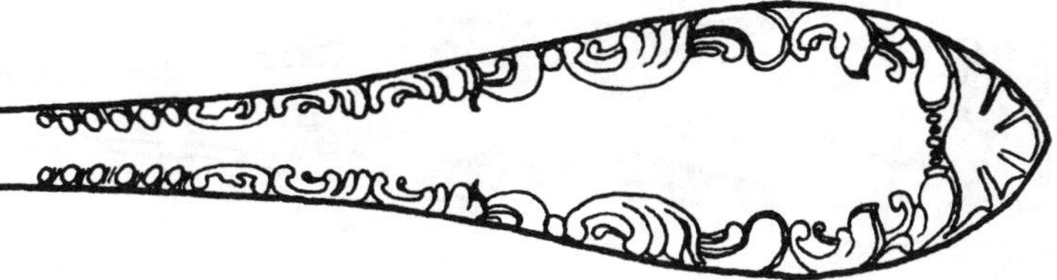

Rhinebeck aka St. Elmo
1900
S

Not a full line.

Vernon
(Niagara)
(R.S. Mfg. Co.)
1900
S

Please refer to "How To Use This Book" page 4.

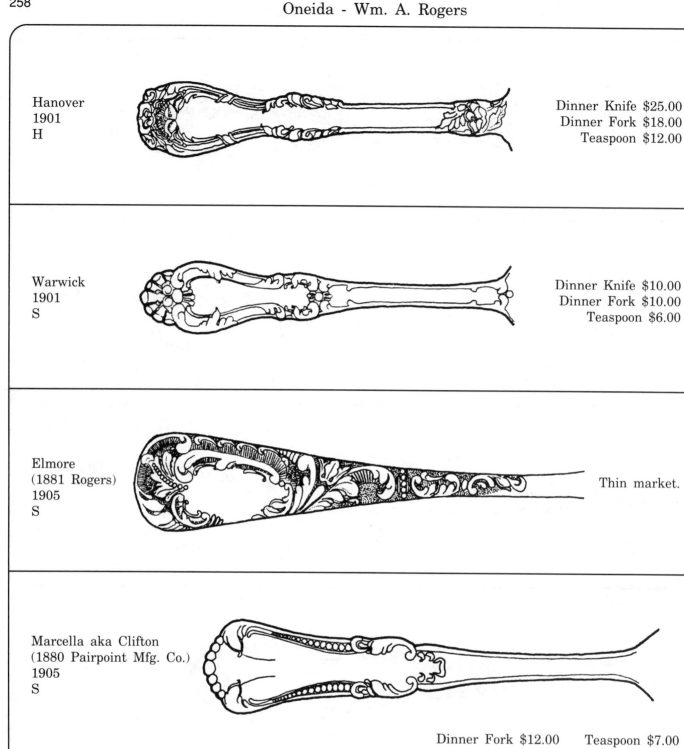

Hanover
1901
H

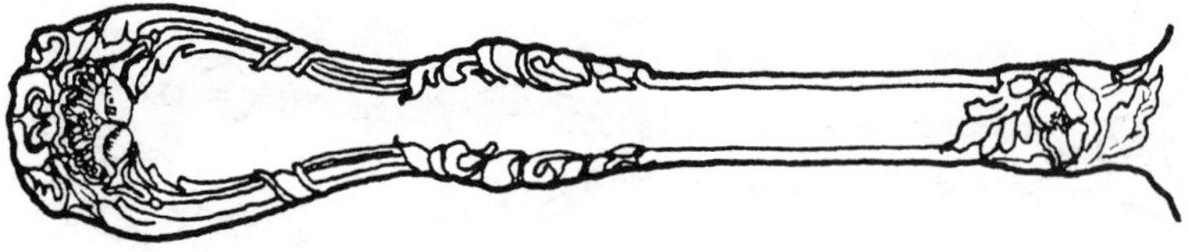

Dinner Knife $25.00
Dinner Fork $18.00
Teaspoon $12.00

Warwick
1901
S

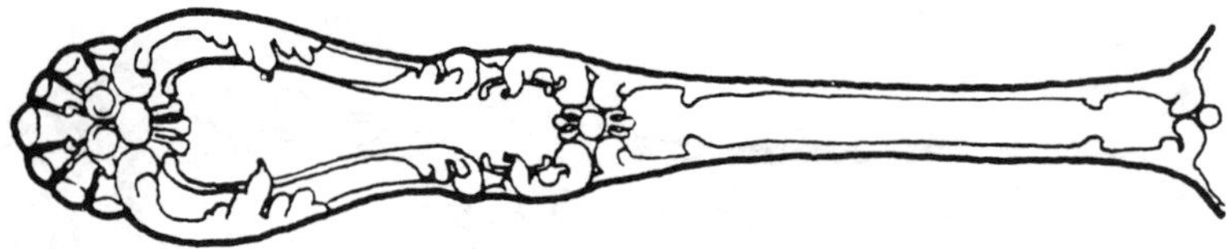

Dinner Knife $10.00
Dinner Fork $10.00
Teaspoon $6.00

Elmore
(1881 Rogers)
1905
S

Thin market.

Marcella aka Clifton
(1880 Pairpoint Mfg. Co.)
1905
S

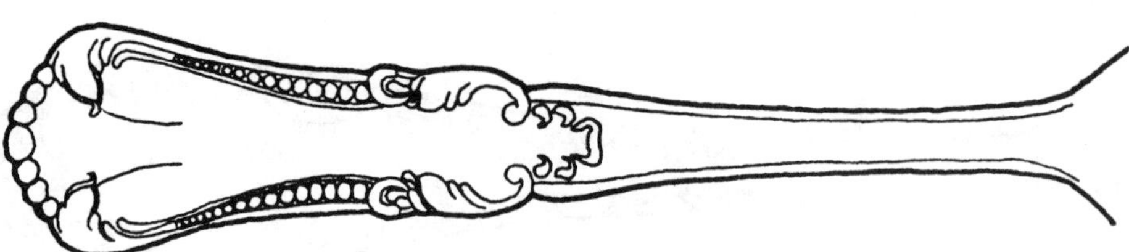

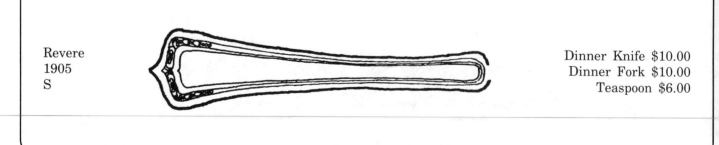

Dinner Fork $12.00 Teaspoon $7.00

Revere
1905
S

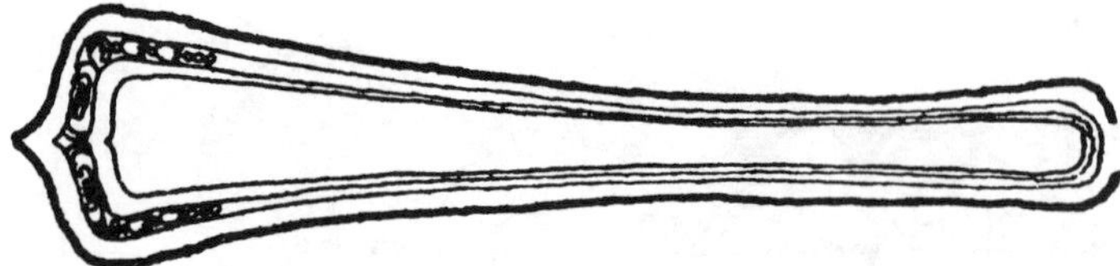

Dinner Knife $10.00
Dinner Fork $10.00
Teaspoon $6.00

Please refer to "How To Use This Book" page 4.

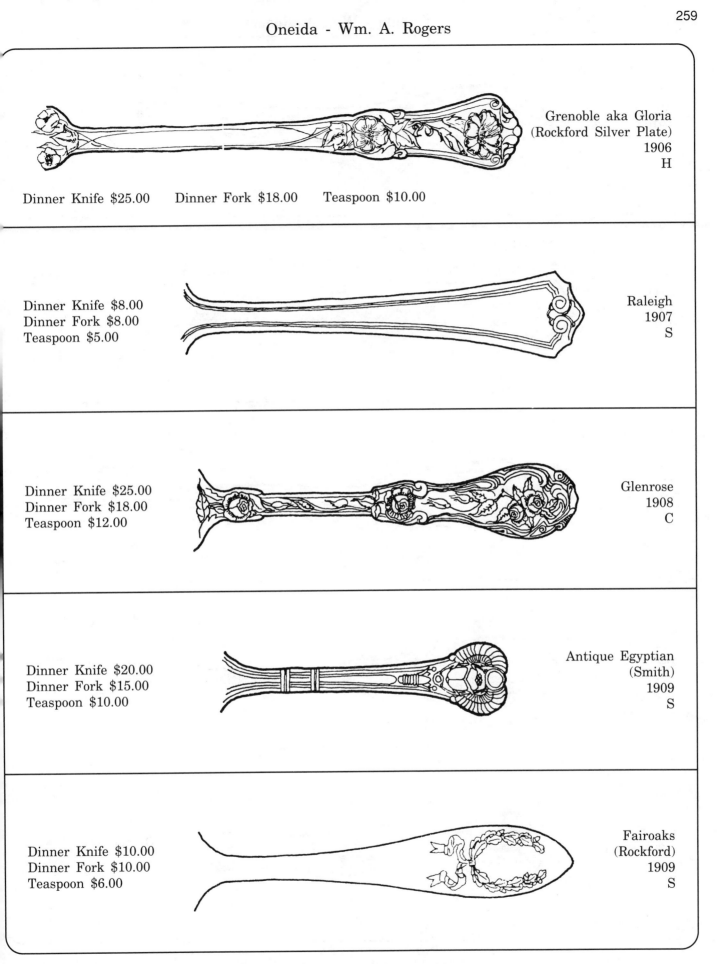

Oneida - Wm. A. Rogers

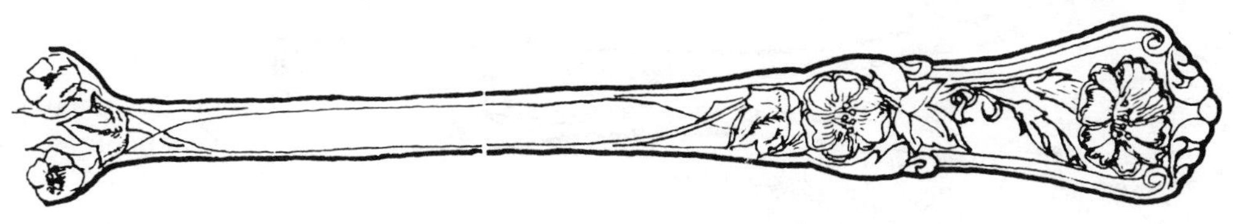

Grenoble aka Gloria
(Rockford Silver Plate)
1906
H

Dinner Knife $25.00 Dinner Fork $18.00 Teaspoon $10.00

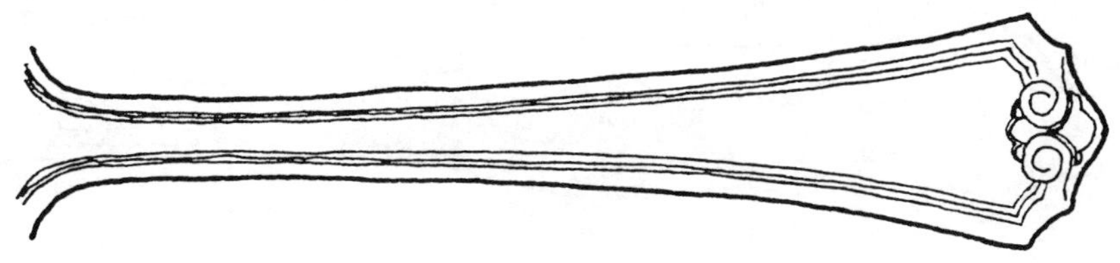

Dinner Knife $8.00
Dinner Fork $8.00
Teaspoon $5.00

Raleigh
1907
S

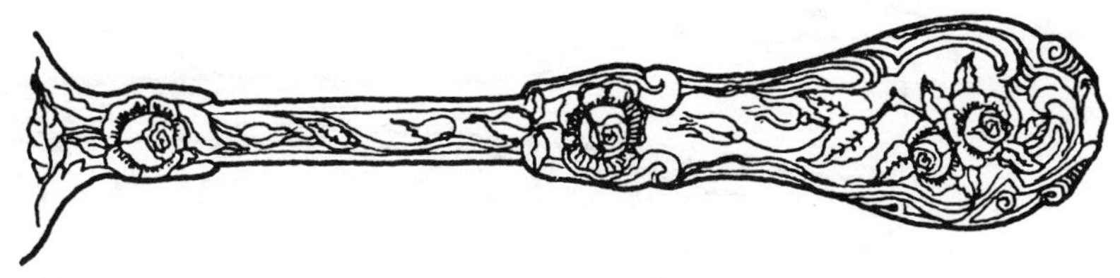

Dinner Knife $25.00
Dinner Fork $18.00
Teaspoon $12.00

Glenrose
1908
C

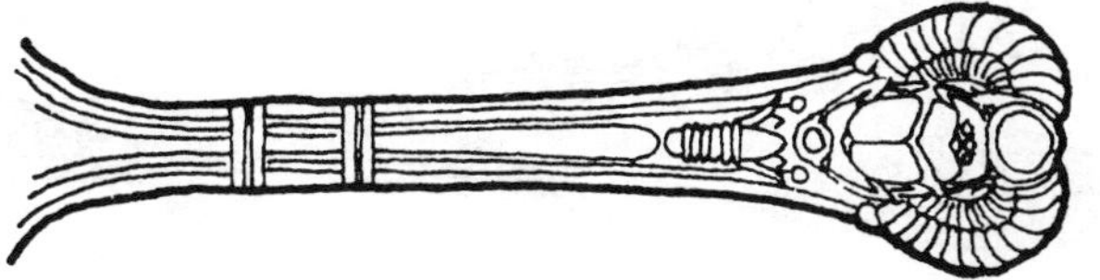

Dinner Knife $20.00
Dinner Fork $15.00
Teaspoon $10.00

Antique Egyptian
(Smith)
1909
S

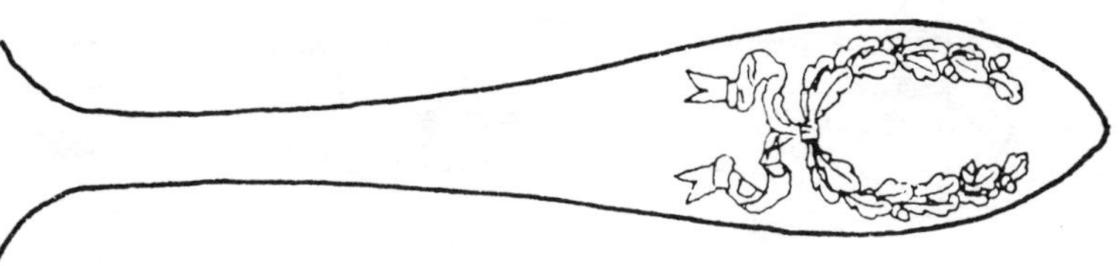

Dinner Knife $10.00
Dinner Fork $10.00
Teaspoon $6.00

Fairoaks
(Rockford)
1909
S

Please refer to "How To Use This Book" page 4.

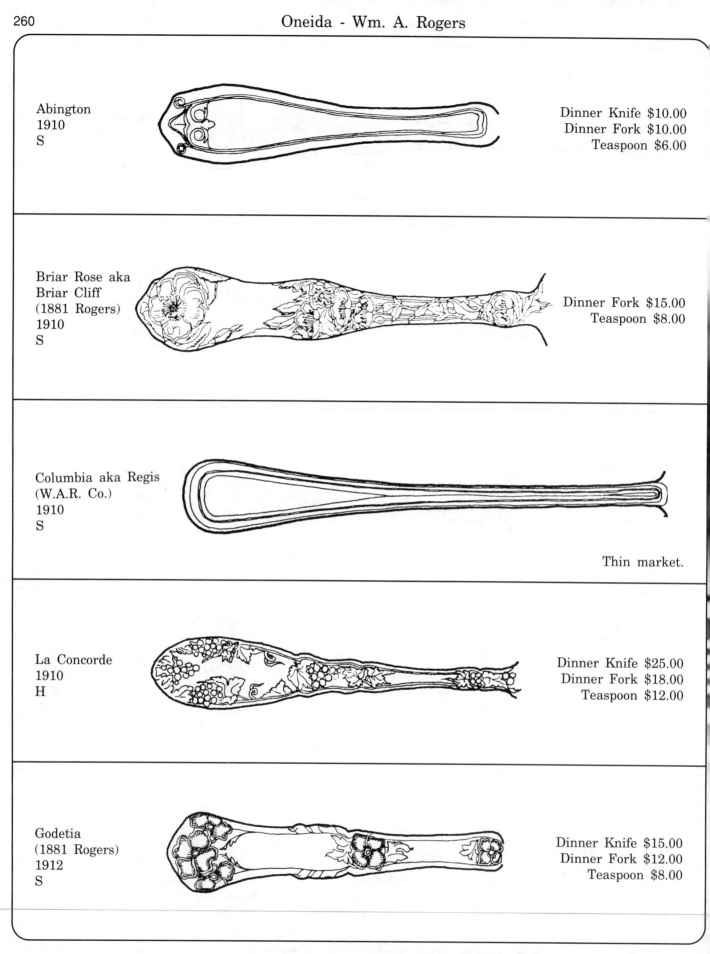

Abington
1910
S

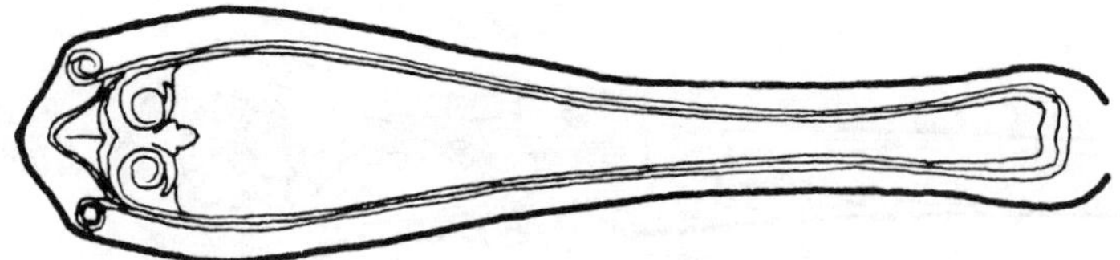

Dinner Knife $10.00
Dinner Fork $10.00
Teaspoon $6.00

Briar Rose aka
Briar Cliff
(1881 Rogers)
1910
S

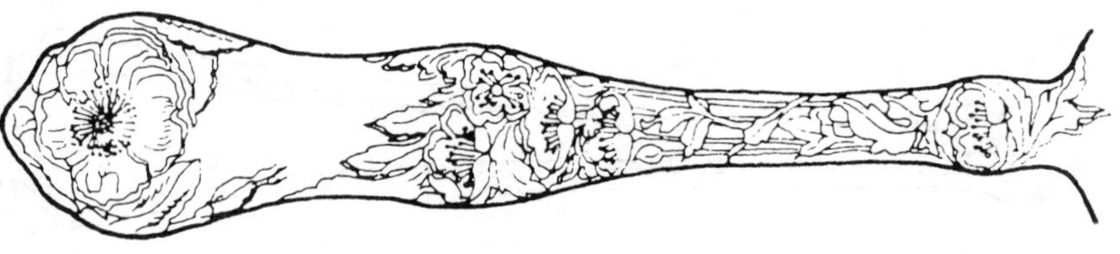

Dinner Fork $15.00
Teaspoon $8.00

Columbia aka Regis
(W.A.R. Co.)
1910
S

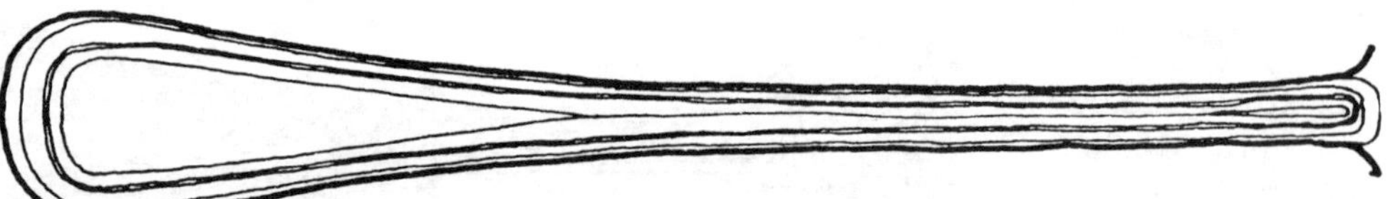

Thin market.

La Concorde
1910
H

Dinner Knife $25.00
Dinner Fork $18.00
Teaspoon $12.00

Godetia
(1881 Rogers)
1912
S

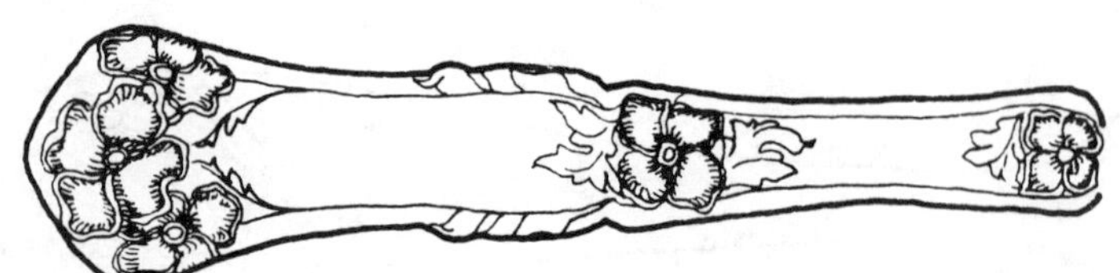

Dinner Knife $15.00
Dinner Fork $12.00
Teaspoon $8.00

Please refer to "How To Use This Book" page 4.

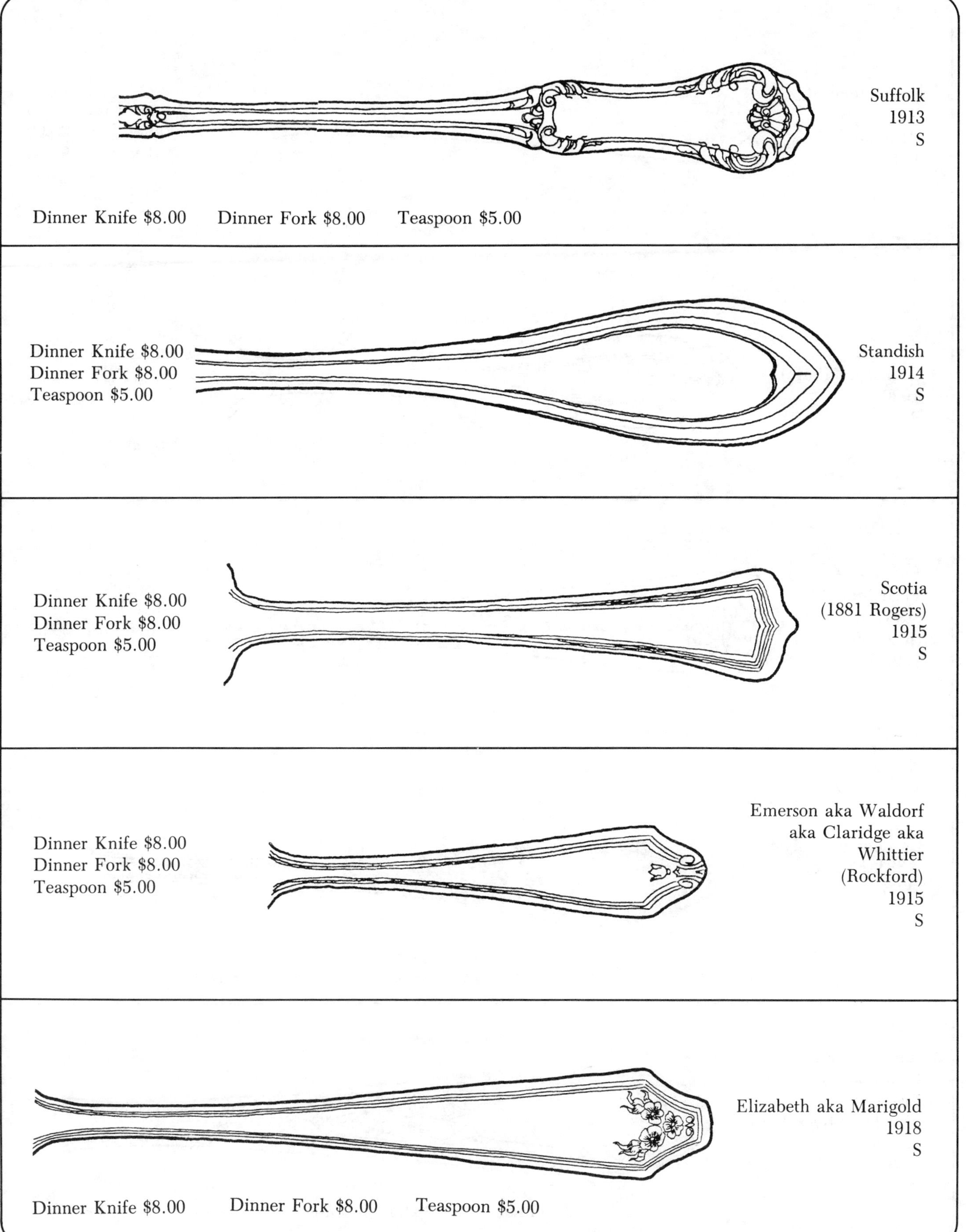

Suffolk
1913
S

Dinner Knife $8.00 Dinner Fork $8.00 Teaspoon $5.00

Dinner Knife $8.00
Dinner Fork $8.00
Teaspoon $5.00

Standish
1914
S

Dinner Knife $8.00
Dinner Fork $8.00
Teaspoon $5.00

Scotia
(1881 Rogers)
1915
S

Dinner Knife $8.00
Dinner Fork $8.00
Teaspoon $5.00

Emerson aka Waldorf
aka Claridge aka
Whittier
(Rockford)
1915
S

Elizabeth aka Marigold
1918
S

Dinner Knife $8.00 Dinner Fork $8.00 Teaspoon $5.00

Please refer to "How To Use This Book" page 4.

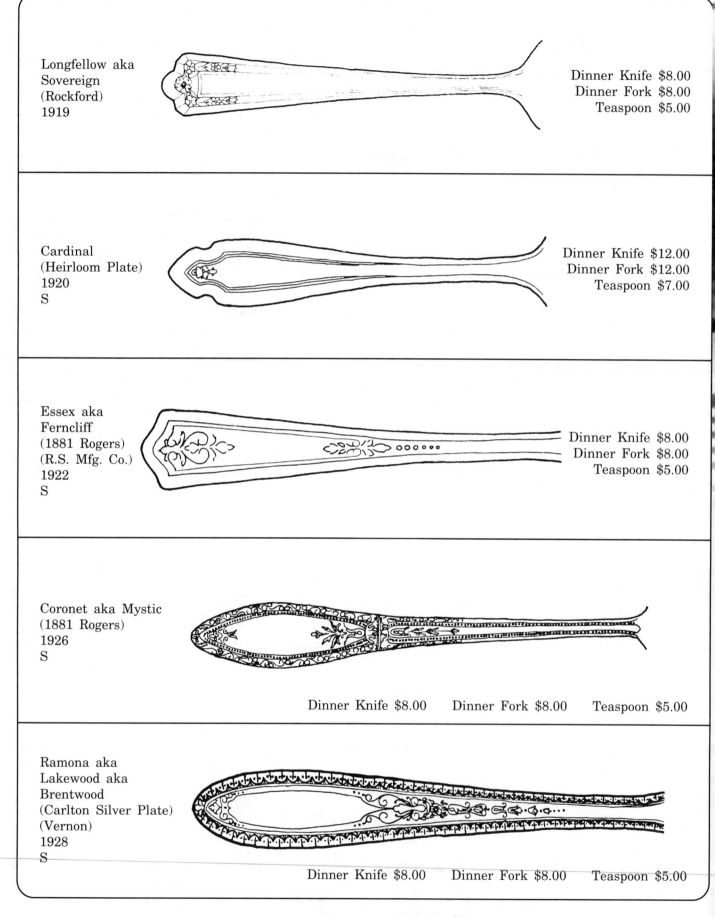

Longfellow aka
Sovereign
(Rockford)
1919

Dinner Knife $8.00
Dinner Fork $8.00
Teaspoon $5.00

Cardinal
(Heirloom Plate)
1920
S

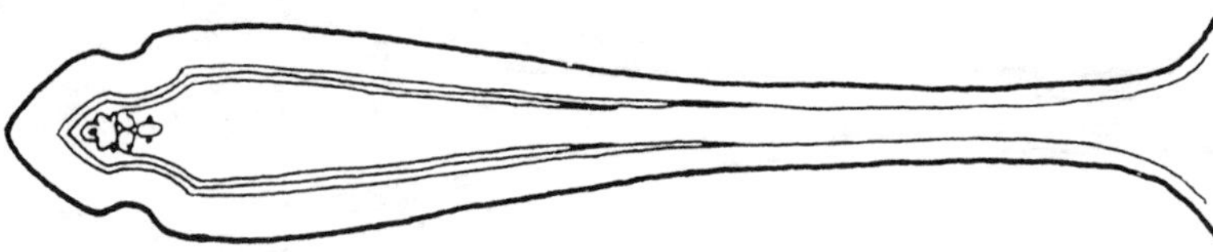

Dinner Knife $12.00
Dinner Fork $12.00
Teaspoon $7.00

Essex aka
Ferncliff
(1881 Rogers)
(R.S. Mfg. Co.)
1922
S

Dinner Knife $8.00
Dinner Fork $8.00
Teaspoon $5.00

Coronet aka Mystic
(1881 Rogers)
1926
S

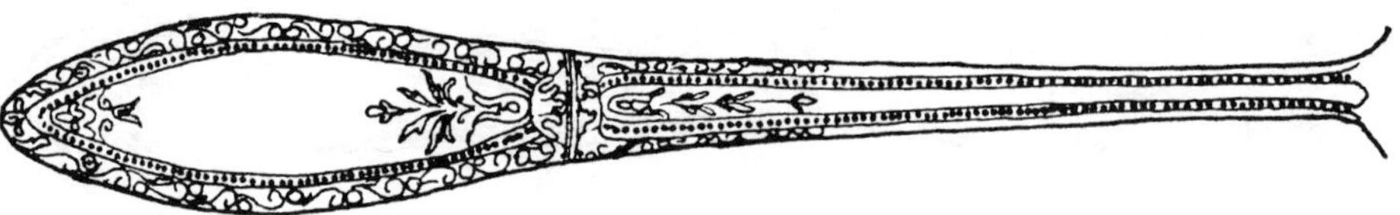

Dinner Knife $8.00 Dinner Fork $8.00 Teaspoon $5.00

Ramona aka
Lakewood aka
Brentwood
(Carlton Silver Plate)
(Vernon)
1928
S

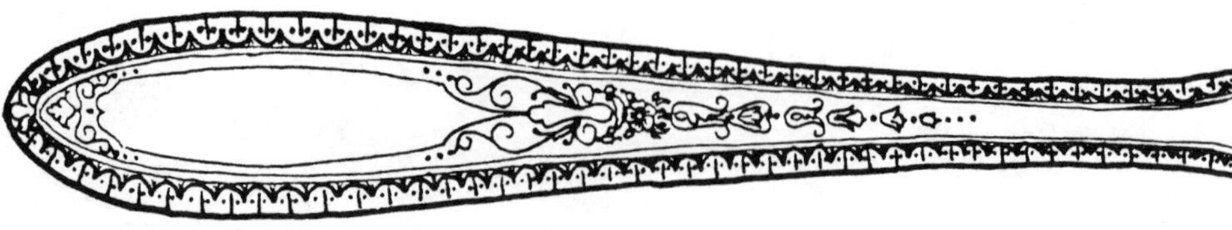

Dinner Knife $8.00 Dinner Fork $8.00 Teaspoon $5.00

Please refer to "How To Use This Book" page 4.

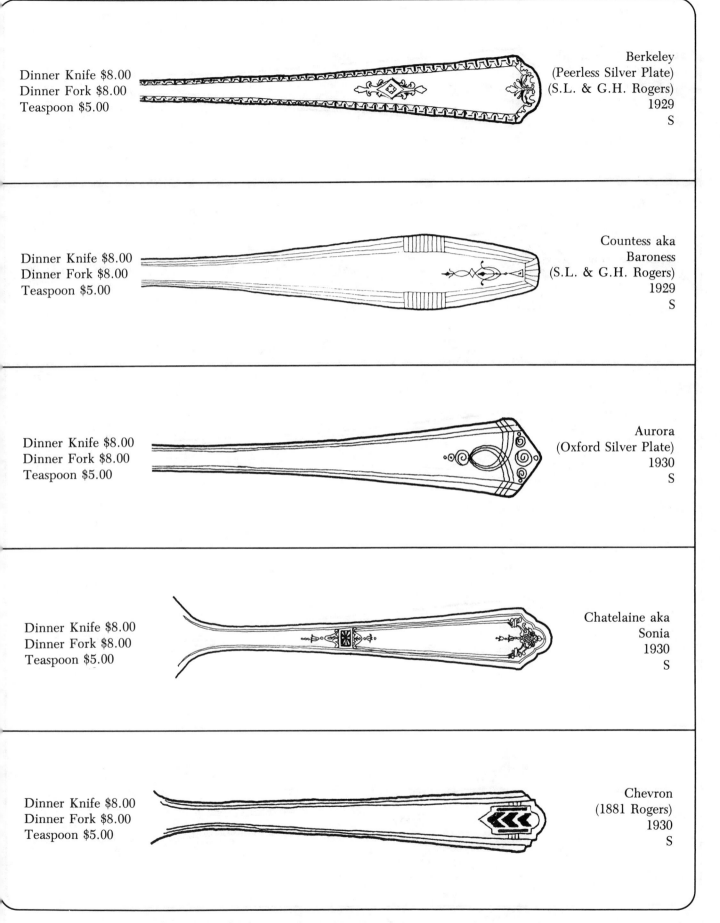

Dinner Knife $8.00
Dinner Fork $8.00
Teaspoon $5.00

Berkeley
(Peerless Silver Plate)
(S.L. & G.H. Rogers)
1929
S

Dinner Knife $8.00
Dinner Fork $8.00
Teaspoon $5.00

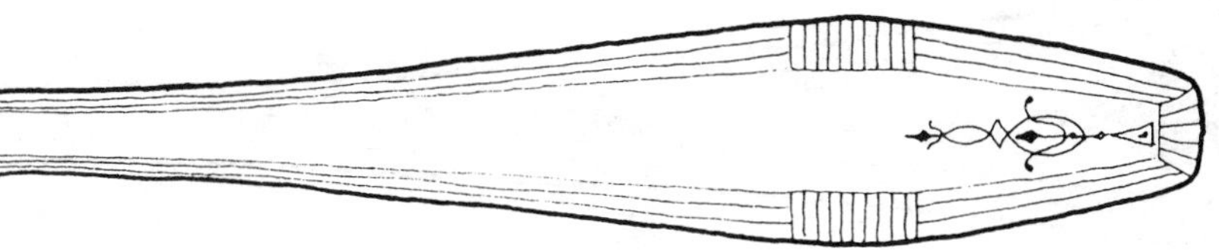

Countess aka
Baroness
(S.L. & G.H. Rogers)
1929
S

Dinner Knife $8.00
Dinner Fork $8.00
Teaspoon $5.00

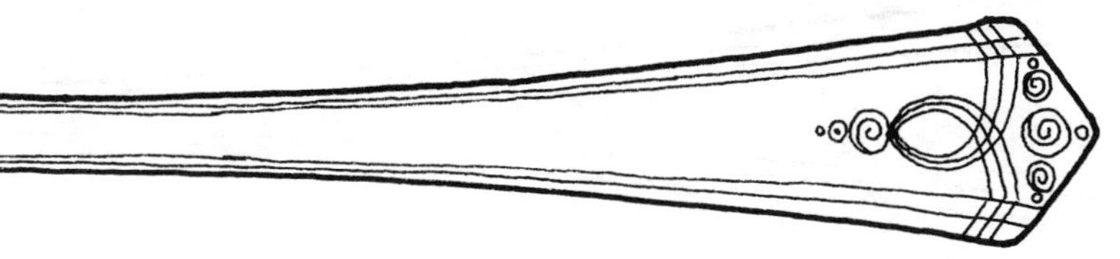

Aurora
(Oxford Silver Plate)
1930
S

Dinner Knife $8.00
Dinner Fork $8.00
Teaspoon $5.00

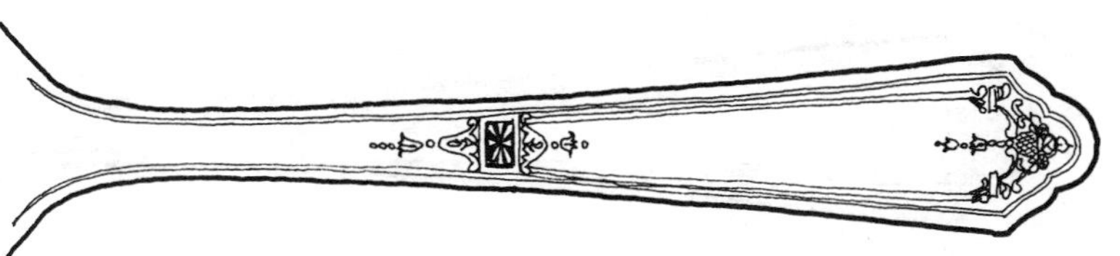

Chatelaine aka
Sonia
1930
S

Dinner Knife $8.00
Dinner Fork $8.00
Teaspoon $5.00

Chevron
(1881 Rogers)
1930
S

Please refer to "How To Use This Book" page 4.

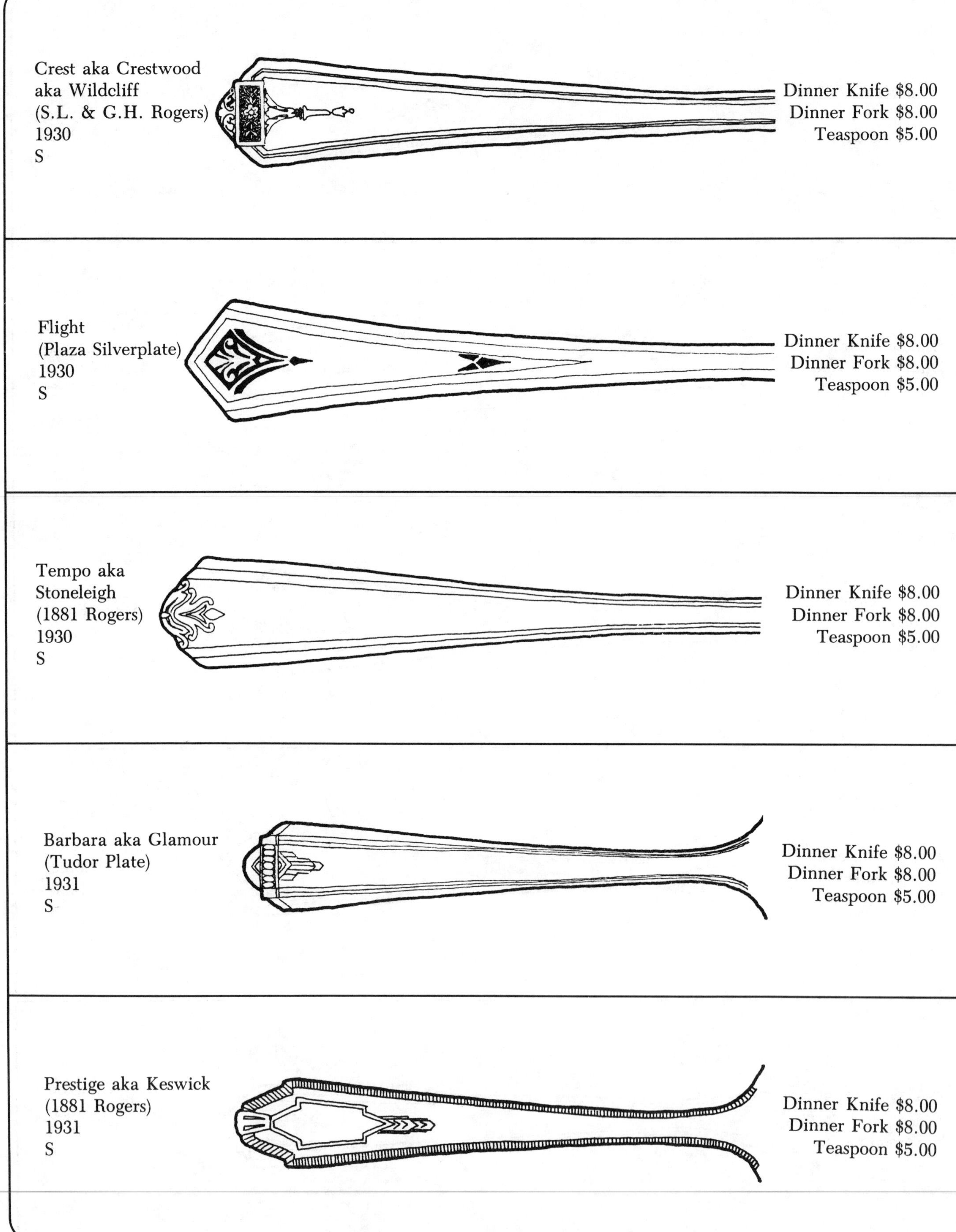

Crest aka Crestwood
aka Wildcliff
(S.L. & G.H. Rogers)
1930
S

Dinner Knife $8.00
Dinner Fork $8.00
Teaspoon $5.00

Flight
(Plaza Silverplate)
1930
S

Dinner Knife $8.00
Dinner Fork $8.00
Teaspoon $5.00

Tempo aka
Stoneleigh
(1881 Rogers)
1930
S

Dinner Knife $8.00
Dinner Fork $8.00
Teaspoon $5.00

Barbara aka Glamour
(Tudor Plate)
1931
S

Dinner Knife $8.00
Dinner Fork $8.00
Teaspoon $5.00

Prestige aka Keswick
(1881 Rogers)
1931
S

Dinner Knife $8.00
Dinner Fork $8.00
Teaspoon $5.00

Please refer to "How To Use This Book" page 4.

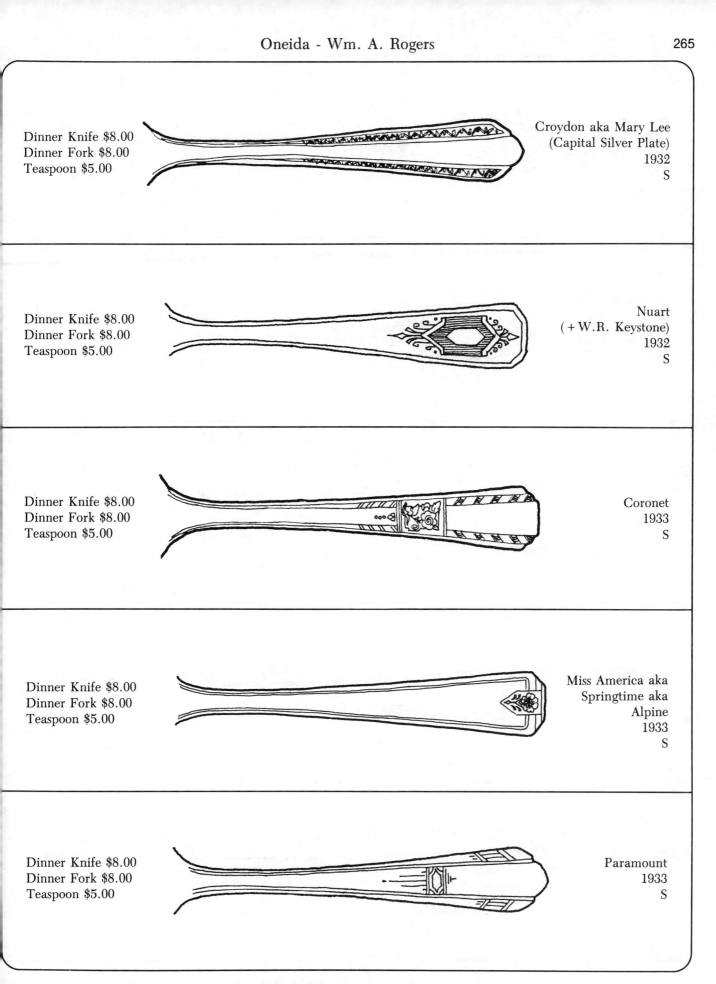

Dinner Knife $8.00
Dinner Fork $8.00
Teaspoon $5.00

Croydon aka Mary Lee
(Capital Silver Plate)
1932
S

Dinner Knife $8.00
Dinner Fork $8.00
Teaspoon $5.00

Nuart
(+ W.R. Keystone)
1932
S

Dinner Knife $8.00
Dinner Fork $8.00
Teaspoon $5.00

Coronet
1933
S

Dinner Knife $8.00
Dinner Fork $8.00
Teaspoon $5.00

Miss America aka
Springtime aka
Alpine
1933
S

Dinner Knife $8.00
Dinner Fork $8.00
Teaspoon $5.00

Paramount
1933
S

Please refer to "How To Use This Book" page 4.

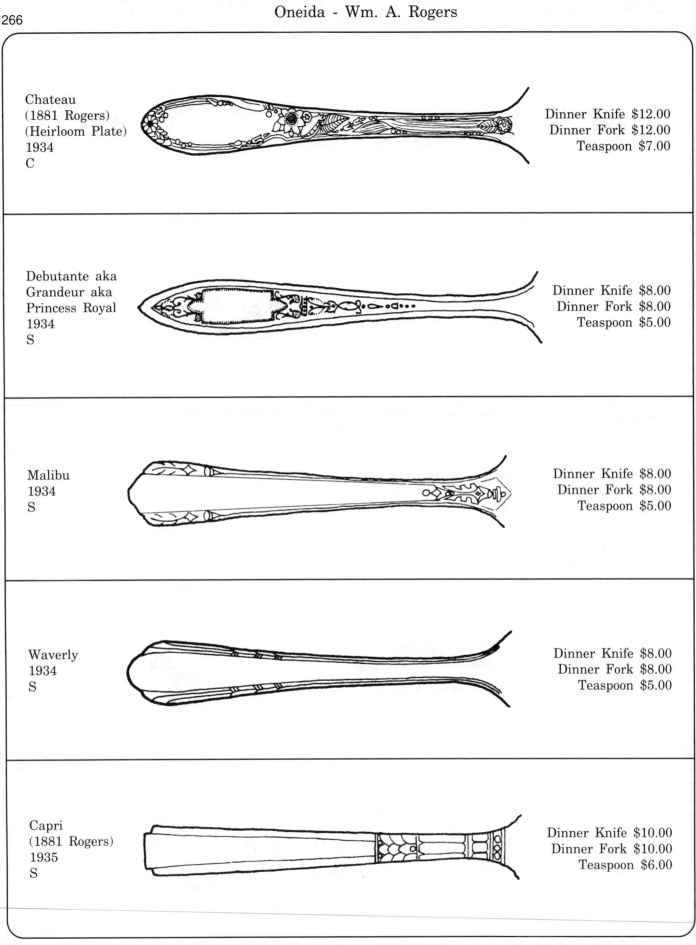

Chateau
(1881 Rogers)
(Heirloom Plate)
1934
C

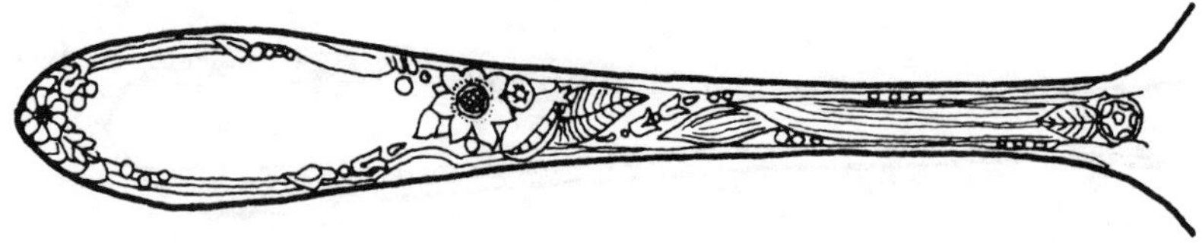

Dinner Knife $12.00
Dinner Fork $12.00
Teaspoon $7.00

Debutante aka
Grandeur aka
Princess Royal
1934
S

Dinner Knife $8.00
Dinner Fork $8.00
Teaspoon $5.00

Malibu
1934
S

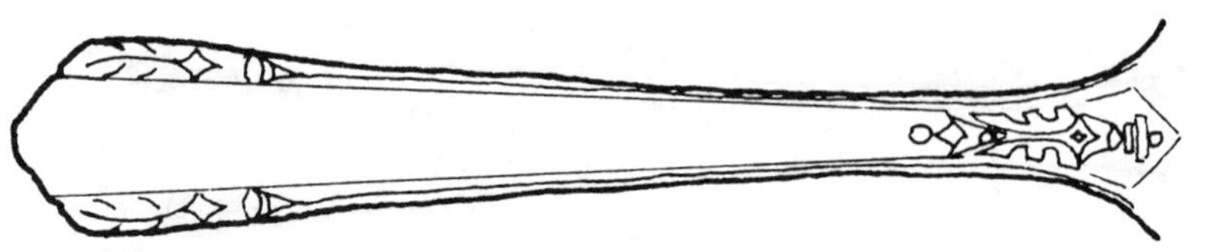

Dinner Knife $8.00
Dinner Fork $8.00
Teaspoon $5.00

Waverly
1934
S

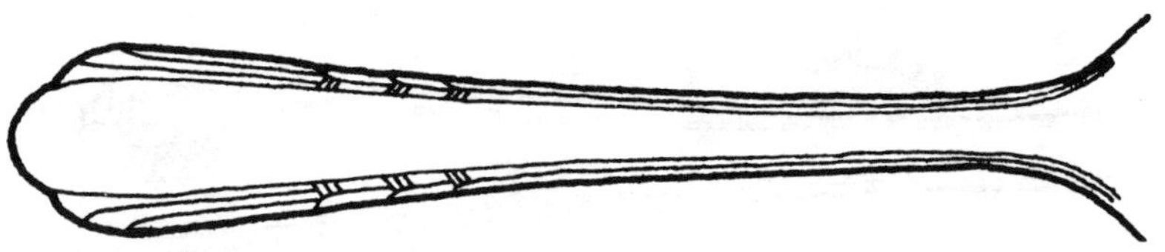

Dinner Knife $8.00
Dinner Fork $8.00
Teaspoon $5.00

Capri
(1881 Rogers)
1935
S

Dinner Knife $10.00
Dinner Fork $10.00
Teaspoon $6.00

Please refer to "How To Use This Book" page 4.

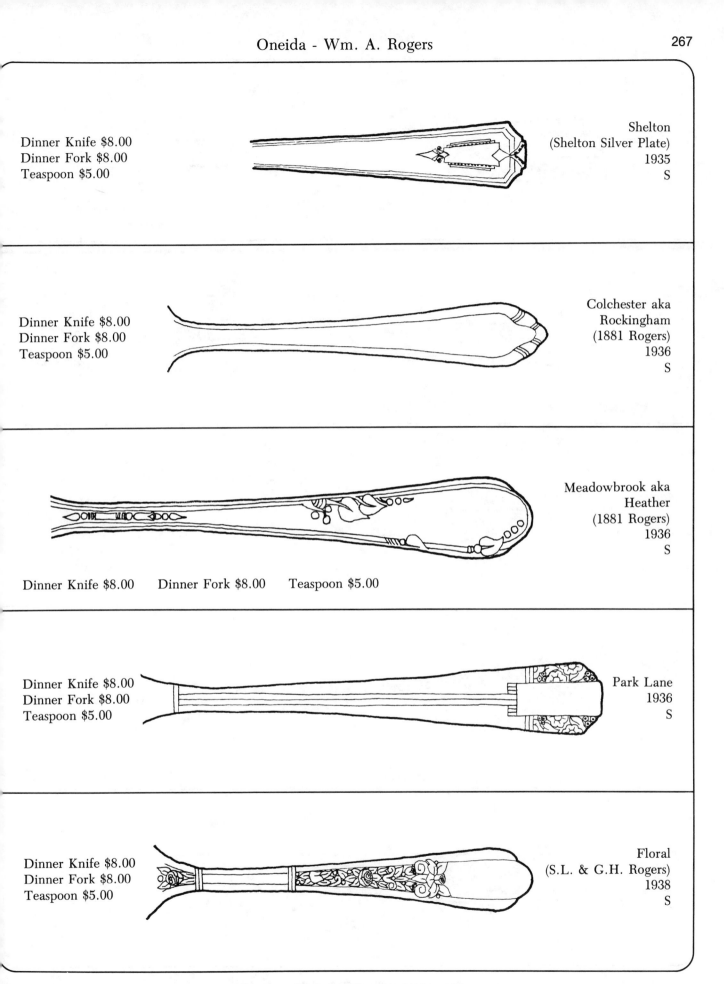

Dinner Knife $8.00
Dinner Fork $8.00
Teaspoon $5.00

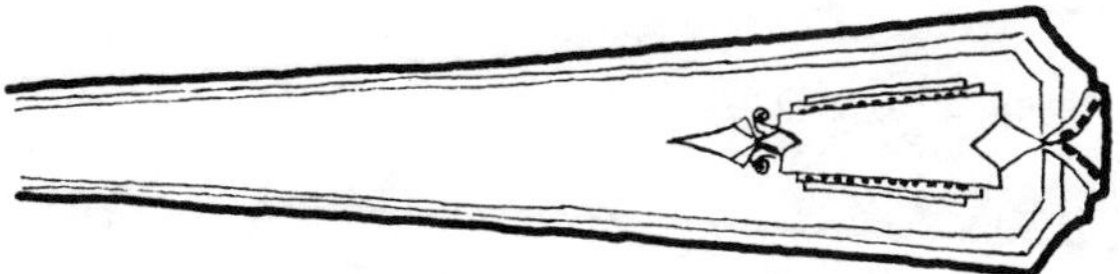

Shelton
(Shelton Silver Plate)
1935
S

Dinner Knife $8.00
Dinner Fork $8.00
Teaspoon $5.00

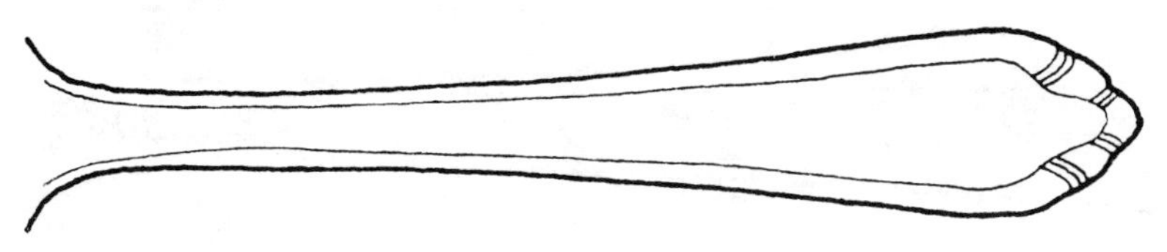

Colchester aka
Rockingham
(1881 Rogers)
1936
S

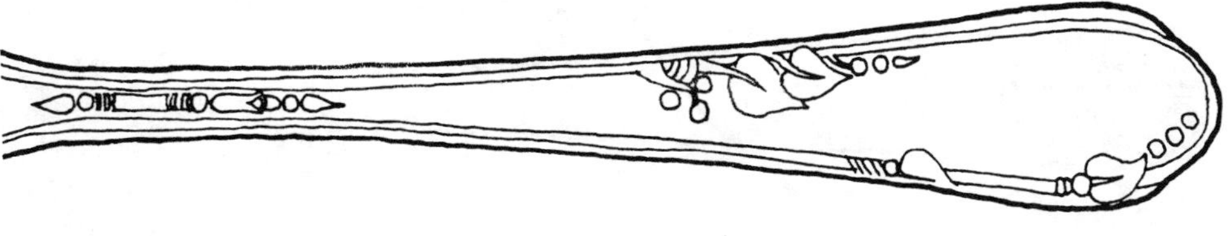

Meadowbrook aka
Heather
(1881 Rogers)
1936
S

Dinner Knife $8.00 Dinner Fork $8.00 Teaspoon $5.00

Dinner Knife $8.00
Dinner Fork $8.00
Teaspoon $5.00

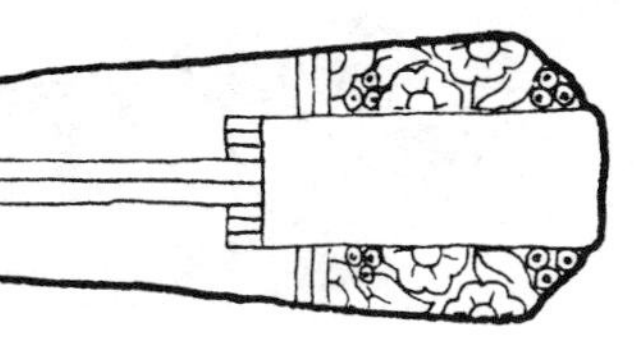

Park Lane
1936
S

Dinner Knife $8.00
Dinner Fork $8.00
Teaspoon $5.00

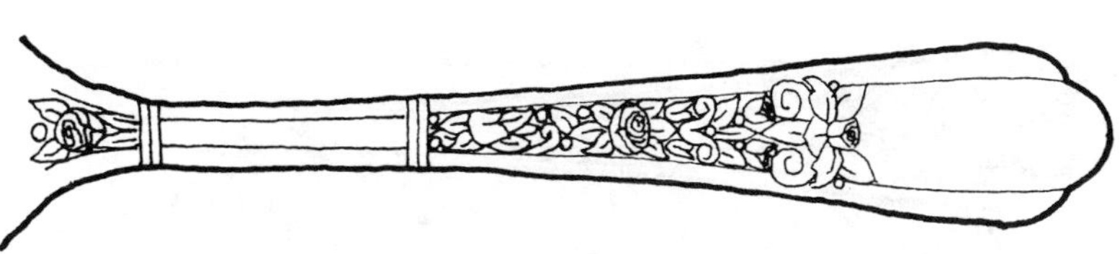

Floral
(S.L. & G.H. Rogers)
1938
S

Please refer to "How To Use This Book" page 4.

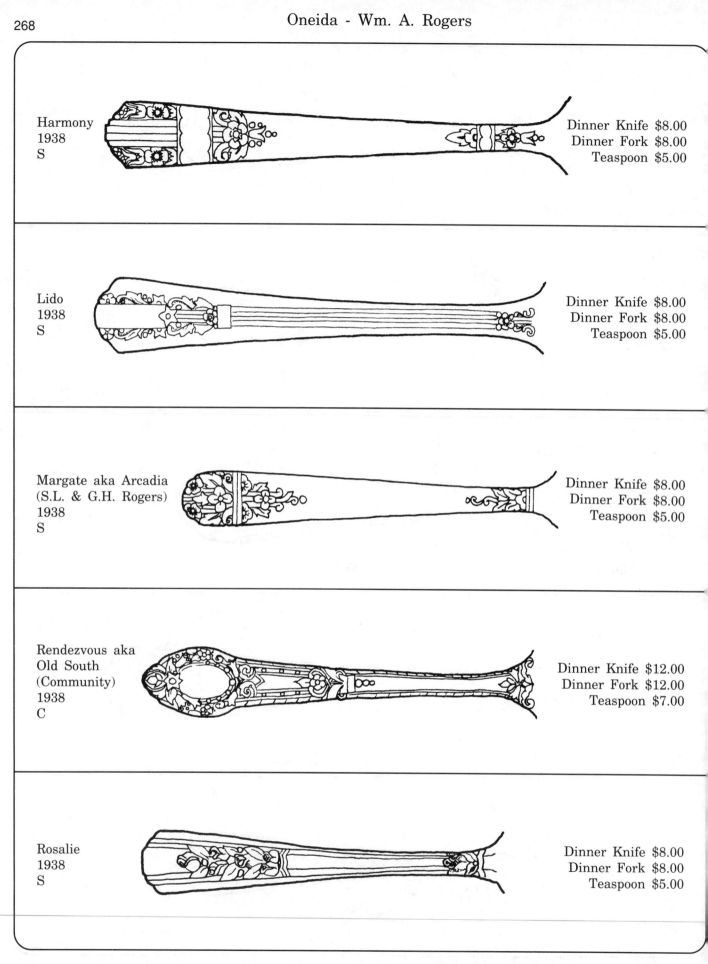

Harmony
1938
S

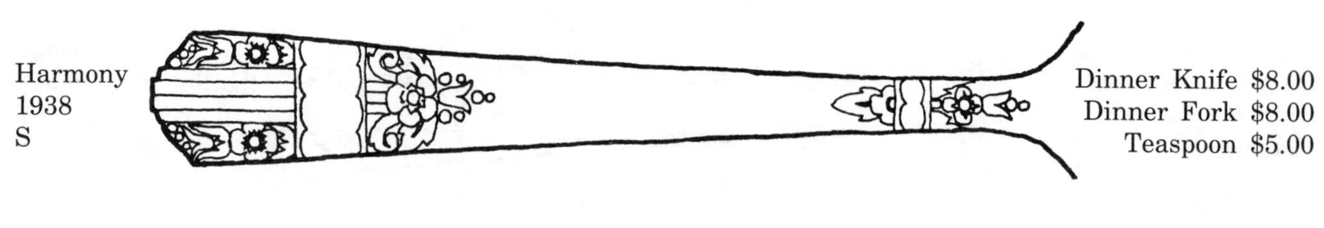

Dinner Knife $8.00
Dinner Fork $8.00
Teaspoon $5.00

Lido
1938
S

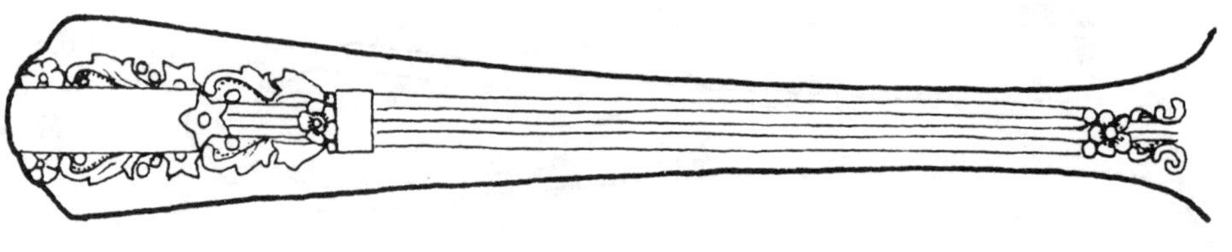

Dinner Knife $8.00
Dinner Fork $8.00
Teaspoon $5.00

Margate aka Arcadia
(S.L. & G.H. Rogers)
1938
S

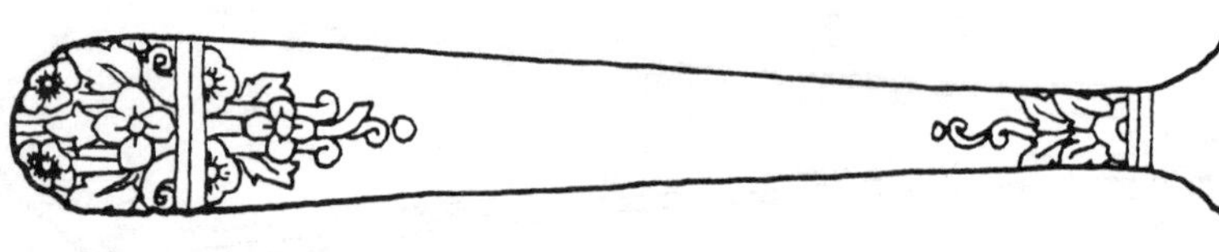

Dinner Knife $8.00
Dinner Fork $8.00
Teaspoon $5.00

Rendezvous aka
Old South
(Community)
1938
C

Dinner Knife $12.00
Dinner Fork $12.00
Teaspoon $7.00

Rosalie
1938
S

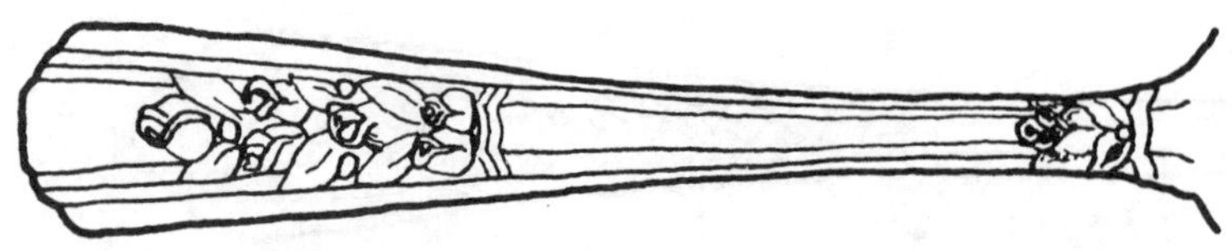

Dinner Knife $8.00
Dinner Fork $8.00
Teaspoon $5.00

Please refer to "How To Use This Book" page 4.

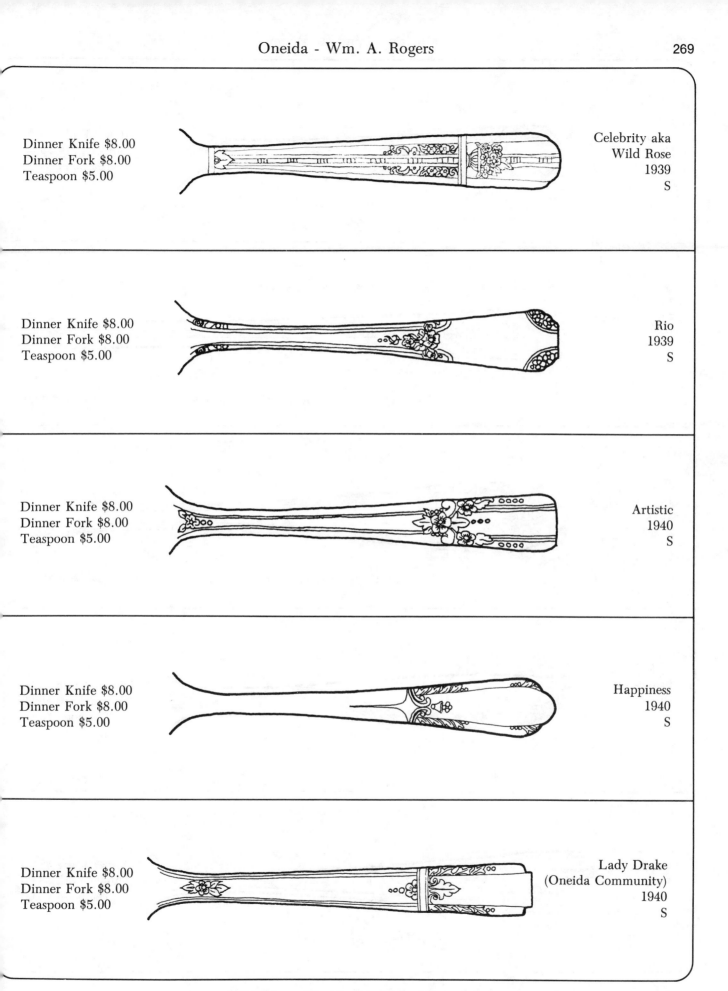

Dinner Knife $8.00 Dinner Fork $8.00 Teaspoon $5.00	Celebrity aka Wild Rose 1939 S
Dinner Knife $8.00 Dinner Fork $8.00 Teaspoon $5.00	Rio 1939 S
Dinner Knife $8.00 Dinner Fork $8.00 Teaspoon $5.00	Artistic 1940 S
Dinner Knife $8.00 Dinner Fork $8.00 Teaspoon $5.00	Happiness 1940 S
Dinner Knife $8.00 Dinner Fork $8.00 Teaspoon $5.00	Lady Drake (Oneida Community) 1940 S

Please refer to "How To Use This Book" page 4.

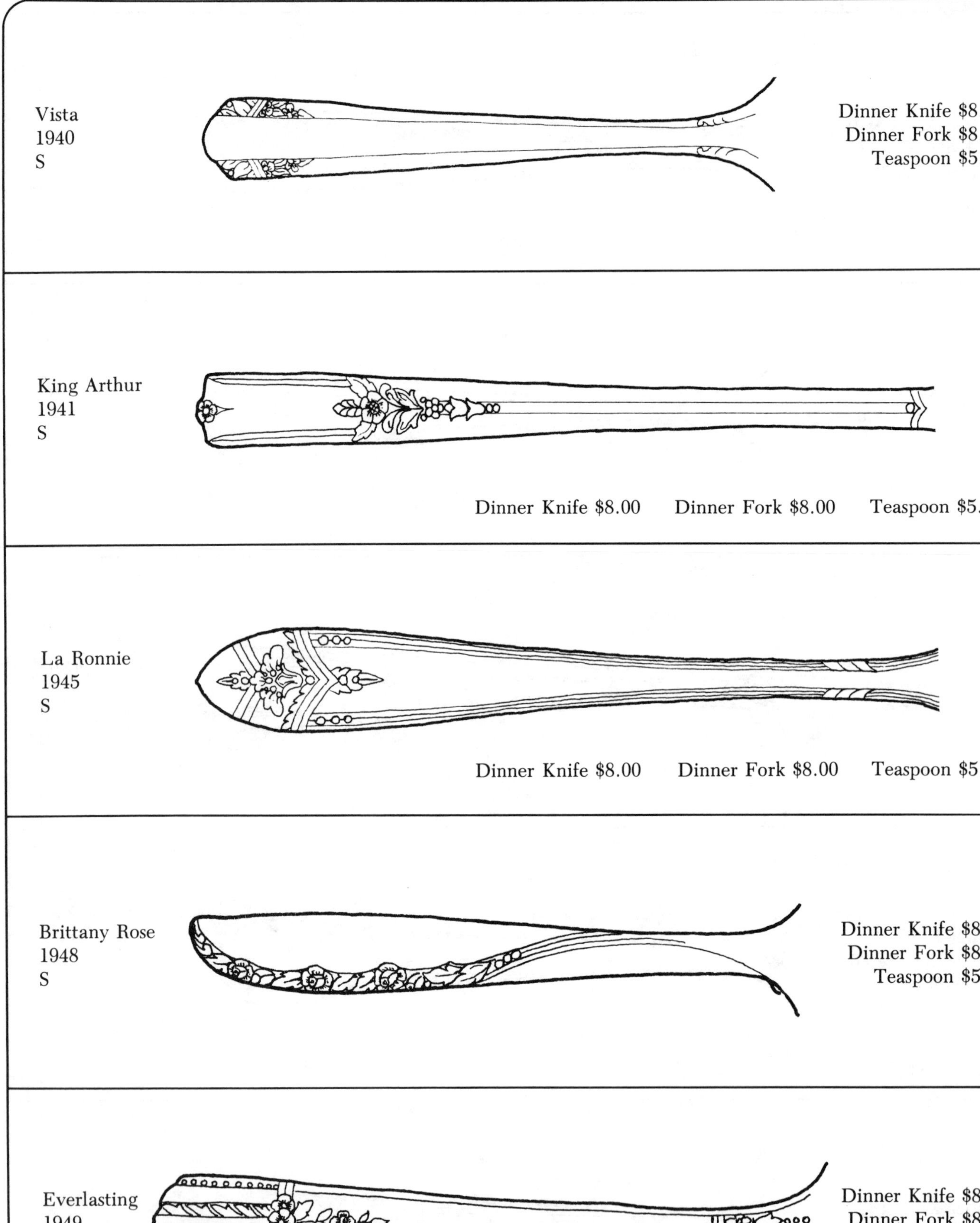

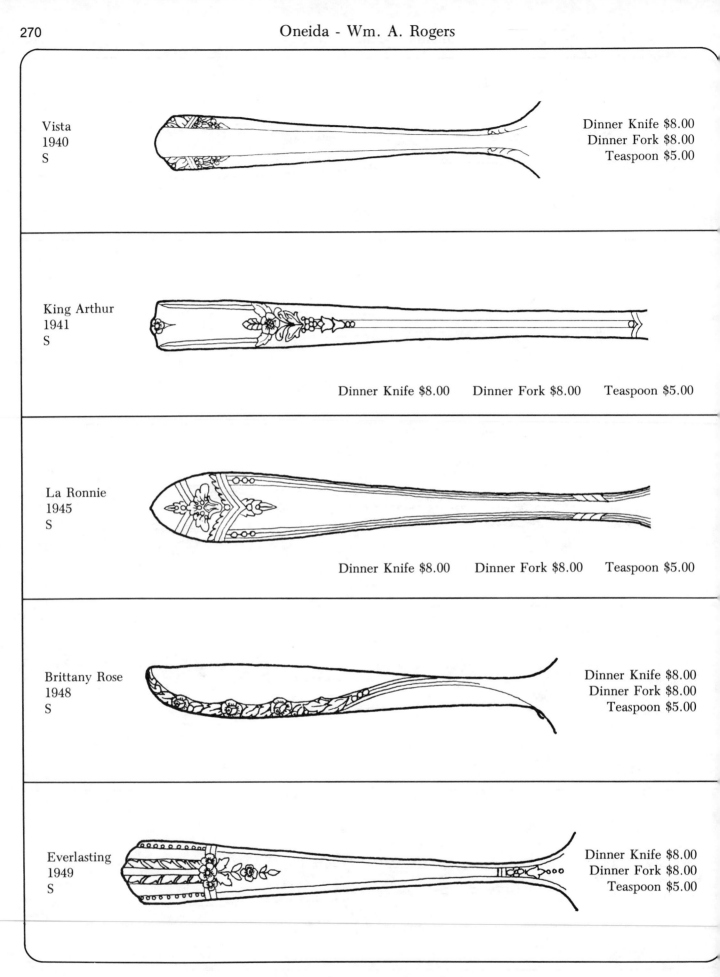

Vista
1940
S

Dinner Knife $8.00
Dinner Fork $8.00
Teaspoon $5.00

King Arthur
1941
S

Dinner Knife $8.00 Dinner Fork $8.00 Teaspoon $5.00

La Ronnie
1945
S

Dinner Knife $8.00 Dinner Fork $8.00 Teaspoon $5.00

Brittany Rose
1948
S

Dinner Knife $8.00
Dinner Fork $8.00
Teaspoon $5.00

Everlasting
1949
S

Dinner Knife $8.00
Dinner Fork $8.00
Teaspoon $5.00

Please refer to "How To Use This Book" page 4.

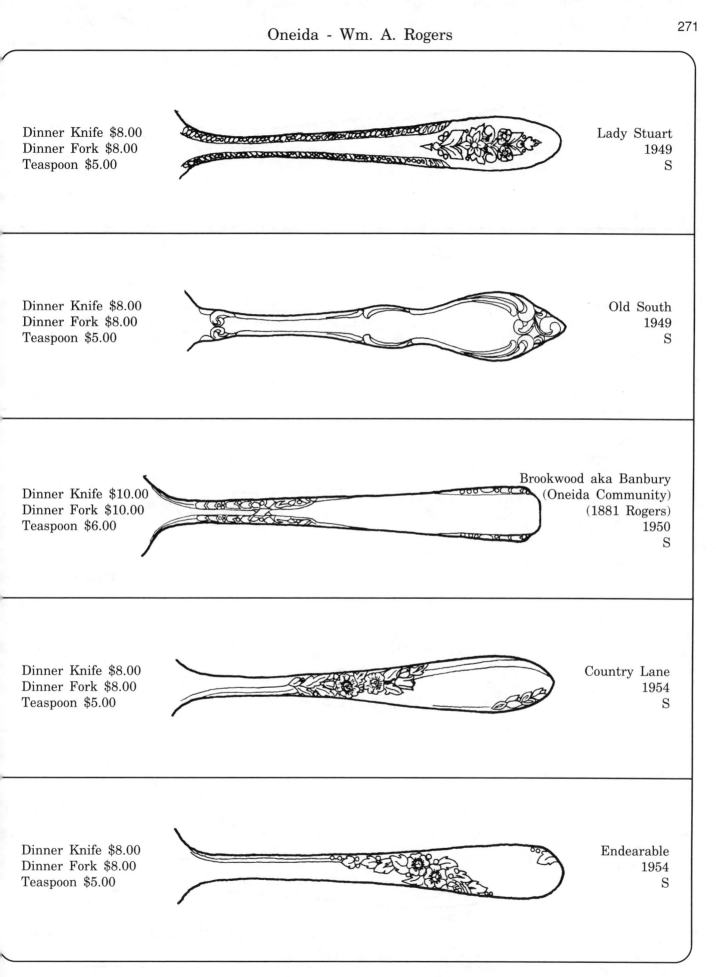

Dinner Knife $8.00
Dinner Fork $8.00
Teaspoon $5.00

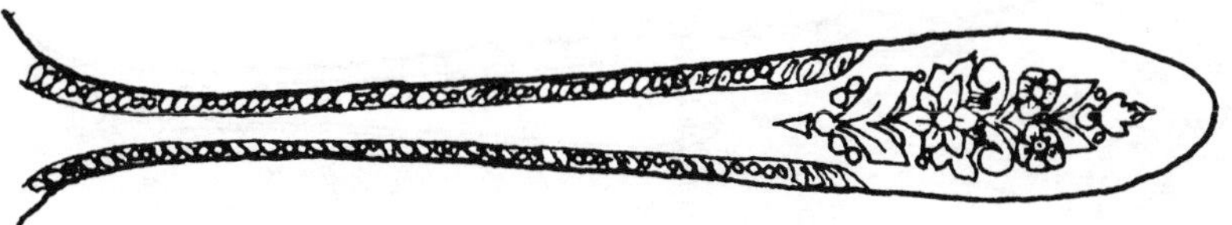

Lady Stuart
1949
S

Dinner Knife $8.00
Dinner Fork $8.00
Teaspoon $5.00

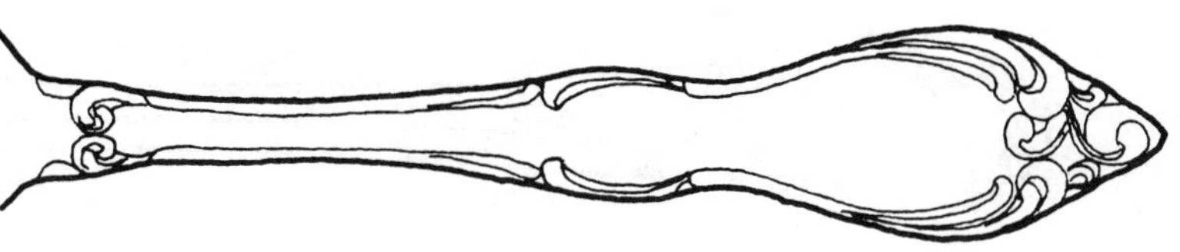

Old South
1949
S

Dinner Knife $10.00
Dinner Fork $10.00
Teaspoon $6.00

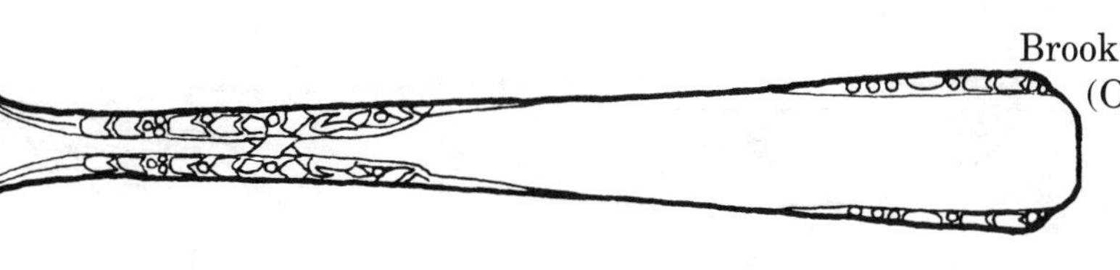

Brookwood aka Banbury
(Oneida Community)
(1881 Rogers)
1950
S

Dinner Knife $8.00
Dinner Fork $8.00
Teaspoon $5.00

Country Lane
1954
S

Dinner Knife $8.00
Dinner Fork $8.00
Teaspoon $5.00

Endearable
1954
S

Please refer to "How To Use This Book" page 4.

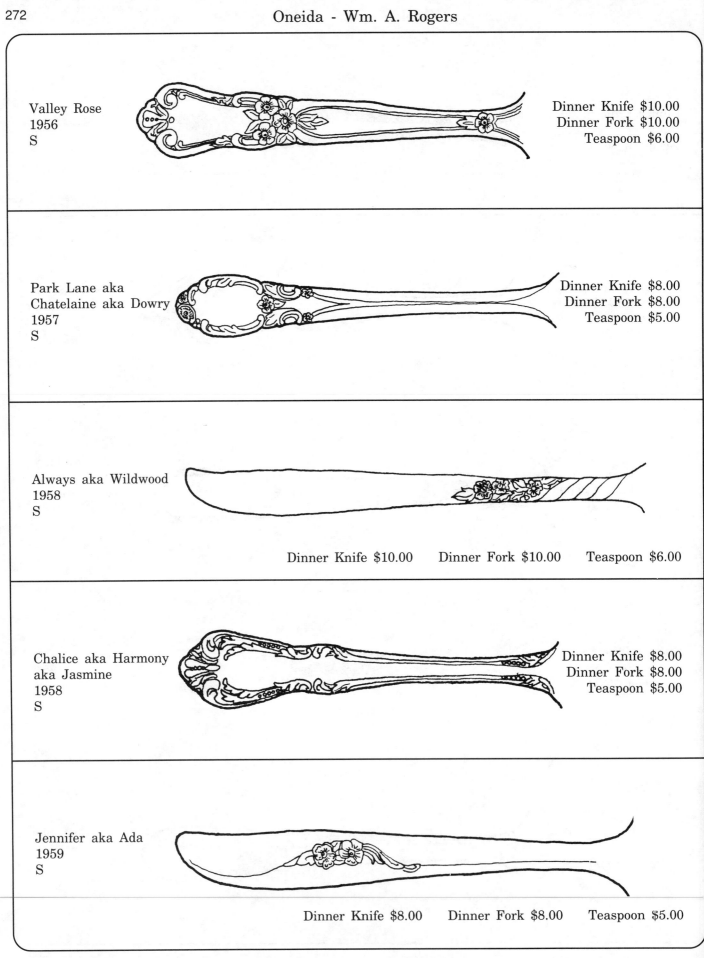

Valley Rose
1956
S

Dinner Knife $10.00
Dinner Fork $10.00
Teaspoon $6.00

Park Lane aka Chatelaine aka Dowry
1957
S

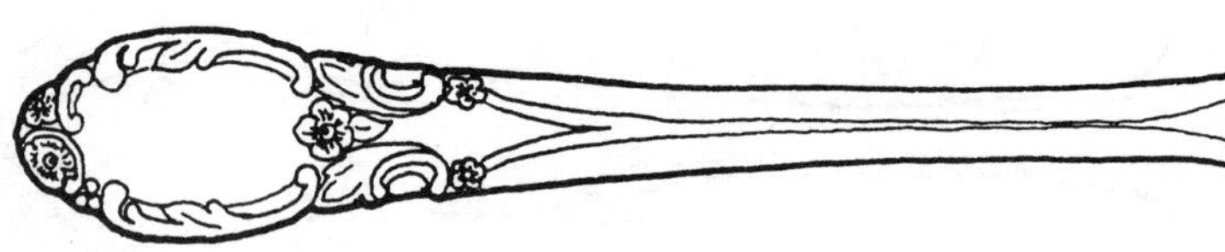

Dinner Knife $8.00
Dinner Fork $8.00
Teaspoon $5.00

Always aka Wildwood
1958
S

Dinner Knife $10.00 Dinner Fork $10.00 Teaspoon $6.00

Chalice aka Harmony aka Jasmine
1958
S

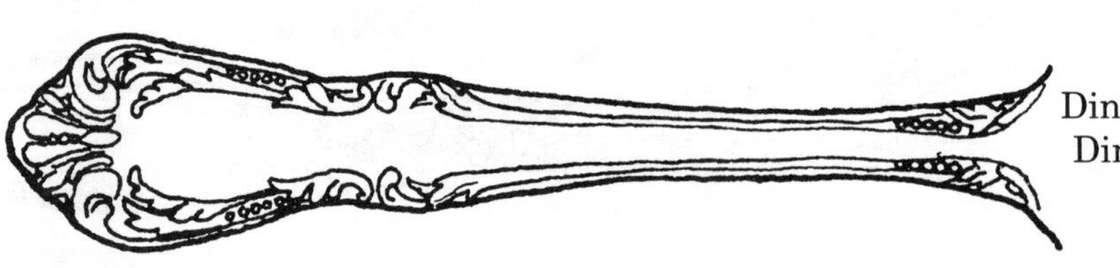

Dinner Knife $8.00
Dinner Fork $8.00
Teaspoon $5.00

Jennifer aka Ada
1959
S

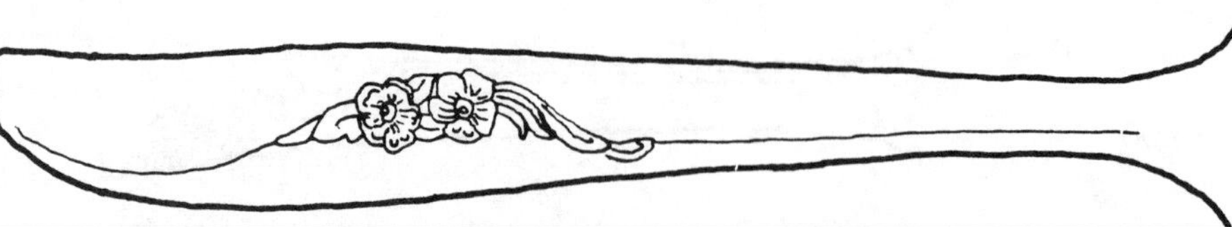

Dinner Knife $8.00 Dinner Fork $8.00 Teaspoon $5.00

Please refer to "How To Use This Book" page 4.

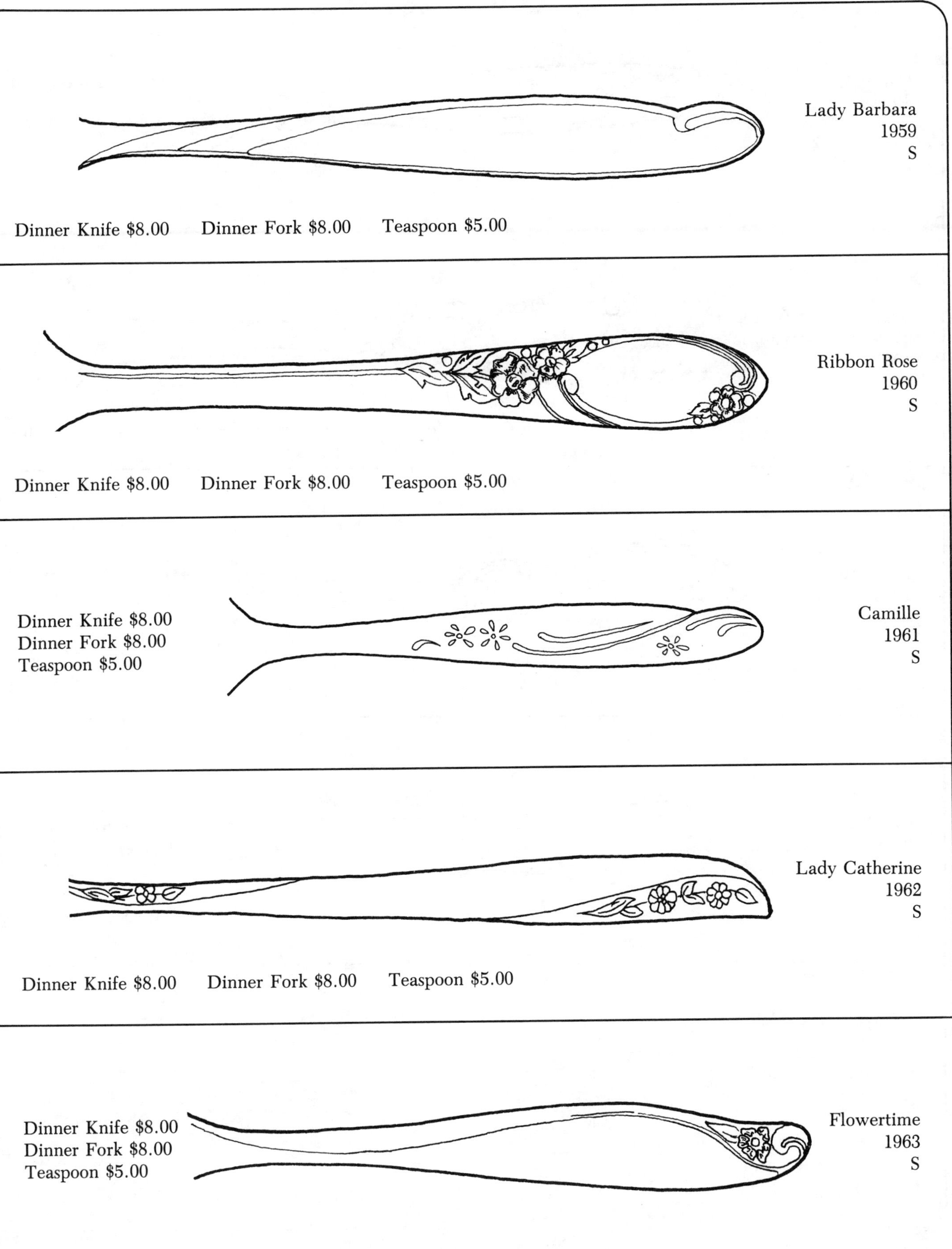

Please refer to "How To Use This Book" page 4.

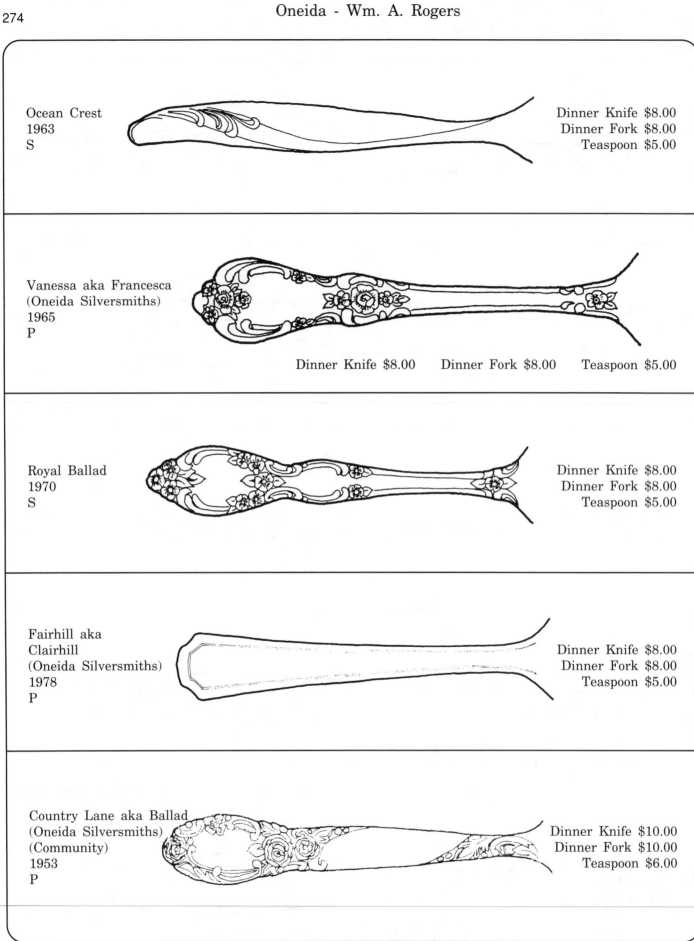

Ocean Crest
1963
S

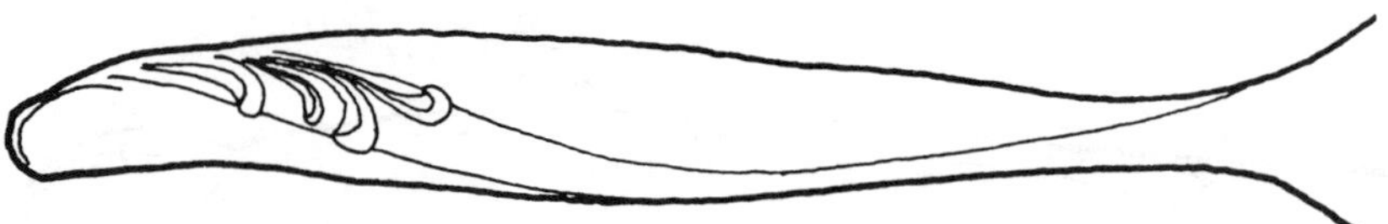

Dinner Knife $8.00
Dinner Fork $8.00
Teaspoon $5.00

Vanessa aka Francesca
(Oneida Silversmiths)
1965
P

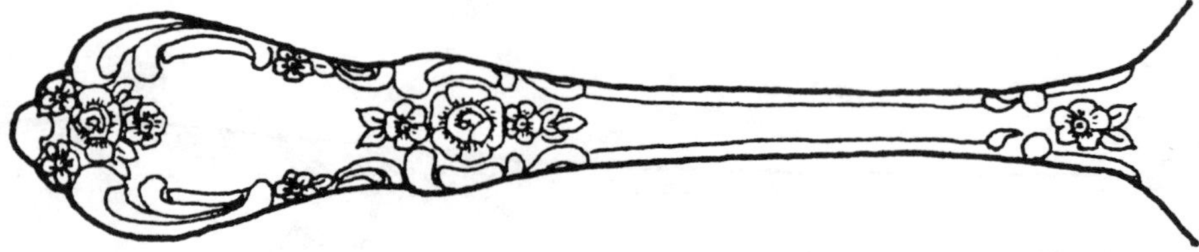

Dinner Knife $8.00 Dinner Fork $8.00 Teaspoon $5.00

Royal Ballad
1970
S

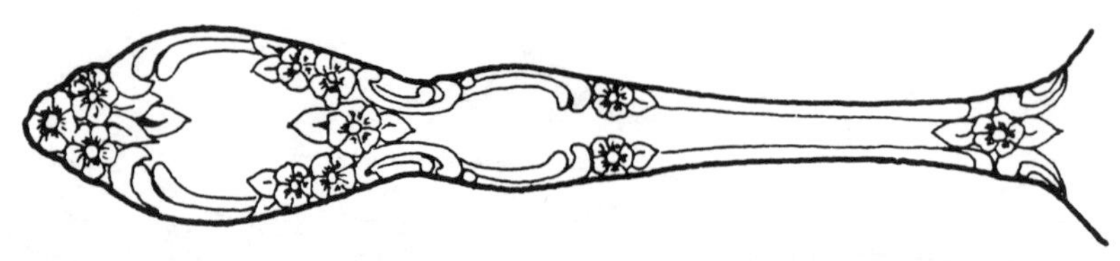

Dinner Knife $8.00
Dinner Fork $8.00
Teaspoon $5.00

Fairhill aka
Clairhill
(Oneida Silversmiths)
1978
P

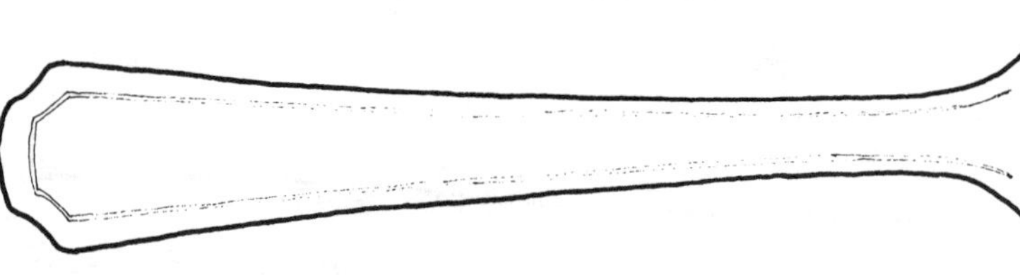

Dinner Knife $8.00
Dinner Fork $8.00
Teaspoon $5.00

Country Lane aka Ballad
(Oneida Silversmiths)
(Community)
1953
P

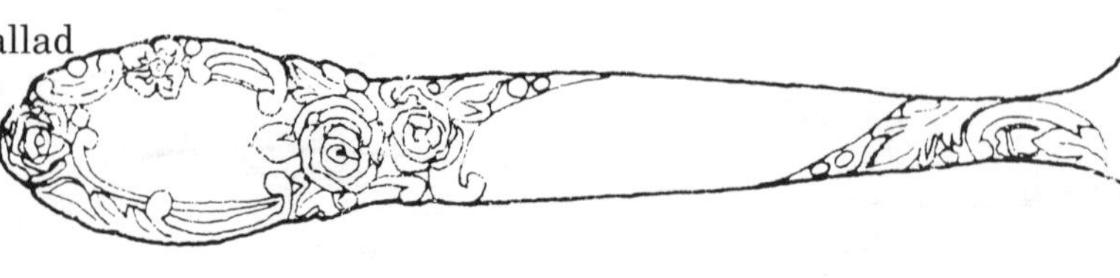

Dinner Knife $10.00
Dinner Fork $10.00
Teaspoon $6.00

Please refer to "How To Use This Book" page 4.

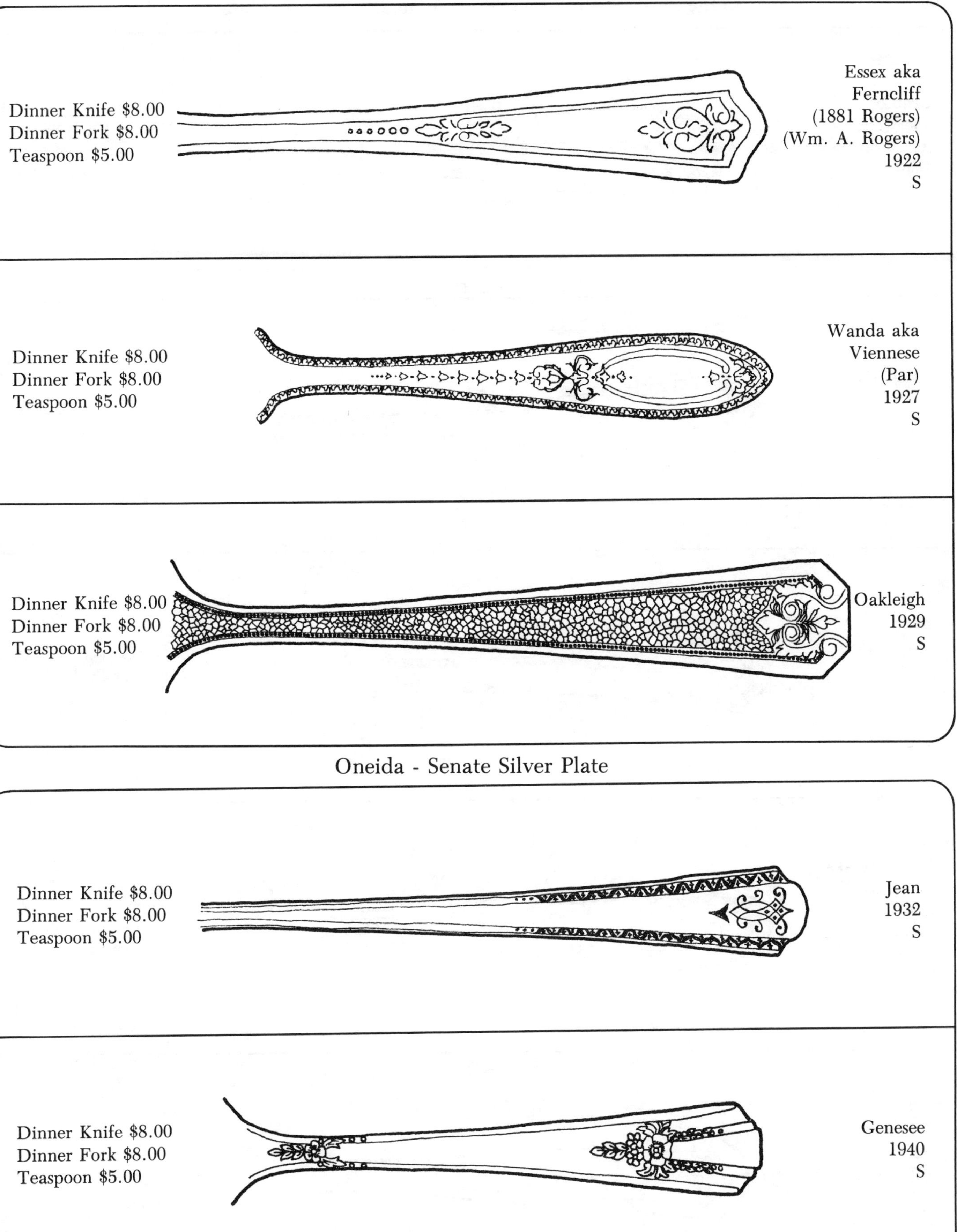

Please refer to "How To Use This Book" page 4.

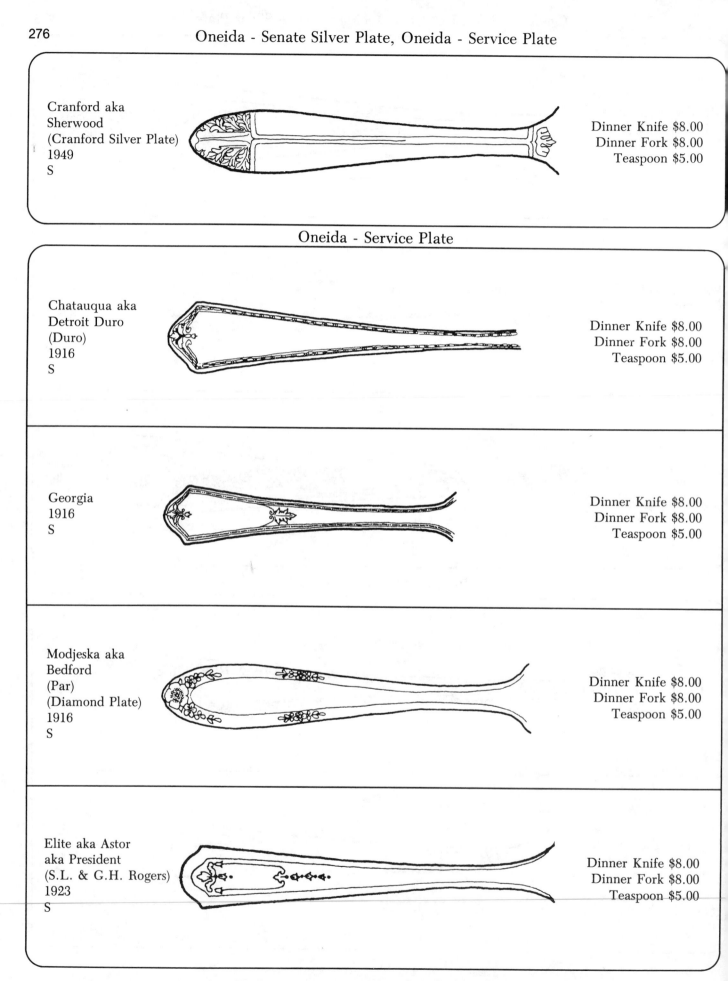

Cranford aka
Sherwood
(Cranford Silver Plate)
1949
S

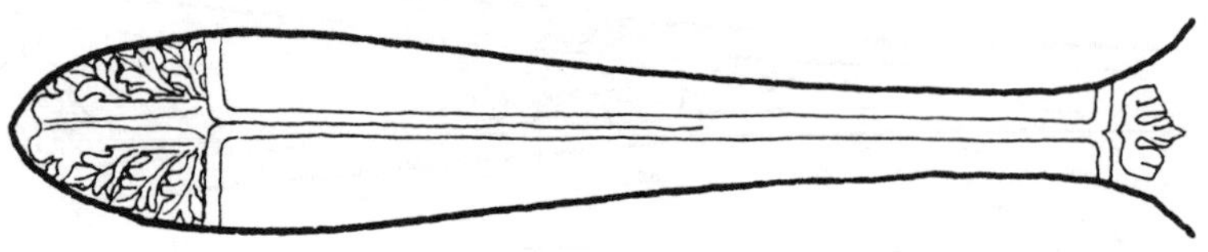

Dinner Knife $8.00
Dinner Fork $8.00
Teaspoon $5.00

Oneida - Service Plate

Chatauqua aka
Detroit Duro
(Duro)
1916
S

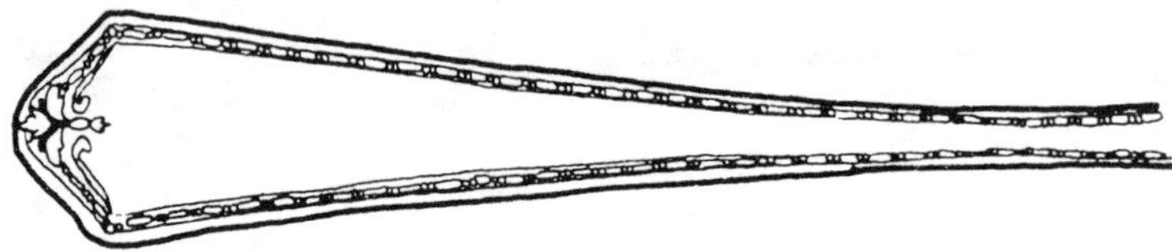

Dinner Knife $8.00
Dinner Fork $8.00
Teaspoon $5.00

Georgia
1916
S

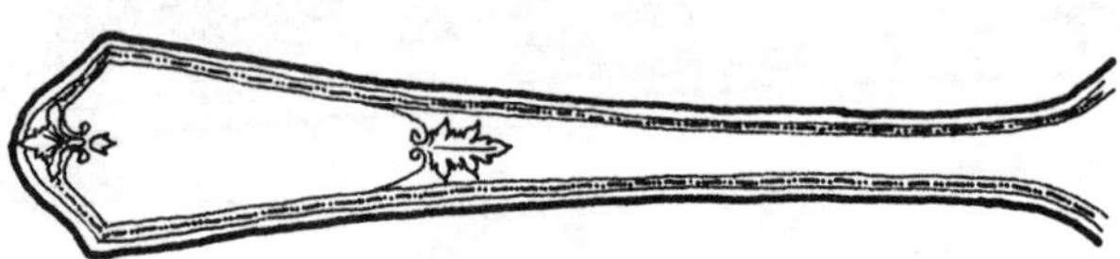

Dinner Knife $8.00
Dinner Fork $8.00
Teaspoon $5.00

Modjeska aka
Bedford
(Par)
(Diamond Plate)
1916
S

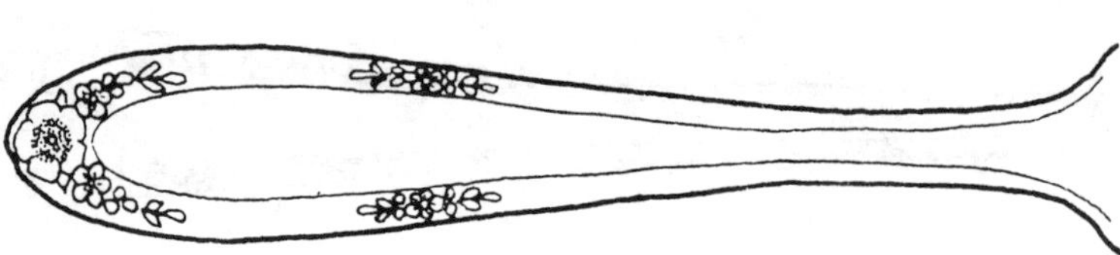

Dinner Knife $8.00
Dinner Fork $8.00
Teaspoon $5.00

Elite aka Astor
aka President
(S.L. & G.H. Rogers)
1923
S

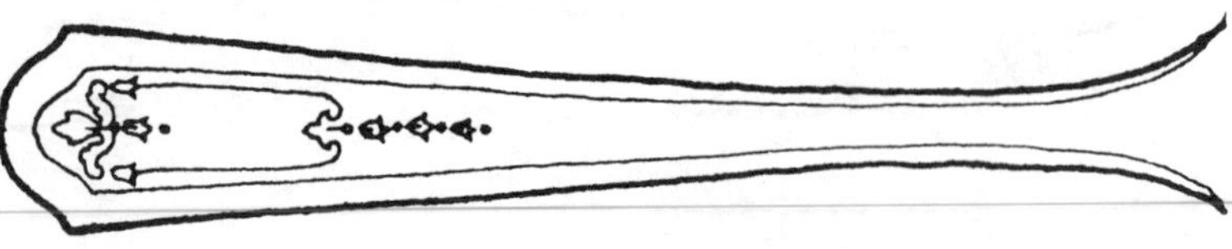

Dinner Knife $8.00
Dinner Fork $8.00
Teaspoon $5.00

Please refer to "How To Use This Book" page 4.

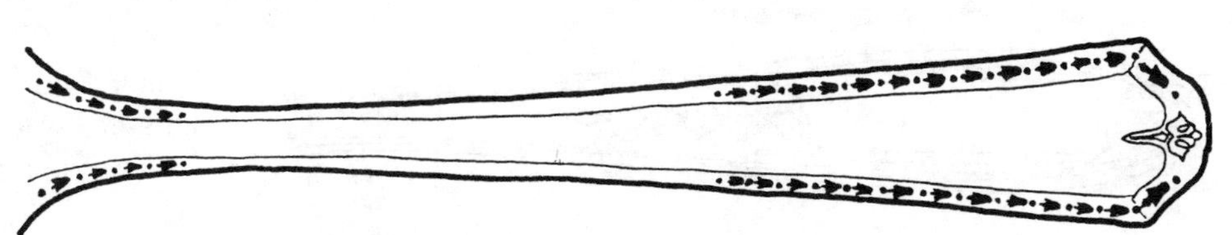

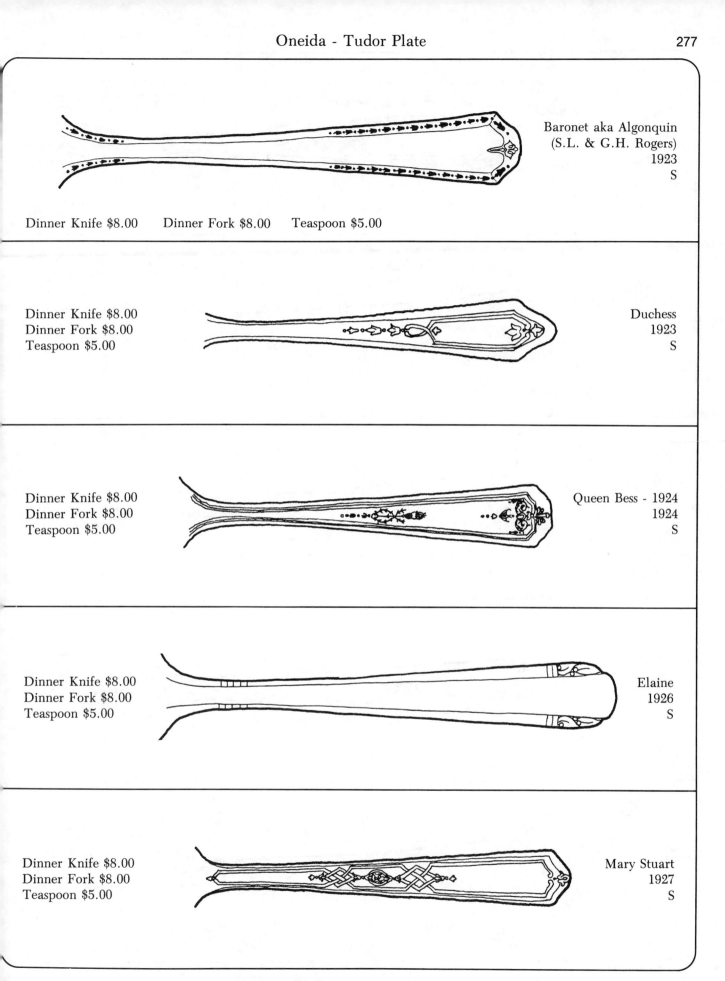

Baronet aka Algonquin
(S.L. & G.H. Rogers)
1923
S

Dinner Knife $8.00 Dinner Fork $8.00 Teaspoon $5.00

Dinner Knife $8.00
Dinner Fork $8.00
Teaspoon $5.00

Duchess
1923
S

Dinner Knife $8.00
Dinner Fork $8.00
Teaspoon $5.00

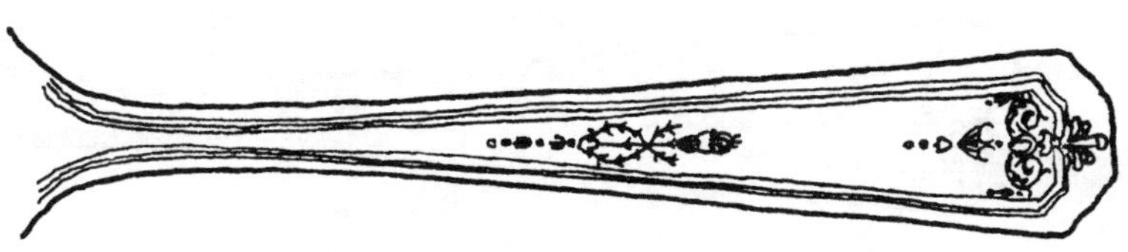

Queen Bess - 1924
1924
S

Dinner Knife $8.00
Dinner Fork $8.00
Teaspoon $5.00

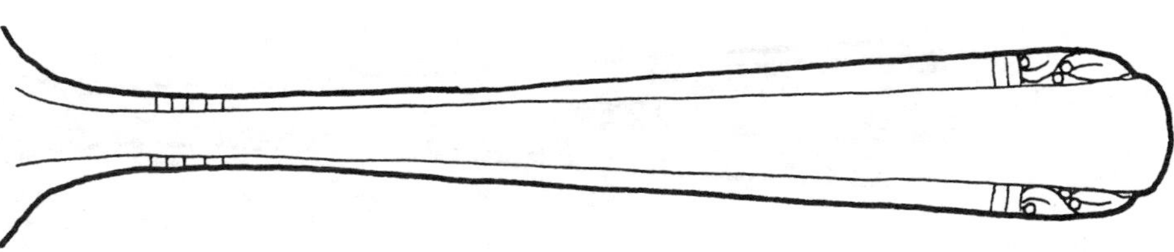

Elaine
1926
S

Dinner Knife $8.00
Dinner Fork $8.00
Teaspoon $5.00

Mary Stuart
1927
S

Please refer to "How To Use This Book" page 4.

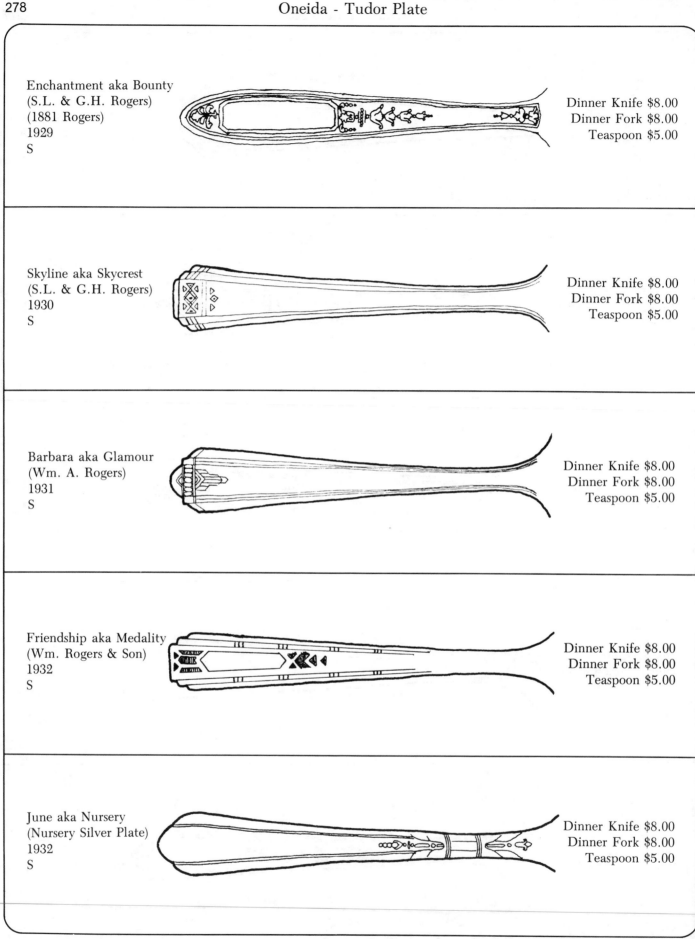

Enchantment aka Bounty
(S.L. & G.H. Rogers)
(1881 Rogers)
1929
S

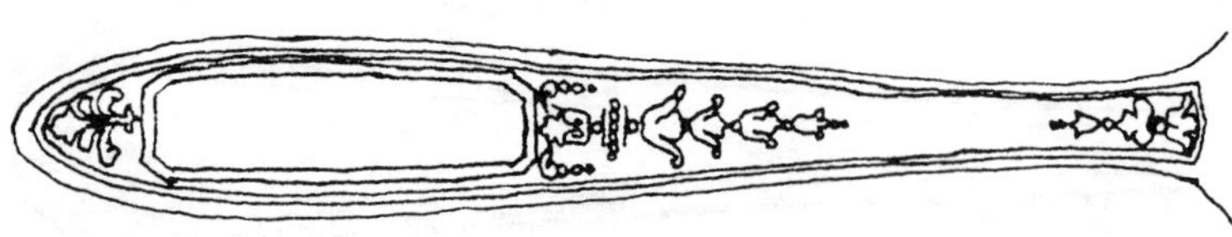

Dinner Knife $8.00
Dinner Fork $8.00
Teaspoon $5.00

Skyline aka Skycrest
(S.L. & G.H. Rogers)
1930
S

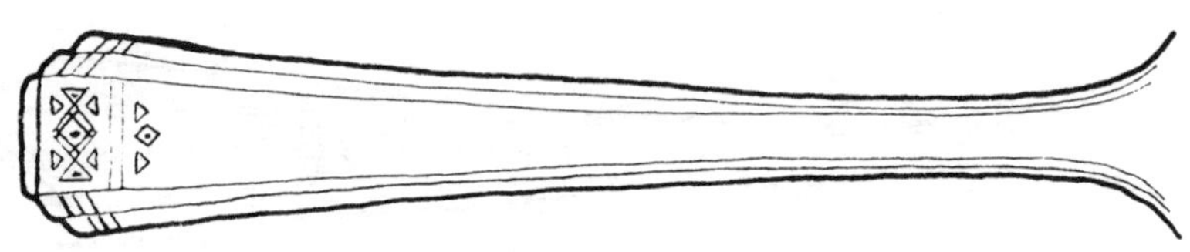

Dinner Knife $8.00
Dinner Fork $8.00
Teaspoon $5.00

Barbara aka Glamour
(Wm. A. Rogers)
1931
S

Dinner Knife $8.00
Dinner Fork $8.00
Teaspoon $5.00

Friendship aka Medality
(Wm. Rogers & Son)
1932
S

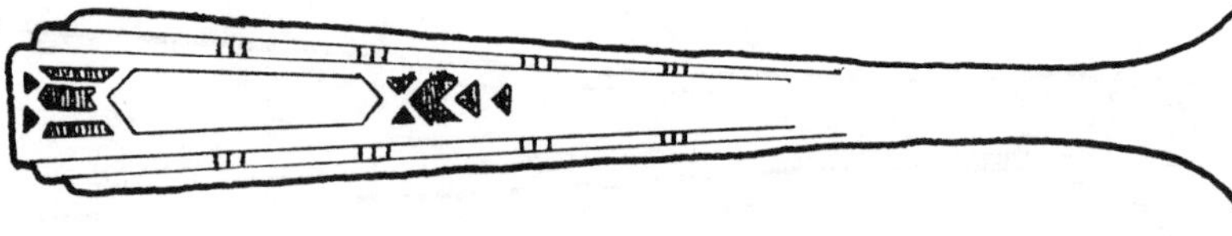

Dinner Knife $8.00
Dinner Fork $8.00
Teaspoon $5.00

June aka Nursery
(Nursery Silver Plate)
1932
S

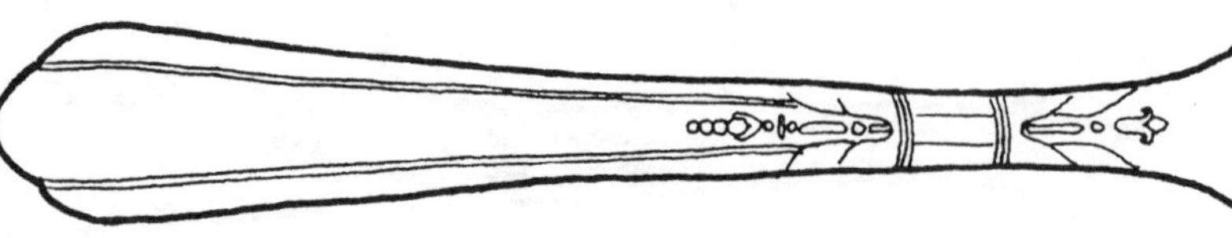

Dinner Knife $8.00
Dinner Fork $8.00
Teaspoon $5.00

Please refer to "How To Use This Book" page 4.

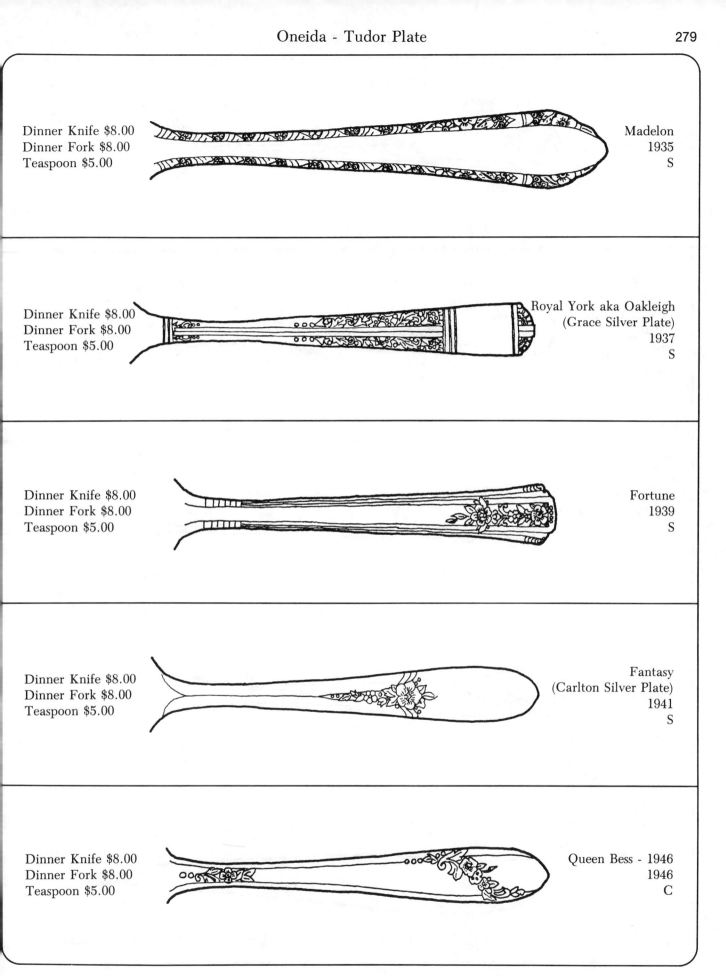

Dinner Knife $8.00
Dinner Fork $8.00
Teaspoon $5.00

Madelon
1935
S

Dinner Knife $8.00
Dinner Fork $8.00
Teaspoon $5.00

Royal York aka Oakleigh
(Grace Silver Plate)
1937
S

Dinner Knife $8.00
Dinner Fork $8.00
Teaspoon $5.00

Fortune
1939
S

Dinner Knife $8.00
Dinner Fork $8.00
Teaspoon $5.00

Fantasy
(Carlton Silver Plate)
1941
S

Dinner Knife $8.00
Dinner Fork $8.00
Teaspoon $5.00

Queen Bess - 1946
1946
C

Please refer to "How To Use This Book" page 4.

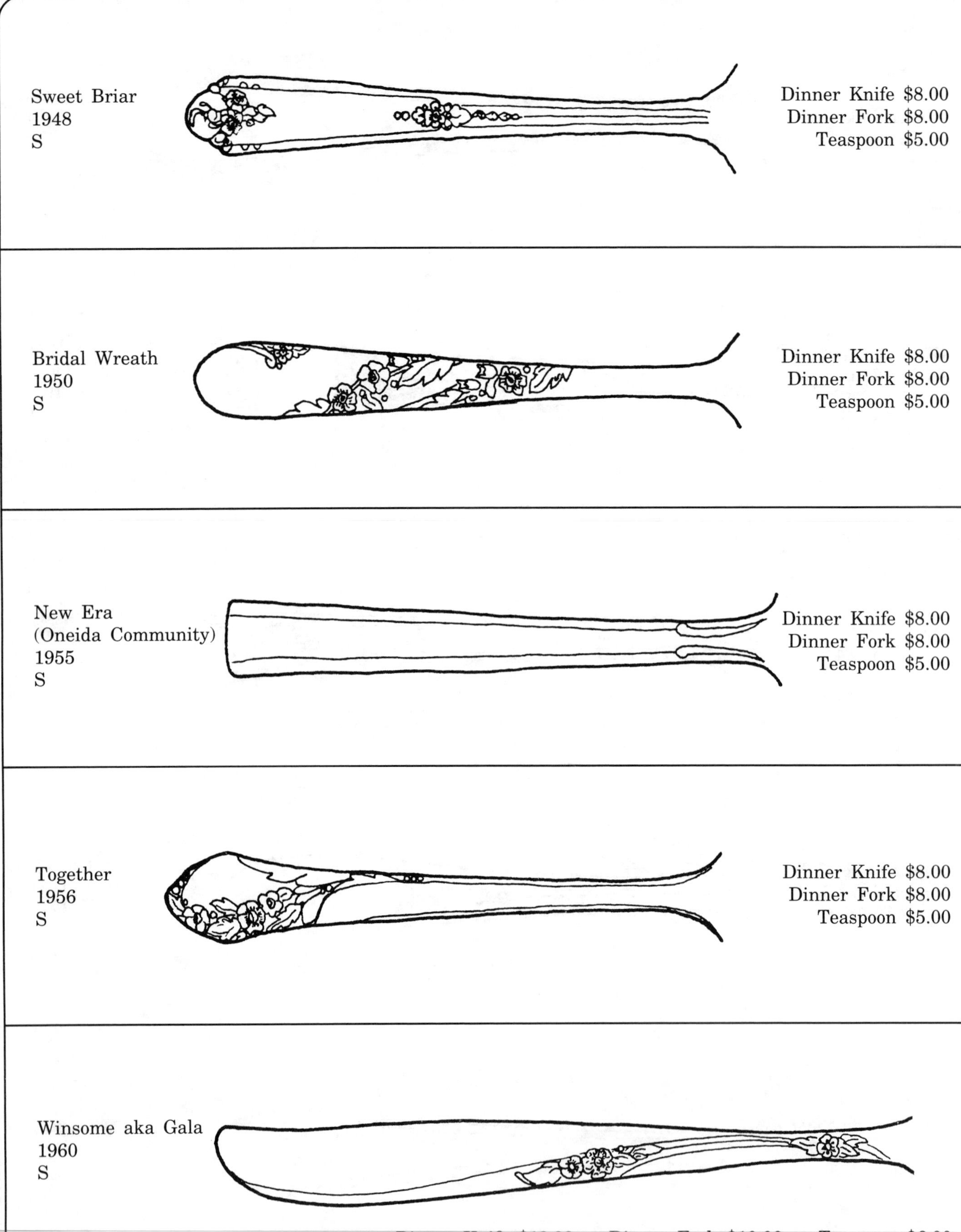

Please refer to "How To Use This Book" page 4.

Thin market.

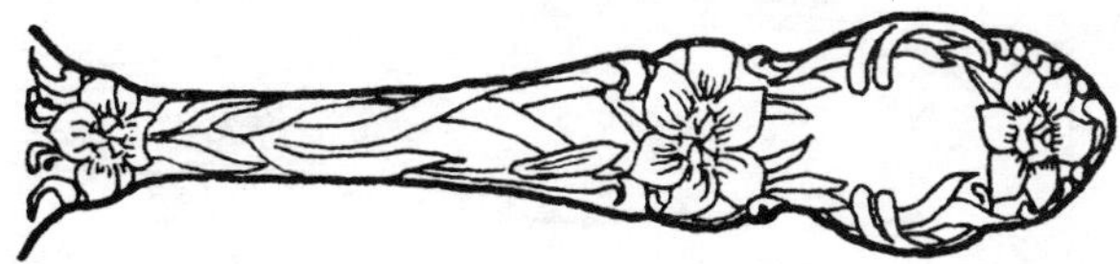

Shraffts
1922
S

Oneida - Vernon Silver Plate

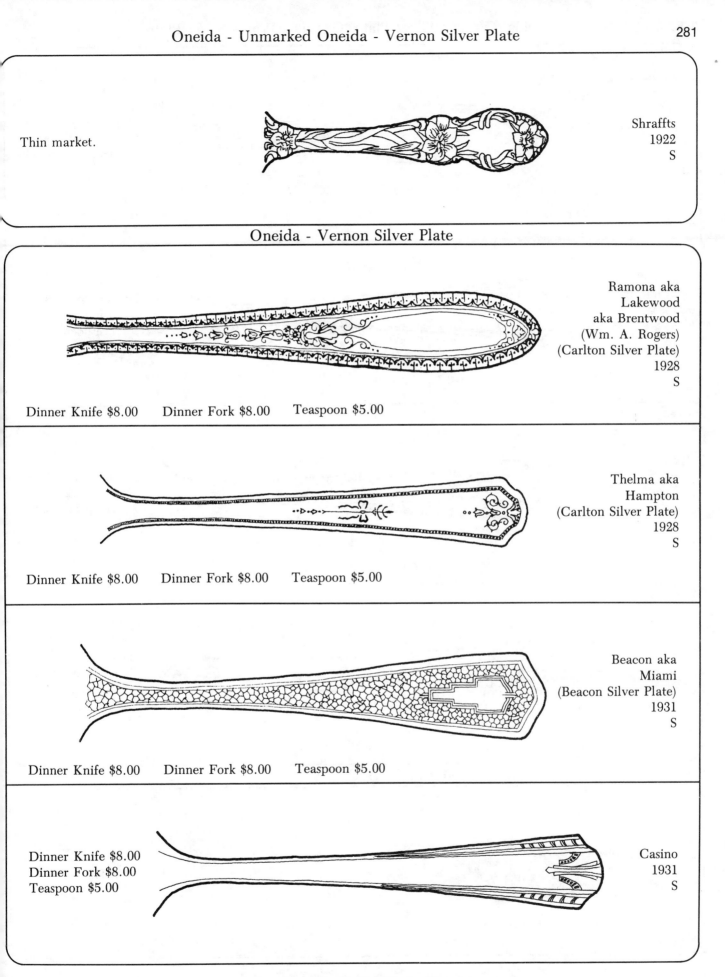

Ramona aka
Lakewood
aka Brentwood
(Wm. A. Rogers)
(Carlton Silver Plate)
1928
S

Dinner Knife $8.00 Dinner Fork $8.00 Teaspoon $5.00

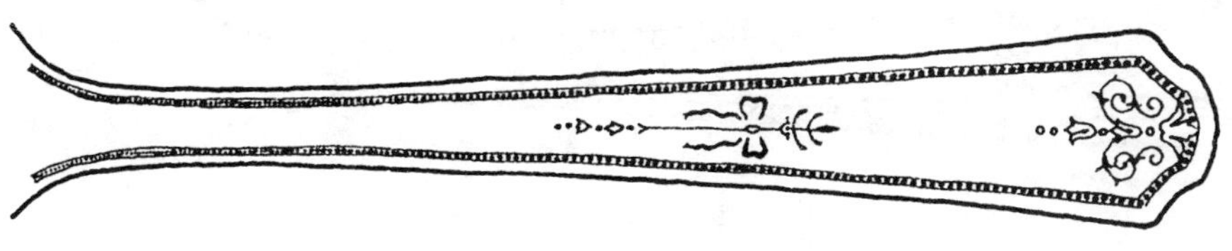

Thelma aka
Hampton
(Carlton Silver Plate)
1928
S

Dinner Knife $8.00 Dinner Fork $8.00 Teaspoon $5.00

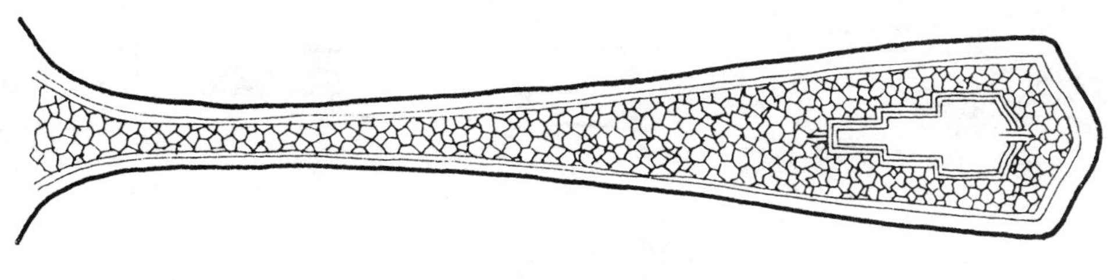

Beacon aka
Miami
(Beacon Silver Plate)
1931
S

Dinner Knife $8.00 Dinner Fork $8.00 Teaspoon $5.00

Dinner Knife $8.00
Dinner Fork $8.00
Teaspoon $5.00

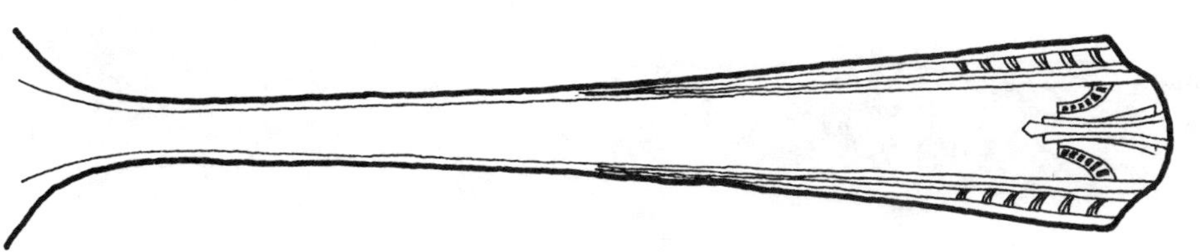

Casino
1931
S

Please refer to "How To Use This Book" page 4.

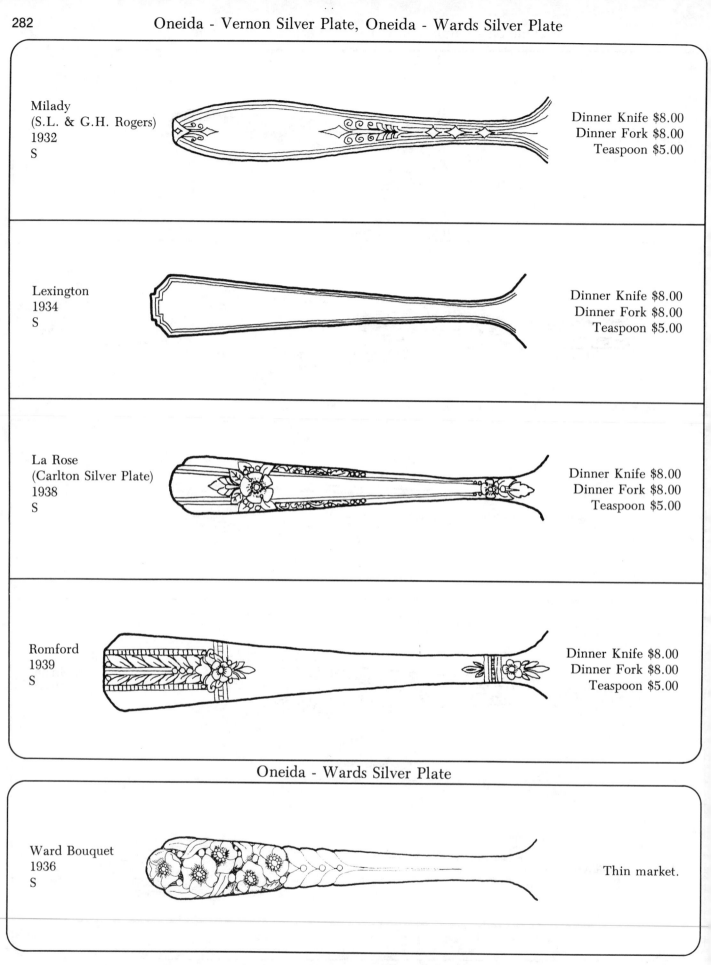

Milady
(S.L. & G.H. Rogers)
1932
S

Dinner Knife $8.00
Dinner Fork $8.00
Teaspoon $5.00

Lexington
1934
S

Dinner Knife $8.00
Dinner Fork $8.00
Teaspoon $5.00

La Rose
(Carlton Silver Plate)
1938
S

Dinner Knife $8.00
Dinner Fork $8.00
Teaspoon $5.00

Romford
1939
S

Dinner Knife $8.00
Dinner Fork $8.00
Teaspoon $5.00

Oneida - Wards Silver Plate

Ward Bouquet
1936
S

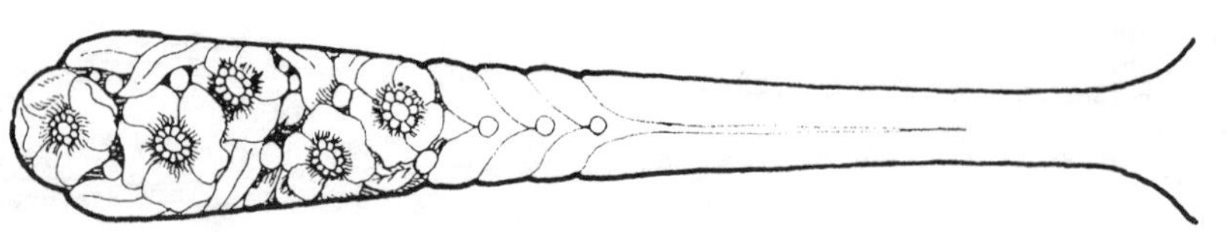

Thin market.

Please refer to "How To Use This Book" page 4.

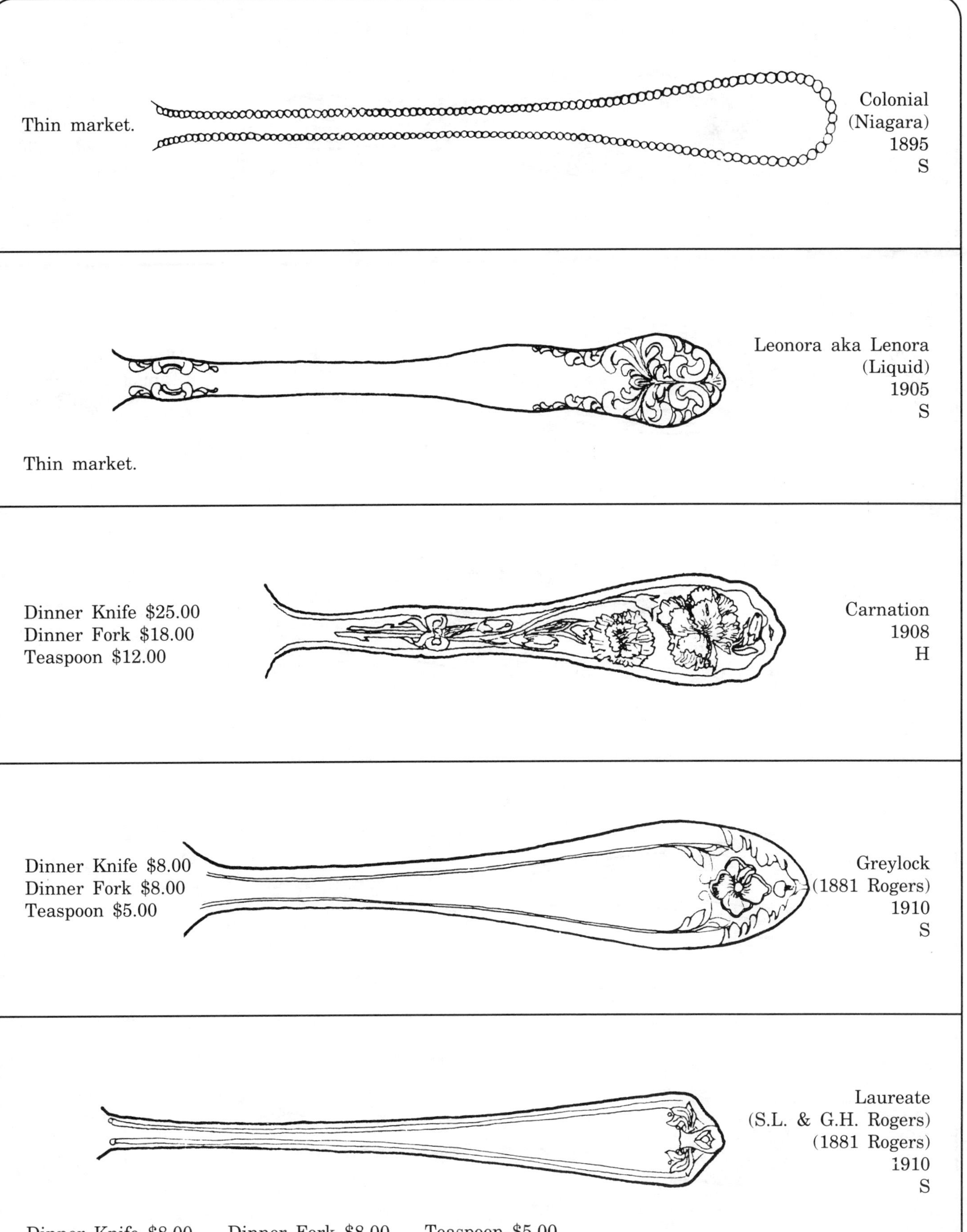

Thin market.

Colonial
(Niagara)
1895
S

Leonora aka Lenora
(Liquid)
1905
S

Thin market.

Dinner Knife $25.00
Dinner Fork $18.00
Teaspoon $12.00

Carnation
1908
H

Dinner Knife $8.00
Dinner Fork $8.00
Teaspoon $5.00

Greylock
(1881 Rogers)
1910
S

Laureate
(S.L. & G.H. Rogers)
(1881 Rogers)
1910
S

Dinner Knife $8.00 Dinner Fork $8.00 Teaspoon $5.00

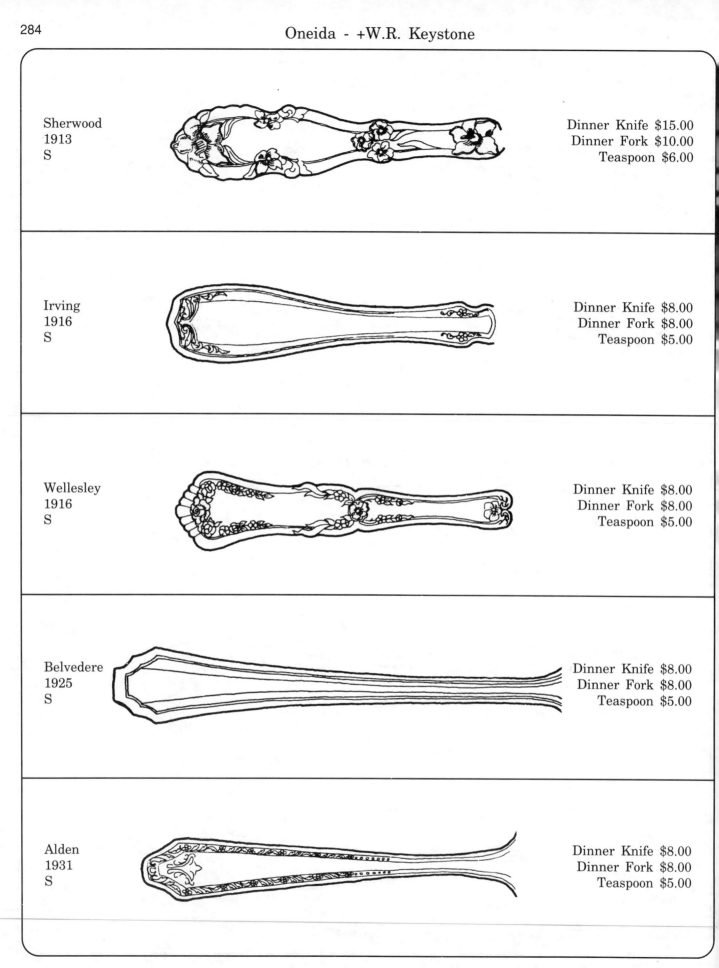

Sherwood
1913
S

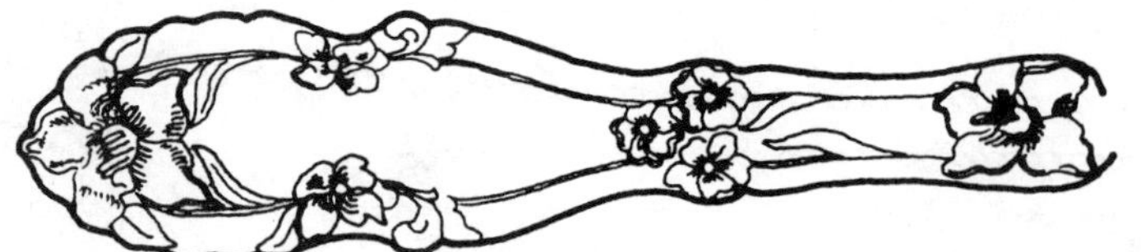

Dinner Knife $15.00
Dinner Fork $10.00
Teaspoon $6.00

Irving
1916
S

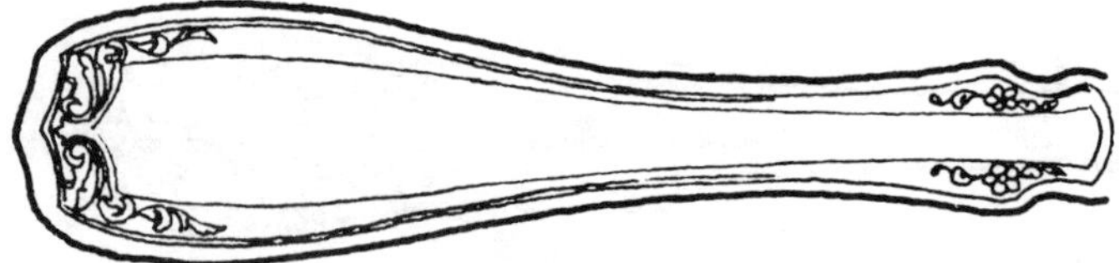

Dinner Knife $8.00
Dinner Fork $8.00
Teaspoon $5.00

Wellesley
1916
S

Dinner Knife $8.00
Dinner Fork $8.00
Teaspoon $5.00

Belvedere
1925
S

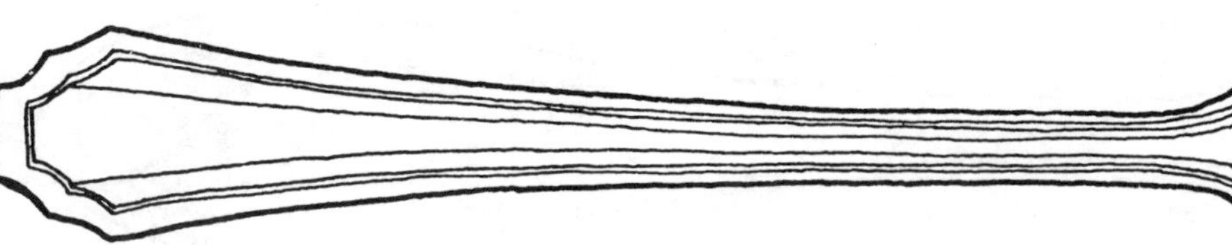

Dinner Knife $8.00
Dinner Fork $8.00
Teaspoon $5.00

Alden
1931
S

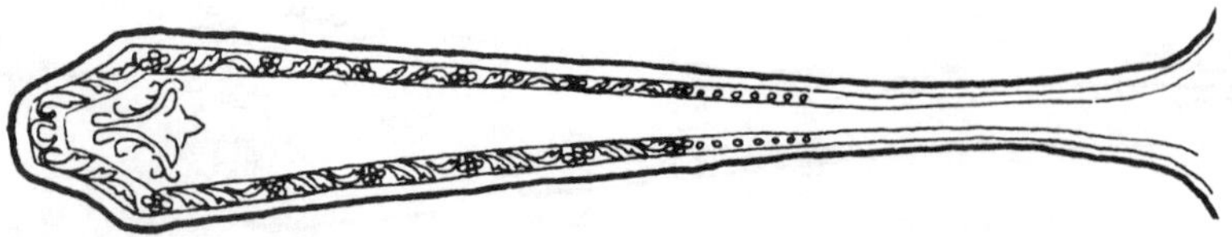

Dinner Knife $8.00
Dinner Fork $8.00
Teaspoon $5.00

Please refer to "How To Use This Book" page 4.

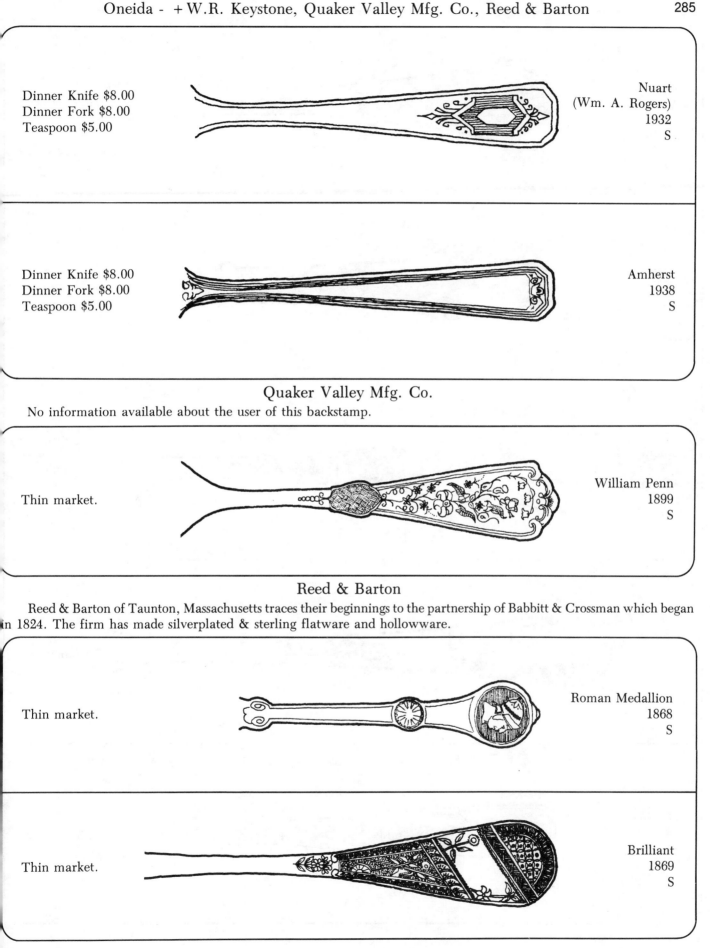

Dinner Knife $8.00
Dinner Fork $8.00
Teaspoon $5.00

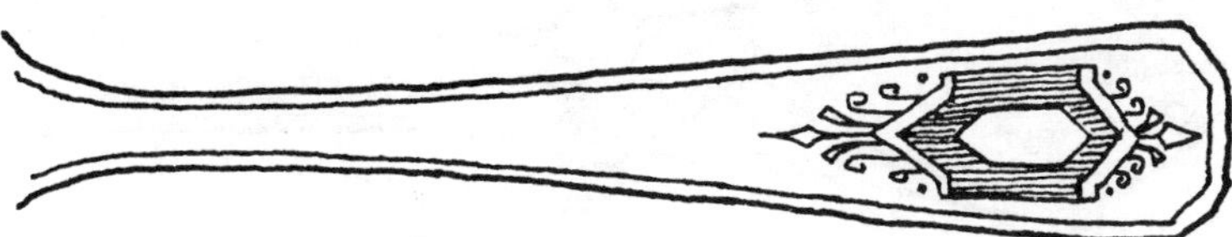

Nuart
(Wm. A. Rogers)
1932
S

Dinner Knife $8.00
Dinner Fork $8.00
Teaspoon $5.00

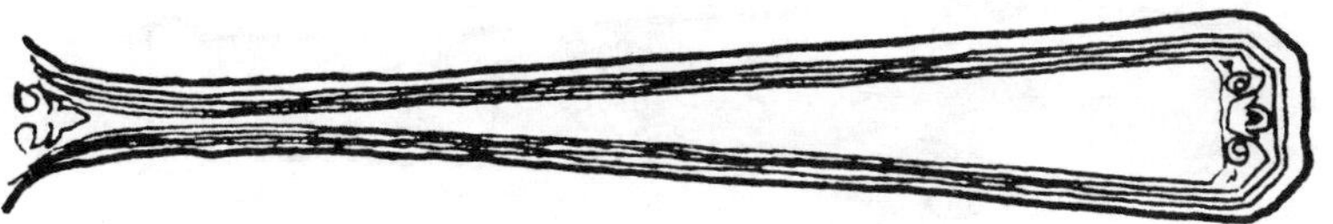

Amherst
1938
S

Quaker Valley Mfg. Co.

No information available about the user of this backstamp.

Thin market.

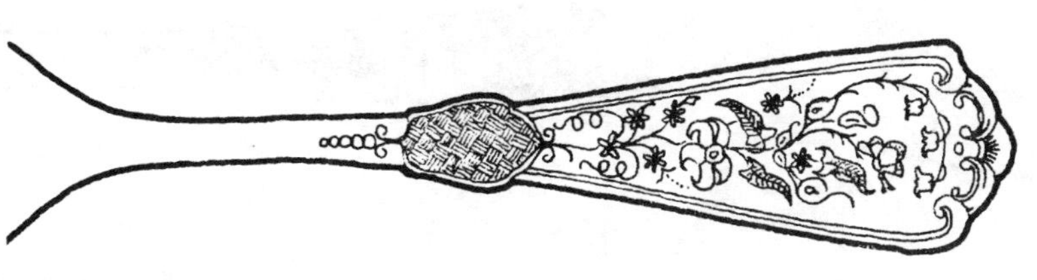

William Penn
1899
S

Reed & Barton

Reed & Barton of Taunton, Massachusetts traces their beginnings to the partnership of Babbitt & Crossman which began in 1824. The firm has made silverplated & sterling flatware and hollowware.

Thin market.

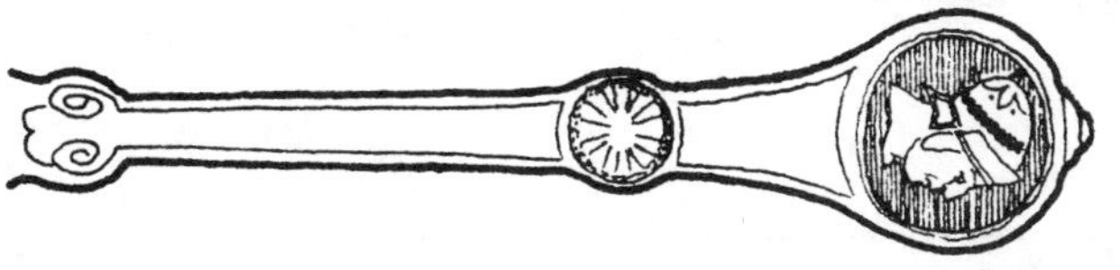

Roman Medallion
1868
S

Thin market.

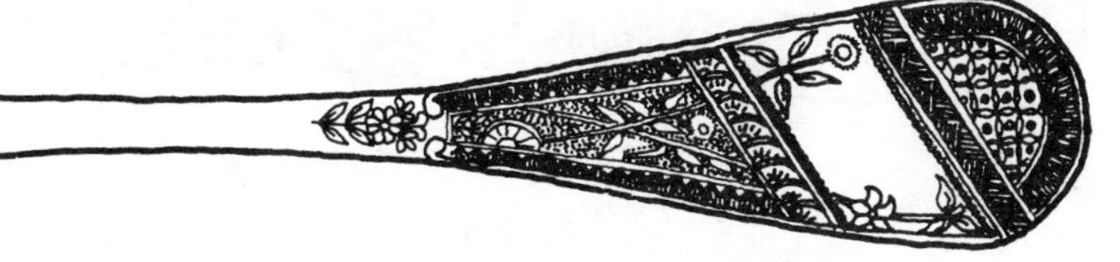

Brilliant
1869
S

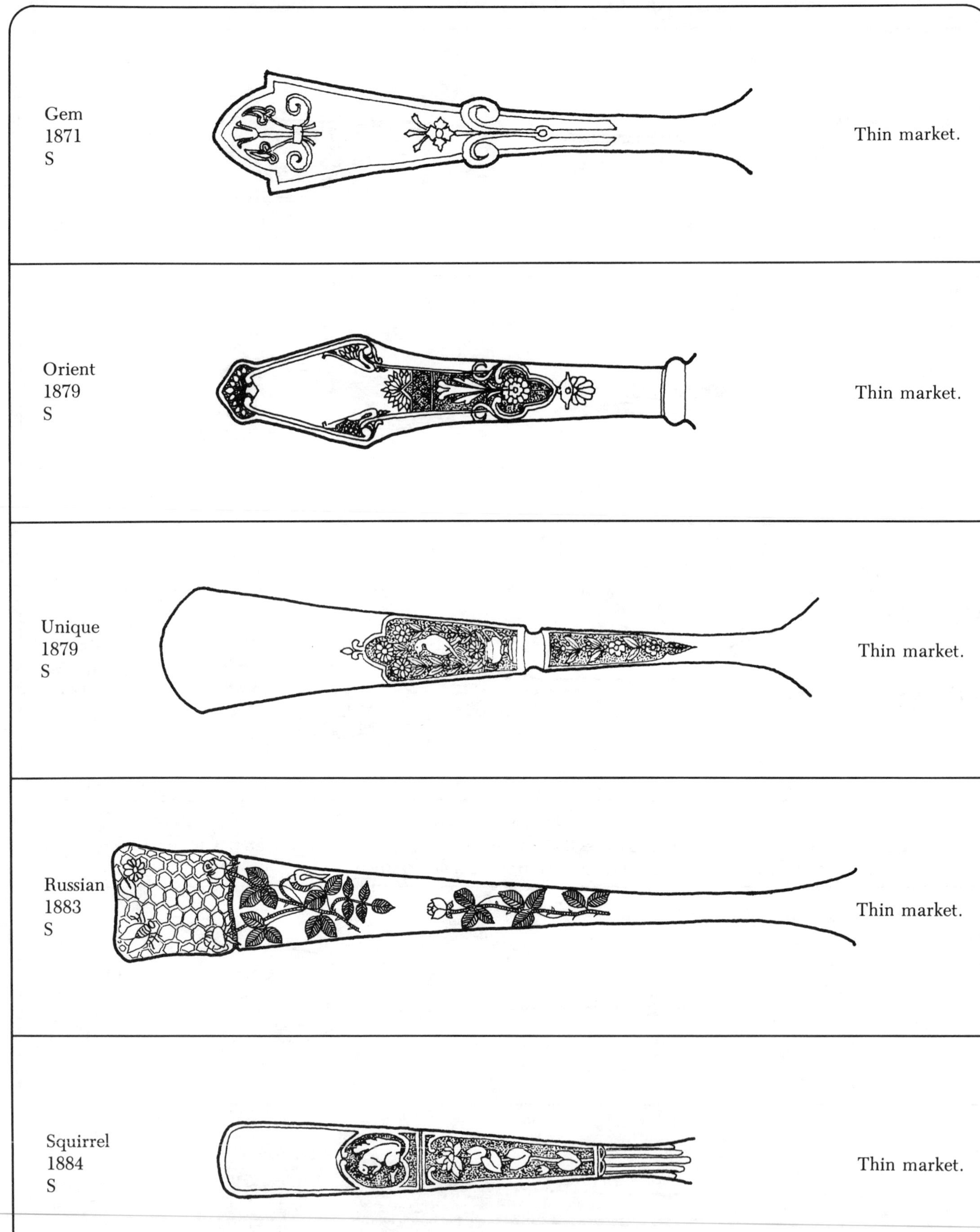

Please refer to "How To Use This Book" page 4.

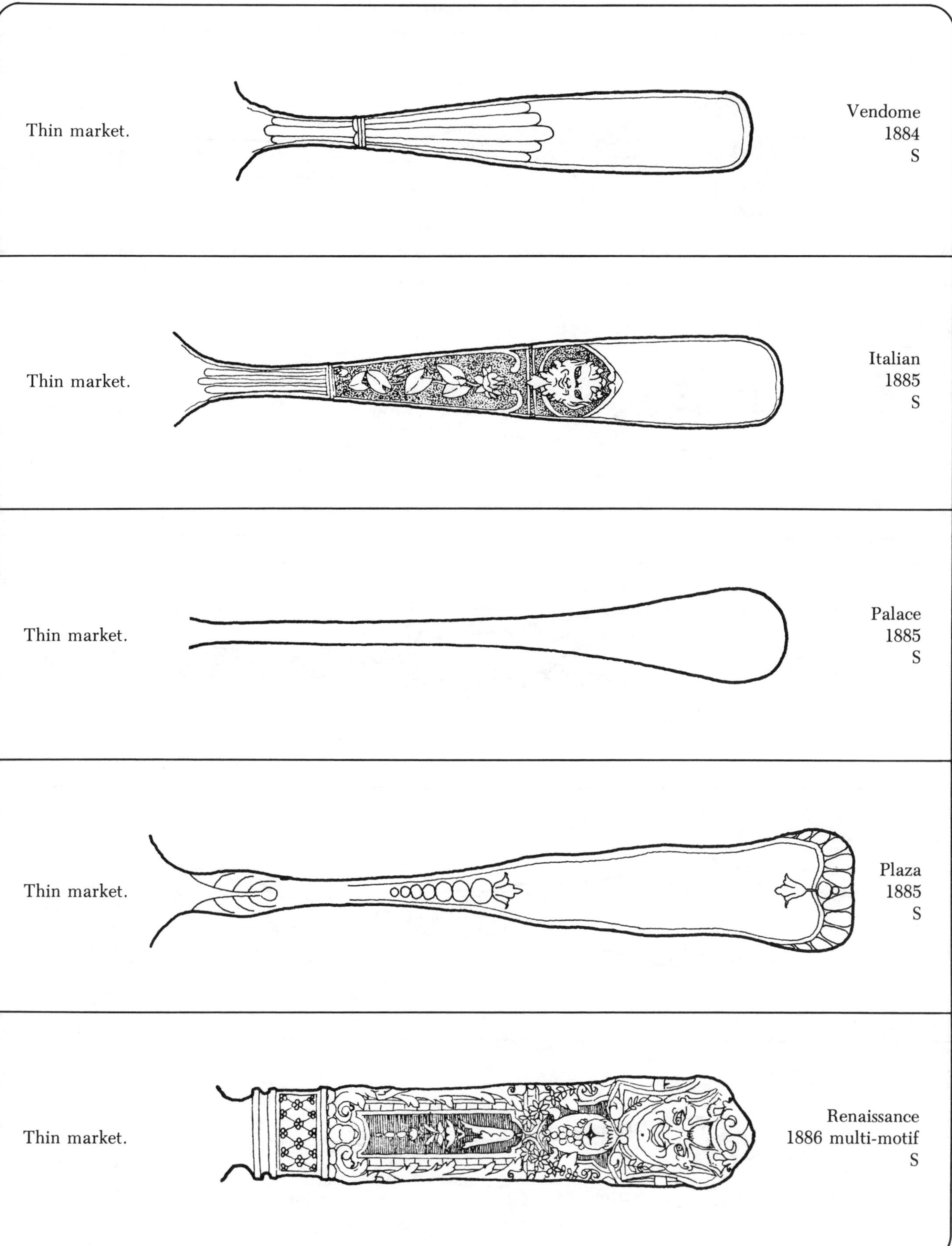

Thin market.

Vendome
1884
S

Thin market.

Italian
1885
S

Thin market.

Palace
1885
S

Thin market.

Plaza
1885
S

Thin market.

Renaissance
1886 multi-motif
S

Please refer to "How To Use This Book" page 4.

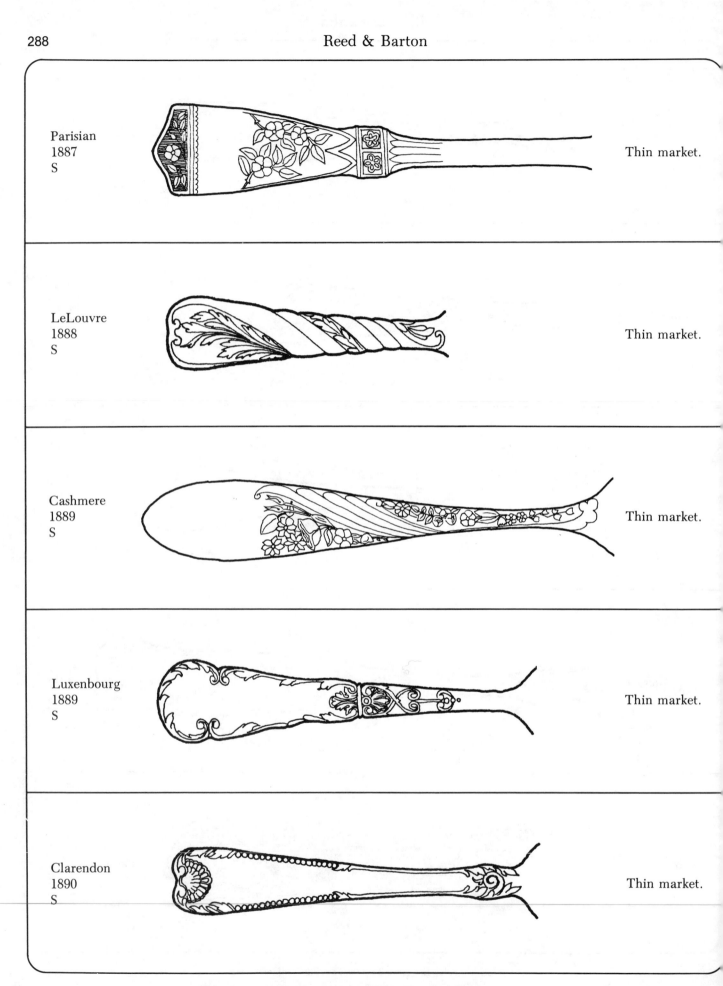

Parisian
1887
S

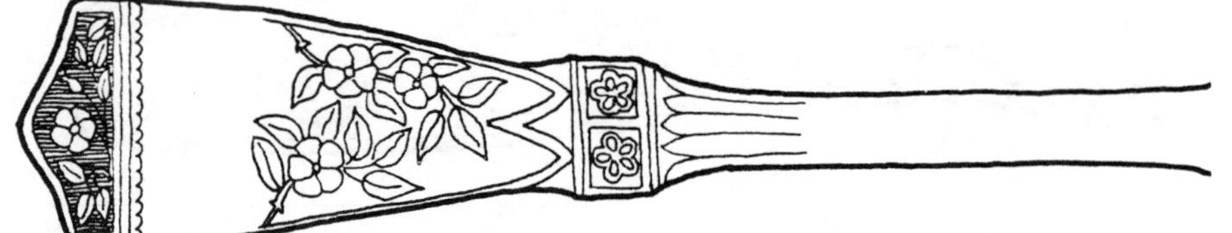

Thin market.

LeLouvre
1888
S

Thin market.

Cashmere
1889
S

Thin market.

Luxenbourg
1889
S

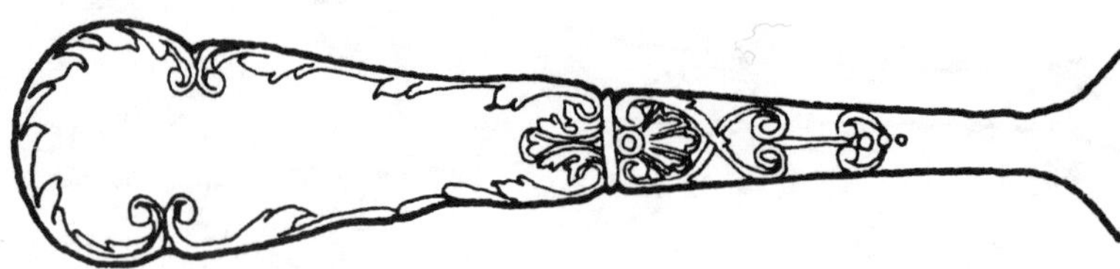

Thin market.

Clarendon
1890
S

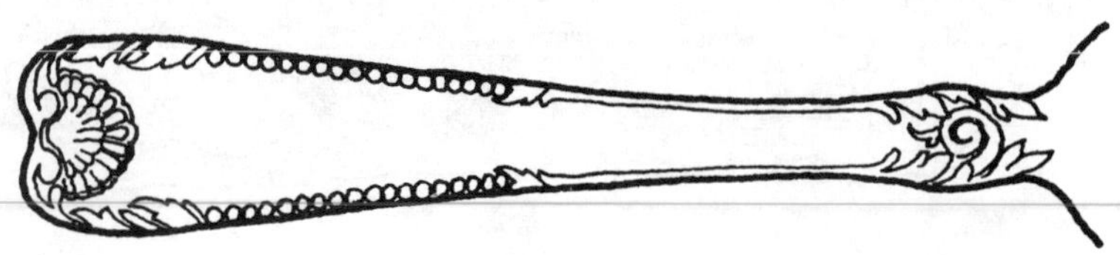

Thin market.

Please refer to "How To Use This Book" page 4.

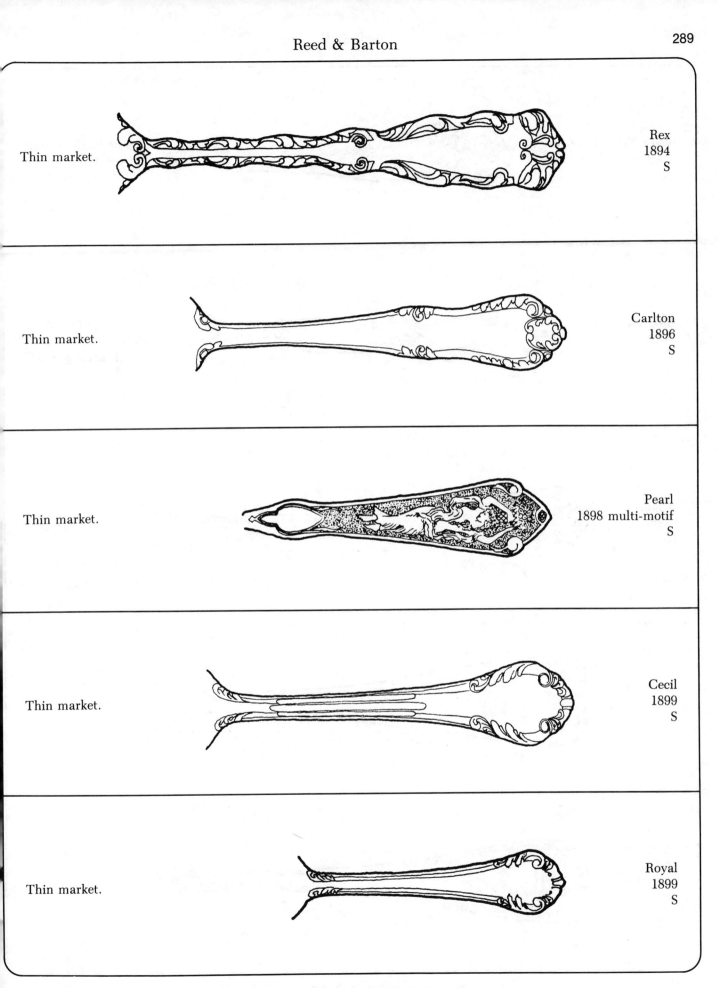

Thin market.

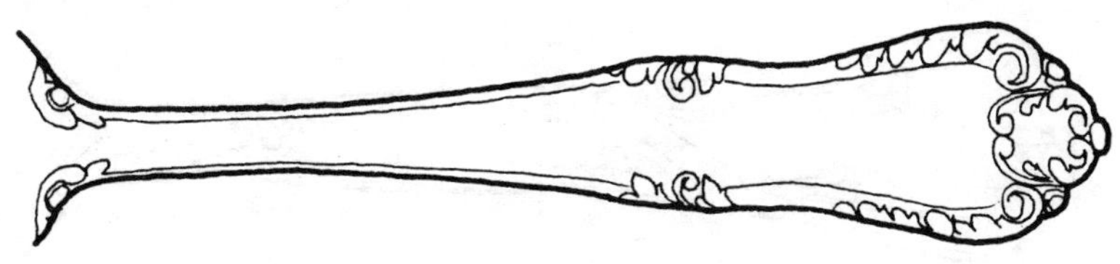

Rex
1894
S

Thin market.

Carlton
1896
S

Thin market.

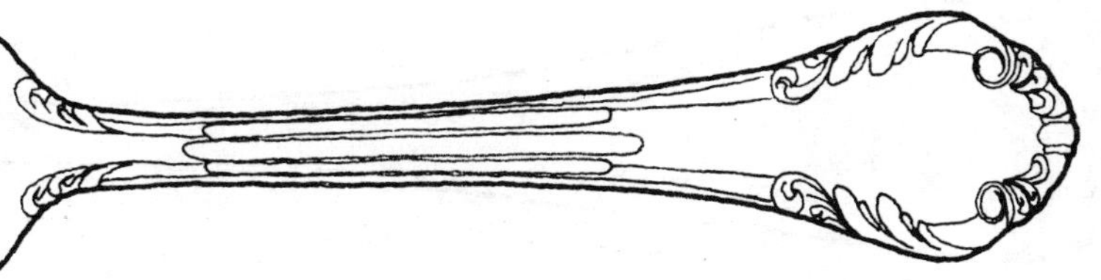

Pearl
1898 multi-motif
S

Thin market.

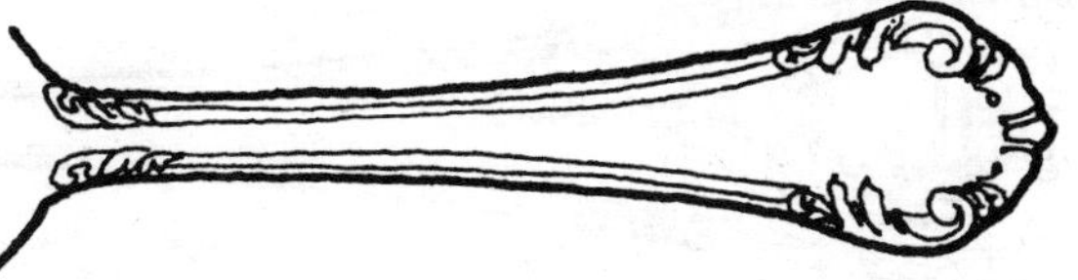

Cecil
1899
S

Thin market.

Royal
1899
S

Please refer to "How To Use This Book" page 4.

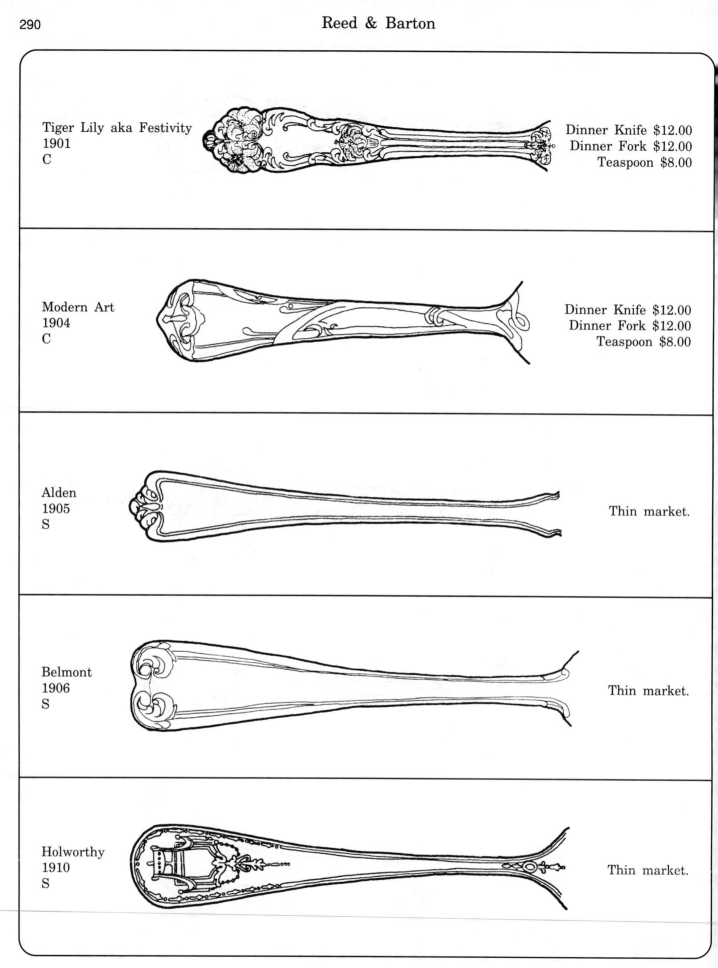

Tiger Lily aka Festivity
1901
C

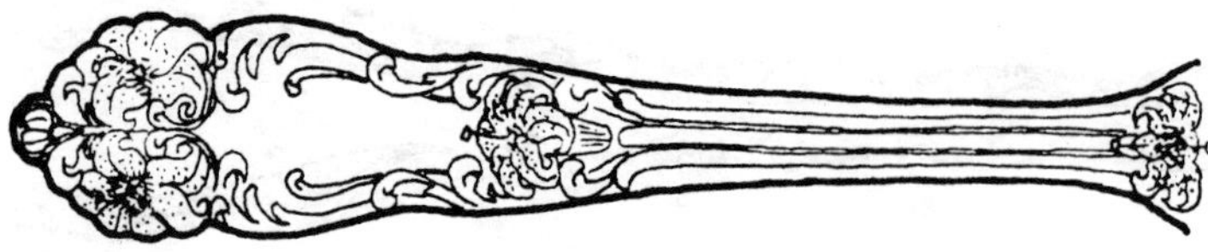

Dinner Knife $12.00
Dinner Fork $12.00
Teaspoon $8.00

Modern Art
1904
C

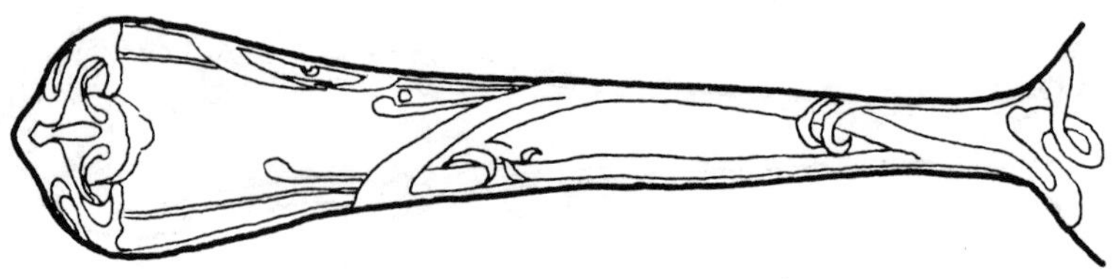

Dinner Knife $12.00
Dinner Fork $12.00
Teaspoon $8.00

Alden
1905
S

Thin market.

Belmont
1906
S

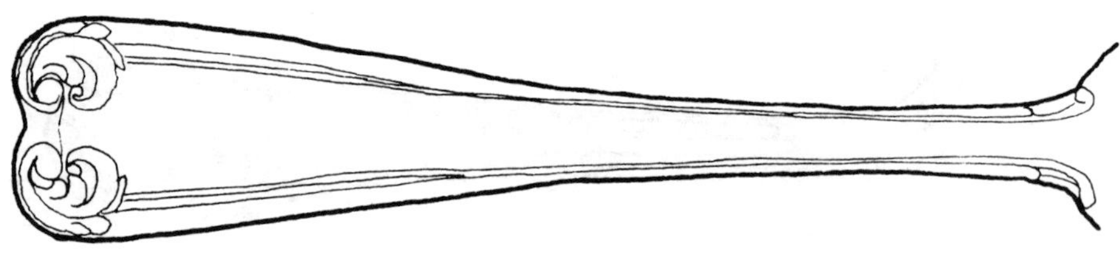

Thin market.

Holworthy
1910
S

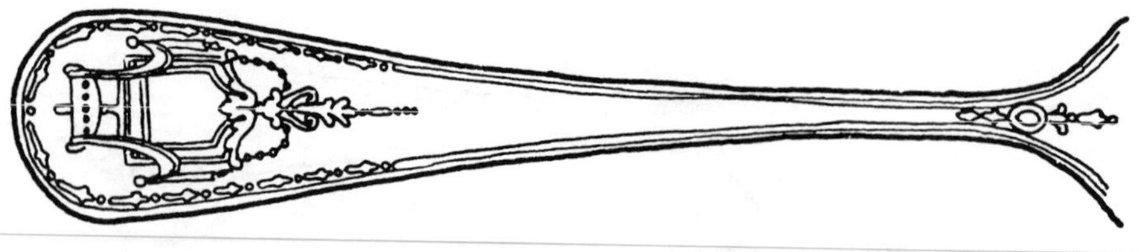

Thin market.

Please refer to "How To Use This Book" page 4.

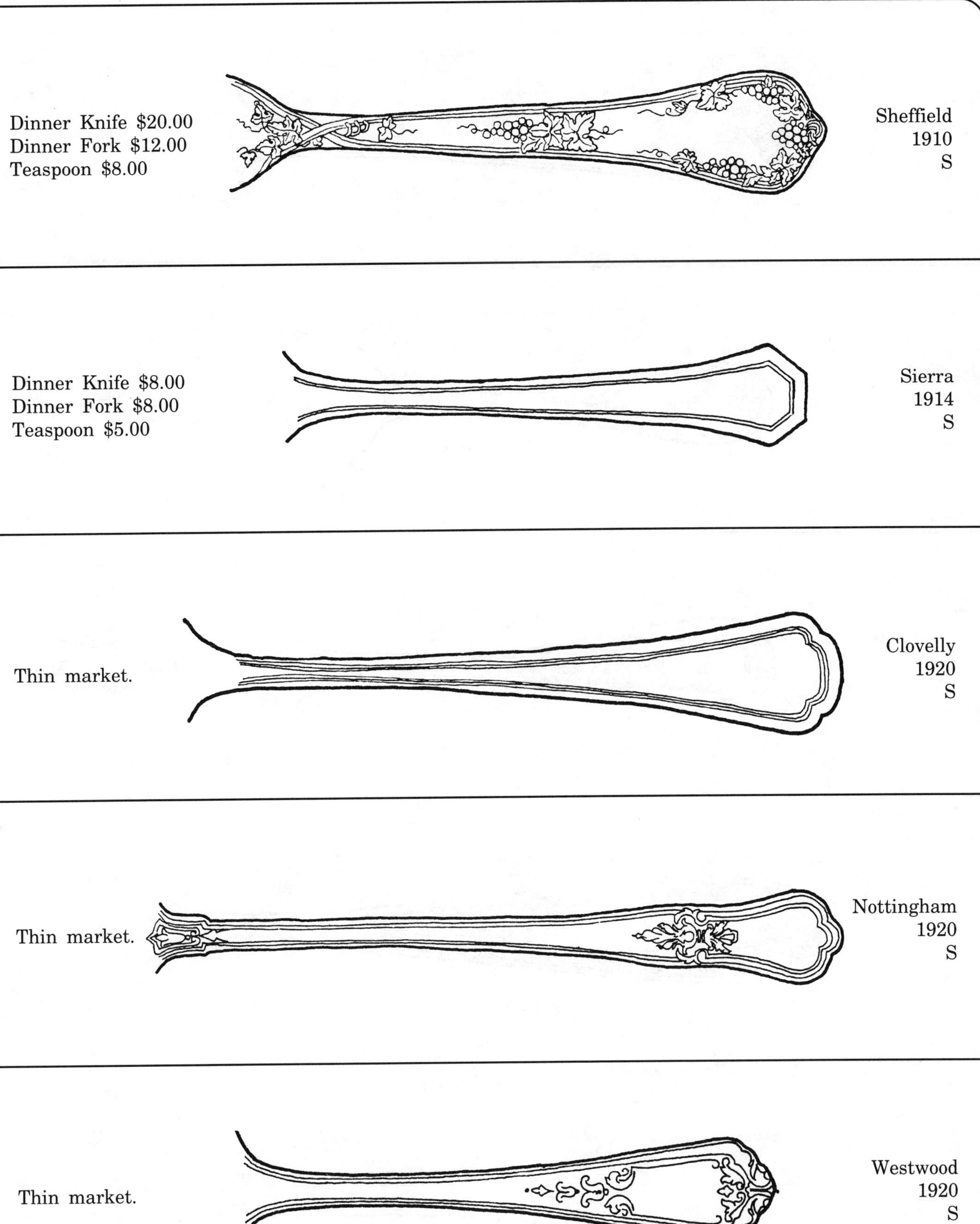

Dinner Knife $20.00
Dinner Fork $12.00
Teaspoon $8.00

Sheffield
1910
S

Dinner Knife $8.00
Dinner Fork $8.00
Teaspoon $5.00

Sierra
1914
S

Thin market.

Clovelly
1920
S

Thin market.

Nottingham
1920
S

Thin market.

Westwood
1920
S

Please refer to "How To Use This Book" page 4.

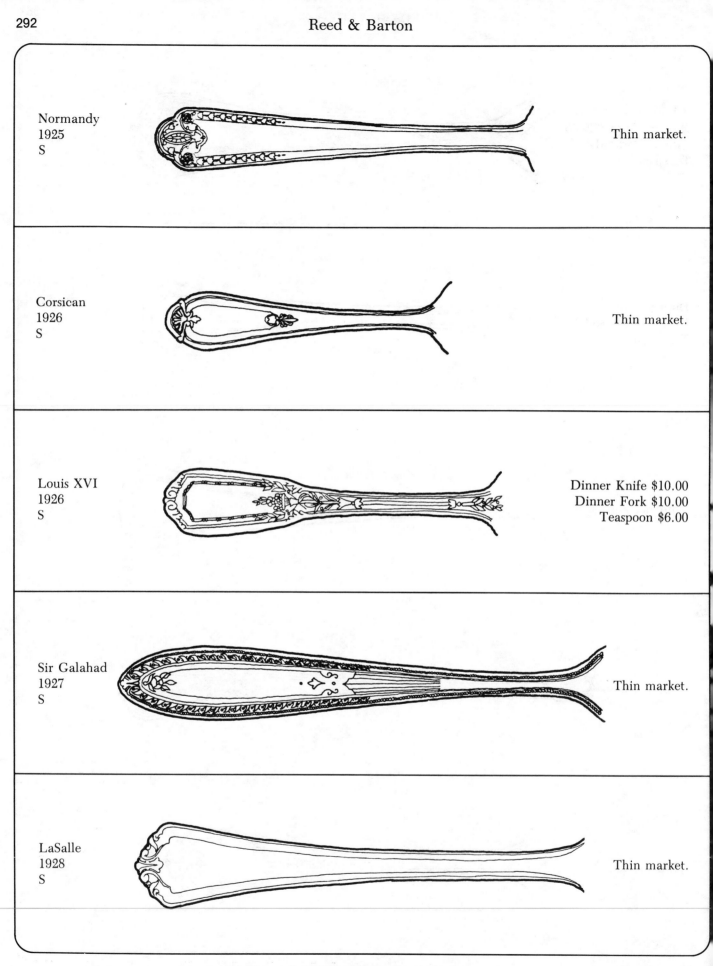

Normandy
1925
S

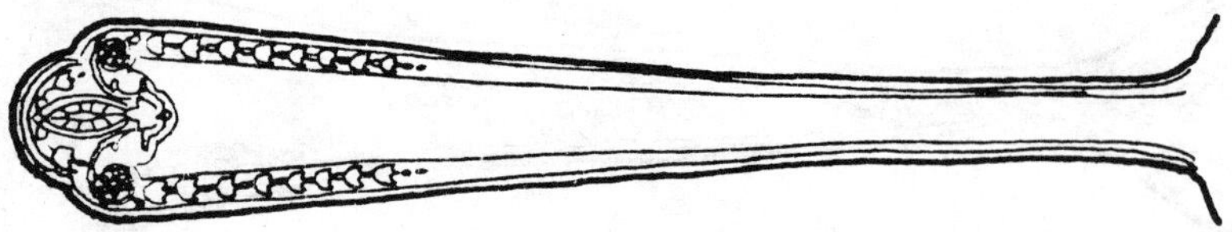

Thin market.

Corsican
1926
S

Thin market.

Louis XVI
1926
S

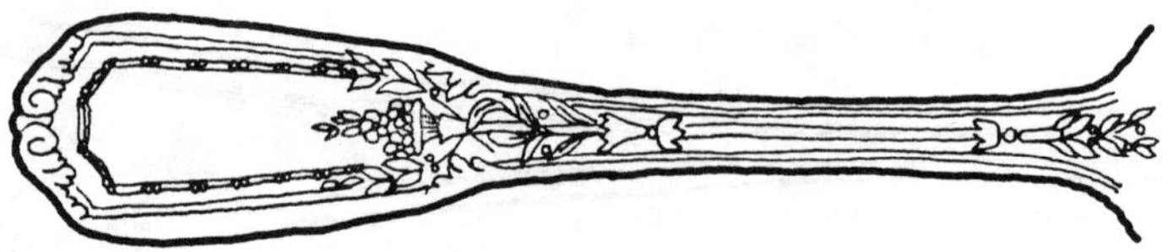

Dinner Knife $10.00
Dinner Fork $10.00
Teaspoon $6.00

Sir Galahad
1927
S

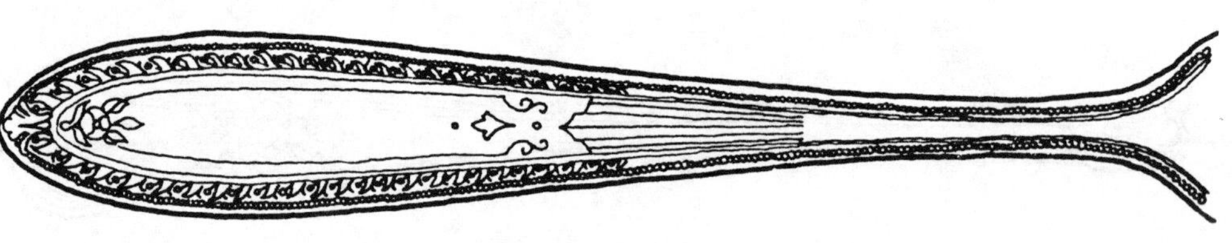

Thin market.

LaSalle
1928
S

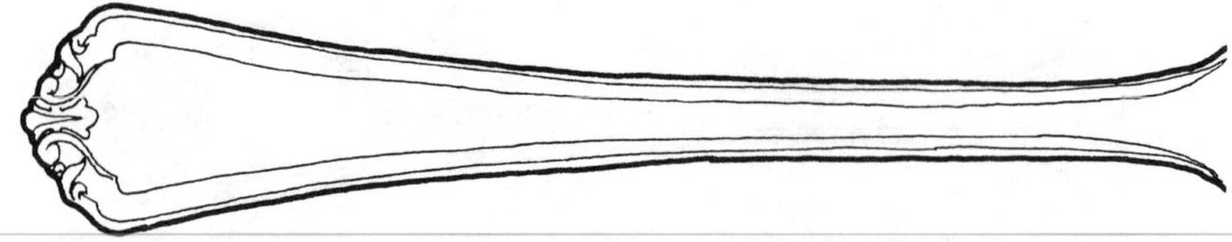

Thin market.

Please refer to "How To Use This Book" page 4.

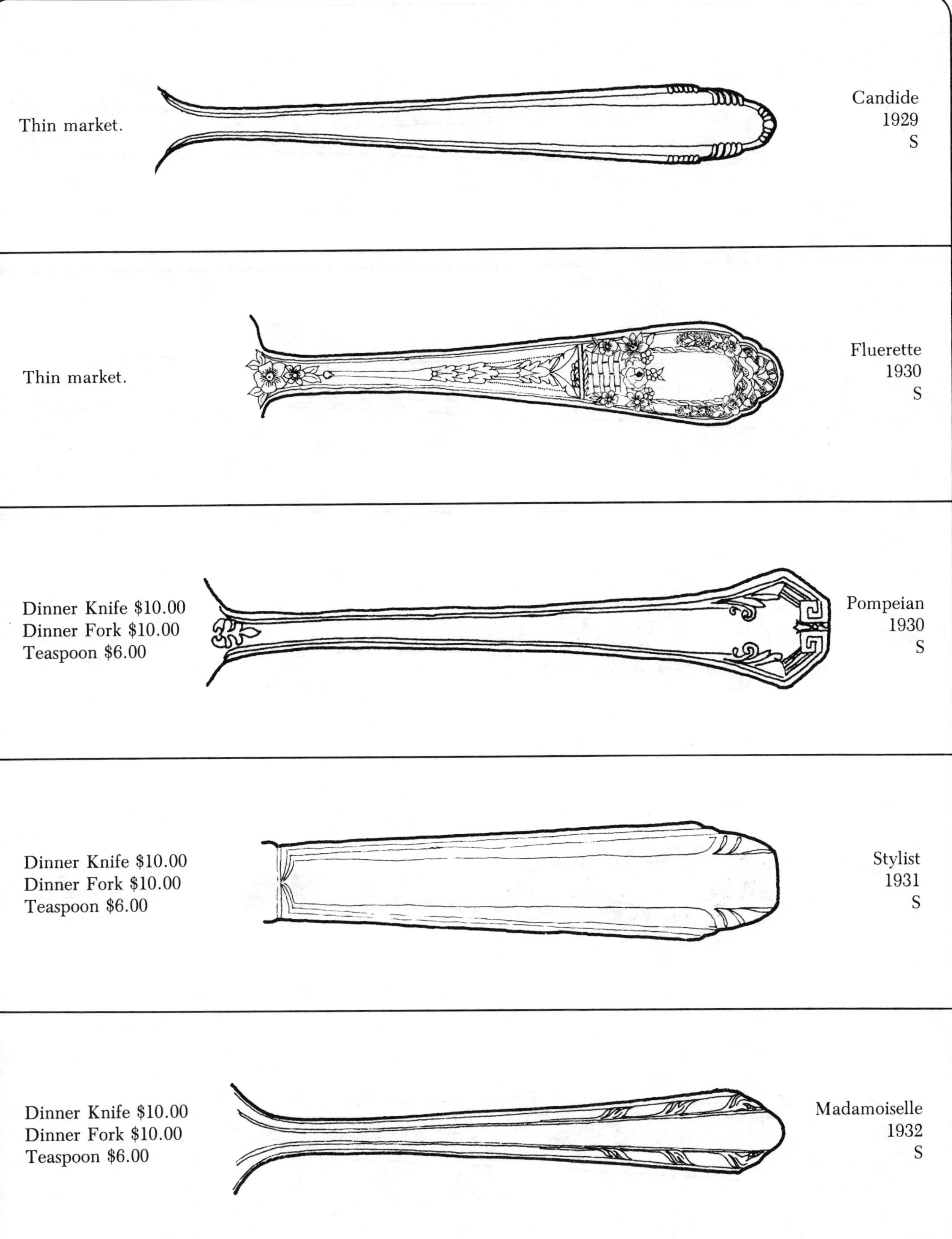

Please refer to "How To Use This Book" page 4.

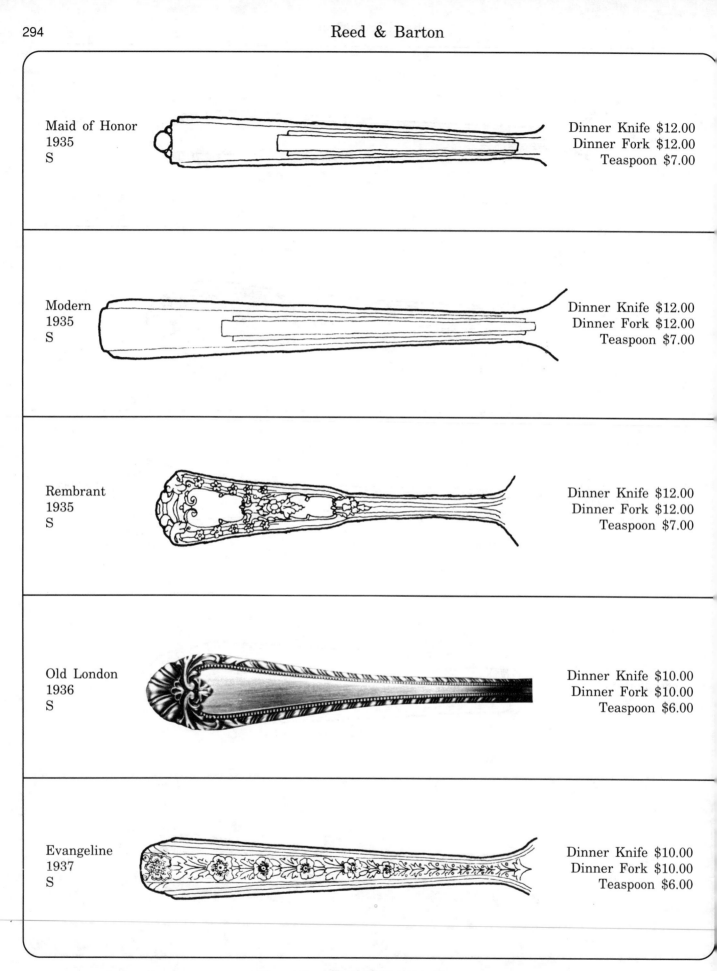

Maid of Honor
1935
S

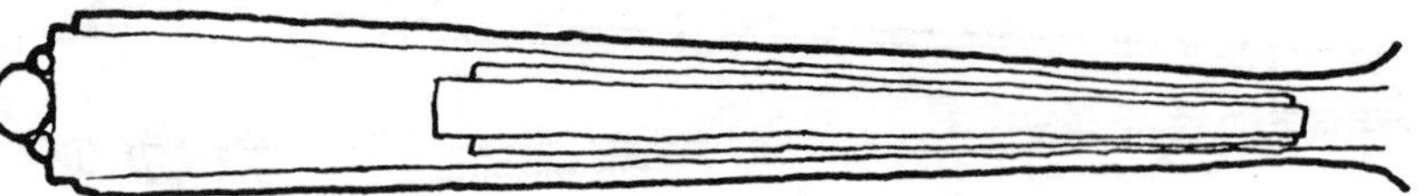

Dinner Knife $12.00
Dinner Fork $12.00
Teaspoon $7.00

Modern
1935
S

Dinner Knife $12.00
Dinner Fork $12.00
Teaspoon $7.00

Rembrant
1935
S

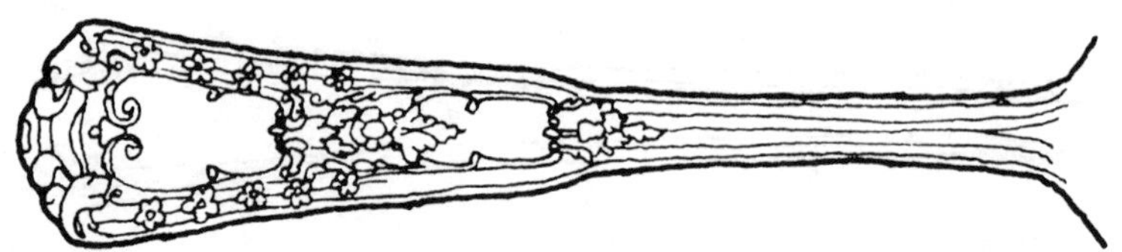

Dinner Knife $12.00
Dinner Fork $12.00
Teaspoon $7.00

Old London
1936
S

Dinner Knife $10.00
Dinner Fork $10.00
Teaspoon $6.00

Evangeline
1937
S

Dinner Knife $10.00
Dinner Fork $10.00
Teaspoon $6.00

Please refer to "How To Use This Book" page 4.

Dinner Knife $8.00
Dinner Fork $8.00
Teaspoon $5.00

Socialite
1937
S

Dinner Knife $10.00
Dinner Fork $10.00
Teaspoon $6.00

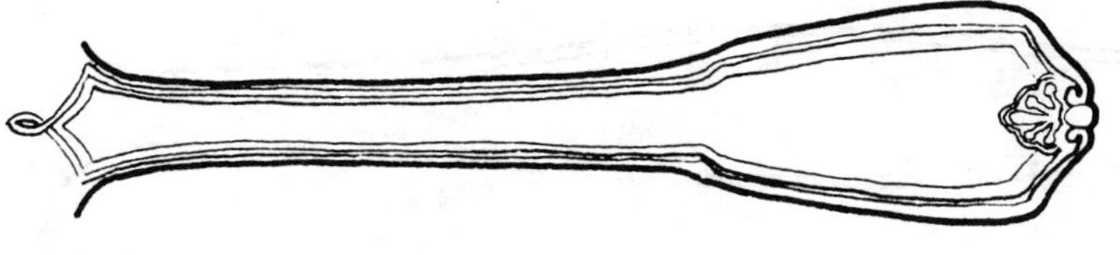

Commonwealth
1939
S

Dinner Knife $8.00
Dinner Fork $8.00
Teaspoon $5.00

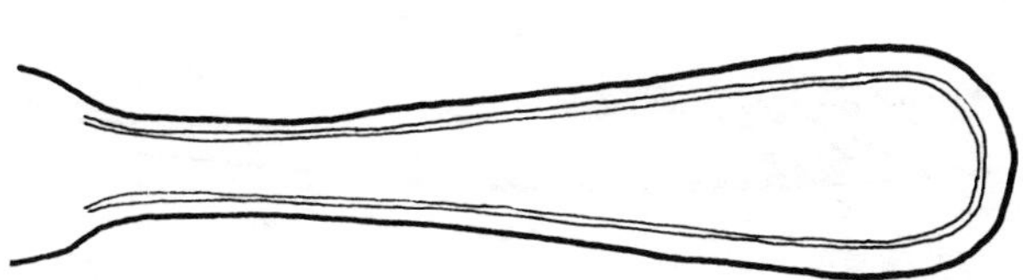

Waverly
1942
S

Dinner Knife $10.00
Dinner Fork $10.00
Teaspoon $6.00

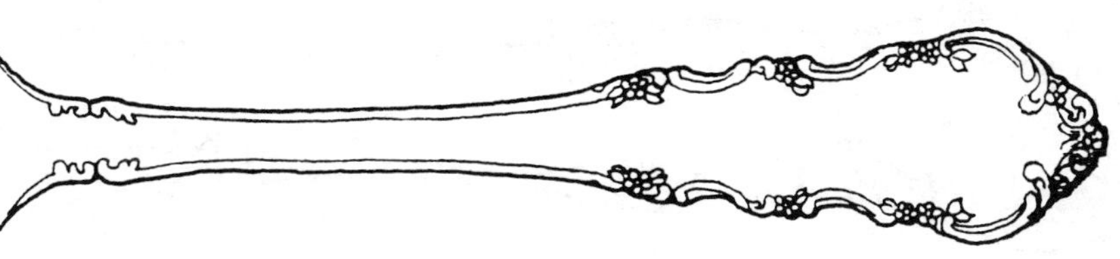

Dresden Rose
1953
P

Dinner Knife $12.00
Dinner Fork $12.00
Teaspoon $7.00

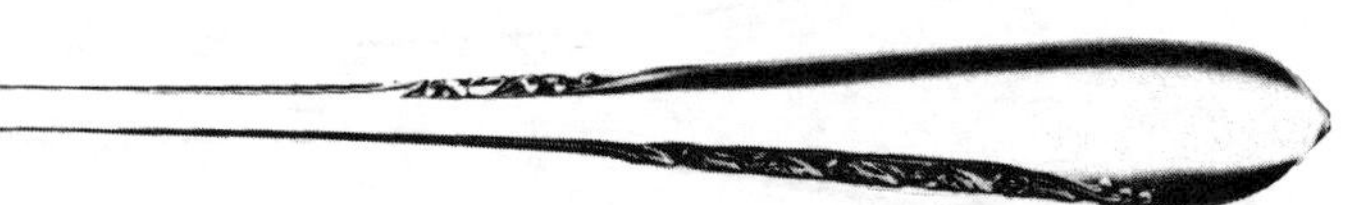

Silver Blossom
1955
S

Please refer to "How To Use This Book" page 4.

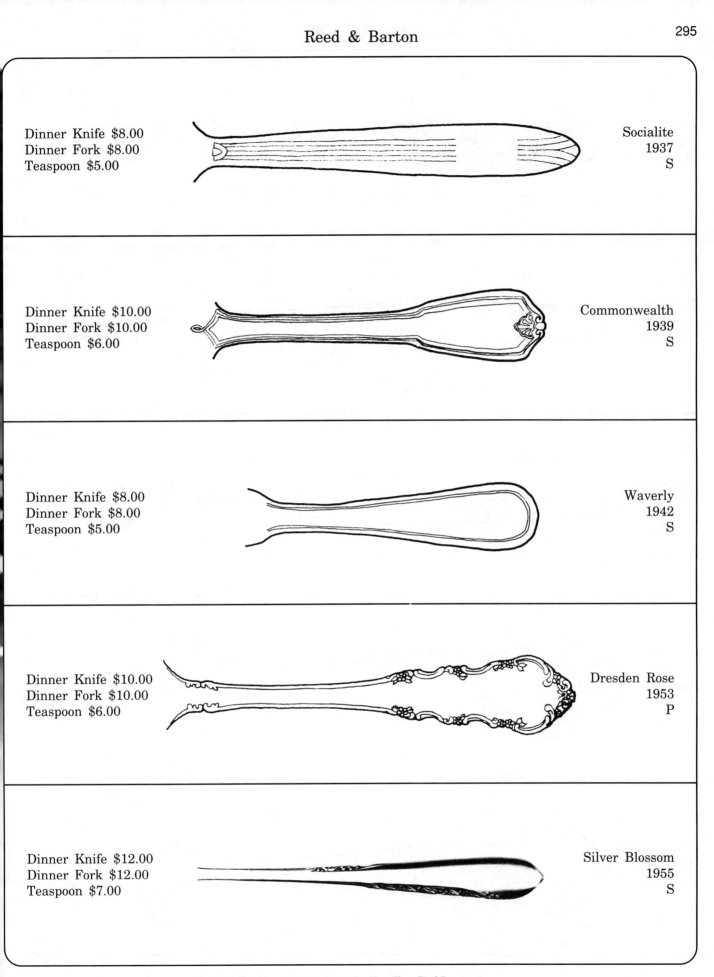

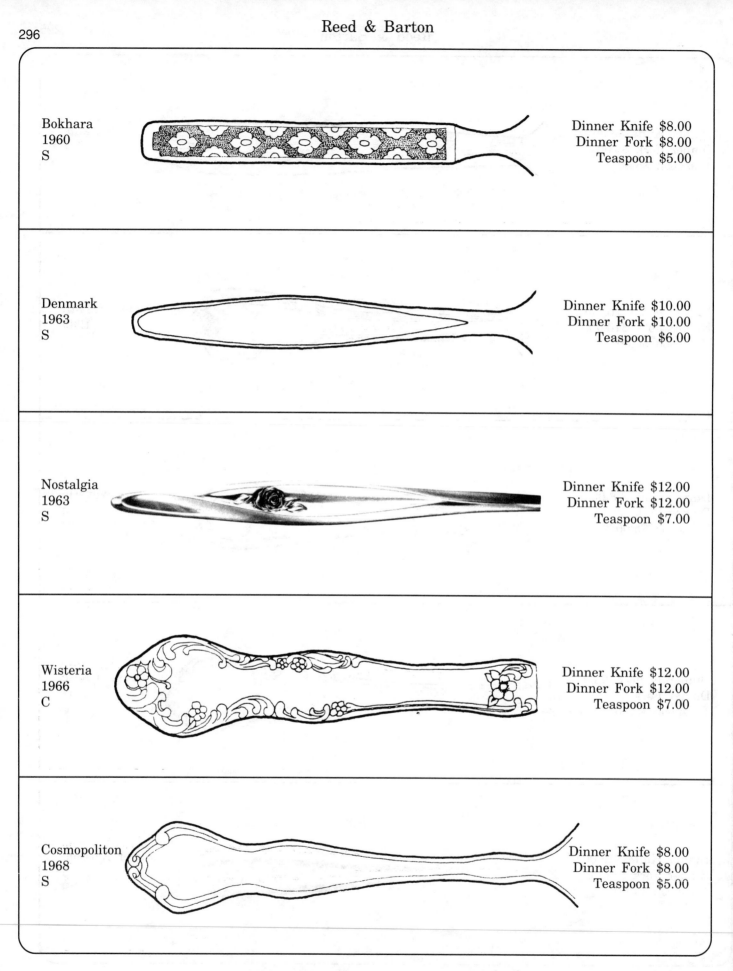

Bokhara
1960
S

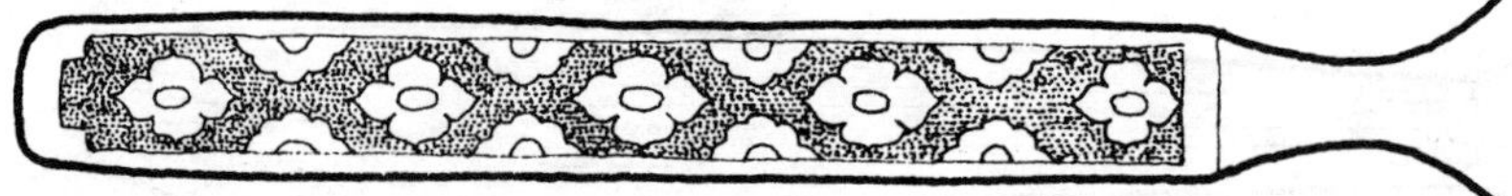

Dinner Knife $8.00
Dinner Fork $8.00
Teaspoon $5.00

Denmark
1963
S

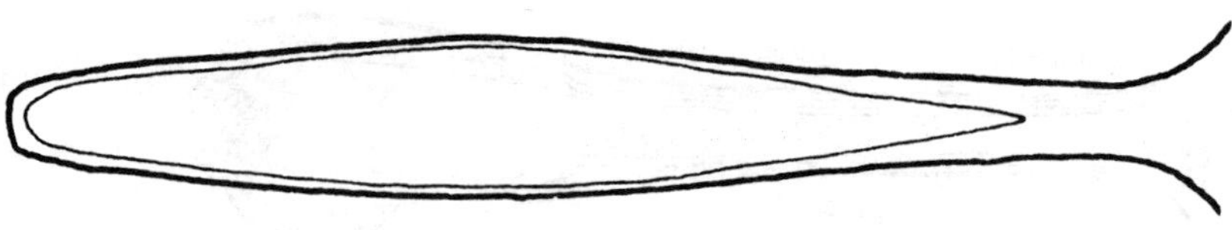

Dinner Knife $10.00
Dinner Fork $10.00
Teaspoon $6.00

Nostalgia
1963
S

Dinner Knife $12.00
Dinner Fork $12.00
Teaspoon $7.00

Wisteria
1966
C

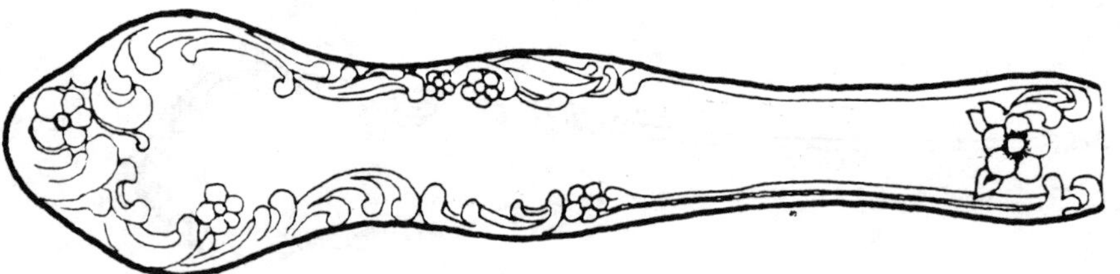

Dinner Knife $12.00
Dinner Fork $12.00
Teaspoon $7.00

Cosmopoliton
1968
S

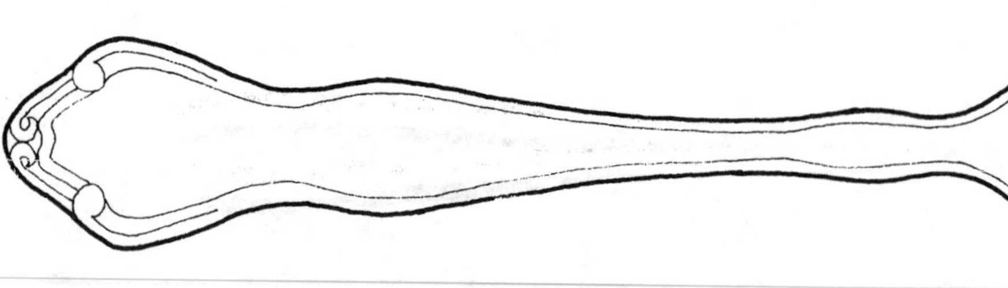

Dinner Knife $8.00
Dinner Fork $8.00
Teaspoon $5.00

Please refer to "How To Use This Book" page 4.

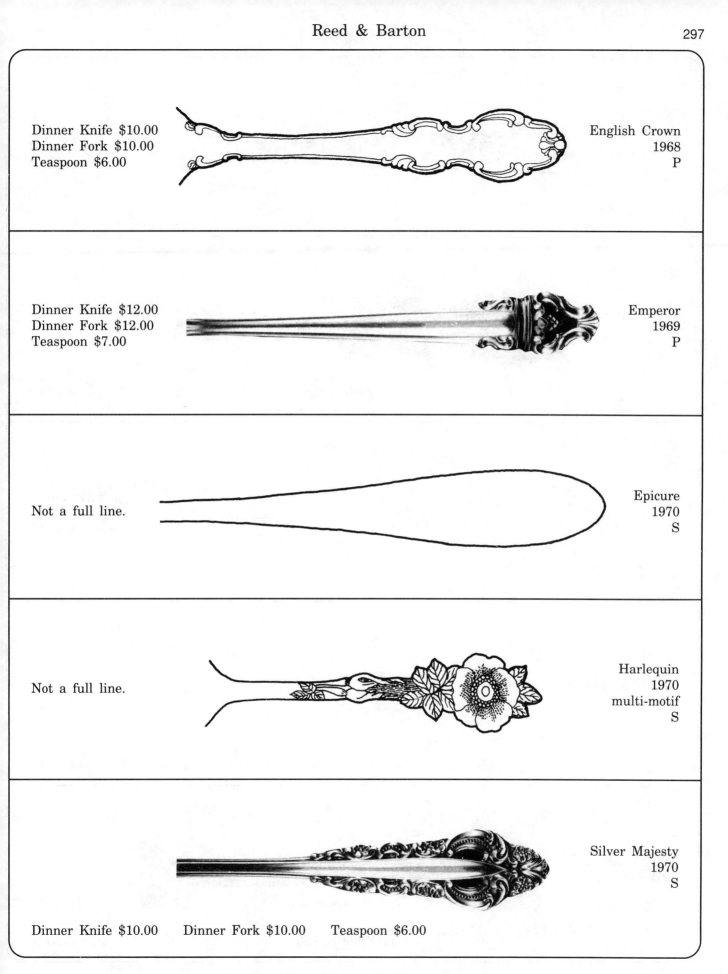

Dinner Knife $10.00
Dinner Fork $10.00
Teaspoon $6.00

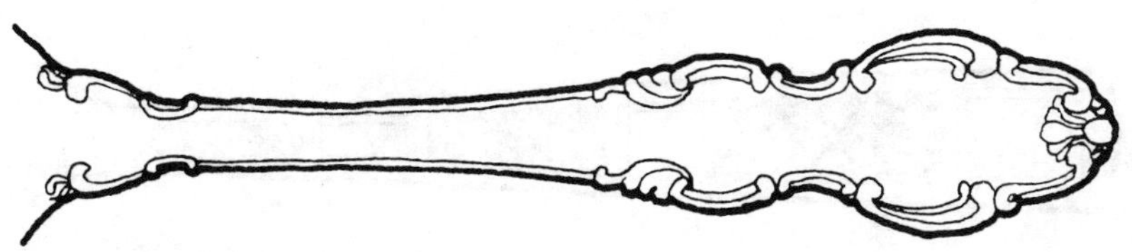

English Crown
1968
P

Dinner Knife $12.00
Dinner Fork $12.00
Teaspoon $7.00

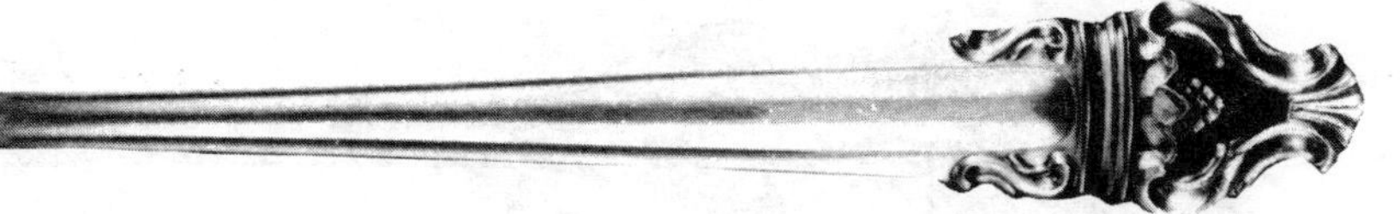

Emperor
1969
P

Not a full line.

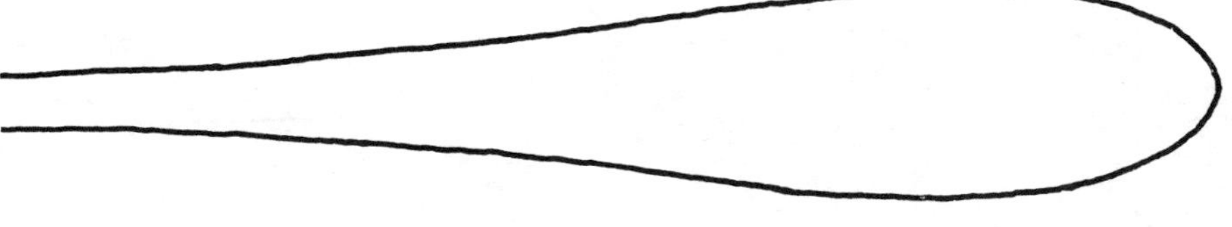

Epicure
1970
S

Not a full line.

Harlequin
1970
multi-motif
S

Silver Majesty
1970
S

Dinner Knife $10.00 Dinner Fork $10.00 Teaspoon $6.00

Please refer to "How To Use This Book" page 4.

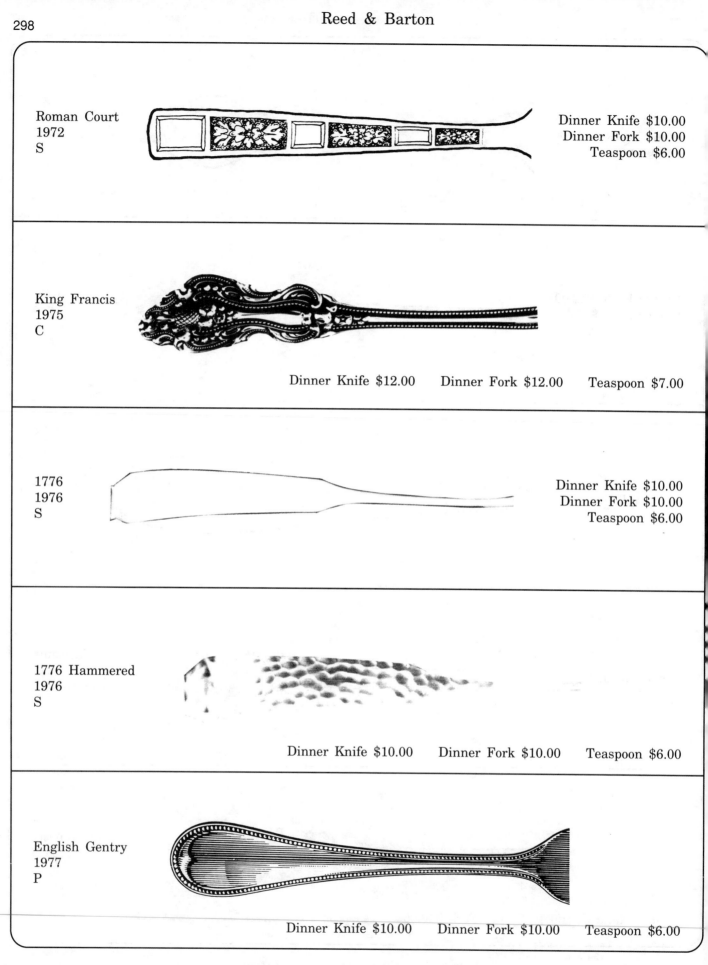

Roman Court
1972
S

Dinner Knife $10.00
Dinner Fork $10.00
Teaspoon $6.00

King Francis
1975
C

Dinner Knife $12.00 Dinner Fork $12.00 Teaspoon $7.00

1776
1976
S

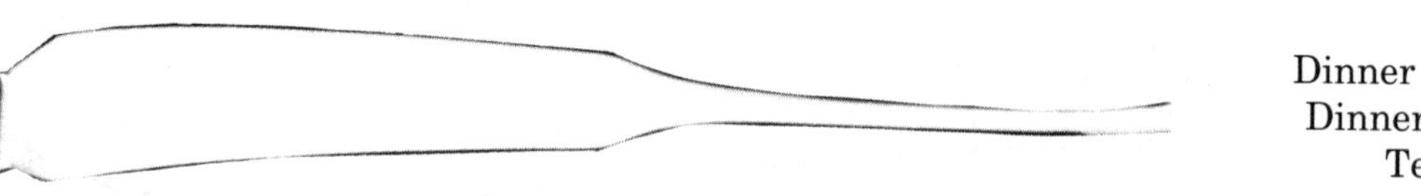

Dinner Knife $10.00
Dinner Fork $10.00
Teaspoon $6.00

1776 Hammered
1976
S

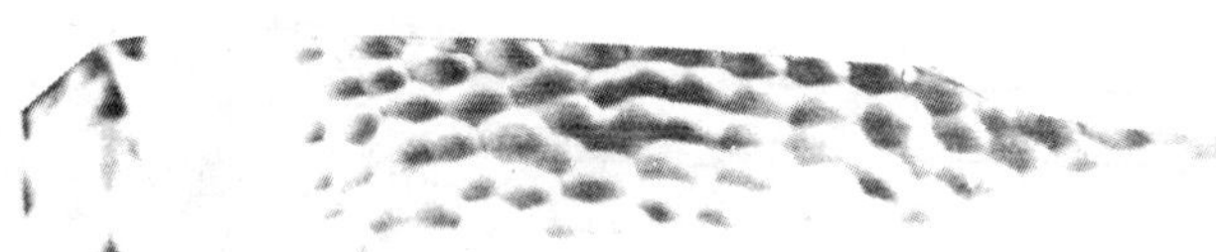

Dinner Knife $10.00 Dinner Fork $10.00 Teaspoon $6.00

English Gentry
1977
P

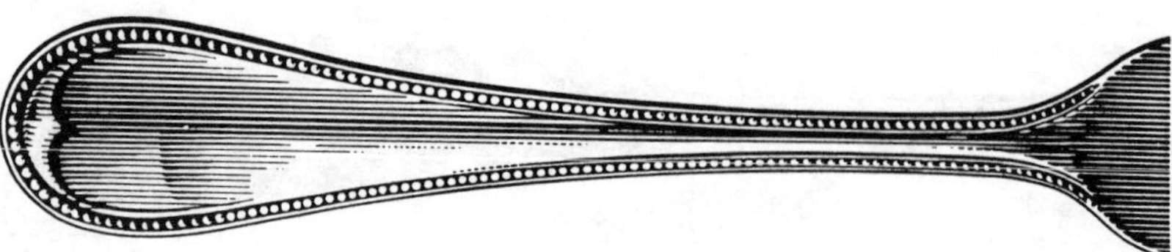

Dinner Knife $10.00 Dinner Fork $10.00 Teaspoon $6.00

Please refer to "How To Use This Book" page 4.

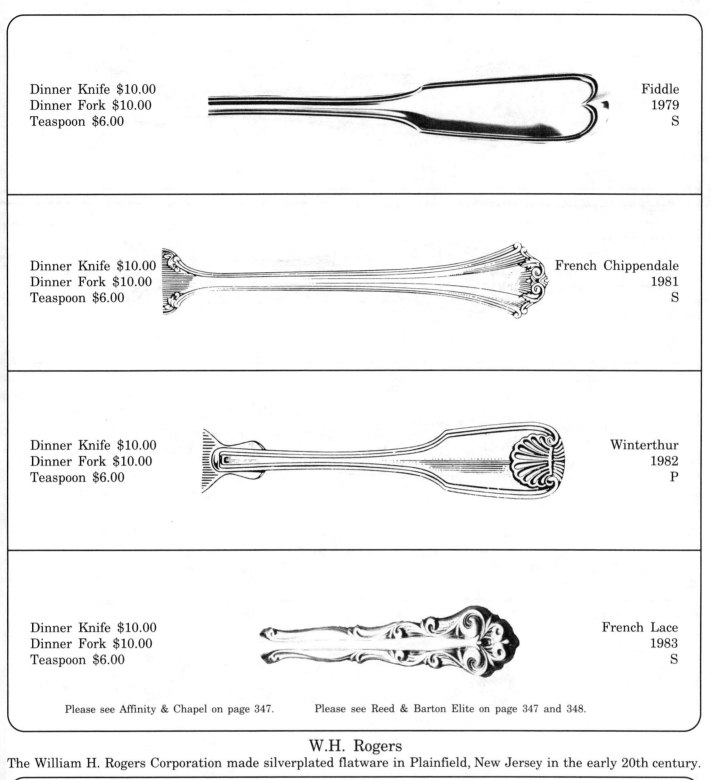

Dinner Knife $10.00
Dinner Fork $10.00
Teaspoon $6.00

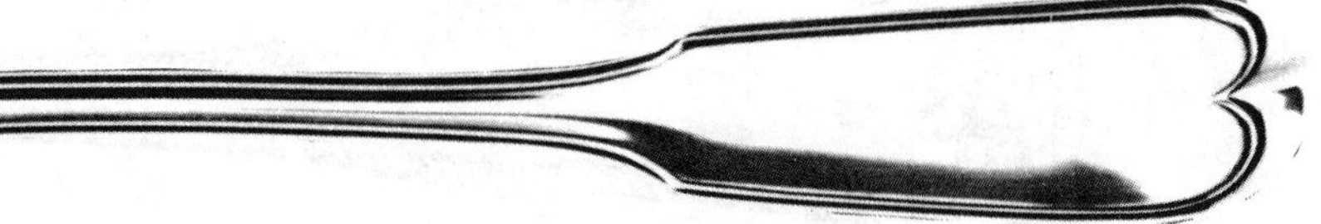

Fiddle
1979
S

Dinner Knife $10.00
Dinner Fork $10.00
Teaspoon $6.00

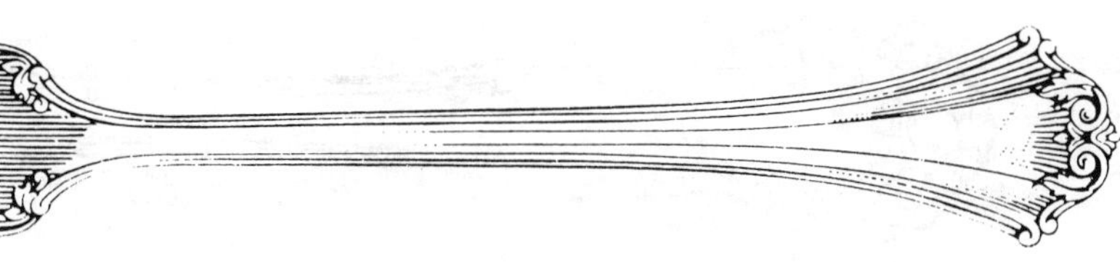

French Chippendale
1981
S

Dinner Knife $10.00
Dinner Fork $10.00
Teaspoon $6.00

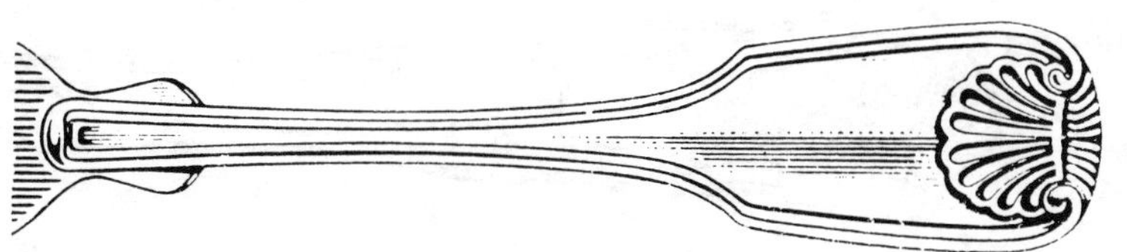

Winterthur
1982
P

Dinner Knife $10.00
Dinner Fork $10.00
Teaspoon $6.00

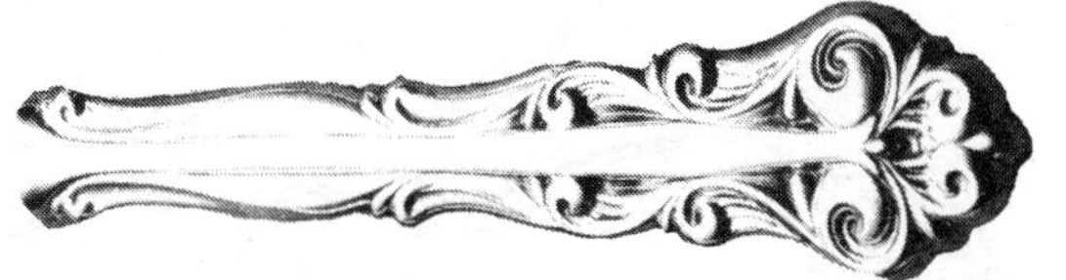

French Lace
1983
S

Please see Affinity & Chapel on page 347. Please see Reed & Barton Elite on page 347 and 348.

W.H. Rogers

The William H. Rogers Corporation made silverplated flatware in Plainfield, New Jersey in the early 20th century.

Thin market.

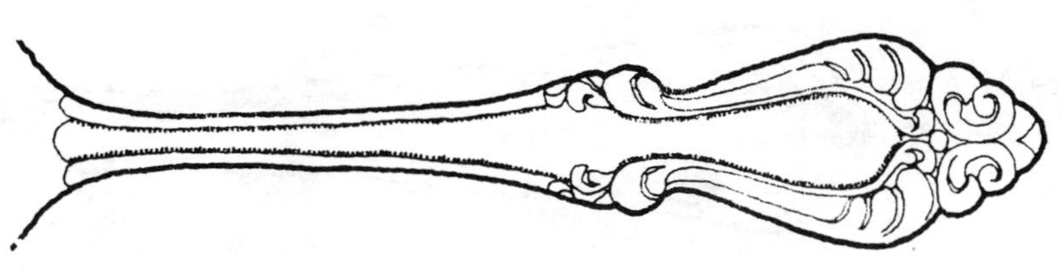

Nordica
1890
S

Please refer to "How To Use This Book" page 4.

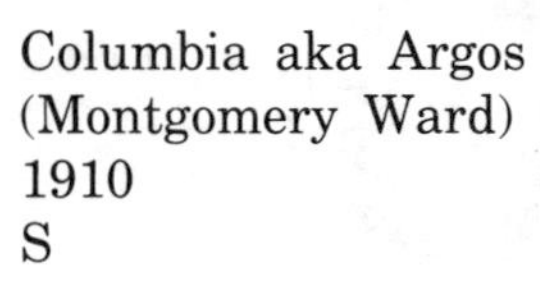

Columbia aka Argos
(Montgomery Ward)
1910
S

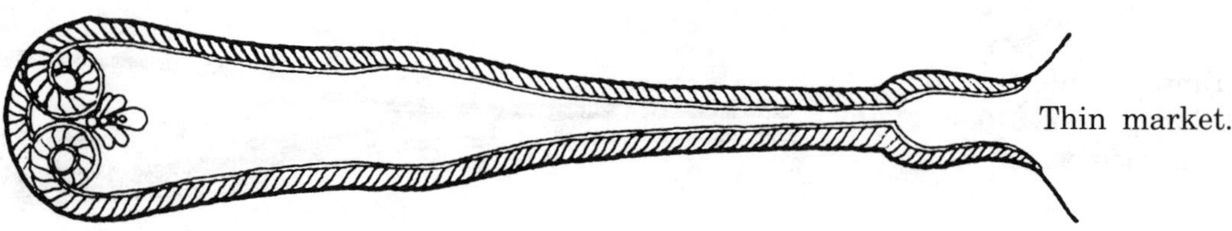

Thin market.

Como aka Erminie aka
Mignon aka Helena aka
Rockford No. 1
(Rockford Silver Plate)
(Montgomery Ward & Co.)
(American Silver Co.)
(Williams)
(C. Guild)
1910
S

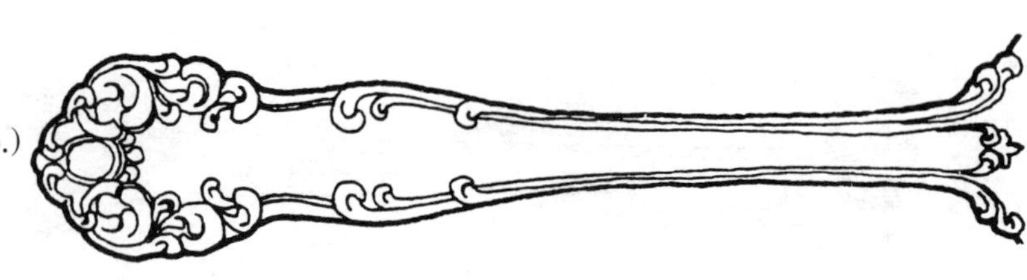

Thin market.

Muscatel aka Vineyard
(Paragon)
1910
S

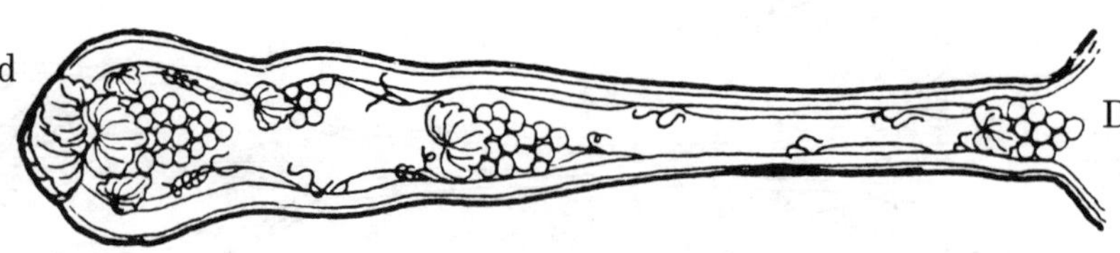

Dinner Fork $15.00
Teaspoon $8.00

Sears Roebuck & Co. - Cambridge Silver Plate

Many different manufacturers of silverplated flatware made flatware for the well-known retailer - Sears Roebuck - to sell through their outlets.

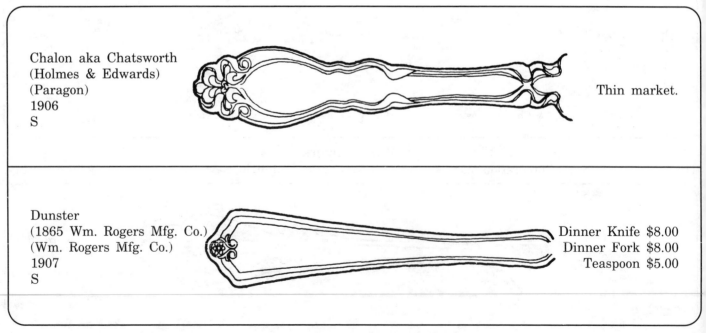

Chalon aka Chatsworth
(Holmes & Edwards)
(Paragon)
1906
S

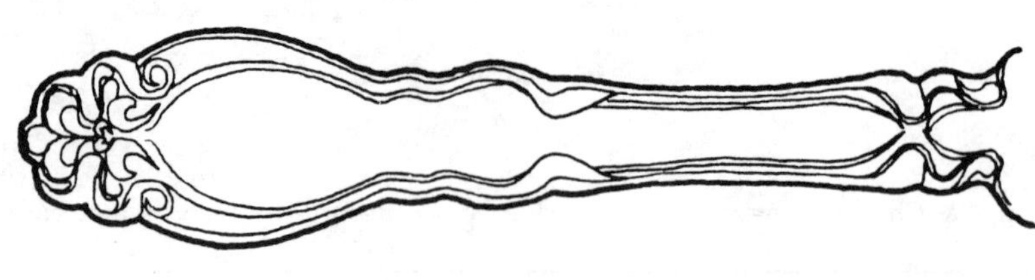

Thin market.

Dunster
(1865 Wm. Rogers Mfg. Co.)
(Wm. Rogers Mfg. Co.)
1907
S

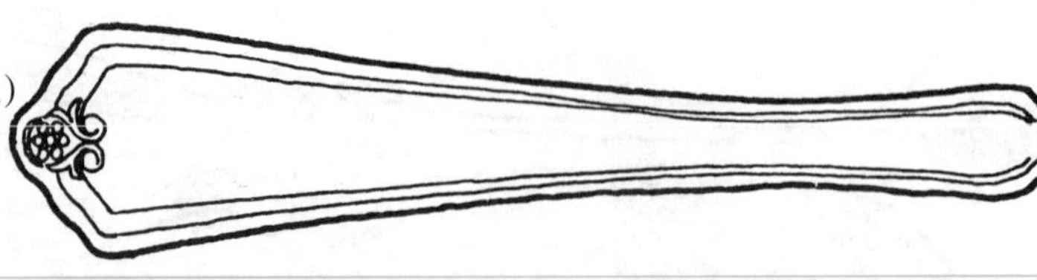

Dinner Knife $8.00
Dinner Fork $8.00
Teaspoon $5.00

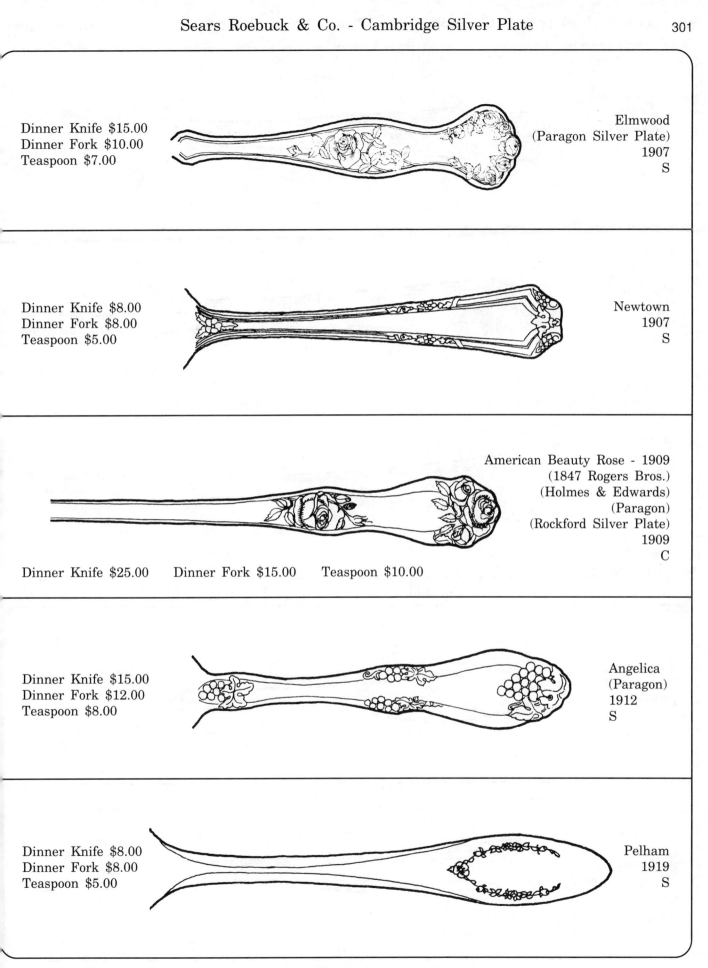

Dinner Knife $15.00
Dinner Fork $10.00
Teaspoon $7.00

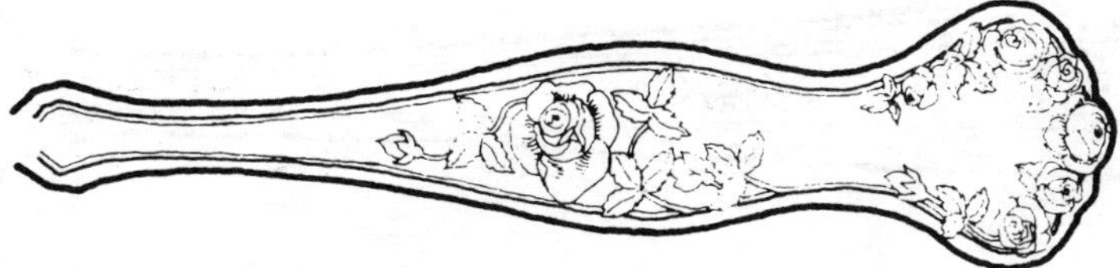

Elmwood
(Paragon Silver Plate)
1907
S

Dinner Knife $8.00
Dinner Fork $8.00
Teaspoon $5.00

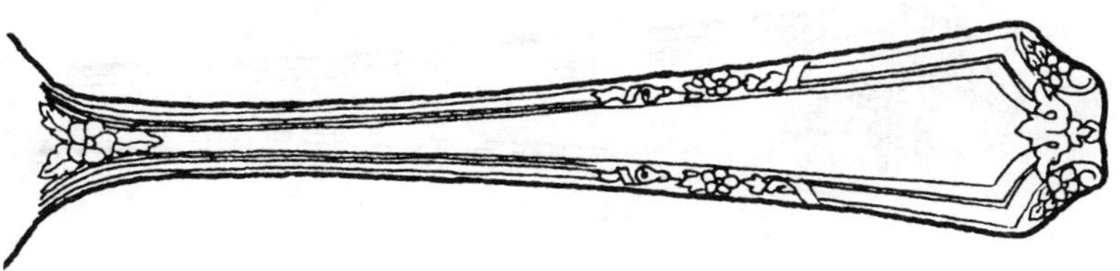

Newtown
1907
S

American Beauty Rose - 1909
(1847 Rogers Bros.)
(Holmes & Edwards)
(Paragon)
(Rockford Silver Plate)
1909
C

Dinner Knife $25.00 Dinner Fork $15.00 Teaspoon $10.00

Dinner Knife $15.00
Dinner Fork $12.00
Teaspoon $8.00

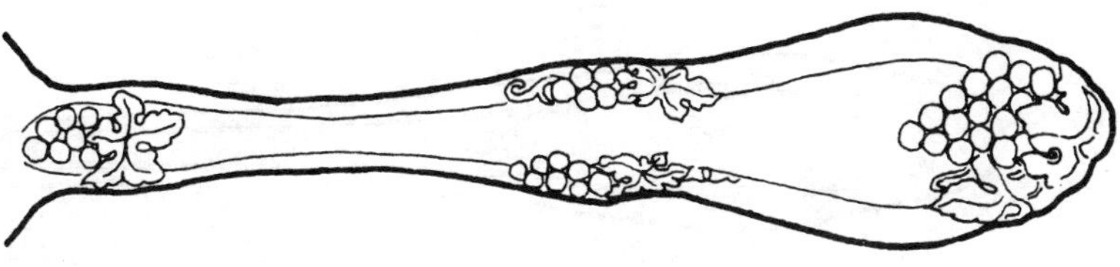

Angelica
(Paragon)
1912
S

Dinner Knife $8.00
Dinner Fork $8.00
Teaspoon $5.00

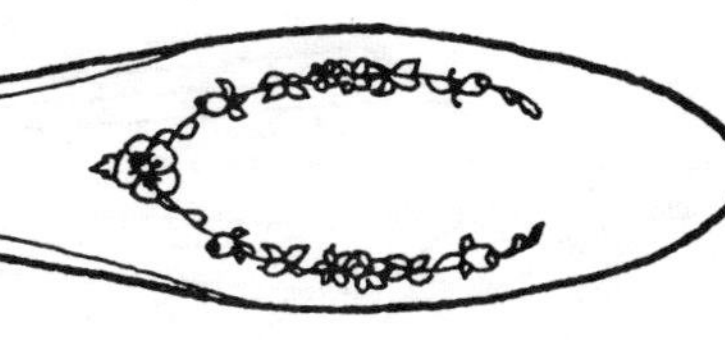

Pelham
1919
S

Please refer to "How To Use This Book" page 4.

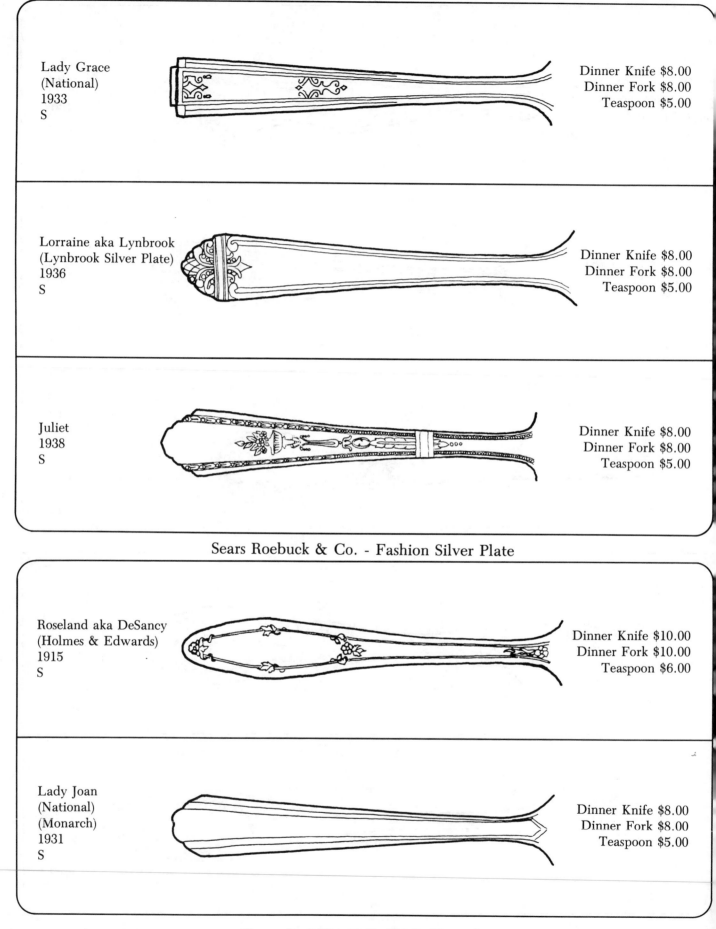

Lady Grace
(National)
1933
S

Dinner Knife $8.00
Dinner Fork $8.00
Teaspoon $5.00

Lorraine aka Lynbrook
(Lynbrook Silver Plate)
1936
S

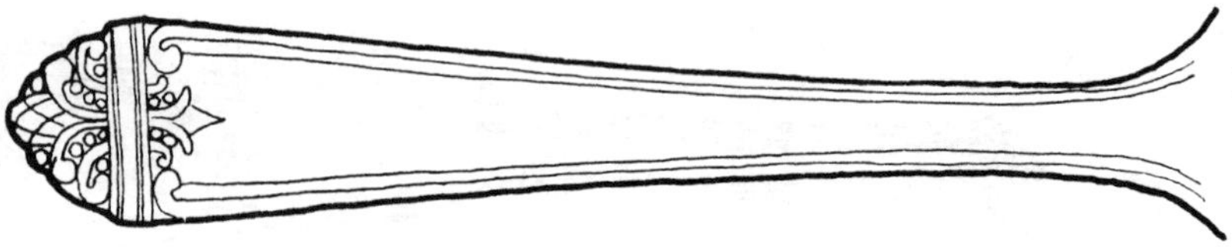

Dinner Knife $8.00
Dinner Fork $8.00
Teaspoon $5.00

Juliet
1938
S

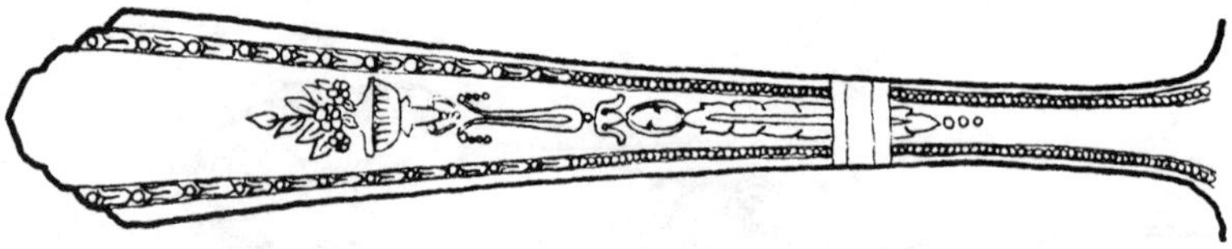

Dinner Knife $8.00
Dinner Fork $8.00
Teaspoon $5.00

Sears Roebuck & Co. - Fashion Silver Plate

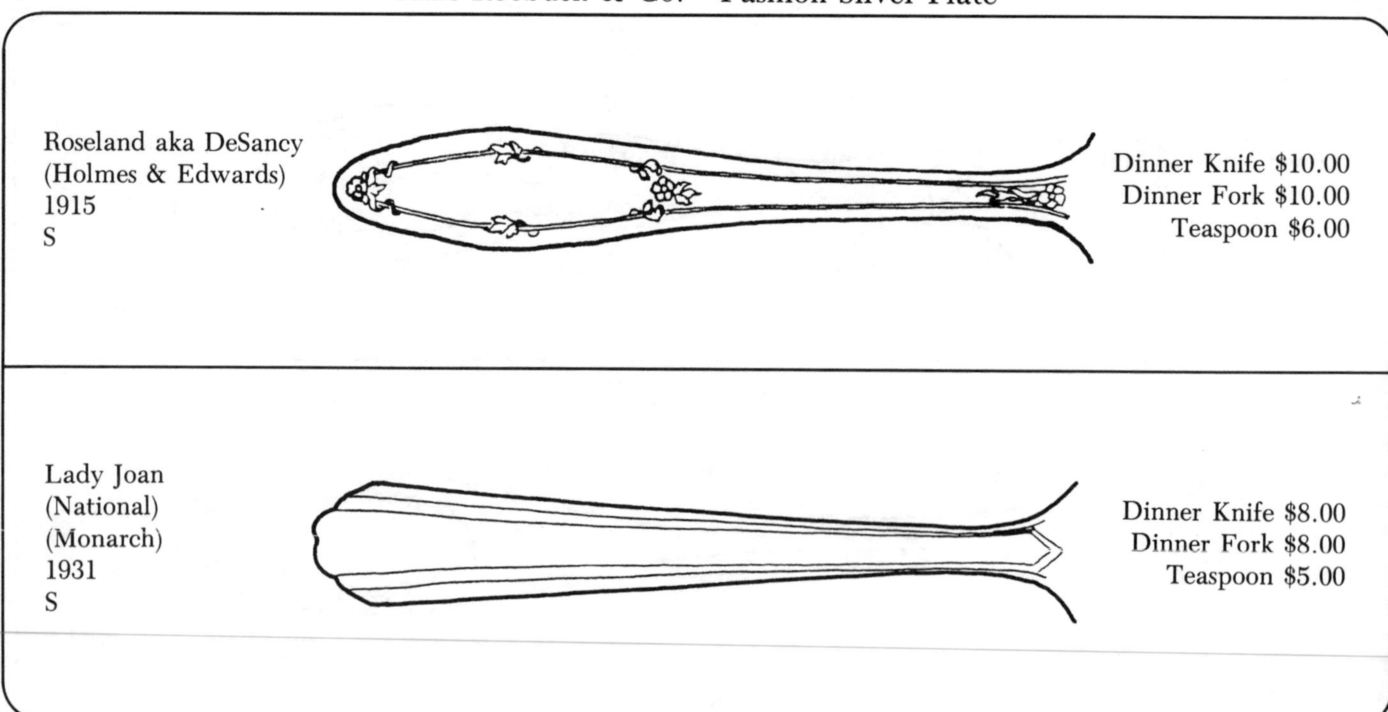

Roseland aka DeSancy
(Holmes & Edwards)
1915
S

Dinner Knife $10.00
Dinner Fork $10.00
Teaspoon $6.00

Lady Joan
(National)
(Monarch)
1931
S

Dinner Knife $8.00
Dinner Fork $8.00
Teaspoon $5.00

Please refer to "How To Use This Book" page 4.

Dinner Knife $8.00
Dinner Fork $8.00
Teaspoon $5.00

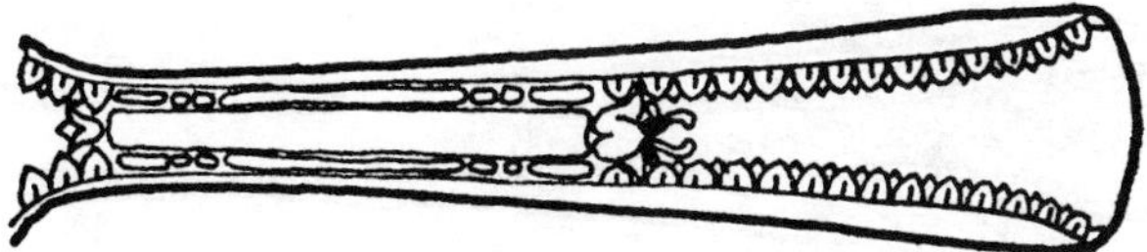

Ascot
1936
S

Dinner Knife $8.00
Dinner Fork $8.00
Teaspoon $5.00

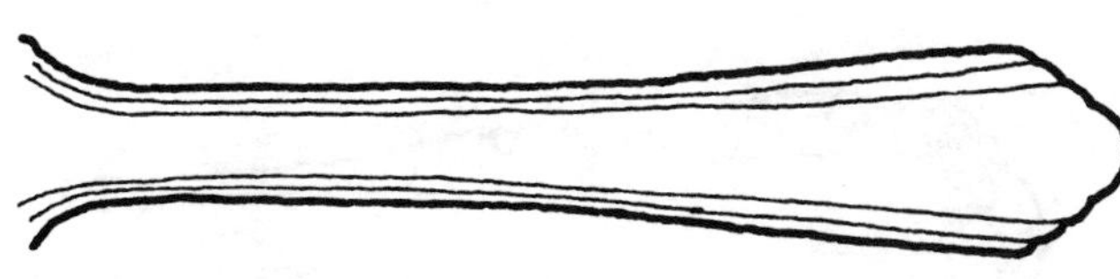

Lady Alice
1936
S

Dinner Knife $8.00
Dinner Fork $8.00
Teaspoon $5.00

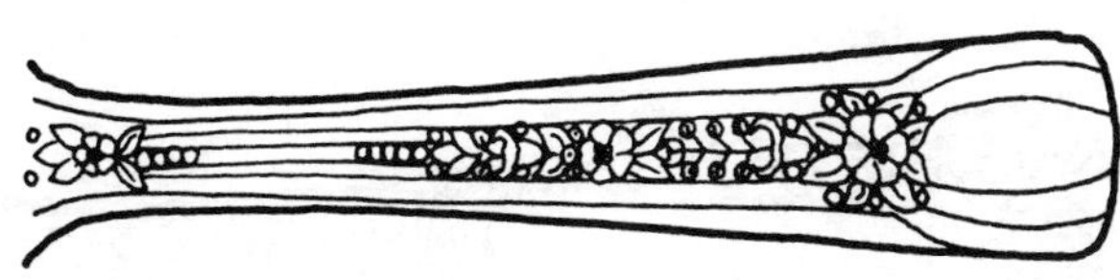

Diplomat
(Master Silver Plate)
1941
S

Dinner Knife $8.00
Dinner Fork $8.00
Teaspoon $5.00

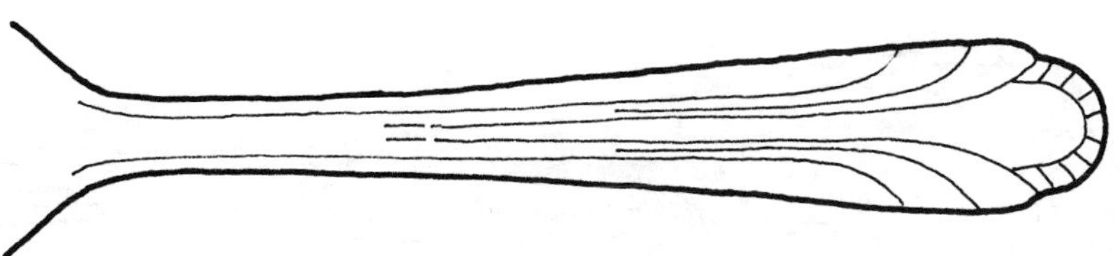

Debut
(Security Silver Plate)
1948
S

Sears Roebuck & Co. - Madrid Silver Plate

Dinner Knife $8.00
Dinner Fork $8.00
Teaspoon $5.00

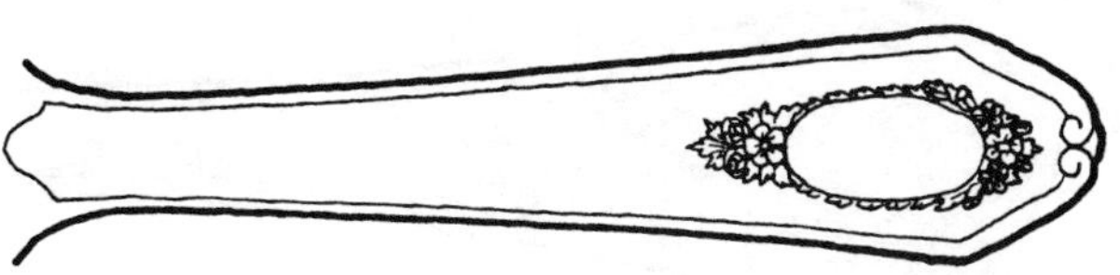

Madrid
1932
S

Please refer to "How To Use This Book" page 4.

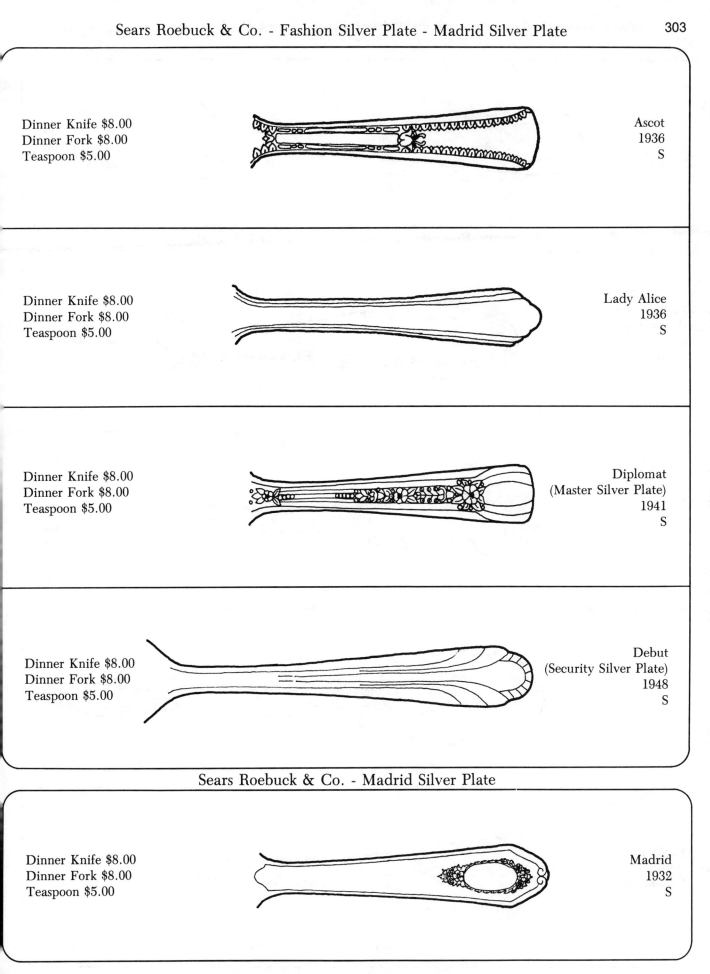

Newport
1946
S

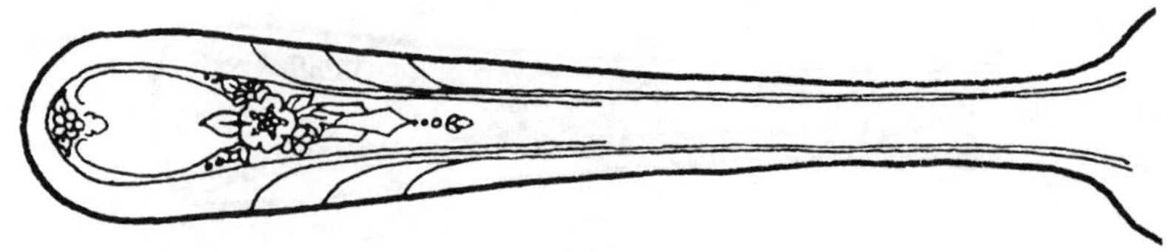

Dinner Knife $8.00
Dinner Fork $8.00
Teaspoon $5.00

Sears Roebuck & Co. - Paragon Silver Plate

Fleur de Lis aka Nassau
(Holmes & Edwards)
(Stratford)
(Sears Roebuck & Co.)
1899
S

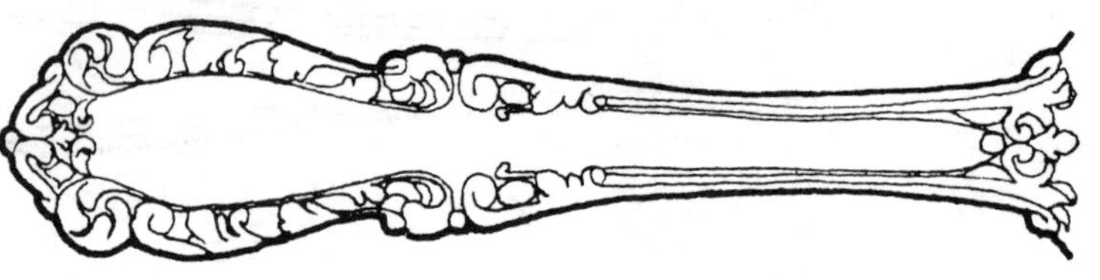

Thin market.

Oxford
(Wm. Rogers & Son)
(C. Rogers & Bros.)
1901
C

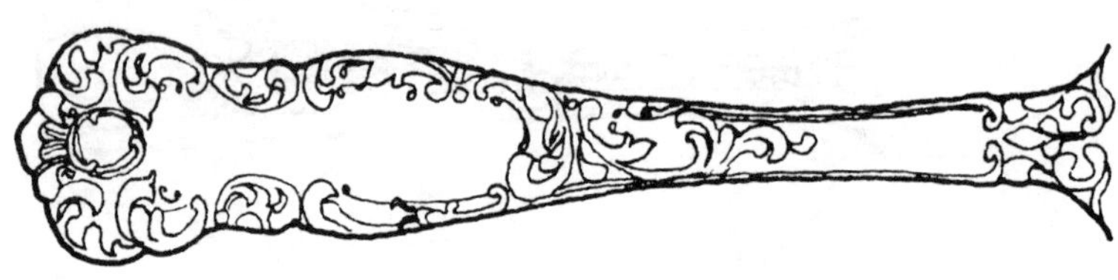

Dinner Fork $15.00
Teaspoon $10.00

Iris
(Smith)
(Salem Silver Plate)
1902
S

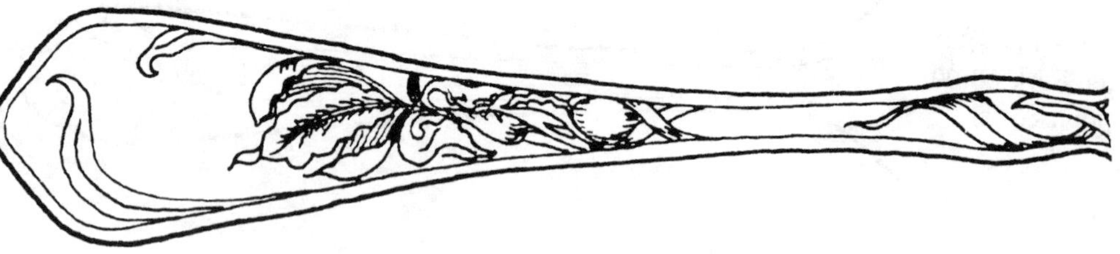

Dinner Knife $20.00 Dinner Fork $18.00 Teaspoon $12.00

Iris Variation
(Smith)
(Salem Silver Plate)
1902
S

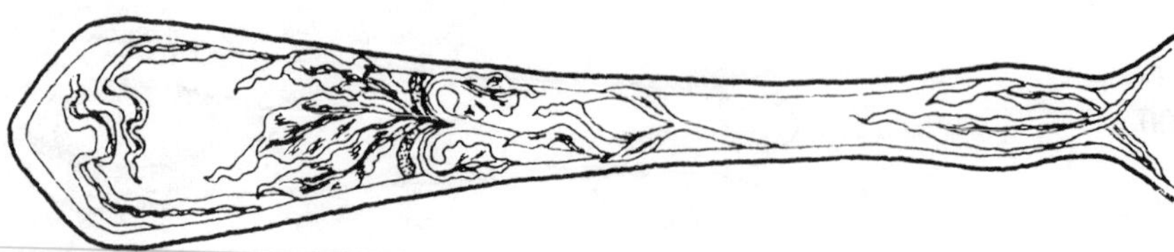

Dinner Knife $20.00 Dinner Fork $18.00 Teaspoon $12.00

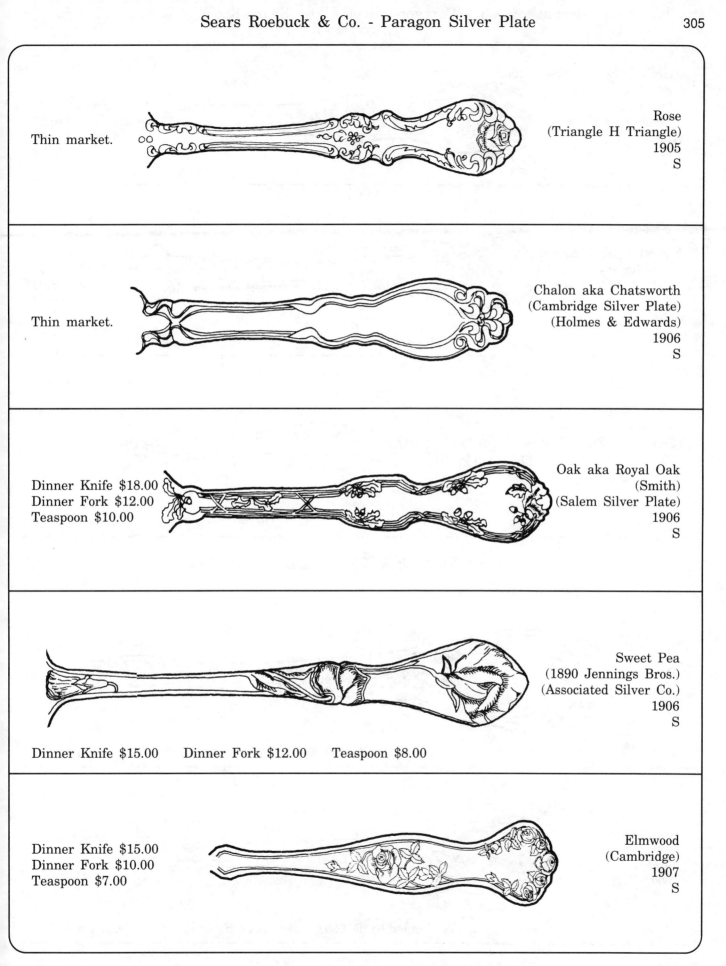

Thin market.

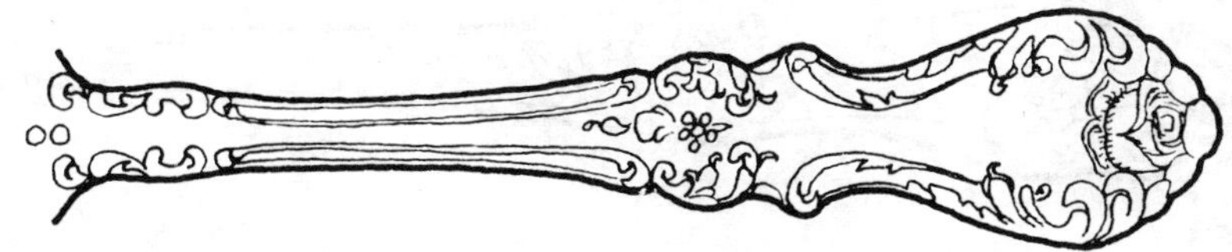

Rose
(Triangle H Triangle)
1905
S

Thin market.

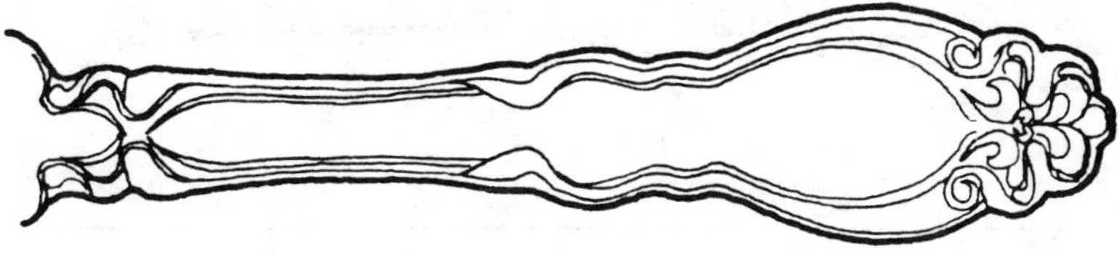

Chalon aka Chatsworth
(Cambridge Silver Plate)
(Holmes & Edwards)
1906
S

Dinner Knife $18.00
Dinner Fork $12.00
Teaspoon $10.00

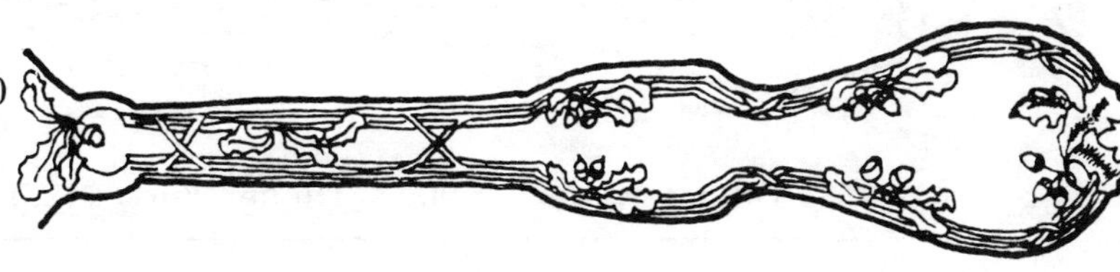

Oak aka Royal Oak
(Smith)
(Salem Silver Plate)
1906
S

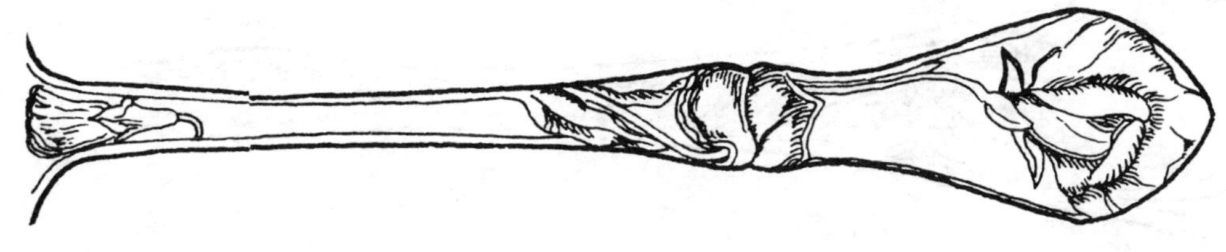

Sweet Pea
(1890 Jennings Bros.)
(Associated Silver Co.)
1906
S

Dinner Knife $15.00 Dinner Fork $12.00 Teaspoon $8.00

Dinner Knife $15.00
Dinner Fork $10.00
Teaspoon $7.00

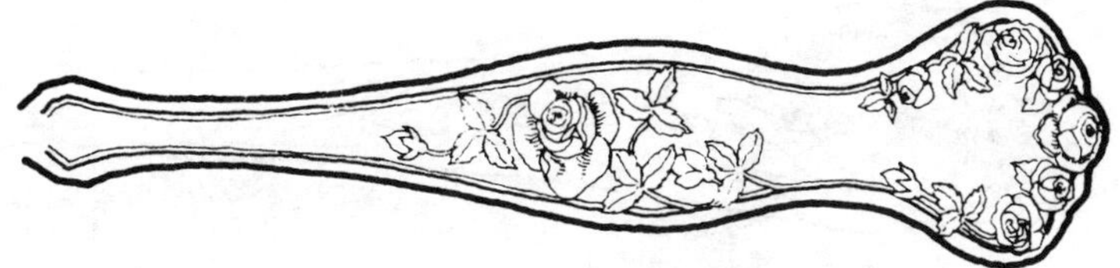

Elmwood
(Cambridge)
1907
S

Please refer to "How To Use This Book" page 4.

Sears Roebuck & Co. - Paragon Silver Plate, Sears Roebuck & Co. - Salem Silver Plate

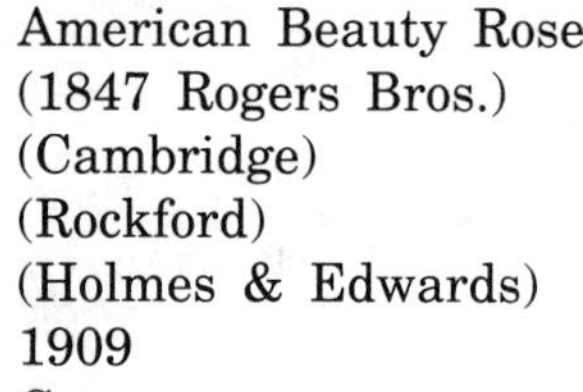

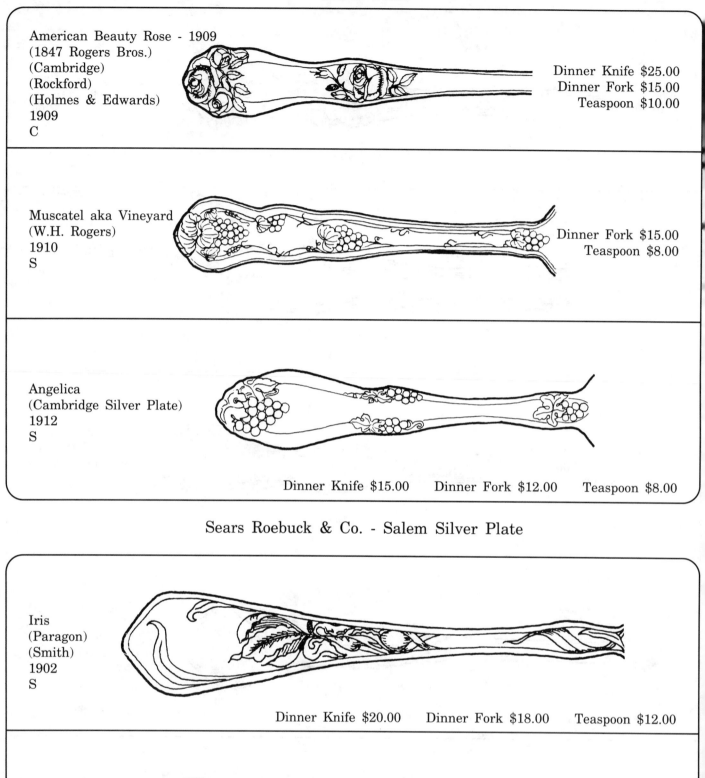

American Beauty Rose - 1909
(1847 Rogers Bros.)
(Cambridge)
(Rockford)
(Holmes & Edwards)
1909
C

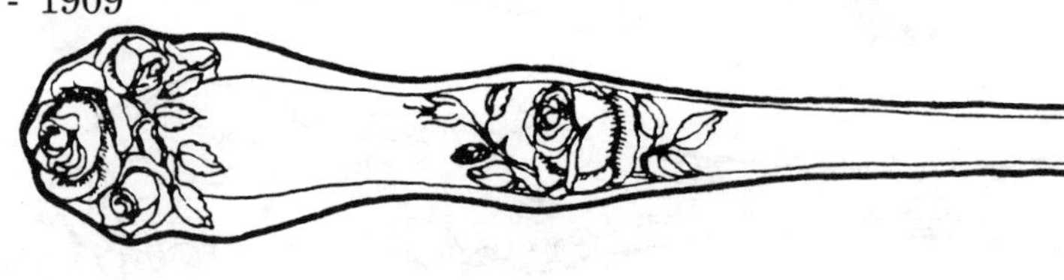

Dinner Knife $25.00
Dinner Fork $15.00
Teaspoon $10.00

Muscatel aka Vineyard
(W.H. Rogers)
1910
S

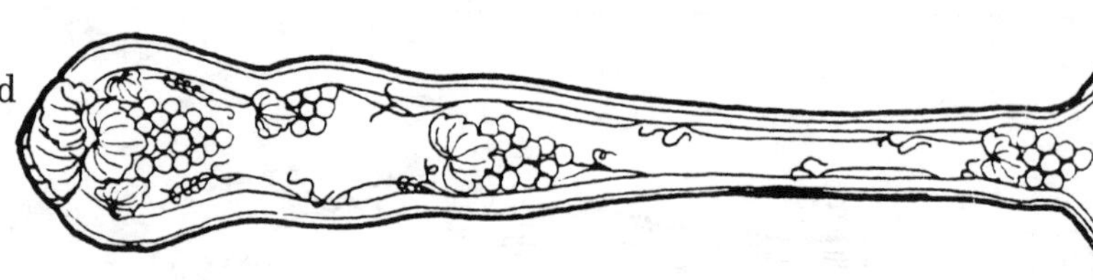

Dinner Fork $15.00
Teaspoon $8.00

Angelica
(Cambridge Silver Plate)
1912
S

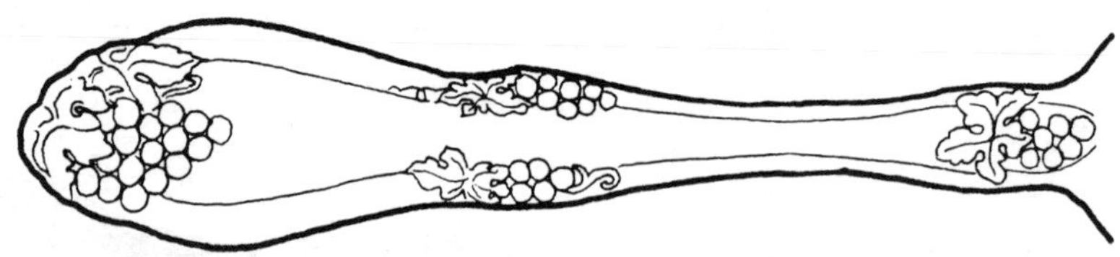

Dinner Knife $15.00 Dinner Fork $12.00 Teaspoon $8.00

Sears Roebuck & Co. - Salem Silver Plate

Iris
(Paragon)
(Smith)
1902
S

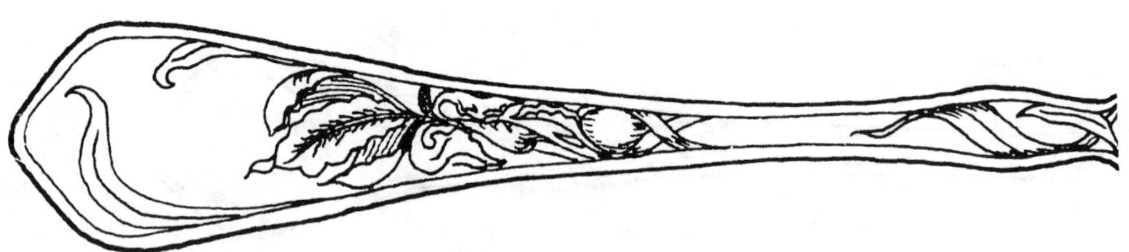

Dinner Knife $20.00 Dinner Fork $18.00 Teaspoon $12.00

Iris Variation
(Paragon)
(Smith)
1902
S

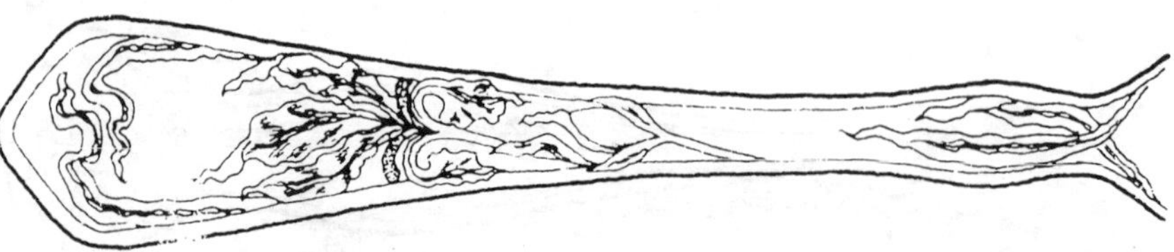

Dinner Knife $20.00 Dinner Fork $18.00 Teaspoon $12.00

Please refer to "How To Use This Book" page 4.

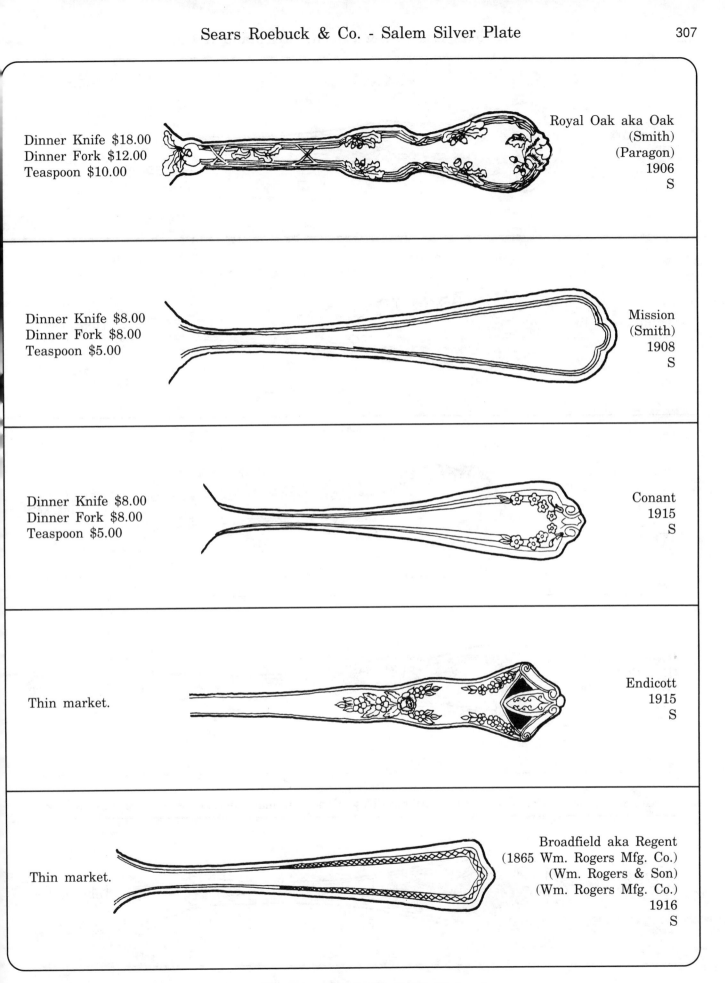

Dinner Knife $18.00
Dinner Fork $12.00
Teaspoon $10.00

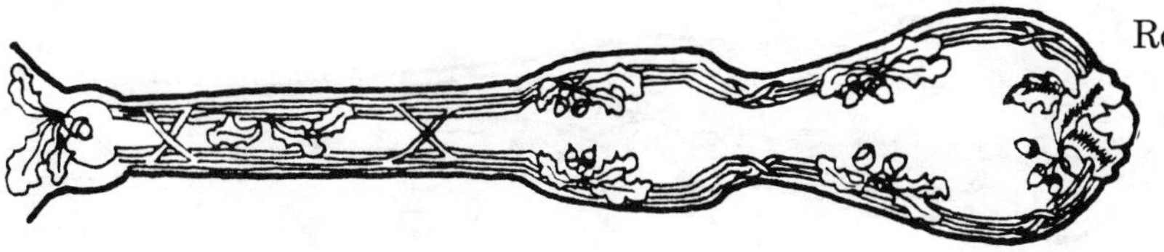

Royal Oak aka Oak
(Smith)
(Paragon)
1906
S

Dinner Knife $8.00
Dinner Fork $8.00
Teaspoon $5.00

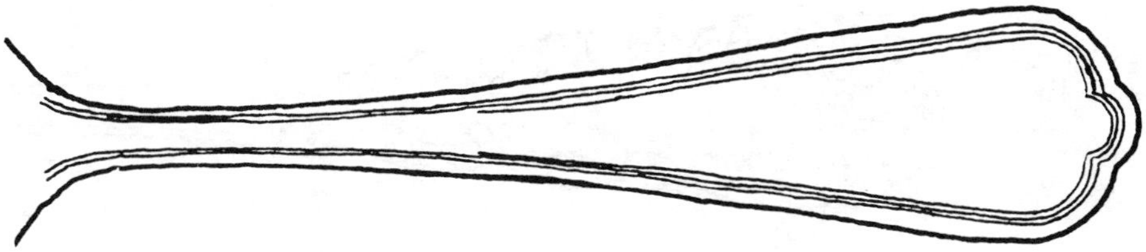

Mission
(Smith)
1908
S

Dinner Knife $8.00
Dinner Fork $8.00
Teaspoon $5.00

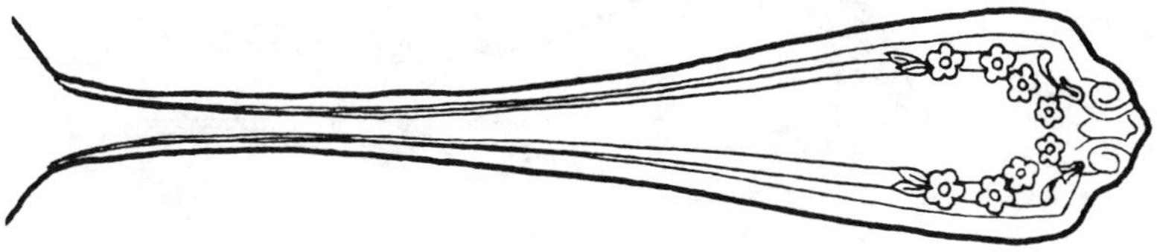

Conant
1915
S

Thin market.

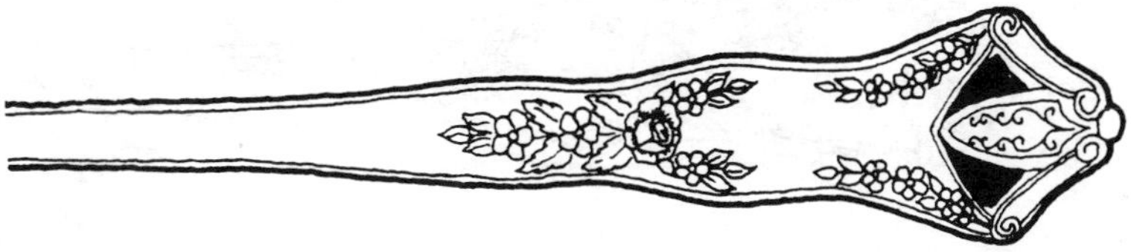

Endicott
1915
S

Thin market.

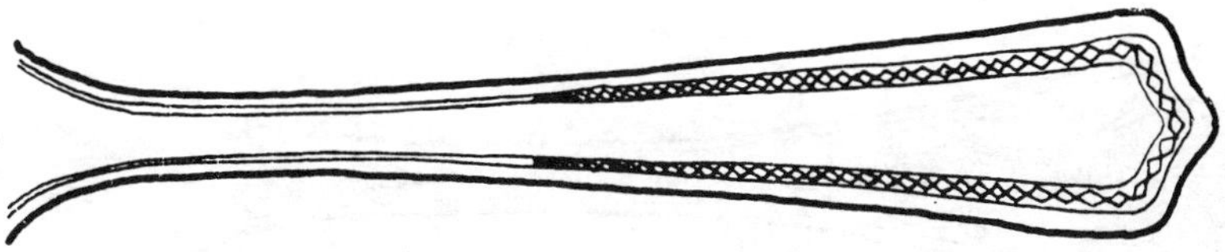

Broadfield aka Regent
(1865 Wm. Rogers Mfg. Co.)
(Wm. Rogers & Son)
(Wm. Rogers Mfg. Co.)
1916
S

Please refer to "How To Use This Book" page 4.

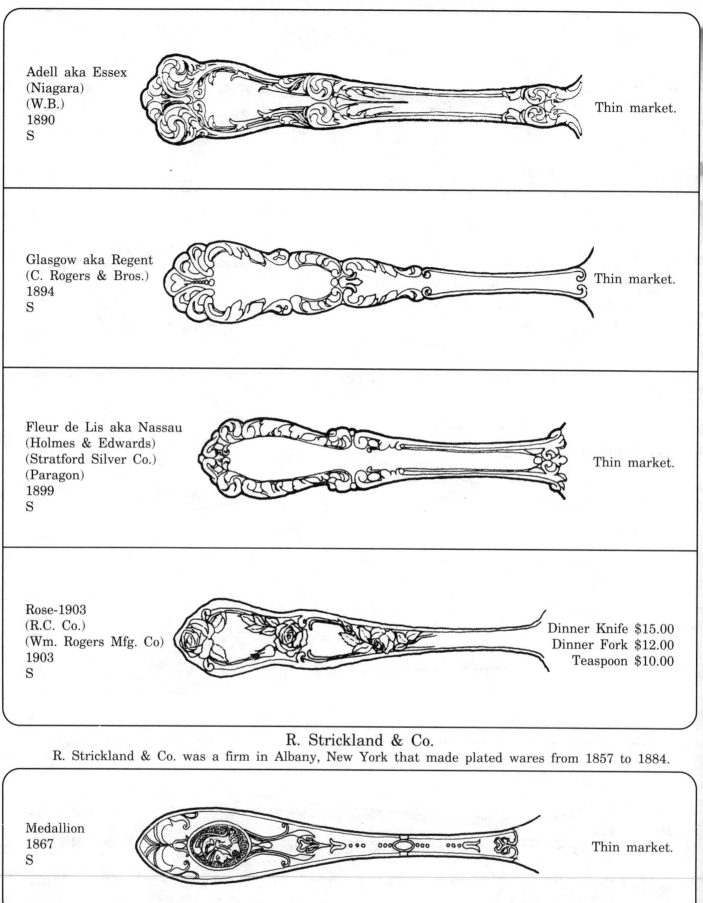

Adell aka Essex
(Niagara)
(W.B.)
1890
S

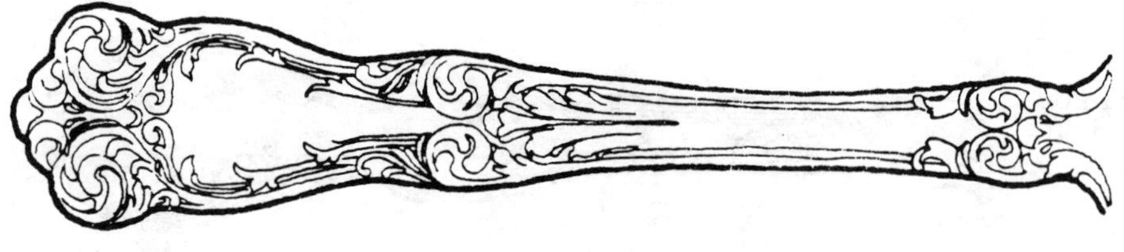

Thin market.

Glasgow aka Regent
(C. Rogers & Bros.)
1894
S

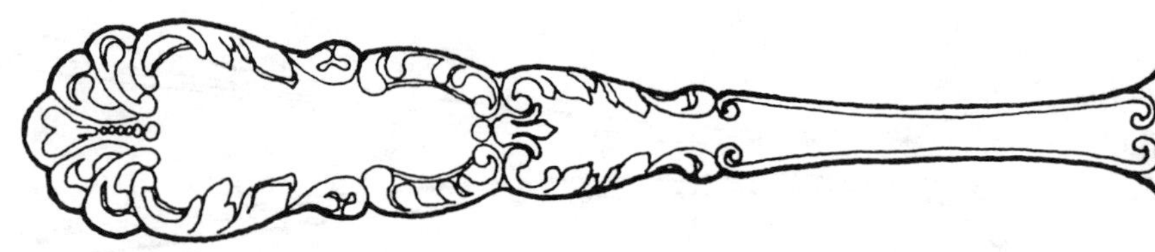

Thin market.

Fleur de Lis aka Nassau
(Holmes & Edwards)
(Stratford Silver Co.)
(Paragon)
1899
S

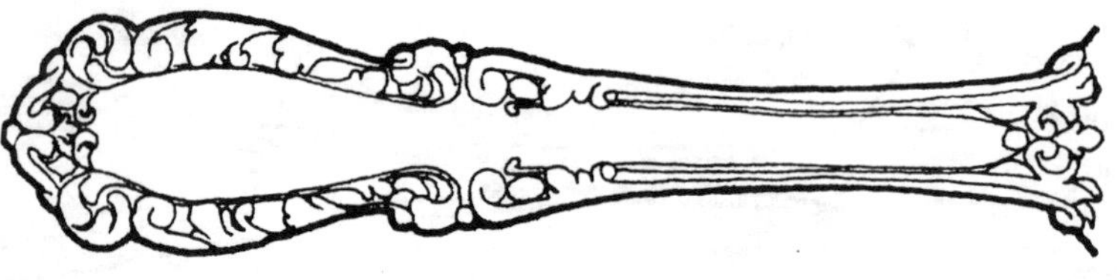

Thin market.

Rose-1903
(R.C. Co.)
(Wm. Rogers Mfg. Co)
1903
S

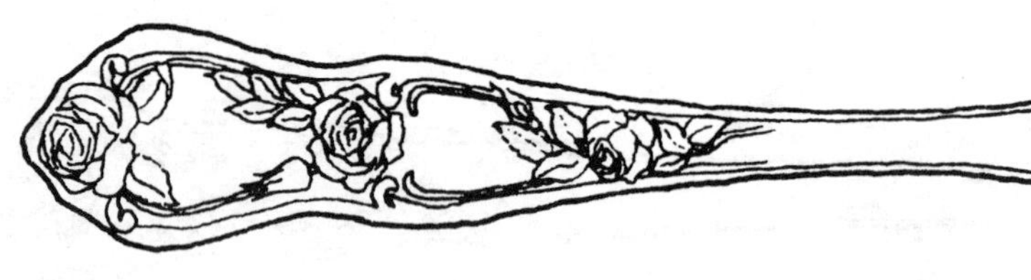

Dinner Knife $15.00
Dinner Fork $12.00
Teaspoon $10.00

R. Strickland & Co.

R. Strickland & Co. was a firm in Albany, New York that made plated wares from 1857 to 1884.

Medallion
1867
S

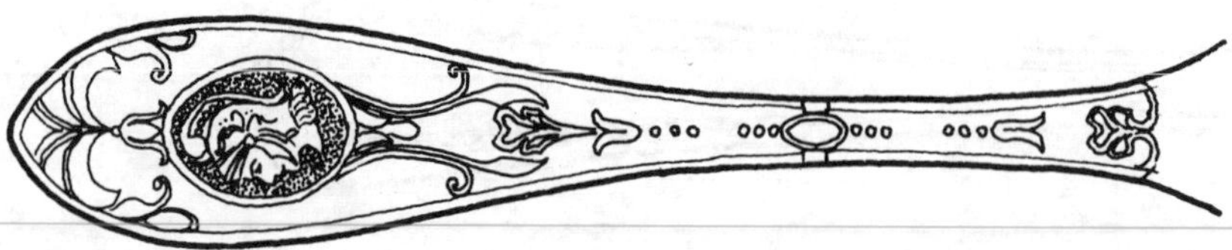

Thin market.

Please refer to "How To Use This Book" page 4.

Tiffany

Tiffany & Co., Inc. of New York, New York is perhaps best known for their sterling silver. However they did make silverplated flatware in the later part of the 19th and the early 20th century.

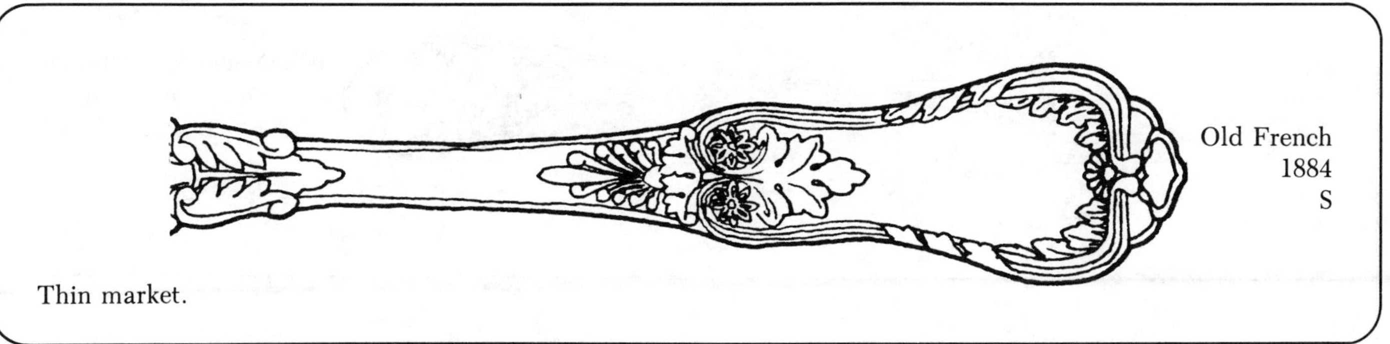

Old French
1884
S

Thin market.

Towle

Towle Silversmiths of Newburyport, Massachusetts can trace their beginnings to 1720. However, the name Towle did not appear in the name of the firm until 1857. This firm makes sterling, silverplate and stainless items.

Towle Silversmiths acquired the William Adams line of silverplated flatware in 1979. The firm has no records of when the William Adams patterns were first introduced. Towle began merchandising these patterns in 1980.

Towle - William Adams

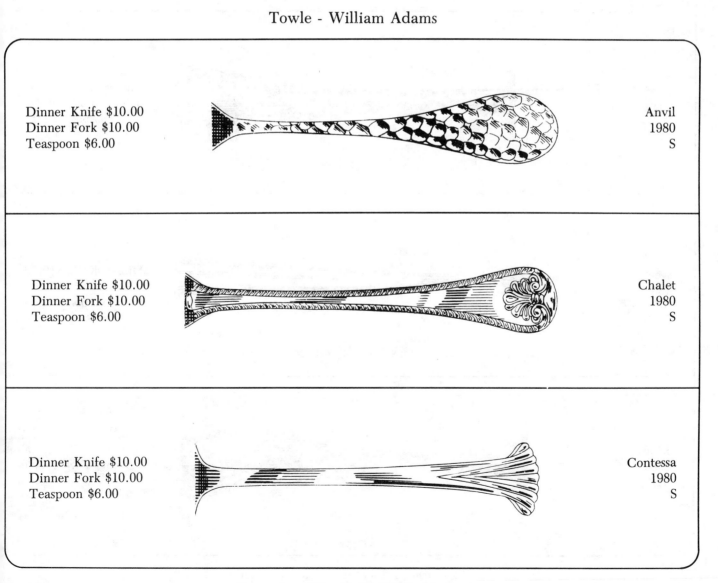

Dinner Knife $10.00
Dinner Fork $10.00
Teaspoon $6.00

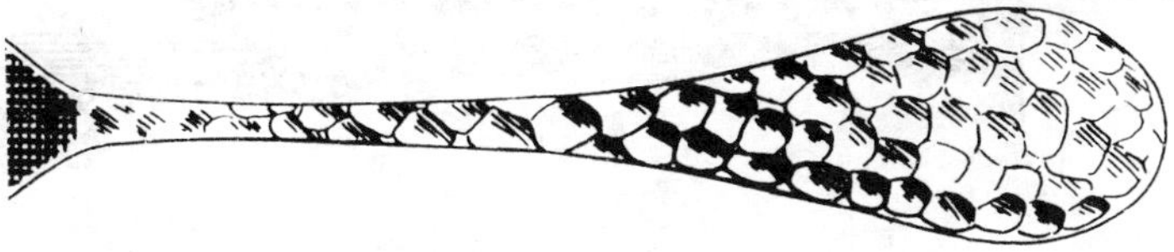

Anvil
1980
S

Dinner Knife $10.00
Dinner Fork $10.00
Teaspoon $6.00

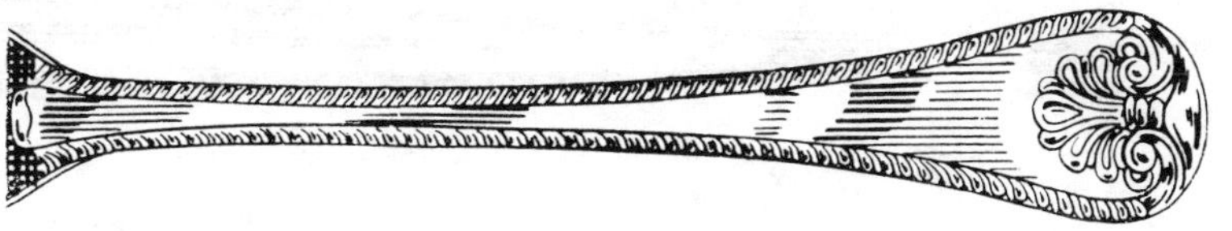

Chalet
1980
S

Dinner Knife $10.00
Dinner Fork $10.00
Teaspoon $6.00

Contessa
1980
S

Please refer to "How To Use This Book" page 4.

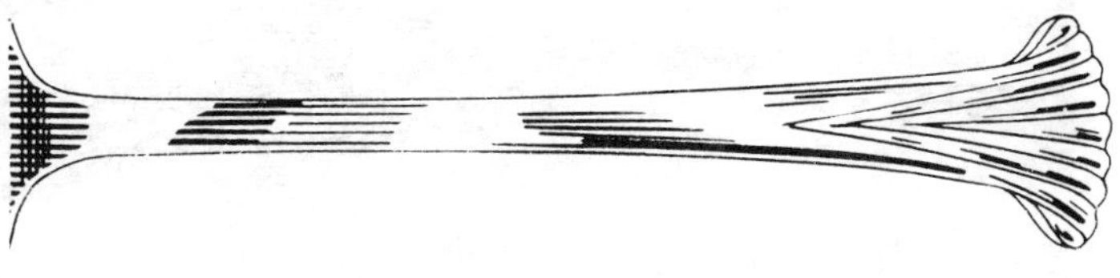

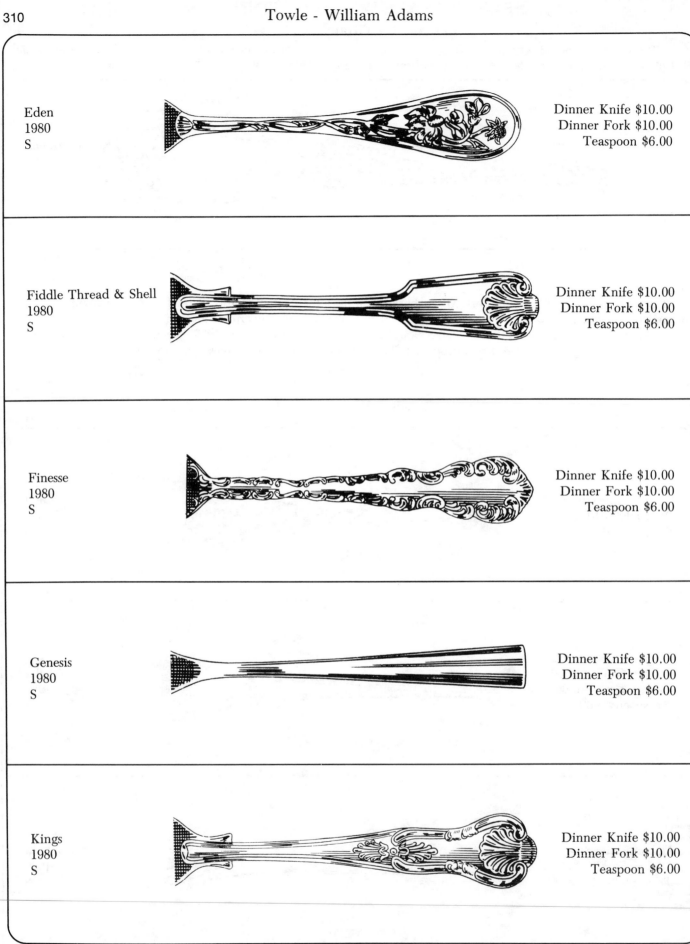

Eden
1980
S

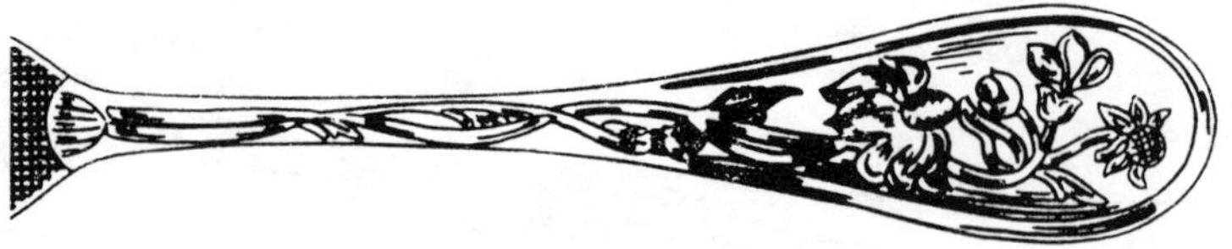

Dinner Knife $10.00
Dinner Fork $10.00
Teaspoon $6.00

Fiddle Thread & Shell
1980
S

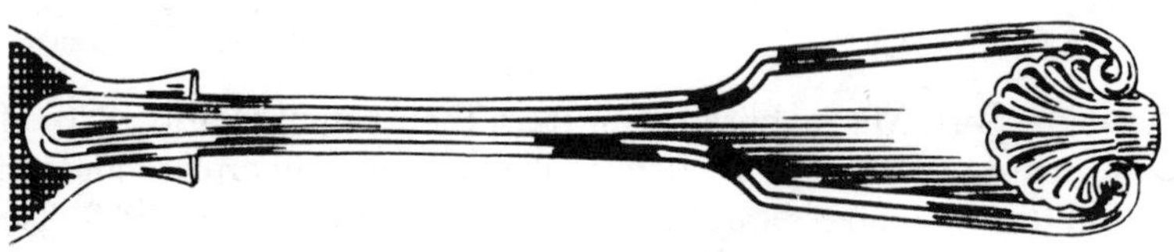

Dinner Knife $10.00
Dinner Fork $10.00
Teaspoon $6.00

Finesse
1980
S

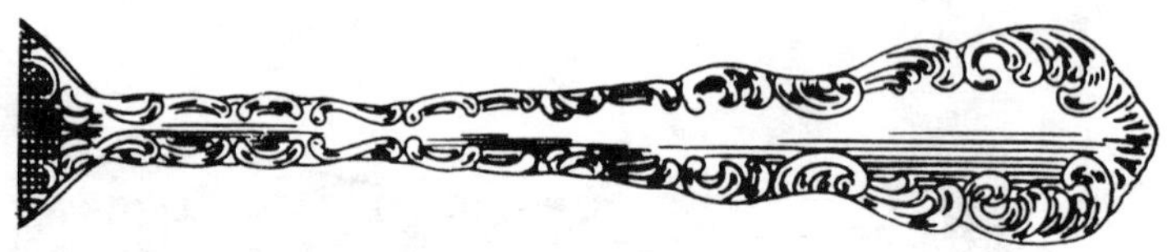

Dinner Knife $10.00
Dinner Fork $10.00
Teaspoon $6.00

Genesis
1980
S

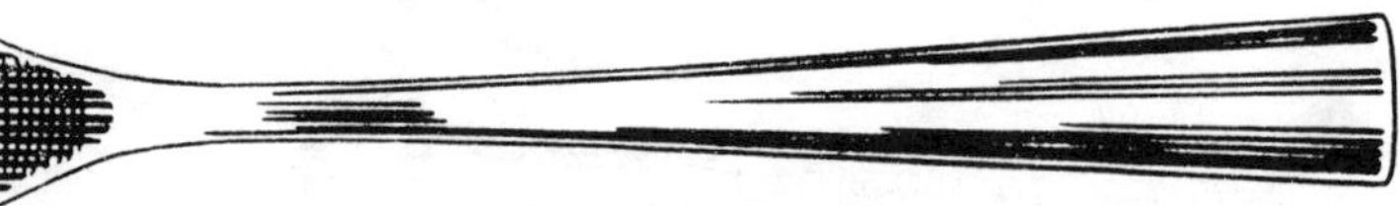

Dinner Knife $10.00
Dinner Fork $10.00
Teaspoon $6.00

Kings
1980
S

Dinner Knife $10.00
Dinner Fork $10.00
Teaspoon $6.00

Please refer to "How To Use This Book" page 4.

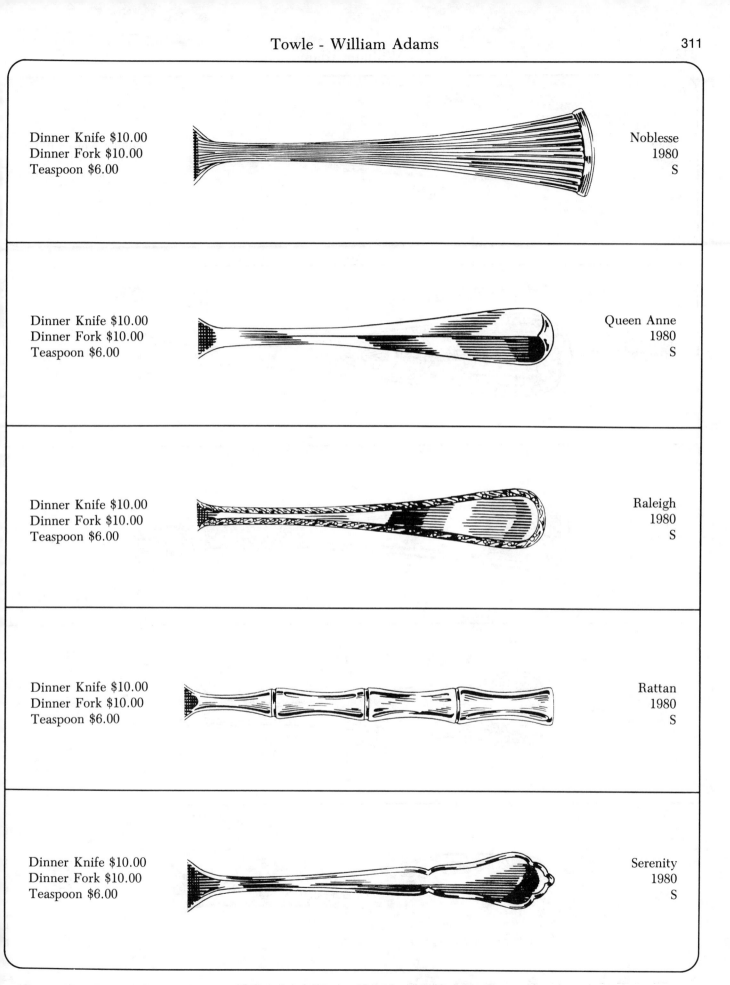

Dinner Knife $10.00
Dinner Fork $10.00
Teaspoon $6.00

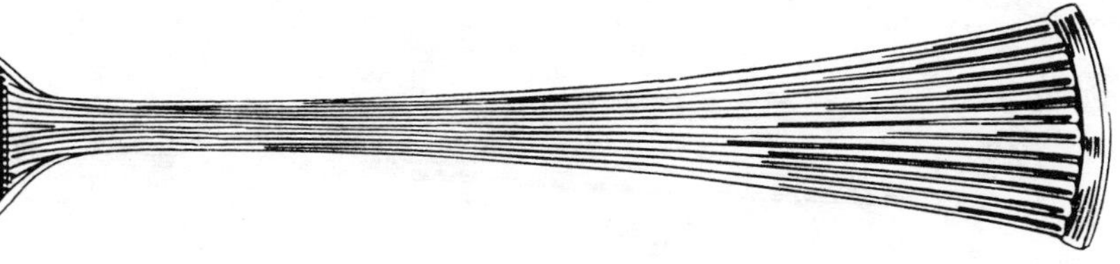

Noblesse
1980
S

Dinner Knife $10.00
Dinner Fork $10.00
Teaspoon $6.00

Queen Anne
1980
S

Dinner Knife $10.00
Dinner Fork $10.00
Teaspoon $6.00

Raleigh
1980
S

Dinner Knife $10.00
Dinner Fork $10.00
Teaspoon $6.00

Rattan
1980
S

Dinner Knife $10.00
Dinner Fork $10.00
Teaspoon $6.00

Serenity
1980
S

Please refer to "How To Use This Book" page 4.

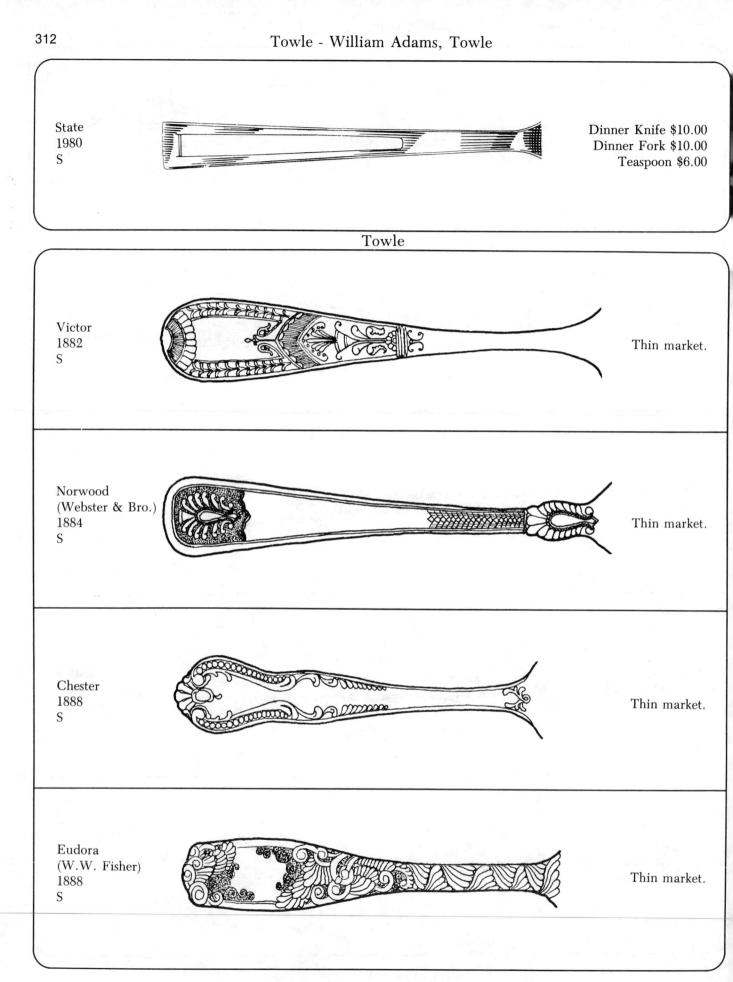

State
1980
S

Dinner Knife $10.00
Dinner Fork $10.00
Teaspoon $6.00

Towle

Victor
1882
S

Thin market.

Norwood
(Webster & Bro.)
1884
S

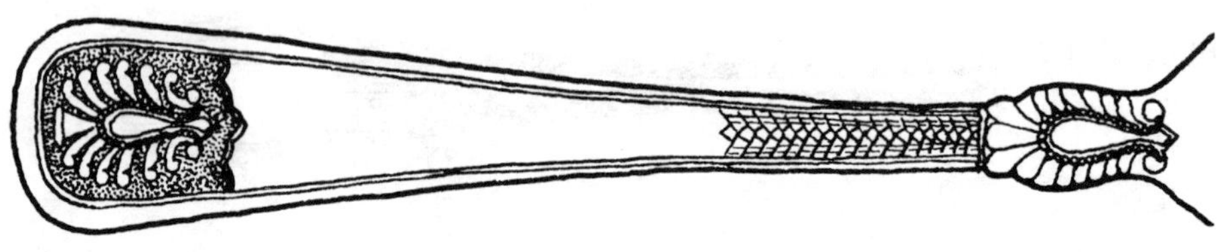

Thin market.

Chester
1888
S

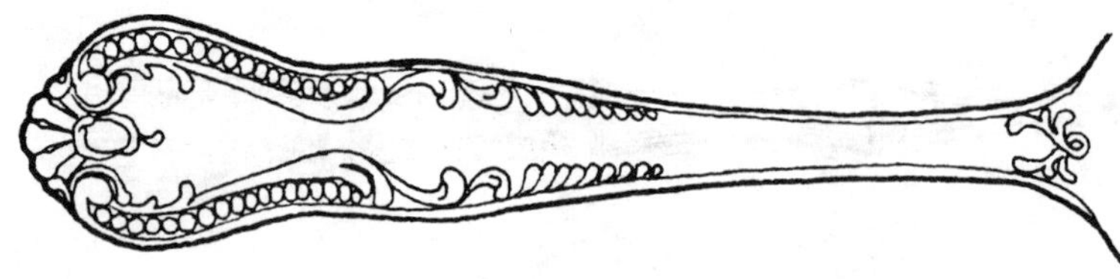

Thin market.

Eudora
(W.W. Fisher)
1888
S

Thin market.

Please refer to "How To Use This Book" page 4.

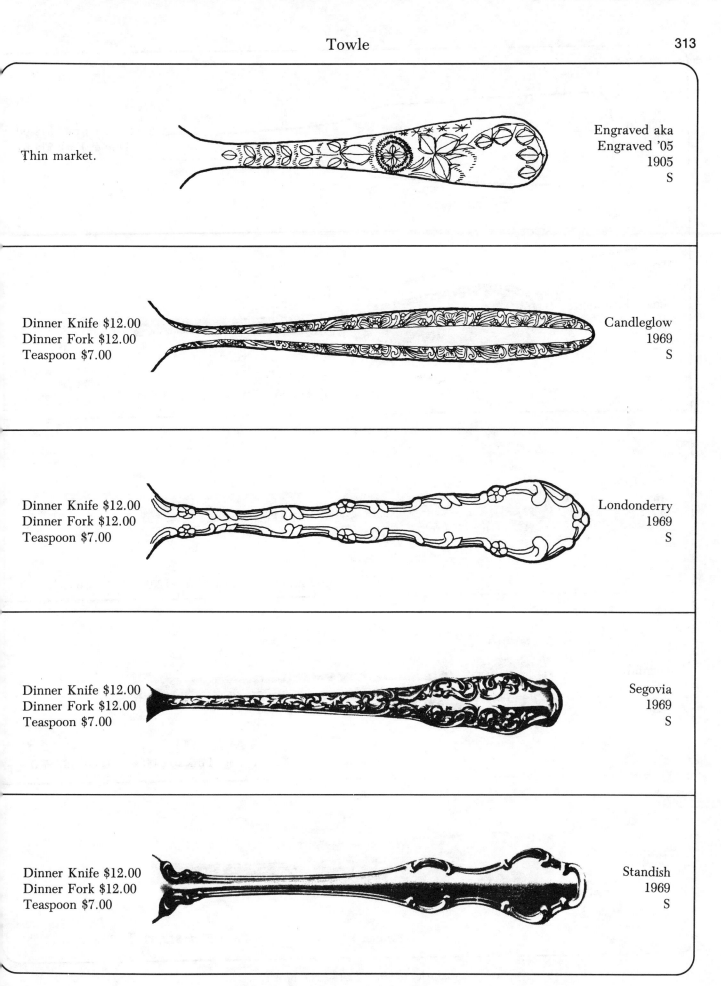

Thin market.

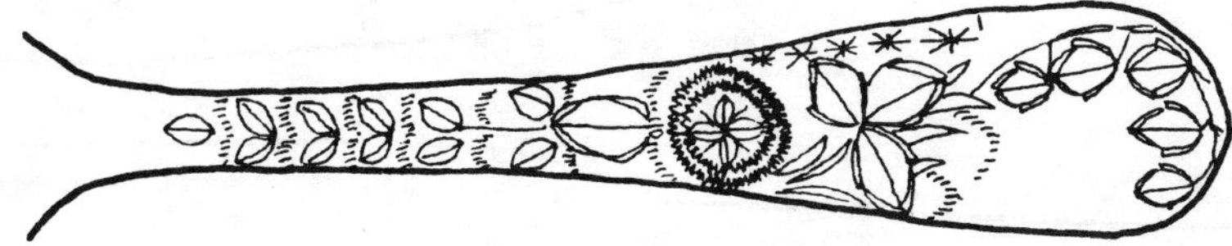

Engraved aka
Engraved '05
1905
S

Dinner Knife $12.00
Dinner Fork $12.00
Teaspoon $7.00

Candleglow
1969
S

Dinner Knife $12.00
Dinner Fork $12.00
Teaspoon $7.00

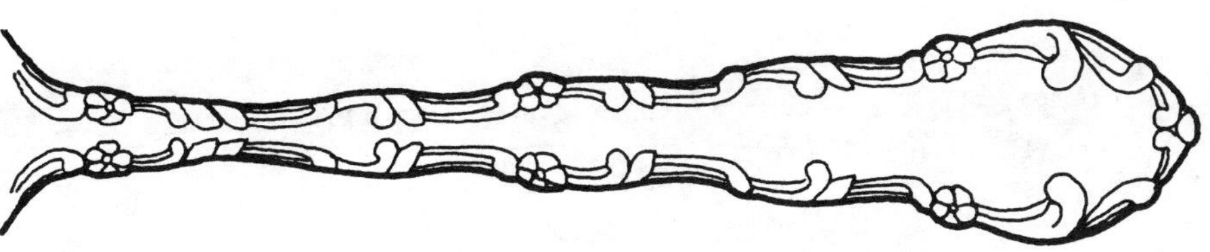

Londonderry
1969
S

Dinner Knife $12.00
Dinner Fork $12.00
Teaspoon $7.00

Segovia
1969
S

Dinner Knife $12.00
Dinner Fork $12.00
Teaspoon $7.00

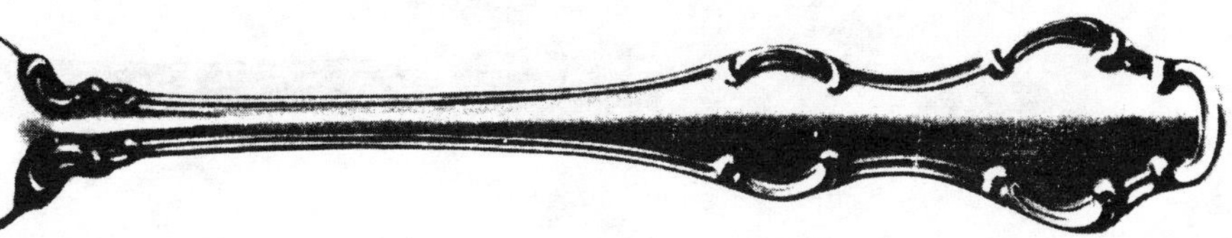

Standish
1969
S

Please refer to "How To Use This Book" page 4.

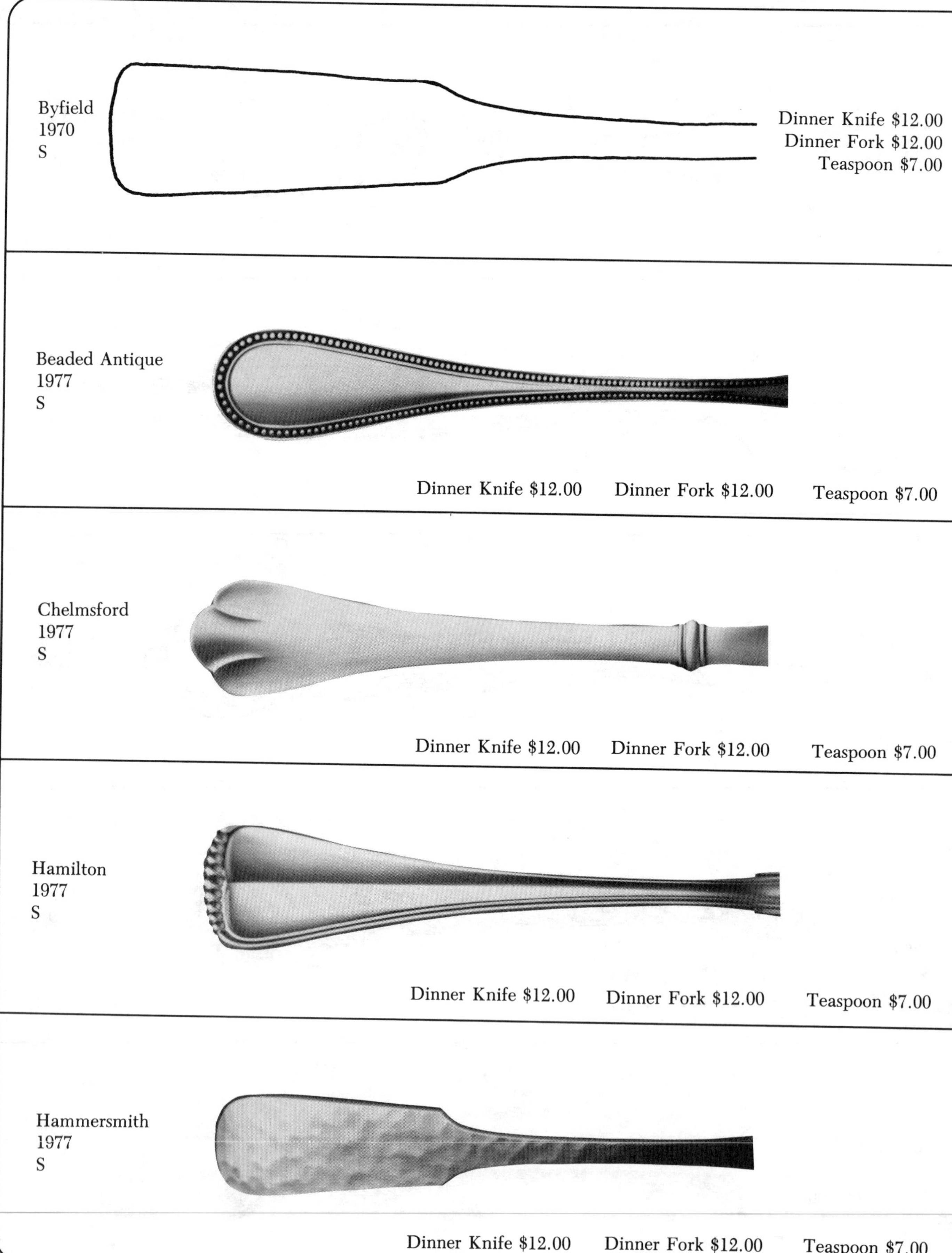

Byfield
1970
S

Dinner Knife $12.00
Dinner Fork $12.00
Teaspoon $7.00

Beaded Antique
1977
S

Dinner Knife $12.00 Dinner Fork $12.00 Teaspoon $7.00

Chelmsford
1977
S

Dinner Knife $12.00 Dinner Fork $12.00 Teaspoon $7.00

Hamilton
1977
S

Dinner Knife $12.00 Dinner Fork $12.00 Teaspoon $7.00

Hammersmith
1977
S

Dinner Knife $12.00 Dinner Fork $12.00 Teaspoon $7.00

Please refer to "How To Use This Book" page 4.

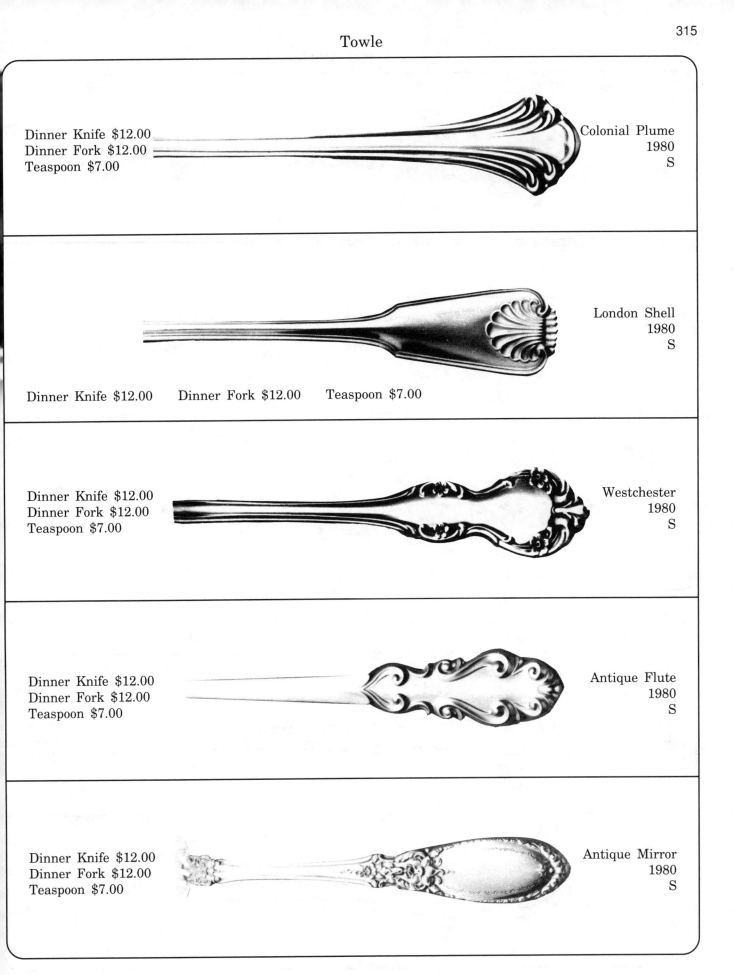

Dinner Knife $12.00
Dinner Fork $12.00
Teaspoon $7.00

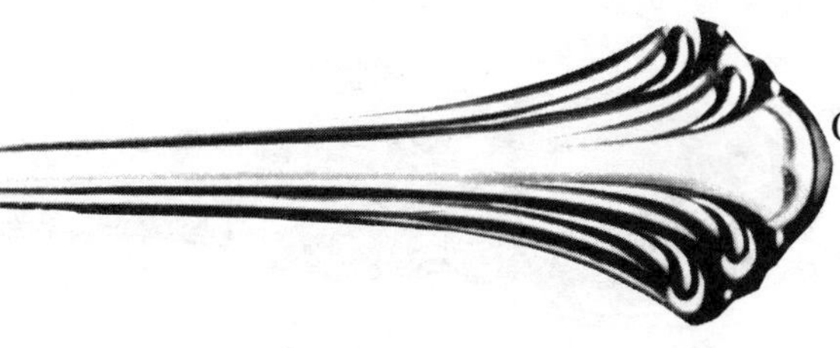

Colonial Plume
1980
S

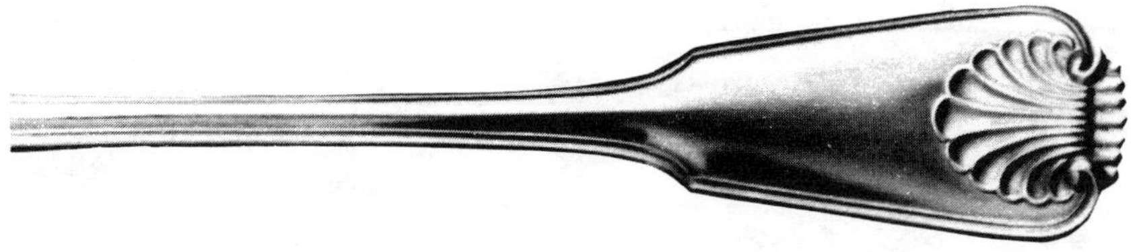

London Shell
1980
S

Dinner Knife $12.00 Dinner Fork $12.00 Teaspoon $7.00

Dinner Knife $12.00
Dinner Fork $12.00
Teaspoon $7.00

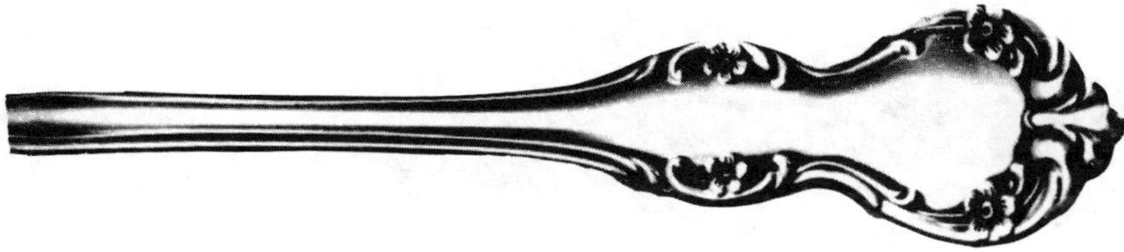

Westchester
1980
S

Dinner Knife $12.00
Dinner Fork $12.00
Teaspoon $7.00

Antique Flute
1980
S

Dinner Knife $12.00
Dinner Fork $12.00
Teaspoon $7.00

Antique Mirror
1980
S

Please refer to "How To Use This Book" page 4.

Towle, Universal

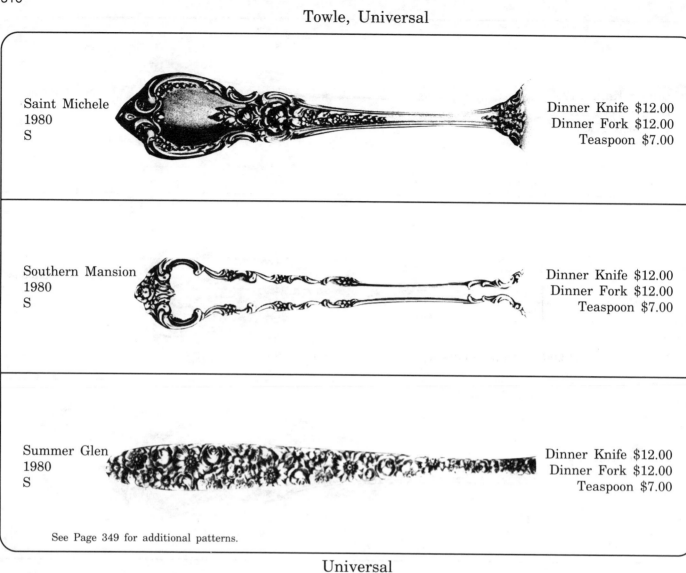

Saint Michele
1980
S

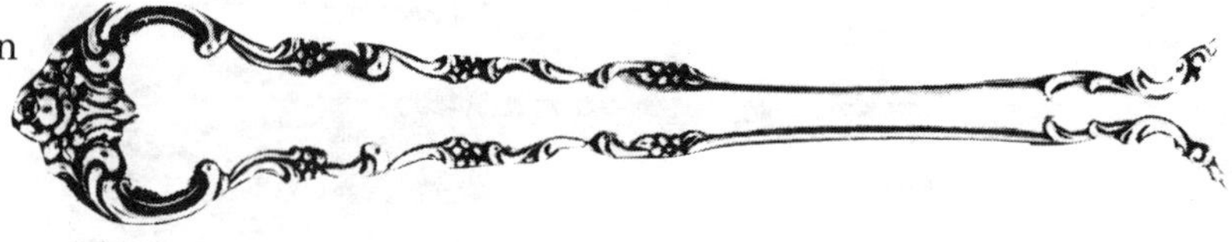

Dinner Knife $12.00
Dinner Fork $12.00
Teaspoon $7.00

Southern Mansion
1980
S

Dinner Knife $12.00
Dinner Fork $12.00
Teaspoon $7.00

Summer Glen
1980
S

Dinner Knife $12.00
Dinner Fork $12.00
Teaspoon $7.00

See Page 349 for additional patterns.

Universal

The Universal mark was used by Landers, Frary & Clark. The firm which is no longer in business was located in New Britain, Connecticut and made flatware for nearly 100 years ending production about 1950.

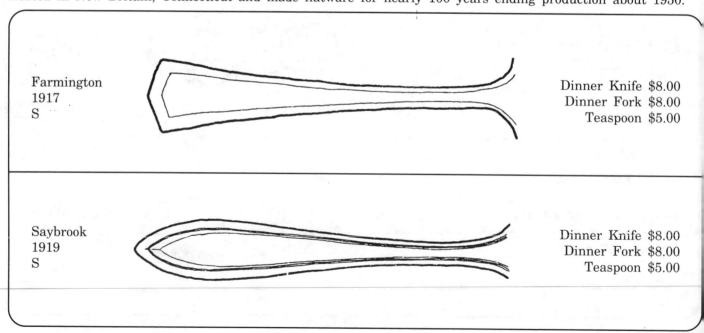

Farmington
1917
S

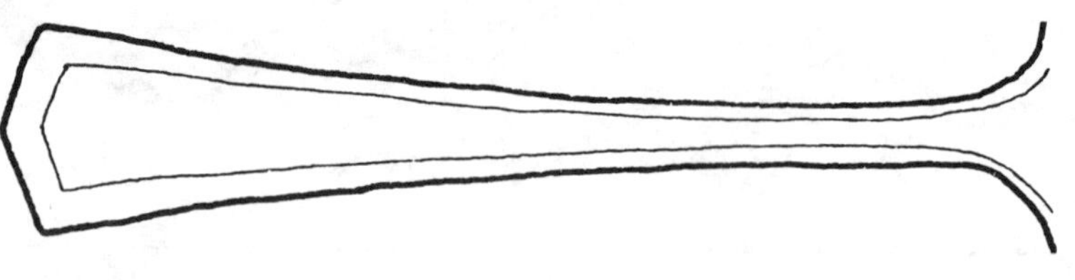

Dinner Knife $8.00
Dinner Fork $8.00
Teaspoon $5.00

Saybrook
1919
S

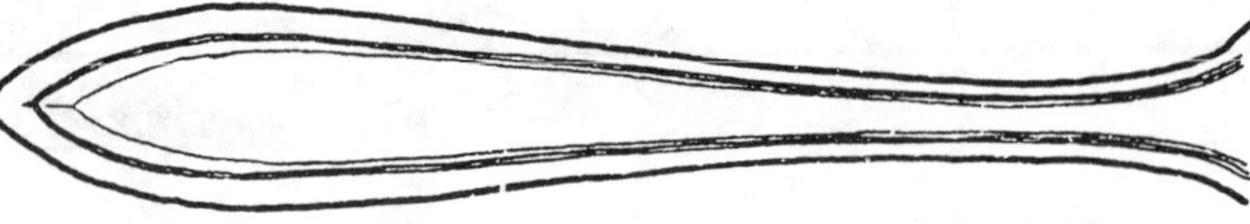

Dinner Knife $8.00
Dinner Fork $8.00
Teaspoon $5.00

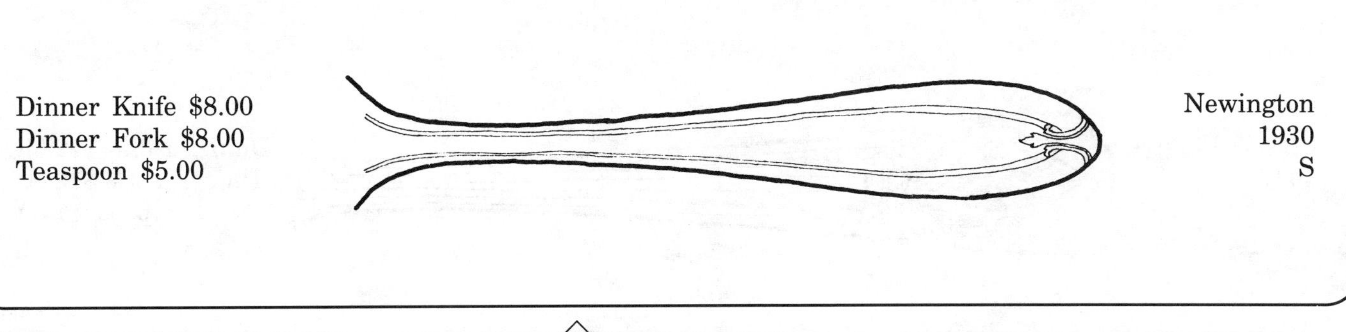

Dinner Knife $8.00
Dinner Fork $8.00
Teaspoon $5.00

Newington
1930
S

◇W Silverplate

There is no information available about the use of this backstamp.

Dinner Fork $15.00
Teaspoon $10.00

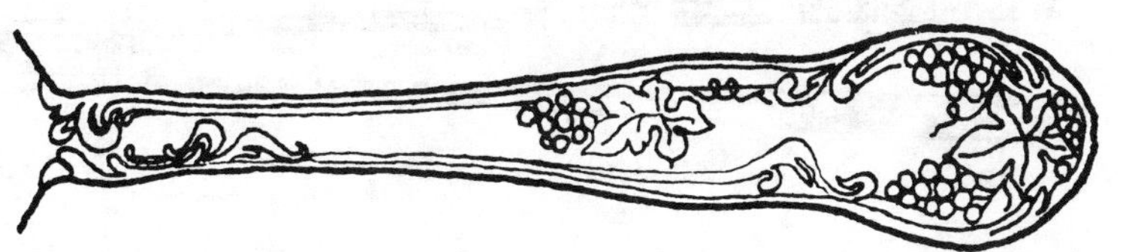

Grape
1910
S

Wallace-International

Wallace-International, Wallingford, CT. Wallace Silversmiths trace their beginnings to 1835. The firm has made silverplated and sterling flatware and hollowware. They discontinued making silverplated flatware in the 1950's and did not resume production until 1980. Both Wallace and The International Silver Co. were acquired by Katy Industries in 1984. Wallace-International was sold to an investor group late in 1986.

Wallace - Fortune Silver Plate

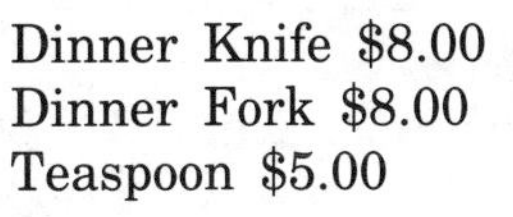

Dinner Knife $8.00
Dinner Fork $8.00
Teaspoon $5.00

Fortune
1932
S

Wallace - Harmony House

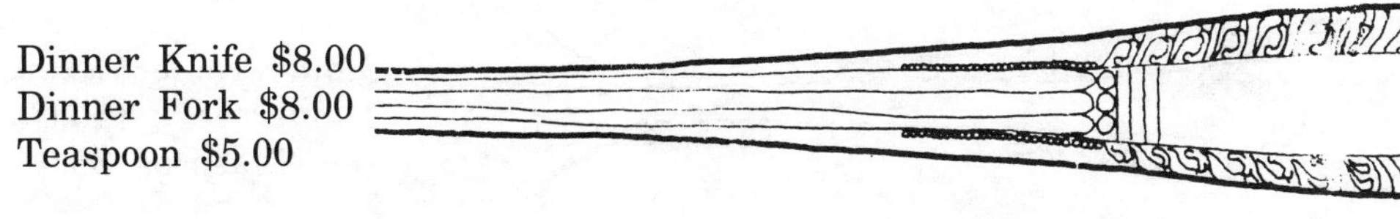

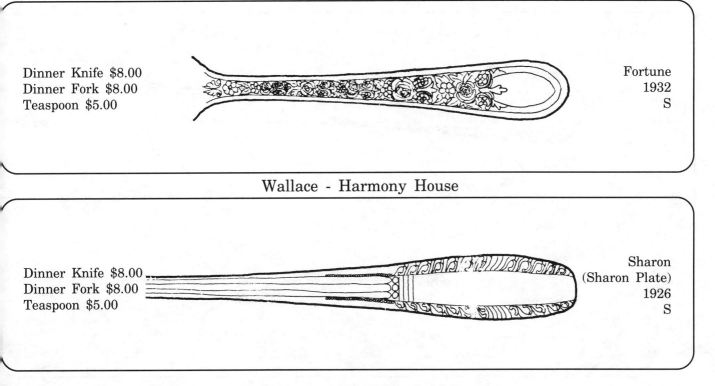

Dinner Knife $8.00
Dinner Fork $8.00
Teaspoon $5.00

Sharon
(Sharon Plate)
1926
S

Please refer to "How To Use This Book" page 4.

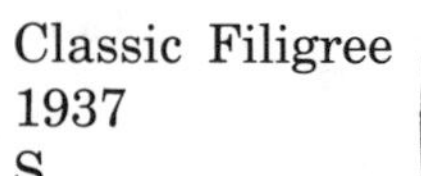

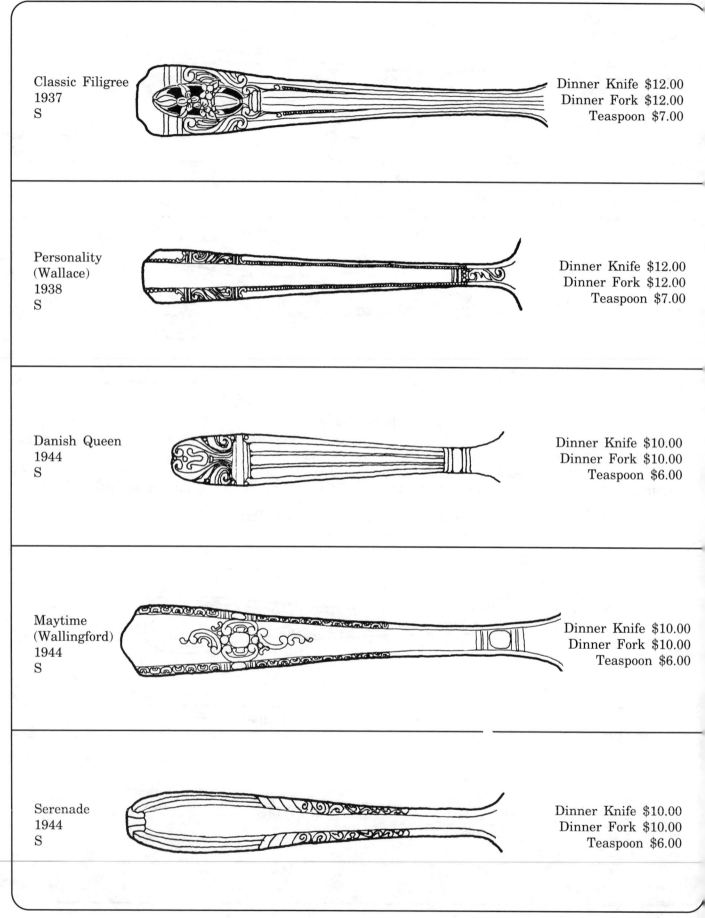

Classic Filigree
1937
S

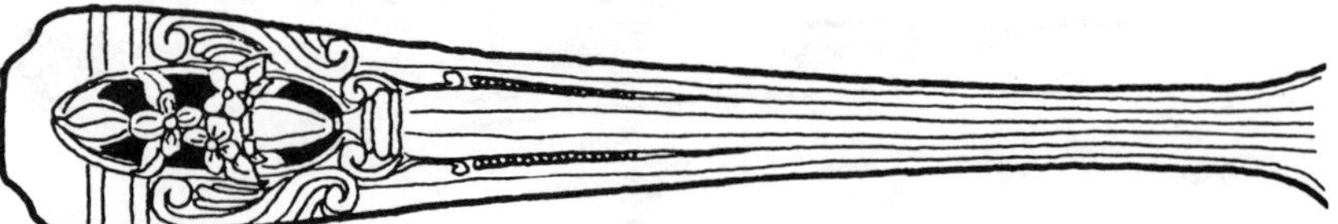

Dinner Knife $12.00
Dinner Fork $12.00
Teaspoon $7.00

Personality
(Wallace)
1938
S

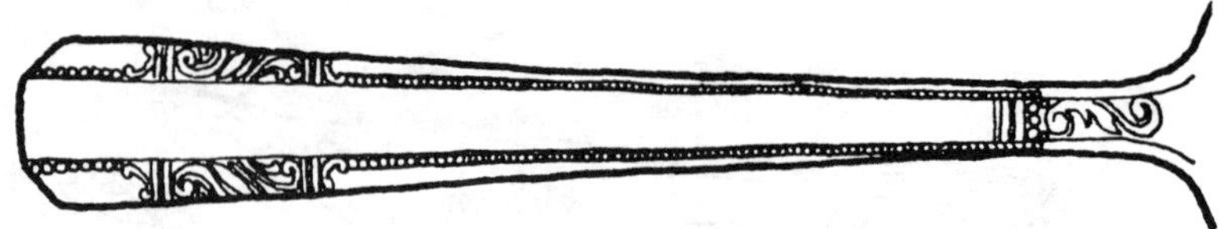

Dinner Knife $12.00
Dinner Fork $12.00
Teaspoon $7.00

Danish Queen
1944
S

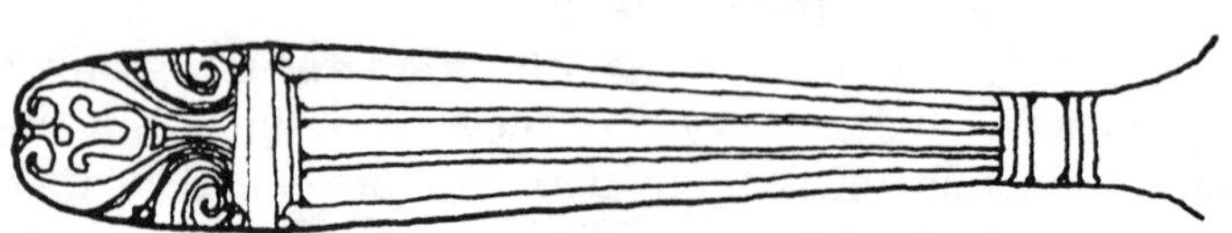

Dinner Knife $10.00
Dinner Fork $10.00
Teaspoon $6.00

Maytime
(Wallingford)
1944
S

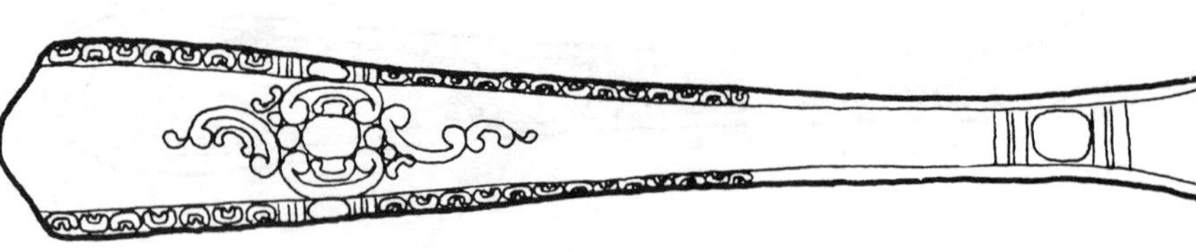

Dinner Knife $10.00
Dinner Fork $10.00
Teaspoon $6.00

Serenade
1944
S

Dinner Knife $10.00
Dinner Fork $10.00
Teaspoon $6.00

Please refer to "How To Use This Book" page 4.

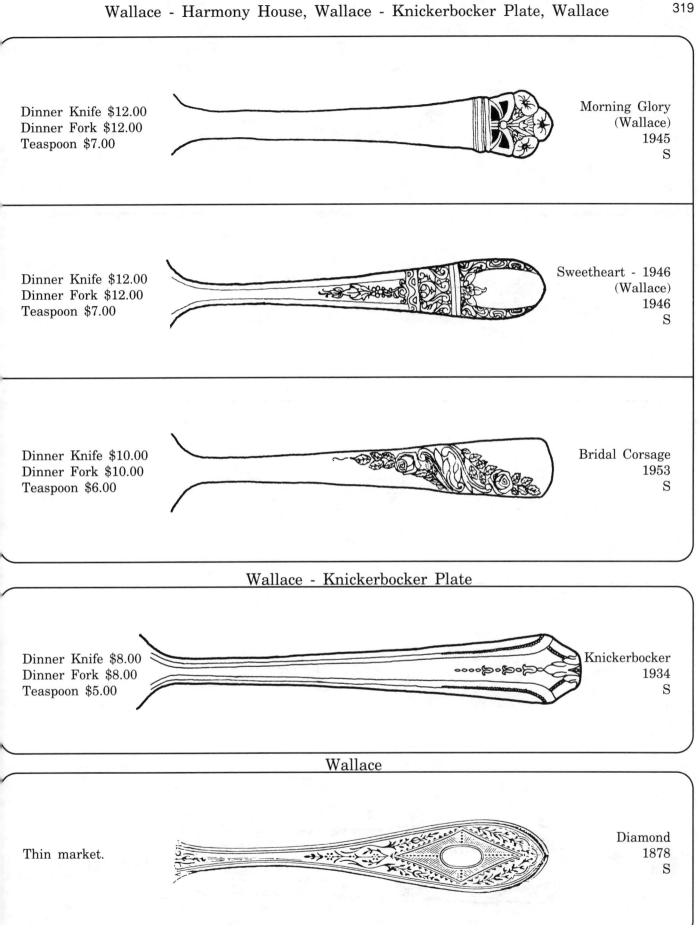

Dinner Knife $12.00
Dinner Fork $12.00
Teaspoon $7.00

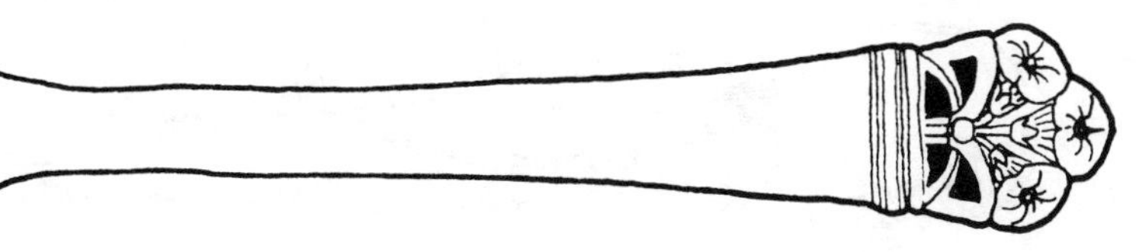

Morning Glory
(Wallace)
1945
S

Dinner Knife $12.00
Dinner Fork $12.00
Teaspoon $7.00

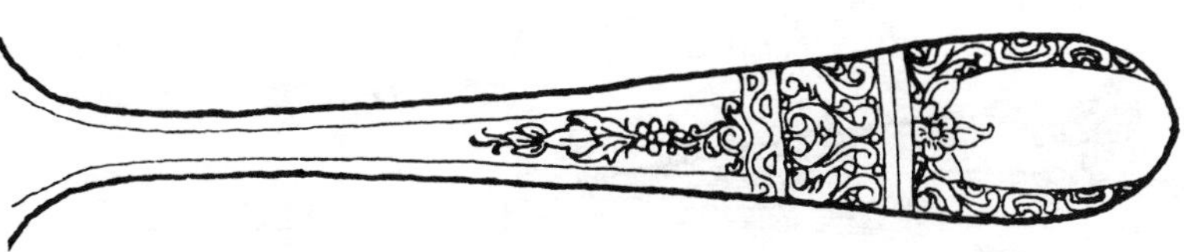

Sweetheart - 1946
(Wallace)
1946
S

Dinner Knife $10.00
Dinner Fork $10.00
Teaspoon $6.00

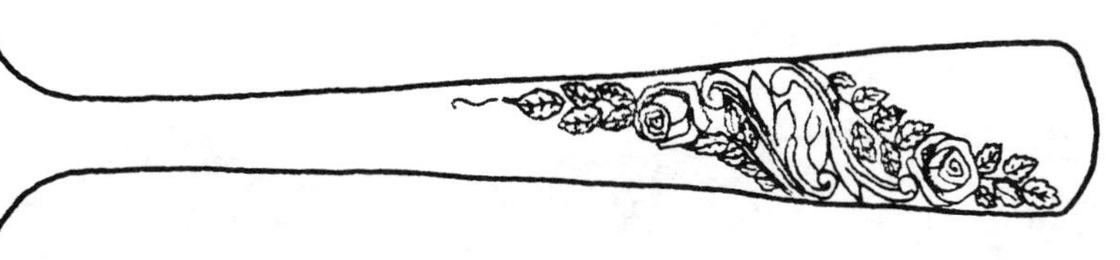

Bridal Corsage
1953
S

Wallace - Knickerbocker Plate

Dinner Knife $8.00
Dinner Fork $8.00
Teaspoon $5.00

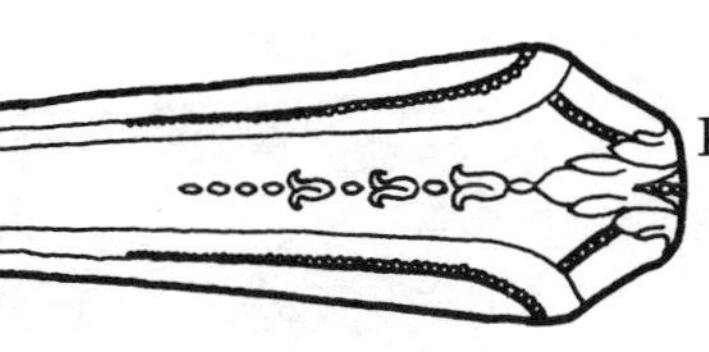

Knickerbocker
1934
S

Wallace

Thin market.

Diamond
1878
S

Please refer to "How To Use This Book" page 4.

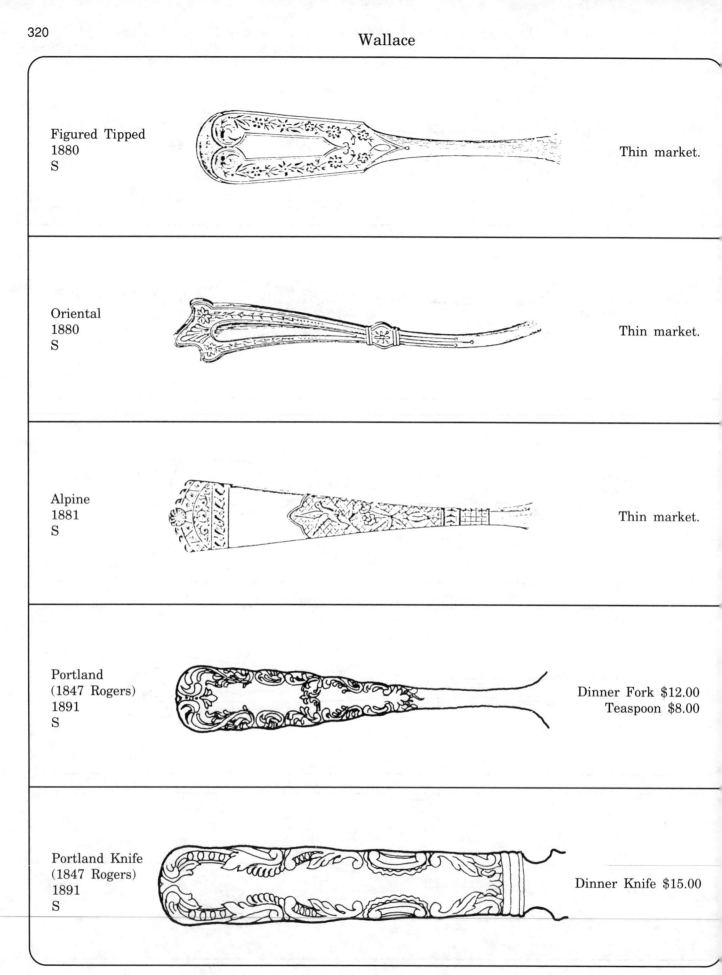

Wallace

Figured Tipped
1880
S

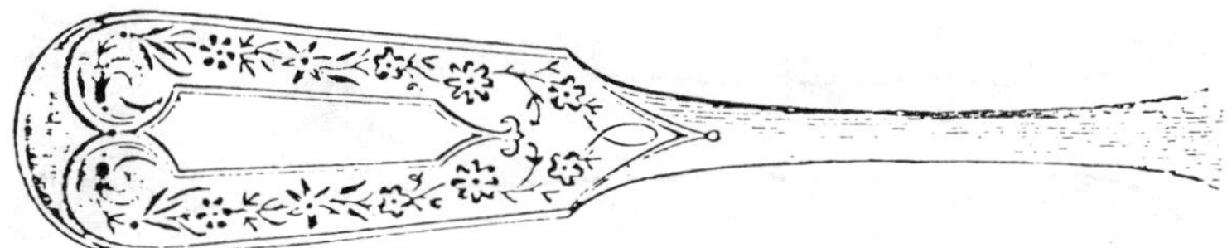

Thin market.

Oriental
1880
S

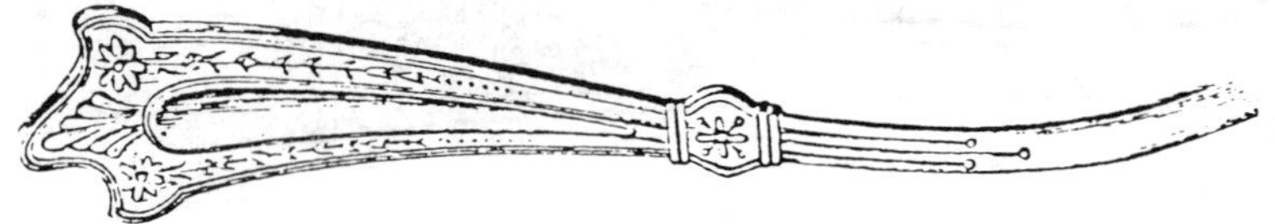

Thin market.

Alpine
1881
S

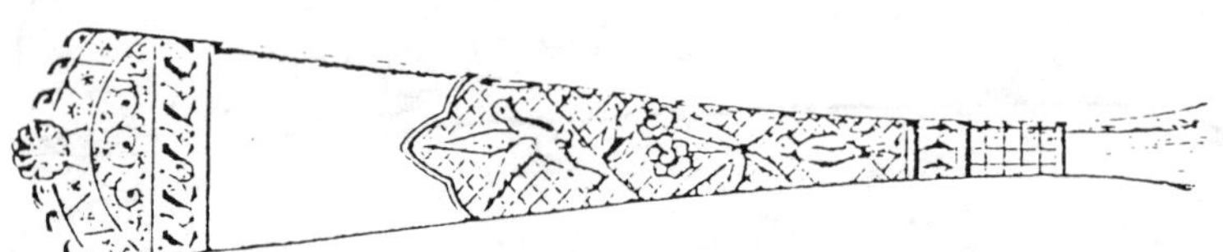

Thin market.

Portland
(1847 Rogers)
1891
S

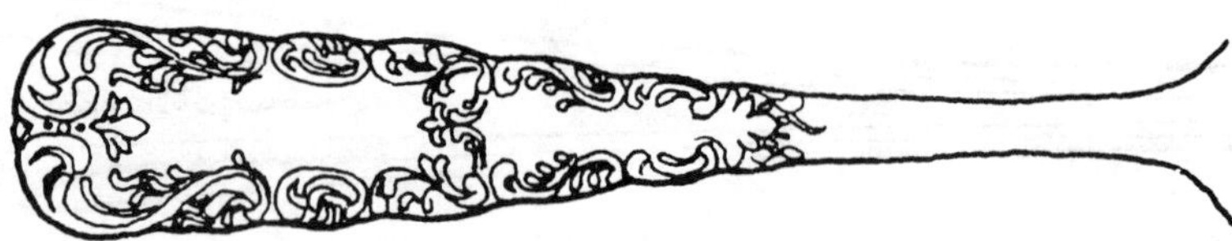

Dinner Fork $12.00
Teaspoon $8.00

Portland Knife
(1847 Rogers)
1891
S

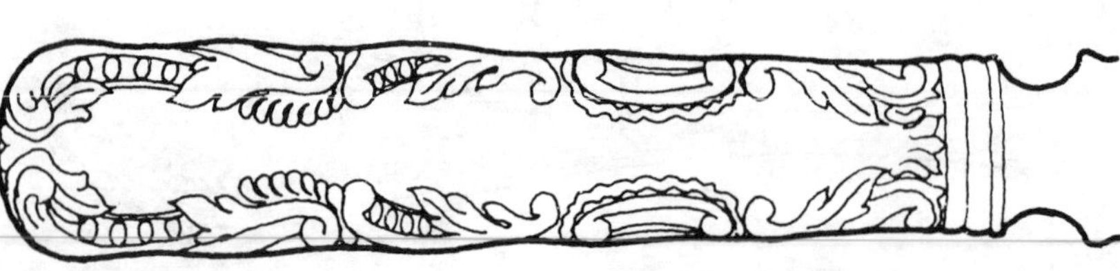

Dinner Knife $15.00

Please refer to "How To Use This Book" page 4.

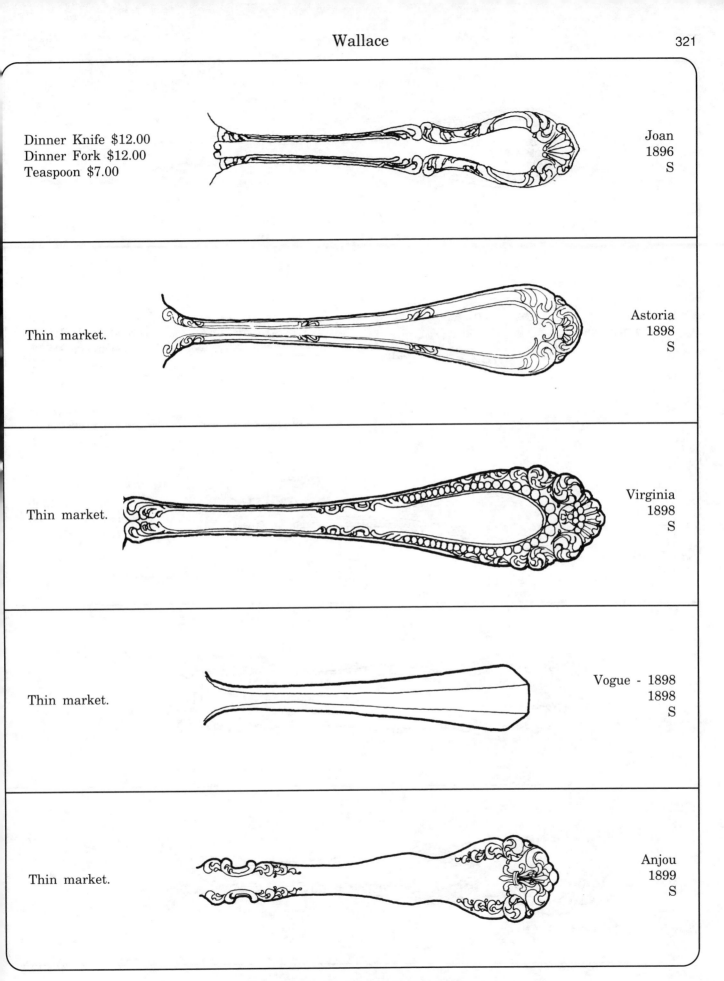

Dinner Knife $12.00
Dinner Fork $12.00
Teaspoon $7.00

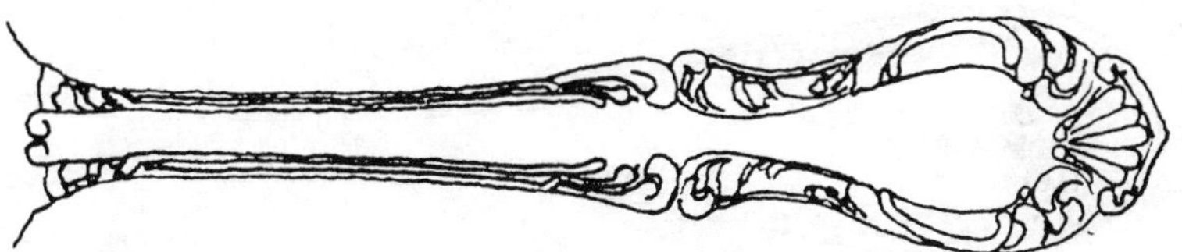

Joan
1896
S

Thin market.

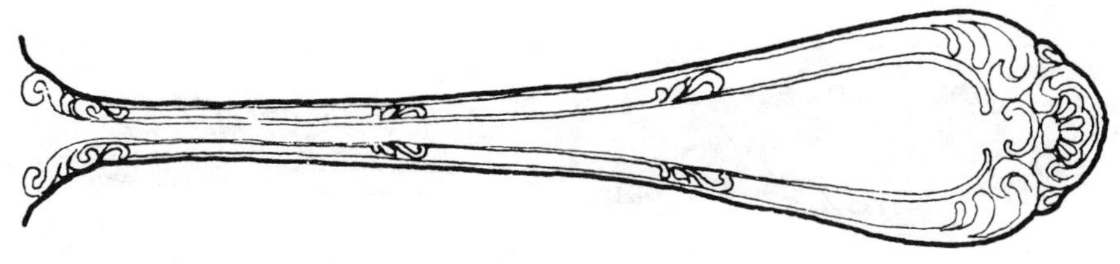

Astoria
1898
S

Thin market.

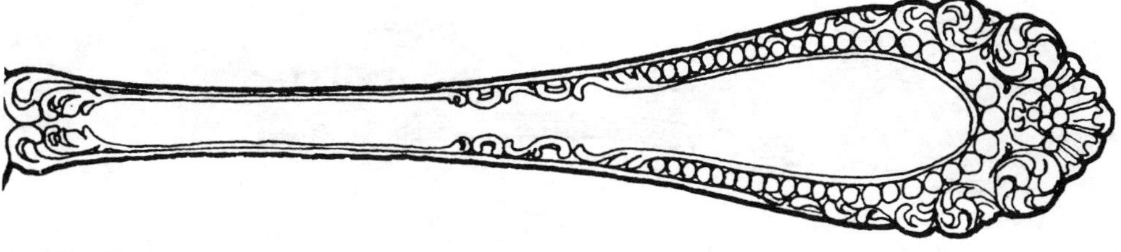

Virginia
1898
S

Thin market.

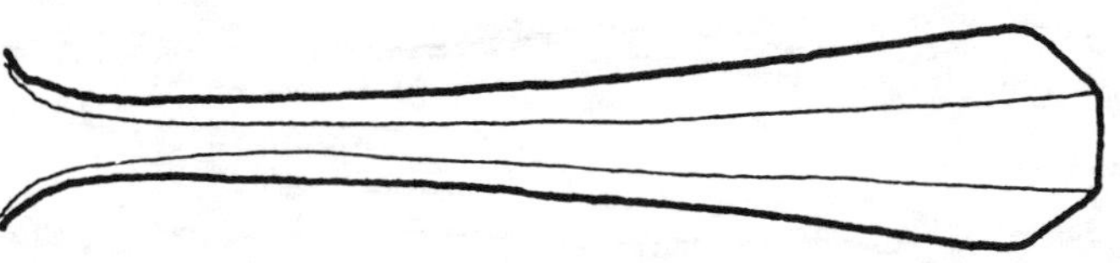

Vogue - 1898
1898
S

Thin market.

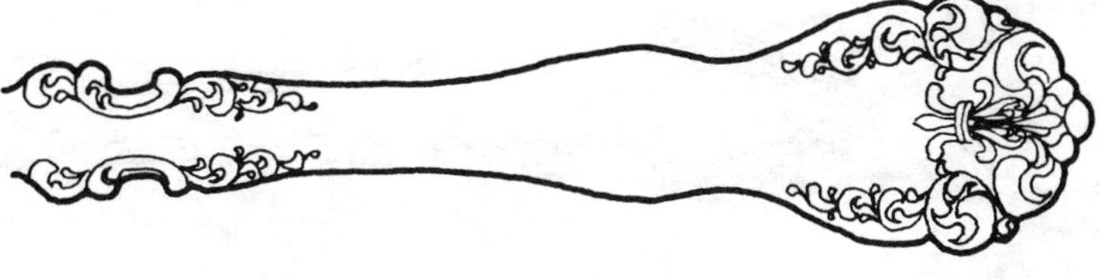

Anjou
1899
S

Please refer to "How To Use This Book" page 4.

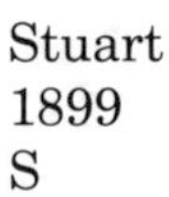

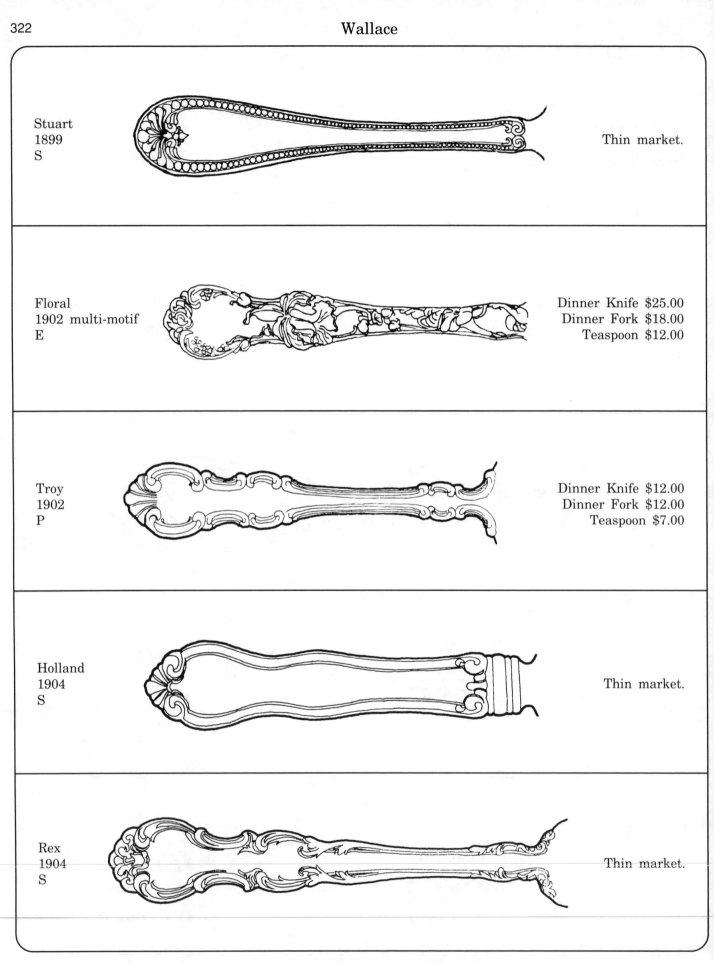

Stuart
1899
S

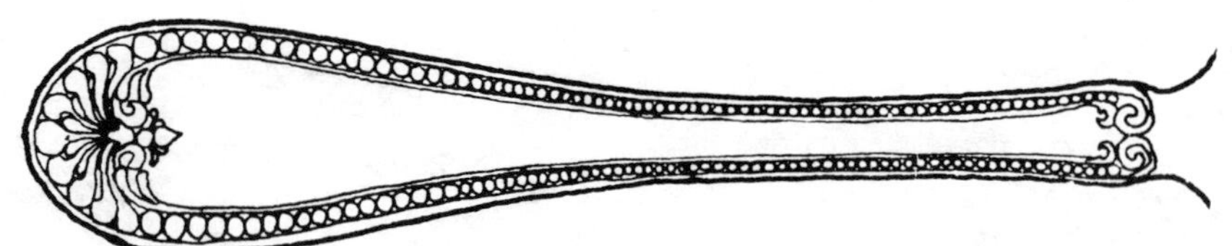

Thin market.

Floral
1902 multi-motif
E

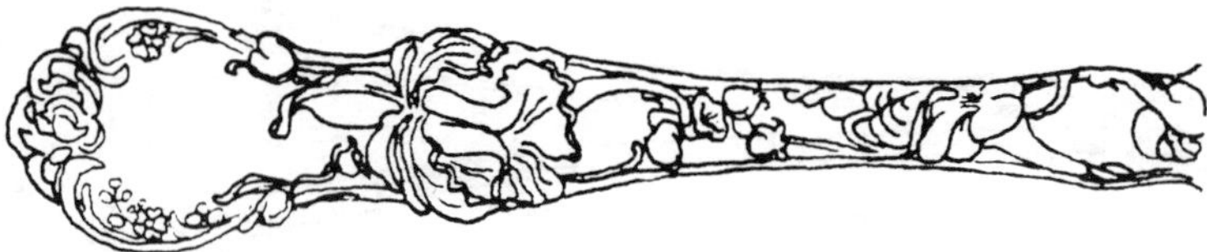

Dinner Knife $25.00
Dinner Fork $18.00
Teaspoon $12.00

Troy
1902
P

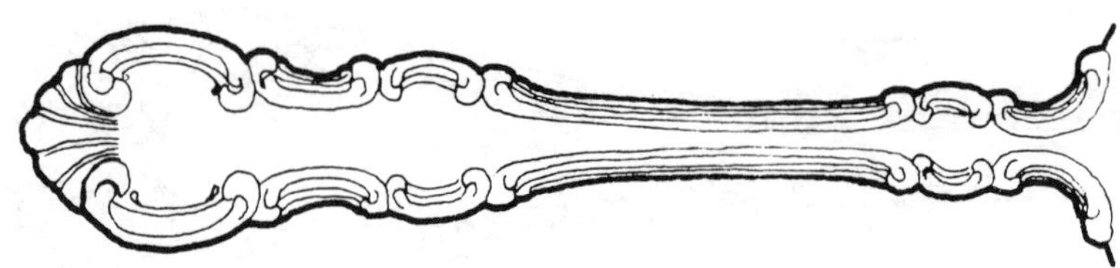

Dinner Knife $12.00
Dinner Fork $12.00
Teaspoon $7.00

Holland
1904
S

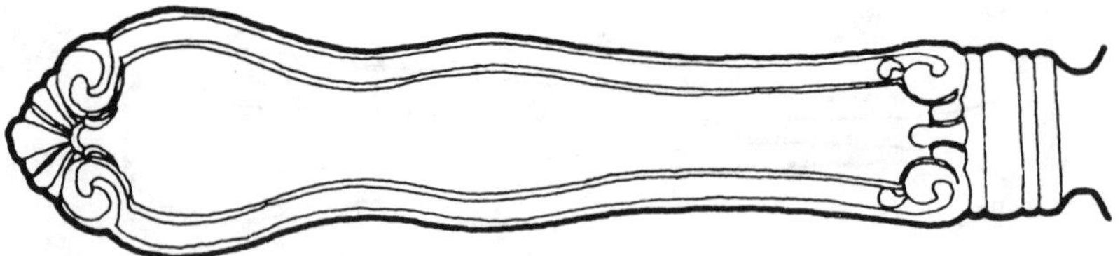

Thin market.

Rex
1904
S

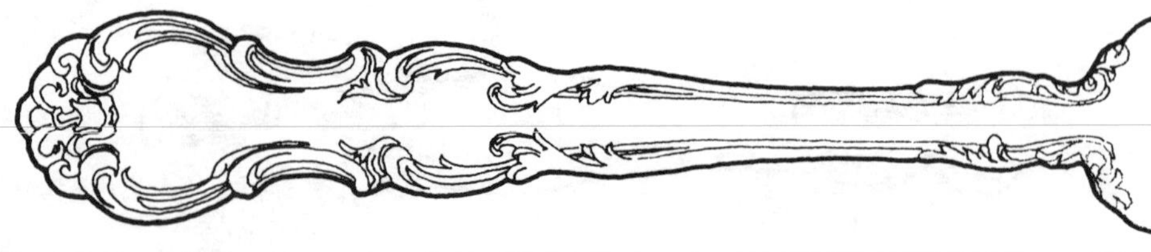

Thin market.

Please refer to "How To Use This Book" page 4.

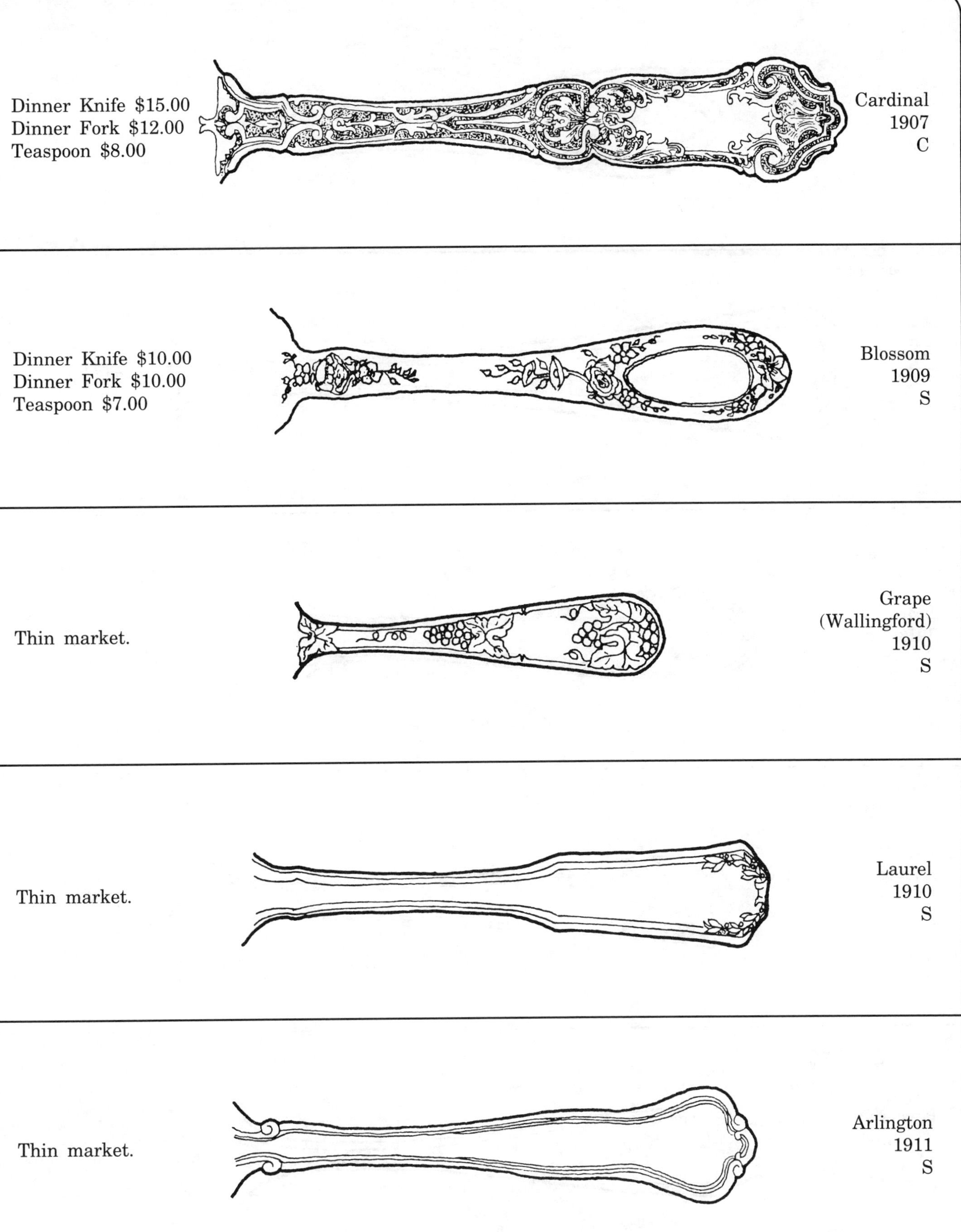

Dinner Knife $15.00
Dinner Fork $12.00
Teaspoon $8.00

Cardinal
1907
C

Dinner Knife $10.00
Dinner Fork $10.00
Teaspoon $7.00

Blossom
1909
S

Thin market.

Grape
(Wallingford)
1910
S

Thin market.

Laurel
1910
S

Thin market.

Arlington
1911
S

Please refer to "How To Use This Book" page 4.

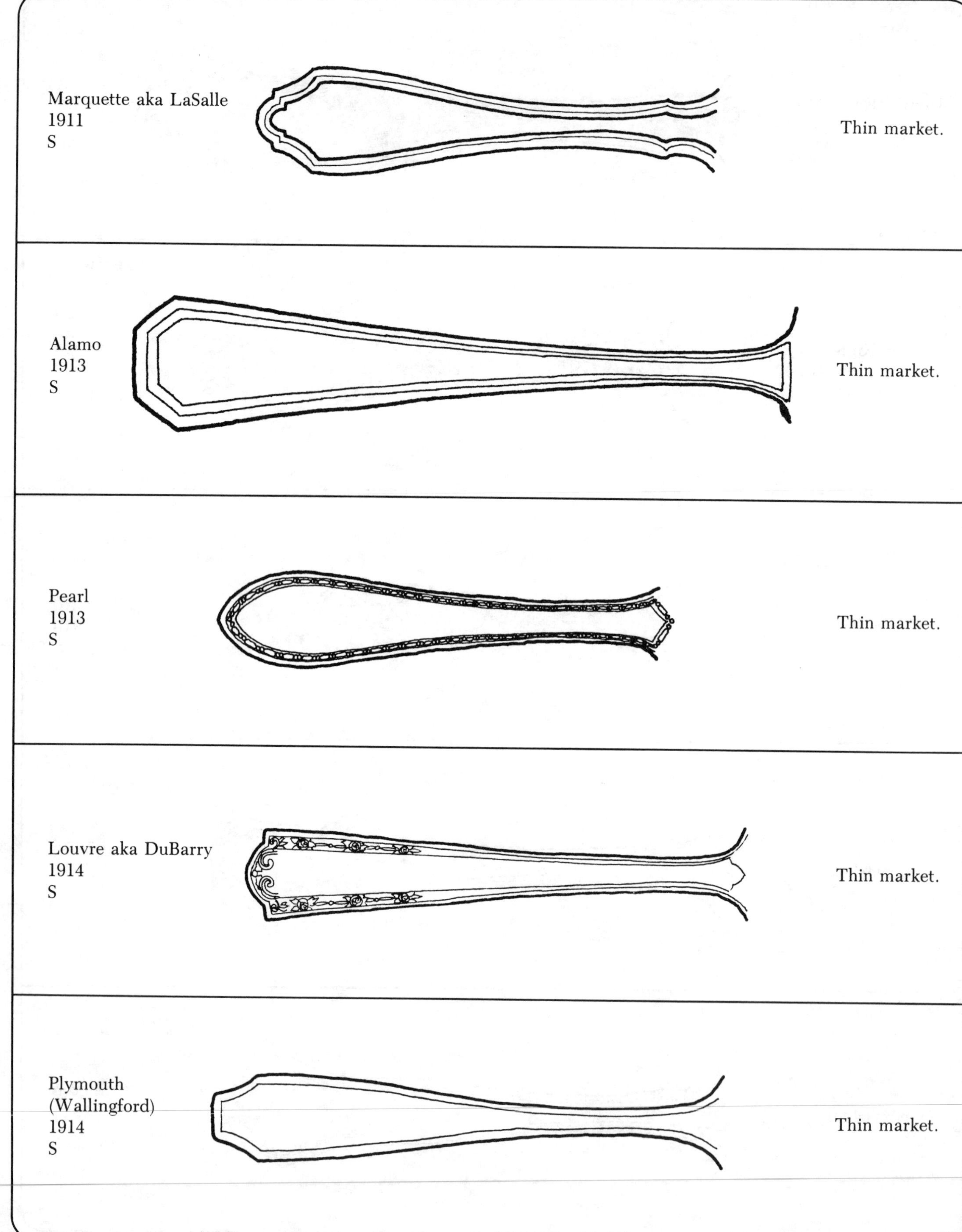

Marquette aka LaSalle
1911
S

Thin market.

Alamo
1913
S

Thin market.

Pearl
1913
S

Thin market.

Louvre aka DuBarry
1914
S

Thin market.

Plymouth
(Wallingford)
1914
S

Thin market.

Please refer to "How To Use This Book" page 4.

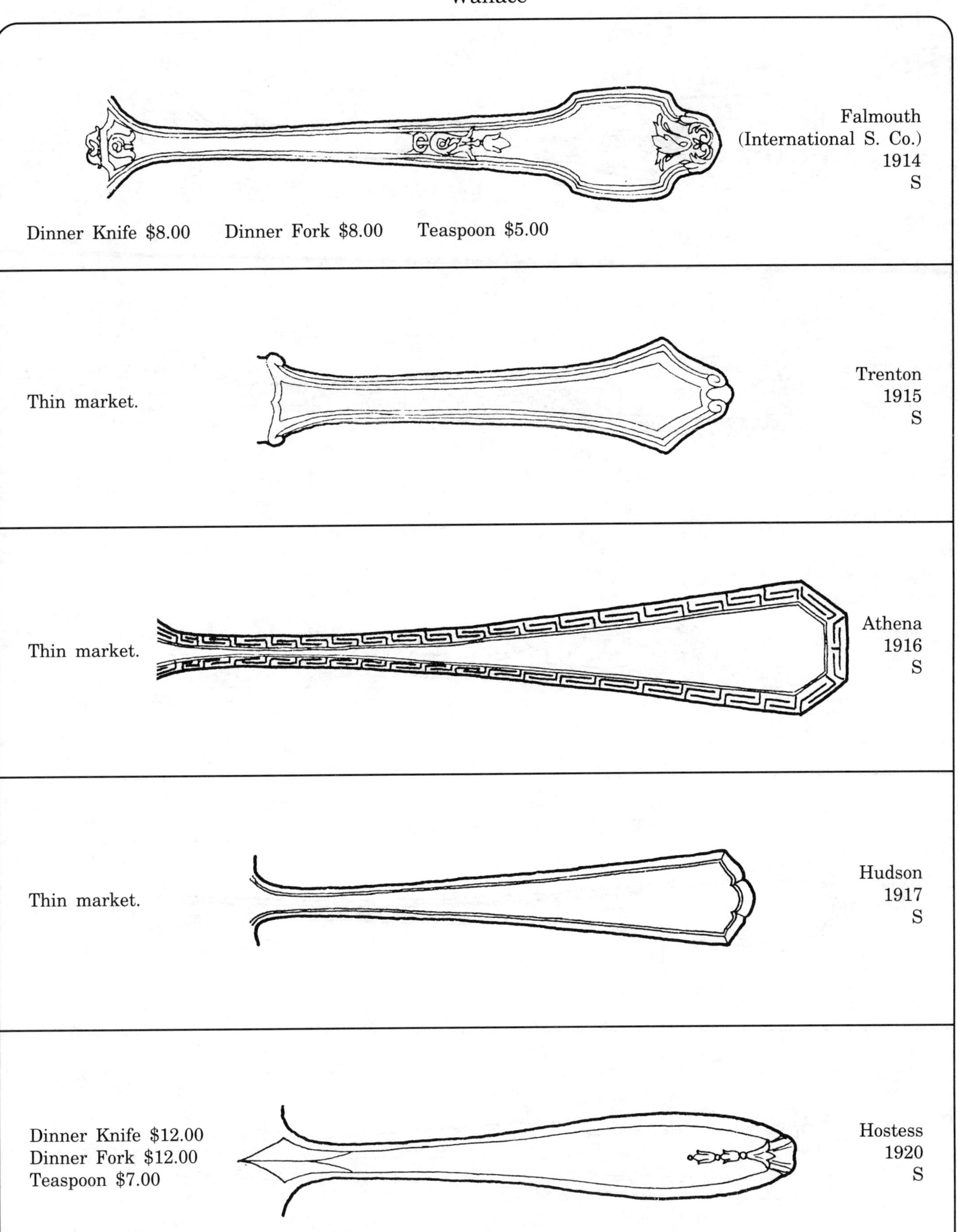

Falmouth
(International S. Co.)
1914
S

Dinner Knife $8.00 Dinner Fork $8.00 Teaspoon $5.00

Trenton
1915
S

Thin market.

Athena
1916
S

Thin market.

Hudson
1917
S

Thin market.

Hostess
1920
S

Dinner Knife $12.00
Dinner Fork $12.00
Teaspoon $7.00

Please refer to "How To Use This Book" page 4.

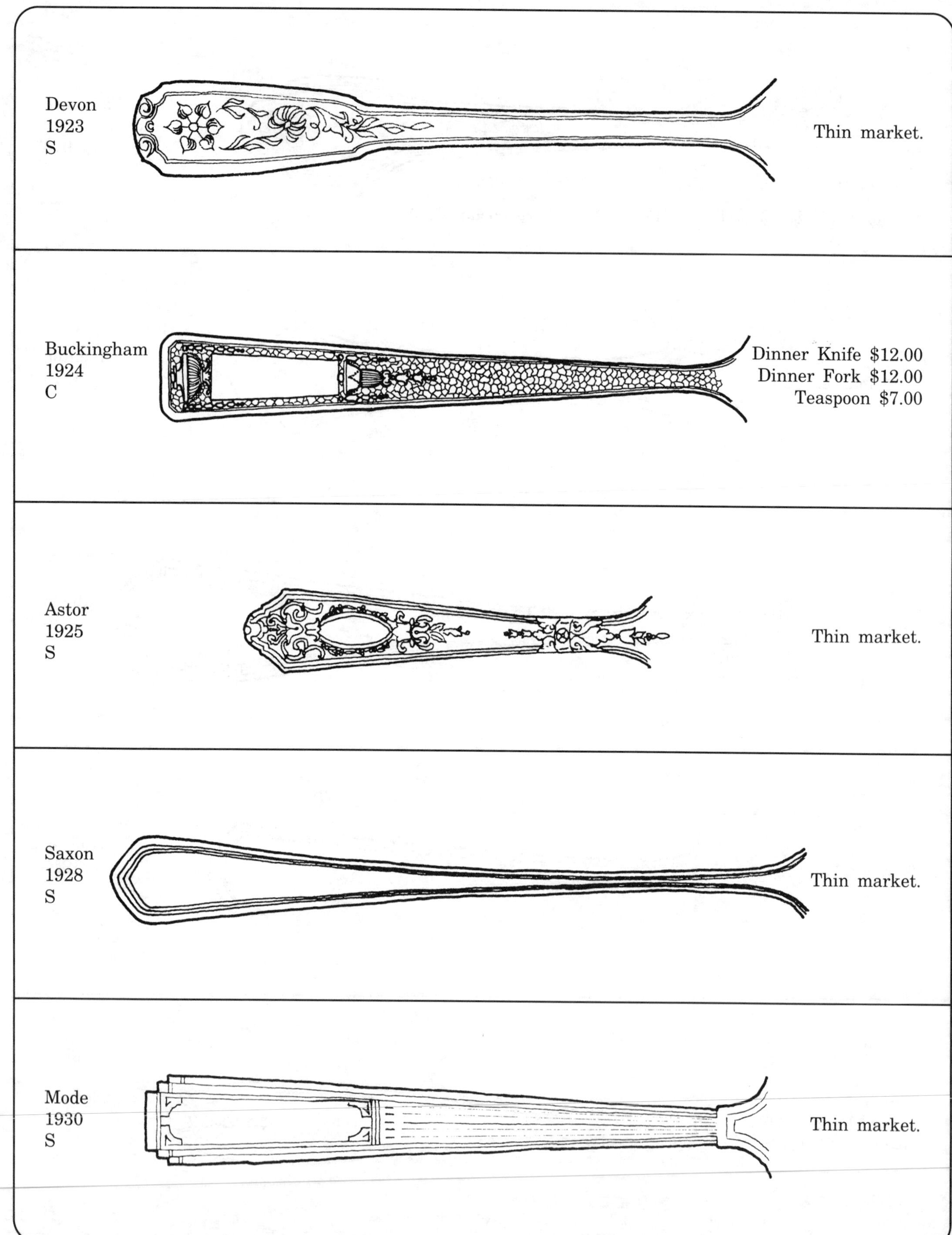

Devon
1923
S

Thin market.

Buckingham
1924
C

Dinner Knife $12.00
Dinner Fork $12.00
Teaspoon $7.00

Astor
1925
S

Thin market.

Saxon
1928
S

Thin market.

Mode
1930
S

Thin market.

Please refer to "How To Use This Book" page 4.

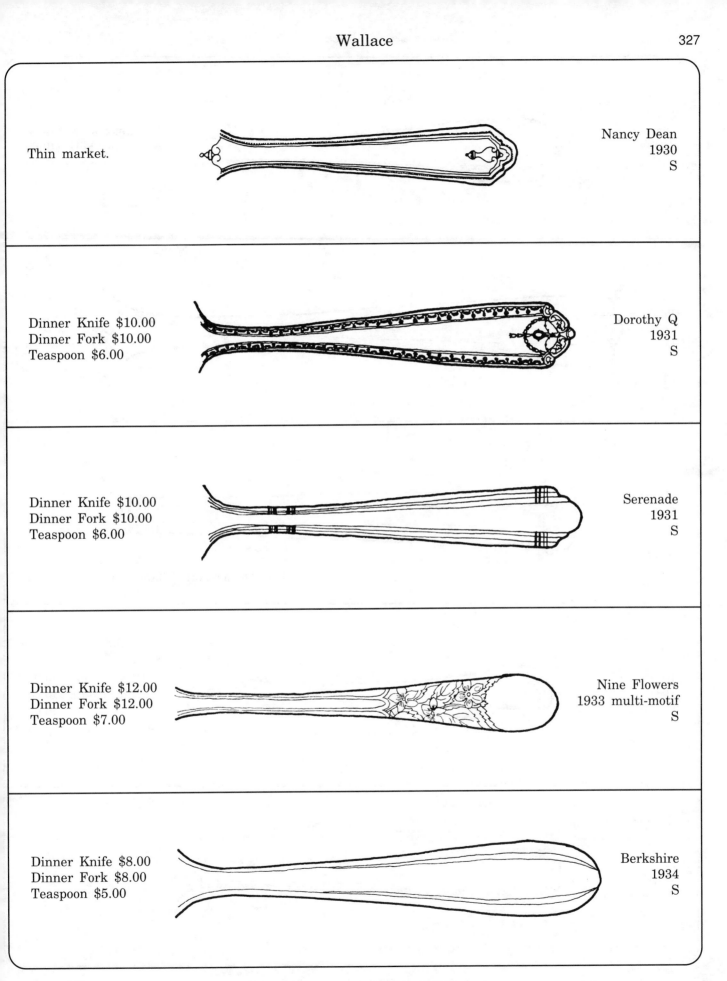

	Pattern
Thin market.	Nancy Dean 1930 S
Dinner Knife $10.00 Dinner Fork $10.00 Teaspoon $6.00	Dorothy Q 1931 S
Dinner Knife $10.00 Dinner Fork $10.00 Teaspoon $6.00	Serenade 1931 S
Dinner Knife $12.00 Dinner Fork $12.00 Teaspoon $7.00	Nine Flowers 1933 multi-motif S
Dinner Knife $8.00 Dinner Fork $8.00 Teaspoon $5.00	Berkshire 1934 S

Please refer to "How To Use This Book" page 4.

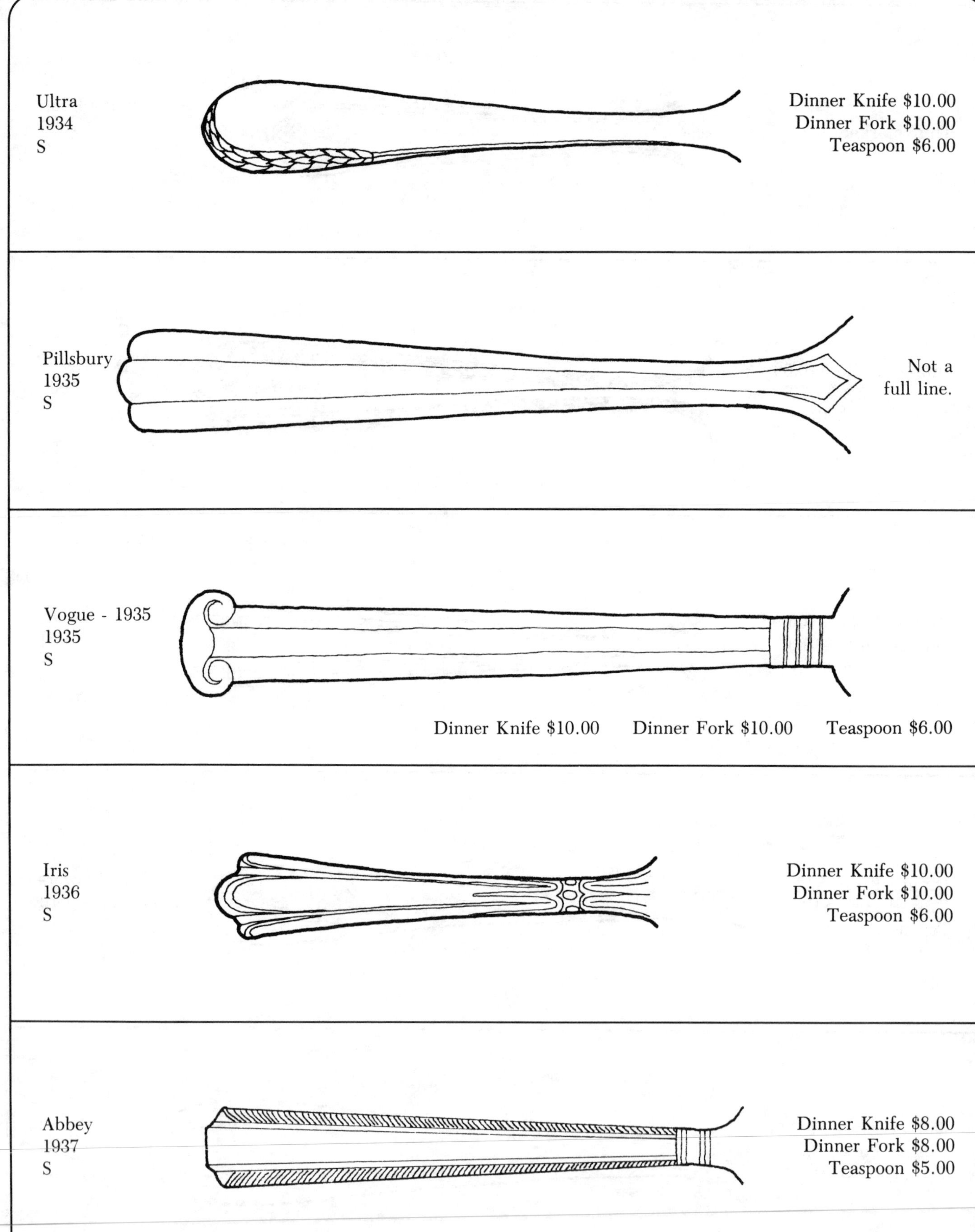

Ultra
1934
S

Dinner Knife $10.00
Dinner Fork $10.00
Teaspoon $6.00

Pillsbury
1935
S

Not a full line.

Vogue - 1935
1935
S

Dinner Knife $10.00 Dinner Fork $10.00 Teaspoon $6.00

Iris
1936
S

Dinner Knife $10.00
Dinner Fork $10.00
Teaspoon $6.00

Abbey
1937
S

Dinner Knife $8.00
Dinner Fork $8.00
Teaspoon $5.00

Please refer to "How To Use This Book" page 4.

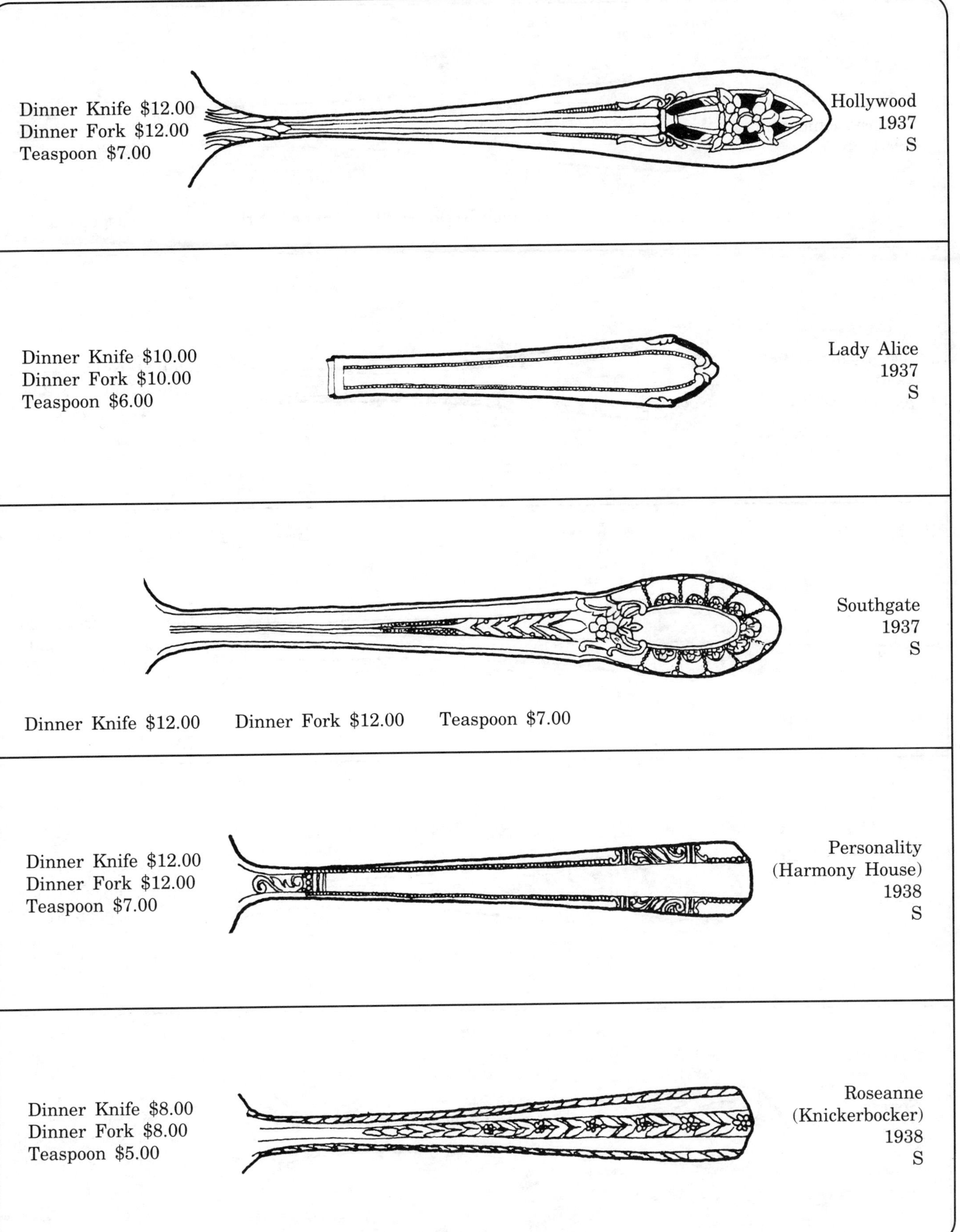

Dinner Knife $12.00
Dinner Fork $12.00
Teaspoon $7.00

Hollywood
1937
S

Dinner Knife $10.00
Dinner Fork $10.00
Teaspoon $6.00

Lady Alice
1937
S

Southgate
1937
S

Dinner Knife $12.00 Dinner Fork $12.00 Teaspoon $7.00

Dinner Knife $12.00
Dinner Fork $12.00
Teaspoon $7.00

Personality
(Harmony House)
1938
S

Dinner Knife $8.00
Dinner Fork $8.00
Teaspoon $5.00

Roseanne
(Knickerbocker)
1938
S

Please refer to "How To Use This Book" page 4.

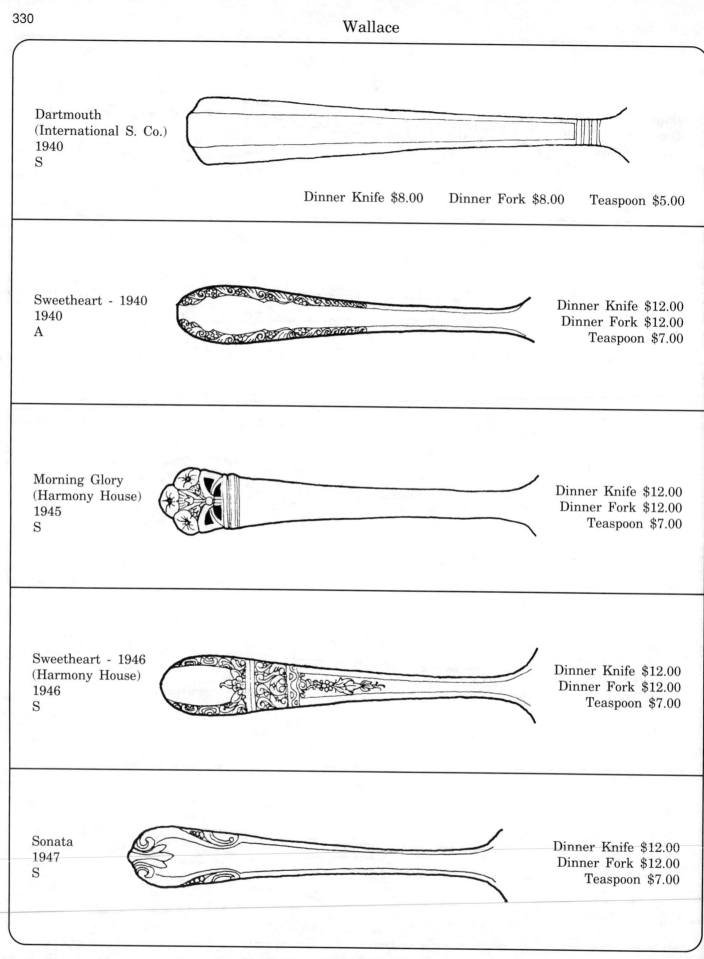

Dartmouth
(International S. Co.)
1940
S

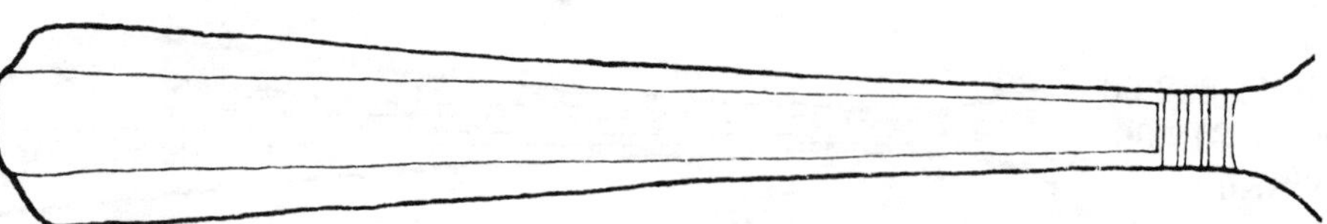

Dinner Knife $8.00 Dinner Fork $8.00 Teaspoon $5.00

Sweetheart - 1940
1940
A

Dinner Knife $12.00
Dinner Fork $12.00
Teaspoon $7.00

Morning Glory
(Harmony House)
1945
S

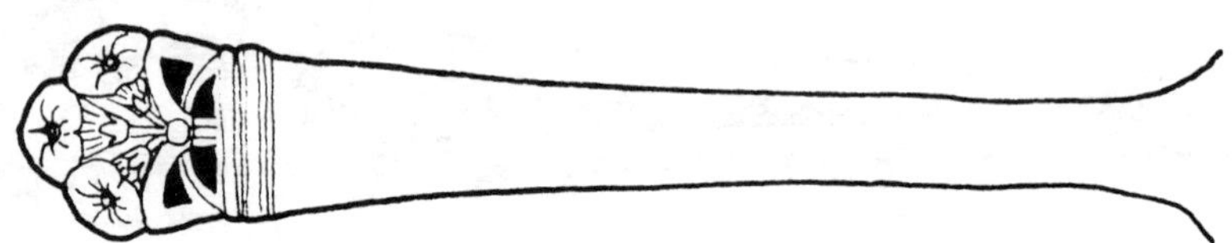

Dinner Knife $12.00
Dinner Fork $12.00
Teaspoon $7.00

Sweetheart - 1946
(Harmony House)
1946
S

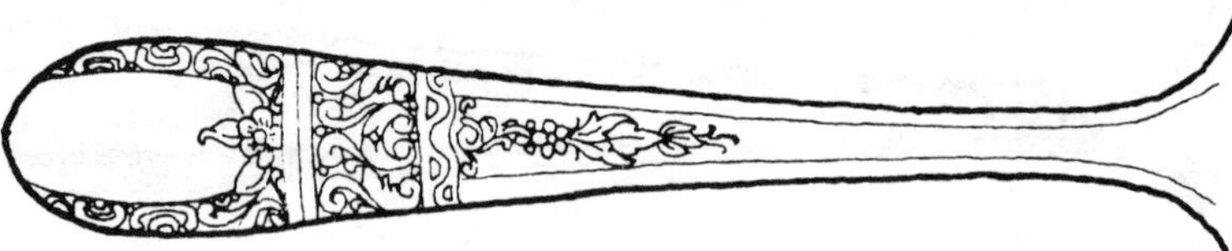

Dinner Knife $12.00
Dinner Fork $12.00
Teaspoon $7.00

Sonata
1947
S

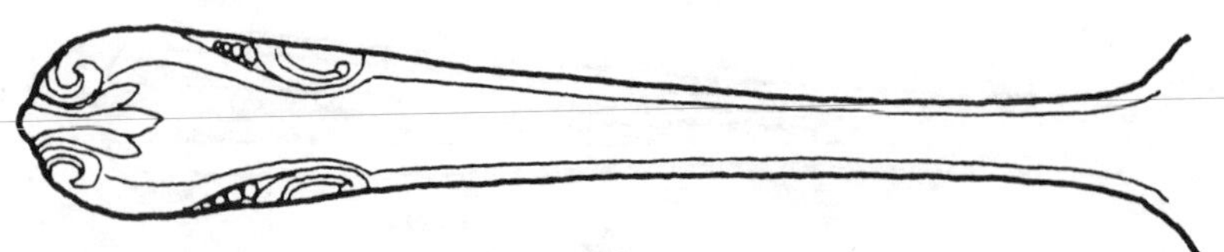

Dinner Knife $12.00
Dinner Fork $12.00
Teaspoon $7.00

Please refer to "How To Use This Book" page 4.

Dinner Knife $10.00
Dinner Fork $10.00
Teaspoon $6.00

Virginian
1956
S

Dinner Knife $12.00
Dinner Fork $12.00
Teaspoon $7.00

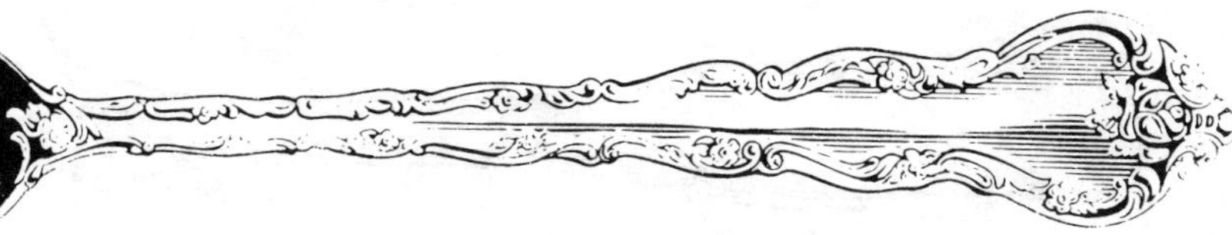

Abbey Rose
1981
P

Dinner Knife $10.00
Dinner Fork $10.00
Teaspoon $6.00

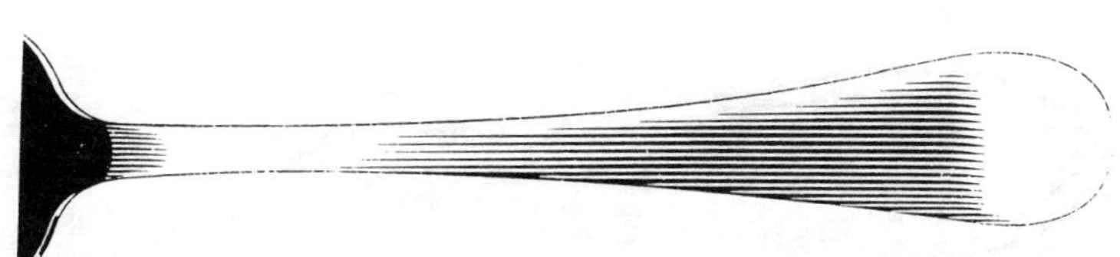

Old Guilford
1981
P

Dinner Knife $10.00
Dinner Fork $10.00
Teaspoon $6.00

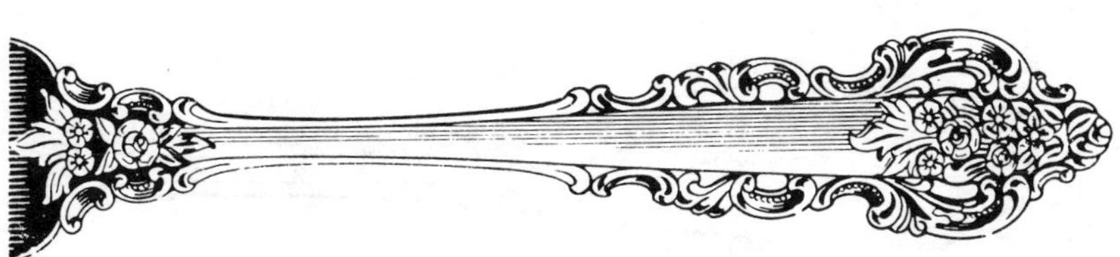

Royal Baroque
1981
P

Wallace - Wallingford Co.

Thin market.

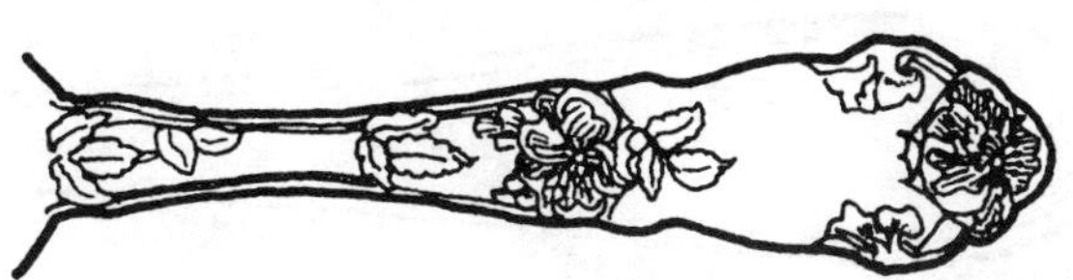

Adams
1906
S

Please refer to "How To Use This Book" page 4.

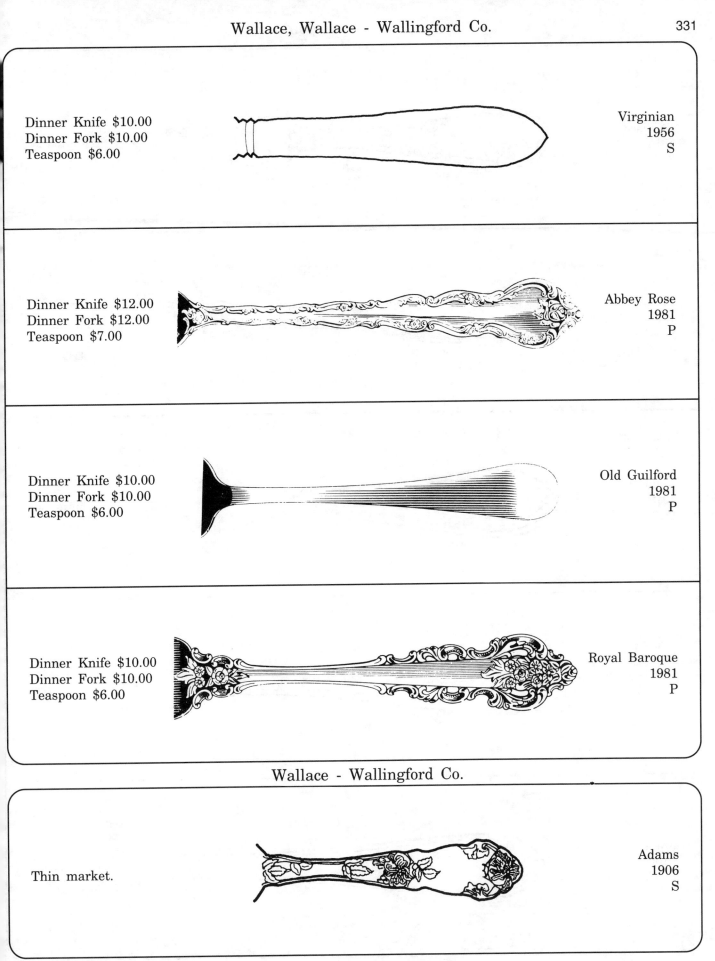

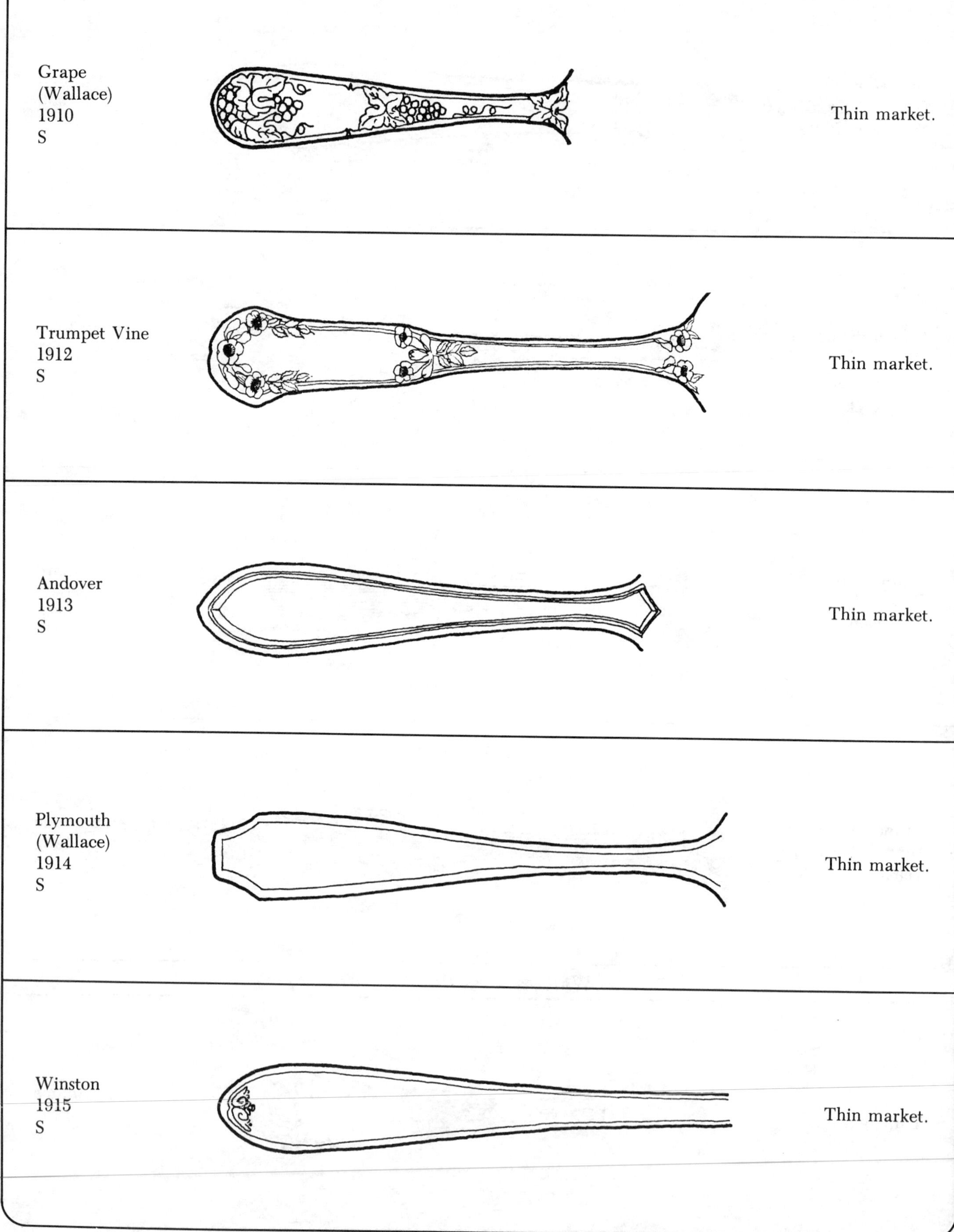

Grape (Wallace) 1910 S	Thin market.
Trumpet Vine 1912 S	Thin market.
Andover 1913 S	Thin market.
Plymouth (Wallace) 1914 S	Thin market.
Winston 1915 S	Thin market.

Please refer to "How To Use This Book" page 4.

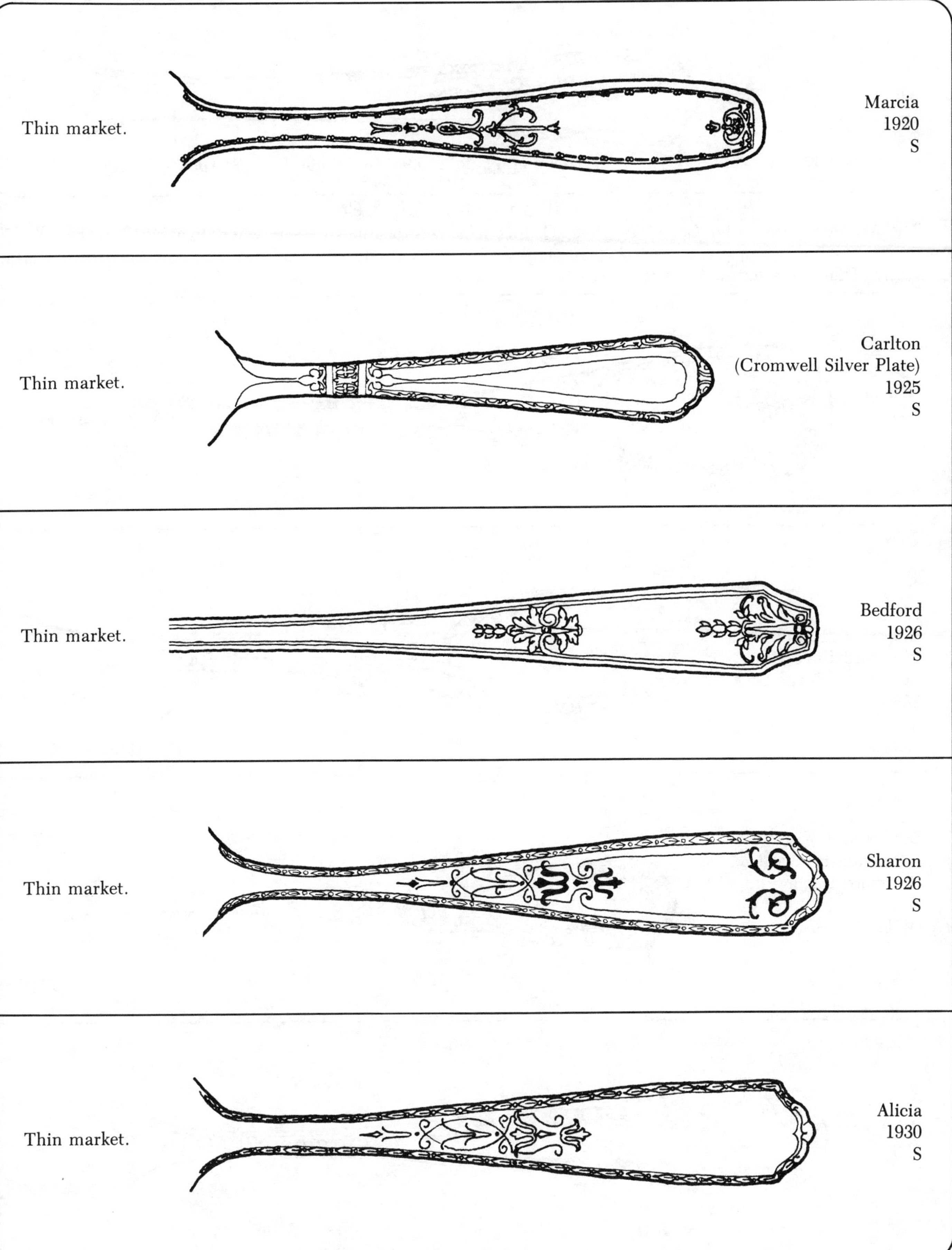

	Pattern
Thin market.	Marcia 1920 S
Thin market.	Carlton (Cromwell Silver Plate) 1925 S
Thin market.	Bedford 1926 S
Thin market.	Sharon 1926 S
Thin market.	Alicia 1930 S

Please refer to "How To Use This Book" page 4.

Maytime
(Harmony House Plate)
1944
S

Dinner Knife $10.00 Dinner Fork $10.00 Teaspoon $6.00

Williams Bros. Mfg. Co.

The William Bros. Mfg. Co. of Naubuc, Connecticut was begun in 1880 when two brothers bought the American Sterling Company. Some of their flatware was marked A.S. Co. standing for American Sterling Company. They were out of business in 1950.

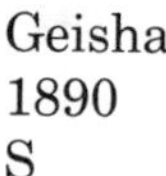

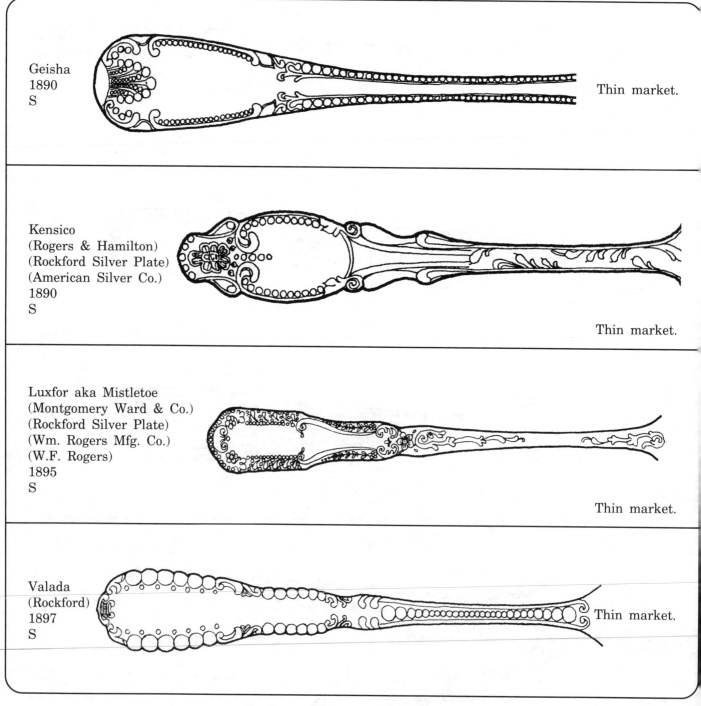

Geisha
1890
S

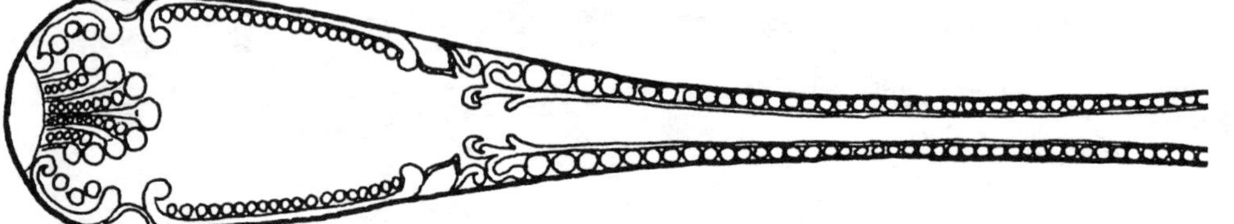

Thin market.

Kensico
(Rogers & Hamilton)
(Rockford Silver Plate)
(American Silver Co.)
1890
S

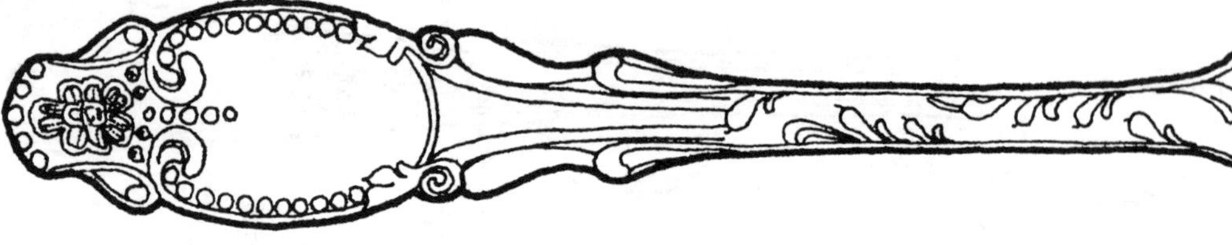

Thin market.

Luxfor aka Mistletoe
(Montgomery Ward & Co.)
(Rockford Silver Plate)
(Wm. Rogers Mfg. Co.)
(W.F. Rogers)
1895
S

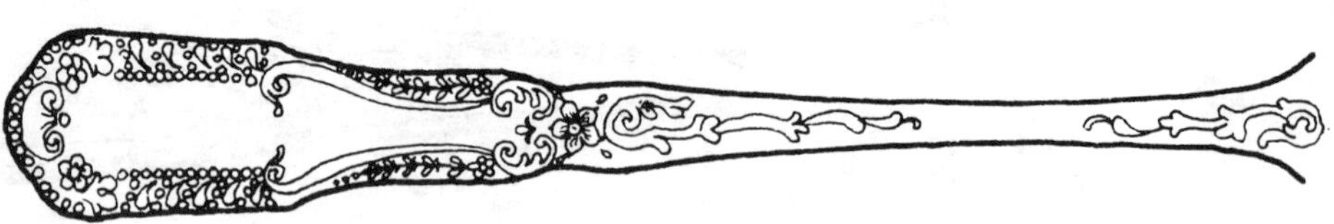

Thin market.

Valada
(Rockford)
1897
S

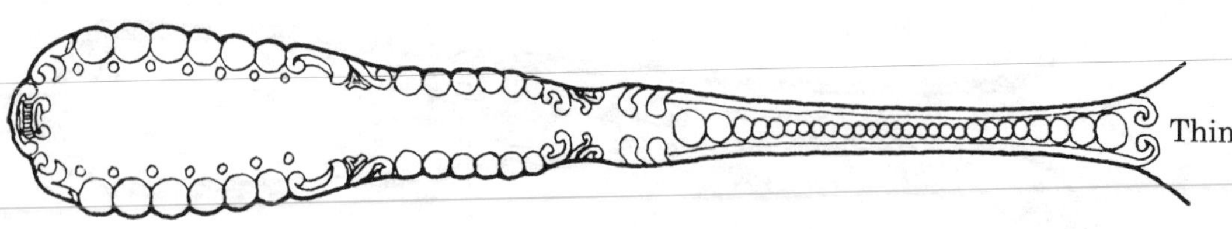

Thin market.

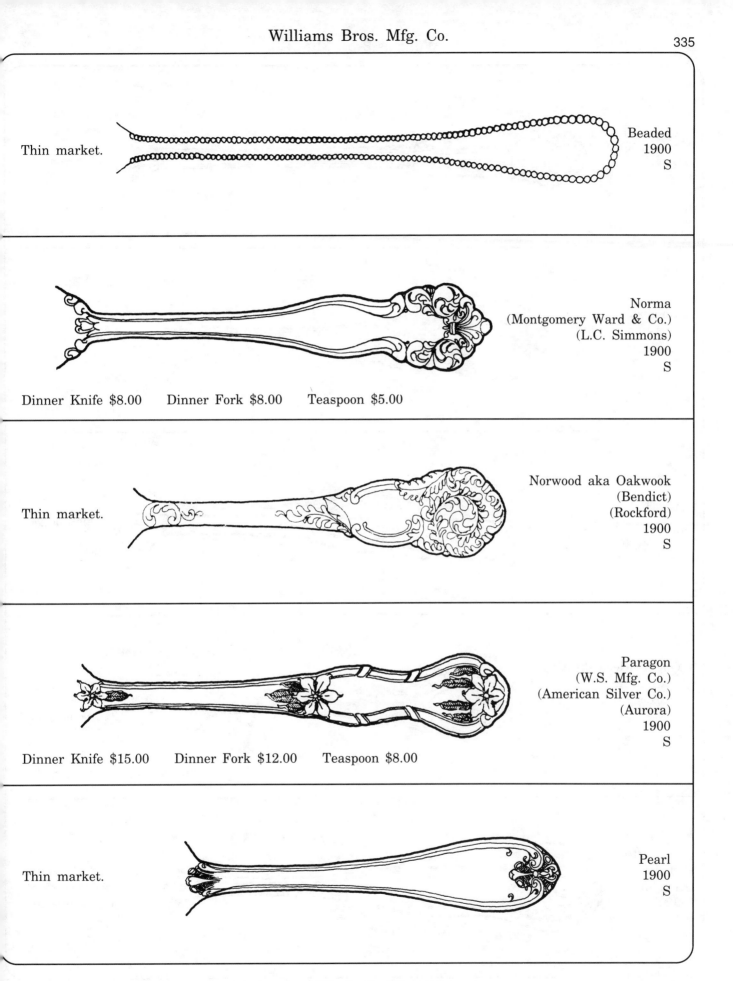

Thin market.

Beaded
1900
S

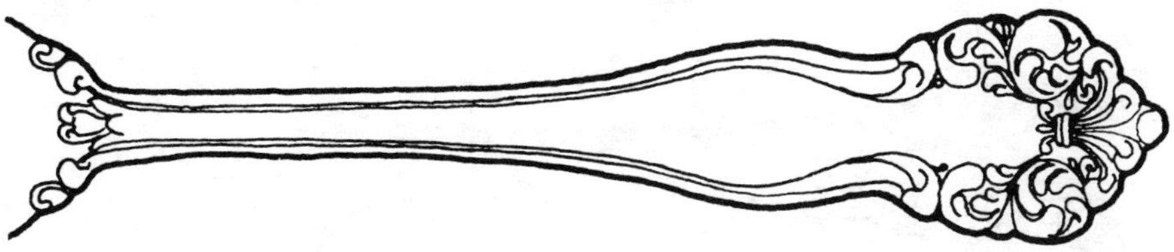

Norma
(Montgomery Ward & Co.)
(L.C. Simmons)
1900
S

Dinner Knife $8.00 Dinner Fork $8.00 Teaspoon $5.00

Thin market.

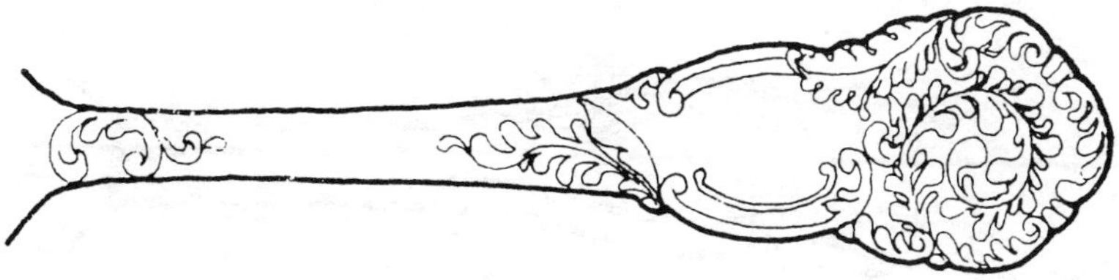

Norwood aka Oakwook
(Bendict)
(Rockford)
1900
S

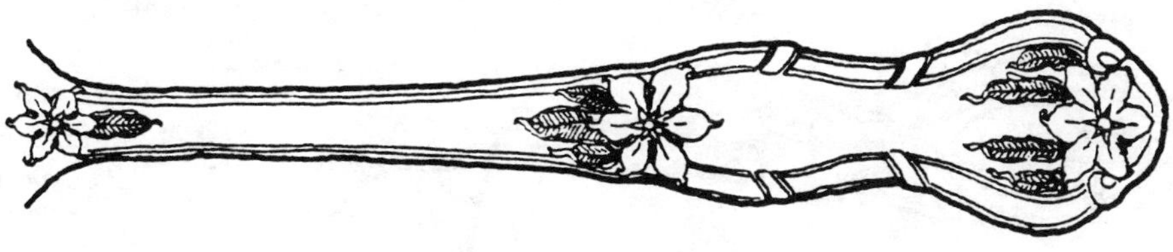

Paragon
(W.S. Mfg. Co.)
(American Silver Co.)
(Aurora)
1900
S

Dinner Knife $15.00 Dinner Fork $12.00 Teaspoon $8.00

Thin market.

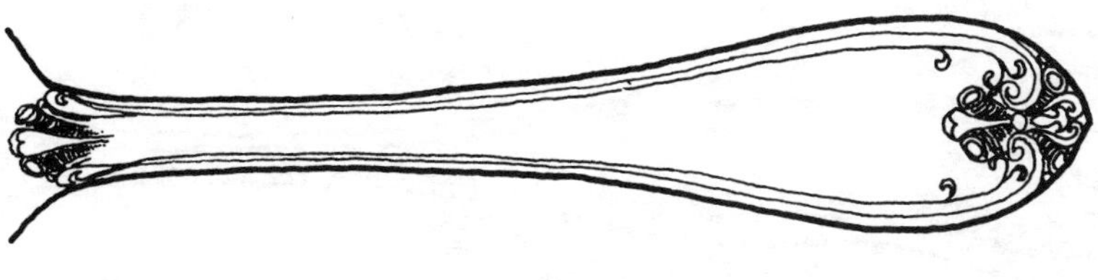

Pearl
1900
S

Please refer to "How To Use This Book" page 4.

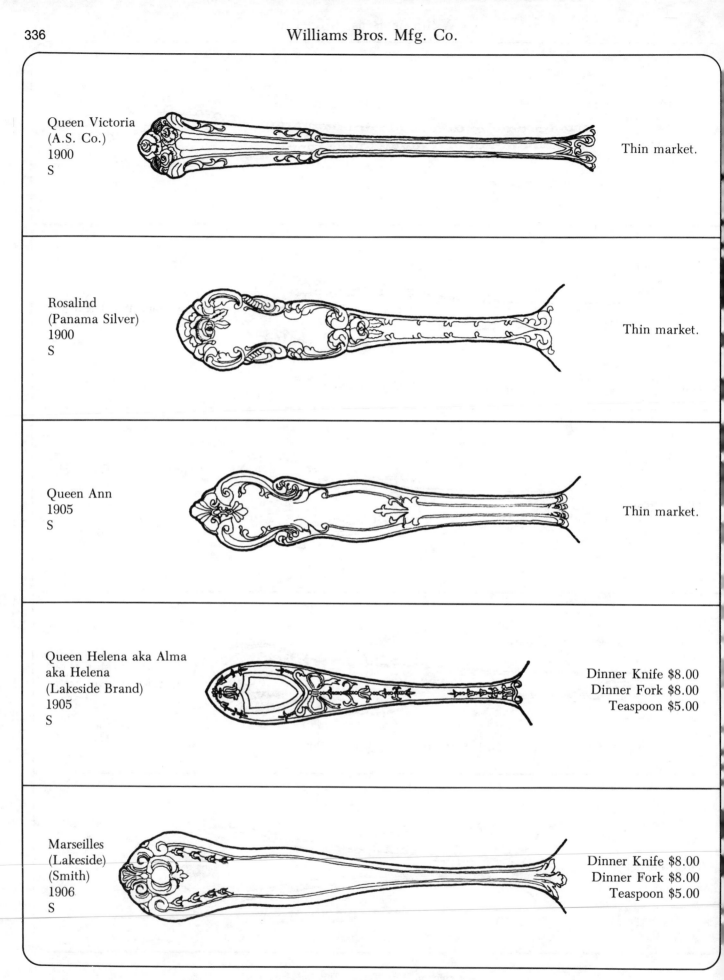

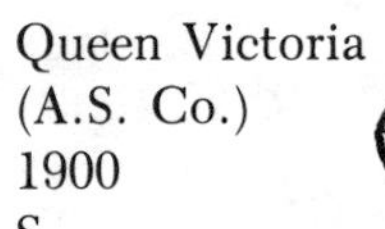
Queen Victoria
(A.S. Co.)
1900
S

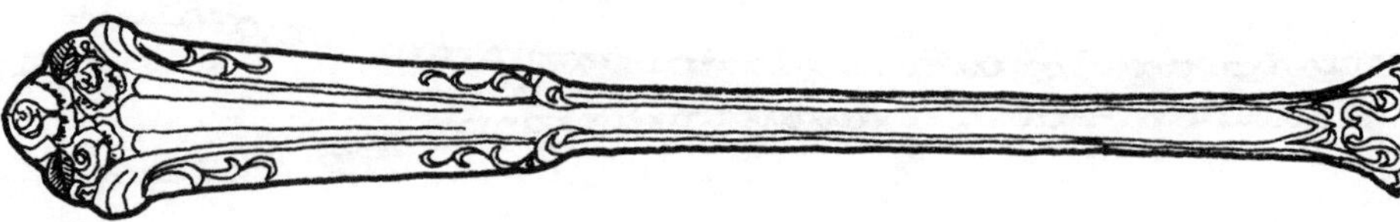

Thin market.

Rosalind
(Panama Silver)
1900
S

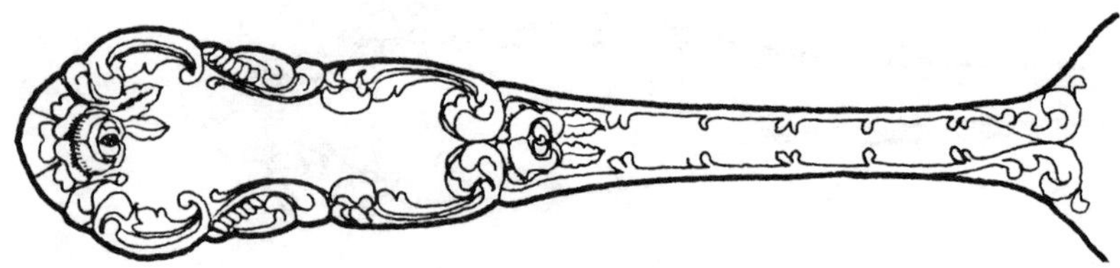

Thin market.

Queen Ann
1905
S

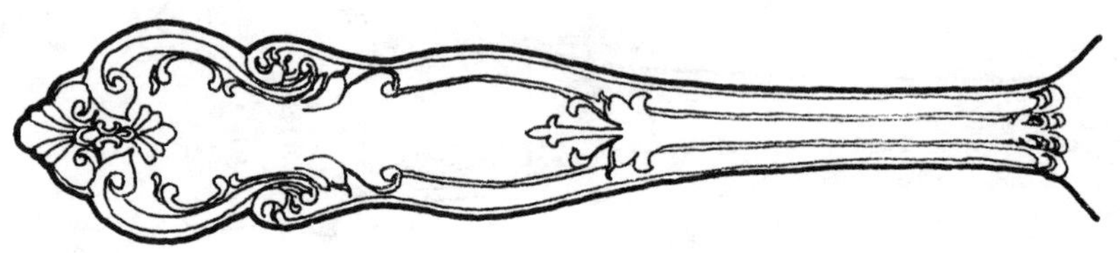

Thin market.

Queen Helena aka Alma
aka Helena
(Lakeside Brand)
1905
S

Dinner Knife $8.00
Dinner Fork $8.00
Teaspoon $5.00

Marseilles
(Lakeside)
(Smith)
1906
S

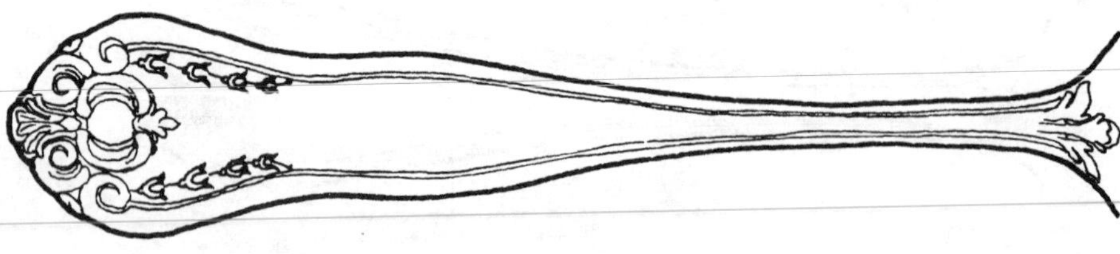

Dinner Knife $8.00
Dinner Fork $8.00
Teaspoon $5.00

Please refer to "How To Use This Book" page 4.

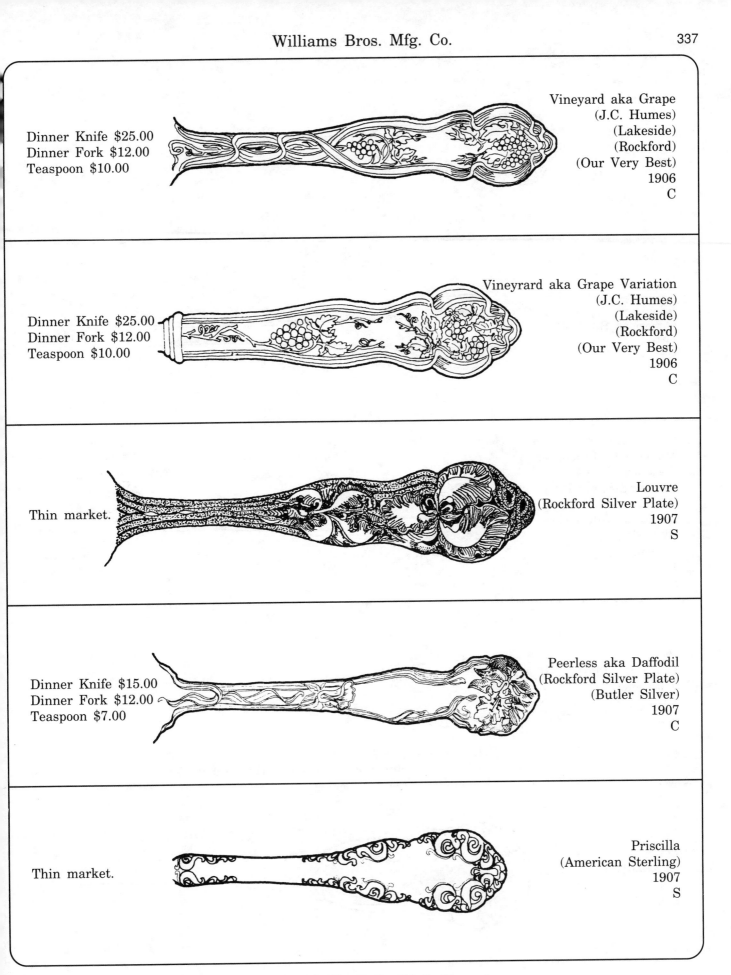

Dinner Knife $25.00
Dinner Fork $12.00
Teaspoon $10.00

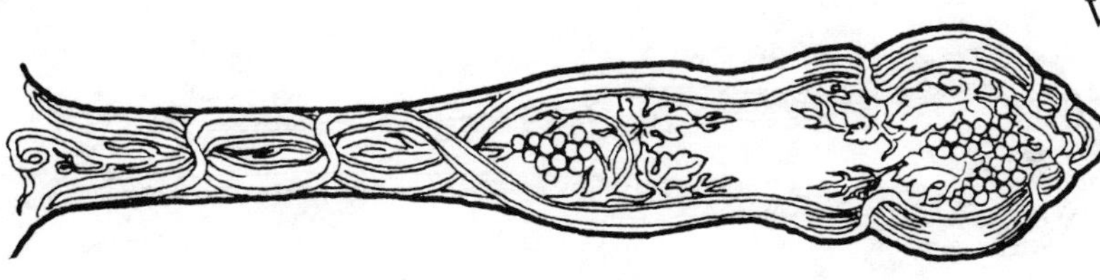

Vineyard aka Grape
(J.C. Humes)
(Lakeside)
(Rockford)
(Our Very Best)
1906
C

Dinner Knife $25.00
Dinner Fork $12.00
Teaspoon $10.00

Vineyrard aka Grape Variation
(J.C. Humes)
(Lakeside)
(Rockford)
(Our Very Best)
1906
C

Thin market.

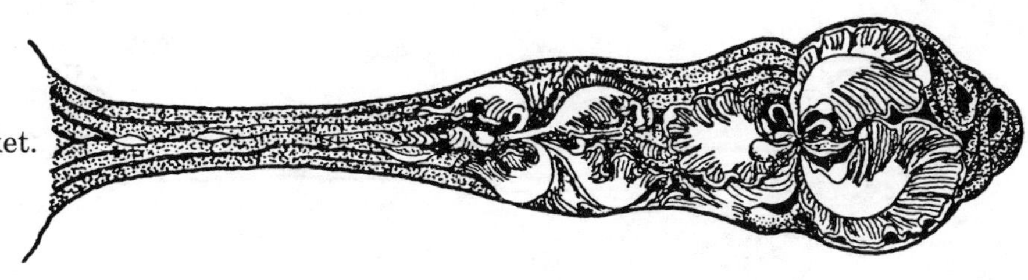

Louvre
(Rockford Silver Plate)
1907
S

Dinner Knife $15.00
Dinner Fork $12.00
Teaspoon $7.00

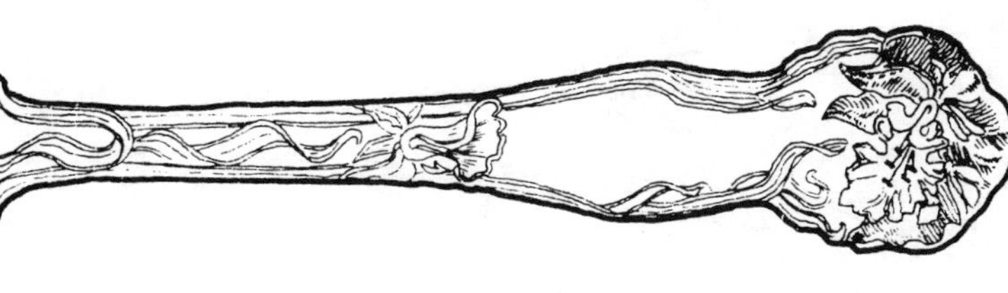

Peerless aka Daffodil
(Rockford Silver Plate)
(Butler Silver)
1907
C

Thin market.

Priscilla
(American Sterling)
1907
S

Please refer to "How To Use This Book" page 4.

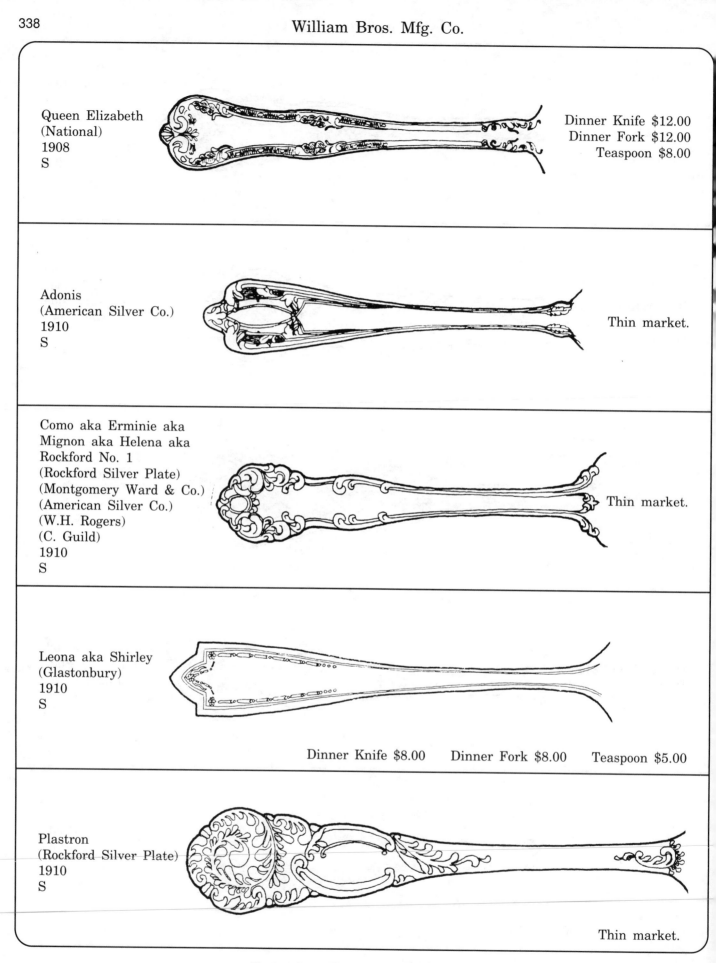

Queen Elizabeth
(National)
1908
S

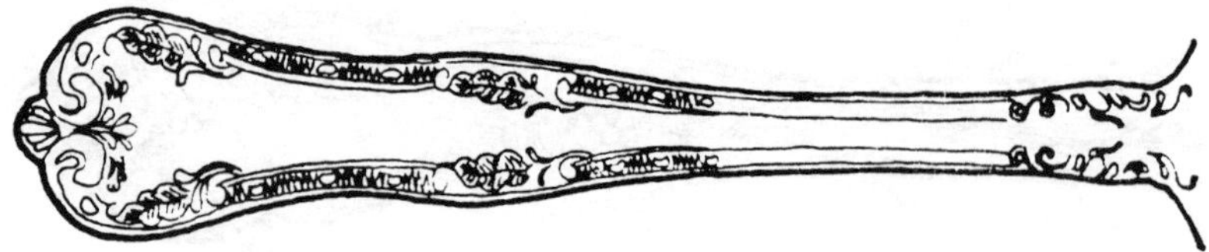

Dinner Knife $12.00
Dinner Fork $12.00
Teaspoon $8.00

Adonis
(American Silver Co.)
1910
S

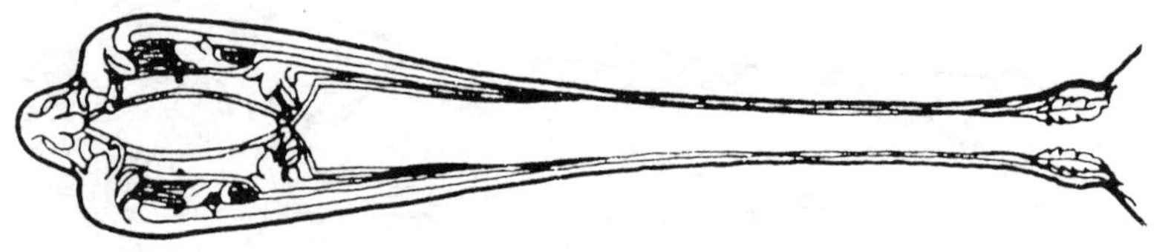

Thin market.

Como aka Erminie aka
Mignon aka Helena aka
Rockford No. 1
(Rockford Silver Plate)
(Montgomery Ward & Co.)
(American Silver Co.)
(W.H. Rogers)
(C. Guild)
1910
S

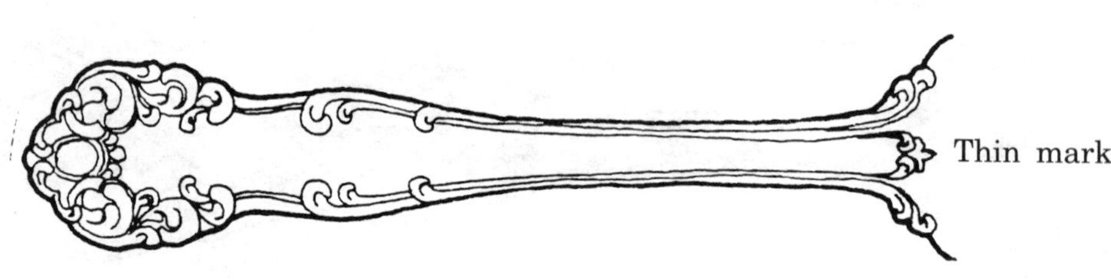

Thin market.

Leona aka Shirley
(Glastonbury)
1910
S

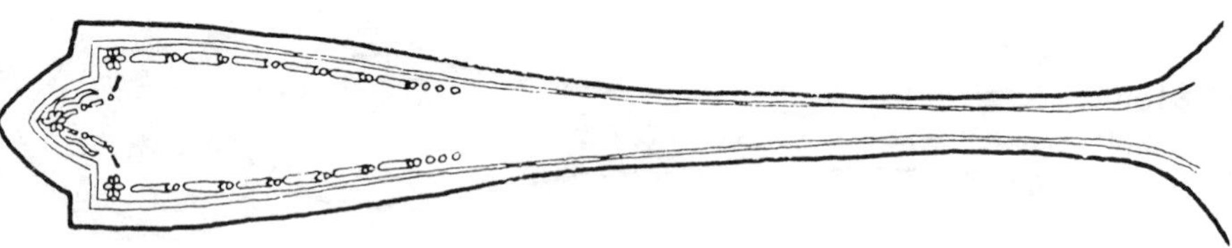

Dinner Knife $8.00 Dinner Fork $8.00 Teaspoon $5.00

Plastron
(Rockford Silver Plate)
1910
S

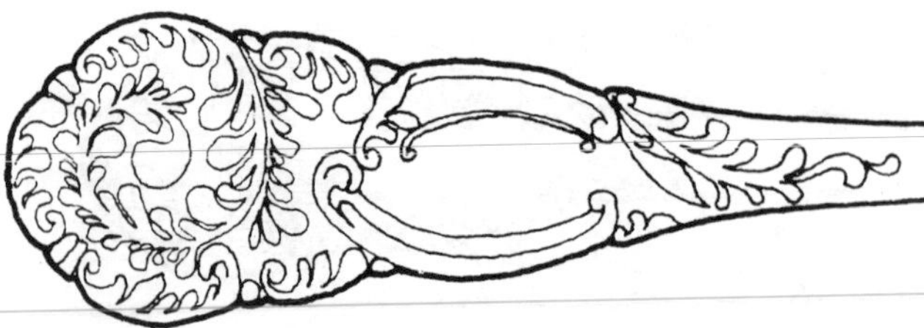

Thin market.

Please refer to "How To Use This Book" page 4.

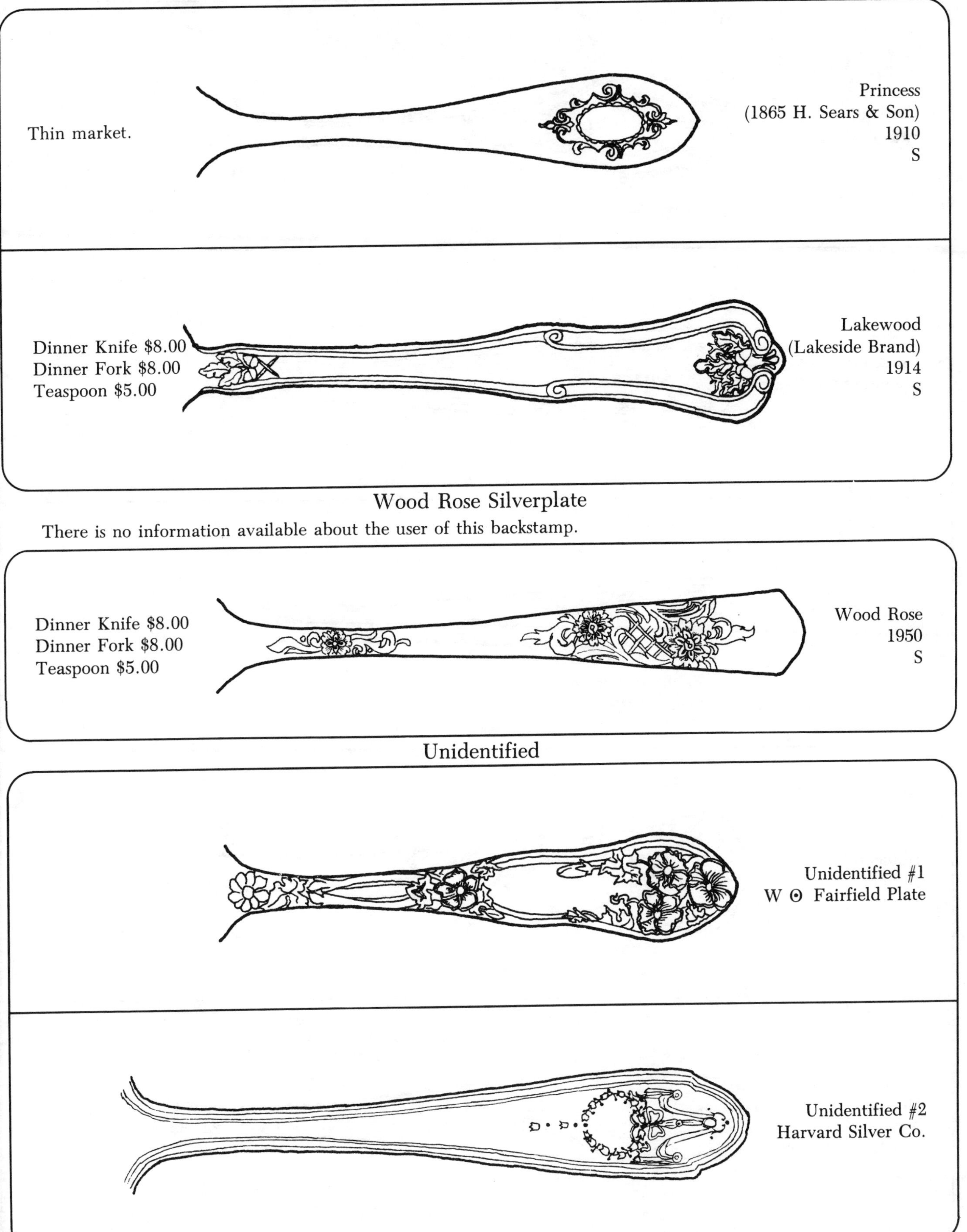

Thin market.

Princess
(1865 H. Sears & Son)
1910
S

Dinner Knife $8.00
Dinner Fork $8.00
Teaspoon $5.00

Lakewood
(Lakeside Brand)
1914
S

Wood Rose Silverplate

There is no information available about the user of this backstamp.

Dinner Knife $8.00
Dinner Fork $8.00
Teaspoon $5.00

Wood Rose
1950
S

Unidentified

Unidentified #1
W ⊙ Fairfield Plate

Unidentified #2
Harvard Silver Co.

Please refer to "How To Use This Book" page 4.

Unidentified

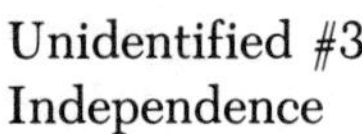

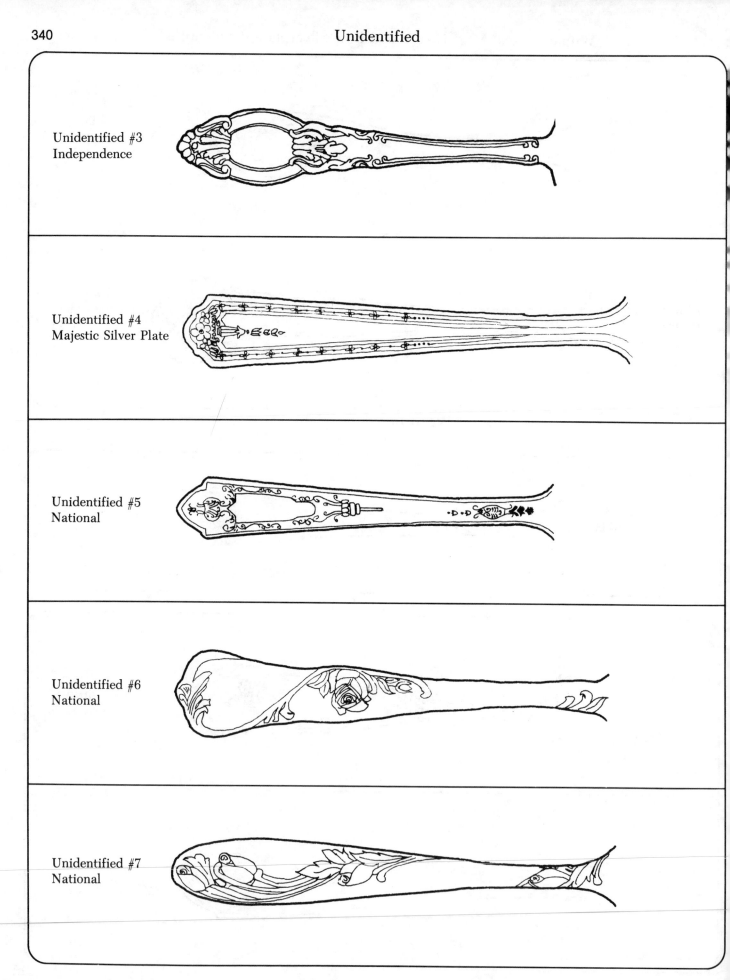

Unidentified #3
Independence

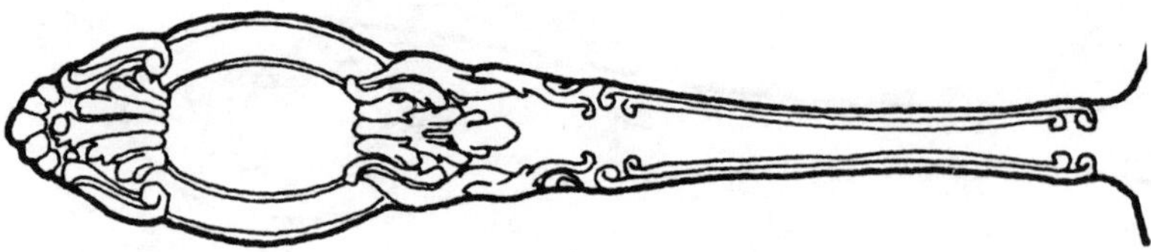

Unidentified #4
Majestic Silver Plate

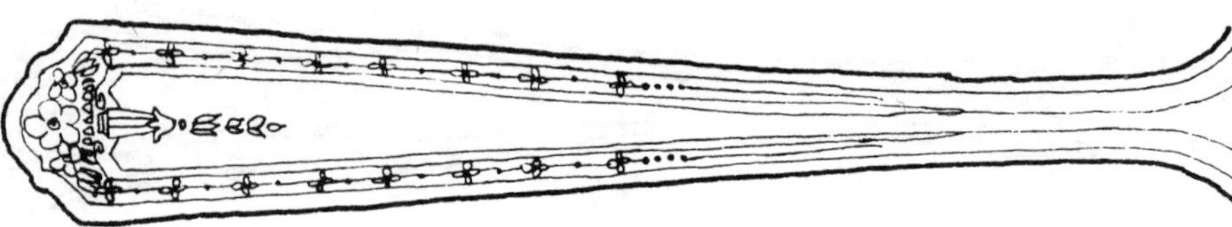

Unidentified #5
National

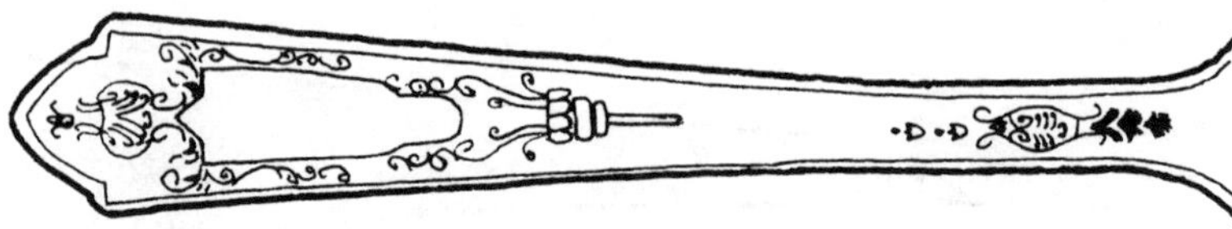

Unidentified #6
National

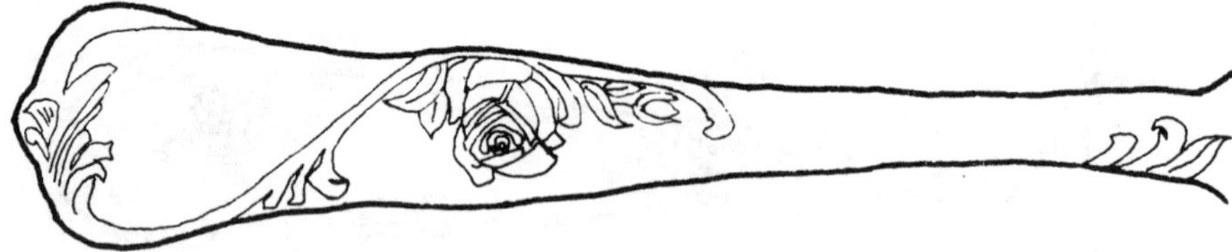

Unidentified #7
National

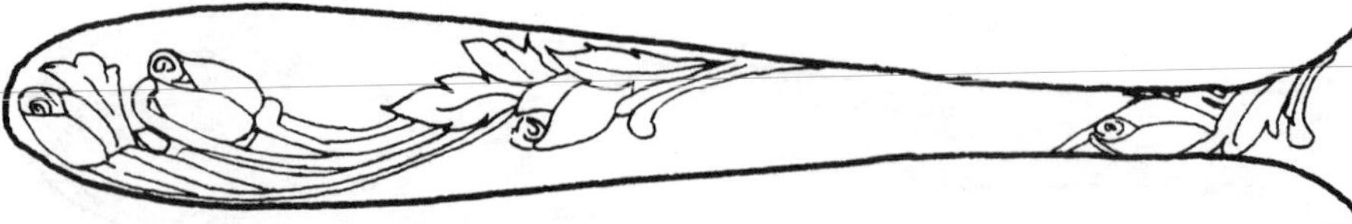

Please refer to "How To Use This Book" page 4.

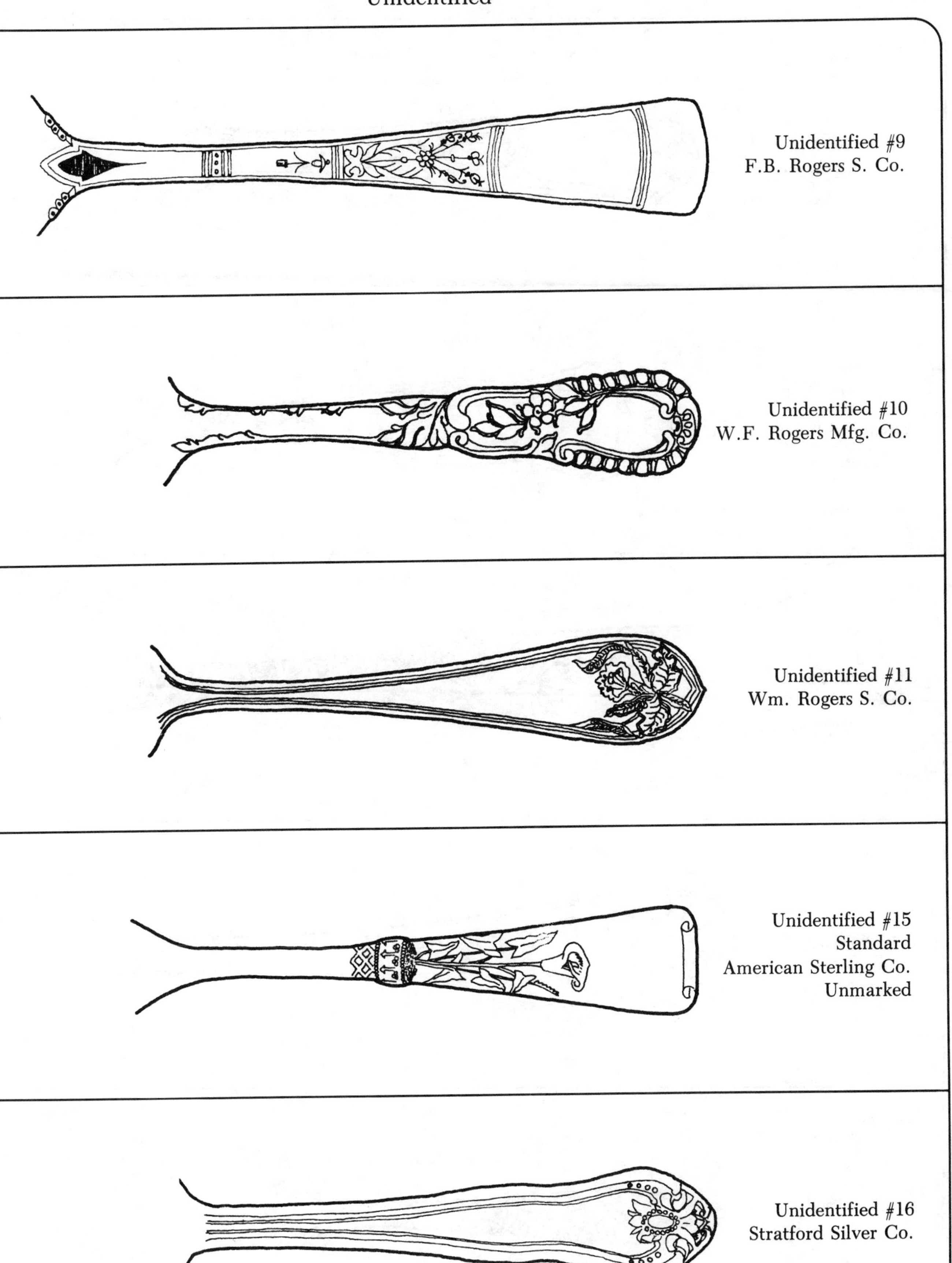

Unidentified #9
F.B. Rogers S. Co.

Unidentified #10
W.F. Rogers Mfg. Co.

Unidentified #11
Wm. Rogers S. Co.

Unidentified #15
Standard
American Sterling Co.
Unmarked

Unidentified #16
Stratford Silver Co.

Please refer to "How To Use This Book" page 4.

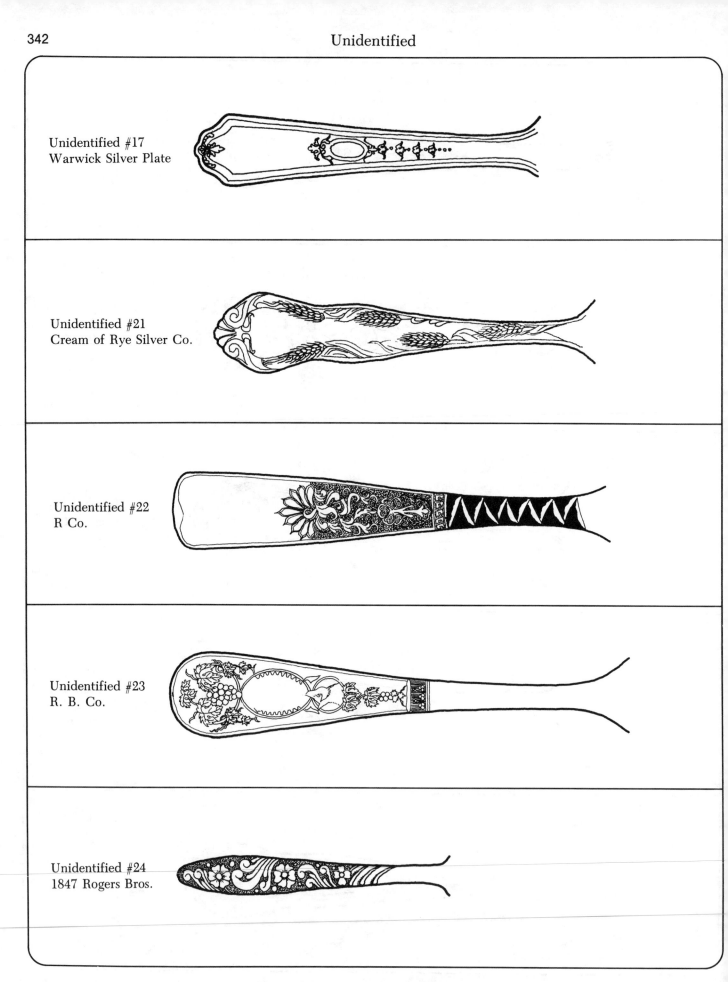

Unidentified

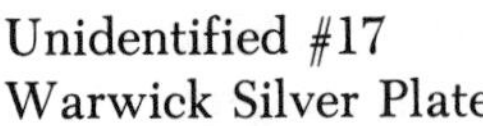
Unidentified #17
Warwick Silver Plate

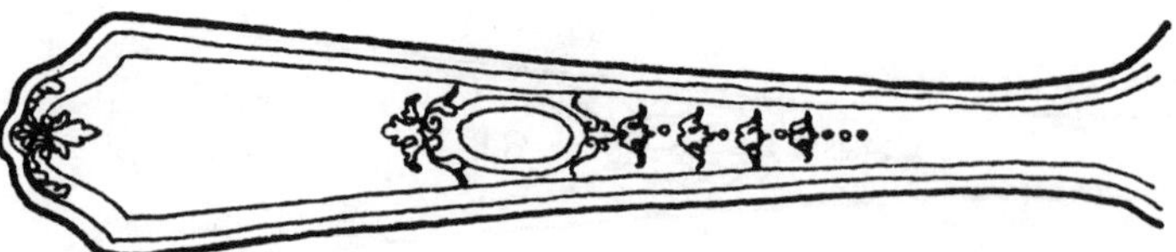

Unidentified #21
Cream of Rye Silver Co.

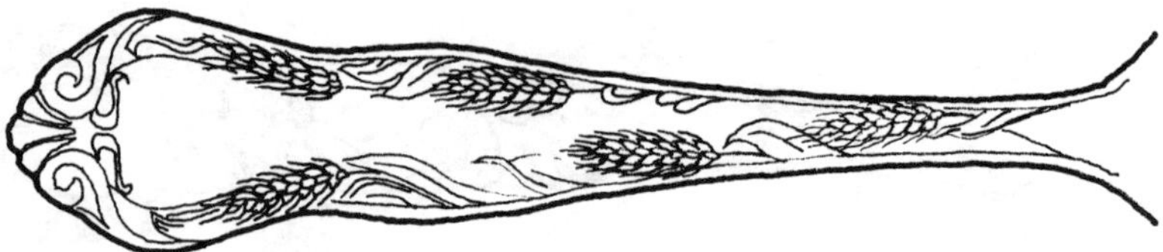

Unidentified #22
R Co.

Unidentified #23
R. B. Co.

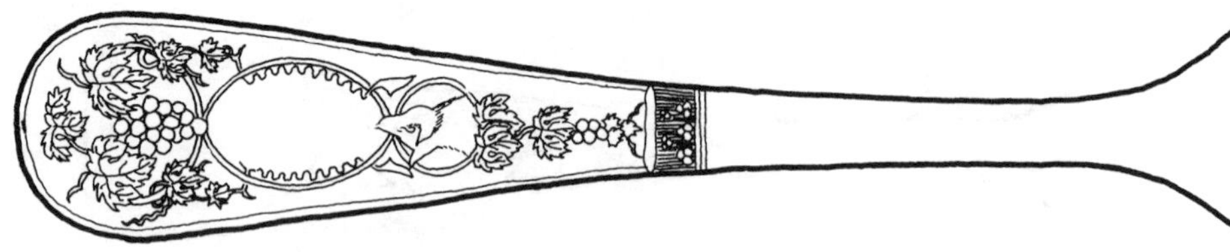

Unidentified #24
1847 Rogers Bros.

Please refer to "How To Use This Book" page 4.

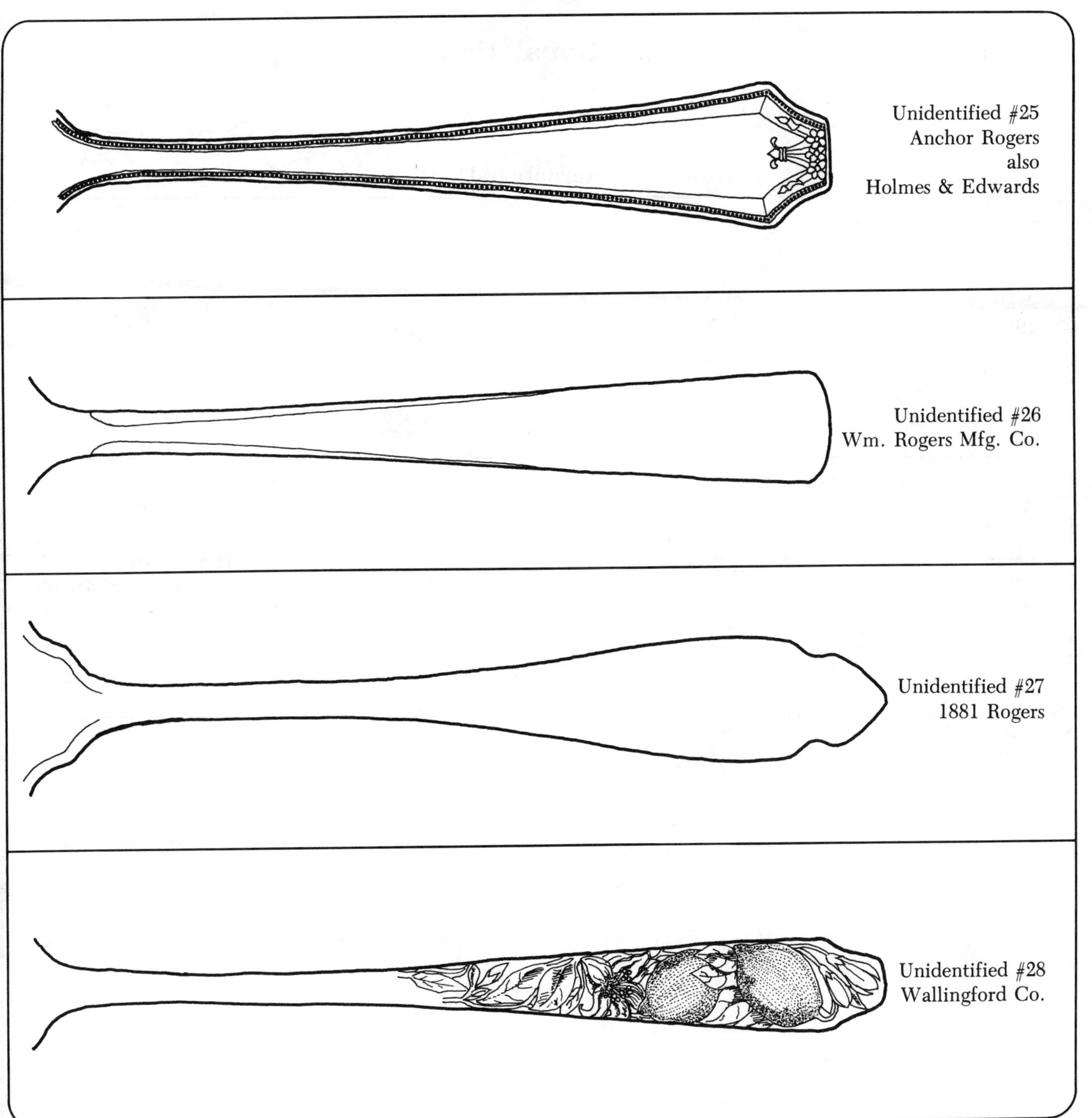

Unidentified #25
Anchor Rogers
also
Holmes & Edwards

Unidentified #26
Wm. Rogers Mfg. Co.

Unidentified #27
1881 Rogers

Unidentified #28
Wallingford Co.

Please refer to "How To Use This Book" page 4.

Additional Patterns

Wallace - International - Deep Silver

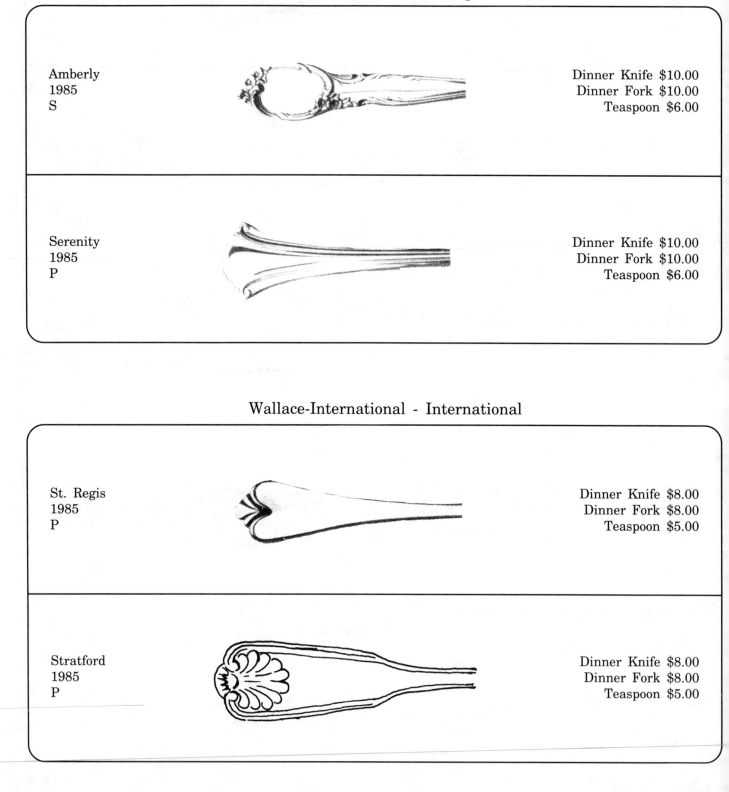

Amberly 1985 S		Dinner Knife $10.00 Dinner Fork $10.00 Teaspoon $6.00
Serenity 1985 P	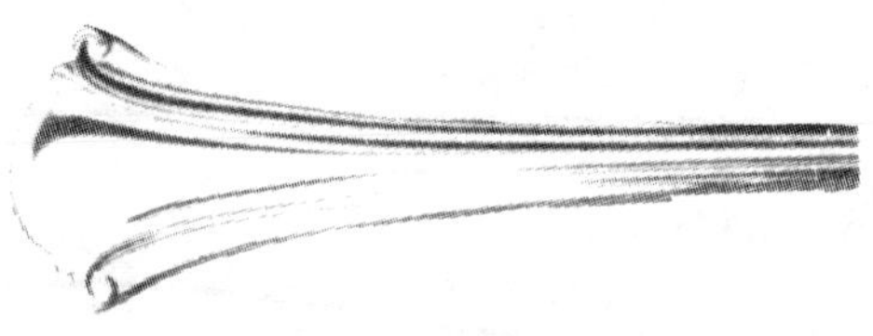	Dinner Knife $10.00 Dinner Fork $10.00 Teaspoon $6.00

Wallace-International - International

St. Regis 1985 P		Dinner Knife $8.00 Dinner Fork $8.00 Teaspoon $5.00
Stratford 1985 P	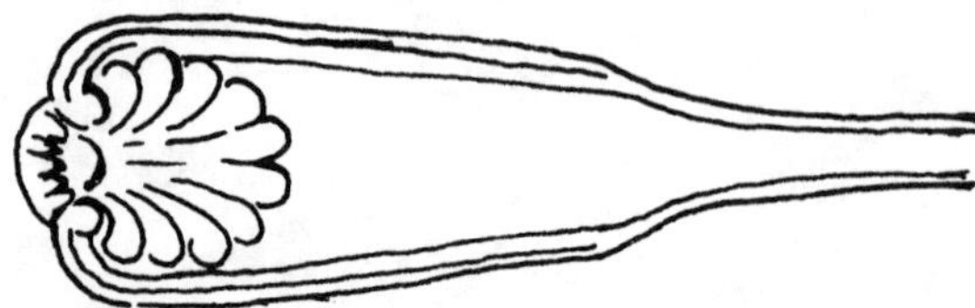	Dinner Knife $8.00 Dinner Fork $8.00 Teaspoon $5.00

Please refer to "How To Use This Book" page 4.

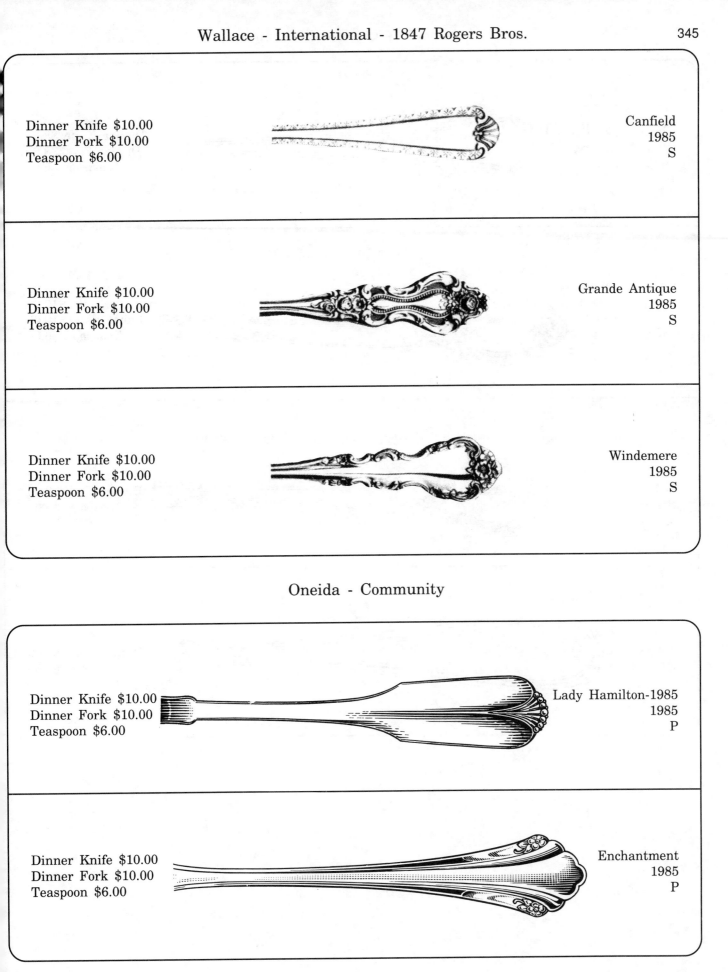

Dinner Knife $10.00
Dinner Fork $10.00
Teaspoon $6.00

Canfield
1985
S

Dinner Knife $10.00
Dinner Fork $10.00
Teaspoon $6.00

Grande Antique
1985
S

Dinner Knife $10.00
Dinner Fork $10.00
Teaspoon $6.00

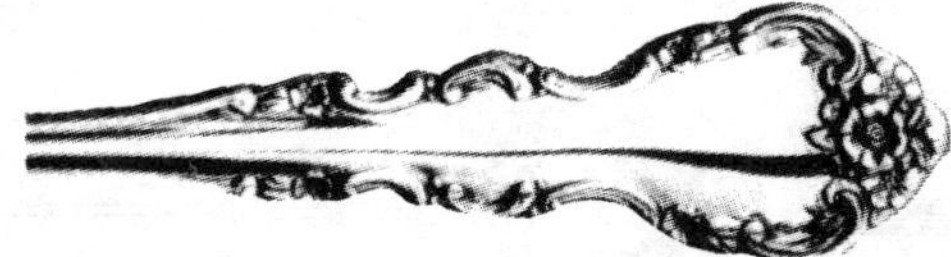

Windemere
1985
S

Oneida - Community

Dinner Knife $10.00
Dinner Fork $10.00
Teaspoon $6.00

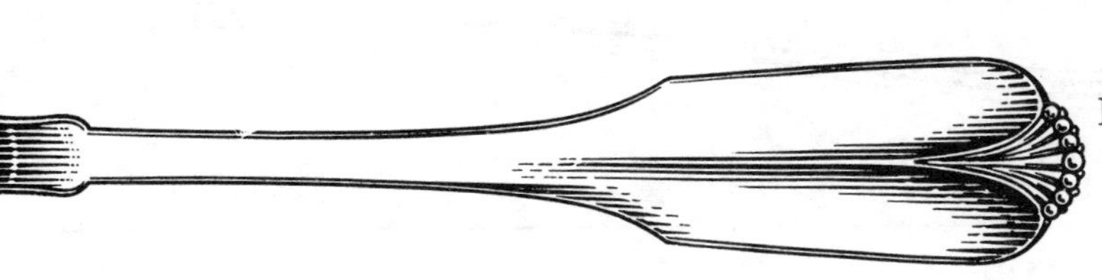

Lady Hamilton-1985
1985
P

Dinner Knife $10.00
Dinner Fork $10.00
Teaspoon $6.00

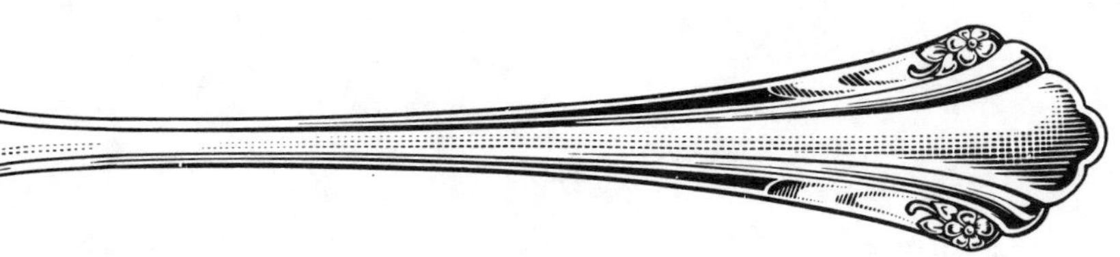

Enchantment
1985
P

Please refer to "How To Use This Book" page 4.

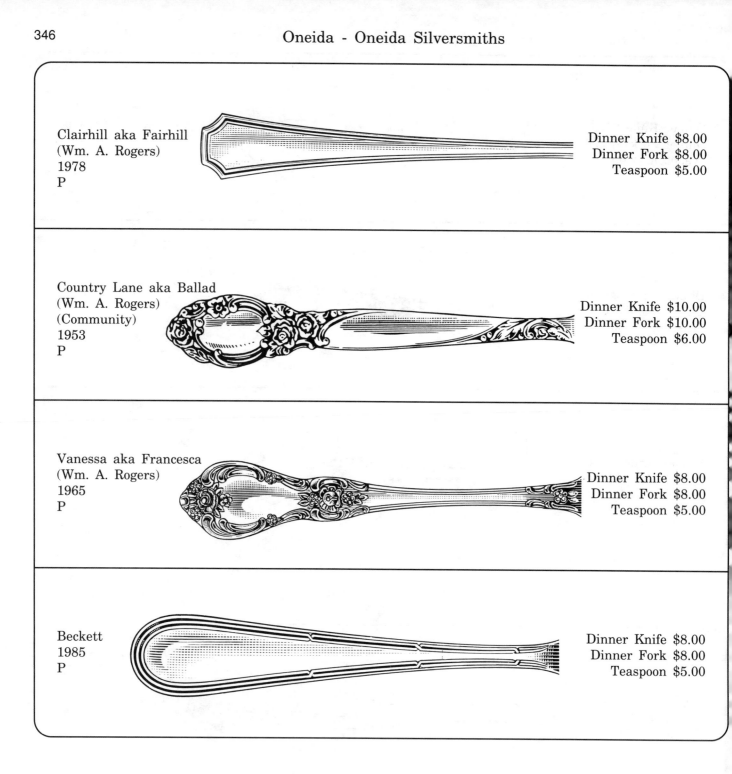

Clairhill aka Fairhill
(Wm. A. Rogers)
1978
P

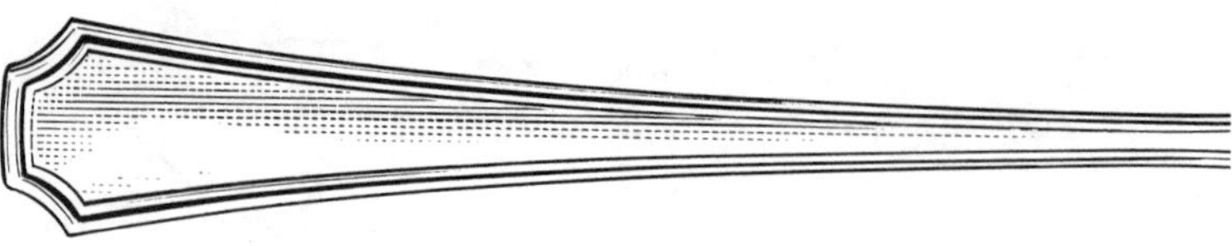

Dinner Knife $8.00
Dinner Fork $8.00
Teaspoon $5.00

Country Lane aka Ballad
(Wm. A. Rogers)
(Community)
1953
P

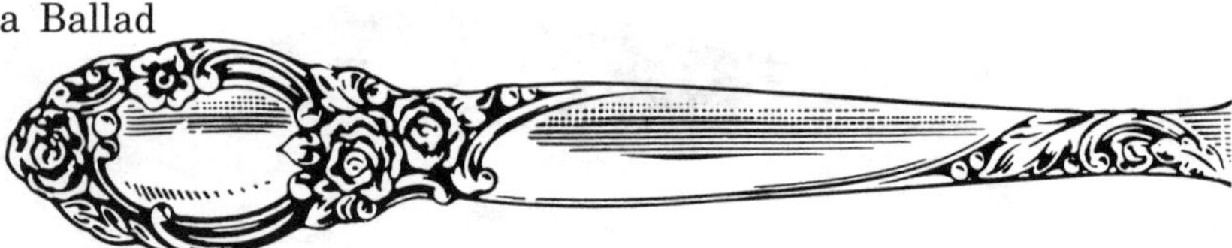

Dinner Knife $10.00
Dinner Fork $10.00
Teaspoon $6.00

Vanessa aka Francesca
(Wm. A. Rogers)
1965
P

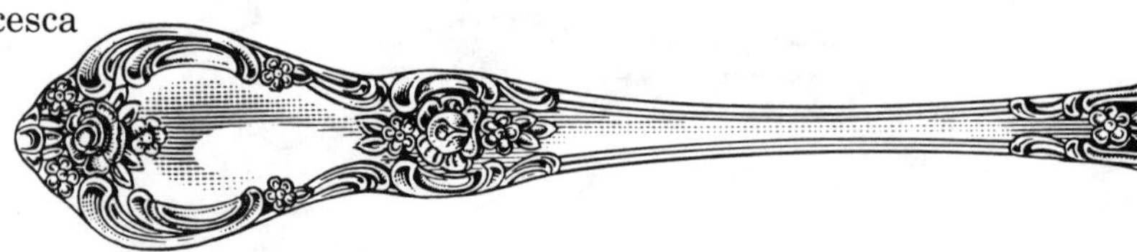

Dinner Knife $8.00
Dinner Fork $8.00
Teaspoon $5.00

Beckett
1985
P

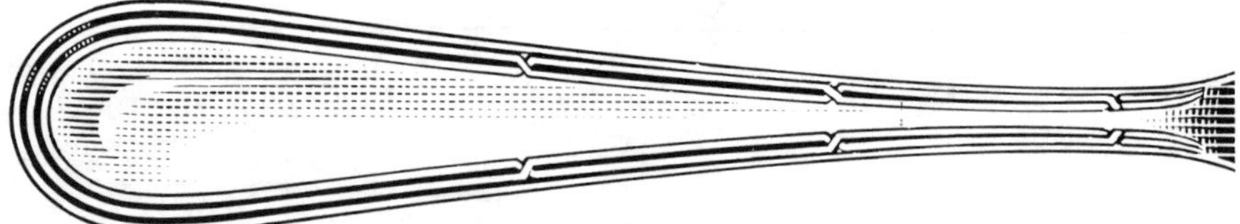

Dinner Knife $8.00
Dinner Fork $8.00
Teaspoon $5.00

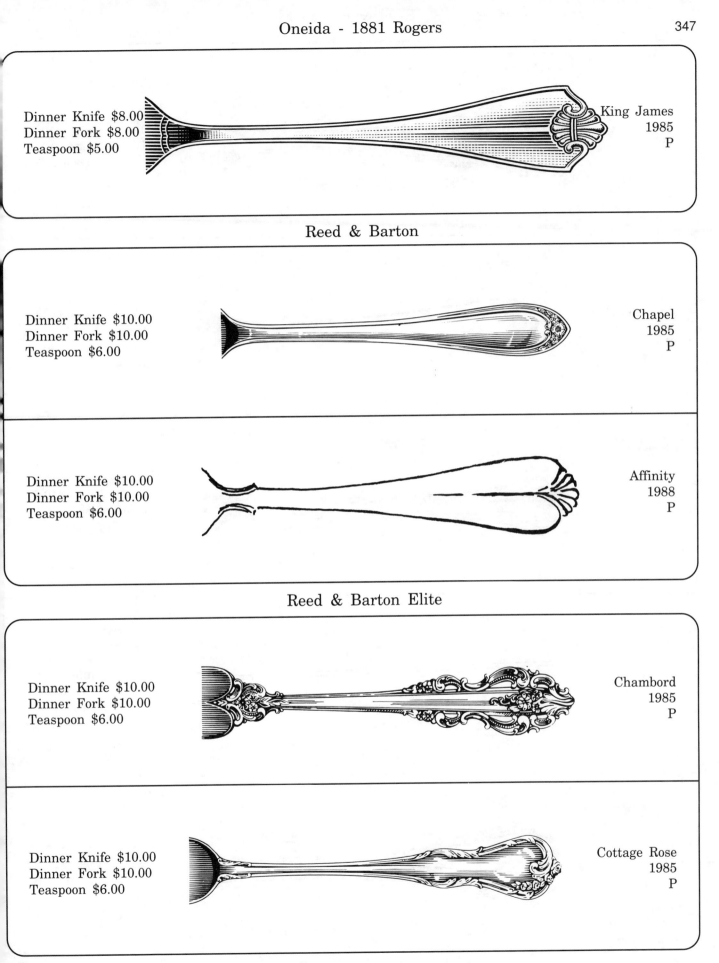

Dinner Knife $8.00
Dinner Fork $8.00
Teaspoon $5.00

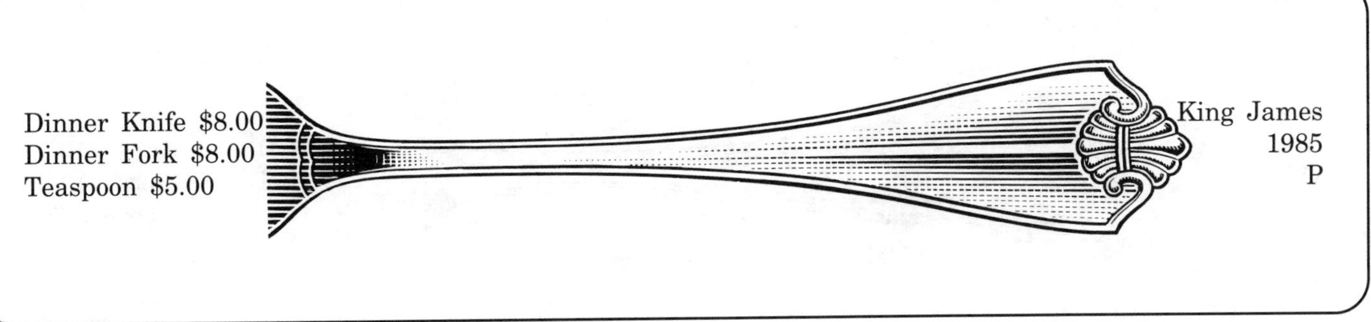

King James
1985
P

Reed & Barton

Dinner Knife $10.00
Dinner Fork $10.00
Teaspoon $6.00

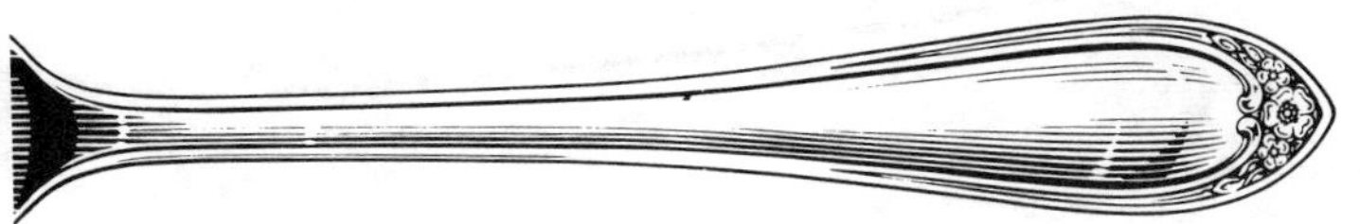

Chapel
1985
P

Dinner Knife $10.00
Dinner Fork $10.00
Teaspoon $6.00

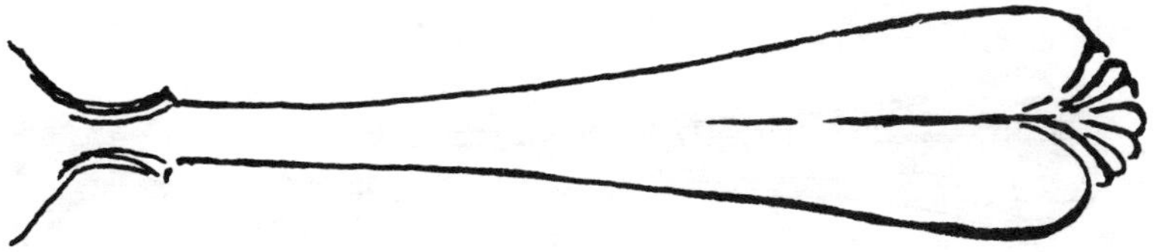

Affinity
1988
P

Reed & Barton Elite

Dinner Knife $10.00
Dinner Fork $10.00
Teaspoon $6.00

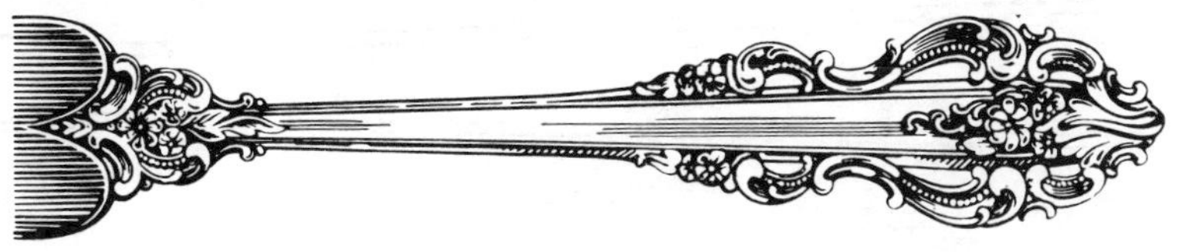

Chambord
1985
P

Dinner Knife $10.00
Dinner Fork $10.00
Teaspoon $6.00

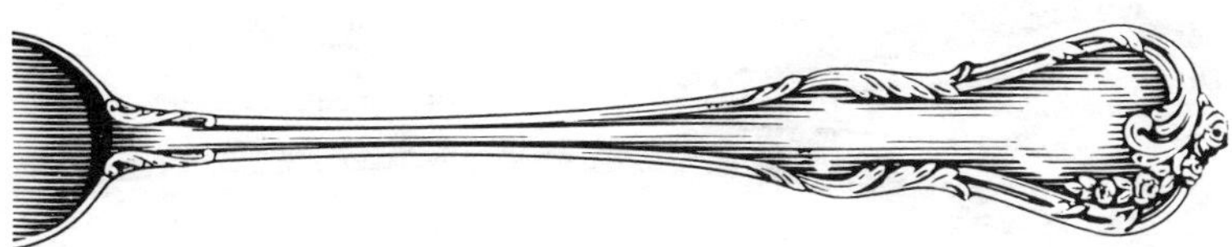

Cottage Rose
1985
P

Please refer to "How To Use This Book" page 4.

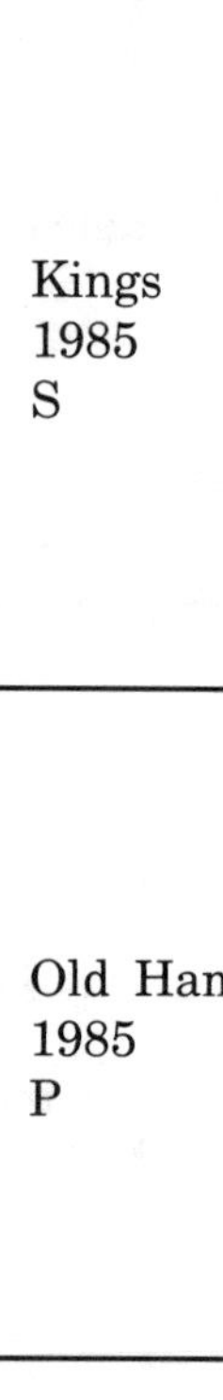

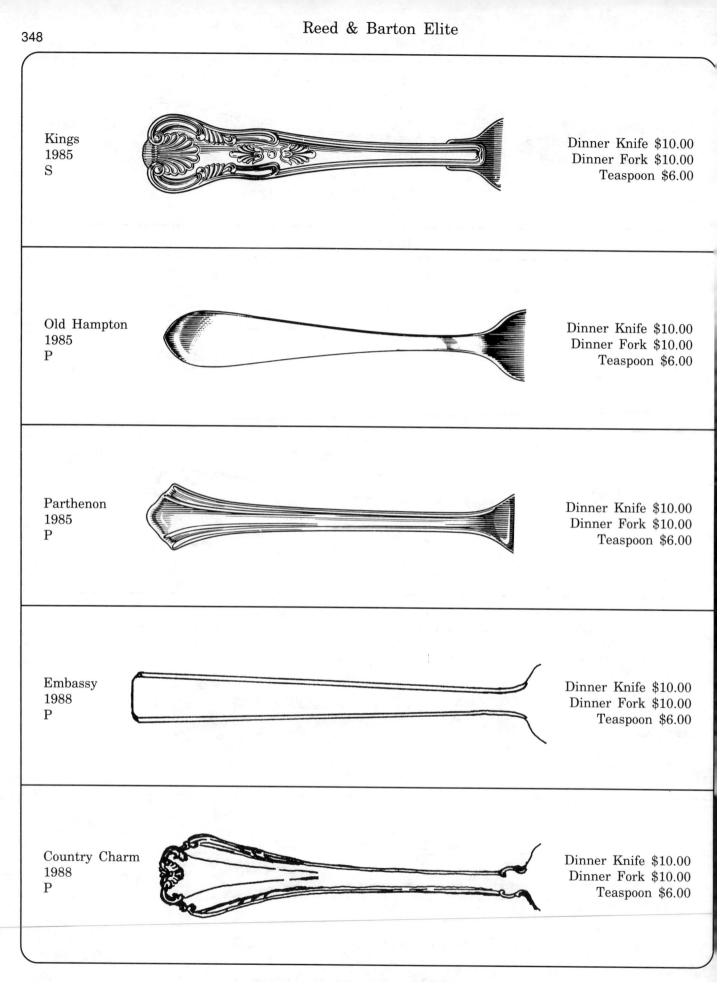

Kings
1985
S

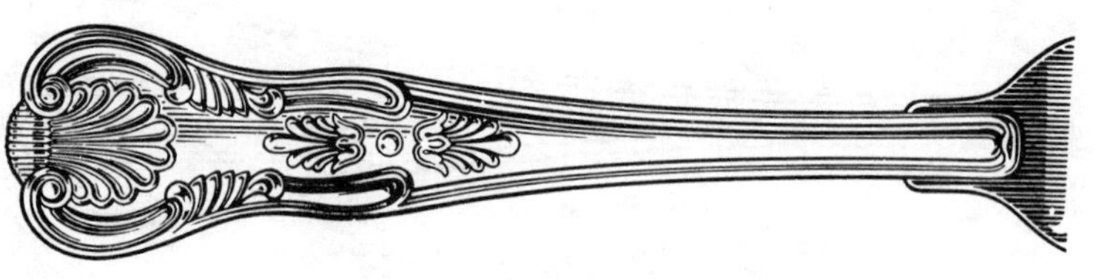

Dinner Knife $10.00
Dinner Fork $10.00
Teaspoon $6.00

Old Hampton
1985
P

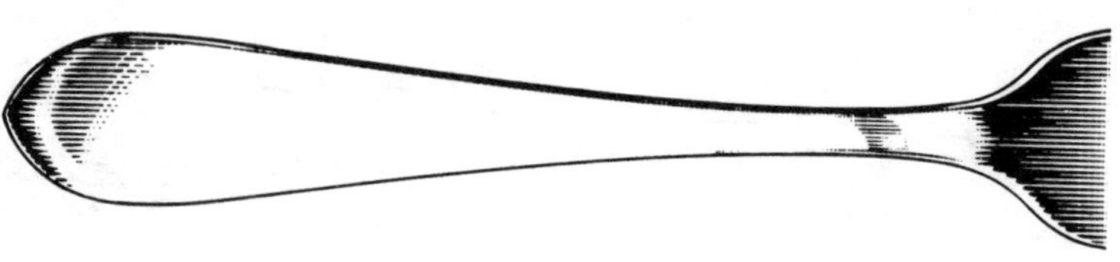

Dinner Knife $10.00
Dinner Fork $10.00
Teaspoon $6.00

Parthenon
1985
P

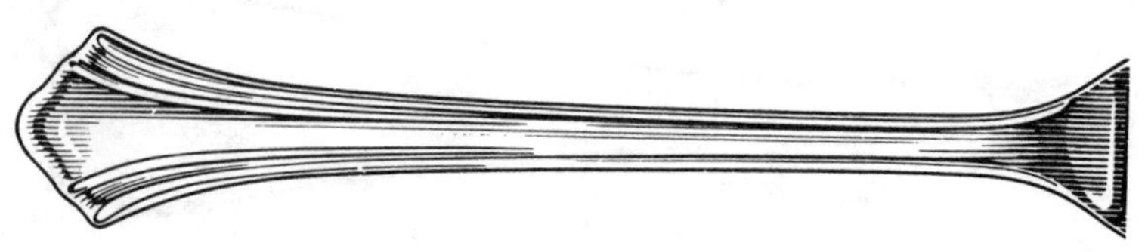

Dinner Knife $10.00
Dinner Fork $10.00
Teaspoon $6.00

Embassy
1988
P

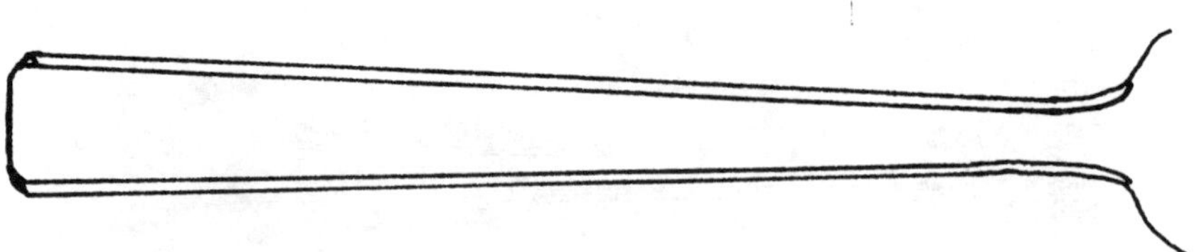

Dinner Knife $10.00
Dinner Fork $10.00
Teaspoon $6.00

Country Charm
1988
P

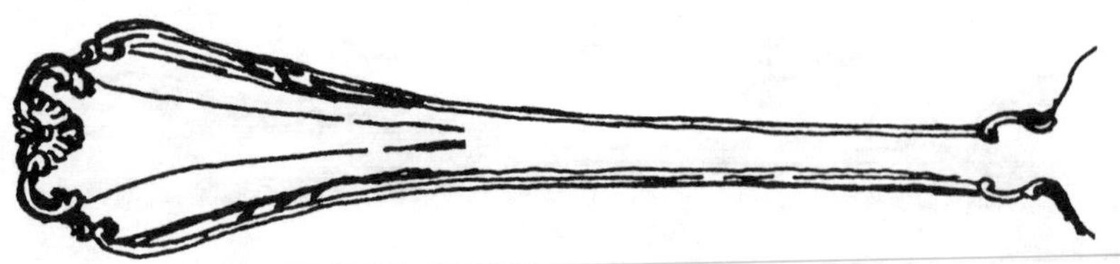

Dinner Knife $10.00
Dinner Fork $10.00
Teaspoon $6.00

Please refer to "How To Use This Book" page 4.

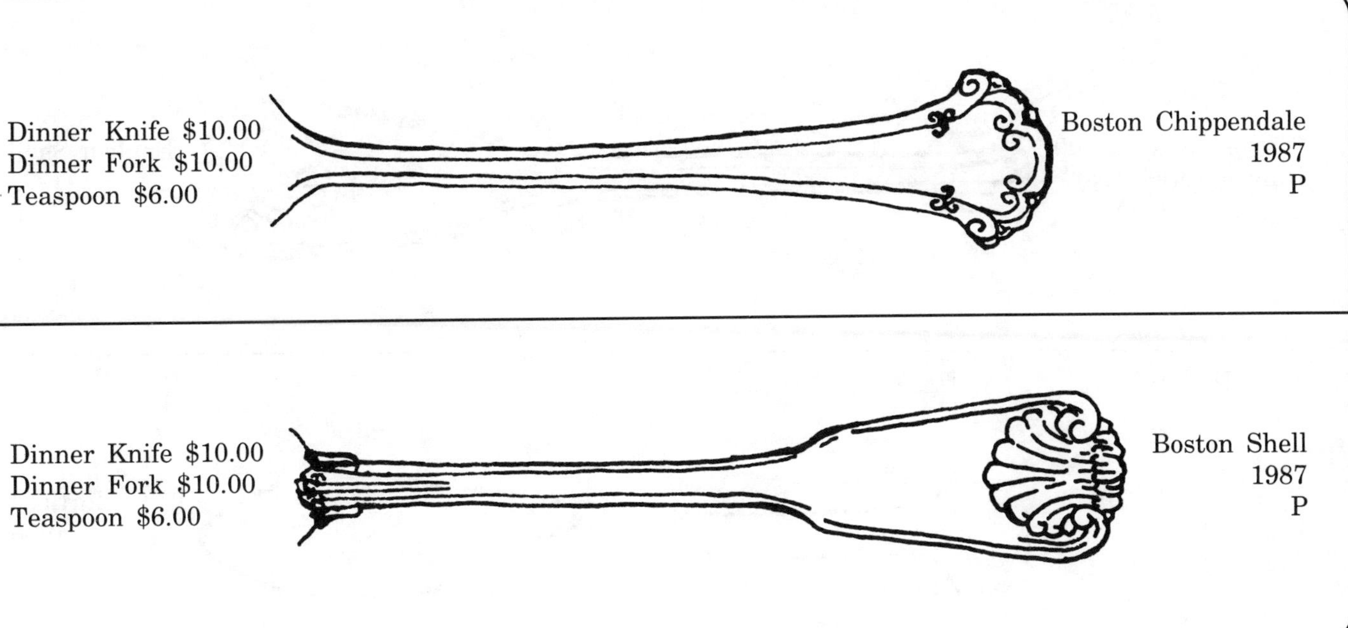

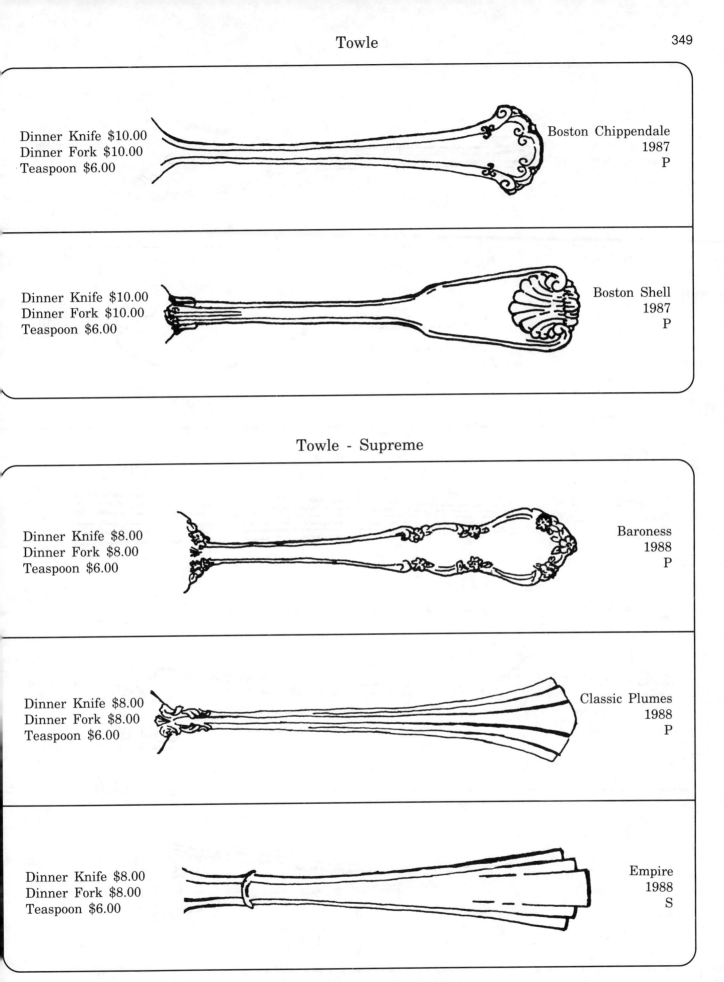

Dinner Knife $10.00
Dinner Fork $10.00
Teaspoon $6.00

Boston Chippendale
1987
P

Dinner Knife $10.00
Dinner Fork $10.00
Teaspoon $6.00

Boston Shell
1987
P

Towle - Supreme

Dinner Knife $8.00
Dinner Fork $8.00
Teaspoon $6.00

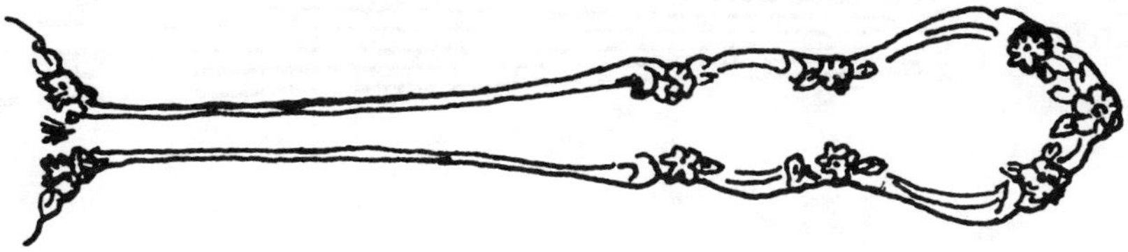

Baroness
1988
P

Dinner Knife $8.00
Dinner Fork $8.00
Teaspoon $6.00

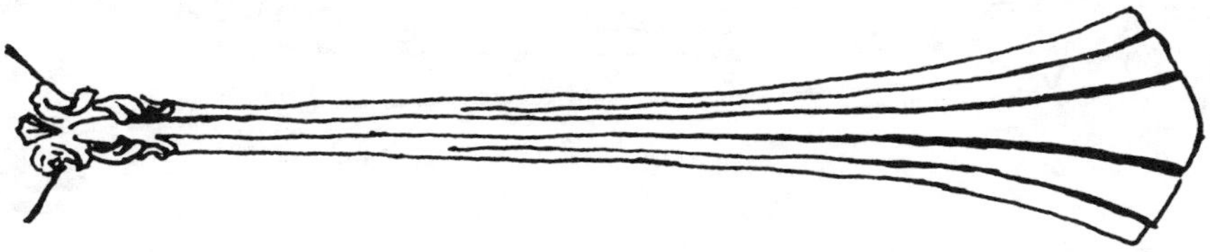

Classic Plumes
1988
P

Dinner Knife $8.00
Dinner Fork $8.00
Teaspoon $6.00

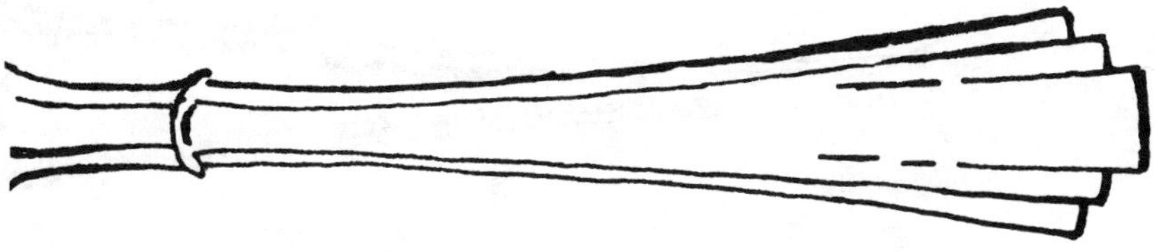

Empire
1988
S

Please refer to "How To Use This Book" page 4.

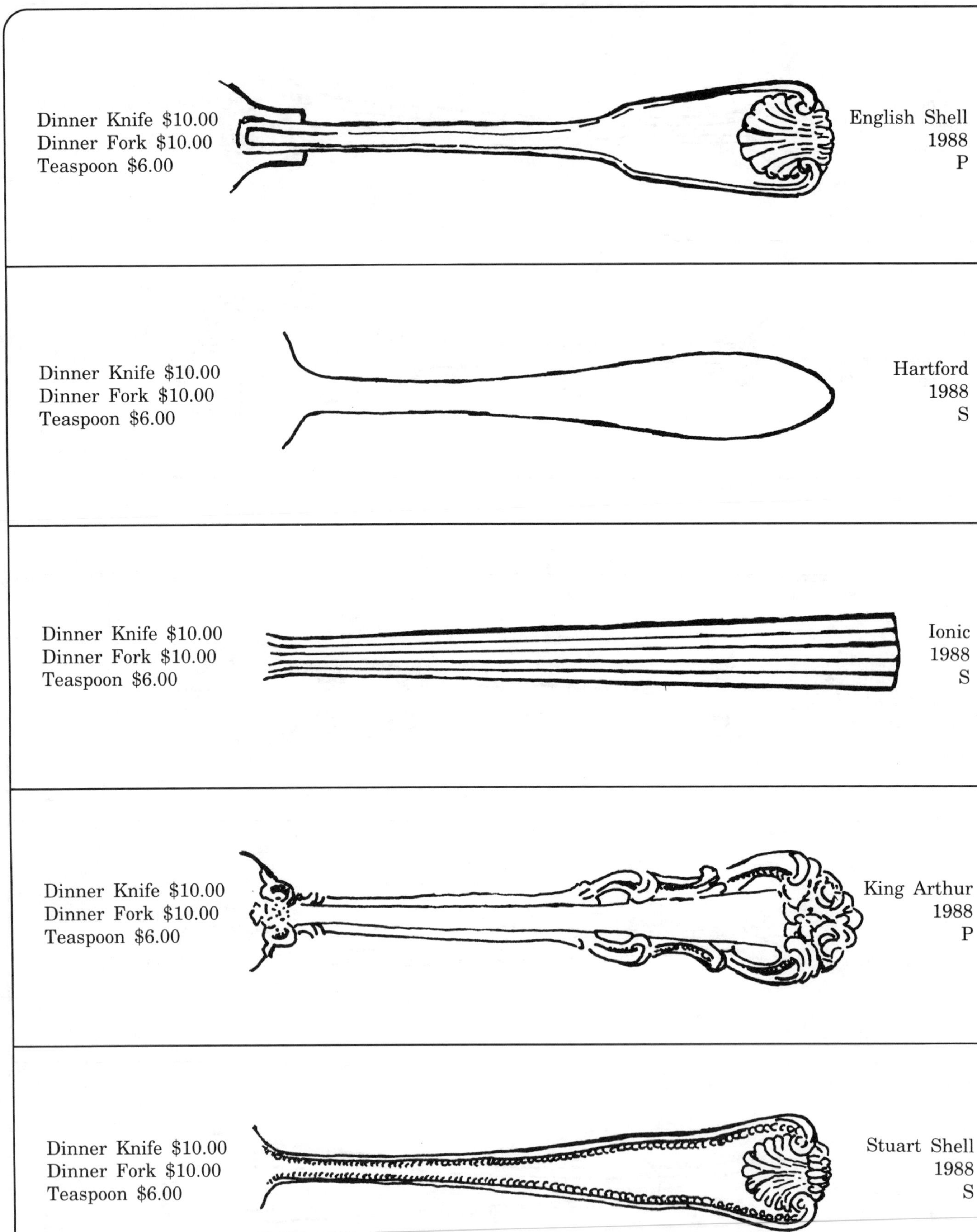

Dinner Knife $10.00
Dinner Fork $10.00
Teaspoon $6.00

English Shell
1988
P

Dinner Knife $10.00
Dinner Fork $10.00
Teaspoon $6.00

Hartford
1988
S

Dinner Knife $10.00
Dinner Fork $10.00
Teaspoon $6.00

Ionic
1988
S

Dinner Knife $10.00
Dinner Fork $10.00
Teaspoon $6.00

King Arthur
1988
P

Dinner Knife $10.00
Dinner Fork $10.00
Teaspoon $6.00

Stuart Shell
1988
S

Please refer to "How To Use This Book" page 4.

CATALOGUE REPRINTS

The following pages were reprinted from a catalogue I acquired. Although not dated, I would put it at the late 1920's. It is a wholesaler's catalogue and I chose for this edition of the book to include some illustrations of hollowware. I am frequently asked what hollowware was made in what patterns.

Since the silver manufacturing companies do not have this information, it is possible to determine only from catalogues such as this or from actual viewing of an item.

Hollowware was also made in a number of patterns from the 1930's until fairly recent times. Illustrations of hollowware of these patterns are not available at this time.

It is likely that other pieces of hollowware exist for the patterns illustrated on the following pages. These were simply the pieces offered by this wholesaler in this catalogue.

Earlier editions of this book have other catalogue reprints to help in the identification of flatware pieces.

COMMUNITY PLATE

The "FOURSOME SET"

Community's Smallest Service for Your Biggest Market

A SERVICE FOR FOUR

A NEW SET based on a big idea—the Foursome, a set for four, selling at the lowest price of any service Community has ever offered. Twenty pieces, in any COMMUNITY PLATE pattern, on a full-size Duo-Service Tray—standard Community quality in slightly less quantity at a much lower price.

It is built for people of good taste but small purse . . . for people who want the best even if they have to take less of it . . . for small families . . . it recognizes *and turns to your advantage* the modern trend toward more intimate entertaining . . . the bridge quartet, the small dinner.

More than a new set, it is a set for a new market—your *biggest*. Far from competing with your present stocks, it will attract new buyers for them. As an entering wedge to new business, as a bait for sales of bigger units, as a builder of later added-piece sales, it has definite dollar value.

20 *Piece Contents*

8 TEASPOONS 4 KNIVES 4 FORKS 2 TABLE SPOONS 1 BUTTER KNIFE 1 SUGAR SPOON

Paul Revere	*Hampton Court*	*Bird of Paradise*	*Grosvenor*	*Adam*	*Patrician*	20 PIECE FOURSOME SET	
14168	13168	12168	11168	10168	6168	with Hollow Handle Dinner Knives, *De Luxe Stainless*	Each $33.88
14170	13170	12170	11170	10170	6170	with Modeled Handle Dinner Knives, Stainless	Each 28.78

COMMUNITY PLATE
THE Paul Revere DESIGN
An Early-American pattern, conceived and executed in the finest manner of what is conceded to be the Golden Age of American Silversmithing.
Bright Butler Finish
DESSERT SPOON
DINNER KNIFE
DINNER FORK
TABLE SPOON
FIFTY-YEAR REPLACEMENT GUARANTEE
SPOONS—Six in Box — Per Doz.
Tea $9.76
Dessert 19.52
Table 19.52
Soup (Round Bowl) 19.52
FORKS—Six in Box
Dinner 19.52
Dessert 19.52
KNIVES (Stainless Blades)
Six in Blue Velvet Lined Gift Box — Per Doz.
Hollow Handle Dinner, De Luxe Stainless . . . $36.80
Hollow Handle Dessert, De Luxe Stainless . . . 36.80
Modeled Handle Dinner, Standard Stainless . . . 21.48
Hollow Handle Fruit Knives, Standard Stainless . 29.80
Modeled Handle Fruit Knives, Standard Stainless 19.12
KNIVES (Plated Blades)
Six in Blue Velvet Lined Gift Box — Per Doz.
Hollow Handle Dinner $31.20
Hollow Handle Dessert 31.20
Modeled Handle Dinner 19.84
Modeled Handle Dessert 19.84
Hollow Handle Tea or Butter 29.80

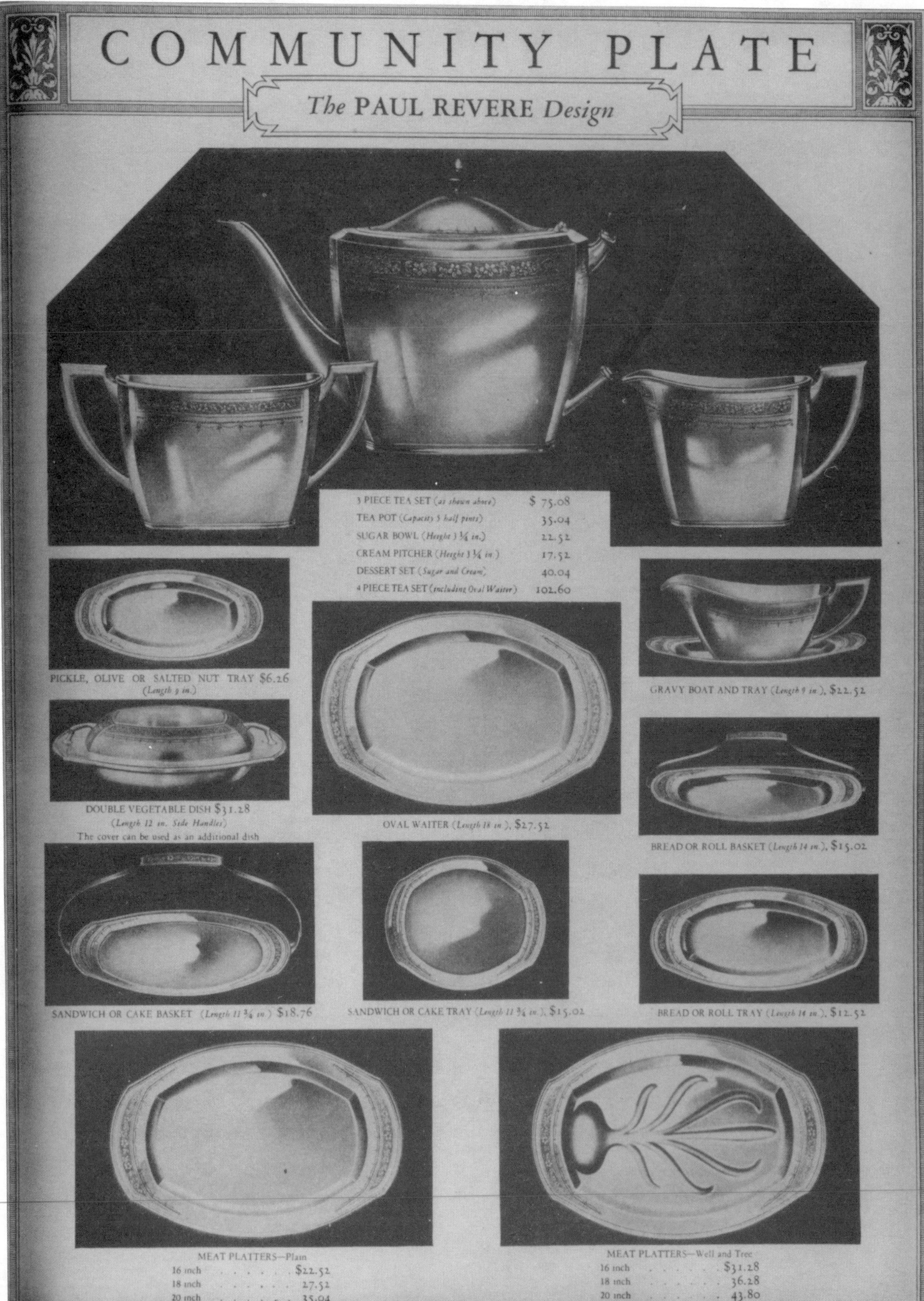
COMMUNITY PLATE
The PAUL REVERE *Design*
3 PIECE TEA SET (*as shown above*) $ 75.08
TEA POT (*Capacity 5 half pints*) 35.04
SUGAR BOWL (*Height 3 ¾ in.*) 22.52
CREAM PITCHER (*Height 3 ¾ in.*) 17.52
DESSERT SET (*Sugar and Cream*) 40.04
4 PIECE TEA SET (*including Oval Waiter*) 102.60
PICKLE, OLIVE OR SALTED NUT TRAY $6.26
(*Length 9 in.*)
DOUBLE VEGETABLE DISH $31.28
(*Length 12 in. Side Handles*)
The cover can be used as an additional dish
OVAL WAITER (*Length 18 in.*), $27.52
GRAVY BOAT AND TRAY (*Length 9 in.*), $22.52
BREAD OR ROLL BASKET (*Length 14 in.*), $15.02
SANDWICH OR CAKE BASKET (*Length 11 ¾ in.*) $18.76
SANDWICH OR CAKE TRAY (*Length 11 ¾ in.*), $15.02
BREAD OR ROLL TRAY (*Length 14 in.*), $12.52
MEAT PLATTERS—Plain
16 inch $22.52
18 inch 27.52
20 inch 35.04
MEAT PLATTERS—Well and Tree
16 inch $31.28
18 inch 36.28
20 inch 43.80

COMMUNITY PLATE
THE Grosvenor DESIGN
Created in the finer mood of those great masters—the Brothers Adam. A fresh, spirited and charming interpretation of the vogue for rich simplicity in tableware.
Bright Butler Finish
DINNER KNIFE
DESSERT SPOON
DINNER FORK
TABLE SPOON
FIFTY-YEAR REPLACEMENT GUARANTEE
SPOONS—Six in Box Per Doz.
Tea . . . $9.76
Dessert . . . 19.52
Table . . . 19.52
Soup (Round Bowl) . . . 19.52
FORKS—Six in Box
Dinner . . . 19.52
Dessert . . . 19.52
KNIVES (Stainless Blades)
Six in Blue Velvet Lined Gift Box Per Doz.
Hollow Handle Dinner, DeLuxe Stainless . . . $36.80
Hollow Handle Dessert, DeLuxe Stainless . . . 36.80
Modeled Handle Dinner, Standard Stainless . . . 21.48
Hollow Handle Fruit Knives, Standard Stainless . 29.80
Modeled Handle Fruit Knives, Standard Stainless 19.12
KNIVES (Plated Blades)
Six in Blue Velvet Lined Gift Box Per Doz.
Hollow Handle Dinner . . . $31.20
Hollow Handle Dessert . . . 31.20
Modeled Handle Dinner . . . 19.84
Modeled Handle Dessert . . . 19.84
Hollow Handle Tea or Butter . . . 29.80

COMMUNITY PLATE
The GROSVENOR Design
PICKLE, OLIVE OR SALTED NUT TRAY (Length 9 in.), $6.26
BREAD OR ROLL BASKET $15.02 (Length 14 in.)
3 PIECE TEA SET (as shown above) $ 87.58
TEA POT (Capacity 5 half pints) 40.04
SUGAR BOWL (Height 6 in.) 27.52
CREAM PITCHER (Height 6⅜ in.) 20.02
DESSERT SET (Sugar and Cream) 47.54
4 PIECE TEA SET (including Oval Waiter) 115.10
DOUBLE VEGETABLE DISH $31.28
(Length 12 in. Side Handles)
The cover can be used as an additional dish
GRAVY BOAT AND TRAY (Length 9 in.), $22.52
BREAD OR ROLL TRAY (Length 14 in.), $12.52
OVAL WAITER (Length 18 in.), $27.52
SANDWICH OR CAKE BASKET (Length 11 ¾ in.) $18.76
MEAT PLATTERS—Well and Tree
16 inch $31.28
18 inch 36.28
20 inch 43.80
SANDWICH OR CAKE TRAY (Length 11 ¾ in.), $15.02
MEAT PLATTERS—Plain
16 inch $22.52
18 inch 27.52
20 inch 35.04

COMMUNITY PLATE
THE
Bird of Paradise
The exotic charm and spirited modern beauty of the admired Bird of Paradise Design, stamps it as one of the most distinctive creations in modern silver.
Bright Butler Finish
DINNER KNIFE
DESSERT SPOON
DINNER FORK
TABLE SPOON
FIFTY-YEAR REPLACEMENT GUARANTEE
SPOONS—Six in Box Per Doz.
Tea $9.76
Dessert 19.52
Table 19.52
Soup (Round Bowl) 19.52
FORKS—Six in Box
Dinner 19.52
Dessert 19.52
KNIVES (Stainless Blades)
Six in Blue Velvet Lined Gift Box Per Doz.
Hollow Handle Dinner, De Luxe Stainless . . . $36.80
Hollow Handle Dessert, De Luxe Stainless . . . 36.80
Modeled Handle Dinner, Standard Stainless . . . 21.48
Hollow Handle Fruit Knives, Standard Stainless . 29.80
Modeled Handle Fruit Knives, Standard Stainless 19.12
KNIVES (Plated Blades)
Six in Blue Velvet Lined Gift Box Per Doz.
Hollow Handle Dinner $31.20
Hollow Handle Dessert 31.20
Modeled Handle Dinner 19.84
Modeled Handle Dessert 19.84
Hollow Handle Tea or Butter 29.80

COMMUNITY PLATE
The BIRD of PARADISE Design
3 PIECE TEA SET (as shown above) $ 68.82
TEA POT (Capacity 3 half pints) 33.78
SUGAR BOWL (Height 3 3/4 in.) 18.76
CREAM PITCHER (Height 3 3/4 in.) 16.26
DESSERT SET (Sugar and Cream) 35.04
4 PIECE TEA SET (including Oval Waiter) 96.34
PICKLE, OLIVE OR SALTED NUT TRAY $6.26
(Length 9 in.)
GRAVY BOAT AND TRAY (Length 9 in.), $22.52
DOUBLE VEGETABLE DISH $31.28
(Length 12 in. Side Handles)
The cover can be used as an additional dish
OVAL WAITER (Length 18 in.), $27.52
BREAD OR ROLL BASKET (Length 14 in.), $15.02
SANDWICH OR CAKE BASKET (Length 11 3/4 in.) $18.76
SANDWICH OR CAKE TRAY (Length 11 3/4 in.), $15.02
BREAD OR ROLL TRAY (Length 14 in.), $12.52
MEAT PLATTERS—Plain
16 inch $22.52
18 inch 27.52
20 inch 35.04
MEAT PLATTERS—Well and Tree
16 inch $31.28
18 inch 36.28
20 inch 43.80

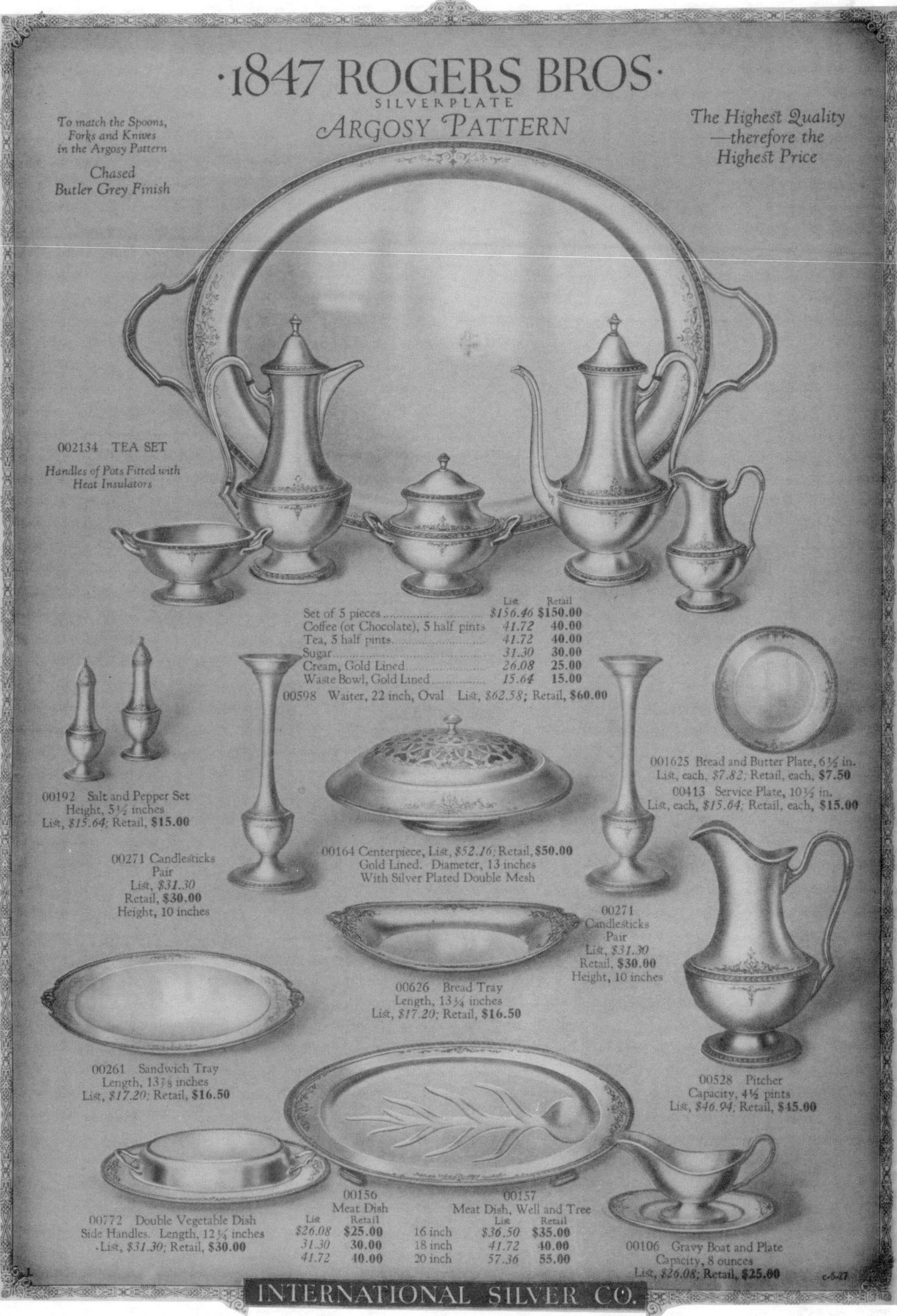
·1847 ROGERS BROS·
SILVERPLATE
ARGOSY PATTERN
To match the Spoons, Forks and Knives in the Argosy Pattern
Chased
Butler Grey Finish
The Highest Quality —therefore the Highest Price
002134 TEA SET
Handles of Pots Fitted with Heat Insulators
List Retail
Set of 5 pieces $156.46 $150.00
Coffee (or Chocolate), 5 half pints 41.72 40.00
Tea, 5 half pints 41.72 40.00
Sugar 31.30 30.00
Cream, Gold Lined 26.08 25.00
Waste Bowl, Gold Lined 15.64 15.00
00598 Waiter, 22 inch, Oval List, $62.58; Retail, $60.00
00192 Salt and Pepper Set
Height, 5½ inches
List, $15.64; Retail, $15.00
00271 Candlesticks
Pair
List, $31.30
Retail, $30.00
Height, 10 inches
00164 Centerpiece, List, $52.16; Retail, $50.00
Gold Lined. Diameter, 13 inches
With Silver Plated Double Mesh
001625 Bread and Butter Plate, 6½ in.
List, each, $7.82; Retail, each, $7.50
00413 Service Plate, 10½ in.
List, each, $15.64; Retail, each, $15.00
00271 Candlesticks
Pair
List, $31.30
Retail, $30.00
Height, 10 inches
00626 Bread Tray
Length, 13¾ inches
List, $17.20; Retail, $16.50
00261 Sandwich Tray
Length, 13⅞ inches
List, $17.20; Retail, $16.50
00528 Pitcher
Capacity, 4½ pints
List, $46.94; Retail, $45.00
00772 Double Vegetable Dish
Side Handles. Length, 12¼ inches
List, $31.30; Retail, $30.00
00156
Meat Dish
List Retail
$26.08 $25.00 16 inch
31.30 30.00 18 inch
41.72 40.00 20 inch
00157
Meat Dish, Well and Tree
List Retail
$36.50 $35.00
41.72 40.00
57.36 55.00
00106 Gravy Boat and Plate
Capacity, 8 ounces
List, $26.08; Retail, $25.00
c-6-27
INTERNATIONAL SILVER CO.

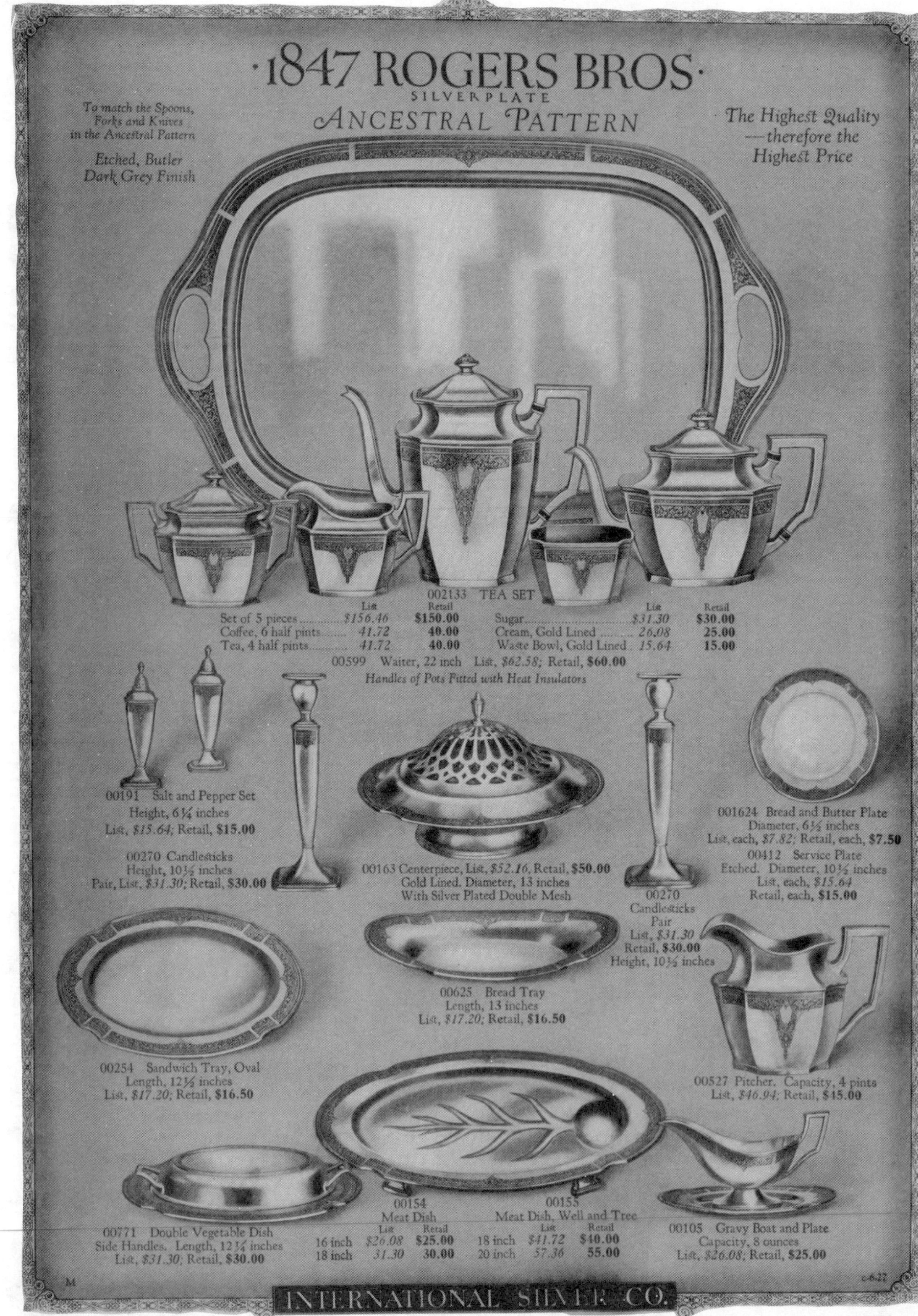
·1847 ROGERS BROS·
SILVERPLATE
ANCESTRAL PATTERN
To match the Spoons, Forks and Knives in the Ancestral Pattern
Etched, Butler Dark Grey Finish
The Highest Quality —therefore the Highest Price
002133 TEA SET
List Retail
Set of 5 pieces $156.46 $150.00
Coffee, 6 half pints 41.72 40.00
Tea, 4 half pints 41.72 40.00
List Retail
Sugar $31.30 $30.00
Cream, Gold Lined 26.08 25.00
Waste Bowl, Gold Lined .. 15.64 15.00
00599 Waiter, 22 inch List, $62.58; Retail, $60.00
Handles of Pots Fitted with Heat Insulators
00191 Salt and Pepper Set
Height, 6¼ inches
List, $15.64; Retail, $15.00
00270 Candlesticks
Height, 10½ inches
Pair, List, $31.30; Retail, $30.00
00163 Centerpiece, List, $52.16, Retail, $50.00
Gold Lined. Diameter, 13 inches
With Silver Plated Double Mesh
00270
Candlesticks
Pair
List, $31.30
Retail, $30.00
Height, 10½ inches
001624 Bread and Butter Plate
Diameter, 6½ inches
List, each, $7.82; Retail, each, $7.50
00412 Service Plate
Etched. Diameter, 10½ inches
List, each, $15.64
Retail, each, $15.00
00625 Bread Tray
Length, 13 inches
List, $17.20; Retail, $16.50
00254 Sandwich Tray, Oval
Length, 12½ inches
List, $17.20; Retail, $16.50
00527 Pitcher. Capacity, 4 pints
List, $46.94; Retail, $45.00
00771 Double Vegetable Dish
Side Handles. Length, 12¼ inches
List, $31.30; Retail, $30.00
00154
Meat Dish
List Retail
16 inch $26.08 $25.00
18 inch 31.30 30.00
00155
Meat Dish, Well and Tree
List Retail
18 inch $41.72 $40.00
20 inch 57.36 55.00
00105 Gravy Boat and Plate
Capacity, 8 ounces
List, $26.08; Retail, $25.00
M
6-27
INTERNATIONAL SILVER CO.

·1847 ROGERS BROS·
SILVERPLATE
ANNIVERSARY PATTERN
To match the Spoons, Forks and Knives in the Anniversary Pattern
French Grey Butler Finish
The Highest Quality —therefore the Highest Price
002132 TEA SET
List Retail
Set of 5 pieces $156.46 $150.00
Coffee, 5 half pints 41.72 40.00
Tea, 4 half pints 41.72 40.00
List Retail
Sugar $31.30 $30.00
Cream, Gold Lined 26.08 25.00
Waste Bowl, Gold Lined 15.64 15.00
00591 Waiter, 22 inch List, $62.58; Retail, $60.00
Handles of Pots Fitted with Heat Insulators
00190 Salt and Pepper Set
Height, 6¾ inches
List, $15.64; Retail, $15.00
00162 Centerpiece, List, $52.16; Retail, $50.00
Gold Lined. Diameter, 11½ inches
With Silver Plated Double Mesh
001623 Bread and Butter Plate
Width, 6 inches
List, each, $7.82; Retail, each, $7.50
00411 Service Plate
Width, 10 inches
List, each, $15.64
Retail, each, $15.00
00269
Candlesticks
Pair
List, $31.30
Retail, $30.00
Height
10¼ inches
00623 Bread Tray
Pierced. Length, 12½ inches
List, $17.20; Retail, $16.50
00269
Candlesticks
Pair
List, $31.30
Retail, $30.00
Height
10¼ inches
00251 Sandwich Tray
Pierced. Width, 10 inches
List, $17.20; Retail, $16.50
00526 Pitcher
Capacity, 4 pints
List, $46.94; Retail, $45.00
00770 Double Vegetable Dish
Side Handles. Length, 11 inches
List, $31.30; Retail, $30.00
00151
Meat Dish
List Retail
$26.08 $25.00 16 inch
31.30 30.00 18 inch
41.72 40.00 20 inch
00152
Meat Dish, Well and Tree
List Retail
$36.50 $35.00
41.72 40.00
57.36 55.00
00104 Gravy Boat and Plate
Capacity, 12 ounces
List, $26.08; Retail, $25.00
N
6-17
INTERNATIONAL SILVER CO.

·1847 ROGERS BROS·
SILVERPLATE
AMBASSADOR PATTERN
To match the Spoons, Forks and Knives in the Ambassador Pattern
Chased, Butler Grey Finish
The Highest Quality —therefore the Highest Price
List Retail
Set of 5 pieces $150.46 $150.00
Coffee, 5 half pints 41.72 40.00
Tea, 4 half pints 41.72 40.00
002131 TEA SET Chased
Sugar $31.30 $30.00
Cream, Gold Lined 26.08 25.00
Waste Bowl, Gold Lined 15.64 15.00
00589 Waiter, 22 inch. Pierced. Chased List, $62.58; Retail, $60.00
Handles of Pots Fitted with Heat Insulators
00189 Salt and Pepper Set Chased. Height, 6¾ inches List, $15.64; Retail, $15.00
001622 Bread and Butter Plate, 6 in. Pierced. Chased List, each, $7.82; Retail, each, $7.50
00409 Service Plate, 10½ in. Pierced. Chased List, each, $15.64; Retail, each, $15.00
00165 Centerpiece, List, $52.16; Retail, $50.00 Gold Lined. Diameter, 12¾ inches. With Silver Plated Double Mesh. Pierced. Chased
00268 Candlesticks Chased Pair, List, $31.30 Retail, $30.00 Height 10 in.
00268 Candlesticks Chased Pair List, $31.30 Retail, $30.00 Height, 10 in.
00620 Bread Tray Pierced. Chased. Length, 13¾ inches List, $17.20; Retail, $16.50
00244 Sandwich Tray Pierced. Chased Diameter, 10½ inches List, $17.20; Retail, $16.50
00525 Pitcher Chased. Capacity, 4 pints List, $46.94; Retail, $45.00
00767 Double Vegetable Dish Lock Handle Pierced. Chased Length, 11¾ inches List, $31.30; Retail, $30.00
00148 Meat Dish Pierced. Chased
00149 Meat Dish, Well and Tree Pierced. Chased
List Retail List Retail
$20.86 $20.00 14 inch — —
26.08 25.00 16 inch — —
31.30 30.00 18 inch $41.72 $40.00
41.72 40.00 20 inch 57.36 55.00
— — 22 inch 73.02 70.00
00103 Gravy Boat and Plate Pierced. Chased Capacity, 8 ounces List, $26.08; Retail, $25.00
c-6-27
INTERNATIONAL SILVER CO.

COMMUNITY PLATE

New Popular-Priced Service Pieces

(MAYONNAISE BOWL—BON BON DISH—CHILD'S CUP—TEA OR SALAD PLATE)

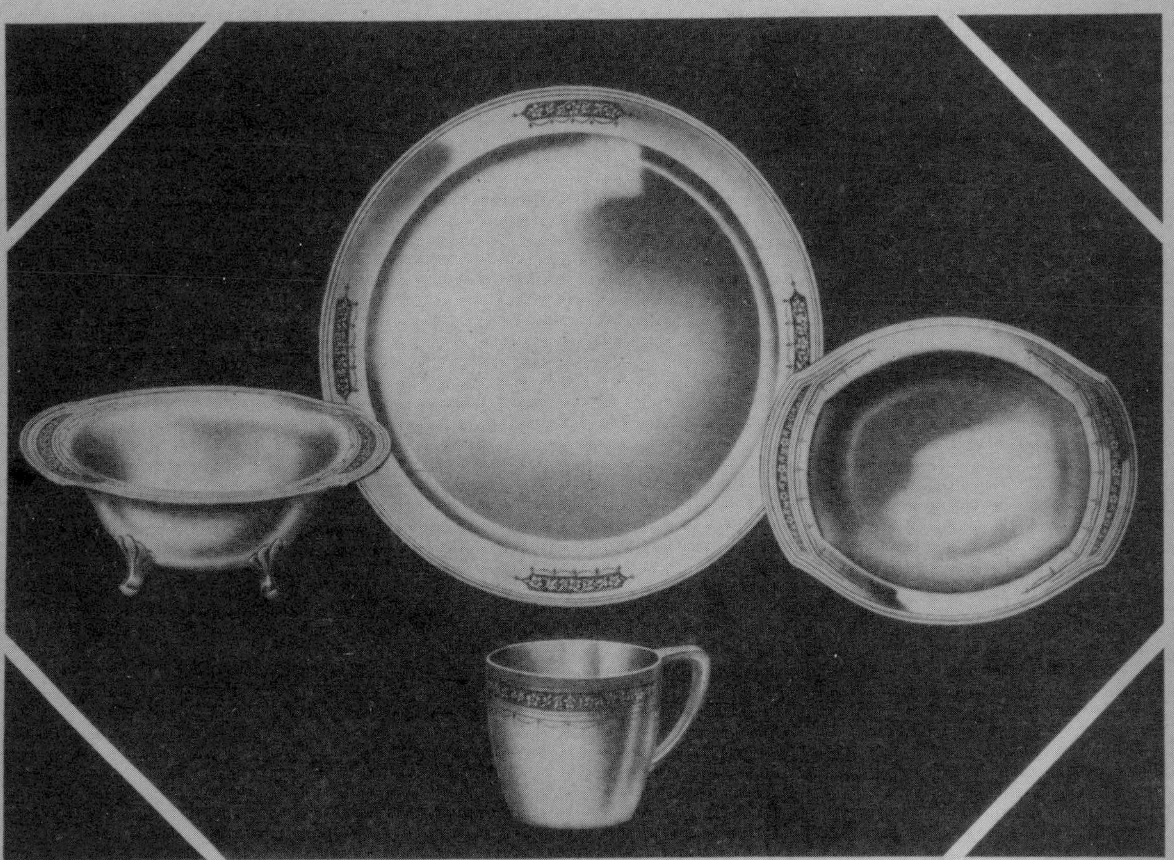

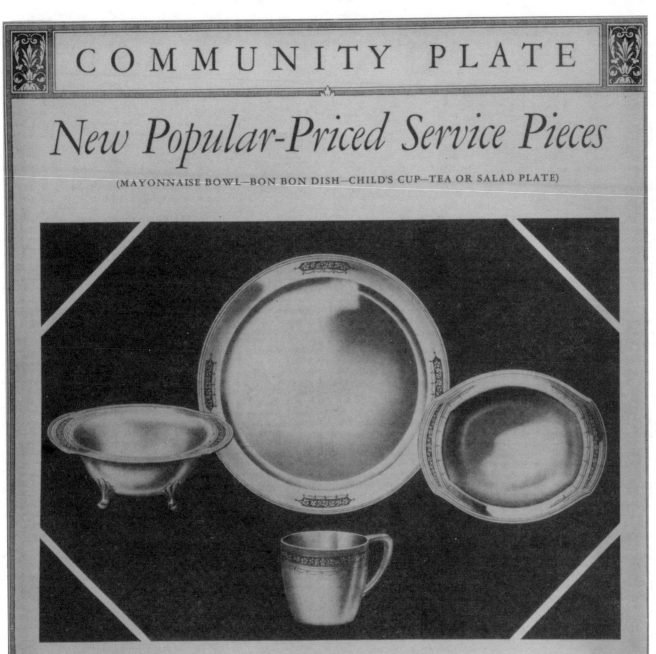

Quick-Selling Gift Leaders—in Three Patterns

These four new numbers by Community craftsmen will enable the dealer to draw added profits from the increasing vogue for silver service of every sort. Fully on a par with previous COMMUNITY PLATE hollowware in design and workmanship, they nevertheless can be sold at prices which should put them in the van of your hollowware sellers. They are available in the *Paul Revere*, *Grosvenor* and *Bird of Paradise* patterns only.

The *Mayonnaise Bowl* is sturdy, graceful, easy to pass, won't tip over. The *Bon Bon Dish* is handsome, flowing of line, capacious. The *Child's Cup* is made with an eye to clumsy young fingers. The *Salad Plate* is a gem of simplicity and utility. All four pieces are finished with typical Community care, and make excellent suggestions for those who seek inexpensive gifts of quality. Display them with the price-tag prominent.

Paul Revere	*Bird of Paradise*	*Grosvenor*		
14948	12948	11948	CHILD'S CUP (*Height 2¾ in.*)	Each $4.38
14977	12977	11977	BON BON DISH (*Length 6¾ in.*)	Each 5.00
14987	12987	11987	MAYONNAISE BOWL (*Length 6¾ in.—Height 2¾ in.*)	Each 6.88
14988	12988	11988	TEA OR SALAD PLATE (*Diameter 7¾ in.*)	Each 5.00

INDEX OF PATTERNS

INDEX OF MARKS

INDEX OF MANUFACTURERS

Books on Antiques and Collectibles

Most of the following books are available from your local book seller or antique dealer, or on loan from your public library. If you are unable to locate certain titles in your area you may order by mail from COLLECTOR BOOKS, P.O. Box 3009, Paducah, KY 42002-3009. Add $2.00 for postage for the first book ordered and $.25 for each additional book. Include item number, title and price when ordering. Allow 14 to 21 days for delivery. All books are well illustrated and contain current values.

Books on Glass and Pottery

No.	Title	Price
1810	American Art Glass, Shuman	$29.95
1517	American Belleek, Gaston	$19.95
2016	Bedroom & Bathroom Glassware of the Depression Years	$19.95
1312	Blue & White Stoneware, McNerney	$9.95
1959	Blue Willow, 2nd Ed., Gaston	$14.95
1627	Children's Glass Dishes, China & Furniture II, Lechler	$19.95
1892	Collecting Royal Haeger, Garmon	$19.95
1373	Collector's Ency of American Dinnerware, Cunningham	$24.95
2133	Collector's Ency. of Cookie Jars, Roerig	$24.95
2017	Collector's Ency. of Depression Glass, Florence, 9th Ed.	$19.95
1812	Collector's Ency. of Fiesta, Huxford	$19.95
1439	Collector's Ency. of Flow Blue China, Gaston	$19.95
1961	Collector's Ency. of Fry Glass, Fry Glass Society	$24.95
2086	Collector's Ency. of Gaudy Dutch & Welsh, Schuman	$14.95
1813	Collector's Ency. of Geisha Girl Porcelain, Litts	$19.95
1915	Collector's Ency. of Hall China, 2nd Ed., Whitmyer	$19.95
1358	Collector's Ency. of McCoy Pottery, Huxford	$19.95
1039	Collector's Ency. of Nippon Porcelain I, Van Patten	$19.95
1350	Collector's Ency. of Nippon Porcelain II, Van Patten	$19.95
1665	Collector's Ency. of Nippon Porcelain III, Van Patten	$24.95
1447	Collector's Ency. of Noritake, Van Patten	$19.95
1037	Collector's Ency. of Occupied Japan I, Florence	$14.95
1038	Collector's Ency. of Occupied Japan II, Florence	$14.95
1719	Collector's Ency. of Occupied Japan III, Florence	$14.95
2019	Collector's Ency. of Occupied Japan IV, Florence	$14.95
1715	Collector's Ency. of R.S. Prussia II, Gaston	$24.95
1034	Collector's Ency. of Roseville Pottery, Huxford	$19.95
1035	Collector's Ency. of Roseville Pottery, 2nd Ed., Huxford	$19.95
1623	Coll. Guide to Country Stoneware & Pottery, Raycraft	$9.95
2077	Coll. Guide Country Stone. & Pottery, 2nd Ed., Raycraft	$14.95
1523	Colors in Cambridge, National Cambridge Society	$19.95
1425	Cookie Jars, Westfall	$9.95
1843	Covered Animal Dishes, Grist	$14.95
1844	Elegant Glassware of the Depression Era, 4th Ed., Florence	$19.95
2024	Kitchen Glassware of the Depression Years, 4th Ed., Florence	$19.95
1465	Haviland Collectibles & Art Objects, Gaston	$19.95
1917	Head Vases Id & Value Guide, Cole	$14.95
1392	Majolica Pottery, Katz-Marks	$9.95
1669	Majolica Pottery, 2nd Series, Katz-Marks	$9.95
1919	Pocket Guide to Depression Glass, 7th Ed., Florence	$9.95
1438	Oil Lamps II, Thuro	$19.95
1670	Red Wing Collectibles, DePasquale	$9.95
1440	Red Wing Stoneware, DePasquale	$9.95
1958	So. Potteries Blue Ridge Dinnerware, 3rd Ed., Newbound	$14.95
1889	Standard Carnival Glass, 2nd Ed., Edwards	$24.95
1814	Wave Crest, Glass of C.F. Monroe, Cohen	$29.95
1848	Very Rare Glassware of the Depression Years, Florence	$24.95
2140	Very Rare Glassware of the Depression Years, Second Series	$24.95

Books on Dolls & Toys

No.	Title	Price
1887	American Rag Dolls, Patino	$14.95
2079	Barbie Fashion, Vol. 1, 1959-1967, Eames	$24.95
1749	Black Dolls, Gibbs	$14.95
1514	Character Toys & Collectibles 1st Series, Longest	$19.95
1750	Character Toys & Collectibles, 2nd Series, Longest	$19.95
2021	Collectible Male Action Figures, Manos	$14.95
1529	Collector's Ency. of Barbie Dolls, DeWein	$19.95
1066	Collector's Ency. of Half Dolls, Marion	$29.95
2151	Collector's Guide to Tootsietoys, Richter	$14.95
2082	Collector's Guide to Magazine Paper Dolls, Young	$14.95
1891	French Dolls in Color, 3rd Series, Smith	$14.95
1631	German Dolls, Smith	$9.95
1635	Horsman Dolls, Gibbs	$19.95
1067	Madame Alexander Collector's Dolls, Smith	$19.95
2025	Madame Alexander Price Guide #16, Smith	$7.95
1995	Modern Collector's Dolls, Vol. I, Smith	$19.95
1516	Modern Collector's Dolls Vol. V, Smith	$19.95
1540	Modern Toys, 1930-1980, Baker	$19.95
2033	Patricia Smith Doll Values, Antique to Modern, 6th Ed.	$9.95
1886	Stern's Guide to Disney	$14.95
2139	Stern's Guide to Disney, 2nd Series	$14.95
1513	Teddy Bears & Steiff Animals, Mandel	$9.95
1817	Teddy Bears & Steiff Animals, 2nd, Mandel	$19.95
2084	Teddy Bears, Annalees & Steiff Animals, 3rd, Mandel	$19.95
2028	Toys, Antique & Collectible, Longest	$14.95
1648	World of Alexander-Kins, Smith	$19.95
1808	Wonder of Barbie, Manos	$9.95
1430	World of Barbie Dolls, Manos	$9.95

Other Collectibles

No.	Title	Price
1457	American Oak Furniture, McNerney	$9.95
1846	Antique & Collectible Marbles, Grist, 2nd Ed.	$9.95
1712	Antique & Collectible Thimbles, Mathis	$19.95
1880	Antique Iron, McNerney	$9.95
1748	Antique Purses, Holiner	$19.95
1868	Antique Tools, Our American Heritage, McNerney	$9.95
2015	Archaic Indian Points & Knives, Edler	$14.95
1426	Arrowheads & Projectile Points, Hothem	$7.95
1278	Art Nouveau & Art Deco Jewelry, Baker	$9.95
1714	Black Collectibles, Gibbs	$19.95
1666	Book of Country, Raycraft	$19.95
1960	Book of Country Vol II, Raycraft	$19.95
1811	Book of Moxie, Potter	$29.95
1128	Bottle Pricing Guide, 3rd Ed., Cleveland	$7.95
1751	Christmas Collectibles, Whitmyer	$19.95
1752	Christmas Ornaments, Johnston	$19.95
1713	Collecting Barber Bottles, Holiner	$24.95
2132	Collector's Ency. of American Furniture, Vol. I, Swedberg	$24.95
2018	Collector's Ency. of Graniteware, Greguire	$24.95
2083	Collector's Ency. of Russel Wright Designs, Kerr	$19.95
1634	Coll. Ency. of Salt & Pepper Shakers, Davern	$19.95
2020	Collector's Ency. of Salt & Pepper Shakers II, Davern	$19.95
2134	Collector's Guide to Antique Radios, Bunis	$16.95
1916	Collector's Guide to Art Deco, Gaston	$14.95
1753	Collector's Guide to Baseball Memorabilia, Raycraft	$14.95
1537	Collector's Guide to Country Baskets, Raycraft	$9.95
1437	Collector's Guide to Country Furniture, Raycraft	$9.95
1842	Collector's Guide to Country Furniture II, Raycraft	$14.95
1962	Collector's Guide to Decoys, Huxford	$14.95
1441	Collector's Guide to Post Cards, Wood	$9.95
1716	Fifty Years of Fashion Jewelry, Baker	$19.95
2022	Flea Market Trader, 6th Ed., Huxford	$9.95
1668	Flint Blades & Proj. Points of the No. Am. Indian, Tully	$24.95
1755	Furniture of the Depression Era, Swedberg	$19.95
2081	Guide to Collecting Cookbooks, Allen	$14.95
1424	Hatpins & Hatpin Holders, Baker	$9.95
1964	Indian Axes & Related Stone Artifacts, Hothem	$14.95
2023	Keen Kutter Collectibles, 2nd Ed., Heuring	$14.95
1181	100 Years of Collectible Jewelry, Baker	$9.95
2137	Modern Guns, Identification & Value Guide, Quertermous	$12.95
1965	Pine Furniture, Our Am. Heritage, McNerney	$14.95
2080	Price Guide to Cookbooks & Recipe Leaflets, Dickinson	$9.95
1124	Primitives, Our American Heritage, McNerney	$8.95
1759	Primitives, Our American Heritage, 2nd Series, McNerney	$14.95
2026	Railroad Collectibles, 4th Ed., Baker	$14.95
1632	Salt & Pepper Shakers, Guarnaccia	$9.95
1888	Salt & Pepper Shakers II, Guarnaccia	$14.95
2141	Schroeder's Antiques Price Guide, 9th Ed.	$12.95
2096	Silverplated Flatware, 4th Ed., Hagan	$14.95
2027	Standard Baseball Card Pr. Gd., Florence	$9.95
1922	Standard Bottle Pr. Gd., Sellari	$14.95
1966	Standard Fine Art Value Guide, Huxford	$29.95
2085	Standard Fine Art Value Guide Vol. 2, Huxford	$29.95
2078	The Old Book Value Guide, 2nd Ed	$19.95
1923	Wanted to Buy	$9.95
1885	Victorian Furniture, McNerney	$9.95

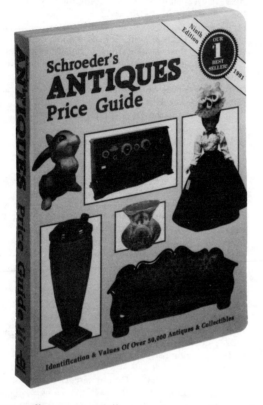

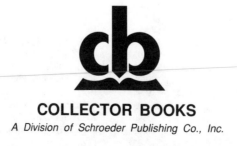